HISTORY OF THE TRIUMPHS OF OUR HOLY FAITH

HISTORY

OF THE TRIUMPHS OF OUR HOLY FAITH

AMONGST THE MOST BARBAROUS
AND FIERCE PEOPLES OF
THE NEW WORLD

BY

Andrés Pérez de Ribas

An English Translation Based on the 1645 Spanish Original

BY

Daniel T. Reff, Maureen Ahern, and Richard K. Danford

Annotated and with a Critical Introduction

BY

Daniel T. Reff

The University of Arizona Press

TUCSON

First printing
The University of Arizona Press
© 1999 The Arizona Board of Regents
All rights reserved
♾ This book is printed on acid-free, archival-quality paper.
Manufactured in the United States of America
04 03 02 01 00 99   6 5 4 3 2 1

Library of Congress Cataloging-in-Publication Data
Perez de Ribas, Andres, 1576–1655.
[Historia de los triunfos de nuestra santa fe entre gentes las mas barbaras y
fieras del Nuevo Orbe. English]
History of the triumphs of our holy faith amongst the most barbarous and fierce
peoples of the New World / by Andres Perez de Ribas.
p. cm.
"An English translation based on the 1645 Spanish original by Daniel T. Reff,
Maureen Ahern, and Richard K. Danford ; annotated and with a critical
introduction by Daniel T. Reff."
Includes bibliographical references and index.
ISBN 0-8165-1720-7 (alk. paper)
1. Jesuits—Mexico—History—17th century.
2. Jesuits—Missions—Mexico—History—17th century.
3. Indians of Mexico—Missions.   4. Missions—Mexico—
History—17th century.   5. Mexico—Church history—17th century.
6. Perez de Ribas, Andres, 1576–1655.
I. Reff, Daniel T., 1949–   II. Title.
BX3712.A1P35   1999
266'.272'09032—dc21
98-40196

British Library Cataloguing-in-Publication Data
A catalogue record for this book is available from the British Library.

Publication of this book is made possible in part by grants from The Ohio
State University, the Program for Cultural Cooperation between Spain's
Ministry of Culture and North American Universities, the Southwest
Mission Research Center, and Cabot Sedgwick, and from the proceeds of
a permanent endowment created with the assistance of a Challenge Grant
from the National Endowment for the Humanities, a federal agency.

CONTENTS

Reference Material

TABLE

MAPS

ACKNOWLEDGMENTS

Major funding for the research and development of this critical edition was provided by The Ohio State University, particularly the College of Humanities and the Department of Spanish and Portuguese, and by the National Endowment for the Humanities. Dr. Susan Wimmer and Dr. Helena Aguera at NEH provided valuable advice and assistance at important junctures of our project. It was a pleasure as well working with the staff of the Newberry Library, which provided both microfilm and a wonderful environment in which to work with a copy of the original 1645 edition of the *Historia*.

Our project would never have succeeded without the help of colleagues at The Ohio State University. Special thanks are due to Professors Nancy Ettlinger and Stephen Summerhill, who provided encouragement, advice, and support throughout the life of the project.

Over the years the project also benefited greatly from the guidance of Professor Chris Zacher, former Associate Dean of the College of the Humanities. Professor Don Dell, former Associate Dean of the College of Social and Behavioral Sciences, and Professor Michael Riley, former Dean of the College of Humanities, were instrumental in getting our interdisciplinary effort off the ground. More recently, Dean Kermit Hall of the College of Humanities and Professors Nicholas Howe, Dieter Wanner, and Thomas Kasulis have helped bring the project to fruition.

Thanks are due as well to the staff of the Humanities Computing Center, particularly Mike Garofano and Diane Dagefoerde, who networked various project members, making it possible for all of us to work together, even when one or more of us was hundreds of miles from Columbus. We also wish to thank Ron McLean and his staff at Graphic Design Services at The Ohio State University for preparing the maps for the edition, which were funded by the Division of Comparative Studies.

The project attracted several graduate students who contributed significantly to the critical edition by drafting, revising, discussing, and otherwise generating translated text. Ileana Chaves Gonzalez, Luis Hermosilla, and Lynn Madison-Olivia all have a rightful share in whatever kind words might be said about the edition. We are thankful as well to Linda Jones, who prepared and double-checked our Latin translations; Linda's contribution was made possible by a small grant from the Center for Medieval and Renaissance Studies at The Ohio State University.

A number of scholars read and commented on the manuscript version of our critical edition. We are grateful to Dr. Thomas Sheridan and Dr. Carroll Riley for their careful scrutiny of the text and for offering a number of suggestions for revision. Dr. David Yetman of the Southwest Center at the University of Arizona also was kind enough to read portions of the manuscript and make suggestions concerning the identification of plants and animals in the *Historia*.

Finally, the publication of this volume was made possible by subventions from the College of Humanities and the Center for Medieval and Renaissance Studies at The Ohio State University; The Southwest Mission Research Center in Tucson, Arizona; the Program for Cultural Cooperation between Spain's Ministry of Culture and United States Universities; and the University of Arizona Press and its benefactors.

HISTORY OF THE TRIUMPHS OF OUR HOLY FAITH

PREFACE
The *Historia* and Its Translation

This is the first complete English-language edition of Andrés Pérez de Ribas' *Historia de los triumphos de nuestra santa fee entre gentes las más barbaras y fieras del nuevo Orbe*. The *Historia* was published in Spain in 1645 and ostensibly is a history of the Jesuit missions of northern Mexico during the period from 1591 to 1643. This fifty-two-year period witnessed the birth and height of development of the Jesuit missions of northern Mexico. The Jesuit mission system continued to expand through the mid-eighteenth century, extending into northern Sonora, Baja California, southern Chihuahua, and finally, southern Arizona. However, except for Kino's efforts and career, this expansion was largely anti-climactic, owing to the fact that the native population had been decimated by Old World diseases.

The preeminent borderlands scholar, Herbert E. Bolton, characterized the *Historia* as "one of the greatest books ever written in the West" (Dunne 1951:120). Indeed, the book is an unsurpassed primary source on the aboriginal cultures of northern Mexico and the dynamics of Spanish-Indian relations in northern Nueva España. It is also a wonderful reflection of the Spanish missionary, and particularly the Jesuit, worldview.

Pérez de Ribas was born in 1575 in Córdoba, Spain, and entered the Jesuit order twenty-seven years later, in 1602. He promptly sailed for Mexico, where he completed his novitiate in June 1604. Pérez de Ribas spent the next fifteen years working as a missionary in northern Sinaloa and southernmost Sonora, first among the Ahome and Zuaque, then among the Yaqui. Because of failing health, he was recalled to Mexico City in 1619. During the ensuing year, while he was convalescing and acting as rector of the Jesuit college at Tepotzlán, he apparently completed a first draft of Part 1 of the *Historia*. The Jesuit archives in Mexico City reportedly contain an incomplete manuscript entitled "History of the Province of Sinaloa by Father Andrés Pérez de Ribas." According to Dunne (1940:224), who examined the manuscript, the history ends abruptly in the midst of recounting events from 1620 (see also Dunne 1951:109).

In the Archivo General de la Nación (AGN) in Mexico City (in Misiones 25) is an unsigned and incomplete manuscript that appears to be yet another, later version of the *Historia*. This manuscript is entitled "History of the Missions Undertaken by the Religious of the Company of Jesus through the Preaching of the Holy Gospel in the Kingdom of Nueva España of the Western Indies." Both Dunne and Bolton (1913) were of the opinion that this unattributed manuscript was authored by Pérez de Ribas. This inference is supported by the fact that both the manuscript and the 1645 edition of the *Historia* are divided into two parts, the first dealing with the missions of Sinaloa and the second dealing with the missions of Topia, San Andrés, Tepehuan, and Parras (Zambrano 1961–1977:3:128). It appears that after completing his history of the Sinaloa missions in 1620, Pérez de Ribas availed himself of Jesuit reports and correspondence in Mexico City and drafted a history of the Jesuit missions covered in Part 2. This section of the *Historia* apparently was written between 1626 and 1637, during the years when Pérez de Ribas served as rector of the Colegio Máximo and the Casa Profesa in Mexico City.

From 1638 to 1641 Pérez de Ribas served as Jesuit provincial, a demanding position that did not leave much time for research and writing. Once out of office, however, Pérez de Ribas apparently spent the years from 1641 to 1645 revising and updating his earlier manuscript history, as evidenced by the fact that the *Historia* has twelve books whereas the manuscript history in the AGN has only eight. Pérez de Ribas also added concluding chapters on the lives of prominent missionaries to some of the books. For example, he noted that he was in Spain at the time he wrote Chapter 41 of Book 10, which deals with the life of Father Juan del Valle. In his letter to the fathers of the Company, which precedes Book 1, he noted that he began the *Historia* in Mexico City and completed it in Madrid. Pérez de Ribas was in Madrid from 1643 to 1645, meeting with Jesuit officials before he proceeded to Rome to represent the Province of Nueva España in the eighth general congregation of the Society of Jesus.

In summary, the *Historia* was written over the course of many years by a man who was intimately familiar with the Jesuit missions of Mexico. Pérez de Ribas was either an eyewitness or consulted eyewitness reports for much of the information he records throughout his work. Indeed, in many chapters he copied letters from the Jesuit annual reports (referred to as the *anuas* or *cartas annuae*) and other correspondence, some of which has not been found or cataloged at major archives in Mexico and Spain.[1] This reliance on the anuas is most apparent in Part 2 of the *Historia*, which quotes extensively from the anuas in recounting the history of the Jesuit missions of the sierras. In particular it is notable that events narrated in Part 2 tend to be more precisely dated than those in Part 1. Pérez de Ribas appears to have relied heavily on his memory when describing the Jesuit experience in Sinaloa, and as a consequence, his narration often lacks dates or other particulars.

Pérez de Ribas stated that he wrote his history for fellow Jesuits, particularly novices and members of the Society of Jesus who were ignorant of the challenges missionaries faced in the New World. The *Historia* was written both to attract newcomers to the missionary vocation and to inform Jesuits bound for the mission frontier. Indeed, the *Historia* is in some ways a textbook on missionary work in the New World. Jesuits who read the *Historia* learned not only about the nature of the mission enterprise, but about the qualities that were required of those who chose a missionary vocation. Pérez de Ribas concluded most books of the *Historia* with one or more chapters on the lives and careers, and often the martyrdom, of exemplary missionaries.

In recounting the lives of individual Jesuits and the history of particular missions, Pérez de Ribas frequently

spoke of *casos de edificación*—instances where missionaries (invariably with divine assistance) "successfully" substituted Christian for native rituals and beliefs. These edifying cases, which often include details about Indian behaviors and beliefs, contribute to the *Historia's* importance as a source of information on the aboriginal cultures of northwestern Mexico, and by extension, the American Southwest. Many behaviors and beliefs that Pérez de Ribas described for groups in northwestern Mexico can be found or have analogues among groups in what is today southern Arizona and New Mexico. This in part reflects a similar adaptation to an arid environment (Ortiz 1983). It also reflects the fact that native groups throughout this "Greater Southwest" traded and communicated with one another for centuries prior to Columbus' fateful voyage (DiPeso 1979; Riley 1987).

In general, considerably more ethnographic data can be found in the first one or two chapters of each of the twelve books that make up the *Historia* (with the exception of Books 2, 7, and 12). In these introductory chapters Pérez de Ribas provided an overview of the aboriginal culture(s) and physical environment of each region where the Jesuits labored. He discussed an enormous number and variety of topics—from the use of peyote and child sacrifice to native ball games and the dress of elites. As was the case with Sahagún (1989) and fellow Jesuit José de Acosta (1894 [1590]), Pérez de Ribas' attention to ethnographic details reflected his belief that one had to understand native idolatry and superstition in order to combat and replace them with Christian spirituality.

At the same time, however, Pérez de Ribas accepted that Native Americans had a rightful place alongside Europeans as descendants of Adam (*de un mismo tronco que es Adan*). He frequently implied that it was the Indians' long isolation from the Old World and an ignorance of the word of God, rather than an inherent lack of reason, that accounted for their "foolish" beliefs and "barbarous" behavior. This guarded acceptance of native peoples as rational beings often empowered him as an ethnographer, predisposing him to cultural rather than abjectly racist or tautological explanations of native values, beliefs, and behaviors. In discussing native warfare, for instance, he emphasized factors such as competition over land, access to salt deposits and hunting territories, and in one instance, a dispute over the rules for playing a native game, *correr el palo*. Such explanations compare well with those proffered by distinguished modern ethnographers (e.g., Spicer 1962:386).

To acknowledge Pérez de Ribas' relativism is not

---

1. At times, especially during epidemics (Reff 1991b:166), Jesuit superiors on the frontier were unable to file annual reports, or the reports that they did file were lost or not copied. In such cases, Pérez de Ribas' own correspondence and his familiarity with these lost reports, which he cites in the *Historia*, are invaluable.

to suggest that he necessarily escaped the cognitive bounds set by his own Eurocentric culture. Arguably, Pérez de Ribas and most of his Jesuit contemporaries never resolved in their own minds the question of Indian identity. Thus, for every explicit recognition of the Indians' natural intelligence there are several explicit and implicit statements suggesting otherwise. As discussed in greater detail in the "Critical Introduction," Pérez de Ribas' disparaging and negative comments reflect a variety of theological, political, literary, and cultural-historical contingencies. More generally, Pérez de Ribas was a product of his age, which reified Aristotelian notions, including the idea that *pulicia*, or "civilization," entailed living in towns or cities with rulers, elites, and "true government" (Corominas and Pascual 1989–1991:4:598; Nader 1990; Pagden 1982). Thus, Pérez de Ribas prefaced his otherwise insightful comments about Cáhita socio-political organization with the observation that "they have neither laws nor kings, nor do they have any form of authority or political government to punish them for their vices and sins." Pérez de Ribas also was a product of late medieval and Renaissance devotionalism and was deeply committed to the notion that the Creator, often acting through his saints, intervened on earth to change the course of events and to combat Satan (Moore 1982; Weinstein and Bell 1982; Wright 1982). Accordingly, the fabric of the *Historia*, which is richly woven with precise ethnographic data, has running through it countless stories of wondrous conversions and miracles. Although some have lamented this woof and warp of empiricism and mysticism, suggesting that the latter detracts from the former (Dunne 1951:128–29), the true wonder of the *Historia* is that they coexist, much as they did in the mind of the Jesuit missionary.

NEGLECT AND PRIOR USE OF THE *HISTORIA*

Although the *Historia* provides a fascinating look at both Spanish and Indian cultures and the clash of two civilizations, a relatively small number of scholars have read and consulted this remarkable primary source. This neglect is attributable in part to the lack of a scholarly edition that would make the work accessible to both scholars and the general public. Although texts of great age can be rewarding reading without the aid of annotation or a critical introduction, this generally is not the case with the *Historia*. Indeed, the title itself

can be misleading, for the work is not a "history" in the Renaissance sense of the term (an objective, empirically based account of the deeds of men). The paradigm that both constrained and animated Pérez de Ribas was that God never abandoned his creation; God and his invisible hand were everywhere to be seen. The job of the historian, as he saw it, was to demonstrate the "in-breaking of the divine" into human affairs. More precisely, his primary concern was to recount the great number and variety of challenges the Jesuits faced and overcame with divine aid, rather than to document their precise chronological order, the names of the participants, and other particulars. Moreover, like medieval historians or hagiographers, he omitted particulars and employed hyperbole whenever he felt it necessary to convey what was essentially ineffable. In other places he compressed events, skipping forward or backward in time without informing the reader. These problems are compounded by highly rhetorical, often obtuse passages and ambiguous, awkward syntax, characteristics of Jesuit and seventeenth-century Spanish discourse, respectively (see p. 434).

Judging from its limited use by historians and anthropologists, the *Historia* has discouraged more readers than it has wooed. Its primary users have been Jesuit historians, many of whom were trained by Herbert E. Bolton and immersed themselves in the anuas from Nueva España—the same sources that informed Pérez de Ribas' own text. During the decades preceding and immediately following World War II, a handful of these Jesuit scholars (e.g., Bannon 1955; Dunne 1940, 1944; Shiels 1934) produced numerous books and monographs on the mission frontier that were based largely on the *Historia*. Although these works exhibit some of the highest technical standards (e.g., translation accuracy, corroboration, cross-referencing), they suffer from negative stereotypes of Native Americans (see Thomas 1989; Weber 1987). Indeed, it is not uncommon in these works to find Native Americans described as "an inferior race" (Shiels 1934:150) or "exceedingly simple and often stupid" (Dunne 1940:57). Significantly, the Jesuits of Pérez de Ribas' era were more ambivalent about Native Americans.

Although several anthropologists, most notably Beals (1932, 1933, 1943), effectively scrutinized the *Historia* for ethnographic data on aboriginal groups such as the Cáhita and Acaxee, this research was principally descriptive (e.g., documenting house types, weapons, clothing). The descriptions do not capture—as the *Historia* does—the dynamic quality of native cultures caught in the sudden collision of the Old World and the New. It provides the only comprehensive picture of native life under what approximated aboriginal conditions, prior to the dramatic changes wrought by Old World diseases during the late sixteenth and early seventeenth centuries (Gerhard 1982; Reff 1991b).

TRANSLATION METHODOLOGY AND PREPARATION OF THIS VOLUME

In recognition of the value and importance of the *Historia*, our team of translators began in the fall of 1992 to produce a critical English-language edition of the work. We obtained a microfilm copy of the original edition published in 1645—a rare copy of which exists in the Ayer Collection at the Newberry Library, Chicago.[2] It contains 756 double-columned pages; a brief index at the end of the book; and another fifty or so pages of licenses, letters, and other front matter.

The original 1645 edition is divided into two parts, containing seven and five "books," respectively. Part 1 is a history of the missions of the Province of Sinaloa; it begins with a brief discussion of the land, climate, and customs of the Indians, followed by a more lengthy review of the history of early Spanish exploration of the region. Pérez de Ribas then recounts the founding of the first permanent mission among the Guasave and Cáhita proper of the Río Sinaloa (Book 2). Books 3 through 6 recount the subsequent northward advance of the Jesuit mission frontier along the Pacific slopes of the Sierra Madre Occidental, among the largely Cáhitan-speaking population of the Río Fuerte (Book 3), Río Mayo (Book 4), Río Yaqui (Book 5), and what in 1643 were the most recent nations to accept baptism, namely the Nébome (Pima Bajo) and Opata of southern and central Sonora (Book 6). Book 7 is a summary in which Pérez de Ribas both reviews and defends the Jesuits' accomplishments in Sinaloa.

Part 2 of the *Historia* details the history of the Jesuit mission experience in the heart of the Sierra Madre Occidental as well as along its eastern slope, among the Acaxee (Book 8), Xixime (Book 9), the Tepehuan and Tarahumara (Book 10), and the Zacateco and Irritilla (Book 11). Book 12 deals only tangentially with northwestern Nueva España and focuses largely on Jesuit

enterprises in central Mexico and La Florida, where nine Jesuits were martyred prior to the arrival of the Jesuits in Mexico in 1572.

There have been two fairly recent Spanish-language editions of the *Historia*, both published in Mexico (see Pérez de Ribas 1944, 1985). The 1944 edition is based on a faithful transcription of the original, which was prepared by Raul Cervantes Ahumada. A systematic comparison of the 1645 and 1944 editions reveals few discrepancies. The editions differ primarily with respect to the modernization of spelling, the simplification of punctuation (e.g., commas deleted or changed to colons), the replacement of abbreviations with full terms, the omission of the original margin notes and references, the rearrangement of the index (as a result of spelling modernization), and a change in the order in which the table of contents and a page of licenses appear. The 1985 edition of the *Historia* also employs Cervantes' transcription. Neither it nor the 1944 edition include critical notes and annotation. Both editions contain only brief introductions, which touch upon Pérez de Ribas and his subject and say little about his sources, Jesuit discourse, or the many issues that have been raised by scholars seeking to understand the clash of the Old and New Worlds.

Likewise no critical, English-language edition of the *Historia* exists. There is only an abridged English translation prepared by Tomas Robertson (1968). Robertson translated less than a third of the *Historia* (91 of 285 chapters). Moreover, by his own admission, Robertson (1968:xiii) relocated phrases, paragraphs, and whole chapters. Robertson also changed or deleted entire sentences,[3] and in at least one instance attributed statements to Pérez de Ribas that do not appear in the *Historia*.[4]

---

2. We also read and consulted the original on site to resolve the usual problems that arise from working with microfilm, such as illegible margin notes.

3. For instance, one passage translated by Robertson (1968:27) reads: "Here they underwent certain ceremonies such as opening the eyes of the children, in this manner emphasizing that they should be vigilant in their own protection." The same passage in the *Historia* (Pérez de Ribas 1645:41) reads: "There they conducted certain ceremonies with the youngsters, such as the one that opened their eyes, making them vigilant to arrows shot at them. Some Indians possess such sight and skill in deflecting enemy arrows that before the arrow can hit or wound them, they turn it from its path with their own bow, so it does not reach its mark" (our translation).

4. Robertson (1968:26) translated a passage from the *Historia* in which Pérez de Ribas (1645:40–41) described an "adoption ceremony" among the Cáhita of the Río Sinaloa. Robertson's translation begins with a sentence that is not in the original 1645 Spanish edition: "Not only because of sickness, but due to constant wars, many Indian children were left orphans." This interpolation distorts the meaning of the entire "adoption ceremony," which is properly understood as a rite of ceremonial sponsorship.

The need for a critical edition of the *Historia* is clear. We considered preparing an authoritative Spanish transcription to accompany our annotated English translation, but this strategy was rejected because it would have resulted in a massive work that would have been prohibitively expensive and would have defeated our purpose of making an underutilized resource available to scholars, students, and the general public. It is also the case that a Spanish-language edition of the *Historia*, albeit one lacking a critical apparatus, is available at many universities and major public libraries.

There are few scholarly experiences as humbling and at times frightening as translating a text that is 350 years old. It is frightening because occasionally we caught ourselves inferring meanings that upon further analysis were not present in the Spanish original. Such interpolations were not simply a matter of carelessness, but a consequence of trying to infer meaning from words and sentences written in a language whose syntax has changed appreciably. Of course, the Spanish semantic world also has changed dramatically in the past 350 years. Modern definitions of reality, based largely on science and empirical observation, differ substantially from Pérez de Ribas' reality, which not only included but often prioritized invisible forces (angels, demons, saints, God). Although the gulf between our world and Pérez de Ribas' is bridgeable most of the time, there undoubtedly were times (of which, paradoxically, we remain unaware) when we misunderstood and, thus, misrepresented the original text. The chances of this happening were increased by Pérez de Ribas' own vague or imprecise usage (his epistemology and worldview not withstanding), which we endeavored to retain, particularly when such usage seemed to reflect the author's ambivalent feelings. There are in fact many hazards in translating Jesuit discourse. Thus we entreat the reader to remain vigilant and, if doubt arises about our translation, to seek out the Spanish original.

To insure that our translation was appropriately "thick" (Geertz 1973) and minimally anachronistic, we familiarized ourselves with the prehistory and ethnology of the native peoples who are the subject of so many of Pérez de Ribas' observations. Knowledge of and participation in archaeological research in Sonora often helped us to imagine what Pérez de Ribas was referring to when he described particular physical environments, geological formations, house types, plants and agave gardens, weapons, etc. Similarly, to understand Pérez de Ribas' perception and representation of reality, including native peoples, presupposed a knowledge of

Catholicism, Jesuit religious culture, and the political and institutional context of the Jesuit mission enterprise in the New World. Of course, the pursuit of these contingencies often raised as many issues as it resolved. Who or what is the "real" Indian to juxtapose against Pérez de Ribas' construct? Can Jesuit or European "culture" be reduced to a set of propositions that adequately encompasses or explains the behaviors and beliefs of the many priests who figure as actors in the drama that is the *Historia?* These are some of the issues we discussed at length during our weekly project meetings.

With respect to the translation itself, we employed a team approach, bringing as many different perspectives as possible to bear on the text: anthropologist, linguist, Latin American literary scholar; certified translator; native speakers, non-native speakers; Latin Americans, Anglo-Americans; Catholics, atheists, and Protestants. Each member of the team was assigned text to translate each week. The text was then revised by another team member and read against the Spanish original at a weekly meeting of project personnel. The principal investigator then recorded the changes suggested by the group, further editing the text while entering it in the computer. In this way the team generated a reasonably polished translation of the entire *Historia* in three years. Then we spent the fourth and fifth years "proofing" the translation, which has meant rereading our most recent English version against the Spanish original. During all this time, as issues were raised and discussed in our project meetings, research was conducted for the annotation and the critical introduction.

The translation that we have produced follows precisely the structure of the original 1645 edition. We have included in brackets indications of where page breaks occurred in the original 1645 edition, with unnumbered pages indicated as [PB] and the remaining pages referenced by number (e.g., [393]).

The structure of Pérez de Ribas' discourse reflects its age, the ideology of the Jesuit order, and his intended readers. Readers with some knowledge of Spanish will agree that the original Spanish text is highly rhetorical and often obtuse, with ambiguous and awkward syntax. The resulting baroque prose is characterized by lengthy, often convoluted sentences in ponderous paragraphs. Methodologically, we have striven for cultural as well as linguistic fidelity while retaining a high degree of readability and naturalness in English. To insure that the English-language reader grasps the meaning of the text, we have often altered Spanish word order and grammatical constructions. When necessary, long

Spanish sentences have been separated into several, briefer English sentences; referents have been specified for clarity; and long paragraphs have been divided to produce two or more logical English equivalents. Throughout the text we have tried to retain Pérez de Ribas' use of negation (e.g., "I can't fail to discuss Yaqui bravery"), rather than naturalize it (e.g., "I must discuss Yaqui bravery") and risk losing any implicit meaning (e.g., apparently some readers might think it unnecessary to discuss Yaqui bravery). We have avoided structures that are "quaint" or anachronistic in English. The subject and contents of the *Historia*, as well as its many embedded voices in the reports that were cited by Pérez de Ribas, impart their own intrinsic flavor without such artificial linguistic devices.

From the perspective of lexical accuracy special attention has been given to the translation of Spanish terms that now have accepted meanings in English or whose meanings have changed significantly over the past 350 years. We have indicated in footnotes Spanish terms or phrases whose English equivalents were arrived at after considerable discussion or research. We left untranslated Spanish administrative terms and titles, such as *fiscal* or *alcalde*. Careful attention has been paid to lexical items such as *doctrina*, which had several important seventeenth-century usages that differ semantically from modern usage. These cultural or temporally bound terms initially are italicized and thereafter appear in normal type. On first usage of a Spanish term we generally provide in a footnote a discussion of the term's significance or meaning. The terms also are defined in a glossary at the end of the translation.

We also retained Spanish place names, such as Nueva España, and personal titles and surnames. The principal investigators drew on their firsthand knowledge of the cultural geography and topography of northwestern Mexico to achieve precise translations of terms used in the *Historia* that might otherwise be misleading, such as *arroyo, monte,* or *ramada*.

Our methodology reflects a recognition that Pérez de Ribas' writing is itself an attempt at cultural translation. In order to achieve translation fidelity, it is as important to be concerned with *how* Pérez de Ribas chose to represent cultural interactions—many of which stretched far beyond his Spanish readers' frame of reference—as with *what* events he reported. Therefore, within the constraints of natural English syntax, we have tried in our translation to preserve representational features, rather than eliminate them. We noted, for instance, that Pérez de Ribas often used more than

one adjective or adjectival phrase when describing phenomena. He sometimes juxtaposed an indigenous term or its Nahuatl equivalent, the language that had become a *lingua franca* among missionaries, with Spanish terms (e.g., *dos casas de petate o esteras* or *los sustentaban con atole, que es lo mismo que puches de maiz*). At other times Pérez de Ribas transcribed a native term such as *cachinipa* along with its referent in Spanish. More frequently yet, he used strings of double or triple synonyms to convey a single concept and to discursively emphasize a point (e.g., *uno de los mayores alborotos, inquietud y estragos de guerra que se vio en la Nueva España*).

Another important discursive feature is the vivid metaphorical rhetoric that the text displays, which appears to be characteristic of Jesuit discourse on missionary frontiers. This is apparent, for example, in Pérez de Ribas' variety of references to the devil, including "the enemy," "the infernal beast," "mankind's most ferocious enemy," and "a demonic kinsman." We have preserved this metaphoric usage, rather than simply rendering all these phrases as "the devil." Similarly, we have retained Pérez de Ribas' use of traditional metaphors of blindness and sight, or darkness and light, to convey the lack or presence of grace or Christian faith.

Our goal has been to transmit the full dimension of Pérez de Ribas' Jesuitical modes of representation. In addition to readability and semantic accuracy, we have striven for a dimension of discursive fidelity. For the same reasons we have retained Pérez de Ribas' frequent asides, which typically appear in parentheses in the original. Other textual criteria that we followed include: retention of the margin notes as footnotes; retention in the text of Latin phrases, which are translated in footnotes; standardization of minor alternate spellings to reflect the most common forms (e.g., Yaqui for Haqui); and the transformation of abbreviations to their fullest terms.

Annotation and Critical Introduction

The *Historia* was written for an audience largely ignorant of the New World, and particularly northwestern Nueva España. A fascinating aspect of the text is the extent to which Pérez de Ribas translates the missionary experience for his audience. The narrative abounds in asides that clarify Jesuit rules, customs, and procedures and native behaviors and beliefs. Accordingly, our edition of the *Historia* has been sparingly annotated. The major problem that modern readers have had with the *Historia* is that Pérez de Ribas frequently failed to identify the participants and dates for various events and observations. He also compressed events, skipping forward in time without informing the reader. Because he relied so heavily on the Jesuit anuas, we consulted these sources in order to supply missing dates, names, etc. Where possible without disrupting the flow of discourse, this information has been provided in brackets directly in the text. Longer clarifications and explanations are supplied in footnotes.

Although the Jesuits and Pérez de Ribas in particular often described Indian behaviors, rituals, etc., in great detail, they often failed to comprehend the emic meaning or significance of certain rituals and customs. This is true, for instance, of the Indians' "drunken revels." We have noted in footnotes alternative meanings suggested by modern research or other colonial observers.

We have retained as footnotes Pérez de Ribas' margin notes, which usually are references to the Bible or exegetical texts. The margin notes in the 1645 edition are in the form of abbreviations for titles and/or authors (e.g., Cor.1. c16 = I Corinthians, Chapter 16;

Cuid. de D. c16 = Chapter 16 of Augustine's *City of God*). We have retained the margin notes in their original form, followed by a clarification of the text and author. Whenever the margin note is associated with a Latin quotation, we have provided a translation of the Latin, using an English-language edition of the Vulgate (Knox 1956), which was considered to be the authentic text of the Bible by Catholic scholars of the seventeenth century (Martin 1993:4). It should be noted that Pérez de Ribas' Latin is often a "free rendering" of the Bible; that is, he often condensed or simplified the passages he quoted. There are times when Pérez de Ribas mentioned or alluded to a particular work and author in the body of the text yet supplied no margin note. In these instances we have indicated the text and/or author in a footnote.

The following critical introduction to the *Historia* and Jesuit discourse elaborates on the variety of contingent factors that governed the Jesuit mission enterprise in Nueva España and Pérez de Ribas' representation of that experience.

CRITICAL INTRODUCTION
The *Historia* and Jesuit Discourse

Daniel T. Reff

During the sixteenth and seventeenth centuries, European missionaries generated an enormous literature on what they referred to as the spiritual conquest of the New World. The Jesuits alone wrote tens of thousands of letters and reports, which are preserved in archives around the world. On occasion missionaries such as Pérez de Ribas took it upon themselves or were asked by superiors to synthesize the observations and experiences of contemporaries.[1] The result was works such as the *Historia*, which provide an invaluable commentary on Native American culture and the dynamics of European-Indian relations during the colonial period in the New World.

CONTEXTUALIZING MISSIONARY DISCOURSE

Although the value of texts such as the *Historia* has long been apparent, significant changes have occurred with respect to how we view and analyze colonial-period texts. Until relatively recently, anthropologists and historians have approached the historical record with what might be described as naive realism (Cowgill 1993:561; LaCapra 1983:17 ff.; White 1973). It generally has been assumed that texts such as the *Historia* mirror reality, except insofar as the author consciously chose to deviate from the facts or failed in what has been construed as an essentially mechanical task of matching the right words to their empirical counterparts. In the wake of

the hermeneutics movement and postmodernism (Foucault 1970; Gadamer 1989; White 1978), it is now generally understood that missionary texts and, indeed, all writing is at once creative and reflective. Between text and world there is a semi-autonomous author whose perception and representation of reality are governed by a host of contingencies, including prior texts and the author's own dynamic, cultural-historical context (Rylance 1987; Tyler 1987; White 1978).

The purpose of this critical introduction is to highlight the principal contingencies that influenced Pérez de Ribas' representation of the Jesuit experience and Indian cultures. As I have discussed elsewhere (Reff 1994, 1995), missionary texts are similar to modern ethnographies. For instance, both are based on participant observation, make use of native informants and the informants' language(s), and attempt to describe behaviors and beliefs for a non-native audience. Accordingly, works such as the *Historia* may profitably be analyzed from the perspective of the critique of ethnography (Clifford 1986; Clifford and Marcus 1986; Geertz 1988; Tyler 1987).

Clifford (1986), in particular, has highlighted several constraints on ethnography (fieldwork and writing) that are relevant to missionary work and texts. In the first instance, both missionaries and ethnographers are bearers of particular values, beliefs, and signifying practices that necessarily affect their perception and representation of themselves and others. With respect to Pérez de Ribas, his epistemology and beliefs were informed by several currents and cross-currents that swept Spain during the Renaissance and Counter-Reformation (e.g., rationalism, devotionalism, Augustinian revival). He was also a member of the Society of Jesus, whose own discourse both complemented and deviated from the much larger system of meanings of which it was a part.

---

1. The fifth father general of the Jesuit Order, Claudio Acquaviva (1581–1615), instructed each Jesuit provincial throughout the world to select a Jesuit to collect historical material and compile a chronicle or history of that province (Morner 1953:10).

One consequence of Pérez de Ribas' dual "citizenry"—being both a Spaniard well-educated in humanism and also a Jesuit imbued with a belief in "the immediate reality of an invisible world" (Moore 1982:100)—is that he often appears to be of two minds. So it might appear from a modern vantage point. The same author who at one moment privileges empirical observation and the rational subject the next moment privileges an invisible reality (e.g., devils, angels), preferring formal and final causes (God's plan/will) over material or efficient causality. It is worth emphasizing that the *Historia* is an explicitly teleological work; the history Pérez de Ribas recounts is as much about God's often mysterious handiwork and the operation of the Holy Spirit as it is about the heroic efforts of Jesuit missionaries. In point of fact, Pérez de Ribas was decidedly medieval in his worldview. As Huizinga (1967) commented, "The Middle Ages never forgot that all things would be absurd, if their meanings were exhausted in their function and their place in the phenomenal world, if by their essence they did not reach into a world beyond this."

Like all ethnographers, Pérez de Ribas also bore the weight of his culture during the actual writing of the *Historia*, when he made often unconscious decisions regarding metaphors, conventions, and other vehicles of expression and meaning. Not surprisingly, the same texts that informed his epistemology and worldview became Pérez de Ribas' primary literary models and sources of rhetorical strategies. Thus, in his "Prologue to the Reader" and at various moments in his narrative he acknowledges the Renaissance ideal of history (i.e., an objective account based on eyewitness testimony), which derived in part from classical notions of history advanced by Livy and Lucian. At the same time his narrative reveals that events were constantly mediated by the Bible, patristic sources, and hagiography, again reflecting his fundamental belief that the Jesuit experience in Nueva España reflected the unfolding of a divine plan. Missionary texts in general differ from texts by non-religious in their privileging of sacred literature as a source of models and conventions and their insistence on a not yet fully discerned divine teleology.

Both the form and content of the *Historia* also were influenced directly and indirectly by Pérez de Ribas' political and institutional context. Modern researchers are well aware that the academic community defines issues and meaning and, furthermore, determines what is published through the publication review process. Similarly, the Spanish crown and the Church—the Vatican, episcopacy, and the religious orders (including th Jesuit order itself)—both licensed the publication of the *Historia* and indirectly influenced Pérez de Ribas' choice of subject matter, its order and extent of discussion, and the rhetoric with which it was constituted or dismissed as unworthy of commentary. Because discourses are never fixed and are subject to contestation (Barthes 1987a:200; Foucault 1978, 1987), Pérez de Ribas voiced hegemonic positions (e.g., the Spanish right to conquer the New World) as well as challenging ideas and practices that were at odds with his own experiences and position as a Jesuit missionary and superior in the New World. Along these lines, by 1640 the vast majority of Jesuits were teachers rather than missionaries. Correspondingly, Jesuit discourse (e.g., rules, texts, letters, public addresses) no longer celebrated exclusively the ministry and career of the missionary. Pérez de Ribas challenged the emerging privileged position of teaching within the Society. He did so in part using a form of "hidden polemic" (Bakhtin 1968), constantly replying to but never quoting critics of the missionary vocation. At the heart of Pérez de Ribas' polemic was his likening of the Jesuit missionaries of Nueva España unto the apostles and Christ's own ministry. Similarly, by likening Nueva España unto the Lord's vineyard, Pérez de Ribas gave new meaning to an otherwise "dead" metaphor (Rorty 1989:16–18), rhetorically rebutting those who devalued the Jesuit missions of Mexico.

Each of these broadly construed and interlocking cultural-theological, literary-rhetorical, and political-institutional contingencies was itself conditioned by Pérez de Ribas' own dynamic historical context (Bruner 1994). However much Pérez de Ribas may have been a "prisoner" of Old World institutions, categories, and signifying practices, he and his Jesuit contemporaries at the same time experienced a New World—a world where sights, sounds, and other human beings did not in fact conform to pre-existing concepts, words, or narratives. The very "newness" of Nueva España became inescapable as a consequence of the Jesuit imperative that all missionaries master the languages of their Indian neophytes. This imperative forced Pérez de Ribas and other missionaries to contemplate and at times give voice to Indian meanings and expression. Pérez de Ribas often employs native terms as well as direct discourse, empowering Indians to express views on topics such as infanticide that a Spaniard could or would not express. Thus, the *Historia* reveals aspects of the mission experience that Pérez de Ribas may never have intended and that were not implied by the cognitive map supplied by his culture (Barthes 1987b).

In the discussion that follows I pursue the cultural-theological, literary-rhetorical, and institutional-political contingencies that governed Jesuit missionary discourse in the dynamic context of the New World. Although for purposes of analysis and discussion the various contingencies are separated out, the reality, of course, is that they were simultaneous, interpenetrating domains: cognitive processes are rarely strictly political as opposed to theological; epistemology is never separate from literature and other texts that inform cognition. True, there are moments in the reading of the *Historia* and all texts when one might perceive that the author is being "political"—casting reality in certain ways for political purposes; however, arguably this is more the exception than the rule.

Because the *Historia* is concerned with native culture and how it was changed through conversion, I conclude with a discussion of how the Jesuits' epistemological and theological culture, literary models and rhetoric, and political and institutional context all governed Pérez de Ribas' portrayal of Indian behaviors and beliefs and the dynamics of Jesuit-Indian relations.

THE THEOLOGICAL AND IDEOLOGICAL CONTEXTS OF JESUIT MISSIONARY DISCOURSE

It was customary when a Jesuit died for those who knew him best to write letters in praise of the deceased. Pérez de Ribas employed these *cartas de necrología* in many chapters of the *Historia* that are devoted to the lives of Jesuits who worked and died in Nueva España. It is somewhat ironic that he who devoted so much ink to other Jesuits apparently was not himself the subject of edifying letters and short biographies. I say apparently because, while no letters have come to light, it would be truly surprising if Pérez de Ribas' life and distinguished career (see table) went uncelebrated. Letters undoubtedly were written and perhaps someday will be found in Jesuit archives in Mexico, Rome, or Spain. Whatever the case, in the absence of such letters, which generally include a discussion of a Jesuit's formative years, we are largely ignorant of the particular circumstances of Pérez de Ribas' early life, when he presumably acquired his most fundamental values and

beliefs. The little we know about Pérez de Ribas' early life comes from performance reports written in later years by superiors who only briefly noted or commented on his education and background. These and other data were compiled by Peter Masten Dunne (1951) in a very informative biography of Pérez de Ribas.

What we do know is that Pérez de Ribas was born in Córdoba, Spain, in 1575. At the time, the centuries of coexistence that Jews, Muslims, and Christians had enjoyed in this city in the heart of al Andalus were largely a memory (Kamen 1985). Interestingly, Pérez de Ribas never mentioned his formative years in Córdoba, nor did he draw comparisons between Indians and Jews or Moors, as did many of his religious contemporaries (Elkin 1993). Moreover, he never reflected on the many similarities in topography and climate between northwestern Mexico, particularly northern Sinaloa and southern Sonora, and southern Spain. When one considers the impact that Arabic had on Spanish, particularly in southern Spain, it is also surprising how few Arabic terms appear in the *Historia*.[2] One almost has the impression that Pérez de Ribas went out of his way to avoid using loan words. It may be significant that the Jesuit college in Pérez de Ribas' hometown of Córdoba was accused by critics of accepting only Jews (O'Malley 1993b:190). As we will see, Pérez de Ribas was quite aware of Jesuit critics. He may well have perceived that it was counterproductive to directly or indirectly draw attention to his place of birth.[3]

As a youth in Córdoba, Spain, in what today we would refer to as high school, Pérez de Ribas studied *Latinidad* (grammar, poetry, history, rhetoric). This early education is reflected in his mastery of Latin; his citation of classical and late antique authors such as Plato, Livy, Cassidoro, Augustine, and Gregory the Great; and his skillful use of rhetoric to teach, please,

2. In Chapter 1 of Book 8 Pérez de Ribas draws from a letter by a fellow Jesuit, Hernando de Santarén. In paraphrasing Santarén's letter Pérez de Ribas used the Arabic term for granary (*alfolie*), which was not used by Santarén; compare Pérez de Ribas:.*les sirven los troncos de los Pinos de alfolies, o alacenas donde guardan su sustento para que no se les pudra*, with Santarén: *haze en un pino seco dies mil agujeros; y mete, en cada uno, una belotal las quales guarda para el ybierno* (Alegre 1956–1960:2:77). Here is one of the relatively few instances where Pérez de Ribas' Córdoban dialect manifested itself.

3. It is possible that Pérez de Ribas was a descendant of *conversos* (Jewish converts). On at least two occasions when he quoted the Bible, Pérez de Ribas for no apparent reason dropped words or phrases that mentioned Jews. In Chapter 7 of Book 2, for instance, he quoted Acts 16:20–21 ("These men, Jews by origin, are disturbing the peace of our city"), omitting the phrase "Jews by origin."

THE LIFE AND CAREER OF ANDRÉS PÉREZ DE RIBAS

1575	Born in Córdoba, Spain
1590–1601	Studies for the priesthood; completes licentiate in philosophy (3-year degree) and four additional years of theology; ordained a priest
1602	Enters Jesuit order; leaves Spain for Mexico
1603–4	Completes novitiate in Puebla
1604	Sent to Sinaloa as missionary
1605	Serves as missionary to the Ahome and Suaqui of the Río Fuerte
1612	Recalled to Mexico City to take the Four Vows and become a professed Jesuit
1616	Sent as envoy to Mexico City to petition viceroy and Jesuit provincial for mission to the Yaqui
1617	Founds the Yaqui mission (with Tomás Basilio)
1619	Recalled to Mexico City
1620	Rector of Jesuit college for novitiates at Tepotzotlán
1622	Secretary to the Jesuit provincial
1626	Secretary to the father visitor from Rome
1626	Rector and president of the Colegio Máximo de San Pedro y San Pablo (premier Jesuit educational institution in Mexico)
1632	Rector of the Casa Profesa (religious community and residence for professed Jesuits, brothers and scholastics in Mexico City)
1637	Rector and president of the Colegio Máximo
1638	Jesuit provincial for the Province of Nueva España
1641	Rector and president of the Colegio Máximo
1643	Elected procurator; travels to Madrid and then Rome
1645	The *Historia* is published
1648	Returns to Mexico with assignment from Jesuit father general to write another history
1650	Rector of Casa Profesa
1653	Completes *Corónica y Historia Religiosa*; publication is suppressed
1655	Dies in the Colegio Máximo in Mexico City

From Dunne (1951:163).

and persuade. At age twenty or thereabouts, Pérez de Ribas began a three-year course in philosophy, which essentially meant studying Aristotle and his later exegetes, principally Thomas Aquinas. After receiving his licentiate in philosophy, Pérez de Ribas studied theology for four years, submerging himself in biblical commentaries, patristic sources, and a vast literature on moral theology and casuistry (de Guibert 1964; O'Malley 1993b). Sometime prior to 1601 Pérez de Ribas was ordained a priest (Dunne 1951).

In 1602, at the relatively advanced age of twenty-seven and with seven years of advanced education already behind him, Pérez de Ribas entered the Jesuit order.[4] Like other novices he began his two-year novitiate by making the Spiritual Exercises of Ignatius Loyola. The Exercises generally required a month and involved a stepwise progression of prayer and reflection on one's life and relationship with God, who was perceived as immediately relevant. This retreat as it was outlined by Loyola (the Spiritual Exercises were first published in 1548) is very much an imaginative exercise; considerable time, for instance, is spent visualizing the historic as well as continuing battle for souls fought between God and the devil. During the Exercises and the novitiate more generally, the novice endeavors to enter into devout conversation with God—a conversation that ideally continues to evolve with regular infusions of grace (Ganss 1991; O'Malley 1993b:37–50).

As part of his novitiate Pérez de Ribas also would have spent innumerable hours reading the lives of the saints, Thomas à Kempis, and other works of a devotional nature, which chronicled and celebrated the immediate reality of the invisible world. Today we say "you are what you eat." Pérez de Ribas and his fellow Jesuits were defined by the sacred and devotional literature they "consumed" during their many years of religious formation. In this regard, perhaps the most striking aspect of the Historia is the extent to which God and the devil played a dynamic role in the lives of Jesuit missionaries and their Indian charges. Supernatural events are recounted throughout the Historia, as in the case of a hungry priest and his neophytes who were satiated by a rabbit that fell from the sky, or that of apostate Indi-

ans who found it impossible to roast the severed arm of Gonzalo de Tapia, the first Jesuit martyr in Nueva España. In his lengthy discussion of the Tepehuan Revolt (in Book 10), and indeed whenever the Jesuits experienced setbacks, Pérez de Ribas invoked the devil as causal agent. Curiously—or so it may seem to us—while Pérez de Ribas had no problem inferring satanic machination or divine will, he appeared oblivious to the ethnocentrism implied by conversion and the fact that the Jesuits were participants in a colonial venture that destroyed Indian peoples and cultures.

In point of fact the Historia is replete with observations as well as "silences" that, when judged by today's standards, raise doubts about Pérez de Ribas' credibility and power of observation. As heirs to the Enlightenment and the miracles of science, modern readers are likely to be frustrated or cynical about Pérez de Ribas' invocation of the devil and his apparent disregard of material or efficient causality.[5] Indeed, modern researchers undoubtedly have ignored the Historia and similar colonial-period texts because the perceived "fictions" appear too numerous to trust the text as a whole. Even fellow Jesuit Peter Masten Dunne (1951:72, 74), perhaps Pérez de Ribas' greatest admirer,[6] became impatient with the latter's uncritical acceptance of miracles.

If the Historia appears to abound in fictions, it is largely because the readers of the text have changed significantly. In the 350 years since the Historia was published, we increasingly have come to believe that God (if s/he exists) has left us to our own devices. The withdrawal of the divine has been coincident with a preoccupation with that which can be seen, measured, and quantified (Crosby 1997). This modern worldview was just beginning to crystallize at the time Pérez de Ribas wrote the Historia, coincident with the rise of capitalism, the first stirrings of modern science, and the Reformation. While many were pushing God and

---

4. Most Jesuits joined the order in their mid to late teens. The fact that Pérez de Ribas completed his education before he entered the Society also was unusual. However, the education itself, which he may well have received at the Jesuit college in Córdoba, was characteristic of the Ratio studiorum or plan of study that Jesuit novices ordinarily pursued (de Guibert 1964:215–19). Pérez de Ribas' seven years of philosophy and theology also were characteristic of professed Jesuits, the highest of the three ranks of the order.

5. It is not that Pérez de Ribas and fellow Jesuits were unaware of material or efficient causality (laws of nature) but rather that they were not terribly impressed with their "explanatory power." If asked why a tree grows, Pérez de Ribas undoubtedly would have acknowledged (following Aristotelian science) that it did so because of water, sunlight, and soil (material and efficient causality). However, given his theology and purpose for writing, which was in large part to demonstrate God's handiwork, he would have emphasized the formal and final causes of why trees grow: (1) because God imprinted in the seed or acorn the plan of the tree, and (2) because God intended that mankind should have shade, firewood, shelter, etc. (Steneck 1976:91).

6. Dunne relied heavily on Pérez de Ribas' Historia and his subsequent Corónica for a handful of articles and books on the Jesuit missions of Nueva España.

his saints and angels to the rear of the stage, others like Ignatius Loyola were championing the notion of God's enduring presence. This is the essence of Loyola's Spiritual Exercises: to cultivate a devout conversation with God that would do away with the distinction between visible and invisible.

The emergent rationalism and deism that pushed humans to center stage (and God to the rear) seems not to have swayed missionaries in the New World until much later in the seventeenth century (Bannon 1955:121; Klor de Alva 1988:32; MacCormack 1991; Pagden 1982). Indeed, many Jesuits may have requested a missionary assignment in the New World precisely because they were disenchanted with trends back home in Europe, particularly the Reformation and the popularization of mechanistic philosophy, both of which seemed to distance God from his creation.[7] Jesuits such as Pérez de Ribas remained committed to a "voluntarist theory of nature": God gives order as well as deviation from order; everything in the world is subordinate to and subservient to the will of God (Heimann 1990:394–95). Arguably, in 1645 the most influential theological exponent of this theory was still Augustine, whose writings appear both in the text and margin notes of the Historia.[8] Augustine held that God's presence and design were everywhere to be seen, including in the laws of nature. Paradoxically, it was the very regularity and predictability of God's creation, implying a designer and engineer, that lulled humankind into a stupor with respect to God's enduring presence (Dods 1948:1:219).

Pérez de Ribas and his Jesuit contemporaries accepted without question Augustine's teachings on the enduring presence of an omnipotent and inscrutable God. It is precisely for this reason that Pérez de Ribas often put invisible "truths" and first and final causes (God and God's often inscrutable intention) ahead of the material causes that we—as heirs of the Enlightenment—have given precedence. Readers will find that the Historia abounds in wonderfully detailed descrip-

tions based on empirical observation, which invariably end with God as their causal explanation. Along these lines it is significant that Pérez de Ribas concluded almost every discussion of the workings of nature in the Historia with an interpretation that posited God's handiwork. In Book 1, Chapter 1, for instance, Pérez de Ribas concluded his description of the physical environment of Sinaloa with a detailed discussion of an unusual bird and tree, noting how both reflected divine truths. With respect to the bird, which becomes a metaphor for the Jesuits and their nurturing mission to the Indians of Sinaloa, he commented:

> Who gave this bird the skill to weave such a deep nest, which is held firmly in place by only a few strands of grass? Even with the continuous weight of the chicks the strands do not loosen or break. The answer to this marvelous puzzle of nature is the wisdom of God, its maker. It is He who endowed this little bird with the capacity and design to rear its chicks in the open air so that the serpents and snakes could not reach its nest, and it is for this reason, some argue, that God gave this instinct and ability to this little bird. To this we can add that through these marvels of nature God meant to delight, entertain, and manifest His divine goodness toward mankind.

Augustine taught that God was constantly tinkering with and at times radically upsetting natural law. In this light miracles were not really a violation of God's laws but a reaffirmation of their existence; they were God's way of reminding humankind that he would never permit the human race to be without his wisdom and power (Dods 1948:1:219). Jesuit missionaries accepted this teaching as well as the scholastic method and text tradition, which shied away from experiment and experience, both of which could be deceptive. Perhaps more important was Saint Thomas Aquinas' observation that reason (inference from observation)—however uncorrupted it might be—could only establish things that already were known. That which we need to know is disguised in mysteries that become intelligible only by increasing the "dim light" of the soul (Wilson 1990:92–93). Other Jesuit favorite writers like Thomas à Kempis (1955 [1427]:195) and such influential figures of the Counter-Reformation as Saint Teresa also advised against too heavy a reliance on the application of reason to experience (Cohen 1957:127; MacCormack 1991; Weber 1992).

As Jesuits, the missionaries who populate the Historia were trained and "formed" to make sense of the world around them only with reference to God; for them to have dropped God from the equation would be analogous to our abandoning the "laws" of nature

---

7. Note that key figures in the development of mechanistic philosophy—Bacon and later Newton—saw God as more than a first efficient cause and believed that a "spiritually informed" reading of the world remained a prerequisite of true knowledge (Wilson 1990). Of course, Bacon's and Newton's privileging of God and "spiritual reading" is not what was celebrated during the seventeenth and eighteenth centuries.

8. Augustine's works as well as those of Gregory the Great and Caesarius of Arles, who elaborated on Augustine's worldview, were prescribed reading for Jesuit novices and scholastics (de Guibert 1964:216). The Jesuits were at the forefront of the revival of patristic studies during the sixteenth and seventeenth centuries (Martin 1993).

or the mathematical models with which we summarize and express causality. Throughout the *Historia*—when churches are destroyed by floods, priests are martyred, or Indians are baptized and then struck dead by lightning—Pérez de Ribas concluded that such events teach us to praise God's judgments, "which are always just, even though human discourse may not always fathom their purpose and exalted ends." The very fact that Pérez de Ribas titled his work a "history of the triumphs of our holy faith" reflects his belief that Jesuit success in Nueva España was in the first instance due to divine providence and only secondarily to the heroic efforts of the Jesuit missionary. As Evennett (1968:37) pointed out some years ago, it was not for nothing that the Jesuits chose as their motto "to the greater glory of God" (*Ad majorem Dei gloria*).

While Pérez de Ribas frequently gave voice to what was essentially an Augustinian or hagiographic conception of the hero as semi-passive agent of God (Heffernan 1988:143), the *Historia* also is filled with narrative scenes of charity and individual choice. The promise of salvation was realized not simply or largely because God chose to cooperate or "descend" but because Jesuits and Indians chose to "ascend" to God through reason and good works. Indeed, the Jesuits' very self-definition as an activist order—preaching the word of God, doing works of charity, and proactively administering the sacraments—presupposed that human beings played a dynamic role in their own salvation and that of others. Human beings could and should do a great deal to save themselves and others, but ultimately they could do so only with God's cooperation.

Of all the laudatory comments that Fray Alonso de la Corte offered in his letter of approval, which precedes Pérez de Ribas' narrative, perhaps the most flattering from a Jesuit perspective was that "the book is a faithful copy of the Acts of the Apostles and those holy missions recorded by the evangelist Saint Luke." As O'Malley (1993a:372) has pointed out, the Spiritual Exercises of Ignatius Loyola encouraged the Jesuit to imagine himself a contemporary of Christ and to see his life as a continuation of the apostolic model. In concrete terms this meant preaching, healing the sick (in body and soul), and living a life of poverty and continual sharing. Consistent with his religious training and formation, Pérez de Ribas absolutely believed (see Book 1, Chapter 7) that the Jesuit experience in Mexico was not a unique historical experience but rather a fulfillment of prophesy and a reiteration of the apostolic model celebrated in the Gospels and Paul's Epistles,

and left "in process" by Luke at the end of Acts.[9] This identification with the apostles is apparent in his "Prologue to the Reader" and his "Letter . . . to the Very Reverend Fathers of the Company of Jesus," where he likened himself unto Paul writing to the Corinthians. Throughout the *Historia* Pérez de Ribas spoke of the "plenteous harvests of souls" and the "abundant fruits of the vineyard," evoking time-honored rhetorical formulas that established an essential unity between the Jesuit experience in Mexico and the nascent Church. As indicated, the *Historia* also abounds in margin notes as well as textual passages where Pérez de Ribas drew parallels between the Jesuit and apostolic experience. He often commented, for instance, on how the Jesuits were able to master Indian languages in a remarkably short period of time, evidencing the gift of tongues that was promised the apostles by the resurrected Christ.

Jesuit identification with the apostles was more than hyperbole. Pérez de Ribas and other Jesuits who served in Nueva España all were volunteers who requested a missionary assignment.[10] In so doing they consciously opted for a difficult life quite unlike the comfortable and secure life enjoyed by many priests in Spain (Defourneaux 1979:106–8). This point is illustrated in Book 2, Chapter 31, where Pérez de Ribas cited a letter in which Father Pedro de Velasco pleaded with the Jesuit provincial not to be recalled from the frontier for a teaching position in Mexico City. Velasco was the son of the former governor of Nueva Vizcaya and the nephew of the viceroy of Nueva España. Velasco's powerful and influential family apparently pressured the Jesuit provincial to have the younger Velasco transferred. Like other missionaries, Velasco knew the chances were excellent that he would die a martyr on the frontier, yet he still opposed his transfer to Mexico City.

Although today we tend to dismiss as fanatics those individuals who pursue or are comfortable with martyrdom, the term obscures rather than clarifies human thought and behavior. Missionaries like Velasco pursued a vocation in Nueva España and accepted martyrdom as part of that because they believed they were

9. Luke ends the Acts of the Apostles with Paul imprisoned in Rome and his fate unknown. As Gundry (1970:210–11) has suggested, the very abruptness with which Acts ends symbolizes the unfinished task of worldwide evangelization.

10. The normal procedure was for a Jesuit to petition his provincial superior for a mission assignment; particularly zealous Jesuits often wrote the father general in Rome (de Guibert 1964:287; Martin 1988; Shiels 1939).

living out their lives in fulfillment of prophecy, continuing the work of Christ and his disciples. The descent of the Holy Spirit on the apostles was not simply a cherished historical event for Jesuits like Velasco and Pérez de Ribas. Arguably, most every Jesuit missionary had experienced a moment (relived each year by making the Spiritual Exercises) when they heard God's voice and felt his grace, prompting them to take up Christ's cross and ministry without regard for their own lives.[11] Death has always been the gateway to life for those who accept Christ's resurrection (Ward 1992:xxii)–even the saints' feast days commemorate the day they died rather than the day they were born. Thus, Pérez de Ribas and other Jesuit missionaries cast themselves as apostles for more than just the rhetorical reason of "pleasing" their audience by using a privileged, authoritative metaphor.

In his "Letter . . . to the Very Reverend Fathers of the Company of Jesus," Pérez de Ribas cited I Corinthians 16, noting how the Jesuits endured the same hardships and battled the same enemies as those identified by the apostle Paul. The chief enemy of Christ and his disciples was, of course, the devil. During the Counter-Reformation, medieval images and concepts regarding the devil's role in promoting sin were reworked and given new emphasis (Aizpuru 1989:98; Cervantes 1991; Cox 1994; Cruz and Perry 1992; de Certeau 1992:261; Evennett 1968; Russell 1984, 1986). The devil's role in human affairs was instilled in the Jesuits during their education and spiritual formation. For instance, in the Spiritual Exercises the novice was encouraged to meditate at length on how the devil and his legion of demons set snares throughout the world, enticing people to sin (Ganss 1991:155). This theme was a constant in Loyola's writings (Martin 1988:159) and was more elaborately developed by Thomas Aquinas (Russell 1984:107, f.206; Trevor-Roper 1967:17–18), whose works were specifically recommended in the Jesuit Constitutions (Ganss 1970:219). In his *Summa contra gentiles* and *Summa theologica*, Aquinas (1945) detailed how the devil and his army of demons were capable of creating innumerable illusions that were observable to the senses, including assuming or possessing a body—all in an effort to promote sin.

Works of demonology such as the *Malleus maleficarum* (Kramer and Sprenger 1971 [1487]) as well as

ecclesiastical rulings (e.g., the papal bull *Summis desiderantes affectibus*) also were important sources of prior interpretation for missionaries (Dunne 1951:131). For instance, in Book 5 Pérez de Ribas acknowledged that the Jesuits used Martin del Rio's *Disquisitionum magicarum libri sex in tres tomos partiti* (Six Books of Research on Magic Divided into Three Volumes) to interpret and describe Yaqui beliefs and ritual.[12] Rio's opus was one of the most influential books on demonology in seventeenth-century Europe (Caro Baroja 1978:56)

The Jesuits and most other religious orders were convinced that the devil was everywhere setting snares and no Christian was safe from Satan's machinations (Aizpuru 1989:98; Benavides 1916 [1630]:30–31; Burkhart 1989:40; Dunne 1951:129; Duran 1971:247; Elliott 1989:59; Keber 1988; MacCormack 1991; Ruiz de Montoya 1892 [1639]:32). This was particularly true in the New World, where Satan had frightened away the holy angels and had ruled unchallenged for millennia (see Book 5, Chapter 20). Throughout the *Historia* Pérez de Ribas quoted Indian informants to the effect that the devil frequently had appeared to them prior to their conversion to Christianity. The devil did not flee with the Jesuits' arrival but rather was a constant source of Indian opposition to baptism and conversion. As discussed in more detail below, this battle with the devil is precisely how Pérez de Ribas perceived and represented the dynamics of Jesuit-Indian relations.

While the Jesuits feared the devil, they never doubted (except perhaps in private) a favorable outcome in their many battles with Satan and his Indian familiars, the dreaded *hechiceros*, or Indian shamans.[13] It was understood that divine providence would come to the aid of the missionary even if it meant the crown of martyrdom. In Book 6, Chapter 15, Pérez de Ribas was quite explicit in this regard:

> It is worth emphasizing here that which often has been noted concerning these missions: God's gentle providence, through various and illustrious means, has freed His preachers from innumerable dangers among these people. And if on some occasions He permits the enemy to attack,

---

11. This is often the most dramatic moment in medieval hagiography, when the saint-to-be is addressed by God or the Virgin, and then embarks on a life of contemplation and good deeds, aided by regular infusions of grace.

12. Although Pérez de Ribas does not indicate which Jesuit(s) used Río's texts on magic, he and Tomás Basilio were the founders of the Yaqui mission.

13. Cervantes (1991) has drawn attention to important intellectual shifts in the sixteenth century that transformed the devil into a more dynamic and insidious opponent, relative to his role in the late Middle Ages. However, the devil's status fluctuated throughout the history of Christianity. During times of uncertainty when Catholic confidence was shaken, such as the Reformation in Europe or Indian uprisings in the New World, the devil became a much more feared opponent.

it is in order to crown His preachers. This dispensation comes from a Lord who knows how to give His servants the strength to scorn death out of love for Him. He is always attentive to whatever affects them, and they are very much under His care and protection. This is of singular consolation to evangelical laborers.

Readers of the *Historia* will find that divine providence did indeed manifest itself in many ways on the mission frontier. For instance, in Book 5 after a lengthy, empirically based account of several battles where the Yaqui soundly defeated Spanish troops and thousands of Indian allies, Pérez de Ribas attributed the Yaqui's sudden change in attitude to their guardian angels, who frightened them into suing for peace and baptism. In the same book Pérez de Ribas drew a parallel between Balaam in the Book of Numbers and Yaqui shamans, suggesting that God himself intervened on the Río Yaqui, transforming its sorcerers from obstacles into proponents of baptism. Elsewhere in Book 3 (Chapters 21 and 22), he recounted how the Jesuits had been favored by the miraculous intercession of Saint Ignatius. Chapter 8 of Book 7 is given over entirely to a discussion of miracles with which God helped the missionaries, including the gift of tongues (mastering Indian languages), protecting them from the Indians' poisoned arrows and concoctions, and transforming the Indians themselves into willing recipients of the word of God.

In sum, Jesuits such as Pérez de Ribas saw themselves as being on a mission from God and were quite convinced that demons, saints, angels, and God intervened regularly in human affairs. Significantly, the Jesuits' epistemology and fundamental beliefs were shared by native peoples, who also believed in an activist God and the inseparability of the natural and invisible worlds. Furthermore, certain of the Indians' own images and symbols, including their mythical portrayal of supernaturals who were black, were consistent with the missionaries' Counter-Reformation notions of the devil and his active participation in human affairs (Reff 1995; Simmons 1980:17). Ironically, the Indians' symbolism and rhetoric concerning supernaturals who were black or who otherwise corresponded to the European image of the devil affirmed the missionaries' self-definition as soldiers sent by God to America to wage a war of liberation against the devil.

LITERARY AND RHETORICAL CONTINGENCIES

It was during his years in the university and as a novice that Pérez de Ribas became enamored of certain literary models and manners of expression that would govern the inscription of meaning in the *Historia*. His manner of expression was prefigured by Latin classics on the wars of Hannibal and the prose of Cassiodorus, the Bible (particularly the Gospels and Paul's Epistles), hagiography, sacred and Renaissance history, and the sermon, which was based on the classical oration. Sacred literature, in particular, provided the building blocks of Jesuit discourse—the concepts, conventions, and other signifying practices that resonated with members of the Society and the much larger political and institutional context of which it was a part, namely the Church and state.

The *Historia* as History

The fact that Pérez de Ribas titled his work a "history" implies that the genre was significant in terms of his perceived authorial function (Mignolo 1982). Historians and anthropologists have assumed that Pérez de Ribas worked with the Renaissance and modern definition of the genre (White 1973:163–90). Judged by this standard—"the unadorned reporting of things" (Nelson 1973:40)—Pérez de Ribas has been found wanting and indeed has been criticized for exaggerating or disregarding the facts (e.g., Astrain 1902:4:xvii; Bancroft 1886:235; Dunne 1951:135–36). Significantly, in his "Prologue to the Reader," which appears to have been written with crown officials in mind,[14] Pérez de Ribas was explicit about his allegiance to the historical-critical method that characterizes modern academic historiography. After citing Lucian's classic work *How to Write History* (Kilburn 1958), he went on to acknowledge that history is a narration of events "that demand that their truth be supported by a clear and truthful style, without affectation, minced words, or embellishments."[15] Anticipating Gibbon and Leopold von Ranke, the founders of modern, empirical historiography, Pérez de Ribas noted:

14. The Prologue to the Reader abounds in military metaphors and goes out of its way to link spiritual and temporal concerns; that is, conversion and conquest. However, its rhetoric and tone are not characteristic of the ensuing narrative.

15. Pérez de Ribas' respect for Lucian clearly applied only or largely to Lucian's views on how to write history, as Lucian considered the Christians of late antiquity credulous simpletons (Barnes 1991:235).

The narrator of this history is an eyewitness to many of the events that are related herein, having touched them with his own hands (as they say). He spent sixteen years laboring in these missions, instructing some of these gentiles. He also accompanied the captains and soldiers from the garrisons on their expeditions to pacify these gentiles, and he dealt with many of the first priests who founded these missions. Furthermore, he learned the languages of these nations and dealt with many of their *caciques* and most knowledgeable Indians. Those things to which he was not an eyewitness he has taken from very reliable original [sources].

Pérez de Ribas did indeed make extensive use of Jesuit correspondence and eyewitness testimony. The *Historia* also is replete with detailed, empirical descriptions of Indian behaviors and beliefs. At the same time and by his own admission, Pérez de Ribas' history is about "the triumphs of our holy faith." In the midst of his rhetoric privileging empirical observation, truthfulness, and clarity, he commented:

> Because this history deals with divine events, it is not merely a dry account recorded by a secular notary concerning some fortunate or disastrous case, nor is it the record of a crime and its punishment. Rather, this history is one of cases involving divine circumstances that were novel, remarkable, and of Christian edification. I do make an effort, however, to keep these asides brief so that they will not impede the flow of this history.

It is debatable whether the asides are brief; their number certainly is not small. The *Historia* abounds in cases of divine "circumstances" as well as demonic interference. Of course, it is difficult to convey the divine in words, as Galahad noted upon peering into the Holy Grail: "For now I see revealed what tongue could not relate nor heart conceive" (Matarasso 1969:283). To convey the presence of God, the Holy Spirit, or demonic possession, Pérez de Ribas had to disregard the Renaissance (and modern) ideal of history as unadorned facts. The immediate reality of the invisible world—miracles, the appearance of saints or angels, and demonic possession—is a nonordinary state. It can be conveyed only using highly metaphorical language and rhetorical strategies characteristic of medieval hagiography, such as hyperbole (exaggeration; e.g., "he never missed his prayers") and *superlatio* (exaggerated comparison; e.g., "whiter than snow") (Heffernan 1988; Nichols 1983).[16]

Because of Pérez de Ribas' paramount concern with

the divine, the *Historia* is both an empirically based and "universal" history. Universal history, which became popular during the late Middle Ages (Nichols 1983), had much in common with hagiography in that it emphasized how historical events rephrased significant past events as recorded in Scripture, thus revealing God's enduring presence and plan.[17] Whereas a modern reader might be put off by the mixing of the two models of history, Pérez de Ribas' epistemology logically permitted discussing the invisible alongside the empirically observable and the supernatural alongside the natural. Like Augustine, Pérez de Ribas appreciated the "disinterested" and empirical imperatives of Livy, Lucian, and Plato. Nevertheless, he was committed to the notion of an omnipotent and ubiquitous God, and thus he privileged the divine in his thinking and writing.

The Influence of the Bible

It is no surprise that the Bible was an important literary model for Pérez de Ribas, who not incidentally divided the *Historia* into twelve books, corresponding with the number of apostles.[18] The manner in which Pérez de Ribas quotes the Vulgate (e.g., occasionally leaving out a word or two, changing verb tenses) suggests that he had studied the New Testament and parts of the Old Testament so thoroughly that he was confident about quoting the Bible from memory. Like medieval theologians, he understood the Bible to be meaningful in a literal as well as a figurative sense; Christ's life and death are both chronicled in the Gospels and anticipated symbolically in the Old Testament, particularly in Psalms and Isaiah (Marrow 1979:190–91; Petersen 1984:25ff.). Similarly, in the *Historia* Pérez de Ribas both chronicled the Jesuit experience and interpreted it typologically (Phelan 1970:6–8), portraying events in Mexico as the fulfillment or reiteration of events described or prophesied in Scripture. For instance, on a number of occasions Pérez de Ribas drew on the Old Testament for metaphors and similes to characterize the Indians' heathen existence prior to the arrival of the Jesuits. This is the case at the outset of Book 2:

> Now for our purposes, I tell you that our Province of Sinaloa was in the same abyss of darkness in which we left

16. As if to betray his reliance on hagiography, Pérez de Ribas used the expression "having touched them with his own hands (as they say)" to establish his authority as an author; the expression was used in early hagiographies such as the passions of Perpetua and Felicitas (Musurillo 1972:109).

17. During Pérez de Ribas' lifetime universal history often was referred to as divine or sacred history (Kelley 1991:375).

18. As Dunne (1951) has noted, the subject matter of Book 12 is somewhat extraneous; one almost gets the impression that Pérez de Ribas felt compelled to write and include a twelfth book.

it in Book I, a veritable kingdom of Satan that resisted the light of the Gospel. Its gentile nations were hardened in their obstinacy, like the statue of stone and bronze that King Nebuchadnezzar saw in his dreams. There thus came a time unknown to mankind when divine will determined to end the tyrannical reign of the devil in Sinaloa. . . . Divine providence arranged for all this by means of a particular knight who, fortunately for the entire Kingdom of Nueva Vizcaya (especially our Province of Sinaloa, which lies within its jurisdiction) began to govern in the year 1590. . . . With the practice of Christianity in which he occupied himself, he seemed to me to be the very image of the patriarch Abraham, whom God had placed in the lands [of Canaan] for the refuge and aid of travelers.

The story of the Gospels—of God sending his only begotten son to humbly preach the good news of salvation, battling the devil, working miracles, and then giving his life for an unappreciative audience—essentially was reproduced by Pérez de Ribas with his narration of each advance of the mission frontier. The Epistles of Paul, the "original" Apostle to the Gentiles, were likewise important as a literary model. Pérez de Ribas' indebtedness to Paul is apparent in his weaving together into one grand narrative innumerable letters of Jesuit contemporaries. These *cartas de edificación*—letters bearing information as well as a message of hope and sacrifice—were a hallmark of the Jesuits and, again, were inspired in part by Paul's Epistles.[19] Throughout the *Historia* Pérez de Ribas explicitly drew parallels between the apostle Paul and the Jesuit missionary, noting for instance that the demons the Jesuits encountered in Nueva España were precisely those discussed by Paul in his letter to the Ephesians.

The Bible served not only as a literary model but also as a source of rhetorical strategies and conventions—a literary "tool chest" with which Pérez de Ribas crafted his narrative of the Jesuit mission experience. Like many New World missionaries (see O'Meara 1992), he was particularly fond of garden and vineyard metaphors, repetitively casting the Jesuits as workers in the vineyard of the Lord.[20] As noted, Pérez de Ribas actually cast himself as Paul writing to the Corinthians. Much like the apostle Paul (Wuellner 1979), he frequently used digression to amass various points in support of an argument (e.g., Book 2 and his defense

of Jesuit reliance on garrisons). And much like Paul as well as the later Doctors of the Church (e.g., Augustine, John Chrysostom, Gregory the Great), he used sophisticated argument and rhetoric (e.g., diatribe, aside) to advance positions that, paradoxically, privileged faith over reason (Cameron 1991:33–35).

The influence of the Bible is further apparent in Pérez de Ribas' extensive use of the "narrative event"—passages where he broke off the narration and shifted dramatically to direct speech. This preferred technique of biblical and Greco-Roman[21] authors (Alter 1981:63ff.) often was used to highlight the rhetorical battles that the missionaries fought (and "won") with Indian shamans. Through this device Pérez de Ribas was able to create the illusion of polyphony, seemingly quoting "informants" while actually orchestrating their appearance in the text (Clifford 1986:15). Also in keeping with the Bible, particularly Luke's rendering of Stephen's death in the Acts of the Apostles, are instances where the direct discourse of Indian converts echoes the sentiments if not the words of Christ himself. In Chapter 10 of Book 2, for instance, Pérez de Ribas quoted a dying Indian woman's last words to her friend—words that echoed Christ's promise to his apostles in John 16:5-19: "Then she turned to another Indian woman who was one of her companions and stated clearly, 'Mary, today thou shalt see me and afterwards thou shalt not see me again. I am going with God, I am going to see God.'" Note the woman's direct discourse ("thou shalt see me"), which serves to drive home Pérez de Ribas' point about the magnitude of the positive change wrought by the Holy Spirit. Elsewhere in the *Historia* Pérez de Ribas employed rhetoric and type scenes from the Gospels to characterize Jesuit martyrs and apostate Indians:

He was thirty-three when he died, in the flower of his youth, at the same age as the Son of God. He left a well-established enterprise, in which he had labored for only four years. The day and year of his martyrdom and the marvelous posture in which his body were found was recorded in Chapter VIII of this book. Father Tapia had a very pleasant appearance and disposition, and due to this and his temperament, they called him The Angel. In fact, a rumor spread among the Indians that he had come from heaven, and they say that one of those who killed him, upon seeing him dead, stopped to speak with him and said, "If you came from heaven, why are you allowing yourself to be killed?" In this we can believe

19. Of course, the Epistle also was a favorite of Greco-Roman authors. Pérez de Ribas' extensive use of it also reflected Ignatius Loyola's directive to his followers always to share their experiences with one another through regular correspondence.

20. Isaiah 5 ("The song of the vineyard") is one of many instances in the Bible where the vineyard metaphor is used (see NJB 1985:1197ff.).

21. Through the convention of the narrative event, Livy incorporated speeches in his historical narratives to portray characters and represent opposing motives; in this way he could present the anti-Roman view without risk of appearing unpatriotic (Bechtel 1906:10-11).

that God has crowned him and raised him to the highest ranks of glory, which he will enjoy for all eternity. (Book 2, Chapter 39)

Note in this instance that Tapia's murderers uttered essentially the same taunt that was leveled at Christ as he was dying on the cross (cf. Matthew 27:40; Mark 15:29–32; Luke 23:35).

Arguably, if we were to interrogate Pérez de Ribas today, he would probably acknowledge that he did not know for a fact whether Tapia's murderers used the direct discourse that he reported. He would at the same time probably wonder why we were so concerned or troubled by such "details." Did we doubt that a Jesuit missionary like Tapia, upon taking up Christ's cross and ministry, endured similar trials and tribulations? It is not important, Pérez de Ribas would perhaps argue, whether Tapia was taunted in the same way as Christ—to indicate as much was simply to convey the "fact" (perceived as such by a Jesuit missionary) that Tapia's life and career paralleled Christ's experience.

What we today might consider "borrowing" Pérez de Ribas would perhaps argue was his best way (given his epistemology, theology, audience, and literary tradition) of conveying truths that were partially ineffable— namely that the Jesuit experience was a reiteration of the apostolic model, which at the level of the individual missionary meant becoming an instrument of God and, thus, Christ-like.

Hagiography as a Literary Model

The quoting of a subject who echoed the words of Christ is a characteristic literary convention of medieval hagiography (Heffernan 1988:78–79). The lives of the saints were enormously popular in Europe during Pérez de Ribas' lifetime, and not insignificantly, it was the Bollandists and other Jesuits who took the lead in publishing sacred biographies for a popular as well as a scholarly audience (Martin 1993:88, 101, 103).[22] The *Vitae Patrum*, which contained the biographies of early

martyrs of the Church and later confessor saints, were prescribed reading for novices and played a central role in Jesuit religious formation.[23] Accordingly, throughout the *Historia* Pérez de Ribas employed metaphors and epithets from hagiography, including references to the devil as "the enemy," "the infernal beast," "mankind's most ferocious enemy," or a "demonic kinsman," among others. References to the devil's snares and prey are as common in the *Historia* as they are in Saint Athanasius' *Life of Saint Anthony* (Keenan 1952:138, 156, 167). So too are metaphors of blindness and sight, and darkness and light, which convey the lack or presence of grace or Christian faith, metaphors that abound in medieval texts (Delehaye 1907; Elliott 1987; Weinstein and Bell 1982).

Hagiography provided not only the most basic units of meaning (e.g., metaphors, similes) but also a narrative structure with which to re-create the lives of pioneer Jesuit missionaries. For instance, in his account of the life and career of Father Gonzalo de Tapia (Book 2, Chapter 39), Pérez de Ribas quoted a letter from Tarascan Indians who knew and loved Father Tapia. The letter's narrative structure and rhetoric are strikingly similar to the Martyrdom of Polycarp, which is among the oldest of the formal Acts of the Martyrs (Glimm, Joseph, and Walsh 1969).[24] More generally, Pérez de Ribas followed hagiographic convention by giving first a chronological (birth, family, education, religious formation, early career) and then qualitative review of a priest's life and career (Robertson 1995:136). In keeping with late medieval/Renaissance trends, which emphasized a saint's exemplary life rather than miracles (Goodich 1982:30–31), the qualitative or topical portion of Pérez de Ribas' narrative emphasized a priest's virtues rather than miracles. Still, there is no shortage in the *Historia* of miracles and other supernatural type scenes, many of which were borrowed from early hagiography (Elliott 1987:63; Weinstein and Bell 1982:147).[25] For instance, one reads of Jesuits who were

22. The Bollandists, named after their leader (Jean Bolland) were a group of Jesuits in Antwerp who around 1640 began compiling, critiquing, and then publishing authoritative lives of the saints. After 1590, when Claudius Acquaviva became the father general and head of the Jesuit order, he urged his fellow Jesuits to be less timid about their illuminism and to write more works of a devotional and meditational nature (de Certeau 1992:250–51; Martin 1993:93). Pérez de Ribas' *Historia* reflects this imperative, as it often speaks of Jesuits who maintained devout conversations with God and who were touched in some way directly by God.

23. This importance stemmed from tradition, beginning with Augustine's account of his own conversion upon reading the Life of Saint Anthony. Of perhaps greater significance was Ignatius Loyola's account of how his own life was forever changed by his reading of Ludolph's *Life of Christ* and the *Flos Sanctorum*, which was a Spanish-language edition of Jacobus de Voragine's compilation of saint's lives (Ganss 1991:15).

24. Another notable parallel between Tapia and Polycarp is that when their respective assailants tried to set fire to them (in Tapia's case, to his severed arm), neither would burn.

25. Early hagiographic texts (e.g., *Vita of Saint Martin*) recount so many miracles that they often have been rejected out of hand as total fictions.

informed of their impending death by bleeding altar-cloths, or of Jesuit martyrs whose bodies—or body parts—remained incorruptible following death. Similarly, the *Historia* recounts an instance where a hungry priest, because of his faith, was satiated by a rabbit that fell from the sky.

Significantly, Jesuit missionaries may well have perceived that hagiography was relevant in a way that modern readers have not appreciated. As Valerie Flint (1991) has pointed out, medieval hagiography recounts more than miracles and the in-breaking of the divine; it recounts a very real struggle between Christian missionaries and non-Christian magi or shamans of pagan Europe. This struggle was coincident with the dissolution of the Roman Empire and profound dislocations resulting from invasions and pandemics (e.g., the Justinian plague), all of which weakened the authority of paganism and the magi. In point of fact the challenges that medieval missionaries confronted and overcame, realizing or evidencing sainthood in the process, were quite similar to the challenges that missionaries faced in the New World (Flint 1991; McNeill 1976; Phelan 1970:92). In Nueva España, for instance, the Jesuits, like their medieval counterparts, worked principally with native societies that had experienced epidemics and other profound dislocations coincident with the conquest. Like their medieval counterparts, the Jesuits' chief enemies were the Indian shamans or magi. The Jesuits directly challenged these religious leaders and just as often employed the favored strategy of medieval saints, substituting Christian for pagan rituals and practices. An example of this parallelism can be found in Book 1, where Pérez de Ribas recounted how Father Gonzalo de Tapia replaced a tree that was being worshiped by the Acaxee Indians with a cross. Sulpicius Severus' *Life of Saint Martin*, which was on the *Ratio studorium* or prescribed reading list for Jesuit novices (de Guibert 1964:216), similarly recounted an incident of tree worship among pagan Europeans, which Saint Martin dealt with in the same way Father Tapia did (Hoare 1954). In Chapter 30 of Book 2, Pérez de Ribas explicitly commented that the Jesuits gave their Indian converts crosses to ward off the devil because the crosses were "the divine remedy that the saints used in their fights with this wild beast." Elsewhere (Book 3, Chapter 21) Pérez de Ribas noted that Jesuits translated the *Flos Sanctorum* (a book of short biographies of saints) into Indian languages. Thus, medieval hagiography served not only as a literary model and source

of metaphors and conventions but also as a guide to what was perhaps the greatest challenge to both Old and New World missionaries—combating shamanism, otherwise termed sorcery (Phelan 1970:92).

The Sermon and *Novelas de Caballería*

The influence of two additional literary models can be perceived in the *Historia*. While not as important as the Bible or hagiography, they nevertheless influenced the form and content of the narrative. The first of these models, the sermon, was all the rage in seventeenth-century Europe (Barnes-Karol 1992). All priests were required during Mass to deliver a homily or brief exposition of a Gospel text. However, it was primarily members of religious orders who gave the sermons, which were generally preached on Sundays and feast days and tended to last thirty minutes to an hour. Importantly, the Jesuits perhaps more than any other religious order instilled in their members the importance of mastering the sermon, particularly sermons modeled after classical oration and consistent with humanist theories of rhetoric (Noel 1985; O'Malley 1993a:98; Smith 1978).

Quite unlike the scholastic sermon (*artes predicandi*), which relied heavily on the citation and explication of authorities, the sermons and "talks" delivered by Jesuit preachers employed a variety of rhetorical strategies that were designed to touch the heart as well as the mind. The goal of the preacher was not simply to inform but to *reform*—to get the audience not simply to ponder alternative truths but to act on them. As Adorno (1986:78) has observed, the sermon is a particularly effective literary model for authors who wish to impress upon their readers certain facts or conclusions. The structure of the sermon is such that the reader is purposefully guided through direct discourse to certain points of view. It is precisely for this reason that Pérez de Ribas used the sermon or classical oration as a literary model. More specifically, the sermon is particularly evident in chapters devoted to "political" issues that were of utmost importance to the Jesuit Province of Nueva España. This is the case, for example, in Book 7, Chapter 2, which is entitled "An examination and declaration of the capacity of these barbarous peoples to receive the doctrine of our Holy Faith." By the mid-seventeenth century many Spaniards, particularly the king's deputies who were struggling with bankruptcy, questioned the huge sums of money that the crown was spending on missionaries in the New World, particularly in light of Indian uprisings and other evidence that the Indians retained many of their "heathen" behaviors and beliefs. At the outset of Chapter 2, Pérez de Ribas implicitly invoked these potential Jesuit critics, noting that it is not surprising that some would question whether people as barbarous as those in Nueva España were capable of grasping Christian truths and thus whether the fruits of Jesuit labor could ever be sufficient to justify the cost. Having raised the issue, Pérez de Ribas responded with the *expositio*, or theme of his sermon/chapter: "God did not exclude any people—great or small, high or low—from the Gospel and salvation; his instructions to the apostles and those who followed them were to go forth and preach to all men." In what is analogous to the *narración* portion of a sermon, Pérez de Ribas cited the major scriptural authority for his sermon, specifically Mark 9, which says, "Go out to the whole world; proclaim the Gospel to all creation." He then proceeded to enumerate various confirmations of this proposition, particularly its inclusiveness with respect to the Indians of Nueva España. In doing so, he employed the rhetorical strategy of *concepto predicable*, implicitly equating, for instance, the angels who were sent to inform the rustic shepherds of Christ's birth with the Jesuits, who brought the message of Christ's birth and salvation to the Indians. After advancing similar proofs that the Jesuit enterprise was sanctioned by Scripture, Pérez de Ribas—in what is in effect the *epílogo*—returned to his opening theme: Christ commanded that his Gospel be preached to everyone, including those who were "rude" and "ignorant."

The *Historia* also bespeaks another very different but no less popular literary model, the *novela de caballería* (parodied in *Don Quixote*). The influence of the chivalric novel is perhaps most apparent in Books 2 and 10, which focus at length on the exploits of Spanish military captains who assisted and defended Jesuit missionaries. In Book 2 Pérez de Ribas wrote at length about the many adventures of his good friend Captain Diego Martínez de Hurdaide. This narrative within a narrative is characterized by vivid descriptions, suspense, miraculous escapes, and joyous returns. Although Pérez de Ribas almost dutifully acknowledges that Hurdaide was favored by divine providence, the effect of his rhetoric is that the captain's many successes were due to his bravery, ingenuity, and knowledge of the Indian, which were acquired through a lifetime of experience on the frontier. Pérez de Ribas did deviate from the chivalric novel, however, in portraying the captain as a

man moved by a love for the Church rather than by a fair maiden or feudal lord.[26]

The chivalric novel was perhaps also the source of the castle metaphor and related military terms with which Pérez de Ribas frequently represented the Jesuit mission enterprise. Throughout the *Historia* he likened the Indians' souls unto castles possessed by the devil; the Jesuits were cast as Christ's militia, cavalry, or soldiers, marching into battle with the standard of the cross and confronting the devil's legions. Both Ignatius Loyola and Saint Teresa (in her influential work *The Interior Castle* [Ramge 1963:89ff]), made use of many of the same metaphors. Arguably, Pérez de Ribas deployed them in part to link the spiritual conquest of the New World with the already celebrated retaking of Spain from the Moors.[27] In Chapter 21 of Book 11, for instance, he commented:

> Those who write about worldly enterprises do not and should not forget the hardships suffered by soldiers in opening and back-filling trenches, erecting fortifications, etc. Although all those things are done to gain control of a piece of land, these other spiritual hardships are undertaken and embraced in order to cast the devil from his throne and gain heaven for souls.

THE POLITICAL AND INSTITUTIONAL CONTEXT OF JESUIT DISCOURSE

Pérez de Ribas' choices of literary models and rhetorical strategies would have resonated with most educated European Catholics of the seventeenth century. The audience for the *Historia* was, however, more narrowly defined by his political and institutional context: the Spanish crown and the Catholic Church (de Certeau 1992:18–19). Pérez de Ribas first became familiar with this political and institutional context as a missionary. In 1612, while he was still ministering to the

26. Pérez de Ribas never discussed the captain's wife or marital situation, although he did mention that the captain had a son. On several occasions in the text he mentions or alludes to Indian women who lived with the captain, apparently as servants. It is precisely Pérez de Ribas' silence or ambiguity concerning the captain's marital situation that is intriguing, particularly as the captain was otherwise discussed at great length and invariably represented as a very devout Catholic.

27. Pérez de Ribas and other Jesuits were no doubt also influenced by the writings of Bernard (ca. 1090–1153), the Cistercian monk and abbot of Clairvaux. In his writings, which were prescribed reading for Jesuit novices (de Guibert 1964), Bernard frequently employed military and chivalric terms (Robertson 1995:152–55). Patristic sources of the fourth century also are filled with military images (Harnack 1981:60).

Ahome of the lower Río Fuerte, he was summoned to Mexico City, where on the invitation of the father general in Rome, he retook his initial vows as well as a fourth vow, essentially committing himself to go anywhere at the request of the pope (Jacobsen 1938:87). With the assumption of these four vows Pérez de Ribas became a "professed" Jesuit, entitling him to leadership positions within the Society of Jesus.[28] The first such position came in 1619, when because of declining health[29] and his demonstrated abilities, he was summoned to Mexico City and assigned the rectorship of the Jesuit college for novices at Tepotzclán. There he remained until 1622, when he became secretary to the Jesuit provincial. In the years that followed, from 1626 to 1638, he served in various administrative positions (see table). In 1638 Pérez de Ribas began a three-year term as Jesuit provincial, the highest-ranking position within the Jesuit Province of Nueva España.

Pérez de Ribas' experience as both a missionary and Jesuit administrator provided him with firsthand knowledge of the missionary enterprise and its relationship to the Spanish crown and the Church, including the papacy, the episcopacy, other religious orders, and the Society of Jesus itself. These institutions, or rather their membership, constituted the audience for the *Historia*. One indication of this audience is the sheer physical volume itself. The *Historia* is in a large-folio format, suitable for a library and scholar's lectern, rather than in the form of an inexpensive pocket-sized *octavo*, targeted to the petty bourgeoisie (Martin 1993:73, 528). Its price (1,005 *maravedís*) was more than a month's wages for the majority of Spaniards (Elliott 1989:230). Upon opening the *Historia* one finds various letters and licenses of approval, testimony to the institutional constraints on Pérez de Ribas' representation of the Jesuit missions of Nueva España. These constraints operated not only with respect to what Pérez de Ribas discussed, and how, but also in terms of the "silences," the subjects he chose to discuss only indirectly or implicitly, if at all.

The Spanish Crown

Through a series of concessions from the papacy known as the *Patronato Real*,[30] the Spanish crown effectively controlled the appointment and financing of both secular and regular clergy in the New World. Regular clergy were those governed by a "rule," such as the Jesuits, Franciscans, and Dominicans. In theory and for the most part in practice, regular clergy answered to the crown and were free from the control of bishops. Secular priests were under the direct authority of bishops who, in turn, were appointed by the king and his deputies.

For both secular and regular priests, the crown, and more precisely the Council of the Indies, controlled who went to the Indies (through the issue of licenses). Along with this right went the responsibility of financing religious activity, including often the cost of travel to the New World.[31] Once he arrived in the New World, each missionary received an annual stipend from the crown; in the case of the Jesuits this generally amounted to 250 pesos (Zambrano 1961–1977:3:650). The Royal Treasury also furnished bells, chalices, vestments, and other costly items associated with priestly ministries and the functioning of a mission.[32]

At the time Pérez de Ribas penned the *Historia*, the Jesuits and other regular clergy had good reason to be concerned about crown policies and decisions that could negatively affect missionary enterprises in the Americas. Spain during the 1630s was in an almost constant state of crisis owing to population decline; a shrinking economy; a slump in the remittance of American silver; and costly wars in the Netherlands, Italy, and with France (Defourneaux 1979:91–96; Elliott 1989:125–33; Maravall 1986:149). In 1640 revolts by Catalonia and Portugal added further to the crown's woes, financial and otherwise. One consequence of Spain's wars and disputes with its neighbors was heightened fears that foreign spies might impede the already diminished flow of silver and other riches from Nueva España. (These fears were not without cause, as English and Dutch pirates

---

28. During the career of a Jesuit, his superior compiles performance reports, copies of which are sent to Rome. Individuals who receive advanced training and who subsequently demonstrate in their ministries good judgment and fidelity to their vows are chosen by the father general to become professed Jesuits. Only they can participate in provincial congregations or general congregations. The highest ranks of the order (e.g., provincial, visitor, general) also are reserved for them.

29. Pérez de Ribas' illness is not known. In a letter of 1622 from the Jesuit father general, he is listed as one of the priests who was allowed chocolate in the absence of medicine (Jacobsen 1938:88).

30. Papal concessions in 1501 and 1508 effectively made the Spanish king secular head of the Church in the New World. Chief among the concessions was crown control over ecclesiastical taxation and appointments (Haring 1947:166–69).

31. Included in this cost of travel was lodging and food for missionaries, who often spent months in Sevilla awaiting the departure of the next fleet.

32. The vestments alone included five different sets of chasubles, maniples, and stoles, each in a different color (black, green, purple, white, and red) for different functions and liturgical seasons (Dunne 1951:49).

regularly intercepted Spanish ships off the east and west coasts of Mexico.) During the 1640s Philip IV and his deputies imposed tighter restrictions on the appointment of non-Spanish missionaries to the New World.[33] These restrictions came at a time when religious vocations in Spain were declining and more and more priests were needed at home in Europe to check the Reformation and deal with mounting social ills (Maravall 1986:149). At the time the *Historia* was published, the Jesuits in Mexico as well as Paraguay, Peru, the Philippines, and other areas of the world faced a serious problem of staffing their expanding mission enterprises (Bannon 1955:118–27; Correia-Afonso 1969; Kamen 1985:200; Shiels 1939; Zambrano 1961–1977:6:572).[34]

As a former Jesuit provincial, Pérez de Ribas was well aware of the crown's power and influence as well as the financial woes that beset the Spanish monarchy. Philip IV and the men he appointed to Council of the Indies—those who passed judgment on Jesuit requests for money and men—were therefore an important part of Pérez de Ribas' audience. It is no coincidence that the title page of the *Historia* is immediately followed by a letter to the king of Spain in which Pérez de Ribas dedicated the work to the Spanish regent. The letter is characterized by a rhetoric of "physical presence" (e.g., "My Lord"), creating the illusion that Pérez de Ribas is actually addressing the king directly.[35] Pérez de Ribas wasted little time in pointing out in his letter that his history dealt with missions that were in lands richly endowed with silver, where peaceful Indian communities had been established under Jesuit tutelage and where both Indians and Spaniards freely worked and enjoyed the fruits of their labor. Philip IV and his deputies were all aware that northern Nueva España provided a large share of the silver that was brought from Veracruz to Spain by the annual treasure fleet.

In emphasizing the pacific nature of the Jesuit missions, Pérez de Ribas implicitly contrasted them with the once war-torn northern frontier, where raiding by bellicose and indomitable Chichimec Indians had previously cost the crown a small fortune in lost revenue (Bakewell 1971; Naylor and Polzer 1986; Powell 1952; Sheridan 1992). The idea that the Jesuits, or more precisely, almighty God *working through* the Jesuits, domesticated and civilized Indians who might otherwise have been as indomitable as the Chichimec runs throughout the *Historia*. Similarly, in his letter to the king, in the "Prologue to the Reader," and in the narrative itself Pérez de Ribas emphasized the Jesuits' close cooperation with civil-military officials. This ideal of Church and state working hand-in-hand was just that—an ideal; the reality was constant bickering and fighting between secular and spiritual authorities.[36] Arguably, the "Prologue to the Reader," which abounds in military metaphors and explicitly links secular and religious motives for the conquest, was written with crown officials in mind.[37] As noted, there are also several chapters in Part 1 that recount the heroic exploits of Captain Diego Martínez de Hurdaide, who invariably is depicted as consulting with and otherwise working closely with the Jesuits.[38] In Book 2 in particular, Pérez de Ribas often commented at length on the important role that governors, captains, and military garrisons played in the conversion of native peoples.

Pérez de Ribas' rhetoric of "domesticated" Indians under the careful stewardship of missionaries and civil-military officials, the latter busily working the silver mines of northern Nueva España, undoubtedly resonated with crown officials who were busy staving off bankruptcy.[39] However, one should not assume that the Spanish monarchy was moved only by promises of silver; such an inference is more in line with our own fully

---

33. During the reign of Charles V and then increasingly during the reign of the Philips (1556–1665) the Spanish crown largely excluded non-Iberians from the New World. Often non-Iberian Jesuits (numbering several dozen) who were granted permission to go to the Indies changed their names before they left Sevilla (e.g., Michael Wadding became Miguel Godínez). This was apparently done to facilitate passage and minimize difficulties once in Mexico (Aspurz 1946; Shiels 1939; Zambrano 1961–1977:6:570–71).

34. By 1628 the number of Jesuits in Mexico had reached 382. Thereafter the number started to decline slowly, declining to 378 by 1638 (Dunne 1951:107).

35. At the time few individuals, including the king's own deputies, had audiences with the monarch (Elliott 1989:148).

36. In 1624, for instance, riots in Mexico City occasioned a dispute between the viceroy and the archbishop (Dunne 1951:86–87).

37. The idea of the Jesuits as a "military order" that was founded to challenge Protestants is *not* characteristic of Jesuit discourse (O'Malley 1993a:45). With respect to the *Historia*, Pérez de Ribas acknowledged in Book 10 that some readers might not read his book chapter by chapter. He may well have assumed that crown officials would read only the prologue, which abounds in militaristic language and metaphors and explicitly links the Jesuits' apostolic mission and Spain's imperial and profane concerns for subjects and wealth. The militaristic tone of the prologue is not characteristic of the *Historia*. The related, negative portrayal of native culture (implying the just use of force) in the prologue also is not characteristic of the narrative as a whole.

38. Captain Hurdaide is a truly heroic figure in the *Historia* and is depicted in much the same terms as the Jesuit missionary; i.e., as an instrument of God.

39. In 1647, two years after the publication of the *Historia*, the reign of Philip IV witnessed its second bankruptcy (Elliott 1989:132).

developed capitalist values. For while "pesos talked" in seventeenth-century Spain, so too did saintly apparitions and relics. Arguably, heavenly discourse, which was being confounded by Protestant heretics, was as much a concern to the Spanish crown as revenue flows.[40] The theory of divine right—that the king ruled with God's approval and scrutiny—was more than an abstraction for Philip IV, who shared the religious zeal of his forefathers. Under the tutelage of the count duke of Olivares, Philip IV became ever more convinced of his popular image as the great upholder of his dynasty's mission to check the forces of heresy and to spread the Catholic religion (Elliott 1989:165–67, 178).

In his "Prologue to the Reader" as well as his letter to the king, Pérez de Ribas gave voice to the king's providentialist view of Spain and its rulers.[41] For both political and cultural-theological reasons, he reminded the king in his letter that the Spanish monarch was fulfilling the prophecy of Isaiah and Christ himself by supporting the Jesuit missions and the preaching of the Gospel in Nueva España. Pérez de Ribas casts the Indians, in turn, as a gift (rather than a financial liability) that God had withheld for thousands of years, at last bestowing it on Philip and his predecessors. Pérez de Ribas reminded the king that while the riches of Nueva España were rightfully his, he was bound by God and the precedent established by his father and grandfather to reinvest this wealth in the conversion of native peoples. The alternative he suggested, with somewhat surprising boldness, was to fall within the ranks of King Herod! On numerous occasions throughout the *Historia*, Pérez de Ribas returned to this theme of the responsible Christian monarch. Indeed, no opportunity was seemingly lost to remind Philip IV of his forefathers' and his mother's charity. In Chapter 36 of Book 2, for instance, he recalled the generosity of Philip IV's mother, whose Austrian kin retained a strong presence at court following her death:

I cannot leave untold a work of great royal piety that is characteristic of the Imperial House of Austria, which

has stood above all the others in the world because of its reverence and devotion to the most Holy and Sovereign Sacrament of the Altar, which it inherited from our Catholic monarchs of all the Spains. Around this time Our Lady Doña Margarita of Austria, mother of Our Lord King Philip IV, may God keep him, learned that the priests of the Company were founding new Christian communities at the ends of the earth, in the Province of Sinaloa, so she ordered royal officials to dispatch a number of gilded tabernacles to Nueva España. These were to be placed in the new Christian churches that were being built in this province. This Catholic queen's piety was so generous and extensive that it reached [even] the most remote parts of the world. . . . With this new enrichment Christianity flourished and daily experienced new growth. (Elliott 1989:117)

When Pérez de Ribas returned to Mexico from Europe in 1647, two years after the publication of the *Historia*, he was accompanied by fourteen new recruits for the Jesuit Province of Nueva España (Zambrano 1961–1977:3:13). The *Historia* had clearly struck a responsive chord with the king and his deputies.

The Church

Although the Spanish crown held the all-important power of appointment and the purse, the Church—here defined in terms of the pope, the religious orders (including the Jesuits), and the all-powerful bishops—also exercised considerable influence on Pérez de Ribas' representation of the missions of Nueva España. The letters of approval from representatives of the holy office, the vicar general of Madrid, and Jesuit superiors, which follow Pérez de Ribas' letter to the king, all underscore the Church's influence and control of religious discourse. Note in this regard that during Pérez de Ribas' lifetime Protestants and Catholics battled in the streets of Europe, in pulpits, and between the margins of pamphlets and books, which were consumed by an increasingly literate population. To counter Protestant "propaganda" and to solidify its own position on various theological issues, the Catholic Church moved to control what was published and read by Catholics. By the mid-1500s various institutions (e.g., the Inquisition, universities, the Vatican) had issued indexes of forbidden books. In 1564 the Council of Trent issued perhaps the most influential index and regulations. Rule 10 required the approval of a priest or other representative of the Church before a book could be printed. The Council also called for the appointment by bishops of inspectors to regularly visit bookshops, levying fines on booksellers caught dealing in prohibited texts (Martin 1993:3–5). Philip II welcomed such

40. In 1633, in the midst of bankruptcy, Philip IV approved 300,000 ducats for wine and oil to celebrate Mass in the monasteries of the New World (Haring 1947:172). It would seem that Philip IV was slightly less religious than his father, Philip II; the latter saw to it that the Escorial was adorned with gold and silver as well as hundreds of relics (Christian 1981:135).

41. Pérez de Ribas was following a tradition that dated back to Eusebius (270–339), who praised Constantine and cast the Church and Roman Empire as part of God's plan for history (Chestnut 1986:139). Eusebius' *Church History* was recommended reading for Jesuit novices (de Guibert 1964:216).

regulations and promoted still others, including an "ex-purgatory index" that excised passages from otherwise orthodox books (Kamen 1985:183).[42]

The fact that religious censors favored the *Historia* — certifying that it contained nothing contrary to the Catholic faith and its "good customs" — is testimony to Pérez de Ribas' skill in negotiating the minefield implied by a work devoted to the triumphs of the holy faith. (It is not known if the *Historia* was expurgated; i.e., whether phrases or passages were deleted by censors prior to publication.) As noted, the *Historia* as well as Pérez de Ribas' "Letter . . . to the Very Reverend Fathers of the Company of Jesus," which precedes the narrative, abound in rhetoric (e.g., the vineyard metaphor), type scenes (e.g., faith healing of the sick) and quotations in Latin from the Bible and patristic sources that affirmed his orthodoxy.[43] In Book 6, Chapter 10, Pérez de Ribas expressed concern about recounting an incident that appeared to go against Church teachings, which involved a woman who was struck dead by lightning after being baptized. He recounted the incident only after first assuring the reader, "I am writing for the faithful, who are familiar with and should venerate and adore God's judgment."

From the perspectives of both the Church and the crown, it was particularly important that Pérez de Ribas affirm the paradigm of beneficent colonization, which Protestant critics at the time countered with the "black legend": a narrative of Spanish atrocities in the New World.[44] The paradigm was explicitly given voice by Pérez de Ribas in his prologue:

> Herein one will read about wondrous marvels wrought by the almighty hand of God in [the Indians'] very nature, confirming the Catholic doctrine preached by His servants and firmly rooting in the Church those tender and newly planted trees. It will be seen that peoples who in the past were little more than wild beasts now live in a Christian republic with well-established civil order.

Passages of this type resonated with Pérez de Ribas' largely religious and elite Catholic audience. Thus Fray Alonso de la Corte noted in his letter of approval that "clear proofs will be given that justify our Catholic monarchs' right to conquer and take possession of the Indies."

Although Pérez de Ribas gave voice to his audience's most fundamental beliefs, including Spaniards' providentialist vision as a chosen people, neither the Catholic faith nor its "good customs" were altogether apparent, as evidenced by the deliberations of the Council of Trent, the Inquisition, and continuing debates over how to distinguish communication with God from that with the devil. Theological disputes often paralleled or masked power struggles between and within the religious orders, the episcopacy, and the Vatican (Wright 1982). The fact that representatives of various elements of the Church sat in judgment on the *Historia*, and by extension the Jesuit missions of Nueva España, meant that Pérez de Ribas had to acknowledge and in some instances ignore controversies and struggles involving the Jesuits.

The Religious Orders

Ever since its inception in 1540, the Society of Jesus had engendered enemies among both secular and regular clergy. The simple fact that the Jesuits were founded as an international order raised suspicions about their loyalty to the Spanish crown—suspicions heightened in 1640 when many Portuguese Jesuits supported Portugal's war for independence from Spain (López 1976:62). The Society's opposition to statutes of *limpieza* (i.e., affirming one's untainted heritage) and its acceptance of converts from Judaism[45] further alienated fellow clergy and Spaniards more generally (Kamen 1985:82, 125). On theological issues the Jesuits also were perceived as a threat to tradition. For instance, in keeping with their Thomistic philosophy and belief that grace perfected nature, the Jesuits advocated frequent reception of the Eucharist as an aid to spiritual improvement (O'Malley 1993b:153; Wright 1991:163). Although this position was adopted by the Council of Trent, the Jesuits were its chief supporters, and they alienated many traditionalists who viewed communion as a rare obligation and privilege.

Both secular clergy and other religious orders also resented the Jesuits' activism, which put a higher value on visiting the sick than passing a night in prayer and mortification (Martin 1988:30). Unlike the rules followed by the other orders, the Formula drawn up by

---

42. As early as 1502 the Spanish crown had required the acquisition of a license before a book could be published or introduced to Spain (Kamen 1985:79).

43. The Council of Trent held that patristic sources carried the same authoritative weight as the Bible itself.

44. It is interesting that Pérez de Ribas says little about the Protestant Reformation, ignoring, for instance, the opportunity to represent Jesuit conversions in the New World as compensating for losses in Europe to Luther and Calvin, which is how one of his censors (Ponce de Leon) valued the Jesuits' New World conversions.

45. In 1593 the Jesuits finally caved in and prohibited the admission of conversos to the Society.

Ignatius Loyola called for no distinctive garb or habit; Jesuit houses also lacked regular "chapter" meetings, conventual masses, and the chanting of the Divine Office by the community as a whole. From the vantage point of other orders, the Jesuits appeared to lack the very structure of a religious order. Equally irksome, the Jesuits (with rare exception) refused tithes or salaried appointments (benefices) (O'Malley 1993b:345). This disdain for any form of remuneration for priestly ministries was particularly irritating to the mendicant orders, which by 1540 had relatively few members who were supported by alms and begging.

What perhaps most irritated and angered other religious orders, particularly the Franciscans and Dominicans, were Jesuit attempts to monopolize various mission fields. At the time the *Historia* was written, the Jesuits were embroiled in a battle with the Dominicans and Franciscans over the Jesuits' insistence that they alone should missionize China. Mendicants who managed to reach China in the 1630s returned to Europe with accusations that the Jesuits attempted to discredit other missionaries and, moreover, that the Jesuits allowed the Chinese to retain many of their superstitions (Cummins 1961). Closer to home in Nueva España, the Jesuits often were at odds with the Franciscans working in New Mexico, who competed with the Jesuits for both crown support and neophytes. During the 1630s the Jesuits and Franciscans each were poised to expand their missionary activities into what is today central and northern Sonora, Mexico. The Franciscans, in a preemptive strike, sent Fray Martín de Arvide to Sonora in 1633 to begin working among the Opata and Pima Alto. Although the friar was killed en route by the Zuni (Kessell 1979:150), five friars succeeded in reaching northern Sonora in 1636 and establishing several missions there. A turf battle with the Jesuits immediately followed, which, while it was soon resolved in favor of the Jesuits, nevertheless symbolized the distrust and competition that characterized Jesuit-Franciscan relations during much of the seventeenth century (Bannon 1955:87; Kessell 1979:150, 158; Polzer 1972; Schroeder 1956).

The Jesuit-Franciscan dispute, which came to a head while Pérez de Ribas was provincial, is never mentioned in the *Historia*. Occasionally in the *Historia* one encounters gratuitous comments about Franciscan martyrs *outside* Nueva España. The reader would never know from the *Historia* that there was a significant Franciscan presence in northern Nueva España. Indeed, when Pérez de Ribas found himself forced to confront this

reality, he transformed it into something else. For instance, in Chapter 8 of Book 1, where he reviewed the history of early Spanish exploration in the north, he incorrectly indicated that Fray Marcos de Niza followed rather than preceded Coronado's expedition of 1540–41. Although a minor error of fact, this nevertheless effectively negated any Franciscan claim to having first discovered and taken possession of Sonora, the Gulf of California, and the Pimería Alta (Reff 1991a). Indeed, Pérez de Ribas stated that "Fray Marcos returned to Culiacán without having obtained anything significant."

Jesuit-Franciscan competition may also help explain why in Book 7, which ostensibly is a summary and defense of the Jesuit mission enterprise in Sinaloa, Pérez de Ribas discussed at great length Jesuit participation in the exploration of Baja California. Chapter 12 includes long quotations from letters written by the viceroy, Jesuit provincial, and Father Jacinto Cortés. Arguably, the letters were cited at length to establish the Jesuit claim to missionize California, which at the time was being eyed by the Franciscans as well as the Dominicans (Reff 1994).[46]

In both Spain and Nueva España the Dominicans and Jesuits also were keen rivals and adversaries (Martin 1993:8). Although Pérez de Ribas broached the Dominicans in much the same way as the Franciscans — largely ignoring them — this was not always possible or advisable, particularly when Jesuit policies and practices were at stake. In Chapter 11 of Book 6, for instance, Pérez de Ribas drew a parallel between the Jesuits in Nueva España and Saint Dominic, effectively silencing Dominican theologians who repudiated the use of force to punish apostate Indians:

> Whoever reads the first part of the history of the holy Order of Saint Dominic will see how for seven years that holy patriarch struggled and suffered, availing himself of both the ecclesiastical and lay arm of the Church to fight the Albigensian heretics in France. He won most illustrious victories over visible and invisible enemies of the Faith, using the sword of the divine word in sermons, disputations, and speeches, together with the sword and weapons provided by the count of Montfort. Saint Dominic did not think it strange to combine the weapons of iron and fire with the divine word and the preaching of the Catholic Faith in order to repress those who rebelled against God and His Church. (Phelan 1970:10)

46. See Alegre (1956–1960:3:344–50) for a copy of a 1649 letter to Philip IV from the head of the Franciscan order in the New World; in the letter the commissary general asks the king to order that the Franciscans be given their due right to missionize California.

Dominican critics also loom large in the concluding chapters of Book 6. Although this book and the others that make up Part 1 of the *Historia* are about the Sinaloa mission, Pérez de Ribas concluded Book 6 with an account of the life and career of Gerónimo Ramírez, who served as a missionary in Zacatecas and Durango and then founded a Jesuit college in Guatemala.[47] Significantly, Pérez de Ribas did not focus on Ramírez's career as a missionary but rather on his successful efforts to overcome the early objections of a Dominican bishop to a Jesuit presence in Guatemala. In Ramírez's case, which Pérez de Ribas presumably held up as a model to imitate, the Dominican bishop quickly came to respect the Jesuit both for his intellect and his sanctity.

Bishops and Secular Clergy

In 1645 the greatest threat to the Jesuit mission enterprise in Nueva España came not from other religious orders but from the episcopacy. The papal bull *Regimini* of 1540, which officially recognized the Society of Jesus, largely freed the Jesuits from the control of the episcopal hierarchy. Bishops and other secular clergy in both the Old and New Worlds resented the Jesuits' independence and their perceived holier-than-thou attitude. Because of their activism and many public ministries, coupled with their often electrifying sermons, the Jesuits often drew people to their churches. This did not sit well with parish priests, who quoted canon law to the effect that Catholics should make confession and take regular communion at their parish church.[48]

In both Nueva España and Europe the Jesuits didn't make things easier for themselves by frequently criticizing secular priests for their lack of education and pursuit of salaries and money for preaching and clerical services (Martin 1988:208; Zubillaga 1968:336). The Jesuits refused to accept the salaried positions that provided secular clergy in the Americas with comfortable if not lavish lifestyles (O'Malley 1993b:286). The Jesuits, however, were somewhat hypocritical because they did accept gifts of money and property (e.g., houses, ranches, farms). These gifts yielded considerable sums,

which were used to fund Jesuit colleges and residences. Not surprisingly, the episcopacy resented gifts to the Jesuit order, particularly as the gifts made it possible for the Jesuits to live as comfortably as those they criticized. Of course, a gift made to a Jesuit residence or college was a gift that might otherwise have gone to a diocese.

Shortly after Pérez de Ribas became Jesuit provincial in 1638, the resentment of secular clergy surfaced during the Palafox affair,[49] when the bishop of Puebla (Palafox) began publicly challenging the Jesuits' exemption from paying tithes on houses, land, and other property. Also in 1638 Pérez de Ribas and his fellow Jesuits faced another, more serious challenge, particularly to their missions in the north. For several years the bishop of Durango, in whose diocese the Sinaloa missions fell, had raised the possibility with the viceroy of creating a new diocese on the northern frontier, which would have meant that the Jesuits as well as the Franciscans would have had to relinquish a significant number of their missions and neophytes to secular priests. In 1637 the king sent a royal decree and questionnaire to all concerned, including Pérez de Ribas as Jesuit provincial, inquiring about the feasibility of creating a new diocese. In 1638 Pérez de Ribas assembled a group of veteran missionaries and fired back a detailed report challenging the viceroy's and bishop's proposal, effectively dashing the latter's hopes of replacing the Jesuits with secular priests (AHH 1638; Alegre 1956–1960:2:581–94; Hackett 1923–1937:3:95–105). This was the first of what were to be frequent challenges on the part of the episcopacy to Jesuit hegemony in northern Nueva España (Alegre 1956–1960:3:214–26).

It is significant that neither the Palafox affair nor the Jesuit dispute with the bishop of Durango over the creation of a new frontier diocese appear in the *Historia*. Both controversies, or their absence from the text, are notable silences. Although arguably the Palafox affair was not directly relevant, inasmuch as the *Historia*

47. Pérez de Ribas averred that he would have liked to discuss the career of the veteran Sinaloa missionary Pedro Méndez but lacked the requisite information. However, there were certainly other Sinaloa Jesuits besides Méndez he could have discussed.

48. The seriousness of this struggle between regular and secular priests is reflected in the fact that approximately one hundred pamphlets were written and published in Paris between 1625 and 1636 arguing for and against the value and dignity of secular versus regular priests (Martin 1993:120–21).

49. The dispute began when a canon of the cathedral of Puebla made known his intention to donate his estate to the Jesuit order, over the objection of Bishop Palafox. Pérez de Ribas, who was provincial, supported the canon's decision, apparently over the objection of fellow Jesuits. Indeed, Pérez de Ribas went so far as to exclude certain professed Jesuits from a provincial congregation because they purportedly questioned the canon's decision and Pérez de Ribas' encouragement of the latter. When the father general in Rome learned of this, he wrote Pérez de Ribas in 1641, scolding him for his behavior. Although Pérez de Ribas apparently was not directly involved in the ensuing debate with the bishop, it nevertheless turned ugly, as Jesuit superiors and the bishop traded insults and excommunicated each other. Near-riots followed in Mexico City, involving supporters of both sides (Dunne 1951:145–151).

is largely about the Jesuit missions of the north, it seems more likely that Pérez de Ribas chose not to discuss the affair because of the power and influence of Bishop Palafox and also the shaky ground on which the Jesuit position rested with respect to their acceptance of alms or gifts and exemption from tithes. As noted later, Pérez de Ribas' sequel to the *Historia*, the *Corónica*, which was completed in 1653, was suppressed by Jesuit superiors precisely because they objected to his polemical discussion of the Palafox incident. Presumably for similar political reasons—fear of alienating the viceroy and the bishop of Durango—Pérez de Ribas chose not to discuss the latter's attempt to wrest control of Jesuit neophytes and missions on the northern frontier. Indeed, in Chapter 16 of Book 3, Pérez de Ribas praised the bishops of Durango for fulfilling their obligation to visit and administer confirmation to the Jesuits' Indian converts in Sinaloa. In a gesture of considerable humility, Pérez de Ribas cast the Jesuits as subordinates (coadjutors) to Bishop Alonso Franco de Luna—the very bishop who suggested to the viceroy that the Jesuits should be replaced by secular priests:

> Doctor Don Alonso Franco de Luna succeeded Fray Gonzalo de Hermosillo as bishop, and he imitated his predecessors in his holy zeal and love for these new Christian communities. His Eminence visited them, confirming and encouraging them to continue in the Christianity they had initiated. He also consoled the missionary priests, who were his coadjutors in this pastoral task.

Arguably, the threat posed by the episcopacy, which grew rather than diminishing during the seventeenth century, also contributed to Pérez de Ribas' rhetoric of heroic sacrifice on the part of the Jesuits, including their mastering of Indian languages. As discussed in more detail later, the threat of turning over their Indian converts to secular priests contributed to Jesuit representation of the Indian as childlike, lazy, and inconstant: Indians with these qualities were incapable of generating surpluses to pay taxes to support secular priests and required years of instruction and constant supervision by priests who could communicate in the Indians' languages.

The Papacy

During the century following its inception (1540–1640), the Society of Jesus was the beneficiary of numerous papal bulls that effectively instructed the episcopal hierarchy to desist in their attacks on the Jesuits. At a time when Catholics as well as Protestants questioned the infallibility of the Holy See, the Jesuits respected and indeed often supported the pope's inerrancy (O'Malley 1993b:296–310). The issue of infallibility notwithstanding, the pope remained in the seventeenth century the ultimate Roman Catholic authority in matters of dogma and the faith. This authority was exercised in part through control of what was published and read in Counter-Reformation Europe. For instance, the Vatican's approval was required for publication of editions of the Bible, liturgical works, and books intended for large audiences (Martin 1993:4–7). Perhaps of greatest significance for Pérez de Ribas, who devoted numerous chapters to Jesuit martyrs and instances of divine intercession, were Vatican prohibitions and guidelines concerning the publication of miracles and the advocacy of sainthood. As a consequence of frequent publicity campaigns mounted by religious orders on behalf of the sainthood of one of their deceased members, Urban VIII in 1625 forbade the publication of miracles or works advocating the veneration of persons of reputed sanctity if they had not been investigated and approved by the Holy See (Dunne 1951:134). This order was followed a few years later, in 1634, by the establishment of the current canonization procedure, which strengthened the pope's authority in matters of sainthood (Goodich 1982:207).

Papal restrictions and authority necessarily posed a challenge for Pérez de Ribas, who sought to demonstrate that the Jesuit experience in Nueva España frequently had benefited from divine intercession. Of course, the more it could be shown that a mission enterprise witnessed divine intercession, the more that mission enterprise would be esteemed (and supported materially) by the crown, the Church in general, and the Jesuit order in particular. At midcentury the Jesuits in Nueva España—like religious orders almost everywhere—faced a shortage of missionaries. Religious orders often publicized the heroic and saintly accomplishments of their members in order to attract new recruits (Cohen 1974; Goodich 1982). Pérez de Ribas undoubtedly was aware that accounts of Jesuits who were favored by God would resonate with novices and scholastics and, he hoped, prompt many to petition their superiors for a missionary assignment in Nueva España.

Pérez de Ribas acknowledged the pope's authority in a formal statement that precedes Book 1 and also in a briefer statement at the very end of the *Historia*. Perhaps more significant are the numerous instances where he denied his intent and authority to pass judgment on miracles or sainthood, then proceeded to do precisely that. Pérez de Ribas seemed quite aware that he was dangerously close to violating Vatican regulations, as his rhetoric implicitly acknowledges Vatican guidelines governing the investigation and demonstration of miracles. Thus, in Book 4, Chapter 10, he gave the names of the Indians who witnessed the miraculous appearance of blood during a Mass celebrated by Father Julio Pascual shortly before he was martyred. Similarly, in Book 2, Chapter 8, Pérez de Ribas enumerated and then systematically eliminated all but one possible explanation for how the lifeless and decapitated body of Father Gonzalo de Tapia could have been found with the hand still making the sign of the cross, made by overlapping the thumb and forefinger:

> There are only three possibilities for when this sign of the Cross was made: either before the blessed priest died; at the moment of his death, when his head was cut off; or following his death. There was no other time when this sign could have been made. With respect to the first possibility, it is known that the body responds to a violent death; if Father Tapia made the sign of the Cross before his head was cut off, then why did it not subsequently come undone with the natural movement of the body? If the sign of the Cross and the raised arm were made at the same time as his head was being severed, how is it that when the lifeless body dropped, the arm did not also fall, particularly given that the soul and life were gone that were required to sustain a heavy arm in that violent position—an arm that was still flexible due to the warmth that it retained? Why wasn't it lying on the ground and why hadn't the fingers of the hand separated, thereby releasing the sign of the Cross? Lastly, if this sign were made after death, then the miracle would be even clearer, because a dead body cannot command its members.

Pérez de Ribas' frequent citing of the works of the Greek and Latin fathers of the Church (e.g., John Chrysostom, Gregory the Great, Augustine) also reflects the Vatican's influence on Jesuit discourse. In an age that celebrated classical pagan skepticism the Vatican enlisted the early fathers of the Church and their apologetics to demonstrate through logic and reason that the Catholic Church of the Counter-Reformation was perfectly in accord with the primitive Church. During the sixteenth and seventeenth centuries the Vatican encouraged and supported an avalanche of patristic studies undertaken principally by Jesuit theologians (Martin 1993:78–80). In citing Ambrose, Basil, Jerome, and other Church fathers, Pérez de Ribas thus affirmed his allegiance to the Church and the pope.

The Jesuit Order

At the time the *Historia* was published there were several hundred Jesuit residences and colleges spread throughout the world. In each, dinner was followed every night with a reading from a book chosen by the superior. Missionary accounts, which were first made popular by the letters of Francis Xavier from India, were particularly popular after-dinner reading (de Guibert 1964:217; O'Malley 1993b:358). Pérez de Ribas was clearly aware of this, as he frequently noted in the *Historia* that his principal audience was fellow Jesuits. The *Historia* affirms and celebrates the Jesuits' unique "way of proceeding" and particularly the missionary ideal upon which the order was founded. Were this not the case the work would never have been approved by Jesuit superiors. Note that the front matter includes an acknowledgement from a representative of the Jesuit order that the *Historia* was read and deemed worthy of publication. Indeed, the father general was sufficiently impressed that he requested that Pérez de Ribas write a second history of the Jesuit Province of Nueva España. As noted, this *Corónica* was suppressed by Jesuit superiors because of its polemical chapters on the Palafox affair. Clearly the stamp of approval from Jesuit superiors was more than a formality.[50]

From the perspective of Jesuit superiors there was very little in the *Historia* that was politically incorrect and that might have jeopardized the Society's dealings with the crown or the Church. As noted, Pérez de Ribas is largely silent or oblique with reference to Jesuit critics and competitors among the Franciscans and Dominicans. He likewise is silent about controversies involving the episcopacy and indeed lauds the bishops of Durango who challenged Jesuit hegemony on the northern frontier. The Vatican is duly acknowledged as the ultimate authority in religious matters and, correspondingly, Pérez de Ribas had only good things to say about the crown or its officers, from the viceroys and governors down to the captains and *alcaldes mayores*.

Jesuit superiors undoubtedly were pleased with not only Pérez de Ribas' tactfulness and appropriate silences on various matters, but also the skill with which he articulated and celebrated Jesuit beliefs and practice. There are many ways in which the *Historia* speaks particularly to Jesuits, including the ubiquitous metaphor of the Lord's vineyard, which Pérez de Ribas em-

---

50. The suppression of Pérez de Ribas' *Corónica* was not unusual. At the time his *Historia* was approved (circa 1645) a fellow Jesuit provincial of Paraguay, Juan Pastor, who had written a history of the Paraguay missions, received word that his history had been rejected for publication by Jesuit reviewers. In a letter to Pastor the father general encouraged him to revise the history, "perfecting it and removing those things that had been identified by reviewers" (Morner 1953:2).

ployed in reference to the missions of northern Nueva España. Although the vineyard metaphor resonated with the clergy in general, it is particularly characteristic of Jesuit discourse (O'Malley 1993b:298). Similarly, Pérez de Ribas gave voice to the particular Jesuit ideal of unquestioning obedience to superiors, often using metaphors and similes (e.g., obedience should be blind, like a corpse) drawn from the writings of Ignatius Loyola (O'Malley 1993a:353). Expressions taken from the Jesuit Constitutions, such as "love poverty as a mother," abound in the *Historia* (Ganss 1991:292). Additionally, the Jesuits whose careers Pérez de Ribas recounts are exemplary because of their adherence not only to their vows, but also to Jesuit customs and rules governing such things as the timing and frequency of daily prayer. In Book 7 Pérez de Ribas quoted almost verbatim the rules governing missions that were drawn up in 1610 by Father Visitor Rodrigo de Cabredo. Arguably, the point of doing this was to remind critics both within and without the Jesuit order that the relative isolation of the frontier did not imply a lack of discipline, quiet prayer, and reflection, all of which were synonymous with a religious vocation.

Although Pérez de Ribas embraced Jesuit ideals and signifying practices, Jesuit discourse has never been stable, and indeed to this day members of the order disagree about the appropriate "way of proceeding" (Martin 1987). For Pérez de Ribas and his contemporaries the most fundamental division centered around the Ignatian ideal of itinerant ministry. Jesuits, particularly in Spain, struggled almost from the Society's inception with the tendency to abandon Ignatian activism in favor of a more contemplative life (Martin 1988:40).[51] During the century following the creation of the Society of Jesus most of its members came to believe that a teaching position, preferably of theology, and life in a Jesuit college or residence was more fulfilling in terms of one's own religious perfection and the "higher good" of awakening in the masses a true understanding and love of God. The Jesuit ideal of itinerant ministry, which was the essence of Ignatius Loyola's concept of the Society, was in effect displaced by the ministry of education (O'Malley 1993a:239, 375;

1993b:483–85). By the time Pérez de Ribas wrote the *Historia* the vast majority of Jesuits were in fact educators.[52] Although many may have enjoyed reading or hearing about the exploits of Xavier, relatively few actually were drawn to a missionary vocation[53] and many saw it as less demanding intellectually (Cohen 1974).

During Pérez de Ribas' lifetime the Ignatian ideal of an international order also was being undermined by nationalistic sentiments. European Jesuits, particularly Spaniards and Italians, who dominated the hierarchy of the order, discriminated against non-European Jesuits. Perhaps even more divisive were the different rights and responsibilities that accrued to the three ranks of the Society: professed, spiritual coadjutor, and temporal coadjutor. Temporal coadjutors were nonordained members of the Society who had little or no formal education and were admitted to the society as cooks, laborers, and other important yet menial positions. Temporal coadjutors were little respected either within or without the Jesuit order. And yet, arguably, without these assistants the Society of Jesus and the missions of Nueva España, in particular, could not have functioned. Ranking above the temporal coadjutors were spiritual coadjutors. They generally were ordained priests with some university training in the humanities and perhaps philosophy and theology. Usually upon entering the Society or during their novitiate they were found lacking intellectually for the more rigorous and lengthier education that professed members undertook. Spiritual coadjutors generally were restricted to low-level positions of authority, as rectors of missions or colleges. Professed Jesuits such as Pérez de Ribas, who generally had several years of training in theology (beyond a degree in philosophy), were entitled to participate in provincial and general congregations and hold the highest positions within the order (O'Malley 1993a).

Pérez de Ribas was mindful of each of these issues, which were immediately relevant to the missions of Nueva España. As a Jesuit superior in the New World facing a shortage of priests, he clearly was moved to exalt the missionary vocation, something he achieved in a variety of ways, including metaphorically likening Nueva España unto the primitive Church. In Book 7, Pérez de Ribas confronted directly the increasingly

51. As early as 1575 the Jesuit father general issued guidelines governing what was to be read by Jesuit novices and scholastics, in an effort to limit their exposure to works and ideas that promoted a contemplative rather than apostolic vocation. Until the end of the sixteenth century Jesuit superiors complained about the rapid spread of Jesuit colleges, which were not considered consistent with the self-definition of the Jesuit order (de Guibert 1964:219; Wright 1982:16).

52. In 1680 the Society of Jesus had more than seventeen thousand members; less than a third were missionaries (de Guibert 1964:288, f.21).

53. Polish Jesuits queried by superiors during the second half of the sixteenth century indicated that by and large they joined the Society not because they were interested in the public ministries idealized by Ignatius Loyola, but "to escape the world and its dangers"! (Cohen 1974).

popular notion that the activism of a missionary vocation was at odds with a life of contemplation and
religious perfection. After devoting several chapters to
a brief in favor of missionary work—showing how it
led to one's own religious self-fulfillment as well as
fulfilling Christ's charge to serve others—he calls as
a witness for the defense Saint Teresa of Avila (see
Book 7, Chapter 13). Although challenged during her
lifetime by Spanish theologians, Saint Teresa became
one of the greatest authorities on spiritual perfection
following the publication in 1583 of her *The Way of
Perfection* (de Certeau 1992:131, 254; Martin 1993:90).
Pérez de Ribas quotes Saint Teresa at length to the
effect that a missionary vocation was preferable to the
contemplative life of a cloister.

Pérez de Ribas' discussion in Book 7 of the life and
career of Father Juan de Ledesma also bespeaks a defense, if not a celebration, of the missionary vocation.
Ledesma was an intellectual giant who was respected
and loved by Mexico City's leading scholars and citizens. However, despite his great intellect and sanctity,
or rather because of it (so Pérez de Ribas would argue),
Ledesma preferred to associate with and care for the
Indians in his church of San Gregorio. As the following quote regarding Father Ledesma suggests, Pérez
de Ribas was not above criticizing academicians with
swollen egos who looked down on Ledesma's activism
and by extension the work of missionaries: "During all
this time his humble manner of proceeding was always
the same. It served him as an anchor with which to
steady a ship so full of rich merchandise, allowing him
to ply the waves of that sea of studies, professorships,
and lecturing, where such swollen typhoons and such
dangerous hurricanes ordinarily arise."[54] Elsewhere in
the *Historia* (e.g., Book 5, Chapter 23), where he reviews
the careers of Jesuit missionaries, Pérez de Ribas made
a point of noting how they excelled in philosophy and
theology, and in some cases were students of Spain's
greatest theologians and philosophers (e.g., La Puente).

In the many chapters of the *Historia* that recount the
lives and careers of Jesuit missionaries Pérez de Ribas
also addressed indirectly the other issues of nationality and rank that tended to divide the order. It was
presumably to attract temporal coadjutors to Nueva
España and allay any fears that they might not be appreciated that Pérez de Ribas devoted Chapter 35 of
Book 3 to the career and life of Brother Francisco de

Castro. Castro was praised not only for his charity and
hard work, but for his wisdom—a trait not typically
associated with temporal coadjutors. Similarly, Pérez
de Ribas devoted Chapter 34 of Book 3 to the life and
career of Juan de Velasco, who was a creole. Recall that
Spanish- and Italian-born Jesuits tended to look down
on Jesuits of other nationalities, particularly those born
and raised in America.[55] In celebrating the career of a
missionary such as Velasco, Pérez de Ribas sent a clear
message to creoles that they were welcome in the Jesuit
Province of Nueva España. Again, this was an important point to make given a shortage of missionaries and
the valuable role that creoles played on the northern
frontier (Reff 1993, 1998). Presumably for similar reasons Pérez de Ribas made a point of acknowledging
(e.g., Book 6, Chapter 3) non-Iberian and non-Italian
Jesuits and their role in Sinaloa and other parts of
Nueva España. However, perhaps because the Spanish
crown was fundamentally opposed to non-Spanish and
non-Italian Jesuits serving in Nueva España, their contribution was discussed in passing rather than in entire
chapters devoted to their lives and careers.

JESUIT IMAGES OF THE INDIAN AND
THE PROCESS OF CONVERSION

We turn at this point to the question of how the
various contingencies outlined here specifically influenced Pérez de Ribas' representation of the Indian and
Jesuit-Indian relations. As an author concerned with
recounting the history of the "triumphs of our holy
faith," it was necessary for Pérez de Ribas to describe
to his largely European audience the Indian "other"
and how the Indian had been positively affected by the
preaching of the Gospel. At the time many Europeans,
apparently influenced by Acosta's *Historia natural y
moral de las Indias* (1894 [1590]), imagined northern
Nueva España as inhabited mostly by "wild" hunter-
gatherers who wore little or no clothing and lived like
animals (Casillas 1964:21–22). Europeans as well as
Mexican creoles, including both secular and regular
priests, had come to believe that Indians in general were
lesser beings.[56] The initial impression of the Indians as

---

54. This turbulent sea metaphor was a favorite of Gregory of Tours
in his *Glory of the Martyrs* (Van Dam 1988:25, f.7).

55. In 1644 the Jesuit father general actually sent a letter to Jesuit
superiors in Nueva España asking that they do something about the dis-
crimination endured by creoles at the hands of European-born Jesuits
(Dunne 1951:144).

56. Although the Indian's humanity had been settled as a legal and
ecclesiastical issue a century earlier, relatively few Europeans ever saw

well intentioned but misguided souls evaporated with Indian rebellions and apostasy and the realization that the Gospel had not supplanted aboriginal religious beliefs and practices. Rather than question their message, most clergy inferred that there was something inherently wrong with the Indian—a lack of intellectual capacity or an unstable nature—or that God had decided to withhold from the Indians the grace required for salvation because of their "sordid" past (e.g., cannibalism, human sacrifice). More and more priests saw the Indians as free agents, choosing Satan over Christ and thus consciously violating the first and greatest commandment of the Decalogue (Cervantes 1991).

It was in the context of increasing demonization of the Indian, and by extension Indian culture, that Pérez de Ribas fashioned his representation of the Indians of northern Nueva España. Pérez de Ribas spoke of the Indians with both praise and disdain; frequently he contradicted himself with respect to aboriginal culture. Arguably, the Jesuits never resolved the question of Indian identity, primarily because they assumed a priori that Indian culture had not benefited from revealed truth, as had European civilization, which they viewed as a proximate albeit imperfect ideal for all humankind. Particular constructs (e.g., lazy, childlike Indians) also were a reflex of political and institutional contingencies such as Jesuit struggles with secular clergy over control of the Indian.

Indian and Aboriginal Culture

Because of the political and institutional constraints on Jesuit discourse, including the very real threat of suppression or expurgation, Pérez de Ribas could not always tell it like it was, even assuming he wanted to and was capable of doing so. Moreover, the reader who attempts to read against the grain, searching for *punctua* that might clarify Pérez de Ribas' true feelings about the Indians, will find the task daunting, owing to his many ambiguous and contradictory statements. Chapters 8 and 12 of Book 12 provide among the most telling reflections of this ambivalence. In Chapter 8 Pérez de Ribas argued against the admission of Indians to the priesthood, noting that the Indians were "inferior in character" and too new in the faith to be entrusted with the sacraments. However, four chap-

ters later he writes at great length about the life of an Indian named Lorenzo who was trained by the Jesuits and became a priest of the highest intellect and virtue. Indeed, Pérez de Ribas relates how on his deathbed Lorenzo was admitted into the Company, apparently with the approval of Pérez de Ribas himself, who at the time was provincial of Nueva España.

Of the various groups with whom he lived Pérez de Ribas spoke most fondly of the Ahome (Book 3), largely it seems because they accepted his authority unquestioningly. He clearly most respected and feared the Yaqui (Book 5). Significantly, there are no asides in the *Historia* about how Pérez de Ribas' respect or affection for his neophytes prompted him to intercede with superiors on their behalf, as he noted that fellow Jesuit Francisco de Castro did. Similarly, while he spoke highly of Father Juan de Ledesma's affection for the Indians, noting how Ledesma preferred the Indians to Mexico City's Spanish elite, Pérez de Ribas never stated or implied that he shared Ledesma's feelings. Rather, he seems to have maintained a patronizing, we-versus-they attitude toward the Indian. Arguably, Pérez de Ribas remained focused on "civilizing" and controlling his neophytes. This attitude often surfaced in the *Historia*, as in the following comment concerning the value of mastering Indian languages:

> There is no means so powerful as speaking to them in their own language for winning them over, dominating them, retaining the great authority required by the evangelical minister, and effectively instructing them, particularly if the language is spoken well. . . . [Through language] the minister convinces them to abandon their superstitions and deceit, and as a result he is more revered than their lying preachers. Last of all I can state on the basis of great experience that sometimes the language enables the speaker who knows it and preaches in it to save himself from the mortal dangers, disturbances, restlessness, and uprisings that the devil causes among these peoples. Speaking to them in their own language calms and controls them; it captures their affection and wins them over, subjugating them in the process. (Book 1, Chapter 6)

Note that Pérez de Ribas did not suggest that language acquisition led to reciprocal understanding; he instead emphasized how language acquisition facilitated the Jesuit's uni-directional program for directed culture change.[57]

---

the Indian as an equal. This generally was true of secular and regular clergy as well, as reflected in their opposition to an Indian priesthood (Poole 1981, 1987).

57. This quote reminds one of the ethnocentric comments of the famous ethnographer Malinowski, which he recorded in his diary and which contradicted his more "understanding" and appreciative comments in his ethnography of the Trobriand Islanders (Herbert 1991:154–55; Stocking 1992:271). Unlike Malinowski, Pérez de Ribas was not

Pérez de Ribas' authority—both real and imagined —limited his opportunities to engage in true dialogical relationships with his Indian neophytes. Still, the very fact that he and other Jesuits were required to master Indian language(s) forced him to venture beyond the confines of his Spanish/Jesuit cultures. If one reflects for a moment on all that is implied by the mastery of another linguistically unrelated language, particularly when it is taught by native speakers, one can begin to imagine how even the most narrow-minded Jesuit was forced to contemplate alternative truths. As Herbert (1991:185–86) has observed, the simple discovery that another's language is rule-based implies that the customs and values to which it refers must also have the same character of a logical or at least systematic organization.

Still, it was very difficult for the Jesuit missionary to acknowledge, never mind accept, alternative behaviors and beliefs. This is evident in Pérez de Ribas' many back-handed compliments of native culture. In Book 1, for instance, he described how "poor, uncivilized" hunter-gatherers living along the coast of Sinaloa used large shocks of grass tied at the top to create ponchos to protect themselves from the rain. Elsewhere he was decidedly impressed with the rationale for Indian behaviors and beliefs. Thus he noted that the Indians often cremated the bodies of warriors who died away from their villages, both to facilitate transporting the remains of the deceased and to deprive the enemy of a corpse with which to celebrate the death. Perhaps more significant are instances where the native perspective is voiced, even when it was diametrically opposed to the Jesuit position:

> Another abuse found among the Mayo that it was necessary to correct was that pregnant women could easily abort their infants. There was some of this in other nations, particularly when a pregnant woman already had a nursing infant. When she was reproached for this abuse and cruelty the response of the Indian woman was, "Can't you see that I am looking out for the life of this child that I'm holding in my arms?" thus making it clear that she was killing one child to raise another. (Book 4, Chapter 3)

This quote is from a letter by Father Pedro Méndez, whom Pérez de Ribas often cited in the *Historia*. Like most Jesuit missionaries, Méndez mastered the language of his neophytes with *their* guidance. In so doing he necessarily came face-to-face with the logic and

complexity of the Indians' values and beliefs (Asad 1986:158–59; Burrus 1979). Indeed, in another letter quoted by Pérez de Ribas, Méndez remarked that he had discovered that the Mayo Indians were familiar with atomistic theory. Clearly Méndez discussed more than the catechism in Cáhita with his Mayo converts.

The Jesuits were empowered as ethnographers by both their acquisition of native languages and their Thomistic philosophy. Aquinas held that all human beings, by virtue of the application of reason to the majesty of creation, were likely to infer the existence of divinity, which they would then endeavor to respect and worship. This knowledge of and worship of God would necessarily be imperfect in the absence of revealed truths (Incarnation, Trinity) and the sacraments (Confession, Communion), which Christ entrusted to his church to insure the greater working of God's grace, the application of which resulted in ultimate wisdom (Pegis 1948).[58]

In the mid-seventeenth century, when Catholic as well as Protestant theologians were standing Aquinas on his head (i.e., nominalism)—seeing predestination as grace—Jesuits like Pérez de Ribas remained committed to the notion that grace perfected nature. Whereas most Europeans believed that Indians and their cultures were fundamentally flawed rather than merely imperfect, the Jesuits assumed that Indian customs were fundamentally sound, albeit misguided. In one sense the Jesuits saw the "glass" of Indian culture as half-full, whereas most Europeans saw it as half-empty.

Pérez de Ribas and fellow Jesuits had much in common with Las Casas (O'Gorman 1967) who wrote a century earlier when many missionaries were still optimistic about the Indian and the rebirth of the Church in the New World. At the outset of the *Historia*, in Book 1, Pérez de Ribas depicted Sinaloa as a land that aboriginally was blessed by God's grace, as reflected in the relative abundance and variety of foodstuffs and the very manner in which nature (e.g., trees and birds' nests) reflected Christian truths such as the Trinity. Pérez de Ribas went on to imply that God's grace extended to the Indians and their culture. Thus he noted the Indians' productive farming and fishing methods and the rather ingenious way they dealt with floods. He likewise noted that aboriginally the women never had

---

constrained by the conventions of modern ethnography to conceal or deny his privileged position with respect to the Indians.

58. Aquinas had a much more positive view of humankind than Augustine, although both held that the sacraments (and the extension of God's grace through them) were of utmost importance in drawing near to and ultimately becoming one with Christ (Cramer 1993:89).

to fear being raped, unlike in Europe, and that theft and greed were largely unknown to the Indians. With respect to the Indians' "barbarous" customs Pérez de Ribas suggested that they were the result of thousands of years of isolation from the Old World and the word of God, not a lack of reason. In Chapter 5 of Book 1, he explicitly accused the devil of introducing cannibalism and drunkenness. Similarly, when mission Indians rebelled and committed the most heinous of sacrileges (e.g., Book 10, Chapter 18), Pérez de Ribas went out of his way rhetorically to blame their apostasy on the devil (e.g., the "misled rebels").

Even in his portrayal of Indian religion, Pérez de Ribas' attitude was closer to Las Casas' than to his fellow Jesuit Acosta's, who tended to dismiss all Indian ritual as satanic mimicry of Catholic sacraments and practice. Most idolatry, Pérez de Ribas claimed, was not "formal" idolatry, but rather a matter of people setting up a stone or pole as a matter of superstition without any real belief that it stood for a deity or supreme power of the universe. Rather than blame or suggest that the people as a whole were responsible for such idolatry, he blamed their shamans for colluding with the devil and for misleading the people through their "sermons." (Even in his condemnation of the hechiceros, however, Pérez de Ribas suggested that some were charlatans or practitioners of magic, rather than actual devil worshipers.) Significantly, Pérez de Ribas noted that the shamans, after they were converted, were allowed by the Jesuits to continue their public speaking. Although the "sermons" now praised Christianity, the very fact that the Jesuits retained this Indian custom was at odds with the more prevalent view among regular priests that all aboriginal practices related to religion should be destroyed.[59]

Neither Thomas Aquinas nor other European philosophers went so far as to suggest that human behaviors and beliefs could take many, equally valid forms (Pagden 1982). To this day it remains difficult to walk the walk of cultural relativism—acknowledging and respecting difference. We should not be surprised, then, that the Jesuits were as convinced as other Europeans (if not more so) that there was but one road to salvation—the road defined by Scripture, which Europeans and Western civilization had followed, albeit stumbling at times. Thus, while the Jesuits as a whole were open to

the possibility and, indeed, often looked for the good in native behaviors and beliefs, they never doubted the superiority of European customs and experience.[60]

As readers of the *Historia* will quickly discover, Pérez de Ribas often spoke of the Indian as childlike, inconstant, and in other ways inferior to Europeans. Indeed, in Book 7 (Chapter 2), where he explicitly addressed the issue of the Indians' intellectual capacity, he implied that Indians were at best on a par with European peasants. Elsewhere in Book 7 (Chapter 11) he commented that the Indian nations that had been converted by the Jesuits "are not comparable to the Spanish nation, which God Our Lord has exalted on earth."

Although one has the impression that Pérez de Ribas' admissions of Spanish superiority were intended at times to disarm his European reader,[61] the fact remains that the Jesuits came to the New World not to discover alternative behaviors and beliefs but to change those that in the absence of the word of God necessarily were imperfect if not depraved. Thus, Pérez de Ribas' positive comments about Indian customs in Book 1 and his allusions to God's grace are overshadowed by lengthy discussions of behaviors and beliefs (e.g., drunkenness, nudity, cannibalism, polygamy) that went contrary to the "good customs" of Catholic Spain. Similarly, whereas the quote concerning infanticide gave voice to the native woman's predicament, elsewhere Pérez de Ribas imposed on native women his own European values and beliefs. In the case of the Mayo, for instance, Pérez de Ribas misconstrued matrilineal residence and classificatory kinship terms as incestual relationships (see Chapter 3 of Book 4). The imposition of European standards and categories is evident as well in Pérez de Ribas' frequent com-

59. Pérez de Ribas' attitude toward Indian religion was shared by other pioneer Jesuits. See, for example, his account (taken from the anua of 1593) of the early efforts of Fathers Tapia and Pérez to substitute their Christian god for native deities (see Chapter 3 of Book 2).

60. In reflecting on the Jesuit attitude toward the Indian and how it differed from that of fellow Europeans, I am reminded of Chinua Achebe's comments regarding the difference in attitude toward Africans of Albert Schweitzer and Joseph Conrad, neither of whom could escape a fundamental belief in the inequality of black and white people. Achebe notes "that extraordinary missionary," Albert Schweitzer, sacrificed brilliant careers in music and theology in Europe for a life of service to Africans, yet all the while Schweitzer believed "the African is indeed my brother but my junior brother." This was very much the Jesuit experience and attitude toward the Indian, who was often cast as a child. Achebe notes that Conrad never used the word 'brother'; the best he could do was suggest some distant kinship with Europeans. Arguably, Conrad's attitude toward Africans paralleled the general European attitude toward the Indian in the seventeenth century (Achebe 1988:256–57).

61. This is particularly true in Book 7, where he made several comparisons between Indians and Europeans that were favorable to Indians; most Europeans probably would have rejected these (along with Pérez de Ribas' larger point about Indian intelligence) had he not gratuitously upheld Spanish superiority.

ments about the "modesty" of Indian women, which he inferred from the fact that Indian women among some groups on certain occasions covered their faces with their hair or danced separate from men. Did the women perceive themselves as being modest, or is this simply how their behavior appeared to Europeans preoccupied with modesty (Schiebinger 1993:99)? It is doubtful that Pérez de Ribas ever asked Indian women what their behavior meant or signified. Although no one in seventeenth-century Europe questioned whether women and children were human beings, it was nevertheless assumed that they did not have the intellectual capacity of men. Pérez de Ribas and his fellow Jesuits never escaped such notions, which were carried over in their dealings with Indian women. Similarly, the idea that women were the "devil's door," particularly susceptible to carnal pleasures and responsible for leading men astray (Sánchez Ortega 1992; Weber 1992:171), often surfaced in the *Historia*. The following quote, for instance, celebrates the power of the word of God to overcome the carnal instincts of weak women:

> Another woman demonstrated no less bravery during a similar incident. When an Indian arrived unexpectedly at her house to declare his rude lust, she turned on her aggressor with such spirit and determination that she was able to get a hold of the bow and arrow he was carrying, and she smashed the arrows to bits so he couldn't shoot and then beat him so hard with the bow that it broke. She repeated over and over, "Don't you know that I am a Christian and that I hear the word of God that the priests preach to us?" With that she drove him off in a state of confusion and was fortunately out of danger. These are the excellent effects of divine grace, which empowers weak women who were used to living freely according to their instincts. It is [also] a sign of how truly these people, although barbarians, embrace Christ's Faith. (Book 2, Chapter 15)

Jesuits like Pérez de Ribas were schooled in Renaissance humanism, which reified Aristotelian notions such as the idea that one had to live in a town or city to be civilized (Corominas and Pascual 1989–1991:4:598; Nader 1990; Pagden 1982).[62] The Aristotelian ideal, which also happened to be the European norm, became the yardstick against which Pérez de Ribas and other Jesuits evaluated Indian cultures. Predictably, Pérez de Ribas had enormous difficulty comprehending hunting

and gathering as a lifestyle. Indeed, he rarely used the term "savage" in the *Historia*, reserving it almost entirely for the Comopori and other hunter-gather groups who exploited the coast of Sinaloa. In Book 1, Chapter 2 he commented:

> Up to this point I have been discussing only the nations that generally live along the banks and shores of the rivers. There are also other nations that are among the most savage ever seen and encountered on earth. These nations do not sow or cultivate crops like the others, nor do they live in houses or protect themselves from inclement weather. And the more different their way of life is from that of other peoples the more deserving it is of being understood. This knowledge is worth possessing so that one can understand the misery that has befallen humanity due to the sin that cost them the Garden of Paradise, where God had placed them from whence to lift them to heaven.

Note in this quote the biblical as opposed to ecological/adaptive approach to understanding human diversity. In keeping with his epistemology and preoccupation with the first cause of things sacred and profane, Indian deviation from European norms was explained in terms of the Bible. In Chapter 6 of Book 1, where Pérez de Ribas explicitly addressed the issue of the Indians' origins and many languages, he invoked Genesis 11, equating the Indians with descendants of Noah who were dispersed from Babel following the deluge.

The Jesuits had as much difficulty with native political systems as they did hunting and gathering, again owing in part to the privileged views of Aristotle and the weight of Western tradition, which held that humanity was "naturally" divided into rulers and ruled. The Jesuits and other Europeans saw the universe as ordered from the top down; the benefit of every doubt was enjoyed by persons of authority, in whom both religious and secular authority were invested with a sacral character (Huizinga 1967:46–55; O'Malley 1993a:353). It was difficult in this regard for the Jesuits to appreciate the relatively egalitarian and democratic nature of Indian socio-political systems. Indeed, throughout the *Historia* Pérez de Ribas seemed to deny that the Indians—sedentary or otherwise—had any government. For instance, in his overview of Sinaloa and its people Pérez de Ribas commented:

> There were no laws or kings among them to chastise their vices and sins, nor was there any kind of authority or civil government that could punish them. It is true that they recognized some principal caciques, who were the heads or captains of families or rancherías. But their authority consisted only in organizing for war or attacks

---

62. Cassiodorus, who is among the classical authors cited by Pérez de Ribas, gave voice to the European and Jesuit ideal of *reducción* when he commented, "Men ought to draw together into cities" (Hodgkin 1886:31).

against their enemies or working out peace agreements with other nations. Such actions were in no instance undertaken without the consent of said caciques, who for such purposes commanded great authority. (Book 1, Chapter 3)

It was not that the Indians lacked government, but rather that it did not conform to the absolute model with which Europeans were familiar. Paradoxically, while Pérez de Ribas often denied that the Indians had government, he and other Jesuits nevertheless described what clearly were sophisticated organizations. For instance, Pérez de Ribas often recounted how native caciques in council or in public speeches endeavored to create a consensus with respect to public policy on matters such as baptism, war, or peace. In Book 5, he noted that each Yaqui ranchería contained groups of kinsmen led by certain *principales* who in turn recognized a "principal chief." The principal chiefs alone decided matters of war and peace, and often raised armies numbering in the thousands. Elsewhere, speaking of the Cáhita in general, he commented that the principal chiefs had the largest fields, which were cultivated with the assistance of their subordinates, and that it was primarily the principales and headmen who enjoyed the benefits of polygamy and differential access to material possessions such as cotton *mantas*.

While native elites in Sinaloa enjoyed differential access to wives and certain material possessions, the accumulation of "wealth" was ameliorated by a cacique's responsibility to redistribute rather than hoard or consume goods and services, as was done by Europe's aristocracy and burgeoning middle class. Similarly, a cacique's power, while perhaps derived in the first instance from membership in a particular clan or lineage, ultimately depended on demonstrated leadership and ability to form a consensus. Pérez de Ribas and other Jesuits could never quite grasp such egalitarian and democratic principles. Thus, in Chapter 11 of Book 2 Pérez de Ribas recounted how the Guasave were at first slow to accept baptism because there was nobody in a position of absolute authority who could order the people as a whole to accept baptism:

Still these Guasave and other populations along the upper Río [Sinaloa] were not completely peaceful, despite the fact that there were Christians among them who had been baptized earlier. The lieutenant and his soldiers repeatedly visited them to establish complete peace. Due to these new nations' instability, because they were governed, or better to say misgoverned, by their many leaders and were unfamiliar with being governed by a single leader, he met with varied success.

Because Indian principales did not behave like European princes or kings—exercising absolute power—they often were seen as powerless. This point is illustrated by a quote from Chapter 13 of Book 5, describing how an Indian cacique was "powerless" to punish an Indian who had threatened Pérez de Ribas:

That night the cacique Don Mateo held a meeting in his house, where all the people gathered. After the customary tobacco he spoke of the ugly incident. He could not punish it, for one thing because the Indian who shot the arrow was not yet reduced to his kin group. Moreover, these caciques (as was previously mentioned) do not have authority over their people to punish them for the offenses they commit. Still he proposed and his people agreed that no one communicate with or go near that Indian who had disturbed and insulted them.

Here is one of many examples where a cacique's power, in this case his proposal to ostracize Pérez de Ribas' assailant, was seen as ineffectual. The fact that native caciques were often seemingly indistinguishable from their "commoner subjects," reflecting principles of reciprocity and redistribution, further confused Pérez de Ribas and most other Jesuits. In Chapter 30 of Book 3, Pérez de Ribas reflected Jesuit surprise that a cacique named Don Bautista behaved like a "commoner": "During the physical construction of churches he took pride in carrying beams, adobes, and mud, encouraging his vassals and subjects through his example. Even though the priest sometimes wanted to excuse him from this task and have him settle for governing the people and overseeing the construction, with a smile he set his hands to work, carrying materials for God's house and thereby inspiring others."

These examples are suggestive of the way in which Pérez de Ribas' perception and representation of aboriginal culture were governed by his European and Jesuit values and beliefs. Quite often the Indian constructed by Pérez de Ribas was a reflex of his most cherished beliefs as well as political and institutional contingencies. As noted, a major reason why the crown invested in missions was so that the Jesuits could "domesticate" the otherwise anarchic and bellicose Indian and in the process create a servile labor force for Spanish mines, haciendas, etc. (e.g., Book 9, Chapter 10). In point of fact it was assumed a priori that the Indians lacked government, which is in part why the Jesuits were sent to the northern frontier—to impart order where none existed. Arguably, the Jesuit failure to perceive Indian government reflects this political imperative as well as cultural-theological contingencies, particularly European ignorance of democratic political forms.[63]

For similar political reasons the Jesuits also had difficulty perceiving and representing native warfare. Pérez de Ribas frequently attributed warfare to either cannibalism (a desire for human flesh) or incursions by one group into another's territory for purposes of rape. This is the case for instance in Chapter 12 of Book 2:

> These nations see the protection that is enjoyed by those who make peace with the Spaniards and who place themselves under the king's protection. They see how much this friendship benefits them in their defense against their former enemies, which they all generally have. They also see that due to this friendship they live peacefully in their pueblos, lands, and fields. Their enemies cannot cast them out or take their daughters away by force or commit offenses against them as they used to do when they were gentiles.

It is difficult to interpret this characterization of Indian warfare, particularly when, as in this case, it occurs in the context of a defense of Jesuit reliance on Spanish soldiers. One may reasonably wonder to what extent Pérez de Ribas was bound to represent native society as both lacking government and troubled by warfare—warfare that was sophisticated enough to require special measures. In this light the Jesuits accomplished what soldiers alone could not: the "domestication" of the Indian.

This said, it would be unwise to dismiss Pérez de Ribas' observations on native warfare. There is considerable archaeological evidence, principally in the form of defensive sites and retreats, which indicates that warfare was in fact common during the protohistoric period (Reff 1991b). The relative ease with which native peoples assembled well-organized armies numbering in the thousands, including armies that defeated or seriously challenged Spanish-led forces, is testimony to the aboriginal prevalence of warfare. Moreover, although Pérez de Ribas often suggested or implied that the Indians went to war almost at the drop of a hat ("for no other reason than the desire for human flesh"), he also indicated in Chapter 3 of Book 1 that it was rare for the members of one nation to fight amongst themselves, committing murder or other acts of violence, as happened in Europe. Equally important, in various books of Part 1 he attributed warfare to competition over land, access to salt deposits and hunting

territories, and in one instance, to a dispute that arose over the rules for playing a native game, *correr el palo*.

In point of fact Pérez de Ribas made contradictory statements about warfare, implying in one moment that it was senseless and in the next, the result of lamentable yet just causes. Similarly, he often stated or implied that the Indians' "drunken revels" were excuses for personal liberty. And yet his text also reveals other "higher" functions, as in Book 6, Chapter 7:

> The storms were so severe that they destroyed what [crops] had been sown, which were already drying up because of a lack of rain. On this occasion this old man, who was a sorcerer, called together some of his sorcerer friends. As a solution to their problems, they arranged the celebration of a famous drunken revel and barbarous dance to placate the storms. The author of these gentile abuses is just like the exercises he teaches them to perform. Although they fooled some Christians who were still tender in the Faith into agreeing to participate in this celebration, God undid the devil's tricks, preventing any [real] damage.

There are many instances in the *Historia* where it is difficult to determine which contingencies—theological, literary, political—influenced Pérez de Ribas' rhetoric. For instance, in recounting how Father Julio Pascual was forewarned while saying Mass of his impending martyrdom by the appearance of blood on an altarcloth (Book 4, Chapter 10), Pérez de Ribas noted that this miraculous occurrence was witnessed by several of Pascual's neophytes, who were "simple people." At first glance the qualification "simple people" appears derogatory. However, when the phrase is considered within its larger context—a chapter in which Pérez de Ribas must acknowledge papal guidelines concerning the documentation and questioning of witnesses to miracles—the argument can well be made that Pérez de Ribas referred to the Indians as "simple people" (i.e., too simple to dissemble) to establish their authority as witnesses.

Similarly, in Book 7 Pérez de Ribas presents a long and intricate defense of the Jesuit missions and the Indians' capacity to comprehend the basic mysteries of the Catholic faith. At the outset he assumed the rhetorical position of the "devil's advocate":

> At first glance what seems to undermine these nations is their limited [intellectual] capacity, which is demonstrated by their inhuman and barbarous customs and their lack of any type of the order that is found in a republic, because they have neither kings nor government. Consequently, one would not expect any fruits—or very limited ones— from the preaching of the divine evangelical doctrine and

---

63. Pérez de Ribas' denial that the Indians had government (despite detailed descriptions of the same) is reminiscent of Evans-Pritchard's (1940:181) comments about the Nuer in his classic ethnography (Rosaldo 1986:94).

holy laws to people who seem to have lost even the natural laws that survived among other civilized peoples. (Book 7, Chapter 2)

This view of aboriginal culture is hardly laudatory, and yet after articulating this negative view of the Indian Pérez de Ribas proceeded to refute it on both empirical and theological grounds.

The fact that Pérez de Ribas' often referred to the Indians as children also reflects more than ethnocentrism. The casting of the Indians as children who needed nurturing was entirely consistent with Pérez de Ribas' theology and the sacred literature that informed his worldview and writing. When asked by his disciples, "Who is the greatest in the kingdom of heaven?" Christ replied, "Unless you change and become like little children you will never enter the kingdom of heaven" (Matthew 18:1–3). The saints of medieval hagiography frequently addressed their religious followers as children (e.g., Keenan 1952:151–52). In I Corinthians 3:1–2, the apostle Paul referred to his neophytes of Corinth in much the same terms used by Pérez de Ribas: "I fed you with milk and not solid food, for you were not yet able to take it—and even now, you are still not able to, for you are still living by your natural inclinations."

The fact that *Historia* was written at a time when the Jesuits were being pressured by the bishop of Durango to release their neophytes to secular clergy also influenced Pérez de Ribas. The bishop and his predecessors had long resented the fact that tens of thousands of Indians under Jesuit tutelage in missions were exempted from paying ecclesiastical tithes, which supported the episcopal hierarchy. In theory, according to the Laws of the Indies (Gómez Hoyos 1961:155–224), once the Jesuits' Indian charges were fully formed in the faith, they were supposed to be released to secular clergy, at which point the Indians would begin paying taxes to support the clergy and bishop. In practice, however, the Jesuits always argued that their neophytes required considerably more tutelage than was anticipated, and thus their charges were never quite ready to be relinquished to secular clergy. The Jesuits pointed out that secular priests rarely spoke the Indians' languages nor would they be satisfied with the meager salary that an Indian parish would furnish (Polzer 1976:6).

There was thus a political reason as well as theological and literary ones why the Jesuits cast the Indian as childlike, in effect requiring the "special education" that the Jesuits provided, principally through their mastery of Indian languages and long familiarity with the Indians' "barbaric" customs.

Arguably, the same contingencies also prompted Pérez de Ribas and other Jesuits often to speak of the Indians in Sinaloa as poor, even while they acknowledged that the Indians enjoyed a relative abundance of food from farming, fishing, hunting, and other subsistence pursuits. Again, Pérez de Ribas' "poor Indians" and "poor land" rhetoric (e.g., Book 9, Chapter 10) were dictated in part by a Jesuit concern with retaining control of their neophytes. Indians who were poor could not pay tithes to support secular priests. No less important is the fact that "poor" Indians were implied by the Jesuits' Christ-like definition of self. As Pérez de Ribas pointedly reminded his reader in Book 7, the first to be told of Christ's birth and the essential message of the Gospel were poor, rustic shepherds, "like our Indians."

It would be a gross simplification to suggest that the Jesuits consciously misrepresented the Indians for political reasons or because they were ethnocentric. Jesuit discourse is a reflection of much more complex processes. This is true with respect to the Jesuits' frequent characterization of the Indians as lazy and inconstant. Despite their vow of poverty and their celebration of the virtue of charity, the Jesuits were very much attuned to the workings of capitalism. Jesuit colleges in Mexico and throughout the world were made possible by rents and other income from Jesuit properties, including ranches, farms, and other concerns that were bequeathed to the order. Jesuits such as Pérez de Ribas clearly saw the Indian as lazy (relative to Europeans) because the Indian often showed little interest in working for more than a few hours a day to accumulate wealth and profits. Similarly, the fact that the Indians operated more along principles of just price rather than "buyer beware," valuing the act of exchange as much if not more than the items bartered, often prompted Europeans to view the Indian as childish or easily impressed by trinkets. The Jesuits never fully understood the complex nature of Indian exchange. Indeed, Pérez de Ribas often commented that the Indians had no commerce aboriginally, owing to their constant warfare. And yet he also noted in passing how various groups exchanged salt, corn, fish, and other items. These seemingly contradictory statements are clarified in Chapter 1 of Book 6, where Pérez de Ribas makes clear that he had been drawing a distinction all along between commerce and barter. Arguably, Pérez de Ribas and other Jesuits made such a distinction because there were in fact real differences between Indian and European "commerce" (barter versus trade/mercantilism). It was also the case, however, that drawing such a distinction made it possible to deny that the Indians had commerce and thus to justify a Jesuit presence on the northern frontier. Spanish law (going back to Vitoria) had long held that conquest and conversion were perfectly justified (indeed required!) in areas of the New World where trade was precluded by warfare, inasmuch as God had intended all nations to trade with one another (Deloria 1992:257).

The Indians' "inconstancy" and "instability" must also be understood as reflecting various truths or meanings. Jesuit neophytes were in fact "inconstant," meaning reluctant to abandon their own behaviors and beliefs in favor of those introduced by the Jesuits. This inconstancy created enormous problems, inasmuch as it implied that the missionaries were not doing their job as teachers, the Indian was incompetent, or God was withholding his grace from both parties. Although Jesuits such as Pérez de Ribas often cast the Indian as inconstant, he and other missionaries in the New World also went out of their way to rebut charges that the Indians were incapable of grasping Christian truths or that God was withholding from the Indian divine inspiration. As the following quote from Chapter 12 of Book 2 suggests, Pérez de Ribas assumed an ambivalent stance regarding the Indians' instability, invoking the devil as well as an inherent flaw in the Indians' character or nature:

> Moreover, there is the matter of the instability of these peoples, especially at the beginning of their conversion. This is when the devil, with his tricks and snares, stirs the coals of the Indians' inherent instability. This fierce lion roars when he sees the flight of the souls that he once possessed and held in tyranny for so long. His obstinacy and that of his familiars, the sorcerers, serves no other purpose than to turn the converted Indians back to their old vices, murders, drunkenness, and barbarous ways. Who can deny the need for force of arms for restraining and frightening such a great number of this type of enemy, particularly when their insolence becomes so uncontrolled?

THE DYNAMICS OF JESUIT-INDIAN RELATIONS

As the preceding quote indicates, Pérez de Ribas represented Jesuit-Indian relations largely in terms of a battle between the Jesuits, favored and aided by God, and the devil and his Indian familiars, the shamans.

Through the use of metaphors (e.g., devil's snares, castle), type scenes (e.g., exorcisms, miracles) and rhetorical strategies (e.g., direct discourse) from the Bible and medieval hagiography, he sought to persuade his audience that the Jesuit experience in Nueva España was not only in keeping with Christian tradition, but was ordained and directed by divine providence. In light of his enculturation, religious formation, and career choice—placing himself in harm's way as a missionary—one has to assume that Pérez de Ribas believed his own story. Today the story may seem surreal because it emphasizes invisible forces such as the God and the devil and ignores what a modern reader might perceive as the "real" forces that affected Jesuit-Indian relations.

Pérez de Ribas' privileging of God and God's will at the expense of material or efficient causality is most evident in his discussion (or relative lack thereof) of Old World diseases and their consequences. Arguably, for both Indians and Jesuits there was nothing more real than epidemics of measles, smallpox, malaria, and other diseases, which were unknown in the New World prior to the conquest. As in other areas of Latin America, Old World maladies devastated the Indian population of northwestern Mexico during the late sixteenth and the seventeenth centuries. The Jesuit anuas as well as the *Historia* itself suggest that native populations were reduced by more than half within a few years of incorporation into the mission system. In a report from 1638 Pérez de Ribas, then Jesuit provincial, noted that of the 300,000 Indians who had been baptized by the Jesuits, only one-third were still alive (AHH 1638). The Indians had never known epidemics of acute infectious disease in any way comparable to the epidemics coincident with the European invasion of the New World. I have argued elsewhere (Reff 1991b) that epidemics of typhus, malaria, and other maladies not only had profound demographic consequences, but undermined the structure and functioning of native societies, including the authority of Indian shamans and other elites, who could neither explain nor prevent the unprecedented suffering coincident with epidemics. The Jesuits generally followed in the wake of epidemics, reconstituting native subsistence practices and socio-political organization, albeit with the resident priest now functioning as "principal chief." This assumption of authority was facilitated by the introduction of Christian beliefs and rituals that had evolved over the course of a millennium in the Old World to deal in part with epidemic disease

(Amundsen 1986; Christian 1981; Flint 1991; McNeill 1976).[64] Although one can question the intrinsic value of relics, rosaries, confession, and blood processions to cure and heal, they nevertheless can have profound benefits for individuals and communities confronting unprecedented suffering. Because the Jesuits coupled prayer with clinical care of the sick, they also had an advantage over Indian shamans, who had little or no experience with acute infectious disease. As Pérez de Ribas noted in Chapter 10 of Book 6, the Jesuits' ritual cleansing of the soul cured more Indians than it killed:

> This case amazed this entire new Christian community, which now believed what the priest had taught them: that this Holy Sacrament does not take lives. Indeed, it had miraculously given life to this sick man when he was in danger of dying. This was also confirmation that even though in His supreme judgment God sometimes arranges for or allows cases that give the devil and his followers the opportunity to challenge the Faith and its ministers, at the same time He does not forget to favor these ministers with other cases of unique providence which support and confirm the Faith, and these [He gives] in greater number and quality.

The conclusion that Spanish-introduced disease played a dynamic role in Jesuit-Indian relations is readily inferable from the *Historia*, and yet paradoxically Pérez de Ribas never really acknowledged that epidemics of smallpox or other maladies could have contributed significantly to Indian interest in baptism and acceptance of the mission way of life. Disease was a lot like Indian government, which the Jesuits also documented even while they rhetorically ignored or denied its existence. More specifically, there are several chapters in the *Historia* (e.g., Book 2, Chapter 6) where Pérez de Ribas noted the great toll in suffering caused by epidemics. However, there are countless other chapters where disease or epidemics appear as what Barthes (1987a) refers to as *punctum*—unplanned narrative details that reflect an irreducible reality obscured by the author's own attempt to inscribe meaning. As a case in point, Pérez de Ribas recounted in Chapter 34 of Book 2 how several hundred Nébome abandoned their pueblos along the middle Río Yaqui in 1615 and traveled more than two hundred miles to reside with other Pima speakers living along the Río Sinaloa. Although he noted that a number of Indians died en route and

another was covered from head to foot with what he referred to as leprosy (the punctum), he concluded that "the principal reasons why these people came [south] were to receive Holy Baptism, become Christians, and enjoy the catechism taught by the priests." Nowhere does he suggest that the Indians were suffering from typhus, which was current in Sinaloa at the time, and had come south hoping that the priests and their ritual cleansing might cure or protect them from sickness.

On numerous other occasions Pérez de Ribas simply declined to discuss disease, claiming he did not want to appear redundant:

> During this visit I spent [only] eight days with the Ahome, because I had to continue on to the Zuaque nation. I left them with orders to build a church that was more adequate, even if it was made of straw, and a similar house where I could dwell when I returned. With this the first formal preaching of the catechism among the Ahome nation was concluded. I will continue discussing the Ahome [below] and then move on to their neighbors, the Zuaque. I will not discuss here the Baptism of sick adults during this entrada. This is to avoid repetition of very similar events that it should be supposed arise at each step in these new enterprises. Such events will be noted only when circumstances worthy of memory form a part of them.

What constituted "circumstances worthy of memory" for Pérez de Ribas were primarily casos de edificación—instances where the sick in the throes of death were besieged one last time by the devil but rejected him in favor of the Christian God. Like early medieval authors who witnessed the plague and its consequences, Pérez de Ribas was preoccupied with the ultimate (God) rather than proximate causes (disease) of Indian behavior (Amundsen 1986:76; Biraben and Le Goff 1975:49, f.3; Van Dam 1993:87). Indeed, the *Historia* abounds in comments such as the following from Chapter 36 of Book 2, which celebrated the salvation of souls and ignored the tragic loss of human life and the destruction of Indian cultures:

> Who would have thought that among such fierce tigers, which is what these barbarous nations were, God would select for His heaven a flock of more than six thousand innocent infant lambs? These infants died with baptismal grace during the first years of this mission and went to heaven, where they joined many other adults who had been baptized on the verge of death, as well as countless other new and old Christians who were saved not through baptismal grace, but rather through the other Holy Sacraments for Salvation that the Son of God left His Church: Confession, Holy Communion, and the holy oils.

64. For instance, the Forty-Hours Devotion was first performed in Milan in 1527 to invoke divine aid at a time of war and plague (Evennett 1968:38).

In Book 4 Pérez de Ribas devoted an entire chapter to the decline of the native population, emphasizing in the first instance Old World disease. However, in characteristic fashion, disease and its consequences were understood almost entirely from a theological perspective:

> And if human judgment is free to humbly inquire after the higher designs of divine providence, what we can understand is that these peoples deserved this punishment because of their sins, idolatries, murders, sorceries, etc. In a single year the most populous Mexican nation [the Mexica or Aztec] sacrificed to devils and their idols twenty thousand of their enemy. This cruelty, as well as the other vices that consumed Sodom, also existed among these peoples, and because of them the Indians deserved to be done away with by God, just as He depopulated the Promised Land so He could introduce His [own] people. Such people deserved to be wiped from the face of the earth by God, as is pondered in Chapters X through XII of the Book of Wisdom. (Book 4, Chapter 5)

Although in some instances in the *Historia* (e.g., Book 3, Chapter 26) Pérez de Ribas cast disease as a punishment from God, more frequently he spoke of it as a gift (e.g., Book 9, Chapter 3). This sentiment is reflected in the previously cited quote where Pérez de Ribas spoke of thousands of infants and countless adults who were fortunate to depart this world with their souls relatively unblemished. In his introductory letter to the king, Pérez de Ribas almost seemed to boast when he commented that the Jesuits had baptized forty thousand infants who had died and gone to heaven. As terrible as disease was,[65] the Jesuits also saw it as beneficial. Epidemics not only saved innumerable modestly blemished souls, but they also provided an ideal battlefield where the missionary could defeat the devil and his Indian familiars, the shamans. As Pérez de Ribas noted in Chapter 20 of Book 5, it was not uncommon after an epidemic for a missionary to find his Indian rival(s) dead:

> It was also noted that God took the lives of other principal Indians who were obstacles to the teaching of the Gospel. He finished them off, to the amazement of others. But at the same time these nations have seen and noticed that the priests among them live long lives. They generally enjoy good health, in spite of the fact that they are destitute of doctors and medicines, for these are completely lacking in these remote lands.

65. Elsewhere in the *Historia* (e.g., Book 9, Chapter 3) as well in the anuas one finds Jesuit admissions that they were greatly saddened by the loss of Indian lives, particularly children.

This is one of numerous observations that clarify how disease and its consequences gave the Jesuits an advantage in their competition with Indian shamans, thus facilitating the process of conversion. Again, from Pérez de Ribas' perspective it was not disease (an efficient cause), but almighty God (the first efficient and final cause) that gave the Jesuits an edge in their dealings with Indian shamans. Significantly, in their battles with the shamans the Jesuits employed sacred literature both as a "practical" guide as well as a source of rhetoric and conventions to represent Jesuit-Indian relations. This is evident in Chapter 12 of Book 2, where Pérez de Ribas noted how the Jesuits mimicked the apostles:

> I also take it to be true, as it is, that the means taken to achieve an objective, in addition to being just, ought to be commensurate with the time, place, and people, as well as the endeavor for which it is intended. This is because different circumstances often call for different means. Means that were convenient and useful at one time and place may be harmful and counterproductive at another time and place. When preaching the Gospel, the holy Apostles were moved by this realization. They tolerated and even made use of some of the ceremonies of the old law, which as a result of Christ's death were no longer relevant. They did this because they wished to avoid obstacles to spreading the law of the Gospel that they were introducing to the world at that time. They also wanted to prevent an aversion to receiving the Gospel in the minds of the Jews.

The strategy employed by the apostles, and later articulated by Gregory the Great and medieval hagiographers, was largely one of redirecting, rather than destroying pagan religiosity. While the Jesuits were gentle with Indian adults, accommodating when possible behaviors and beliefs that did not violate Christian truths, they worked closely and intensely with Indian children, making sure that they acquired few of the parents' "sinful" ways. One of the first things the Jesuits did when they arrived in Sinaloa was establish a boarding school where the sons of native elites were educated. Because most Indian groups often had to wait years for a resident priest, it was common for a group in the meantime to send a handful or more of their children to the Jesuit college at San Felipe to be educated. The children often returned as young (Christian) adults to their nation, where they assumed positions of authority and assisted the resident priest (see Book 2, Chapters 26 and 36).

It was with the children that the Jesuits enjoyed their greatest and most lasting success as agents of culture change. By the time the *Historia* was published in 1645, almost every Indian pueblo in Sinaloa was governed by Indians who had been instructed as children in Christian ways. During the century following the publication of the *Historia*, the vast majority of native cultures in Sinaloa ceased to exist as distinct cultural entities. This loss of native languages and lifestyles was due only in part to Jesuit programs for directed culture change. Throughout the seventeenth and much of the eighteenth centuries, the native population of Sinaloa continued to decline, principally from disease (Gerhard 1982; Jackson 1994; Reff 1991b). At the same time increasing numbers of Indians and mestizos from the south migrated northward to Sinaloa and Sonora, merging with the resident population (Radding 1979; Sheridan 1992).

Of course, Pérez de Ribas was oblivious to the Jesuit role in the destruction of native peoples and cultures. Indeed, what we term destruction he saw as salvation. Where we see Indian communities fleeing disease, he saw God bringing them back into the fold. Significantly, the *Historia* embodies both realities and worlds of meaning.

CONCLUSION

The fabrication of an Africanist persona is reflexive; an extraordinary meditation on the self; a powerful exploration of the fears and desires that reside in the writerly conscious. It is an astonishing revelation of longing, of terror, of perplexity, of shame, of magnanimity. (Morrison 1993:17)

The Jesuit construction of the Indian was every bit as reflexive as the Anglo-American fabrication of the Africanist persona. The Indians who populate the *Historia* originated in the Jesuit imagination, which was both thoroughly European and yet opposed to what Europe was becoming. The Reformation, deism, and budding capitalism made for sleepless nights. Jesuits like Pérez de Ribas eagerly departed the Old World for the New, hoping to relive a biblical past and participate in the rebirth of the Church. As is apparent from the *Historia*, the Jesuits found what they were looking for, and not insignificantly, they employed the same strategies as the apostles and medieval saints, accommodating as much as destroying pagan beliefs and ritual. In both early Christian Europe and the New World, epidemics and social upheaval (e.g., collapse of the Roman and Mexican Empires) paved the way for the missionaries and monks (Flint 1991; McNeill 1976). This, however, is a modern inference; although both monks and mis-

sionaries made note of disease and culture change, they had meaning only as manifestations of divine will.

In casting Nueva España as the primitive Church Pérez de Ribas not only gave voice to the hopes and dreams of Catholic reformers, but he deployed for political purposes privileged and authoritative metaphors and literary conventions, which helped to assure continued crown and Church support for the Jesuit mission enterprise in Mexico. Pérez de Ribas' discursive strategies were simultaneously a reflection of political and institutional contingencies and his most cherished beliefs and epistemology, which in turn were informed by sacred literature. The very complexity of his audience (e.g., kings, bishops, Jesuit novices), coupled with the weight of Western tradition and the actual experience of the New World and its native peoples, resulted in different and often contradictory images of the Indian as well as the Jesuit enterprise. Sinaloa was both the Garden of Eden and the devil's castle; the Indians were ingenious as well as childlike, pacific yet warlike; the Jesuits never coerced the Indians, yet garrisons were essential to missionary success; missionaries were not to tempt God by expecting miracles, yet God never abandoned his ministers.

Pérez de Ribas and fellow missionaries endured an intellectual wrestling match between the Indian implied by Western experience and Christian theology and the Indians who showed up at the priest's abode each morning for religious instruction. As is evident throughout the *Historia*, Pérez de Ribas firmly believed that God never abandoned his creation. The Indians may have strayed and been taken prisoner by the devil, but they were never forsaken by God and left without some measure of his grace. This fundamentally positive and hopeful attitude toward native peoples, coupled with the intellectually jarring experience of learning Indian languages and residing with native peoples, enabled and forced Pérez de Ribas to transcend the bounds of his own cultural categories and experience. True, this transcendence was partial and infrequent, but it nevertheless made for moments in the *Historia* when Indian voices were heard.

Pérez de Ribas' chief concern, however, was not Indians, but how God's grace flowed through his missionaries to the Indians, changing them from fierce and barbarous peoples into true Christians. The reality with which he was preoccupied is only knowable indirectly; it is the effects of grace that are visible. Thus the fabric of the *Historia* is woven of countless instances of wondrous conversions and miracles, *alongside* ethnographic data worthy of the most positivist science. In this regard the *Historia* is very much a reflection of the Jesuits' seemingly curious blend of Renaissance humanism (particularly the philological imperative of close attention to detail) and late-medieval devotionalism and mysticism. Pérez de Ribas valued and was quite good at empirical observation, describing in great detail Indian rituals, military engagements, and other events and processes. However, whereas today we in-terpret and explain human behavior on the bases of material or cultural constraints, Pérez de Ribas emphasized invisible forces, chiefly God and the devil.

In reading the *Historia* the key challenge is to avoid anachronistic judgments; that is, evaluating Pérez de Ribas' account of the Jesuit mission enterprise from a wholly modern perspective. A context-sensitive reading of the text provides a window on both the encounter and our own modern predicament.

THE HISTORIA

HISTORIA

DE LOS TRIVMPHOS DE NVESTRA

SANTA FEE ENTRE GENTES LAS MAS BARBARAS
y fieras del nueuo Orbe: confeguidos por los Soldados de la.
Milicia de la Compañia de IESVS en las Missiones
de la Prouincia de Nueua-
España.

REFIERENSE ASSIMISMO LAS COSTVMBRES,
ritos, y fuperfticiones que vfauan eftas Gentes: fus pueftos, y temples:
las vitorias que de algunas dellas alcançaron con las armas los Ca-
tolicos Efpañoles, quando les obligaron a tomarlas: y las dichofas
muertes de veinte Religiofos de la Compañia, que en va-
rios pueftos, y a manos de varias Naciones,
dieron fus vidas por la predica-
cion del fanto Euan-
gelio.

DEDICADA A LA MVY CATOLICA MAGESTAD
DEL REY N. S. FELIPE QVARTO.

ESCRITA POR EL PADRE ANDRES PEREZ DE RIBAS,
Prouincial en la Nueua España, natural de Cordoua.

Año IHS 1645

CON PRIVILEGIO

En Madrid. Por *Alōfo de Paredes*, jūto a los *Eftudios de la Cōpañia.*

HISTORY

OF THE TRIUMPHS OF OUR

HOLY FAITH

AMONGST THE MOST BARBAROUS
AND FIERCE PEOPLES OF
THE NEW WORLD,

Achieved by the Soldiers of the Militia of the Company of J e s u s in
the Missions of the Province of Nueva España.

An account is also given of the customs, rites, and superstitions of these peoples; their lands and
climates; the military victories won by Catholic Spaniards when these [peoples] forced them to take
up arms; and the glorious deaths of twenty religious of the Company who, in various places and at
the hands of various nations, gave their lives for the preaching of the Holy Gospel.

Dedicated to His Most Catholic Majesty,
Our Lord King Philip IV

Written by Father Andrés Pérez de Ribas,
Provincial of Nueva España and a native of Córdoba

* *
Year   * * * * *   1645
* *

With Privilege

[Published] in Madrid by Alonso de Paredes, next to the offices of the Company. [PB]

To His Most Catholic Majesty, Our Lord King Philip IV

(My Lord), I have assembled in this history the accomplishments of the sons of the Company of JESUS—Your Majesty's most humble chaplains—which have been wrought through the preaching of the Gospel to the most barbarous and indomitable peoples in the New World. These people, who are likewise the most humble and unknown, have been granted the protection of Your Majesty's most Catholic favor. Although in their former natural and political state these people were humble, unknown, and base, they are presented in this history, which is dedicated to Your Majesty, in the supreme and noble state of children of God, within the flock of His Holy Church. Through them is proclaimed that divine herald celebrated by a great Prophet-king [David]. He announced that the Prince of Ages, the only begotten Son of the Father, would descend from His royal throne to favor the humble and the poor, granting them entry into the greatness of heaven among princes and great men. He also said that we would see the Lord who was spoken of in Psalm 112, which says, *Excelsus super omnes Gentes Dominus*[1]—He is the Lord who lives on high, exalted and eminent over all peoples. He lifts from the dust those who were humble and scorned, placing them among princes—*Suscitans á terra inopem, & de stercore erigens pauperem: vt collocet eum cum Principibus, cum Principibus populi sui.*[2] In accordance with Saint Jerome,[3] I can clearly understand who the princes of God's people are in the courts of heaven. In this very same canticle the Prophet-king gave signs of when such amazing works would come to pass, saying, *A Solis ortu, usque ad Occasum, laudabile nomen Domini;*[4] that is, when the nations of east and west are united and they all join in singing praises and acknowledging the divine name of the true God. The present account discusses the western nations, [PB] whose human and temporal condition is poor and humble. These nations are presented to Your Majesty here in this history, asking for your royal protection and favor. They are now improved in divine and heavenly matters and are well on their way to joining the courtiers of heaven, singing praises to the name of He who is the sovereign and only God, whom before they did not know.

(My Lord), the courtiers and assistants to Divine Majesty did not scorn poor and humble shepherds. Rather, they happily descended from heaven to serve as escorts and guides, inviting the shepherds to acknowledge and adore their Heavenly King. Nor did these seraphim hold their Divine King in low esteem because He came down from the incomprehensible supremacy of His throne, leaving His everlasting Father's side to firmly embrace humanity, which had sunk to the state of poor, mortal beings. Instead, these [angels] were greatly moved that their Divine King should favor humanity with the most outstanding acts of kindness and humility that human reasoning and angelic knowledge could comprehend. These are the lengths to which He went in order to exalt humanity *Cum principibus populi sui,*[5] that is to say, so that they could be seated at His table along with the angelic courtiers of His heaven.

In the commandment that Our Lord gave His ministers in His divine parable He could not hide the kindness that welled up within Him for the poor and the scorned. Specifically, He ordered His servants to invite to His royal banquet (where the delicacies were nothing less precious than grace and glory) all whom they should happen to meet—no matter how poor or oppressed. By way of Saint Matthew He said, *Ite ad exitus viarum, & quoscumque inveneritis vocate.*[6] Saint Luke expounded on this even further, saying, *Pauperes, ac debiles, & caecos, & claudos.*[7] This includes those who are blind in their heathenism, as Saint Ambrose well understood.[8]

Obliged by the rules of their order and dispatched under orders from Your Majesty or your glorious fore-

---

1. Psalm 112:4: "The Lord is sovereign king of all the nations" (Knox 1956:525).

2. Psalm 112:7–8: "Lifting up the poor from the dust he lay in, raising the beggar out of his dung hill, to find him a place among the princes, the princes that rule over his people" (Knox 1956:525–26).

3. Pérez de Ribas is apparently alluding here to Saint Jerome's influential commentary on the Gospel of Matthew.

4. Psalm 112:3: "from the sun's rise to the sun's setting let the Lord's name be praised continually." (Knox 1956:525).

5. Psalm 112:8: "Among the princes that rule over his people" (Knox 1956:525–26).

6. *Margin Note*: Matthew 22[:9]: "go out to the street-corners, and invite all whom you find there" (Knox 1956:23).

7. *Margin Note*: Luke 14[:21]: "the poor, the cripples, the blind and the lame" (Knox 1956:73).

8. *Margin Note*: Ambr. Sup., Luc. ca. 14. The apparent referent here is Ambrose's influential commentary on Luke 14 (see Farmer 1992:20).

fathers and your Royal Council, the sons of the Company of JESUS, ministers of this Lord, have led many of these nations, albeit scorned and humble, into God's royal palace. Some have entered the palace of the Church militant and others the Church triumphant.[9] Moreover, [PB] having submitted to the yoke of evangelical law, they have simultaneously declared themselves vassals of the Catholic monarchs, placing themselves under their protection and care. Many [nations] did so during Your Majesty's reign; for our sake may God keep you for many happy years. These peoples have recognized this favor as both divine and royal. In the first instance they have benefited from the divine law that they have accepted and [now] profess. Second, they have benefited from secure temporal defense against the enemy nations on their borders, who wish to disturb their peace. Because this is all pleasing news, Your Majesty should be the first to receive it. And because it is this history that conveys this news, both it and its author hope that it will be granted permission and favor. For this same reason the author of this history begs Your Holy Royal Majesty's pardon for the boldness of dedicating this work to you. What other protection could I seek than that of he who among all the kings and princes on earth is such a supreme and superbly Catholic king? God chose you to be the prince and custodian (just as the greatest potentates in heaven are) of the many provinces and kingdoms that are now being formed and multiplied in the New World. Because these highly numerous peoples and nations had been unknown and forgotten, they were destitute of the light of the Faith and the knowledge of its true God. This Lord (who is King of Kings) had preserved these nations for centuries and thousands of years so as to place them under the protection and crown of Your Majesty and your glorious forefathers, who always have protected them with their royal orders and favorable provisions and decrees.

(My Lord), along with the news of spiritual success related in this history, I cannot nor should I fail to include here a most singular attending circumstance of divine providence. Although the nations of which this history speaks were poor in temporal and earthly respects, divine goodness nevertheless willed through His amazing providence that their fields, mountains, and lands be very rich, productive, and fertile in their outstanding silver deposits. As a result many of Nueva España's rich mining centers are located in these poor peoples' lands. So that these do not become confused, I will name them here: the mining camp called El Parral, which was just discovered and is very rich; Guanaceví; and San Andrés and Topia. Additional mines have also been discovered [PB], which are presently being explored. All of these are located in the lands and fields of these peoples, as this history relates.

Efforts are also being made to locate pearls in the Sea of California. Your Majesty has ordered the far coast of that gulf to be settled if things go well, as they are expected to, on the basis of some trial runs. This very rich treasure will [eventually] be maintained by the nations that have already been converted and those that are now being converted in this extensive Province of Sinaloa, which is discussed at length in the present account. God had reserved all these riches for the Catholic monarchy of the kings of Spain because He knew how well they would employ them in the expansion and preservation of His Divine Faith throughout the entire world.

Besides tending primarily to the religious instruction of these peoples, the sons of the Company, Your Majesty's most humble chaplains, also labor in Your Majesty's service to domesticate and preserve them in Christian friendship with Catholic Spaniards, so that your vassals and the Indians can live in great peace and unity and so that all might enjoy the great treasures that have been mentioned. (My Lord), this history does not fail at many points to provide irrefutable testimony of the glorious use made of such riches. This is done not only because the subject matter demands it, but also because it is right that the [whole] world and all its peoples should know and acknowledge that the nations of this [new] world extend only as far as your royal Catholic generosity, piety, and holy zeal for spreading the Divine Faith throughout all those places that have been, are being, and will be discovered. In this history the sons of the Company of JESUS, Your Majesty's humble chaplains, will bear witness to and proclaim the benefits of royal generosity that we have experienced in the execution of this glorious endeavor.

[We] have been dispatched from Spain many different times over the years with this royal provision and generosity to convert the peoples of the American Indies. The most fortunate part of this is that there have been clear demonstrations of the successful results of this labor. At present, in Nueva España alone, to which the present account is limited, there are sixty-five priests from the Company working outside colleges, sustaining religious instruction in the nations they have converted, which number more than twenty. In their

---

9. The Church militant refers to living Christians; the Church triumphant are those in heaven (Attwater 1949:97).

pueblos they have built more than eighty churches and Christian temples. [PB] With baptismal grace an army of forty thousand infants (a number based on written records) from among those who have been washed and cleansed in the Savior's fonts are already reigning with Christ. They have safely ascended to heaven from this corner of the world, resembling the angels in not having stained their robes with actual sin.

What may please Your Majesty is to have this army pleading with Divine Majesty for the prosperity of your crown and monarchy. Out of gratitude they will undoubtedly acknowledge that they entered to reign with Christ, unlike those other innocents murdered by order of that other king [Herod] [10] in an attempt to keep Christ from reigning. Rather, they were protected by a Catholic king who, desirous of extending that divine kingdom, yearly sends ministers at his own royal expense to expand this kingdom of the Church militant and triumphant. Others of these ministers are currently working to pacify and reduce [11] to friendship and peace numerous other barbarous nations that are [still] gentiles, with the intention of raising above them the glorious standard of the holy Cross, which your Catholic Majesty's loyal Spanish vassals have always defended and continue to defend with the weapons that you provide. As is recounted in this history, in raising this standard among the peoples that have been converted up to the present time twenty of these evangelical ministers have spilled their blood at the hands of these barbarous infidels, thus consecrating their lives for the preaching of the Gospel and the exaltation of our Holy Faith. We deal here only with what has happened in the Kingdom of Nueva España, leaving what the [sons] of the Company have accomplished and endured in other kingdoms and provinces in America to be recorded by those who have firsthand knowledge of those matters.

Thanks be to God that, despite the fact that those courageous preachers of the Gospel ended their lives in such a glorious labor, and although those currently employed in that labor are none too free of that danger, both groups have nevertheless achieved very glorious triumphs. Christ's doctrine and holy law have prevailed

and are now esteemed, obeyed, and worshiped by a good number of barbarous nations. According to baptismal registries, 300,000 souls in these nations have received our Holy Faith, not counting those who are currently being baptized.

(My Lord), he who writes this account, laying both it and himself at Your Majesty's feet, [PB] set out for Nueva España forty-two years ago, in 1602, from our Company's college in Córdoba, his city of birth. He was sent by holy obedience in the company of others under orders from your Royal Council. He spent sixteen years among these peoples, giving them religious instruction and dealing with many of these nations in their [own] languages. Then, as a duty of his office [as Jesuit Provincial] he later visited them and gained very precise knowledge of that which he records herein, without which he would not dare to present this account to Your Majesty, for to do so would be an impertinence most worthy of punishment.

(My Lord), having heard these arguments, who could disapprove of such a work and report being dedicated to Your Catholic Majesty and of your favor being requested, because all that is right is to be favored by your royal protection? If temporal and political matters in the Indies make it necessary to seek and resort to royal protection on a daily basis, how much more appropriate would it be to request and seek your favor for the publication of an account of cases and enterprises that are glorious for both Divine and human Majesties? And given Your Majesty's great piety and clemency, who can doubt that this work and its author should be quite confident of being well received and favored? May God on high keep your royal personage for the good of your kingdoms, the New World, and the entire Catholic Church, just as we, Your Majesty's most humble servants and chaplains, continually beg of the Divine Majesty. Madrid, July 15, 1645.

Your Catholic Majesty's humble chaplain,
Andrés Pérez de Ribas

[PB]

10. See Matthew 2:16.

11. Throughout the *Historia* Pérez de Ribas uses the term *reducción* with a connotation that is close to the original meaning of the Latin verb *reducire* 'to lead back'; that is, to gather into settled communities (McNaspy 1984:53). This connotation is consistent with the Jesuits' theological perspective on Native Americans, namely that they were descendants of people who many centuries earlier had strayed from the Old World and God's truth.

Approval of the Reverend Father Monsignor Fray Alonso de la Corte, of the Order of Saint Augustine, retired university professor of advanced theology in the Royal College of Saint Augustine at the University of Alcalá de Henares.

By commission of Don Gabriel de Aldama, Vicar General[12] of Madrid and its district, I have examined and read this book, the title of which is *History of the Triumphs of Our Holy Faith, etc.*, by Father Andrés Pérez de Ribas, of the Company of JESUS, Provincial of the Province of Nueva España. I do not find herein anything contrary to the Catholic Faith or good customs. Rather, the book is a faithful copy of the Acts of the Apostles and those holy missions recorded by the Evangelist Saint Luke. The religious of this outstanding order who have been sent to these missions are a living example of JESUS Christ, because (as Tertulian said) imitating Christ means principally preaching, toiling, and suffering death. These were the tasks that occupied the Son of God while He was on earth, and this was the continual labor of these zealous ministers [in Nueva España]. *Est & illa Dei voluntas* (he says) *quam Dominus adminstravit praedicando, operando, sustinendo, ad quae nunc nos velut ad exemplaria prouocamur, ut & predicaemus, operemur, & sustineamus ad mortem usque.*[13]

In this history Gospel laborers will find a guide for governing their actions when, with divine aid, they introduce, propagate, and maintain the Catholic Faith in the remaining provinces [of Nueva España], which are so extensive that their boundaries remain unknown. Illustrious examples of apostolic men of this holy order will [also] be given. As heirs to their great father Saint Ignatius' spirit and zeal for the welfare of souls, some of them, through their heroic virtues, were a true portrayal of the Gospel. Others augmented these virtues by spilling their blood in defense of the Faith, triumphing gloriously among extremely fierce nations that belonged to the enemy of mankind, and thereby freeing those souls from the slavery, idolatry, and superstition through which he had oppressed them.

Herein one will read about wondrous marvels wrought by the almighty hand of God in [the Indians'] very nature, confirming the Catholic doctrine preached by His servants and firmly rooting in the Church those tender and newly planted trees. It will be seen that peoples who in the past were little more than wild beasts now live in a Christian republic with well-established civil order. The edification of all the long-time faithful will be great, seeing such steadfastness in the Faith and such shining virtues in many of the newly converted.

The subjects of the [Spanish] crown will be encouraged anew by the portrayal of valiant feats undertaken by Spanish captains and soldiers who, with their invincible weapons, expanded and defended the boundaries of the Church. Clear proofs will be given that justify our Catholic monarchs' right to conquer and take possession of the Indies. Last of all everyone will greatly enjoy reading about the variety of subjects and events that are contained within this history.

Up to the present time [news of] these missions has been confined to the boundaries of Sinaloa. Henceforth, however—to the author's credit—such news will extend to the ends of the earth. [Before,] these evangelical laborers' heroic works benefited only some Indians, but [now] they will benefit all of Christendom. To date these deeds ran the risk of {PB} being forgotten, but [now] they are indebted to the author for perpetuating their memory.

The author complies with all the rules of history, especially the principal rule, which is truth and exactitude in what is recounted. He incontrovertibly sur-

---

12. A vicar general, also referred to as *provisor* (Poole 1981:640), is a deputy appointed by a bishop, who acts on behalf of the bishop and takes precedence of all clergy of the diocese (Attwater 1949:516).

13. *Margin Note*: Lib. de oratione cap. 4. The referent here is chapter 4 of Tertulian's *Book of Prayer*. Tertulian was a Carthaginian theologian of the early Christian era (A.D. 160). "There is also that will of God (he says) that the Lord administered by instructing, toiling, and enduring [suffering], which we now are called forth to exemplify, so that we too may instruct, work, and endure [suffering] until our death."

APPROVAL OF FRAY ALONSO DE LA CORTE 55

passes almost all historians, who ordinarily record what they have heard or found written [elsewhere]. The author of this history either drank from the primary sources—the individuals he discusses—or was present at the events he records. He himself plays no small role in this history, and its veracity is thereby confirmed. The law gives more credence to a single eyewitness than to many who only heard something. Plato elegantly advanced this argument when he said *Qui audiunt audita dicunt, qui vident plane sciunt*.[14] He thereby elevated the sense of sight above all the others; it is more noble because it is the least susceptible to deception, and from nothing else does understanding receive more certain information than from the eyes.

So that the richness of the gold of truth is not left without its enamels,[15] these are provided by the author through the great erudition that he demonstrates in his interpretation of Scripture and the writings of other priests with which he adorns this work. I cannot fail to offer many congratulations to Córdoba, who throughout the centuries has had sons who have given her such great fame. She now enjoys the fame given her by this author, who is no less than any of her other sons. I will not sing his praises because it might place me under suspicion, because we share the same homeland and blood. I will content myself by providing the reader of this history with the same single commendation that Cassiodorus offered when he was unable to praise another as he would have liked *Est enim* (he says) *quoddam speculum morum agentis oratio, nec maius potest esse mentis testimonium, quam qualitas inspecta verborum*.[16]

Therefore, I feel that not only should the author be granted the permission he has requested to bring this history to light, but also that he should be given many thanks. This is my opinion and I place my signature upon it in this, the Convent of San Felipe, Madrid, December 14, 1644.

Fray Alonso de la Corte

[PB]

14. *Margin Note*: Citado por Barcio in adversarijs ad Claudianu Mamercum, lib. 50. c. 3. Barcio and his work, "against those opposed to Claudianus Mamertus" (d. ca. 474), are unknown. "Those who hear speak things heard, those who see know them clearly."

15. 'Enamels' refers to the vitreous varnish that often was added to metal (often gold or silver) objects, particularly religious ornaments.

16. *Margin Note*: Lib. 5. variar. c. 22. Book 5 of the *Variae* or Various Letters of Cassiodorus, a devout Christian statesman and philosopher of the sixth century. Chapter 22 is a letter entitled "King Theodoric to the Senate of the City of Rome," recommending the appointment of a young official named Capuanus (Hodgkin 1886:277–79). "Indeed (he says), speech is a certain mirror of the way things are done, it can be an indication of the mind more than the scrutiny of words."

Approval of the Most Reverend Father Fray Juan Ponce de León, of the Order of the [Friars] Minor of Saint Francis de Paul, Censor of His Majesty's Council of the Holy and General Inquisition and Visitor to the Bookstores of Spain[17]

Your Highness has ordered me to examine *History of the Triumphs of Our Holy Faith amongst the Most Barbarous and Fierce People of the New World, Achieved by the Soldiers of the Militia of the Company of* JESUS *in the Missions of the Province of Nueva España*, which was written and prepared with remarkable erudition by the very reverend Father Andrés Pérez de Ribas, Provincial of the Company of JESUS in the aforesaid province and a native of the city of Córdoba. Having studied this history with the attention and care that Your Highness's supreme orders require of me, I find it to be a work that is worthy of its author. In it he informs both the [Old and New] Worlds of the marvels wrought by God among those gentiles, using as His instrument the highly illustrious sons of the great Company of JESUS *per quos* (as Rupert said on a similar occasion) *veram Dei magnitudinem cognouit mundus*.[19] The Company's major concern is the most assured fulfillment of its most holy Institute,[20] as discussed by Bozio, Caussin, Francisco Montano, Luis Richeome, Maximiliano Sandaeus, Jacobo Silvanio, Martín Sis-

coria, Pedro Estebarcio, Sangaverino, and many others, as well as in chapters 1 and 3 of the *Super Cantica* and in Paulo Leonardo's history of middle science.[21]

However, among all those mentioned, it is Father Antonio de Vasconcelos who provides us with the greatest notice of the marvelous deeds wrought by the sons of this great order in compliance with its holy Institute.[22] He says that from the time the cornerstone of the Company of JESUS was laid up until 1610, its sons had reduced 1,370,000 believers to the flock of the Church in the Orient alone. As Luis de Urreta discusses at length, between 1610 and 1628 in the remote kingdoms of Ethiopia,[23] which were subjects of Prester John of the

---

17. The visitation of bookshops was an important element of official attempts by the church and crown to suppress heterodoxy in Europe. In 1564 the Council of Trent called for the appointment of inspectors to regularly visit booksellers and assess fines against those selling prohibited material. As early as 1551, lists of banned books were drawn up by the Holy Office and theological faculty at various universities in Europe (see Kamen 1985:78–79; Martin 1993: 2–4; McGrath 1988:15; O'Malley 1993a:313).

18. M.P.S. stands for Most Powerful Lord (*Muy Poderoso Señor*), referring to the king.

19. *Margin Note*: Ruperto. The referent here apparently is Rupert of Deutz (1075–1129), who authored a number of influential commentaries including one on the Song of Solomon. "Through whom (as Rupert said on another occasion) the world knows the true greatness of God."

20. The Jesuits often referred to the way they lived and worked as their Institute, which was outlined in the Formula or fundamental charter of the order (what the "Rule" is to other religious orders) drawn up by Ignatius Loyola and his followers and subsequently amended and elaborated as the Jesuit Constitutions (O'Malley 1993a:5–8).

21. *Margin Notes*: Bozio de signis Ecclesia, signo 4. c. I, & sequentib; Causino lib. 14. c. 17; P. Paulo Serlog. & P. Paul. Leonard. tom. I. & 3. Super Cantica. The authors cited here in the text and in the margin notes include several well-known Jesuits. Tommaso Bozio's (1548–91) *De signis Ellesiae Dei Libri* was published in 1591. Nicolas Caussin was the Jesuit confessor to Louis XIII and author of *The Holy Court* (3 volumes: 1625, 1629, 1630) and *Spiritual Guidance According to the Spirit of Blessed Francis de Sales* (1637) (de Guibert 1964:350, 370–71). Louis Richeome (1544–1625) was a French Jesuit who authored a number of mystical and historical works about the Jesuits, including, in 1596, *Apologia . . . pro Societate Iesu in Gallia contra Antonii Arnaldi . . .* and, in 1606, *Victorie de la vérité catholique . . .* (see Martin 1993:94; Stalker 1986:107–8). Maximilian van der Sandt, better known by his Latin name Sandaeus, authored numerous works including *Key to Mystical Theology* (1640) and *Song of a Century*, in which he tried to show that during the Company's first one hundred years it had a succession of eminent mystics (de Guibert 1964:33).

22. *Margin Note*: P. Ant. Vasconcel. tom. 2. de Angel. Custode p. 4. lib. 6. cap. 6. The referent here is Antonio Vasconcelos' *Treatise on the Guardian Angel* (1621), which furthered devotion to angels; this was an important devotion encouraged by the Jesuits in the early seventeenth century (de Guibert 1964:392).

23. *Margin Note*: Luis de Urreta lib. 3. fol. 590. Although Fray Juan apparently is referring here to Luis de Urreta's *Historia eclesiastica, politica, natural, y moral, de los grandes y remotos reynos de la Ethiopia, monarchia del emperador, llamado Preste Juan de las Indias . . .*, this work was published in 1610, and thus could not recount events from 1610 to 1628. Moreover, Urreta was a Dominican friar who was apparently critical of the Jesuits. Fray Juan may have confused Urreta's history with the Jesuit, Almeida's *Historia Aethiopiae*, which covers the period 1610–1635 (Caraman 1985:129, 159).

Indies,[24] in the provinces of Gezira, Musa, Travancore, Hormuz, Cochin, Indalcanez, Monomotapa, Meale, Vaciano, Filando, Malabar, Coulan, and in many of the others under the jurisdiction of the Patriarch of the Indies [Francis Xavier], the priests of this Company, by way of their missions, converted more than two hundred thousand people to our Holy Faith. By the same year, in Bohemia and Hungary and their neighboring provinces, the Jesuits, who had been preaching against the errors of Luther and Calvin and a host of Huguenots, had reduced more than forty thousand heretics to the flock of the Church. Paul Laiman testifies to this in his defense of the Order of Saint Benedict in response to the elimination of its monasteries in [PB] Palatine.[25] At present the sons of Saint Ignatius have converted more than thirty thousand infected heretics belonging to a great variety of sects, as is recounted by Gabriel Patreolo.[26] In France Father Emond Auger preached in the fields because his listeners would not all fit inside the churches, as Florimond de Raemond and Cornelio de la Piedra testify.[27] He alone converted more than forty thousand Lutherans. This son of the Company was so great in all things, especially in preaching, that, shouting, people called him *Tuba Franciae*,[28] because his voice was like the voice of wisdom and moved [even] those who lived very steadfastly.

Because of the preaching of the sons of the great Company of JESUS, and by way of their heroic deeds, heaven has been enriched with a new glory, the Church with abundant children, Christendom with believers spread far and wide, and the world with a singular light. Demons experience particular confusion and suffering when they see that, because of the highly illustrious sons of Saint Ignatius, hell is becoming poorer

and the number of heaven's inhabitants is growing. As Bozio points out, the most glorious father Saint Francis Xavier reaped great fruits in Japan, converting three hundred thousand believers, and in the Moluccas [Spice Islands], in the districts of Tholo, another twenty-five thousand idolaters. In the eleven years that he spent preaching in the Indies, *Plus homines ad Christi caulan reducit, quam innumera Hereticorum millia, ex omni gente, & Natione, & toto Orbe terrarum per annos mille & quingenta, ad suas sectas traduxerunt*.[29] Accordingly, Bozio wonderfully stated, *Vnum huius sodalitij validissimum Ducem Franciscum Xauerium Nauarrum plures Christo aggregasse de idolorum veneratoribus, quam suos traduxerunt ad errores, quot quot unquam extiterunt Haeretici, a Saluatore passo in hunc usque diem*.[30] The fruits that this great order of the Company of JESUS has wrought in Christendom are greater than the insults that the Calvinist and Lutheran heretics have made against the Church Universal. Bozio, Posevino, Botero, Sandero, Surio, Alano Copo, Simón Mayolo, Valdés Fernández, Puente, Torquemada, and many others testify to this in various places.

That which is recounted by Nicephorus Callistus is very pertinent here.[31] He discusses the great city of Constantinople, noting that the earth shook so hard that the tallest buildings toppled over and the city was razed. However, on that occasion the prefect Syrus' industriousness was so great that he rebuilt the city and returned it to its former splendor. For this reason everyone in Constantinople publicly thanked him, saying *Constantinus condidit, Syrus restaurauit*.[32] Let the Lutherans and the Calvinists attempt to devise new ways to undermine the Church; let the gentiles in Java, Malaysia, Bengal, Makassar, Buzareta, Ende, and many other places wage war against her by means of their idol worship; let those from Persia, Zaradia, Tiberias, Hircania, the Caspian, Semaclite, Sarazene, Ethiopia, Lagos, Sana, Anasgos, Sauromatia, Rhaetia, and Mos-

---

24. A legend still current in the seventeenth century held that a former king, Prester John, had ruled a vast Christian empire somewhere in Asia, which was thought to have evolved in isolation from the Christian kingdoms of Europe during the Middle Ages. The Christian community that was found in Ethiopia in the sixteenth century following Vasco de Gama's voyage of discovery was thought to be a part of Prester John's legendary empire (Caraman 1985:4–7; Neill 1964:120–21).

25. Palatine here apparently refers to the region of southwestern Germany.

26. *Margin Note*: Gabr. Patreolo. The referent here is unknown.

27. *Margin Note*: Floremund. Ramund. lib. 5. n. 6 fol. 24 & Cornel. de la Piedra tom. I in Prophetas maiores ad initium Isaiae fol. 11 (*On the Greater Prophets going back to the beginning with Isaiah*). Florimond de Raemond was a Bordeaux jurist and influential critic of the Calvinist heresy in France. Emond Auger was one of the most important Jesuits in sixteenth-century France. Known as the 'Canisius of France', he founded a number of Jesuit colleges, authored a celebrated catechism, and was a confessor to Henry III (Gilmont 1961:295–301).

28. "The trumpet of France."

29. *Margin Note*: Bozio de signis Ecclesiae lib. 6. c. 3. The referent here is Tommasso Bozio's (1548–91) *De signis Ellesiae Dei libri*, published in 1591. "He led more humans into Christ's flock of sheep than the innumerable thousands [removed by] Heretics; [people] from every race and nation and from the whole world were won over to the [Christian] way of life after fifteen hundred years."

30. "One of the most powerful leaders of this religious brotherhood, Francis Xavier of Navarra, added more to the flock of Christ from among those who worship idols than they [Protestant heretics] won over to their errors, as many heretics as ever have existed, stretched from our Savior's day to this."

31. *Margin Note*: Nicephoro Calixto lib. 14. c. 46. The referent here is Nicephorus Callistus Xanthopulus (ca. 1256–1335), apparently Xanthopulus' *Paradise*, an account of the Slavic Church.

32. "Constantine built, Syrus rebuilt."

cow attempt to undermine the Church through their errors and sects. JESUS will raise His great Company so that through their lives, example, and continual preaching in all the aforementioned nations, they can reduce to the flock of Saint Peter all the believers who lacked His light.

All these fruits are obtained through the great missions that the author of this book and others on different occasions recount, saying that the great Order of the Company of JESUS rebuilds the ruins of the Church, returning it to its former beauty. If one considers the Company as it was and has been since the glorious patriarch Saint Ignatius founded it, then Christendom can shout [PB] that Christ founded His Church but the sons of Syrus (who is the same as he who produces fire) restored it to its original beauty.[33] In this way one can rightfully say along with Bozio, *Formosam faciem eius, pulchrioreque apperere, quam erat ante a, quam ab Haereticorum perfidia deformata fuisset.*[34] As proof of this the *Gloss*[35] indicates that when Daniel was being held captive he rebuilt a fallen temple. This caused great amazement because *Ut mutatione temporum, ac si nouiter instructum fuisset, omnibus cerneretur.*[36] The *Gloss* also states that the wonder of this deed was so great because *quod quacunque die cernitur, eadem constructum putatur, quia sic pulchritudo noua, & materia solida.*[37]

All this is experienced in the apostolic missions of the Company of JESUS. Through their preaching they restore life to those who were dead in sin, leaving them with a new splendor and glory. These ministers offer their lives in holocausts in the most remote regions of the world, and their only goal is to lay at the feet of the Pontiff the green branches that once were dry. Once these ministers separate from their brothers they offer themselves as bloodied sacrifices to God, just as He ordered in the first book of Leviticus.[38] Because of this, Florimond de Raemond, Counsel of Burgundy, spoke with wonder of the Company of JESUS, *Quis non dicet Societatem Iesu auxiliarem esse manum e caelo contra nouum Senacherib summissam, quam etiam firmiter sperandum est, non prius defecturam, quam omnes Haereses sint extinctae: diuinitus ad hoc mmissa est Societas, ut mundo faelicitatem, Ecclesiae salutem, sibi gloriam pararet, & adferret.*[39] Within this great order there is no other motive for all these things than their great love for dutiful compliance with their holy Institute, as is illustrated by the heroic deeds of each [of its sons]. The same thing was discussed on a different occasion by Saint Basil concerning Musonio, his predecessor in the church at Neo-Caesarea. He says, *In se ipso videndum praebuit priscam Ecclesiae formam, velut ad sacram quandam veteris status imaginem Ecclesiae, sibi commissae faciem effingens.*[40]

There are twenty-nine provinces, eleven vice-provinces, three hundred colleges, twenty-three professed houses, thirty novitiates, and one hundred residences that are all made illustrious by the religious of this great order. And one will find that the more than fourteen thousand Jesuit priests who live in all these different dwelling places have no other goal than that of preparing the world [for salvation], in fulfillment of their Institute, thereby restoring to God the images that the devil has taken from Him by way of various deceptions. This upsets the perfidious heretics so much that, as Florimond de Raemond says, *Quod Melanctonem morti vicinum, tam anxium habuit, ut audiens Iesuitas flumina, & maria transmittere, & culta omnia, atque inculta peragrare, nec quemquam fere iam Orbis esse angulum, quo non penetrarint, & ubi non semen sanquine suo non raro tinctum, ac rube factum relinquerint, ductis es intimo cordis suspirijs exclamauit. Ab quid hoc esse dicam. Video sane totum mundum breui iesuitits repleturi iri.*[41]

33. *Margin Note*: Assi lo dize Marcelin. de Pise in serm. de S. Ignacio sobre aquellas palabras de Iob 38. *Numquid producit luc ferum in tempore suo, & vespere super filios terrae consurgere facis, &c.* "And so Marcellin de Pise speaks of Saint Ignatius' sermon on those words from Job 38." "He never brings forth the light-bringer before its time; in the evening you [our Lord] make it rise over the sons of the earth, etc." Marcellin de Pise is perhaps best known for a history of the Capuchins, begun by Zaccaria Boverio.

34. "His beautifully formed face seemed even more beautiful than it was before it had been disfigured by the treachery of the heretics."

35. *Margin Note*: Glos. in c. I. Iudic. The *Gloss* (*Biblia Sacra cum gloss ordinaria*, 1617) is a scriptural commentary in the form of footnotes, clarifying obscure words in the Vulgate, and based on Walafrid Strabo's authoritative work of exegesis compiled in the ninth century (Attwater 1949:211).

36. "Even as time passed it still appeared to all as if it had been newly built."

37. "Regardless of when it was built, it appeared as if it had been constructed that very day, because it stood firm and beautiful."

38. Leviticus 1 is an account of God's orders to Moses concerning the procedures that the Israelites are to follow when making a burnt offering.

39. *Margin Note*: Florem. Ramund. de origine omnium Haeresum, tom. 2. fol. 5. n. 4. f. 13. The referent here apparently is a work entitled *Concerning the Origin of All Heresies*. "Who will not say that the Society of Jesus is a helping hand sent down from heaven against the new Senacherib [Assyrian king, d. 681], which one must also firmly expect will not fail before all heresies are extinct; the Society has been sent by the Divine to obtain and bring about good fortune for the world, salvation for the Church, [and] glory for itself."

40. "In him can be seen the ancient Church that provided the sacred image a place in which to revel." Basil the Great (A.D. 379) was archbishop of Caesarea and a Doctor of the Church; he apparently succeeded Musonio as archbishop of Caesarea in A.D. 370.

41. *Margin Note*: Florem. Ramund. lib. 5. de orig. omnium Haere-

If the Company was still in its infancy, still in its diapers, and caused the heretics such concern, then how much greater concern must it cause them now, a century later, when they see how prosperously fecund the Company is and how illustriously grand both it and its extremely famous sons have become? As Vicencio Lirense said, no other order is as blessed by its sons as this one *qui ex sinu suo innumeri Doctores, innumeri Sacerdotes, Confessores, & Martyres extiterunt*.[42] This is affirmed by Ribadeneira, Andrés Scoto, and Felipe de Alegambe, in his recently published *Biblioteca*.[43] Many others [PB] have also attempted to recount the grandeur of the Company of JESUS, but they have been unsuccessful in fully capturing the heroic deeds of its sons.

These deeds are so great that omitting them or relegating them to silence would be a clear offense, as Pedro Harisio said when he was telling the world about the Jesuits' wondrous deeds and was unable to restrain himself, *Cum nefas sane meo quedem indicio, fuerit posteritatem tam illustrium gestorum, facinorumque tam inclitorum, que in bello hoc spirituali, contigere cognitione fraudare, & quadammodo furtum, aut sacrilegium potius, honorem supreme bonitati a que omne emanet bonum, & Iesu Christo summo nostro capiti, cuius gloria imprimis expectatur, debitam quadam tenus surripere, denique & Ecclesiae gaudium subtrahere*.[44] This is in accordance with what the Holy Spirit says, *Si tacuerimus, & voluerimus nunciare sceleris arguemur*.[45] This is in agree-

ment as well with the comments concerning this matter offered by Nicolás Renton, Daniel Arculario, Felino Videmba, Mauricio Helincio, Andrés Miguel, Mateo Hostio, Luis Labaterio, and other expositors, who consider it a sin to fail to recount and record succinctly the apostolic acts of the sons of this most illustrious order.

Their due praises shall be sung by Florimond de Raemond, who took them in turn from the mouth of a great heretic named Schluselb. In the preface of his *De sectis Iesuitarem* he speaks of the Jesuits, and unable to remain silent about their grandeur, he says, *O inuicti, & indefatigabiles Acacide Coelitos vos missos credimus, ut tam longo, ac funesto bello sinem imponatis vobis, ut a Mercurio olim Vlyssi, diuina illa berba moly a Deo data est, ut tantum miserorum hominum a benefica illa Circa Haeresi excantatorum, & in bestias transmutatorum multitudinem pristine formae restituatis, aliasque quas mali illius vis nondum attigit, praeseruetis a vobis Duces fortissimi, ultimus ille ictus Laerneo monstruo infligendus expectatur: in fatis nempe est, ut sicut Troia su Pyrrho, sic sub vobis Heresis pereat, atque exscindatur: quamuis autem merita vestra, & labores, non ut par est, ab omnibus accipiantur, & compensentur, ne tamen cessare victorias vestras persequi, donec hostis plane prostratus, & deuictus in triumphum a vobis ducatur*.[46] With these words there is nothing left for me to say concerning this great order. On this occasion I wish I had at my disposal an even greater knowledge of the Company to employ in fulfilling my obligation and in praising the Company and its great sons.

The marvelous deeds that the Company of JESUS has wrought by means of its sons among the most fierce and barbarous nations of the world in its new orb are described by the author of this history with precise factual details, adorned with singular erudition. He portrays to the world the outstanding deeds that those great fighters, the Jesuits, have wrought in those parts [of the world] in the service of their two Majesties. They have worked for the greater glory of God and for Your

---

sum, fol. 34. n. 4. "When Melanchton [apparently Melanchton—German religious reformer d. 1560] [was] near death, he became so upset upon hearing that the Jesuits crossed oceans and rivers, traveling through all lands, cultivated and uncultivated, and that there was now almost no corner of the world where they did not go, leaving behind seeds moistened and made red by their plentiful blood, that he cried aloud in deep breaths drawn from the deepest part of his heart. Let me say that this is indeed so, for I see the whole world in a short time will be filled with Jesuits."

42. *Margin Note*: Vicenc. Lirens. de orig. omnium Haeresum, cap. 23. The author is unknown, although the work in question is the previously cited *Concerning the Origin of All Heresies*. "who in his fold counts innumerable Doctors, priests, confessors, and martyrs."

43. The referent here apparently is an earlier edition of *Bibliotecha scriptorum Societatis Iesu* (Rome, 1676), co-authored by Pedro de Ribadeneyra, Phillipo Alegambe, and Nathaniel Southwell (see de Guibert 1964:217, 288, f.22).

44. *Margin Note*: Petr. Harisio in tom. 1. Thesauro Indico, fol. 11. The referent here is unknown. "Indeed, in my judgment it is surely sinful that posterity has been cheated of the knowledge of illustrious deeds and acts of renown during this sacred war; in some ways it is theft, as a certain wealth, the joy and copper of the Church, has been stolen from our most sacred head, whose glory is especially awaited."

45. *Margin Note*: 4. Reg. 7. (In the Vulgate, 1 and 2 Samuel were considered 1 and 2 Kings, thus 4 Kings in the margin note.) 2 Kings 7:3–8 tells of four men who, sick and hungry, debated whether to enter a famine-stricken city; the men concluded that they would die either way, whether they entered or remained outside the city. "Whether you are silent or speak you are accused of a crime."

46. *Margin Note*: Floremund. Ramund. to. 2. lib. 5. c. 3. ad fin. nu. 4. fol. 35. "Oh unconquerable, and untiring one, we believe that you have been sent from heaven by the Guileless One, so that you may put an end to a war that has been so long and deadly for yourselves. As once God working through Mercury gave Ulysses that divine herb, moly, so may you restore at last the multitude of wretched humans who have been enchanted by that generous Circe heresy, which has transformed them into beasts. May the strongest among you observe beforehand—you who have not yet been touched by that evil—that the last blow is expected to be struck by the Lernaean monster. It is certainly fated that, just as Troy perished under Pyrrhus, so will this heresy be destroyed and perish under you. Nevertheless, let those deserving the praise and labor be accepted by all, lest your victories cease to follow through to the end and the enemy is entirely defeated and you lead him subjected in triumph."

Majesty (God keep you), seeking new vassals who bow to you in obeisance and proclaim your grandeur. Christendom could say of the sons of the glorious patriarch Saint Ignatius the words spoken by Saint Anselm on a similar occasion: *Gratias agimus Deo, & vobis, pro bono selo, quem habetis, & quia ordinem vestrum strenue custoditis, & ut alij illum obseruent strenue studetis.*[47]

In this history the author recounts the great advances that his order has made among these gentiles, subjugating the most isolated nations in the New World to both [Divine and human] Majesties. He also demonstrates how loving the Jesuits are toward those uncivilized nations, which is something for which these people love and respect them. Therefore, because of the continual benefits that they receive from the sons of the Company, these Indians can rightfully say the same words spoken by Saint Bernard to the Abbot William: *Unum sancti Ignatij Ordinem opere teneo, caeteros abaritate.*[48] [PB]

This book can be read confidently: events are recounted in great detail, and the erudition with which they are seasoned is most exquisite. Whoever reads it will benefit so greatly that the words of Pedro Selense will be relevant: *Comede igitur, quicumque librum legis panes appositos, & non corrodas sudore cauponentis valde laboriosos, potius pro obsequio gratia debetur, quam invidia.*[49] Whoever reads this book will find herein much for which to be thankful to its author, and also much for which to be envious of him. The reader will also note what Simon Aldenardense said concerning the life and works of the great father Saint Benedict and his family: In reading these apostolic acts *attentus fueris anxietates a te depellet, cordi tuo inseret incredibilem voluptate sublata malitia radices virtutum affiget anima: opus est omni acceptione dignissimum, & quod eruditoram, & maxime Religiosorum omnium mereatur applausum: opus (dico) foelici, & acuto partum ingenio, summa elaboratum industria, maturo iuditio, & grauissimo ordine concinnatum, nec non coelesti-*

bus sententijs, & exemplis refertum.[50] Finally, this book is pious, erudite, varied, elegant, pure, *in omnibus celebre, in singulis singulare. Et vbique sua laude difusum.*[51] I feel that one can rightfully say of its author the same thing Saint Ennodius said in approval of some of Saint Epiphanius' works: *Pingebat vir sanctus actibus suis paginas quas legebat.*[52]

This history is of such high quality that there is no topic in it that might be subject to censorship, neither theological nor political. There are many passages that are very rich in moral lessons, and these are presented so skillfully, without the author tiring or sinning in digression, that his narrative serves as both instruction and history. Throughout, he maintains piety in his emotions and speech, in great accordance with his lineage, age, position, and state as a religious. Therefore, I feel that the Holy Order of the Company of JESUS, especially in the provinces of Nueva España, should offer him the thanks due him, as was done on a different occasion by Saint Ennodius in the panegyric that he wrote regarding Theodoric, king of the Astrogoths, saying of him (as can be seen in the *Biblioteca of the Fathers*,[53] vol. 12, p. 2): *Refundat tibi Religiosorum generalitas rebus obligat a sermonem, cum in aequalis vicisitudo compensat laudibus, quod adoptata est sudore.*[54]

In this history we find not only what the author presents to us with his quill, but also what he actively carried out through his deeds. Therefore, it is with most justifiable license that one can speak of him using the same words that Peter the Venerable, Abbot of Cluny, pronounced when he saw the history of his own Bene-

47. *Margin Note*: S. Amselm. lib. 3. Epistolarum, epis. 91. The referent here is Saint Anselm's Epistle 91. Anselm (d. 1109), who was archbishop of Canterbury and a Doctor of the Church, was a great theologian ('father of scholasticism') notable for his kindness and opposition to slavery (Thurston and Attwater 1956:2:138–41). "We give thanks to God, and to you, for your good zeal, and because you guard your order vigorously and are eager that others observe it rigorously."

48. *Margin Note*: S. Bernard. The referent here apparently is William of St. Theirry's *Vita prima* of Bernard (Casey 1988:4). "I consider the Order of Saint Ignatius unique in the charitable work it does for others."

49. *Margin Note*: Petr. Selense Epistola ad Salisbariensem, in prologo de panibus. The referent here is unknown. "Therefore eat the nearby loaves of bread, you whoever read a book, and may you not gnaw away at those laborers who certainly serve it up with their sweat; thanks rather than envy is owed indulgence."

50. *Margin Note*: Simon Aldenardense. The referent here is unknown. "You will notice that it drives away anxiety and fills your heart with incredible pleasure; when you endure malice, it will fasten the roots of virtue within your soul. It is a work most worthy of all acceptance and rather instructive; it especially deserves the applause of all religious. It is needed (I say) by the blessed, and is brought forth by an intelligent nature, worked out by great diligence, mature judgment, and arranged by the most serious order. It is reported as well with heavenly thoughts and examples."

51. "Renowned among all, unique among individuals. It is spread everywhere by its own praise."

52. *Margin Note*: S. Enodio. tom. 12. Bibl. V. PP. 2. p. Ennodius (A.D. 541) succeeded Saint Epiphanius (A.D. 496) as bishop of Pavia and authored a panegyric for Epiphanius (Thurston and Attwater 1956:1:139). "The holy man embellished the pages of his text through his actions."

53. Apparently an edition of the *Bibliotecha Patrum* or collected works of the 'Fathers of the Church'. The Jesuit hagiologist, Heribert Rosweyd, compiled an edition that was published in 1615 and again in 1628 (Robertson 1995:77).

54. *Margin Note*: S. Enodio. "Your broad comments on religious matters overflow when change is equally balanced with praise, because it is with sweat for things desired."

dictine order. Therein, one can read of the deeds that the sons of Saint Benedict executed for the greater service of God and for the honor of their holy habit. With holy affection he thus says of the author, *Tanto enim tempore, etiam post mortem tuam apud Deum extendetur lucrum operum tuorum, quanto, ut ita dicam durare potuerit vita librorum tuorum.*[55]

I feel the same, and I pray that Your Highness will be served by granting the author the privilege and necessary funds for the printing of this book. At [Our Lady of] Victory, Madrid, Order of the [Friars] Minor of Saint Francis de Paul, February 3, 1645.

Fray Juan Ponce de León

[PB]

Author's Declaration

On March 15, 1625 our Most Holy Father [Pope] Urban VIII delivered a decree to the Holy Congregation of the Holy Roman and Universal Inquisition. This decree, which was confirmed on July 5, 1634, prohibits the printing of books dealing with deceased men who were renowned for their holiness or their fame as martyrs, as well as books containing descriptions of miracles, revelations, or other benefits obtained from God through these deceased men's intercession, unless they have received the recognition and approval of the Ordinario [i.e., a bishop]. Things of this nature that have already been printed without this approval should in no way be considered as approved.

On July 5, 1631, the same Pope had decreed that praise of a saint or beatified person is absolutely prohibited, although praise that is a matter of opinion or custom is permissible, provided a disclaimer is given at the beginning of the book indicating that such praises do not have the authority of the Roman Church, but rather only whatever validity the author gives them.

In recognition and confirmation of this decree, and with due observance and reverence, I profess and declare that I do not myself consider nor do I want others to consider any of the things that I relate in this book to have any meaning other than that which is customarily assigned by human authority, as opposed to the divine authority of the Roman Catholic Church or the Holy Apostolic See. Exception is made for only those individuals whom the Holy See himself has placed in the Catalog of Saints, Beatified Persons, and Martyrs. [PB]

---

55. *Margin Note*: Petr. Venerabile lib. 1. epist. 20. ad fratrem Hislibertum, tom. 12. Bibliotec. V. PP. 2. p. The referent here is Epistle 20 ("to my brother Hislibertus") in a collection of Peter the Venerable's letters (*Bibliotheca Cluniacensis*), an edition of which was published in Paris in 1614 (Martin 1974:12). The collection is perhaps Peter's best known work (Constable 1967:70). "Indeed, long after your death the profit from your works will spread in the house of God, for as long, if I may say so, as the life of your books."

Prologue to the reader and an introduction explaining the *History* and its contents

God Our Lord inspired our holy patriarch Saint Ignatius Loyola, founder of the Company of JESUS, to employ its sons in several different ministries, enlisted under the banner of its captain, Christ JESUS, in His service and in the service of His bride, the Holy Church. One ministry that was very central to the Institute of this holy order was missions among both the faithful and infidels and among both civilized and barbarous peoples. With favors from heaven this ministry has been carried out quite successfully since the Company's founding.

The triumphs that this history discusses were won in just such enterprises, and for that reason I call them 'missions'. I must explain why I use this term and what it means, because some might find this usage unusual. First, one should not think it odd that the name given these enterprises does not have its origin in the word 'Apostles'. This is the name the Son of God Himself gave His first twelve disciples whom He chose to be captains in the spiritual conquest of the world. They were to scatter to all parts of the earth and to all towns and cities, spreading the rays of the light of His Gospel and dispersing the shadows, teaching all men and opening the way to their salvation. As the Evangelist Saint Luke writes, *Apostolos nominavit*.[56] He gave these illustrious conquerors of the world the title 'Apostles'. This is the same as 'ambassadors on a mission' or, as Saint Jerome interprets it, the same as the Latin *Missos*,[57] or 'missionaries', which means the same thing. Christ Our Lord confirmed this title when He said, *Apostolus non est maior eo, qui missit illum*.[58]

This is the source of the names 'missionaries' and 'missions' instituted by the holy founder of the Company of JESUS. He did not intend to endow his sons with the supreme title and renown of Apostles, which pertain principally and foremost to those whom the Son of God chose to be the original preachers of the Gospel in the world. Rather, he wanted to make it understood that the Company's institution of this ministry of missions was very much in line with the Institute of Christ Our Lord's divine apostolate. The latter was the norm and basis for all evangelical religious orders, in which they all take justifiable glory. Moreover, even though the title 'Apostles' pertains foremost to those whom Christ chose for that supreme ministry, the Holy Church nevertheless has also used this title to grant honor and renown to apostolic men, particularly those sent by the Supreme Vicar of Christ to preach the Holy Gospel in provinces throughout the world. This is why Saint Gregory the Great, who secured and prepared the promulgation of the Gospel in England, is called 'the Apostle of England', and why Saint Boniface, who preached in Germany, is called 'the Apostle of Germany'. Our father, Saint Francis Xavier, preached in the Indies of the Orient and was the first to introduce the Gospel and to found missions in Japan. Accordingly, when he was canonized as a saint in a bull issued by Pope Gregory XIII, he was granted the title 'the Apostle of India'.

This ministry, which was founded and instituted by Christ, is so divine and supreme that the Evangelist Saint Luke found the assignment and circumstances of these missions to be most worthy of being recorded and celebrated in his Acts of the Apostles [PB] (which is a history of the Apostles' missions, particularly those of the Apostle of the People,[59] Saint Paul). Thus, he often noted how during these missions unusual orders came from heaven and even from the Holy Spirit. This happened not only in those missions that the Son of God ordered the holy Apostles to undertake with Him in the various cities and towns of Judea, as recorded by the holy Evangelists, but also in other missions to other peoples following His ascent into heaven and the coming of the Holy Spirit. Saint Luke focuses specifically on these missions, saying that the Holy Spirit itself

---

56. *Margin Note*: Luc. c. 6. Luke 6:13: "these he called his apostles" (Knox 1956:60).

57. Translation: 'sent'.

58. *Margin Note*: Ioann. 13. John 13:16: "no slave can be greater than his master, no apostle greater than he by whom he was sent" (Knox 1956:103).

59. Pérez de Ribas refers to Paul as the *Apostól de las gentes*, which we have translated here and throughout the text as Apostle of the People. It seems that Pérez de Ribas went out of his way to refer to Paul as such, rather than as the Apostle to the Gentiles, which is how Paul is commonly known.

chose Saints Paul and Barnabus for missions: *Segregate mihi Saulum & Bernabam in opus, ad quod assumpsi eos.*[60]

God is so concerned with the ministry of these missions that He wills that His own hand and counsel determine even the time, place, and peoples among whom they are to be carried out. He arranges and decides everything Himself. Accordingly, Saint Luke writes that once Saint Paul and his companions had passed through the region of Phrygia the Holy Spirit forbade them from departing for Asia: *Vetatisunt ab Spiritu Sancto loqui verbum Dei in Assia,*[61] because the time and opportunity had not yet arrived that His divine providence had arranged for preaching the Gospel to those people. When they reached Mysia Saint Luke writes that they encountered another new order from heaven, saying, *Tentabat ire in Bithiniam, & non permissit Spiritus JESU.*[62] They attempted to proceed with their ministries and missions into Bithynia, but the Spirit of JESUS did not permit it. By saying that the Spirit of JESUS prevented this Saint Luke made it very clear that the Lord uses His Spirit (which is the Holy Spirit itself) in planning and preparing His evangelical missions. He finally writes that they went down to Troas, and while they were there, *Visto per noctem Paulo ostensa est.*[63] Saint Paul had a unique revelation. A man from Macedonia appeared to him, who (in the opinion of holy Doctors) must have been the guardian angel of that province. Through him the holy Apostle was sent notice from heaven that he should go to Macedonia to preach the Holy Gospel. Subsequently, Saint Luke writes: *Statim quaesivimus proficisci in Macedoniam, certifacti, quod vocasset nos Deus evangelizare eis.*[64] We immediately directed our journey and mission to Macedonia, certain that for the time being God wanted us to preach the Holy Gospel to these people, not others. In order to get the Prince of the Apostles, Saint Peter, to baptize some gentiles who had sought him out, the angels lifted him in ecstacy to heaven. There they presented him with a divine revela-

tion, telling him that it was God's wish that he should administer Holy Baptism to those gentiles.[65]

I confess that I have gotten carried away and have dwelt at length on such divine demonstrations. But because they deal with the topic of the Apostles' missions, which were undertaken on orders from heaven, and because the missions that this history relates are so much like them, and because I have placed the word 'missions' in its title, it has been necessary to state how much they please Our Lord and how much His divine providence cares for them. Given such special and divine orders, who could fail to clearly see how much God and His divine Spirit care about these enterprises and missions for reducing gentiles to Christianity? Or, because they are so important to Christ and His Church, how attentive divine providence is to selecting the time, place, and persons to be employed in them? It can be of great consolation for those whom God chooses for such apostolic enterprises to reflect on these matters.

Our holy patriarch wanted his sons to labor in this ministry that is of such concern to God, and he also wanted his sons' devotion to parallel [PB] as closely as possible that of the holy Apostles in seeking the welfare and salvation of souls (a goal which, along with self-perfection, the Company intensely pursues). One means he chose for attaining this supreme goal was missions among the faithful and infidels like those carried out by the holy Apostles. These means and ministry are central to the Institute of the Company of JESUS, as was declared by its Vicar, Pope Gregory XIII, in his [papal] bull, which begins *Ad perpetuam rei memoriam,* and then it continues *Ipsa Societas, inter omnia Religioniam Instituta expeculiari, & solemni voto, specialem curam habet salutis proximoru, pertitum Orbem discurrendi.*[66] Through these words the Supreme Pontiff declared that under-

---

60. *Margin Note*: Actor. c. 13. Acts 13:2: "I must have Saul and Barnabas dedicated to the work to which I have called them" (Knox 1956:128).

61. *Margin Note*: Actor. 16. Acts 16:6: "the Holy Spirit prevented them from preaching the word in Asia" (Knox 1956:132).

62. *Margin Note*: Ibidem. Acts 16:7: "they planned to enter Bithynia, but the Spirit of Jesus would not allow it." (Knox 1956:132).

63. *Margin Note*: Ibidem. Acts 16:9: "Here Paul saw a vision in the night" (Knox 1956:132).

64. *Margin Note*: Ibidem. Acts 16:10: "we were eager to sail for Macedonia; we concluded that God had called us there to preach to them" (Knox 1956:132).

65. This is the story in Acts 10:9–48 of Peter's vision of a linen cloth that descended from heaven, which was filled with beasts that God commanded Peter to eat. Peter did not want to consume anything that was unclean, but God told him that he was not to consider unclean anything that He had made. Therefore, when Peter was later called to the house of Cornelius in Caesarea to preach to the gentiles, who were subsequently filled with the Holy Spirit, he did not refuse to baptize them because he understood from his earlier vision that God willed that even the gentiles should receive God's grace.

66. "For perpetuity," and then it continues, "this Society will be distinguished from all other religious by a solemn vow to hasten anywhere in the world for the special care of the salvation of its neighbors." Gregory XIII was pope from 1572 to 1585. It was Pope Paul III, in 1540, in his bull *Regimini militantis ecclesiae* who first acknowledged the Jesuit order and its specialized function and mission (O'Malley 1993a:5).

taking missions throughout the world, placing souls on the road to heaven, is a ministry that is very much a part of the Company's self-perfection. It is noteworthy that the words of Christ Our Lord agree with those of His Supreme Vicar, for Christ ordered His Apostles: *Euntes in universum mundum praedicate Evangelium.*[67] Travel throughout the entire world; the Supreme Pontiff, too, commanded the Company to disperse over the entire globe.

The sons [of the Company] have done so in the missions of the Indies of the east, where they have labored for the glory of the most holy name of JESUS. Other authors have written about the glorious victories these missionaries have achieved through the favor of that divine name. In the present history I will relate only those deeds that their brothers have achieved in the Indies of the west through that same divine grace. I do not discuss all of them, but rather only those that Our Lord deigned to provide in the western portion of the Kingdom of Nueva España. There, trophies were won that were just as glorious as those that have been won in other, more civilized nations.

I must also explain the other title that I included in the name of this history, calling it "The Triumphs of the Faith." I thought this appropriate because the triumphs and victories won in these missions are certainly worthy of being remembered. These involved battling and reducing to Christianity peoples who were wilder than the lions and bears whose jaws David and Sampson broke. However, without breaking these fierce peoples' jaws or taking their lives, their barbarous, indomitable, and unheard of customs were destroyed and uprooted, and in their place were introduced the holy Christian customs that are preached in Christ's gentle Gospel. Those who were fierce and inhuman were transformed into gentle lambs in Christ's flock; simultaneously they were introduced to the celestial wisdom of the one God, Creator and Redeemer of the World.

Because these are the victories [won in these missions], I do not feel I have gone too far in giving this work the title "The Triumphs of the Faith." These victories were achieved among fierce nations in the recently discovered New World, and I attribute them to the Faith of Our Redeemer Jesus Christ, to whom this glory belongs. In order to give this history such a title, I can certainly cite the authority of that greatest of [Church] Doctors, Saint Jerome, who said, *Trium-*

phus Dei est martyrum passio, and shortly thereafter, *Hic triumphus est Dei, Apostolorum que victoria.*[68] With these words this great Doctor designates the martyrdom of saints as "triumphs of God and apostolic victories." And martyrdom is part of the subject matter of this history, because in addition to the other triumphs related herein, accounts are also given of twenty apostolic men whose blood was shed preaching the Gospel in pursuit of felicitous victories among barbarous peoples.

All the missions recorded in this history are grouped into five principal missions. The first of these is the Sinaloa mission, which is the most extensive and the first that the Company undertook in Nueva España. The second is the Topia mission, the third is the mission of San Andrés, the fourth is the Tepehuan, and the fifth is the [PB] mission of Parras. They are each composed of various districts and *doctrinas*,[69] and more than sixty priests from our Company labor therein. They are geographically contiguous, spread out over a distance of two hundred leagues[70] within the diocese of the Bishopric of Guadiana and under the political jurisdiction of the government of the Province of Nueva Vizcaya, which is in the Kingdom of Nueva España.

In the history of these missions the means employed by divine providence are so intertwined with human and political means that I must not, nor am I able to separate them. And I have no doubt that the reader will enjoy seeing them united. We find examples of divine authors employing this practice, particularly in the historical books of Divine Scripture, such as Judges, Kings, and the Paralipomenon.[71] Therein are recounted the wars, campaigns, and triumphs of God's [chosen] people over the barbarous peoples whom they conquered. At the same time are recounted the vices, unholy customs, idolatries, superstitions, and rites of

---

68. *Margin Note*: Hier. epist. ad Hebdil. q. 11. The referent here is one of Jerome's epistles, perhaps to Helvidius. "The triumph of God is the suffering of martyrs," and shortly thereafter, "This is the triumph of God and the victory of the Apostles."

69. The term *doctrina* had a precise legal meaning according to the *Recopilación de Leyes de Indias*. Doctrinas referred to gentile communities that had accepted the faith and were receiving religious instruction but that were not fully formed in the faith. Because doctrinas were exempted from ecclesiastical tithes, Jesuits such as Pérez de Ribas were careful to refer to them as such, particularly in the mid-seventeenth century, when there was pressure to "reclassify" the doctrinas as parishes (*parroquias*), which would have forced the Jesuits to relinquish their authority to secular clergy and the Indians to pay tithes (Polzer 1976:5–7).

70. A league equaled approximately 2.6 miles or 4.2 kilometers.

71. The Paralipomenon consists of chronicles that were originally ignored but were later added to the Old Testament books of Samuel and Kings.

67. Mark 16:15: "go out all over the world and preach the Gospel to the whole of creation" (Knox 1956:52).

those who inhabited the Promised Land that God wished to return to His people.

In our time we have seen much of this wrought by God's sweetest providence. He used the Catholic Spaniards' victories and the enterprises they undertook for seeking and discovering new peoples, lands, and riches as a means of introducing His Christian people to unknown and distant provinces. Through this same means He conveyed the riches of His grace to infinite numbers of people, who were ignorant of them and had never had anyone to tell them about them. This is why spiritual enterprises cannot be separated from temporal and political ones, why the pacification of fierce and warlike peoples cannot be omitted, and why one cannot keep silent about the desires and efforts of men to find mineral deposits and treasures of silver and other similar things. These means are all directed and guided by God's supreme providence. Through them He delivered countless nations from the darkness of heathenism, barbarity, and unheard-of customs. The devil had held them captive and tyrannized them, but they were reduced and subjugated to the gentle yoke of Christ's holy law, and the glorious standard of His Cross was raised where [before] it was unknown.

It will also be necessary to record the heroic deeds of outstanding and memorable virtue performed by evangelical laborers and soldiers of Christ's militia, which will also serve as pleasing and edifying examples. These men labored in their apostolic ministry and spiritual conquests to free the souls that God had redeemed with His blood and to destroy the fortresses where the devil held them captive. Some of these valiant soldiers spilled their blood at the hands of infidels for preaching the Gospel in these enterprises and missions. Others risked their lives for the same cause, exposing themselves to these and countless other dangers, including being killed by poisoned arrows or having their heads split open by a *macana* (a cruel weapon used by these barbarians) and then being eaten by them, as has in fact occurred. They are also exposed to an infinite number of other hardships, including hunger, thirst, very rough roads, etc. However, all these things did not overwhelm or intimidate them or keep them from offering themselves for these evangelical enterprises. In recognition of this, at the end of each book of this history, the lives and joyous deaths of some of these apostolic men will be recorded. In addition, throughout the course of the *History* we will find many other [men] who travel through the dry and terrible wilderness without any water, or through dense and thorny thickets, or through swamps

and burning sand dunes, thirsting for the welfare of these souls. [We will find] others who sprint like deer across high mountain peaks that are inaccessible even to birds and [watch them] descend into the deepest gorges, traveling along rivers [PB] that flow for many leagues, which they must ford countless times. They all [proceed] with the same glorious and apostolic purpose: saving souls and placing them on the road to heaven.

He whose eyes peruse this history in its entirety will see all these things in full, but it is impossible to discuss everything all at once. I also add that even though this history is more ecclesiastical than secular or political, nevertheless, the deeds of some of our Catholic Spanish captains and soldiers who were zealous in their Christianity should not be entombed in oblivion. They labored and assisted in both the temporal and spiritual conquests of the many nations which, upon receiving the light of the Gospel, were reduced and simultaneously placed under the protection of the Catholic kings of the Spanish monarchy. Because these monarchs enjoy the great glory of that title, it is their duty to favor and protect the Faith in the known world as well as in the world that is yet to be discovered. These Catholic Majesties have done so in the past and continue to do so today, with holy zeal for the universal expansion of the Church.

The present history must observe the style shown to be appropriate by important authors and writers. Pliny commented *Habent quidem Oratio, & Historia multa communia, sed plura diversa in his ipsis, quae communia videntur: narrat sane illa: narrat haec; sed aliter: huic pleraque humilia, & sordida, & ex medio petita; illi omnia recondita, & splendida, & excelsa conveniunt.*[72] The style of history and oratory may coincide in some ways (he says), but the requirements of history and those of oratory nevertheless differ. History is constrained to speak of things as they occurred, without affectation, in such a way that the information conveyed is effortlessly understood and its meaning is clear and intelligible to everyone. If the style of history is violated, it is separated from the language required of it, being transformed instead into panegyric and praise, which primarily seek to elevate and adorn. In the book that Luciano wrote concerning the style that history should observe he laughs at those

---

72. *Margin Note*: Lib. 4. epist. 8. Actually Book 5, Epistle 8 of Pliny's correspondence. "Indeed, history and oratory have many common features; yet in these very apparent resemblances, there are several contrasts. Both deal in narrative, but each after a different fashion. Oratory must concern itself as a rule with the low and vulgar facts of everyday life; History treats only what is recondite, splendid, elevated."

histories which, in an attempt to rise on the wings of eloquence, become a panegyric prayer, and he adds these words *Unum opus est Historae, & unus finis, utilitas, quae ex sola veritate conciliatur.*[73]

The prudent and knowledgeable individual cannot deny that because history is a narration of events and cases that have taken place, they demand that their truth be supported by a clear and truthful style, without affectation, minced words, or embellishments. History does not need these things to be beautiful, nor are they appropriate. Rather, these stylistic devices might compromise the truth. As much as possible I have attempted to adhere to this truth so that an accurate account might be rendered concerning matters that on the one hand are very new, and on the other most illustrative of God's remarkable works in the conversion of new peoples. For this reason throughout the course of this history, which is ecclesiastical and deals with the preaching of the Gospel, some brief references to divine and human authorities are included from time to time to support a point. Because this history deals with divine events, it is not merely a dry account recorded by a secular notary concerning some fortunate or disastrous case, nor is it the record of a crime and its punishment. Rather, this history is one of cases involving divine circumstances that were novel, remarkable, and of Christian edification. I do make an effort, however, to keep these asides brief so that they will not impede the flow of this history.

Finally, I note that the narrator of this history is an eyewitness to many of the events that are related herein, having touched them with his own hands (as they say). He spent sixteen years laboring in these missions, instructing some of these gentiles. He also accompanied the captains and soldiers from the garrisons on their expeditions to pacify these gentiles, and he dealt with many of the first priests [PB] who founded these missions. Furthermore, he learned the languages of these nations and dealt with many of their *caciques* [chiefs] and most knowledgeable Indians. Those things to which he was not an eyewitness he has taken from very reliable original [sources].

The first part of this history contains seven books, which parallel the seven expeditions that have been undertaken by the Gospel [ministers] among the nations of the extensive Province of Sinaloa. The five books of the second part [of this history] will recount the spread of this same Holy Gospel throughout the nations that have been converted to our Holy Faith in the other principal missions. [This is done] with no other wish or purpose than to glorify God Our Lord through the admirable and compassionate deeds that He has performed in our times. May He be given His due glory throughout all eternity. Amen. [PB]

---

73. "History is a unique labor and has a single goal, utility, which is made acceptable by reasoning of truth alone." Lucian of Samosata (ca. A.D. 125–200) authored one of the earliest (if not the earliest) extant ancient analyses of historiography, entitled *How to Write History* (see Kelley 1991:64–68; Kilburn 1958:2–73).

Letter from the author to the very reverend fathers of the Company of JESUS, my dearest brothers in Christ

(Very Reverend Fathers and dearest Brothers in Christ), the Apostle of the People, Saint Paul, considered it a great duty of Christian love to send to the faithful who had already received Gospel preaching and doctrine an account about not only the hardships, but also the fortunate events [that took place] during his divine preaching. He thereby allowed them to partake of the fruits of his missions and to participate in the pilgrimages on which the Lord had sent him. At the same time he requested the assistance of their holy prayers. From Rome he sent word to the Colossians that everywhere he traveled throughout the world the Gospel had been just as fruitful as it had been in Colossus *In universo mundo est, & fructificat, & crescit sicut in vobis.*[74] He sent word to the Philippians not only about his incarceration, but also about his hopes of succeeding in defending the Gospel cause, telling them that he wished to have them as companions in his hardship as well as in his joy: *Eo quod habeam vos in corde, & in vinculis meis, & in defensione Evangely, socios gaudij mei, omnis vos esse.*[75]

The holy Apostle undoubtedly had two goals in mind when telling the faithful children of the Church about what was happening with him and the Gospel. The first was allowing his brothers and companions (the name he gave the faithful) to share the consolation that they might receive from learning the happy news of the exaltation of Christ's Faith and the glorification of His holy name throughout the world. His other goal was to request the aid of their prayers for success in his enterprises and for [overcoming] hardship—for God to smooth the roads and ease the difficulties that he encountered in preaching the Holy Gospel.

From Ephesus he revealed the first of these motives in his first Epistle to the Corinthians, giving them the good news that God had opened a great door for him to preach the Gospel in that famous city, where the idolatrous worship of the goddess Diana reigned and where her celebrated temple, one of the seven wonders of the world, was frequented by many. He gives the Corinthians this good news, saying, *Permanebo Ephesi usque ad Pentecostem, ostium enim mihi apertum est magnum, & euidens, & adversarij multi.*[76] I will remain here in Ephesus, where a great door has clearly been opened for the doctrine of the Gospel, and where there are also many adversaries. There is no lack of mystery in the holy Apostle's linking, on the one hand, the great door that was being opened to the Holy Gospel and, on the other, the adversities, enemies, and hardships that he expected [to encounter] in his evangelical efforts. These two things were always linked in the Apostle's missions and enterprises.

Saint Paul's second goal, that of providing the faithful with an account of his Gospel preaching, was revealed to the Colossians when he said, *Oratione instate vigilantes in ea in gratiarum actione; orantes simul, & pro nobeis ut Deus aperiat nobis ostium sermonis ad loquendum mysterium Christi; propter quod etiam vinetus, ut manifestem illud.*[77] Persevere in prayers of thanksgiving, principally for the compassion God has shown you. Then pray that He open a door for us and that He open our lips to announce to the people the mysteries of Christ's Faith, for which I am imprisoned and in chains.

(Most reverend Fathers), these two goals of the Apostle Saint Paul, to whom preaching to the gentiles had been entrusted, have inspired me to write *The Triumphs of the Faith* and to record the successful results that Your Reverences' brothers have obtained through preaching the Gospel. And they have done so not in populous and haughty cities such as Ephesus, nor among wise peoples such as the Greeks, but rather

74. *Margin Note*: Colos. c. 1. Colossians 1:6: "which now bears fruit and thrives in you, as it does all the world over" (Knox 1956:207).

75. *Margin Note*: Philip. 1. Philippians 1:7: "you are close to my heart, and I know that you all share my happiness in being a prisoner, and being able to defend and assert the truth of the Gospel" (Knox 1956:203).

76. *Margin Note*: Cor. 1. c. 16. 1 Corinthians 16:8–9: "Till Pentecost, I shall be staying at Ephesus; a great opportunity lies open to me, plain to view, and strong forces oppose me" (Knox 1956:179).

77. *Margin Note*: Colos. 4. Colossians 4:2–4: "Persevere in prayer and keep wakeful over it with thankful hearts. Pray, too, for us; ask God to afford us an opening for preaching the revelation of Christ, which is the very cause of my imprisonment, and to give me the right utterance for making it known" (Knox 1956:210).

among those who, of all the peoples ever discovered in the world, were farthest from the light and the most entombed in darkness.

The sons of the Company have done battle using the weapons of the Gospel, fighting against very fierce nations who were the devil's familiars and quite fond of continual dealings and communication with him. They have domesticated and transformed these nations into Christ's gentle sheep, who now recognize His voice and follow it through the whistling of their shepherds, your brothers. God opened the door for them and gave them passage to the far reaches of a New World. We can say that they go forward in the vanguard of the Church, and like [PB] courageous soldiers they endure great hardships in the fight against heathenism in an effort to raise the standard of the Church, Christ's Cross, among people who have never even heard His glorious name. Even though no haughty temples of Diana have been found among these peoples, the devil, the Prince of Darkness, has been found here. He has fortified himself in castles of superstition, sorcery, and barbarous customs, and he predominates here more than in other nations in the world.

Even though the splendors of which the other nations in the Old World boast—civil order, letters, and material opulence—did not shine here, there have nevertheless been many conversions. In them God's divine grace and clemency, the riches of His worth, and the divine blood He shed for them shine even brighter. In accordance with this, the Apostle Saint Paul says, *Que stulta sunt mundi eligit Deus, ut confundat fortia; & ignobilia mundi, & contemptibilia elegit Deus, & ea que non sunt, ut ea que sunt, destrueret.*[78] Here, boasting of divine grace, he writes that God deigned to allow even the most scorned and oppressed people in the world to partake of His glory.

Your Reverences will see these boasts fulfilled to the letter in this history. Herein will be seen how the most ignorant people in the world acquire the intellect[79] and receive the [very same] knowledge of the Faith and its mysteries that was cast aside and misunderstood by those [the Greeks] whom the world considered wise. It will also be seen how those who are weakest in the world become strengthened in the Faith in order to steadfastly defend and preserve it in the midst of the clashes and conflicts of war and the stratagems of sorcerers and demons; in some cases they even shed their blood for the Faith. Finally, the peoples whom the Apostle Saint Paul called *"Quae non sunt"*[80] will be seen to be chosen by God and admitted to His kingdom. I do not know to which nation this name *"quae non sunt"* is more aptly applied or suited than those described in this history.

When the holy Apostle was preaching the people of the New World did not exist, or if they did, it was as if they did not. At least that is what the ancient historians supposed, for they did not believe that such nations could exist hidden away somewhere in a new world; nor was there any way of finding them for many, many centuries and thousands of years; nor was there any point of entry to these regions; nor any tracks left by those first conquerors and famous captains whom the Son of God had sent throughout the entire [known] world. God reserved for our time and for the sons of our Company the conquest of these peoples who did not exist and had never been heard of; and the Lord Himself opened the door for their entry.

I have no doubt that it will suit Your Reverences when I now call you by the same name that the Apostle Saint Paul used for those he wanted as companions in his joy and hardship: *Socios gaudij.*[81] Companions and brothers, sharing the consolation and delight of news of the successes, trophies, and victories won by your brothers, many of whom have spilled their blood and given their lives in this conquest.

In addition to being a manifestation of the compassion and the wonderful ways in which God sent His light to these blind peoples, this history also provides some news and insight for those whom His divine goodness selects for these enterprises, especially those from our Company, which is dedicated to such undertakings. Some of the means will also be seen by which victories were achieved among people who seemed indomitable, unconquerable, and almost without hope of salvation. These means were employed in order to drive the Prince of Darkness from the fortress that was his empire. The devil has already been defeated in many

---

78. *Margin Note*: 1. Cor. 1. 1 Corinthians 1:27–28: "God has chosen what the world holds weak so as to abash the strong. God has chosen what the world holds base and contemptible, nay, has chosen what is nothing, so as to bring to nothing what is now in being" (Knox 1956:165).

79. *Capacidad*. Here Pérez de Ribas gives voice to the more positive of the two seemingly contradictory positions that he takes throughout the *Historia* concerning the Indians' ability to reason (see Book 7).

80. Repetition of a portion of 1 Corinthians 1:28: "what is nothing" (Knox 1956:165).

81. "Companions of joy."

of these nations, and in those that are presently being discovered, he is being combated with the weapons of our Holy Faith and the divine word.

Of its will, as if by centripetal force, this history is drawn to Your Reverences' hands. And just as the core welcomes with pleasure that which is a natural part of it, so I hope that you will welcome this work with your great love and affection. This history also requests that Your Reverences favor your brothers' enterprises with the aid of your holy sacrifices and prayers. If the Apostle of the People [Saint Paul] requested this of the faithful, then those who preach the very same Gospel in the most distant and remote regions of our Province

of Nueva España also have reason to request this from you. They send greetings in Christ's love to their absent, dearly beloved fathers and brothers, and they also provide you with an account of the joyous labors for which they were destined by holy obedience. This enterprise is recorded by he who is the least of all of them, and even though he is unworthy, he labored there for some time. He who offers this account hopes that it will be given favorable reception, and he begs pardon for his limited knowledge and style. He, too, commends himself to Your Reverences' holy sacrifices and prayers. Madrid, where this book was completed (although it was begun in Mexico City), July 22, 1645. [PB]

Permission from the superiors of the Company of JESUS

I, Pedro de Avilés, Father Provincial of the Company of JESUS in the Province of Andalucía, with a commission from our most Reverend Father General Mucio Vitelleschi, do hereby grant permission for the publication of a work entitled *History of the Triumphs of Our Holy Faith {amongst} the Most Barbarous Peoples of the New World, Achieved by the Soldiers of the Militia and Company of JESUS*, written by Father Andrés Pérez de Ribas of our Company. This work has been approved by important and learned persons of our order, and in testimony of this I hereby place my signature, etc. Sevilla, January 24, 1645.

Pedro de Avilés

Permission of the Ordinario[82]

Don Gabriel de Aldama, Esq., counselor of the Holy Office of the Inquisition and Vicar General of the Villa de Madrid and its district, etc., has ordered an examination of this book entitled *History of the Missions of the Company of JESUS*, written by Father Andrés Pérez de Ribas, a religious of the Company of JESUS. It contains nothing against our Holy Catholic Faith and good customs. Thus, as regards the Holy Office, permission may be granted for its publication. Madrid, December 11, 1644.

Don Gabriel de Aldama, Esq.

82. Ordinario in this case refers to the bishop of the Diocese of Madrid. Aldama, as vicar general, was an appointed deputy of the bishop.

Summary of Privilege

License and privilege are granted for a period of ten years to Father Andrés Pérez de Ribas, of the Company of JESUS, Father Provincial in the Kingdom of Nueva España, to publish the book entitled History of the Triumphs of Our Holy Faith {amongst} the Most Barbarous and Fierce Peoples of the New World Achieved by the Soldiers of the Militia of the Company of JESUS in Nueva España. Anyone who publishes this book without said permission is subject to the penalties outlined in the *prematica*. These are further enumerated within said permission, which was issued in writing by Juan de Otalora Guevara in Madrid, February 17, 1645. [PB]

Errata [83]

On page 66, column 1: change *de carga* to *descarga*. On page 181, column 2: change *este mismo tiempo* to *por este mismo*. On page 109 in the chapter title: change *serranias* to *serranas*. On page 552 in the chapter title: change *jornnada* to *jornada*. On page 635 in the chapter title: change *la conversione* to *las conversiones*. On page 683, column 2: change *Maastro* to *Maestro*. On page 731, column 2: change *novi* to *novicios*.

With these errata, this book, entitled *History of the Triumphs of Our Holy Faith, etc.*, written by Father Andrés Pérez de Ribas, Provincial of the Company of JESUS in the Province of Nueva España, is correctly and faithfully printed from the original. Madrid, July 27, 1645.

Doctor Francisco Murcia de la Llana

---

83. The *Historia* contains many more errors than are here acknowledged.

Assessment

I, Don Diego de Cañizares y Arteaga, notary of Our Lord the king's chamber and a member of his council, certify that the members of said Royal Council have examined this book entitled *History of the Triumphs of Our Holy Faith amongst the Most Barbarous and Fierce Peoples of the New World Achieved by the Soldiers of the Militia of the Company of JESUS*, written by Father Andrés Pérez de Ribas of the Company of JESUS. I certify that the book was published with the approval of said council. They assess each folio of said book at five *maradís*.[84] The book appears to have 201 folios, which at the aforementioned rate amounts to 1,005 *maravedís*.[85] The sale price of this book must not exceed that amount. This assessment must appear at the beginning of each book that is published. In accordance with the request of Father Andrés Pérez de Ribas, I do hereby issue this assessment. Madrid, August 1, 1645.

Don Diego de Cañizares y Arteaga

[PB]

Table of Books and Chapters for This History

84. A folio was a sheet of paper folded to create four pages of printed text. *Maradís* is an abbreviation of *maravedís*. The common gold coin in Spain (the *castellano*, which came to be known as the *peso de oro*) was valued at 450 maravedís; the silver piece of eight (the *peso de plata*) was valued at 275 maravedís (Polzer, Barnes, and Naylor 1977:36).

85. At such a price the *Historia* clearly was published with an institutional (e.g., Jesuit college) or wealthy audience in mind. In 1623 a poor man's daily expenditure was thirty maravedís (Elliott 1989:230).

86. Here and throughout the text we have retained the word 'entrada' when it was used as a referent for what was in a sense a "formal visit," implying a Jesuit commitment of men and resources (if not the actual establishment of a new mission), which required the approval of Jesuit superiors and the viceroy. An entrada generally involved the baptism of infants and a commitment on the priest's part to follow up these baptisms with religious instruction for the children as well as their parents and other adults, who, once informed of their religious obligations, also would be baptized.

END OF TABLE OF BOOKS AND CHAPTERS

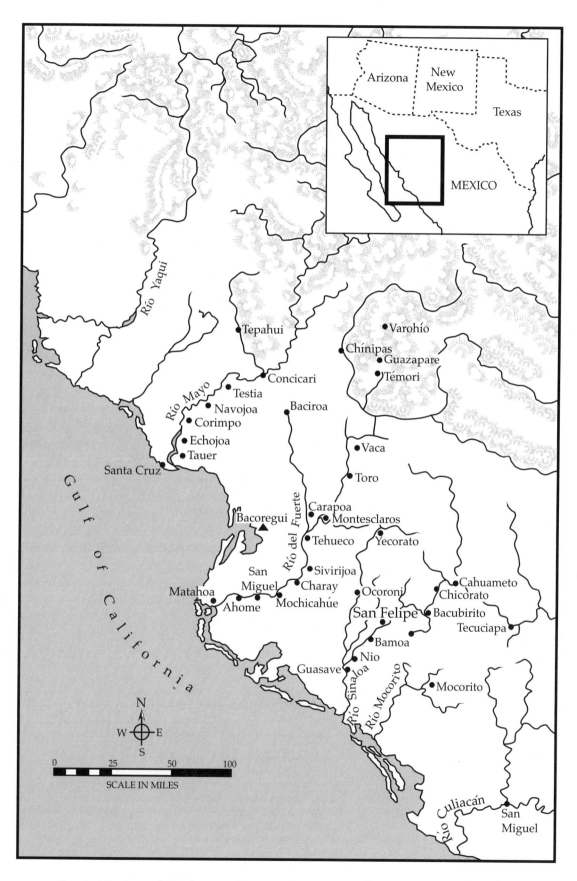

MAP 1. Jesuit Missions of Sinaloa to 1645

BOOK I

Description of the Province of Sinaloa, the Nations That Inhabit It, Their Customs, and the First Penetration of the Region by Spaniards

CHAPTER I The boundaries, climate, characteristics, rivers, mountains, and animals of the Province of Sinaloa

As stated in the prologue I begin this history of the missions of the Company in Nueva España with the Province of Sinaloa. It was founded before the other mission provinces, which will be discussed later, and also had the greatest breadth of nations reduced to our Holy Faith. Before I discuss the spiritual endeavors and conversions that have brought people into the flock of the Holy Church, it will first be necessary to write about the nature and location of this province, its characteristics, and the customs of the wild peoples that inhabit it. The latter constitute the temporal subject matter of this history, whereas the former constitute those matters dealing with the spirit and the soul, namely the means by which divine wisdom guided these people to the light of the Gospel, the admirable results and changes that divine providence wrought among them, and the spiritual fruits harvested by the evangelical ministers.

The Province of Sinaloa lies three hundred leagues to the north and west of the great city of Mexico, seat of the kingdom and extensive empire of Nueva España. I call Sinaloa a province because it encompasses a large area and has many nations. It is forty leagues wide and extends 140 leagues in longitude, to what are presently the northern limits of evangelization. To the east are the [2] high mountains of Topia, which descend northward. To the west Sinaloa is bounded by the arm of the sea called California [the Gulf of California], which also extends to the north. The former Villa de San Miguel de Culiacán is at the center [of the province].[1] To the north are lands that have innumerable nations but whose boundaries are unknown. The prov-

1. The Villa of San Miguel de Culiacán was originally located on the Río San Lorenzo; sometime prior to 1564 it was relocated to the Río Culiacán (Gerhard 1982:261).

ince begins at twenty-seven degrees north and extends as far as thirty-two degrees [north], which is as far as the Holy Gospel has been preached.

The climate of Sinaloa is extremely hot. This is especially true near the South Sea [Pacific Ocean], as it is hot all along the [west] coast [of Mexico]. Nevertheless, it is usually very cold during the months of December and January. The rest of the time it is usually excessively hot, so much so that even the animals suffer greatly. Many times livestock become so tired while walking that the heat melts the fat in their bodies and they drop dead; other times the heat makes them so stiff that they cannot be used for a long time, and then only if they are bled immediately. The rains are few, especially along the coast, where the skies send only three or four good storms per year. In other areas the rains begin in the month of June and end around September. God thereby makes tolerable the most difficult months of the year.

The land itself is healthy. The rays of the sun, although not unhealthy, are hot. The heat is the cause of the dryness of the earth, which would be uninhabitable for human beings if the land were not watered by many large rivers that cross it en route to the Sea of California. There are barely any springs or water holes, only the rivers.

Most of the province is flat but full of dense thickets and native trees, including some red brazilwoods and ebonies.[2] These wooded areas are so extensive that some cover three, four, or six leagues. They are so thick that birds cannot fly through them, and they serve only as lairs for wild animals. But along the banks of the rivers there are pleasant valleys full of green groves of poplars[3] that are free of thorny underbrush. In the valleys and hills there are many game animals and birds. In the dense thickets there are many peccary, deer, and rabbits. There are also some leopards, although they are not as big or as fierce as the African variety. There are very powerful tigers, but they are not man-eaters because they rarely leave the hills, where they find their prey.[4] There also are a number of bobcats, coyotes (an animal very similar to a fox),[5] and many lizards, serpents, and poisonous snakes. In the valleys there are a great

variety of fowl and birds; partridges, doves, and grouse are very abundant. At times during the year there is also an abundance of cranes and a variety of parrots and macaws. The latter are colored like parrots but are much larger and have plumage that is very prized for ornamentation. There are also many other small birds.

Because of its dryness, this land of Sinaloa would be completely uninhabitable for human beings, and even for animals, if it were not traversed and replenished by the rivers that run through it and into the Sea of California. The length and breadth of the rivers and the lands through which they flow will be noted when the conversions of the peoples living along their banks are discussed. All the rivers originate in the high mountains of Topia. Some have very strong currents, and during the rainy season or when the snow melts they flow with such great force that the rising waters entirely flood the fields, spreading out over one or two leagues at the mouth of the river. Due to [3] the loose soil of the floodplain, the rivers sometimes even change course. For this reason it is very difficult when the Gospel is first introduced to find a safe place to build a church or settlement. During these floods, which do not ordinarily subside for four, six, or eight days, the Indians remain safe by using a particular means adapted to their way of living. Because there are no hills or knolls where one can seek safety, they erect platforms made of poles in the low crowns of scrub trees. They cover these with branches and then dirt so they can build a fire, and there they live while the fields are flooded. The priests who have gone to preach to these people have frequently had to endure this hardship (as I will later relate). In some of the Christian pueblos where churches had been built on the best spots that could be found, the rivers rose with such force that the churches were destroyed along with the houses, and the priests were forced to resort to these refuges in the trees. They would remain there for days and nights, suffering from a lack of food and sleep. Sometimes the rivers rise so quickly that there is no time for warning. The Indians have occasionally saved the life of a religious who has been instructing them by carrying him on their shoulders through the water for nearly two leagues.

In the rivers there are wild ducks and an abundance and variety of fish that enter from the sea, especially when they lay their eggs. Many caimans or crocodiles[6]

---

2. Presumably Pérez de Ribas' "brazilwood" is what is today known in Mexico as *brasil* (*Haematoxylon brasiletto*); his "ebony" is probably *ebano* (*Chloroleucon mangense*).

3. Apparently cottonwoods (*Populus mexicana*).

4. It is not clear to which animals Pérez de Ribas was referring when he spoke of leopards and tigers; the former were probably cougars (*Felis concolor*) and the latter jaguars (*Felis onca*) (Beals 1943:13–14).

5. Pérez de Ribas may be alluding to the kit fox (*Vulpes macrotis*) (Cornett 1987:169).

6. *Cocodrilos*. According to Beals (1943:9), who incorrectly speaks of alligators, fifty years ago crocodiles were still found in great numbers in the Río Fuerte and Río Sinaloa.

enter the mouths of the rivers in schools, fishing for food and even for men, whom they occasionally catch. Therefore, the Indians do not dare to fish alone in the inlets where these beasts are found. Instead, they fish in groups, making noise to frighten these wild animals, whose fangs and teeth are so strong that once they bite it is impossible to free the victim without severing the body part clenched in the crocodile's jaw. Many have died trapped in this way.

The Sea of California and its shores are also very beneficent to these Indians, especially those living in settlements near the mouths of the rivers that empty into it, which abound in several varieties of fish, especially mullet and bass. It has happened at times that some Indians have been sent out to fish and have returned in two hours with fifty arrobas[7] of fish. They fish with nets, sometimes out on the high sea and other times in the estuaries, of which there are many along this coast. Some fish with bow and arrow, especially in estuaries where the water is low. There one also finds oysters, clams, and other types of seafood that they eat.

The coast has many saltbeds. Some consist of crystallized salt from water that floods the land during the summer months. When this salt dissolves with the first hard rains the Indians turn to other kinds of saltbeds that are found in deep pools of seawater, where rock salt forms. Because it is so hard, they break it with long, hard poles, diving beneath the water and retrieving large chunks. This salt is highly prized, not only for their own use, but also as a trade item; they make large blocks of salt and trade them with pueblos that have none in exchange for mantas[8] and other things they need.

To conclude our discussion of the Sea of California, which is so beneficial to this province, I note that its boundaries remain unknown. Nor is it known whether it turns toward the North Sea [the Atlantic Ocean], if it is connected to it, or if it ends in this land. It is true that this sea has become famous because of reports that pearls grow here. [4] Sometimes they have been gathered as far as thirty-two degrees [latitude] up the coast.[9] Presently the coast of Sinaloa is being fully explored, as is the opposite coast [of Baja California],

which is also inhabited by barbarous people. It is said that in this past year of 1644 on orders from our king, Philip IV (may God keep him), Admiral Pedro Portel de Casanate was sent [from Spain] to Nueva España to explore this gulf and to colonize the far shore.[10]

There are many silver deposits in Sinaloa, so when Spaniards explored this region (as I will discuss later) they made great efforts to find them. They have discovered some rich deposits from which they have extracted silver, but they have not pursued this endeavor because of the scarcity of native labor for building mills, which initially are expensive. Here in the Indies there is a saying that one mine requires another. This is particularly true in remote regions where, due to the great distances, prices are very high for the equipment and clothing required for mining. Fortunately, Our Lord keeps these riches hidden in the bowels of the earth for the occasion chosen by His divine providence, just as He kept others hidden for hundreds and thousands of years in Nueva España, where each day brings a new discovery.

To conclude this chapter I will discuss two unique wonders of nature that I have frequently observed in this land. These are so marvelous that they deserve mention. They concern a bird and a tree. There are some birds that look like and are the size of thrushes.[11] When they build their nests to raise their chicks, however, they do so in a manner different from all other birds. The nests of these birds are shaped like a sack or a long mesh bag, and they hang from a branch or the knot of a tree limb that is usually very high. This net is narrow at the neck, which is the opening or door; at the base it widens to become round. From top to bottom it measures one-half or two-thirds of a vara.[12] Even though this nest is hanging and exposed to breezes or winds there is no danger of it coming loose. Many times I have observed that when nesting time is over it still resists the winds, until it finally falls, rotted by the rains.

Now comes the most marvelous part, which invites praises to the Lord, the Author of Nature, who created this little bird and gave it such artful skill. There are two things about it that are marvelous. First, this nest,

---

7. An arroba equaled 11.5 kilos (Polzer, Barnes, and Naylor 1977:43).

8. Mantas were woven from cotton or pita (agave) and used for breechcloths and blankets.

9. In Book 7, Chapter 12, Pérez de Ribas copies a letter of fellow Jesuit Jacinto Cortés, who in 1642 accompanied the commandant of the garrison of Sinaloa, Luis Cestín de Cañas, on a month-long exploration of the California shore. Cortés' letter was probably a key source for Pérez de Ribas' information about California (Bancroft 1886:181).

10. Portel de Casanate left Cádiz in June and arrived at Veracruz in August 1643. In January 1644, having prepared the frigate *Rosario* on the coast of Nueva Galicia, he set sail, principally to warn the Manila galleon of the danger of raids by Dutch pirates. Portel de Casanate spent five days exploring the outer coast of the Baja peninsula (see Bancroft 1886:177ff.).

11. Pérez de Ribas' description of the bird's nest suggests it is an oriole, which is a common species in the tropical deciduous forest (David Yetman, personal communication).

12. A vara equaled 0.84 meters or 33 inches (Polzer et al 1977:39).

net, or sack is woven entirely of long, firm grasses that the bird knows how to locate and select. The second and more unusual aspect is how this little bird with only its beak can weave such a long net using only grass, without daubing it. No mud is used at all, only blades of grass that serve as fibers. For a man to make such a net he would need two hands, ten fingers, a needle, and knowledge of the art of weaving. It is even more amazing that when the bird begins collecting grass for the nest and places it on a branch that has been chosen for its exposure to a cool breeze, the grass is not blown off; rather, it remains in place until the bird returns with other blades to weave into the nest. When the bird completes the nest it makes the bottom just wide enough for the mother and chicks. Moreover, because there is no branch to perch on, the bird completes the nest while hanging in midair.

Who gave this bird the skill to weave such a deep nest, which is held firmly in place by only a few strands of grass? Even with the continuous weight of the chicks the strands do not loosen or break. [5] The answer to this marvelous puzzle of nature is the wisdom of God, its maker. It is He who endowed this little bird with the capacity and design to rear its chicks in the open air so that the serpents and snakes could not reach its nest, and it is for this reason, some argue, that God gave this instinct and ability to this little bird. To this we can add that through these marvels of nature God meant to delight, entertain, and manifest His divine goodness toward mankind.

Let us turn to another natural wonder worthy of consideration, which is a tree often found in the valleys of Sinaloa and in other warm places. This tree, which has a very large crown, is called *tucuchi* in the language of this region.[13] Its fruit is a small, sweet fig; some of its branches are very long and large, extending so far that they could no longer sustain themselves without forked branches to hold them up. The Lord aided them in a very unusual way: some trunks that are separate from the main trunk of the tree grow straight up out of the earth and under the tree branches. They do so in such a way that forks are formed, and these hook onto the main branches and support them. Most noteworthy here is that the supporting branch is so smoothly fused to the main branch that it does not even evidence a knot, as is usually the case with a graft. Secondly, the branch that is supported by this fork extends with its buds, leaves, and growth, extending from two separate trunks that are one to two *brazas*[14] apart. One grows from the tree of which it is a branch; the other grows from the fork. It is difficult to understand whether this forked branch grew down from above and entered the ground, as some think, or whether it grew up out of the earth from the roots of the plant, joining itself to the extended branch when the latter pleaded for help. Whatever the case may be, the growth or sprouting of a single branch from two separate trunks, one distinct from the other, is a very unusual event but one that we see frequently here with our own eyes. We can therefore say that God wanted to leave in nature a sign of how the Holy Spirit flows from the Father and the Son, persons who are truly distinct, whom these works praise.

13. Tucuchi is perhaps a corruption of *hutuqui*, one of sixteen terms for trees with edible fruit in Cáhitan (Buelna 1891:138). More specifically, it may be a referent for one of several species of the genus *Ficus* (fig), which abound in the region. David Yetman (personal communication) has suggested *Ficus cotinifolia* or *Ficus insipida*, both of which have enormous pole-like aerial roots and produce edible fruits.

14. A braza equaled 1.67 meters (Polzer, Barnes, and Naylor 1977: 39).

CHAPTER II The many nations that inhabit this province, the fruits of the land that they enjoy, their mode of dwelling, and their livelihood

When I refer to the peoples that inhabit this province it is not my intention to give the impression that they are as numerous as Europeans, whom we refer to as the Spanish nation, the Italian nation, etc. There is no comparison between them. Nevertheless, I consider them to be different nations, albeit not as populous, because they are divided in their relations with one another. Sometimes they speak totally different languages; in other instances they speak the same language. Whatever the cause, they are divided and opposed; they kill one another in continuous warfare in order to maintain their territorial boundaries and lands, which each recognizes as its own. Thus, anyone who dared to enter the other's territory did so at the risk of leaving his head in the hands of whatever enemy he happened to meet. The end result was that this large number of people were totally divided in their dealings with one another.

The settlements of these nations are usually located along the banks of the rivers, because if the [Indians] left the rivers they would have neither drinking water nor fields to sow. In their gentile state they lived [6] in *aldeas*[15] or rancherías that were not very far apart. In some places, however, the distance between rancherías was two or three leagues, depending upon access to holdings and cultivated land, which they usually tried to keep close to their houses. They made the latter by first taking poles from the *monte*[16] and sticking them into the earth. These were woven together and tied with reeds that are very strong and durable, like the branches of the greenbriar.[17] The framework for these walls was strengthened with mud plaster to keep the sun and wind out. The exterior of the house was covered with brush; the roof was made of earth or clay, and with this they were content. Other groups made their houses out of *petates*,[18] which is a type of mat woven from split canes sewn together to serve as walls and roofing. For this purpose they are laid over the tops of arched poles that are staked into the earth. When it rains the houses are like the covered carts found in Spain, as there is no danger of leakage from running water. In front of their houses they erect ramadas, which serve as a kind of porch where they store produce from their fields. This is also where their daily activities are carried out, in the shade. During the summer they sleep there at night, using the aforementioned reed mats as their mattresses. They neither used nor knew what locks or keys were, nor did they fear theft. When they occasionally left their homes they were content to lean some tree branches in the doorway; this was their only safeguard. When they left their crops in the fields they protected them, too, in this manner. To keep weevils from getting into the food, they stored it on a ramada covered with thorny branches.

The seeds these people sow and the foods they process and eat are primarily maize, which in Spain is called 'wheat of the Indies'. Maize gives such high yields that a *fanega*[19] sown usually yields one hundred–fold or more. Among the maize they also sow various kinds of squash, which are sweet and tasty. Some are cut into slices and dried in the sun; these last for most of the year. All these people use the *frijol*, which is a seed similar to the broad bean of Castilla but even softer, as well as other types of seeds that they have in abundance. They also eat a type of *algarrobilla*, or carob bean, which comes from a native tree called a *mesquite*.[20] These beans are ground

---

15. An aldea is perhaps best understood as a village intermediate between a ranchería and a pueblo, having upwards of several dozen houses and no public architectural features such as a ballcourt. A ranchería is a smaller grouping of upwards of a dozen or so houses. The term 'pueblo' generally was applied to a settlement of several hundred people that was an economic and political center, and that had some public architectural feature(s) (Gibson 1964:32–33; Nader 1990).

16. Pérez de Ribas generally used the term monte(s) to refer to the dense, thorny-plant vegetation that abounds in the foothills and near the coast of Sinaloa and Sonora.

17. The Spanish is *sarsaparilla*, the common name of which is greenbriar or smilax. The English 'sarsaparilla' is not used here in order to avoid any confusion with the soft drink of the same name, which takes its flavor from the oil of the sassafras tree.

18. This word derives from the Nahuatl *pétlatl*. Its first documented usage in Spanish appears in a 1531 narrative referring to Culiacán (Corominas and Pascual 1989–1991:4:510). Petates apparently were woven from a cane-type grass (*Phragmites australis*).

19. 2.58 bushels (Polzer, Barnes, and Naylor 1977).

20. Mesquite (*Prosopis velutina*) beans are still a valued food item in northwestern Mexico.

and made into a drink with water, and because they are somewhat sweet, they are for these Indians what chocolate is for Spaniards.[21] Their montes and wooded areas abound in these and other similar kinds of fruit.

The *mescal* plant,[22] which in the shape and form of its foliage is like a large aloe, is also a source of food and enjoyment. It is thought that there are many varieties of this plant; the one referred to here is that which is celebrated in certain histories of Mexico. Wine, honey, and vinegar are made from it. Thread and twine are also extracted from the tender blades of the plant, the sharp points of which are used for needles. Although it is true that the plant provides all these products, these peoples use it mainly for food. When it is in season they cut it at the base of the trunk and roast it in a pit into which heated stones have been placed and subsequently covered over with branches and dirt. After the slow heat has softened the trunk and a portion of the blades they are made into a type of preserve, which is very sweet because of the way in which the plant has been roasted. This is the only beneficial plant they are in the habit of raising near their houses;[23] they do not utilize others. There are many prickly pear cacti that bear *tunas*, called 'figs of the Indies' in Spain, as well as another plant that grows wild in the montes (which I will discuss later) called the *pitahaya*.[24] Plants brought from Castilla grow well in these [7] regions, especially orange and fig trees. Melons do so well that you rarely find one that is not pleasing.

Up to this point I have been discussing only the nations that generally live along the banks and shores of the rivers. There are also other nations that are among the most savage ever seen and encountered on earth. These nations do not sow or cultivate crops like the others, nor do they live in houses or protect themselves from inclement weather. And the more different their way of life is from that of other peoples the more deserving it is of being understood. This knowledge is worth possessing so that one can understand the misery that has befallen humanity due to the sin that cost them the Garden of Paradise, where God had placed them

whence to lift them to heaven. Thus, in these peoples the words of the royal Prophet are fulfilled to the letter: *Homo cum in honore esset non intellexit, comparatus est iumentis insipientibus, et similis factus est illis.*[25] Some of them live in the mountains and foothills, others along the seashore and sand dunes of the coast. The former survive by hunting, gathering roots and wild berries, and drinking from puddles or pools of rainwater. The coastal peoples subsist on fishing and sometimes on shellfish, snakes, and other odd animals. Their bread consists of raw, dried, or salted fish. It is a fact that at the time of the maize harvest, some of these people go up [river] to trade fish in the pueblos of their friends who are agriculturalists; at other times they collect a small seed from a plant that grows below the water,[26] which they use for bread. It must truly seem incredible to European nations that most of the year these peoples survive without any bread or other grain substitute, eating only fish or wild berries, as we have mentioned. Most of the year they use the pitahaya, which grows abundantly here. It is an unusual plant in European terms or even compared to other trees in the world. Its branches are like green grooved candles growing straight up from the trunk, which grows short and robust, making a very striking crown. It has not a single leaf, but the fruit appears on the branches like nipples. Because of its thorny surface, this fruit looks something like the chestnut or the prickly pear [fruit]. Its flesh is similar to that of the fig, but softer; the flesh is very white in some plants, red or yellow in others. It is very delicious, particularly when grown in the dry soil along the seashore in the Province of Sinaloa, where it rains very little. These trees are so abundant that there are groves that stretch for two, three, and up to six leagues.

These are the foods of some of these unusual nations. It is worth noting that in spite of such sparse and simple foods these people are very corpulent (especially the coastal and mountain dwellers). They are very agile and are the tallest of all the nations of Nueva España or even Europe. With such meager and minimal sustenance they live many years, to the age of decrepitude.

Now that I have written about their unusual sustenance I will also write about how they shelter themselves from the rain and harsh weather. If they want to take shelter from the rain, they take a shock of long

21. Chocolate from the New World was relatively inexpensive and was consumed as a beverage in large quantities by Spaniards of all classes (Defourneaux 1979:153).

22. Agave (*A. angustifolia*). Pérez de Ribas appears to use *mescal* and *magüey* interchangeably for agave.

23. In Book 6 Pérez de Ribas provides a more detailed discussion of agave cultivation among the Nébome.

24. Pitahaya here refers to *Stenocereus thurberi*, commonly known as organ-pipe cactus, which produces abundant fruit.

25. *Margin Note*: Psalm. 48. Psalm 48:21: "Short is man's careless enjoyment of earthly goods; match him with the brute beasts, and he is no better than they" (Knox 1956:497).

26. Eelgrass (Felger and Moser 1985:379).

straw from the field and tie it at the top. Then they sit down, open the shock of straw, and place it [8] on their heads. Their bodies are covered as well, so it serves as a cape against the rain; it is just as effective as a roof, house, or camp tent, even when it rains all night. This is their shelter from the rain. There is likewise no better protection in this region from the very strong sun. All one has to do is insert some branches in the sand, sit down, and live and sleep under their shade. There is no shelter from the wind except the naked body. On some of the bitter nights of the two coldest months of the year (which we said are December and January), they use firebrands,[27] which they light and place in the cold sand next to them. They use this means of warmth when they travel through uninhabited regions, placing the firebrands in a row, each a short distance from the next (wood is never lacking because of the many montes in this province). They lie down to sleep between the firebrands and take care to extinguish them when they awake. Lastly, if one of these scantily dressed Indians wants to travel four or six leagues at night in spite of the intense cold, he takes a burning firebrand in his hands and places it near his stomach for warmth, leaving the rest of the body exposed to the wind. These strange people are much fewer in number than those who farm. Nevertheless, they live as happily as if they had all the riches and palaces in the world.

CHAPTER III   The vices and barbarous customs that were prevalent among these peoples, as well as those that were lacking

I warn the reader that before he finishes reading about these peoples' wild and barbarous customs, which may seem an inappropriate subject that degrades and debases this history, he should consider that the same people depicted here were greatly favored by God, who raised them to the status of His own children by way of Christ's grace and His Divine Sacraments. They are transformed in both civil and divine aspects, and in them is ratified that outward sign that God Our Lord so highly values, saying: *Creavit Dominus omnes gentes inlaudem et nomem et gloriam suam.*[28] Thus, I do not exclude any nation or barbarous people upon whom His glory may not yet have shone. God sanctifies those who seemed to be dragons, basilisks, and serpents; His angels take them by the hand and escort them to heaven. The Prince of the Apostles, Saint Peter, was repulsed by these creatures during his mysterious vision. This is recounted in Chapter 10 of the Acts of the Apostles.

When the Apostle saw that mysterious sheet in which venomous and repulsive beasts were cast down from heaven, it caused him to understand that despite their appearance the Lord had purified them and made them worthy of His heaven. With these words uttered from above, *Quod Deus purificavit, tu comune ne dixeris,*[29] the Lord commanded Saint Peter never again to be repulsed by them. All this has great bearing on the nations of which we are speaking. Although they appear wild because of their barbarous vices and customs, they were not excluded from Christ's redemption, nor from His heaven. As we will soon see they are converted to God and incorporated into the flock of His Holy Church.

The most widespread vice among nearly all these peoples was drunkenness. They were intoxicated for days and nights on end. Instead of drinking alone in their houses, their drinking occurred in [9] continuous, well-publicized festivities that were held for the purpose of inebriation. Whenever anyone in the pueblo made wine, he made large jars full of it, inviting to

27. *Candeladas.* Apparently made from branches of the pitahaya (see Book 4, Chapter 3).

28. *Margin Note*: Deuter. 26. Deuteronomy 26:19: "His will is to exalt thee high above all other nations he has made, for his own glory and renown" (Knox 1956:170).

29. Acts 10:15: "It is not for thee to call anything profane, which God has made clean" (Knox 1956:125).

these festivities the men from his ranchería or pueblo and sometimes the entire surrounding region. There were so many people that there were celebrations each day and night of the week. Thus, these drunken celebrations were never-ending.

Their wine was made from various native plants and fruits such as pitahaya or prickly pear, which in Castilla is called 'fig of the Indies'. Sometimes the wine was made from the carob beans of the mesquite tree, which I previously mentioned. It was also made from other plants, such as the mescal and its stalks when it is in season and bears fruit. When these plants are ground or crushed and added to water they soften up in two or three days and take on that pleasing taste that snatches away whatever judgment these rational souls still possessed. Among all the wines they made, the most popular and flavorful was made from honeycombs, which are harvested at a particular time of the year. It should be noted that there was one thing that tempered this vice of intoxication: women, young men, and children did not participate.

These drunken celebrations were well-publicized and common when they prepared for battle or assembled for war. They were held to whip up fury or when they had been victorious or had cut off an enemy's head, which for them was sufficient reason to celebrate. These inebriations were accompanied by a communal dance to the beat of huge drums that could be heard for more than a league. Women participated in this dance, which they celebrated in the following manner: the head or the scalp of the dead enemy or some other body part such as an arm or a leg was hung on a pole in the middle of the plaza. They danced around it, unleashing a barbarous cry as they hurled insults at the dead enemy; they also sang songs that referred to the victory. In a way it had all the appearances of hell, with throngs of devils, which is who ruled these people.

During these celebrations there were also offerings of tobacco, which is commonly used by all of these barbarous peoples. When one nation invites another to forge an alliance for war they convey the invitation by sending a number of reed canes filled with tobacco. They light these, enjoying the same habit of smoking that originated with these people and has now spread throughout the world. To accept this offering was to accept an invitation to forge an alliance for war.

The other related vice that was prevalent among these nations was constant warfare. One group would attack and kill its neighbor, either in the open coun-

try, in their fields, or in *albazos* (a term that is used in war zones to refer to attacks that occur at daybreak). No age or sex is spared. At times in the past they honored themselves by taking as a name in their own language something such as he-who-killed-women or -children, he-who-killed-in-the-monte or -in-the-field. They celebrated such victories, or savagery, as if they were something great, and it was rare that they were satisfied solely with enslaving their captives. This continuous warfare resulted in their having no news of or commerce with other peoples at any distance beyond their own lands. With no truces they were usually hemmed in by their enemies. This continued until Christ's law reached them, a law of peace that resolves differences and binds them in the love that His divine kindness brought to the world.

For weapons they usually use the bow and arrow, carrying large bunches of the latter in quivers over their shoulders. They handle this weapon very skillfully because [10] they practice using it from the time they are small. As soon as a little boy is able to walk, they put a small bow in his hands and teach him to shoot reeds as arrows. Then when he is a bit older they teach him to shoot lizards. Thus, they become so skillful and rapid in shooting arrows that in the same time it takes a Spanish soldier to load and shoot his harquebus they can shoot eight or ten arrows. Most of these arrows are smeared with an herb so venomous that, as long as it is somewhat fresh, there is no antidote or remedy that can save the life of anyone who has been wounded, no matter how little venom has entered any part of the body. In wartime the paths are sewn with barbs of very hard wood that have been smeared with this poison. They bury these in the grass to pierce the feet of enemy Indians, who usually go barefoot. No matter how slight the wound, if the poison enters the bloodstream it will take the life of the victim. These poisons are certainly to be more feared than the shot from a harquebus, which if it hits an arm or a leg, can be cured and is not mortal. No antidote has been found to combat this poison, regardless of where it has entered the body.

When they fight in hand-to-hand combat they use another weapon called the macana, which is like a hard wooden club. It can split open a human head with a single blow. Some also use a kind of pike or pointed pole. Because they had no iron and were unfamiliar with it, they made the point or sometimes the whole weapon from brazilwood. These pikes are used by the Indians who have a role similar to that of our captains, who carry short lances.[30] The most important leaders used small shields made from caiman or crocodile hides, which are very tough. These shields resist arrows as long as they are not shot at close range or by someone with a very powerful arm. We must also mention the defensive gear they wear on their left wrist, which is struck by the bowstring after an arrow is shot. In order for the wrist not to be bruised, they bind it (and wisely so) with the soft pelt of a martin;[31] this absorbs the blow of the bowstring. Their bows do not have a stock as the crossbow does, but rather an extremely strong shaft. They shoot with such force that if they are using their strong arm, the tips of the bow almost meet. As I noted earlier they also handle the bow with great speed and ease.

To go to war they decorate themselves with a kind of paint that is made from the fat of worms and red ocher or soot from their cook pots. They paint their bodies and faces in such a way that they appear to be ferocious devils from hell. They decorate their heads and hair with bright feathers and crests from birds that they either raise or hunt in the montes. These nations take great delight in killing people. Some principales[32] who acted as captains used to go to war wearing a type of doublet with sleeves or a blue cotton cape adorned with shells of mother of pearl that shine brightly.[33] They also wore other charms around their necks. When they fight they move their bodies a great deal, rising, stooping, and changing places so as not to become a target. Other aspects of their wars will be mentioned in the course of this history.

In a land where there is so much drunkenness the vice of adultery was, of course, present. As the Apostle Saint Paul noted with respect to wine, *In quo est luxuria*.[34] This vice, too, is caused by the demons whom Christ ordinarily called 'the unclean or evil

spirits'. These demons have overpowered these people. I can nevertheless state that I often observed [11] that in spite of the blindness in which they lived, this fire did not burn so fiercely nor had it taken hold among them as freely as it might have.

The taking of several wives was not common practice among everyone, but rather only among the principales and chiefs. In some nations those who contented themselves with a single wife were much more numerous than those who had many. Because their marriages were ordinarily dissoluble, they were actually concubinages, lacking the permanence required by a true marriage contract.

The marriage of a virgin was celebrated with some solemnity. First of all it was not contracted without the parents' permission; if it was, the union was considered scandalous. Accordingly, such [cases] were uncommon. Among some nations when a virgin bride was handed over to her husband they removed from her neck a carved shell that the young women wear as an emblem of their virginity. It is considered dishonorable for a woman to lose her virginity before marriage. Another sign of temperance among these people, which I confess amazed me, was how safely the women and girls walk around alone through the fields and along the roads without being attacked by anyone.[35] I do not know whether they could have done this as safely in some Christian countries. Lastly, this vice was not as uncontrolled as it sometimes is among people who have received the light of Faith, nor are these Indians so barbarous that they do not admire the evangelical ministers' purity and cleanliness in their lives and customs. Indeed, the Indians are so scandalized by the slightest slip in a priest's conduct that they loudly spread news of it.

The other variation on this filthy vice, which because of its indecency will not be named, was occasionally practiced by these peoples. But because it was worse than bestial, being absent even among the brute animals, it was considered very vile and shameful by these nations, even though they were so blind and so far from the light of reason. This was especially true for the passive partners, who were known and despised by everyone.[36] Such individuals were labeled with an in-

---

30. *Gineta*. At one time this short lance was the insignia of Spanish infantry captains (Larousse 1983:407).

31. Probably otter, as martins are not known today in northwestern Mexico.

32. Principales were respected individuals who exercised varying degrees of power and influence. Later in this chapter Pérez de Ribas states or implies that they were heads of lineages or clans (also see the "Critical Introduction").

33. The second anonymous account of Diego de Guzmán's entrada of 1533 describes a Yaqui[mi] cacique: "Among them came an Indian more conspicuous than the others, wearing a black cloak like a scapulary decorated with ornately worked pearl shells in addition to many small figures of dogs, birds, and deer among other things" (Hedrick and Riley 1976:47).

34. *Margin Note*: Ad Ephes. 5. Paul to the Ephesians 5:18: "that leads to ruin" (Knox 1956:201).

35. *Sin que nadie las ofendiese*. The phrase in this context appears to refer to a man raping or otherwise physically abusing a woman, as opposed to a woman suffering verbal taunts.

36. This "adultery" involving "passive partners" presumably refers to men assuming female roles while having sex with other men, rather than to women assuming male, or what to Pérez de Ribas' way of think-

sulting word in their language, and they did not carry bows and arrows; rather, some dressed like women.

The vice of those who are called anthropophagists (those who eat human flesh) was introduced to all these peoples in their gentile state by the devil, the principal enemy of all humankind. Some practiced it more than others. In the high mountains and among the Acaxee this inhuman vice was as common as eating meat from the hunt, which was a daily occupation. They used to go out to hunt an enemy in the montes or fields just as though they were hunting deer. They ate their prey after it was cut up and boiled or roasted. Other nations did not do this except when an enemy was killed who was known for his bravery in battle. By eating his flesh they thought they would increase their own courage. But thanks to the acceptance of the Gospel of Christ Our Lord this barbarous and ferocious vice has been eradicated and stamped out, along with all the others.

There were no laws or kings among them to chastise their vices and sins, nor was there any kind of authority or civil government that could punish them. It is true that they recognized some principal caciques, who were the heads or captains of families or rancherías. But their authority consisted only in organizing for war or attacks against their enemies or working out peace agreements with other nations. Such actions were in no instance undertaken without the consent of said caciques, who for such purposes commanded great authority. It was at their houses [12] that the well-known drunken war revels were held. In addition, their subjects helped cultivate their fields, which were usually larger than those of others. These caciques acquired this authority not so much through inheritance, but rather through their bravery in war, the number of children, grandchildren, and other relatives they had, or at times because they were orators or preachers. This will be discussed throughout the course of this history.

Finally, these blind nations did not possess any kind of literature, painting, or art. The only agriculture they understood was that of the fields they cultivated, which was previously explained. The only tools they had for sowing and harvesting the fields were long, wide, wooden knives, which they used to hoe the ground, a task in which both men and women participated. The women also practiced the art of spinning and weaving

cotton or other native fibers such as Castilian hemp or pita.[37] They made mantas from it, but they did not use looms, for they did not possess even this invention. Instead, these mantas were woven by means of very laborious handiwork, placing stakes in the ground for use in producing the cloth.[38] Their customary clothing was scanty; men wore barely anything at all. The women covered their bodies from the waist down with a cotton manta, which as we said, they wove. Those who did not have these cotton mantas wore short skirts made of buckskin. This is a material that they know how to work well, and they drew designs on some of them with red ocher, especially the young women. They also painted their faces and wore stones as earrings and charms. The girls, no matter how poor or young they are — even the newborns — are covered with a small manta, and this demonstrates these peoples' modesty. As for the men we can say that they went about totally nude, because even though some of them covered themselves with cotton or fiber mantas, they freely cast them off.

These were the people who still retained some human civility,[39] for other poorer or wilder nations wore even less clothing, except for the women, who always wore something, even if it was only grass and tree leaves. They thus reveal themselves to be children of our first parents, Adam and Eve, who protected themselves with tree leaves out of shame for their original sin, until God covered them with animal skins.

Both men and women grow their hair long and value it highly. Many women wear it loose over their shoulders; sometimes it is tied back or braided. Men usually wear it tied back, with bangs or crowns that they decorate with palm leaves and colored feathers. When they go into the monte to hunt they wear buckskin caps so that their hair will not catch on the trees and branches.

Because I have made note of these peoples' barbarous customs and vices, I must also discuss those vices that were lacking in spite of their blindness. These same vices and customs are found frequently among very civilized and wise peoples; for in the kingdoms and countries of this world that possess evangelical law

---

37. This fiber (*ixtle*) probably was derived most often from the narrow leaves of *Agave angustifolia*.

38. This manner of weaving was described more fully by Father Juan Nentvig (1980:68).

39. Pérez de Ribas used the terms *policia humana*. People who had policia generally were considered "civilized" by European standards; they wore clothing and lived in towns or cities, with elites whose differential access to goods and services was manifested in clothing and other visible signs of power (see Corominas and Pascual 1989–1991:4:598; Pagden 1982:98ff).

---

ing would have been "assertive" roles, with passive male partners. Beals (1943:53), who cites Pérez de Ribas as well as other sources, notes that homosexuality was fairly common among the Cáhita, principally among men.

and the laws of Christ no one escapes theft, stealing, and robbery, no matter what people or country or however civilized they might be. Is there a country or city where one does not encounter false testimony, blasphemy, and illicit dealings and abuses, or where one does not find quarrels and strife that lead to the bloodshed or murder of a compatriot, a neighbor, or a relative? It was rarely or never that such things happened among these peoples; instead, there was agreement and peace among all those of a single nation, [and they lived] without deceit, fraud, or theft. When theft [13] did occur it involved only a gourd, a melon, or some ears of maize. And if anyone says that the lack of such vices in these people was due to the lack of any material goods and wealth to warrant the occasion, my reply is this: They generously shared with each other the little that they did have. Whenever a hungry person needed food, even if he were only passing through, he would find it at any house he went to, as long as he was not an enemy, and he would sit down to eat just as if he were in his own home.

CHAPTER IV These peoples' unique games, diversions, and hunting practices

Among these peoples' customs, some of which are good and some of which are bad, there are yet others that I wish to discuss which are neither. These include their diversions, games, and hunting practices, all of which they participated in without giving offense. They hunted a great deal, in part because the montes and woodlands (as previously discussed) abound in deer, peccary, hares, rabbits, and other odd creatures. Moreover, one does not need to travel very far to find them. Indeed, we could say that these peoples' dwelling places were the same as those of the deer and wild animals and that they all lived together. On their hunts they sometimes killed tigers, lions, wolves, and foxes, although the latter they sought not so much for their meat as for their pelts. Another reason they hunted so much was because they lacked their own source of meat. Lacking domesticated livestock such as goats, sheep, or cattle, they were forced to seek out the wild game of the monte, and their taste for this sustenance called them to the hunt. Last of all hunting developed their skill in using the bow and arrow and was, therefore, practice for warfare.

Some hunts are communal and bring together one or many pueblos or rancherías. On occasion the individual Indian hunts for his own diversion and benefit. Boys often hunt by themselves, particularly for doves and quail. These are very abundant, so they kill many. The manner in which they conduct their communal hunts is to encircle a thicket. If it is the dry season, they set fires all around it and then circle it with their bows and arrows in hand. The fire forces all the fowl and wild animals, even the serpents and snakes, to flee the monte, and nothing escapes their arrows. If an animal escapes with a fatal wound, they go to find it the following day at the spot where they know for certain that it has fallen dead. Because they normally use poisoned arrows (even for hunting), it takes no longer than twenty-four hours for an animal to die. It is remarkable that the meat is not poisoned when the animal is killed with these venomous arrows. They find the place where the animal has dropped by looking up to the sky, where the *zopilotes*,[40] or buzzards (a type of eagle that feeds on carrion, of which there are many in this land) are flying in circles. When the hunters spot them they know where their prey has fallen. When they find it they carry it back to their houses to gorge; all the venison is cooked together and the residents or relatives are invited to the feast.

These Indians also hunt two other kinds of small animals that abound in the montes. Both are prized as food. The first they call *iguanas*,[41] a reptile very similar to a lizard but uglier in appearance. It inhabits the hollows of trees and also the water, so it is both terrestrial and marine. For this reason its flesh can be eaten even

40. This term is derived from the Nahuatl *tzopílotl*, a compound of *tzotl* 'filth, dirt, nastiness' and *piloa* 'to hang' (Corominas and Pascual 1989–1991:4:108). Because the Nahuatl term was not known in Spain, Pérez de Ribas coupled it with a Spanish term, *buitre* 'buzzard'.

41. Probably the spiny-tailed iguana (*Ctenosaura hemolipha*).

on fast days. It is a healthy and delicious food source. The little stones these animals produce (like bezoar[42] but whiter) are very medicinal and highly prized as a remedy to aid in the retention of urine.[43] They are not, however, found in all iguanas. To catch these animals in the hollows of trees, the Indians first reach very carefully for them with their hand, breaking their jaws so they cannot bite down on the hand like they usually do. They bring back bunches of live ones with their jaws broken, and these can be kept alive for eight to fifteen days in this way, thrown into a corner until they are ready to be eaten. But the Indians refrain from this and all other hunting when their wives give birth, because in their barbarous superstition they believe that the infant will die if they do not stay at home and fast.

Another hunt I will discuss is for the honeycombs from wild beehives with which God endowed their wooded areas and montes. Although their bees do not produce wax, being no larger than flies, they do produce a very fine honey. In softness, sweetness, and aroma it is better than the best honey from Castilla. The hive is round and measures two-thirds of a vara in length or, if full of honey, a full vara. The material covering the hive where the combs of honey are stored is similar to a leaf, like wasps' nests in Castilla, and there is an entrance that is just large enough for the bee's tiny body. The way the hives are designed and built is also marvelous because they construct them high up on a branch that has some kind of hook to hold the hive so the wind cannot blow it down. Because the honey is made from sweet-smelling flowers, it, too, smells good. [14]

It is now time to describe how the Indians harvest this crop that God provided for them in the brambles, which is where they are usually hidden. In the spring, the season when they are found, the Indian who is looking for honey searches for a pool of water, often in areas of the monte where the streams have overflown. There he waits for the bees to arrive to drink the dew they need to make honey. When a bee flies off he runs after it, keeping its flight in his sight until he locates the hive. When he finds it he cuts down the branch from which the hive is hanging and carries it off to his house. There he savors its contents, not only the honey but also the bees' larvae, which are still shapeless, fragile little worms in their tiny houses in the comb. He places these on the coals and, when roasted, they are eaten as a delicacy. All of this is reason to praise the most generous Creator, who took such great care in providing sustenance for these poor peoples. The Indian who searches out the hives must possess good eyesight in order to be able to see the little bee in the wind. For the same reason one should not try to find them on a cloudy day.

Now that we have discussed the hunting pastimes of these nations, we will go on to the topic of their unusual games. The one they call *patoli* is widespread among them. It corresponds to cards or dice, but instead of these items they use four short reeds that have been split open, each less than a *geme*[44] in length. Little figures and points are drawn on the reeds to indicate their value or a loss. The reeds are cast onto a small stone slab so that they bounce and fall by chance, giving the player a win or loss. They draw a line on the ground for each point that they win, until they reach the set number that has been wagered. The bet is for a string of small sea snail shells that they prize and wear as ornaments. They also wager bows or arrows, as well as knives and hatchets that they have obtained. These same items also serve as stakes [15] in other games, but patoli is the game they play most often.

Another important game for them is called the running stick game.[45] This is played by all these nations, and it serves as exercise for war. For this game a large number of Indians assemble, sometimes one or two hundred, and entire pueblos challenge each other. The players divide into two teams. Each one carries its stick, which is a rounded piece of rather heavy wood no longer than a geme. It is thinned at midpoint so that when it is on the ground the bare foot can fit under it and it can thus be tossed by the players. Each team throws down its stick at the same time, and from this starting point a player from each team begins to advance it. This is done so skillfully that it could not be hurled farther by the arm of a good archer. The rule of the game is that the stick cannot be touched by the hand, only by the foot. Players can help it along, however, using a small stick carried in the hand. They use this latter stick to

---

42. Concretions that develop in the digestive systems of deer and other ruminants, which were thought to have magical properties. During the early seventeenth century the Jesuits in Peru sent to Europe thousands of bezoar stones from the llama and the vicuña; the latter were prized as an antidote (Martin 1968:100–1).

43. It is not clear from the Spanish whether the stones were a remedy for incontinence or for treating the retention of urine caused by something such as kidney stones. *Uña de gato* or cat's claw (*Acacia greggii*) when made into a tea of sorts purportedly was used by the Opata to relieve urinary retention (Nentvig 1980:52).

44. A geme was the distance between the end of the thumb and the index finger when both were fully separated (Alonso 1986:2:2127), which would be approximately six inches.

45. *Correr el palo.*

place the former on the instep of the foot. The player with the small stick hurls it forward to his advancing teammates, who move it to the end-line and then back again to the starting point. The first team to get back to its starting point wins the bet. The distance covered in advancing and returning the stick is so great that the players usually run two, three, or more leagues. In this way they become very swift for battle, where they never stop and are continually in motion. Because they sweat profusely while playing this game, they then jump into the river, which makes them very happy. These nations are generally more courageous, lively, and daring in this sport than the other nations of Nueva España, although the Mexica do not play this game.

Quite a few of these nations play another game with a ball that is larger than the one used in Europe. This ball is made from a special kind of rubber obtained from a tree called the *ulle*.[46] It is very solid and bounces so easily off the ground that it barely stops. They play this game in a plaza that they call a *batei*,[47] which they sweep in order to keep it flat and clean. There are two teams of four, six, or eight Indians lined up facing each other, and they kick the ball back and forth. Each time the ball is advanced the opposing player closest to it kicks it back. The rules of this game allow the ball to be hit only with the shoulder blade or the bare thigh. Sometimes the shoulder or thigh hits the ball so hard that it travels thirty or forty paces or flies so high that the opposing team cannot return it. Even so the ball is so heavy and solid that if it happens to hit a player in the stomach it will kill him, as has happened. When the ball bounces along the flat earth an opposing player will move with

great skill and swiftness to bounce it off his hip until it passes the opposing team's end-line, where the game and wager are won. In this game as well as the running stick game the players finish excited and covered with streams of sweat, because the weather is hot. Their solution (the river) is right at hand, however, and throughout the day they jump in to cool off and bathe. All of them, young and old, men and women, swim like fish.

While discussing these peoples' pastimes I also want to add something about the unusual way they carry burdens. The weight is borne on the bare shoulder, across which is laid a pole of smooth, strong wood that has a long net at both ends, like a scale. These nets are large enough to hold a *fanega*[48] of maize and with it, if need be, two small children, just as if they were in a cage. At times they carry such a heavy load that it makes even a strong pole bow. [16] The Indian will nevertheless walk with it for three, four, or more leagues. Sometimes I was afraid that such a huge weight might break their shoulder bones. But rather than breaking, a callous forms on the shoulder that is as thick as a nut. Today this way of carrying loads is used less frequently because the Indians have many horses, which they buy from Spaniards. They use them for travel as well as for carrying produce that they harvest or acquire through trade in distant places.

Enough has been said regarding the pastimes of these nations. Although these lesser subjects need to be discussed, I want to begin discussing more substantial and rewarding topics. As this history unfolds, there will be no lack of matters that praise and glorify God.

46. This term comes from the Nahuatl *ule*, which refers to rubber.

47. Although Beals (1943:79, f.38) suggested that the term 'batei' was introduced by the Spaniards from the West Indies, Pérez de Ribas implies here that it was a native term. This is consistent with the construction and use of ballcourts in prehistoric times (see Scarborough and Wilcox 1991).

48. A fanega equaled 2.58 bushels.

CHAPTER V Whether formal idolatry existed among these peoples or if they were atheists; also their sorcery, superstitions, and renowned sermons

No one can deny that atheists are the most hopeless and lost people in the world, and also the most distant from divine light, for they close their minds and ears to the principal truth of all divine doctrine, the basis of eternal salvation. They have no one to fear or love, so they take as much license as they want in their evil deeds and commit as many abominations and sins as one can imagine. This is why the devil, the principal enemy of humankind, strives to attract men to this state of utter ruin, just as he is doing today with more than a few heretics of our times. Because they cannot defend their errors, they go from heresy to atheism, slamming the door on any understanding of sound truth. They fear neither a God who punishes nor a law that forbids, becoming brute animals who recognize only the visible, the corporeal, and the worldly, paying no heed to the blessed and eternal purpose for which God created man. They thus arrive at the wretched condition that the royal Prophet lamented: *Dixit insipiens in corde suo: non est Deus*,[49] which he went on to explain *Corrupti sunt et abominabiles facti sunt*.[50] They reached (he says) an abominable state of corruption of customs.

Let us turn now to the barbarous peoples who are the subject of this history. I paid close attention to the matter of idolatry during the years that I spent among them, and it is accurate to state that whereas traces of formal idolatry existed among some of these peoples, others did not have any knowledge of God, nor of any deity, not even a false one; nor was there explicit worship of a Lord who held dominion over the world. They did not understand the providence of a Creator and Governor from whom in another life one might expect rewards for their good deeds or punishment for evil ones, nor did they collectively worship any divinity. Any worship that was to be found was reduced to bar-

barous superstitions or sorcery,[51] knowledge of which was acquired by certain persons who had intimate dealings with devils. This knowledge was a heritage passed on from their elders. The latter taught it to others at the hour of their death, charging them to practice some of the ceremonies of sorcery and superstition, which they used to cure, kill, and deceive. Such sorcerers are usually healers, and they are the most sinful and feared people among them, because they know that their sorcery can kill whenever they want. [17] Because these sorcerers deal so much with the devil, it is they who are most opposed to Gospel preaching and most persecute its ministers. They are the instruments most used by Satan to introduce whatever evil he wants among these blind peoples. Whenever it happened that God wished to take some lambs to heaven as pleasing first fruits of this new Christianity, these sorcerers spread rumors, just as they have often done, that the waters of Baptism kill children. They were also the source of something else that I observed at times while serving in these doctrinas. When gentile mothers brought their children to be baptized and the moment came in the ceremony when the blessed salt was placed in the infant's mouth, the mothers became frightened because the sorcerer had persuaded them that it was a kind of spell that the priests used to kill infants.

These demonic healers are also the source of the speeches (which they call *tlatollis*)[52] promoting uprisings and rebellions in the pueblos and the burning and razing of churches. When the devil sees that the light of the Gospel and the catechism are undoing the healers' deceitful tricks, diminishing their authority and the peoples' interest in them as healers, and putting an

---

49. *Margin Note*: Psal. 14. Psalm 13:1: "There is no God above us is the fond thought of reckless hearts" (Knox 1956:483).

50. Continuation of Psalm 13:1: "warped natures everywhere and hateful lives!"

51. We have translated *hechizos* as sorcery to reflect Jesuit thinking that the practitioners (*hechiceros*) obtained their knowledge and power from evil spirits, namely the devil.

52. Tlatolli, meaning language or discourse, is from the Nahuatl verb *tlatoa* 'to speak'. The Mexica monarch was called *tlatoani*, which reflected the fact that his power and effectiveness as a ruler were dependent on his speech-making ability (Soustelle 1961:87).

end to the Indians' vices, then the enemy of human-kind marshals all his efforts through the sorcerers to persuade the pueblos to rebel, to burn the churches, and to return to the montes to live as they please.

The way these bedeviled doctors cure is by blowing on those parts of the body that are infirm or painful. They blow with such force of purpose that the noise they make is heard far away. At other times they suck the wound. Although we could say that this action had the natural effect of a suction cup that concentrates or diffuses the humor, it is so cloaked in superstitions and lies that we cannot be sure that it is entirely safe, nor that it is free from deceit or a pact with the devil. They make the patients believe that they remove from their bodies the sticks, thorns, and pebbles that caused their pain and illness. All this is a ruse, because they carry these things hidden in their mouths or hands, and once they have cured the patient they show them to him and pass this off as the truth. This is, however, all a hoax and a lie. They are even so bold as to display these items that they have removed from the body, just as tooth-pullers fashion strings of teeth to show off the skill of their art. They also cure arrow wounds by sucking out the poison. This is an effective remedy, provided they renounce the customary pact they have made with the devil. When they suck the wound they also suck out the poison, but the tongue is not harmed provided they spit the poison out. It is not lethal as long as it does not enter the bloodstream.

Usually, the pact that these sorcerers make with the devil is kept bound up in small pieces of rawhide made from the pelts of animals similar to the ferret. They make small pouches out of this material, in which they keep colored pebbles or nearly transparent marbles. They guard this little pouch as though it held relics, so when they hand it over at the time of their Baptism, it is a good indication that they are truly receiving Christ's Faith and divorcing themselves from their intimacy with the devil.

The devil frequently spoke to the Indians when they were gentiles, appearing to them in the form of animals, fish, or serpents; he has not forgotten how successful he was in assuming this same shape to cause the downfall of our first mother. The Indians greatly respected and feared him whenever he appeared, and [18] as a title of respect they called him 'Grandfather'. They did so without distinguishing whether he was creature or creator. Even though they recognized the shape of the animal or serpent in which the devil appeared to them, painting it in their own fashion or sometimes erecting a stone or

pole as an idol, they clearly did not seem to recognize a deity or supreme power of the universe. Most of the idolatry found among these people turned out to be of this kind. However, among other peoples who will be described later, greater evidence of formal idolatry did exist, as we will see. Thanks be to God and His mercy that these people are being freed from all this blindness, lying, and deceit. As this history unfolds many unusual events concerning this matter will be recounted.

One of the duties of the sorcerers of whom I have spoken was to preach and deliver extraordinary sermons and speeches. Because this is a matter of false or true religion, I will write here about the sorcerers and their role and customs. It was very common practice among all these nations to have such preachers. They were ordinarily their principales or caciques, especially if they were sorcerers. The role played by such individuals paralleled somewhat that of the priests of the gentiles' idols.[53] These sermons were preached most frequently at the outset of a war, during peace talks with another nation or with the Spaniards, or when they celebrated a victory or the taking of enemy heads. On these occasions the old principales and the sorcerers would meet at the house or ramada of the cacique. They would be seated around a torch, where they would proceed to light some of their tobacco-filled reeds, which they would then pass around to smoke. Then the Indian who held the greatest authority would stand up, and from his standing position he would chant the beginning of his sermon. He would start by walking very slowly around the plaza of the pueblo, continuing his sermon and raising the tone of his voice, shouting so that the entire pueblo could hear him from their bonfires and houses. This circling of the plaza and sermon would take more or less half an hour, depending on the preacher. When this was done he would return to his seat, where his companions would welcome him with great acclaim. Each one would express this individually, and if the preacher was an old man, which they usually are, the response went like this: "You have spoken and advised us well, my grandfather. My heart is one with yours." If the person congratulating him were an old man, he would say, "My older or younger brother, my heart feels and speaks what you have said." Then they would honor him with another toast and round of tobacco. Next, another orator would get up and give his sermon in the same manner, spending another half an hour circling the plaza.

---

53. The reference is to biblical accounts as recounted in Paul's Epistles and the New and Old Testaments more generally.

These sermons took most of the night, especially if they were discussing an important declaration of war or peace. That which they preach in these sermons conforms to their barbarous intellect, so they repeat things many times, often presenting the same arguments. If they wanted to incite warfare, the speakers would depict the bravery of their archers; the [importance of] defending their lands, women, and children; and the deeds of their valiant captains, naming those who at that time were warriors in their nation, etc. If they were negotiating peace with the Spaniards, they preached the advantages of peace, how they would be able to enjoy their lands and river valley, and how they would benefit from Spanish protection. When [19] it was a matter of priests coming to instruct them, they added other reasons that I will discuss at the appropriate moment in this history.

The usual epilogue of these sermons exhorted all members of the pueblo, young and old alike, invoking them in terms of kinship, saying, "my grandfathers, my fathers, my older and younger brothers, sons and daughters of my brothers, let us be of one heart and mind." This is how they concluded their sermons. They truly had a great capacity to move people to do whatever they wished, be it good or evil. For this reason, so that they might promote the divine word and Christian customs, they are still permitted to deliver sermons even after they are baptized and converted. To accomplish this they repeat many times, "The word of God has reached our lands; we are no longer who we were before." There are many other things that pertain to these peoples' customs and their increased capacity, which has resulted from their being educated and instructed in the catechism. This will become clearer during the course of this history, as will the fruits of this labor in both the divine and human spheres.

CHAPTER VI What has been learned about the origin of these peoples and the route they took to come and settle this region; the variety of their languages and how important it is for evangelical ministers to learn them

It is difficult to determine (and many erudite persons have written about this) what route these peoples took to reach the lands of the New World, which is so isolated from the Old and was so unknown to all the historians and writers of past centuries. These writers believed that Hercules' Columns, erected in Cádiz or along its coasts, marked the end of the earth and its settlements. Moreover, they added that if land should be discovered beneath the Torrid Zone,[54] it would be uninhabitable due to the rigors of its climate and would thus have no people. After thousands of years, nevertheless, such peoples have now been discovered. When that which the past had never known was discovered in our times God manifested His greatness by opening the eyes of mankind, demonstrating that He can make habitable regions and climes that men had declared wild and unbearable. Moreover, He populated them with the great number of nations that have thus far been discovered, and it must be stated that they descend from the same single branch as the rest of mankind, that is, from Adam.

Much has been studied and written concerning how these peoples reached the New World, separated as it is from the Old by such immense seas. I will not pause here to relate the ideas and debates on this subject. These can be reduced to the most likely opinion, which is that these people arrived from Asia overland to the

54. What today we know as the equatorial region between the Tropics of Capricorn and Cancer.

north or crossed some narrow stretch of sea that was easy to cross and remains as yet undiscovered. In ancient times, unlike today, there existed neither the skill nor the knowledge required to navigate the immense stretches of the high seas. The ancients had no knowledge of the compass, nor did they have maritime charts showing how to navigate and cross the high seas.

To this I will only add something that will shed light on a subject that until now has been very obtuse. I learned this through my dealings with and instruction of some of the nations that inhabit the Province of [20] Sinaloa, which are the most remote of all the nations discovered and populated by Spaniards in Nueva España. More than a few times I very carefully questioned the eldest and most intelligent of these Indians, asking whence they had come and when they or their ancestors had settled the places that they presently occupy. Every one of them consistently responded that they had come from the north, abandoning places that they had held and settled. These had been taken from them in warfare and subsequently occupied by those other nations that had overcome them.

I found evidence of the truth of all of this during the expeditions that Spanish soldiers conducted into the interior for the purpose of pacifying peoples and other necessary causes. I accompanied these expeditions to provide whatever was necessary in the way of Christian ministries, and in [reviewing] the reports that I wrote concerning these expeditions I found clues that all the nations that are being peacefully settled in new missions came from the north. This is what is constantly said of the great Mexican nation, that they came from the same region and experienced hardship, as is often reported in their histories. These people say that the Spaniards are the only ones who came from the east, and that they know of no other nation that came from that direction. This argument is supported by the fact that most of the nations of Sinaloa refer to Spaniards as *Yoris* or *Doris*. Although this word means 'brave' in the language most commonly spoken by these people, the term also refers to the lion, the tiger, and other rarely seen wild animals. It was because the Spaniards came to their lands from the east, whence no other nation had come, and because they considered them to be brave that they gave them the aforementioned name.[55]

When I was learning some of these peoples' languages I noted additional evidence that they as well as the Mexica came from the north. Almost all of these languages (and there are many) have words, or what are primarily called roots (of which I could provide an extensive glossary here), that either belong to the Mexican language [Nahuatl] or derive from it, retaining many of its syllables. From all this two things can be inferred: the first is that nearly all these nations [once] communicated with and occupied the same lands as the Mexican nation. Even though their *artes*[56] and grammars are different, many of their rules are the same. The second is that all these nations, including the Mexica, came to settle the New World from the region to the north. There they found an overland route across the continent to America (although this has yet to be discovered). Alternatively, America is separated from the Old World only by some narrow stretch of sea, one that men as well as wild animals could easily cross to this New World. If so, then God has reserved the discovery of this route or stretch of sea for a time known only to His divine and inscrutable providence, which has been seen to be so wondrous in the discovery of the New World.

Now that we have begun discussing the different languages of these nations, it can also be said that their variety and confusion were punishment for the sins of those who tried to erect a tower of confusion against God, as is related in the Holy Scriptures.[57] Just as the sins of these peoples have been multiplying, so have their languages multiplied and become confused. Because the devil is the master and prince of confusion and division, from the very first time he caused this to happen among the angels in heaven, he has not ceased in doing [21] the same on earth by dividing peoples and languages. By this same means he also makes the preaching of the Gospel more difficult. But Our Lord, who in His mercy derives good from evil, has transformed this vast number of languages into material for greater rewards for His evangelical preachers.

To accomplish their holy enterprise and aspirations, these preachers, with their holy zeal for saving souls and introducing them to their Creator and Redeemer, have overcome great difficulties in learning an infinite number of barbarous languages. This fulfills and verifies the magnificent promise that Christ Our Lord made to His Apostles and those who succeeded them in Gospel

---

55. It is more likely that the Indians likened Spaniards unto lions and other wild animals because the first Spaniards that the Indians encountered were slave raiders/soldiers who participated in Nuño de Guzmán's conquest of Nueva Galicia in 1531.

56. An *arte* was a grammatical synthesis of a native language (Pennington 1979; Shaul 1990).

57. The Tower of Babel (see Genesis 11).

preaching. He pledged that they would speak in new and unknown tongues: *Linguist loquentur novis*.[58] When we reflect on the fulfillment of this promise today we see that it has a particular meaning. When Christ Our Redeemer declared that His disciples would speak in new and varied tongues His disciples had not yet learned them nor did they know that such languages were spoken in the world. The languages that were spoken in the Old World at the time the promise was made were not, therefore, particularly new or unknown. Much newer and unheard of were those languages that were later invented, multiplied, discovered, and subsequently conquered by our evangelical ministers, with holy zeal for the salvation of souls. These new and unknown tongues have not always been imparted to the preachers of this New World by the Holy Spirit. They have normally been learned through hard work and study, accompanied by the charity and love infused in their hearts by this very same Holy Spirit. It is also true (and we have examples that are verified by the sons of the Company of Jesus and by other holy religious devoted to the preaching of the Gospel) that they often received singular favors of divine grace that enabled them in two or three days to acquire enough competence in a very strange language to preach to a pueblo, some of whose people God had undoubtedly predestined. This grace was bestowed not only on the Apostle of the Orient, our father Saint Francis Xavier, in whom this talent shone brightly, but also on many others who were endowed by divine goodness. It was also found in other ministers of the Gospel whom I could list, who (to their astonishment) found at times that they possessed enough skill in a given language to preach the deep mysteries of our Holy Faith to these new peoples; their teacher was obviously the Holy Spirit.

The number of languages found among these nations is almost infinite. Although at times many pueblos are found to speak the same language, it also happens that different languages are spoken in different *barrios*[59] of a single pueblo. It thus becomes necessary for many of our religious to learn (as they do) two and three different barbarous languages, without books, papers, grammars, glossaries, or dictionaries. And even though these languages might be barbarous, it is amazing to see how they nevertheless follow rules for the formation

of tenses and cases and the declension of nouns, as well as other grammatical rules that [characterize] refined languages. It is difficult to understand how each one of these nations, when adopting a language distinct from the others, could uniformly agree to form and invent as many words as there are in a single language. Each one requires its own vocabulary and all the regular and irregular rules ordinarily found in a grammar, [arrived at] without disagreement among those who invent the language. Although this problem was [22] resolved in those [instances where] languages were derived from others, such as Romance from Latin, this same solution does not hold for languages that were different from the start, as is the case among these many nations, where neither vocabularies nor grammars match one another. As a solution to this problem I see that one can answer that change in language does not occur suddenly or by summoning together an entire nation to agree upon it. Instead, it occurs gradually over time, in the same way we can see that the Castilian spoken today differs from the Castilian spoken in earlier times. But all this does not entirely diminish the problems that occur when a nation completely changes all its words, terms, phrases, and grammatical rules, becoming totally different from the language from which it separated. These problems are augmented by the fact that these languages, or most of them, are not among those that God in His power divided suddenly among the peoples who built the Tower of Babel. It is said that there were seventy languages then, but the languages here are countless. Consequently, it must be confessed that many of them have been newly invented. Whoever is not satisfied with this solution to the problem can choose whatever alternative best suits him.

What I can say about our evangelical workers is that not only have they overcome the immense challenge of learning such difficult and numerous languages, but they have also made these languages easier for future missionaries to learn by reducing these tongues to grammars and rules. So great is their zeal and love for the welfare of souls that they have already written texts concerning the Christian mysteries and customs in some of these languages. They have also preached in these languages so eloquently that sometimes the Indians were heard to say that they did not speak their own language as well as the priests. The latter have learned the new tongues so effectively that at times they have forgotten their own native language as a result of learning the foreign one. There is another observation that must be included here, which can only encourage the ministers

58. *Margin Note*: Marc. cap. 16. Mark 16:17: "they will speak in tongues that are strange to them" (Knox 1956:52).

59. Apparently areas within pueblos that were occupied by distinct lineages or kin groups.

who come to instruct these nations in the catechism: There is no means so powerful as speaking to them in their own language for winning them over, dominating them, retaining the great authority required by the evangelical minister, and effectively instructing them, particularly if the language is spoken well. It is when the minister so teaches *tanquam potestatem habens*[60] that the preaching of the Gospel takes root among those who hear it. The minister convinces them to abandon their superstitions and deceit, and as a result he is more revered than their lying preachers. Last of all I can state

on the basis of great experience that sometimes the language enables the speaker who knows it and preaches in it to save himself from the mortal dangers, disturbances, restlessness, and uprisings that the devil causes among these peoples. Speaking to them in their own language calms and controls them; it captures their affection and wins them over, subjugating them in the process. It was not without reason that Christ Our Redeemer stated the following about the gift of language: *Serpentes tollent*,[61] they will handle serpents, which these peoples were.

CHAPTER VII The first news is received concerning the Province of Sinaloa; the first explorations carried out there and its nations and boundaries

In the year of Our Lord 1521 the Spaniards subjected the great Mexican Empire to the crown of the Catholic monarchs of Castilla. They did so for the greater glory of both the Divine and human Majesties, as well as to extend to the New World the [23] boundaries, settlements, and holdings of the Catholic Church. God had clearly promised this to them through His evangelical Prophet Isaiah, saying, *Dilata locum tentorij tui et peles tabernaculorum tuorum extende: ne parcas, longos fac funiculos tuos, et clavos suos consolida; ad dexteram enim, et ad laevam penetravis, et semen tuum gentes heriditabit, et civitates desertas inhabitabit.*[62] That all these magnificent promises pertain to the time of evangelical law is confirmed by the Apostle of the People, Saint Paul. He wrote to the Galatians in Chapter 4, explaining the words of the evangelical law that came from the Prophet himself. I do not know where the words of this most illustrious prophecy are so completely fulfilled as in the discovery of the New World,

for the greater happiness and redemption of infinite souls whom the devil had commandeered from their Creator.

What most serves our purposes in this prophecy is that it shows many signs of being fulfilled in the reduction to Christ's church of the barbarous and uncultivated peoples discussed in this history. What else can be meant by those words that announce that Christianity must extend not only to walled cities and splendid buildings, but also to nations that live in tents and out in the fields? *Dilata locum tentorij, ne parcas.*[63] Do not spare the work of converting the most fierce and barbarous nations of the world, who live in the fields, for I will subject them to you. What else could be meant by those other words: *Semen tuum gentes hereditabit?*[64] Your descendants and successors, heirs to the Apostles' institution, will populate once-deserted cities with Christians who acknowledge and adore God. In other words, *Semen tuum civitates desertas inhabitabit.*[65] What deserted cities can these be but the very settlements or deserts

60. "As if strengthened"

61. Mark 16:18: "They will take up serpents in their hands" (Knox 1956:52).

62. *Margin Note*: Isaí. 54. Isaiah 54:2–3: "Make more room for thy tent, stretch wide—what hinders thee?—the curtains of thy dwelling places; long be the ropes, and firm the pegs that fasten them. Right and left thou shalt spread, till thy race dispossesses the heathen, peoples the ruined cities" (Knox 1956:671).

63. Isaiah 54:2: "Widen the space of your tent, . . . do not hold back!" (Knox 1956:671).

64. Isaiah 54:3: "till thy race dispossesses the heathen" (Knox 1956:671).

65. Isaiah 54:3: "Till your race . . . peoples the ruined cities" (Knox 1956:671).

inhabited by these peoples? In numbers they constitute cities, but in terms of buildings and government they were deserts inhabited by wild peoples, those whom the Prophet called 'children of the desert'. To whom does this correspond more perfectly than to these children who are born to the Church in these wild, barren places? It is clear that the Prophet's words and divine metaphors fit these inhabited deserts even more perfectly than they fit Rome or Athens. In the end it cannot be denied that Isaiah's remarkable prophecy is fulfilled to the letter when the Gospel is introduced to the New World and to the unknown peoples that we are discussing. Indeed, because this was such an extraordinary work, one can clearly understand that God did not fail to reveal it and others to His Prophets, particularly because this discovery and conversion of a new world was so marvelous.

Let our digression end here and let us return to the topic of our history and the discovery of the nations of the Province of Sinaloa. These nations did not form part of the Mexican Empire, nor were they subject to it when it was conquered. Rather, they inhabited the mainland adjacent to the Mexican nation. News of them was received very shortly after Mexico was conquered. As soon as Mexico had been subjugated by the Spaniards, they began to reduce the surrounding nations and provinces, reaching Jalisco, which lies 130 leagues to the west of Mexico City. From there they advanced another 140 leagues to found the Villa de San Miguel de Culiacán, the first [Spanish] inhabitants of which were very noble and valiant in battle. They helped to establish Christianity [24] and founded the aforementioned villa through the pacification of the gentile nations in the valleys and along the powerful rivers of the region. Twenty leagues beyond here begin the settlements of the Province of Sinaloa, the initial exploration of which took place in the following manner:

At that time there was a captain who was motivated by greed and heeded neither king nor law (for greed tramples everything else).[66] Knowing that this province was populated by many barbarous peoples, he decided to explore it with some of his comrades for the purpose of capturing slaves to sell, thereby depriving them of their God-given freedom. In the course of these manhunts there occurred one of the strangest

cases ever told in history. I will sum it up here in a short narrative only as it bears on the exploration of the Province of Sinaloa; I refer those who wish to learn about it in its entirety to the history written by the official royal chronicler of the Indies, Antonio de Herrera,[67] particularly Decade IV, Book IV, Chapter VII, and Decade VI, Book I, beginning with Chapter III.

It happened that those four comrades, namely Alvar Núñez Cabeza de Vaca, Andrés Dorantes, Benardino del Castillo Maldonado,[68] and a black man named Estebanico, were the only survivors of the expedition of Governor Pánfilo de Narváez. Of the four hundred men who had set out to explore La Florida in 1527 all but these four died either in battle or from hunger, hardship, and illness. Divine providence protected them during the ten years that they traversed the lands of countless barbarous nations, among whom they worked miracles with the sign of the holy Cross. Through virtue and divine will they healed innumerable sick persons by making this divine sign over them and uttering a prayer. Because of such marvelous events, they were accorded immense respect and reverence by the nations among whom they sojourned. The Indians viewed them as men who came from heaven or as children of the sun. They looked upon them with such affection and fear that they did not kill and eat them but instead gave them lodging and food and asked them to stay with them. When these travelers declined due to their desire to return to Christian lands the Indians accompanied them until they reached another group. Thus, they never took leave of their benefactors (because beneficence commands, subdues, and tames even fierce and barbarous peoples). Therefore, the four pilgrims always traveled accompanied and defended by troops of Indians. God protected them during this strange journey, saving them from many misfortunes and seeing to it that they ended their quest in our Province of Sinaloa.

There[69] they encountered Captain Alcaraz (the name of the soldier who had been raiding for slaves). One of

66. The time was March 1536 and the captain was Diego de Alcaraz; Alcaraz was one of Nuño de Guzmán's followers, who were each awarded an *encomienda* in the region surrounding the Villa de San Miguel de Culiacán along the lower Río San Lorenzo. Guzmán's men made a living plundering native settlements for slaves, who were then taken south to Mexico (Reff 1991b:30, 197; Reff 1996).

67. In 1596, Antonio de Herrera y Tordesillas (1559–1625) became the chief historian (*cronista mayor*) for the Council of the Indies; he authored the first official history of the Indies, which was published between 1601 and 1615 (Haring 1947:103, f.6). Note that Pérez de Ribas errs in his citation of Herrera; Herrera's discussion of Spanish exploration of northern Nueva España occurs in Decade 4, Book 3, Chapter 5 (Cabeza de Vaca); Decade 4, Book 5, Chapter 4 (Fray Marcos de Niza); and Decade 4, Book 6, Chapter 5 (Coronado).

68. Pérez de Ribas is in error; the correct name is Alonso del Castillo Maldonado.

69. Sauer (1932:20) was of the opinion that this encounter occurred along the Río Ocoroni, a tributary of the Río Sinaloa.

his soldiers who had gone ahead saw Alvar Núñez and his companions in the distance, and thinking that he had run across the Indians they were looking to capture, he sounded the call to arms and summoned Captain Alcaraz. Here were four unknown travelers who in dress and appearance were indistinguishable from the Indians. They had not worn clothes for years and were just as sunburned and long-haired as the barbarians with whom they were traveling. Alvar Núñez Cabeza de Vaca recognized the Spanish soldiers by their weapons and uniforms, so he went up to the front of his company of Indians. Wishing to defend them, he got down on his knees, and using whatever language he could remember in order to be recognized, he spoke in halting Castilian, which [25] he and his companions had nearly forgotten. They stated who they were and whence they had come. This speech kept them from the slave chains and collars, but it did not stem the captain's greed, and he continued his efforts to capture Indians.

This abuse was prohibited in 1531 and condemned as unjust by the illustrious Archbishop of Santo Domingo, Sebastián Ramírez de Fuenleal, who was president of the Real Audiencia de México and governor of Nueva España.[70] Loyal to divine law and his king, this subject liberated those who had been born free, placing them under the protection of the Catholic king. Although Captain Alcaraz neither welcomed nor treated kindly these four travelers and their companions, he finally let them continue on to the Río Petatlán[71] and to what is today the Villa de San Felipe y Santiago, the seat of the Province of Sinaloa.

There the four travelers met Captain Lázaro de Cebreros, a resident and conqueror of the Province of Culiacán, which (as we said) is not more than thirty leagues from Sinaloa. When he recognized that these

men were Spaniards, despite the fact that their dress and appearance belied it, he proceeded to treat them with special pleasure and attention. Then he and the others who were with him shared their own clothes with the poor wanderers, whom he decided to take to the Villa de San Miguel [de Culiacán]. There they were very well treated and attended by the good people of that villa. When they had rested and made known their miraculous journey, they were given horses, provisions, and everything they needed to proceed the one hundred leagues to the city of Compostela. At that time His Majesty's Real Audiencia was located in that city; it was later [in 1560] moved to Guadalajara. In Compostela they were well received by the judges[72] of the high court and the king's ministers. When they considered this unusual case they decided that the viceroy who governed all of Nueva España should hear the news. Thus, they commanded that the travelers should be given whatever was needed for their journey, and they were sent to the great city of Mexico to present themselves to His Excellency. What happened when they arrived there will be related in the following chapter.

We should not forget, however, the troop of Indians from the interior who had accompanied our travelers. When they understood that their benefactors were taking leave of them for distant lands, they begged them to work out a secure situation for them with the Spaniards in that region; they wanted the latter to favor rather than enslave them. Cabeza de Vaca and his companions did so out of gratitude to the people who had been such faithful companions and escorts on such a dangerous journey. They arranged for their friends to be given a place to settle where they could cultivate fields. This was on the Río Sinaloa four leagues downriver from the present-day Villa de San Felipe. There they founded a pueblo called Bamoa, which is now inhabited by people of a language and nation [Nébome or Pima Bajo] located one hundred leagues farther inland. Later, at the appropriate time, we will discuss the conversion of this entire nation, which was marvelous. Because this nation was the source of an unusual devotion that will be discussed throughout this history, I will include it here.

The people of Sinaloa retained their memory of the sign of our redemption, the holy Cross, in this manner. When the troop of Indians that had accompanied the four Spaniards very regretfully took leave of them, they asked them for aid in the form of a sign with

---

70. The audiencia was a court of law that exercised both judicial and legislative functions, in conjunction with the viceroy and the royal exchequer. The first audiencia in the New World was established at Santo Domingo in 1511. Additional bodies were established on the mainland, the most important being the Audiencia de México. Sebastián Ramírez de Fuenleal succeeded the first president of the Audiencia de México, Nuño de Guzmán, in 1530, while at the same time retaining the archbishopric of Santo Domingo. As president, he was charged with implementing the orders and decrees of Charles V, including those issued in 1530, which forbade the enslavement of Indians under any pretext (e.g., "just war") (Haring 1947:54, 84).

71. Today known as the Río Sinaloa. The first Spaniards who reached the Río Sinaloa around 1531 "saw that in all of the Indian towns the houses were covered with mats which they call in the language of Mexico, *petates*, and therefore we named it Petatlán" (Hedrick and Riley 1976:39). In keeping with modern usage, all subsequent references to the Río Petatlán have been changed to Río Sinaloa.

72. *Oidores*, members of the audiencia.

which they could protect themselves from attacks by Spaniards. The sign that Cabeza de Vaca and his companions gave them was the Cross. They were told that whenever they happened to get word that Spaniards were coming to their lands, they should meet them [26] with a Cross in their hands. They were also to erect Crosses at the entrance to their pueblos, and the sight of these Crosses would protect them from harm. This healing sign made a deep impression on them, and they [still] wear Crosses made of mother-of-pearl around their necks or on their foreheads. Some nations erected Crosses in their pueblos even before they were converted. It is true that the sight of this divine sign should strike the heart of a Christian with piety and mercy, for at the sight of it even devils, with their infernal rage, control and repress their impulses.

And using this holy Cross to perform wondrous signs and miracles (as some histories tell), God Our Lord liberated those who had wandered lost through unknown and strange lands, among so many and such fierce nations. This was how divine providence provided the first news of the peoples who inhabited the interior of the great Province of Sinaloa, the northern limits of which (as we have said) remain unknown. To this day there is no clear indication of where the northern boundaries of the Province of Sinaloa lie, although it is true that heading eastward the land forms part of the mainland with Nuevo México and La Florida, whence our travelers came walking overland. The nations that live farther inland are likewise unknown, except for those that are discovered and civilized with the advance of Gospel instruction. It has been the good fortune of the Company of Jesus that the Lord gave to His sons such extensive fields, with innumerable nations, in which to cultivate the seed of the Gospel. Today there are thirty-five priests employed in Sinaloa, with nearly the same number of ministers working in the other missions that I will discuss. All of them are working for the glory of God and the spread of His Gospel.

CHAPTER VIII   Alvar Núñez Cabeza de Vaca and his companions reach Mexico City and report to the viceroy, who as a result dispatches an expedition to Sinaloa; the events of this expedition

When our travelers reached Mexico City and presented themselves to the viceroy (who at that time was Don Antonio de Mendoza, the first official to govern Nueva España with the title of viceroy), they provided a lengthy account of the many events (some happy, some sad) of their marvelous journey. They related what they had found along the way, as well as the peoples, nations, lands, and signs of mineral deposits that they had discovered. There was great amazement and interest in what they recounted because at that time the territories of the Spanish crown were not very extensive in the New World, nor had the many rich silver mines that God later provided been discovered yet. These new discoveries were received with great excitement, and God employed them for His exalted ends. It was on the basis of these new reports that the viceroy ordered an expedition to explore all the lands about which the travelers had brought news. Antonio de Herrera writes about this expedition in his *History of the Indies*, Decade VI, Book IX, Chapter II.[73]

In 1540 a draft was levied to recruit upwards of four hundred men for this expedition. Some of them were to be foot soldiers and others cavalry, because in those days there were not enough horses for everyone. The viceroy named Francisco Vásquez Coronado as governor and captain general of the troops and the expedi-

---

73. Coronado's expedition is actually discussed in Decade IV, Book 6, Chapter 5 of Herrerra's *Historia*.

tion. Don Pedro de Tovar, [27] who was an extremely important gentleman and a resident of the Villa de Culiacán, was appointed *alférez real* [second lieutenant]. It is still told how the viceroy himself traveled to Compostela to muster the expedition and dispatch it to the field. They drove cattle before them to provide for whatever need might arise on such a long expedition. The army and its general also had orders to explore the region—its settlements, valleys, and rivers—and assess the lay of the land. They were instructed to return with a report and account of everything. The viceroy also charged the most Holy Order of Our Angelic Father Saint Francis to appoint four religious to accompany the army in this endeavor, just as all the expeditions that have been conducted to spread the Holy Gospel in the New World have been the enterprise and occupation of religious orders.

Once mustered this squadron of Christian soldiers departed Compostela and marched northward, following the route indicated by Cabeza de Vaca and his companions. They did, however, take some detours inland, which seemed more appropriate for the new discoveries that were the objective of their expedition, which lasted more than two years. They traveled across the Province of Sinaloa and continued to search for a very populous city called Quivira,[74] which they had heard had houses that were seven or more stories high. In the reports I can find no solid evidence that they actually found it, although some people affirm that they did. At any rate they reached places at more than forty-two degrees north that were so cold that the rivers froze solid.

They crossed lands belonging to those who, because they live off hunting *cíbolas*,[75] are called 'the people of the bison'.[76] This already well-known animal is very similar to our European cows. In the end this expedition failed, because unfortunately its general, Francisco Vásquez, died from a fall from his horse.[77] The soldiers and other members of the squadron decided to return because of the disagreements they had with one another; they had not found the riches they were seeking and they were very tired of traveling. When the expedition reached Culiacán the army disbanded and the members of the expedition scattered; everything fell apart and was forgotten. The only thing achieved was that some Spaniards (although only a few) remained to settle the Villa and Province of Culiacán. A few others settled in Sinaloa, hoping to discover new mines there. The alférez, Don Pedro de Tovar, established herds of livestock at a location that seemed well suited along the banks of one of the rivers of Sinaloa so that in the future they could serve the settlers of this province.

Shortly thereafter the governor of Nueva Galicia came to the aid of the Villa de Culiacán, which was besieged in a war waged by a very powerful cacique.[78] The governor pacified the land, and under orders from Viceroy Don Antonio de Mendoza, the governor sent Fray Marcos de Niza, of the Order of the Angelic Father Saint Francis, back to the Province of Sinaloa to initiate a search for Quivira. The friar took Estebanico, the black man who had accompanied Cabeza de Vaca, as well as some Indians, and they proceeded without soldiers or weapons in search of the famous city, where they were to pacify the people and prepare them to receive the Gospel. The religious Father de Niza traveled into the interior, where after many leagues and great travail he discovered many nations and large settlements. Although some people received him well, others rose up, killing Estebanico and some of his [Indian] companions. Thus, Fray Marcos returned to Culiacán without having obtained anything significant. This was because the time determined by God had not yet arrived for the reduction of these peoples to the Gospel, which is the purpose for which His exalted providence commands and ordains these explorations. [28]

74. Pérez de Ribas here confused Quivira with Cíbola.

75. The name *cíbola* was first used by Fray Marcos de Niza in 1539 in reference to the Zuni province in New Mexico, where the friar was led to believe there existed seven large and wealthy cities. This idea was dispelled by Coronado and other explorers, who encountered the magnificent bison (*Bison americanus*) during their search for the cities of Cíbola. Over time, cíbola (or síbola, zíbolo) came to be used in reference to the bison (Hodge, Hammond, and Rey 1945:229–30).

76. *Vaqueros*.

77. Pérez de Ribas is in error: Coronado was badly injured, but he did not die from the fall (Hammond and Rey 1940:266).

78. Pérez de Ribas is in error with respect to the timing of the events narrated in this paragraph. The uprising suppressed by the governor of Nueva Galicia (Coronado) and Fray Marcos de Niza's journey to Cíbola occurred in 1539, prior to, not following Coronado's 1540 expedition. Note that Herrera, whom Pérez de Ribas cites, correctly has Coronado follow rather than precede Fray Marcos (see Herrera's Decade 4, Book 6, Chapter 5).

CHAPTER IX Francisco de Ibarra, governor of Nueva Vizcaya, explores the Province of Sinaloa and founds a villa

Around 1563 Francisco de Ibarra, governor of Nueva Vizcaya, decided to explore the Province of Sinaloa, which fell within his jurisdiction.[79] He was motivated by the news that was still circulating [concerning wealthy native lands], as well as by his desire to discover what others had not. He departed the city of Guadiana[80] (which is the seat of government [for Nueva Vizcaya]) with a fair number of soldiers and crossed the very high mountains and valleys of Topia, thereby reaching Culiacán and the Province of Sinaloa. He traveled throughout the province, visiting its nations. They received him in peace, and he promised them the same in return. Seeing that the province was inhabited by so many people, that it had such strong rivers, and that the colors with which the Indians painted themselves indicated the presence of mineral deposits (from which they make their paints), he decided to found a villa on the river they called the Zuaque [now the Río Fuerte], at a location called Carapoa. He established the villa, giving it the name of San Juan Bautista. This villa was settled by sixty Spaniards who had accompanied him, several of whom were married; the remainder were bachelors. He gave them lands and water sources and entrusted them with the care of several nearby Indian pueblos. He designated a very brave soldier named Esteban Martín Vohorquez as captain and *justicia mayor*.[81] The residents, their houses, their churches, and everything else were all very poor because it was a such a new settlement and the land was so distant and poor. A cleric named Hernando de la Pedrosa remained with them (they say),

serving as priest. Three friars of the Holy Order of Saint Francis also remained. After arranging all this Francisco de Ibarra left the province with the remaining people, hastening his departure because news had reached him that some very rich silver mines had been discovered in Chiametla (which fell outside both his jurisdiction and Sinaloa, on the road to Mexico City). Near these mines he founded another villa called San Sebastián. At first these mines yielded great riches, but in time their production decreased and they were eventually exhausted.

Returning to the Villa de Carapoa,[82] the settlers there received news of mineral deposits within the Province of Sinaloa. They explored and assayed some that seemed promising, but they were unable to continue because of disturbances and skirmishes with neighboring Indians, which resulted in several fatalities. Within a short time the newly founded Villa de Carapoa was itself endangered by unrest and assaults from neighboring Indians. Each side blamed the other for the unrest, and both are sure to have had their share in the blame. It is nothing new for soldiers to aggravate the nations they conquer with their harsh treatment, nor is it anything new for Indians to flee the vicinity of Spaniards and to refuse to work, preferring instead to enjoy their freedom. Finally, for one reason or another the Indians of the Zuaque nation, who figure very prominently in the course of this history, took action. When a group of the leading residents of the villa went to Zuaque lands to trade for maize, the latter received them peacefully. The Zuaque, however, acted falsely, inviting the Spaniards to a feast of game and fruits of the earth. As they sat eating, however, the Zuaque killed them and cut off their heads. One of the Spaniards who was taken alive was tied up, and they danced around him in a drunken victory celebration before finally cutting him to pieces. Another Spaniard who escaped brought the sad news

79. At that time Sinaloa actually fell outside of Ibarra's jurisdiction (Nueva Vizcaya) and was part of Nueva Galicia. It was only after Ibarra's successful reconquest of Chiametla, his pacification of the Culiacán region, and the founding of San Juan Bautista (all in 1564–65) that the Province of Sinaloa was removed from Nueva Galicia and became part of Nueva Vizcaya.

80. Guadiana subsequently became known as Durango. In keeping with modern usage, we have substituted Durango for Guadiana throughout the remainder of the text.

81. An individual who served at the behest of the governor as his deputy in a given settlement or municipal corporation (Haring 1947:151–52).

82. Pérez de Ribas jumps ahead here twenty years, overlooking the fact that the original villa founded by Ibarra in 1564 was destroyed within a year or so, along with its inhabitants. In 1583, Pedro de Montoya founded a second villa on the Río Fuerte. It is the destruction of this second villa (San Felipe y Santiago de Carapoa) in 1584 and subsequent events that Pérez de Ribas focuses on here.

to those who had remained in the villa. They bewailed the events and managed to withdraw [29] with their women and children to a small fortified palisade that they had erected out of brushwood. They notified their good friends and neighbors at the Villa de Culiacán of the dreadful events. They even made plans to abandon Carapoa and go to Culiacán to settle, which is what they in fact did.

At this point it is not fair to keep silent and fail to demonstrate how much the Province of Sinaloa owes the noble Villa de San Miguel de Culiacán and its residents. Beginning with the very first discoveries and explorations, they helped with the pacification and settlement of Sinaloa, treating its settlers as though they were brothers (indeed some were very close relatives), assisting them in person as well as with material goods and weapons. They supported them in every situation of need, serving as good brothers, just as they have continued to do up to the very day when this history is being written.

In confirmation of this the inhabitants of Culiacán held a town meeting as soon as they received the unfortunate news of the murders committed by the Zuaque and the continuing danger to the surviving inhabitants of Carapoa. At this meeting they recruited twenty-four very brave young men, who enthusiastically offered to go immediately to the rescue, taking along some of their servants. They took their weapons and horses, which when armored and used on a level battle field (as we will mention on another occasion), can be used for attack and are a great defense against Indian arrows.

Gaspar Osorio, a well-respected resident who knew the region very well, was named leader of this foray. They departed at full speed and arrived at the Río Sinaloa, where they found some Indian settlements that had remained at peace, as well as others that had declared themselves partisans of the Zuaque. While they were at the Río Sinaloa they learned that the Zuaque were celebrating the massacre and destruction of the Spaniards with a dance. They forged ahead, and on the road to Carapoa they met the surviving Spaniards from the villa. These individuals had already abandoned Carapoa and had no intention of returning, planning instead

to settle in the Villa de Culiacán. One can well imagine the emotions that overcame the two parties when they met. The residents of Culiacán were informed of and could see the terrible events that had befallen their friends and relatives, founders of the unfortunate Villa de Carapoa, only a few of whom had managed to escape. The survivors demonstrated their heartfelt gratitude to those who, like faithful brothers, had come to rescue them, risking their own lives in such a terrible and sorrowful situation. They all spent that day resting at the place where they met. Afterwards they held a meeting, and there were many opinions and different ideas about whether they should return and rebuild Carapoa so as not to give the Zuaque the pleasure of thinking that they had driven the Spaniards away. After much discussion the decision was made that the Spaniards should not abandon the Province of Sinaloa entirely, but that they should relocate along the Río Sinaloa, where some of the Indian settlements were calmer, and they would be closer in times of need to their loyal friends and neighbors from Culiacán. This plan was carried out, and those few Spaniards who fled the ruins of the Villa de Carapoa settled where today stands the Villa de San Felipe y Santiago. The Spaniards who had come from Culiacán returned to their own villa, waiting for time to reveal how to proceed with the conversion and settlement of the province.

During all this time of Spanish exploration [30] religious instruction could not be purposefully introduced, nor did events lend themselves to the preaching of the Gospel or anything related to it. The only Indians who were baptized were those who demonstrated friendliness toward the Spaniards and who learned some prayers in Latin, as was common practice at that time. The three religious of the seraphic Order of Saint Francis died violently in the aforementioned attacks, and we can well imagine that they must have received a glorious crown in heaven for having given their lives for the divine enterprise of preaching the Holy Gospel which, as we all know, is a task so typical of this holy order. [As a result of their deaths] the region was left without a single priest.

CHAPTER X Governor Hernando Bazán's expedition to punish the murderers of the residents of Carapoa

Agentleman named Hernando Bazán[83] succeeded Francisco de Ibarra as governor of Nueva Vizcaya, and when he got news of the crimes and outrages that the Indians of the Province of Sinaloa (mainly the Zuaque) had committed in the murder of the Spaniards at the Villa de Carapoa, he decided to undertake a mission to punish them and rein in their pride, thereby recovering the Spaniards' good Christian name and reputation.[84] These were all well-justified reasons. He gathered a company of more than one hundred Spanish soldiers (not a small number for those days, when there were not as many Spaniards living in the Indies). When he had armed them and his squadron was prepared, he named Gonzalo Martín, a very courageous soldier, to be their captain. Then he marched with them to the Province of Sinaloa, taking the route to the lands and settlements of the Zuaque. Along the way he fought some skirmishes with other tribes, who ambushed them and who did not dare to fight out in the open. He and his men finally reached the lands of the Zuaque, who had withdrawn to their dense thickets and woodlands, which are vast in that region. The governor halted his troops at a suitable place for the men and horses. Then he decided to send Captain Gonzalo Martín with a squad of eighteen or twenty of the most seasoned soldiers to scout the land and determine where the enemy had withdrawn. They began the march on horseback, and when they came across tracks and a narrow trail where it looked like the pack mules had entered, they left the horses and went in to get them. They came out into a small open field that had been cleared of trees, although it was still enclosed. The openings in the trees had been blocked off with many cut branches with which the Zuaque warriors had fortified the enclosure. As soon as the Indians heard the Spanish soldiers they summoned one another with great shouting and noise making. They encircled the Spaniards so that they could not escape and then unleashed a shower of arrows upon them. It was learned that many of these Spanish soldiers defended themselves very bravely and ravaged the enemy with their harquebuses for as long as the gunpowder lasted. When it ran out they drew their swords and embraced their *chimales*[85] (small shields), determined to die fighting like valiant soldiers. The Indians finished the Spaniards off with some long stakes that they cut, as well as with their arrows. By some stroke of good luck two Spaniards escaped; the rest of the [31] squad, however, died. The Indians cut off their heads and later used them for their *mitotes*[86] and dances. The insolence and pride of the victorious Zuaque were so great that as a sign of their triumph they carved figures of the headless bodies of their victims in the bark of the trees in that place where they had trapped the Spaniards. I can testify to this because years later, when by God's will I came at this nation's request to instruct them in the Gospel and baptize them (as I will later recount), I repeatedly saw these figures, which were still carved into the trees.

It would be wrong to remain silent here about the meritorious bravery of Captain Gonzalo Martín. His enemies were themselves witnesses to this, and they still talk about it. They say that when the captain saw his soldiers dead and himself surrounded by the enemy, he backed up against the trunk of a huge tree to protect his back from the arrows. Then for many hours he stood there fighting with his sword and shield against all those who pressed in on him. To this day they still remark how he slashed away at arms and heads, even as he was hit by arrows shot from a distance, until he finally dropped dead from his wounds. Moreover, the Indians said that the captain fought for such a long time that they were constantly sending groups to a distant river to cool off

---

83. Bazán was governor from 1583 to 1585 (Polzer, Barnes, and Naylor 1977:106).

84. Bazán's expedition was undertaken in 1585.

85. These apparently were shields used by the Mexica and other Nahuas, which the Spaniards adopted for battle along with their Nahuatl name.

86. A mitote was a dance made famous by the Nahuas involving a large number of people who were colorfully adorned. They would hold hands and dance in a circle around a banner, next to which there was a vessel filled with an alcoholic beverage. They would drink from this vessel every so often until they finally became intoxicated and lost their senses (Santamaría 1974:728).

and quench their thirst, all because of a single Spaniard. This demonstrated this famous captain's bravery. As soon as he fell as a result of his many wounds, his enemies descended on him, and they were not content simply to cut off his head like they did others. Because they had seen how brave he was, they cut all the flesh off his body, leaving only the bare bones. All the pueblos and rancherías wanted to celebrate their dances with a piece of flesh from such a brave man, or even to eat it or drink his blood, in order, as they said, to become brave.

When the news of the disastrous end of his scouting party reached Governor Bazán's military encampment, he became terribly upset. He armed all his remaining troops and set out very angrily the following day, intent upon destroying the enemy. But the Zuaque could not be found because they had broken camp and withdrawn to their dense and impenetrable thorn thickets. When the governor reached the clearing and corral where the catastrophe had occurred he found the remains of the dead, as well as the captain's bones. Along the way he ordered the enemies' crops cut to stubble, and then he went back upriver to the abandoned Villa de Carapoa. It broke his heart to see that the proud Zuaque had not received the punishment they deserved for having depopulated the first villa in Sinaloa and more so for this recent massacre of the Spanish scouting party, who were killed by approximately one thousand warriors. After the governor stopped briefly in Carapoa he continued

through the province to see whether he could engage the enemy or their confederates. When he reached the Río Mayo, which was twenty leagues from Carapoa, the Mayo received him peacefully. He nevertheless seized some prisoners from among them and threw them in chains, for it seemed to him that they had been accomplices in their dealings with the Zuaque. Later when these prisoners reached Mexico City, during the tenure of the marquis of Villamanrique,[87] their arrest and its justification were reviewed. Such matters were of utmost concern to our Catholic monarchs, [32] who with great Christian zeal command that the exploration of this New World, which God has placed in their care, proceed with complete fairness on behalf of all peoples. The Mayo Indians were found to be deserving of their freedom and were ordered to be released.

Governor Hernando Bazán and his company departed the Province of Sinaloa and returned to his province [of Nueva Vizcaya]. I wish to warn the reader not to be saddened or to hastily suppose that the treacherous Zuaque, enemies of Christ's name, will escape the punishment merited by these outrages and others that they subsequently committed. God saved their punishment for another time, to be meted out by another courageous captain of whom I will make honorable mention in this history, whose enterprise brought great honor to the Spanish nation.

CHAPTER XI The condition of the Province of Sinaloa and its five Spanish residents following Governor Bazán's departure

Given the adverse events in the Province of Sinaloa and the pride that the enemy nations had acquired, nearly all the Spaniards left because they no longer felt safe. Some went to settle at the Villa de San Miguel de Culiacán while others left for lands that were already pacified. Only five Spaniards remained at the site of the [future] Villa de San Felipe on the Río Sinaloa. We can say that this was due to a special provision from heaven so that later (at a time when Our Lord decided to com-

municate the light of the Holy Gospel to these peoples with greater assuredness) those few people could aid in this effort. And this they did, becoming the means by which the province was restored and a great Christianity was established, as will be seen in the following six books, where the conversion of these peoples and nations is recorded. But the bravery and perseverance

87. Alvaro Manrique de Zúñiga, viceroy from 1585 to 1590 (Polzer, Barnes, and Naylor 1977:99).

of the five poor soldiers who remained in this land merit that their names be inscribed here: Bartolomé de Mondragón, Juan Martínez del Castillo, Tomás de Soberanis, Antonio Ruiz, and Juan Caballero. These men had participated as brave soldiers in all the events of the conquest and pacification of Sinaloa and the search for mineral deposits, and they remained among the Indians of the Río Sinaloa. By treating them well they managed to gain and preserve friendship with those in some of the nearest pueblos, where there was still a Christian here and there who had been baptized earlier. These poor Spaniards lived like paupers in straw houses, and they also erected a church of the same material. They lived off game that either they killed themselves or their Indian friends shared with them. They also ate maize and beans, which they cultivated. They dressed in the local fashion, in buckskins and shirts made from cotton mantas. The Indians were very pleased with their company, because whenever there was an enemy attack their good friends the Spaniards came to their aid with their harquebuses and weapons. These friendly Indians did the same for the Spaniards.

The rebellious tribes (particularly the Zuaque) did not cease in their attacks. Even though they were twelve or fourteen leagues away, at times their squads would come to the [Río] Sinaloa. Because they could not capture the Spaniards, whom God kept safe in the midst of these dangers, they would instead go up and down the river attacking and killing horses. At this time [33] the Spaniards were extracting small amounts of silver ore from mines that were not very far from their settlement, and with this they were able to purchase goods from the Villa de San Miguel de Culiacán. They usually went there once a year for Holy Week, for there was a priest there who administered the Holy Sacraments. No priests had dared to remain in a place as desolate as Sinaloa, where their lives were exposed to such great danger. Therefore, in order to observe the celebrations of the Christian mysteries and the Holy Sacraments, these five Christian Spaniards would go to the neighboring Villa de San Miguel de Culiacán, and once they

had fulfilled their obligations they would return to their own settlement.

Around this time [circa 1589] the residents of San Miguel de Culiacán learned of mineral deposits in Sinaloa (particularly those in Bacaburito and Chínipa), so they went as a group to explore and work them. Each time they went exploring, however, they met with bad luck. The Indians always attacked them, and they had no chance to assay or work the mineral deposits. The nations of Sinaloa were still gentile, entombed in their barbarous vices and customs. Sinaloa was a woodland of wild animals and a cavern of devils, inhabited by thousands of sorcerers. It was a place where plants grew that yielded only thorns and brush. It was worse than an Egypt,[88] shrouded in palpable darkness. But in spite of all this God did not forget the uninhabited deserts that were mentioned earlier. Through the Prophet Isaiah He had promised His Church that these deserts would be populated with His Crosses, temples, and altars. He reserved this enterprise for the year 1590, when the standard of the holy Cross was raised in Sinaloa and the emptiness was filled with Christian settlements and churches that were consecrated to Christ and His saints. It was then that God sent His priests, some of whom would fertilize these barren fields with their blood (which was shed for Christ).

To conclude this book I wish to prevent those who read this history from reaching any premature conclusions before they have delved very far into it, or from doubting whether fruits can be harvested from the preaching of the Faith and Gospel to people who were as barbarous and seemingly incompetent as those whom I have depicted in this book. To dispel any doubts I refer the reader to the discussion of the Sinaloa mission that follows, as well as to Book VII, beginning with Chapter III, which specifically addresses this issue [of the Indians' competence]. As will become evident in the following book, the means by which divine providence wrought the introduction of its Holy Faith in such peoples is marvelous and delightful.

END OF BOOK I [34]

---

88. More specifically, the Egypt of the Jewish exile as recounted in the Old Testament.

BOOK II

The Sinaloa Mission

Priests from the Company of JESUS Arrive in Sinaloa and Begin Their Ministry

CHAPTER I The governor of Nueva Vizcaya asks the Father Provincial of the Company to send religious to convert the gentiles of that kingdom; priests are dispatched

Book II recounts the many events of a human and divine and worldly and spiritual nature that occurred during the first twelve years of the conversion to our Holy Faith of the nations that populate the first three rivers of Sinaloa. The first of these rivers is called the Sebastián de Evora or the Mocorito, the second the Sinaloa, and the third the Ocoroni. The distance from the first to the third river is eighteen leagues. Although these rivers are the least powerful, they were nevertheless well populated by peoples who spoke several languages.[1] The introduction of Christianity and the establishment of peace were achieved at the expense of great hardship. However, once they were introduced and established among these first nations their example greatly helped in their expansion among peoples farther inland, who live along rivers that are more powerful and more densely populated.

The manner in which divine providence determined that its sons of the Company of Jesus should embark on such a holy enterprise was most unusual and worthy of praise to divine goodness. It was just like the time when the arrogant [35] Nebuchadnezzar pressed the holy Prophet Daniel to interpret his dream and reveal the mystery of the statue that had appeared to the king of Babylon. After the Prophet had prayed to God and had asked Him to reveal how he should respond to the tyrant, Daniel emerged singing these wonderful words of divine praise that are so pertinent to us: *Sit nomen Domini benedictum, a saeculo, et usque in saeculum; ipse mutat tempora et aetates, transfert Regna, atque constituit, ipse revelat profunda et abscondita et novit in tenebris constituta, et lux cum eo est.*[2] May God's name be blessed forever and ever. He is Lord of the centuries and ages, and He changes them according to His divine will; He also destroys and establishes kingdoms according to His

---

1. Powerful rivers carried lots of sediment and water, overflowing their banks in the spring and creating extensive areas for farming. Thus, Pérez de Ribas' implied logic: powerful rivers tend to be lined by large populations.

2. *Margin Note*: Cap. 2. Daniel 2:20–22: "Blessed be the Lord's name from the beginning to the end of time; his are the wisdom and the power; change and chance of our mortal life he rules, crowns one man and discrowns another. Wisdom of the wise, skill of the skillful, what are they but his gift? The hidden depths he can lay bare, read the secrets of the dark; does not light dwell with him?" (Knox 1956:790).

divine will and reveals the most hidden things to the discourse of mankind whenever and however it pleases Him; ultimately the light is His and is with Him.

Now for our purposes, I tell you that our Province of Sinaloa was in the same abyss of darkness in which we left it in Book I, a veritable kingdom of Satan that resisted the light of the Gospel. Its gentile nations were hardened in their obstinacy, like the statue of stone and bronze that King Nebuchadnezzar saw in his dreams. There thus came a time unknown to mankind when divine will determined to end the tyrannical reign of the devil in Sinaloa, dispossessing him of those many nations that he had taken from their Creator. God wanted to grant possession of them to His Most Holy Son, as He had promised Him, saying, *Dabo tibi gentes haereditarem tuum, et possessionem tuam terminos terrae.*[3] The works of My omnipotence and mercy will not cease until the ends of the earth recognize and obey You. Today these ends of the earth are here in the Province of Sinaloa, where God introduced the rays of the new light of the Gospel that drove away the shadows: *Et lux cum eo est.*[4] He destroyed the statue that was made of as many different metals as there were nations in this land, and they were converted to one law and one Baptism and recognize only Jesus Christ. Certainly we can say, *Sit nomem Dominini benedictum, a saeaculo, et usque in saeculum.*[5]

Divine providence arranged for all this by means of a particular knight who, fortunately for the entire Kingdom of Nueva Vizcaya (especially our Province of Sinaloa, which lies within its jurisdiction) began to govern in the year 1590.[6] Because of his great Christianity, bravery, and prudence, he merits mention here, particularly as Our Lord made him the instrument of the great compassion wrought in the Province of Sinaloa. This knight's name was Rodrigo del Río y Losa, a native of the Villa de Arganzón, in the Bishopric of Calahorra in Castilla. He served the king for a long time in the wars to pacify the Chichimeca and other wild peoples,[7] learning a great deal in the process about Nueva

España. He was a participant in the expedition that was led by Governor Francisco de Ibarra to the Province of Sinaloa, which was discussed in the previous book. During this expedition he showed such bravery that the governor granted him an encomienda[8] of pueblos. Later, when he was needed for the pacification and restraint of the Chichimec nations, he proceeded to that enterprise under orders from the king. He subdued and restrained the Chichimeca with such bravery that when His Majesty Philip II, of glorious memory, received news of how well he had been served, he rewarded him with the Habit of Santiago.[9] He was also granted ample lands and ranches, which he stocked with cattle and horses that reproduced [36] so abundantly that each year they branded 24,000 yearling calves.[10] I do not want to go on at length, but I will note that he did not keep them solely for his own use; the poor and needy received a large portion of this abundance. At his ranch on the plains, between the cities of Zacatecas and Durango, his home was a refuge, shelter, and source of sustenance for travelers, passengers, and individuals traveling through the interior. I passed through there on the way to Sinaloa in 1604 with a captain and a squad of gentile Indians from Sinaloa, having gone to Mexico City to petition the viceroy for more missions and priests.[11] I saw with my own eyes this knight's generosity and magnanimity. With the practice of Christianity in which he occupied himself, he seemed to me to be the very image of the patriarch Abraham, whom God had placed in the lands [of Canaan] for the refuge and aid of travelers.[12] When this knight took over the government of the province, he was mindful not only of service to the king, but also to God (the two of which can be combined with admirable harmony). He found himself in charge of some gentile nations in the Province of Guadiana, or Durango (which is one and the same), in the high sierras of Topia and San Andrés, and throughout the wide Province of Sinaloa, with which

3. Psalm 2:8: "Ask thy will of me, and thou shalt have the nations for thy patrimony" (Knox 1956:479).

4. Daniel 2:22: "does not light dwell with him?" (Knox 1956:790).

5. Daniel 2:20: "Blessed be the Lord's name from the beginning to the end of time" (Knox 1956:790).

6. Rodrigo del Río y Losa, governor from 1589 to 1595.

7. Chichimeca is the Nahuatl term for various semi-sedentary groups (mostly Otomí speakers) to the northwest of the valley of Mexico who were considered barbarians by the Mexica. Spaniards adopted the same attitude, particularly after 1550, when Chichimec raids threatened silver mining and the movement of silver southward from Zacatecas to Mexico City (Powell 1952).

8. A grant of land and Indian labor for which the recipient, or *encomendero*, agreed to protect his charges as well as support their conversion to Christianity (Gibson 1964:48–67).

9. The Order of Santiago was a military and religious order that combined the ideals of monasticism and chivalry. It was founded by Pedro Fernández and approved by Pope Alexander III in 1175 to defend Christendom against the infidels. By the fifteenth century members of the order no longer held to ascetic practices (e.g., chastity, simple clothing), and the power of appointment shifted from the pope to the Spanish monarch (O'Callaghan 1975:239, 632–33; Rades y Andrada 1572).

10. In 1586, 42,000 head of cattle were branded on the newly appointed governor's hacienda (Bancroft 1886:112, f.31).

11. This trip is discussed further in Book 2, Chapter 28.

12. See Genesis 11:31–25:11 for the life of Abraham.

he was already familiar. To discharge these obligations, he wrote to the Father Provincial of the Company, who at that time was Father Antonio de Mendoza, begging him to send some religious to cultivate the new fields that God offered His Church in the Kingdom of Nueva Vizcaya.[13] The Father Provincial granted his request very willingly as a work of great glory for God and the salvation of so many souls. For this enterprise he chose two individuals who were outstanding in religion, learning, and prudence, and both labored gloriously in this work. One of them, as I will later relate, gave his life, spilling his blood in pursuit of Gospel preaching. The men whom God chose for this great enterprise to effect an extension of Christianity were Father Gonzalo de Tapia and Father Martín Pérez. The Father Provincial dispatched them with orders to report to Governor Rodrigo del Río y Losa and to offer themselves on behalf of souls for whatever task the governor might choose, no matter how difficult it might be.

The first two missionary fathers of Sinaloa, founders of its Christianity, departed in the year 1590. At the city of Durango, located at a distance of 150 leagues from Mexico City, the governor received them with great pleasure. He saw that his wishes to realize the salvation of the many helpless souls that God had placed under his jurisdiction were already being fulfilled. The priests presented him with the orders that they had brought from their superior, and the governor (undoubtedly moved by God) responded that although his intention had been for them to instruct the Indians around Durango, he had changed his mind. He felt that they would reap a greater harvest in the Province of Sinaloa, of which he had received a good deal of news.[14] He knew it to be inhabited by many gentile nations, so the

priests could be of great service to Our Lord by converting them to His Holy Church. This assignment from the governor was consistent with the priests' great desire to convert souls, so they took their leave of His Lordship.

Even though the shortest and most direct route would have been through the mountains of Topia, [37] the Indians in those valleys were at war,[15] so the priests took a detour (albeit enduring great hardships) through the Province of Acaponeta, crossing the rugged and uninhabited mountaintops until they joyfully arrived in the Villa de Acaponeta, on the eve of the Feast of the Holy Spirit.[16] They occupied themselves preaching and hearing the confessions of Spaniards and Indians of the area, who had gathered in large numbers. Then they continued on to the Villa de San Miguel de Culiacán, one hundred leagues farther ahead. All along the way and in the pueblos through which they passed they continued their ministering. Everywhere a large audience of Spaniards and Indians turned out. The fruits of that journey were therefore plentiful, and it seemed that this is what God had hoped to accomplish by keeping them from going through the mountains of Topia, where the harvest would not ripen until later, as we will later see.

When the priests reached the Villa de San Miguel, they were received with even greater demonstrations of pleasure and kindness, so much so that they were obliged to remain in that noble villa for several days, ministering to the resident Spaniards and a large number of Indians from the area, all of whom they comforted. The [residents of the] villa were particularly joyful because the moment had arrived for the conversion of their neighbor, the Province of Sinaloa, something which they had always desired.

---

13. The letter apparently was written late in 1589, after Río y Losa observed or learned of the work done that year by Fathers Tapia and Arnaya in Zacatecas and Durango. In 1590 Mendoza was succeeded as provincial by Pedro Díaz, who was reluctant to send missions to the north. It was Diego de Avellaneda, the Jesuit father visitor, who pressured Díaz to favor Río y Losa's request (Shiels 1934:71–82).

14. Early in 1591 Antonio Ruiz traveled to Chametla to meet the new governor; Ruiz apparently convinced Río y Losa to send the Jesuits to Sinaloa (Bancroft 1886:115).

15. The route is discussed by Shiels (1934:93ff). The war was apparently an inter-"tribal" dispute involving the Acaxee in the valleys around Topia (Alegre 1956–60:1:364). The reason for the war is unknown, although it may well have stemmed from factional disputes over whether to cooperate with or resist Spanish encroachment on Acaxee land (see Reff 1991b:88–89).

16. Apparently May 30, 1591 (Shiels 1934:94). The Feast of Pentecost occurs on the seventh Sunday after Easter and commemorates the descent of the Holy Spirit on the apostles.

CHAPTER II The priests depart Culiacán for Sinaloa; how they were received along the way and their arrival at the Villa de San Felipe[17]

These two fervent evangelical laborers could hardly wait to find themselves employed in the fields to which they had been led by the Supreme Father of Families, Jesus Christ. Once they arrived at the Villa de San Miguel de Culiacán, they sent word to the five Spaniards who were still living in Sinaloa. God had preserved them in the midst of so many dangers so that Christianity could be greatly extended from that Villa de San Felipe, as was later seen in this province. They notified them that they had been sent by the Father Provincial of the Company of Jesus and the governor of Nueva Vizcaya to wholly dedicate themselves to the spiritual and temporal good of their far-flung province. Their wishes were to spare no labor or diligence in attaining this end. And even though they were not accompanied by soldiers, as in the past had been the case in that land, they trusted that the Lord would assist them in introducing the peace of the Holy Gospel. I warn he who reads this statement not to judge it as contrary to what will be noted later, because in time it did become necessary for the viceroys of Nueva España to place garrisons[18] in Sinaloa. The reasons why they were obliged to do so will be given later.

When news [of the Jesuits' impending arrival] was received by the residents of Sinaloa, there was great joy among those who had spent so many years in that desert. They saw that the time had come when they would have amongst them those who would be their refuge in temporal as well as spiritual matters, for they had lacked just such a refuge for many years. They then sent word to the small pueblos of their Indian friends and allies. They were also very happy with the news, especially those few Christians who, as mentioned before, had been baptized when the Villa de Carapoa was settled, as well as a few others who had taken Christian names but were Christian in name only.

It was immediately agreed that two of the Spaniards [38] would go to the Villa de San Miguel de Culiacán to accompany and guide the priests.[19] They were joined by some of their Indian friends, Christians as well as gentiles, who wanted to go and meet the priests. They set out immediately and met the priests along the road at a pueblo called Capirato, eight leagues from Culiacán. There they welcomed the priests, who were overjoyed to meet the two Spaniards who had emerged from the ends of the earth. They were even happier to see their first fruits, the Indians who were a sign of the great harvest that God had promised them in this region, so far removed from the world. When the Indians approached the priests, they kneeled to kiss their hands, and remaining in this position, they asked for Holy Baptism and religious instruction for their people. The priests embraced them and explained their intention of helping them in all that would be of benefit to their souls and the order and peace of the province. This was their only desire in coming from Mexico City, and they sought no other riches than the Indians' salvation.

The priests remained that night in Capirato and traveled the next day to the first river of Sinaloa, called the Sebastián de Evora. This name was taken from the first encomendero to have a pueblo on this river, called Mocorito.[20] Three leagues before reaching the river, they had to stop to sleep at a watering hole, where they were detained for the reason I will explain here.

Among the Indians who went with the two Spaniards to welcome the priests was the son of a Christian cacique of the pueblo of Mocorito. Joyful at the priests' arrival, the son went ahead to inform his father. The cacique responded by gathering all his people, and even though they were gentiles, he ordered them to gather all the unbaptized children. The people cooper-

---

17. Pérez de Ribas' primary sources for this chapter are the anua of 1593 (AGN 1593) and the *relación* of Antonio Ruiz (Nakayama 1974).

18. We have translated *presidio* as garrison. A presidio was a small garrison of soldiers who were sometimes accompanied by their families; they joined with friendly Indians to protect frontier settlements (e.g., missions, mines) from hostile Indians (see Naylor and Polzer 1986:15–19).

19. The two Spaniards who escorted Tapia and Pérez were Juan del Castillo and Antonio Ruiz; the latter was the *alcalde mayor* and, in effect, the political leader of San Felipe.

20. Sebastián de Evora was a Portuguese conquistador who was awarded an encomienda in the 1530s. This encomienda was subsequently acquired by Pedro de Tovar, a prominent citizen of San Miguel de Culiacán (Gerhard 1982:274). In keeping with modern usage, the Río Mocorito is used henceforth in this text rather than the Sebastián de Evora.

ated, and he set out with the children and his people to where the priests had stopped to sleep. He arrived around midnight, and it was, indeed, a good night for the priests, because the cacique brought a few things to eat and presented the children for Baptism. Although they did not understand it as such, this was a request for Christ to be reborn in their souls. As I said, this was a good night for the priests, whose hearts broke out in songs of joy (and it must have been the same among the angels) to see so soon those first fruits that this uncultured land was yielding, which they offered to God.

At this place the Indians built a ramada, or arbor, as poor as the one in Bethlehem, with an altar. There Mass was said and those lambs were baptized and cleansed. Afterwards, they departed for the Río Sinaloa and the Villa de San Felipe (which was twelve leagues away). When the few Spaniards and the Indians from friendly pueblos who had gathered heard that the priests were drawing near, they celebrated their arrival by spreading large amounts of sedge and grass along the road and arranging and decorating it with many tree branches,

which served as tapestries and canopies. They did the same in the plaza of the pueblo, which was really a field. One cannot express the delight and happiness with which everyone embraced and congratulated one another—the priests for having arrived at the ends of the earth to help such defenseless souls,[21] and the others for the arrival of those who would be their priests and the means to their salvation, for (as we said) they had never had a priest of their own. Once the people were assembled, the priests made known the purpose of their long journey. They considered it worthwhile that God had brought them to this destitute land on which He now wished to bestow His mercies. With this [39] they withdrew to a small house made of poles covered with straw that had been prepared for them. This was the best house in the pueblo and they entered it happier than if they were in a royal palace. Here they were most certainly able to sing that psalm, *Hec requies mea in saeculum saeculi*,[22] because both of them (as we will later see) concluded their blessed lives in this place and mission.

CHAPTER III The priests make arrangements to begin religious instruction and Baptisms in the Villa de San Felipe and neighboring pueblos; a gentile abuse is described that was eradicated

The priests reached the Río Sinaloa and the Villa de San Felipe y Santiago, which, as we mentioned, was inhabited by those five lone Spaniards and a few Indians who had joined them. Then, without resting from their long journey, they undertook the work in the vineyard that Our Lord had entrusted to them, notwithstanding that it was uncultivated and full of underbrush and thistles. Trusting in divine favor, they initiated this enterprise by outfitting the villa's little straw church with the modest ornaments that they had brought with them so that they could say Mass. They remained here for some fifteen days, preaching in Castilian and Mexican [Nahuatl] to those few who understood it.

Both Spaniards and Indians came to confession and received the Most Holy Sacrament, which they finally had in their land. This got their task off to a good start and was an inspiration to all to attend to its completion. The priests then gathered information about the many pueblos and nations that were settled along the river, all the way down to the Sea of California. They divided their ministerial duties between them in such a way that they could attend to the people in the Villa de San

21. According to a letter written by Tapia to Father Claudius Acquaviva, prepositus general of the Company, Tapia and Pérez arrived in Sinaloa on July 6, 1591 (Alegre 1956–1960:1:571).

22. Psalm 22:6: "through the long years the Lord's house shall be my dwelling-place" (Knox 1956:487).

Felipe as well as the nearest pueblos, which were better disposed to receiving Gospel teachings. Father Martín Pérez took charge of the pueblos of Cubiri (one league downriver from the villa) and Bamoa, which, as noted, was settled by the Indians who had left the mountains with Cabeza de Vaca. He also took charge of some other smaller pueblos. Father Gonzalo de Tapia was in charge of the pueblos upriver called Baboria, Tovoropa, Lopochi, Matapan, and the pueblo of Ocoroni, which is on the bank of another small river five leagues farther on. They ordered churches constructed in these pueblos, and at that time these were quite modest, consisting of ramadas. Their houses and shelter consisted of straw huts, and their table and bed were made of woven rockrose branches.[23] At the beginning of such missions, there is neither skilled labor nor anyone with the knowledge of how to erect other types of buildings.

Their normal diet was maize, beans, and squash, which they boiled in water or roasted in embers. Once in a great while they had some small fish from the river or game from the monte and maybe *chapulines*, which are locusts. I can testify to this because some time afterwards while I was in the company of one of these priests, they offered me a blackened dish of these roasted locusts as a great delicacy and their finest supper. Because of either the novelty of the food or the poor seasoning, my nature rejected it until I saw my companion (who, out of necessity, had grown accustomed to it) eating it with such pleasure that it awakened my own senses and I was reminded that it had also been the food of that great penitent of the desert, Saint John the Baptist.[24] Such were the extremes in which these apostolic men began their preaching. They took pleasure in their poverty, as they remembered Our Lord, who, being rich, *pro nobis egenus factus est*,[25] as the Apostle [Saint Paul] said.

In the end the priests were happy in their work of [40] establishing some civil life in those pueblos, principally through the Christian religion, beginning with the Baptism of the children.[26] This is their first concern, to safeguard the welfare of those youngsters, who are at risk regardless of the ailment. Furthermore, their salvation is secured with baptismal grace when they depart for heaven.

Later, the priests sought to obtain basic information about the languages that were necessary [for them to learn] at the time. They endeavored to compose the catechism in these languages, and although it was difficult and demanding work because the languages were so unusual, the priests were assisted by the Spaniards who had lived among the Indians, who acted as interpreters. They [then] started to teach the catechism to the adults so that they would be prepared to receive Holy Baptism, which they had begun to request insistently, with the necessary respect for that sacrament.

The first adults to be baptized were women and men who were married to or, better said, cohabited with Christians. They were married with the blessings and ceremonies of the Holy Church, which they admired as well as revered. Later, other adults were baptized in groups of twenty and thirty at a time, depending on their disposition and preparation. The Spaniards went to the Indian pueblos to act as godparents.[27] The Indians valued this highly, making much of the spiritual relationship that they contracted with the Spaniards (and perhaps because this relationship signified an improvement with respect to another that they had practiced as gentiles). This gentile custom, which the priests learned about at this time, is worth describing here because it is peculiar to some of these nations.[28]

These Indians used to hold a celebration for adopted children,[29] during which all the orphans in their nation were placed in the homes of kinfolk, who received them as their own children in a solemn celebration. They held just such a celebration the year the priests arrived, in the following manner. First, the Indians searched out and gathered together the orphans who were to be adopted.

---

23. The Spanish says *zarzos de jara*, with the former referring to woven constructions and the latter to members of the species *Cistus*, commonly known as rockrose.

24. See Mark 1:6.

25. II Corinthians 8:9: "he impoverished himself for your sakes" (Knox 1950:186). Note that the Latin cited by Pérez de Ribas actually says "for *our* sake."

26. It was Jesuit practice to baptize infants and children immediately (with the permission of their parents). Adults were baptized only after they had been instructed in the mysteries of the faith, or if they were in danger of dying and had accepted the most basic teaching of Christianity, namely the incarnation.

27. *Padrinos del pila*. Individuals, in this case adult males, who act as sponsors during the baptismal rite. Sponsors assume responsibility along with the child's natural parents for the training and rearing of the child as a Christian.

28. The "gentile custom" that Pérez de Ribas is about to describe is taken from a letter by Martín Pérez that is quoted in the anua of 1593 (AGN 1593; Zubillaga 1973:98). Interestingly, page 1 of the anua, in the Archivo Historico de la Provincia de Mexico, reportedly contains a margin note with Pérez de Ribas' signature, indicating that he consulted the document. The note reads: "I have taken what there is to take [pertaining] to the mission of Cinaloa . . ." (Zubillaga 1973:49).

29. This "adoption ceremony" for "orphans" was apparently a rite of passage involving young boys who, depending on their kinship affiliation, became members of a religious, warrior, or some other society or sodality, as is found among the Pueblo (Tewa).

Then they erected two houses made of petates, or mats, houses similar to those in which they resided. The two houses matched each other and were separated by a distance of a hundred paces. In one house they placed the orphaned children, who remained there for eight days, during which time they were fed *atole*, which is the same as maize gruel.[30] In the other house (which was larger) they sprinkled loose sand in the middle of the floor, creating a circle two and one-half varas in diameter. The Indians moved in and out of this circle, singing and dancing, adorned or painted, with rods in their hands. At times they sat on the sand and painted different figures with loose sand of varying colors, which they placed within lines they traced with a thin reed.[31] They painted mainly two figures that appeared to be human; one they called Variseva. The other was called Vairubi, who was said to be the mother of the first figure. They spoke with much confusion about what these figures represented, like the blind who lack divine light. It even seemed that they spoke of them with a glimpse of God and His Mother, for they referred to them as the first beings from whom the rest of mankind was born. Nevertheless, everything they said was confusing.

Around these two figures they painted maize stalks, beans, or squash, and among these plants they painted snakes, tiny birds, and other creatures. They continued painting until the circle, where they conducted their ceremonies with some degree of reverence, was filled with painted sand. This celebration lasted eight days, during which time they entered and left the house each morning and night, [41] solemnizing it through the diversion of their dances. One thing in particular must be noted: during all this period they did not allow women to enter that house.[32]

News of this celebration reached the priests, who attempted to learn more about it in order to banish these people's errors and ignorance. One of their leaders took the priests to the place where the celebration was held, and taking a reed in his hand, he pointed to the figures that his ancestors revered, those whom they asked to safeguard their planted fields from the snakes, toads,

and animals that were painted there. The devil kept these poor unfortunates distracted in this blindness until the priests disabused them of these and similar superstitions, making them understand that such superstitions did little or no good.

To conclude the celebration of the adopted children, as soon as they finished the dances, which were held for eight days, they danced to the house where the adopted youngsters were housed. There they conducted certain ceremonies with the youngsters, such as the one that opened their eyes, making them vigilant to arrows shot at them. Some Indians possess such sight and skill in deflecting enemy arrows that before the arrow can hit or wound them, they turn it from its path with their own bow so that it does not reach its mark. They also gave weapons to the adopted children, and then each one chose his youngster to take home and raise as his own son,[33] having first gone to the house where the paintings were, which they erased by rubbing his body with sand.[34] Afterwards they fed the children abundantly, and when the meal was over everyone went to bathe in the river. With this they concluded the gentile celebration, which (thanks to God's mercy) they no longer remember at all.

This custom has been described here as it pertains to the esteem in which godparents were held during the Baptisms that were conducted by the priests shortly after they began their labors in the pueblos that they divided amongst themselves. Mention must also be made of the results of the religious instruction that was imparted to the Indians who participated in the aforementioned celebration. Subsequently, during the Feast of the Nativity [Christmas 1592], which was being celebrated with much solemnity and joy in another pueblo, the priests noticed that the Indians had another ramada similar to those used in the ceremony for the adopted children. Within it they found another circle with sand paintings of a river, lions, tigers, serpents, and other poisonous creatures. Now instead of the two figures of Variseva and Vairubi, however, the Indians had painted something different. One figure was of a man, another of a woman, and another of a child. When the priests

---

30. Atole is a thin porridge made of ground corn that was boiled in water; condiments were sometimes added to it, such as the fruit of the nopal (genus *Opuntia*) (Nentvig 1980:37).

31. This "sand painting," apparently depicting the Cáhita origin myth, appears similar to those produced by the Navajo (Gill 1983:503).

32. Among the Cáhita and other patrilineal societies, where men frequently enjoyed differential access to and control of goods and services, women were often excluded as performers or played only minor roles in public rituals. This is still the case today among groups such as the Yaqui (Spicer 1980).

33. Judging from the experience of other southwestern groups (see Ortiz 1969; Titiev 1944:11–12), it is likely that the children spent only a brief time with their ceremonial sponsors and then returned home to their biological parents. With this rite of passage, however, the boys presumably began a long association with their ceremonial sponsors, which meant, in effect, less time with their biological parents.

34. The Spanish is ambiguous in that it does not specify whose body was rubbed with sand, although presumably it was the child's.

asked what it all meant, the Indians responded that one figure was God and the other His Mother; the figure of the child was Jesus Christ, Their Son, all of whom they asked to safeguard them from those wild animals and the rivers that flooded their planted fields. The Indians added, "We are teaching this to our children so that they will do likewise from now on."

The priests praised the Indians' worthy efforts to recognize God and His Most Holy Son as the authors of all our well-being, as well as the Virgin, who intercedes to achieve it. They told them that they should seek recourse in them during times of need and tribulation. However, because it seemed that this ceremony touched too closely upon their former celebrations, the priests wished to remove it from their memory. Therefore, they ordered that one day during Christmastide (having abandoned those figures) the Indians should enter the church dancing and asking God and the Virgin (whose image was there with her Son in her arms) for the same things they had formerly sought through their worthless superstitions. They were thus instructed and content. [42]

CHAPTER IV The Spaniards at Topia petition the priests to visit their mining camp[35] and the neighboring gentile Indians; what happened to the priest who went, as well as other events in Sinaloa

Our glorious father Saint Ignatius, founder of the Company of Jesus, who was inspired and ruled by the Holy Spirit, founded his order to be like a squadron and company of soldiers. They were to be like fast horses (as the saint himself used to say and as is written in his autobiography), always ready for the call to attack whenever there arose the need to help souls. This was the practice of Father Gonzalo de Tapia, who had gone to the Sinaloa mission as superior. Even though what is written in this chapter appears to pertain more to the Topia mission, it will be discussed here because it deals with Father Gonzalo de Tapia himself and the holy deeds of his mission that were carried out from Sinaloa.

It happened that four months after the priests had arrived in Sinaloa, the Spaniards who had been exploring and working the mines at the Topia mining camp (fifty leagues to the east) got news of the good deeds that the priests were performing in Sinaloa and how they were spreading peace and baptizing its nations. Wishing to see the same for the Indians of their own area (who were still gentiles), the Spaniards wrote to the priests, urging one of them to be so good as to come to their mining camp and visit the Indians in those valleys, who were in great need of instruction. Heeding their pleas and with a burning desire for the salvation of every person (even though he was so busy), Father Gonzalo de Tapia left the fields in Sinaloa for a short time to visit the fields that God offered him in Topia. The Spaniards went to meet him on the road, very glad to see that the door was opening to the spiritual remedy and salvation of those souls.

Now to those who observe from afar (and more so those in foreign nations) Spaniards may appear to have no other goal in their exploration of lands in the New World than their own interests and lust for silver and

35. The *real* (*de minas*), in this case that of Topia, was an officially sanctioned permanent mining community or town generally involved in vein mining (as opposed to placer or surface deposit mining). This community was sustained by outlying farms and ranches and generally served as a provincial administrative center. In the 1580s, the real de minas of Santa Cruz de Topia was a burgeoning mining center and a resting place for muleteers hauling wheat, chile, cloth, mercury, and other products over the sierras from Durango to San Miguel de Culiacán (Reff 1991b:122; West 1949; West and Parsons 1941).

the extension of the frontiers of their monarchy. The truth, however, is that they never lack the zeal of faithful Catholic Christians. Their desire is for all peoples, whom both they and their Catholic king value, to join the flock of the Roman Catholic Church. Therefore, when the zealous Spanish miners of Topia learned that an evangelical minister was walking to their mining camp, they traveled quite a few leagues to meet Gonzalo de Tapia. He arrived and spent several days there preaching to and hearing the confessions of the residents.[36] He reaped a great harvest from his ministries, particularly among a good number of Tarascan Indians whom he found working in the mines. They had a special love for the priest because he had preached to them before in their own lands and spoke their language with distinction.[37] After consoling them and administering the Holy Sacraments, he went down to tour the Valle de Topia. This is where the main Indian settlements were located, although they were not as populous as those of Sinaloa. He found some Indians who had been baptized due to the proximity of Spaniards, but they were so ignorant of matters of the Faith that they were not very different from gentiles. He reformed them as best he could, baptized some sick adults and children, and gave those people as much information about the Faith as time allowed. He was being called back to the greater harvest that God had offered him in his mission in Sinaloa, so he reserved [43] their fuller instruction for another time, which the Company provided, as will be told later.

Before he departed, they reported to him that on a nearby mountain underneath an immense tree the Indians used to have an idol to whom they offered maize at planting time and weapons in time of war. The Spaniards had already knocked it down and smashed it. The priest gathered together all the people he could and had a handsome Cross fitted out. Then they went to the site of the tree singing the Christian doctrine.[38] There he had the tree destroyed, and in its place he planted the very beautiful Cross.[39] He blessed that place and

in so doing erased the memory of that tree and those other superstitions.

After consoling those people with the hope of receiving priests who would come specifically to teach them the law of [the] one [true] God, Creator of heaven and earth, he started back to Sinaloa, leaving matters as they were. He passed by the supportive sister Villa de San Miguel de Culiacán, where he made the case for some singers to accompany him [to San Felipe], bringing their musical instruments to celebrate the joyous Christmas season, which was drawing near. The people of Culiacán heeded this request with goodwill, so the priest set out quite content with his company of singers. He reached Sinaloa around Christmastide, where his return was very eagerly awaited.

The work that his companion, Father Martín Pérez, had undertaken at this time in Sinaloa, where he had remained, must not be omitted. In addition to visiting all the pueblos where instruction had already been initiated, he decided also to visit the rest of the nations that inhabited the [lower] Río [Sinaloa] as far as the sea. There were many Indians living along the river for a distance of seventeen leagues, including the Bamoa, the Guasave, the Sisinicari, the Ure, and other lesser rancherías. He busied himself winning over and encouraging these Indians to imitate their neighbors in accepting peace and the doctrine of the Holy Gospel, for the example of their neighbors' conduct carries weight among these people, as does the Gospel. They became very well disposed after this visit and brought some children [to Bamoa], who were baptized along with some other sick adults.

With these visits Father Pérez was reaping a harvest, pulling out the weeds, and planting new seedlings in the fields of the Church. God came to his aid and sent His saving water down from heaven, as will be seen in a portion of a letter written by one of the priests who ministered in this garden. The letter reads as follows:[40]

36. Tapia reached Topia during Holy Week of 1592. Note that he left for the mountains after experiencing a bout of fevers, apparently a resurgence of malaria. Father Pérez convinced Tapia to visit the mining camp in order to experience a change of climate, which was thought to be beneficial (Shiels 1934:126–27).

37. Pérez de Ribas explains this in greater detail in Chapter 37 of Book 2.

38. The Jesuits used a version of the catechism developed by the Council of Trent and prepared by Father Gerónimo Ripalda (*Doctrina Cristiana*), which they then translated into Indian languages; the various prayers or teachings of the catechism often were sung (Aizpuru 1989:52; Buelna 1891).

39. Certain trees figured prominently in Acaxee religious beliefs

and ceremonies (Beals 1933:27–29). Hernando de Santarén, who had worked for five years among the Acaxee, noted in a letter in the anua of 1604 that in order to insure victory in war the Acaxee placed offerings of arrows or enemy bones at the foot of a zapote tree, which grew in the plaza of their ceremonial houses (Alegre 1956–1960:2:80).

40. This letter was written by Pedro de Velasco, one of two new missionaries who joined Tapia and Pérez at San Felipe in March 1592. The letter is found in the anua of 1593 (AGN 1593; Zubillaga 1973:102). Significantly, in copying Velasco's letter, Pérez de Ribas left out an important line (in italics below) that makes it clear that an epidemic was in progress. The anua reads: *Son tantos y tan maravillosos los effectos que, cada día, se ven de la divina predestinación, en esta peste, que se tiempla, con esso, el dolor de ver morir tantos. Y se hace suavissimo el trabajo que se passa en andarlos a buscar por los montes, especos arenales y sementeras, donde se desparraman en*

The results seen daily from the divine predestination of some of these souls are so numerous and marvelous that the labor of going out to find them in the thick montes, sand dunes, and cultivated fields where they are scattered is made easy. I went to pueblos of gentiles whose language I did not know, and when I arrived they eagerly offered me more than 250 children for Baptism, which I administered. Then, in order to help the adults *in extrema vel gravi necessitate*,[41] I composed a brief catechism in their language with the help of an interpreter who knew it. They listened very attentively to the few words that I spoke to them about Our Lord and the rest of what I read from the paper. Then because of their insistence I began to baptize some sick people. They became very distressed when I delayed baptizing some of them because their sickness did not seem life threatening and I wanted to baptize them later after more thorough instruction. They and their relatives begged me to baptize them because they, too, were sick and had come to be baptized. Therefore, I administered that Holy Sacrament to a good number of those who appeared to be in danger. Nearly all of them died and God took them to Him.

This was this priest's report, and [44] I add that in spiritual terms (more so than in terms of bodily health) the promise of Christ, the ultimate martyr, was being fulfilled: *Super aegros manus imponent, et bene habebut.*[42] Even though their corporal life was ending, when those hands sprinkled that heavenly water on their heads they suddenly found themselves improved, enjoying the divine life of heaven.

CHAPTER V   The priests celebrate the first Christmas;[43] two other priests arrive from Mexico City, which Father Gonzalo de Tapia decides to visit

Father Gonzalo de Tapia returned to Sinaloa from Topia around Christmas, bringing with him singers and musical instruments. He wished to celebrate with all possible solemnity the first Christian festivity in that poor and faraway land, in order that those people new to the Faith would have a better idea of the Christian mysteries. Because the church of the pueblo of Lopochi (which was not even a full league from the Villa de San Felipe) was larger, he ordered that the celebration take place there.

Spaniards as well as Indians were convened for the festivity, and the number of baptized Indians who were present was more than one thousand; many gentiles also attended. Mass was celebrated with music, which amazed and awed the Indians, as it was something very new to them. The priests ordered a procession that day outside the church, in which some dances took place to celebrate the gathering. The result was that everyone was very happy, and the gentiles were more eager to receive Holy Baptism. They esteemed that which they saw celebrated with such solemnity, and this was something of great importance during the early stages of this new Christianity. I will not pause here to discuss two expeditions that were carried out around this time by some Spaniards from Culiacán and others who joined them. They went in search of mineral deposits near a pueblo called Cahuemeto and in the Chínipa mountain range.[44] The goal of these expeditions was not realized because of the trouble caused by neighboring Indians, who forced the Spaniards to abandon their plans to work those mineral deposits.

What is more relevant to our history is that at this

---

semejantes tiempos. Pérez de Ribas' version replaces this missing line with *de algunas de estas almas que*, also replacing the conjunction *y* with *que.*

41. "In extreme or grave need"

42. Mark 16:18: "they will lay their hands upon the sick and make them recover" (Knox 1956:52).

43. This actually was the priests' second Christmas in Sinaloa (1592); it was the first "real" Christmas in the sense that it was celebrated by the Indians with music, pageantry, and other formal and informal activities characteristic of Christmas celebrations in Spain.

44. The earliest of these expeditions was in 1589 (Bannon 1939).

time, in the year 1593,[45] two more priests reached Sina-loa to help with the great enterprise that had been ini-tiated by the Company of Jesus. Once Father Gonzalo de Tapia became aware of the great door that was being opened to the Gospel, he informed the Father Provincial of the great opportunity that Our Lord was offering. The spiritual fishing of souls was so abundant and so many were entering the net of the Gospel that it was necessary *Annuere focijs, ut ivenirent, & adiuvarent.*[46] According to Saint Luke, this is what Saint Peter did when, by Christ's order, he spread his nets, which filled with such an abundance of fish that he had to ask for companions to help gather them all.

After he was informed of the situation in Sinaloa, the Father Provincial sent two individuals to help, Father Alonso de Santiago and Father Juan Bautista de Velasco. Both were welcomed with great joy. The former was entrusted with some pueblos where he instructed the people for some time, but due to poor health he had to be moved from Sinaloa to Mexico City,[47] where he undertook tasks of great service to Our Lord. Father Juan Bautista, [45] who spoke the Mexican language very well, worked with great praise for many years in this province, up to the end of his life (as we will see further ahead). He was placed in charge of the pueblos of Mocorito, Bacaburito, Orobato, and their *visitas*,[48] where there were some Indians who were very *ladino*,[49] due to their proximity to and dealings with the resi-dents of Culiacán, who aided in their conversion. Father Gonzalo de Tapia, a man who showed spirit in great enterprises and was not worn down or intimidated by difficulties and labor for the glory of God, decided to re-turn to Mexico City to discuss the settlement of Sinaloa with the viceroy of Nueva España and our Father Pro-vincial. He also wanted to request many more workers for the great and ripe harvest that could be seen there. In addition, he asked for monetary assistance for the few

poor Spanish residents of the Villa de San Felipe, who had maintained the villa during very difficult times, and for anyone else who wished to settle there (something which had been desired for years and which had not yet been achieved). He also requested some alms for the sustenance of the religious ministers of the Gospel who were working there among such poor people and in such a barren land. Although His Catholic Majesty in his royal generosity had ordered his viceroys to aid all ministers of the Gospel in the Indies, those in Sina-loa had not enjoyed this assistance up to that time.[50]

Father Tapia left Mexico City with things in good order. He also obtained from the viceroy some orna-ments for those new and poor churches, as well bells and musical instruments for celebrating feast days with the appropriate decency. When he left for Mexico City Father Tapia had taken with him some native Sina-loa Indians so that the viceroy and the priests could see a sample of those peoples—unknown [in Mexico City]—who were receiving the Gospel. He also wanted the Indians from Sinaloa to see other newly [con-verted], populous, and rich Christians who adored as their God the crucified Lord preached to them by their priests. He did this so that when the Indians returned to Sinaloa they could relate what they had seen to their nations, which were isolated in Sinaloa. This is with-out a doubt a very useful strategy, and it also provides these new peoples with credible evidence [of what is being preached to them]. The viceroy received these poor Indians with love, treating them well so that they would receive the catechism with pleasure. He gave them gifts of clothing, with which they returned to their land very comforted. As soon as possible, Father Tapia hurried back to his beloved Sinaloa, to which he was drawn by his love and desire to rear the children he had engendered in Christ and to acquire new ones as well. These were the saintly intentions of this most religious priest, but as will be seen two chapters ahead, Our Lord was leading him to spill his blood for his love, for the salvation of his fellow men, and to con-summate the course of his works and triumphs.

45. The anua of 1593, which was written in March of that year, states that the two priests had arrived in Sinaloa the previous year (AGN 1593).

46. Luke 5:7: "and they must needs beckon to their partners . . . to come and help them" (Knox 1956:59).

47. Santiago left for Mexico City in August 1594, shortly after two new priests reached San Felipe. He apparently became an educator and was one of forty professed Jesuits who participated in the sixth provin-cial congregation in 1603 (Zambrano 1961–1977:5:63).

48. Missionaries were generally assigned to districts (*partidos*), which included a pueblo where the priest resided (a *cabecera*) and other nearby pueblos or rancherías that he visited on a regular basis. The latter con-stituted visitas.

49. Indians who were "ladino" were familiar with Spanish language and culture and, indeed, often emulated Spaniards in various ways (e.g., clothing, language, values).

50. As discussed in the "Critical Introduction," under the terms of the *Patronato Real*, the Spanish crown subsidized religious in the New World; it is not known why Jesuits in Sinaloa were not receiving their stipend.

CHAPTER VI Two noteworthy cases in the Province of Sinaloa following Father Gonzalo de Tapia's return from Mexico City

Father Gonzalo de Tapia left Mexico [City] and returned to the Province of Sinaloa, where he was sorely missed because the people had come to love him very much. The most important Christian Indians joyfully met him thirty leagues from San Felipe. It was with a special happiness that he received the beloved children that he had begotten in the catechism of truth. He acknowledged their role in the welfare [46] of their province and the establishment of the missions, which made everyone happy. For their part, the Indians who had accompanied Father Tapia returned well treated, with gifts and a great deal to relate about what they had seen in Mexico City.[51]

The establishment of Christianity was given greater impetus after Father Tapia's arrival, aided by two things of note by way of which God appeared to be warning and pressuring the people to receive the catechism of the Gospel and to take advantage of the means for salvation that was so close at hand. The first was a cruel epidemic, which although only of smallpox and measles,[52] was nevertheless so contagious and pestilent that it carried heaps of Indians to their death. It was pitiful to see houses full of suffering people left with no one to offer them relief or food and to see bodies covered with sores that gave off a noxious stench. The epidemic quickly became horrific as flies landed on the open sores of the ill, where they laid their eggs, which turned into worms (as happens in warm climates), boiling within and spewing forth from peoples' mouths and noses. They said that it was the most pitiful and distressing thing that they had ever seen.

This was a good opportunity for the priests to show their untiring charity toward so many sick bodies and souls in the pueblos, which had become great hospitals of suffering people. As Christ commanded, the evangelical ministers sacrificed themselves to aid the poor. They gave assistance to everyone at all times, sparing no labor or possible diligence during this time of great need and affliction. They attended to some with the sacraments in order to insure their salvation, while others were sustained with food. The priests were in continual movement; day and night, in pueblos, rancherías, fields, and gardens—wherever people had fallen ill—they heard confessions, baptized, and anointed, and also helped the few survivors to bury the dead. They said that this latter task became so tiresome that some were left where they had perished in the monte. Still it was marvelous how the priests, who were so few in number, were able to minister and attend to so many people in need. It was also a special favor that with divine assistance all, or nearly all, who died received the Holy Sacraments and were thus well prepared for death. One can therefore conclude that God had ordained this illness, which provided so many souls with eternal bliss and salvation.

The sickness spread not only to the pueblos neighboring the Villa de San Felipe, where missions had been established, but also to distant gentile pueblos among groups such as the Guasave nation (ten or twelve leagues from the Villa de San Felipe). The encomendero[53] (which they already had) understood the urgent needs of his pueblos and wrote to Father Juan Bautista de Velasco, asking that he extend his charity to the Guasave. The priest set out [from the Río Mocorito for the lower Río Sinaloa], where the people were in a miserable state. There he exercised the same charity, baptizing large numbers of infants, who subsequently died. He also instructed and baptized sick adults, who died leaving behind fond hopes that they were going to heaven. Altogether there were more than three hundred souls [who were baptized and/or perished].

The second event (with which it appears that God

---

51. Pérez de Ribas neglects to mention that all but one of the children who accompanied Tapia to Mexico City died during the return trip, in Valladolid, where they contracted smallpox (Reff 1991b:133).

52. This epidemic began in January 1593, and killed thousands of Indians in the area around the Villa de San Felipe (Reff 1991b:133ff.). Smallpox and measles had become diseases of childhood for Europeans and were no longer the great killers they once had been. Thus Pérez de Ribas' use of "although only."

53. The encomendero is unknown; apparently he was one of the five Spaniards resident in San Felipe when the Jesuits arrived in 1591 (see Gerhard 1982:275; Nakayama 1974:30, 58).

wanted to prepare and pressure these people to receive the law of the Holy Gospel) was an extremely frightening and unusual earthquake. Although the Indians did not have buildings of plastered adobe, but rather only humble buildings made of poles, this earthquake did {47} cause a hill of bare rock next to the principal Zuaque pueblo, called Mochicahue, to violently shake, crack, and then open, spewing forth torrents of water from its mouth. The blind and ignorant Zuaque cast into this water large quantities of mantas, blue-green stones,[54] beads, and other things that they valued, thinking that this would placate whomever was the cause of these tremendous horrors. They did not yet recognize their author, the Lord, who causes all creatures to tremble. In the end, however, this event caused the arrogant heart of the Zuaque to tremble in such a way that they were forced to turn their eyes to heaven and to recognize that there was a Lord there who could destroy and finish them off and that His power was greater than that which they bragged came from their bows and arrows.

A group of their principales went to see Father Gonzalo de Tapia because they had heard that he preached about this God, or (as others said) because they were convinced that Father Tapia had caused these events because he was unhappy that they made no efforts to become baptized or to receive God's word in their lands. To appease him, they offered him some fruits of the earth such as beans, *coali*,[55] young ears of maize, and others that they valued. The priest disabused them, preaching to them about God's power and great works, and he exhorted them to receive His word and Holy Baptism. They agreed to this, but the promise was forgotten once that warning and threat had subsided. So it is with some men, born in the midst of Christianity and raised in the light of the Holy Gospel, who promise mountains of gold and make great promises when they find themselves at death's door, yet once the moment [of danger] has passed, all is forgotten. The truth is that years later the Zuaque did take advantage of this warning, as I will later relate.

The Sinaloa nation proper (which is a companion and very good friend of the Zuaque nation) also felt the shock of the earthquake. This inspired them to visit Father Gonzalo de Tapia and offer a gift similar to that offered by their Zuaque friends. They asked more directly and with greater insistence than the Zuaque that

he visit their lands and pueblos to baptize them, even if he were to baptize only the children. They understood that the Baptism [of children] was an easier matter and that with it the adults could begin receiving the catechism [that was required for their own Baptism]. They had already heard a little about Baptism, dating back to the time of the Spaniards' Villa de Carapoa. Due to their insistence, Father Tapia decided to take advantage of the occasion to visit their pueblos, which were twenty leagues from the Villa de San Felipe. After walking ten leagues, he came to a large Cross erected along the road. He was greatly consoled to see that trophy and emblem of our redemption, which foretold success. Upon inquiring about who had erected the Cross, he learned that there was a nearby rancho of Indians, who had heard of our Holy Faith and the Christian mysteries, so he sent for them. Some gentiles arrived, and they told him that they had erected that Cross because there were a few Christian Indians from Culiacán living among them. These Indians had either fled from Spaniards, who at times mistreat them, or had come in search of arable land to farm and settle, and they had taught something of the Christian catechism to those gentiles. The latter had heard that the priest would be passing their way, so they built a ramada where he could rest. Later, the Christian Indians from Culiacán arrived and asked him to spend the night and say Mass, for which they would prepare another ramada. The priest granted their {48} pious request and said Mass, which they had not heard in years. He also consented to baptize some children and promised that he would return soon to give them their own priest who would care for them. This was eventually carried out and this rancho became the site of a pueblo called Cacalotlán, where these Indians received religious instruction.

The priest continued on with his Sinaloan escort, reaching their lands and finding a large number of people distributed among twenty-four aldeas or rancherías.[56] The people were pleased that he had come to their lands, and they received him with great demonstrations of joy and kindness. They brought him some children, whom the priest baptized, and then he preached to them, telling them to depart the blindness in which they were living and to prepare themselves for receiving the catechism on which their salvation depended. After learning something of the land and the

---

54. *Aguas marinas.*

55. This may be tepary beans (*será wi*) (Beals 1943:10).

56. In 1533 Diego de Guzmán reported that the Sinaloa were living in twenty or twenty-five pueblos, each with one hundred to three hundred houses (Hedrick and Riley 1976:41).

large number of people who inhabited it, he promised he would return and see to the matter [of a priest for their salvation]. He then left for the pueblo of Ocoroni, where he was headquartered.

A few days later Father Tapia went to fulfill the promise that he had made to the Sinaloa. Upon his return, however, he found that they were no longer as well disposed as he would have liked. To begin with, he found the people in the first pueblo quite enjoying themselves and drinking wine; they were very lukewarm to hearing the word of God. What he understood even better was that the principal cacique was planning to kill him. Heaven soon punished this man, because later, during another drunken revel to which he was invited, he was affected by the wine or the devil, who played the role of constable in divine justice. He was incited to jump off the top of a high cliff as a test (because he thought he was brave), whereupon he fell into the depths of hell and lay there dead. He thus paid for the sin of having attempted to kill the one who had come to give life to their souls. In the end the priest realized that because of drunkenness the pueblo was not ready to hear and receive God's word. Despite the fervor that burned in his breast for the salvation of those poor souls, he decided to go on to the other pueblos, where he was better received. They brought him some infants to baptize, and these, along with the others that he had previously baptized, brought the total to six hundred. With the passage of time and as a result of the adversities that will be discussed later, this number remained the same for ten or eleven years, except for those whom God took with baptismal grace. His divine goodness ordinarily selects its first fruits from these Baptisms.

After Father Gonzalo de Tapia returned to his pueblos, he fulfilled the promise he had made to the Indians who had erected the Cross along the road to the lands of the Sinaloa. Because he was the [local] superior, he ordered Father Martín Pérez to take charge of the rancho and its inhabitants, which [Father Pérez] did with great enthusiasm. He visited them, and after a while he moved them to a better location, where a very steadfast Christianity was founded.

These were the results of the warnings that heaven gave these people. Through great and pestilential sickness and a tremendous earthquake it seems the Indians were called to conversion. And still another event was to occur that on the one hand is pitiful, yet on the other is a real blessing for the priest who initiated and founded Christianity in Sinaloa. Through this incident, he earned the glorious palm of a martyr, watering those sterile fields with his blood.

CHAPTER VII   The Indians of the pueblo of Tovoropa murder Father Gonzalo de Tapia

The ministries of Gospel instruction advanced very propitiously, [49] making great progress during the four years following its inception in the Province of Sinaloa. There was a very abundant harvest of Indian conversions, Baptisms multiplied daily, and our Faith began taking root. Gentile customs declined, and Christian customs flourished in such a way that the new Christians traveled during the winter on foot for two or three leagues to hear Mass, arriving at church at sunrise with only their scanty clothing or covering. Those residing in pueblos came to pray morning and evening; catechism was attended by gentiles as well as those who were baptized. Those who were already Christian were preparing to receive the Holy Sacrament of Confession.

But the more this primitive Church grew in Christian customs and the more gentile customs declined, the more the devil's rage grew. This principal enemy of mankind saw himself being stripped of the souls that he had dominated and possessed uncontested for so many years. On the occasion of the epidemics many of the souls of baptized infants and newly baptized adults no longer entered his infernal caverns as they used to, but instead went to heaven. He saw how the priests' talks revealed the web of lies with which his sorcerers and familiars (who are his tools) entangled and deceived so many people. The devil understood that if he did not stem the course of the Gospel, he would soon be stripped of all the souls in Sinaloa. He realized that Father Gonzalo de Tapia, as captain of the conquest, was the principal person waging war against him. Therefore, he fired all his shots at the priest. It seemed to him that with Father Tapia dead, all the soldiers who accompanied him would lose heart. He could then raze the churches and altars dedicated to the true God and knock down the Crosses. Drunkenness would once again rear its head, along with the savage dances and sorcery with which he entertained these peoples until he carried them off to hell.

In order to put this diabolical plan into action he chose a famous sorcerer, and through him he used a clever trick similar to the one related by Saint Luke in the Acts and Missions of the Apostles. The devil attempted to cast the Apostle Saint Paul and his companions out of the Province of Macedonia because he saw that *Confirmabantur fide, et abundabant numero quotidie,*[57] each day the faithful multiplied in number and became more confirmed in the Faith. When Saint Paul and his companion Timothy arrived at the city of Philippi, the devil moved the spirit of the masters of a bedeviled pythoness,[58] through whom they had made their evil gains, to proclaim to the people, *Hi homines conturbant civitatem nostram, et annunciant nomen, quod non licet nobis suscipere, nec facere, cum simus Romani.*[59] This is precisely what happened when Father Gonzalo de Tapia was killed and snatched away from Sinaloa.

At a pueblo called Tovoropa, half a league from the Villa de San Felipe, there was a bedeviled old Indian called Nacabeba, which means 'wounded or marked on the ear.' [He was given this name] because of a blow that he had received, and it seems that the devil had already branded him, closing his ears so that he would not hear God's word. He never entered the church with

the others for religious instruction, always remaining instead in his fields. There he held his drunken celebrations and meetings with his companions and accomplices. The speeches of these pythons were very similar to the voices of the masters of that other pythoness: "The priests who have come to our land (they would say) are strangers to us; every day they baptize more people; [50] the baptized and the churches multiply, and now all we hear is talk of going to church to pray. They introduce and teach customs that are unknown to us, which neither we nor our grandparents knew. They no longer allow those who have been baptized to have more than one wife. Our entertainments and pleasures are coming to an end. Let us do away with this Father Tapia, who leads the rest, and we will be left in peace."

Father Tapia realized the evil plan that Nacabeba was plotting and the great stumbling block that it represented to Christianity. First, with gentleness and softness (in which the priest was very talented), he attempted to persuade the Indian to hear God's word and change his ways, which were scandalizing his nation. These affectionate and fatherly admonitions continued for almost a year without results. Then, in order to put an end to the grave scandal this Indian was causing in the region, especially among the new Christians, Father Tapia reported what was happening to Miguel Maldonado, alcalde mayor of the Villa de San Felipe, who also held the position of captain. He asked him to take more effective steps to stem the harm caused by this obstinate Indian's speeches. When the alcalde mayor learned of the case he sent for Nacabeba. After verifying his crimes and the degree of his guilt, [Maldonado] ordered that he be flogged. This punishment did not mend Nacabeba's ways; instead, he became even more obstinate and possessed by the devil. He finally decided to kill Father Gonzalo de Tapia, thinking that it must have been [Tapia] who had reported his crimes to the alcalde mayor. He began to summon accomplices to execute his evil deed, but no matter how hard he tried he could not win over as many persons as he wanted, nor did he even dare to communicate his plans to everyone. Many people loved Father Tapia like a father and were resolute in the catechism that he had taught them. Nacabeba was able to gather only nine Indians, including two of his sons, a son-in-law, the son-in-law's brother, and three other relatives. They all took up their weapons and agreed to set upon the priest early in the evening because it was more likely that he would be alone then.

When they arrived at the priest's little house, which

57. *Margin Note:* Actor. 16. Acts 16:5: "They found the churches firmly established in the faith, and their numbers daily increasing" (Knox 1956:132).

58. Pérez de Ribas uses the term pythoness with reference to a woman who was possessed by a divining spirit in Acts 16:16–20. The woman's masters made a profit from her ability to predict the future. Saint Paul cast the divining spirit out of the woman, hence her masters' proclamation against him and his companions.

59. Actor. 16. Acts 16:20–21: "These men, Jews by origin, are disturbing the peace of our city; they are recommending customs which it is impossible for us, as Roman citizens, to admit or follow" (Knox 1956:132). Note that Pérez de Ribas' Latin version leaves out "Jews by origin."

was a straw hut, they found him saying the Rosary of the Most Holy Virgin.[60] Nacabeba entered the hut as though he meant to kiss the priest's hand, and being the traitor that he was, he began to strike up a conversation. Then, after two more of his accomplices came in, Nacabeba took a macana, which is a weapon like a bludgeon, short-shafted with a head of very hard wood, and struck a strong blow to the priest's head. It split his forehead, but not enough to cause him to fall. Realizing that he was wounded, Father Tapia got up and went out toward the church, which was nearby. He knelt before a Cross in the cemetery, like someone who wished to die in the manner of his crucified Lord, and Nacabeba and his cohorts came from behind. Adding more cruel blows with axes and short clubs, they finished off his life.[61] Because these wild beasts' rage and cruelty were not satisfied with having killed the priest, they also cut off his head and left arm. Furthermore, they stripped him of his meager clothing, leaving the trunk of his body lying chest-down on the ground. Then those wolves savored the blood remaining on their lips from that innocent lamb whom they had ripped apart. They took his head and his arm to celebrate their savage victory, and it was later learned that they put the arm on the coals to roast it for eating. But Our Lord did not allow the flesh of His holy servant to be transformed into the flesh of those bedeviled people. It was set on the spit to barbecue (the previously discussed invention that they use to roast the meat of the animals they kill),[62] but despite [51] three attempts by those savages to roast the arm, each time they tried to eat it, it came out as raw as when they had put it on the fire. Because they were unable to satiate their hunger with it, they skinned the arm and stuffed the skin with straw down to the tips of the fingers of the hand with which Father Tapia used to say Mass. The killers and their allies also dressed up in his priestly vestments and drank wine from the skull of that holy head. They held a great victory celebration, accompanying this with dances, drunkenness, and superstitions, [all] of which are very clear indications of the motives of the devil and his ministers for taking the life of such a saintly man.

---

60. The rosary is a devotion whose origins date to the twelfth century, when a nun who was in the habit of saying 150 Hail Marys was visited by Mary, who told her she needed to say only fifty of the prayers, albeit with greater devotion and more slowly. Subsequently, the rosary developed into a well-defined devotion involving meditation and the recitation of prayers, using a string of beads (Kieckhefer 1987:93). The meditation and prayer are divided into decades, each celebrating a "mystery" (e.g., immaculate conception, glorious assumption) or "major moment" in Mary's life. Reflection on each mystery is accompanied by an Our Father, ten Hail Marys, and a Gloria. Often these "required" prayers, said in decades, are supplemented with other prayers and concluded with the Act of Contrition.

61. Tapia was in the pueblo of Tovoropa, a league from San Felipe. Pérez de Ribas' account of Tapia's death is taken largely from letters by Fathers Pérez, Velasco, and Méndez in the anua of 1594 and a report by Father Martín Peláez, who immediately after the murder went to San Felipe to conduct an investigation (see AGN 1594a, 1594b; Shiels 1934; Zambrano 1961–1977:2:400ff).

62. Pérez de Ribas is in error here, as there is no previous discussion of any barbecue.

CHAPTER VIII News of Father Tapia's death reaches the Villa de San Felipe; a search is undertaken for the body, which is found in an unusual position; the body is buried

At the time the Indians murdered the venerable Father Gonzalo de Tapia, two boys who served in the church at Tovoropa happened to be outside. The boys managed to hide in some nearby thickets, escaping the fury of those savages. The latter even went so far as to kill the priest's little dog, shooting it full of arrows. This is an animal of which the Indians are very fond; sometimes dogs are taken as payment for a day's work. At dawn the boys ran to the Villa de San Felipe to relay word of the priest's death and related events. Everyone was shocked and saddened by the news. The alcalde mayor, Captain Miguel Ortiz, summoned the few residents of the villa and ordered three of them[63] to arm themselves and ride to the pueblo of Tovoropa to assess the state of the people and to search for Father Tapia's body. He gave them a clean blanket in which to collect and return it, and the men departed. Upon reaching the plaza of the pueblo, where the church was located, they found only the trunk of the priest's body. It was stretched out in front of a Cross, with the right arm, which had been left by the killers, in an amazing position. When the trunk of the body landed face down (I mean, with the chest facing the ground), the right arm was elevated above the elbow and the thumb and index finger were making the sign of the Cross;[64] the remaining fingers were tightly closed. Although dead, the priest's arm and hand raised high the standard of the holy Cross.

This action and posture would appear to make it impossible for us to deny this marvelous deed or obvious miracle, for there are only three possibilities for when this sign of the Cross was made: either before the blessed priest died; at the moment of his death, when his head was cut off; or following his death. There was no other time when this sign could have been made.

With respect to the first possibility, it is known that the body responds to a violent death; if Father Tapia made the sign of the Cross before his head was cut off, then why did it not subsequently come undone with the natural movement of the body? If the sign of the Cross and the raised arm were made at the same time as his head was being severed, how is it that when the lifeless body dropped, the arm did not also fall, particularly given that the soul and life were gone that were required to sustain a heavy arm in that violent position—an arm that was still flexible due to the warmth that it retained? Why wasn't it lying on the ground and why hadn't the fingers of the hand separated, thereby releasing the sign of the Cross? Lastly, if this sign were made after death, then the miracle would be even clearer, because a dead body cannot command its members. [52]

From all this we infer that it was God who moved and sustained this venerable priest's arm, just as He moved the voice and tongue of His Apostle Saint Paul, who, after his head had been severed, called out three times the most holy name of JESUS, which he had preached. From this it was understood that following Paul's death the glorious name that the holy Apostle celebrated would continue to be preached throughout the world. In this way, God wanted to glorify the arm of this evangelical minister, preventing those infidels from cutting off both the hand and fingers with which Father Tapia had taught those people to make and revere the sign of the holy Cross. The fact that his arm remained erect and retained the sign of the Cross was a sign of its victory and triumph over the enemies of the Faith. Although the devil and his squad had hoped to seal the mouths of those who recited the Christian doctrine and to rid Sinaloa of the preaching of the holy Cross and of He who had died on it, this sign indicated that they would not succeed, but rather that through God's mercy Christ's Cross and His Gospel would be triumphant in the Province of Sinaloa, as has been the case. Even though this adverse event and the persecution of that primitive Church were something of a

---

63. Antonio Ruiz, Sebastián de Acosta, and Juan Pablo went for the body with a "Mexican Indian" named Pedro Hernández (Nakayama 1974).

64. Reportedly a Spanish custom of the time (Dunne 1940:237, f.8).

setback, in time the land bore fruit. It was watered with the blood of this apostolic man who so desired the spread of Christ's glory in Sinaloa, where new Christian communities were being founded and new churches erected, as we will later see.

At the sight of the dead body holding high the standard of the holy Cross, the soldiers began to give many thanks to God and to mourn the loss of such a priest (as was written by the commander of the soldiers[65] who went after the body). When they turned the body over, they found a reliquary filled with blood-stained relics. That those barbarians had not taken it was amazing. It appeared that those relics attracted and admitted to their company the blood of he who had just spilled it for Christ. As a result of the cruel blows, the bloodied body was covered from top to bottom with bruises and welts. The soldiers also found two short cudgels covered with blood with which the Indians had apparently finished off Father Tapia. It was also understood from the marks left by the blows to his body that the savages had attempted to sever his right arm. God did not allow this, however, out of reverence for His holy Cross and as a sign that Father Tapia had died for its sake; this man held it on high and exalted it in death. One can certainly believe in the ferociousness of such peoples, for they did not even spare the priest's right hand, which he had used to teach them to make the sign of the Cross in church. This was what those ministers of Satan so abhorred. To further confirm that this and no other motive was indeed what had incited those bedeviled souls to murder Christ's minister, they did not lay a hand on his humble bedclothes, although they greatly prize anything of this type, even a poor blanket. They did not, however, spare the holy vessels with which he said Mass, or even the consecrated chalice, for the devil was aware of the war that the holy priest waged against him on the altar.

At last the three soldiers wrapped the body in the blanket they had brought with them, and with the help of some servants who had accompanied them, they carried it to the Villa de San Felipe. It was buried with the grief and tears of all those gathered in the rustic church there. Father Tapia's joyous death occurred on July 11, 1594.[66]

The Indians of the pueblo of Tovoropa, [53] where the priest was killed, immediately fled to the monte (although not all were accomplices in the crime) out of fear over the events that had taken place in their pueblo. Indians in the pueblos near the Villa de San Felipe also fled, fearing that the Spaniards would take them for accomplices in the evil deed. They withdrew and hid in the rock-strewn hills and montes. The alcalde mayor was mindful of the danger to which the other two priests, Martín Pérez and Juan Bautista de Velasco, were still exposed. At the time of Father Tapia's death they were in the pueblos of their districts, some distance away. Therefore, he sent word to them that they were to return to the villa until the storm had passed and the state of things could be assessed. God willed that they should arrive before the burial of their holy superior, which was set for the following day. The captain also set up a day and night watch with the few soldiers he had in the villa and sent word of what had happened to the sister Villa de San Miguel de Culiacán, asking for whatever help might be necessary.

During this time the Indians of the pueblo of Ocoroni, whom Father Tapia had baptized and instructed, learned of their priest's death and the delinquents' uprising, so they took up their weapons in revenge and tried to catch the killers. Although they could not find the actual murderers, with little discussion they killed two innocent people whom they found in the pueblos where Father Tapia had provided instruction.

The [residents of] Villa de San Miguel very promptly sent help to their friends in Sinaloa. They recruited twenty armed men, led by Alonso de Ochoa de Galarraga, a leading citizen of that villa, and they promptly arrived in Sinaloa. There they joined the alcalde mayor in the search for the criminals, but they could not catch them, so they returned to protect the Villa de San Felipe, which had remained unguarded. Then those who had come from Culiacán returned to their homes.

The life and heroic virtues of the remarkable and venerable Gonzalo de Tapia, whose martyrdom we have just recounted, will be recorded at the end of this, Book II, in compliance with what I promised in the prologue.

---

65. Here and elsewhere we have translated *caudillo* as commander of the garrison or troops. The reference is to Antonio Ruiz (Nakayama 1974).

66. The complete date was Sunday, July 11, 1594 (Shiels 1934:158, f.16).

CHAPTER IX Two other priests arrive in Culiacán at this time; the work they did on their way to Sinaloa

At the time that God Our Lord, as the provident and divine Master of the Vineyard, took His fervent evangelical minister Father Tapia to heaven, He brought two other laborers to Sinaloa to do the work of planting in that province. They were sent from Mexico City at the request of the deceased [priest], who before he died had asked our Father Provincial to send additional help in the form of laborers for the great conversion that this province offered. These men were Father Pedro Méndez and Father Hernando de Santarén. The latter's blood was shed years later for the preaching of our Holy Faith, at the hands of those unholy apostates, the Tepehuan (as will be duly told). The former succeeded to the position of administration of the mission [that had formerly been held] by the apostolic Father Tapia. Father Méndez carried the mission forward and was a pillar of support for [all] the missions of Sinaloa.

When these priests reached the Villa de Culiacán, the residents were greatly bereaved by the news of the death of the captain of that new Christian enterprise.[67] Aware of the unrest and danger that remained in the province [of Sinaloa], they tried to keep these priests from moving forward, [54] persuading them to wait for the storm to die down and for times to improve. The two fervent missionaries struggled with whether they should proceed. On the one hand, they were compelled by their desire and holy zeal to aid in the salvation of the nations of Sinaloa for which God had chosen them and to die in this pursuit (if need be) with their brothers who still remained there. On the other hand, the residents of San Miguel strongly insisted that they stay. Perhaps they were moved by that holy Archangel [Saint Michael], just as he had aided God's people on another occasion in their escape from captivity so that they could celebrate their feast days at the temple in Jerusalem.[68] The delay of the priests at that time resulted in fortunate fruits and results.

The residents of San Miguel finally prevailed, and the priests stayed and visited the thirty pueblos in the lower Valle [de Culiacán]. There, they busied themselves with a great harvest. Although these people were Christian, they had received [Baptism] only a few years earlier and were not yet mature in their Faith. They were in great need of instruction and the sacraments, and were so hungry for divine sustenance that entire pueblos followed the priests, hoping to receive the bread of life. The fruits that they harvested in that valley were so abundant that there was not a single man, woman, or child who had use of reason who was not well instructed in the Faith and had not received the Holy Sacrament of Confession.

The priests had to use the Mexican language to instruct these people, and although this was not the language of the region, some of the Indians knew and understood it. The priests also added that they made a great effort during the month and a half they spent in this mission to learn some of the basics of what they needed to know to minister to the Indians in their own language, which was Tahue. Divine aid provided nearly miraculous assistance, and one of the two priests suddenly discovered that he possessed sufficient competence to hear some confessions in this language and to instruct penitents. What was even more remarkable was the fervor with which those [Indians] who did not know the Mexican language sought out those who did understand it so that the latter could teach them and relate to them what had been preached in the priests' sermons and talks. Others willingly brought their own interpreters with them to confession, which is something they had never done before. Those who were not present when the priests visited their pueblos subsequently

---

67. Méndez and Santarén arrived at Culiacán on June 29, 1594—eleven days before Tapia's death. It was en route to San Felipe from Culiacán, at the pueblo of Capirato, that the priests got word of Tapia's murder, at which point they returned to the Villa of Culiacán.

68. See Daniel 12, which discusses Michael's deliverance of the Israelites from the hands of the king of Syria, who held them captive in Babylon. See also Exodus 14:19–20, which discusses the role played by an angel of God in the Israelites' flight from captivity in Egypt (note that the Exodus passage does not state that this angel was necessarily Michael).

went looking for them, no matter how far, in order to confess. Some did this two or three times, often walking many leagues to reconcile the most trivial things.

When the priests entered the pueblos all the people, young and old, came out to greet them with Crosses raised on high. They sang songs and escorted them to the church, where the priests declared their intentions and desires to help their souls and to prepare them for the [extraordinary] jubilee[69] that the Supreme Pontiffs had granted the members of the Company of Jesus [to commemorate] their time as missionaries. The Indians received this message from heaven with such affection and esteem that they followed the priests from pueblo to pueblo. Some people followed them the entire time they were in the valley, which consoled them greatly. Thus did they realize that it had been the counsel and will of heaven and the negotiation of the angels of the Province of Culiacán and its patron, Saint Michael, that they should stop there before going on to the Province of Sinaloa.

At the end of this period [August 1594] two Spanish residents from Sinaloa arrived and [55] safely guided and escorted these priests to their desired province, where they were received with special consolation by their brothers. The priests who were there were very happy with the new assistance of these companions, who came to continue the enterprise that had already been initiated. The new missionaries set about preparing themselves by studying the languages in which they were to preach the Gospel; they were not intimidated by the death of he who had given his life for it only a few days earlier.

CHAPTER X The condition of the missions and Christianity in Sinaloa following the death of the venerable Father Gonzalo de Tapia

The devil certainly thought, and better to say incorrectly thought, that he had achieved a victory with the death and removal from earth of the founder of the Sinaloa mission—he who had laid the foundations for that extensive Christianity. But the devil's plans had the totally opposite effect, just as they did when he spilled the blood of the [ancient] martyrs. The latter's blood always fertilized the fields of the Church; each additional [sacrifice] multiplied the evangelical harvest. And so it was in Sinaloa: The tempest subsided and calm returned to those pueblos; neither Father Martín Pérez, cofounder of the Sinaloa mission, nor the three other priests lost spirit. Instead, their energy was renewed, and they buckled down to begin anew the task entrusted them by God, that of watchful shepherds bringing in the sheep who had strayed. Even though it was rainy and miserable, the priests searched the montes and rock-strewn hills for several days for gentiles and Christians who were in hiding out of fear [of Spanish reprisals]. The first Indians they encountered fled. They had to hurry to overtake them, just as Saint John the Evangelist did when he went after the young man whom he had baptized and borne in Christ who fled and joined a company of bandits. Father Martín Pérez caught up with those who were fleeing and calmed and dispelled their fears, reassuring them that he was seeking not revenge, but rather to protect them, for he loved them as his own children. These Indians returned to the mission settlement and began calling others. Little by little a good number of people were gathered into the pueblos that were closest to the Villa de San Felipe. There were only a few Indians who were unable to overcome their fear of Spaniards, saying (although I do not know whether it was true) that in the past the Spaniards had not kept their word. In the end, with diligence and perseverance, the priests overcame the difficulties posed by the Indians, and those places were once again settled.

---

69. An extraordinary jubilee is a plenary indulgence (remittance of sin) granted by the pope on special occasions for a limited time through certain confessors (Attwater 1949:269).

Those in the pueblo of Ocoroni, which was the venerable Father Tapia's very own mission, came to see the priests, expressing great sorrow over what had happened. Subsequently a priest went to visit them and found them celebrating a dance in their limited capacity, using the scalps of some dead Indians whom they had killed because they thought they were accomplices in Father Tapia's death. Finding them participating in such an activity, the priest threatened never to see or visit them again unless they gave up such barbarous customs and lived like Christians. They heeded this warning and repented, promising to reform.

Of still greater edification is the example of a Christian Indian who was a principal cacique. [56] During these troubled times the cacique's followers had killed some other Indians, either justifiably or without cause. Therefore, the cacique and his household came to live among the Christians of the Villa de San Felipe. The cacique said that he would rather be alone, separated from his vassals, than risk his Holy Faith and fail to fulfill his obligations as a Christian.

The Christian pueblos near the Villa de San Felipe returned to their Christian practices with renewed fervor. On feast days it was a sight to see the Indians enter the pueblo in two groups, one coming from downstream and the other from upstream. Wearing wreaths of flowers on their heads and carrying tall Crosses adorned with feathers, the Indians sang prayers with great dignity all the way to the church. There they heard Mass and the Christian catechism, and at the conclusion of this Christian exercise they returned to their pueblos.

Those who were gentiles began considering Holy Baptism, which meant that Christianity was improving and growing. At this time [1595] Our Lord showed on various occasions that there were many among these people who were predestined, whom He selected for heaven. I will choose here [only] a few of the many cases of edification.

At the time of Father Tapia's death there was a very old Christian Indian woman whose predestination was revealed. Although ordinarily it is not easy to instill the Faith in such women, she retained much of the catechism that Father Tapia taught her, and she made sure that her house was near the church. She also heard Mass every day it was offered in her pueblo, even when she was sick, and it was difficult to find anything that required absolution in the confessions that she made. She raised her children with the catechism that she had learned, and during the general uprising she remained in her pueblo at home with her husband; the rebels

were powerless to make her join them. When she became ill and was near death, two old gentile women came to decorate or paint her face and body (which is what superstitious gentiles do at the hour [of death]). The sick woman wholeheartedly resisted and, turning to Christian relatives, she begged them that in the event she lost consciousness they not consent to anything that she would not voluntarily do herself or that would be alien to their professed Faith. She believed in one true God with all her heart, and she felt in her soul that she was ready to see Him. Then she turned to her husband and pleaded with him not to forget the catechism and teachings that he had heard from Father Tapia. She told him that once she was dead, if he wanted to remarry, he should marry a Christian who respected God's law. Then she turned to another woman who was one of her companions and stated clearly, "Mary, today thou shalt see me and afterwards thou shalt not see me again. I am going with God, I am going to see God.[70] Do they not say that those who believe in God shall see Him? I believe in Him with all my heart." She repeated with special devotion, "Lord, when shall I see Thee?" Saying this with great tenderness, and with the tears of all those who were present, she made two Crosses with the fingers of both hands, imitating the blessed Father Tapia, whom she dearly loved. She kissed these Crosses many times and repeated the sweet name of JESUS, drawing her final breath in great peace and calm. It can and should be believed that a soul that demonstrated such a lively faith, even though raised in the midst of this heathenism, went on to enjoy the sight of God, just as she had predicted and desired with such confidence. How well God knows, and this is nothing new for Him, to pluck roses for heaven from among the thorns of these montes.

Somewhat similar is the following case, [57] although the circumstances were different. It happened that a priest discovered that there was an old Indian in a ranchería who was so close to the end of his life that his relatives had stacked the kindling to burn his dead body (a custom they sometimes used for their deceased, especially when they died in the fields or away from their pueblos). The priest heard about this and went to visit him. When he arrived it appeared that the man had less than an hour to live. The priest hurriedly

---

70. Note the parallel here between what this woman is saying to her friend María and what Christ said to his disciples several times in the Gospel of John, in particular John 16:16: "After a little while you will see me no longer . . . I am going back to the Father" (Knox 1956:107).

went over the catechism, baptized him, and placed a rosary in his hand. The Indian kissed it many times with special devotion and would not let go of it. He placed it on his eyes, and displaying his sorrow over the sins of his life, he drew his final breath, leaving many assurances of the salvation, achieved in such a short space of time, of a soul that an hour earlier had been in the darkness of heathenism. The women who earlier had wanted him to be cremated [now] placed a Cross in his hands and buried him like a Christian.

Faith was hard at work at this time, despite the efforts that the devil made to extinguish it. Some Indians who had been baptized at the time of the first Spanish entradas into the region, who had been prevented from making a confession because of the disturbances, came to do so after twenty or more years. Their fervor reached such high levels that two Christian Indians from a pueblo close to the Villa de San Felipe, who had squandered their lives in sin and scandalized others, entered the church and knelt before the public. Of their own free will, or better to say by the will of Christ's grace, they asked for pardon and atoned for their sins by scourging themselves in public. I do not know whether I should say that this was more remarkable than if individuals of greater status had done so. This will be judged by He who knows how haughty these people are, raised in their fierce and barbarous freedom, without recognizing subordination to God or man.

Although the priests lived with the consolation that their labor was yielding prosperous fruits, there was no shortage of violent eruptions that disturbed the peace and kept them busy. Nevertheless, even in these disturbances they could recognize the favor of ever-watchful divine providence, which warned and protected them. [For example, there was] a very fierce and bellicose Indian who was plotting to kill one of the priests. Even in the most orderly republics it is common to bring one evil person or bandit to justice only to find it necessary to bring yet another person to justice within a few weeks. Therefore, it is not surprising that another Nacabeba should appear like the first, but God foiled the efforts of this second [assassin]. Learning of what was going to happen, some other good Indians from the district of Ocoroni set out at midnight for the priest's place [to warn him of the impending attempt on his life]. When they arrived, the priest asked them why they had come at such a late hour, and they told him that they had learned of the perverse intentions of that fierce Indian and that they had come to protect him from danger and, if necessary, to die with him. But this is not what happened, for once the would-be murderer learned that his plot had been discovered, he desisted from his intended harm and the priest remained unharmed.

CHAPTER XI The residents of the Villa de San Felipe ask the viceroy of Nueva España and the governor of [Nueva] Vizcaya to send reinforcements for the preservation of the province; a garrison of soldiers is established; an account is given of a unique case of an idol

Although on the one hand the affairs of Christendom were prospering and peace and tranquility were returning to the Province of Sinaloa, in some places the storm of restlessness and its vestiges still lingered. This was [58] because delinquent Indians, together with their allies, went about stirring up trouble, even daring to assault and set fire to the Villa de San Felipe. When they were unsuccessful, because the residents of the villa were always on guard, they attacked horses and other animals that they encountered. They shot them full of arrows and cut off their manes and tails, which they hung from the trees to taunt the Spaniards. Through other insolent acts, they stirred up the baptized [Indians] near the Villa de San Felipe; neither the Indians nor the inhabitants of the villa were safe, nor were the priests who ministered to the Christian pueblos. This forced the few Spaniards in the Villa de San Felipe to send an account of the state of the province to the viceroy, the count of Monterrey, and to Rodrigo del Río y Losa, governor of Nueva Vizcaya. They begged them to send some aid in the form of either Spanish settlers or a presidio of soldiers, who could secure the province and suppress the arrogance of those who disturbed it and prevented the further preaching of the Gospel. This task had been entrusted by our Catholic monarchs to their viceroys and governors ever since Christ's Vicars had granted them the patronage and protection of the New World. As proof of this truth I will relate here what His Majesty, the gloriously remembered and most triumphant emperor Charles V, wrote in the way of instructions. These instructions were dispatched to the governors of these newly discovered [provinces] and were cited by Don Juan de Solórzano [y Pereyra], of His Majesty's council, who quotes the Most Holy Emperor as follows:[71]

If the Indians maliciously obstruct or cause delays in welcoming those persons who undertake the teaching of the Faith; or if they hinder their presence among them, not allowing them to continue preaching and teaching good habits and customs; or if they refuse resettlement in missions or block conversion of their relatives or those residents who desire conversion; or if they arm themselves or come in war to kill, steal, or cause other damage to the aforesaid discoverers and preachers; then, in such cases, war can be waged with appropriate moderation, after first consulting whatever religious or clergy are present, as well as the Real Audiencia if there is time, regarding its justification and appropriate form, and also filing whatever other documents, protestations, and requests are deemed appropriate.

I end here my quotation of this imperial order, which fits our case perfectly, as if it were written in response to it.

Thus, knowing the pressing need for a military force in Sinaloa to resist the rebels and restore peace, the viceroy ordered the governor of Nueva Vizcaya to dispatch some soldiers to the Villa de San Felipe to help the residents defend themselves and to punish those who were guilty and delinquent. The governor sent twenty-four paid soldiers, led by Alonso Díaz, a greatly honored resident of Durango who was given the title of lieutenant general.[72] One might argue that this seems to be a small force and number of soldiers for a province with so many nations, so I will address this and

71. *Margin Note*: Lib 2. de Indiarum jur. The referent here is Juan de Solórzano y Pereyra's *Política indiana*. Solórzano was one of the most learned and distinguished jurisconsuls of his day. He was a judge of the Audiencia de Lima and compiled a colonial code and legislation for the New World (Haring 1947:104).

72. Díaz was actually lieutenant captain general, the highest ranking provincial military commander. Although the position often was held by the governor, the latter could appoint an officer or enlisted man to the position (Polzer, Barnes, and Naylor 1977:140).

related issues in the following chapter. For now I [wish to continue my narrative] by noting that the lieutenant reached Sinaloa around 1596,[73] finding it in the state just described. The spirits of the few residents of the villa were lifted and they were encouraged by this new aid. Therefore, they attempted to negotiate peace with some neighboring pueblos whose inhabitants were still restless, such as Nío and Vacayoe. These were about five leagues from the villa and had some five hundred families. Another three leagues farther downriver were the pueblos of the Guasave. This nation extended as far as the mouth of the river as well as along the coast, where there were many people; the number of Indian archers [in this nation] totaled [59] three to four thousand.[74]

Now that there was a greater [Spanish military] force in the province to repress troublemakers and those who were restless, the priests began anew to visit these nations, pacifying them and laying the foundations of Christian doctrine. Although priests had previously visited [the Guasave], baptizing some during an outbreak of disease (as was mentioned earlier), there was no opportunity at that time to begin teaching the Christian doctrine. This they began to do, along with building churches, albeit of brush[75] and straw.

The cacique of the pueblo of Nío was baptized and married in the Christian rite, and it appears that these divine sacraments inspired him with particular fervor and zeal to help the priests bring his people to the Christian religion. He searched out his followers, treating them very well and helping them according to their capacity with their catechism. The teaching of the catechism was also begun among the Guasave nation, with the help of a Christian Indian woman who spoke Spanish and years earlier had been a slave to some Spaniards in the Villa de Culiacán. Her fervor for teaching the catechism was so great that she made her people come to church twice a day to repeat this exercise. Now even at night, a time that they used to set aside for their superstitious dances, they assembled of their own free will to chant the catechism.

Still these Guasave and other populations along the upper Río [Sinaloa] were not completely peaceful, despite the fact that there were Christians among them who had been baptized earlier. The lieutenant and his soldiers repeatedly visited them to establish complete

peace. Due to these new nations' instability, because they were governed, or better to say misgoverned, by their many leaders and were unfamiliar with being governed by a single leader, he met with varied success. On one occasion when the priest who was catechizing the Guasave was away visiting other pueblos, they gave free rein to their ancient bouts of drunkenness. Because the devil did not waste any opportunity to recover the prey that had been taken from him, he incited and infuriated these people in such a way that they inhumanely killed the good Christian woman who was teaching them the catechism and the way to salvation.[76] Once the Guasave were stirred up they and their allies living along the coast [the Batucari] fled to the monte. When the priest found out about this, he wanted to go after them by himself and bring them back, but the captain would not allow him to place himself in such clear danger. Instead, he and eighteen Spanish soldiers accompanied the priest, and they calmed the storm somewhat, as many of the Indians returned to their pueblo. This was not, however, the final disturbance among these nations, and through it all, both gains and losses, God continued to select the chosen and predestined from among those who were lost and damned. In the end peace and a good Christianity were firmly established among them.

I will not be silent here about a particular case that happened at this time which shows how the devil raged against Christ's doctrine. It happened that the priest who had begun catechizing the Guasave[77] was returning to the Villa de San Felipe, accompanied by some Spaniards. The priest noticed that an Indian who was walking ahead of them left the road and followed a path into the monte. He followed the Indian and saw him stop and make some demonstrations of reverence at a stone shaped like a pyramid, crudely inscribed with certain figures. The priest declared to him the deceit of that idolatry or superstition and ordered him to knock down the stone, for it made no sense nor could it help him in any way. The Indian answered that he did not dare touch it, as he would die instantly. The priest and the Spaniards who were with him took hold of the stone, and even though it was heavy and measured more than a vara in length, they brought it to [60] the plaza of the villa. There they assailed it, dragging it about and stomping on it, so as to free the Indian of the fear he had of touching it. Some Indians who

---

73. The anua of 1595 indicates that they arrived in that year.

74. Presumably adult males aged 15–60, perhaps a third of the total population (see Reff 1991b:211).

75. *De prestado*.

76. This event occurred in July 1596.

77. This was Santarén, who after this incident in 1595 was replaced by Martín Pérez (Alegre 1956–1960:1:451).

were present expressed extreme indignation and predicted a punishment of sickness and death because of the great disrespect shown the stone. Specifically they predicted that that very night there would be a tempest and hurricane of winds that would topple houses and the church, for they had overthrown he who gave them good weather and favorable results in war. They also added that the devil answered them through the stone, and they trusted in it for help during spells of bad weather and times of war, sometimes carrying the stone with them on journeys of one or two days.

The priest was forced to gather all the people of the pueblo at the church. There he preached the catechism of the one and only true God, along with other truths of the Faith that appeared appropriate for such an occasion, which dissuaded them of those gentile superstitions. In spite of all this, Our Lord still allowed something unusual to happen. When the people left the church following the priest's sermon, a furious dust- and windstorm suddenly picked up, causing great damage. The wind smashed houses to the point that it appeared it wanted to pull them up and carry them off through the air. This was an event that greatly disturbed many people who were still very new to the Faith. If they had been more enlightened and possessed greater capacity, they would have concluded that this was a demonstration of the devil's rage at seeing himself trampled upon and cast from the stone and banished from the Province of Sinaloa by the catechism that the priest had just preached, thereby untangling his web of deceit.

The same thing happened when evil spirits were exorcised from bedeviled bodies; they came out furious, still leaving their hosts in torment. We have a good example of this bedevilment in the story told by Saint Mark of how a father brought his child to Christ to be cured. Once the boy found himself in this divine presence, the Evangelist says, *In terram volut abatur spumans*,[78] [the child] was thrown to the ground by the devil, possessed and spewing foam from his mouth. After the Lord commanded the devil to come out and never enter that body again, upon leaving (as the Holy Scripture states) *diserpens eum, & factus eft sicut mortuus*,[79] his body was so ravaged that he appeared dead. The Lord had to allow this to happen in order to reveal the guest that this demon-possessed boy harbored in his own home. Afterwards, the Most Benign Liberator took him by the hand and helped him to stand, [completely] healed. We can say that the same thing happened in our case: seeing himself banished from that stone and from the Province of Sinaloa, where he had ensconced himself, the devil demonstrated his furious feelings in those whirlwinds and gusts of wind that he had raised.

He was not content with this, for he then left for the pueblos of the Guasave, which still had some sorcerers. Working through them, he once again stirred up the Guasave, taking them back to the monte and away from the church, which they tried to burn. The priests were not disheartened, however, by these setbacks; instead, they worked diligently to bring the Indians back together and calm them down, even at great risk to their own lives. They also received some assistance from the soldiers who had arrived to subdue the restless, as they eventually did. In the end, the devil did not remain in that stone, nor in the Guasave pueblos, as will be seen in due time, after discussing an important topic in the following chapters. [61]

78. *Margin Note*: Marc. c. 9. Mark 9:19: "he fell on the ground, writhing and foaming at the mouth" (Knox 1956:42).

79. Mark 9:25: "he lay there like a corpse, so that many declared, 'He is dead'" (Knox 1956:42).

CHAPTER XII Arguments for placing garrisons on the frontier for the protection and defense of new nations that are being converted to Christianity

I am obliged at this point to address an important issue which, although it might not seem pertinent to history, is nevertheless very closely related to the subject matter of the present work and is a circumstance of it. This subject is one that will also come up later, so it needs to be examined here. The problem, as some have noted, is that the endeavors recounted in this history involve the evangelical and apostolic preaching of Christ's Gospel, which the Lord Himself intended should be freely and spontaneously received, without discord or force of arms. That is, Gospel preaching was to be accomplished only through the strength of the divine word, as He made known when He entrusted this responsibility to his holy Apostles, using precisely those words quoted by Saint Mark: *Praedicate Evangelium omni creatura.*[80] They were to convert all people solely by preaching His word, and He indicated no other means. If this is indeed the case, then why does this history of the preaching of the Gospel so often mention garrisons, military escorts, and weapons? It is imperative that I address this issue here.

This matter has been dealt with by very serious authors, and whoever wishes to read such treatises should consult [the work of] Doctor Don Juan Solórzano, of His Majesty's Council of the Indies, who wrote so knowledgeably about this subject.[81] I will add here my own experiences, based on my years in the Sinaloa missions, which confirm Doctor Solórzano's arguments. There, I learned about the spiritual and material fruits produced by the garrisons that were established under His Majesty's orders for these types of frontier enterprises. They do not contradict the manner and spirit in which the Gospel should be preached according to the teachings of Christ Our Lord, the Divine Legislator, who entrusted this to His Supreme Vicars and Pon-

tiffs. They, in turn, are in charge of dispatching Gospel preachers to all the peoples of the world.

First, I take it as a truthful and undeniable argument that the reception of the Faith and Holy Baptism by adults must be spontaneous and of their own free will. In this, there is not, nor could there be, doubt or dispensation. This was the manner and spirit that Christ observed in His own divine preaching, which the Apostles learned from Him and which the Church has preserved since it was founded. The clear consequence of this teaching is that if the establishment of garrisons on the frontier among barbarous nations is for the purpose of violently and forcefully imparting the Faith and Holy Baptism, then this is very alien to our evangelical and apostolic ministry. Once this undeniable truth has been established one must clarify the motives and causes for the establishment of garrisons on the frontier for the conversion of barbarous peoples. It is not surprising that those unaware of these objectives might have trouble with this proposition, but if the reasoning is made clear, they will clearly understand that garrisons do not contradict evangelical laws; rather, they are a means that is both advantageous and necessary (at least at certain times and in certain places, when they remove obstacles to the Gospel and offer [62] stability and safety for its teaching).

I also take it to be true, as it is, that the means taken to achieve an objective, in addition to being just, ought to be commensurate with the time, place, and people, as well as the endeavor for which it is intended. This is because different circumstances often call for different means. Means that were convenient and useful at one time and place may be harmful and counterproductive at another time and place. When preaching the Gospel, the holy Apostles were moved by this realization. They tolerated and even made use of some of the ceremonies of the old law, which as a result of Christ's death were no longer relevant. They did this because they wished to avoid obstacles to spreading the law of the Gospel that they were introducing to the world at that time.

---

80. Mark 16:15: "preach the Gospel to the whole of creation" (Knox 1956:52).

81. Again, Pérez de Ribas is referring here to Solórzano's *Política indiana*.

They also wanted to prevent an aversion to receiving the Gospel in the minds of the Jews. At the present time, however, the observance of these ceremonies might not be beneficial, but rather mortally dangerous. The very same holy Apostles, at the council that they held in Jerusalem, established laws of *sanguine, et suffocato*.[82] At that time these laws were advisable as well as obligatory; now, however, they are neither. Because theologians have examined this issue extensively, we will not detain ourselves here, inferring only that it is appropriate to use whatever means are helpful in preaching the Gospel, as long as they are just and licit and do not deny or contradict the Gospel. All of this will be demonstrated more clearly by recording here in our history the events and times when these garrisons served some of these missions to the greater benefit of evangelical preaching.

It often has happened that one of these barbarous pueblos or nations, which had neither government nor civil life, was spontaneously moved by the force of the divine word to convert and receive God's word. He emphasizes such events through His Prophet Isaiah, saying, *Verbum meum non revertetur ad me vacuum: sed faciet quaecunque voluit, et prosperabitur in ijs adquae missi illud*.[83] These marvelous results are experienced countless times in these missions, and we acknowledge that it is this divine word which must produce conversions. Once these people are moved by it, they receive and embrace the Faith and Holy Baptism. Nevertheless, it also happens on these frontiers that these baptized Christians and those who were converted earlier live among infidels and in the midst of false Christians and even some apostates. At times Saint Paul, the Apostle of the People, and the other holy Apostles suffered a great deal from apostates, as he wrote when he said that he had suffered more than a few dangers *in falsis fratribus*.[84] Such unfaithful people are not satisfied with their own betrayal of Christ's law. Both spiritually and materially they stir up those who have received it and do not allow them to live in peace in their homes and pueblos. Therefore, I now ask, who can doubt that it is a very holy endeavor for our Catholic monarchs, who through their appointed guardianship[85] have been entrusted with the promotion and protection of the Holy Gospel in the New World, to suppress this insolence and to aid those who, of their own free will and moved by the light of the divine word, enter and join the Catholic Church? Or, I ask, when the Catholic monarchs come with weapons to the aid of a persecuted Christian community, does that depart from or deny an apostolic preaching of the Gospel? We must confess that it is the divine word {63} that will overcome and subject mankind to Christ and achieve the conversion of these peoples, but in order to obtain these marvelous results, it is necessary to hear the divine word, and for this reason the Apostle said, *Fides per auditum*.[86] For it to be heard, however, someone must preach it. So if the infidels impede some people from preaching it and others from hearing it, and not content with rejecting it themselves, their rebellion reaches the point where they unjustly persecute those who, moved by God, do receive it, well, in such a case who is to defend the afflicted people and combat the others? The evangelical ministers cannot; they do not have the power. They work alone, accompanied only by divine aid. [And what if] they are unable to preach the divine word, which was the weapon with which they were to make war and by which they were to subject nations to Christ? So, do such cases deny the apostolic preaching of the Gospel, given that the Catholic monarch, for whom God reserved the protection of the conversion of the New World, was commanded to employ his forces, wealth, and arms for removing obstacles in the form of irreverent barbarians who attempt to impede the preaching of the Gospel, which Christ (the Supreme Emperor) commanded be preached to the entire world? It was for this very reason that God granted His Church the power and might to remove impediments to divine preaching, as was gloriously done by the Most Holy Roman Emperors Constantine the Great and Theodosius. At other times evangelical men who were preaching the Gospel and converting gentiles to our Holy Faith found protection with all those who considered themselves Christian princes.

But let us turn to another frequent case in this history involving evangelical missions. These nations see the protection that is enjoyed by those who make peace

82. *Margin Note*: Salas de legib. q. 103. tractit. 14. disp. 23. The referent here apparently is an unknown commentary on Acts 15:20: "only writing to bid them abstain from what is contaminated by idolatry, from fornication, and from meat which has been strangled or has the blood in it" (Knox 1956:131).

83. *Margin Note*: Isaias. C. 55 Isaiah 55:11: "So it is with the word by these lips of mine once uttered: It will not come back, an empty echo, the way it went; all my will it carries out, speeds on its errand" (Knox 1956:672).

84. II Corinthians 11:26: "from false brethren" (Knox 1956:189).

85. *Patronazgo*. As noted in the "Critical Introduction," a series of papal bulls at the turn of the fifteenth century gave the Spanish crown extensive rights and responsibilities with respect to the introduction and propagation of Christianity in the New World and other newly discovered lands.

86. Romans 10:17: "faith comes from hearing" (Knox 1956:157).

with the Spaniards and who place themselves under the king's protection. They see how much this friendship benefits them in their defense against their former enemies, which they all generally have. They also see that due to this friendship they live peacefully in their pueblos, lands, and fields. Their enemies cannot cast them out or take their daughters away by force or commit offenses against them as they used to do when they were gentiles. Often, some of these people recognize these benefits even before they have received the Gospel or are baptized, so they come willingly to settle in peace and place themselves under the protection of the Catholic monarch. This is carried out in public, before the captain and the garrison and in the presence of the notary and witnesses. On behalf of their nations the caciques pledge reciprocity and promise not to aid those who attempt to contaminate Christians. If delinquents should come to their lands, they pledge not to admit them, but rather to turn them over to the person who is governing the province. They are also to aid the Spaniards in whatever enterprises should arise, and the Spaniards promise to defend their nation from the affronts of their enemies. All of this yields great benefits for both parties.

This agreement is similar to the one that the brave captain Judas of Maccabee made with the Roman people, as is told in the Holy Scriptures.[87] In this way the gentile nations are made ready to receive the Gospel of their own free will and to become domesticated, tractable, and tamed. For the king and his vassals it is also better to keep gentile nations calm, for when they are quiet these Christian nations are able to attend their churches and peaceably practice their Christian religion. Thus, the king is saved the expense of defending them when opposing nations create disturbances, for in a province like Sinaloa, which extends more than one hundred leagues and is uninhabited by Spaniards, the recently converted [Indians] are bounded by countless gentile nations. Now, [suppose that] one of the nations that had made [64] such an agreement with the Christians came to request protection from its aggressors. If there were no arms or garrison to protect these Christians and their friends and to suppress their enemies, then what peace, Christianity, or safety could one expect?

Moreover, there is the matter of the instability of these peoples, especially at the beginning of their conversion. This is when the devil, with his tricks and snares, stirs the coals of the Indians' inherent instability. This fierce lion roars when he sees the flight of the souls that he once possessed and held in tyranny for so long. His obstinacy and that of his familiars, the sorcerers, serves no other purpose than to turn the converted Indians back to their old vices, murders, drunkenness, and barbarous ways. Who can deny the need for force of arms for restraining and frightening such a great number of this type of enemy, particularly when their insolence becomes so uncontrolled? The cases mentioned here have actually happened and are not fictitious, and they have been observed many times among these nations. These insolent and malicious deeds have even prompted some of them to place their sacrilegious hands upon that which is sacred, to set fire to churches, to profane holy vessels, to mock blessed vestments, and to commit outrages against holy images. Having done so, they have then withdrawn to a stronghold in the monte or to an enemy nation to celebrate their impious victories, inviting other outlaws and even apostates from the Faith to participate in these irreverent acts. In a similar case the valiant Mathias could not be held back, as is celebrated by the Holy Spirit in the Holy Scriptures. Instead, risking his own life and that of his children, the brave Maccabees, as well as his fortune and homeland, he took up his arms in plain view of the squad that the unholy king of Antioch had sent to petition the people of God to renounce their holy law, and there and then he slit the throat of the first person who failed to keep the holy law by attempting to make a sacrifice to the idols and return to the law of the gentiles, as is told in the first book of Maccabees.[88]

In cases such as these why should Christian soldiers and arms not be made available to strike fear and suppress such treachery against Christ, His flocks, and the Church? What other weapons can be borne by priests who apostolically preach the Gospel? The Apostle of the People, Saint Paul, preached the Gospel apostolically, and even though the swords and scimitars [to which he resorted] belonged to gentile judges and governors, he still wanted them to be feared by those who had become Christians. Therefore, he taught the following doctrine to the Romans who had become Christians: *Non est potestas nisi a Deo, quae autem sicut a Deo, ordinata sunt, dei enim minister est vindex in riam, ei qui malum agit, non enim sine causa gladium portat.*[89] With these words the

---

87. I Maccabees 8.

88. *Margin Note*: Cap. 2. See I Maccabees 2.

89. *Margin Note*: Cap. 13. Romans 13:1, 4: "authority comes from God only, and all authorities that hold sway are of his ordinance. . . .

holy Apostle recorded the suitable causes and reasons for bearing arms where the Gospel was being preached: to suppress abuses, evil deeds, and crimes. From this we deduce that the holy Apostle would not be surprised to find that arms are borne for the same reason where Indians are being converted to the Faith. When that same Apostle who was chosen by Christ suffered the false accusations of the Jews, even on matters of faith, he saw that the president of Judea would not protect him or grant him justice, so he appealed his cause, attempting to make use of the authority of Caesar, as Saint Luke notes, saying, *Ad tribunal Caesaris sto ibi me oportet iudicari.*[90] Thus, if authority and the power of justice to [65] right wrongs, punish criminals, and render justice were lacking among these peoples, how could the civilized government that all republics of the world need in order to live in peace be introduced among them? If this justice should lack the force of arms and ministers, what house would be safe, whose honor would not be at risk, or what chalice would be secure upon the altar? The garrisons protect all this, and it is for such justified ends that they are established among these nations, who on their own did not have any government or civil life.

CHAPTER XIII Response to the challenges that could be made to the arguments [in favor of garrisons] given in the previous chapter

The nature of this New World's conversion to the Gospel and the manner in which it is conducted are in plain view or, at a minimum, are [things of] which all the nations of the world have heard. Therefore, this conversion is subject to judgment by the inhabitants of the New as well as the Old World. Because of its importance and gravity, I am obliged to linger longer than I would like on this topic, even though there is much that I could write that I will omit. In this chapter I will respond to certain criticisms which, if they were to remain uncontested, might appear to weaken the brief presented in the previous chapter. In the process it will become clear how garrisons should be used in this remote part of the world, which is a topic that pertains to this history.

The first objection that could be raised to the arguments in favor of the garrisons is that they do not appear to be a sufficient force to repress so many nations, which are so warlike, restless, and ferocious. The garrison in the Province of Sinaloa presently has only one captain and forty-six soldiers. There are twenty or thirty thousand Indian warriors who could be fielded if the [different Indian] nations were to unite. What can forty-six soldiers do against an enemy force of thirty thousand? To oblige Our Lord the king to continually maintain garrisons in these conversions would also seem to be a huge expense to his treasury and a detriment to his royal resources, and this should concern all his loyal vassals.

I respond to the first point by noting that when something happens and help is needed from the garrison to pacify or punish rebels, etc., the Spanish soldiers do not go alone. Rather, depending on the needs of the expedition, they are helped by a greater or lesser number of Indian allies, who are never lacking. Although these Indians would not dare to attack another group by themselves, nor would they know how to organize themselves for such an enterprise, they are not afraid to do so when accompanied and directed by Spanish soldiers. It should be noted as well that, in terms of self-defense, an armed [Spanish] soldier riding an armored horse[91] is a castle to which an Indian archer cannot com-

---

The magistrate is God's minister, working for thy good. Only if thou dost wrong, needst thou be afraid; it is not for nothing that he bears the sword" (Knox 1956:160).

90. *Margin Note*: Act. Apost. cap. 25. Acts 25:10: "I am standing at Caesar's judgement-seat, where I have a right to be tried" (Knox 1956:143).

91. Here and throughout the text we have translated *caballo de armas* as 'armored horse'. From Pérez de Ribas' comments further on it would

pare. A horseman can cause great damage and destruction if the battle is waged on level ground, where he can charge and overtake the enemy. When the [battle] site is hilly and the horses are brought to a halt in an appropriate location, the Indian allies, like foot soldiers, do not hesitate to pursue the enemy into the monte and forests. They know that their backs are covered and that they can fall back under the cover of the Spanish harquebuses (the shots of which reach farther than the enemy's arrows). And when they are pressed down upon they retreat under the cover of harquebus fire, which is there for their defense. This is why in the company of only a few Spaniards Indian allies will take to the field against a large army of barbarians. From this one can clearly infer the importance of [66] these garrisons, even though they may not be manned by a large number of soldiers.

It is true, as experience has shown, that soldiers and armored horses are the principal strength and defense in these enterprises. Because they are loaded down with armor, the horses are ridden only during battle; [the rest of the time] they are led so that they do not become tired. The Spaniards are very clever at making the armor for these horses, fitting them with double layers of rawhide. The horse may be at risk, however, if the archer is brave and his aim is accurate, or if an Indian dares (as they often do) to dive under the horse's armor and cut its hamstring with a machete, or if many Indians together pull the horse down by the tail, or if the horse happens to fall on rocks or step into a hole. These are all risks that are taken in these wars, just like those taken in wars and battles elsewhere in the world. In such cases [when a horse falls] the soldier and the horse are both in very great danger because the Indian is very swift in his attack and the horse and horseman are too weighted down by weapons to get up. When one least expects it the Indian can land a blow to the head or helmet with a macana or a cudgel (which they also use in war) and one never rises again.

In spite of all that has been said, however, I am happy to have the chance to write about something marvelous that is worth making known to the world, for which I give infinite thanks to divine kindness. During the discovery of the many nations of this New World, which were brought forth from darkness and

imparted the light of the Gospel, the Catholic Spanish nation has been favored countless times with singular aid from heaven and from God's powerful arm, as He is the God of their armies. The truth is that without heavenly assistance it would have been impossible for such a small number of soldiers to pacify the large number of fierce and barbarous peoples who are being brought into the Church today. I have been an eyewitness to this truth many times over, and many such cases and their proofs will be found in this history. Taken together, they are signs that God approves the garrisons of soldiers that the Catholic monarchs establish for such justified ends and purposes. It is only fair to add here that divine providence must also be recognized for providing such valiant soldiers and captains. It seems as though these men were chosen to perform memorable deeds in defense of the Faith and evangelical preaching. God also wants, however, for us to help ourselves by human means for His works, just as He wished for His ancient people to go out onto the battlefield with their weapons and fight while He Himself led their armies by choosing their captains.

As I do not want this to go unaddressed, [I will reply here] to the other point that was mentioned at the beginning of this chapter concerning the expense that these garrisons incur to His Majesty's treasury. To make it understood what a good investment they are, even though a fortune may be necessary to maintain them, I respond that this is a glorious expenditure for the millions of converts and other innumerable souls who desire the Church's protection (a reason which in itself is sufficient to make this a glorious expense). Moreover, the funds are very well spent with respect to the material possessions and wealth that God has given His Majesty for this purpose. If the garrisons did not keep these nations at peace, the many mining camps in their territory or along their borders could not function, nor would new mines continue to be discovered daily [67] in their lands. When a nearby nation rebels, the Spaniards and the people who work the mines can expect the Indians to attack at dawn on any given morning, and on any given night they may watch their machinery go up in flames, see their livestock shot full of arrows and, finally, observe the sacking and razing of the king's vassals' ranches. This constitutes an irreparable loss of the Indies' riches, which God has given to them and to His Majesty. As testimony and proof of this, I offer the example of the revolt of the Tepehuan nation, whose pacification cost the king 800,000 pesos. This figure

---

appear that these horses were ridden *a la brida*, in the manner of medieval Spanish knights, rather than ridden *a la jineta*; that is, in the manner of light cavalry, which was introduced to Spain by the Moors and also became popular in the New World (see Denhardt 1975).

does not include the value of his vassals' ruined and lost properties, as I will discuss in the history of the Tepehuan mission [Book X], to which I refer the reader.

It is clear from all this that the expense of the garrisons is neither superfluous nor unnecessary. Rather, their maintenance represents a huge material profit, which is understood by those who concern themselves with material goods and the wealth of land. For the glorious Catholic kings of the Spanish monarchy, however, upon whose coat of arms and emblems God has engraved the Plus Ultra [Great Beyond] of the ancient world and to whose crown He has added a new one, no other reason is necessary to expend its treasures and kingdom than the promotion of Christ's kingdom throughout the entire world. This holy zeal, so noble

and royal, should be proclaimed and made known. Let all nations know that the invincible Catholic kings of Spain transfer this holy zeal along with the crown that is passed from father to son, as the unvanquished Charles V demonstrated in the letter that I previously cited. His son, the great monarch Philip II, who inherited this zeal, wrote to a governor of the Philippine Islands (as was related to me by a royal official) that he would send the treasures of his own patrimony if royal funds did not cover the cost of the conversion and promotion of our Holy Faith in the principality of those islands. This is worthy testimony to his holy and most devout zeal, for which he will find the most glorious reward in heaven.

CHAPTER XIV It is proven that the use of the garrisons does not contradict the apostolic mode of preaching the Gospel

The arguments that have been discussed up to this point in favor of garrisons have dealt not with evangelical preaching, but rather with the defense and support of property and Indian allies, the punishment of delinquents, and other temporal goals. Although it cannot be denied that these temporal ends are related to the spiritual benefits of evangelical preaching, they are not as closely related as what now follows. I will attempt to prove that the missions should not be stripped of their glorious, evangelic, and apostolic title because of the fact that they are conducted with the support of garrisons.

I will begin with the command that Christ, the Sovereign Master, gave His holy Apostles and first evangelical preachers, whom He sent to preach to all peoples: *Sicut oves in medio luporum*,[92] like lambs in the midst of wolves. Although He advised them in their preaching to be as tame as doves, He also added that

they should be as astute and prudent as serpents: *Estote prudentes sicut serpentes, et simplices sicut columbae*.[93] [68] This is not the place to discuss the nature of these symbols, but the Lord Himself explained this wisdom a bit later, saying, *Cum persequentur vos in civitatem ist fugite in aliam*.[94] If you are persecuted, take refuge in another city or town. The Apostle Saint Paul observed this rule when the enemies of the Gospel were looking to kill him and he lowered himself in a basket down the wall of the city of Damascus. He wrote to the Romans, asking them to pray to God *Ut liberer ab infidelibus*,[95] that he be saved from the snares and persecution of the infidels. Saint Paul was not trying to escape death, which he actually desired for Christ's sake; rather, he was motivated by what he later accomplished, saying, *Ut*

92. Matthew 10:16: "to be like sheep among wolves" (Knox 1956:9).

93. Matthew 10:16: "you must be wary, then, as serpents, and yet innocent as doves" (Knox 1956:9).

94. Matthew 10:23: "Only, if they persecute you in one city, take refuge in another" (Knox 1956:10).

95. Romans 15:31: "that I may be kept safe from those who reject the faith" (Knox 1956:162).

veniam ad vos in gaudio per voluntatem Dei.[96] He wished
to see himself preaching the Gospel in Rome, and he
did not intend to die and cut short his life's work, nor
the fruit that he could win by preaching to new nations
and peoples. He judged it to be for God's greater glory
and the welfare of souls to preserve his life rather than
let himself be killed. Assuming this to be true, I now
turn to our evangelical ministers in these missions and I
ask, if a priest is instructing a nation and they warn him
that they intend to burn him alive in his hut, fomenting rebellion and inciting the people (which is what
frequently happens in new missions), then in such cases
would it be of Christian prudence and in agreement
with Christ's instructions to allow oneself to be killed
when one could escape death and the disruption and
harm that usually follow flight, uprisings, and other irreparable damage? Once this danger has passed, he who
has attempted to free himself can then aid the same
peoples and others. Thus, it is clear that accepting death
would not be in agreement with the order that Christ
gave His Apostles (who were the model for preaching
the Gospel), for the Divine Master told them that if they
were persecuted they should flee to another city. This
is particularly true if the reason for withdrawing and
looking for a garrison is not simply to escape death, but
rather to insure that evangelical preaching continues
and indeed is intensified once the furor and persecution
have subsided, which at times happens quickly.

To continue, if in accordance with Christ's mandate to His Apostles our evangelical missionaries were
to flee persecution, to what city would they turn for
refuge in such a distant and isolated land if not to the
fort of Spanish soldiers? There are no other Spanish
settlements, and even if there were, on such occasions
they still need the protection and safety of the garrison.
Furthermore, our missionaries do not ask the soldiers
for help except on rare occasions, during emergencies,
when the soldiers accompany the priests to the pueblos
where they reside and work. The priests ordinarily
travel alone in their districts, without an escort. Many
priests are thirty, forty, and even eighty leagues from
the garrisons; they may be eaten before the captain and
the Spanish soldiers learn of their deaths. On those occasions when they need an escort it is only for a few days,
and even then they are accompanied by only four to six
soldiers, which is enough to control a few troublemak-

ers. Even the caciques who govern the pueblos and their
own people ask the captain for soldiers and protection.

The benefit of a garrison is confirmed by Saint Luke
in the Acts of the Apostles, which if you look at them
carefully, are the history of the holy Apostles' missions.
[69] When the Apostle Saint Paul preached the Gospel in Jerusalem, the priests and the Pharisees raised
such a ruckus and became so furious that they grabbed
the holy Apostle and were about to kill him. When the
tribune[97] of the Roman garrison saw the danger of this
disturbance, the Holy Book says, *Timens Tribunus ne dis-
cerperetur Paulus ab ipsis iussit milites rapere eum de medio
eorum, ac deducere eum in castra.*[98] Nothing could be more
relevant to our present discussion than what the tribune did on this occasion. Seeing the risk to Paul's life
and the threat of an uprising, he ordered his soldiers to
rescue Saint Paul from the clutches of those furious persons who wanted to tear him to bits, *Ne discerepetur.*[99] He
then sheltered him inside the garrison: *Deducere eum in
castra.*[100] Saint Paul was not surprised by this favor or by
the support of the tribune and his soldiers. When one of
the holy Apostle's nephews warned him that four hundred Jews had hatched a new plot to treacherously take
the holy Apostle's life,[101] the Apostle arranged through
a centurion for his nephew to meet with the tribune.
His nephew informed the tribune of the situation and
requested his protection. After listening, the tribune assembled two hundred foot soldiers and seventy horses
ut Paulum salvum perducerent ad feolicem Praesidem,[102] to
save Saint Paul and place him under the protection of
the governor, who was in Caesarea. It is clear that evangelical preaching was not contradicted when the holy
Apostle to the People occasionally made use of a garrison of soldiers. He felt that it would be to the greater
service of God to save his life so that he could preach
the Gospel elsewhere, as Christ Our Lord demonstrated
on this occasion and as the Holy Scripture states.

---

97. A Roman official who was charged with protecting the rights of
plebeians before patrician magistrates.

98. *Margin Note*: Act. cap. 13. Acts 23:10: "and the captain, who was
afraid that they would tear Paul in pieces, ordered his troops to come
down and rescue Paul from their midst, and bring him safe to the soldiers' quarters" (Knox 1956:141).

99. Acts 23:10: "tear [Paul] in pieces" (ibid).

100. Acts 23:10: "bring him . . . to the soldiers' quarters."

101. Nowhere in this episode recounted in Acts 23 of the Vulgate
is such a high figure given for the number of Jews involved in the
conspiracy against Paul. In Acts 23:21, Paul's nephew tells the Roman
tribune, "Some of them will be lying in ambush for him, more than
forty in number."

102. Acts 23:24: "so that they can mount Paul and take him safely
to the governor, Felix" (Knox 1956:141).

96. Romans 15:32: "so that I may reach you, God willing, glad at
heart, and make holiday with you" (Knox 1956:162).

All of the aforementioned does not advocate preaching the Gospel by force of arms, nor is it at odds with the apostolic mode of preaching. To this one can add that the Apostles and apostolic preachers often took some faithful with them when they went to preach among the peoples, as is deduced from the Acts of the Apostles and ecclesiastical histories.

I am aware of what can be argued concerning the difference between a company of soldiers and those who accompanied the Apostles and apostolic men. The soldiers' freedom, pride, and behavior usually disturb these new peoples, and their arrogance and excesses do more harm than good. In response, it cannot be denied that the customs of the military cause disturbances and damage. When such problems are weighed against the benefits of the garrisons that have been discussed, however, the latter clearly outweigh all these shortcomings. I will prove this point with examples drawn from experience. Because they pertain to our history, they grant me the freedom to expound on this matter at greater length.

When a priest enters one of these missions that are totally isolated from the world, he does so to preach the one Faith, some of its mysteries, and new laws that have never been heard or thought of by these nations—nations which were totally ignorant of the fact that there were other people in the world who observe these laws. The [priest] preaches to them about religious acts that require great veneration and reverence and are observed and adored by the rich and powerful civilized nations of the world. The preachers of the Gospel should make use of all of these credulous arguments that link the Faith and evangelical preaching, for the Apostle of the People, Saint Paul, made use of these [arguments] himself. [70] That is why I often invoke his authority. At the beginning of his letter to the Romans, he gives thanks to God and the people of Rome, which was the center of the world, because due to their belief and illustrious example of the Christian religion, this same religion had now been received and venerated by the entire world. His words are these: *Gratias ago Deo meo per Iesum Christum, pro omnibus vobis, quia fides vestra annunciatur in universo mundo.*[103] The rich, the wise, and the powerful of the world celebrate the Christianity of the Romans. In this way he made them understand that these people valued the Faith, which was an argu-

ment for other nations to receive it and to venerate and revere its mysteries. The holy Apostle gives thanks to God and the Romans for all of this.

Let us now turn to our barbarous nations, which were entombed in the deep darkness of ignorance not only of divine matters, but also of political and human affairs. They were hidden in the corners of the rock-strewn hills of the earth and did not know that there were republics in the world, or even in Nueva España, nor were they aware of organized religious practices. As we stated previously, because of the continuous wars that all these nations waged with their neighbors, they had no dealings or knowledge of distant nations. They sometimes think that the priest who comes to preach to them is a poor man who is seeking maize for food. Their limited knowledge even leads them to think that the evangelical minister is more ignorant than they are, particularly when he does not yet speak their language. The term or word that they use in their language to refer to him means that he is an ignorant or stupid person. This being the case, who can doubt that when these people saw Spaniards, whom they consider courageous (which is the only thing they value), attending church, kneeling and adoring the Holy Sacrament, revering the priests who say Mass, kneeling in front of them to confess their sins, receiving the consecrated Host with the greatest reverence, and adoring holy images, who would doubt that that which they see with their own eyes frequently makes a greater impression on these barbarians than the words that they or their ancestors had never even heard, thought, or knew were spoken in the world?

This, then, is how the garrisons directly aid in the preaching of the Faith. Because this is one of His works, God has most certainly taken care to provide many good and pious Christian soldiers for these missions, although there have been some who were not. And I can state that I often saw soldiers from the garrison in Sinaloa who were very good examples and who furthered these peoples' esteem for the Christian religion. I saw in particular the brave and pious Captain Diego Martínez de Hurdaide (whose zeal for the salvation of souls will be described later in great detail) as he practiced these religious exercises, often kneeling in plain sight of the Indians to confess at the priest's feet. He would then receive Holy Communion with the greatest reverence, setting an example that his soldiers followed. The brave Cortés, conqueror of the New World, provided the same example to everyone when the friars of the Holy Order of Saint Francis reached Nueva España. In front of the entire New World, he knelt to welcome

---

103. Romans 1:8: "And first I offer thanks to my God through Jesus Christ for all of you, you whose faith is so renowned throughout the world" (Knox 1956:148).

them with singular reverence. All these are very religious and devout acts and they validate, enhance, and exalt Christ's Holy Faith, thereby allowing it to be received with veneration.

With this, it can certainly be seen how garrisons [71] greatly assist in the preaching of the Gospel, especially where there are no other Spaniards. Garrisons are not only a convenient, but also at times a necessary means.

Now, the final proof of all that has been said: to refuse to make use of those means that God's providence ordinarily offers and makes available to realize some good end is the same as asking for extraordinary miracles and tempting God. A miracle is unusual; it goes beyond the ordinary. However, God wants us to use the means that His ordinary and gentle providence has placed at our disposal (even in the matters we are discussing), just as those with great and holy zeal for preaching the Gospel find a ship to come to the Indies, with a pilot and provisions. If they were to throw themselves into the water in order to walk upon it, who could doubt that it would be an extraordinary pretension, asking for a miracle and tempting God? Didn't the holy Apostles, who performed extraordinary miracles, use boats to preach the Gospel? And didn't the very Son of God Himself sail at times? On one occasion, in order to demonstrate His divine command over the waters, this sovereign and supreme God did walk upon them. Saint Peter also dared to do this because he was overcome by his desire to reach his beloved Master, but he first asked permission. And not only did he ask permission, but he also requested that the Lord explicitly command him to walk on the water, saying, *Domine, iube me venire ad te super aquas.*[104] He wanted Christ to explicitly command him to proceed before he would dare to use a means as extraordinary as a miracle. He did not dare to step onto the water until he heard the word from the mouth of the Lord, *"Veni."*[105] Moreover, even though this same holy Apostle had superb faith, a storm suddenly blew up and his faith began to waiver and he began to sink. Not wanting to use a miracle to save Peter, Our Lord used a common and ordinary means of saving this sinking man. He extended His divine hand to sustain him and remove him from that danger, as the Gospel says, *Continuo Jesus extendens manum apprehendit eum.*[106] The omnipotent Lord could very well have commanded the swollen waves to sustain him, but He no longer wished to use this miraculous means, preferring instead a common and ordinary one. Therefore, the Lord sustained Saint Peter with His hand, thereby teaching us that when we have human means at hand, we should not look for extraordinary and miraculous ones, which God dispenses when and as it pleases Him.

I will close with these instructions and memorable words from Pope Nicholas, which confirm all that was stated above. He decreed that when it is necessary to take up arms for just defense, then this should be done, even though it may be during Lent; also, we should not seek miracles for a just defense: *Ne videlicet videatur homo tentare, si habet, quod faciat, et suae ac aliorum saluti consulere non procurat, et sanctae Religionis detrimenta non praecavet.*[107] It seems that these memorable words were written specifically for our case, which if not identical, is very similar. I will not pause here to ponder this, for I feel that what I have said is sufficient to prove and proclaim [the following]: First, in no way are the garrisons established to introduce the Faith through violence, nor were they ever used for that purpose in our missions. Rather, they were used for the benefits described herein. Second, we deduce that in the conversion of barbarous peoples said garrisons neither contradict evangelical preaching and its endeavors, nor are those who are employed therein undeserving of the title of apostolic and evangelical preachers. [72] Indeed, in these endeavors our missionary priests are exposed to countless hardships, difficulties, and mortal dangers for preaching the Faith to these peoples. As a result of this preaching to date eleven have shed their blood in Nueva España, as have many others in other parts of the West as well as the East Indies.[108]

---

104. *Margin Note*: Matt. c. 14. Matthew 14:28: " 'Lord, . . . bid me come to thee over the water' " (Knox 1956:15).

105. Matthew 14:29: " 'Come' " (Knox 1956:15).

106. Matthew 14:31: "And Jesus at once stretched out his hand and caught hold of him" (Knox 1956:15).

107. *Margin Note*: C. si nulla 23 q 8. The referent here is a papal bull apparently issued by Pope Nicholas V (1447–55). "Lest a human not see clearly how to attempt what he should do, if he has [it], he takes care to take counsel for the salvation of himself and others, guarding against losses of the Holy religion."

108. The West Indies being the New World and the East Indies referring to India, China, Japan, and Southeast Asia.

CHAPTER XV The positive results of the garrison that was established in the Province of Sinaloa

In Chapter XIII, I began to discuss the group of soldiers that was dispatched to Sinaloa under orders from the viceroy. I will now return to that topic, providing pragmatic proofs of the arguments that were previously set forth. As soon as the garrison reached [Sinaloa], the troops were dispatched for the first time to the Guasave, where some bellicose and rebellious Indians were plotting to kill the two priests who had come to instruct them. Because there are faithful even among infidels, some of them warned the captain of the plot, and he immediately dispatched fifteen soldiers to arrest the leaders. The Spaniards were met by an Indian principal bearing a lance, and even though he was accompanied by two hundred warriors, the Spaniards' tactics were so clever that they were able to capture the rebel leader. They tied this Indian up, pardoned his followers, and then brought him back to the Villa de San Felipe. There he was punished, and the crime they had plotted was thus prevented.

Nevertheless, there were still some Guasave who remained restless and tried to convince the rest of the people to flee to the monte, after first setting fire to their wooden churches. But God willed that after a few days these same Indians grew tired of the difficult life they were experiencing away from their homes and lands (because they were farmers), and after further consideration and by the grace of God, who was working in them, they returned to their homes. Some even began to visit and enter the Villa de San Felipe,[109] and when they saw the example set by the other Christians they expressed a willingness to remain settled in their pueblos. To insure that this happened, the lieutenant-captain visited them in the company of Father Hernando de Villafañe (who ministered to that nation for many years). A great Christian community was established there, one of the most splendid in the province in terms of quality and numbers.

The Guasave are the best and most docile of all the nations of Sinaloa; civilized life has been very well established among them. These people have always pro-

vided the Spaniards of the Villa de San Felipe with the best and most regular service.[110] Lastly, since the time this nation accepted missionization, they have helped whenever war parties have been needed, showing more loyalty [than other groups].

And so the lieutenant-captain and the priest went to visit this nation. They found the pueblo [of Guasave] nearly deserted, so they decided to proceed to another called Ure. More than four hundred armed Indians came out to meet them, and although not intent on war, they were uncertain about whether the Spaniards had come in peace. When the priest assured them that they had, they laid down their arms and requested [religious] instruction. The priest assured them that they would attain this and indicated appropriate sites for their churches. This made the Indians very happy and they put their good intentions into action. Five churches were erected in the five pueblos [73] in which the Guasave settled, and the number of people was great, with some two thousand residents. Once this was done the priest returned alone and was warmly received. Indian parents joyfully brought 240 infants to be baptized, and the priest offered them to God with even greater joy, for they were the first fruits of the great harvest that was being promised and gathered in that nation.

With the help of alms from Spaniards at the mining camps at Topia and San Andrés the priests ordered the construction of another church in the Villa de San Felipe that was more secure than their [original] straw church. This was done to further strengthen religious instruction and Christianity and to provide greater safety for the people who had congregated at the villa, including the Mexica and Tarascan Indians and other faithful who had settled there at the time of previous disturbances.[111] Although this new church was made of adobes, it turned out to be very large and strong. In case of enemy attacks and assaults it could serve as a

---

109. By the end of 1596 all but a handful of the Guasave had returned to their pueblos.

110. Pérez de Ribas is presumably referring to Indian compliance with labor requests from Spanish encomenderos.

111. Note that it was Spanish practice to encourage acculturated Nahua-speaking and Tarascan Indians from central Mexico to settle in frontier communities, where they served as "examples" for local Indians and acted as interpreters for both priests and lay Spaniards.

fortress and refuge for all the people of the villa. This was a much-needed project that subsequently proved to be of great importance.

There were many spiritual fruits harvested at this time [1596–98] among the Indians of the Villa de San Felipe and the pueblos closest to it that were receiving instruction. This encouraged the priests to continue in their endeavors without being dismayed by the obstacles and dangers surrounding them. The example of the more veteran and most devout Christians was taking root among the new Christians, so during the holy Lenten season they attended church with greater frequency. To make the stations of the Cross, they erected Crosses in the most appropriate sites, for there were not many churches or shrines to visit. On the designated day they conducted processions to each station, singing hymns and doing penance by scourging themselves and drawing blood. When there was no public scourging many flogged themselves in church while singing the *Miserere*.[112] In addition to these exercises conducted by true Christians, there were many who devoutly heard Mass each day. This was admirable given that they previously cared only for their bows and arrows and for hunting in the monte. Both young and old were especially fervent in making their confessions, and even the young became very competent in terms of the integrity of their confession,[113] the order of its presentation, and its circumstances. The following case is one among many examples.

A priest heard the confession of a very young boy, and afterwards, in order to explore the child's concept of that sacrament, he asked who the boy thought could cure and heal his soul of those ills. The child responded that it could be no one other than God and, through His word, the priest. What a remarkable answer for one who was so young and new in the Faith! In this and other similar cases it is amazing to see what God secretly works in souls through His divine grace, which is more than what we achieve with our entradas.

The effects of the divine word were felt not only among the Christians near the Villa de San Felipe, but also among those at a distance, where priests had preached in passing. An Indian from the mountains got sick and subsequently became dangerously ill. Because

there was no priest [available] to hear his confession, he set out on the road, fearful of dying without Confession, although he might well have feared dying along the way, for it was a long journey. Our Lord favored his good intentions not only by giving him the strength to endure and confess, but also by granting both his soul and his body complete health.

With regard to the vice of drunkenness, which was so deeply rooted in these people at the beginning of their conversion, there continues to be progress in amending this problem, as the following case shows. In a nearby pueblo an old Indian made wine from honey and invited some friends to celebrate. [74] Of course, someone notified the priest of what was going on, and he effectively reprehended this deed in church, where all the people had assembled. When the nine or ten men who had been drinking heard the sermon they got down on their knees before the entire pueblo and willingly confessed their guilt and then publicly scourged themselves as penance. It happened that one of the guilty individuals was absent. An old man who noticed this called him and obliged him to kneel down and do as the rest of his companions had done. Who would expect this from a people who were so warlike, indomitable, and fierce?

Let us [now] add examples of other virtues, including the notable virtue of chastity displayed by a married Christian woman. An Indian who was a stranger to the region found her out alone in the monte (this must have led him to dare to do something that he would not do in his own territory). He threatened to kill her if she didn't satisfy his unbridled appetite. In this moment of crisis the woman bravely resisted, giving as a reason that she was a Christian whose law forbade this sin against divine law, which she defended at the risk of her own life. But she did not escape easily from that encounter, as she was badly beaten and injured. Moreover, the baby she had with her was badly wounded when she risked their lives in defense of her virtue.

Another woman demonstrated no less bravery during a similar incident. When an Indian arrived unexpectedly at her house to declare his rude lust, she turned on her aggressor with such spirit and determination that she was able to get a hold of the bow and arrow he was carrying. She smashed the arrows to bits and then beat him so hard with the bow that it broke. She repeated over and over, "Don't you know that I am a Christian and that I hear the word of God that the priests preach to us?" With that she drove him off in a state of confusion and was fortunately out of danger. These are the excellent effects of divine grace, which empowers

---

112. Psalm 50 in the Vulgate. Historically this psalm has been considered the ultimate psalm of penitence; often it was sung by religious while mortifying themselves (Attwater 1949:324).

113. The Jesuits and other priests were encouraged by the Council of Trent to make certain that confession was integral, i.e., that the penitent confessed all sins according to kind and number (Polzer 1976:43).

weak women who were used to living freely according to their instincts. It is [also] a sign of how truly these people, although barbarians, embrace Christ's Faith.

This [then is what] happened in the pueblos near the villa at the beginning [of their conversion]. As we will see later these are the same pueblos that prospered and where the number of Christians increased greatly, although they were not free of the difficulties and enemy disturbances that have always been present wherever there is evangelical preaching.

CHAPTER XVI The disturbances that Nacabeba and his accomplices caused among the Christians, the efforts made to capture them, and their unfortunate end

We have not [yet] finished relating the good results and fruits produced by the garrison of soldiers that was assigned to the Villa de San Felipe, as will be seen more clearly in what follows. As we just mentioned, Christ's law and catechism were taking root in the souls of the Christians, producing more fruit each day in the peaceful pueblos that were close to the Villa de San Felipe. Nevertheless, the devil tried to disturb and unsettle this peace through the Indian Nacabeba and his consorts and outlaw allies, who had murdered Father Gonzalo de Tapia. After this perverse Indian committed this crime he withdrew with his band to a very harsh, densely wooded area [along the upper Río Sinaloa]. Even there, however, he could not feel safe from Spaniards [75] nor from faithful Indians, who were greatly upset by the priest's death. Nacabeba did not dare to sleep at night with his companions in the monte, where the Spaniards might happen to find them. Instead, he chose a safer place, deeper in the brambles, where he could escape if necessary. Nacabeba fulfilled that divine proverb that says of the infidel, *Sequitur eum ignominia, & opprobrium*,[114] and another that says, *Fugit impius nemine persequente*.[115] The infidel flees but he does not feel safe; even when no one is searching for him, he is pursued by his own wickedness.

The captain did not hesitate to take steps to get his hands on Nacabeba not only to punish him for the grave crime he had committed, but also because Nacabeba's companions had relatives among those who were peaceful, and the latter were becoming agitated. Once the captain received news of the place to which Nacabeba had retreated, he sent a well-equipped group of Spaniards and Indians to apprehend him.[116] This barbarian had not dared to wait for them, so the Spaniards and Indians captured some women. Among them was Nacabeba's wife. Before anyone could stop him an Indian cut her throat, and thus she could not be taken alive. She was the one who had donned the priest's chasuble and danced during their mitotes and drunken revels, and was therefore the first to pay for her crime. All the others who had not been accomplices in the offense were promised freedom.

Hiding among them was an Indian apostate who had been one of the chief aggressors in Father Tapia's death. This Indian had been very well treated by the priest, whom he ordinarily accompanied. Indians from his own pueblo recognized him and told the captain, who captured him and pressured him to reveal where Nacabeba and the rest of the renegades had withdrawn. The first day he stubbornly refused to cooperate, but when he saw that they were going to apply force he said he knew where [the fugitives] were and would turn them over to the captain. The captain believed the man, and taking

114. *Margin Note*: Proverb. 18. Proverbs 18:3: "shame and reproach go with him" (Knox 1956:550).

115. Proverbs 28:1: "Bad conscience takes to its heels, with none in pursuit" (Knox 1956:558).

116. The events of this and the succeeding chapter occurred in 1599.

him along as a guide, he set out one evening with twelve soldiers. They were led to a hill with a deep precipice, where the guide tried to throw himself over the cliff. The soldiers acted quickly and managed to deter this desperate attempt, but later as they were returning with him to camp, he saw a poisonous herb, which he grabbed and ate. He fell asleep, and it was impossible to bring him back to consciousness. He finally died twenty-four hours later, having punished himself with a well-deserved death for the crime he had committed, in spite of the fact that the captain had promised him his freedom if he would expose the delinquents.

When Nacabeba saw from these events that he was not safe in the monte he decided to take refuge with his remaining people among the bellicose Zuaque nation, who boasted of being killers of Spaniards. They admitted him to their pueblos and were so haughty and insolent that their boldness went so far as to once again assault the Villa de San Felipe. They attempted to set fire to the houses of the Spaniards and their Indian friends. However, when they realized they could not attack the houses or the residents, who were very vigilant, they attacked horses and pack animals, taking some of them for their own use and wounding others with arrows. They also committed other abuses and insolent acts, even on Christmas Eve {1599}. Thus, it can be clearly seen how well employed and necessary the garrisons are, as was previously noted.

In the end {76} {with a word} from the mouth of Christ, Judge of the Living and the Dead, the killer is immediately sentenced to death, no matter where he is: *Omnes enim qui acceperint gladium, gladio peribunt*.[117] This sentence was executed in the following manner. Some Indian allies were hunting and found two of the killers. One was Nacabeba's son and the other was said to have dealt the second blow to the blessed Father Tapia. The allies attacked them with such fury that they cut off their heads, which they then presented to the captain. He was very pleased that the band of outlaws who had disturbed the province was diminishing and being eliminated.

Only Nacabeba, the principal aggressor and evildoer, remained. The captain's sole concern was to capture him and do away with this very bad seed, but he did not dare enter Zuaque territory to look for him, for the Zuaque were very bellicose and had many warriors. Moreover, the forces at the garrison did not seem suffi-

cient at that time to risk {such an operation}. But then God took it into His own hands to punish this very harmful Indian. It happened that one of Nacabeba's relatives who was hiding among the Zuaque happened to find a Tehueco Indian along the road. The Tehueco are neighbors and mortal enemies of the Zuaque nation, and this relative of Nacabeba's killed this Tehueco Indian and cut off his head, which he then brought to the captain to sell and gain favor, claiming that it was Nacabeba's. The Tehueco found out what had happened, that the dead Indian was not Nacabeba but rather an Indian from their own nation, and they were moved by revenge. This is very common among these nations, for they do not desist until they have cut off one enemy head to avenge each head that has been taken.

A very important and courageous Tehueco Indian named Lanzarote (who must have taken this name when the Spaniards lived in the original Villa de Carapoa) summoned as many people as he could to attack the Zuaque to avenge the death of his fellow Tehueco, as well as to capture Nacabeba. He struck one morning when the Zuaque were unprepared, at a time when one of their preachers was on top of an *enramada*[118] fervently exhorting the outlaws to continue in their victorious campaign against the Spaniards because they had so many Christian heads in their possession.

Lanzarote shot an arrow so accurately that it brought the preacher to the ground, and he then rushed in to cut off his head. The preacher implored him with many pleas and prayers to spare his life, and although life is of little value to these people, Lanzarote finally heeded his request. He did not crack open his skull, which they do with great ease and dexterity, twisting the head off and then splitting and separating the skull from the brain. If they do not have a knife to cut the meat, they do so with their thumbnail, which they grow long. But Lanzarote did not take this Indian's life; instead, he held him down on the ground and stuffed handfuls of dirt into his mouth, telling him, "Now I'll see if you are able to preach against Spaniards and Christians, as you so greatly boast!" At that moment a great number of enemy Zuaque charged Lanzarote, wounding him and forcing him to retreat, leaving behind the prisoner he had so valiantly captured.

Although this may seem to be a digression, the actions of this Tehueco Indian were remarkable and must be recorded. As time went by he showed himself to be a

---

117. *Margin Note*: Mat. 26. Matthew 26:52: "all who take up the sword will perish by the sword" (Knox 1956:29).

118. An enramada was a ramada enclosed on three sides with walls of woven mats or brush, which at times were plastered with mud.

good friend to the Spaniards and a great means to converting his nation. He and his wife and children were baptized before religious instruction reached his river, which is eighteen leagues from the Villa de San Felipe. It was singular and edifying how divine grace enabled him to overcome the hurdles to receiving the Faith and Holy Baptism, for he greatly regretted having to separate from his five wives. When he was with Spaniards and a gentile Indian would pass by [77] whom he knew to have but one wife, he would say, "This one will be a good Christian." To become one himself, he continued cooperating with grace and put aside some of his concubines. If one of the women happened to pass by, he would say to the Spaniards so that they would understand that he was preparing for Baptism, "She used to be my wife, but I have dismissed her because I want to be a Christian." He had a young son, and when the child and his mother happened to pass by, Lanzarote told the Spaniards, "This child is the possession that I most love. I dearly wish for him to become a Christian. If I should die in war, I hereby give him to you so that when he is older you will make him a Christian, even if it is against the will of his mother and his relatives." God's grace eventually prevailed over nature in this Indian, and he chose one wife from among the five women. After leaving the others (it was a heroic deed for him to separate himself from what was so ingrained in him and had become one flesh and blood with his own) he was taught the catechism and baptized with his wife and son. This occurred long before religious instruction came to his nation; therefore, he was baptized on the condition that he and his wife and child come at certain times of the year to the Christian pueblos near

the villa to hear the preaching of the catechism and to fulfill the obligation of making confession during Lent. He did everything he was told, and I saw him several times when he came from his pueblos to visit us. These visits continued until a mission was established in his nation, and then he was of great assistance in securing the Baptism of the entire [Tehueco] nation.

Returning to our history, the captain and the Spaniards continued in their efforts to capture Nacabeba and to do away with this individual who was such an obstacle to the progress of the Faith and such a scandal to the province. God willed that the Tehueco should finally capture him, for following the aforementioned skirmish when the Indian Lanzarote failed to capture Nacabeba, he and his companions came and walked right through the Tehueco's front door. Apparently they were not safe among the Zuaque, against whom the Tehueco had been launching cruel dawn attacks. The Spaniards had also been making great overtures to the Zuaque to turn Nacabeba and his accomplices over to them, offering clothing and other rewards to anyone who would bring them their heads in the event that they could not be captured alive. Nacabeba decided, therefore, to take refuge among the Tehueco, placing himself and the few people he had left in their hands. The Tehueco admitted him on the barbarous condition that they could do as they pleased [119] with the wives and daughters they brought with them. This unfortunate Indian agreed to this because it was now apparent that there was nowhere else to turn. The Tehueco admitted him on this condition, which was the means by which he finally came to pay for his crimes.

119. *Hazer francas.*

CHAPTER XVII Nacabeba falls into the hands of the Spaniards and is brought to justice

Because Nacabeba had acted traitorously in killing the blessed Father Tapia, God wanted him to pay for his sin with a similar punishment. Although the Tehueco offered him protection under the infamous condition that they be able to do as they pleased with the women they brought along with them,[120] they did not keep their word. Once they had Nacabeba they tied him to a stake so that he could not run away. With him under guard they sent word to the Spaniards in the Villa de San Felipe, saying that they would turn him over to them if they would come for him. The captain, who was Lieutenant General Alonso Díaz, was absent when this offer reached the villa,[121] but he had left Diego Martínez de Hurdaide in his place as head of the garrison.[122] [78] As we shall see, Hurdaide was a brave man. He ordered that twelve armored horses and an equal number of soldiers be readied, and without waiting for Indian allies he departed as quickly as possible for one of the Tehueco pueblos. As he approached the pueblo the cacique Lanzarote came out to meet him. Seeing so few soldiers, who previously would not have dared to enter his lands in such small numbers due to the fact that there were more than one thousand Indian warriors who were still gentiles, he asked the leader, "Is that all the men you have brought with you?" This brave leader knew how important it was not to allow these Indians to see any cowardice, and he was also suspicious that the Tehueco had simply plotted to lure him out onto the open field in their own lands so they could declare war. With daring bravery, therefore, he responded to Lanzarote, "Indian dog, if you have called me under false pretenses with the story that you want to turn over Nacabeba, and your intention is actually to fight and kill Spaniards, then call all your people and I will fight them all by myself, even without the help of the soldiers I have brought with me." Seeing that the commander was upset, the Indian calmed him, saying, "Do not become angry. I really do want to turn Naca-

beba over to you." Then, pointing to a certain house in the pueblo, he said, "He is in there, tied up. Come and see for yourself and you can take him with you." The commander and some of the soldiers dismounted, while the others remained on horseback [to respond] to whatever might happen among such untrustworthy people. The commander came within sight of Nacabeba, who upon seeing the Spaniards, exclaimed to the Indians who were present, "Alas, Tehueco, did I not ask you to kill me rather than turn me over to the Spaniards?" The Spaniards found him ravished by hunger, for he had not eaten in three days. The commander calmed him and ordered that he be untied from the stake and given something to eat. The Spaniards then bound him once again and returned to the Villa de San Felipe. They also took along one of Nacabeba's daughters and some other women who had accompanied Nacabeba and were being held by the Tehueco. When they reached the villa, a trial was held and Nacabeba and one of his nephews, who had been an accomplice in his crimes, were sentenced to be hanged and quartered. His daughter was condemned to perpetual servitude and was exiled from the province to Mexico City. When the priests heard about the sentencing they went to help the two who had been condemned to death to prepare them for that difficult moment. Because he had never wanted to become a member of the Church and had not been instructed in the ways of our Holy Faith, they taught Nacabeba the catechism in order to baptize him. Now, in that difficult moment, he finally began to listen and willingly received the priests' word. His nephew, who had been baptized, made his confession, and when the one at the foot of the gallows had been baptized and the other had completed making his confession, they both died with great repentance for their sins. Without a doubt the blood of Father Tapia, which they had shed, worked to the benefit of his enemies, as did his pleas and merits in heaven. Thus, the commandment that Christ Our Lord left with us on earth is also observed in heaven.[123] The two delinquents died giving great signs of their salvation, and the Province of Sinaloa was freed from the scandal that had plagued it and had hindered the extension of the Holy Gospel.

120. *Que les hiziessen francas las mugeres que consigo traían.*

121. Pérez de Ribas appears to be in error, as Díaz left Sinaloa for other duties in 1596 at the behest of the governor. Pérez de Cebreros succeeded him as captain and was promptly replaced by Diego de Quirós, who was in office in 1599 (Dunne 1940:48).

122. Hurdaide came to Sinaloa with Díaz in 1596 as Díaz's first lieutenant and commander of the troops.

123. The reference here is to Matthew 5:44.

CHAPTER XVIII Religious instruction is begun in two gentile pueblos; several cases of edification among those who were baptized

The Lord, who is Master of the Vineyard, not only cares for the labors of His Church, [79] cleaning and uprooting the weeds that impede progress, but also sees to the planting of new vines so that the desired fruit can multiply. Once that weed, the restless Indian, had been pulled up, God moved other gentile pueblos to ask for missionaries to preach the catechism that the Christians enjoyed. These people were from the foothills of the mountains and what they called the 'valley of the crow', or Cacalotlán, fourteen leagues from the Villa de San Felipe. After these mountain people had built their churches, which were made out of brush and straw, they came to petition Father Martín Pérez, who was the [local Jesuit] superior. He had once visited these pueblos in passing, [but had been unable to stay] due to time restrictions, so he now began their catechism in earnest. This took a good hold among them because of their better nature, which is not as fierce as that of some others. Father Martín Pérez writes about these peoples' conversion:[124]

I received (he says) word of some Indians who lived in the mountains in caves and on the mountain summits and who cared not at all about the other life. Afterwards, I sent some well-meaning Christian Indians of their nation to call on them, and thirty-eight adults came to see me with nineteen of their children, who were like small mountain deer in the way that they ran and hid so as not to look at me. I spoke to them with kindness, telling them that they should take advantage of the opportunity they now had so readily available to see to the salvation of their own souls and those of their children. After hearing this speech they immediately decided to remain in the pueblo and be baptized. The infants were the first to receive this Holy Sacrament, and on the day of the Baptisms, a few long-time Christians held a great feast and celebration, giving the newly baptized food to eat. To make the celebration even greater, that same day some of the adults were married in *facie Ecclesiae*.[125] A few days later thirty more Indians came down from the mountains, and once they had been instructed I baptized them. Each day more people come down from the mountains, moved by the good example and the improvements they see in the bodies and souls of their neighbors. Those who have been Christians

for the greatest length of time are very good about coming to confession, from which all seem to benefit. There are some women who, pursued and attacked by the enemies of their chastity, are very strong, regardless of the valuable and prestigious presents they are offered or the threats made against them. There was one woman who, remembering what she had heard in the sermons, fled the bad company of a man who had deceived her. She traveled thirty leagues by herself to the pueblo where I was and threw herself down on her knees. Then with great repentance she asked me amidst many tears to give her the penance and punishment that her grave sins merited.

I end here my quotation of Father Pérez's letter. These two pueblos [Cahuemeto and Chicorato], which [today] have some three to four hundred residents, have always persevered as very faithful Christians. They have been and are to this day a fine example of Christian customs and practices.

With this increase in churches, at this time (which was around 1600) the number of baptized persons in the Province of Sinaloa reached more than seven thousand souls. Of these a good number of infants as well as adults went to heaven with baptismal grace. Those who remained fervently followed Christian practice, and with their example others began asking once again for Holy Baptism. There were consoling cases of which Father Martín Pérez himself writes in another letter, which I will refer to here, because one sees in them how divine predestination saves some [80] of these poor people's souls. And so he writes,

They came quickly to call me concerning an old faithless woman who was close to death. I went to her, and as long as I have been in this land I have never seen such a miserable and ulcerated body, nor have I seen such a willingness and desire to receive Baptism, nor a greater liveliness in understanding and giving an account of the matters of our Holy Faith. I baptized her, and she died immediately, leaving me with a special consolation to see the soul of that blessed old woman win heaven in an instant. It is noteworthy that she had been the most adverse and negative of all the people in her pueblo with respect to matters of our Holy Faith, so much so that it had never been possible to get her to go to church. But who can oppose the superiority of predestination?

Father Pérez also adds the following case:

---

124. This letter was written in 1611 but relates events that happened some ten years earlier, around 1600.

125. "According to the Church."

They came to tell me that a faithless sick Indian, who was in his field, was calling for me, saying that he wanted to be baptized. I went and found him quite exhausted but noticeably happy to see me. I taught him the catechism, but even though he completely understood the matters of the Faith, I decided to wait another day before baptizing him because the illness was not getting any worse and I wanted to better prepare him for receiving that sacrament. The following morning I sent [some people with] a horse to bring him to the church. They were to notify me if he was not up to making the trip, in which I case I would go to him. However, they encountered him along the way, in high spirits, with staff in hand, being helped along by his wife. When he reached me I baptized him, fulfilling his fervent desire, and he received Holy Baptism with great joy and devotion, both his and my own. Our Lord rewarded him with double favors for the task he had undertaken, for by means of this celestial and holy bath he achieved the total health of his body as well as life for his soul. This Indian feels so grateful that he regularly travels one and a half leagues to see me, and in gratitude for having been allowed to join the congregation of Christians he always brings whatever his poverty allows, which is usually a watermelon or a squash.

I will omit other similar examples, adding instead one that pertains to a different matter which served to further confirm the faith of these new Christians. At this time, the Spaniards as well as the Indians were seriously affected by a severe drought that caused their fields to dry up. The Indians informed the priest who was administering religious instruction, and he gave a sermon in which he advised them to pray to God for three days asking for relief (these were the three days immediately preceding the Nativity of the Most Holy Virgin).[126] He also advised them to go to confession and, for those who were able, to receive the Supreme Sacrament of Communion. The following day, which was the feast day of the Virgin, he said a Mass for their cause, and a large number of them turned out for this [religious] exercise, which was followed by three days of scourging in front of an image of Our Lady that they had in the church. On the last day they carried her in a procession, and on that very same day the sky, which had been calm and clear, suddenly clouded over. Then she who is the Mother of Compassion created an abundance of clouds that unleashed a heavy rainfall that lasted for two hours, gladdening the sown fields and even more so the hearts of those who were afflicted. They were greatly consoled by this relief from heaven and were confirmed in the truths of our Holy Faith, as they saw with their own eyes the results of their devotion.

There was also another good that came from their devotion, which was the following: After seeing that it had served them well to plea and turn to God and His Most Holy Mother in their affliction they brought to justice a woman who had misled them. She had told them that it had not rained because she did not want it to and that with certain words she had dispersed the clouds because she was angry [81] with them. They brought this liar to the church, where she was questioned in front of the whole pueblo. She confessed her guilt and the fraud with which she had deceived the people, and the fiscal of the pueblo remedied this by publicly punishing her. These were the means by which those people became more enthusiastic each day about our Holy Faith, and also by which they emerged from the deceit and darkness in which they had been entombed by the devil.

126. This Marian feast day is celebrated on September 8.

CHAPTER XIX The commander of the garrison of Sinaloa is dispatched to Mexico City to report to the viceroy on the state of the province; its state upon his return

The affairs of Christianity and its establishment in the pueblos near the Villa de San Felipe were going well. The number of baptized persons was increasing and the number of churches being built had grown to eight. Nevertheless, unrest and disturbances still persisted, caused mainly by the Zuaque and other gentiles on the frontier. To pacify and settle the province, Lieutenant General Alonso Díaz decided to send Commander Diego Martínez de Hurdaide to Mexico City to give a report on the state of the province to the count of Monterrey, viceroy of Nueva España, so that His Excellency could order whatever would be most advantageous to the service of both the Divine and human Majesties and the aid and preservation of that land. He departed with great speed and, upon his arrival in Mexico City, he gave the viceroy an extensive account of that far-flung Province of Sinaloa. His Excellency listened to the commander with pleasure, and being very zealous in his service to the king and in the principal concern with which His Majesty had charged all his governors in the Indies, spreading the Gospel, it seemed to him that Hurdaide would be the appropriate [person] to tend to these matters. Moreover, due to his advanced age Captain Alonso Díaz was asking to retire to his home and hacienda in Durango. The viceroy therefore decided to give the title of captain to Diego Martínez de Hurdaide, along with a commission to add ten soldiers to the garrison, bringing the total number to thirty-six. In time as the reduction of peoples in the province expanded, ten more soldiers were added and this presidio became permanent. The garrison still exists today and has forty-six soldiers, a captain, and another squad leader [127] or commander.

The viceroy's decision was right on target, as if it had been sent from heaven. God had chosen this outstanding captain so that through him He could bring about the marvelous conversion to Christ's law of the savage nations of almost the entire Province of Sinaloa. This will be seen throughout the course of this history, especially in the following chapter. One can say of this man what the Holy Scriptures say of the Maccabees, which was, *De semine virorum illorum, per quos salus facta est in Israel*.[128] We can apply this to this Christian community and our captain, who was one of those chosen by God for great works in such a remote area of the Indies.

The new captain returned to Sinaloa with his ten additional soldiers around 1599 and assumed his new office, which he soon had to exercise. On his return from Mexico City he found that some restless and bellicose Indians, who had been incited by the devil, had persuaded the Guasave nation to rebel. They had burned the churches that had been built, led principally by a cacique who was highly [82] esteemed and of great bravery. When the new captain learned of the Guasave uprising he armed his soldiers and horses, and together with some Indian allies he went in search of the rebels. They had gone into the montes and rock-strewn hills, which are their stronghold, so he followed and caught up with them and captured the leaders of the disturbance. He executed those who were the most guilty and settled the others peacefully in their pueblos. He pardoned the principal cacique because he was so esteemed by his nation and, if this cacique were converted, he would be of great use in helping his people and governing them. This is what happened, because later the cacique ordered his people to rebuild the churches and receive their priest and minister in peace. He was later baptized and christened Don Pablo Velázquez and was a great supporter of the Christianity of the Guasave nation, governing in peace for many years until his death. This flock was thereby gathered together and remained so. Thus, this military undertaking turned out to be very important because all the pueblos along the Río Sinaloa where the Guasave lived

---

127. *Cabo*, which corresponds to the modern rank of corporal (Naylor and Polzer 1986:28).

128. I Maccabees 5:62: "of that race they sprang that should afford Israel deliverance" (Knox 1956:867).

were settled. There was no one who could disturb them, and in all these pueblos the number of Christians grew and multiplied every day.

This chapter will close with a case concerning the cacique of the Guasave, of whom it was said that the captain had made the right decision in pardoning his life for the sake of the great fruits of the Guasave nation. It is not uncommon for the wild brushlands to produce abundant and advantageous fruits once they have been cleared and planted with good seed. It is worthwhile to note here the turn to Christianity taken by he who was bellicose and brave in a gentile fashion. Governor Don Pablo Velázquez was an Indian of great [intellectual] capacity (of which there are actually quite a few among these people), and having become a Christian, he lived with great concern for his soul. He maintained his people in close observance of God's law and civil order, and his subjects showed him great obedience. He confessed very carefully, closely scrutinizing his conscience. God wrought a marvelous work in him that made quite an impression on his people. At one point he was so close to death from an illness that it was necessary to give him the Holy Sacraments. He had [his people] take him very clean and well-groomed to the church on a litter with blankets. He received the Most Holy Sacrament and Extreme Unction and then they took him back home. This is not an unusual practice among the Indians who, no matter how sick they are, usually go out into the countryside and the open air. Within a short while, and when it was least expected, Don Pablo, who had been on the verge of death, appeared before the priest healthy and well. The priest asked him how he had recovered so quickly. He responded that due to the severity of his illness he had already lost his sight before he received the Holy Sacrament, but the moment he received that Supreme Sacrament he suddenly found that his sight had been restored. When he got back home he began to improve, and now he was happy and healthy. If the Holy Scriptures recorded the case of what happened to Jonathan, who had his sight returned to him as he feasted on a honeycomb that he found, *Et illuminati sunt oculi eius*,[129] then we can recount as equally famous the case of our Indian Don Pablo. This case was so renowned among the Guasave that as the priest preached to the entire nation on the following Maundy Thursday about how the benefits of Holy Communion extend to the body

as well as the soul of those who properly receive it, the people's attention was focused on the example of their cacique, who was present before them in church. They admired in him the obvious effects that this Supreme Sacrament had achieved, which [83] Don Pablo had publicized. He died years later, having been of great assistance to the Christianity of his nation. His life ended in a very Christian fashion, and he was one of the most distinguished Christians in the Province of Sinaloa.

Lest the fruits of this new Christian community seem sparse, which at the outset they were not, I will write here about the fruits that the father superior [Gonzalo de Tapia] of these first missions gathered among these people while he was still alive; others that were harvested after his death will be recorded later. He says:

Among these nations one sees the spiritual fruits generally harvested among native peoples, as well as how pleased Our Lord is by their good wishes. The flames of our Holy Faith are being stoked every day, and they are developing great capacity in that which is taught and preached to them, memorizing whatever they are taught about virtue and mending their ways. Thus, it is of notable comfort to see and experience the benefits reaped from the great care and watchfulness that is taken in instructing them on how to proceed on the path to heaven and salvation. They eagerly aid themselves through the means for achieving this end, especially through the use of the Holy Sacraments. Confession, of which they often partake, is highly esteemed, as is seen in that they go to confession and cleanse their souls of sin whenever they feel it necessary and are able to do so. They show great pain and remorse for their sins, often breaking into tears of sorrow. It is remarkable the value some of them place on the soul; because the Lord had selected them Himself, they come to understand the end that awaits the soul: that God has promised eternal joy to those who do good works, but for those who do not take advantage of the priest's catechism and allow themselves to be won over by sin, there awaits a hell of everlasting fire. These people speak of this with great admiration, and this esteem in which they hold the mysteries of our Holy Faith results in their seeing as evil any vice they observe in others. Consequently, they reprehend any such behavior on the part of others and report it to the priest. Their fondness for the Most Holy Sacrament of the Altar is very great. They praise it and bless it and prepare themselves in their souls as best they can to receive Holy Communion, which is offered frequently and as a great example. They take Communion many times throughout the year, on the designated days of the Most Holy Sacrament and on the feast days of Our Lady the Virgin. In some places on any given day of devotion there are three hundred, four hundred, and even six hundred Indians taking Communion. They benefit greatly from these and the other heavenly remedies that Christ left His Church. To satisfy their needs and free themselves of worldly adversities, they confess (generally in great numbers) and take Communion. It has

---

129. *Margin Note*: I, Reg. 14. I Kings 14:27: "his eyesight grew clearer at once" (Knox 1956:239).

been seen that God Our Lord has confirmed these poor people's hopes by granting that which they desired. One year in particular they sowed great fields of maize and other seeds. When they saw the days were growing longer and the months were passing and their fields were going to waste because of a lack of water, they turned to placating Our Lord, who they thought was punishing them. They confessed and flogged themselves with true devotion and penance, and then Our Lord came to their aid with copious downpours and continuous rainfall.

CHAPTER XX The virtues and outstanding bravery of Diego Martínez de Hurdaide, Captain of Sinaloa

In the following chapter I will write of the extraordinary punishment [of the Zuaque rebels] and other outstanding victories in the Province of Sinaloa by Captain Diego Martínez de Hurdaide (who undoubtedly received aid [84] and counsel from heaven). In order that they be well received, I want first to summarize the captain's enormous bravery, wisdom, virtue, and other qualities, which make him without a doubt worthy of consideration among the outstanding men who have fought and served God and their king in the New World.[130] His works are worthy of an illustrious memorial because they have been responsible in large part, if not entirely, for the incorporation into Christendom of innumerable souls and nations, particularly in the Province of Sinaloa. I also promised in the prologue that I would write about those outstanding individuals who assisted in the enterprises of the Faith that are recorded in this history.

Captain Diego Martínez de Hurdaide was born in the city of Zacatecas in Nueva España,[131] which is rich with numerous and copious mineral deposits. His father was Vizcayan and his mother was born in Nueva España; both were very honorable persons. From the time he was a boy, he was very lively and high-spirited. This gave him an inclination to the military, which he joined at a young age. In fact, I once heard a great soldier under whom he first served, the governor and captain general of Nueva Vizcaya, Don Francisco de Ordiñola, say that other soldiers considered Hurdaide too young so they asked the governor why he had allowed him to join the military. The captain general answered, "Let him be, he is going to be a devil," meaning he was going to be brave and courageous. Pleased that his predictions had been correct, the governor told me this story long after Captain Hurdaide had accomplished brave feats. Early on he saw signs of [Hurdaide's] bravery, skill, and dexterity, as well as the prudence and discipline with which he carried out his missions. On numerous occasions he was victorious because he relied on military strategy rather than on simple force of arms. He took great pains to think through any military undertaking, particularly if it might lead to the ruin or downfall of a Christian community or threaten the restoration of peace among some nation. He was even more cautious when the honor of his God and king and the spread of the Christian religion were at stake. When it was necessary to act quickly to overwhelm the enemy he was like a bolt of lightning from the sky, acting before the enemy had time to think. When rebellions occurred he would say, "I must not allow the enemy to savor victory; I must snatch it from their hands before they have a chance to think about it; I cannot give them an opportunity to prevail." And as he was saying this he went into action.

On many occasions the enemy felt the force of arms and saw themselves overwhelmed by the man whom

---

130. It was Hurdaide who returned to Sinaloa from Mexico City in 1604 with two new missionaries, Fathers Pérez de Ribas and Villalta. During his years as a missionary, particularly among the Zuaque and later the Yaqui, Pérez de Ribas developed a great attachment to the captain.

131. Hurdaide was born in 1568 (see Johnson 1945).

they thought was still preparing to search them out. This is the origin of the Indians' opinion and name for him, 'Sorcerer'. Yet when the captain saw that the enemy attack was going to fail he did not use excessive force, opting instead for military prudence and halting the use of arms. He [preferred] to intimidate the enemy and wear them down. This is the same means used by the Roman captain and dictator Fabius, who wore down Hannibal's forces. As Livy writes, Fabius waged war, but not [in major confrontations but] by *sedendo et cunctando*.[132] According to Michael Verino, in his *Disticha moralia: Plus cunctatoris Fabj mora profuit urbi, Flaminij, et Grachi, quan vatiere man?*[133] Hannibal, who had conquered the fortresses of the Flaminians and the Grachans, could not win after Fabius V's retreat. This is the strategy that Captain Hurdaide sometimes used, but his most common strategy was to respond quickly and diligently, as a captain must, rather than [85] proceeding slowly, which results in lost opportunities and momentum.

Early in his military career, Captain Hurdaide served His Majesty on the frontiers of Nueva Galicia, Nueva Vizcaya, and Zacatecas, as well as at the mines of Guanaceví, Santa Bárbara, and Mazapil. He also participated in the wars and pacification of very savage nations, which taught the Spaniards in Nueva España many things. In all these endeavors, he demonstrated great bravery, which made him highly esteemed and very renowned. He demonstrated his bravery and prudence in all these places and conquests, but he was most outstanding in the Province of Sinaloa, where he pacified and reduced nearly twenty nations. The authority and dominion that he held over them demanded admiration, not just among Christian nations and their neighbors, but also among distant and fierce nations. They were all so won over and subdued that he was able to govern them with only four wax seals, which were impressed on a small piece of paper. This was the sign

that accompanied his orders, and it was like a royal provision, requiring no letter or writing. The Indian who carried this paper placed it in a small split reed, which was then placed in the little ring that, as noted, they used to pull back their hair. This person traveled alone, to and from his land and through enemy nations that in previous times would not have hesitated to cut him to pieces. Now, however, when they saw the paper and seals it was as if they were seeing the captain himself, and accordingly they served the messenger and assured him safe passage through their lands. A threat was made to all the nations that if any ambassador or other Indian set out to see the captain and happened to disappear, then the nation through whose lands he had passed would have to turn him over. Otherwise, the captain would go in person to look for him, and if he should fail to find him, they would pay with their heads. He fulfilled this threat whenever it was necessary, but in order to avoid such consequences they rolled out the red carpet for any and all messengers. Thus, one could walk in total security across all one hundred leagues of the province.

Although Captain Hurdaide's bravery was quite outstanding, it cannot be denied that he received great favor from heaven, with which he cooperated. He carried out the duties not only of a soldier, but also of a very Christian captain. He attended Mass and received the sacraments frequently, revering divine worship and the priests and thereby teaching the Indians to revere them as well. Indeed, his unique zeal for spreading the Holy Gospel and conversions was such that he spent his entire fortune squelching disturbances that might interfere with the promulgation of Christ's law. This zeal was so great that when he went to Mexico City to obtain permission to extend missions to the nations of the great Río Sinaloa (as will be told), a very important and holy priest from our order heard him speak of the matter and said, "God has given this man the vocation and zeal that He normally gives His apostolic and evangelical laborers." From this fondness was born the great kindness that he showed the Indians, which together with his bravery wrought great feats among them. He never used the Indians for his own interests, nor did he bother them with planting fields for him or busying themselves in other labor, as was done by other exploitative governors who were a burden on the Indians. Rather, he distributed among them quantities [86] of clothing and large numbers of colts, particularly to the principal caciques, which led to their faithfulness in times of need. They highly prize horse racing, even if it

---

132. *Margin Note*: Decade 2 Lib. 2. The referent here is Titus Livy's monumental history of the Roman people (*Decades*), which includes an account of the Second Punic War, otherwise known as the war with Hannibal, during which Fabius "the delayer" and the equally patient (yet ultimately victorious) Hannibal ended their confrontation with what amounted to a battlefield chess match (Bechtel 1906). "Sitting and waiting."

133. "The city [Rome] and the Flaminians and Grachi benefited more from Fabius' delays [or patience] than his troops." Verino's (d. 1514) *Disticha moralia* (Latin version) was first published in Salamanca in 1496. As an aside, Verino's name appears on a list of authors whose works were approved for printing in Nueva España by the viceroy for use by Jesuit scholastics (Zambrano 1961-1977:16:266-67).

is done bareback, and although the only rein they have is a cord tied to the [horse's] lower jaw, they greatly enjoy this and are entertained by it.

The fact that the captain enjoyed his post for more than thirty years is proof of his liberality and kindness. The viceroys never dared remove him from the province, which he had won over, settled, and expanded. Once when the marquis of Montesclaros tried to remove him from office,[134] Governor Don Francisco de Ordiñola wrote him (as was told to me by His Lordship) that even though he considered himself a good soldier, he did not consider himself to be on a par with Captain Hurdaide. Although Captain Hurdaide had received highly honored remunerations from His Majesty, when he died he was in debt rather than rich because of all he had spent on smoothing the path for the preaching of the Gospel. His desires were well reflected in his happiness when a nation that he had just settled was baptized, which led in turn to his desire to see another nation converted, as he manifested by saying, "Now we must give the devil another shove here in Sinaloa."

Among all the things that can be said of such a distinguished captain there was one thing that was quite outstanding (although it is true that I am omitting many things so as not to draw out his history, of which an entire book could be written). Although one might think that this diminished the authority of such a brave person, it could also be that God wanted to emphasize his uniqueness. The fact is that the captain had a very small body with crooked, or twisted, pigeon-toed feet. Even so, he had such great upper-body strength and was so quick that he could run up a hillside after an Indian like a hare and he did not let go once he got a hold of him, as we shall see in the memorable account in the following chapter, as well as in others throughout most of this history. These will provide proof of all that has been written about this outstanding captain, of whom I will discuss one last thing that was a unique example of his bravery, prudence, and good fortune.

This is something fortunate that can be said of very few captains who have spent a long time in campaigns, and it is also something at which the captain worked very hard. Specifically, in the more than thirty years of skirmishes with the enemy, and in more than twenty very dangerous battles with them, the enemy never captured one of the captain's soldiers or took any of their heads. Although many were badly wounded and some eventually died, there was never an occasion during the captain's tenure when the enemy gloried in dancing with the head of a Spaniard, and certainly not with the head of the captain himself. Governor Don Rodrigo del Río considered it some kind of a miracle that despite many encounters and battles, the enemy had never managed to do so. This was something that many of the enemy desired, even if it meant buying it with their own heads, and they were amazed and discouraged because they were unable to accomplish their goal. They attributed to witchcraft what was undoubtedly divine providence, which chose such a brave captain for these holy enterprises in the service of both the Divine and human Majesties and as the means to the salvation of so many people. What is true is that the two go together well, as is seen in the example given [by Captain Hurdaide].

By order of the Real Audiencia de México, reports of the captain's merits were compiled for [87] presentation to the Royal Council [of the Indies] to secure thanks from His Majesty. However, the recounting of these merits was halted by the captain's death so that Divine Majesty could double his glorious rewards in heaven, as those of us who knew him and dealt with him are sure has happened. God granted him a very quiet and Christian death in bed. He prepared for this at our college in the Villa de San Felipe (where he died), where he spent eight days in retreat, performing the [Spiritual] Exercises of our order.[135] He spent this time in prayer and penance, a sure preparation for the final journey he made to heaven. With this we will move on to one of the many journeys he undertook here on earth.

134. The marquis of Montesclaros, Juan de Mendoza y Luna, served as viceroy from 1603 to 1607. He may have suggested removing Hurdaide after learning of the latter's rather severe punishment of the Zuaque and Guasave converts who rebelled in 1603–4.

135. The Spiritual Exercises of Ignatius Loyola are at the heart of Jesuit spirituality. Individuals are guided through these exercises, which vary in length from a week to a month depending on one's spiritual state. The exercises involve considerable visualization of Christ's passion and other religious themes, together with reflection on one's own life. This is all done in an effort to come to a better knowledge of self and to engage God in "devout conversation," in effect to experience a religious revival (Ganss 1991).

CHAPTER XXI The famous and extraordinary punishment that Captain Hurdaide meted out to the fierce and warlike Zuaque nation

At this time [1600–1] in this new land, which was on the frontier of so many nations, there occurred some disturbances and riots that the brave Captain Hurdaide had to quell by force of arms. The greatest cause of concern and unrest in the province was the haughtiness and arrogance of the insolent Zuaque nation, which prided itself as a killer of Spaniards. The Zuaque nation was the shelter and breeding ground for all the outlaws and troublemakers in the province, summoning and gathering them together to strengthen their valor. A few months prior to the punishment that I will recount here this matter had reached an extreme of excess and license. When the lieutenant captain-general[136] was still in the province and Diego Martínez de Hurdaide was his commander, an Indian arrived at the Villa de San Felipe with a message from the Zuaque, challenging the lieutenant captain-general to enter their lands. Thinking that the situation conformed to orders from the viceroys to avoid war at all cost unless he were forced into it, he answered the Indian in a moderate manner. The impatient spirit of the [future] captain, however, could not endure such a thing, so he grabbed the Indian and threw him down at his feet, saying to him very angrily, "Run, Indian, and tell the Zuaque that one of these days they will see me in their lands, where I will seek them out and put a stop to their boldness and pride." He turned to his superior to justify his actions, which could have appeared to be too hasty or excessive, and said, "General, sir, it is not right that the Indians should treat Spaniards this way. As long as these people scorn us and fail to acknowledge the reputation for bravery that Spaniards have earned with their weapons, then peace and safety cannot be expected in this province and we might as well give it up for lost." After the Indian left, the Zuaque continued in their arrogance and boldness, coming to the very gates of the Villa de San Felipe, as has been told.

The time finally arrived when Diego Martínez de Hurdaide returned to Sinaloa with the rank of captain and thirty-six soldiers. The first thing he saw to was the punishment and humiliation of the arrogant and harmful Zuaque nation. He deliberated his strategy alone, commending it privately to God and without sharing it. It truly seems that the unusual tactic and strategy that he attempted came from heaven, because the whole plan worked out [88] just as he had imagined it in his mind. It was precisely as if it had happened just as he had visualized it. The first thing he decided to do was to enter the feared Zuaque's lands. He knew that they would come out to do battle with him, so he disguised his entrance as something else. Days before he departed he very secretly prepared neck chains and shackles. At night, locked alone in his house, he hid the chains in sacks, wrapping them up in cloth and straw to conceal them so that the soldiers would not learn of his plan, for they feared this ferocious nation. In spite of everything, the plan came to light when some soldiers noticed that the captain was closing himself up in his house; they realized he was preparing one of his usual daring plans, and like good soldiers they obeyed him. When his plan was readied he told them that he thought they needed to make beef jerky, so they should go after the wild cattle that had been roaming free in the montes near the Zuaque ever since the first Villa de Carapoa had been abandoned. At that time there was no domesticated livestock and they needed provisions, so he commanded the soldiers to ready themselves and their armored horses for whatever might occur, which they did. Hurdaide then departed the Villa de San Felipe with only twenty-four soldiers and some Indian servants. Before they reached the Zuaque lands, he delivered a prepared speech, setting out the arguments and reasons that, for the welfare and peace of the province, had obliged him to punish such a rebellious nation, which had caused so much trouble and had so disturbed Christianity. He told them that they should take courage in the fact that they were returning to Zuaque lands, where the Spaniards' reputation had nearly been destroyed. What he wanted was for each of the soldiers to seize and bind two Zuaque Indians. He told them to be prepared for

---

136. Apparently Alonso Díaz who, as noted, appears to have retained the title of lieutenant captain general until 1599, although he served as captain in Sinaloa only until 1596.

his signal, which would be the Spaniards' "Santiago!" [137] and to have ropes handy so they could bind the Indians until they could be thrown into chains. He planned to execute this plan at a time when the Indians would be spread out around the camp. Once they had grabbed the Indians the soldiers were not to let go, and he added that for the plan to be executed smoothly the Indians had to be dispersed, so the soldiers should attempt to distract them until the cry of Santiago was sounded. The captain knew that because of their extreme curiosity the Indians would be spread throughout the camp looking at the saddles, bits, etc., that the Spaniards had brought with them. [He proposed that] some [of the soldiers] give them leather belts; others [he suggested] should take out *cozcates*,[138] or strings of blue glass beads, which they greatly prize, and break the strings so the Indians would be busy picking them up. Some of the soldiers who heard this strategy thought it very difficult and too ambitious, so they asked as a group whether the captain would be satisfied if each of them delivered only one bound Indian. They thought it no small matter to bind one wild Indian, and that one would need four hands to hold down and bind two Indians at the same time. The captain told them very firmly that they should get their servants to help them and that no one should deviate from his plan or he would order them garroted right there in camp. He also told them that he himself, just like the rest of the men, would be obliged to tie up two Indians, and with this the soldiers acquiesced to his order.

When they reached Zuaque lands, they set up camp in a clear place in the monte, keeping the armored horses nearby in case they were needed. [89] The Zuaque were unaware at first that the captain's expedition had penetrated their territory, but as soon as they heard about it they took up their weapons. Then, loaded with bows and arrows, they marched to the Spaniards' camp to offer the captain a false welcome. They thought that because they now had him in their lands, they were sure to have his head with which to dance. When all of the leaders of the nation had assembled they went to Hurdaide and said, "Captain, why have you come?" "I come," he responded, "with these sons of mine (as he called his soldiers) to kill some

cattle for food, which we will share with you." I point out here a special circumstance which, although minor, will serve to indicate how well prepared the captain was for anything that might arise during this military operation. A very important woman named Luisa, who was a Christian, had come with the Zuaque caciques. She had been captured by the Spaniards during their first exploration of Sinaloa [139] and had been a slave for some years at the mining center of Topia, where she was baptized. When given the opportunity, however, she had fled to her own land. From time to time she would come with her two daughters to visit the captain at the villa, and she served as his interpreter because she knew the Mexican language. The captain maintained her friendship with gifts of clothing. Seeing that she had come to the camp with the caciques, he placed her near him and ordered one of his Indian servants that if she were to flee in the event that war broke out, then he was to go after her and bring her back to the camp.

At this point the Indians asked the captain why the cattle hunt had not begun. He told them that they needed wood in the camp to roast the meat for eating. "Well, wait," they said, "we will go get some." Then the captain said, "There is no reason for you, the principales, to go and fetch it. Send your *macehuales*" [140] (which is what they call their vassals). The captain's intentions were very pious and he always tried to punish not the innocent, but rather those who were most guilty, the leaders of the disturbances and killings. Because he knew that the most guilty parties in the trouble that the Zuaque had caused the Spaniards were their warlike caciques, he made sure that the punishment did not fall upon the others. When the caciques heard the captain's proposal they remained in the camp and sent troops of their macehuales to get wood. The latter left the camp shouting wildly, without putting down their bows and arrows, because they thought they would soon be eating the meat of both the cattle and the Spaniards. As they were leaving they said to each other, "Let's go get wood to roast the captain." An Indian who served the captain as an interpreter heard them, and proving himself to be faithful, he informed him, "Do you know

137. Santiago or Saint James (the patron saint of Spain) miraculously appeared during the reconquest in a battle at Compostela, favoring the Spaniards against the Moors. Subsequently the cry "Santiago" was invoked whenever Spanish forces engaged an enemy.

138. *Cosca* is 'glass bead' in Cáhita (Buelna 1891:152).

139. Luisa became the interpreter for Ibarra's expedition in 1564–65; at the time she was living in Ocoroni and previously had learned Nahuatl. According to Obregón, Luisa ruled and governed the pueblo of Ocoroni and was the wife of the leader and chief of this territory. Interestingly, Obregón also represents her as the mistress of various caciques of the region (Hammond and Rey 1928:79, 83, 86, 99, 152).

140. The term to designate commoners in Nahua society was *macehual-tin* (pl.) or *macehual-li* (sing.) (Karttunen 1983:126).

what those men are saying? They are going to roast you with the wood they bring." The captain pretended he knew nothing and kept the most principal caciques with him. One of them was a very famous man named Taa, which means 'the sun'. He allowed the other caciques free range among the soldiers' campsites. God was arranging everything exactly as the captain wanted (because it seemed that He had inspired the plan). The Indians would do exactly as he wanted, and before they realized it they would endanger themselves through overconfidence. It seemed to them that the Spaniards, who had already experienced their macanas and bows and arrows, would be afraid to fight a thousand Indians in their own territory, but the truth was that the time had come when God wished to punish them. When the captain saw that the moment had come, he called out "Santiago" and grabbed two of the caciques who were with him by their hair, giving the signal to his soldiers. {90} These men acted very bravely, and nearly all of them seized and bound two *gandules*;[141] two did escape, however. One of those whom the captain seized was Taa, a very tall Indian who towered over him in stature by half a vara. This Indian, who was being held by the hair, lifted the captain off the ground, but his courage was such that when he told me about this later, he said, "The Indian could very well have torn my arm off, but my hand was not going to let loose of that hair." In the end forty-three captives were placed in the iron chains and collars that the Spaniards had brought with them.

At the moment of the capture the Indian Luisa took off running, just as the captain had thought she would. The Indian servant who had been forewarned captured her, and she began to wail, saying to the captain that the captives were her brothers and relatives and making a great show of her sorrow over their capture. He calmed her, telling her that she should realize that those prisoners were harmful to her nation and to the entire province. They were the authors of the many murders committed by the Zuaque against Spaniards, and they persevered in keeping all her nation in a state of unrest. He would pardon her nation by punishing the delinquent leaders, and to please her he would set free the prisoner who was her closest relative, which he proceeded to do when she pointed him out. He was a very brave and corpulent Indian who, because of this stroke of luck, was named Buenaventura by the Spaniards. A few years later when religious instruction was introduced to that nation, I gave him that name when I baptized him, and he was a great help in the reduction and settlement of his people.

While the Indian prisoners were being put into neck irons, the two who had escaped from the soldiers had run to the monte to warn the other gandules who had gone to gather wood. Taking up their bows and arrows, they ran to the Spanish camp, but when they reached the outskirts they saw that all their captains had been taken prisoner and that they were without leadership. Even though their blood boiled with rage and they were filled with anger and indignation, they did not know what course to follow. Confounded by God, they remained paralyzed at the sight of the camp. The captain spoke to Luisa in the Mexican tongue (which he knew and she understood) and asked her to counsel and persuade her Zuaque people not to start a battle because all of them would pay for it. He would not leave without first destroying their homes and fields and burning their pueblos. He said he would be satisfied with punishing their criminal leaders and would leave the rest of them and their children and women unharmed. As proof of this he gave permission for them to come safely into the camp to bring food to the prisoners. The Indian Luisa urged her nation to accept these conditions and, trusting in the word of the captain (who always managed to keep his word with these peoples, who valued it), the prisoners' wives began to come into the camp and bring food to their husbands, who were all in irons and guarded by soldiers. Stunned by what had happened to them when they had least expected it, the rest of the Zuaque withdrew to their pueblos, which were two or three leagues away. In order not to draw out this chapter, we will relate in the following one the culmination of this extraordinary military operation. {91}

141. *Gandul* had the meaning of 'young, bellicose Moor or Indian'; in modern times it is used to refer to someone who is a vagabond or lazy. It derives from an Arabic term used to refer to a young man of modest means who feigns elegance and attempts to please women, living without working and quick to take up arms (Corominas and Pascual 1989–1991:3:76).

CHAPTER XXII The topic of the previous chapter is continued and the punishment of the prisoners is recounted

Diego Martínez de Hurdaide always demonstrated the spirit of a very pious and Christian captain, as well as a brave one. This time he demonstrated it once again, for he could have slit his prisoners' throats and returned to the Villa de San Felipe and the fort that had been built there, having successfully concluded his campaign to punish the Zuaque nation. He need not have remained in a place where a thousand Indian warriors could gather (and more if the Zuaque summoned their allies), whereas he had only a few soldiers to assist him. (He had not brought along very many soldiers so as not to call attention to his expedition.) Even so, he paid no heed to the valid fears that might have stirred in his breast, fears which were overcome by piety and his desire that those souls not be lost. Thus, he decided to remain there for four days and nights, the latter being more dangerous among these peoples, until he notified the priests so that two of them might come and prepare those gentile prisoners to receive Holy Baptism before they died. He sent a messenger to the priests in the villa, which was sixteen leagues away.

In the interim something extremely dangerous happened that placed the prisoners and the campaign at great risk. The Indian prisoners secretly told their wives to bring stones hidden in the food when they brought them their meals. They did this very cleverly, for when they brought them *guamuchiles*,[142] a wild fruit that they eat, in *jícaras*,[143] which are a type of bowl made from a gourd, they filled the jícaras with stones; the latter were very well hidden under the fruit. One night after each of the prisoners had gathered together a number of stones and the Spaniards had allowed them to make fires because of the cold, the men in chains rebelled and began to throw stones and hot coals at the soldiers on guard. They did this with all the force of those who are fighting for their life and liberty. The soldiers on watch sounded the alarm, and the captain and the rest of the soldiers were awakened. When they saw the stones they ran to the prisoners in neck irons and forced them to sit down again. This was not easily accomplished, and some of the prisoners were so rebellious that two ended up being killed by the stroke of the sword because they showed such resistance. In addition, there was concern that the main Zuaque force would receive word from the prisoners and return to help them and attack the encampment. The captain was so worried by what had happened that night that every time he lay down to rest a bit, he would start from his sleep and grab his sword, slashing at the air.[144]

Undoubtedly heeding the captain's piety and desire for the salvation of those souls, Our Lord saw to the swift arrival of the two priests whom they were awaiting. These were Fathers Pedro Méndez and Juan Bautista de Velasco, who understood the Zuaque language. The captain was very glad to see them, and he charged them with immediately instructing those Indians and preparing them to die as Christians, for they were all to be hanged from the trees. The priests took the proper death and salvation of those souls very seriously, and the first thing they made the prisoners understand was the necessity of Holy Baptism for their eternal well-being. They exhorted them to take advantage of that opportunity and not to lose the life of their souls along with that of their bodies. They taught them everything else that is required {92} for an adult to receive Holy Baptism, and God moved their hearts to request it. After the priests had spent two days teaching them and preparing them for death there were only two Indians who remained hardened and obstinate. The captain ordered two large trees to be readied where they would be hanged, and as the prisoners arrived the priests began baptizing them just before they were hanged, thus helping each one at the moment of death. They were

142. Guamúchil refers to members of the genus *Pithecellobium*, e.g., *P. dulcis*, which bears the common name in English of ape's earring or blackbead bush. This is a relative of the soap-bark tree and has an edible fruit that is contained in twisted, coiled pods. Both its pod and flower resemble those of the acacia (Schoenhals 1988:54).

143. Nahuatl term for a semi-hemispherical bowl made from a gourd.

144. Pérez de Ribas clearly heard this story firsthand from the captain.

surrounded by an escort of soldiers on armored horses, until forty-two of those gandules, who had made the entire Province of Sinaloa tremble and had worried the entire Kingdom of Nueva Vizcaya, had been hanged. The priests had assurances and satisfaction that those souls had been saved, except for two or three of the most stubborn who were executed.

The reader might think that the punishment I have recorded here was too harsh or cruel, and it was judged as such by some people at that time.[145] They did not know the reason for hanging so many barbarous Indians, and they were unaware of what these Indians do. Recall the insolence of the Zuaque that was recorded earlier: At a feast they treacherously killed nearly all the residents of the first Villa de Carapoa, which was subsequently razed and abandoned. Recall also the massacre they inflicted upon Governor Hernando Bazán's squad of soldiers (as was told in Book I); as trophies, they painted the headless trunks of the soldiers' bodies on the trees. Moreover, recall that they attacked the Villa de San Felipe with insistent arrogance and mocked the Spaniards by hanging the manes and tails of the horses they had shot with arrows on the gates of the villa and in the trees. Remembering all these and other acts of insolence and unrest, you will not judge as too severe this punishment of a people who, even with this blow, were not entirely humbled.

In the end the well-deserved punishment of hanging forty-two Indians was carried out. Once it had been executed the captain sent word to the Zuaque nation through the Indian Luisa that if they took down the cadavers without his permission, he would turn on them and they would pay for it. He ordered them to remain quiet in their pueblos and told them that henceforth their wars and uprisings should cease because, although he could have destroyed the women and children, he had instead made sure that they were not touched. What he asked was that they remain at peace in their pueblos and fields and that they not disturb the Christians who were under the protection of his king. Through some presents and gifts he was able to console Luisa and preserve her kindness toward the Spaniards so that she would continue her good work of pacifying and taming her nation, which she did; she was truly an Indian of great worth.

As time passed the Zuaque were taught the catechism, which I had the good luck to preach to them. Living among them for a period of eleven years, Luisa was a great help to me in the Baptism of the entire nation. After they had been baptized they settled down and preserved the peace that the Gospel brings, and a great Christianity was established. As we shall see, however, there were first other arrogant outrages that occurred in that nation, which had not been completely subdued by this blow. And Captain Hurdaide was once again successful, just as he had been in the foregoing disturbance. Things went so well that he not only successfully executed the punishment of the Zuaque nation, but also had handed over to him some Indian outlaws and wrongdoers who had taken shelter among the Zuaque. [93] In order to avoid excessively bloodying his sword, he pardoned them and returned to the villa, leaving the memory of his name with all those nations.

---

145. These critics may have included the viceroy, the marquis of Montesclaros, who, as previously noted, tried several years later to remove Hurdaide from office.

CHAPTER XXIII The progress of Christianity at this time[146] and the gentile abuses that were being eradicated

We have already written about the land and secular matters concerning the soldiers' endeavors, so let us now return to the spiritual soldiers of Christ and the fruits and victories of evangelical preaching in the midst of persecutions by the devil, the common enemy of mankind. What Christ Our Lord said through Saint Matthew will be fulfilled: *Porte inferi non prevalebunt adversus eam*.[147] He assured us that even if the gates of hell were thrown wide open and the infernal furies should issue forth to oppose evangelical preaching, they would not be powerful enough to prevent it or to sing victory over it.

Our five evangelical preachers[148] were divided and employed in the religious instruction of the pueblos along the first river, the Río Mocorito, and also along the Río Sinaloa and the rivers in the sierra and Valle del Cuervo. There were thirteen pueblos along these rivers, each with two hundred, three hundred, or five hundred male heads-of-household[149] and their families, not counting those scattered in the montes, valleys, and fields. With each passing day these people were added to the pueblos and churches where the Baptisms of infants and adults were celebrated. Every day gentiles came in greater numbers to hear catechism and prepare to receive Holy Baptism. This excluded those who were ill, whom it was necessary to instruct more hastily. Because God wishes to take some adults to heaven quickly, it is not only children who enter with baptismal grace and obtain with its flower the fruit of this Holy Sacrament. This will be declared in a portion of a letter written by a priest [who was working in these pueblos] at that time.[150] [Writing letters] was the custom of the priests who labored in this solitude, and while far from their brothers they consoled and encouraged one another with the positive results of their enterprises. The letter says:

> I went to a pueblo where I found a great number of sick people. They took me from one house to another; some came looking for me half dragging themselves, insisting that I baptize them. It was amazing to see that if some of them were unable to concentrate on what I was teaching because of their pain and sickness and they were slow in answering, then their relatives would encourage them to respond affirmatively to everything the priest taught them. Because of their diminished capacity, it was not necessary that they understand the same concepts that are [ordinarily] required of adults for receiving the Sacrament of Baptism. Nevertheless, I waited for the sick to respond themselves. Once I felt they understood all that was necessary concerning the principal mysteries of our Holy Faith, I baptized them. Our Lord took for Himself a great number of them, but not all, for He also left seed that would bear fruit in the future.[151]

There was one Christian woman (adds the priest) who consoled and cared for the sick, making sure that the dead were buried. She contracted the disease herself, and when I later returned to the pueblo, I found her exhausted, quite nauseous, and in agony from the hard work and foul odor she had endured with the sick and the dead. I had her face washed and I comforted her with [94] a little bit of the wine that I had for Mass (there was no other). Then I told her a Gospel story, and it was Our Lord's will that she should promptly regain her health. This strengthened the faith of all those who witnessed it.

Another Indian from the same pueblo was suffering from a constriction of the throat that was causing him a lot of pain. I had some holy water brought and, making two Crosses over the place where it hurt, I told him to trust in the Lord who had died on that Cross. Through this divine remedy (for there are few human remedies in this land), he and other sick people were healed.

Up to here I have been citing the priest's letter, and although I omit other similar cases, there is a singu-

---

146. 1601. As this chapter suggests, during this and the following year the Sinaloa missions and their gentile neighbors, including the Zuaque, were devastated by an epidemic of measles and several other maladies (Reff 1991b:142ff.).

147. *Margin Note*: 16. Matthew 16:18: "and the gates of hell shall not prevail against [the Church]" (Knox 1956:17).

148. Pérez, Méndez, Velasco, Villafañe, and Brother Castro; the anua of 1601 notes that Santarén had left Sinaloa in 1598 to work in the sierras among the Acaxee in the new mission of Topia.

149. *Vecinos*.

150. This letter was written in 1601 by Father Juan Bautista de Velasco (AGN 1601b).

151. Thousands died during this epidemic (Reff 1991b:144–47).

lar one I will not leave out that took place in a small pueblo of gentiles the first time the priest visited it. The people made a ramada of straw and forked branches from the monte, and there they gathered to hear the priest preach the main articles of our Holy Faith. When his talk ended two of the principales stood up, and on behalf of the entire pueblo they thanked him for the benefits he brought by coming to their land and teaching them God's catechism. They asked him for Holy Baptism, and the priest consoled them by saying that they would receive it in due time, provided they continued to learn the catechism.

Around that time he baptized some infants who were brought to him, and then he began to baptize the adults. One of the first people [to be baptized] was the principal cacique, who had three wives, or concubines. He gave up two of them and was baptized with the one he chose to marry in *facie Ecclesiae*. This so consoled him that he became the one to most encourage his pueblo to receive Holy Baptism and live as Christians. In this way the flock of Christ and of His Holy Church grew; wherever the priests went the harvests of souls increased.

At the same time, to better introduce Christian customs and the holy ceremonies of the Church, the priests were careful to remove from this field the weeds of the monte and the wild grasses of abuse and gentile superstition. They proceeded slowly and cautiously, according to the teachings of Christ, who stopped the hurried servants who wanted to uproot the weed that had grown among the unripened wheat. He conveyed this through Saint Matthew in that memorable maxim: *Ne forte colligentes zizania eradicetis simul cum eis, & triticum, sinite utraque crescere, usque ad messem.*[152] It is well to pull up the weeds, but do so in due time so as not to harm the good seed. It is important that actions on which the salvation or preservation of entire nations depends be undertaken with care. For this reason our priests proceeded with great care and caution, tending to the preservation of this field without neglecting their work.

These people had quite a few superstitions concerning the burial of their dead. One consisted of placing some food and drink in the grave along with the body to serve as provisions for the journey it would make. In this they showed many signs that they understood [the idea of] another life or the immortality of the soul. This was good reason for us to preach the truth of the Faith concerning the other life that awaits mankind. Concerning their knowledge of where souls went, what they did, and where they remained, they were foolish, confused, and blind. They placed the body of the deceased in a cave that they dug for a tomb, either sitting up or lying down, but raised off the ground in case it attempted to walk. With their catechism and talks the Gospel missionaries uprooted these people's deception and nonsense. Concerning [95] the souls' need for corporeal food, the priests told them what the Faith teaches about the place where they go, etc. They introduced the Christian practice of burying the dead, which became well established. The [Indians] very devoutly attended Lenten exercises and confession, as well as blood processions during Holy Week. Their drunken revels have become largely controlled. Some gentile pueblos asked the priests for an Indian or a knowledgeable boy who could teach them the Christian catechism, and all this was attended to very carefully. The evangelical ministers had progressed considerably in learning the native languages, and they were already able to preach more fluently. This gave the Indians great pleasure, and large audiences gathered for their sermons. They listened to the priests speak on all subjects in their language, and they enjoyed the profound mysteries of the Faith even more. Our diligent laborers were not content simply with knowing these languages, so they also made note of and recorded the rules and precepts of their grammars. To do this well, it is necessary to have penetrated the Indians' extraordinary modes of speaking, and with care and [hard] work these ministers accomplished a great deal. The challenge of learning these languages was thereby made easier for future priests so that within a short time they, too, could employ themselves in the holy ministry of preaching and aiding souls.

152. *Margin Note*: Matt. c. 13. Matthew 13:29–30: "No, or perh while you are gathering the tares you will root up the wheat with the... Leave them to grow side by side till harvest" (Knox 1956:14).

CHAPTER XXIV By order of the viceroy, Captain Hurdaide leads an expedition inland to search for mineral deposits

The count of Monterrey, viceroy of Nueva España,[153] received word from knowledgeable sources that there were potentially valuable mineral deposits in the Province of Sinaloa. Their discovery would be very good for the king and his vassals, and this would [also] be a means to populate that faraway land, thereby alleviating expenses to His Majesty in Sinaloa and furthering the preaching of the Gospel. As a result of these reports His Excellency dispatched an order to the captain of Sinaloa, whose bravery had already become well known. He was instructed to organize an expedition to explore the aforementioned veins, in particular in the Chínipa mountains, which were famous for their rich ores. This was more than seventy leagues from the Villa de San Felipe, and to get there it was necessary to pass through nations that were not yet at peace, including the Chínipa, in whose lands the explorations were to be carried out. In spite of all of this, in fulfillment of the viceroy's order the captain quickly prepared himself and his soldiers for the journey, even though it was a dangerous one.[154] He was joined by some who were greedy for mines, and he also recruited some Indian allies. Some of them were Sinaloa, through whose lands his troops would have to pass. He also took along some equipment, as well as rations for everyone's nourishment.

Marching along, he reached the Chínipa's lands, where a trap was discovered. This had been plotted by the Chínipa and their allies, the Sinaloa. They set this trap in a narrow and dangerous pass created by [some] very high mountains. There the enemy lay in waiting, and once the vanguard had passed they started to throw rocks from above. They threw so many that they did not need to use bows or arrows, and they threw them with such force that the trees were knocked down. This forced the troops to split, with the vanguard breaking away from the main body of soldiers. [96] The captain ordered all the remaining people to take refuge under some high cliffs, which deflected the rocks thrown by the enemy.

The troops were so isolated and divided during the two days of the enemy assault that those in the vanguard did not know what had happened to those in the rear guard. During all this time neither group had access to provisions nor any way of replenishing their food or drink. But God willed that the enemy should also lack food, so they dispersed and departed, thereby allowing the Spaniards to reunite. They congratulated one another and thanked God for rescuing them from such great danger, as well as for [the fact] that none of the soldiers had been seriously injured, for both groups had already given the other up for dead. There is no bravery or resistance against rocks and crags, and it was an [act of] immense mercy by God that all of them were not smashed to pieces right there.

Many of the beasts of burden perished, along with their cargo, which included the holy vessels that Father Pedro Méndez had brought along. He had accompanied the army to help with whatever spiritual needs might arise and had saved himself by huddling close to a boulder. Among the provisions stolen by the Indians was a copper pot, which they made into a drum. Throughout the battle, they sang to its beat and boasted of their victory, saying, "You will not get out of here, captain." But the captain, brave as always, organized his people, for he did not want to return without descending to one of the Chínipa pueblos to execute the viceroy's orders and searching for the mineral deposits that he had heard existed in that region. The captain also wished to capture some Chínipa, not to make them slaves, but rather to utilize them in the discussion and establishment of peace with that nation. He found the pueblo abandoned, but he did discover some silver deposits which, when assayed, did not contain as much silver as had been originally thought.

He had another [stroke of] good luck when he captured a woman and her child. He treated them very well and took them with him to the Villa de San Felipe. He took care of them for several years in his home so

---

153. Gaspar de Zúñiga y Acevedo, viceroy from 1595 to 1603.
154. The year was 1601.

that they might learn the catechism and be baptized. If with the passage of time a door should be opened to preach the catechism to that nation, the mother and her child could teach and serve as interpreters of their language for the priest who went there to preach. This was something the captain always desired in all of his expeditions and journeys.

Having done this, he still did not forget the punishment merited by the delinquent and traitorous Sinaloa, disturbers of the peace. His troop had been greatly ravaged in this last attack, and he lacked supplies. (But when he had no other nourishment the spirited captain knew [quite] well how to survive on the roots and trunks of the wild mescal.) In spite of this he left

Chínipa and retraced his steps through the pueblos of the Sinaloa, where he destroyed the cultivated fields and tried to get his hands on some of the leaders of that treacherous [plot]. He succeeded, and so they did not escape the punishment they deserved; he hanged four or five of them and thus taught the others a lesson. Once back at the villa he reported to the viceroy concerning his expedition, and the further pursuit of mineral deposits was suspended. A few years later on a better occasion the time arrived to provide these two nations, the Sinaloa and the Chínipa, with religious instruction. The priests went to preach the Holy Gospel with joyous success, as will be told ahead at the appropriate time and place. [97]

CHAPTER XXV The priests begin building churches and introducing civil order in the Christian pueblos; the results of these efforts among the Guasave are recounted

We will leave for the time being the Chínipa pueblos of which we spoke in the last chapter and return to the Christian pueblos of the Río Sinaloa, where the Villa de San Felipe is located. Here at this time {1602–3} our priests were employed in an ambidextrous fashion, for they were using their hands to tend not only to matters of the spirit and soul, but also to secular and civil affairs. It cannot be denied that the one helps the other, for man is made of body and soul, half spirit and half clay. And because the functions of the soul in this life are dependent on those of the body, by arranging the body's disposition, man is more easily subjected to God's law. In recognition of [the importance] of that which is civil and human God gave that maxim: *Reddite quae sunt Casaris Casari & quae sunt Dei Deo*.[155] Thus, our priests induced the Indians to cover their barbarian nakedness and to be more concerned

with clothing. They exhorted them to be more diligent and careful about planting cotton, which the women were exhorted to spin and weave into more mantas with which to clothe themselves. They gladly accepted this advice and [soon] came to enjoy clothing so much that they began buying it. To obtain woolen cloth, they traded the seeds that they gathered and harvested from their fields, which they even expanded for this purpose. On a number of occasions they took the food from their own mouths, using the seeds they harvested for buying clothing. In doing so they were forced to spend part of the year eating roots from the monte. At other times they went to look for work outside the province, as they do today.

For his part the captain sought to establish civil government in the pueblos. He did so by appointing governors and municipal officers somewhat in the form of a republic,[156] and he charged them with inform-

---

155. Matthew 22:21; Mark 12:17; Luke 20:25: "give back to Caesar what is Caesar's, and to God what is God's" (Knox 1956:23, 46, 79).

156. Although technically it was the captain's right and responsibility to appoint Indian governors and other officials, the Jesuit mission-

ing him of any disorderly conduct or unrest. Because those whom he appointed usually came from the same nations and families [as those whom they were to govern], they adapted easily to this government and it was successfully established.

This was the state of affairs when Father Hernando de Villafañe, who was entrusted with the great Guasave nation, finished baptizing the pueblos' inhabitants and began construction of permanent churches to accommodate all those who had been baptized. This undertaking was new to the Indians, who had never seen or labored in such an enterprise. However, because the people of this nation were more malleable and dedicated to working than others, and because these were works of great importance and would make the pueblos more permanent, the priest managed to get the Indians to build these churches. They were made of adobe and were well covered with flat earthen roofs,[157] which freed them from the fires that affect churches made of wood and straw. Hands were put to work, and great quantities of adobes were made in each of the three principal pueblos. Work was begun erecting the walls, and as they rose higher, so did the Indians' desire to see such a novel work completed. They cut and carried on their shoulders large numbers of trees, which they made into lumber (they carry such loads extremely capably). Three very large churches were built,[158] and although they were not of stone masonry, they were nevertheless a sight to see in that land, particularly [98] as the priest endeavored to adorn them by whitewashing and painting them with local pigments that he was able to find. These people view their churches the same way Europeans view what they call their "wonders of the world." The Guasave were very pleased, and they boasted of being the first and only ones who could view such buildings from their meager homes. But God's judgments, although always just, are inscrutable, and that same year in which the churches were finished [1604][159] He

arranged for or allowed them to be destroyed before they were even consecrated. Even though the churches were built on sites that were thought to be safe from the flooding rivers and other dangers, it rained for five days straight (an unusual occurrence in this land). The river overflowed its banks with such fury and force that it violently destroyed pueblos and churches, forcing the Indians to take refuge in the montes and trees, which as previously mentioned, is a refuge on such occasions.

One could say that with this event God intended for the Indians to experience and become accustomed to work, forsaking idleness, for they were now obliged to build new churches. It is well known in all the republics of the world that work is of great utility and benefit to man, whereas idleness is the cause of infinite harm and can become the plague of a republic. God wanted to remove these people from the uncivilized life in which they had been reared, just as He wanted to do for His ancient people, whom He punished for their licentious idleness. He corrected their behavior by delivering them to nations who subjected them and made them work, as happened in Egypt and among other nations such as the Canaanites and Medianites, of which there are plenty of examples in the Holy Scriptures.

In the end the recently finished churches of the Guasave were demolished by God for reasons that only His Majesty knows. True, they required a lot of work, more on the part of the priest than the Indians, who had little knowledge of [building] such structures. Likewise, there were no artisans here, and the priest himself was often forced to lend a hand in the construction. The river flooded so strongly that it entirely covered the pueblos, and not a piece of ground was left where refuge could be sought. The priests who were catechizing the people of that river had to seek refuge like the Indians in the tree branches of the monte. One priest [Pedro Méndez] spent two days in the branches of a tree without food or even sleep. Although he was at risk of drowning, some Indians were so loyal that they remained with him in the event that he should need help. Another priest [Pedro de Velasco] was [trapped] in the corner of a sacristy for five days. He could not get out and surely would have drowned from the raging floodwaters if the Indians had not swum to where he was to rescue him. I have written about this here so that others will understand the great variety of hardships and dangers these apostolic men endured for the good and salvation of these poor souls, particularly at the beginning of their conversion.

The river's floodwaters inundated the Villa de San Felipe as well, and although the church and the Jesuit

---

ary assigned to a particular pueblo identified and made recommendations regarding capable individuals, whom the captain then appointed. The Jesuits and Captain Hurdaide followed crown policy, consulting with and appointing native caciques or other elites (e.g., lineage heads) as governors, provided, of course, that these elites cooperated with the Spaniards.

157. *De azoteas y terrados*, which here and subsequently in the text we have translated as flat earthen roof(s) (cf., Covarrubias 1943; Real Academia Española 1969:1:528).

158. Churches were built in the three main Guasave pueblos: Guasave, Tamazula, and Sisinicari.

159. Note that the anua for this year (AGN 1604:139) indicates that four churches were destroyed among the Guasave; perhaps the fourth was an older, more perishable structure.

residence at the college were at grave risk, Our Lord spared them.[160] Still, the river washed out all the planted fields and that year's harvest, and the devil seized the opportunity to stir up these poor people (he doesn't miss a single one). Once the people had witnessed the destruction of their fields he employed renegade Indians to stir up trouble in the pueblos. These Indians exhorted the people to flee to the monte for food and, more importantly, for freedom of conscience. This unrest was remedied after a while, however, and they returned to their pueblos, where they were encour-aged to build churches that were even more beautiful than the previous ones. In the end and with the help of God and the patience of [99] His ministers, works and fruits that appeared to be very difficult were attained among these people through the preaching of the Holy Gospel. The Guasave's constancy and tirelessness not only aided in the rebuilding of their churches, but also set an example for the pueblos of the Río Mocorito as well as other Indians, who were encouraged to build churches in their own pueblos that turned out to be very beautiful.

CHAPTER XXVI The importance of rearing the youth of these nations with the catechism and good habits; another means introduced by the priests to establish civil order is discussed

A maxim repeated by all the ancient and modern writers is that the rearing of children with the catechism and good habits is fundamental to the welfare of a republic. For one thing childhood is an impressionable period; youth, like a soft, malleable material, can be imprinted with virtues. Childhood is also the beginning, when the foundation is laid for the rest of a man's life, and a building erected on this [proper] foundation is more durable and lasting. If this is the case and has been verified in the youth of the civilized nations and republics of the world, then an even stronger argument can be made with respect to the necessity [of educating the youth] among people like those we have discussed here, who were totally destitute of catechism and civil order. Accordingly, to insure that the Faith and good customs of these nations would persevere, our evangelical ministers were particularly concerned with the education of the young people. At this time [circa 1602–4] there were already a good number of gifted young Indians from all these nations at the college in the Villa de San Felipe.[161] There they learned the catechism, good habits, and to read, write, and sing, which would [later] enable them to help the priests in their mission districts. They were like yeast, enabling Christianity to mature in their pueblos. As proof of how well things have gone I will discuss in this chapter some of the many examples that reflect and confirm how this nurturing yields great fruits.

In the last chapter we discussed how a group of restless renegades fled their pueblo for the monte.[162] The previous afternoon the priest had sent the young singers and the people who served in the church of the pueblo to another pueblo, where he was planning to meet them the following day. While this group was encamped in the countryside for the night an Indian unexpectedly arrived. He was sent by the children's rebellious parents and relatives with a message for the children to join them in the monte. The young Indians confounded the

160. These colleges were essentially boarding schools for Indian boys and young men.

161. The anua of 1602 indicates that there were thirty boys at the college in San Felipe.

162. The "renegades" were from Father Pedro Méndez's pueblo of Ocoroni.

messenger, politely dismissing him. They forsook their biological parents for their spiritual father, whom they [then] searched out, determined not to leave him. They persisted in staying with him, so great was the love that those little barbarians had for the priest. Their fidelity did not end there, for they became the means and motive for their parents' and relatives' return to the quiet life of their pueblo.

To this case was added another with peculiar circumstances. It happened that while the priest was traveling with his company of loyal young singers, they encountered a woman with her school-aged son, whom she was taking to the monte. He was a classmate of the others and had been absent on this occasion, but when he saw [100] the priest and the other children he joined them. His mother was not powerful enough to separate him or convince him to continue in her company, and this is no small thing among people in whom there reigns a fervent love for their children.

This [same love] won a woman her salvation. She had a Christian son who had been gone for two years, so she went to see him. Upon arriving, much to her good fortune, she became gravely ill. When the missionary priest learned of this he visited her and begged her to prepare herself to receive Holy Baptism. Her son added his own loving advice to this petition, and it was agreed that she would be taught the catechism. During the day and a half that her life endured the priest instructed her, baptizing her just before she died. She left assurances of having gone to heaven, inasmuch as God had brought her to where her son was, where she became sick and where, with her son's help, she received Holy Baptism before dying.

In the case that follows another of these children was the means to the salvation of another old gentile Indian. A priest visited this sick Indian and started to instruct him [in preparation] for Holy Baptism. Because the man's illness [was not that serious], there was still time to better instruct him in the mysteries of our Holy Faith. Therefore, the priest left a youngster with him to continue the catechism. After he had spent some time with this sick person the youngster decided to leave, and as he was going the feeble man called out, "Come back soon to teach me, because I want to die as soon as I am baptized." The boy went straight to the priest and told him what the sick man had said, and the priest listened and became concerned. Therefore, he went back to the sick man to finish catechizing him. Then he baptized him, and the Indian was true

to his word, for he died, leaving great assurances of his predestination and of having gone to heaven. As Saint Luke preached,[163] the Divine Shepherd said that it was right to search for a single lost sheep, even if it meant leaving the remaining ninety-nine.

Other innumerable cases similar to those above will not be recounted here, but through these cases God continued to remove the old, who are ordinarily an obstacle to the religious instruction of these people. He satisfied Himself by winning many of them over in the final moments of their lives, leaving the youth to be reared as the seed of the Gospel, which produced more abundant fruit. Some of these young men who were reared in the seminary turned out to be so skilled and devoted that, confident of their excellent intellectual capacity and virtue, the priest sometimes entrusted them to give speeches to the pueblo under his supervision. They did this in church, appropriately dressed and standing on the steps of the altar. This means was extremely effective because the same catechism taught by the minister of the Gospel was received with special pleasure and had a greater effect and impact, becoming more ingrained in their hearts, when it came from the mouths of their sons and relatives in their own style and language. All of the aforementioned means contributed to the salvation of these souls.

Finally, so that all of the fruits that are harvested from the rearing of these youths might be recounted, because these young men have greater [intellectual] capacity, they are the first among these new Christians to be introduced to the practice of Holy Communion, which requires more preparation than the other Holy Sacraments.

I will conclude this chapter by noting that around the year 1600 the priests had baptized and properly instructed approximately eighteen thousand souls in Sinaloa. To this number [101] already born in the arms of the Holy Church should be added the fruit that God continued to produce in the midst of this Christianity, as well as those who will be born in the future. This fruit should be attributed to the evangelical ministers who planted the Faith in these nations, just as the extremely fortunate growth of the Spaniards' Catholic Faith should be recognized and acknowledged as a fruit of the preaching of their glorious patron, Saint James, even though many feel that he converted only

---

163. *Margin Note*: Luc. 15. Luke 15 (The parable of the lost sheep).

a few of them to this Catholic Faith.[164] Although I acknowledge the great difference between this saint and the missionaries in Sinaloa who are being compared to him, it cannot be denied that all these souls were redeemed at the same price of Christ's divine blood, and that God selects many from among these people for heaven. The fruits of the vineyard planted by the glorious Saint James that are being harvested in Spain today are fruits of this holy Apostle's toil. In the same way we must confess that those that are harvested and will be harvested in the future from the vineyard of Sinaloa should be attributed in great measure to the six or seven evangelical workers who were chosen by God to plant His Holy Faith in Sinaloa. This fact should encourage those who labor in these enterprises, even though at the present time they are unable to see the full fruits they desire from their labors.

CHAPTER XXVII The captain goes to the Río Zuaque to pacify two warring nations; the rebellious Zuaque and one of their famous sorcerers are punished

Because this was a frontier at war, there were always acts of aggression that Captain Hurdaide was obliged to respond to with force of arms. After the expedition to Chínipa, the Ahome nation, which inhabited the lower part of the great Río Tehueco, came to him [in 1602] to register a complaint. The Tehueco nation (which is very fierce and warlike) had left its lands along the upper part of the river and had moved down into the river valley of the Ahome, where they stripped them of their land and usurped it for their own cultivation. They were not content with this, so they also took the Ahome's wives and daughters, whom they abused.[165] The captain was very upset by this, for although both nations were gentile, the Ahome had always been at peace with the Spaniards. They had placed themselves under the king's favor and protection and were very docile and obedient, even though they were more than twenty leagues from the villa.

Seeing that other measures had failed to bring the Tehueco to justice and reason, the captain was obliged to go in person to defend his allies, the Ahome, and to repair the damage that had been inflicted on them. After he armed his troops and some Indian allies he traveled to the pueblos of the Zuaque, through which he had to pass to reach the lands of the Ahome and the Valle de Mathaoa, where the Tehueco had usurped Ahome land. The Zuaque received word that the captain and his expedition would be traveling through their pueblos, and having failed to learn a lesson from their previous punishment, on this occasion they summoned their friends and comrades in arms, the Sinaloa, who had also experienced the punishment referred to earlier following the treachery that they had plotted with the Chínipa.

After reaching Zuaque [territory] the captain and his troops camped at a pueblo called Mochicahue, which had five hundred male heads-of-household and was located on a wide, flat plain. The Zuaque did not wish to battle the Spaniards when they entered the pueblo; they waited instead for a better opportunity [which arose] when the soldiers dismounted. However, the captain always was prepared and had some men

164. Pérez de Ribas is alluding here to serious doubts raised by theologians that James the Great, apostle and martyr (d. 44), ever preached the Gospel in Spain, or if he did, whether he converted significant numbers of people. From the twelfth through fifteenth centuries the cult of Saint James of Compostela mushroomed as miracle stories abounded of James' intercession as a defender of Christianity against the Moors (Farmer 1992:250).

165. It is not clear from Pérez de Ribas' usage (*usavan mal de ellas*) how they were abused; that is, whether they were raped or otherwise violated.

ready with armored horses [102]. While the captain was seated in his tent with Luisa, the Christian woman who was mentioned earlier, a troop of Sinaloa Indians came walking toward his tent with their bows and arrows in hand. They were led by a brave and warlike Indian who was a renowned sorcerer. He was very respected and revered by the Sinaloa and the Zuaque, as well as by other nations whom he incited with his tricks and diabolical arts. His fame spread far and wide, and it was common knowledge that he once mounted a horse and then raised it in the air, boasting, "When the priests who preach to you can do the same thing, you can believe what they teach you." Because of these tricks, ostentatious displays, and diabolical arts with which he stirred up so many nations and caused trouble among them, the captain wanted very much to get his hands on him, which is what happened on this occasion. The woman Luisa spotted the sorcerer approaching and told the captain, "Taxicora (which was the sorcerer's name) and his people are headed this way." The captain knew very well that these nations spring their ambushes quickly, and he suspected that they were being deceitful in coming to greet him, to see if they could capture him through treachery. Thus, in that brief moment when the sorcerer was nearing his tent, the captain deliberated whether to seize him or, given the present danger, let his capture go until another time. The entire Zuaque nation was there on top of him, and worse yet, there were the Sinaloa, whom Taxicora had brought to the verge of war. Moreover, the captain found his troop blocked from above by the Tehueco, who had set up rancherías eight leagues farther on, whence they could be summoned. The captain went over all of this in his mind, and he told me later that in that perilous moment he turned to himself and said, "Oh, Vizcaya, where are you?" He said this because he was the son of a Vizcayan and prided himself on having inherited the spirit displayed by that valiant nation on such occasions. It was with that courage, then, that he resolved to take the prisoner himself. With dissimulation he told the soldiers who were near his tent to secure and prepare the armored horses. Then he waited as the Indian sorcerer approached. He was carrying a bow and arrows, which is a sign of Indian arrogance. The captain, however, pretended not to recognize him and asked him who he was. Still talking and looking busy, he grabbed hold of the Indian's bow, stepping on the bowstring with his foot. Then he grabbed the Indian by the hair and had him bound and guarded. At the same time the captain ordered his soldiers to get ready for a possible attack. Fortunately, the Indians and Taxicora's

people withdrew. They did not attack because they feared that their leader, who was being held prisoner, might be killed. When they and the Zuaque withdrew, however, they divided into groups and encircled the pueblo, ready to fight at the moment the captain and his soldiers broke camp. At this point the captain could have been satisfied with his prisoner, which he had so wanted, and he could have left the campaign against the Tehueco for another time and returned to the villa. Instead, due to his great spirit and valor, he resolved to go forward and liberate his friends, the Ahome.

He gave the order to break camp and told Luisa to advise her people to remain quietly in their pueblo and not to shoot any arrows. He would be content with taking Taxicora prisoner. They were warned that if they started a fight, he would make them pay. The captain then commanded that Taxicora be placed on a mule in the center of the troop, along with a soldier as a guard, and they commenced to march. [103] As soon as the Zuaque and the Sinaloa heard about this, they gathered all along the way (which was somewhat blocked with trees and thickets) and proceeded to attack the Spaniards with such a great volley of arrows that the captain, who had had many skirmishes with the nations of Sinaloa, had never found himself or his soldiers in any greater danger. Because the path was so narrow and difficult, the soldiers could not make use of their armored horses, and they were kept plenty busy protecting themselves with their shields from the arrows that rained down on them. Their harquebuses could not harm the enemy, who fought with bows from behind the trees, where they were protected from the shots. The captain told the soldier who was guarding the prisoner to take out his sword and threaten to kill Taxicora right there on the mule if he did not tell his people to stop shooting arrows. The soldier knew the [Indian's] language well and threatened the prisoner with his sword in hand. Looking death in the eye, the prisoner shouted to his people, "Sons, do not shoot or they will kill me on the spot." The Indians were fighting so furiously that they ignored Taxicora and angrily continued shooting. Meanwhile, a soldier who was next to the captain had fallen on a rough stretch [of the trail]. Now, due to the weight of the armor, it is difficult to get up and remount a horse once you have fallen. At that moment the captain spurred his horse, grabbed an Indian, and proceeded to do something that, because of his pious spirit, he had never done before: he took an Indian's life without first preparing him to die as a Christian. There on the spot he put a noose around that Indian's neck and hanged him from a tree. When the others saw their companion hanged, their fury subsided somewhat. The troop, therefore, was only slightly affected and was able to escape danger and move forward with its prisoner.

Upon reaching the Valle de Mathaoa, where the Tehueco had settled in rancherías, the captain attacked them before they realized what was happening. They did not dare to face off with him in the open country, which is what characterized that valley. Therefore, he captured all the lesser people, of whom there must have been two hundred Tehueco women and children. He kept them under guard in camp and later sent a message to those who had retreated to the monte that they must give the Ahome their freedom and immediately leave those lands, which belonged to the Ahome, and return to their own. Although he could have done so, he had no intention of spilling the blood of innocent women and children. Instead, he would return all the prisoners, and he assured whoever came for them that he would allow them to enter his camp, provided they complied with his order to withdraw from Ahome territory. They trusted his word (because he always kept it) and accepted his conditions, pledging to comply with them, and they came to gather the prisoners and departed with their belongings, leaving the Ahome to enjoy their lands. The latter were very grateful to the captain and the Spaniards and asked that priests be sent to their pueblos so they could receive the word of the Holy Gospel and be baptized. As I will later discuss they received both of these with singular demonstrations of their desire to become Christian.

For now it remains [to be told] how the captain went once more after the rebel Zuaque, who had not yet been subjugated. We will see that he employed one of the most remarkable military strategies against barbarous nations that anyone has ever read about; notwithstanding that the prudent and brave Captain Hurdaide employed many such strategies.

He broke camp in the valley of the Ahome and proceeded with the Indian sorcerer [Taxicora] until he had reached the center of the same pueblo where he had taken him prisoner. The Zuaque understood very well that the captain was quite indignant with them because of their perverse stubbornness and their desire to continue waging war against the Spaniards. [104] Therefore, they did not dare to meet him on the open battlefield; instead, they withdrew to their strongholds—the montes that surround their pueblos, which horses cannot enter. They then sent Luisa to present

their excuse for having waged war and taken up arms: they had been incited by the Sinaloa when their principal sorcerer, Taxicora, was taken prisoner.

Readying his troops for attack, the captain replied to the woman that it was not his intention to spill Zuaque blood or burn their pueblo and houses which, because it was harvest time, were full of maize. They were to understand, however, that he would not leave without punishing them for their ferocity and boldness. He would be content if the Zuaque agreed to come forward to be whipped and to have the hair that they so esteemed cut. Each of them was also to contribute some of the cozcates, or beads, with which they adorn themselves to the Indian allies who had accompanied the captain. If they did this, he agreed not to touch their houses or fields, and they would finally understand how much they would benefit from peace and friendship with the Spaniards.

The Indian Luisa gave this message to her nation, and because this was a very difficult pact for some [to accept], they remained in the monte with their weapons in hand, watching to see what would happen. Seeing the danger they were in and knowing that the captain was now master of their houses and their food [supply] for the entire year, others began to surrender and submit to being whipped with the reins from a horse's bridle. The captain made sure they were not whipped vigorously, and then these Indians yielded their hair to the scissors. It was not cut too short, only to the top of the shoulder, leaving hair in the back to protect them from the sun. They also gave beads or bows and arrows to the captain's [Indian] allies, and then each was allowed to return to his house to guard it and keep it safe.

There were still those in the monte who watched and refused to lay down their weapons, so the captain commanded some of his soldiers to go through the pueblo and set fire to any house of which the owner remained unpunished. These houses caught fire easily because they were made of wood and woven reed mats. When the recalcitrant Indians understood the captain's resolve and saw the flames leap from the houses of those who had remained rebellious, they finally surrendered. Luisa yelled to persuade them to submit to punishment, and when this was done the captain broke camp. With his troop in formation he then set out for the villa with his prisoner, the sorcerer [Taxicora].

I want to comment on how frightened the proud Zuaque were at this moment. When the captain was executing his punishment he was heard to say that he would recognize by their hair those rebels who had not submitted to punishment and that he would mete out an exemplary punishment once he [finally] found them. This threat caused so much fear that those who had not been punished ran after the captain along the road once he had departed, saying to him, "Captain, I must still be punished. Do not come after me, here are my hair and my back." For those who have never experienced the Zuaque's hostile and warlike nature these tactics and the subjugation of this nation will not seem so impressive, but those who did know [the Zuaque] felt that it was remarkable how God stepped in with special aid for the captain. Hurdaide was satisfied to allow the Zuaque to keep their hair, and those who caught up with him along the road he sent home safely.

This expedition was concluded when the captain and his party reached the villa. Taxicora, the notorious sorcerer who had stirred up these nations, was brought to trial, and the captain sentenced him to hang. This was a well-deserved punishment, and the priests attended him at the hour of his death. He prepared well for this, as he received the Holy Sacrament of Baptism, thereby providing assurance of his salvation. [105] And as a result the province was rid of a great and troublesome obstacle to the preaching of the Holy Gospel.

CHAPTER XXVIII The captain of Sinaloa goes to Mexico City to give an account to the viceroy of the state of the province and to ask for religious and permission to catechize the Zuaque and other nations

In addition to those remarkable military operations that have [already] been credited to Captain Diego Martínez de Hurdaide, there were yet others that arose with the arrogant Zuaque, Sinaloa, and Tehueco nations. In each instance, with singular assistance from God, who clearly favored his Christian efforts, he always demonstrated the same bravery and skill. I will pass over them so as not to draw out this history with worldly events and enterprises, spiritual ones being my principal concern.

After the fortunate outcome of his many skirmishes with the nations of Sinaloa, the captain managed to tame and settle the three main nations—the Zuaque, the Sinaloa, and the Tehueco. The caciques of these three nations came to the captain and the priests to ask that they come to their lands and provide them with religious instruction. They finally wished to have the stable peace of those who were Christians, and they offered to build churches and to reduce their pueblos to convenient locations. This was happy news for the captain, and even more so for the religious, whose burning desires were to spread the glory of Christ's name throughout that entire province, especially among these three nations, for they were the doorway and passage for the Gospel to enter many other nations.

Two difficulties arose in carrying out these three nations' request. First, there was a lack of ministers who could take specific charge of these new missions and the extremely large number of pueblos and people found therein,[166] for the priests were busy in their own districts. The second and greatest difficulty was that there were orders from the viceroys that no more entradas to establish missions among nations were to be made without first reporting to His Excellency, without whose

---

166. At this time, 1604, there were still only four priests (Pérez, Méndez, Velasco, Villafañe) and one brother (Francisco de Castro) working in Sinaloa.

order the captain of the garrison cannot support such enterprises.[167] The captain must first provide information about the readiness of such nations to receive the catechism of the Gospel, for this also brings them under royal protection for their stability, preservation, and defense. This order is well reasoned and conforms to the advice that Christ Our Lord gave His disciples, charging them not to throw the pearls of His Gospel to unclean animals nor that which is holy to the dogs: *Nolite dare sanctum canibus, neque mittatis margaritasvestras ante porcos, ne forte conculcent eas pedibus suis & conversi dirumpant vos.*[168] By this Our Redeemer, who so desired the salvation of souls and the spread of His Gospel, caused it to be understood that one should be attentive to the disposition of those to whom he is preaching, as will be told in the case at hand. If you enter (as if the Divine Master Himself were speaking) to preach to a nation that has not been stripped of the fierceness and anger of dogs or one that does not wish to abandon the barbarous and filthy customs of unclean animals, then those precious pearls—the Divine Sacraments, the heavenly mysteries, and the venerable and holy jewels of the Church, which you offer to them without their understanding—will be tread upon, stepped upon, and rooted around. And those of you who offer them these things and preach to them will be trampled upon and [106] torn to pieces by their teeth and weapons: *Dirumpant vos.*[169] This perfectly describes these nations, who are accustomed to eating those whom they cut to pieces. Thus, this is a warning from the Master of Heaven.

The captain and the priests conferred on how to overcome the difficulties that might arise among nations that had been so savage as the three we have described here. They also discussed how to teach them the catechism, for a great deal of labor and blood had been spent reducing them to their present state of peace. With mature counsel it was resolved that the captain should go in person to Mexico City to report to the viceroy on the state of the province and the advisability of providing these nations with priests so as not to frustrate the willingness they had demonstrated to receive religious instruction. It was also resolved that he should take along some of these nations' Indian caciques so that they could personally implore the viceroy to grant them the favor of missions. This decision was carried out, and the principales of the three nations were notified. They joyfully accepted the trip to Mexico City in the company of the captain and four of his soldiers. The captain left his lieutenant behind with those in the villa.

The captain arrived in Mexico City [in the spring or early summer of 1604], where he was well received by the viceroy, the marquis of Montesclaros, who was satisfied with the captain's motives for making the journey. After consulting with the Father Provincial of the order concerning the wishes of the Tehueco, Zuaque, and Sinaloa Indians the viceroy resolved that the captain should return to Sinaloa with two priests, who were to be assigned to these nations. Once they had determined that these Indians were ready to receive the catechism of the Holy Gospel they were to begin by baptizing the infants and, if more ministers were necessary, they would be sent later to help them. In addition to this the viceroy ordered that the royal officials make a withdrawal from His Majesty's treasury for a complete set of ornaments for the priests and the altars, as well as chalices, bells, and musical instruments. He also ordered that the Indians whom the captain had brought be given clothing and swords, with which they returned quite contented. He also gave them alms for provisions for the return journey to their lands. The Archbishop of Mexico, Don Fray García de Mendoza y Zúñiga, who greatly enjoyed seeing these Indians, also helped out. The Most Illustrious [Archbishop] indicated to the viceroy that he supported the request for missions and also believed that the Indians should return well treated. In spite of all the gifts and favors that were bestowed on these Indians, some of them failed in their good intentions and in the loyalty of believers, as will be told in the following chapter. These are inconstancies to which these nations are subject in the beginning. Still, there were others who remained steadfast in their good intentions and later assisted greatly in the settlement and catechism of their nations.

---

167. As noted, under the terms of the Patronato Real, the crown and its agents (the viceroys) had the authority of ecclesiastical appointment, including the assignment of missionaries, whose stipends were provided by the crown.

168. *Margin Note*: Matth. 6. Matthew 7:6: "You must not give that which is holy to dogs. Do not cast your pearls before swine, or the swine may trample them under foot, and then turn on you and tear you to pieces" (Knox 1956:6).

169. Matthew 7:6: "tear you to pieces."

CHAPTER XXIX The captain returns to Sinaloa; events along the way; the unrest that he found in the province and how he calmed things

Captain Hurdaide was very pleased with what he had accomplished on his mission and by the fact that he was returning with two more preachers who would bring the Gospel to additional nations, which he so desired to see Christian.[170] He and his company left Mexico City and traveled eighty leagues to the city of Zacatecas. There one night four of the Indians who had been treated and cared for so well unexpectedly fled for no reason other than their inconstancy, and even more for the good that ultimately came of their flight. This concerned the captain not because they were necessary to him, but rather because he knew from his great knowledge of these nations the ease with which their restless leaders could foment rebellion. He suspected (and rightfully so) [107] that those who had fled would lie and brag, embellishing their flight as they generally do, stirring up their people and causing them to rebel. As soon as the captain learned of their flight he set out that night on horseback to look for them. The Indians, however, were shrewd and took a path off the main road. It must be pointed out that even though they were two hundred leagues from their own lands and were traveling through territory with deep gorges and mountains that were often uninhabited, they never got lost or perished. They had traveled the main road [from Sinaloa to Mexico City] only once before, and on their return they avoided it, eating nothing but grasses and wild roots.

The captain was unable to capture his prisoners and became very concerned about what those who had fled might plot once they reached their lands. Therefore, he increased the distance he traveled each day en route to the Topia mining center, which is sixty leagues from Sinaloa. There he received news of even greater concern. First, the Indians who had fled had encountered three Indians from Culiacán near the border between Sinaloa and Culiacán. These Indians had stopped to rest for the night in an arroyo, where they were killed by the fugitives who, according to their old customs, wanted

scalps with which to dance and celebrate an uprising. Their plan was to persuade the Tehueco nation to rebel, so they cut off their victims' heads and left the trunks of their bodies. Then when they reached their people, they agitated everyone and everything came to pass just as the captain had feared and imagined it would. These nations did not entirely believe the braggarts, however, and when they saw that the captain was not going to leave their crime unpunished they retreated with some of their supporters to the gentile mountain nation of Tepahue.

The second piece of news the captain was given was that two other pueblos, Ocoroni and Bacaburito, had rebelled and burned their churches. The pretext and reasons for doing so were partially true, but mostly false,[171] and there were still some good Christians who had remained calm and had not supported the rebel cause. These bits of news reached Captain Hurdaide at Topia on the very day he had taken a purge for a bout of illness.[172] No sooner had he consumed the purge than he set off for Sinaloa, despite the efforts of miners at the camp to detain him. To fulfill the duties of his office, he was prepared to confront the rebels' poisonous barbed arrows. On this occasion it seemed to him that in order to halt the uprising before it got started and before the leaders could retreat to distant nations, where it would be more difficult to retrieve them, he was bound by duty to risk death from the copious purge he had taken. Those who had remained calm did not follow the [rebel] leaders, and God favored this good enterprise because the purge did not harm the captain as he made long journeys across the harsh and extremely frigid peaks of the Topia mountain range.

When the captain finally reached Sinaloa with the two priests, they were welcomed with great joy by the priests who were already there and the rest of the

---

170. Curiously, Pérez de Ribas makes no mention here that he was one of the two priests; the other was Cristóbal de Villalta.

171. Pérez de Ribas presumably is alluding here to the Indians' doubts about the efficacy of Christianity in the wake of the epidemic of 1601–2 and then floods and famine in 1604, the same year when Hurdaide made his trip to Mexico City.

172. Like many Spaniards Hurdaide probably suffered from quartan malaria or typhoid (Reff 1991b:107).

people in the villa. Events in the province had caused the priests to suffer greatly during the captain's absence, but now that he was back they were certain that his bravery and prudence would [108] remedy all the unrest. And they were not disappointed, because afterwards the first thing that he tried to do was to provide security for those Indians who had remained calm. He then sent messages of peace to the rebels and a pardon to those who were innocent. Some took advantage of these offers, but the captain and his soldiers had to go after those from Bacaburito. Despite some dangerous skirmishes he was able to capture them; those who were [true] rebels and had authored the uprising paid with their heads. He ordered some to hang and obliged the others to rebuild the churches they had burned. As a result, this pueblo became well established and has been very steadfast in its peace and Christianity ever since.

The captain did not forget about the Indians who had fled at Zacatecas, who had cut off the heads of the Indians from Culiacán. These Indians had retreated to the mountain lands of the gentile Tepahue nation, with whom they had a long-standing alliance. When the captain heard about this he sent for the leaders of the Tehueco nation, to which the fugitives belonged. He reasoned and explained to them how unfounded and unreasonable their relatives' and fellow Tehueco's flight and attempted rebellion had been. He also told them of how well they had been treated on the trip to and from Mexico City and of the murders they had committed. The people of Culiacán were complaining and demanding satisfaction, so he told them he was obliged to search out the delinquents and bring them to justice, even if this meant entering the Tepahue's mountains, which they considered inaccessible and impenetrable.

I want to refer here to a saying that the captain often repeated, which is worthy of his bravery. It goes like this: Whenever they came to tell him about Indian outlaws who had gone into the montes or gorges, where they bragged that neither the captain nor his horses could enter, he would ask this question of whomever brought him these types of messages: "Does the sunlight reach those lands?" They answered that it did, and he immediately responded, "Well, then, I will go where the sunlight goes." Because they knew that the captain's protestations and threats were not mere words, they became concerned whenever he spoke. Once the Tehueco learned of the captain's resolve, in order to prevent a destructive search of their settlements by his soldiers, the Tehueco agreed to send a sizable squad of Indians

to capture those who had fled and to help convince the Tepahue to relinquish the fugitives. Five hundred Indians were dispatched, who negotiated well, returning with the four who had fled. They turned them over to the captain, who had them executed in the same place where they had killed the Indians from Culiacán. The people from Culiacán were satisfied with this, and it also taught others a lesson about challenging the captain.

Although the captain had punished the attackers and had taken care of the uprising by the Bacaburito, he still had to deal with the rebellious pueblo of Ocoroni. The reduction of these people provided much more of a challenge because there were very few of them left after they fled their pueblo. Those who rebelled numbered around four hundred, about two hundred of whom were archers. They had fled inland, where they took refuge with nations that were enemies of the Spaniards; this made it very difficult to seek them out.

In order to say something of peace and edification in the midst of all these wars and uprisings, it is well worth recounting here the display of [109] fidelity and the establishment of Christian catechism in those whom God chooses from among these people, especially those of a tender age. It happened that Father Pedro Méndez, who was catechizing this rebellious pueblo as well as others that were at peace, had gathered for religious training and education as many as sixteen young men and boys, who were learning to read, write, sing, serve in the church, and teach the catechism in the priest's absence. Following the Ocoroni uprising, the fathers, mothers, and relatives of these boys and young men worked diligently to badger these boys into rebelling and fleeing with them. All of them bravely resisted these attacks, and for even greater security they ran from their natural parents and sought out those who had engendered them in Christ and had reared them in virtue and holy customs. Throughout the entire uprising, which lasted a long time, they did not part the priest's company, which amazed everyone, both Indians and Spaniards. They saw people who were very tender in age and the Faith who were not stripped of reason by their love of their fathers and mothers, which is ardent and lively among these nations.

In the end the Ocoroni persisted in fleeing. This had both favorable and adverse consequences, and although these results were contradictory to each other they were nevertheless joined by divine providence. The negative result of the Ocoroni's flight was that it led to the most pitched battles between Spaniards and Indians in the

Province of Sinaloa since the time of its discovery.[173] The favorable consequence of this uprising was the conversion of two of the most populous nations in Sinaloa, the Mayo and the Yaqui. All of this will be seen later in this history, in Book V. There it will be necessary to refer to the reduction of the Ocoroni, which was achieved along with and linked to that of the famous Yaqui nation.

CHAPTER XXX The founding and conversion of pueblos and rancherías in the mountains near the Villa de San Felipe

Much of the Province of Sinaloa is made up of extensive plains, and up to this point I have written only about the nations and missions on the plains near the Villa de San Felipe. I have waited until now to write about the establishment of Christianity among nations whose pueblos and rancherías are no more than eight, ten, or twelve leagues from the villa, but which are very difficult to reach because they are located in rough mountains. These nations, including the Chicorato, the Cahuemeto, and other neighboring rancherías,[174] were the last in the vicinity of the villa to receive the Gospel and be reduced to peace. Years ago Spaniards looking for mineral deposits had visited them, but these forays were short-lived. The Indians stirred up trouble and showed little friendship and peace toward the Spaniards and also caused unrest in neighboring Christian pueblos. It was for this reason—to establish peace—that the captain entered their lands, and through deft reasoning and without bloodshed he was fortunately successful. He made a deal with them to expel some Christian Indians who were living among them as they pleased, with freedom of conscience. [110] He then succeeded in having more than fifteen hundred of them settle in a suitable place.[175] To further oblige them to leave the summits and rugged mountains he had their maize and other foodstuffs carried on mules and pack animals to where they were to be reduced. Finally, with the Christian spirit and generosity with which he dealt in such matters, he bought farmland from their Christian neighbors for them to cultivate and gave them fruit trees to enjoy. He also entrusted their Christian neighbors with helping them build new homes, and with this assistance what was previously a desert was transformed into a great pueblo [of Cahuemeto]. To insure that they remained there, the captain had their old homesteads burned, after which the Cahuemeto remained contented.

After this episode the captain returned to the villa, where he met with the Father Rector of the college. Together they decided that because these people were related to old Christians and were so well disposed, it would be possible to immediately instruct them in the catechism. They were entrusted to Father Pedro de Velasco, who had recently arrived from Mexico City [in February 1607] to help the other missionary priests. This priest, who was so willing to endure many difficult tasks to spread the Faith of Christ Our Lord, eagerly accepted the enterprise, even though it was in those rugged mountains and among peoples much poorer and worse off than those of the plains. These Indians are also shorter and less corpulent and are very swift walkers and climbers of cliffs and rocks. They are very adept with the bow and arrow, the heads of which they work from flint. Although the flint is not strong enough to penetrate chain mail armor in the same way as the fire-hardened wooden tips of the plains Indians,

173. Pérez de Ribas is alluding here to later battles involving the Yaqui, discussed in Book 5.

174. The Bazapa, Hoguera, Gozopa, Oronirato, and Bayacato. Little is known about the Chicorato, the Cahuemeto, or these other groups; all are thought to have spoken the same language, Comanito (Dunne 1940:97ff.; Sauer 1934, 1935).

175. This relocation apparently took place toward the end of 1607.

and although they make less use of the poisonous herb, their flint tips nevertheless cause a wound that is more difficult to heal. When these flint arrowheads, which are shaped like a harpoon, enter the flesh the flint stays inside when the arrow is removed. If the wound is deep it is impossible to extract the point without great harm and danger. Whereas the Spaniards fear this type of arrow less because of their defensive weapons, the Indian allies, who fight in the nude, do so at greater risk.

Because this also relates to the difference between the nations of the mountains and those of the plains, I note that the mountain women work harder, mainly carrying loads. One Indian woman carries what would be a burden even for a pack animal. They climb cliffs and peaks, loaded down with maize, jars of water, and other valued possessions. They wear a sash around their head that extends down their back, forming a long basket of sorts, in which they carry one or two children. With staff in hand they climb those mountains and walk many leagues. The women begin training for this type of labor and transport when they are young and are first able to walk. Just as boys are equipped at an early age by their fathers with a small bow and arrows so that they will become skillful archers, so mothers hang small loads of greater or lesser weight from the heads of young girls according to their strength. In this way they become very skilled at crossing the mountains and are readily able to transport their households and valued possessions.

It was in this vineyard, the plants and labor of which had been entrusted to him by God, that this religious priest began to work. This labor began with abundant first fruits and prospered [111] with the hundreds of infants that he baptized. In order not to repeat what has already been said about the conversions of other nations, I will not recount in detail here the general Baptism of adults. Once this was completed [in 1611][176] almost all these extremely poor mountainous people were baptized, numbering up to six thousand souls. With this marvelous expansion of Christianity in the province those who appeared to be mountain deer were domesticated and transformed into tame lambs of Christ. They were so obedient that they did not even go to their fields without first letting the priest know, for fear that the latter might find them absent from church. They accepted the catechism with enormous pleasure; indeed, whenever there was a celebration in a neighboring pueblo of established Christians they would assemble as a group, and wearing garlands on their heads and following a Cross, they would enter that pueblo singing the catechism. This amazed and gladdened the established Christians, who only a short time before had known them to be so wild. All of this served to encourage everyone in the Faith.

A singular salutation that was very famous among them, which had been introduced by their priest and minister and which still remains today, is to greet each other with the extremely sweet names of Jesus and Mary. Indeed, it is a cause of great happiness to pass by another's rancho and to be welcomed by loud voices saying, "Jesus and Mary." This is a practice introduced by their priests, who look upon these poor little things as their own children. Just as Christian children's real parents teach them to parrot and pronounce these beneficent names, in the same way this priest reared these infants in the Faith on this milk so that they would articulate these divine names and their hearts would be imprinted with the love and knowledge of those to whom they belonged. This might appear to be childishness, but we see that the Son of God was pleased when, upon entering Jerusalem, the children acclaimed Him with *Hosanna filio David*.[177] Moreover, He silenced the scribes who were upset with this salutation, making them understand that the children's greeting was very agreeable to Him, saying, *Numquam legistis, ex ore infantium, and lactentium perfecisti laudem*.[178] This was fulfilled in those who were children in the Faith.

A very good Christianity was established among these people, characterized by adherence to Christian practices, just as in all the other [nations]. When called to say the Hail Mary, they all gathered in their homes to pray. They took this so much to heart that they would remain in prayer for more than an hour, and everyone knew the Christian catechism. What they had great difficulty changing with respect to their old customs was growing their hair long, for at the time of Baptism it had to be cut. They also had difficulty refraining from burying their dead in the countryside and placing some reeds full of water at the side of the deceased for the imagined journey (as was told before)—all superstitions and abuses. The priest was obliged to deliver a long speech on this point and to explain to them the

---

176. The anua of 1610 has several of Velasco's letters, which Pérez de Ribas draws from for this chapter.

177. *Margin Note*: Matth. c. 21. Matthew 21:9: "Hosanna for the son of David" (Knox 1956:21).

178. Matthew 21:16: "have you never read the words, 'Thou hast made the mouths of children, of infants at the breast, vocal with praise?'" (Knox 1956:22).

meaning of the customs and rites that the Church commands be used for the burial of Christians. They were greatly enlightened and rewarded by this instruction and were so happy with burying the dead at the church that when the priest asked whether there were any gentiles who wanted to be baptized, instead of answering, "Yes," they responded, "Well, will you bury me in the church?" What had once been an impediment to Baptism was now motivation.

The priest's talk also served to eradicate another abuse dealing with the dead that was practiced by this nation in particular. [112] When someone's wife, sons, or close relatives died and the person was buried, the widower, widow, or the deceased's next of kin was taken to a river, and there facing west, he was submerged in the water three times. This was done for three consecutive days, and afterwards they locked him up in a house for eight days, where he was unable to eat game or fish and was given only a small amount of maize flour and water. During this time he was not allowed to be seen by anyone, nor could he go to church to hear Mass, even if he was a Christian. Once the priest learned of this superstition he taught them how to help their dead with prayers and good deeds, thereby banishing this superstition.

There was a very singular case that is worthy of mention here because it is a declaration of the virtue of the holy Cross. This case involved a sorcerer who had a very close relationship with the devil. When the priest baptized him he admonished him to renounce and discontinue all the pacts he had established with such a great enemy of humankind. The Indian gave his word that he would, and he was baptized. His word and good intentions fell short, however, and he allowed the devil to visibly appear to him several times, persuading him to return to his diabolical arts. The distressed Indian asked the priest for a remedy, which he gave him, charging him to renounce the devil and his dealings with him. In addition, the priest ordered him to place several Crosses in his house and to make the sign of the Cross whenever the devil appeared. One time when the Indian was lying on his bed the devil began calling from outside in a terrifying manner, telling him to remove the Crosses if he wanted him to come inside. The Indian responded that he could not come in or see him, that he was not going to remove the Crosses, and that the devil should go away, for he never wanted to share in his friendship again. The devil was driven away by this response and never returned, and the Indian was left quite contented for having achieved victory by means of the holy Cross, the divine remedy that the saints used in their battles with this fierce beast.

CHAPTER XXXI A disturbance, rebellion, and uprising in these pueblos and how it was suppressed; the priests' steadfastness in ministering to these pueblos

The devil was furious to see himself exiled from those mountains where he had made his stronghold. Stripped of the vassals that he had so subjugated, he searched for ways to return to the castles that he had lost. He managed to do so on the occasion that I will relate here. A pueblo of Christians was celebrating a feast day, which attracted many people from all around. They had decided to play correr el palo (a game that was previously described), and a disagreement arose between the two groups that had come to play concerning the rules of the game.[179] This disagreement reached the point that some took up their bows to settle matters (a rare thing among these people). The priest was present at the time and managed

179. This dispute is recounted in a letter of January 13, 1613, by Father Juan Calvo, which was copied into the anua for that year. Calvo had arrived in Sinaloa in 1611 to assist Pedro de Velasco. The Chicarato and the Cahuemeto, long-time enemies, were the two parties involved in this dispute, which took place at the recently founded Chicorato mission of San Ignacio.

to settle their differences, making them put down their weapons. Still, some sparks of rancor remained and the devil attempted to fan them into flames, inducing them to ignore the priest's exhortations and return to their barbarous freedom. To take revenge [113] on their opponents, the troublemakers withdrew to neighboring gentile pueblos, where they were supported in their decision to go and kill the priest. They would have executed their perverse intent if they had not encountered en route some other gentile Indians who knew the priest and had benefited from his good deeds. They sang in their own manner very high praises of the priest, relating how well he had treated the people of their pueblos. Thus, they made the others change their minds and decide to turn back. Their having decided against taking the evangelical minister prisoner did not mean, however, that their angry spirit had been quieted. They captured two Christian Indians whom they found fishing at a river and cut off their heads, taking them to celebrate their feasts and drunken revels. The priest tenderly regretted the death of his Christians, whom he loved as his [own] children, but it was of some consolation to him that one of them had confessed shortly before [he died]. The priest went to recover the bodies and give them Christian burial at the church. Although there was great sorrow among the rest of the Christians, he managed to calm them with sound reasoning so that they would not rise up against the killers and search them out in vengeance, as they generally did in their heathenism.

These are the dangerous circumstances in which the ministers of the Gospel frequently found themselves, especially in the beginning of these missions. So that one might note the special providence with which more than a few times God Our Lord protected His faithful servants in the midst of innumerable troubles and mortal danger, I will write here about an unusual case that happened to a priest of this mission at this time. At nightfall he[180] was saying the Rosary under a ramada at the door of his little brush house when suddenly, without any warning whatsoever, such a terrible fear overcame him that his entire body began to tremble and he was forced to go inside his poor hut to finish saying the Rosary on his knees. At that very same moment a boy who had gone for a firebrand was hit by an arrow in the very same spot where the priest had been; had the priest remained there, he would have been

killed. In truth, on innumerable occasions the Sovereign Virgin is quite able to save the devotees of her Holy Rosary from such dangers.

Although the infernal wolf was foiled in his attempt to kill this shepherd of Christ's flock, he did not desist in his plans to destroy the flock itself. To this end he encouraged the gentiles and bad Christians who had killed those two Indians to set fire to the churches in the Christian pueblos. They burned the churches and a large number of houses, and also attempted to get the rest of the Indians to accompany them in their rebellion and uprising and to be accomplices to their crimes. In one of the pueblos the good Christians resisted very bravely and clashed with the rebels in a bloody battle in which one of the aggressors was killed and some of his comrades were wounded. None of the Christian defenders was killed; after sending the captain a request for help they fortified themselves on a small hill near their pueblo and buried their [church] bell so that their enemies would not smash it. In addition, they took the [holy] image from their church to the monte until the aforesaid help could arrive. After the captain reached their pueblo with his soldiers [in 1614] he pursued the enemy and seized some of the delinquents, whom he executed. The rest he reduced, thereby restoring peace and quiet to the pueblos and church of this [114] Christian community.

The devout Father Pedro de Velasco labored here for many years.[181] He advanced and promoted this Christianity through his great spirit and zeal for the welfare and salvation of these poorest of souls. This is revealed in his own letter[182] to our Father Provincial, who was calling him to Mexico City to assign him to a more prestigious ministry in letters, in which he was quite talented. The priest would also have excelled at this job because of his illustrious bloodline: He was of the house of the commander-in-chief[183] of Castilla and was the son of Don Diego de Velasco, former governor of the Province of Nueva Vizcaya.[184] His written reply

---

180. Although below Pérez de Ribas implies Pedro de Velasco was involved in this incident, it was Father Juan Calvo, who was in his mission of San Ignacio.

181. From 1607 to 1621, at which point Velasco left the frontier for Mexico City, where he taught Scripture and moral theology at the Colegio Máximo of San Pedro y San Pablo. As Velasco's letter below indicates, he at first resisted this transfer which, contrary to Pérez de Ribas' assertion, did occur in 1621. From 1646 to 1649 Velasco served as Jesuit provincial of Nueva España.

182. This letter was written in 1610 to Nicolás de Arnaya, the Jesuit provincial.

183. *Condestable.* Title of the dignitary official in charge of all military forces.

184. Diego Fernández de Velasco was governor of Nueva Vizcaya from 1595 to 1598 (Polzer, Barnes, and Naylor 1977:106). At the time

to the Father Provincial is of great edification; it reads as follows:

> I received Your Reverence's letter, and although its paternal affection is of special consolation to me, my heart cannot help but regret what has occurred to me. On the one hand, I see a great chance to serve Our Lord, as well as the grand opportunities in this region for His greater glory. On the other hand, looking my faults straight in the eye, I felt that if I should suffer some penance and punishment because of them, it would be that the Lord would strip me of such great employment (as if I were a base individual) and place me elsewhere. Thus, as I see that this is coming to pass I must pay great heed to it. When I see this punishment carried out I believe that the Lord is remembering my sin. My Father Provincial, I feel tenderly and most eagerly about helping these poor little ones. I am inclined to this ministry and am adverse, for my part, to the Spaniards' pretenses. All of this should be of little consequence with respect to my not wanting to surrender promptly. And yet, although it causes great distress on my part to [fail in] holy obedience, I nevertheless present them to Your Reverence, as one who is an affectionate father and superior. It occurs to me to point out that a consequence of my transfer would be the loss of a great amount of glory to Our Lord. This can be deduced from the thousands of souls who have been baptized in this place. In the first three years more than three hundred people died who had just been baptized or had just received the sacraments. It seems to me that as a result, more glory will have been rendered to God than would be in the same amount of time required for me to teach a course in the literary arts. There are still a great number of gentiles to be baptized and many dry-boned elderly people scattered among those peaks who must be brought down from the mountains, gathered together, and given spiritual life. It seems that this must be done through the voice and tongue of some prophet, and although I may not be

> the one, I have been the first priest and minister among them. There are three languages spoken in these pueblos, and I did everything possible to learn two of them and am now learning the third. The position of reader and lecturer can be filled much more satisfactorily by other ministers in Mexico City. When I think of leaving this ministry my remorse returns, thinking that I have to exchange the book of the Gospel of Christ and His Apostles for one written by Aristotle. This is all due to my own faults, for not having known how to read the book of the Holy Gospel with the necessary willingness and reverence. Going to live near my relatives will only serve for lesser calm, so I trust that the lord viceroy, who is so pious and prudent, will allow me to remain here. That would be of great service to Our Lord and to the welfare of these peoples, who are so defenseless, as I will write to His Excellency. May Our Lord keep Your Reverence, into whose holy sacrifices and prayers I commend myself, requesting with the necessary resignation that you please consider my proposal if possible.

This was the priest's letter, and because it demonstrates the apostolic spirit in which it was written, it needs no commentary. I note only that the lord viceroy would [in the end] be satisfied, for His Excellency had asked [115] the Father Provincial to bring this priest to Mexico City because he was a relative.

To his most religious reply I could add other very similar ones concerning other very talented individuals and ministers who have worked in these enterprises that are of such glory to Our Lord. In the end all the offers which were made to Father Pedro de Velasco were not powerful enough to move him from these crags and brambles, nor from the dangers in which he lived out his beloved evangelical career.

Pedro de Velasco assumed his mission post in Sinaloa his uncle, Luis de Velasco II, was viceroy. It appears that Pedro's great uncle was Luis de Velasco I, the eighth viceroy of Nueva España (1590–95) (Polzer, Barnes, and Naylor 1977:99).

CHAPTER XXXII An account of the great loyalty [shown] by these peoples on the occasion of an attack by the Tepehuan rebels

The unusual case that follows will definitively illustrate the steadfastness of these mountain people, the proof of their loyal Christianity, and how rooted their priest's instruction remained in their hearts.[185] At the time when Father Pedro de Velasco was quietly instructing his already pacified pueblos the Tepehuan Rebellion took place. This uprising, which will be written about at great length elsewhere,[186] was very famous in Nueva España. When this extremely bellicose nation rebelled the Spaniards declared war against them and sought to punish them for their terrible crimes. The Tepehuan then tried to defend themselves by asking other nations to take up arms and join the rebellion. They devoted great effort to the Christian mountain peoples whom we are discussing, encouraging them to burn their churches and return to their former lives as gentiles. They dispatched several messengers, at times with threats, at times with promises, asking the mountain people to carry out their perverse plan. They offered the bloodied clothing of Spaniards whom they had killed, including a bloodstained shirt from one of the eight holy priests, ministers of the Gospel, whom they had murdered. They also unsheathed the swords that had been taken from dead Spaniards to persuade these Christians to become accomplices in the attempted general uprising. However, all the Chicorato Indians and most of the Cahuemeto remained faithful to God and their Faith. They rejected the rebel and apostate Tepehuan, ignoring their perverse arguments. This reply so angered the rebels that they decided to destroy them. They decided to attack one of the Christian pueblos [San Ignacio] on a feast day at a time when everyone was gathered in the church, unsuspecting and unarmed. They planned to set a fire and thereby put an end to the church and the Christians.

They tried to implement their strategy as planned on a Sunday morning, when there were more than six hundred persons in church. [After the congregation had] finished praying and had heard the sermon, and while the priest was putting on his vestments to say Mass, a band of furious Tepehuan suddenly entered the pueblo, intent upon burning the church and killing whomever they found. This would have been dreadful if God had not intervened through His divine providence. As it happened, a boy who was up in the bell tower spotted the enemy and raised the alarm. The people, who were unarmed, were very concerned because the enemy was already in the plaza of the church. The men raced out of the church to take up their bows, even though they were exposed to great danger. In the end those whose houses were nearby were able to get their weapons. They were aided by two soldiers with harquebuses who happened to be in the pueblo. Once the good Christians gathered their weapons they attacked the enemy, and the fight lasted for a good while. [116] God helped the Christians, and although some were wounded, these were taken to the priest's house, where he treated them and heard their confessions. In the end the good Christians decapitated some of the apostate Tepehuan and wounded others, pushing them back until they finally had to retreat.

God granted this marvelous victory to these steadfast Christians who, unwarned and unarmed, were hearing Mass in a church made of straw. They would have all burned if God Our Lord had not interceded. He also delivered the priest from clear danger, for just as he emerged from the church to shelter the women and children in his nearby house, which was made of earth and not in danger of burning, the Tepehuan shot an arrow that came so close that it was good fortune that it did not pierce him.

Even though this danger passed and God saved this Christian pueblo, they still feared greatly that the Tepehuan would return and attack again. For this reason the priest decided to secure the church's [holy] images by sending them to the villa until things quieted down. The good Christians, however, would not permit him to do so, promising that they would guard them with their weapons and lives, as they did. They stood watch

185. Velasco's letter recounting the events of this chapter appears in the anua of 1617.

186. This rebellion, which began in November 1616, is discussed at length in Book 10.

over their church for a long time until the trouble subsided, which was proof of their constancy and perseverance in their faith in God and His minister who taught it to them. Even in the midst of the fight, they endeavored to console the priest's anguish at seeing his faithful and constant flock in such danger. Afterward, the captain protected them by sending some soldiers,[187] who searched for the Tepehuan and blocked their passage through that region into the Province of Sinaloa, although some (as will be told further ahead) attempted to gain entry by other routes.

This happy event also served some neighboring Indians who had not yet converted to the Church. Upon seeing the misguided Tepehuan and the evil life and restlessness that went along with their rebellion, they reconsidered conversion, coming in groups of three hundred with Crosses in their hands as a sign of peace.

They settled in the Christian pueblo of San Lorenzo, and the devil lost what he had set out to win. The inhabitants of other pueblos near Tecuchuapa also came down [out of the mountains] to settle there, for greater safety and to receive instruction. Thus, this Christian community and district where Father Pedro de Velasco labored with great effort for many years, tending to it with unusual care and building very handsome churches, was greatly augmented. He aided in the salvation of the great number of souls that we can understand were saved by his instruction, as well as in the salvation of those whom God continues to select. This very diligent Christian community perseveres greatly improved today, and it was this priest who laid its first foundations. Therefore, he has a large part in all that is built upon those foundations and is subsequently gathered for heaven.

CHAPTER XXXIII Indians from another mountain nation called Tubari come to request missions and Holy Baptism and return with hopes of receiving them

With the present discussion of the Tubari nation, we will leave for the time being those who inhabit the sierra, returning to the plains of Sinaloa to conclude the first enterprise and triumphs of [117] the Faith that were achieved in this province, which were followed by even greater ones. The Tubari nation is not very populous and lives two days' journey from the nation discussed in the previous chapter [the Cahuemeto]. They inhabit several rancherías along the upper part of the great Río Sinaloa. Even before they were Christian these Indians always showed a kind heart toward Spaniards. (This is an expression they use to make it understood that they are friendly and loyal to other nations.) The Tubari were never unfriendly to the Spaniards, and they have never made war on them or harmed them on those

occasions when Spaniards entered their lands. Rather, they punctually came to Captain Hurdaide's aid during the explorations that he undertook.

They sometimes had contact with Christian Indians with whom they traded for salt, which they do not have in their lands. Father Juan Calvo, who cared for the neighboring Christian nation, said the following of the Tubari nation:

> I had (he says) a good opportunity to speak with the Tubari and to discuss their salvation through Baptism, which was very important to them. I have done this many times with many of them, and they always gave me good answers and expressed a desire to put into action that which was discussed. However, because the mountain region has been so restless during these years due to the Tepehuan Revolt, so much so that we were not even secure here in the pueblos that had been settled and Christianized, I did not push the issue [of their conversion]. The superior had instructed me that for the time being it was not advisable to put a

---

187. Six soldiers were temporarily lodged at Chicorato.

lot of energy into this, so I was content with having and keeping them as our friends, as they always have been, even when the whole mountain region had taken up arms and was at war. This was clearly seen during the Tepehuan uprising, when the latter came to Tubari lands asking for food, arrows, and people to help them in their evil efforts. The Tepehuan threatened the Tubari with death and the ruination of everything if they did not comply with all their requests. They offered them rewards and gifts that they had stolen from the churches and Spaniards. But the Tubari were not interested in the Tepehuan's gifts or in helping them. They remembered (as they themselves later disclosed) what I had told them to say just a few days earlier after I had heard that the Tepehuan had revolted and were making their retreat through these mountains. In the event that they should reach Tubari territory the Tubari were not to grant them entry nor were they to give them any provisions. If they did so and showed them favor, they could be sure that the captain would punish them. With this warning they did not dare to give them anything, placing a higher value on the friendship of the Spaniards than on that of the Tepehuan. When the Tepehuan arrived, therefore, the faithful Tubari sent Indians to notify me.

Now that the Lord has established calm throughout this mountain region, the Tubari have come down to our Christian pueblo more frequently, always showing greater signs of wanting to be baptized and become Christian. They have also gone to Fort Montesclaros, where Captain Diego Martínez de Hurdaide resided, to request a mission and priests to instruct them. This year, 1620, in the month of January forty of the most principal Indians from all the rancherías of this nation came down to the pueblo of Yecorato to see me. They began presenting their case by telling me that their hearts were saddened and disconsolate [118] because they realized that other distant nations already had priests and churches and were Christian, whereas they, who are closer, have not yet been baptized and are without a priest. They therefore requested that I come and baptize them, because I knew how many times they had asked me to do so. My heart went out to them because on the one hand I saw with how much reason and truth they spoke, and on the other I saw that I could not attend to their good wishes as quickly as they wanted and hoped because I had to wait for the viceroy's order and permission. Therefore, I sent them to the Villa de San Felipe to present their good wishes to the Father Rector and to Captain Diego Martínez de Hurdaide. They were received with great kindness and given gifts and staffs of *topiles*,[188] which is a type of office like a minister of justice. These were given to ten of the most principal Indians, who appreciated this gift. With this and the high hopes that superiors would soon give them a mission they returned very consoled and encouraged.

They promised that as soon as they reached their ranchos they would gather everyone together in three places. There they would build churches and a house for the priest, thus obliging the superiors to establish missions more quickly. One of them added, "So that you understand, Father, that this comes from the heart and that we speak in truth, upon reaching our lands we will send you four of our sons to be taught the catechism and baptized. Then they can teach us when they come back with you." They did just as they had promised, because when they reached their lands, four of the aforementioned topiles sent me four of their sons, adding that if I wanted more, they would send them. The four boys were quite content in the village of Yecorato, where they are being taught the catechism.

I had known for a long time about the large number of Tubari people, having been told of their numbers by the many Indians from this mission district who go to trade with the Tubari for mantas, of which they have a great abundance. I wanted to find out more precisely [how many there were], so I sent an Indian who spoke Spanish well who was also of their same tongue and nation. He had been born in one of the pueblos in the area where I am and, accompanied by others from the same pueblo, he was instructed to visit all these rancherías and to observe the lay of the land and the number of people. I gave him a piece of paper on which to indicate all the rancherías; [next to] each one was a large line to record the number of married Indians in that ranchería and settlement. He brought back a figure of 1,123 married Indian males, and he says that there are many more. Because he was there for only a short time, however, he was unable to visit all the households and count everyone. This is quite a number of people for the sierra, and they say that they can all be reduced to three or four good places with good land within a distance of one day's walk. The same Indians say that those who live in the high sierras not too far from there can also be reduced to this place. These Indians have two languages that are totally different; the one that is more widespread and has the most speakers is spoken here in my mission district [Comanito]. When I speak to them, they understand me, and I understand them just as I do those in this district. The other language is totally different.

Up to this point I have been citing the priest's letter. I add that later on many of these people joined the Church and were baptized. I have jumped ahead to finish telling about the reduction and conversion of these first mountain peoples so that I can return to conclude my discussion of the people of the plains near the Villa de San Felipe. This was the first task our priests had during the first twelve years following their arrival in this province. With this we will move on to the account of the conversion of a most outstanding people. [119]

---

188. The word 'topil' is from the Nahuatl term *topilli* (*vara de justicia*) and refers to an Indian who acts as *alguacil* in the councils and lower courts of the pueblos under his authority; he is also ordinarily in charge of taking care of the churches in the pueblos and rancherías (Santamaría 1974:1073).

CHAPTER XXXIV The notable reduction of a group of people who left their [home]land and walked many leagues to request Holy Baptism and settle near the Villa de San Felipe

I have saved for here some unique cases [of edification] among the first Christian communities of Sinaloa that are deserving of memory and beg for their own chapter in this history. The first case is an outstanding, if not a miraculous, flight from Egypt and heathenism to the holy land of the Church. A group of people from the Nébome nation left their homeland and customs some eighty leagues inland and came to settle along the river four leagues from the Spaniard's Villa de San Felipe.[189] The principal reasons why these people came [south] were to receive Holy Baptism, become Christians, and enjoy the catechism taught by the priests.

To understand the means employed by divine providence and the orders of His most supreme predestination, it is necessary to recall what was discussed in Book I concerning the discovery of the Province of Sinaloa. It was noted in that book how groups of Indians followed and accompanied Cabeza de Vaca when he set out from La Florida and how they remained on the Río Sinaloa, where they founded the pueblo of Bamoa. Once they were baptized they became the best Christians near the villa and in the region. After a few years had passed and there was peace in the land, the Bamoa remembered their relatives and countrymen whom they had left years earlier. Some of them went to visit them to give them the news of their successful transmigration. They told them that they were living quite happily and that they had been baptized and had become Christians, with a knowledge of the true God and His word. Their speeches and reasoning moved the gentile Nébome so much that they decided to send some of their principales to the villa to ask that priests come to their lands to teach and baptize them, as they had done with their relatives [in Bamoa].

The priests and the captain (to whom they also presented their demand) received them warmly. They hesitated, however, in their response to the Nébome's request because it was difficult at that time to fulfill the Indians' wishes. Their land was eighty leagues from the villa and there were other nations in between with whom it was first necessary to secure and maintain peace. The Nébome (which is the proper name of this nation) perceived that they would have to wait a long time for priests and Baptism, so God moved the hearts of 350 people who, in a memorable act, loaded up their children and belongings and came to live with the Christians of Bamoa, thus attaining Baptism and salvation.

This company of pilgrims—men, women, and children—suffered great hunger and tribulation because they all traveled on foot, loaded down with their valued possessions and children, who were carried by the women. Although they had brought some provisions, there were not enough for such a large number of people on such a long journey. Furthermore, they did not pass through the lands of allies who could assist them, but rather through the lands of bellicose enemies. If the latter had not been afraid of the captain, who had threatened a rigorous punishment for those who harmed any Indians from gentile nations who were coming to see him, these people would have been cut to bits by their enemies, who would have triumphantly celebrated with the scalps of men and women. Thus, their journey was even more dangerous than if [120] they had walked across the desert. But God brought them along and favored them, so this blessed company passed safely through many dangers. Three adults died from the labor of the journey. It can be understood that Our Lord showed them compassion by deeming it appropriate for them to receive that holy, heavenly water through *flaminis*[190] Baptism because of their intentions

---

189. This exodus in January 1615 is recounted in a letter by Father Diego de Guzmán in the anua for that year (AGN 1615). As Pérez de Ribas' comments at the end of the chapter suggest, the Nébome apparently left their homeland after being struck by an epidemic of typhus, which raged on and off in Sinaloa between 1612 and 1615 (Reff 1991b:154–58).

190. By virtue of a burning desire, which is one of three means of baptism required for salvation—the other two being by water and blood (Attwater 1949).

and willingness to be baptized and because they had been taught the Christian catechism by a knowledgeable Indian who had made the journey with them.

This blessed company reached the villa on the first of February 1615. They went to visit the captain and the priests at the college, who received them warmly and paid them special attention. They welcomed these gentiles who, even if they had not been drawn by a star like the holy magi, had at a minimum been called or moved by divine inspiration. God had brought them out of their shadow-filled lands in search of the divine light, and they remained where it shone.

From the villa they then went down[river] to the pueblo of the Christian Bamoa, who were their relatives and spoke their language. The priest in that mission district considered the people worthy of being received with joy and celebration, just as the angels received the poor shepherds who went to adore Christ. Therefore, he ordered the whole pueblo to gather and organize a procession to receive these pilgrims. With the priest dressed in a choral cape and with chapel music, the tolling of bells, musical instruments, and arches made from tree branches, they all sang the *Te Deum Laudamus*,[191] which was composed upon the Baptism of the great Doctor of the Church, Saint Augustine. The priest received them with general joy and elation as a new flock for the Church, taken by such a marvelous means from the midst of the heathenism of Egypt.

When the pilgrims saw that they were being received with such pomp and joy, they formed their own procession in the same fashion in which the Christians were receiving them. They proceeded men with men and women with women, as if they were already very well instructed and civilized, and they all entered the church in this order. Afterwards, they prayed and gave thanks to God with several prayers, which were chanted by the priest, who remained standing while everyone else knelt. In a brief sermon the priest explained to his guests that all this rejoicing and celebration were so they would understand how happy the Christians were to receive them. He further told them that they should feel the same joy for having been brought by God to a land where they were received and baptized as brothers. As a sign of their faith and good intentions he asked them all to approach and adore the holy Cross that he

held in his hands, which was the symbol of Christianity and our redemption. They all came forward in a most orderly and concerted fashion, giving many signs of the devotion with which they had been drawn by God.

When this act was concluded the residents of the pueblo offered an invitation to their prodigal brothers who were being reduced to the house of God the Father. Each one took to his dwelling as many guests as he could provide with the type of food they enjoyed. They were very generous and both the young and old, who had suffered so greatly on such a long journey, were satisfied and restored. The following day the children, who numbered 114, were baptized. These Baptisms were celebrated with great joy by all the people and the invited guests and sponsors. Eight days later the priest assigned them land for fields and gave them a large quantity of maize to sow. They received all these benefits with [121] many thanks, and within a short time five of the newly baptized died, as did several infants. Thus, there were first fruits from among these people in heaven, whence they could aid those who were still here.

The new flock that God had brought with a desire to become Christian regularly joined the rest of the people in the pueblo for church and catechism so that they could soon be baptized, as they were. They developed such a love for the priest who instructed and baptized them that they came to him in times of need with great confidence, and the priest looked upon them with special affection, as people brought [to him] by such a marvelous means. They also brought their children to the priest to be blessed, particularly when they had some minor illness. This affection was born in them because of what happened to the first child who was baptized. This child had a dangerous abscess, but once the child was baptized it burst, leaving the child happy and healthy.

Our Lord showed His special compassion with another who was not a child, but rather an old man more than ninety years of age. This man had come with the rest of the people in the transmigration, and even though he was weak in his bones and was lame and nearly blind, God gave him the spirit and strength to walk the eighty leagues. His relatives had cared for him en route so that he would not die without the water of Holy Baptism, and God granted him the time to receive it. The priest who had instructed him in the catechism had many assurances that God had shown him compassion and had safeguarded him so that he could receive this sacrament of health. Although it was pure divine compassion [that saved this man], it did not hurt that he had always maintained a good moral life.

191. "Thee, God, we praise," a psalm-like hymn, called the Ambrosian hymn and attributed to Saint Ambrose (A.D. 339–97), the bishop of Milan, who was instrumental in the conversion of (Saint) Augustine of Hippo in 386 (Attwater 1949:488; Farmer 1992:19).

This was an opportunity for divine compassion to grant him the time to obtain the only means for his salvation, which is Holy Baptism. To this we can add that his good morals during his life did not preclude divine aid.

The following case of another member of this group seems even more miraculous. It seemed that even after God had brought them out [of the wilderness] He continued to work miracles with His powerful arm, as was the case when He brought His people out of Egypt. Among the Indians who came [south], there was one who was so leprous that there was not a single part of his body from his head to his toes that was not affected by this plague, which had brought him to the brink of death.[192] He showed unusual signs of pain for his sins and had learned the catechism very well, responding skillfully to questions concerning that which he had been taught. He requested Holy Baptism, which the priest granted, giving him the name of Lazarus, for the leper.[193] Holy Baptism worked in such a way that from Lazarus the leper he became Lazarus the risen.[194] He healed in such a fashion that the following day the leprosy dried up and the scabs came off, leaving almost no sign. That very same day he came to the church sound and strong to give thanks to God for the benefit he had received. This is similar to what God did with Constantine the Great,[195] for His infinite compassion extends to both great and small; in fact, it shines even more brightly in the latter.

I conclude this [portion of] the history by noting that the populous settlement of Bamoa was further increased by the new arrivals, not one of which backslid or tried to return to the Egypt that was their land or the gentile customs in which they were born and raised. This is a rare thing in such an inconstant people. However, with the continual catechism and teaching that they have had they persevere to this day as a very good example of Christianity. Their church is well adorned, and in order to acquire even more adornments, every year the residents plant a [special] field. From the sale of the harvest, which they easily market because of their proximity to the Spaniards in the Villa de San Felipe, they are able to acquire ornaments and other items pertaining to [122] divine worship. They are quite contented with this, and there are good signs that quite a few souls go to heaven.

CHAPTER XXXV A notable case of the devil's ostentation, preaching against the Christian doctrine; his plot was undone. An account is [also] given of military action [taken] against rebel Indians

It was noteworthy that one of God's Son's most admirable and steadfast activities during the time in which He preached His Holy Gospel on earth was to combat demons and those whom they possessed. The devil [even] dared to accost the Redeemer of the World at the beginning of His preaching when He was in the desert. From there His preaching took Him to the pinnacle of the temple, where the devil accosted Him with another temptation. From there He went to a lofty mount, where the devil accosted Him a third time. Although this enemy was foiled in all these attacks, he retained a fortress of souls, and because the devil's strength increases with the number of

---

192. As previously noted the Nébome may have suffered from typhus, which produces skin lesions that could be confused with leprosy.

193. See Luke 16:19–31.

194. See John 11:1–48.

195. After suddenly becoming ill the emperor Constantine (274–337) requested baptism. However, he died shortly thereafter, rather than recovering as Pérez de Ribas seems to imply.

souls [he possesses], one of the marvelous and frequent tasks in which Christ Our Redeemer and His Apostles busied themselves was casting demons out of those who were possessed, thereby driving this savage tyrant out of men's souls and bodies. For this reason there were more discoveries and manifestations of demons and possessed people during the time in which Our Lord preached His Gospel than during all the time of the old law. During the latter period the most that was ever spoken of was a pythoness whom King Saul consulted in the holy books of Kings.[196] In the New Testament, however, innumerable accounts are given and repeated. Saint Luke tells how the Lord cast a legion of demons out of a single man.[197] Something else worthy of note that is recounted by the same Evangelist in the following chapter was that when Our Redeemer sent His holy Apostles to preach the Gospel, the first thing Saint Luke says He charged them with was to cure the possessed: *Convocatis duodecim Apostolis, dedit illes virtute & potestatem super omnia demonia.*[198] From this we can understand that preaching the Gospel leads to the discovery of possessed people and to encounters with demons. One of the signs that the Gospel being preached is Christ's is the discovery of possessed people, with whom there is frequent combat. This has been brought up so that we are not surprised by the frequent repetition in this history of cases of bedeviled sorcerers that were encountered by the priests who were preaching to these people. It confirms that the Gospel preached by the priests in these missions is the same as that preached by Christ Our Lord. It shows the same signs and conforms to the sentence pronounced by the Eagle of the Evangelists in his first canonical statement: *In hoc apparuit Filius Dei, ut dissoluat opera diaboli.*[199] This will be seen throughout the course of this history and in the following case, which is unique among all the innumerable apparitions that the devil used to mislead these people.

The case that is recorded here was quite public and should not be kept silent. It involved Father Alberto Clerici, who was in charge of the mission to the Guasave

nation.[200] On the eve of the feast day of our father Saint Ignatius [July 31], as Father Clerici was preparing for the celebration, the man who taught the children catechism came to tell him, quite excitedly, that the devil had been preaching for more than two hours in the home of a sick woman who had been baptized. Upon hearing the news many people had congregated to listen to all that the devil was saying. The priest thought that it was probably [123] some Indian liar or sorcerer, but the Indian who brought him the news insisted that it could not be so, and he gave him enough reasons to make it understood that no man could speak that way. Neither the husband nor any of the other relatives who were standing at the doorway had seen anybody enter or present in the home. Furthermore, he who spoke exceeded the most skilled Indian in his speech and eloquence. He told the woman that, of course, she knew that he was her father and her lord and her former god and that she was to believe in him once and for all. He promised her pleasures and abundance and eternal life if she believed in him, and he told her that her disbelief was why she was always sick.[201] He asked why she did not stop fooling herself and go with him into the monte to her former dwelling places, where each person lived as he wished, instead of here, where the priest deceived them with his inventions. "Understand," he said, "that the priest and I are not going down the same path. He says one thing and I say another. Come, then, do not be stubborn, for if you are, it will be at your [own] expense and you will lose your life." In the midst of these words, he struck her many times and mistreated her, bragging that he feared neither the captain nor the priest, nor the heavens nor the earth. The anger with which he said this amazed those who were outside listening. The priest came, and as he arrived he was told through signs by those outside that the devil was still inside, even though they had heard the devil say, "I am going. You stay." The priest went inside and found the sick woman alone, lying in a different place than where her family had left her, despite the fact that she did not have the energy to have moved all by herself. The priest deduced that the woman's trouble stemmed from something in her past, so he blessed the house and said a few prayers. The sick woman, who was con-

---

196. This story is recounted in I Kings 28 of the Vulgate (note that in the Vulgate I and II Kings are also known as I and II Samuel). The pythoness referred to in I Kings 28 acts as a spirit medium, calling Samuel back from the grave for Saul. Pérez de Ribas also uses the term "pythoness" to refer to a slave girl possessed by a divining spirit whose story is recounted in Acts 16:16–20 (see Chapter 7 of the present Book).

197. *Margin Note*: Luc. 8. Luke 8:26–39 (Knox 1956:64).

198. Luke 9:1: "And he called the twelve apostles to him, and gave them power and authority over all devils" (Knox 1956:65).

199. 1 John 3:8: "If the Son of God was revealed to us, it was so that he might undo what the devil had done" (Knox 1956:254).

200. Clerici worked for many years among the Guasave, apparently beginning in 1609; the anua for that year misidentifies him as Andrés Perecio.

201. The woman may well have suffered occasional bouts of fever and delirium caused by malaria, which became endemic or semi-endemic along the coast of Sinaloa during the colonial period (Reff 1991b:106–8).

fused and tormented, regained consciousness, and the priest exhorted her to confess, which she did through acts of faith, renouncing the devil. She did this without hesitation while adoring and kissing a crucifix. The priest questioned her in order to discover the cause of this event, and the woman responded that she believed that the man who was mistreating her was the same man who used to appear to her forty years earlier in the monte where she had lived, and she said no more.

Then the priest left her, for it was already dawning and he had been there since early evening. He left orders that she be cared for that day. The following night they sent word that the devil had returned. With the same anger as before he was trying to persuade her again, quite pleased that many people would hear him. He mistreated the sick woman and threatened those outside, saying that he would have to kill them if they did not follow his teaching. However, the people outside kneeled and prayed with their Crosses in their hands. As they did this the devil threw dirt in their eyes from within the house, reprimanding them because they were praying and repeating the sweet name of Jesus. While this was taking place the Indian who taught the catechism rose up from among the others, where he had been kneeling, and said, "Let's go get the priest and we will see how brave you are, if you want to wait for him." Here, the devil said a word in their tongue which is like saying "shoo" in Spanish, adding, "So you even want to threaten me with the priest? Well, then, go for him and we will see what he will do to me. I will be waiting for him here." Later, the sick woman said that as soon as the devil said this he barricaded himself in the room, making himself visible with a bow and arrows and making great threats as if prepared to fight.

Those who were outside heard more noise, and then the priest arrived with one of our brothers, Francisco de Castro. While the two of them were nearby under a ramada in the midst of the throng, the devil continued making a racket. Then, having donned a surplice and bearing a lit candle in one hand and the Book of Exorcisms in the other, the priest went inside. [124] Immediately, the devil made such a loud noise that it astonished him. However, without hesitating the priest went to the sick woman, reciting the exorcisms, which caused all the racket to cease. The priest tried to find out in more detail the cause of this incident, but was unable to learn anything. He asked the sick woman whether she had in fact been baptized and learned that she had. Furthermore, he was reasonably satisfied with her conduct, good habits, and the fact that she

confessed frequently. Finally, because the event had occurred on the first and second nights of the [feast] day of our father Saint Ignatius, he placed a medal of this saint around her neck. The following day's Mass was offered to him, and the priest and everyone else begged Our Lord on their knees to be served by favoring the sick woman through the merits of the saint.

With this the priest went to bed, leaving her well prepared that night. He had exhorted her to give herself over to the glorious saint and had told the others to do the same. At daybreak he received word from some Indians and the catechism teacher that even though the devil had come, he had not dared to touch the sick woman or say a word. Nevertheless, when they went to give the sick woman a little holy water to drink the devil had kicked over the vessel, spilling the holy water. The priest went back and questioned her more diligently about whether she knew of any [possible] cause or origin of this event or her suffering. She was moved by God (after seeing that the image around her neck of our holy father Saint Ignatius had made the devil less daring), and she responded that it was an idol in the monte who was persecuting her. Her ancestors, who forty years earlier had lived in the monte twenty-six leagues away, used to resort to this idol. When they were at war with their neighbors, the Zuaque, he appeared to them in human form and told them to believe and trust in him because he was their lord. He said he would aid them and give them victory over their enemies. They then accepted him as their god, and from that point on he appeared to them in a hooded cape covered in rich plumage, although it had a noxious odor. He spoke and the bows and arrows trembled in their quivers, as if he were forcefully shaking them. This was proof and an argument of what he could do, and he ordered them to worship a stone. She said this stone was in his image, and they offered not only themselves, but also carved staffs, arrows, lances, and other things. She also said that her father had been the sacristan and guardian of this idol. When he died his daughter was very young and the devil appeared to her in this same suit and comforted her, telling her not to cry but rather to be happy because he had taken her father's place and would provide her greater protection and consolation. Since then he had appeared to her often, asking her to believe in him, scaring her with apparitions and whipping her when she was still a gentile because she did not believe in his words. Once she was baptized he had left her alone for many years, but six years earlier he had returned to bother her. He frequently took her out into the monte and appeared in her house when she believed him to be many leagues away. This continued until that day when she had finally found the remedy for such a great evil, and the devil fled from the image of our father Saint Ignatius and from the Cross and the holy water. He was greatly angered by these things, as has happened throughout the world on numerous other occasions when this fierce beast has confessed that he finds them unpleasant. The most important result of all this was the discovery of the idol, which the priest had four of the most trusted Christians retrieve. Afterwards, unusual things happened as the devil threatened [125] to persecute the priests and the Christian communities where they were preaching. There were indications that these threats were later carried out during the uprising by the Tepehuan nation, which will be recorded later. In the end the idol was retrieved and burned and the ashes were thrown into the river. God was glorified, and from then on this woman was free.

To this spiritual battle and victory over the devil and his lies I will add another temporal battle and victory that was achieved by Captain Hurdaide at that time [in 1608], in which he proved to be just as brave as on the other occasions we have discussed. This encounter involved some groups of wild Indians who had settled among the Christian Guasave. They were called the Toroaca. After some of them had received religious instruction and Holy Baptism, they were perverted by their judge[202] and mainly by the devil, who does not cease in stirring up these people. Having significantly damaged their Christianity, they retreated to an island almost two leagues from land (where they used to live). They thought that the Spaniards would not be able to reach the island to which they had swum. These Indians did not use sailing vessels, nor were they familiar with anything other than some rafts made from poles lashed together with straw, which were only good for use on rivers and small inlets.

The captain was always of the opinion that those who were delinquent renegades should not believe that there was anywhere they could flee to, so he attempted something very difficult and succeeded. [Because there was no one in that land who knew how to build sailing vessels,] he and his soldiers and some Indian allies constructed some large rafts, which were much larger than those used by the Indians. Once these rafts were made he and his soldiers sailed those two leagues to the island and caught up with the renegades. He took them back to dry land as prisoners and ordered that the seven leaders who bore the most guilt be hanged. He pardoned the others and spread them out among the pueblos of the good Guasave, who were to care for them and settle them into their homes and lands, which they did in good friendship. This plan worked out well because it led the wild Toroaca to become domesticated, settle down, and come to love the catechism. After baptizing the remaining gentiles, they all finally applied themselves to living in great peace and Christianity.

202. Pérez de Ribas uses the term *juez*, which in this instance probably refers to a senior male clan or lineage head, who acted as a judge or arbitrator of disputes.

CHAPTER XXXVI The progress to date of Christianity among the first nations converted in the Province of Sinaloa

ere in Book II I have written about the nations of the first rivers of Sinaloa, which will not be specifically dealt with again in this history. Before turning to new conversions and enterprises of the Faith, I will conclude this book with a discussion of the status of this first Christianity, which has persevered up to the time when this history is being written. In doing so I will provide a clearer idea of the fruits that have been harvested through so much of the aforementioned hardship and persecution. This discussion will help those whom God has chosen for similar tasks, principally from among the Company of Jesus, to whom this work is dedicated. It will comfort and encourage them, helping them to see the abundant harvest that was reaped for the granaries of heaven by only six missionary priests during the first twelve years. These priests entered the mission field at different times, laboring among very fierce and barbarous people. [126] By 1604 they had baptized about forty thousand souls in this primitive Christianity; this figure does not include the full harvest that has been reaped since that time. They married thousands of couples according to the rite of the Holy Church, and these couples live in the holy state of matrimony, conjugally faithful, as Christ's holy law commands. They have forgotten their former appetite and unchecked license for many wives, contenting themselves with only one legitimate spouse. These priests raised the standard of Christ's Cross in the montes, plains, and pueblos where formerly devils, superstitions, and idolatries triumphed. They built and have maintained in this first Christianity fourteen churches with very well-decorated altars, sacred silver vessels, and ornaments. The people of the pueblos—for not an Indian remains in the montes—very frequently attend Mass and Christian instruction, from which they have benefited greatly. Indeed, when the priest asks them in church and in the presence of the entire pueblo (as is commonly done) about the mysteries of our Holy Faith, they give an accurate account of everything, doing so in words that differ from the catechism, which they learn by heart. They attend the Holy Sacraments with great care and confess every Lent, with great understanding of the components of this Holy Sacrament. They confess frequently throughout the year, and either because of their individual devotion or for greater peace of mind, many make general confessions.[203] Now they all [have] the capacity and disposition required to receive the delicacy that communicates celestial life, the Bread of Angels. They receive it with unusual devotion and reverence, as though they were long-time Christians instead of recent converts.

I cannot leave untold a work of great royal piety that is characteristic of the Imperial House of Austria, which has stood above all the others in the world because of its reverence and devotion to the Most Holy and Sovereign Sacrament of the Altar, which it inherited from our Catholic monarchs of all the Spains. Around this time[204] Our Lady Doña Margarita of Austria, mother of Our Lord King Philip IV, may God keep him, learned that the priests of the Company were founding new Christian communities at the ends of the earth, in the Province of Sinaloa. She ordered royal officials to dispatch a number of gilded tabernacles to Nueva España. These were to be placed in the new Christian churches that were being built in this province. This Catholic queen's piety was so generous and extensive that it reached [even] the most remote parts of the world. Once royal officials in Mexico City received the tabernacles they sent word to the priests in the missions, followed by the tabernacles themselves. These, along with the Sovereign Sacrament, were placed with great care and solemnity in the extant churches of Sinaloa. This occurred at a time of great peace among nations, when it was safe and there was no danger that the Divine Treasure might suffer some irreverence. With this new enrichment Christianity flourished and daily experienced new growth.

203. Pérez de Ribas uses "general confession" as it was spoken of by Ignatius Loyola in his Spiritual Exercises (Ganss 1991). A confession of this type involved reflection on and scrutiny of one's entire life, to effect a better understanding of self and to move closer to God (O'Malley 1993a:137).

204. This was sometime prior to 1611, when Queen Margarita died.

The feast days of the mysteries of Christ Our Lord, those of His Mother the Most Holy Virgin, and those of the major saints are celebrated with solemnity by great crowds of people. They take special care with Holy Week exercises, Confession, Communion, and Penance. To make apparent the fervor of such a new Christianity I will present here a few cases, which will serve [127] as examples so it can be understood how well Christian law and religion are established among these people.

One Holy Thursday when a pueblo was conducting a procession, a deformed, one-armed Indian who had been crippled since birth came to the priest's house, asking to be flagellated with a scourge containing metal spurs.[205] He said that he, too, was a sinner and wanted to do penance, so the priest administered it. Due to the man's infirmity, however, he did not use the aforementioned scourge with metal spurs. After he was flagellated, the man went to church, and because he could not stand, he was seated. He continued to flagellate himself the entire time the procession lasted, and did so with such great fervor that even though the scourge did not have metal spurs, it nevertheless removed his skin and he lost a great deal of blood. Only when the whip finally broke did he cease; afterwards, it took several days for his wounds to heal.

This person was joined by another, equally fervent, who whipped himself with a dozen spurs and made the stations of the Cross in leg irons. He was so exhausted after doing so that he collapsed at the threshold of the church portal. When out of pity the people who were present tried to remove his leg irons and take him back to his house, he got up with a great stir, telling them that he had not yet finished his penance and that they should help him over the threshold. He entered the church and prayed there for a long time. Afterward he continued flogging himself on his way back home. Those who saw him were frightened to see that he did not diminish his harsh penance. Later when they asked him why he had been so hard on himself, he answered, "Because of the many sins I committed when I was a barbarous gentile, and so that God might have mercy on me." This action would have attracted great attention even were it taken by a long-time Christian, yet this man's offense was not so remarkable. But for a barbarian upon whom the light of Faith had barely dawned, and who had not yet shed the barbarous habits and liberties in which he

had been reared, it provides a clear demonstration of the unusual change and affection with which some of these gentiles receive the doctrine of the Gospel.

To illustrate not only their remorse for past sins, but also how they live in fear of committing even more [I present here] another brief case as an example. A priest went to hear the confession of an Indian of advanced age, who was very sick. The priest began the confession and asked the man about his sins. He answered, "Father, when I was a renegade, or Chichimec (a name they apply in Nueva España to the most fierce and barbarous Indians), I used to commit many sins. But from the time I was baptized, which must be about fifteen years ago, I don't remember committing any sins, unless it was on one feast day when I started to weed my field because it was going to ruin. However, because I only worked a little, I could say that I didn't really commit a sin, or if I did, it was a minor one." Thus, in fifteen years of living an Indian who had been reared in drunkenness and other vices had committed no mortal sin. Who could doubt that it was God's singular grace that [was responsible for] such a change and amendment of life?

Another Indian came to confession and astonished the priest when he indicated that he had no sins to confess. The priest expressed doubt, and the Indian answered sincerely, "Father, don't be amazed. Don't you see that I already fear God and that it is not as it used to be?" This is the difference one finds among these gentile peoples once they become Christians.

We could add to these examples of their careful observance of God's law much more about how Christ's law makes a strong impression on young women and other people. So that it may also be seen, however, how the weak who break the law have learned to resolve their weaknesses, the following case is presented.

A married woman [128] succumbed in a moment of carnal weakness, which enraged her husband to the point that he had decided to kill her. To effect this end in greater secrecy, he took her to the river. Once there, the poor woman realized her husband's intentions, and she pleaded with him, "Because you want to kill me for my sin, at least let me confess first." It was truly something remarkable for her to be more concerned about dying in a state of sin than about death itself. She did not beg him to spare her life, but rather only to allow her to make her confession, even if he was going to kill her. But the Indian man kept to his plan and was about to drown her when she shouted out, "This sin will be yours, not mine, because God knows that I wanted to confess and obtain His pardon." With this, divine mercy

---

205. *Diciplina de rosetas.* A scourge for flagellating oneself that apparently had small, round pieces of metal in the form of flowers attached to the leather straps.

rescued this poor repentant woman. As she was struggling a sound rang out like people were coming. Fearing he would be discovered, the Indian fled, leaving his wife half dead. She managed to regain consciousness and went to the priest, begging him to hear her confession, which she made as though she were preparing to die, for she was not safe from her husband. Our Lord took pity on her contrition and arranged for her husband also to repent of his evil attempt. He forgave her and lived peacefully with her, and both their lives were amended.

Continuing our discussion of this Christianity, I note that feast days are celebrated with song and skillfully performed musical arrangements. The priests have gone to great efforts to introduce ecclesiastical music. Accordingly, in the pueblos on these first rivers there are church choirs that can compete with those in the great and civilized pueblos in and around Mexico City. The priests searched for and hired at a salary of five hundred pesos a choirmaster to train the Indians. Today these schools where singing is taught serve purposes other than training singers. They are also where the students are instilled with the most important civilized and proper customs. One can choose from among the students individuals to govern their pueblos who will exercise that office with great wisdom. Others are chosen to be fiscales for the churches, keeping them clean and caring for their property. They also advise the priest when he has been absent if someone is sick and in need of the Holy Sacraments, or if a scandalous sin has occurred that needs to be corrected. The priest carries out all these tasks so that in the civil and spiritual spheres these pueblos are governed very peaceably, and their ancient wars and tumults are entirely uprooted.

In the midst of this primitive Christianity is the Villa de San Felipe y Santiago. When the priests first arrived it had only those five poor Spaniards who, as we mentioned at the end of Book I, wore buckskin and lived alone in poverty. Because God preserved them among such fierce people without a church or priest to administer the sacraments or sustain them with the bread of the divine word, it is necessary to talk about the Villa de San Felipe's present condition and the fruits of great Christianity that have been harvested there. Through God's mercy the religious of this mission have played a great role here, and whereas it was once very destitute of settlers, with the priests' support a good villa developed here, with more than eighty honorable residents. Many of them are very courageous soldiers who have great experience in warfare and the enterprises of this New World. They are sustained by many cattle ranches,

as well as cultivated fields, from which the surrounding mining camps get supplies, for which they pay the residents of the villa in silver. [129] In addition to the aforementioned Spanish residents, there are also a good number of Spanish-speaking Indians who have congregated at the villa. Our Company of Jesus has founded a college in this villa, where there are two or three religious who are continually occupied. There are also fourteen other suffragan priests who attend to their own individual districts. Twice a year they all congregate to discuss religious topics as well as matters concerning the proper administration and fruits of the souls in their districts. The two or three priests who continually attend to the villa are charged with administering the Holy Sacraments to its residents and the soldiers and captain [at Fort Montesclaros, on the Río Fuerte], who stop there at different times throughout the year. A very large and beautiful temple has been built in the villa, where feast days are celebrated by great crowds of Indians from nearby pueblos, who recognize it as their principal church and house [of worship]. With frequent sacraments, jubilees, sermons and all the other exercises of Christian virtue, Christianity flourishes greatly among the villa's residents and soldiers. Thus, the vices that are so prevalent among military men—swearing, gambling, etc.—are not observed here. These men consider themselves evangelical soldiers, and they desire to have a part in the conversion of these peoples and the propagation of our Holy Faith.

In conclusion I note that it may not be possible to appreciate the fruits of this first enterprise in Sinaloa without comparing the Indians' present condition to their gentile state, for which I refer the reader to the last chapter of Book I. Who could have known that in the thick woodland of thorns and brush in which these people lived, seeds would be sown that would grow and ripen, and that such a fertile harvest of Christianity would be reaped? And who would have thought that among such fierce tigers, which is what these barbarous nations were, God would select for His heaven a flock of more than six thousand innocent infant lambs? These infants died with baptismal grace during the first years of this mission and went to heaven, where they joined many adults who also had been baptized on the verge of death, as well as countless other new and old Christians who were saved not through baptismal grace, but rather through the other Holy Sacraments for salvation that the Son of God left His Church: Confession, Holy Communion, and the holy oils [of Extreme Unction]. In the end what is apparent and shines so brightly is the efficacy of the grace of Christ Our Lord and the merits of His precious blood. With confidence in Our Lord the priests continue today without rest in the labor that has already begun of instructing their faithful and baptizing those who are thus reborn. They are happy to see themselves in those deserts, far from the populous cities in which they could have brilliant and esteemed duties. They consider it even more glorious that God has chosen them for the exaltation and preservation of His Holy Faith and the spreading of His holy name among these poor gentiles. By this reasoning I have derived my justification for writing this book which, as stated in the prologue, is dedicated to evangelical laborers, who cannot help but be consoled by news of the abundant fruits of these enterprises. Consider as well the fact that the holy Evangelist Saint Luke, when writing the history of the glorious enterprises and conversions that the holy Apostles achieved, judged it worthwhile to record and contemplate the

case of the holy Deacon Philip, who was a disciple of the Apostles.[206] The Holy Spirit gave Philip special inspiration to approach the chariot in which an Ethiopian eunuch of Queen Candace was riding, and right there on the road in the open countryside, he was told [130] of Christ and was baptized, which was a deed worthy of the Holy Scriptures. Similarly, we have pondered here how the Holy Spirit, through holy obedience, took five of His laborers and others who have since gone to the ends of the earth to illuminate and bring the light of heaven to the souls of these numerous barbarous infidels, who were entombed in darkness. They gave them a knowledge of Christ and promoted the reverence and adoration of His name, which today is worshiped and revered by the nations of the first three rivers of Sinaloa. This is what has been discussed here in Book II, and (as I wrote in the prologue would be done at the conclusion of each book) it will [now] be followed by the lives and joyous deaths of two holy missionaries.

CHAPTER XXXVII The life of the venerable Father Gonzalo de Tapia and the ministries in which he occupied himself before he went to establish the Sinaloa mission, where he died for preaching the Gospel

It is worth writing here about the heroic actions and evangelical labors of the venerable Father Gonzalo de Tapia, founder of the Sinaloa mission. Even from his tender years, God had prepared Father Tapia for the very glorious end of his saintly (albeit brief) life. He was thirty-three, the same age as Christ Our Redeemer when He died, having taught the world His divine doctrine. With respect to the short life of the blessed Father Tapia, we can particularly affirm what the Holy Spirit said about the just man who was agreeable to Him among sinners and the impious: *Placens*

Deo, factus est dilectus, et vivens inter peccatores translatus est, and then, Consumatus, in brevi explevit tempora multa.[207] These [words] aptly describe this apostolic laborer, who in a few years established many barbarous and fierce nations in peace and reduced them to the Gospel. This had not been achieved [previously] in Sinaloa during many years of expeditions by captains, companies of soldiers, religious, and other ecclesiastics. Father Tapia achieved victory with the glorious triumph of his holy

206. Philip was one of seven deacons and became an able evangelist (Acts 6:5; Acts 8; Acts 21:8–10).

207. *Margin Note*: Sap. cap. 4. Book of Wisdom 4:14: "So well the Lord loved him, from a corrupt world he would grant him swift release;" 4:13 "With him, early achievement counted for long apprenticeship" (Knox 1956:576). Note that Pérez de Ribas reverses the order of these verses.

death. The account of his life recorded here is taken from the one given by three very solemn priests of our order. They accompanied him on several occasions and were very close to him. One of them, Father Francisco Ramírez, Prepositus of our professed house[208] in Mexico City, had known him since childhood.[209] He later had contact with him on several occasions and was his superior at the college in Pátzcuaro.

Father Gonzalo de Tapia was born [in 1561] to noble parents in the city of León, in Castilla. His father, named Gonzalo de Tapia (like his son), married a very illustrious woman of equal nobility, and they had several children. The older sons were attracted to the military, where they were outstanding. However, Christ Our Redeemer chose the youngest to be another David, a captain of His militia and evangelical enterprises. [Tapia] devoted himself earnestly to the humanities and the study of Latin at our college in León, where because of his rare talent, ability, and memory, within a short time he surpassed his fellow classmates.[210] From this time forward he was very careful to complement his studies with all types of virtue. He was an example of this, such that the type of frivolity or mischief proper to those of his age was never observed in him. Rather, he was an example of maturity and angelical modesty. When he was old enough to become a religious he asked to be received into the Company at our college in León, and he was [131] accepted [in 1576] with the endorsement and applause of all the priests. During his novitiate he improved the virtues that had begun to sprout during childhood. He subsequently [1578 to 1584] undertook advanced studies and theology, in which he distinguished himself. He was held back from the priesthood because he was not yet old enough when he completed his studies. Around this time Father Antonio de Mendoza, who was on his way to Mexico City to act as Provincial, was recruiting individuals in the Spanish provinces to labor in the copious missions of the Indies. When the superiors realized that Father Gonzalo had callings from heaven that directed him to the missions, they chose him, along with other outstanding individuals, who then accompanied the Father Provincial to Mexico City. When they arrived in 1584 the priest who taught the grammar course at our college in this populous city could not continue teaching anymore because of illness. Therefore, the Father Provincial, who knew of Father Gonzalo de Tapia's great talent, entrusted him to complete the course, which he did, giving such great proofs of his knowledge that the priests judged him capable of occupying a higher position teaching theology. The Father Provincial had just made this decision when God, for His part, chose His servant for the apostolic ministry of preaching His Gospel among barbarous peoples. Around this time He arranged for the grave illness of three priests at our college in Pátzcuaro who spoke the Tarascan language and were laboring in the abundant harvest in the Province of Michoacán and its environs. In this hour of need the Father Provincial sent Father Gonzalo de Tapia to help these spiritual workers.

He arrived at his post, and in the beginning, at the insistence of the prebendaries at the churches of Pátzcuaro and Valladolid, where the cathedral of this episcopate is located, he preached to the Spaniards, who unceasingly celebrated his magnificent talent, judging him to be illustrious, as he truly was. But this did not affect his apostolic spirit and the purpose and longing with which he had come from Spain to the Indies, which was to devote himself to the poor Indians. He avoided the illustrious posts and ministries that were forced upon him, and three days after reaching Pátzcuaro he began to devote himself to the study of Tarascan, the language of that province. The Father Rector (who knew Tarascan eminently well) noticed that Father Tapia was learning the language quite rapidly, even though he had studied it for no more than fifteen days. Therefore, he told him to give a sermon in [Tarascan] at our refectory. Using a language that was still so new to him, he preached this sermon with such skill and good pronunciation that the priests who spoke Tarascan well said that it was as if he were speaking Romance [i.e., Castilian or Spanish] and that they would not dare to attempt to do the same. Thus, the superiors recognized the grace and talents that Our Lord had bestowed upon Father Tapia and immediately entrusted to him the densely populated missions and districts of the Sierra de Michoacán. He began his ministries of preaching, teaching the Christian catechism, and hearing confessions with such ability that the local Indians became quite fond of him. They developed such a love for him and his ways that they did not let him out of their sight, proclaiming that he spoke their language better than they did. He

---

208. This was a permanent residence supported by alms for fully formed Jesuits (in contrast to residences for scholastics or novices) (O'Malley 1993a:356).

209. The other accounts of his life and death were written by two of Tapia's companions in Sinaloa, Alonso de Santiago and Martín Pérez (Shiels 1934).

210. Tapia entered the college at age ten and spent five years studying Latin (Shiels 1934:35–37).

preached nearly every day, and he had such a soft and gentle manner (which was always excellent and very distinguished in [132] this priest) that almost everyone sought him out for confession and did as he instructed.

He returned from that mission and reported his accomplishments to his superiors. Beneficiaries[211] were moved and amazed by the priest's fame and the abundant fruits that he had harvested in the places and pueblos where he had ministered. Therefore, they soon began asking that he return to visit their districts. The Father Rector of Pátzcuaro learned of the need that existed among the cannibalistic[212] Chichimec Indians, who (because of their fierceness) appeared to be the most indomitable of all the nations of Nueva España. They were in the midst of a revolt at this time,[213] and he felt that it would be of great service to Our Lord for this priest to employ his holy zeal, charity, and grace among such a fierce nation and in some other places in that region. The priest undertook this journey [in 1587], and everywhere he went he was welcomed as an angel from heaven. To the great consolation of all, the harvest was also great. With the great confidence he had in Our Lord and with an intrepid spirit for divine service, this priest entered Chichimec territory. The Indians were frightened [at first] and said, "Who is this man that seems not to fear us?" He began to talk with them, which they enjoyed, and he learned their language so skillfully that in less than seventeen days (as confirmed by Father Francisco Ramírez *in verbo sacerdotis*[214]), he was speaking their unusual language like one of them. He gathered a great number of them in a settlement where some had already begun to congregate, because at this time their peace and settlement were being discussed. There he began instruction in the Christian catechism, leaving them well prepared for

settlement [in missions]. This was later accomplished, as will be told when the Company's house and mission in the pueblo of San Luis de la Paz are discussed.

Because this mission had been so successful, our Father Provincial decided [in 1589] to send Father Tapia to minister at the college in Zacatecas. The Chichimec Indians had reached this city and had carried out major assaults along the Camino Real, which stretches some fifty leagues from Mexico City to Zacatecas. They had killed many travelers and had stolen great quantities of the silver that is taken from the rich mines of that city to all of Nueva España and the entire world. When the priest reached Zacatecas he found a large number of Tarascan Indians who were working in the mines. These people care little about the welfare of their souls, and many of them are renegades who have left their pueblos to live more freely in the mining camps. The priest found a field that was in great need of a zealous, courageous, and very spirited minister of the Lord who would undertake great works and enterprises in His service. He was aided a great deal by his many previous dealings with the Tarascan Indians when he carried out a mission among them in their province, where he had so won them over. The attendance at his sermons and speeches was great. Large numbers of these Indians also came to him for confession. He found that many of them had left their legitimate wives and were living in sin with other women. Also, the women who were left behind in the pueblos, abandoned by their husbands, had taken up with other men. The priest tried hard to eradicate this abuse, and in the end many returned to the good graces and service of God. [133] By letter he notified the priests of Pátzcuaro to help him in this effort by working with those he was sending there. Thus, the number of Indians who changed their ways was great. It was common knowledge in the pueblos of Michoacán that Father Gonzalo de Tapia restored fugitives to their pueblos, which thereby became peaceful and well populated.

He undertook another equally difficult task in Zacatecas that was of no less service to Our Lord, and he was extremely successful. A deeply rooted abuse among the various nations that come to work in those mines is for the many work gangs to challenge one another on feast days. They go to the countryside with weapons, darts, arrows, and knives; those lacking weapons use stones. At these fights many die in extremely cruel ways, for those who are wounded and fall are not spared by their opponents. To make themselves more fierce for the challenge, they drink wine and become drunk. Although the authorities and even the ecclesiastical

211. Clerics or religious who received a salary ("a living") for what was generally a lifetime appointment as pastor of a parish. These priests were primarily secular clergy; the Jesuits were prohibited by their constitutions from accepting such positions.

212. *Caribe.* This term and its negative connotation stemmed from Columbus, who stereotyped the Indians of the Caribbean as cannibals. The term stuck and was used elsewhere in the New World in reference to cannibals.

213. This "revolt" actually had begun during preconquest times, when the Chichimec resisted Mexica incursions. After the conquest and the discovery of silver at Zacatecas (1546), the Chichimec turned their attention to Spaniards, raiding mines, related settlements, and Spanish wagon trains traveling the Camino Real, or Royal Highway, which linked Mexico City with Zacatecas and Guanajuato. The Chichimec actually belonged to many distinct groups, although most apparently were Otomí speakers.

214. 'In the words of a priest'.

arm tried several means to uproot this barbarous and long-standing abuse, they were not powerful enough to eradicate it. On those occasions when the authorities, accompanied by ministers, tried to repress the Indians' fury, all the combatants united against them and this caused the fire to spread. It was not sufficient to punish some of them afterwards, for on the following feast day the wine was warmed again and the flames were kindled anew. Because this fire had been so violent, Our Lord decided to give our Father Gonzalo de Tapia the grace and authority to deal with such unrestrained and fierce people. The moment they saw him with his staff ascending the hill that was the arena for the battle they desisted and laid down their arms. The improvement that was seen around this time was exceptional.

All this was achieved through the preaching and voice of this apostolic man. In this instance his voice resembled that of God, of which the royal Prophet [David] sings, *Vox Domini in virtute; vox Domini in magnificentia, vox Domini confringentis cedros Libani, & commovebis Dominus desertum Cades*.[215] For the priest to speak to these people about the catechism was (as they say) like a voice crying out in the desert. In their arrogance they were like proud cedars, which the voice of the Lord broke and humbled through the voice of His minister, Father Gonzalo de Tapia. These were the ministries in which he employed his holy zeal before going to Sinaloa, where God had saved for him the triumph of and reward for his holy labors.

CHAPTER XXXVIII   Father Gonzalo de Tapia's other religious and heroic virtues

Although I have discussed the ministries in which this evangelical man employed himself from the time of his ordination until his glorious death, we should not forget the very religious virtues with which God adorned his soul. God made him an example of the virtues that a minister of His Gospel should have, and those who knew him celebrated these as rare and eminent. He never failed to practice humility, which is the foundation of a saintly life, and everyone—superiors, inferiors, and his brothers—found him to be humble. Nor were the great talents that Our Lord had given him an obstacle to the practice of this holy virtue.

From the moment he became a religious he practiced evangelical poverty, loving it as he would a mother. He renounced his paternal and maternal inheritances, which he generously spent in the rescue of four priests from [134] our Company who, while walking to Rome in 1573, fell into the hands of heretic Huguenots.[216] They were imprisoned in a fortress and badly abused, and as a result of this mistreatment, one of them died. This was Father Martín Gutiérrez, who was known for his sanctity.

Throughout his life Father Tapia was meticulous in the poverty that he had professed, particularly during his long pilgrimages, which he undertook without concern for provisions or any type of comfort. In the Sinaloa mission, where there was so much to endure in terms of continual travel, heat, and rendering assistance to the sick in countless pueblos, his daily sustenance was either maize tortillas or atole, which is like a gruel made with maize flour. On those days when he indulged himself it was with some beef jerky sent to him as [a gift of] charity from Culiacán. He was extremely punctual, observant, and constant in his obedience, which he very clearly demonstrated in the arduous and difficult work in which he always busied himself. Our Lord had given him superior willpower to confront difficulties.

215. *Margin Note*: Psal. 29. Psalm 28:4–8: "The Lord's voice in its power, the Lord's voice in its majesty. The Lord's voice, that breaks the cedars, the Lord breaks the cedars of Lebanon. . . . The Lord's voice makes the wilderness rock; the Lord, rocking the wilderness of Cades" (Knox 1956:489).

216. Apparently only three priests were imprisoned by Calvinists in Cardeat during the winter of 1572–73. Tapia, who was only eleven years old, ransomed the two who survived the ordeal (Shiels 1934:37–38).

His purity and chastity achieved the highest form, for it is considered a certainty that he died a virgin. This was confirmed by a very important priest who was very close with him and ordinarily heard his confession. This virtue was also evident in his very reserved and composed behavior. No matter where he went, people spoke of seeing an angel from heaven, because the angelic purity that he possessed showed in his face and composure.

The hours he spent in prayer and conversation with God were long, particularly in the morning, when his prayers went beyond the rule of the Company.[217] The remainder he left for midday, and he followed this rule even when he was traveling and was away from the Jesuit colleges.

This servant of God always accompanied his prayers with mortification. He did not sleep on a mattress, but was instead content with a blanket or a woven reed mat. He also endured other innumerable discomforts, for in them he found freedom for contemplation, through which Our Lord communicated to him the singular light for his ministerial endeavors.

He told his companion, Father Martín Pérez, that it was Christ Himself who had taught him how to preach, and from this same model he had learned the virtue of patience, which was invincible in this blessed priest. The importance he placed on this virtue was reflected in his [frequent] comment, "Oh, invincible patience." He never showed signs of anger or fury on occasions when they were warranted, because he always remembered the lessons of the most gentle Master.

His zeal for the salvation of souls, which is so characteristic a vocation of the sons of Saint Ignatius, is quite clear in what has been written at the beginning of this book concerning his laborious efforts and peregrinations, which he undertook for the love of his fellow man and the glory of God, for whom he gave his life. The many languages he learned—never tiring of this rather dry and tasteless exercise—are proof of his great zeal for saving souls. The love he felt for souls made learning languages delightful, and he knew not only his native language and Latin, which he spoke equally well, but also six other foreign and barbarous languages: Tarascan, Mexican [Nahuatl], Chichimec, and three others spoken by the nations of Sinaloa. The Father Rector of Michoacán, Francisco Ramírez, once heard him talk-

ing to Indians from several nations of Sinaloa, whom Father Tapia had brought to Mexico City when he came to discuss {with the viceroy and Jesuit superiors} the founding of missions. The Father Rector noticed the different manner in which Tapia spoke with each of them and asked whether he had spoken to them all in the same language. Tapia responded {135} that he had spoken in three. Then Father Ramírez asked, "So, does Your Reverence know all three of them well?" Father Tapia replied, "Do you think I know the language of Michoacán reasonably well?" "Yes, eminently," responded Father Ramírez. "Well, it seems to me that I know any one of these other three better." He added sincerely that if it meant saving souls, he would learn as many additional languages and would do so, with the help of Our Lord, in only twenty days' time. This is a clear indication that God's spirit dwelled in his soul, just as was said of the holy Apostles: *Repleti sunt Spiritu, & caeperunt loqui variys linguis*.[218] Once they were filled with the Holy Spirit, they found themselves moved to speak and teach the doctrine of Christ in several languages. And of this same Holy Spirit it is said in the Book of Wisdom that *scientiam habet vocis*;[219] that is, it is the master of voices and languages. Father Tapia's mastery of languages was not so much the result of the great talent that he possessed to learn them, because God had also given him the same talent for the higher activities of the pulpit and the podium, which he declined. Rather, this mastery was due to the zeal that the Holy Spirit ignited in the heart of this evangelical laborer to make known the name of Christ and to guide poor souls to heaven. He often spoke of the missions in terms of rescuing souls from hell to send them to heaven. He looked upon those who were in the state of mortal sin as if they had fallen into hell. Whence sprang his relentless courage to hear confessions, even when it meant seeking out penitents when they did not come.

His charity was not confined to matters of the soul, but [extended] to the body. He imitated Christ Our Lord, for whom there are many examples in the Gospels of His restoring the health of the body along with that of the soul among the crippled, the maimed, and the lepers. The first thing the priest did when he arrived in a pueblo was to take a staff in his hand and go from house to house, consoling and feeding the sick with his own hands and charging others to care for them and

217. The Jesuits were governed by "rules" laid down in the Jesuit Constitutions, which were modified and supplemented over time. A rule enjoyed the force of a "precept;" that is, a Jesuit's failure to observe a rule constituted a serious sin against his vow of obedience (Polzer 1976:14).

218. *Margin Note*: Actor. 2. Acts 2:4: "and they were all filled with the Holy Spirit, and began to speak in strange languages" (Knox 1956:115).
219. *Margin Note*: Sap. c. 1. Book of Wisdom 1:7: "it takes cognisance of every word we utter" (Knox 1956:574).

cure them. He responded to this ministry with singular affection, joy, and goodwill. The poorer and more repugnant the sick were, the more the flame of his charity was kindled; never did he question whether he should risk his life for his brothers, fearing that he would catch their illnesses, even though they might be contagious.[220]

When he first traveled to Sinaloa and stopped at the Villa de Culiacán, some people told him about the violent nature of the Sinaloa nations, who had killed three religious from the Order of the Seraphic Father Saint Francis who had accompanied the first discoverers of that land.[221] He was not frightened by these fearful accounts; instead, there is no lack of evidence that this blessed priest knew his life would end cruelly at the hands of those whom he wanted to lead to salvation. He gave indications of this when he was returning from Mexico City in the company of some Sinaloa Indians, as was mentioned previously. When they stopped at the college in Pátzcuaro, he showed the Father Rector of the college the weapons the Indians were carrying, and while the Father Rector held the macana in his hand, studying and observing how strong this weapon was, Father Tapia commented as if future events were passing before his eyes, "Look it over very carefully, Your Reverence, so that you are not surprised when you hear that I have been killed by one of these weapons." He said this with great feeling and reflection, and after he had been killed and the Father Rector {136} held the skull from his holy head in his hands and saw the mark of a blow from a macana, he reflected deeply on what Father Tapia had said. Thus, the priest was not intimidated by any of the suspicions and fears he faced, and they did not keep him from proceeding to Sinaloa to help these people. Although his love for them would cost him his life, each hour that his death was postponed seemed like another year in which to help the poor and barbarous Indians.

The priest subjugated the Indians to the yoke of Christ by treating them with singular affability and gentleness, traits that were bestowed on him as a gift from the Lord. Although he daily saw their rusticity, faults, and miseries, his love for them was such that he never expressed disappointment, anger, or weariness. He also understood how important it was to moderate this love with that other grace, authority, which he was careful to reserve and employ when necessary so that

they did not forget their love for him and the obedience and respect that were due him. The best testimony to all this is a letter that was written in their own language and style by some Tarascan Indians who were working in the mines of Topia. This letter was written after they had received word that the Sinaloa Indians had killed Father Tapia. They addressed the letter to all the Indians of the [Tarascan] nation in the Province of Michoacán, where the light of Father Tapia's preaching and catechism had first shone. This letter will also serve to demonstrate how he was still loved even though many years had passed since he first made the rounds of their pueblos as a missionary. For this reason I thought it appropriate to retain the letter's sincere style, faithfully translating it into Castilian. The envelope containing the letter reads, "Indian Governors, Municipal Officers, Members of the Cabildo, and other Principales of Michoacán: Read this letter and send it to all neighboring pueblos. We, the Tarascan Indians of Topia, write to make it known to all that some Indians in Sinaloa have martyred the holy Gonzalo de Tapia, father to us all." The letter inside reads:

> Most honorable gentlemen, residents of Pátzcuaro, Sivina, Navatzín, Charano, Arantzán, and all the other pueblos in the Province of Michoacán where our language is spoken, we inform you and ask that you inform all the smaller pueblos that our very reverend Father Gonzalo de Tapia is now dead. He had been sent to teach Christ's Faith to the people of Sinaloa, who killed him and made him a great martyr, chopping off his head and left arm. [He was found] lying on the ground with only his right arm, which was making the sign of the Cross as if to bless himself. There he lay after his death with his bloody right hand, with which he blessed his entire body and made Crosses as far up as his left shoulder, where they had chopped off his arm when he was still alive. His body remained like this outside his house until he was buried. The name of the pueblo where our very reverend Father Gonzalo de Tapia was martyred is called Tovoropa. We inform you of his death so that all of you might pray an Our Father, just as we are all preparing to have a Mass said. Do not doubt what we are saying, for he really has died, and we implore you to inform everyone. This letter was written by Juan de Charán and the principales of the area. God and the Virgin Mary be with you.

Here ends the letter in its simple style.

The Tarascan Indians of Topia learned of Father Tapia's death from a member of their nation whom the priest had taken from Michoacán to Sinaloa. The letter was taken to the Indian governor, municipal officials, and principales of the pueblo of Arantzán in Michoacán, {137} who gave it to Father Francisco Ramírez, who had gone to preach to them in their language on the feast day of Saint Geronymous, to whom that pueblo

---

220. Caring for the sick and poor (and giving one's life in the process) was an important Jesuit ministry; the Jesuit Constitutions required novices to do at least one month of hospital work (O'Malley 1993a:171–73).

221. These friars apparently died during the destruction of the first Villa de Carapoa on the Río Fuerte.

is dedicated. He received this letter in the presence of their beneficiary, Juan Pérez Pocasangre. The multitude of Indians who had come for the celebration immediately gathered together, expressing great sadness over what had happened. The priest told them that because it was late they should come back to church the following day for Mass, when he would read the letter in public and preach about the incident. The next day a great number from the pueblo assembled, and ascending to the pulpit, he started to read the letter. The tears, cries, and clamors of grief were such that the priest could not read, nor could they hear him, and he had to pause for a good while. After the people quieted down he finished reading the letter and tried to console them, saying that he who had been such a [wonderful] father when he was alive would continue to be such in heaven

because he had departed in such a glorious death. Then the principales asked for the letter, and with great care they dispatched the original, just as they were asked to do, throughout the region, where there was no less sadness. In the other pueblos Masses were said with great solemnity for the souls in purgatory, who it was said they now entrusted to he who was enjoying heavenly bliss and whose memory remained fixed in their hearts. Father Alonso de Santiago, who was Father Tapia's companion when he worked in the Tarascan missions, wrote that he could not persuade himself to say the Masses on Father Tapia's behalf that our Company ordinarily offers for one of its deceased. Instead, he asked that the Lord receive those Masses for whatever would be to His greater glory. At the same time he asked God to pardon his own sins in light of the merits of His chosen servant.

CHAPTER XXXIX [222] The veneration of the bodily remains of the blessed Father [Tapia], the fate of his murderers, and the fruits of his death

The first thing I assume in this chapter is that I am not speaking here of public veneration by the faithful of the relics of saints, which (as is known) requires the approval of Christ's Supreme Vicar. He alone declares and certifies for the Catholic Church those who should be venerated as saints and implored for favors and intercession with God.[223] I am not speaking here of that [type of] veneration, which to date has not been shown Father Gonzalo de Tapia or the remains of his body. I am speaking instead of the personal veneration taught by the Doctors [of the Church] [224] that each individual can show

toward him who, with good and prudent reasoning, the individual judges to have been of distinguished sanctity.

It has already been discussed how the soldiers gathered the remains of Father Tapia's body that this servant of God left here among us. They went for him and brought him to the Villa de San Felipe, where he was buried in the simple church that existed at that time, which was made of poles and straw. His bones were later moved to the church at our college in Sinaloa, where they have been reverently guarded. It was later learned that his skull was in the possession of friendly Indians, who had taken it from the murderers, who had dyed it with red ocher and used it as a drinking vessel during their drunken revels. Once Father Pedro Méndez and some other Spaniards gained possession of it, it was held in great esteem [by the Christians]. Eventually, Father Martín Peláez, of our Company, went as Visitor to the missions [225] and brought it to the college

---

222. The original is incorrectly titled Chapter 38.

223. Beginning in the thirteenth century the Holy See increasingly took control of the process of sainthood (Goodich 1982). By the seventeenth century there were strict rules governing the publication and veneration of would-be saints, as is suggested by Pérez de Ribas' comments at the outset of this chapter.

224. Theologians and ecclesiastical writers noted for their holiness who have been recognized with a Mass and office by the Holy See. Pérez de Ribas often cites the great Greek and Latin Doctors of late antiquity and the early Middle Ages (e.g., Ambrose, Jerome, John Chrysostom,

Basil and Gregory the Great, Augustine, Peter Chrysologus (Attwater 1949:154; Wright 1991).

225. A visitor is a member of the order who is sent by a Jesuit su-

in Mexico City, where it is guarded in equal reverence in a [138] decent place. In addition, the chalice [from the church at Tovoropa] was found, although broken, as were a portion of the ornaments that those fierce murderers had taken.

A portrait of this venerable priest is found in a chapel dedicated to Santa Marina in the Tapia's own parish in the city of León, in the priest's homeland of Castilla. Not only do his relatives have him in their church, but so do their vassals in a place called Quintana de Raneros. This is not, however, public veneration. The priests of our Company of Jesus in León also have a *retablo*[226] of Father Tapia, to which the entire city shows particular devotion. Some years after his death the city of León insisted that it have one of his relics, so Father Hernando de Villafañe, Visitor of the Sinaloa missions, gave them one [in 1622]. It was received with great enthusiasm and joy as the symbol of a very great servant of the Lord who had been born in that city. It was welcomed by all of our priests at the Jesuit college in León, as well as by the most eminent people of the city, both ecclesiastical and secular, who all wanted to honor their blessed compatriot. This relic, which was accompanied by the Archdeacon of that holy church in León, was welcomed a quarter of a league from the city at Castro's bridge by Father Gabriel Sánchez, who was wearing a surplice.[227] Father Sánchez, who had been this apostolic man's grammar teacher, received this relic, the arm that had raised the holy Cross, with many tears of consolation and devotion. It was then taken and placed in the Jesuit church.

Father Tapia's vassals, the residents of Quintana de Raneros, also joined [in the ceremony]. They boasted of having such a holy gentlemen as their sixth successive lord, and they upheld him as an illustrious martyr. The city of León [likewise boasted of] having such a man as a [native] son, one who so amplified Christ's name.

With the exception of Nacabeba the priest's murderers all met a disastrous end. Not only their descendants, but also the entire pueblo where the crime was committed were consumed and eliminated.[228] Father Tapia, who had a burning love for his murderer, Nacabeba, achieved a far more glorious triumph with his death than any he had been able to achieve in life. That which he had failed to achieve with Nacabeba during an entire year of admonitions, which [in the end] cost him his life, exhorting him with fatherly love to recognize his sins and vices and to refrain from being a stumbling block to other souls, all this he achieved in heaven before Nacabeba died. When Nacabeba was finally captured by Captain Diego Martínez de Hurdaide, who ordered that he be executed for his great crimes of murdering the priest and agitating the province, he prepared himself so well at the hour of his death and showed such great signs of remorse for his evil deeds that those who attended him were left with great reassurances of his salvation. At the hour of death he gave even greater confirmation of this when he affectionately asked the priests to carefully teach the Christian catechism to his relatives and children. He thus provided some satisfaction for the scandal he had created in distancing his relatives and children from the doctrine of the Church. He told his relatives to use the priests as a means to salvation and to keep from committing the same evil deeds that he had committed, which now caused him great sorrow. Without a doubt these were all effects of the prayers of this holy priest, who in heaven attained from God what he had so greatly desired while on earth: the salvation of his murderer. He thereby fulfilled that precept from Christ, that we love our enemies and pray for them.

I can appropriately add here another marvelous effect that was achieved following Father Tapia's death (I believe, as do all the priests in these missions, that it can be called a miracle worked by this great servant of God). [139] Once the storm of his death had passed and the missions were back to normal the Indians began to amend their barbarous drunken revels. These had blazed in the province, and (as we said) it was during these revels that the death sentence was discussed and passed on that zealous priest who preached against them. This [practice] was so completely uprooted that it has never again been seen or heard among these people, and this is a most unique and miraculous thing, for you will not find among all the many nations in the extensive Kingdom of Nueva España a single one that is more abstinent or freer from this vice [than this one]. It seems that this unique and marvelous effect has also

perior, in this case the provincial of Nueva España, and acts with the full authority of that superior in the investigation or consideration of affairs in a given mission. Peláez had Tapia's skull and arm sent to Mexico City in 1610 (Dunne 1940:38).

226. A painting generally done in watercolors on wooden panels (Steele 1974:10–11).

227. A loose-fitting, white outer vestment worn during religious services.

228. Tovoropa disappears quite early from Jesuit censuses and re-

ports. Pérez de Ribas' use of "consumed" probably reflects Tovoropa's fate during the epidemics of 1593, 1601–2, and 1606–7.

been wrought by God in honor of this priest's skull, because they used it (as was said) to drink the wine for their inebriation. The blessed skull extinguished and did away with that pernicious and evil vice, and if it was this [vice] that took the priest's life, then he took its life [in return].

It is also worthwhile to note another unique effect that can be attributed to Father Tapia's death, which (as I said) was plotted by the devil by means of sorcerers and their assemblies. It has been a marvelous thing the number of sorcerers (the most difficult to convert) who have converted and been baptized in the Province of Sinaloa since the devil busily plotted to employ the hand of one of them to kill he whom God has glorified with such works.

Finally, we can recount one of the many other miracles achieved by the merits of the holy father and founder of the Sinaloa missions. Since his death innumerable souls and nations in this province have been reduced to the Holy Gospel, which he so desired to propagate. The abundant fruits that will be seen throughout this history have been harvested, and Christ's Cross has been raised (just as this blessed priest raised it with his arm and hand in his holy death) in the sixty churches that have been erected to date in Sinaloa. From there innumerable souls have departed for heaven, having been taught the catechism of Christ that was introduced by this apostolic man. And if, according to the catechism of our holy fathers, the conversion of a sinner is a more marvelous work than the resurrection of a dead man, how many miracles of this type can we count that were worked by this evangelical laborer in so many souls and converted peoples?

The brilliant insight of Saint Peter Chrysologus provides the finishing touch to the life of this apostolic man. Meditating on the arrival of the three wise men from gentile nations who were guided to Christ, whom they adored and revered, this saint felt it a greater miracle that those gentile wise men should recognize Christ than that a new and previously unseen star should appear in the heavens. His words are these: *Plus caeleste de Magis, quam de stella signum est, quod Iudaeae Regem, quod legis auctor em Magus scit*,[229] as if to say, "When I see the

wise men come guided by a star, what I find most marvelous is that those gentiles recognized as their God and King He whom they had never known, surrendering to His laws, of which they were ignorant." *Plus de Magis, quam de stella signum*.[230] It is known that this word *signum* is the same as *miraculum*. In this regard, if the blessed Father Gonzalo de Tapia had been surrounded or crowned by stars in life or in death, then the number of miracles might not appear to have been so great, nor would they have been of such value. [140] We can piously believe, however, that his miracles were both, because during his life he planted the Faith and reduced a great number of gentiles in Sinaloa who recognized and adored Christ as their God and Redeemer, and after his death he interceded with his prayers to change such deeply rooted and barbarous customs and so many sorcerers, or magi. Although this word 'magi', which the Scriptures use to refer to the holy kings, may have another meaning, here I can use 'magi' in its strict sense for the great number of sorcerers converted to Christ. These people renounced their pacts with the devil, abandoning the rancherías where they were born and their caves and dwelling places in favor of settlements with churches, where they adored and revered Christ and the trophy of His most holy Cross that was raised by the preaching and death of His faithful servant, Father Gonzalo de Tapia, of the Company of Jesus.

He was thirty-three when he died, in the flower of his youth, at the same age as the Son of God. He left a well-established enterprise, in which he had labored for only four years. The day and year of his martyrdom and the marvelous posture in which his body was found were recorded in Chapter VIII of this book. Father Tapia had a very pleasant appearance and disposition, and due to this and his temperament, they called him 'The Angel'. In fact, a rumor spread among the Indians that he had come from heaven, and they say that one of those who killed him, upon seeing him dead, stopped to speak with him and said, "If you came from heaven, why are you allowing yourself to be killed?"[231] In this we can believe that God has crowned him and raised him to the highest ranks of glory, which he will enjoy for all eternity. Having dwelled at length on the blessed life and death of he who was the founder of these missions, I will let this serve as the two biographical summaries that I said I would record at the end of each book. [141]

---

229. *Margin Note*: Serm. 156. This sermon on Matthew 12:1–12 is entitled "Epiphany and the Magi" (Ganss 1953:265–70). "The Magi themselves are more of a heavenly sign than the star, for a Magus recognized the King of Judaea and the Author of the Law." Peter Chrysologus (d. 450)—Peter the Golden Orator—was declared a Doctor of the Church in 1729 by Pope Benedict XIII (Farmer 1992:392; Ganss 1953). Sermon 156 is characteristic of his allegorical interpretation of Scripture, which undoubtedly attracted Pérez de Ribas, who also was

fond of interpreting and representing events and facts as symbols.

230. "The magi themselves are more of a heavenly sign than the star."

231. Note this taunt parallels the taunt leveled at Christ as he was dying on the cross (cf. Matthew 27:40; Mark 15:29–32; Luke 23:35).

BOOK III

The Triumphs and Conversion to Our Holy Faith of the Three Principal Nations of the Great Río Zuaque [Fuerte]

CHAPTER I Description of the great Río Zuaque and the nations that inhabit its lands and valleys

The nations that were to receive the word of the Holy Gospel after those discussed in the previous book inhabit the banks of the great Río [Fuerte] of the Province of Sinaloa. If divine wisdom and clemency were admirably demonstrated in the reduction and conversion of those first nations, supreme providence showed no less mercy and an even more marvelous faith toward this second group. It tamed the most warlike and arrogant nations in the province, nations that were the most obstinate in their opposition to Christianity. These nations had killed many Spaniards and had destroyed the first Villa de Carapoa, as has already been told. As a consequence they rebelled for a period of forty years against receiving the Holy Gospel, but such as they were, divine goodness subdued and tamed them to the sweet yoke of Christ. In the end Christianity flourished among them in such a way that very abundant fruits were harvested from the seed of the Gospel.

These nations inhabit the banks of a great river, the fourth of those mentioned at the beginning of this history. It descends from the very high mountains of Topia, crossing and watering the plains of the [142] Province of Sinaloa before entering the Sea of California. It takes its name from the nations that inhabit it, and as these are several, its name changes accordingly.

Sometimes it is called the Río Sinaloa for the nation that lives where [it flows], who are also called the Sinaloa. In fact, the entire province took its name from this nation. For the same reason this river is [sometimes] called the Tehueco, because the Tehueco inhabit its banks. At other times it is called the Río Zuaque, for the same reasons. But all those names refer to a single river, which flows faster and stronger and floods more than the Guadalquivir in Andalucía.

Even though the point where this river emerges from the mountains of Topia is known, its source is uncertain because it must rise at a point far into these mountains, which are vast and nearly inaccessible. This river extends for a length of thirty leagues through the Province of Sinaloa, and it runs from the foothills of the mountains until it reaches the sea. It fertilizes stretches of very beautiful valleys with its floodwaters, which usually rise twice a year, once during the rainy season and again during the winter months. During these periods a fine rain falls steadily for two or three days. This melts some of the snow on the mountainsides, and such a mighty force of water is produced that on some of the plains the river overflows its banks for two or three leagues. It irrigates the fields in the same way the Nile is said to do in Egypt. The nations that live in some of its valleys are left with irrigated lands that are then ready for sowing once, twice, or three times a year. The first crops need no moisture from the skies because even without any rain the irrigation water that the course of the river leaves behind is enough to supply abundant harvests of all the crops the Indians sow.[1] But the fields are barren during those years when there are no high waters.

The nations that inhabit the banks of this river (which from here on we will always call the Río Zuaque, because this nation has the best valleys) are several, but they will be reduced to four principal nations. Even though each of them has other allies, the latter are less populous and joined the larger settlements when mission instruction and districts were established. The four main nations are the Sinaloa, the Tehueco, the Zuaque, and the Ahome.

The Sinaloa inhabit the upper part of the river where it emerges from the high mountains. In this nation there are more than one thousand families, with an equal or greater number of warriors. The Tehueco nation has settled six leagues downstream from the Sinaloa's last pueblo. They are very brave and fearsome, and together with their allies they could send fifteen hundred archers to the battlefield. Five leagues downstream from that nation are the settlements of the fierce Zuaque, which extend for ten leagues and have about one thousand households. Finally, four leagues farther downstream toward the sea along a length of eleven leagues are the settlements of the very docile Ahome and their allies, with one thousand or more families. Some of these allies are maritime fishermen whereas others live off hunting in the monte and fishing from the sea; none of them work the land. As I said at the beginning of this history the latter were the most barbarous people ever discovered in the Indies.

All these nations shared the famous Río Zuaque and all enjoyed its benefits and waters, which are very sweet and beneficial. They boasted of this in their gentile speeches, which I already mentioned. Even now, after they have received the Faith, they still use this rhetoric, although for different reasons. Whenever fugitives have gone to them and attempted to disturb them the principales and those who are at peace in the pueblos preach against them. [143] In doing so, I have often heard them shout the following proposition, "Here we enjoy the water of our river in peace. What do we have to look for in the montes? Let those who are not content go to the montes and search for water to drink."

In addition to the water itself, these nations also enjoy a great abundance of fish that breed in the river. There are even more fish from the sea that enter the mouth of the river and inlets and go upstream to spawn at the appropriate time. Great quantities of mullet, bass, and other types of fish remain after spawning to enjoy the fresh water. Then when the waters recede, especially during the summer heat, the Indians hold their communal fishing in its deep pools. They summon the neighboring pueblos to gather large bundles of *barbasco*,[2] with which they then beat the surface of the water. All the fish in the deep pool become intoxicated from the herb's juices and float to the surface of the water. There they are easily caught, and the poison from the plant does not harm those who eat them.

All the nations that inhabit this river have more or less the same customs and rituals as depicted at the beginning of this history, where they were mentioned in general terms. Each of the large settlements in which they were reduced when the priests came to instruct them will be discussed individually. Their pueblos are located at a distance of some fifteen, eighteen, and twenty or more leagues from the Spaniards' villa and garrison at San Felipe, according to their location and the turns taken by the river through their valleys.

---

1. The anua of 1602 notes that the Zuaque provided five hundred fanegas (approximately one thousand bushels) of maize to Captain Hurdaide and Brother Francisco de Castro; the maize was apparently sought for the pueblos of the Río Sinaloa, which were devastated by the epidemic of 1601-2.

2. Apparently from the tree *Jacquinia macrocarpa* of the family Theophrastaceae. According to Schoenhals (1988:20), the term barbasco can be a referent for a variety of plants that may be thrown into the water to stun fish, including members of such genera as *Croton, Piscidia, Paullinia,* and *Teophrosia*, which have narcotic properties.

CHAPTER II The nations of the Río Zuaque come to ask the captain of the garrison and the priests to enter their lands to baptize them and preach to them Christ's Faith

After the nations of the great river learned that Captain Hurdaide had returned from Mexico City with two priests who were to establish new missions, they went to the villa to discuss the order in which the priests would come to their pueblos to instruct them and make them Christians. Along with other principales from the Zuaque nation came Luisa, the famous Christian Indian woman (who was previously mentioned), and also the Indian Ventura [Buenaventura], whom Luisa had freed from chains from among those who were hanged. Some of their relatives also came. The famous Lanzarote, who was already a Christian, came with his wife and other principales of the Tehueco nation. Principales also came from the Sinaloa nation. Those of the Ahome nation, who were as docile as the others were fierce, were allies and long-time friends of the Spaniards and had always demonstrated their good will and desire to receive the Holy Christian Faith. They all displayed great joy at the arrival of the priests who were to instruct them, and on behalf of their nations they discussed their petition and the time and manner of its execution with the captain and the priests. They offered to gather their homes in locations that would accommodate churches and established pueblos, because some of them still followed their old custom of living in their ranchos and fields. They were ordered to carry out the plan and to jointly erect *xacales*³ for churches in the plazas of the pueblos. These are like large arcades with walls of [144] wood and large forked beams erected in the middle to support the roof made of brush. Alongside each church they were to build a similar yet smaller lodging for the priest. They were also asked to notify all the people from their pueblos to prepare themselves to receive those who were coming to preach to them God's word. They were also to communicate with their allied nations that they, too, should try to resettle in the pueblos of their friends so that all of them could be instructed together. With this the ambassadors of all those nations were dispatched. When they reached their lands they joyfully celebrated the priests' decision with many sermons and meetings according to their custom.

It turned out to be inopportune for the priests who had come to Sinaloa from Mexico City with the captain to hasten their entrada and begin as quickly as they would have liked.⁴ They did not remain idle, however, and immediately began learning the languages of these Indian nations, who later stood firm and did not go back on their good word. In order to better secure their objective and guarantee their steadfastness, therefore, each nation chose some of the most suitable boys and young men from their pueblos to be sent to the villa. They took them and handed them over to the priests for the school that is there for all nations. Having learned the doctrine well, these students could then accompany the priests when they went to their lands, where they could teach the doctrine in their pueblos. Through this careful preparation God's powerful arm wrought a great change in these peoples.

Father Martín Pérez, superior of the Sinaloa mission, called all the priests together to assign them to these new missions. It was decided that the pueblos would be distributed among three priests, because the two priests who had come from Mexico City would not be sufficient to attend to the many pueblos and their large populations. Father Pedro Méndez, a veteran missionary who was in charge of the mission district of Ocoroni, was appointed to the Tehueco nation and their allies and friends. Father Cristóbal de Villalta and he who is the author of this history had just arrived from Mexico City. [We] were assigned, respectively, the Sinaloa nation and their allies and the Zuaque nation and their neighbors, the Ahome. As soon as these nations

---

3. A Nahuatl term for a hut or other perishable structure made of local plant material.

4. There apparently was a delay in receiving formal viceregal approval for these new missions, which did not come until the fall of 1606. Shortly thereafter (November), the priests went to live with their neophytes.

received news of the minister that had been assigned to them, they visited the villa with tokens of gratitude for the priests and to give an account of the preparations being carried out in their pueblos. They pressured the priests to visit them, which the priests earnestly desired because they could not wait to see themselves employed in such a glorious apostolic enterprise. Therefore, the happy day was set when the light of the Gospel would be borne to those peoples who lived in the shadow of death. Some Indians from the pueblos offered to accompany and guide the priests to their lands (which they did), and then they all went back to their pueblos.

To retain clarity and avoid confusing the specific cases of the conversion of large settlements that are worthy of memory, the establishment of missions, general Baptisms, the erection of churches, and everything else that was necessary to complement the Christianity of these nations, each will be discussed in turn, tracing their development up to the present time when this history is being written. We will begin with the Ahome. They have always maintained peace and friendship with the Spaniards, and are very temperate. They waited the longest for ministers to instruct them and thus deserved to be the first to receive this benefit. [145] Subsequently, I will write about their neighbor, the Zuaque nation. I cannot help but mention that the Spaniards in the villa, who were both fearful and hopeful, joyously celebrated this people's conversion. On the one hand, they had experienced the Zuaque's warlike nature; on the other, they hoped that once that battle was won, the door for the Gospel would be opened wide and many other nations would receive it, as fortunately happened through divine grace.

CHAPTER III The location, settlement, and unusual customs of the Ahome nation

The Ahome nation and its principal pueblo [Ahome], which has three to four hundred male heads-of-household, is four leagues from the Sea of California. It is on a plain surrounded by rock-strewn hills and woods, which served as a fortress and refuge during enemy attacks. They enjoy beautiful valleys with poplar groves and land for farming. Their elders used to say, or better said, were persuaded by the devil to brag that the souls of the deceased lived in these valleys. This was their paradise, where they delighted in great drunken revels, which brought them happiness; such is the heaven that the devil promised. The people also had an [oral] tradition that was passed down from their ancestors that they had settled these lands following a pilgrimage from the north. Another group of people called the Zoe, who spoke a different language, had come with them and had settled along the upper part of the same river. Because of this tradition, the Ahome always maintained friendship with the Zoe, even though they were separated by thirty leagues. The Zoe nation will be discussed later, along with its neighboring nation, the Sinaloa. The Ahome are also friendly with, related to, and speak the same language as the Guasave, who live on the Río [Sinaloa] where the Villa de San Felipe is located. They undoubtedly came together on their pilgrimage from the north.[5] The Ahome were also allied to and spoke the same language as some bands of more barbarous peoples. As we said at the beginning [of this history] these peoples have no established pueblos and sustain themselves on the fruits of the monte and fish from the sea.

The Ahome are docile by nature and learn very easily whatever they are taught; their children read, write, sing, and play musical instruments. I can attest to the gentleness, good nature, and fidelity of this nation (a marvelous thing in the midst of the many fierce nations in this province). Whenever I think about the many dangerous occasions when I saw that the entire province might riot and rebel, in such instances

---

5. Items of material culture (e.g., overlapping manos, shell ornaments) recovered from limited archaeological research in the 1930s at Guasave suggest the prehistoric inhabitants may have had ties to the Hohokam of southern Arizona (DiPeso 1979; Ekholm 1942).

my best chance for safety was to flee with my loyal Ahome, even if it was into the monte, until the storm and danger had passed. This provided me with greater security than any other place in that land. Such is the love and respect this nation has for its spiritual fathers. During the eleven years I lived with them teaching the catechism I never sensed any unrest or inconstancy. Nevertheless, there was plenty of danger among the other wild nations[6] who were their allies.

The [Ahome] people are of better character than the other Indians of the province. Consequently, their barbarous customs of getting drunk and waging war were not as savage as in other nations. Cohabitation with, or marriage to, many women was rare among them. Rather, the Ahome had a laudable custom that was inviolably maintained of protecting their young daughters' virginity. As was said at the beginning, the latter wore a small conch shell around their neck as a sign of their virginity until the day of their marriage. [146] They removed this medallion from a maiden's neck when they handed her over to her spouse. Thus, if in any nation there was evidence of true marriage contracts, it was in this one.

The women of this nation dress more modestly than in any other. Their clothing was made from cotton mantas that they wove and in some instances decorated with curious designs and colors. They had very few sorcerers and very little sorcery. They had only one custom that was nearly intolerable and excessive, and that was their crying for their deceased. This wailing lasted for a year in the home of the dead, and the screaming was so loud that it seemed more like the howls of the damned. They would wail for an hour every morning and evening, and this was done in several tones of voice that brought forth responses from other houses. This custom was so deeply rooted that it took a long time to moderate and amend it. Their wars did not stem from attacks on other nations; they waged war only to defend themselves from outsiders. They maintained perpetual peace and unity with the Spaniards. Finally, because the devil had not corrupted this nation with vices and savage customs, there was a greater willingness to receive the Faith and the sweet law of Christ Our Lord. As we will soon see, they received it and it settled into their souls with ease.

CHAPTER IV The arrival of the first priest among the Ahome nation and a singular event that followed his arrival

Seeing myself so fortunate as to prepare and instruct the Ahome nation for Holy Baptism, I sent word of the date of my arrival so the people could assemble at their main pueblo.[7] Upon arriving, I planned to tell them my motive and goal for coming to the ends of the earth where they lived. This speech is very important because they are thereby persuaded that the minister of the Gospel is not going to ask them for anything, not even food, which is their

only wealth. I also advised them to have all the mothers assemble with their little children so that I could baptize the latter when I arrived. Christ Our Lord and His Church take these children as security to thus win over their parents.

I departed with some Indians from the Jesuit college in the Villa de San Felipe for the pueblo of the Ahome, which was twenty leagues away. It was necessary to travel along the seacoast, away from the road, through an area where there were some wild Indians called Caribes. Having never laid their eyes on a priest before, some of them came out to see me as I passed by. I received them warmly, giving them some food, which pleased them. At this time an unusual thing happened,

---

6. *Montarazes*, which Pérez de Ribas later describes as those who "live on the game and fruits of the monte"; hunter-gatherers in modern parlance.

7. This visit occurred in 1605.

and because it was unusual, it is recorded here. As I was sitting with a group of them there in the countryside, telling them about God, the Creator of all things, He willed that the earth should suddenly begin to tremble. When the Indians felt this they got up. Taking advantage of this event, I made them sit back down and I explained [the earthquake] to them. I spoke of God's power and the importance of receiving the Holy Faith and the divine word, which other nations who were their neighbors had already received. [I explained that] with the passage of time these nations had settled in Christian pueblos and continued to benefit from catechism.

A few leagues beyond this place, as we were nearing the pueblo of the Ahome, the principal cacique came out [to meet us] on a horse that Captain Hurdaide had given him. He was an Indian of very good disposition and [intellectual] capacity and was later of great support to this Christian community. With him came others who were his vassals, [147] whom he called sons. He welcomed me with great joy and accompanied me to the pueblo. Along the way there were arches made of green tree branches, which they commonly erect to welcome a respected person; this is a sign of being welcomed with love and joy. When we reached the plaza of the pueblo a large throng of men, women, and children of all ages had assembled. What was most amazing and a cause of great joy was that they came out in a procession, led by a Cross that was adorned with their richest decorations, which are colored feathers and tree branches. Although they were gentiles, they all sang the Christian Gospel and divine praises loudly in their language. They were so orderly and sang with such harmony and recall that they seemed like long-time Christians. This was an amazing act for a people who had never had a priest in their land to teach them. It was in all respects like Christ Our Lord's entry into Jerusalem, when the people welcomed Him in triumph with branches and palms. The children acclaimed Him with divine praises, for by means of the Cross He was going to strip the prince of this world of the kingdom he had tyrannized, claiming it as His own. Thus, it seems that when the priest came in Christ's name to this poor Ahome nation, the Lord wanted him to be received by them and to take possession of their souls, rescuing them from the power of Satan, who had possessed them for so many centuries.

In order to respond to doubts that may arise here concerning how or by what means this gentile nation, which was the farthest from the Spaniards and had never been visited by priests, had learned the Christian

catechism and prayed and sang with such order and harmony, I will discuss the means and unique providence by which God sent them the first rays of divine light. There happened to be a blind Christian Indian among the Guasave nation, an ally of the Ahome, who knew extremely well all the prayers and questions of the catechism and the mysteries of our Holy Faith. Our Lord had given this blind man a most remarkable and unselfish inclination for teaching the Christian catechism. He spent a lot of time and many nights teaching the young and old, not only in their houses in the pueblo, but frequently in their homes in the fields. He was not content to practice such great Christianity among his own people, so he went to the pueblos of his friends and relatives, the Ahome. Because he took his duty of teaching the catechism so seriously and because the divine seed fell on such good soil, the Ahome by nature being pliant, it yielded the abundant fruit that has been discussed.

[When I arrived at the Ahome pueblo] I was overjoyed by such an unusual reception. I was amazed when I sat with the people under a ramada they had made of tree branches and asked their gentile children, "Who is God? Who is the Most Holy Trinity? Who is Our Lord Jesus Christ?" They responded with answers that were better than those that are usually given by long-time Christians who have been raised in a Christian community. Afterward, we went into their poor church, which was an enclosed ramada, where they finished praying and singing the heavenly canticles.[8] They were given the usual sermon and then, because they would not all fit inside the ramada, all the mothers sat in a circle with their children in the plaza of the pueblo, which was a field in front of the ramada. The flock of little lambs, of whom there were almost three hundred, were offered to God and given rebirth in Christ through the water of Baptism. I gave them Christian names, which they welcomed with singular pleasure, and I divided them among the three or four Christians present there, who acted as godparents. I recorded [148] their names in the book of Baptisms so I could remind them of their [new] names in case they forgot these strange words that were new to their language. They were baptized with the greatest solemnity and ceremony possible in such a poor land, and once the Baptisms were concluded on that joyous day, some of them returned to their homes and others to their fields. The godparents took their

---

8. Liturgical songs from the Bible such as the Magnificat or the Psalms.

godchildren's parents to their homes and gave them their greatest gifts, which are tortillas and tamales, a type of maize roll. They gave the same gifts to the priest, and when night fell we might say that it became a joyful day, for there were speeches and public sermons all night long, celebrating the arrival in their lands of the word of God and the priest who would preach it. They congratulated one another for this, as well as for the fact that they now had protection and defense from their enemies. It was a well-established order of the captain of the garrison that anyone who caused unrest in any nation or pueblo where a priest was attending or preaching God's word would be punished. They took the priest to the mountain passes to show him where their enemies, the Zuaque, would sometimes attack them and assault their pueblo, which was surrounded by montes. They said very joyfully, "Our Father, now that you are with us, the women will be able to safely come to this river for water, whereas before it was necessary for us to accompany them with our bows and arrows."

During this visit I spent [only] eight days with the Ahome, because I had to continue on to the Zuaque nation. I left them with orders to build a church that was more adequate, even if it was made of straw, and a similar house where I could dwell when I returned. With this the first formal preaching of the catechism among the Ahome nation was concluded. We will continue discussing the Ahome [below] and then move on to their neighbors, the Zuaque. I will not discuss here the Baptism of sick adults during this entrada. This is to avoid repetition of very similar cases that it should be supposed arise at each step in these new enterprises. Such cases will be noted only when circumstances worthy of memory form a part of them.

CHAPTER V The priest returns to visit the Ahome, building a church and formalizing religious instruction

After a short time I paid the Ahome another visit [in the fall of 1606] and found this new flock very happy. They were waiting with dressed wood to erect a church that would be more appropriate for Christian ministering and Baptism. It was necessary for me to help them, even assisting with my own hands, because such construction, although humble and poor, was still great and out of the ordinary for them. It certainly appears that Christ, the Redeemer of Mankind who wished to enter the world and be born in a poor manger covered only with straw, also wanted the arrival of the Gospel and the salvation of these poor nations to occur in churches that were as poor as these straw-covered shelters. The Ahome, men as well as women, joyfully hauled wood and straw and thus their church was quickly completed. They were so satisfied that it was as if they had a beautiful royal palace in their pueblo. They gathered all the children who had not been baptized during the first entrada and all those who had been born recently, totaling almost five hundred, and they were baptized.

Afterward, the principal cacique and his entire family agreed to be baptized: his wife and children as well as his father, who was a strong and venerable old man of very high intellectual capacity. He was also a great pillar of [149] this Christianity, and in his own fashion he delivered very sensible sermons and arguments about peace, stability, and the value of God's word. Because they had already memorized the catechism, they were all prepared for Baptism in just a few days. These Baptisms were celebrated with the greatest possible solemnity, and they were given Christian names. They were permitted to retain their gentile name as a surname, although this nation barely remembers the latter. Unlike in other nations that glorified taking [enemy] lives, the Ahome's gentile names did not refer to taking human life.

This old cacique was named Don Pedro and his son

Don Miguel, a name he lived up to on many occasions, assuming the office of captain and guide for his pueblo.[9] Captain Hurdaide made him governor of those nations, and a list was made of all the families[10] so that they could be reduced to the Church and catechism. They made sure that they attended church every morning, where the principal mysteries of our Holy Faith were explained. A good number of the most able children were chosen to serve in the church and to learn to read, write, and sing. [The children's parents] gladly volunteered them [for this training]. A fiscal was appointed to notify [the priest] of those who became ill and to make sure that the people went to church. Some of them who had their ranchos and houses in their fields moved to the pueblo, and thus both Christian and civil governance were established in this nation.

The good Ahome were so happy with their new lives that they came to me one day and asked permission to hold a traditional dance so that their young people could have fun. They understood that there could be no drunkenness, which was ruled out by their acceptance of the catechism. I told them that I would agree to their request so long as the men and women did not dance together. The wise Ahome understood my misgivings, which was noteworthy in a nation so new to the Faith. They answered me, "Our Father (they have no other title for their minister, whether he is present or absent), you will see how modestly the maidens and young men dance and how the maidens dance separately with particular dignity." Their petition was granted so as not to sadden people so new [to the Faith] over a matter that had been so carefully planned to avoid problems. The dancers came to the plaza of the pueblo and celebrated with an order and modesty such as had never been seen before in these nations' many celebrations. Although the young women danced in sight of the young men of the pueblo, they did not raise their eyes to look at them, nor did they touch the clothing or mantas with which they danced. In the same way a young maiden of this nation does not raise her eyes to look at the boy or young man whom she knows her parents have chosen for her to marry in due time. In a gentile and barbarous nation this prudence in matters of modesty is noteworthy.

Afterwards, some caciques from the wild fishing nations allied to the Ahome, who spoke the same language, came to me to inquire about what decision had been reached concerning where their people were to settle. They were received with particular kindness and given some small things, which it is necessary to have on hand for this purpose. Although these items are of very little value, it is through them that many are won over to God. Because these [Indians] are poor and have never seen such things, they value, for example, colored glass beads, with which they adorn themselves; knives, which they lacked; horseshoes, which they sharpen and make into hatchets; and needles, with which they sew their nets. A lot of work was required to make these items when they were gentiles, so the caciques were very happy with these meager gifts. [150] I asked them to advise their people to come to see me and to exhort them to settle in places where I could visit and teach them God's word and where they could enjoy the peace and security of their friends, the Ahome. The latter also helped me with advice and gifts for their allies, offering them farmland and friendship should they decide to join their pueblo. Thus, they happily departed to discuss these offers with their own people.

9. Pérez de Ribas is alluding here to Don Miguel's similarities to his namesake, the archangel Michael.

10. Here as elsewhere Pérez de Ribas uses "families" in the sense of kin or descent groups.

CHAPTER VI Nations allied to the Ahome come to choose a place to settle and the pueblo of Bacoregue is formed

The caciques mentioned in the last chapter, along with others who had previously remained along the shore in the rock-strewn hills and thickets, returned to see the priest and inform him of what they had decided concerning their reduction and religious instruction. They decided that the Batucari, who lived in the monte, would join the pueblo of Ahome, building homes in one of its quarters. They would be governed by their own cacique (these people hate any government that is not their own) and would adapt to farming the land that had been offered them by the Ahome. The maritime fishing people of the coast, however, found this very difficult to do. It appeared to those who had been born and raised in the sand dunes by the sea that they would be too far from their daily sustenance, fish, which they had right at hand. Also, the pueblo of Ahome was five leagues from their old rancherías. With regard to receiving the Christian catechism, however, they were quite willing. So that this could be done and in order for the priest to come and preach to them, they would choose an acceptable place to gather and build their houses, forming a pueblo of their own.

I willingly agreed to their solution, so as not to upset them, and a satisfactory place was chosen three leagues below Ahome. It had good land and was close to the sea and their fishing sites, and I accompanied them in order to gather these lambs who had so strayed. The place that had been chosen was on a beautiful airy plain above the river. It was cleared of unnecessary underbrush and trees, particularly where the church was to be built, and there they chose homesites and distributed the land. Once this was done they returned to their rancherías for their meager belongings. They came back with some children, but because these people do not always uproot themselves all at once from the places where they were born and to which they were accustomed, it is necessary to proceed patiently and at their own pace. During this first entrada it was difficult to get them to reduce themselves and form a congregation. Nevertheless, they offered God a good number of infants and nearly two hundred were baptized. The care of this pueblo was entrusted to its principal cacique, an Indian of good character who was noted for his massive body. He was like a giant and had such great strength that he [even] dared to seize a caiman, or crocodile, an animal well known for its ferocity, and lift it out of the water with his hands. It was a particular [act of] providence by Our Lord to choose him to guide this ranchería, for on the one hand he possessed great valor and strength, yet on the other he was very docile, calm, and well loved by his people. He had such a good heart that after he was baptized he used to say, "Father, when I go fishing I say, 'Father God, give me fish to catch.'" Even though he was new to the Faith and had only a short time before been ignorant of God in heaven and on earth, he made his request for fish in faith, [151] and it was apparent that God heard and was pleased by this petition from His son because He granted him great abundance whenever he fished. This Indian became the means for achieving the reduction of the most difficult nations of the New World to [permanent] settlements with some form of civilization and political order.

With the aid of Our Lord and this Indian this [reduction] was accomplished. The results of this first entrada were that some of the new residents were gathered in homes, a humble church was built, a fiscal was appointed to assemble the people for catechism, and the aforementioned blind man who had taught the Ahome was appointed teacher. With all this the Bacoregue (their own name for their nation) were very contented, and as a sign of their happiness, they said that they wanted to go fishing so that they could give what they caught to their priest, who had come to teach them God's word. After a few hours they returned with a huge quantity of fish, which were extremely abundant along that coast. There was [even] enough to share with those who had accompanied me. After this new pueblo was settled we returned to the Ahome. We did so with great happiness on both my part and theirs, because God Our Lord had made it easier for these people who were so lacking in humanity to receive the light of the Gospel. Soldiers would be of little help reducing [people] such as these, for they have no houses or homes; it would be like hunting deer in the monte.

CHAPTER VII The general Baptism of adults among the Ahome and the reduction of two other wild nations to the Ahome pueblo

There was little difficulty in preparing the Ahome for Holy Baptism because they were very well instructed in the mysteries of our Holy Faith and had embraced instruction with great affection. Nor [was it necessary] to defer the Baptism of adults for as long a time as is generally the case with other nations. Of their own free will and encouraged by their cacique Don Miguel groups of adults came to church to request Holy Baptism and to give their names so that they could be recorded with the other catechumens, just as was done in the early Church. They assembled mornings and afternoons for eight days preceding [Baptism] to hear the principal mysteries of our Holy Faith explained slowly and in great detail. In this way groups of approximately forty were prepared for Baptism. These Baptisms were then celebrated with the greatest possible solemnity. Once those who were married had been baptized, they ratified or contracted matrimony as a sacrament of our Holy Mother Church. They very eagerly received the blessing while attending Mass, and it is true that all these holy ceremonies confirm them in the Faith and in the indissolubility of holy matrimony. They recognized that they were no longer subject to the inconstancy from which they had suffered in their heathenism, when neither the husband nor the wife could be sure of the perpetuity of their marriage. They contracted matrimony as Christians with such solemnity that they knew their marriages would endure.

With these Baptisms of adults almost the entire [152] Ahome nation was baptized within a year; the number exceeded one thousand, not counting infants. They were joined by another wild nation called the Batucari, who as we said, live on the game and fruits of the monte. Although they had no houses, they resided four leagues from the Ahome pueblo among thickets, near a little rainwater lagoon that was present year-round. Because the Batucari were at peace with the Ahome, they came at harvest time to the pueblo to trade and barter (which is the way commerce is conducted among these nations) whatever little things they happened to have for some maize, which they ate at this time of year. Because they were happy with their wild foods, they did not make provisions for the rest of the year.

By the time I returned Don Miguel had already congregated some of the families of this nation, or ranchería. I tried to show them affection, especially their captain and cacique. We made an agreement for him to finish bringing all of his people out of the monte. Given their good reception in the pueblo of their allies, the Ahome, they were to begin farming, an important means by which nations whose life consists of wandering among deer and rabbit burrows and even among serpents and vipers become settled and rooted. The cacique accepted this proposal in the name of his people and went after those who had remained in the monte. He reduced almost all of them, even though there are always some whom the devil has hardened and made obstinate, particularly the elderly, who find it difficult to change the wild and barbarous life in which they have grown old. In the end, with endurance and patience, about three hundred people congregated at this ranchería. The cacique was entrusted with governing and executing the office of fiscal, and the Batucari attended religious instruction, following the example given by the Ahome. One hundred infants were baptized and a list of the families was made so that they could be monitored. Despite all this effort the Batucari remained rooted in their [former] lands and returned to that Egypt. They were drawn by the monte, where at times they would celebrate their drunken revels. Because they were exiles in the Ahome pueblos, they sought their former solitude, where they would not be seen by Christians and could have freedom of conscience. God punished this nation for these retreats with illnesses that struck them in the monte[11] and that obliged the priest to come to their aid with the sacraments. Because they had already acquired Christian customs from their Ahome friends, and perhaps be-

---

11. In 1606–7 the Jesuit missions of northwestern Mexico were again hit by measles, smallpox, and other maladies. As Pérez de Ribas later indicates (but never details), thousands of the Jesuits' newest converts along the Río Fuerte perished (Reff 1991b:147–54).

cause they had attended instruction and sermons, they already had some idea of the necessity of Baptism for their salvation. Their cacique was sure to advise me of those who were ill, so on several occasions it was necessary [for me] to go back and forth through the monte, visiting and helping them in the midst of those briars. Those in greatest need were baptized, and we can say that this became an enjoyable hunt for the souls living among those rocky hills and thickets.

In addition to this ranchería, another ranchería of fishermen of even greater number was reduced to the Ahome pueblo. They were reduced with greater ease than the Batucari and in a short time more than one hundred of their children were baptized. The adults, meanwhile, applied themselves to hearing the Christian catechism in order to [also] receive Holy Baptism. With this the Ahome pueblo had five hundred male heads-of-household[12] living in great harmony and brotherhood, with easy access to water, monte, and farmland. Although these flocks were not as large as those among the nations that will be discussed later, there is nevertheless no doubt that Christ, the Supreme and Divine Shepherd, enjoys having them gathered together and, moreover, that He wants [153] them to praise Him for having discovered them. He also wanted the holy Apostles to gather up the leftovers from the bread He had abundantly distributed to the crowds who had followed Him into the countryside. He willed that His holy Evangelist should make mention of this,[13] which is proof of the generosity that the Lord shows these people, who it seems are the remnants of the populous peoples of the world. Through all this, He wants and wills that they be given the sustenance of life, the bread of His divine word.

CHAPTER VIII The singular reduction of the most barbarous and savage nation in Sinaloa

Although we have just written about the reduction of some of the many rancherías of savages who lived in those vast and wild thickets and swamps, I have saved for this chapter the recounting of the reduction of another ranchería that occurred in an unusual way that revealed how divine providence placed it on the road to salvation. The nation discussed in this chapter, the Comopori, was as wild and fierce as the Zuaque, whose pride and fierceness have already been recorded. One time the Zuaque dared to attack the Comopori in the open field, and many Zuaque were left dead. Those who survived lived for many years, acknowledging and fearing the strength of the savage Comopori, whose reduction to life as humans and docile Christians is herein related just as it happened.

When I was in the pueblo that I wrote about two chapters earlier, where the Bacoregue fishermen had recently settled, I was informed that the fierce Comopori lived among the sand dunes in rancherías along the shore of an isolated peninsula seven leagues farther on. Although they spoke the same language as the docile Ahome, they were not friendly toward them, instead killing them whenever they got the chance. I also learned, however, that a few Christian Indians enjoyed safe passage among the Comopori, which sometimes happens among these nations even though they contend with one another. Because of individual circumstances or kinship ties that they have previously contracted, a few persons have entry to the enemy nation, and so I found a Christian who was accepted by the Comopori. Because I desired their reduction and the salvation of their souls, I sent this Christian Indian with a message of kindness, inviting some of them to come to see me; they would be very well received, in peace and with safe passage. Trusting in my word, a few came to see me, in particular their leaders. From the outset I attempted to show them affection by giving them some of the little

12. *Vezinos.* Pérez de Ribas' population figures (one thousand Ahome, three hundred Batucari, and one thousand of this last group), totaling twenty-three hundred, are consistent with five hundred households (4.6 persons per household).

13. Matthew 14:15–21; Matthew 15:34–38; Luke 9:12–17.

things they value. At the same time I invited them to come to trade for maize at harvest time. In this way they were won over so that both men and women now came to the Christian pueblos, which was a very reassuring sign. I invited them to the Christians' feast days and Easter and Christmas celebrations. The Christians also treated them affectionately and invited them to their houses. This moved them, or better said God moved them, to request the Baptism of their little children.

With the Comopori thus disposed the Christian Indian who had established this stronger friendship with them came to tell me that they would like me to visit their lands to see all their people. I consulted [154] the Father Rector of the college in the Villa de San Felipe about this, because (as I have said) there is an order not to undertake new entradas without orders from superiors. The Father Rector replied that because this visit was to be made with a military escort and in the company of two dozen brave and ever-loyal Ahome Indians, I should determine whether these poor people could be won for Christ. Therefore, I decided to visit this nation. When the date was set the Comopori were notified and I called the Ahome cacique Don Miguel and ordered that on the appointed day he come to present himself with about twenty of his Indians so that we could all go together. He very willingly carried out all I had asked of him, and he and his people readied themselves for the trip to a land where they had once fought and where many had died. Even during this present visit the Ahome were exposed to danger, but the Lord's providence is manifested whenever these people risk their own lives for that of the minister of the Gospel. The expedition was prepared to set out, but the afternoon before it was to leave the wife of the cacique Don Miguel came to me very sad and distressed, saying that she had received news that the Comopori did not have a good heart (a phrase they use to indicate that they were traitors). Their intention was to get me to visit their lands so they could kill me and my companions. As evidence of this she had learned from one of their confederate groups in the monte, who virtually filled the swamps and were going to join the Comopori, that there were rumors of the Comopori's restlessness and lack of loyalty. This warning made me cautious, but my experience with these people has taught me not to show fear or cowardice; much of the authority that a minister needs is lost by doing so. On this occasion, because I could find no reason to cancel the visit, I encouraged the worried woman not to discourage her

husband. I entrusted the enterprise to Our Lord and asked His divine favor in this matter that was of such service to Him and to the salvation of those souls who were [now so] near the light of the Gospel.

I said Mass before dawn and we started on our way. When we had crossed the river, on the banks of which lay the pueblo whence we had departed, I found myself surrounded by more than one hundred Ahome allies, equipped and ready for war, loaded down with quivers, bows, and arrows. I stopped for a minute and called Don Miguel, asking the reason for such a large and boisterous group. I knew that he had asked no more than two dozen of his kinsmen to accompany him. We risked trouble once the Comopori learned that we were going to their lands in such an uproar, with so many armed people. He answered me, "Father, I only called those people you told me to call, but those who are your sons say they do not trust the Comopori very much. They know them very well, and they do not want their priest to run the risk of being killed. No matter how much I tried, it was impossible to hold them back."

To prevent the alarm that so many armed people would cause among the Comopori, I sent an eighteen-year-old Ahome boy ahead. His spirit and bravery were outstanding and he was like a Spaniard, fearlessly entering strange lands. His safe passage was also due to the fact that he was Captain Hurdaide's servant and, above all, because he skillfully commanded several languages. In order to make [155] this boy's spirit understood, I note that on this particular day when he came to accompany me, he did so on a good horse he had, and because he could not arm it like Spanish soldiers do, he covered it with an armor that was painted in red ocher. This boy rode as skillfully as the best Spanish horseman.

I sent this very bright Christian Indian ahead with a message for the Comopori that they should offer safe conduct to my sons (this is what the priests call those whom they have baptized, who have only one name for him, Our Father), who were accompanying me in peace and friendship and with a [good] heart. Once this messenger was dispatched, we continued on our way, much of which took us along the seashore, where there were plenty of fish for the Indians to shoot with their arrows. We finally reached the Comopori, who did not have any kind of dwellings or pueblo, neither hearth nor home, living instead like wild animals out in the open. In the sand dunes they had erected an enramada made out of tree branches stuck in the ground for my shade and protection from the extremely hot sun that we have here [in Sinaloa]. Then I found out something that made me fear for my safety: very few of the Comopori had come to meet me with their cacique (Cohari, who was famed as a great warrior). It also seemed that they had come without their women and children. I thought this very strange, because when these people withdraw to the monte or their women and children do not show themselves, it is a clear sign that they are at war. Noticing this, I asked the cacique why the women and children did not come out so I could see them and give them gifts of some small items of food and the other things they enjoy. I added that I considered them to be my children and that I would not leave without seeing them. He replied that they had gone to a nearby pool or inlet for fish to feed me and my people. After a little while just three or four women appeared with some small nets of fish and oysters that they had collected.

The day went by and the rest of the women and children had still not appeared, which revived my suspicions and concerns for my safety. The Indian allies became wary, and thus the day passed. Later four other Indians appeared, who showed us their catch and some inlets where they had fished. At nightfall the cacique Cohari came with a few of his companions and began to make a speech, saying, "Father, we wish to build a church here. You will come to instruct us and baptize us in this place, like you do with the other nations, because we cannot leave our fishing and our lands (or better said, sand dunes) to go to a strange place." Now I finally understood why he had received us so strangely. He feared that I had come to force them to leave their beloved sand dunes. I know from experience that such a nation must be won over through planning, time, and patience, because in this way they finally give in. The first thing I said to him was that I had not come to take him away from his lands. Because of the disadvantages of that location, however (the lack of a permanent source of fresh drinking water and [a place to grow] maize to feed people), it was impossible to grant their request to build a church among the sand dunes where I could visit, instruct, and baptize them. Furthermore, I would not be able to visit them because I might be cut off by the river, which rushes so furiously and in a such a wide swath across those flats during most of the year that not even they dared to try to cross it. Finally, I said that for now I was satisfied to have seen them and that just as [156] they had done up until that time, they could continue to come to see me from time to time at the pueblos of the Christians, who were their friends and

relatives. If some of them wished to settle with them and work the land, I would accept them very willingly. They were relieved and very glad to receive this reply and peacefully went back to their ranchos to sleep.

Here I must tell about the loyalty and steadfastness of Don Miguel, the Ahome cacique, who watched over the safety of the priest and minister. The cacique and his people suspected some treachery or trouble that night (and not without reason) when they saw that the women and children never appeared. When the talk I had with the Comopori was concluded around midnight I called Don Miguel and asked him how or where his sons were lodged. This prudent Indian answered me, "Father, you can rest here in your enramada without worrying, because some of my sons and I will be sleeping nearby, and I have made ready and distributed all the rest of my people to sleep at the Comopori's own hearths because we know that is where they make their treacherous pacts. Whatever trouble they might try to cause, we will be warned and they will not be able to carry it out without our first hearing about it and defending ourselves." With all due preparation and care this loyal cacique had set up this warning system. Actually, it turned out to be unnecessary because the Comopori had gone away very satisfied and reassured with the reply I had given them earlier that evening. It calmed them and gave them ample opportunity for their reduction at a better time and place.

In the end this was all successfully achieved, because in the morning all the people appeared with the women and children. They were shown much attention and afterwards they came frequently to see me at the Christian pueblos. They began to apply themselves to working the land and sowing some fields, putting aside the lives they had led as savages. When they were in the pueblos of the baptized people they went to the church with them to receive Christian doctrine and sometimes a few of them were baptized. Thus, they were finally settling down, and within two years [1607–9] these groups of people who had seemed untamable were reduced on a peninsula where they had gone to keep company with the fish in the sea. This seems to fulfill what Christ said to His disciples, that He would make them fishers of men. This was a catch of men who made their life by fishing. They entered the apostolic nets of the Gospel doctrine and were washed in the sacred waters of Holy Baptism. About six hundred persons congregated in Christian pueblos, and today they are among the best of those peoples who have received instruction. They established great friendship and brotherhood with the docile Ahome, who had once been their mortal enemies.

This account will serve to make known the nations of these provinces that the sons of the Company of Jesus have domesticated through His grace, no matter how fierce and barbarous they might be. Further ahead we will encounter many nations that are more populous and civilized. All of them belong to the crown with which Christ Our Lord said He would adorn His church. In Chapter 4 of the mysterious [Song of] Songs,[14] the handsomely portrayed Holy Spirit invited His bride, the Holy Church, to abandon the beautiful mountain of Lebanon and its beautiful plants, whose blossoms were to be her crown. He desired that this crown also should be interwoven with branches from the thickets where the lions and wild beasts dwelled: *Coronaberis de capite Amana, de vertice Sanir, & Hermon, de cubilibus Leonum, de montibus pardorum.*[15] All these words clearly manifest the dwelling places and nature [157] of the peoples we are now discussing, just as there is no lack of holy scholars who have understood them to be gentiles.

With regard to the people we are discussing here I found a kind of superstition or quasi-idolatry. Along the seashore and among the sand dunes where they lived they had erected in certain places some high stakes at the base of which they piled human bones. Near them they placed some skeins of *iztli*, which is like Castilian hemp but made from a wild plant.[16] They use this fiber to weave their fishing nets. When I came upon these places I asked the cacique Cohari about their meaning and purpose. This gentile answered that those were the bones of some Indians who had died in the jaws of sharks, trying to cross that inlet of the sea. They greatly fear these fierce fish that swim along these coasts. He added that those bones had been placed there so that whoever had to cross the inlet could first place a skein of twine next to the bones so that the sharks would not catch him. This is a lie with which Satan had entombed them in darkness. I managed to disabuse them of it and make them understand that we must ask God alone to free us from the dangers of life, because He is the author of it and grants it to us and preserves it. For the purpose of enlightening his people I asked Cohari to knock down those poles and bury the bones. These words scared the cacique to death and he began to shake, telling me that if he did such a thing he would die. I then turned to a Christian Indian and told him to knock down those poles and bury the bones. He did so immediately, and the rest of the Indians were no longer tricked by that devil's snare because they saw that the person who had buried the bones had suffered no harm.

The preceding event alone made this dangerous journey very worthwhile, but it also produced many other outstanding results, and God was served to protect us and provide us great consolation and success.

14. Pérez de Ribas' reference to the "mysterious Songs" (*sus misteriosos Cantares*) is an allusion to the allegorical nature of this book, which is unusual in that it makes no explicit mention of God. It is instead a very passionately worded discourse on God's love for his people, and vice versa, presented poetically through images of a relationship between a husband and wife.

15. Song of Songs 4:8: "my queen that shall be! Leave Amana behind thee, Sanir and Hermon heights, where the lairs of lions are, where the leopards roam the hills" (Knox 1956:570-1).

16. Iztli is a generic term derived from Nahuatl used to refer to any kind of plant fiber, particularly that of the agave (Santamaría 1974:622). The fiber known as pita is made from the leaves of the agave (Johnson 1950:13).

CHAPTER IX The Ahome's allies are baptized and another pueblo is founded; the state in which this Christian community has persevered up to the present time

As discussed in the previous chapters, the wild fishing nations settled in the Ahome pueblos. These reductions were carried out so completely that there was not a single person, large or small, young or old, who remained in the monte or along the shore, not even those who had most burrowed themselves away. Then general Baptisms began among all those rancherías. God had prepared them through His divine grace such that they received and understood the Christian doctrine very well. Throngs of them fervently requested Holy Baptism and within a year about two thousand souls were baptized. This Divine Sacrament, in which men are reborn as children of God, wrought a marvelous change of customs, bringing peace and joy to their new lives. All of them, young and old, attended the lessons and talks concerning Christian doctrine. They attended Mass even on weekdays. Those who became sick requested the Sacrament of Confession, and men who had previously had numerous wives married only one legitimate spouse. The women whom they cast aside came to ask to be admitted to Baptism in order to contract legitimate, Christian marriages with other men. Gentile dances and drunkenness were no longer seen or heard among them. [158] They busied themselves cultivating fields and sowing their seeds. When they did not have any of these seeds, the priest bought them for them. Once they had a taste of these fruits they became more settled in their pueblos and attended Christian exercises more readily.

In the pueblo of Ahome, which was the principal settlement [in this mission], a choir was formed, and with time and practice it was perfected. Sunday Mass and the other major feast days, as well as the services of Holy Week, could then be celebrated with great solemnity. This allowed the [Indians] to understand more clearly the mysteries of our Holy Faith and provided entertainment at Christmas, Easter, and especially the feast days of the saints for whom their pueblos are named. It is an established custom that when a pueblo is settled, they take as the name for their newly founded church or pueblo one of the mysteries of Christ Our Lord or His Most Holy Mother or the name of a saint. On this feast day (which they also call *Pascua*)[17] they also hold celebratory dances. These are decent dances, to which pueblos of their own and even neighboring nations are invited, gentile or not. Wishing to give their guests gifts on such occasions, the fishermen usually go fishing collectively. Although two or three thousand Indians usually attend these feast day celebrations, these fishermen catch such a large number of fish that there is enough to distribute to everyone.

Even before Lent they had begun attending to their confessions, each day becoming more capable in the steps required in this Holy Sacrament. Those persons who demonstrated the greatest [intellectual] capacity were prepared for Holy Communion, beginning with talks about the supreme nature of this Holy Sacrament. The use of this sacrament was introduced by choosing a group of people in each nation who set a good example by observing God's law and learning Christian doctrine. The undeveloped [intellectual] capacity and barbarous customs of these peoples do not allow them to receive this Divine Bread immediately after they have been baptized. Rather it is reserved for those who are strong and robust in the Faith. They also apply themselves very readily to the Lenten acts of penance by administering blood scourges. They do so with great devotion and concert while crowds accompany the procession and sing the litanies.

Although these things would be considered very ordinary in long-time Christian pueblos, in nations so new in the Faith that were [previously] as free as the deer in the fields, as fierce and warlike as lions and tigers, as wild as feral boars, and as hidden as fish in the sea, it is like a miracle to see them now subordinated to these practices and to see such a change. Who can doubt that the change in such customs is the work of the Almighty

17. This is the Spanish term used in reference to the Christian holidays of Easter, Christmas, Pentecost, and Epiphany.

and that it is just as worthy as it was for the blind to see, the dead to rise, or the possessed to be healed?

With the Ahome nation and their allies in this state, and having baptized all their people, the principales were approached about building permanent, more decent churches that would be more spacious than the brushwood shelters they were currently using to celebrate the holy services and their feast days. They listened to this speech with pleasure. Because it seemed to them that this task would be an honorable one for their pueblo, they offered their labor. Even though the construction would be simple, using adobes, it was so new to them that it was necessary to seek tradesmen to train them and also someone to teach them how to cut and dress large trees for framing a large, spacious church. They applied themselves to this [task] with such high spirits that a hundred or more Indians would carry a huge beam on their shoulders. What would have taken many yoke of oxen to pull [159] these Indians did joyously. This was in part because they were used to carrying loads on their shoulders. Moreover, they had no other means of bringing the beams to the construction site at that time. Men and women, young and old, worked on the church, and when it was completed it could accommodate two thousand people. Once it was whitewashed and painted it was dedicated with a great celebration that was attended by a large number of people from neighboring nations. They were astonished to see something so novel, and it kindled their desire to have a similar church in their [own] pueblos.

The pueblo settled by the Bacoregue fishermen, whom we mentioned before, was inundated by a flood.

Through the intervention of the priest's pleas, and after they had seen the church erected in the pueblo of Ahome, they were moved to come and settle there. This was done without opposition from the Bacoregue, who settled with the Ahome. This pueblo then had some six hundred houses, which were very well laid out. Later on, some of the people who had remained in the coastal areas, who were very numerous, set up another large pueblo two leagues upstream from the Ahome. More than four hundred families congregated there and it was named for the Archangel Saint Michael, whose favor was apparent in the successful settlement of such wild people. Even though this reduction cost Father Vicente de Aguila (whom I will mention later) great tribulations in coming and going to the swamps to mold [the people] to human and Christian laws, he accomplished his work very well.[18] All these new people were congregated, and they learned the doctrine and were baptized. They erected another very beautiful church like the one in Ahome, and to this day a noteworthy Christianity shines in this pueblo.

I will not detain myself here with details of their progress because such an account would be very similar to the previous ones. At the present time one priest ministers to the district containing these two pueblos, where from its beginnings to the present day ten to twelve thousand souls have been baptized and added to the Church, not counting those that are born each day. Of these there are good signs that many now reside in heaven. With this we have recorded the reduction of the Ahome and their allies. This will be concluded with the account of a ship that reached their shores at that time.

18. Aguila succeeded Pérez de Ribas as missionary to the Ahome and Zuaque in 1616. That year Pérez de Ribas went to Mexico City. When he returned to Sinaloa in 1617 he and Tomás Basilio initiated the reduction and conversion of the Yaqui.

CHAPTER X How and why a ship commanded by Captain Juan Iturbi reached the coast near the pueblo of Ahome

I have decided to record here the arrival of a ship while I was in the aforementioned pueblo of Ahome. In 1615 Captain Juan Iturbi came from the South Sea into the Sea of California with two ships. He was commissioned by Tomás Cardona, a resident of Sevilla, to whom His Majesty Philip III had given permission to equip two ships with divers to search for the many pearl beds that were rumored to be found in the Sea of California. As was previously mentioned, this sea runs along the coast of the Province of Sinaloa.

At this time it also happened that the some Dutch pirates [19] had passed through the Strait of Magellan into the South Sea and up the coast of Nueva España. Before they entered the Sea of California near its mouth at [Cabo] San Lucas, they encountered Iturbi's ships. One ship was captured, but the captain escaped with the other. [160] He then sailed into the Sea of California and spent several days sounding shell beds and testing and assessing them. They found many rich ones, and the captain and his companions and soldiers recovered a fair quantity of pearls. The captain told me later that although there was an abundance of shells, there were not many pearls in them. Perhaps this was because it was not the time when they grow; if I remember correctly, it was at the beginning of the spring.

Captain Iturbi spent some time sounding this sea and advanced along the coast to thirty degrees north. There he ran out of provisions and found himself in a critical situation, without knowledge of a port along that coast, which was so new to navigation, where he could replenish his supplies. Around this time word spread among the Indians of a sighting on the sea, far from land, of something like a house, or *teopa*, (the name they give the xacales that are used for churches).[20] When I was notified of this I suspected that it might be a Spanish ship that had entered the sea in search of

pearls, because there were many greedy people at this time. Because I had not received news of Dutch pirates in the South Sea, and thinking that the wooden house the Indians said was sailing the sea might be a defeated and lost Spanish ship, in which case they would be in need of help and information about the coast, I decided to write a short letter to the Spaniards who were sailing out there. It would inform them that if they were in need of some fresh provisions, they should know that the coast was populated by friendly Christians, among whom there were priests from the Company of Jesus who would help them.

I gave this letter to an Indian who was a great swimmer, charging him to remain on the coast for a few days and if he should see such a house or teopa on the sea, he was to approach the ship and give the note to the Spaniards without being afraid. He placed the letter in the band with which they tie back their hair, inside a little reed so that it would not get wet. Although the Indian had accepted this task, it was unnecessary for him to carry it out because while I was relaxing in my house in the pueblo of Ahome, two Spaniards appeared, causing a great commotion among the Indians because of the novelty of that event. They arrived in such bad shape that they were about to faint from hunger. When they saw me they raised their voices and hearts to heaven, giving thanks to God for finding themselves in Christian lands.

I immediately had them fed, which is what they first needed in order to be able to speak. Then I asked them about their journey and how they had come upon this pueblo of Ahome, which was four leagues inland through dense brush and thickets. They told me of their trip and how, when they were very low on provisions and nourishment, the captain had sent them [ashore] in the ship's skiff. Although they had no information about the people who lived along the coast, they were instructed to look for a place where they could replenish [their supplies] so that they would not perish from hunger. Actually, if they had landed a little farther up the coast of the Sea of California, they would have disembarked at a place where the Indians would

---

19. *Pechelingues* (see Corominas and Pascual 1989–1991:4:529). In the late 1500s Dutch pirates, following in the wake of English pirates such as Sir Francis Drake, plied the waters of the southern extreme of the Gulf of California awaiting the Manila galleon.

20. The word for church in Cáhita is *teepo* (Buelna 1891:166).

have eaten them.[21] The [Spaniards] added that God had directed them to the trail they had so fortunately followed, which consisted of fishermen's footprints and led from the sea through the thickets and to this pueblo. They added that the ship remained anchored one or two leagues from shore because of a lack of knowledge of a safe port. [161] The captain had remained there awaiting the return of the skiff, which they had left at a point along the coast that they described.

I called the Indian principales of the pueblo, in particular the cacique Don Miguel, and I charged him with getting some people ready by the following morning with as many fresh provisions for the exhausted Spaniards as could be carried. The Indians could not wait to leave to go and see the wooden house that sailed through the water. I made them pack beef jerky (which is our nourishment in these missions), maize flour, and other fruits of the earth. We departed early the following morning with a large number of people who were summoned to guide us through those dense thickets. We were unable at first to find the path the Spaniards had followed, and lost our way. In the afternoon we found ourselves blocked by some estuaries, of which there are many along this coast. However, from what the Spaniards said concerning the place where they had left the skiff, it was not far away. The Indians said we could not cross the estuaries on horseback, so in order to help those who were in very great need I asked the Indians to go ahead with the fresh provisions, even though it was through the water. The two Spaniards decided to accompany them, leaving behind the horses they were riding. They also removed some of their clothes to cross the pools and estuaries [more easily], and they thus continued on their journey.

That night I remained in the monte so that the following day a path could be found that led to the captain, and he could be welcomed and informed of a place where he could anchor his ship. The Indians finally reached the skiff, which was loaded with the fresh provisions and taken to the ship by the [two] Spaniards. Captain Juan Iturbi received them with great happiness and gratitude and sent word that he would send the skiff for me the following day. The Indians told me they would carry me on their shoulders through the

pools, which is in fact what they did. I very willingly made this trip in order to help the voyagers, and also so that the many Indians who had accompanied me could see the ship, as they so greatly desired. This would also let the inland nations know that the Spaniards knew how to sail upon the sea and along the coast, which they considered impenetrable. I knew as well that this would also help tame ferocious nations that were ignorant of another world.

When I reached the ship [I found] the captain waiting; he had seen the skiff approaching when it was more than a league away. After the greetings demanded by Christian charity I asked him to allow me to board the ship with as many Indians as possible because they wanted to see it. Everyone who could fit got into the skiff, and afterwards we realized there were more than we wanted, for the wind blew very strongly and the waves swelled to the point that we were in danger of sinking before we reached the ship. But God willed that we should finally arrive, and upon boarding the Indians were stunned to see something so novel, the likes of which they had never seen or imagined.

Once we had rested and eaten something I told the captain that thirty leagues down the coast was the mouth of the Río [Sinaloa], where the Villa de San Felipe was located. There or somewhere nearby they could find a port and replenish the provisions they needed for their journey. He could be assured that the captain of the garrison and the priests who were there would willingly assist them. With this the Indians and I returned most joyfully to our pueblo. The Indians were especially happy to have seen such a miraculous thing, and this was confirmed by their words to me upon our return, which are noteworthy given their limited capacity: "Father, we are now confirmed in all the doctrine that you preach to us in the church [162] because we have seen with our own eyes what you have told us, that you had come from your land to teach us God's law by crossing the sea in a house of wood, and now our eyes have seen it."

I had told them this sometimes to endear them, and I was not saddened by what they told me. They did not mean to say that they had not believed the catechism preached to them in the church, which they had in fact received and believed in as the truth. Rather, this served to strengthen them, just as new circumstances and events serve loyal long-time Christians as credible evidence that confirms the Faith they already possess. There is also a need for this among people so removed

---

21. Pérez de Ribas may be alluding here to events a century earlier, in 1532, when one of two ships that were commanded by Diego Hurtado de Mendoza went aground near the mouth of the Río Fuerte and its crew was killed by the Indians (Reff 1991b:35).

from and ignorant of the truth of the catechism that is being taught to them. In spite of the fact that this catechism, which is so alien to them, is valued by more civil nations, they were ignorant of this fact.

The ship remained anchored there for two to three days, during which time groups of Indians unceasingly came to see it, bringing provisions of seeds and trading for some of the Spaniards' clothing. Once these days passed, Captain Iturbi set out with his ship for the Río [Sinaloa] and the Villa de San Felipe. There he anchored and sent word of his arrival to Captain Diego Martínez de Hurdaide, who provided him with all the necessary assistance. At this time Dutch pirate ships were still sailing along the coast of Nueva España, because the ships from the Philippines [the Manila galleons] were expected at the port of Acapulco. When the viceroy, the marquis of Guadalcazar, heard that a ship had landed along the coast of Sinaloa he quickly sent orders for Captain Bartolomé Suárez, of the garrison of San Andrés, which was not far from Sinaloa, to board the ship with some soldiers and to set sail in search of the ships from the Philippines. They were to warn the Philippine ships to protect themselves from the enemy by taking a different route and proceeding to a port other than Acapulco.

The viceroy's orders were carried out, but Iturbi's ship did not find the Philippine vessels. Nevertheless, God willed that they should reach the port of Aca-pulco without encountering the Dutch pirates. Captain Iturbi's ship returned to a safe port that he had found earlier (which he named the port of Saint Ignatius), a short distance from the mouth of the Río [Sinaloa] and the Villa de San Felipe. There he built another large ship and loaded it with provisions. Then with this ship and his other one he set sail once again into the Sea of California, looking for new pearl beds. He found some while navigating to thirty-two degrees latitude, at which point he turned around and pursued more purposefully the [pearl diving] enterprise he had suspended some years earlier. Other subsequent expeditions were undertaken there (although not for the purpose of finding pearl beds), and they all discovered pearls and made friends with the Indians of California. The settlement of California by Spaniards would serve the Province of Sinaloa by providing an outlet for its produce.

The arrival of the ship that we have discussed here was very opportune because it left all the nations of the province with greater respect for the Spaniards and greater fear of their weapons and valor, as will be told in Book V when the conversion of the bellicose Yaqui is discussed. It was recorded earlier that Our Lord King Philip IV (may God preserve him for the good of all Christianity) had sent Admiral Don Pedro Portel de Casanate, a knight of the Order of Santiago, to settle California.[22] May Our Lord grant him joyous success. [163]

CHAPTER XI The priest's first entrada to establish a mission among the brave Zuaque nation

The time established by divine providence finally arrived for the surrender and subordination of the Zuaque nation to the sweet yoke of evangelical law. For many years they had rebelled against divine law, opposing the brave Spaniards, who so often were forced to take up arms against them, [albeit] without making a dent in the hardness of their rebelliousness, treachery, and arrogance. But in the end God made them understand that it was His arm, not a human arm, that was at work. He saved His victory, the conversion of such a fierce nation, until after the Zuaque's barbarous rebellions, which have been discussed in several parts of this history.

It has already been told how [in 1604–5] they asked for a priest to come to their lands to instruct and baptize them. The good fortune of instructing and baptizing the Zuaque and the neighboring Ahome nation

22. Pérez de Ribas discusses the exploration and settlement of Baja California in Book 7, Chapter 12.

fell in large part to me, under orders of holy obedience. Once the Ahome had been settled I began my spiritual enterprise among the Zuaque nation. The entire province desired to see them at peace and Christian, for they had been a concern and source of continual terror. This [labor] was begun in the year 1605 in the following way. The Christian Indian Luisa, whom I have previously mentioned, went with her relative Ventura [Buenaventura] and some other principales to the Villa de San Felipe to accompany the priest on his announced visit to the pueblos. Entrusting myself to divine protection, I went with my Zuaque to their pueblos, of which there were three within a distance of six leagues, with about a thousand heads-of-household and their families. The principal pueblo, called Mochicahue, was on the banks of the river on a beautiful plain in the most fertile valley in all of Sinaloa. When we arrived we were greeted by crowds of joyous people. Men and women with their children welcomed me and kissed my hand; others asked me to place my hand on their heads, which as I have said is a sign of reverence that they use to greet their ministers. They also demonstrated their reverence and affection by not carrying bows or arrows, which were the source of their arrogance and pride; ordinarily, they would not lay their weapons down. I found that they had erected some enramadas for a house and church, so as soon as I arrived I went into the church and gave the customary speech, explaining why I had come to their land. It was not to wage war, for I did not carry weapons, nor was I accompanied by soldiers. Rather, I came to help them, to be a father to them, and to show them the way to salvation. Afterwards I told them that to do so I first had to baptize their small children, as had been done with other nations. I told them that this would insure peace and would show that their request for instruction in God's word was genuine.

They received this speech very well. The Indian Luisa, who was very familiar with this custom, had informed and gathered together a great number of mothers with their infants and toddlers. Thus, this flock of lambs was made ready there in the fields not for slaughter, but to be offered to God and to be given life. Through Holy Baptism they were marked with the seal of the Lamb [of God], which takes away the sins of the world. This flock reached three hundred in number and was divided among the few Christians who were present, who acted as godparents.

I do not want to omit one particular thing that was more evident among the people of this nation than others. It pertains to the Sovereign Queen of the Angels [164] and to the singular grace that was bestowed by her Son. [Specifically] any female child who received the glorious name Mary was feted and received with special applause and joy. They called her *laut teva*,[23] which is an important title given to women. The person who most celebrated this custom was the Christian woman Luisa, who explained its significance. It was a sign that manifested the favor that this Sovereign Mother of Mercy had worked and would continue to work from then on in softening hearts that were as fierce as those of this nation.

The Baptism of infants in this first pueblo was celebrated with great joy, for this was a great harvest for heaven from a field that had previously been sterile. I then proceeded to the other two pueblos, with the Indian Luisa always preceding me. It seemed that God made her the instrument of that nation's salvation. When she entered a pueblo she began the job of gathering the children for Baptism, shouting to the people in a loud voice, inviting them to assemble. Because she knew them and recognized when they were absent, she sent for those who were out working in the fields and did not rest until they were brought to the church and baptized. She offered herself as a godmother to many of them and made her three daughters, who were already Christians, do the same. She was so anxious for everyone to be baptized that if the priest rejected some children because he felt they were too old and would have to learn the catechism [first], this Christian Indian lowered their age by subtracting years, insisting that they be baptized. Baptism was celebrated in these two pueblos in the same manner as in the first pueblo, and in the course of two visits eight hundred Zuaque children were baptized.

In their own way the very old are like infants, at considerable risk of dying without Baptism. For this reason, and because they were decrepit, I did not hesitate to baptize twenty-five adults. If I had waited a while, not only might death have overtaken them, but they would also have gotten older (which is an infirmity) and more inept at understanding what little they had been taught and [would thus be unable to] receive that Holy Sacrament. They were assembled at the ramada and a fire was built for them because of the cold. So that hunger would not take away what little sense they still had left at this age, they were also regaled with food. For this they gladly came morning and night, and during each session one of the most essential articles of Faith

---

23. The meaning of this expression is unknown.

was explained. Their religious instruction took a lot of effort because some of them were half-deaf and others nearly half-dead. Nevertheless, God kept them alive so that He could show such poor people the richness of His mercy. They came to understand the most basic elements of the catechism, and with this their Baptism was celebrated. This was followed by the ratification of the marriages of those who were nearly one hundred years old (which was quite entertaining to those who were present). This allowed them to receive matrimony as a sacrament, for one often doubts the validity of their former marriage contracts. In the end that holy ceremony was explained to them and these souls who seemed so desperate for a remedy were brought into the state of salvation. While teaching the catechism to those old people it sometimes happened that they were joined by others who desired Baptism who were not so old. Because there was time for them to learn the catechism, however, their Baptism was postponed until that of the infants and the elderly had been completed.

Once a foundation was laid and the initial steps were taken to convert the Zuaque, they often came to me with great happiness, saying to me, "Father, we are very happy in your company." When I asked them the reasons for their former rebellion and past wars, [165] they would reply that they had feared dealings with the Spaniards, of whom their preachers and sorcerers had spoken very badly. But now that they had a priest in their company they were free from fear and deceit and were very content. For my part I tried to treat them affectionately, and through divine grace their preachers' sermons changed. Now every night in the plaza at dusk [24] they congratulated themselves for having God's word in their land and a priest who preached it living among them. They added that they no longer feared enemy attacks and concluded by repeating the refrain that they often use, that from then on all should use good judgment and have a good heart.

I have gone to great lengths to relate the beginnings of the conversion of this nation, which was so difficult to reduce, because I am writing this history principally for the priests of our Company of Jesus who are working in these holy missions so that they might have news of the wonders that God works in overcoming the difficulties they face in winning over fierce rebel nations like this one. It is in God's hands to humble the harsh and haughty mountains and fulfill that promise that was made for the time when His Son's Gospel would be preached: *Omnis mons et collis humiliabitur, et erunt prava in directa, et aspera in vias plana.*[25] God thus brought an end to the harshness of this nation, which during this first visit surrendered so tamely and became so gentle that from this time forward no uprising or rebellion was ever seen here again. This is something that was not accomplished in other nations even after they were converted.

CHAPTER XII The entire Zuaque nation is baptized; the solemnity of the dedication of the churches built in their pueblos

There were nothing more than enramadas to serve as churches during the first entrada to preach the catechism in the Zuaque pueblos. Saying Mass there was like saying it out in the fields; there was no protection from wind or rain. The Zuaque realized this and were aware that other Christian pueblos had churches. Therefore, they built some large xacales made of poles and covered with straw, in the manner discussed previously. Once these xacales were finished a fervent effort was made to get all the people to come both morning and evening for religious instruction. They did this to the sound of bells that had been brought at the king's expense; their sound was as joyful to the Indians as it was novel.

On the pretext of bringing their baptized infants

24. *Prima*, which Pérez de Ribas uses in a military sense to refer to the first quarter of the night.

25. *Margin Note*: Isai c. 4. Isaiah 40:4: "Bridged every valley must be, every mountain and hill levelled, windings cut straight, and the rough paths paved" (Knox 1956:659).

and very small children, mothers also attended and enjoyed Mass whenever it was said. Although they were still gentiles,[26] they were allowed to attend because they were catechumens and were learning Christian doctrine in order to be baptized when their time arrived. We could even say that everyone in those pueblos was a catechumen, for all of them were continually in church, and their barbarous and gentile customs were continually being uprooted. One did not speak of or hear any discussion of drunkenness or war. Rather, their principales were constantly preaching sermons against these things in the plaza.

With things going so well it was decided to begin baptizing the adults, namely the most important Indians in the nation, so that they might serve as a guide and example for the masses, who greatly follow their leaders. [166] Even though it was difficult for some of them to leave their many wives and be happy with just one inseparable spouse, the grace of Christ Our Lord nevertheless worked wonders. A good number of adults gathered and gave their names for the catalog of catechumens and then withdrew to consider and discuss Christian doctrine both morning and evening. They enjoyed this so much that they did not leave the church during the entire day.

When the day of their Baptism finally arrived, it was celebrated with great joy in the pueblos. One of those baptized was the cacique to whom the Spaniards had given the name Ventura [Buenaventura], and he was indeed fortunate that his kinswoman Luisa had freed him from the noose that the others experienced, as was stated earlier. Once he was baptized he aided in the Baptism of his nation and lived and died as a good Christian.

Among the Indians baptized at this time was one of the most outstanding in all the province in terms of his bravery and valor. He was the point man in battle, for which he had won great authority and renown in his nation. He was an Indian who, if he became restless, had the power to stir up many other nations. For this reason the captain and the other Spaniards made an effort to win him over completely. This was achieved, because even though he had many wives, he chose one with whom he was baptized and married according to the Church. He was named Don Cristóbal Anamei, and he turned out to be a great supporter of the conversion

and Baptism of the Zuaque nation. Once he became a Christian he governed them for many years and aided in their construction of a proper church, before finally dying like a true Christian.

With this first [round of] Baptisms the Zuaque were greatly encouraged to follow up with more abundant Baptisms, overcoming the difficulties that this posed. Proof of this is a particular case that occurred with a principal Indian. He came with one of his little children to greet the priest, wanting to kiss his hand. At first the priest was going to allow him to do so, but then he told this Indian that he did not want him to kiss it because he had two wives and had made no effort to become a Christian like the others. This act and these words were the means by which God moved this Indian to go home and throw out one of his concubines, even sending her away from the pueblo. He then returned with the other, saying, "Father, I want to be baptized and live as a Christian with only this woman." The priest accepted his offer and the two of them were catechized, baptized, and married. They then persevered as a good example for the others.

An effort was then made to choose and gather together a good number of boys to learn to read, write, and sing for service in the church. The Zuaque quite willingly agreed to this and some of the principales gladly offered their sons. They felt such contentment in the new state God had granted them that they repeatedly said in their speeches, "Oh, Father! We were right when we asked for you to come to our land. While our children were unbaptized, we could not be secure or happy."

Christ's sweet law was taking possession of them and their ordinary greeting was "Jesus Christ be praised!" This is how they concluded their [daily] religious instruction in the church and also how they greeted both the priest and one another. It seemed that as this sweet and good name resonated, the air of that land was purified. Before, it had been polluted by the gasps of the infernal serpent who had so blinded them.

Both young and old came in throngs to request Holy Baptism. Parents did not want to give their young daughters of marrying age permission to do so unless they were baptized at the same time with their husbands. They already knew that in contracting marriage as [167] Christians, they were assuring its perpetuity and perseverance.

During each visit made to the pueblos some were greatly comforted with Baptism and others were pre-

---

26. As this statement implies, gentiles ordinarily were not allowed to participate in Mass, particularly the celebration of the Eucharist.

pared to receive it during the following visit. Within one year [by the end of 1606], therefore, the Zuaque nation had been baptized and cleansed in the water of Holy Baptism. This flock joined the Catholic Church, with more than three thousand Christians being reborn therein. By that time they all came very fervently and frequently to the church on Sundays [to hear] Mass and the sermon. In their devotion they even came on week-days before going to their fields. For this reason, they were called 'those of the morning'. Finally, in order to enjoy these Christian exercises even more, as well as for other reasons, they reduced their three pueblos to only two. There were eight hundred male heads-of-household in these two pueblos, which were two and a half leagues from each other. This made it easier for the priest to spend time with them and to visit their neighbors, the Ahome.

Once the general Baptism of the Zuaque was completed the people were inclined to build proper churches like their neighbors. This matter was discussed with the principales, who agreed to build them. Then I proposed it to the pueblo in church, encouraging the women to aid in the labor. The churches needed to be large and spacious enough to hold many people, including separate groups of boys and girls, who have their own distinct places. It would have to accommodate not only all the people of the pueblo for Mass, but also those from neighboring pueblos, who normally come out of devotion even though they are not obliged to do so because of the great distance. For these reasons it was necessary that the churches be very large and that large amounts of material be used in their [construction]. The Zuaque Indians offered themselves very willingly to help build it, and every day that there was construction fifty or a hundred of them carried water. It served as no small encouragement to tell the barbarous Zuaque women that this house was for Mary, the Mother of God, whose name they considered glorious and kind (as I already stated). Even the boys and girls helped quite a bit in the labor. Some days there were four hundred or six hundred people of all ages working, although the work only lasted for half a day so as not to tire them out.

The churches in the pueblos were finished, white-washed, and adorned with paint, and a very tall and beautiful Cross was erected in front of each church to mark the cemetery. Once they were finished the proud Zuaque discussed the celebration of their dedication, desiring that this be done with great solemnity and that the neighboring nations be invited. This pleased me

greatly because they could see that with Christ's law they were not being stripped of festivals and honorable and holy celebrations, which replaced their former pro-fane and atrocious ones. Care was taken to solemnize this celebration through all possible means of joyful and pleasing spectacle, for the spiritual conquest of the Zuaque constituted the most difficult-to-defeat for-tress of the many that the devil possessed in this prov-ince. Therefore, nothing was spared in terms of music, dances, and fires that could be had in such a poor land.

The Zuaque women were so spirited in the con-struction of their principal church that they decided also to build a small chapel to the Most Holy Virgin. It was erected next to their pueblo at the top of a pretty little pinnacle of rock, the base of which was bathed by their river. This pinnacle was mentioned earlier when it was told how it broke open due to the unusual trem-bling through which God had threatened to punish this nation for their rebelliousness. Therefore, [168] this chapel and church were a sign that this nation's hearts had softened and that they had dedicated themselves to God.

The church and chapel were solemnly dedicated at the same time. The night before, two trios of flutes and trumpets were placed at the chapel, and another two trios were placed at the top of the church. These trios answered each other with their music, and there were many luminaries and bonfires lit in many differ-ent places. In addition to this, standards and pennants made of Chinese silk were raised on the churches, which for here was like having three-story brocade tapestries.

In the plaza of the pueblo [of Mochicahue], which was large, more bonfires were lit. In the midst of these bonfires the dances and drums that once called the Zuaque to war against the Christians, which they trium-phantly celebrated with severed heads, were now cele-brating festivals for Christ and His Most Holy Mother. Many nations came to this celebration, some of them from a great distance. They were amazed to see the brave Zuaque nation, which they no longer recognized.

The following day a procession was organized to en-ramadas that were erected in every corner of the plaza. These were made of freshly cut green branches from the monte, which were also used to adorn the altars within the enramadas. The streets through which the procession passed were adorned with the same tapes-tries made from trees from the monte. Mass was sung with solemn music and a sermon was preached by a priest who had a great command of the Zuaque language.[27] He had come to this celebration with many of his people from another district.

Once this was finished the Zuaque invited their guests to eat. For this meal, which is very sumptuous and consists of what they most like, the priests give them some of the cattle sent to them from the college for their own sustenance and for the sick.[28] In these parts there is no beef to be found or purchased. The Zuaque's maritime neighbors, the Ahome, also attended and contributed to the celebration with a large amount of fish.

With everyone satisfied, this solemn celebration was concluded and the guests returned to their lands, greatly edified and most joyful. The Zuaque remained in their own lands and did not tire of seeing their churches, which were the work of their [own] hands. They were so taken with the adornment and beauty of divine worship (which is very attractive to these

nations) that they decided to plant some fields of maize, which the pueblo worked collectively, selling the fruits of their labor to Spaniards and soldiers. They planned to use the proceeds to buy items to adorn their church, and they did in fact put this into practice.

These celebrations have been recorded here because even though they may not be the triumphal celebrations of emperors and may not be held in the courts of princes, there is no doubt that these triumphs and conversions are celebrated by the angels in heaven, and by the Catholic monarchs in their courts as well, because so many infidels have been successful in their conversion to our Holy Faith and have come to recognize and adore Jesus Christ, the King of Kings, as their God. Finally, this conversion of thousands of barbarous people who before lived in darkness was accomplished through divine grace.

CHAPTER XIII The case of a penitent cacique and the state of Zuaque Christianity up to the present time

The case of the Indian Don Cristóbal Anamei, whose bravery and Baptism were mentioned in the last chapter, is worthy of discussion here. Shortly after he was baptized and had conquered his former passion for many wives, or concubines, [169] the devil, who does not sleep, roused his passion one night while he was in another pueblo away from his home and legitimate wife. At midnight he went into a house that was not his own and took another man's wife. Her husband was unable to de-

fend her, for Anamei possessed great authority and was feared by his people.

The fiscal of the pueblo came to tell me about Governor Anamei's outrageous behavior. He was greatly concerned about the event, because if but one person hears something, it becomes public [knowledge] among these people. I dismissed the fiscal for the time being, and two days later when the case had become public I wrote to the captain of the garrison about what had happened, noting that this seemed unlike the Indian Anamei. I asked that he take appropriate measures to prevent other caciques from committing similar effronteries. Doing so would also prevent other problems that might arise among people so new in the Faith should there be no punishment of a crime that was so scandalous and contrary to the commandments from God that were being introduced and preached in these early days. I added that because the person who had committed this crime possessed such great au-

27. Either Juan de Velasco, who had prepared a grammar of Cáhita (see Chapter 34 of this Book), or Pedro Méndez, another gifted speaker of Cáhita who was working upriver among the Tehueco.

28. The Jesuits established a cattle ranch near the Villa de San Felipe shortly after they arrived in Sinaloa. A portion of the herd was slaughtered each fall and the meat was then jerked and apportioned among the priests in the outlying missions (Treutlein 1949:99). As the missions increased in number and distance from the villa it became more efficient for each priest to take thirty or so head with him when he went to establish a new mission (Hackett 1923–1937:3:122–23).

thority and spirit and was their governor, I did not dare to amend it [myself], nor was it my place to do so.

When the captain learned of this case it greatly pained him. He replied that although this scandal grieved him and he desired to amend it, he was concerned about the danger that might arise if he were to punish Anamei. If he withdrew to the monte and its evil ways, he was capable of inciting two or three nations to revolt. There was also other significant damage that might result from riotous acts by such a bellicose Indian. The very daring captain added that I should consider [other] measures that might subdue this Indian and provide the punishment that seemed least likely to cause serious problems.

The Indians of the pueblo were waiting and watching to see what kind of an example would be made of such an important person in such a serious case. Three or four days went by and neither he who was being investigated nor his concubine appeared. I commended the incident to His Majesty, Our Lord, who as expected, dealt with it with His almighty hand. At the end of the four days, around midnight, Anamei arrived at my house and told one of the altar boys who was sleeping there to notify me that he wanted to speak with me. I allowed him to come in, although I feared that he who had been blinded by his passion might commit some outrage. But God, with His providence and compassion, prevented this from happening. The fierce Indian came in very changed and peaceful and threw himself at my feet, begging forgiveness. He said that the devil had tricked him into the crime he had committed. With gentleness I welcomed the repentant man, even though I did not fail to speak to him of the poor example that he had set for his nation, of which he was governor. I reminded him of the benefits he had received and also that he had been entrusted with aiding me in the conversion and Christianity of his people. I also presented him with other arguments provided by Our Lord on that occasion, all in order that this Indian should subject himself and give the pueblo some public satisfaction, which I deemed necessary to prevent people of such good faith from committing similar effronteries against the Christian laws that were being established. Finally, I told him that because the people of his pueblo were aware of his sin and the husband of the woman whom he had abducted was very upset, he needed to do public penance for his crime.

This Indian was dumbfounded by my proposal, which he undoubtedly felt to be harsh and rigorous, for he had been reared in liberty as a barbarous and daring individual. At this point, in order to soften him and make the penance easier, I told him he did not have to receive it at the hand of another nor publicly in church, as was done with others who committed public crimes. It was enough that [170] he receive a scourging by his own hand, and to satisfy the pueblo two principal fiscales would have to witness his repentance. I was well aware, however, that only one was needed for the whole pueblo to find out about it.

God overcame this lion, and those who know of and are familiar with the fierceness of these nations will appreciate that what was wrought was a wonder of His divine hand, which softened and subjected this Indian's brave spirit. He finally accepted the conditions that I proposed, so I stayed with him and sent an altar boy to get two of the principal fiscales from the pueblo so they could witness his penance. When they arrived I told them that Don Cristóbal Anamei had come to me repentant, that he was on his knees asking for forgiveness for his sin and the bad example he had set for his pueblos, and that he was prepared to do penance in their presence. Once this was done he would confess in order to receive a full pardon from God for his sin.

Once I had said this the kneeling penitent removed the jacket and shirt he was wearing. He was dressed very much in the Spanish style, for the captain ordinarily gave governors clothing and a sword. He took the scourge he had been given in his hand and began to vigorously beat and lash his back, and I confess that I was amazed by such a change. I removed the whip from his hand and encouraged him to confess and return to the pursuit of the fulfillment of his Christian duties, as he had done in the past, thereby setting a good example for his pueblos. He put this into practice from then on, and the pueblo was satisfied, edified, and confirmed in the loyalty of Christian matrimony.

I gave many thanks to Our Lord for having resolved such a difficult case and also to see such a change in a subject who held himself in the same esteem (albeit barbarous) as a person with many responsibilities, even though he was not of the same bearing and grandeur as a governor or a very noble person from a very civilized nation. The subject with whom we are dealing here is worthy of much greater esteem because of his more limited understanding of the seriousness of his sin. The pueblo learned of his penance and was quite edified, and the captain of the garrison was very pleased with the fortunate outcome of the case.

To conclude this chapter on the Zuaque's Christianity (for there are others that are calling us), I note that up to the time at which this history is being written, this Christianity has persevered and will continue to persevere in its great enjoyment of Christian customs. During the eleven years that I lived among the Zuaque and catechized them [1605–16], I did not perceive any unrest worthy of concern, nor has there been any since then. Rather, on the occasions of war and expeditions to other nations when the Spaniards have drafted people from the Zuaque pueblos, these people have faithfully come to their aid. The many sorcerers found in this nation, who were the principal enemies of the Gospel doctrine, were finally all baptized. Some of them even preached about good Christian customs, which silenced the demons such that they were no longer heard, and their lying, rituals, and barbarous customs disappeared. Little by little the use of Holy Communion was introduced and it was considered a great honor to be permitted to partake of this sacrament. Today all of them enjoy this supreme benefit, and to receive it they place crowns of flowers on their heads. These are all ceremonies which help them understand the invisible effects that this celestial sustenance has on the soul.

Turning now from spiritual matters, the Zuaque have also improved in terms of civil matters. They built suitable homes for their ministers and homes of adobe for themselves, thereby forming streets and plazas in their pueblos. They notify the priest so that he can resolve any disorder or scandal that arises in their communities. [171] They have reformed greatly in their attire, and many of them buy and keep horses for riding and carrying loads.

The fame of the Zuaque's Christianity became very widespread because of their churches and pueblos and the stability and peace they enjoyed. Indeed, a good number of caciques from the very populous Mayo nation, who were all gentiles and had never had dealings or friendship with the Zuaque, came forty leagues to see the Zuaque's churches and houses and to watch the assemblies for Christian instruction.[29] After they saw all this they became so enthusiastic about and desirous of seeing the same in their own pueblos that they asked me to instruct them just as I had taught the Zuaque. Some of them even came and offered to live among the Zuaque until priests went to their lands. I treated them well, giving them some of the small things they value, and for the time being I told them to persevere in their good intentions, requesting a mission and priests to preach to them. I also gave them hopes that priests would eventually come and show them the way to salvation. They spent a few days here [in Mochicahue] and could not help but be amazed at the joy and happiness with which the Zuaque entered the churches and performed the rest of the Christian exercises. They returned to their land, telling their people of what they had seen, speaking so favorably that later large groups came to visit these Christian pueblos. This was the beginning of the conversion of the Mayo nation, which will be discussed later.

All of this would eventually increase the joy of the Zuaque, whom we will now leave, concluding their history by saying that today one priest ministers to their two Christian pueblos. Because their people are so numerous, they make up their own mission district. With this nation and the preceding one, the Ahome, as well as those who joined them, a good count of those who have been baptized from the beginning up to the present day would be more than fourteen thousand souls, of which Our Lord undoubtedly has many in heaven. We turn now to a discussion of the Tehueco nation.

---

29. The anua of 1613 notes that the Mayo came south in 1605 and that same year Father Juan de Velasco paid a reciprocal visit.

CHAPTER XIV The location and particular customs of the Tehueco nation and Father Pedro Méndez's entrada to establish a mission[30]

The pueblos of this nation, which were originally three, began three leagues upstream from the last Zuaque pueblo. They were settled within a seven-league stretch on beautiful plains along the banks of the same great river. Their pueblos were free from floods because they were located above the river, surrounded by the thick growth of the monte, which abounded in game. These pueblos are sixteen leagues from the Spaniards' Villa de San Felipe and not more than three leagues from the former villa [of San Juan de Carapoa], which we noted was razed by the Zuaque.

As mentioned, the Tehueco had requested a mission and priests to teach them [the catechism]. Father Pedro Méndez, a truly apostolic and experienced minister, was chosen. He was just what was needed for the Tehueco nation, where gentile and barbarous customs predominated more than in others. This was especially true of their sexual behavior, as many of them had three, four, or five wives. It was often the case that one of these wives was the mother, the other her daughter, and the other her sister.[31] This vice had taken such hold of this nation that it was greatly feared that it would disrupt their conversion and the introduction of the Christian religion. That is why such a minister was chosen [172] to take charge of this task. It will be necessary to mention Father Pedro Méndez at many points throughout this history because he worked so gloriously in the conversion of many other nations and in the founding of many other missions in Sinaloa, as will later be seen. The reader will find these other nations just as interesting, thanks to their greater numbers and their singular cases of conversion.

Once the time had arrived when the Tehueco desired a permanent priest to instruct them and make them Christians, a few of their principales came to the Villa de San Felipe for Father Pedro Méndez. The Tehueco were a very bellicose people who had fought with all the other nations of the province, and their enemies did not dare set foot in their territory. Nevertheless, the priest entered their land without an escort of soldiers.[32] Although on occasion the Tehueco had shown friendship toward the Spaniards and had aided them in wars and expeditions, at other times they had been changeable and inconstant and had clashed with the Spaniards. Trusting in God's protection, however, this priest set out from the Villa de San Felipe in the company of his Tehueco [escort] and traveled to their pueblos. He himself will speak of the joy and pleasure with which he was received and what happened during this first entrada. The letter in which he gives an account to his superiors, as priests usually do, reads as follows:

> Our Tehueco welcomed me with many signs of joy and turned out in larger numbers than we might expect, bringing their small children for me to baptize. Although the river was running very full and strong, those on the other side swam across. Those who acted as godparents treated the baptized children well, giving them all they had. The homes of the newly baptized were full of people all day long. They lived in such great peace and security that from the time I arrived until the time I left, I did not see a single Indian with a bow or an arrow.
>
> Although they were still gentiles, accustomed to dances and drunken revels, there was not a single sign of these things. It greatly amazed me to see that they could abstain [from drinking] for such a long time, giving no sign of their former custom and passion. They came from two and three leagues away, mainly on Sundays, to the pueblo where I was attending. Bringing their small children to be baptized, they came in such great numbers that the fields were filled with people. They gave me gifts of whatever they had, including wax for the altar, food, and cotton, which they also used for clothing the children they gave me for service in the church. This was all done with great affection. In addition to other things, they asked me how they should bury their baptized children if they died, thereby showing their good intentions.
>
> Two groups who were neighbors of the Tehueco and spoke a different language—although they know a little Tehueco—were so inspired by the Baptism of the Tehueco

---

30. Méndez's visit occurred toward the end of 1606 and was coincident with yet another epidemic, which spread well up the Río Fuerte (Alegre 1956–1960:2:120; Reff 1991b:147–54), as suggested by Méndez's letter, which is quoted in this chapter.

31. It is more likely that the Jesuits misconstrued the Tehueco's practice of sororal polygamy.

32. A letter written by Hurdaide indicates that Méndez actually was escorted by eleven soldiers (Dunne 1940:90).

children that they crossed the river and came with great enthusiasm to beg me to baptize their children as well. They offered to accept whatever conditions were proposed, such as settling among the Tehueco and even abandoning their language and learning to speak Tehueco so that they might be more easily instructed. When I gave them my approval they showed great joy. Later one morning the women came loaded down with their children and with food made from *piñole* (which is maize flour) and other small things for the godparents. I baptized more than seven hundred children in all and never even made contact with two other rancherías that were not yet settled.

Up to this point, I have been citing Father Pedro Méndez's letter concerning the positive results of his first entrada to establish a mission among the Tehueco.

[173] Once the first Baptisms of children were completed the Tehueco set to building brushwood churches. They completed these churches and also a house for the priest made of wood from the monte. The priest began gathering the people who were still in the fields and countryside, and they were all reduced and built their houses in the form of pueblos, with a regular street plan, church, and plaza. The Indian cacique Don Diego Lanzarote, who was mentioned before, was of great assistance in all this. The baptized children visited the priest often, frequently being brought by their mothers. He gave them gifts of whatever he had. This was how this highly barbarous nation began to be tamed and prepared for general Baptism, as is later told.

CHAPTER XV The general Baptism of Tehueco adults is begun; proofs of their Christianity

Now that the Tehueco had a permanent priest they were convinced that everyone, both young and old, should be prepared to receive Holy Baptism and become Christians, as had been the case with other nations. With the Indians so well disposed, the priest decided first to baptize those elderly who had best learned the Christian doctrine and presented fewer impediments to receiving it. Within a few months several general Baptisms were celebrated. Once there were a good number of Christians this vineyard began to bear first fruits, as was related in another letter by Father Pedro Méndez. Although some adverse winds later damaged these fruits, with respect to the present the priest noted:

God Our Lord has been cultivating and refining our uncouth Tehueco, who were entombed in the vices of their heathenism. They receive Baptism with a great enthusiasm that must be maintained. One-half of the people are already baptized and are very good Christians, obedient to God's commandments. I spent this entire Lenten season [of 1607] with them, and although many of them are still gentiles, to my knowledge not a single one of them ate meat or went hunting for deer or rabbits. One Friday they all gathered to go hunting and were about to leave with their bows and arrows, but when they realized that it was Friday they immediately returned to their homes and put away their bows.

Because those who had been baptized were new to the Faith, I doubted whether I should speak to them about [their need for] confession. After seeing their fervor and good disposition, however, I resolved to do so. Everyone confessed, with more fervor than I could have expected from people so new [to the Faith]. They knelt for one or two hours, waiting their turn, and on the day of scourging they knelt for a long while, listening to the sermon of the Passion. When I started to talk about the flogging of Christ Our Lord, they grabbed their scourges and started whipping themselves. I was surprised by their fervor, which I respected, and this warmed my feelings toward them.

When the [Lenten] procession passed throughout the pueblo almost as many gentiles as Christians participated. There were so many torches that it was breathtaking; all the Indians kept silent and were fascinated by what they saw. Throughout the pueblo there were Crosses and stations made of branches where they would kneel, begging for mercy as if they had been doing this for a long time. [174] When the general procession was finished another was started by those who had not participated in the first one, and they, too, showed this same order and devotion.

Good results were obtained from these [religious exercises]. Four long-time Christians who were in sinful relationships left their infidel women, and these women were then baptized and married to other men. There were two sisters among five women married to an Indian cacique who withdrew from this evil arrangement. Another two of these women chose husbands and were baptized and legitimately married. He who had five [wives] was now unfettered and very happy, so he prepared himself for Baptism and marriage to the fifth woman. In this way there have been seven pairs of Baptisms and marriages that have been of great importance to this Christian community and of great service to Our Lord. It is very edifying that those such as the Tehueco, who were so gluttonous in the vice of sensuality, live in Christian continence once they are baptized. They do so to the benefit of the pueblo and without going back to the women they have left, even if they had children together.

On one occasion I baptized twenty-six old women, some of whom were very old, blind, maimed, sick, and decrepit. They received Baptism with so much emotion and happiness that they answered the mysteries of the Faith in loud voices and gave proof of contrition and penance for their past sins. Some of them died shortly after being baptized.

The case that follows was no less notable. A blind Indian was baptized along with his wife (who was older than he was). They were so devoted to the catechism that they spent most of the day teaching each other. After they were baptized they were so happy and devout that when I went to another pueblo the following Saturday, that good old blind man came to me, guided by his wife, and they threw themselves at my feet with great joy and reverence. When I asked him why he had come he answered that it was to hear Mass on Sunday. The previous day he had crossed a creek that I had to cross on a raft because the water had risen

two *estados* [three meters]. This good blind man stayed for a whole week, each day hearing Mass with great emotion.

There was another Indian who came to church to hear Mass with his face and body painted. I told him that this was no way to enter God's house and to go wash in the river and then return to the church. He promptly obeyed, and it is [now] a rare thing for any Christian to paint himself. This habit is as difficult to eradicate among them as it would be to prohibit European women from procuring the makeup they love.

They listen to sermons with great attention, particularly those pertaining to the miracles performed by Christ Our Lord or His sayings. One time the Passion was preached to them for three hours, and they were so attentive and pleased that not a single soul left the church during this [entire] time. This is a rare thing for Indians who do not know how to remain still for fifteen minutes.

Up to this point I have been quoting the priest who sowed the Christian religion among the Tehueco nation, and he described its beginnings. He ends his letter saying, "Although I have done a great deal in the service of Our Lord, I confess that His Majesty has rewarded me very well, considering the happiness I feel at narrating any one of these events. May He be blessed forever."

CHAPTER XVI The Baptism of the Tehueco nation is completed and two Bishops make entradas to confirm this Christianity; one of the Prelates dies in Sinaloa

The Tehueco nation generally attended Christian instruction very fervently, [175] so except for a few who were very set in their old ways, the Baptism of the entire nation was completed. The sorcerers, who were famous in this nation, were of particular concern to both the captain of the garrison, who knew them well, and the priest, who was with them and tried to win them to God by whatever means possible so that they would not be an impediment to the salvation of others. Those who were baptized very faithfully attended the Christian devotions of Mass, catechism, sermons, etc. They were governed politically by their principal caciques, who were ap-

pointed by the captain. At this time [1610] some groups of the wild Bacabachi were also reduced.[33] They were called rat killers because they lived on these nasty animals. These people were very wretched, but finally the clemency of Christ Our Benefactor prepared them to enjoy His redemption.

It is necessary at this point to break away from the discussion of the development of this Christianity,

---

33. The Bacabachi were hunter-gatherers who lived along the coast north of the mouth of the Río Fuerte. After petitioning unsuccessfully for a priest and baptism a large number of them followed Jesuit advice and relocated near the Tehueco (Alegre 1956–1960:2:210).

postponing it for two or three chapters, so as to record here events that happened at this time and place. The Christian communities of Sinaloa fell within the extensive Bishopric of Guadalajara, in the Province of Nueva Galicia. Therefore, Bishop Don Juan del Valle, a Benedictine monk who was a very learned and exemplary individual, decided to visit and become familiar with the new Christian flock that God had entrusted to him.[34] He was to confirm them in God's Faith through the Holy Sacrament of Confirmation, for up until that time no other Prelate had administered this sacrament or even traveled to the Province of Sinaloa.[35]

His Eminence departed Guadalajara, which is two hundred leagues from this province, and overcame the difficult roads and strong rivers blocking his path. En route to the Villa de San Miguel de Culiacán he administered the Sacrament of Confession in the many pueblos of long-time Christians. At the Villa de San Miguel he performed this same pontifical task. From this place His Eminence proclaimed the great favor of a visit that he wished to bestow on the Province of Sinaloa. The one priest in the Villa de San Felipe[36] (the rest were in their mission districts) received news of the Bishop and went to the Villa de San Miguel to welcome His Grace in person and to thank him for the great favor of coming to such a poor and isolated land, encouraging this new Christianity by his very presence. The Bishop left the Villa de San Miguel for the Villa de San Felipe. As he was approaching the latter, Captain Hurdaide came out to welcome him with his garrison of soldiers and the residents of San Felipe. As part of the welcoming festivities the captain arranged for a large company of Indians with their bows, arrows, and feathered headdresses to ambush the Bishop along the road, with the din and commotion of warfare. This was not to give His Eminence a sudden fright, but rather to demonstrate how happy they were with his arrival. It was also to show him the kind of people that God had brought as meek sheep into His flock and had given the Bishop as parishioners.

At first sight this war stratagem was somewhat disturbing, particularly as the soldiers of the garrison also came out on their armored horses. When their pretense soon became clear, however, the Bishop was extremely happy and moved by this spectacle. He gave them his blessing, which they received kneeling down, and then he continued on his way, which was lined with triumphant arches made of green branches. He dismounted at our college in the Villa de San Felipe and entered the church, where a crowd of Indians from the neighboring pueblos had assembled. Here His Eminence gave a very important speech [176] in which he expressed his love and joy at seeing the new Christianity that God had sown in His church. He added that he considered his difficult trip worthwhile because they could [now] enjoy the new waters and episcopal sacrament that would confirm them in the Faith, which he would begin administering on the following day of his pontifical ministry.

All the priests in the province were informed so they could prepare the Indians of their districts to receive this Holy Sacrament. Great multitudes from all the nations and languages and of every age and sex flocked with the priests to the villa. The number of people who gathered to see and be confirmed by this great prince and father (which was what they called the Lord Bishop, whom they had never seen before) was so great that he worked for five days, mornings and afternoons, to complete the confirmations. The Indians enjoyed and were amazed by his authority and pontifical robes, which all served to confirm them not only in the Faith, but also in the reverence and adornment with which divine matters and circumstances were administered, which move these people greatly.

Out of respect clean cotton mantas were prepared so that the many Indians who came without clothes could approach the Bishop in decency. This pious Prelate received them with unusual kindness, regardless of their appearance, and if at times one of them hastily came forward and knelt down naked, he was affectionately escorted by a priest to the Bishop, who then administered confirmation. He told the soldiers who were keeping order not to speak rudely to anyone nor to slight or turn anyone away. Two or three priests acted as interpreters and helped in the church, organizing the various nations of different languages that had gathered to receive this sacrament. The priests also told them the effects of the grace that it imparted and inspired them to receive it with contrition for their sins.

Although not all of the Christian Indians from the interior could come, eight thousand souls were confirmed over the course of five days in our church in the Villa de San Felipe. The Lord Bishop was very happy

---

34. Bishop del Valle visited Sinaloa in 1611.

35. Years before Bishop del Valle's visit the Jesuits in Mexico had asked the father general in Rome, Claudius Aquaviva, to petition the pope for the right to administer confirmation, a privilege limited to bishops. Aquaviva rejected the request of his inferiors in Mexico. Del Valle was the first bishop willing to travel to the northern frontier to administer this sacrament to the Jesuits' neophytes (Dunne 1940:141).

36. The superior of the Sinaloa mission, Father Martín Pérez.

to have exercised such a holy act in that Christian community, and he gave many thanks to Our Lord for seeing Christianity sown in a land so sterile, destitute, and isolated from the world. He also gave many thanks to the missionary priests for the care and work with which they nourished His lambs. However, he was not content to thank only the priests. After he had returned from his journey, having also visited the other missions of Topia and San Andrés, he wrote a letter of thanks to the Father Provincial, Rodrigo de Cabredo. These are the words that were born of His Lordship's kindness:

> I have seen (he writes) almost all of the priests in these missions and I have returned extremely consoled and greatly edified. I have seen that the Church, His Majesty, and the Company all owe them a great deal for the notable improvement they are effecting in these places and for all they endure among these gentiles who are under their care. Therefore, wherever I go I will proclaim this and the other good things I have seen and touched with my own hands, which I will not mention here in order to be brief. Our Lord would be served if some day we should bear witness to them when we speak, and as much as I can I will be a great protector of these missions and their priests. I returned very tired but very happy to have undertaken this long journey. And even if I should die now, I hope in Our Lord that His Divine Majesty will be greatly served by what has been accomplished.

These are all the [177] words of this holy Prelate, and being such, as well as a successor of the Apostles, he wanted to personally visit his entire diocese, which involved immense hardships because it is so extensive and spread out. For this reason a few years later in 1621, with a papal brief from His Holiness Urban VIII, His Majesty the Catholic King Philip IV ordered that this bishopric be divided into two: Guadalajara and Durango. The Sinaloa missions remained in the Bishopric of Durango, whose first Bishop was Lord Don Fray Gonzalo de Hermosillo, of the Order of Saint Augustine, a professor of Holy Scripture who had taught for several years at the Royal University of Mexico City. The visits of the saintly and zealous Prelates with whom God Our Lord has favored the new Christian communities of Sinaloa will be told together here.

Wanting to provide a felicitous beginning to the foundation of this Christianity's church, and in imitation of the Bishop of Guadalajara, Lord Don Fray Gonzalo de Hermosillo visited his diocese some years later. He suffered great hardships in crossing the rough and high mountains of Topia, where he became very fatigued due to their harshness. He was also astounded that Spaniards had penetrated and conquered them out of greed for silver and that evangelical ministers had overcome them with their zeal for the good of the souls that were hidden therein. With great suffering this holy shepherd finally overcame the difficulties of the sierras and [in January 1631] reached the Province of Sinaloa. There he was received with the same demonstrations of happiness that were shown His Eminence Don Fray Juan del Valle. He went on to conduct confirmations in the Villa de San Felipe and afterwards crossed the Río [Sinaloa] and traveled to the principal pueblo of the Tehueco, called Macori. There he was received with unusual happiness by a large assembly of people and conducted additional confirmations. He confirmed eleven thousand Christians in all. For the greater consolation and confirmation in the Faith of such a new Christianity, one feast day he also deigned to celebrate a Pontifical Mass.[37] He also happened to be there on an ember day,[38] when he celebrated the holy ordination of some of the clerics who had accompanied him and others who had joined him in Sinaloa. All of these acts were beneficial in that they provided these people with a better understanding of the sublime nature of our Holy Faith and also of the ministers who preached the Holy Gospel and administered the Holy Sacraments.

Divine goodness wished to reward the acts of such an apostolic Prelate without further delaying his glorious reward. When he had concluded his pontifical ministries in Tehueco and was returning to the Villa de San Felipe he was suddenly stricken by a serious illness. This made it necessary to carry him in a chair to our college, where the religious and all those who understood curing tried to heal him. He did not improve from any of the remedies that were available in a land so destitute of doctors and medicines, and with unusual patience, inner peace, and consolation at seeing himself surrounded by the many religious and apostolic preachers of our Company who attended him, he surrendered his blessed soul to the Lord.[39] To the great favor of the province and its Christianity, the remains of the holy body of the first Bishop of the Diocese of Durango remained in our church, where it was hoped

---

37. A Pontifical Mass is one of four types of Mass. It is solemnly sung by a cardinal, bishop, or abbot in his own abbey and involves more pomp and ritual than a regular Mass. The celebrant generally is assisted by other priests and at least nine acolytes (Attwater 1949:387).

38. Apparently December 13, 1630. Ember days are those set aside for prayer and fasting at the beginning of each of the four seasons of the year. These include the Wednesday, Friday, and Saturday following the first Sunday in Lent, Whitsunday, Holy Cross Day (September 14), and Saint Lucy's Day (December 13) (Attwater 1949:167).

39. On January 28, 1631 (Dunne 1940:258, f.30).

he would favor the prayers of that new Christian community for which we can say he gave his life.

In this Prelate was fulfilled what Christ Our Lord said of the good shepherd, who gave his life for his sheep: *Bonus Pastor animam suam dat pro onibus suis.*[40] This holy shepherd gave his life here for his sheep. [178] His body rests next to the high altar on the Gospel side,[41] with a portrait set above his sepulcher. His soul is crowned with that everlasting wreath that the Prince of the Shepherds (as His first Pope, Saint Peter, wrote) has prepared for His loyal and diligent ministers, the stewards of His families. His Eminence Lord Don Fray Gonzalo de Hermosillo was one of these and therefore his memory deserves to be celebrated. In doing so, this history is also honored.

Doctor Don Alonso Franco de Luna succeeded Fray Gonzalo de Hermosillo as Bishop,[42] and he imitated his predecessors in his holy zeal and love for these new Christian communities. His Eminence visited them, confirming and encouraging them to continue in the Christianity they had initiated. He also consoled the missionary priests, who were his coadjutors in this pastoral task.

I will conclude here the favors that these new children of the Church have received to date from their Prelates, now turning to the fourth Prelate (of the said Diocese of Durango, who at present is Lord Fray Diego de Evia, a Benedictine monk). After he came to his church from Spain he, too, wished to visit this new and distant Christianity. His Eminence was very happy to have seen it and he also noted in a letter to the Father Visitor of the missions and the Father Provincial of Nueva España that despite its being far away it was [entirely] possible to visit this Christian community. With regard to the religious who administered it he added that it was as though he had met and communicated with saintly hermits. For this reason he felt that the travails of his long journey were most worthwhile.[43] These are all words born of the piety of saintly Prelates who love these new flocks.

CHAPTER XVII By order of the viceroy a fort named Montesclaros is built near the Tehueco nation

Christianity continued to progress and prosper in Sinaloa through the conversions that have been and will be recorded here. However, because we are discussing the Tehueco nation, in whose land a fort named Montesclaros was built, the reasons for its construction and the benefits that ensued from it must be told. The principal end that moved Captain Hurdaide to present the benefits of building the fort to the viceroy (the marquis of Montesclaros, for whom the fort was named) conformed to what our Catholic king had ordered in his most holy and pious zeal and had entrusted to his governors in the Indies. These forts were to work for the extension of the Holy Gospel in the provinces that are being discovered as well as for the security, peace, and stability of those who have received it.

The Christian nations of Sinaloa had expanded and would expand again with other requests for instruc-

40. *Margin Note*: Ioan. c. 11. John 10:11: "The good shepherd lays down his life for his sheep" (Knox 1956:99).

41. The Gospel is read on the right side of the main altar during the Roman Catholic Mass.

42. Franco de Luna was bishop from 1632 to 1639. As is perhaps apparent from the brevity of Pérez de Ribas' comments, he was not a friend of the Jesuits. In 1636 or thereabouts the bishop suggested to the viceroy that the Jesuits were, in effect, living comfortably off their Indian charges and that it was time that the Jesuits turn over at least some of their missions to regular clergy and the bishop of Durango. In 1638 Pérez de Ribas, who was at the time Jesuit provincial, responded rather forcefully to the bishop's allegations in a letter to the viceroy (AHH 1638; Alegre 1956–1960:2:581–94; Hackett 1923–1937:3:95–105).

43. Despite Pérez de Ribas' kind words, in 1646 (a year after the original publication of his *Historia*), the bishop successfully gained control of the Jesuit missions of Parras (the subject of Book 11), excepting Parras itself.

tion and Holy Baptism. The garrison at the Villa de San Felipe was far away in the event of an attack or trouble, when flames might rise that would need to be extinguished immediately before the fire could spread. Establishing new garrisons in other locations meant increasing the number of weapons and soldiers, and subsequently the expenses to the king. All of these concerns were resolved by moving His Majesty's garrison at the villa to a more suitable location, whence the soldiers could depart when the call came or the alarm was sounded. It was also believed that it would be advantageous for the fort [179] to be situated where soldiers and other settlers could find suitable places to live, land for farming, water, firewood, pasture for cattle, and horses for defense in case the Spaniards should be attacked.

Once the viceroy was presented with these arguments, he dispatched orders and money to Captain Hurdaide to build the aforementioned fort.[44] He also ordered that the garrison, or some portion of it with a squad leader, reside permanently next to the fort, protected by it. The place found to be most suitable for this purpose was a small hill two leagues from the main pueblo of the Tehueco. This was near the location of the original Villa de Carapoa, which had been destroyed. The fort was built above the river and had a view of the extensive plain, which was free of brush and thorns and where many head of livestock could graze and the Indians could not launch ambushes. Even though the fort was made of adobes, it turned out to be so spacious that all the horses could be kept safely inside whenever war broke out. When there is warfare the first thing the enemy shoots at are the horses grazing in the fields, because they know that when the horses are lost, so are the Spaniards. Living quarters for the soldiers were also built within the fort, and its four corners were fitted and secured with four towers, which served not only as a lookout over the cultivated land but also to frighten the Indians, as was soon seen by the effect they had.

Within a short time after it was finished, four caciques of some wild and barbarous peoples from farther inland[45] came to see the captain, who was staying at the fort at the time. They requested peace, offering him as a gift and a sign of friendship nearly a thousand arrows, in addition to wildcat and martin pelts. They said they had come to see the churches that the Christians had built and the priests who were with them, for they wanted them in their lands, too. They also relayed other news of the many nations who were their neighbors. The captain welcomed them warmly, giving them some of the things that they value. They went to see the churches in the nearby pueblos, and the priest treated them well, giving them high hopes that in good time other priests would go to their lands so that they could hear God's word, as was later done. With this they returned to their pueblos contented.

The fort also served to instill new terror in the Chínipa, with whom the captain fought a dangerous battle when he went on an expedition to search for mineral deposits, as was discussed in Book II [Chapter XXXIV]. The principal cacique of these nations sent one of his sons to see the captain, requesting pardon for the treachery they had plotted with the Sinaloa on that occasion.[46] He promised to settle peacefully and in friendship; this was carried out after some time had passed, as will be told later. These were the effects of love and friendship that resulted from the building of Fort Montesclaros.

Another effect of the fort was terror and fright. While the captain and his soldiers were occupying the fort, he received a warning that some gentile Indians,[47] along with some troublesome Christians who were their neighbors, were trying to start a rebellion and wage war against Captain Hurdaide. This officer, who was as astute as he was brave, ordered a number of knives to be dipped in cattle blood, which he then sent with messengers to the restless Indians. In addition to the threat implied by those bloody knives, they were to understand the punishment they would receive if they did not calm down or if they disturbed the peace. Together with the sight of the fort, which was already completed, this threat served to subdue their pride. All of these good results, as well as others that will be seen later, were obtained from this strong fort, [180] which was staffed by soldiers and a squad leader who are at hand for whatever need should arise. Some Spaniards have already settled within the fort's protection, and when the captain carries out an expedition to visit this land his garrison has a safe place to rest.

44. Although the fort was approved during the viceroyalty of the marquis of Montesclaros (1603–7), it wasn't until the fall of 1609, following Captain Hurdaide's defeat at the hands of the Yaqui, that Viceroy Luis de Velasco gave the go-ahead to begin construction of the fort, which was completed in 1610 (AGN 1610; Dunne 1940:129–31).

45. Probably the Baciroa, Témori, Tubari, and Huite.

46. In 1610, the year the fort was built.

47. It is not clear who these Indians were. They may have been the Tepahue, who subsequently provided refuge to Tehueco rebels.

CHAPTER XVIII The Tehueco attempt to revolt, burn churches, and murder a missionary; how part of the nation fled

Before we can finish discussing the conversion and Christianity of the Tehueco we have another event [to record]. Although it may seem that this case somehow weakens the reasons and motives that we have just recorded in support of [Fort] Montesclaros, the truth is that it does not undermine them. Although it is true that armies and the fortifications they build are not always useful and do not always produce favorable results, this is no reason to abandon or raze them. Rather, the case recorded here confirms the benefits cited in Book II regarding the reasons why garrisons should be established on these frontiers.

It must be supposed that even though it is a well-known and proven fact that these nations receive the Gospel well and enjoy the peace it brings them, the devil does not like it nor does he like to lose the vassals he once possessed. Rather, he does all he can to create and sustain war against those who are on the side of Christ, and he always has some cohorts who follow his lead. Throughout history we read of many revolutions and uprisings that are instigated among new Christian communities by this enemy of humankind. Thus, it should not surprise us that the Tehueco, who (as we just wrote) had enthusiastically received Gospel instruction and were content to have been baptized, had entirely changed: They were now attempting to kill the priest who had engendered them in Christ and loved and treated them like [his own] children (although not all of them took part in the plot).[48] Nor should we be amazed that some who had enthusiastically come to church were now trying to set it on fire and do away with Christianity and, if they could, the Spaniards and the soldiers who defended it. The fire they started was large and the uprising they attempted was among the most dangerous that had occurred in this province. These events took place in the following way.

Some of the Tehueco were very upset that the missionary priest in their mission [Pedro Méndez] had discovered some sorcery and what was more or less the worship of some stones that were like idols. After these inventions of Satan were destroyed the sorcerers got together, and with their diabolical arts they conjured a prediction of the future based on the stars.[49] They announced to the people that a tremendous sickness would strike them and that they wished to prevent it and cure it (all these sorcerers practiced as doctors, or diabolical healers, which is how they profit, taking everything the sick people have in payment for their cure). Without the priest's knowledge they assembled a large number of people and organized one of their gentile dances. At the end of the dance they took a manta, or cotton sheet, by the four corners and threw some of the things into it through which the devil makes his pacts. Making faces and performing other ceremonies, blowing in all different directions, they went to all the houses in the pueblo saying that they were gathering up the illness to take it to the monte, where they also repeated these superstitious [acts].

All this had the effect of preparing the people to rise up and return to their gentile freedom; to do away with the priests, churches, and instruction once and for all; and ultimately to do away with the captain and the Spaniards [181] who defended these things. It was learned for certain that one of the sorcerers, the main one among them, had promised to give them the captain's head. To assure them of his fraudulent deception, some evenings he would summon people to his house. Then when he was alone inside in the dark, he would tell them he had the captain's head there in a pot and that they could hear his shouts and how he cried out when they cut off his head. They said that you could in fact hear painful moaning on those occasions. It is, however, nothing new for the devil to play these tricks, which he was already using to stir up and perturb these people.

Because there are always good people among evil ones, there was a good and faithful Christian who told

---

48. This revolt occurred in 1611 and was coincident with an outbreak of smallpox among the Tehueco's neighbors, the Sinaloa (see Chapter 25; Reff 1991b:154–55). As the present chapter suggests the Tehueco harbored doubts about the efficacy of Christianity, particularly in dealing with what were unprecedented epidemics. This and subsequent chapters are based on the anua of 1611, which includes a lengthy letter written by Pedro Méndez, who was in charge of the Tehueco mission.

49. *Levantaron figura.*

the priest that those people were talking of very evil things and that soon something would happen. He advised the priest to retire to his house early in the evening and, "Even though they should come calling," he said, "do not open the door or they will kill you." The priest took notice of this warning and also noted signs of restlessness in the people. Nevertheless, he waited for some time without letting on that he knew what was happening, entrusting to God the means to calm the storm that was brewing.

The sorcerers who were the authors of this uprising were the principales of the nation and commanded great authority. The captain had received some news of what was going on and he personally tried to prevent the outbreak of war, fearing that this could disturb other nations.[50] Because of this, he sent the priest an escort of four soldiers, in case there happened to be a nighttime attack on his house by some of the most daring of these Indians, for not all of the people had turned against the priest.

The priest finally decided to give a sermon to the pueblo, talking to them about how important peace and calm were to their pueblos, as was the church. He explained to them the great harm caused by uprisings, etc. Although it appeared that this talk had calmed and quieted the people, they actually had depraved intentions. Late one night the Indians came two or three times to force open the door of the priest's house to kill him. When the priest and the soldiers who were with him heard the aggressors, who were few, the latter withdrew. God Our Lord wished to thwart their evil intentions because, if the soldiers had emerged from the house, they and the priest would have been pierced by arrows and bludgeoned to death.

At the same time there were some delinquents hiding out among the gentile mountain nation of the Tepahue, who were allies of the Tehueco. These were some of the Indians who had joined the Tehueco fugitives who had fled from Captain Hurdaide on their way back from Mexico City, as we recorded in Book II. The rebellious Tehueco sympathized with these fugitives and maintained contact with them. It seemed to those who were in Tepahue that this was a good opportunity to destroy the Tehueco's Christianity, so a squad of them decided to go to the Tehueco [pueblos] and set fire to the churches (which is where the devil focuses his evil eye).

Once assembled the group of rebels traveled by night, reaching the first Tehueco pueblo, where they set fire to the church. To accomplish this in greater secrecy (because they still feared some of the faithful Christians who lived in the pueblo), they [remained] outside the pueblo and fired an arrow with a burning cob of maize on its tip into the xacal that served as a church. Because it was made of brushwood, it easily caught fire. However, some good Christians hurried to the church and removed a painted image in a large frame, which they then moved to a safe place.

The priest was in another pueblo at this time, and when he got news of this event he came a second time to calm the spirits of the good and peaceful Christians. He did not want them to get carried away by the angry troublemakers, [182] for they were already gathering their belongings to go join the Tepahue in the free life they promised. He persuaded them with good arguments to remain calm in their pueblos, for they did not have to fear the punishment of Captain Hurdaide, who would instead protect them from the rebels. God willed that this talk should serve to detain a good number of people who were already preparing provisions for the journey to Tepahue, which was forty leagues away.

Other dangerous attacks on the priest occurred during the half a year that this uprising lasted. During this time this good shepherd did not abandon his flock, and there were always some faithful who wished to enjoy peace in their pueblos and churches. At this time the good priest, who guarded his flock at the risk of great danger, received his payment and reward from Our Lord by way of the salvation of the soul of a gentile Indian who was one of those who had fled to Tepahue. They had sent word to the priest that he was becoming very sick and wished to be baptized, and that he was coming with his wife and four children. The priest dispatched some Indians to bring him back, and they returned with the news that the sick man could not walk, at which point the priest sent a horse for him. Once he arrived and was catechized the priest baptized him, and shortly thereafter he died. Then his wife and their four children were baptized. This event served to console the zealous minister, seeing that in the midst of the persecutions of the infernal dragon, God knew how to snatch from the craw of the beast those whom He wished to take to heaven.

Other similar opportunities for service to Our Lord on behalf of these souls were offered to the besieged minister at this time, in spite of the fact that the storm had not subsided. The last and most dangerous of these storms was that the devil incited the spirits of his famil-

---

50. Namely the Yaqui, who a year earlier had made peace with the captain after soundly defeating him in several battles.

iars, the sorcerers, along with some other corrupted individuals, to put into action the general uprising of the entire nation. This was during Lent, when the good Christians, in demonstration of being just that, confessed and held a procession, flogging themselves until they bled. At that time and with great anger (just as he had demonstrated at the time of Christ's Passion) the devil inflamed the spirits of the leaders of the rebellion. On the evening of the Friday before Passion Sunday while the priest was sleeping, four Indians came to wake him and very secretively warn him to leave immediately for the Villa de San Felipe. He was to flee the impending danger, for at that very moment the devil was pronouncing a death sentence against the priest, the soldiers in his escort, and the captain, who was at Fort Montesclaros. This plot had advanced so far that the rebel Indians had divided into troops to attack him and his soldiers and had blocked the roadways so that they could not escape. These Indians had come not only to warn the priest, but to help him escape using a route other than the road. To confirm their loyal warning, one of them added that the conspirators had taken him prisoner and had tied him up because they feared he might warn the priest, but he had skillfully freed himself and had fled to inform the priest.

Because of his many long years of experience as a missionary, the priest was very familiar with the Indians' nature. He suspected from certain signs that the warning was false and that they intended to take him outside the pueblo to kill him (because there were still some good Christians in the pueblo who would help him). He decided to take refuge in the church and beg for divine aid and protection, which does not fail God's servants in their hour of greatest danger. The Christians of the pueblo learned of the danger the priest was in and came very loyally to be with him. [183] To keep watch over him that night, they built many bonfires all around the church.

The enemy had sent spies ahead to assess the situation of the priest and the pueblo's residents. They realized that their treason had been discovered; when this is understood the perverse intentions of these nations are usually halted. Thus, the rebels stayed their hand for the time being. However, because they thought that the captain would find out about their crime and punish them, they decided to go back to their friends, the Tepahue, which they did, taking with them many deceived people from the Tehueco nation. When the captain heard about this he sent word to alert those who had stayed behind that if they remained quietly in their pueblos, the rebels' uprising would not jeopardize them; rather, he would defend them if the rebels returned to cause trouble. Then he attempted to bring back those who had fled and to punish the leaders of the uprising, especially those who had set fire to the church.

CHAPTER XIX The captain and his troops journey into the sierra to the Tepahue nation to punish and reduce the rebel Tehueco

The Tehueco Rebellion [of 1612] gave Captain Hurdaide much cause for concern; he had plenty of reasons to fear the possible consequences of the revolt. First of all, the nation was very bellicose, and there was no assurance that the people who had remained calm would not become restless and follow their relatives who had fled. Second, the location, lands, and nations where they had taken refuge were very far away and in very rough mountains and gorges, where the armored horses, which are the Spaniards' greatest weapon, would not be very effective. Moreover, the army would have to pass through lands belonging to other friends and allies of the Tepahue, with whom the Tehueco had taken refuge. Finally, if this dangerous undertaking failed, as could very well happen, there were other nations—Christian (where there are still some who are evil) as well as gentile—waiting [and watching] who might also become emboldened and rebel. All these considerations alerted the captain and priests to the possibility of a general uprising in the Province of Sinaloa. At the same time, leaving these restless and pernicious peoples' insolent deeds unpunished also posed grave consequences.

The captain and priests conferred about a solution, and with fervent prayer the latter asked God to intercede. Following this consultation it was decided that peaceful means would first be employed to amend things with the rebels and their Tepahue hosts. For this purpose the captain dispatched some Christian Tehueco with messages [of peace]. The messengers were ignored by the rebels, and indeed they were lucky to come back alive. Realizing that he had no other remedy but force of arms, the captain readied his troops for the expedition. I can speak of this as an eyewitness because I accompanied the army under orders of holy obedience. I was to aid with spiritual ministries to any Spaniards or Indian allies who should happen to find themselves in danger [of dying] in battle.

The captain ordered forty armored horses to be readied. Although this is a small force when compared with the number used in Europe, in wars on the frontier a soldier riding an armored horse {184} is like a castle against the Indians' offensive weapons. Still, everything aids in defense, and it cannot be denied that to remain steady one needs Spanish valor, particularly at the sight of a shower of arrows. In accordance with their obligation to keep peace in the land, the captain obliged some of the encomenderos who lived near the Villa de San Felipe to accompany the forty Spanish soldiers from the garrison on the expedition. He entrusted the protection of the villa to those who stayed behind and drafted two thousand Indian warriors from several Christian and allied gentile nations. In exchange for their service the latter asked to be allowed to take enemy scalps with which to dance, saying that they would be content with this as payment. The captain agreed to their request but made a counterproposal that was very akin to his pious Christian heart. For every enemy that was captured alive, particularly women and children, he promised a horse in exchange. They accepted this proposal, but to the captain's great regret they did not comply with it.

The captain then immediately set about provisioning the expedition, which would be gone a long time and involved a large number of people. The messengers he had sent with an offer of peace had told him that the rebels and the Tepahue firmly believed that even if the captain and his army should enter their lands, they would not be able to continue the war for more than four or six days because of a lack of food and supplies. They [on the contrary] could continue to fight from their mountain peaks, where they had gathered {abundant} provisions in a short period of time. To break their spirit, the prudent and astute captain sent them a message that he did not plan to leave their lands without first punishing the delinquents, even if he died there. He planned to drive a large herd of cattle ahead of the army to feed his people and he would not return to the villa without at least punishing the leaders of the uprising. This severe resolution caused the enemy great concern and, even if it did not eliminate the need for the expedition, it at least served the purpose that will later be recounted here.

To make them understand that he meant what he said, the captain ordered that four hundred head of cattle be taken from his ranch to a suitable place to be ready when his troops began to march. He gathered his people and then provisioned the expedition with maize in a pueblo of the Sinaloa nation, where he spent several days preparing for battle and making a strong show of force with military exercises, at which he was quite experienced. He kept the people he had gathered fed and did not announce the day he would march, as they were still four or five days' journey from the enemy.

The enemy had gathered their own people and neighboring gentiles and were waiting each day to do battle with the captain. Hurdaide's [own] troops asked him when he planned to march and he answered, "[Be patient] no time is being wasted." He had sent spies to find out where the enemy was encamped and they brought back news that they and their allied nations were waiting for him in the mountain peaks. "Well, let's make them wait (he would say). I know that their provisions and maize will run out and they will be forced to scatter because of hunger." This was an important means for weakening the enemy.

They also brought news that one of the nations along the way, called the Conicari, had promised to finish off {185} the captain and his people as they passed through a very narrow and dangerous stretch that had lots of crags and rocks. Although this was their plan, a cacique of this nation, who thought the captain knew nothing of their plan and had noticed that the expedition was moving very slowly, came to see the captain under the pretense that he and his people would help the expedition move through the pass. The captain realized that this offer was a sham, but he received the cacique indulgently and with a friendly countenance at his tent. Then after he had listened to him he took a short pistol and fired two shots in front of the Indian, making a hole in the tent in two places. He told the cacique, "I am aware of your intentions and your people's plan to wait for me in a place where you boast that you have a bunch of stones to throw at me. Go back to your people and wait for me. If I had wanted to kill you, I could have very easily done so with those two musket shots, but go on back and pile up your stones because I am going to come looking for you and you had better not be hiding when I get there."

This Indian was flabbergasted by the captain's response and the fact that he had discovered his intentions. He returned to his land so bewildered that later when the army reached the pass, he came out to receive the captain peacefully. After ordering his people to retreat and not join the Tepahue, he remained at the captain's side. The overwhelmed cacique asked the captain not to harm his rancherías, which were nearby, and the captain granted this request, ordering the entire army not to touch those rancherías. When he felt it was time to depart he broke camp and continued on his journey, driving ahead the four hundred head of cattle he had brought along for sustenance (as we said).

We all walked at the pace of the cattle, and after walking for two days a large group of people, including a smaller group of women, was seen coming down a slope. When the captain saw them he turned to me and said, "Those are the Christians who fled. Now that they see things are serious, they are returning to their pueblos. They should receive some punishment because they have caused such a great commotion and expense. When I attempt to punish them Your Reverence should intercede on behalf of the women. For them the [mere] threat [of punishment] will be enough. As for the men who followed the uprising and did not remain at peace like the other Christians, they will not learn any lesson if they do not receive some kind of punishment." Actually, a moderate punishment was fine because a more rigorous one would not have made them any more fearful.

The troops halted there and the Indian men arrived with their bows, arrows, and macanas, claiming that they had been deceived by the Tepahue, who assured them that the captain would not be able to enter their lands. They were disillusioned and were returning to their pueblos. The captain, however, first ordered the Indians to surrender their bows, arrows, and weapons. Then a great bonfire was built and everything was immediately burned. He commented to the soldiers, "Now there will be fewer of these bows with which they

can shoot us, even if they try to go back by another route and help their people, as they are wont to do." Their handsome bows, which were very coveted by the allies, were consumed in the fire along with their quivers and arrows.

The captain then ordered each Indian to be bound with leather straps, albeit loosely. Turning to the Indian women, he started to scold them, saying that they could have quieted their husbands and prevented them from revolting and dragging them off through the mountaintops tired, wretched, and hungry. He made other similar arguments that from his great experience he knew would be appropriate given the nature of Indian women. Then he started to threaten [186] them with flogging. At this point I came out of the tent in which I had been waiting and interceded on the women's behalf. With this they were free and very grateful, as was the rest of this large group of three hundred people, who with safe conduct returned to their pueblos.

As he often did, the captain had sent a piece of paper with peace seals on it to an Indian leader of the uprising who was nevertheless respected by the Spaniards because he had helped them on previous occasions. This Indian came with the aforesaid group, and in order to feel safer, as soon as he entered the camp he asked where the priest was lodged. He came to me directly, and kneeling down he begged me to intercede on his behalf. I did so, reassuring him and then taking him to the captain. Thus, he and his other companions were also freed of punishment, for they knew that we priests intercede on their behalf.

The following day the troops departed, and when we encountered another group of Indians that was smaller than the last one, we dispatched them in the same manner. There were still a large number of outlaws, however, and as we approached enemy territory the mules, cattle, and horses began to suffer from a great lack of pasture. The enemy had set fire to the fields which, because it was so dry, had burned completely. Only a small bit of green remained along the banks and niches of some streams. We continued at this disadvantage, advancing little by little until the army finally reached a place in the mountains of the enemy, who were located in the surrounding area of three high mountains and peaks. The outcome of this expedition will be left for the following chapter.

CHAPTER XX Continuation of the Spaniards' expedition to the sierra of the Tepahue

The captain chose to camp with his troops in a valley through which the river of the Tepahue [Río Cedros] flowed and where there was an abandoned Tepahue pueblo. When the Tepahue packed up their households they took their maize and food to the top of the mountains that surrounded them, which the troops had in sight. Here the captain ordered his soldiers to await his signal before pursuing and battling the enemy. Likewise, they were not to kill them. They were only to capture an enemy Indian to obtain an interpreter or information about how or where the Indians were camped. The captain wanted to send some new demands for peace with the condition that they surrender those who were the principal delinquents in the uprising.

He gave his Indian allies permission to search for and confiscate the enemy's hidden maize, in the event that the war continued, because the maize they had brought along was not sufficient to sustain them. The allies busied themselves gathering the maize that was hidden on the mountaintops and among the crags, and they also harvested the agave that was planted in their enemy's abandoned ranchos. The Indians roast these plants and consider them a delicacy. Then they broke the pact they had made with the captain when they had agreed not to behead anyone, particularly women and children. They had agreed instead to bring the prisoners back alive, and for each one of them the captain would give them a horse. He did not want to enslave them, but rather wished to free the innocent. In any event the agreement was broken, because along the road we came across the bodies of two women who had just been [187] beheaded by gentile Indians who were traveling ahead of us.[51]

Returning to the topic of the sustenance of the expedition, the main food consisted of six or eight cattle that were butchered each day and distributed among the people. Although it was Lent, it is well known that the Church's rule about fasting does not apply when no other food is available.

In the six or eight days that the captain spent here

he sent several formal demands to the Tepahue, making them understand that it was not his intention to wage war against them. Instead, he wanted to invite them to peace, as long as they surrendered to him the guilty rebels who had set fire to and burned down the church at Tehueco. These announcements did no good, so it was decided to wage war against them. He gave permission for his allies to fight with whomever they met, and he broke camp and went farther into the sierras in search of the enemy. All the roads were sown with thorns and sharpened stakes that were set in the grass and rubbed with the most poisonous herb known in those lands. They removed all those they could find in order to insure safe passage for the Indian allies, who walked barefoot or at best wore flimsy sandals.

They reached a dangerous narrows with a river flowing through it that they had to ford. It was not possible, as is ordinarily the case, to cross the river elsewhere or avoid the roughness of the steep cliffs that rose on either side. The Spaniards had their Indian allies, who were sprier and faster, ascend the heights. They could then guard them so that the enemy could not roll boulders and rocks down on the troop while the long baggage train and the cattle were passing underneath. This danger greatly concerned the captain and his soldiers (I speak here as an eyewitness), because the passage was so narrow that the people and the horses could only go through in single file. They might perish even if only a few boulders were rolled down on them by the enemy. On this occasion, however, God obscured their vision so that they would not do so. In the end the captain decided that he could not abandon the pursuit of the enemy because it would allow them to commit even more treachery and would risk everything that had been won.

This decision put the troops on high alert, as we entrusted this plan to the Most Holy Virgin. On the [feast] day of her Most Holy Annunciation [March 25] the soldiers heard Mass and confessed. They wanted to receive Holy Communion but we had been delayed for so long that there were not enough Hosts to consecrate for everyone. Therefore, the men promised to receive Our Lord when they returned to the Villa de

51. These gentile Indians were probably Guazápare, Huite, or members of one of the other nations who lived in the sierras.

San Felipe. They would also jointly celebrate the feast day of the Most Holy Virgin, Protector of Christians, in thanksgiving for the fortunate outcome they expected to achieve as a result of her intervention. Merciful Mother that she is, she granted this and the troop train passed confidently through the narrows. Even though the distance was not great, this took two hours, but God willed that there was no danger.

The enemy awaited the troops in our vanguard at the mouth of the gorge. From their high perch they began to rain arrows down on the Indian allies who were in the lead, who then shouted to the captain, who was back among the body of the troops with me at his side. He immediately spurred the mule he was riding, and with the harquebuses that he always carried on his saddlehorn (and without even thinking to take the armored horse that his servant was leading along beside him) he called to the nearest soldiers and they began the battle. When the Indians heard the harquebuses so close backing up the Spaniards' allies, they did not dare to wait around.

Because the allies were quicker, they pursued the enemy into the gorges and when they caught up with them they cut off a number of heads. They brought them back to camp [188] hanging from cords and I confess that it horrified me to see how they carried them. The Indians had cut off their skin and scalps, which because they were gentiles, they had saved for their dances. They hung them by the nostrils on strings made of roots and, although it was very distressing to see this, such are the customs of war. The following evening when the troops halted there was so much uproar and dancing with the heads that the sounds seemed to boom across that meadow from hell itself. There were a lot of people and they lit a thousand torches, celebrating victory with such shouting and screaming that their dissonant songs thundered all night long through those mountains. I tried to stop those who were Christians (who always stayed near the captain's tent and another one where I said Mass) from joining in the gentiles' dances, but there were so many of them that it looked like the very picture of hell. Also, it was sometimes necessary to remain as much on guard with these gentile allies as it was with the enemy, for if they should collaborate in some treasonous act, they might do away with all the Christians right there on the spot. The captain prevented this by not bringing too many people from one single nation with him. Instead, he selected people from various nations so that they could not hatch any treachery.

The sentries on guard duty carried out their night watches on their armored horses with harquebuses in hand. I include all these details in order to provide information about warfare among such strange peoples.

To conclude the discussion of this expedition, I can say that in the various battles that were fought with the enemy, seven of the most harmful Indians who also bore the greatest guilt for the uprising were captured and taken prisoner. Some of them were Christians, but they were corrupt and had been deceived by devils and sorcerers. The captain sentenced them to hang and the two most guilty were garroted. They were all burned in the same lands in whose incomparable fortresses they had placed their confidence. I tried to prepare them well for death and to hear the confessions of those who were Christian. The rest of them were baptized and nearly all of them showed signs of their salvation, except for two who persevered in their stubbornness. The Tepahue's fields were also destroyed.

Now hunger and lack of supplies pressed so hard on the troops that the Spaniards ate meat without bread or with cooked maize that served as bread. Even the salt had run out. For this reason people began to get sick and as a result the captain decided to go back. He granted a general pardon to the remainder of the rebels and the few remaining Christian Tehueco returned to their pueblos. They realized that they had been deceived by their famous sorcerer when he vowed to deliver them the captain's head. The Tepahue who had harbored the delinquents recognized how beneficial peace with the Spaniards was and later came to request it.

It was also a favor from the Most Holy Virgin that among the allies only a single gentile was killed in this battle. He was a very brave Indian who writhed in agony for twenty-four hours before he died from a wound caused by the mere tip of an arrow that had lodged in his foot. He was baptized with such desire for salvation that he himself urged me to baptize him, saying to me, "Father, I will consider myself a miserable wretch until you baptize me." I went slowly so that he could understand the principal mysteries of our Holy Faith, which he had never heard, for he was from a very distant nation. But seeing that he was so exhausted, I had to hasten his catechism and Baptism. In this case I based my decision on what I could hear in his voice, which was racked with pain from the mortal poison from the herb on those arrows. Even a tiny wound made by one [189] of these points on the tip of his foot, so far from his heart, was enough to kill this Indian, who was as big as a giant. It took his life after twenty-four hours of agony, and his relatives burned his body so that the enemy could not hold a victory dance with his head or bones.

I will add here another spiritual fruit that was harvested on that occasion. Among the gentile Indians who had accompanied this expedition there was a large troop from a very loyal nation. Among them was a cacique, with his wife and son, whom she carried in her arms. The cacique strongly insisted that I baptize his son, saying that he was afraid he might die without Baptism on the way back to his own land. I had to grant his request because he was an Indian who had come many times to the Christian pueblos to ask for priests to go to his nation. He returned to them very comforted because his son had become a Christian. Later he aided greatly in making his entire nation Christian as well.

This expedition lasted for a month and a half, and when the captain took leave of the gentiles who had accompanied him, he very generously gave them the remaining beef cattle from the original herd of four hundred. These served not only for food, but also to break trail in the mountainous areas. There must have been about twenty of them left, which made the Indians who had assisted in the war very happy. The captain set out for the Villa de San Felipe, and when he reached the Tehueco pueblos along the way he left them safe and settled.

To conclude this expedition, he did something which demonstrated the reverence and fear that these people should have for sacred things. In Tepahue he had captured the horse (a very handsome and coveted specimen) ridden by the Indian who set fire to the Tehueco church. When they reached Tehueco the zealous captain took this horse and tied it to a pole. He had the people who had gathered shoot it full of arrows. Then he had it burned, saying that even the animal upon which that sacrilegious Indian had dared to assault the House of God had to be shot and burned and would not escape punishment. All of this helped to keep any infidels in check.

When the captain and his soldiers reached the villa they fulfilled their vow of thanksgiving to the Most Holy Virgin, by whose intervention God had worked such good effects. The great success of such a dangerous expedition had cost the life of only one Indian (who had been baptized, for it seemed that his predestination had been reserved for this occasion). The few remaining Christians among the Tepahue returned to their pueblos and if there were any remaining rebels, the Tepahue themselves cut off their heads and sent them to the captain. After peace was established this nation requested that priests come to their lands to instruct and baptize them. A very solid Christian community was established there, as will be told further ahead in Book IV. For now we will return to the Christianity of the Tehueco, which had been interrupted by the various events related here.

CHAPTER XXI The Tehueco nation remains calm following the Tepahue campaign; they continue in their Christianity and build churches

The expedition to Tepahue was concluded. This campaign had been necessary because the Tehueco had rebelled, believing the sorcerers' false promises that they would have the captain's head and thus be quite secure in their barbarous freedom. The delinquents who had burned [190] the church in Tehueco were punished. Once this nation was enlightened (although some of the Tehueco had remained calm), and the storm had passed and the evil [caused] by the sorcerers' scandals had been uprooted, Christianity began to bloom anew and the Gospel began to yield abundant fruits. In order to govern themselves better and to benefit more from catechism, the three Tehueco pueblos were reduced to two [Macori and Sivirijoa], in which there were about eight hundred or one thousand families.

Because the churches they had built previously were made out of brushwood and straw, the Tehueco decided to build [new] ones made of adobe with flat earthen roofs, which would be safer from fire and more durable. They went to work on this, and many people—men, women, and little children—joined happily in the task. They erected two very handsome and spacious churches, which they dedicated with great solemnity, just as their neighbors, the Zuaque, had done. Once the churches were dedicated and all the people had been baptized, the Tehueco nation experienced a marvelous peace and calm, which has endured. A government was established and mayors were appointed to govern them. This was accomplished in such an orderly fashion that none of the long-established Christian pueblos around Mexico City have any advantage over them.

Once the people were better prepared and instructed, the use of Holy Communion was introduced to select persons who understood its meaning, for this is a sacrament that requires greater [intellectual] capacity. Those who were permitted to partake of it readied themselves through great preparation. Through the use of this Supreme Sacrament there was such a great change that barbarous and gentile customs were forgotten.

There is one young man from this nation who is worthy of memory here as a singular fruit of this Christianity and an aid in introducing and expanding it. He was raised by one of the priests, and while serving in the church he was this man's inseparable companion. He was very faithful during times of rebellion in discovering the treachery and abuses that have been mentioned. Above all he possessed such great [intellectual] capacity and displayed such good habits that the priests had named him 'The Discreet One'. He was greatly inclined to matters of piety and was a great help to the priest [Pedro Méndez] in establishing the Christian religion in his district. He assisted not only with these things, but also with the translation into their language of the *Flos Sanctorum*,[52] or lives of the saints. This was of great advantage not only to the Indians, but also to the priests who later came to preach in their language.

This young man fell ill from a seizure so violent that four men could not hold him down. He nevertheless broke loose, and at the height of his suffering he ran looking for the priest, who was absent. Having already confessed, he wanted to ask the priest to administer the holy oils. When the priest was informed of what was happening, he came as quickly as possible to see his companion, the son whom he had engendered in Christ and had reared himself. Because it appeared to him that the young man was on the verge of death, he administered the holy oils. The boy himself responded just as he did when he was attending the priest in this ministration. Having received these oils, he became so calm that he appeared to be sleeping. Desiring good health for he who was so helpful and such a good example for his nation, the priest asked our father Saint Ignatius for health for that sick young man. He took him an image of the saint, and as soon as he placed it in front of him, the young man recognized and adored it,

---

52. The *Golden Legend* is a thirteenth-century compilation of short biographies (five to fifteen pages) of various saints, arranged according to the sequence of their feast days during the Church year. (The word flower in the title, *Flos Sanctorum*, really means the best or most important) (Ganss 1991:16). Pedro de Ribadeneira, an early and influential Jesuit, compiled a version that was widely read in Europe and elsewhere (Martin 1993:104).

praying for good health and making a vow. Our Lord granted the saint this [favor] and the young man was soon well enough to play the flute at a feast day celebration. He who had already been anointed for death was there giving thanks for his health, very mindful [191] of our holy patriarch, whose singular favors are experienced not only by his sons who administer these missions, but also by the faithful of their flocks.

There are two marvelous things that we can attribute to the favors that this glorious saint has worked in this province. One is snatching from the devil's clutches the souls of bedeviled sorcerers, who have had dealings with this fierce beast for many years. The devil has confessed (as is told in several histories) that it is Saint Ignatius who wages the greatest war against him in the world. The second is the great reform that one can see with respect to the vice of sorcery, which these nations, especially the Tehueco of whom we are now speaking, used to be so fond. Even though this has been touched upon in other parts of this history, the following chapters will recount some of the most unusual cases and clear testimonies of this matter. These cases manifest the fruits that are reaped from preaching the Gospel among these peoples.

CHAPTER XXII Cases of edification involving sorcery that occurred among the Tehueco and other nations; favors that the priests of the Company have received from their glorious patriarch Saint Ignatius

With regard to the veracity of the cases that are told here it is worthwhile to note that they are truths confessed by those who were the very enemies of Christ's Faith. This infallible truth has forced them to confess outright the lies and tricks by which the devil had fooled them. In addition, it should be noted that these same witnesses would not accuse themselves of the same such deep-rooted vices if they had not been illuminated by the light of the Gospel that now shines in their hearts. The following case was witnessed by, among others, an Indian who was famous in the diabolical art of sorcery. The priest managed to enlighten this Indian and bring him to truly renounce the pact, superstitions, and dealings he had with the devil.

This Indian had been baptized, and upon hearing the priest preach on this matter, his heart was touched by God. He came to make a very good confession. Once this was finished the priest asked him about the means by which the devil so deceived them, with the intention of using his teaching to undo these tricks. The converted Indian replied that he appeared to them in a thousand different forms. When he wanted to persuade people to war and vengeance he appeared to them as very fierce, and in their language they called him 'the fortress'. And just as if he were the lord of this fortress they offered him bows, arrows, shields, and other weapons. To those he wanted to incite to crimes and obscenity he appeared in a peaceful and delightful form, and these people called him 'Delight' and offered him feathers, mantas, and other soft items. On other occasions he told them that he was the lord of the rains and that as such they were to call upon him so that their crops would be successful and they would have prosperous harvests. At other times he appeared to them as a bolt of lightning or a sword of fire that shook and struck the air with great fury, suddenly killing whomever he wished from among those who were present. Then they called him 'the Lord of Life and Death', and they feared him more than death itself. In order to placate him, they would offer him something and beg him not to unleash sickness on their lands. Finally, he sometimes appeared to them in the form of what we call here the 'Angel of Light', revealing to them things that had already happened or had been lost. For this reason they called him 'Light of Midday' in their language. Whenever they [192] lost something or something was missing, they called on him and he came to wherever they were.

Not everyone had the ability to see these figures, only the most famous sorcerers. Nor did these sorcerers communicate with all of these figures. They had some of these figures, or quasi-idols, made from stone and gnarled poles. These were ugly and were kept hidden in the monte, which is where they practiced their abominable sorcery. The priest worked diligently to find them, and when he did he smashed them to pieces, burned them, and then buried them in an extremely deep hole. In their place he ordered a Cross to be erected so that the devil would no longer remain there.

The devil later appeared to the Indian of whom we are speaking, as well as to others, frightening them and telling them in loud voices and screams that if they denied him, he would kill them and burn their church. In addition to this, he threatened no longer to find lost objects for the Indian who had formerly been his familiar. If he wanted the former friendship to continue, he was not to enter the church or make the sign of the Cross or believe what the priest was teaching. But the enlightened Indian sent him away, saying that he no longer wanted to know about his arts or benefit from the knowledge that he used to share with him. This is what the priest, whom he loved very much and whose words from God he greatly revered, had advised him to do. He heeded the man who had placed the Cross on his forehead when he was baptized.

In the end this Indian was so changed by divine grace and the priest's exhortation that he went to church and heard Mass often. He greatly commended himself to God, asking to be freed of that infernal dragon. He rejected the spells that the devil had taught him for taking the lives of others—which he had [in fact] done, even those of his own children when they were born. The fierceness of the enemy of humankind reached such lengths that he [even] taught his disciples this type of cruelty. The priest comforted the rest of the people and confirmed them in the Faith, and he advised them to arm themselves with the sign of the holy Cross and to pray the Creed. They obeyed him, and Satan was overcome and his fraud revealed. These new Christians were enlightened and had renewed energy to serve their true God.

The following case also helped. During a time of illness a sorcerer caused a young gentile who was twenty years old to flee to the monte. The sorcerer told him that if he became sick [while he was] in the pueblo, the priest would find out about it and would come to baptize him, which would cause him to die. But the opposite happened, for after he had fled to the monte, he became sick and reached the point that the relatives who were caring for him thought he was dead and had dug a grave to bury him. The priest happened to arrive at that time, having been called by other sick people. He asked who that grave was for and they told him that it was for that young infidel who had just died. All of them said that he had withdrawn to the monte to flee Baptism.

The priest approached the place where the young man was [lying]. He was already wrapped in a woven reed mat for burial in their fashion (they did this so quickly that even before the dying person had expired they normally had him prepared for the grave). The priest then ordered that the mat be untied, and he called the sick young man by name. Immediately, he whom they had wanted to bury arose, saying, "Father, I came here fleeing you. My soul was being carried off by coyotes, who wanted to swallow it up." (These are animals like dogs or foxes.) "Baptize me," added the sick young man, "so that they don't rip me to pieces." The priest catechized him very slowly and gave him the name Buenaventura, for his good fortune on this occasion of being plucked by God from the jaws of hell. Through Holy Baptism he was healed in body and soul and survived and became a preacher against the sorcerers. He persecuted them and [193] revealed both them and their deceit.

One night a demon entered a woman, or perhaps it was many demons. This notably afflicted her and caused her to grimace horribly. Word was sent to the priest, who then went to her aid. He said the Church's holy exorcisms over her, added the litanies, and in addition placed a reliquary with several relics in it around her neck. Nevertheless, the devil was still rebellious and persistent. As a final remedy the priest brought an engraving of our blessed father Saint Ignatius. He showed it to the poor woman and told her to commend herself to that saint. Then he placed it on her head, and she began to calm down immediately. Once she was free and had completely recovered she confessed. She showed great devotion and thanks to the saint who had freed her from her captivity.

Our Lord also freed another woman from the hands

and cunning of sorcerers. Even though she was a Christian, she led a free and dissolute life. During a time of drought and hunger she was in her house preparing some squash to give her husband to eat when he returned from the field. At that time two strangers happened to arrive, brought there by the famine that had spread throughout the land. They asked her to help them by [giving them some of] the stew she was preparing. She refused to do so, saying that she did not have anything else to give her husband. The Indians, who were sorcerers, with which the earth swarms, said certain words to her that caused her to fall suddenly to the ground as if she were dead. Her hands and feet began to shake and her body made other extraordinary movements. Then she lost her ability to speak. This lasted all night and into the following morning, when they [finally] called the priest.

This was the state in which he found her. He wanted to anoint her, but before doing so, he remembered the power that God has given our holy patriarch [Saint] Ignatius against demons and possessed people. Therefore, he placed a medallion of the saint on her heart, and immediately the woman took a deep breath and began to stutter. Little by little, through the intercession of the saint, her speech was restored and she was able to confess, which she greatly needed. She declared that the mere words muttered by those bedeviled Indian sorcerers had caused that incident and placed her in that trance. She had been freed and healed by the image of the saint and also greatly enlightened and confirmed in the Faith.

Because there were so many demons wandering about Sinaloa, it is no wonder that there were so many people possessed by them. The following case was notable, and occurred with an Indian who was a herdsman.[53] One day when he was going out to round up the herd the devil appeared to him in the form of a mulatto.[54] Speaking kindly, he asked the cowhand to serve him in the abominable trade of sorcery. The agreements were made and the mulatto devil gave him a little piece of roasted meat and a drink from a nearby *jagüey* (which is what they call little puddles of rainwater). He told him that he would shortly make the water turn red (entertaining him with such colors and lies). Then he began to persuade him not to enter the church or [attend] Mass. If he did go to church from time to time so as not to be missed, he was not to look upon the consecrated Host.

After the Indian had eaten and drunk that which the devil had given him, he became ill and fell unconscious. The false mulatto, who had not left his side for a minute, then dragged him along by the feet, and it seems like he could not wait to drag him off to hell. The affliction worsened to the point that [194] he became delirious; however, the following day he awoke, having recovered somewhat. He called for the priest, who immediately went to see him. When he arrived he found him with his eyes open, but he was senseless and could not see. The priest sprinkled holy water on him and he regained consciousness, as if coming out of a deep sleep. Then the bewitched man said, "Now the mulatto has finally left me. The priest has drowned him, for due to his presence, he withdrew to the cave at the lake. If the priest had not come, he most certainly would have killed me."

No sooner had he regained consciousness than he confessed. He made a new declaration of faith and renounced [any] dealings with the devil. He was left so thin and weak that he could not stand on his own for twenty days. After that he was completely healed and the devil never appeared to him again, leaving this Indian quite confirmed in the Faith and abhorrent of dealings with demons. In this case it might seem that our father Saint Ignatius had intervened, but the truth of the matter was confessed by the Indian who had been fooled by the mulatto. [He said] that the moment the priest came, that fierce serpent fled the mere presence of a son of Saint Ignatius, withdrawing to his cave at the lake. Never more did he appear, nor did he tempt that sick man whom he had poisoned.

The favor of our holy patriarch was even more apparent and the benefit he worked even more illustrious in the following case. There was an Indian, one of the first to be baptized, who lived a good life. He had been ill for many days and feared that he had been bewitched. He was slowly being consumed, a common effect of the spells used by those who practice this perverse craft, which is why they are feared by all. Even though this sick man was on his feet, one day he was suffering so much from the illness that they sent word to the priest to come and hear his confession. When the priest arrived the sick man said to him, "Father, you should know that a priest like yourself has appeared to me, in

53. *Baquero.*

54. Note that the devil often was represented in late medieval and early Renaissance literature and art as being black or having dark skin; Pérez de Ribas and his fellow Jesuits continued this tradition (Reff 1995:76).

your habit, together with four other priests who were his companions.[55] They were bathed in light, and with a serious look on his face the first one asked me why I did not confess as often as I used to. He told me to do so soon because I needed it. I did so and began to recover, but the devil caused me to fall prey to a sin which I later regretted. To have soiled my soul caused me greater pain than the illness from which I am now suffering, which is quite great. Three days ago that saint appeared to me again, and he could barely stand to look at me. When he did it was with a furious look, saying from a distance, "Because you lost God, you will go blind and become lame, so much so that you will not be able to see or get around." And this is exactly what happened, for at this time the sick man's biological father came to see his son, and when he asked whether he could see, the son answered, "No, father, don't you see that I'm blind?" The son told his [other] father, the priest who had come to hear his confession, that the saint who had appeared to him had said, "Confess, for in a few days you will find yourself in heaven. I will take you there. Why would you want to continue in this mortal life?" [The Indian said,] "I answered, 'Take me right now.' He did not want to and this made me very sad."

Upon hearing this the priest prepared him in case he should die. He then left him for the time being. Later he returned to visit him and found out from the Indians who were attending him what the sick man had said. They told him that all he said was, "God gave me this illness and I most willingly receive it for the love of God and Holy Mary, His Mother." Shedding tears, he said, "It burdens me more to have offended Him than to suffer as I do." These were effects that clearly demonstrated themselves to be from heaven. They were proof of the veracity of the apparitions of which he had spoken and of the fact that the devil never changes nor will he ever change the pain of sin.

Finally, the sick man told [195] the priest that the saint had returned and, looking at him with a kind face, had said, "Aren't we going?" With this, he began ascending towards heaven with his companions and the Indian saw them no more. A day later, after having received the Holy Sacraments, the sick man died and was taken to Our Lord, as can be expected given the circumstances surrounding his death. He left a will made in his fashion, ordering that all his valuables be given to the Church and the poor. He was given a solemn burial, which was attended by the [entire] pueblo. This caused great devotion in the Indians, in particular to see the many tears that the sick man had shed for his sins up to the time when he turned his soul over to God, who protected him with such unique favors and with visits from our father Saint Ignatius, who singularly favors his sons in these enterprises, as is seen on many and varied occasions.

If one had to record here all the marvelous and singular favors that the invocation or image of our glorious patriarch has worked in terms of freeing both mother and child from dangerous births and breeched babies, an endless number could be gathered. These will be passed in silence, however, so as not to draw out this chapter. What is certain is that the type of benefits that are commonly experienced in the rest of the world thanks to [our] blessed father [Saint Ignatius] are [also] commonplace in this new Christian community in Sinaloa. Other good results will be spoken of in the following chapter.

---

55. The fact that they were bathed in light suggests that they were Jesuit saints, namely Ignatius Loyola, Francis Xavier, Luis de Gonzaga, Stanislas Kostka, and Jean Berhmans. Loyola, Xavier, Kostka, and Gonzaga were the subject of a "lives" (abridged) by the French Jesuit Etienne Binet, which went through many editions during Pérez de Ribas' lifetime (Martin 1993:94, 103).

CHAPTER XXIII The sorcerers confess that their powers and pacts with the devil have been weakened by the preaching of the Holy Gospel; the present flourishing state of the Tehueco nation

It is known from experience with these new Christian communities that when the sun rises the darkness flees, and with it the wild animals and enemies of the light, who return to their caves. And so it is that the devils, Princes of Darkness, are exiled from and made to flee those places where the Holy Gospel is being preached. They withdraw to gentile [lands], as this is the only place where their snares and lies can endure. This was confessed by a famous sorcerer and healer who, when asked to cure a sick child with his devilish arts, responded with these words: "I do not know what is happening. We are no longer any good at healing. After we were baptized our familiar spirits left us."

Traces and sparks of sorcery [nevertheless] persisted in one pueblo where the devil tried as hard as he could to fan the smoldering flame (for there have always been some devils who are more stubborn than others). It was a time of great drought and some Indians sought out a sorcerer to make it rain. The sorcerer sought to fulfill their desire by making great promises of abundant water, but his conjuring and diabolical invocations were in vain, as was the case with the priests who invoked the idol Baal. These priests requested fire from heaven for their sacrilegious sacrifice, but the fire was not forthcoming.[56] The Tehueco sorcerer was likewise unsuccessful with his invocations and actions to produce rain. [196] When the persons who had trusted in such a false prophet realized that they had been deceived, they recognized their sin and advised the priest of the liar's guilt. The priest had him punished for his crime and bad example, and so that those who were new to the Faith would know God (the true Lord of the rain), the priest ordered that a procession be held to ask for His aid. The Lord condescended to such

pious pleas with an abundance of water, and with this the Indians were consoled. They realized how little the devil can do and how valuable the favor of the true God and Creator of all things is.

I will conclude here by relating how the preaching of our Holy Faith triumphs over devils—and those possessed by them—binding them in chains. I cannot keep silent about a very singular instance of divine providence that was noted in this Province of Sinaloa and its conversions. Among these people there are so many sorcerers possessed by the devil that it can be said that the priests are in the midst of veritable gangs of demons. Moreover, their acts of sorcery are both frequent and powerful, as has been told in many parts of this history. Add to this the fact that the said sorcerers and their familiar demons view the priests and ministers of the Gospel as their capital enemies. This is because the priests are the ones who reveal and destroy the lies whence they have obtained their pernicious profits. During these many years when there have been so many priests ministering among these diabolical sorcerers (and there are thirty-five in the Sinaloa mission alone), divine providence has so tightly bound the hands of the latter, while protecting the former, that up until now not a single sorcerer has been able to use his diabolical arts to cast a true spell or harm a single one of these evangelical ministers, neither through the use of [poisoned] food or drink nor by any of the other means that the devil teaches them. Undoubtedly, if God had not tied the devil's hands and those of such ferocious enemies, they would have killed all the missionary ministers who have come to these peoples. One can see here the fulfillment of the divine promise that was made to those who trust in the [Lord's] protection, as was foretold in the Ninetieth Psalm: *Super aspidem, et basiliscum ambulabis, et conculcabis Leonem, et Draconem.*[57] It promised them that they would walk safely among

---

56. In III Kings 18 of the Vulgate, Ahab assembled the prophets of Israel on Mount Carmel to debate whether Yahweh or Baal was God. The prophet Elijah alone challenged the 450 prophets of Baal to prepare a sacrificial bull and to call upon their god to send fire from heaven as a sign. Baal never responded; Yahweh did and a celebration ensued (Knox 1956:303–5).

57. *Margin Note*: Psalm. 90. Psalm 90:13: "Thou shalt tread safely on asp and adder, crush lion and serpent under thy feet" (Knox 1956:516).

serpents and basilisks[58] and would tread upon lions and dragons without being harmed. These are the demonstrations and proofs of how the preaching of our Holy Faith weakens the devil's strengths.

The discussion of sorcery in this and the previous chapter was prompted by the fact that sorcerers and sorcery were so prevalent among the Tehueco nation at the time of their conversion to our Holy Faith. The instigators as well as the supporters of the rebellious flight to the sierras of the Tepahue were sorcerers who had been scorned and punished (as was told). I will conclude here the discussion of this nation's Christianity and how it presently flourishes both spiritually and civilly, for in both respects the change has been marvelous, especially in the spiritual [realm].

There have been a great number of general confessions, covering many years [of the confessants' lives]. The reason these people gave for doing so is that when they were new in the Faith, they did not have as much knowledge of the integral nature and circumstances of this Holy Sacrament. Once they had acquired this knowledge they wanted to make a good confession and atone for the sins of their past life. These confessions were very precise in terms of the number, distinction, and circumstances of their sins. If their sins had been a bad example to others, [197] those who knew how to write (for some of them had learned to do so) wrote them down on a piece of paper, which they then took to these general confessions. Those who did not know how to write recorded their sins on strings, marking them with spaces and knots.[59] Therefore, even very wise Spaniards who had been born and raised in Christianity had no advantage over the Indians in this respect, even though these seemed like things that surpassed the [intellectual] capacity of Indians.

Beyond this, and of even greater esteem, is the fact that they made these confessions with great sorrow, tears, and remorse for their sins. The priest who heard their confessions was moved to the verge of tears. At the same time he was particularly consoled to see the fruits that the Faith produced in those who were so new to it and who so recently had lived like wild animals and barbarians. The integrity of these confessions was not surprising, given that they prepared for them over the course of several days, attending church for two hours

in the morning and another two hours in the afternoon. The men met in the choir loft or tower and the women in the nave of the church. The priest who was in charge of this mission said that over a period of five years there were four hundred of these general confessions.

Holy Communion, which had been introduced earlier to the Tehueco nation, is now practiced with more remarkable signs of devotion and reverence. It is considered a great favor and honor to be admitted to this Sovereign Sacrament. The method used by the priest to effect the change required by Christian life in the habits of people accustomed to more freedom or boldness was to tell them that if within a certain amount of time they corrected their sins or faults, he would admit them to Holy Communion. This means has had other unique results as well.

They are obligated to receive Communion on the principal feast days of the Mother of God.[60] On the afternoon preceding such feast days, as soon as they return from their fields, they assemble in church to hear a sermon by the priest about the mystery [pertaining to that particular feast day]. They are already in church before sunrise, where they remain to hear the singing of her Mass and to receive Communion. Afterward, they say her Rosary.[61]

Another custom that was introduced was to have the people from the two Tehueco pueblos gather together to celebrate Holy Week services, one year in one pueblo and the next year in the other. The pueblo where Holy Week was not celebrated in a given year later got to celebrate the Feast of the Most Holy Sacrament,[62] which was revealed for twenty-four hours and accompanied by lights, altar ornaments with greenery, and many flowers. Numerous pictures of the Passion of Christ Our Lord were also hung inside the church. They liked very much to hear sermons on the Passion, listening to them with many tears of devotion. What is to be most esteemed about this feast is that the people hardly leave the church the entire day and night during

58. A legendary reptile with fatal breath and glance.

59. This knotted string brings to mind the Andean *quipu*. It is not known whether the Cáhita used such knotted strings aboriginally, or whether they were something introduced by the Jesuits.

60. These feast days are the Immaculate Conception (December 8); the Annunciation (March 25); Our Lady, Queen of Heaven (May 31); The Assumption (August 15); and the Nativity of the Blessed Virgin Mary (September 8).

61. Following the lead of Saint Ignatius, who purportedly had a vision of Mary and the infant Jesus on the night of his conversion, the Jesuits were (and still are) especially devoted to Mary (Tylenda 1984:109–11).

62. The Feast of Corpus Christi, celebrated on the Thursday after Trinity Sunday (in June), was an important focal point for Jesuit spirituality and devotion and often was celebrated with processions and elaborate ceremony (O'Malley 1993a:156–57).

the twenty-four hours that the Most Holy Sacrament is revealed (the same happens on Holy Thursday, between the time the Sacrament is shrouded and when it is revealed). The priest has nevertheless assigned the wards of the pueblo a turn at prayer in church, which (because there is no clock) is signaled by the sound of a trumpet. They pray on their knees with rosaries and in great order, such that the men are separate from the women. They do this with such devotion and silence that not a disturbing word is heard. Even the mothers take great care that their small children do not cry. [198]

Spaniards from Fort Montesclaros who came at times to attend these feast days and Communions were amazed to see how orderly and devout the Tehueco were, for at one time they had been so warlike. The Spaniards would emerge [from church] saying [it was worth] traveling fifty or sixty leagues to see such a change and to see such Christian piety. They remarked especially on the Indians' composure and the way the Christian Tehueco kept their eyes lowered.

Other unusual demonstrations of Christianity have been observed during the twenty-four hours of prayer [associated with the Feast of the Holy Sacrament] and during Holy Week, but it need not be Holy Week for them to conduct processions. They do so in threes, one for men, another for women, and another for boys and girls. The first is a blood procession, for which they respectfully wear tunics and capes to cover themselves decently. It is a rare man, the exception being those who are ill, who does not flagellate himself to the point of bleeding; the women do so as well, separately. The fervor of this holy exercise is such that the priest has to stay the hand of people who are disabled. Those who are too disabled to participate in the blood scourging walk at the head of the procession, praying in silence with great devotion and carrying a Cross in one hand and a rosary in the other; gone is the jewelry that both the men and women once wore.

The boys and girls in the third procession walk in separate lines, with crowns of thorns on their heads and a small Cross carried on their shoulders. They pray the Rosary they are carrying with great devotion, and they do so without talking or raising their eyes from the ground. They are followed by the older children, who flagellate themselves. They are instructed in this by their fathers and mothers. When the children no longer have enough strength to walk, the parents carry the child and the child's Cross.

As a last word on this demonstration of Christianity, I will add here what was affirmed to me by a very devout priest who administered this mission for many years.[63] He was born in Italy and had been in Rome and many other European cities. He commented to me, "It would bring tears to the eyes of those in Rome, Madrid, Mexico City, and many other large cities to witness such actions by the Tehueco; it seemed that heaven was instilling wisdom and devotion [by way of] their childlike sincerity."

Devotion to the Most Holy Virgin has also been firmly planted in this nation. Young and old alike wear her rosary around their necks and recite it in their homes, along the roads, and in the fields. Some even confess if they ever happen to fail in this [devotion]. The first words they teach their little children when they begin to babble and talk are "Hail Mary," "Our Mother," and other sweet and loving words addressed to this Sovereign Lady.

One of a number of cases told to me by the aforementioned priest that offers proof of this involved one of these boys. He was being held by the hand by his biological father, who was talking to the missionary priest. The child stared very fixedly at the sky, causing the priest to stop and take notice. He asked the child, "What are you staring at?" Jumping for joy, the little angel immediately replied, "I'm looking at my home." "Well, do you want to die?" asked the priest. "Yes," answered the simple child. Then the priest asked, "And where will your soul go?" "Up there to heaven," said the little innocent, "where Holy Mary my Mother is." The priest continued his questions, "And who up there will feed and dress you?" The child answered with great joy and laughter, "My Holy Mother Mary will give me everything." Hanging on the priest's robes, the child unceasingly jumped for joy, imitating, it seemed, that other child, [John] the Baptist, both in the presence of the Mother of God and at her sweet memory. [199]

Those who were present noticed this tender child's unusual affection for this Sovereign Lady, and the *temachtianos*,[64] who are in charge of instruction in the church, said to the priest, "Father, this child almost always attends Mass, and he hears it with his eyes fixed on the image of the Virgin in the church. When it is

---

63. If by "this mission" Pérez de Ribas means the Sinaloa mission as a whole, then perhaps he is referring to the one-time superior, Hernando de Villafañe.

64. As Pérez de Ribas indicates in Chapter 26 of the present Book, temachtianos were Indian catechists who in theory understood the catechism very well and assisted the priest in teaching it to other Indians. In the priest's absence they also conducted religious instruction and regular prayer services (Polzer 1976:42, 49, 101).

time for the Hail Mary, which he prays with extraordinary devotion, he immediately kneels and makes the other boys do the same." Thus, we see the devotion to the Mother of Mercy that has been so impressed upon this nation. This is the present state of the Tehueco, who [only] a short time ago were barbarous, warlike, and governed by sorcerers, rebels, criminals, church-burners, and murderers. Thus are noted the remarkable victories of the Faith, which continue today.

In terms of civility, they live in their houses almost like Spaniards, along very orderly and clean streets. With respect to dress, both men and women cover their entire bodies. The tables at their banquets and feasts as well as the weddings of their children are arranged in such a manner that men and women are divided and men serve men and women serve women. This is done with outward modesty and composure, so much

so that when the Lord Bishop Don Fray Gonzalo de Hermosillo came to administer the Sacrament of Confirmation to these pueblos, and His Eminence and the Father Visitor wanted to tour the pueblo to see people so new [to the Faith], they confessed that they were amazed to see the Indians' good behavior and the reverence and courtesy of both the men and women.

The men have come to learn various arts, including writing, painting, and other skills. There is a carpenter who, for lack of another tool, uses a knife to carve candlesticks or a vase for the altar, which look as though they were made on a lathe. On feast days they play a cane-throwing game on horseback[65] as though they were born to it.

With this we will leave the Tehueco and proceed to the next nation, where we will find other similar triumphs of evangelical law.

CHAPTER XXIV The establishment of a new mission among the nation called Sinaloa; their location and particular customs

Sinaloa is this nation's name for itself, and it is [also] the name of the entire province, because these Indians were the first with whom the Spaniards traded in the early days. Furthermore, the Villa de Carapoa, which was destroyed, was founded not far from here. The Sinaloa's seat and settlements are on the same river as those of the Tehueco and the Zuaque, at its highest point and closest to the slopes of the Topia mountains. Their pueblos begin six leagues upstream from Fort Montesclaros.

These Sinaloa were not steadfast in preserving peace and friendship with the Spaniards. Rather, because of their instability, there were at times disturbances and war. This was because they are of a more hostile and restless nature than other nations. But in the end, by the example of those who had been reduced, they requested a mission and priests to teach them. Captain Hurdaide had received permission to do so from the viceroy when he went to Mexico City. Several months after he reached the Villa de San Felipe, having accom-

panied the captain from Mexico City, Father Cristóbal de Villalta was chosen to found this mission.[66] The principales of the Sinaloa nation came to the Villa de San Felipe to escort him to their pueblos, where he was welcomed with the same demonstrations of joy and celebration that were recorded for priests who established earlier missions among [200] other nations. In this regard the Indians always emulate one another so as not to be seen as inferior. Thus, there were many arches and branches along the way, and throngs of people from the pueblos gathered to welcome the min-

65. *Cañas a caballo*, also known as *juegos de cañas* ("cane play"), was a game introduced to Spain by the Moors, which simulated battle with javelins. Horsemen threw cane sticks at one another, and the object of the game was to catch these canes without being hit (Denhardt 1975:21).

66. After reaching San Felipe in 1604 Villalta in 1605 paid the Sinaloa one or more visits. In November 1606 he began a permanent mission among them; this was at the same time that Méndez went to reside among the Tehueco and Pérez de Ribas began working with the Ahome and the Zuaque.

ister whom God was sending them. They even gave him some of their meager food. The priest treated them well, giving them some trinkets in return.

Then he began discussions of Holy Baptism, of its supreme nature, and of the necessity of [receiving] it in order to attain salvation (for he had learned their language [Cáhita][67] with distinction upon his arrival in Mexico City). They were so eager to be baptized that they immediately set to work on receiving that Holy Sacrament. The priest told them that the adults would first need to take the time to learn the Christian doctrine and God's law and commandments, which they would have to keep. He would, of course, begin baptizing the infants, so their mothers and fathers immediately brought them [to him], with great demonstrations of their desire to see them as Christians. This fervor was so great that even though some of them were far away and on the other side of the river, they swam across with their little children, without being deterred by the high, fast-running waters. At this time five hundred were baptized, four of whom were sick and went to heaven after having been baptized.

Four things that the priest noted as unique in these people were reported in a personal letter in which he gives an account of his visit. The first was that they were very organized and pacific in their pueblos, having gathered there from their ranchos.[68] The men were very dedicated to their fields of maize, cotton, and other grains; the women cared for their houses, wove mantas, and made woven reed mats and baskets. They worked so well together that they appeared to be people of some civility. The second thing was the way they obeyed their principales, their elders, and the priest, doing whatever he ordered. This obedience was such that the priest barely opened his mouth to give an order when it was

already being carried out. One word from the principal cacique and they were all gathered in church. The third thing was the eagerness and pleasure with which they listened to God's word, without tiring even if they were called to hear it often. The fourth thing was the facility with which they understood that which was taught to them. This was such that within four or five days of the priest's arrival in the pueblo, they knew how to make the sign of the Cross and were singing the prayers. They finished the latter with a "Jesus Christ be praised!" that was as clearly pronounced as if they were Spaniards, even though it is quite difficult for them to pronounce this because of the syllables of their language.

When he arrived the priest ordered that he be informed of who was sick, even if they were in the monte or the fields. Because these people were in danger, he would baptize them right away, even if they were older. Along the way he pointed out that those who died after being baptized should be buried as Christians at the church, which was nothing more than an enramada. They received all this very well.

The priest won them over, on the one hand because of his good speaking abilities and on the other because of his peaceful manner (which was very pleasant). He progressed so well with the Sinaloa that upon learning of his arrival in these pueblos and of how happy the Sinaloa were with his company, a neighboring nation of a different language, called Zoe, sent one of its principal caciques to the priest, saying that they would like to see him in their lands. If he went, they would congregate in pueblos and live as Christians. The priest gave them high hopes, with which the cacique and his companions returned very happy. This reduction will be addressed later. [201]

67. Apparently a draft or completed copy of Juan de Velasco's grammar of Cáhita was already available in Mexico City for study by missionaries bound for the northern frontier.

68. It is not clear what Pérez de Ribas means to imply with this statement that the Sinaloa "gathered there from their ranchos." Because he was committed to the "civilizing" effects of Christianity, it may well be that he had difficulty acknowledging the fact that the Sinaloa had lived in nucleated settlements aboriginally. Diego de Guzmán reported in 1533 that the Sinaloa lived in twenty or twenty-five pueblos with one hundred or three hundred houses made from woven reed mats. When Tapia visited the Sinaloa in 1592 he noted that the Sinaloa were living in twenty-five populous rancherías (AGN 1593; Hedrick and Riley 1976:41). It could also be that in the wake of epidemics the Sinaloa had abandoned some or many of their pueblos in favor of rancherías and ranchos.

CHAPTER XXV The entire Sinaloa nation is baptized; a very grave illness strikes; the fruits that were harvested from this and the singular superstitions that were uprooted

Our Lord greatly advanced the good that was begun among the Sinaloa nation with the Baptism of its infants. All the adults also desired to receive that Holy Sacrament, so they came to the church quite frequently for talks and religious instruction. Those who had many wives began turning some of them away (which was no small task) and chose others with whom to be baptized. The clamor raised by the women who had been cast aside was great. The men who abandoned them also suffered because they were thereby separated from the children they had had with these women. It is customary for the mothers to take these children with them, especially if they are not yet grown. The [children's paternal] relatives, along with their demon familiars (especially if they were sorcerers), flew into a rage.

One can clearly understand the degree to which God's favor was necessary here for the battle against such a large number of enemies. This battle was stressed by the Apostle Saint Paul, who had converted the Ephesians. He wrote to them, telling them to take note that their fight was not against enemies made of flesh and blood who can be seen with the eye or felt with the hand. Rather, both he and they were combating powerful invisible princes who had fortified themselves and taken control of the world and were evil incarnate: *No est nobis colluctatio adversus carnem, & sanguinem, sed adversus principes, & potestates, adversus mundi rectores tenebrarum harum, contra spiritualia nequitia.*[69] I know of no other people than these of whom it can be better said that demons had taken control of them. They were governed by these demons, their familiars, and by innumerable sorcerers; it is they who have authority in these pueblos.

It is added here that in this fight the battle was not only against demons and bedeviled people, but also

adversus carnem et sanguine.[70] These weak Indians had to fight against their own flesh, stripping it of that which had become a part of them: *Erunt duo in carne una.*[71] They fought against their own blood, which was that of their children. This blood was drawn from their hearts when they separated themselves from their children, who went with their mothers. Therefore, the battle amounted to being against flesh, blood, the rulers of darkness, and disguised demons. Thus, one could correctly say that at the time in which the general Baptism of adults began, the favor of heaven and the grace of Christ were quite necessary for the battle.

This divine assistance was greatly felt, for through it the priest began the general Baptism of adults. Within a year the whole Sinaloa nation was baptized, to the number of nearly one thousand families. They were reduced to three pueblos [Toro, Vaca, and Chois], [all] within a distance of eight leagues. The evangelical minister was continually out visiting, explaining to them more clearly the mysteries of our Holy Faith, and each day the Sinaloa were developing greater [intellectual] capacity. The newborn children were baptized, those who were reaching the age for contracting holy matrimony did so, those who were sick were ministered to, those who died were buried, and many other [Christian] rites were practiced.

There is a need for Christian charity when conversions are newly begun, and there are certainly opportunities to exercise it among these converts. At this time [the winter of 1606–7] a general illness struck. It seemed that God wanted to begin to reap fruits from this new young vine, and thus the priests' labors increased. Before this illness began there was a full lunar eclipse,[72] which led to the performance of [202] old superstitious ceremonies, particularly by the sorcerers.

---

69. *Margin Note*: Ephes. 6. Ephesians 6:12: "It is not against flesh and blood that we enter the lists; we have to do with princedoms and powers, with those who have mastery of the world in these dark days, with malign influences in an order higher than ours" (Knox 1956:202).

70. Repeating Ephesians 6:12: "against flesh and blood."

71. Mark 10:8: "and the two will become one flesh" (Knox 1956:43).

72. Apparently on September 16, 1606 (Meeus and Mucke 1983: 195).

At the time of the eclipse, in a pueblo where the priest was, the Indians came to the plaza with their bows, arrows, and clubs, shooting arrows toward the sky and furiously beating the woven reed mats covering their houses. This, they said, was in defense of the moon, which they considered to be a living thing. When it eclipsed [they believed] it was dying in a battle with one of its enemies up there in the heavens. They thought, or dreamed, that the moon was constantly at war with this enemy.

The priest emerged [from his house] because of this noise and tried to rescue them from this deception that still persisted from their gentile state. They told him that the eclipse foretold an epidemic of thorns[73] from which many would die. The devil, who persuaded them, added his [own] lies, telling them to surround their houses with thorny branches, which they did. Realizing that this superstition was going to continue, the priest explained more clearly how they were being deceived by the devil, telling them that God alone gave them health and life. Being Christians, they should turn to God for relief and to the Holy Sacrament of Confession to attain pardon for their sins. His speech was somewhat effective at that time, and they burned the thorns. Nevertheless, in people who are so new to the Faith and still living among gentiles it took a lot of effort to completely uproot their superstitions.

As the priest was walking to another pueblo, the principales came out to meet him in the form of a town council to ask that he keep the plague (which they call *cocoliztli*)[74] from reaching them. This is a [type of] request that they had made on other occasions for rain. At the same time those who were already Christians offered to confess in order to placate God. The priest accepted this latter offer, taking them several times to the church to pray and to speak to them so as to completely disabuse them of these lies. He repeated to them that God alone is the author and Lord of life and death. In all of this one can clearly see the continuous battles God's ministers faced among these peoples, both spiritual and temporal. In the end God draws good from

them, and this good was experienced at this time, because the priest's speeches worked in such a way that those who still had instruments of superstition—such as bones, hair, skins, seeds, and stones carved in different figures—brought them to the priest, and they were thrown into a bonfire and burned in the presence of the entire pueblo.

One of the many who had heard these speeches imagined death so vividly that he would not leave the priest's side. He made a general confession, with great sorrow, regret, and remorse for his sins and their circumstances, thus seeming like a long-time Christian. Finally, when he was completely enlightened, he told the priest how the devil had possessed him for twenty years, during which time he had always committed great sins. And another circumstance was added to this unique conversion. When he began his confession, which lasted for several days, he felt happy and healthy, but as he was finishing he felt pangs of death and he himself pressed the priest to administer Extreme Unction. The priest did so because of the Indian's insistence, even though it did not seem to him that he was so near the end. He finally died three days later, with great relief, saying, "Let's go see God." He left great hopes that he was predestined, for the Lord had shown him such compassion, bringing him out of the great darkness in which he had lived for so many years.

In spite of this the serpent attempted to place snares in every path and in all the means to salvation, just as he had done with the forbidden tree, which in and of itself was good. He tried to set his snare in the Sacrament [203] of Extreme Unction, which struggles against this enemy during the rigorous moments before death. He led them to believe that it was through this sacrament that the priests took their lives. For this reason they hid the sick people from the priest, covering them with woven reed mats so he could not see them. And because they were so young in the Faith, they sometimes faltered in their practices. The priest worked very hard to undo other trickery, and Our Lord assisted in particular cases so that they would lose their fear of this Holy Sacrament. They were eventually persuaded that, on the contrary, it was often a means of attaining bodily health (which it is).

One principal Indian was so close to death that it was thought he had no more than an hour to live. He received Extreme Unction, and despite being more than sixty years old, he immediately began to improve and soon felt as healthy and strong as a young man.

73. *Enfermedades de espinas*, which is perhaps a Spanish rendering of a native term or terms for what was probably malignant smallpox, measles, or typhus, each of which produces a rash that, from the Indians' perspective, may have been analogous to the inflammation and swelling that can occur with puncture wounds from cholla or other cacti that abound in the monte.

74. This is a Nahuatl term for epidemic disease or great sickness. It was often used in reference to the most virulent (fulminating) form of smallpox (Reff 1991b:127).

There was another Indian who could no longer speak, which made the priest very sad because he could not make his confession. He administered the holy oils, and then the Indian's speech and senses returned and he confessed. I could write of many such cases in which Our Lord was served so that these peoples might be completely removed from their deception.

This illness caused great damage among them. One day in just a single pueblo three hundred people woke up sick. There were deaths by the thousands and there were unspeakable hardships that the missionary priests of this and other districts had to endure, attending to the Indians both day and night. In addition, there was a lack of human resources as well as food for both the sick people and the priests,[75] who had to take care of everything. They worked non-stop day and night, with no time for rest. These apostolic men carried out all of this with great conformity to divine will, which has as its supreme end sending these tribulations upon recently converted nations. Even though the advantages of these supreme ends are often secret, glimmers and signs of them are always revealed. These are worthy of mention here so that thanks may be given to God.

Among the fruits that God reaped from this illness was the Baptism of sixty-three elderly men and women who, being more hardened to the introduction of Christian ways, had refused Baptism when they were healthy. They had been persuaded by the devil that Baptism would make them sick and cause them to die. The illness struck them even though they were not baptized, and seeing that they were going to die without Baptism, they asked the priest to baptize them. Once he had prepared them he baptized and cleansed them in those heavenly waters. Then within days God took them all in a state of salvation.

There was another Indian, more than eighty years old, who had fled Holy Baptism. She was so obstinate that she had withdrawn and hidden twelve leagues from her relatives, who were trying to persuade her to be baptized. But divine compassion went and sought her out, for her relatives sent word to the priest of what was happening. He sent for her and, having brought her back, he showed her kindness and treated her well. Even though the only sign of illness she showed was some swelling in her feet, he persuaded her to be baptized. God moved her heart in such a way that she affectionately asked for that which she had once so adamantly refused, which amazed those who had seen her former hardheartedness and obstinacy. Having prepared her, the priest [then] baptized her, and it seems God had nothing more in store for the salvation of this poor soul, for within two hours He took her to heaven (as we can imagine). Indeed, His Majesty used a great many means of singular providence so that she [and others] might attain the one means for salvation.

Another gentile Indian was plagued by the devil in [204] several ways. One time in particular he assumed the form of a misshapen snake. This was God's curse, that he should pull himself along the ground like a snake, where he was to live out all the days of his life. The Indian came to request Holy Baptism, which he received, freeing him of this fierce beast from then on. He was very grateful to the Lord, who had granted him such a unique benefit, and he mindfully came to church. With these favors from heaven, this Christian community blossomed and produced more fruits every day.

---

75. Note here Pérez de Ribas' implicit acknowledgement that the epidemic affected other groups (e.g., Tehueco, Zuaque) along the Río Fuerte. Actually the epidemic affected thousands of Indians in Sinaloa as well as in the heart of the Sierra Madre and along the eastern slopes of the great divide (Reff 1991b:147–54).

CHAPTER XXVI The Sinaloa build churches; the outstanding Christianity and civility in which they have persevered to date

Divine grace overcame the aforementioned obstacles to the final establishment of Christianity among this nation. Once they had been baptized, the priest spoke with the principales about replacing their temporary pole churches with more durable ones; the former is what they usually have in the beginning. The principales agreed to this request and built very attractive churches, making sure that they were not inferior to those of their neighbors, the Tehueco and the Zuaque. These churches, where all their major feast days were celebrated (their gentile festivities having already been forgotten), were dedicated in great solemnity. They also dedicated two retablos that had been brought from Mexico City. One was of the Annunciation of the Blessed Virgin Mary and the other was of Saint Christopher. Although they were not rich or sumptuous, they were nevertheless admired and greatly applauded in that Christian land. When they looked at the altar with the Virgin Mary they would say, "How wonderful it will be to see this Lady in heaven!" With that attitude and with frequent visits to church, their love for the matters of our Holy Faith continued to grow. Their great desire to fully learn the catechism was such that the priest could hear them from his house sometimes praying until midnight. The frequency with which [they prayed] was such that children who were nursing started to mouth the words of the Christian doctrine that they had heard spoken by their parents.

There were two remaining obstacles that the priest had to overcome to complete this nation's conversion to Christianity. One was an old, very influential, and much-loved cacique who was very stubborn and hostile toward Holy Baptism. He had always remained hidden in the montes, protected by others, notwithstanding that the captain had wanted him captured because he knew he was a scandal to his nation. Divine providence, however, arranged another way to remedy this situation. The cacique had a son whom the missionary priest tried to win over so that he could learn his father's whereabouts. The son was finally conquered by the priest's pleas and revealed where the cacique had

retreated. He added that he was very ill and that he would accompany the priest if he wanted to go see him. The priest accepted the son's offer and went with him to see the cacique, who had the ferocious countenance of an Indian of great valor even though he was near death. The priest attempted to convince him to listen to the doctrine of the Faith and to receive Holy Baptism. God changed the cacique, who became very well disposed to the Holy Sacrament of Baptism, which he received. Three days later he died. God thus liberated the captain and the priest from having to worry about this cacique who, because of his great authority, could have disrupted the Sinaloa nation with a single word.

The other obstacle that the missionary priest worked hard to eliminate was suicide, which was carried out by eating the [205] leaves of a weed[76] that is readily found in the monte and which even grows among their houses. It is easy to eat, and with the same facility it causes a loss of consciousness; you can also die from it within twenty-four hours or less. An Indian man or woman did not need a significant reason to use this type of evil and desperate means; a fight between a husband and wife was sufficient. God, however, wanted to banish this abuse, and in the end the priest conquered this gentile custom with good words and speeches. Then Christian customs and laws became well established in this nation, and once this jungle was razed and the weeds were uprooted, the evangelical seed began to spread and yield happy fruits, as did the divine word and frequent participation in and respect for the sacraments.

Since the time they were baptized, many have made general confessions, assuring for themselves what at the beginning of their Christianity they affirmed by chance, without completely understanding (as they do now) the integrity of this wholesome sacrament. It was very common for them to prepare for these confessions by spending two to three weeks going over their entire lives. The use of the Sovereign Sacrament of Holy

76. There are a large number of desert trees and shrubs such as the *yerba de flecha* tree (*Euphoria biloculare*) that yield potential poisons (Nentvig 1980:50).

Communion was also introduced very successfully, and they received it with great preparation and reverence. Our Lord mercifully punished an Indian who failed in this regard when he dared to receive Holy Communion after concealing a sin in confession. The Indian was unable to pass the Sacred Host for a long time and became ill as a result. He then called the priest and made a good confession, revealing what had happened and learning a lesson in the process.

The devotion to the Virgin's Holy Rosary was also established with special affection in this nation. The custom of wearing that beautiful jewel around the neck was the first devotion introduced to both men and women. So as not to go without it, they collected a small wild fruit that was suitable for making rosaries, and they made others from another colored wood. These rosaries were so beautiful that they also attained temporal gains from them.[77] They are generally very careful in the practice of this sweet devotion to the Mother of God, from whom Christendom has received many benefits. They do not forget it, even when they travel, for they have often been encountered on the road carefully executing this wholesome exercise. They walk along the road in groups, forming two choirs,[78] praying the Rosary as they go. This custom is born of another they had established in their pueblos, where on Saturday afternoons the people pray as a group in church. They are led by the temachtianos (who oversee catechism), who divide the men and women into separate choirs. The captain and his soldiers witnessed these happy devotions on the roads when they undertook military expeditions in which there were people from several nations. When the troops would stop, the Sinaloa would retire apart from the others to pray the Rosary in the manner previously described. The captain and the soldiers told the priest of the Sinaloa's unusual actions, and not without reason, for they were struck by such a change in a people so new to the Faith who had been raised with ferocious customs that were so distant from divine light.

The replacement of barbarous customs with holy Christian ones does not end here. Another no less pious example involves what has become a well-established custom among the Sinaloa involving the deceased and the souls in purgatory. When the bell is rung at the appointed time of the evening for the souls of the dead (as is the practice in all the pueblos), all the Sinaloa immediately kneel and begin praying aloud two decades of the Rosary, regardless of where they are or what they are doing. In this way each week they complete their devotion and prayers [206] for their dead.

As the following small yet worthy case indicates, they did not tolerate any interruption of this pious devotion. Two Spanish soldiers who came from far away, tired and hungry, arrived at a Sinaloa pueblo called Toro. They were looking for food and shelter and happened to go to the house of some Indians who were praying for the souls [in purgatory]. They spoke to those inside, but no one answered. The Spaniards spoke insistently, but the Indians apparently felt that the travelers should wait until they had finished their devotion. One devout woman who grew tired of the soldiers' disturbing behavior angrily interrupted them, "These could not be our Spaniards, they must be demons who want to impede our prayers for the deceased." Turning to the disturbers, she said, "If you are truly Spaniards, you will wait until we have finished praying, and then we will help you." The woman spoke sincerely and with reason, for the trouble endured by the souls in purgatory and the help they need has no comparison with that of a traveler, even if he is very tired and dying of hunger.

The Sinaloa's devotion to the dead continues [today], and all of them gather as a community to pray the Rosary for the deceased on the eve of All Souls' Day, which the Church has established for their commemoration. On this night many scourge themselves in church. The following day they bring offerings as alms to the church. After someone is buried the relatives frequently go to the church and scourge themselves; others confess and receive Communion on behalf of the deceased, aiding him with this holy supplication.

Their behavior during times of sickness and drought, when their newly planted fields lack water, is also testimony to how their Christian customs are well rooted in the Faith. There is no recollection of asking their sorcerers (as they used to) for help with sickness and drought; instead they turn to she who is the Mother of Mercy. They recognize her as such and do not know her by any other name than their Mother, so they call her 'Our Holy Mother Mary', in the same way that we call her 'Most Holy Virgin'. They go to her with the aforementioned needs, praying the Rosary collectively in choirs, marching in processions with her holy image, and doing other acts of penance. The Sovereign Queen of Heaven has demonstrated such propitiousness to this, her devoted nation, that a priest who catechized

---

77. Presumably using them as items for sale or trade.

78. That is, antiphonally—one group would say the first part of the Hail Mary and Our Father and the second group would chant the second half of each prayer.

them for twelve years asserts that in times of need they never lacked the aid of this merciful Lady and Mother.

Although I have just related the virtues of this nation, because of the law of history I do not want to keep silent about how it sinfully strayed at this time [1611]. In the sacred Evangelists' holy history they did not pardon the fall of Saint Peter,[79] who was fervent in his Faith and love for his Sacred Master. Everything serves to teach a lesson, as the present case shows. Some gentile and barbarous Indians cruelly killed (as they usually do) some of the Sinaloa's relatives. Accordingly, once Captain Diego Martínez de Hurdaide captured the murderers, he sentenced them to death. He sent for the Sinaloa's missionary priest, who was nearby and knew the language of those who were being executed. The captain asked him to come to Fort Montesclaros to prepare the murderers for death, and the priest presented himself for this very pious task. The Sinaloa learned that those who had killed their relatives were going to be executed, and being ill advised and mindless of the piety they should maintain as Christians, in the priest's brief absence from their pueblos they [207] celebrated the deaths of those who were to be executed with one of their former gentile dances. If God had put up with their doing so in the past, it was because they and other gentiles who behaved similarly were not part of His flock and still lived in darkness. But once they were His children He, as their Father, was careful to punish them, in conformity with what was written by the Apostle [Saint Paul]: *Quod si extra disciplinam estis, ergo adulteri, et non filij*.[80] As punishment for this celebration, God sent a sudden outbreak of smallpox that affected almost all of their children. When the priest returned at the end of three days he found three hundred boys and girls afflicted with this illness. Because it is like the plague for them, the majority of the children died. It was understood that this was a punishment from God, because it only struck the pueblo where the gentile celebration took place; another Sinaloa pueblo nearby that did not celebrate remained untouched by the illness. It was noted that those who were most responsible for these barbarous dances suffered the most because more of their children died.

Just as God often pleases parents by doing good by their children, He also punishes the parents through their children, although He is merciful toward those

who are most innocent. Thus it happened in our case, because the priest wrote that it was marvelous to see how the children accepted illness and, in the case of those who died, death. "When I went to administer the sacraments to those who were able to receive them, it brought (he says) tears to my eyes to hear their filial dialogue, which was full of cordial familiarity with Our Lady the Virgin, whom they called 'Our Dear Mother, Our Sweetest Mother', whom they wanted to go see and enjoy." These devout pleas were at times so loud that the priest, who was walking through the pueblo visiting the sick, could hear them from the plaza and the streets.

So that the conversion and Christianity of the Sinaloa nation are not concluded with the sin they committed when their knowledge of Christian obligations was limited, I return to the recognition that this nation deserves. I wish to contrast the previous case with another of great edification that is characteristic of long-time Christians, and even of the early Church. The Huite (a gentile nation), whose reduction will be presented in two later chapters, were inspired to become Christians by the example of their neighbors, the Sinaloa. The latter were very happy to see the Huite (who were their mortal enemies in their heathenism) converted to our Holy Faith. Several obstacles arose in the [conversion] of the Huite; they spoke a different language and lived in inaccessible mountaintops, in rancherías on the other side of the Río Sinaloa. The pious Sinaloa overcame all of these obstacles through an act that was very typical of loyal Christians and worthy of memory: they helped their former enemies. The priest notified and exhorted the Sinaloa to do their part in this pious task, so [in 1612] they invited the Huite to their pueblos, bringing three hundred of them so that they could learn the Sinaloa language and the priest could learn Huite, thereby facilitating their Baptism and religious instruction. This Christian charity shone even brighter when the Sinaloa received their guests (although gentiles) with great revelry and rejoicing. They were very generous with them and treated them with great love, supporting them for a long time as if they were their brothers, until they were ready to be baptized. This would have been a notable act even for long-time Catholic Christians. [208]

The Sinaloa also gave land to farm to those Huite who wished to settle in their pueblos, and they gave the Huite children clothing and even their own personal adornments. They considered them their own children and treated them as such. Indeed, their affection for them was so great that they even removed the adornments from [their own children] and gave them

---

79. Specifically, Peter's three denials of Christ.

80. *Margin Note*: Ad Hebr c. 12. Hebrews 12:8: "you must be bastards, not true sons, if you are left without [correction]" (Knox 1956:238).

to these foreign children.[81] A notable Christian cacique of the Sinaloa, who will be referred to later when the complete settlement and religious instruction of the Huite are discussed, made a great effort in the aforementioned acts.

The history of the conversion of those who are truly Sinaloa and the state in which their Christianity perseveres today will be concluded by recounting [here] the opinion of the priests who minister to these missions. Their feeling is that in considering all the Christians in this province, the Faith of Christ Our Lord and His Gospel have been most firmly established, developed, and fruitful among the Sinaloa. Their progress has been great and these improvements have been not only spiritual and divine, but also human and civil. In their pueblos they have all built flat-roofed adobe houses. Many have dedicated themselves to learning trades, which is necessary in a republic. There are even some among them who are so skillful that they have learned to make musical instruments such as flutes, as well as altarpieces such as ciboria[82] and other vessels. In the end there is no land so wild that it cannot be improved by cultivation. This is a truth that is experienced in these missions in terms of both the human and the divine. It is an experience that can greatly encourage the evangelical ministers among these peoples, [convincing them] that their labors are not in vain. Let us now move on to other conversions that are calling us.

CHAPTER XXVII The gentle way in which the Zoe nation, which borders the Sinaloa, was converted to our Holy Faith

When we traverse the Province of Sinaloa, we invariably encounter the nations that inhabit the sierras surrounding it to the east and north. The Zoe were mountain Indians whose settlements were along the upper part of the same river as the Sinaloa, in the foothills of its mountains.[83] They were a wilder people and spoke a different language than the Sinaloa; there must have been about five hundred families or male heads-of-household in their rancherías. This nation received word that their neighbors, the Sinaloa (who were seven leagues away), had welcomed Father Cristóbal de Villalta into their pueblos and were very happy with his instruction and company. Therefore, the Zoe sent a cacique to ask this priest to come to their lands to instruct and baptize them as [he had done with] the Sinaloa.[84] Although the priest, who was a very fervent laborer, gave them firm hopes of granting their wishes, he had to postpone this for a more convenient time when he was not so busy. God began preparing them through a most gentle means that was very consonant with the law of grace. As the Doctors of the Church have explained in detail with respect to the peoples who join the Church, God would convert the hillsides and fields through the whistling of the Shepherd: *Sibilabo eis, et congregabo illos, quia redemi eos, et multiplicabo*,[85] they come not because of the blows of a staff or a rod or with a shepherd's hook, but because of the soft and gentle whistling of a loving Shepherd, which is what the word *sibilabo* indicates. With this whistling

---

81. This act of removing adornments from their own children and giving them to strangers was probably a ritual act of fictive kinship. Recall that the Sinaloa had just lost several hundred of their children to smallpox.

82. *Sagrarios*. The ciborium is a sacred vessel shaped somewhat like a chalice, which is used to distribute the consecrated Eucharist to large numbers of communicants (O'Brien 1879:77).

83. Very little is known about the Zoe and many of the sierra-dwelling groups that Pérez de Ribas discusses in this and subsequent chapters. The Zoe, Huite, Guazápare, Tubari, and Témori, who all lived along the headwaters of the Río Fuerte, were largely destroyed by disease between 1612 and 1660; by 1700 they ceased to exist as distinct cultures (Reff 1991b:225–28; Sauer 1934, 1935).

84. This was apparently in 1610, when a Zoe delegation visited and made peace with Captain Hurdaide.

85. *Margin Note*: Zach. c. 10. Zacharias 10:8: "Flock of my ransoming, see how they gather at my call! Thriving now as they throve long since" (Knox 1956:851).

God called the mountain nations (which are recorded in this and subsequent chapters) to leave the mountains and cliffs. Their conversion was accomplished without warfare, conflicts, or disturbances, for *quia redemi eos*,[86] He redeemed them with His blood. [209]

It was while the priest was instructing the Sinaloa nation that the Zoe heard the holy whistles of the Christian doctrine, which their neighbors learned and sang with pleasure. And it was by this means alone that God gently brought them to the priest, asking him to come to their lands and rancherías to share with them the teachings that they would so willingly receive. The priest went to visit them [87] with the same goodwill. He preached our Holy Faith, emphasizing their duties toward it and simultaneously letting them know that it was necessary for them to settle in pueblos where they could be instructed and have churches like the rest of the nations. They gladly agreed to everything that was proposed to them. He baptized a good number of infants who were offered to him, in order to take possession of that new flock in the name of Christ, and from that time on it belonged to Him.

At the outset of the conversion of these mountain peoples, there were two special cases that demonstrate the particular providence by which Our Lord protects His evangelical ministers. The priest recorded them in the following way:

When I was with my mountain people, a tlatolli, or speech, was made concerning an uprising during which the Indians were going to take up arms and kill me. When one of the boys from the church who was with me heard about this, he went to one of the caciques who accompanied me and told him in great secrecy that some Indians were speaking evil and that they wanted to kill me. As soon as the cacique heard this, without saying anything to me, he went to notify his [fellow] Sinaloa of what was happening. Of their own initiative they immediately took up their bows and arrows and other weapons of war to defend and protect me. They declared that this news had worried them so much that when they heard it, they immediately set out to rescue me, without even eating. I thanked them for their goodwill, and it amused them when I told them that if the mountain people had taken up their bows, it must have been to hunt game or fish for me and those in my company. So that the mountain people would not be angered by this display [of force], as well as to show them that I trusted them, I intentionally stayed with them several days more, and with this the trouble subsided. Through it, whether by truth or by lies, the devil was attempting to stir up these people whom God wanted to save.

The priest further added:

In the second case we can see the supreme paths taken by predestination in some of these souls. I found a very sick old man who was nothing but skin and bones, and furthermore he was deaf. When I went to see him he was doing so poorly that he seemed more dead than alive. I spoke to him, but he did not respond. I made an ear trumpet out of a reed and a funnel of paper and placed it next to his ear. When I spoke to him through it he barely seemed to hear me. In spite of everything, I persisted for half an hour with him and, commending him to Our Lord, I asked him if he wanted to go to heaven to experience great joy, consolation, and the sight of God. He finally gave some signs of being able to hear, and little by little he began to understand me, even when I took the ear trumpet away and spoke to him not loudly, but in a low voice. Like anyone with good hearing, he responded to what I asked him, and finally, through God's will, he was able to learn the mysteries of our Holy Faith. I baptized him, much to his consolation as well as my own. If this Indian was in fact deaf, then the word of Our Lord is able to overcome this and more, for it was written that with His coming, the sealed ears of the deaf would be opened. And if his deafness was feigned, it was even more beneficial for God to cure him of that which arose from his rebellious will. The following day I had him brought to the church, where I anointed him with the holy oils, performed the rest of the holy rites, and administered Extreme Unction. Then God Our Lord took him away.

Thus wrote the priest, who was correct in his conclusion, [210] because it is clear that such singular providential acts by God for placing this soul on the road to salvation would not be thwarted.

The priest was very busy with the great harvest among the Sinaloa. Because some of the rancherías of this nation were on the other side of this river, which was very wide, particularly at flood time, the priest could not get across to assist them at times when the sacraments were needed or on other occasions. Therefore, he proposed to the Zoe that they settle in a place that was more convenient for these purposes. Although there were problems at first, these were eventually overcome and they congregated in a place that was assigned to them. There they formed a pueblo of five hundred male heads-of-household, where the priest finished baptizing the entire nation, which numbered fifteen hundred individuals.

Although at the outset these people were converted through the aforementioned gentleness, after a while Satan (who never sleeps and whose barrage of artillery never falters or ceases) invented various pretexts and whims to stir them up. He reminded them of their montes and wild fruit trees as well as other freedoms of their heathenism. This stirred them up and turned some

---

86. "[Flock] of my ransoming" (see note 85).

87. Villalta apparently made this trip in 1612.

of them back to their Egypt, to which they withdrew for a time. During this period [88] the priest's life was in danger because many times even when the priests are among docile nations, these blessed ministers hear their death sentences, which are a glorious herald of their labors. But through rewards and praise and then by endurance and patience and the means born of his fervent charity, this priest converted these lambs and they settled in their pueblo.

Another priest [89] who came later to instruct the Zoe got them to agree to build their church for the express purpose of increasing their fondness for this place. This is in fact what usually happens when they see their own handiwork. There they built a church that was so beautiful and so decorated with paintings, which they like very much, that when it was finished the majority of those in the pueblo did not emerge from it during the entire day. When they did, it was with great admiration and boasting that there was not a single nation in the province that had enjoyed a church that was so beautiful, which it truly was. It had taken a great deal of work to drag the forty large handsome cedar timbers for the roof down from the mountains on their shoulders. The church was dedicated with great solemnity in a celebration attended by many people from the surrounding nations. Mass was said by Father Julio Pascual (a holy man), who, as will be told, later died a martyr [in 1632] at the hands of another mountain nation not far from there.

The Zoe were not content with having built a church that they were fond of looking at, especially those who had been reared and uprooted from the montes. Therefore, they all gladly built adobe houses with flat roofs, forming streets and a plaza in the pueblo. This nation completed its settlement in such a way that they never again attempted to rebel or move. Instead, they remained there very peacefully, just as they do today. They also attend religious instruction, and just like the most veteran Christians in the province they also attend the other Christian exercises, including feast days, Christmas, Epiphany, Easter, Pentecost, Holy Week ceremonies with blood processions, Confession, Communion, and devotion to the Rosary. The fragrant flowers of infants that are plucked for heaven now grow where once there were thorns.

I will not pause here to write about the unusual cases of the fierce Indians of this nation who were transformed into gentle lambs, or about sick persons who departed for heaven with baptismal grace, or about the barbarous superstitions and customs that were uprooted and forgotten, because these cases were similar to those that have just been recorded for other nations. Such cases were not lacking in this nation, whose prosperous harvest I am happy to declare. In this little corner of Sinaloa [211] fifteen hundred souls were baptized, and they live in exemplary Christianity; not included in this number are the fruits that will later be produced and harvested. We will now go on to another nation that was transplanted from even rougher sites and cliffs.

88. Pérez de Ribas jumps ahead here to the year 1624; Captain Hurdaide ascended the Río Fuerte and quieted the Zoe.

89. In 1620 Juan Castini replaced Villalta, who had gone to replace Pérez de Ribas among the Yaqui. The anua of 1626 notes that the Zoe had built one of the finest churches on the Río Fuerte.

CHAPTER XXVIII The conversion to our Holy Faith of some rancherías and people who inhabited cliffs and precipices

The name for the Huite nation in the Sinaloa language is the same as [that for] 'archers' (these people's archers must be outstanding).[90] They lived in huts at rancherías or in caves among the high cliffs and sharp precipices, which only a deer or a bird could penetrate. To reach them they helped one another by pulling themselves up, one over the other. These places were so dry that the only water they had to drink was rainwater that collected in shallow depressions in the rock. The best-situated ranchería was in a little valley where there were two hours or less of daylight, for the sun was blocked by the high mountains and formidable peaks. About three hundred families lived in these dreadful places. Even though they were only seven leagues from the Sinaloa nation, they did not trade or communicate with them except when they killed one another with bows and arrows. They had no knowledge of any other world except their own among the cliffs. These people ate the flesh of their enemies whenever they could, and the person who hung the most enemy skulls over his doorway or cave was considered the bravest in the nation.

These people were to find divine grace by the special means of a Huite boy, whom the Sinaloa had captured and given to the priest for him to rear and teach the Christian doctrine and the Sinaloa language. When the priest who attended the Sinaloa nation got news of these withdrawn people,[91] he was moved to send some Christians to that nation. He risked sending them (because he was unable to enter that place) so that they could discuss peace and friendship with the Huite, whom he sent some small gifts. The good Christian Sinaloa agreed to make the journey because they wished for their cliff-dwelling neighbors to enjoy peace in the doctrine of the Gospel in the same way they did.

Fortunately, the journey was successful. The Sinaloa were well received by those mountain people (who previously killed them). They distributed gifts, including bows, arrows, salt, and knives. Furthermore, in order to assure a more peaceful settlement, the Sinaloa got the Huite to send some of their children to the priest to grow up among the Sinaloa and learn their language and the Christian doctrine. Afterward they could return to their own lands to teach their nation. The Sinaloa promised to treat these children as if they were their own. The Huite agreed, and so it was that gifts broke down the barrier of the cliffs. These barbarians were softened by the Sinaloa's gifts and kindness. We can say that the Huite gave parts of their own flesh, their children, to those whom they feared as mortal enemies and whose flesh they once had eaten. Therefore, through divine grace God encouraged the Sinaloa to invite their enemies (which is what the Huite were) to become friends and to trust them. This is the plan that God laid out for recovering this flock.

The Sinaloa ambassadors returned very happily to the priest. [212] Afterward, many Huite followed and brought some of their children to learn the doctrine and the Sinaloa language and to prepare themselves for Holy Baptism and Christianity, which they said they now desired. Our Lord [saw to it] that these good beginnings prospered. Three hundred individuals, young and old, left their cliffs to come live among the Sinaloa, who received them in their pueblo and homes with such great displays of affection and kindness that they took the adornments from their own children and placed them on the children of their new guests, just as we noted they had done with the Zoe. For his part the priest also celebrated their arrival, showing much paternal affection to these little children whom God was bringing to his home.

The infants were the first of these three hundred people to be baptized. They were followed by the adults, who were baptized in two groups with all possible solemnity. The Sinaloa showed great piety and joy during these Baptisms, which they celebrated with feasting and dances. Some soldiers who were present fired a round [of shots] with their harquebuses. The angels

---

90. Buelna (1891) lists the following Cáhita words: *huicori* 'bow for shooting arrows'; *huihua* 'arrow'. Note that these both have the root *hui-*, as does the name Huite.

91. The priest in this and the subsequent chapter is Cristóbal de Villalta, who describes the events of this time (1611–12) in a letter in the anua of 1612.

surely fired another round to match it, for we have it on faith that the angels hold similar celebrations whenever even a single sinner is converted. Thus, within a short time part of the three hundred Huite were baptized. On numerous occasions they visited their relatives who had remained among the mountain peaks, telling them how well they were doing and how they enjoyed the catechism, church, and life among the Christian Sinaloa.

Several years went by and there were still some Huite who remained in their inaccessible homeland. Nevertheless, they were so fond of communication with the priest and the Christians that they came down often from their high peaks to visit and see their baptized children. They made an agreement with the priest that even though [at that time] they chose not to settle in a place where they could be instructed along with the rest of their group, they would stay in touch with the priest and obey all his requests. They made the same agreement with the captain of the garrison, whom they went to visit. What is more amazing for such an intractable nation was that during the years that this nation remained in its mountaintops, many gentiles would of their own free will bring their newborn children to the priest to be baptized. For his part, throughout the year the priest would send some well-trained youths from the church who were very well instructed in the matters of the Holy Sacrament of Baptism to catechize and baptize whoever was ill or in danger of dying. In addition, the temachtianos would bring those who had previously been baptized as infants and were now seven years old and ready to learn the catechism to the pueblos of the Sinaloa so that they could become members of the Church. The Huite handed them over very willingly, and it was amazing to see how the children left their biological parents to go to live among those who so shortly before had been their mortal enemies, trusting that they were under the protection of their spiritual father.

This nation wavered in its decision to move from such a harsh and inconvenient place, but the priest was moved by his desire for the welfare of these reluctant souls, so he finally decided to go himself to seek them out in the hillsides and cliffs, even if it meant he would have to overcome many difficulties, imitating that shepherd in the Gospel who left his other ninety-nine sheep to go and rescue the one who was lost in the thickets. Accompanied by some of his Christian Indians, the priest went to the one Huite locale that he was able to reach. [213] He had sent word ahead of his impending arrival and they received him with great joy, providing him and his companions with maize, beans, and squash. They had also prepared two enramadas, one that served as a church and another as the priest's house.

During this visit, which led to the complete reduction and conversion of these people, the priest first preached to them about Christian doctrine and the necessity of Baptism for their salvation. He also discussed how beneficial it would be for them to settle in a place where they could be instructed. They finally agreed to leave their very harsh lands. The second thing [the priest did] was to baptize some children who had not received this Holy Sacrament, as well as some old people and some of the sick who were in danger of dying. The Indians celebrated these Baptisms and the priest's arrival with great feasting in their fashion. The final thing, which gladdened the priest and made his journey so worthwhile, was that when word spread that a priest had come to the ensconced Huite, great numbers of people from other nations much farther inland came to see and meet the man who was instructing Christians. The priest treated them very kindly and gave gifts to all these people. He encouraged them as well by telling them that some day priests would reach their lands to teach them how to live like human beings and to preach to them the word of the Gospel, which all men throughout the world need for the salvation of their souls. This preaching was the foundation of the reduction and conversion to the Faith of these other peoples [the Guazápare, Témori, and Varohío], who were even more remote than the Huite. These peoples will be recorded further ahead. After the priest had spent several days in this holy task he happily returned to his district among the Christian Sinaloa.

CHAPTER XXIX The priest prepares to reduce the Huite; the remarkable journey made by a principal cacique who assisted with the reduction of this and other alien nations

The priest's zealous desire and concern to see the Huite nation reduced to God did not diminish. He knew that to achieve this it would be necessary for them to leave those cliffs and gather in a suitable place where they could be taught the doctrine, build a church, and form a civilized pueblo and dwelling place for men. He was determined to work very diligently to put this into action. Therefore, he placed several Christian faithful who were familiar with the entire region in charge of looking in utmost secrecy for a place with good lands and water where the Huite could settle. Once they found a place he ordered them to build some enramadas for a church and a house. The following day he gathered some Sinaloa and Huite Christians, as well as some of the gentile Huite who lived in the peaks of the mountains, and he went to this place. After he said Mass with all those people gathered together, he spoke to them, explaining the advantages of that reduction, which would provide the Huite with better lands. He was [trying] to persuade those who had not come down from their harsh mountains to follow the example of their relatives who, in order to become Christians, had come to live among the Sinaloa, where they were treated very well. Many of them now desired to have [the other Huite] close by as brothers in the Faith. These and other advantages were presented to them, and they were asked to [214] have a look around and see with their own eyes the aforementioned conveniences. If they were satisfied, they were to clean and remove from that field all the weeds and trees that stood in the way. They were [also] to open a path for the priest to go and visit them from the Sinaloa pueblos, because this was impossible without a path through such rough terrain.

The Huite accepted this proposal and later a good number of them came down from their peaks and cleared a place [for a settlement] and opened a path, cutting down trees and clearing the rough terrain. They built a wooden church and a fair number of families made their homes there. Within a short time the priest began baptizing the adults, who were steadfast in coming to church to learn the doctrine and Christian practices. They were becoming quite well molded in their [new Christian] customs and were forgetting their old ones, which was no small thing given that their former way of life was [still] so fresh in their minds.

On this occasion God offered another means that was very useful for finally winning these people over. This was a favor from the priest in response to their petitions and pleas. They asked the priest to negotiate with people of the Chínipa nation, which had already been reduced, to turn over certain slaves to him.[92] These were women and children who had been captured when these people were at war with the Huite (who rarely spared their lives).[93] The priest was to bring them out of captivity to the Christian pueblos. He set to work on this most pious task, and in order to please the Huite, he begged the Chínipa to hand those captives over to him. They responded to this petition very willingly, turning over all the slaves, men as well as women. The priest settled them in the homes of good Sinaloa Christians, who were to rear them, teach them the doctrine, and mold them in good customs so that they could be baptized and brought into a state [of grace]. All this was carried out and everyone was baptized. This action on the Huite's behalf made them more affectionate toward the priest and helped to win them over.

Even with things in this state there were still a few reluctant souls in their sierras and peaks, for not everyone obeys divine calling with the same promptness. Divine providence provided a means worthy of being

92. Here and elsewhere we have translated *piezas de esclavos* as slaves. The Spanish original better reflects the European likening of slaves to livestock or other movable property.

93. Pérez de Ribas may exaggerate the murder of women and children taken captive, as more often than not his own examples are of women whose lives are spared (see, e.g., the woman captive who marries Don Bautista in the present chapter). It seems more likely that women and children were spared (provided they were cooperative) because they contributed significantly to the productivity of the lineages or kin groups into which they were assimilated.

recorded here that was the only way of completing the reduction of all of this nation's rancherías. In the Sinaloa nation there was a principal Indian who was their governor and an exemplary Christian, deserving of the memorial I will give later concerning his virtues. His name was Don Bautista. The priest saw in him a great capacity for assisting in the reduction of the neighboring gentile nations because the latter thought highly of him. He was a widower, so the priest persuaded him to consider taking as his wife a wise and chaste young maiden from the Huite nation who, even though she had been one of the slaves taken captive by the Chínipa, had been raised in total chastity. The governor agreed, and with his own pleasure as well as that of his people, he was married to the one whom the priest had told him would be good company for him. The Huite were content to be related to an Indian whom they so highly esteemed and from whom they had received good works.

With this good opportunity the priest asked Don Bautista to go with his Huite wife to visit her relatives and try to win them over so that they might all finally be reduced to a church and pueblo. The priest offered all of them a warm reception and told Don Bautista to advance and penetrate the sierra to try to establish friendship and peace with the nations that (as was said) lived in that extensive mountain range. God was preparing them for that which we will be told of. Don Bautista agreed to the journey most willingly for the good of those peoples. [215] He carried it out [in the winter of 1619–20], taking along his wife and some of his closest Christian relatives. This journey started out well, for they were received by the gentile Huite with great joy. They had invitations from their relatives in all the nation's rancherías. The gentile Huite were not content with this alone; they also wanted to escort them to the gentile nations who were their allies, which were spread out across the space of six days' journey into the mountains. These were the Guazápare, the Chínipa, the Ihío, the Témori, and others of whom I will write in their own time.

Everywhere the couple went they were received with joy, festivity, and a multitude of people. Each group emulated the other in their gatherings and willingness to abandon the mountains to come and see the Christians whom they had heard about from so far away. They had especially heard about the Huite woman who was the governor's wife, who had previously been a slave to the Chínipa. Now they saw her very much loved, adorned, and honored, married to the governor of the

Christians who was very famous among those nations. They insisted on bringing them all types of small gifts, and they hung on their words until midnight, listening to speeches about the customs and lifestyle of the Christians and the priests who taught them the catechism. The [couple] spoke of the peace, friendship, and security in which they lived, the churches they erected in their pueblos, etc.

What most amazed those people and was a singular proof and example of Don Bautista's Christianity is that every morning, according to their instructions from the priest, the Christians gathered together away from the gentiles and knelt to say the prayers of the Christian doctrine. At dusk they would assemble to recite the Rosary that they wore around their neck, as well as prayers for the dead. They never missed a day of this devotion, to which we can attribute the fact that God Our Lord gave these devout Christians success in their journey. And through this [journey] His divine providence began preparing many of these people who would later receive the Gospel.

These Christians found something of particular consolation farther into the mountains, in [the territory of] one of those distant nations. In a concavity like a niche they found three painted Crosses. From this they deduced that some Christians had passed through the area. These could have been left by the men we mentioned in Book I [Cabeza de Vaca and his companions], who came to Sinaloa from La Florida following their failed expedition. Alternatively, they could have been left by Christians from the Province of Santa Bárbara, which lies on the eastern slopes of that mountain range.[94]

Don Bautista and his people had found a very warm welcome in those nations, and in the end they returned most happy. They brought along some ten or twelve caciques to see the priest, along with many other Indians from the caciques' territories. When the people in the Sinaloa pueblos learned that these strangers were coming with their governor, many went out to meet them on horses, which their guests had never seen. The Sinaloa had been busy preparing a welcoming celebration with arches of branches, food, dancing, drums, and all types of merriment. This was along the way; when they arrived at the pueblo [Vaca] they found new festivi-

94. Spanish miners and ranchers flocked to the Santa Bárbara region in the closing quarter of the sixteenth century. During this time they made forays into the mountains to the west looking for additional silver deposits (Griffen 1979).

ties, with bells, flutes, trumpets, and dances. The Christian Sinaloa women, along with the Christian Huite women (who lived among the Sinaloa), went to the pilgrim gentile women and embraced them. They gave them gifts and celebrated their welcome with a charity very much in the fashion of Christian women. They did this with [an] incredible [amount of] joy for people who not much earlier barely showed any sign of humanity.

The priest [Cristóbal del Villalta], who was waiting for the pilgrims at the door of his home, was full of joy at seeing those new flocks that God was bringing out of the most hidden mountains and valleys to be reduced to His Church. [216] When the pilgrims spied the priest from a distance they were told by the Christians who accompanied him that he was the father of the Christians. All at once they broke out in joyful shouting and noisemaking and ran to him as fast as possible, gathering around him. Kneeling, they clung to his clothing, and without taking their eyes from him they repeated over and over, "*Nono, Nono,*" which means, "Our Father, Our Father." Standing, they began to speak loudly to the priest in their own tongue. The priest called an interpreter and discovered that these gentiles were trying to convey their joy at having come from such distant places to see Christian pueblos and the priest who taught the doctrine and considered them his children. They added that even though they had traveled for very many days, enduring unusual hardship, they deemed it worthwhile to see the man who loved everyone. Trusting in the fact that he was a father to all those nations to whom he taught the doctrine, they had dared to travel through the lands of their former enemies, whom they no longer feared, knowing that they all looked upon and obeyed him as they would a father.

The priest responded to them with similar statements full of love and affection. Then he ordered that the men enter his house and be given food and treated as well as possible. The women were taken to an enramada outside his house and given the same treatment. Once the meal was finished the principales of the pueblo took these guests to their homes and treated them with singular affection and kindness. Sermons were heard almost the entire night from all different parts [of the pueblo]. They spoke of establishing friendships in perpetual brotherhood so that they might treat each other as brothers and communicate with one another from that time forward. As a sign of this one group gave the other some cotton mantas, beaded adornments, and little trinkets.

Once the pilgrim guests had rested for a few days in this Sinaloa pueblo the priest took them to another pueblo [Toro] of the same nation. There all the people, both men and women, came out to welcome them with the same demonstrations of joy as in the first pueblo. They came out to meet them two leagues from the pueblo. Many of the Sinaloa were on horseback and performed their mock skirmishes to the accompaniment of banners and drums. They gave the [pilgrims] lodging in their own homes and showered them with all possible love and charity. After they had rested here for a little while the priest judged that it would be good for the newcomers to visit the Villa de San Felipe and meet the captain, the priests, the Spaniards, the residents, and the soldiers. Thereby, when they returned to their lands they could take news and give testimony of the good treatment they had received everywhere they went, all of which would serve to establish peace with more finesse.

The priest appointed the man who had brought them from their lands, Governor Don Bautista, to be their guide. He also sent word to the pueblos along the way so that they might welcome them and take them in with great love and kindness. They came out to meet them with the same festivities as in the pueblos of the Sinaloa. The arrival of these new people was truly like a principal feast day [celebration].

The group reached the villa [on Easter 1620], and the captain welcomed them with singular pleasure and warmth, as he had often done with many nations. He offered them his protection, stating that their neighbors would all understand that they were now under his protection. He gave colts to the ten principal caciques, and so that they could govern their people, he also gave them the staff of justice,[95] which they greatly esteem.

One person who went to great lengths to [217] favor and show affection to this troop of gentile pilgrims was the Father Visitor of the missions, Diego de Guzmán,[96] a veteran missionary in Sinaloa who at that time was at our college with some other priests who had assembled there. These pilgrims were well treated at our house, and as they took their leave they were given high hopes that some day priests would go to their lands to teach them the doctrine and God's word. They were provided

---

95. *Vara de justicia*, which formally recognized a cacique's rights and responsibilities as governor of a pueblo or group of rancherías.

96. Pérez de Ribas errs here. At that time Diego de Guzmán was superior of the Sinaloa mission. He did not serve as Jesuit visitor until 1628.

with abundant provisions for the journey and sent off quite won over. As they departed for their return journey through the pueblos of their friends, the Sinaloa, they told the Father Visitor how much they still desired to be baptized and soon see priests in their lands.

Among all the small gifts they were given, which they greatly appreciated, they particularly appreciated a large amount of salt. They valued this greatly because they lived so far from the sea and lacked this item that is so necessary for human life. They barter mantas for chunks of salt with anyone who happens to reach their lands.

They were specifically told to inform their people of how well they had been received by the priests, the captain, the Spaniards, and all the Christians, and of the love and kindness with which they had been treated, the churches they had seen, and anything else that could help these nations become enthused about the Christian Faith and way of life. The Father Visitor also told them that both they and the rest of their relatives, as well as neighboring nations, should try to return to the villa from time to time and that he would receive them with great love and happiness. They took their leave and departed quite content with all these favors.

They were very encouraged to maintain friendship and communication with those from whom they had received so many benefits. They later took advantage of the Father Visitor's offer, for on several occasions many caciques and ordinary people returned to visit him, especially from the Guazápare and Témori nations. They insisted that he send priests to their lands to baptize them, and asked the same of the captain. This was eventually carried out, as we will see when we conclude the reduction and perfect settlement of this Christianity, which was begun with the mountain-ensconced Huite. There were still several rancherías among their peaks, so the complete reduction of the Huite remained to be accomplished by Governor Don Bautista.

CHAPTER XXX The entire Huite nation is reduced and baptized; a church is built and an exemplary Christianity is founded; the cacique Don Bautista's exemplary Christianity

Our Lord was served by the means referred to in the last chapter such that the resistant rancherías of Huite among the rugged mountains were softened and uprooted from the place where they had been born. All of them were finally reduced to the place the priest had chosen for them, and there they were all instructed, prepared, and finally baptized. This was to their own great pleasure, and the even greater pleasure of the priest, who appreciated the strength and perseverance with which they settled, not returning to their mountain peaks.

The Baptism of the Huite was coincident with an act of great edification that was proof of a very true Christianity. A mountain ranchería and group called the Calimona, who were already reduced and living among the Sinaloa, had been the principal enemies of the Huite in their heathenism. When the priest celebrated the Baptism of the Huite he called the Calimona principales, appointing them as the godparents of the Huite who were being baptized. This spiritual kinship united these two groups in such great love and friendship that from [218] then on they loved each other more than brothers.

When the Huite were all baptized the priest talked about having a suitable church built. They received this petition with so much pleasure that they started to work right away; men, women, and children all helped. They cut cedar beams and covered [the church] with a flat roof. It was very spacious, with three naves, and was adorned with images and altar ornaments. When it was finished, painted, and perfected it was one of the most beautiful and spacious churches in that province.

Although there are similar churches, the church of the mountain Huite, who were born and raised among the cliffs, exceeded all others [in beauty].

When all of this nation was gathered together in the place that had been chosen by the priest and their church was built, the Christian fervor with which they applied themselves to the Christian exercises was marvelous; [at the same time] they forgot their gentile and barbarous rites. Therefore, the priest who was instructing them [Cristóbal del Villalta], who had dealt with several nations of the [coastal] plains and mountains of Sinaloa, was of the opinion that the Huite had become the most skilled and docile of the many nations he had instructed. They were steadfast in their attendance at church and [religious] instruction. Those who had appeared to be beasts and mountain deer became gentle lambs. A particular devotion shone in them to hear Mass, even on weekdays, and to confess and receive Communion during Lent, when they scourged themselves. They gathered every Saturday in church as a community to pray the Rosary in unison in their own language. Every night the music of the Christian doctrine was heard in their houses, where they lived in absolute peace. The religious minister confessed that this nation's success brought tears of joy [to his eyes], for he had expended great effort in reducing them and had suffered a great deal for their total conversion. Today this pueblo has three hundred male heads-of-households, not counting those of other nations whom they attracted [to their pueblo] by their example. They all persevere so peacefully that there has never been any uprising or occasion for disturbance, as there has been in other newly converted nations.

Governor Don Bautista played a major role in the reduction and settlement of this nation and was a great example in the material as well as moral construction of this Christian community. He was a singular Indian who had converted to God a few years earlier and he deserves special mention, as do the fruits of the Gospel among these people. Even in his gentile state this Indian possessed great [intellectual] capacity and a good disposition and was loved and respected by everyone. Therefore, before his Baptism and that of his Sinaloa nation, Captain Hurdaide appointed him governor, knowing how able he was. In the thirty years that he served in this office Don Bautista showed great loyalty and love for the Spanish nation and the ministers of the Gospel, for whom he risked his life, protecting and defending them. He also displayed great zeal in making Christianity known everywhere.

Don Bautista was baptized at the young age of twenty-six. He and his people were the safest escort, company, and protection that the priests had during the many and grave dangers that arose in the conversion of his own Sinaloa nation, as well as that of the Huite, Chínipa, Guazápare, Témori, and others. He was the leader of all exercises of piety and the Christian Faith, and he was singular not only by virtue of the sermons he gave in his manner, but also by his example, which drew others to the Church, religious instruction, Mass, Confession, Communion, Penitence, and the practice of scourging. During the physical construction of churches he took pride in carrying beams, adobes, and mud, encouraging [219] his vassals and subjects through his example. Even though the priest sometimes wanted to excuse him from this task and have him settle for governing the people and overseeing the construction, he set his hands to work with a smile, carrying materials for God's house and thereby inspiring others.

Generosity and mercy were his most outstanding virtues. The needy found succor in him; he owned nothing because it belonged to whomever asked for or needed it, whether they were of his own nation or a foreign one. Above all his constancy and perseverance in his harmonious and Christian behavior were admired and made him loved and respected by all. Brave Captain Hurdaide paid great heed to his advice concerning entradas and enterprises, and he sought his help as if this Indian were a Spaniard of great importance. The priests did the same with respect to the governance and organization of their districts. Don Bautista responded to this with such gratefulness and reasoning that he did not seem a barbarous Indian, but rather a fine and noble Christian. No matter how much he did for the priests it never seemed enough to him. He responded by saying that he owed everything to the priests, whom he considered parents, loving them as father and mother.

One time a Spanish soldier was very rude to [Don Bautista], and the soldier feared that the captain would hang him for his behavior. He was freed from this danger by four words spoken by the priest to the governor, who was easily calmed and placated and forgave the offender. If on some occasion the priest gave him some warning or minor reprimand (which was rare), he withdrew tearfully to his house until he had satisfied the priest. This noble Indian's behavior was not born of cowardice or a lack of spirit, because he showed strong courage when in danger. It was born instead out of reverence for the minister of the Gospel who preached God's word. He lived this way for many years, with a concern for the expansion of Christianity in Sinaloa, which he expressed through speeches, good works, and his example. He heard Mass every day, confessed and received Holy Communion throughout the year, and was very good company for the priests.

Even though he had prepared diligently for a general confession when he was in good health, when he was taken ill he prepared particularly well for death.[97] When he was already very faint but still possessed all his senses, he received the holy oils with great devotion. Because they loved him a great deal, the entire pueblo of Toro came to his home at the time of his death. Weak as he was, he gave them a very Christian speech. He spoke of how grateful he was to the priests, renewing in everyone's memory the many benefits they had always received from them. He charged [his people] to respond to the priests like true children and Christians, as he had tried to do throughout his life since the time he first met the priests. He made his will, as is the custom once they become Christians, and this was recorded by the schoolmaster. When they reached the matter of his sword, which is the emblem of government among them, he said, "I leave this sword to the priest so that he or the captain can entrust it to some Spaniard, in order that he may serve with as good a heart as I always have." This is an expression used by these people to signify their fidelity, which is divorced from all treason. He died shortly after concluding his will.

We can piously believe that this man received great glory in heaven—a man who had been born and raised in the midst of the most barbarous heathenism in the world and who became a loyal and exemplary Christian, truly helping to spread the Holy Gospel. Thus, in writing to the Philippians, the Apostle of the People, Saint Paul, [220] makes important mention of those people who in their measure and manner helped him, adding that their names were written in the book of life: *Cum caeteris adiutoribus meis, quorum nomina sunt in libro vitae.*[98] The holy Apostle meant by these words that those who aid in the ministry of evangelical preaching are predestined. Good Don Bautista was one of them, for he was an aid to the most loyal Christians converted in the Province of Sinaloa, advancing their Christianity very steadfastly for many years.

His funeral was attended by many people including the caciques from the neighboring pueblos, who carried him on their shoulders to the church, where they made a funeral bier in their fashion. The Mass was accompanied by music and many tears were shed by all the people, who had lost a father and protector. The funeral Mass was sung and the sermon preached, and the good example of his life remained in everyone's memory. Through the diligence of Don Bautista, the conversion to our Holy Faith of the unyielding Huite nation was finally concluded and their castle and fort finally surrendered to Christ. We now leave this nation to continue with the propagation of the Gospel in another mountain range that is located nearby.

97. Don Bautista became ill and died shortly after his visit to the Villa de San Felipe in the spring of 1620. At this time many Indians in Sinaloa died from what were described as "great and vicious fevers" (Reff 1991b:161).

98. Phillipians 4:3: "as much as Clement and those other fellow-labourers of mine, whose names are recorded in the book of life" (Knox 1956:205–6).

CHAPTER XXXI The reduction of the Chínipa nation to our Holy Faith is begun

We have strayed somewhat from the conversion of the most populous nations on the [coastal] plains of Sinaloa and have entered the foothills of the sierras, where the Chínipa nation is found. In Book II it was recorded how Captain Diego Martínez de Hurdaide, under orders from the viceroy of Nueva España, undertook an expedition in search of silver deposits that were purported to exist in these mountains. The Chínipa opposed and disrupted this expedition. Then in Chapter XVII of the present book it was recorded that when Fort Montesclaros was built, this nation reconsidered and sent one of its caciques to establish peace with the captain and request priests to give them religious instruction. These were ways in which divine providence was marvelously preparing the salvation of the Chínipa. These Indians insisted and made new efforts to get the captain of the garrison and the priests to send a priest to their pueblos to baptize them and make them Christians.[99] Their perseverance obliged the superiors to order the missionary priest of the Sinaloa and the Huite to go and visit the Chínipa. In the event that he should find the necessary willingness, he was to begin their religious instruction, baptizing their infants. In this way he would take possession of the nation on behalf of Christ Our Lord.[100]

This nation was three days' journey into the mountains beyond the Huite nation. The trail ascended three leagues into extremely rough mountains and ravines and the descent was extremely dangerous. But neither these nor other greater difficulties disheartened the priest, who would add this new enterprise to earlier ones. To fulfill the orders of superiors, he sent word to the Chínipa that he would soon come to visit them, to receive them as his children and to fulfill their wishes. Before discussing his arrival it is worth recounting a case that took place at this time, which is exemplary of these people. The Chínipa did not consider themselves Christians, and in fact they were not Christians at this

time. Perhaps because they were bidding farewell to their gentile drunken revels and believed that by the time the priest arrived they should have no more of them, [221] they celebrated one of these revels. During this celebration, for what reason I do not know (although the wine was sufficient reason for him to have lost his senses), the principal cacique of this nation shot an arrow at one of his kinswomen. This is a rare occurrence in these peoples' drunken celebrations, because such excesses do not usually occur, particularly among relatives. Perhaps God permitted this because of the good results it produced.

When the cacique came to his senses he deeply regretted his disgrace. He also feared that when the priest found out what had happened it might give him justifiable cause to delay his arrival. Therefore, he went flying along a very rough trail, and in just one day he covered what was [normally] three days' journey. He went to the priest and threw himself at his feet, telling him about what had happened, and with great remorse he confessed his crime. On the one hand, the priest felt kindness because this gentile and ignorant Indian was already repentant. On the other hand, he of course felt zealous about uprooting this pernicious vice, which can so disrupt the introduction of Christianity in these nations. God obliged or moved him to impose a penance on the delinquent that might seem rigorous but was effective. He was to return to his pueblo, and in an enramada that they had built to serve as a church, he was to gather all the caciques and tell them of his remorse for what had happened and for the bad example he had set. Then as punishment for his sin, he was to ask each of them to administer two blows to his back with a scourge.

The Indian heard the penance imposed by the priest and accepted it (an unusual case in a barbarous man who is not accustomed to this kind of humiliation, which is very foreign to his haughty and bellicose nature). He accepted his penance so wholeheartedly that he immediately departed to carry it out. Once he had reached his pueblo he promptly did as instructed and received his whipping (and there was a great desire among his relatives and the people of his nation to attend his punishment). Then he stood up and said

99. The anua of 1620 indicates that the Chínipa, Guazápare, Témori, and Varohío sent delegations to San Felipe that year (the winter of 1619–20) to request priests.

100. Father Juan Castini undertook this entrada in 1620.

to those who were present, "As you are all aware, I, your principal cacique, behaved as a delinquent during our drunken revel. Because we were trying to become Christians, in which case we should abandon such celebrations, I have subjected myself to this punishment, as you have seen. Rest assured that from now on no one should dare to make wine, for I myself will rigorously punish him and there will be no pardon." Through this case the deeply rooted vice in which these people had been reared, that of [getting drunk on] wine, was buried forever.

Upon hearing of this noteworthy act the priest hastened his journey to this most willing nation, notifying them of the day of his departure. Once the Chínipa had learned of this, nearly one hundred of the most principal Indians came to accompany the priest. He departed with them, and they took such great pains to show their pleasure at his coming to their lands to give them religious instruction and make them Christians that along the way, which was extremely rough with rocky outcroppings and trees, some of them went along clearing the trail and cutting branches. Others did what they could to remove rocks so that the priest could pass. They had also prepared some enramadas along the way, with food for all the people who were with him. There he could say Mass and spend the night.

The priest and his company reached the first pueblo after three days. There he found all of the people of the nation gathered, which would have been some five hundred families. They were divided among five settlements, but would later be reduced to one. The priest found a church made of wood. To better celebrate the hold that the Gospel was taking on this new church, he entered dressed in a choir robe that he carried with him for Baptisms. The children accompanied him bearing a very beautiful image of Our Lady of El Pópulo, so that she might receive [222] her Son's new pueblo under her care. The residents celebrated their minister's arrival with great solemnity and dancing. When he left the church they took him to a little house they had built for him. Even though it was made of wooden poles, he was quite pleased with it, for he could see the good disposition of that new flock to receiving the divine word. Then they gave the priest some presents in the form of their meager food, and in return he gave them gifts out of his own poverty.

He then ordered, as he had been charged, that the children be baptized. About four hundred of them ages seven and under were gathered and baptized, to the great pleasure of their parents. Of these, God took His

first fruits to heaven within a few days, even before the priest had departed. These children were buried with solemnity as Christians. Once the Baptism of the Chínipa children was completed their parents performed a singular demonstration of devotion with the sign of the Christians, the holy Cross. Each household in the pueblo, which was well laid out and had flat-roofed adobe houses (at which this nation excelled), raised a Cross on their home. In addition to these, they raised other large Crosses at the intersections of their streets.

This act of such great affection for Christianity was later followed by another, which was of no less esteem, that served as a sign that they were truly welcoming the Faith. The Chínipa were surrounded by enemies, with whom they were continually at war. For this reason there was barely a home that did not have some of the customary skulls and bones of the dead with which they had celebrated their victory dances. In addition to this, they still had some little idols and other instruments of superstition. Because the priest wanted to begin uprooting these weeds in order to sow the seed of the Gospel, he gathered together the most principal Indians and made them understand that the law of God and the Christians prohibited and abominated such superstitions and trickery by the devil, who was the principal enemy of mankind. [He told them that] they no longer needed to have human enemies, for no enemy nation would dare [to attack] them because they were [now] under the captain's protection and had a priest in their lands. These and other similar arguments worked with them, such that the principal Indians took their leave of the priest and went back to their pueblos, where they gathered forty-eight *chicubites*, or baskets, full of enemy bones and skulls and other instruments of sorcery and superstition. They brought these to the priest, who told them that it would be good if all those things were burned and forgotten. No more words were necessary, for the Indians themselves built two bonfires, and before the priest's eyes they threw these things into them. There is no doubt that as the devil watched the burning of the trickery and deceit by which he had misled those poor souls he also felt himself burned along with those cursed instruments.

The priest saw how God with His grace had favorably disposed and prepared these people so that the adults could receive religious instruction and Holy Baptism. He also saw that he could spend no more time there for the moment because the fields of the Christian pueblos of his own district were calling him. Therefore, he asked the Chínipa to choose a few young men and boys whom he could take with him to be raised in his Christian pueblos, where they would learn the Christian doctrine and customs, as well as to read, write, and sing. This was a means which (as we have stated elsewhere) was very useful in introducing Christianity among these people. These boys would later return to their pueblos, and there they would teach the others and prepare them all for Baptism. The Chínipa raised no objections to this proposal and immediately gathered a number of boys so [223] that the priest could choose those whom he deemed best suited. He took twenty-four, some of whom were the sons of caciques. They happily accompanied him and lived among Christians until the time came when another priest went to settle this nation and baptize all its people.[101]

CHAPTER XXXII Another unique outcome and benefit of the first entrada to the Chínipa by this minister of the doctrine

Although the first visit to the Chínipa bore abundant fruit, Our Lord granted that this nation should prosper further before the priest [completed his visit and] returned to his district. It is clearly seen from the circumstances of this event that it was arranged by unique providence and intercession from heaven. When the priest was about to return to his Christian pueblos, he got up one morning at the hour of prayer (which is the rule of the Company), and as he was praying he was overcome by an extraordinary desire to remain with the Chínipa and try to establish peace between them and some mountain nations eight leagues away. These were their mortal enemies, the aforementioned Guazápare and Témori. While the priest was among the Chínipa he had heard that fifteen days earlier these other Indians had cut off the heads of some Chínipa and had danced with them in celebration of their barbarous victory.

The priest was moved by this extraordinary impulse, as well as by the fact that it seemed to him that those misguided people who now had the light of the Gospel so near might be reduced to our Holy Faith by way of this peace. With most loving affection he asked the guardian angels of these poor souls (whom God does not deprive of this singular benefit, even if they are gentiles) to favor him with their aid and intercession in this effort. After the devoted priest had said this prayer he went to the door of his little house. There he found a Chínipa Indian waiting to inform him that he had seen a Guazápare Indian not far from there behind a little hill. This Guazápare was the brother of a cacique of that nation. He had told the Chínipa Indian that he wanted to see the father of the Christians but did not dare to enter [the pueblo] for fear that the Chínipa would kill him. It was through God's special providence that upon seeing a mortal enemy in his land this very same [Chínipa] Indian who had come with the message had not himself killed the Guazápare. But God and His angels were at work here, preparing the way for the salvation of these souls.

This case is paralleled by what happened to the glorious Saint Peter. As he was praying, the [angels] showed him that linen cloth from heaven that was full of fierce animals, a representation of the gentiles who were coming from Caesarea in search of this holy Apostle so that he might bring them into the Church. After he finished praying he found them at the door of his lodging place, as is told in the book of the Acts of the Apostles [Acts 10:11–21]. We find similar circumstances in our case, and because they are obvious I will not pause to ponder them here.

In the end, when the priest had finished the prayers in which he had felt such unique impulses and desires for the Guazápare's salvation and when he had heard the news brought by this Chínipa, he sent some loyal Christians to safely bring the Guazápare Indian to him.

---

101. In 1626. The priest was Julio Pascual.

Once he was brought before the priest the Guazápare declared the intentions and desires with which he had come to see the father of the Christians. At the risk of his life but with the assurance of the priest's presence, he had come to speak of peace between the Chínipa and the Guazápare so that [his nation] might obtain Christian religious instruction and a minister to teach them. The priest's pleasure is well manifested here, [224] for he saw that God was revealing the purpose of the impulse that He had conveyed to and ignited in the priest while he was praying.

In order to begin the execution of these ends, he sent for the Chínipa principales. He persuaded them that as a sign of peace they should embrace the Indian who came to request this [peace], forgetting all their past wars and deaths (even those that were so recent). Given that the Guazápare wanted to be Christian, the Chínipa were to consider them friends and brothers from then on. The good Chínipa people agreed to everything asked of them by the man whom they now respected as their own father.

To insure greater peace and stability, which were of such great service to Our Lord for the salvation of so many lives in both body and soul, the priest decided to stay on for another four days, even though he had already been prepared to leave. He gave the Guazápare Indian a message to take to his nation: that he would wait for them if they wanted to come and see him and

they could come without fear of being attacked to confirm the friendship that had been agreed upon. The Indian departed so quickly and contentedly that within two days more than one hundred Guazápare men, women, and children joyfully came to see the priest. He and the Chínipa received them with great signs of love, and the good Chínipa people treated them well and welcomed them warmly.

After the peace was confirmed anew the [Chínipa] loaded them down with maize, which the Guazápare needed. They also gave other gifts to those who at another time they would have chopped to pieces. The priest bid these guests farewell, ordering them to tell their people about the warm reception both he and the Chínipa had given them. They were also to profess their friendship and brotherhood as Christians, without attempting or even remembering vengeance or death against the Chínipa or any other nation. They were to tell the rest of their allies in that mountain range the same thing. This had such a good effect that during the following two months large numbers of people from all those nations regularly accompanied the Guazápare during their visits to the Chínipa. All these nations were later tamed and reduced to the flock of Christ, and the priest returned to his district most happy with the joyful fruits of his journey and the foundations he had established for that new Christian community.

CHAPTER XXXIII The priest goes to the Chínipa a second time;[102] the noteworthy peace established among other warring nations

We do not leave the Chínipa nation as a completed [enterprise] or even with an established mission. Rather, they are only very much in the early stages, albeit steadfast in their good intentions of having a priest permanently in their company and of everyone receiving Holy Baptism. The priest could not fulfill their desires because he was very busy with his own Christian pueblos of the Sinaloa and Zoe. These pueblos required his presence because their Christianity was new and not yet completely formed. Added to this was the fact that the Chínipa, along with the rest of the nations of whom we have spoken, were at least three days' journey from the priest's district. This was all an impediment to founding a mission among the Chínipa. Moreover, the [priests] were still waiting for new ministers to come to Sinaloa from Mexico City for the fields that God was preparing and ripening for the harvest.

At that time this shortage was compensated for through various means, on one hand by the Indians and on the other by the priest. The Indians persevered and steadfastly came to visit him and request Baptism. For his part the zealous minister supported their efforts through good speeches. From time to time he also sent some good Christians to their district to visit and [225] teach them. He told these Christians to fulfill this responsibility with good judgment and Christian counsel and to maintain the established peace. Satan always made an effort to disrupt this, but God, who had mercy on these peoples, supplied them with such fervor and desire to become Christian that the Chínipa, the Guazápare, and the Témori were all moved to undertake a journey to the Villa de San Felipe, almost eighty leagues away, to insistently ask the priest's superior and the captain to order that a priest be sent to their lands to reside there permanently and instruct and baptize them. There was no way at that time to fulfill such desires other than for the priest who had made the first entrada to go back a second time to these nations, baptize their infants, and prepare things as much as possible for the arrival of a minister from Mexico City who could take more permanent charge of their religious instruction.

The piety of Captain Diego Martínez de Hurdaide, whom we have already given a deserving memorial, must not be forgotten here. The captain wrote the priest a letter and entrusted him with this enterprise. He says in this formal manner, *"They considered me to be blessed for being able to kiss the ground upon which Your Reverence treads while carrying out such a great and needy enterprise."*[103] This is clear testimony of this brave and zealous layman's honor for God and the salvation of souls. He clearly knew from experience how many of these people went to heaven.

With orders from his superior the priest prepared for a second entrada. He reached Chínipa and was welcomed with the same demonstrations of joy as before. He himself was joyful to see those whom he had baptized the year before and to realize the desire and willingness the Chínipa had to learn the Christian doctrine.

Because I have not yet discussed the particular customs of this nation, which are worthy of being known, I will summarize them here. The Chínipa women are very chaste, timid, and modest, especially the young single women. Their dress is more decent than that of other nations, and it was rare for a man to have more than one wife. The houses (as I have said) have walls and flat roofs, and these are people in whom gentile barbarism had not predominated as much as in other nations.

The priest ordered that all the children that had been born that year be brought together along with others who had not yet been baptized. The Chínipa

---

102. The date of this second visit is unknown. Near the outset of this chapter Pérez de Ribas suggests that it followed the first visit by a year. Toward the end of the chapter, however, he suggests that Castini's second visit occurred in 1624, two years before the Ihío and Varohío were assigned a permanent missionary (Julio Pascual), which was in 1626. A date of 1624 for the second visit would seem to be more consistent with the suggestion early in the chapter that from time to time between the first and second visits Castini sent "good Christians" to instruct the Chínipa.

103. This quote was italicized in the Spanish original. Presumably Pérez de Ribas wished to emphasize the fact that he was quoting directly from Hurdaide's letter to Castini.

brought them with great pleasure, and with the same pleasure the priest consecrated them with the holy water of this Divine Sacrament. He also baptized some old men and women who were in mortal danger because of their advanced age. These people received this remedy of life without the same difficulties presented by others who have become hardened in their years.

Because the priest realized that it would not be possible for him to remain there (without consequently neglecting his own district and flock), he decided to leave a Christian Indian who was traveling with him to make up for this need until someone else arrived who could take charge of them. This Indian was very wise and knew how to read and write. He was to teach the Chínipa the doctrine and Christian customs. In cases of urgent necessity he could baptize those who were in mortal danger, for he was well instructed in matters of the Faith and had been raised in the schools that are established for these young men. This Indian was not married, and to ensure that he settled among this foreign nation that not much earlier had been an enemy, the priest decided to marry him to a Chínipa woman. Being thus related to her, he could better attend to this task.

The young man agreed to the priest's plan. The Chínipa were so pleased that he would be staying behind to teach them the doctrine that they offered him any maiden he wished from among all [226] those in the pueblo. He chose one who was so chaste that when the priest asked her biological father to approve her marriage to that young man, who was very wise and virtuous and would be staying in their pueblo to teach them the doctrine and Christian customs, his answer was, "Father, my wife and I would be most pleased by this marriage, but our daughter is so frightened by the company of a man that if you yourself do not speak to her and persuade her to marry him, I fear that we will not be able to do so." This is good testimony of the previously mentioned chastity that is found among the maidens of this nation.

In the end the priest persuaded her to take as her spouse this man who would be good company for her and of great assistance to her nation. The marriage was performed and the Chínipa were so pleased that all the principales took the newlyweds to their homes to celebrate this wedding with several celebrations [in honor] of their matrimony, which turned out to be very wise. This woman was an inseparable consort for her husband when he went to the pueblos and rancherías teaching the doctrine. Throughout the year they often returned together on the three days' journey to see their spiritual father and to confess and take Communion. This virtuous young man was not content with the work he carried out among those who were now his relatives, the Chínipa, so he also went to the Guazápare and the Témori, who had been chief enemies. He maintained the peace that had been established with them and prepared them well for Holy Baptism. As we discussed in the last chapter, the priest had arranged for all of this when he was in the Chínipa pueblos, whence he made an effort to travel farther [into the mountains] to visit the Guazápare and Témori nations, as they had requested.

Among these Indians was a very famous cacique named Cobameai. He had never come with the others to see the priest or the Christian pueblos. The priest had sent him some messages through his relatives, saying that he wished to see him. Finally, he sent word to Cobameai that he had reached Chínipa with the hope of coming to his lands to visit his children, as he had earlier promised the other caciques he would do. He wanted to know what Cobameai's wishes were and he hoped that the two might meet. Upon hearing this, Cobameai came with a large number of people to meet the priest. The day he arrived was one of great pleasure and joy for the Chínipa because they were now seeing in their lands the man who was head of the nations that had been so opposed to their own during previous wars. They also now were seeing at peace he who had once been the terror of all nations.

Cobameai was an Indian of large build, robust but well proportioned. He had a fierce countenance and horrendous stare. He was fifty years old and wore a blue manta that reached his feet. His ears were covered with the earrings they wear, which go all the way around the ear and consist of carved shells of mother-of-pearl strung on blue threads. The priest treated this Indian and all his people very affectionately, and the Chínipa caciques accompanied him throughout the pueblo. When they reached the center Cobameai went up to the roof of a house, whence he preached a sermon in his manner. This sermon lasted for an hour, and with great energy and in a loud voice he spoke of the permanent peace and friendship that was being established among these nations. He invited the Chínipa to come into his lands from that time forward now that they all had a priest and should treat one another as brothers and have marriages among their nations.

After this they spent the whole day entertaining themselves in feasts and dancing and festivities of great merriment. Once the celebration had ended the priest charged Cobameai and his people with opening the way so that he could pass through to their lands (they had not [yet] done so because these nations had communicated so little with one another in the past). He also told them that [227] once they informed him that the way was ready and that the people had been gathered together, he would set out to see them. They carried all of this out very carefully, and Cobameai himself, along with his sons, built an enramada along the way where the priest could rest. They also erected a Cross inside so that he could say Mass for himself.

The priest reached the Guazápare settlements, or rancherías, and they welcomed him with great joy and festivity. He found a church made of wood and straw, for they had invited some Christians to come and teach them how to build it. The same thing happened with the Témori, who were three leagues away. Between these two groups there were about five hundred families.

These peoples' lands were stony and their maize fields were planted among rocks. The climate was very cold because they were farther north and subject to snowfall. The priest gave thought to these peoples' places and the locations [of their settlements]. The mountain range was tortuous, harsh, dry, and sterile. They lived in high places among horrible crags, lacking water and decent places for settlement. Also, they were of a more fierce and bellicose nature than other nations. At that time, therefore, he decided to administer Holy Baptism only to those children who were more or less one year of age. In this way the [Guazápare and the Témori] would be contented and would have some assurance that they were going to become Christians. This field would also begin to ripen more and there would be time in which a priest might arrive from Mexico City who could specifically take charge of them. In addition, with the intention of maintaining their good wishes, he also left it established that in time some of them were to

visit his Christian pueblos, as they did. Finally, he gave orders for the Christian Indian who had gotten married in Chínipa, and who was a teacher of the doctrine, to instruct them in Christian customs and, when necessary, to baptize the sick who were in mortal danger. This was all carried out to the great benefit of the Guazápare and the Témori, who were mindful of gathering in their poor church to pray and learn the prayers.

It is in this state that we must leave these nations, until the time arrives for their total conversion and [the establishment of] their mission. We only add here that when the priest visited them, two other mountain nations called the Ihío and the Varohío came in peace to see him to request that he also come to their lands and baptize their children. But he did not have an order from his superiors to extend his labor to such distant nations, where it was still unknown whether there was the [necessary] ripeness and willingness to safely employ the pearls of the Gospel. He did not, however, entirely dismiss their good intentions, for he gave them good hopes that in time there would be a priest available to attend to them. After treating them affectionately he sent them off. These Ihío and Varohío, along with the other nations, were so persistent in their demands and efforts that they finally attained their goal two years later [in 1626]. They were catechized, and thousands of souls were baptized. This cost the lives of two priests,[104] who spilled their blood in this enterprise and earned themselves the prize of the crown of martyrdom. This will be recorded in Book IV, after discussing the conversion of the populous Mayo nation, which was converted before their not-so-distant neighbors, the Ihío and the Varohío. Book III will now be concluded with an account of the lives, labors, and exemplary virtues of the two religious who labored for many years and died in the holy missions of which we have written up to this point. [228]

---

104. Julio Pascual and Manuel Martínez, martyred in 1632.

CHAPTER XXXIV Examples of Father Juan Bautista de Velasco's great religion and zealous desire for the welfare of souls, which he showed at the time of his death while catechizing these nations

The outstanding virtues, glorious hardships, and apostolic tasks of those Gospel ministers who labored for many years and sacrificed their lives are worthy of being remembered and recorded here. Although they did not lose their lives to the blade of the sword and were not [mortally] wounded and filled with arrows, they nevertheless suffered great and lengthy hardships in the enterprises of these holy missions, which are of such great glory to God and do so much good for the welfare of souls. Furthermore, this is an appropriate topic for this history, just as it is appropriate to write about and celebrate the conquests and secular battles of virtuous captains and soldiers who distinguished themselves through memorable actions and heroic accomplishments. These serve as an example and promote strength and courage in those who read them, and the same is true of the deeds of our apostolic men. In addition to adorning our history like precious jewels, they also marvelously invite imitation. This was expressed quite elegantly by [Saint] Basil the Great, who said, *Quemadmodum ex igne naturaliter emicat splendor, & ex unguento diffunditur odor, sic ex Sanctorum commemoratione gestorum ad omnes proveniunt utilitates.*[105]

Having thus written in Book II about the blessed martyrdom of the venerable Father Gonzalo de Tapia, founder of the Sinaloa missions, I will record here in Book III the notable virtues and saintly death of Father Juan Bautista de Velasco, as well as his reward for his holy works. He was one of the first evangelical laborers whom the Lord of the vineyard selected and led at the hour of prime[106] to labor in Sinaloa. Following the violent end met by the founder of these missions, the venerable Father Gonzalo de Tapia, this very religious man was the first to die of natural causes. He went to heaven to receive payment for his work. This payment was not for just one day's work, as was the case with those depicted by Christ Our Lord in the divine parable in [the Gospel of] Saint Matthew [20:1–16]. Rather, he received payment for twenty-two years of immense hardship and fatigue cultivating the nations of the first river of Sinaloa, the Río Mocorito and its salt marshes.

This evangelical minister was born of honorable parents in the city of Oaxaca, Nueva España. He had been a student at the Jesuit [college] there and entered the Company at the age of sixteen. He finished his studies, excelling in letters and virtues, as is characteristic of a son of the Company. Because of his competence, superiors chose him for the new mission in Sinaloa, where he was sent at the age of twenty-nine. He suffered, or better said enjoyed, its most difficult aspects and remained joyful and at peace during the entire twenty-two years that he worked in this mission. When the infidels were in control of almost all the land and were on their own, free and barbarous, with nobody to fear and unrestrained in their vices and drunkenness, he was one of the principal ministers who in the midst of these and many other toils and hardships, with the aid of Our Lord and with his zeal and preaching, reduced the land to the state that it now enjoys. He suffered great discomforts and became sickly from this enterprise, which was lacking in human comforts. Yet he gathered his flock and always tried to advance and [229] refine them in all [matters of] Christianity, thereby serving as a model and example for other [missions] that were later founded.

---

105. *Margin Note*: Basil, orat. in Gordian. "In the same manner that brightness gleams forth naturally from fire, and a scent is spread about by perfume, so all profit from the mention of the deeds of the saints." The referent here is apparently a speech or panegyric in praise of Gordius, the ancient king of Phrygia in Asia Minor. Basil the Great (ca. 330–379), bishop of Caesarea and a Doctor of the Church, was considered one of the most eloquent orators in Church history. He formed the first monastery in Asia Minor and authored various works in which he outlined the principles of monastic life (Thurston and Attwater 1956:2:539–42).

106. Prime is the first occasion for the reciting of the Divine Office, usually around 6 a.m. Here it is used as a metaphor for the dawn of the Sinaloa mission.

Every Sunday and on all the feast days throughout the year he gave a sermon and sang Mass, never allowing illness or his ailments to hinder him. In his zeal for the salvation of souls he imitated the Apostle Saint Paul, who was not satisfied with promoting virtue in his public sermons alone. To these he also added private and holy conversations, as is attested in his correspondence with the priests of Ephesus, in which he said, *Scitis quomodo nihil subtraxerim utilium, quominus annuntiarem vobis, & docerem vos publicé, & per domos, testificans poenitentiam, & fidem in Dominum nostrum Jesum Christum.*[107] Our zealous Father Bautista practiced this a great deal, giving private talks[108] to those of the greatest [intellectual] capacity. He reprimanded their vices and on occasion praised their virtuous actions. He did this with such skill and gentleness that very good results were obtained in those who listened to him. He loved his children tenderly, and like a father he always came to their defense. He was their spiritual and corporal doctor, healing them many times with his own hands. He spent part of his stipend on this and requested that medicines be brought from Mexico City that were appropriate to his needs.

This priest spoke the two main languages of this province extremely well and reduced them to a grammar.[109] He preached in them as if he were preaching in Romance, and he said that it cost him no more effort to speak these languages than a desire to preach. Therefore, he became a teacher for the others who [later] came to this mission.

He was especially careful about his church services and the Divine Office, which were celebrated with the appropriate ritual and decorum. Due to the extreme poverty of the land, he built and adorned the churches of his pueblos at his own expense and personal sacrifice. The poverty he endured was such that after twenty-

two years he was still using the same blanket that he had brought with him from Mexico City.

Among Father Velasco's many virtues there was one that shone very brightly. This was the virtue that the Son of God had very specifically commended to His first preachers of the Gospel: *In patientia vestra possidebitis animas vestras.*[110] The priest endured adversity with great patience, suffering, and evenness of temper; no one ever saw him get upset, even on occasions that warranted it. On the contrary, he controlled himself and did everything with a very serene face. He never forgot this virtue, which was strongly commended by Christ Our Lord. He frees His servants with the long-suffering virtue of patience, making them masters of themselves and their own proper conduct. This guarantees good results and victories; it also increases the fruits within oneself and within one's fellow man, as was the case with Father Juan Bautista.

This virtue was paired closely with a humble resignation to execute the most difficult orders from superiors. Both these virtues were very noticeable and endured for a very long time in Father Juan Bautista, who remained hidden and forgotten for so many years in such a remote land. He possessed excellent talents with which he could have been successful elsewhere. He was among those chosen to teach the most advanced courses, and many times superiors had suggested that he return to Mexico City for a good [teaching] position. In spite of this he never wanted to abandon his flock, which he loved so tenderly. For important matters he had [230] the gifts of prudence and good judgment. Diego Martínez de Hurdaide, captain of Sinaloa, frequently turned to him for advice in important cases in this province. He also always chose Father Juan Bautista as his confessor.

Two other things excelled beyond measure in this very religious man. The first was the virginal purity that he maintained throughout his life. Proof of this was given at the time he received the oils [of Extreme Unction]. He gave thanks to our God for this gift and the grace of His divine hand, saying, "*Indulgeat tibi Dominus quidquid peccasti per ardorem libidinis*"[111]—because of the Lord's kindness, I have done nothing of a grievous nature since birth that I now need to confess. The sec-

---

107. *Margin Note*: Actor c. 20. Acts 20:20–21: "and how I have never failed you, when there was any need of preaching to you, or teaching you, whether publicly or house by house. I have proclaimed both to Jew and to Greek repentance before God and faith in our Lord Jesus Christ" (Knox 1956:137). Note that Ribas' Latin does not include the segment 'both to Jew and to Greek'.

108. The practice of private or devout conversation (engaging others in discussions of matters of the faith and spiritual fulfillment and correction) was commended in the Jesuit Constitutions. Although not a ministry per se, like preaching, lecturing, or caring for the sick, it was considered an important and effective means of spreading God's word, particularly if the conversation was with an individual of influence and power (e.g., a European prince or an Indian cacique) (O'Malley 1993a:110–11).

109. The two languages were Guasave and Cáhita; a version of Velasco's grammar of Cáhita was published by Buelna in 1891.

110. *Margin Note*: Luc. 21. Luke 21:19: "It is by endurance that you will secure possession of your souls" (Knox 1956:80).

111. "May the Lord be indulgent toward you in whatever sin you have committed through the passion of desire."

ond way in which he excelled was revealed in what he said to a fellow priest a few days before he died. He said that he could not remember having knowingly lied in his entire life. This is convincing proof that Our Lord preserved him in original baptismal grace, safeguarding that which could be easily and quickly lost.

He died when he was fifty-one. For seventeen of those years he was a professed member of the Company, having taken its four vows. Our Lord prepared him for death with a three-month illness, which started with an abscess that [eventually] killed him. He endured his illness and suffering without creating hardship. Despite being very thin, he honored his vow of obedience and traveled from his district to the annual meeting that the priests hold at the college in the Villa de San Felipe.[112] Once he had fulfilled this obligation, and in spite of the fact that he should have been in bed resting rather than on a ten-league journey (the distance from the villa to one of the pueblos in his district), he returned. It was there that God willed he should consummate his holy life.

Like a good shepherd he cared for the sheep he had been entrusted with by Christ Our Lord until the time of his death, which he awaited like a good soldier on guard. When his illness worsened two priests who were the closest to his district came to him. They found him so weak and exhausted that they told him it was evident that the end of his life was drawing near. The priest responded by asking, "If I die of this illness, will I be saved? Will God have mercy on me?" They answered that he could be sure of this, thanks to God's mercy, the good life he had led, and the fact that he had joined the Company at such a young age. Then the blessed priest said, "Well, if that is the case, let us die and go see God." He frequently invoked the extremely sweet name of JESUS, asking for relics, rosaries, and holy water. When he saw himself very close to death he asked for a crucifix. He remained unconscious for quite a while, and then regaining consciousness he said, "Let us hope that I have been able to arrange with Our Lord to have my purgatory in this life." And in conformity with this he lived for [another] three days, which we can piously believe to be the time he needed to purge [his soul of its sins]. During the first day he received the *Viaticum*[113] while kneeling in bed. The next two days he spent in prayer, preparing for the moment of death. During this time he did not forget the souls that God had entrusted to him. He had the most principal of his Indians brought to him. He ordered them to make good use of what he had taught them and to have great love and reverence for the priest who would replace him. Finally, after talking with Our Lord and being in a sweet state of mind, he departed for heaven on Monday, July 29, 1613, twenty-two years after the foundations of the Sinaloa missions were laid.

The children whom he had engendered in Christ showed their grief and how much they owed their great priest and protector. When he died the people [231] of the pueblo gathered in the church, mourning his absence and crying out in grief, "Our father is dead. Who will defend us and take care of our needs?" In the manner in which they ordinarily mourn their dearly departed the women raised cries and pitiful screams throughout the pueblo.

Father Velasco's body was taken to the Villa de San Felipe by the two priests who had assisted him, accompanied by all the Indians from Father Velasco's pueblo. The captain and his entire garrison came out to receive the body more than two leagues from the Villa de San Felipe. The captain was the first to grab hold of the litter and carry it to our church. Eleven priests, who had congregated from all over, performed the [funeral] rites, [and afterwards] Father Velasco's mortal remains were buried in the church of Sinaloa. The memory of such an apostolic missionary is perpetuated in that province, and his examples remain alive for others. In the pueblos of his faithful very good fruits are being harvested to this day from the Christianity that he established with such care, zeal, and vigilance.

---

112. In 1610 Father Visitor Rodrigo de Cabredo issued a set of rules for missionaries on the frontier. These are presented in Book 7, Chapter 14. One of these rules required that the priests assemble twice a year for a minimum of eight days to discuss mission strategy, outline individual material needs for the coming year, observe as a group the religious exercises carried out in Jesuit colleges, and perform the Spiritual Exercises of Ignatius Loyola. It proved impractical for all the priests (or even a majority of them) to meet as a group twice a year. Indeed, during some years individual priests found it impossible to attend even one such gathering (see Polzer 1976:16–17, 64–65).

113. This term is from Latin and literally means "provision for a journey." It is Holy Communion that is given to a person in danger of dying (Attwater 1949:515).

CHAPTER XXXV The life, labor, ministries, and joyous death of a brother coadjutor[114] of our Company of Jesus who assisted the priests of the Sinaloa missions

[N]ow that I have] related the departure and death of the very religious Father Juan Bautista de Velasco, this chapter will relate the life, virtues, and death of a brother of our Company named Francisco de Castro. God chose him to aid in promoting and sustaining Christianity in Sinaloa from its early days. For thirty-three years he exercised his great virtues and endured countless hardships, working untiringly as a temporal coadjutor. He was to be a relief from the greatest hardships that the ministers of the Gospel experienced as they cultivated this vineyard, the fruits and merits of which were due in very large part to this great servant of Our Lord. The remarkable examples of virtue that he left for us to imitate also merit discussion here, along with an account of his death [and life], which he so felicitously concluded in Sinaloa.

Brother Francisco de Castro was a native of a village near Sevilla called Ginés. He was the son of honorable parents who were in charge of the properties of the marquis of Villamanrique.[115] His father gave him to the marquis as a servant when the latter went to Nueva España as viceroy, which demonstrated the esteem in which the marquis held him. Father Antonio de Mendoza, who was the [Jesuit] Provincial [of Nueva España] asked the viceroy for permission to receive Francisco into the Company. After granting this request and after Francisco's good credentials were verified, the viceroy commented, "Your [Reverend] Father will not regret having received him."

Francisco de Castro entered the Company at the age of twenty-five and promptly applied himself to his vocation as brother coadjutor. Because of the wisdom with which he was endowed, he had always esteemed

this vocation and was filled with a desire for the ministry for which divine will had chosen him. After he left the novitiate he served with great humility as a cook for five years at the [Jesuit] college in Mexico City. He performed that lowly job (which was highly esteemed in the house of the Lord) with great edification and became an example at the college, where he left a vivid memory.

Our Lord took him from there to perform very great service in the Province of Sinaloa, where he did much good. As previously discussed, when holy Father Gonzalo de Tapia traveled from Sinaloa to Mexico City [in 1593] to discuss matters concerning the establishment of this mission, the Father Provincial [232] sent Brother Francisco, who was well suited for this task, to aid those priests who were continually busy with spiritual ministering. Thus, he entered the Province of Sinaloa at its very beginnings, doing his part for its establishment and growth, both materially and spiritually. The abundant spiritual fruit that has been harvested here is due in large part to his care, great prudence, and perseverance. Much of the zeal that the holy founder of the mission, Father Tapia, had for converting all gentile nations to God was passed on to Brother Castro. He never held himself back in his job and offered whatever assistance he could, exposing himself to many dangers in the course of this enterprise. When his beloved Father Tapia so cruelly lost his life (as was previously discussed), I heard him afterward lamenting the fact that he had not been there when it happened: "If I had been there, I could at least have died embracing the holy priest."

Brother Francisco arrived in Sinaloa at a time when the priests did not have a church or a house or anything to call their own. He immediately and completely applied himself to the [temporal] tasks for which he alone was responsible in that community. He made it possible for the priests to labor as hard as they did in cultivating this new vineyard. He worked with whatever was available in those difficult times, making sure the priests had the support they needed. He built the

114. Francisco de Castro was technically a temporal coadjutor. As such, he was considered an auxiliary or 'helper,' someone who cooked and did other forms of manual labor on behalf of the missionary priests (who were either spiritual coadjutors or professed) (O'Malley 1993a:346–47).

115. Alvaro Manrique de Zúñiga y Acevedo, viceroy from November 5, 1595 to October 27, 1603 (Polzer, Barnes, and Naylor 1977:99).

[Jesuit] house and two churches, personally working on their construction. He continued this line of work for thirty-three years, whenever the need arose. Even when he was an old man he never let up, working with the same spirit and perseverance as when he was young. It was amazing to see him go without breakfast in such a hot climate, where the sun's rays shone like fire, helping the Indians (who, while naked, still perspired streams of sweat) raise beams and lay adobes.

In order to specifically relate the virtues of this servant of God, I will begin with what must be the first, the pure and holy intention of his acts, which is what makes them so valuable. Although this must be an interior quality, as Saint Gregory said, with faith it is revealed; it could be seen in his face and in the attention that he paid to his daily work, taking care to please the Lord Our God, without human pretensions. His goal was simply to do what he understood to be of divine service, first of all because he was a truly spiritual man and second because in his acts there was not the slightest hint of self-interest or self-esteem or any other worldly consideration. This holy purpose encouraged and raised the good brother's spirits with a continual desire for the salvation of the many souls that were converted to God in Sinaloa. He undoubtedly received a large part of the reward for those who were saved because his continual concern was that new nations receive the light of the Gospel.

Once he was in a populous pueblo of gentiles where he heard them say that they were now ready to ask for priests and religious instruction. He immediately had a large and beautiful Cross decorated, and kneeling down, he had it raised with great ceremony in the plaza. He made all those barbarians kneel down before it and worship this divine sign of our redemption. This made them very happy, and afterward they received our Holy Faith. Because of this zeal and attentiveness to spreading the Holy Faith, [233] he always worked with unusual care, anywhere and with any missionary. When he arrived in a mission district or pueblo where there was a missionary, he promptly applied himself to any construction that was underway or to any other task in which he could be of assistance. When he was in our college in the villa, which was his ordinary assignment, he was the one to whom the priests turned when they were in need. Because they had so many needs, the letters and errands rained down on this charitable brother, in whom they always found the comfort of a loving and caring mother.

This perseverance in holy deeds and words sprang

from and was maintained by prayer and devotion, in which he spent whatever time he had left after he had tended to his other duties. He particularly spent a large part of the evening in prayer (as I will tell further ahead), but this never caused him to miss community prayers in the morning. He attended the Divine Office with the same or even greater fervor, serving at ordinary Masses and whatever High Masses he could. He also had a notable talent for decorating the altars, and he arranged the church for feast days as though it were the only thing he had to do. He attended the ecclesiastical ceremonies that pertained to him as if he were a sacristan and nothing else, arranging every single thing for every service. Each year he urged his superiors to send to Mexico City for ornaments and items for divine worship so that they would always have new or better ones. The best news that the priests could give him was to tell him that the yearly supplies from Mexico City, which originated in Spain and were brought by the fleet, included some ornaments for the church.

It is known that in spiritual men the practice of pure prayer is accompanied by penance and mortification. Our devout brother always took great care in combining these two virtues. He scourged himself daily and his meals were very moderate and limited (in spite of the fact that he worked so hard). He did not concern himself with eating during the countless trips that he took throughout the province. When he was at home [at the college in the villa], one almost had to force him to eat the modest and meager sustenance on which he survived. Because the climate was so hot and made one listless, he did not eat in the mornings, nor did he drink wine or chocolate, even though the latter is used quite commonly in Mexico.[116] This mortification was even more remarkable and unusual with regard to sleep. He not only slept very little, but also always slept in his clothes. During the thirty-three years he spent in that mission, he never slept in a bed, nor did he even lie down to rest on the ground. His permanent bed was a chair. He would sleep sitting up in it for a little while, and then get up again to go into the church and be in the presence of the Holy Sacrament. This is how he would spend the night, alternating between prayer and resting

116. The drinking of chocolate, which was very popular in Spain at the time, was considered too satisfying or pleasurable an experience to be consistent with the self-denial celebrated by authors such as Pérez de Ribas. However, missionaries who were ill or aged were permitted chocolate for "medical reasons." Indeed, Pérez de Ribas' name appears on a list from 1622 of Jesuits who, in the absence of medicine, were permitted chocolate by the father general (Jacobsen 1938:88).

somberly in his chair. When he traveled in the country-side and camped for the night he would sit against a tree or whatever was at hand, spending the night without lying down. Thus he always practiced the same penance everywhere until his death, as we will later recount.

His poverty was admirable for the clear example it gave. His habit was always worn and mended; his con-solation was to enjoy poverty in material things and riches in eternal matters. When he was working on construction he always wore a cassock of dark woven serge, with such consolation that his joy overflowed.

His humility was as extreme as his poverty. He dis-dained no job, exercise, or task, no matter how humble or lowly. [234] He embraced everything completely and willingly and never spoke of himself or his own personal matters, nor of the many hardships he suf-fered in such holy occupations; he did not even men-tion them. His unusual humility was demonstrated by the great respect and reverence he had for the priests, whom he always addressed with his hat off, standing with his eyes lowered and his face with a very modest and humble countenance. When he took leave of them he would bow his head in recognition of the priestly state, and even though the act I will now relate may seem trivial, it is significant of that reverence. In the refectory he did not wash his hands with the water that was set out for the priests. As a sign of special reverence for their holy hands he washed after them, using the water that had fallen from their hands into the basin.

His charity with [people of] all stations and condi-tions was so remarkable that he did not ignore anyone. All found solace in Brother Francisco, even the needy from outside the house. Because people in such a re-mote land are so needy, there are many opportunities to practice charity. He was so gentle toward everyone, so kind to his fellow man, so helpful to the poor. Be-cause of his gentle manner, it seemed, and it was said, that he was the mother of the province. In his duties as procurator[117] he gave freely or lent whatever was in the house. He came to the rescue of the hungry and the sick, according to the permission he had received from his superiors. One time a poor person was being sent away without what he had requested because the su-perior felt that it was needed in the house at that time.

When Brother Francisco heard about this he went to the Father Rector with tears in his eyes, begging him not to let that person go without aid. "Because (he said) no one must go without solace from this house." The sick person received help, and Brother [Francisco] received the title of 'everything for everyone'.

The charity, love, and attention with which he treated even the Indians was indescribable. He cured those who were ill and gave food to countless Indians who came to the college from various places. When he was in their pueblos he would dress their wounds or bleed them when it was necessary and there was no one else to do it. For this reason the Indians of the province had a great and unusual affection for him. Indeed, for them it was a day for rejoicing when he came to their pueblos. Although they were gentiles, when he entered the pueblos to buy or trade maize for the college he did so with such great security that everyone came up to him as though they were looking at their priest.

Other virtues can be added to those that we recog-nize in Brother Francisco de Castro, all of which he prac-ticed with great prudence, good judgment, frankness, sincerity, and truth, without affectation. Everything he did was especially praiseworthy and did not diminish his persistence and charity, which were his crowning virtues. That maxim of Christ, the Master of Life, took root in his breast: *Qui perseveraverit usque, in finem, hic salvus erit.*[118] He persevered to the end in the virtue with which he had begun, always playing the role of an exemplary, discreet, penitent, and holy religious, in ac-cordance with God's wishes. Therefore, Our Lord deter-mined that he should die as he had lived. He took him quickly while he was busy in a task for the college, and he died as he had lived, without any material comforts.

Although he was not more than two leagues from the college, [235] he died without help after suffering for three hours from a fierce stomach pain. It seemed that God wished to hasten his reward for such hard work, because although a good man who was with him advised him to go back to the college, when the good brother realized from the pain that he was dying, he said that it was better to stay put than to die some-where along the road. They made a bed for him using the bedclothes they were able to find there. However, because he had not slept in a bed for so many years, he could not get comfortable. Therefore, they laid him down on a woven reed mat on the ground, but he could

117. In this instance, the individual responsible for managing the supplies and property of the mission and compiling and filling requests (with the permission of the mission superior) for wine, knives, candle wax, cloth, and other material goods that were requested by missionar-ies in outlying districts.

118. Matthew 24:13: "but that man will be saved who endures to the last" (Knox 1956:25).

not rest there either. He wanted to die in his old bed, which was a simple chair, so he asked to be seated. Once he was seated he asked for a crucifix and a holy candle, and entrusting himself with great serenity to Our Lord, he offered up his soul. Two days earlier he had confessed and taken Communion at the college. Whenever he was there he received the Holy Sacrament on Sundays and Thursdays, and thus his entire life was a continual preparation for death. We can very rightly say of this faithful and prudent servant that he was one of those whom Christ Our Lord depicted in His divine parable, referring first to their ministerial duties: *Quis putas est fidelis seruus, & prudens, quem constituit Dominus super familiam suam, ut det illis cibum in tempore*,[119] and then to their canonization as blessed, provided they worked and gave a good account of their duties.

We can say that God had reared and selected our Brother Francisco in order to care for and sustain His ample new family in Sinaloa. The Lord found him with his hands busy in his labor, hard at work, as was stated by the many missionary priests who knew and dealt with him for many years. They said, "If our father Saint Ignatius were alive today and happened to meet Brother Francisco, he would put his arms around him and say, "This is precisely the type of brother for our Company of Jesus, just like I demand in my rules." Thus we can clearly understand that the Lord kept the promise that He had made to His faithful servants: *Beatus ille seruus, quem cum venerit Dominus eius invenerit, sit facientem, quoniam super omnia bona su constituet eum.*[120] So God has rewarded His servant in heaven for his great and holy works. And from heaven His divine kindness has watched over His new vineyard in Sinaloa, continually sending laborers like Brother Francisco and others who will be written about in this history. We will now go on to another new and abundant field in this province, which this same divine clemency prepared to receive the light of the Gospel. [236]

---

119. *Margin Note*: Math. c. 24. Matthew 24:45: "Which of you, then, is a faithful and wise servant, one whom his master will entrust with the care of the household, to give them their food at the appointed time?" (Knox 1956:26).

120. Matthew 24:46–47: "Blessed is that servant who is found doing this when his lord comes; I promise you, he will give him charge of all his goods" (Knox 1956:26).

BOOK IV

The Mission to the Río Mayo in Sinaloa and the Reduction of the Mayo and Neighboring Nations to Our Holy Faith

CHAPTER I The location of the Río Mayo, the number of its inhabitants, their customs, and how they requested religious instruction

The reduction of the Mayo nation, as they are called in their own tongue, follows both chronologically and geographically the reduction of the [nations of] the Río Zuaque, which were recorded in the previous book. Mayo is also the name of the river that they inhabit. This nation is more numerous than any of the others that have been discussed up to this point. In their language [Cáhita] the word 'Mayo' means *término*, or boundary. This is because their river is between two other rivers populated by enemy peoples who constantly waged war against them, thus making it difficult for them to leave their territory. One of these enemy peoples was the extremely bellicose Yaqui, who will be discussed in the following book. The others were the Tehueco and other nations who lived along the Río Zuaque. As will be seen throughout the chapters of this fourth book, the Christian religion has been victoriously advancing throughout all these nations. In the process the glorious standard of Christ's Cross has achieved new triumphs and the Gospel has spread new splendors. The reduc-

tion and conversion of lesser nations will also be recorded. These people joined the Mayo and were settled along the upper part of their river, in the foothills of the mountains. This book will be concluded with the glorious triumphs of two ministers of the Gospel who spilled their blood and gave their lives for its preaching.

The Río Mayo is about forty leagues from the Villa de San Felipe on the Río Sinaloa and about twenty-four leagues to the north of the large Río Zuaque. It is the fifth river in the Province of Sinaloa and has its headwaters in the mountains of Topia, just like all the other rivers in the province. [237] The river runs through flatland and some valleys for sixteen leagues, and then through montes and into the Sea of California. It is not very swift or powerful, and almost the entire year one can wade across it, provided that it is not at the time of year when the water rises. Then, it takes on a lot of water and overflows, just like the others, and in this way it irrigates and fertilizes some of its valleys. Even though the river is not swift and powerful, it was one of the most densely populated in all of Sinaloa. For this reason one could gather eight to ten thousand Indian warriors from among the people who lived there, where the total population was about thirty thousand.[1]

Their language is the same as that spoken by the people on the Río Zuaque and Río Yaqui. The Mayo, however, are not as fierce as these other nations. Rather, they are more tractable and gentle. They all work the land except for the few in one ranchería or another who were wild.[2] In terms of the rest of their customs—their foods, homes, lifestyle, weapons, the use of drunken revels and dancing, and the multiplicity of wives or concubines—the Mayo were similar to the rest of the nations we have described. Many of them were fishermen, especially those who lived close to the sea, for both the sea and the river abound in fish. Their settlements consisted of rancherías along the banks of the river.

In the beginning the Mayo had very little contact with Spaniards because they were confined within their borders; commerce and dealings with other nations were cut off on all sides. They waged war against some of these nations, particularly the Yaqui. The normal case was that they were the attacked rather than the attackers. In time, however, Captain Diego Martínez de Hurdaide opened the way and made travel safe for them (as was stated earlier). Once they had free passage they came in large numbers to see the captain and the priests.[3] They [also] went to Christian pueblos, where they enjoyed seeing the arrangement of houses and churches, and the peace they enjoyed. This was how they came to wish for the same thing in their own pueblos and for both them and their children to be Christians.

When Christians went to their lands and rancherías the Mayo welcomed them with special kindness. By that time Christians were already enjoying a great deal of security with all nations, even those that were gentile and with whom they previously had been at war. To enter these nations and be well received, they needed no other safeguard than to say, "I am baptized." With this, they were assured of being well treated and given safe passage (except through the lands of the Yaqui, who were a fortress that was difficult to conquer).

When Fort Montesclaros, which was referred to earlier, was being built [in 1610] a great number of Mayo volunteered to help. At about the same time, and before they were missionized, whenever the captain had to undertake an expedition or military action, a large number of Mayo would respond when he ordered them to draft men to accompany him. On many occasions they faithfully assisted him, especially in his full-scale battles with the Yaqui, which will be mentioned later. The captain reciprocated this loyalty with good deeds. He decreed in writing that they were under the crown's protection and gave their caciques horses and other things. In this way he had them quite won over and they felt safe in their lands, without fear of other nations disturbing or invading them.

This was the state of this nation when divine grace moved them to insistently and effectively request priests to provide them with religious instruction and illuminate them with the light of the Gospel. The Mayo were notably diligent in their efforts to get priests to minister to them as [priests] did other Christian nations in the province. They frequently went to the Villa de San Felipe to see the priests and the captain, [238] offering to reduce themselves to large settlements with churches, so that they could more easily receive religious instruction.

There were some families at that time who felt that ministers were being delayed in reaching their lands, and so they decided to come and settle where there were priests. I was instructing the Zuaque when a large group of Mayo offered to come and live there in order to benefit from my teaching. They would have done so had I not assured them that within a short time they would have priests in their own lands. According to royal orders and decrees, this nation could not be reduced without an order from the viceroy. There was also no priest in Sinaloa who could attend to the Mayo without neglecting his own district. Furthermore, everything had to be arranged first in Mexico City.[4]

Once this proposal was made to superiors and the advantages had been recognized of providing religious instruction to such a willing nation, the viceroy, who was the marquis of Guadalcazar,[5] gave his permission for the founding [of the Mayo mission]. His Excellency

---

1. As noted in the "Critical Introduction" Pérez de Ribas' aboriginal population estimates generally are low and reflect his failure to acknowledge pre-missionization losses from introduced disease. The Mayo may well have lost upwards of half their population between 1591 and 1614 (Reff 1991b:214–18).

2. *Montarazes*, meaning that they were hunter-gatherers rather than agriculturalists.

3. As noted in the previous Book the first Mayo delegation came south to the Río Fuerte in 1605.

4. Pérez de Ribas is referring here to the fact that permission (and a commitment of funds from the royal treasury) was required from the viceroy before a priest could assume missionary responsibilities on the frontier.

5. Diego Fernández de Córdoba (1612–21) (Polzer, Barnes, and Naylor 1977:99).

wrote to the captain of the garrison, entrusting him to carefully keep the Mayo under royal protection. He ordered the Father Provincial of the Company to send priests to take charge of this new enterprise, which was of such great service to Our Lord. This was difficult because of the large number of people and the location of their settlements. The Mayo were farther from the garrison than the other nations that were being instructed. They also bordered many gentile nations, especially the brave Yaqui, who are no more than fourteen leagues from the Mayo. These were all reasons that obliged the Father Provincial to find a minister who was highly experienced in similar enterprises. God, who governs with His divine providence and sees to all things, especially those dealing with the conversion of people and their reduction to His church, provided an appropriate subject. This was Father Pedro Méndez, the veteran missionary of Sinaloa who was mentioned earlier. He had given the Ocoroni religious instruction and had also founded the Tehueco mission. After laboring apostolically for twenty-four years, superiors called him back to Mexico City to rest and find relief, for he was weakening from age and the great hardships that he endured in the missions.[6]

This most religious priest was in Mexico City at the time discussions were taking place concerning a minister to found the Mayo mission. The Father Provincial was certain of Father Méndez's tireless spirit in the service of God, but he feared for his bodily strength, inasmuch as Father Méndez was nearly seventy years old. All the same, because of special impulses from heaven (which I omit for the sake of brevity), the Father Provincial offered him the enterprise. The priest accepted the proposition as soon as he heard it, as if he were willed and ordered by God Himself. And so he returned to Sinaloa.

He promptly made the journey of three hundred leagues [to the Villa de San Felipe]. There, he was so anxious to see the Río Mayo and help those poor souls who awaited him that he departed the villa and our college before the other priests, who loved and venerated him as a father and companion, could welcome him, for they were all in their districts.

Because this was an undertaking that the viceroy had specifically entrusted to the captain, he, too, wanted to accompany the priest to the Mayo. The captain had come to love these Indians, who had assisted him in previous enterprises. Therefore, he quickly ordered that thirty soldiers be readied, as well as armored horses, because the Mayo were bordered by other gentile nations. They all set out in good company for the Río Mayo where, as is told in the following chapter, they were welcomed. [239]

6. Méndez had left Sinaloa for Mexico City in 1611, after his life was threatened by some of his rebellious Tehueco neophytes.

CHAPTER II Father Pedro Méndez arrives accompanied by the captain; they themselves relate the welcome they were given by the Mayo and the establishment of their mission

The Mayo had already been informed by the captain that he was bringing a priest who would reside permanently among them, baptizing them and teaching them God's word, thereby fulfilling their desire to be Christians. The Mayo received this news with great pleasure. The priest's and captain's personal letters to the Father Rector of the college relate how they were welcomed by the Mayo.[7]

Father Pedro Méndez says the following:

In this [letter] I will give Your Reverence an account of our arrival, which to the glory of Our Lord was quite prosperous. The fact that the captain had taken this [visit] so seriously was very important, for no other person would have done half of what he did. He first notified the Mayo of our coming, [the purpose of] which was to give them Holy Baptism, which they had requested many times. He told them that they should gather together to receive it. Although they had dispersed because of famine, they paid the captain great heed, gathering in the pueblo that he had indicated in his orders. The most important cacique came to inform us of this ten leagues before we reached them. Farther on, before reaching the first pueblo on that river (which we named the River of the Holy Trinity), fifteen more principal caciques came forward, as did more than four hundred Indians with their wives and children. They welcomed us joyfully, with their heads adorned in abundant plumage of several colors. They had erected Crosses along the way, which certainly caused us to spill many tears of devotion. They had erected arches as well which, although not triumphal (like those in Mexico City), certainly did well to declare the glorious triumph that Christ, the King of Kings and Lord of Lords, was winning over His enemies. Large numbers of people streamed out on horseback and on foot. They were organized so they could be counted, the men and boys in their lines and the women and girls in theirs. They had built enramadas in the form of churches where the infants would be baptized.

We reached the first pueblo and from there to the coast of the Sea of California, along a distance of eighteen leagues, we congregated seven pueblos. With the good help of the caciques the captain and soldiers counted about twenty

thousand people.[8] They were careful not to count in one pueblo those who had already been counted in another. Because the famine was great, there was a large number of Indians missing who had stayed in the monte searching for food. There were other maritime groups at the mouth of this river who were not counted because they were dispersed among the inlets, although their caciques did follow the captain's order. They promised to come and settle wherever he told them as long as it was close to their fishing sites. These people together with those who live along the river will form a large settlement.

To the glory of Our Lord and the consolation of the superiors who sent me here, in the first fifteen days I baptized thirty-one hundred infants, five hundred adults, and a large number of old men and women. Of all those baptized some five hundred infants and adults later died, going quickly to be with Our Lord with great assurances of their salvation.[9] Blessed be the Lord, who has so rapidly granted these people that which I have desired for so many years and because of my sins cannot achieve.

It happened that, having just arrived from my journey and being very tired, I [found myself] baptizing five hundred and six hundred people without ceasing so that they would not disperse until they had all been baptized (the captain's patience in all this was very edifying). Since then other solemn Baptisms have been carried out here. [240]

As soon as they were baptized, I married some seventy couples in facie Ecclesiae. They came to me with a wife chosen from among the many they usually have, and they keep only this one. They take to this well, and will do so even more once they are reduced and willingly abandon their drunken revels and former profanities. It is most comforting to see them in the church removing the discs they wear in their ears from one another. There have been pueblos in which (without my mentioning it or even remembering to do so) they have asked me to cut their hair to make a ponytail like [that worn by] the Christians near the Villa de San Felipe. Although the churches here are not like those

7. Hurdaide and Méndez reached the Río Mayo in January 1614. Méndez's letters and Hurdaide's letter to Martín Pérez, the rector and superior of the Sinaloa Mission, are in the anua of 1614.

8. Méndez's letter in the anua of 1614 says nine thousand. Pérez de Ribas was not exaggerating the size of the Mayo population, however, as is borne out by the anuas from subsequent years (e.g., AGN 1616, 1620).

9. This is a sizable number of deaths. In the following chapter Pérez de Ribas cites another of Méndez's letters written in 1614 that further suggests that the Mayo were affected by the epidemic of typhus and other diseases that hit the northern frontier in 1612–15 (Reff 1991b:154–58).

in the villa, I have seven made from xacales, where I trust in Our Lord many souls that are pleasing to His Divine Majesty are gathering and will gather in the future.

The people of this river are (generally speaking) of a very good nature and display the least degree of idolatry that I have observed to date. It is true that these people behave differently than those of other nations. In fact, some of these nations of the Río Mayo even understand atoms;[10] those who do are not as mistrustful [as other nations].

Going into one pueblo, I found a sick man who was dying and nearly unable to speak. I baptized him because I had learned earlier that he had requested Baptism and through many means had tried to get someone to find me. As I understand it, Our Lord took him away just after I had baptized him, which was a great comfort to me. In a different pueblo prior to this one, an old Christian woman died and they buried her outside the door of her house. But then one of her sons arrived from outside the pueblo and dug her up and took her to the church, saying that if she was a Christian, why should she not be buried in the house of the Christians? I have not found any repugnance for Baptism on the part of old men or women, nor on the part of those who are sick and then recover and want me to baptize their companions and marry them in facie Ecclesiae. Among other nations this is usually difficult to accomplish.

Some time later [still in 1614] the priest wrote the following:

I did not know what the Mayo were [really like] until I began baptizing adults, and the Lord be praised, I have baptized seventeen principal Indians. I can say of all of them that they are the best Christians I think I have had in all the missions I have been in. They are attentive and devoted to the matters of God Our Lord, and at night I hear praying in all the houses. They never miss Mass for any reason and they are very obedient. From the change they have undergone since the days when they lived in liberty it seems a good thing that Our Lord has come into their souls. These are the good beginnings that promise Our Lord great glory in the end.

Up to here [I have been citing] the priest's [letters]. What follows is Captain Hurdaide's letter, which is included here because of the information it provides concerning the variety of nations that inhabit this extensive province. [The letter] says:

My Father Rector, because it was a time of great famine, I used up all [the provisions] I had brought with me when we reached the Mayo and began their reduction. Because I was in charge of maintaining such a large [number of] people and Indian allies, I was forced to send my muleteers

in search of maize in the sierras of the Nébome and Nure. Without my authorization these muleteers went fifty-five leagues farther ahead, and I received word that they were in peril, surrounded by enemies. I myself was in greater peril from hunger, for the soldiers and I were eating nothing but grass. Nevertheless, I felt obliged to go as quickly as possible with my twenty soldiers to save the muleteers. I went into the high mountains of the gentile Nébome, who are [my] allies and have always been faithful, having promised me their friendship five years ago [in 1610].

They welcomed us with great demonstrations of love, with enramadas and Crosses placed here and there. Some older Indian women took [241] large pots of water, and sprinkling it on us, they said, "There are as many of you Spaniards coming to live in these lands as there are drops of water that we are sprinkling on you." Once they had performed this ceremony with me, they went to the place where we had slept and did the same. There I found the muleteers who had fled the aforementioned danger. I continued on for three days through settled lands in that mountain region, and before I had reached the last settlement the people came to [our] rescue with large amounts of food. I found Crosses in place, [as well as] arches, enramadas, and an infinite number of Indians from the region, with their wives and children. They asked me to place my hand on their heads, saying, "Now that you have touched me, I will live many years because of the great desire I had to see you."

These nations are settled on some very large plains which are formed in the middle of the widest part of the mountain range, to the north between the Río Mayo and the Río Yaqui. They are a settled people of a very gentle nature and are given more to laboring and cultivating the land than to war. They are great farmers and cultivate using irrigation. They manage [their] reservoirs and canals as skillfully as Spanish farmers. They also have many chickens from Castilla.[11] Their settlements are much more orderly and compact than those of other nations outside the mountain range. Their buildings are very sturdy because they are not temporary like those along these rivers, which are made from woven reed mats. Theirs are made of poured earth,[12] like adobes. The Indian

10. *Atomos*; Méndez is presumably referring here to the atomistic theory of Greek philosophers such as Aristotle (later discussed by Ambrose and Augustine), which held that matter was made up of simple combinations of elements (Steneck 1976:31–33).

11. *Gallinas de Castilla*. The Nébome had visited the Villa de San Felipe and their relatives at Bamoa for years, so it is possible that they had obtained chickens, which were introduced to Mexico by the Spaniards. It is also possible that Pérez de Ribas was referring to domesticated turkeys, as the Nébome (Pima Bajo) raised several birds aboriginally (see Hammond and Rey 1928:161; Pennington 1980). However, if he was in fact referring to domesticated turkeys, one would expect him to have used a native word or the usual Spanish term *gallinas de la tierra*.

12. *Terrados de tierra*. Archaeological research in Sonora (Pailes 1978; Reff 1981) indicates that the Opata and Pima Bajo built rectangular, flat-roofed structures of "puddled adobe." Upon a foundation of stone set in adobe, a wall several feet high would be formed and allowed to dry, and then another layer of adobe would be added; this process was repeated until the desired wall height was realized. Adobe structures of this type date to at least the eleventh century in Sonora (Pailes 1978; Pailes and Reff 1985). A Spaniard viewing such a structure in the seventeenth century might well have described it as one of layered earth.

women are very chaste in their dress. They cover themselves all the way to their feet with well-tanned buckskin, which they consider so valuable that they refuse to give it up at any price.

Two caciques from farther inland came to see me because they had heard that I was there. They said they wanted to pledge obedience and be my friends. I treated them well and they returned [to their lands]. When I asked them about the nations of Nuevo México, none of them had any news concerning Spaniards, although they did know about the bison of Cíbola and other large settlements.[13] I experienced their good nature and docility and their great willingness to receive the Holy Gospel, especially the Nébome, who with demonstrations of great regret said to me, "We will all be gone before a priest comes to baptize us." I told them they had been missing out on the benefit of having a priest because they had not been as insistent as the Indians on the Río Mayo. They repeatedly promised that they would come soon to make their request. This will be a great tool for keeping the Yachimi [Yaqui] Indians, their enemy, in check. By giving these Yachimi religious instruction at the same time as the Nébome, it can all be done with greater security.

Upon learning that I was there, another Indian nation in that region called the Nure came down (according to what they said) to help me. Six years earlier they had pledged me their peace and obedience. They have lain fallow long enough to be well ready for the planting of the holy word and to carry forth the Holy Gospel. Your Reverend Father, ask Our Lord to aid in their cause and ask our Father Provincial to send laborers for this large field that promises overflowing fruits. May the Lord bring them to ripeness.

Up to here [I have been citing] the letter of this brave Christian captain, who always accompanied the priests so well. I add that some years later these nations of which he speaks were reduced to our Holy Faith. This will be recorded in Book VI of this history. All these happy beginnings of the foundation and establishment of the Mayo mission were a good omen of similar advances that the Mayo would later make in our Holy Faith. [242]

CHAPTER III Cases of edification and the progress of this new Christianity

The devil did not cease to regret the loss of his great prisoner, the populous Mayo nation, which was taken from him. Vice had taken deep root among the Mayo, particularly in the matter of marriage, or better said, cohabitation with women who were closely related, such as mothers and daughters or sometimes sisters.[14] The devil returned with his snares, pointing out to the Mayo that this was a custom of their ancestors into which they had been born and raised. This was an obstacle that prevented more than a few of them from attaining Baptism. The priest needed the special favor of Our Lord to overcome this, and divine providence intervened in several cases, which for the sake of brevity will not be told.

Another abuse found among the Mayo that it was necessary to correct was that pregnant women could easily abort their infants. There was some of this in other nations, particularly when a pregnant woman already had a nursing infant. When she was reproached for this abuse and cruelty the response of the Indian woman was, "Can't you see that I am looking out for the life of this child that I'm holding in my arms?" thus making it clear that she was killing one child to raise another. The following case helped to provide a solution to this pernicious abuse. Just as there are midwives who help women in the birth and delivery of their children, there was an old Indian woman who had the diabolical job of making pregnant women abort, exhorting them and providing them with the means to do so. God had mercy on her soul, for he moved her heart to request Baptism. She prepared herself and received it, and then the following morning she was found dead. It seems that God wanted to insure her salvation, for He gave her no chance to fall back into the detestable vice that she used to practice. He removed this scandalous woman from the pueblo so that pregnant women would learn a lesson regarding this abuse.

13. These were probably Opata from Sonora, Batuco, or Sahuaripa, all of whom would have known about Cíbola from trade.

14. Here again it would seem that Pérez de Ribas and his fellow missionaries misconstrued the Mayo's classificatory kinship system and practice of matrilineal residence.

At the beginning of their conversion God Our Lord favored these Mayo materially with very fertile [fields] and abundant harvests. Even those who were gentiles noticed this. When they were gentiles the entire nation suffered from great hunger because there were so many people and [arable] land was scarcer than on the other rivers. Nor did the Mayo dare to leave [their territory] for food, because their enemies were very close and surrounded them. But after the Mayo became Christians their fields yielded such abundant harvests that they could then help other neighboring nations. This made them happy with the new law of God that they had received, and with it so many divine favors in material and human matters.

A special case happened regarding this matter. A gentile Indian came to the priest, leading a horse that he said belonged to a Christian. He showed fistfuls of maize stalks to demonstrate the damage that the horse had done to his fields and to complain about the Christian owner. The priest called the owner and learned that the damage had been very slight and that the Christian did not have anything with which to pay for it. Therefore, the priest turned to the gentile Indian and said: "Our Christian law commands that no one do wrong to another person. This Christian, or his horse, did wrong to you, but he cannot pay you. I will pay you for him." The priest then satisfied him with some iron implement or a hatchet or a knife, which these Indians highly prize. [243] But more highly prized was what resulted from this minor case. The gentile Indian went back to his house and brought sixteen of his relatives, saying to the priest, "Well, if this is what your law commands, it surely is from God. For this reason these relatives of mine and I have come to be baptized in order to live in the good law." All of them prepared [for Baptism], and once they had been baptized they persuaded others to do the same and become Christians.

Divine grace overcame a serious problem through the conversion of a sorcerer who came to ask the priest to baptize him. The priest responded that he certainly would not do so unless he first handed over the tools of his sorcery and renounced them, for these were things that were highly forbidden by our holy law. (This is a very difficult matter to overcome in people who are very accustomed to and trained in familiar dealings with the devil. Nevertheless, God concurred here with His grace.) The Indian demonstrated the validity of his request for Holy Baptism, because he immediately went to his house and brought back four kinds of sorcery that he used for various effects and events: one to prevent the fields from drying up, another to prevent the river from flooding, and others for similar frauds. Because this Indian was a famous sorcerer, the priest was somewhat concerned that there might still be some traces of superstition left in his house. Therefore, he exhorted him to make sure that none of these diabolical tools remained. The Indian answered that the priest should be satisfied that he had willingly brought these things and desired to be a true Christian. The priest baptized him, and he gave many signs of having sincerely received God's law.

These were signs that this new Mayo Christianity was beginning to flourish, the blossoms being the actual fruits of this Christianity. In the first four years more than sixteen thousand souls were baptized. In the years that followed almost the same number [were baptized], not including those in distant rancherías. Although these Baptisms have been discussed only briefly here, it should not be understood, as some might think, that they are performed in a mad rush or that the sacrament is administered and received blindly, without the Indians understanding what they have received and what their duties are as subjects of the law of Christ Our Lord. All this helps the Gospel to become better established, and they understand as well that the holy bath [15] of Baptism is not simply any bath like the ones they take in their river.

Thus it was that once Father Pedro Méndez had [baptized] a good number of Christians, he celebrated the first Lenten season, explaining to them in various talks the meaning of the holy season and how the Holy Church celebrates it, particularly the precept of annual Confession, which is the obligation of all Christians. These new Christians applied themselves so well to the fulfillment of this precept that they surpassed what one would expect from people so new in the Faith in regard to the integrity and orderliness of their confessions. They devised means to aid their memory so that people would not forget a single sin. Some of them made little bundles of colored sticks, setting out a certain number for each kind of sin; others made knots on little cords at certain intervals; others were helped by the fingers on their hands, which is how they count.

The priest remained in each pueblo for fifteen days in order to finish hearing confessions, and he marveled at the fervor of these new Christians, as the church was never empty the entire day. Moreover, it was something to see how carefully all those who had made their confession participated in scourging processions, using

15. *Lavacro.*

a rope scourge made from [the fibers of] the mescal plant. These processions took place in each pueblo after confessions had been heard. The Indians forged the rowels [of their scourges] by sticking either broken needles or thorns from the thickets into little wax balls. [244] There was not a single old man or young boy, principal or *macehual* (which is what they call vassals), who did not scourge himself. They marched in a very orderly procession, in groups of two hundred by two hundred, carrying countless torches. These are makeshift, because they do not have large candles made from wax (which is scarce in this land). Instead, they use the branches of the pitahaya cactus, which grows in the monte. When they are dry they burn like a torch and illuminate the plazas and fields. One can well understand that God would welcome the enthusiasm of these poor Indians, for these [processions] astonished many gentile observers, moving them to tears.

The Redeemer of the World willed that during the first Lenten season in this new Christian community there was a converted Magdalene in whom the power of His divine grace could be made known, in a fashion similar to the conversion the Lord wrought in the other Magdalene in the Gospel when the Son of God walked among men.[16] It is thus seen that the effectiveness of His divine word and clemency still works. It happened that in this nation there was a gentile Indian woman who was given the name Magdalene when the priest baptized her, because her exterior beauty was the most extraordinary that had ever been seen among these people. The Indian woman enhanced her beauty with all kinds of finery, paints, and colors. She was a fallen woman and the temptation and scandal of all the pueblos. Just as she herself was lost, she also had led many married Indian men astray. Her profession was to rob other women of their husbands, and she usually had two or three beguiled men who were caught up in her wiles and with whom she entertained herself.

She did everything possible to avoid the priest and to keep him from seeing her. God willed that one day he should meet up with her along the road in the company of some other Indian women. She was all dressed up, and although she tried to hide herself, she was unable to do so. The priest asked her why she made no effort to be baptized when there were so many Christians in her nation. She answered impertinently and scornfully that it was because she didn't have any man she could marry. The priest could very well have said to her what Christ said to the Samaritan woman—that she had at least five husbands but not one was her own. Instead, he ignored this so as not to irritate her, replying simply that as she was going to the same pueblo as he was, he would specifically look for a husband for her, one with whom she could be baptized and married.

At that time these statements made no impression on her, but later when the priest went to hear the confessions of people in another pueblo, he renewed his efforts to find the lost Indian woman and have her brought to him. They found her and she came to see him with no less trappings and paint than she usually wore. She was so furious that her heart seemed to leap out of her body. The priest, with his usual calmness, began to exhort her to change her life and choose a husband with whom she could settle down and live in God's service. She responded to this very angrily, "I've had one for three days, and he'll be just like all the others that I have discarded." Moved by God, the priest then changed his style, and demonstrating his anger, he raised his voice and with great authority reprehended her for speaking so impertinently to a man who was a priest and who taught them God's word. He ordered her to get down on her knees and remove the finery she was wearing. Divine grace then began to demonstrate its effectiveness, for this women who was a fierce lioness was transformed into a lamb, and getting down on her knees and removing her finery, she very humbly requested Holy Baptism.

Not wanting to lose this opportunity, the priest set to work to find her a suitable husband. God sent a young man who wanted to marry her and whom she also wanted to take as her husband. The priest gave them both a talk concerning the state into which they were entering and the faithfulness that they were to observe. Once he had instructed them in the catechism he baptized them, and to the great pleasure of their souls they remained [245] in this new state, in which they persevered as promised, setting a good example in their pueblo. To this was added the fact that once those men who were lost or rebellious due to their relationship with this woman, who was the devil's snare, were freed by this couple's example, they also sought to be baptized and to marry and live in God's service, as they did. This event demonstrated the mercy God has shown these peoples, and the following chapter will further confirm this.

---

16. Pérez de Ribas appears to have in mind here Luke 8:2 and 7:36–50 ("the woman who was a sinner"), which today, and apparently in the seventeenth century, often is incorrectly thought to refer to Mary Magdalene.

CHAPTER IV Another letter from Father Pedro Méndez relating the fervor with which the Mayo nation was accepting conversion

No one can speak or write more precisely about things than the individual who has them in front of him or can touch them (as they say) with his own hands. For this reason in this chapter I have copied word for word a letter from the very religious Father Pedro Méndez, who returned to Sinaloa from Mexico City (as we said) to Christianize the Mayo.[17] As a most obedient son, and because this was a new Christian community, he gives the Father Provincial who sent him an account of events and of his ministries and mission. He writes:

I was greatly comforted by Your Reverence's letter and by its encouragement for whatever difficulties and hardships arise in this or any other mission and conversion in the service of Our Lord. When I consider the wonders that He works with the Mayo and how much He loves them, I want to write to you at length for the edification and consolation of those [in Mexico City].

In the previous letter, which I wrote a short time after our entrada, I said that the [number of] persons baptized reached into the thousands. Now as I write this letter, because of the Lord's kindness and love for those whom He has redeemed, the number of baptized is much greater, as is the number of couples married in facie Ecclesiae. They are all very good Christians and are very fond of matters concerning Our Lord and the Church. They are also very obedient to the priests. I have never instructed people who learn the catechism so quickly and who pray without tiring. Those who are catechumens at one Baptism are teachers at the next. They come running [to religious instruction] with as much excitement as if they were coming to take their seats at the theater.[18] At night one hears nothing from their houses but their praying in unison, not only boys but the adults and topiles. It is a great comfort to see them hear Mass on their knees, as silently as if they had been raised throughout their entire lives to do so, and also to see them worship the Most Holy Sacrament by beating their breast when it is raised or to watch all the Christians genuflect and bless themselves when they enter a church. When the [bell] is sounded for the Ave Maria in the evening they stop whatever they are doing, whether they are out under their ramadas or in the doorways of their houses. Since the very beginning of Baptisms, they have made a habit of very devoutly saluting the priests who have baptized them. As a sign of recognition both young and old would greet them in the morning and again at vespers.

It is amazing to see toddlers three or four years old sitting in small groups and saying their prayers as best they can. When the older children are tardy in the morning they come to excuse themselves by saying, "Pardon me, Father, I overslept," or, "It was so cold that I waited before coming." A name has been coined for these children. It is [246] *Paretabuseme*, which means 'the priest's guard' (because they see me walking accompanied by them). Although the Mayo use this term in jest because they see that I have no other guard or escort, I take it in the way that it should be taken—that through them the Lord is protecting me. Although such matters may seem insignificant, these children are not. From the time they are small they are greatly inclined to the old customs in which they are raised. During the day or at night with a light they go out into the monte with their little bows to kill lizards and rats. The older children play with a knife from sunrise to sunset, or they sleep during the day with it stuck into the ground as a headboard. Now, however, one sees them going about in the cold of the morning, making the stations [of the Cross] and kissing the hand of a person whom only yesterday they did not know.

It greatly consoled the Father Rector, who came to visit me, to see the joy, peace, and serenity that everyone—young and old—enjoys on this river. I certainly confess that one of the greatest difficulties of coming here, which it was mentioned I might find, was the noise—the all-night drumming and dancing—which disturbed me for several years in similar districts.[19] It seemed to me that these things that the infidels do are a thing from hell. But Our Lord has decided to confound my faintheartedness, and due to Your Reverence's holy assistance, I have not found any trace of what I had feared; rather, at night there is only the sweet sound of prayer. Among all the people that I have instructed I have not seen such evident proofs of grace and the Holy Spirit as I have in these people following their Baptism. Those who were clothed in their distinctive and barbarous customs are overcome by extraordinary joy when they are baptized. The old and lame seem to acquire feet and the agility to run to the church, while the dumb acquire tongues to give thanks to the priest for the favor received.

I baptized the principal of a pueblo who on many occasions had avoided me. He was very given to profanity

---

17. This letter was written in December 1614 and addressed to Rodrigo de Cabredo, the Father provincial.

18. *Comedia*.

19. Méndez may be alluding here to his stint among the Tehueco, whose rebelliousness forced him to retire to Mexico City several years earlier.

and painting himself, but as soon as he surrendered to the voice of the Lord he removed everything, and it was as if he had never worn it. The same day this man was baptized he accompanied me [when I went] to [visit] a sick person who was very far from the pueblo. He was riding a very good trotting horse and got quite a way ahead of me, but he frequently stopped to wait and once in a while would turn and say to me with a laughing voice: "Father, I'm very happy," "Father, what is this new happiness that I feel in my soul?" and other similar things. I would answer him with whatever struck me as appropriate.

I baptized another old principal who subsequently accompanied me to the homes of newly baptized persons. While we were all talking in the doorway he would kneel for nearly half an hour, refusing to rise. He continually explained with words and gestures that he felt great happiness in his soul to be a Christian. He would have returned to his house on his knees if I had not ordered him to stand up.

Even with all the adults that I have mentioned who have been married and the many women who have been put aside, I do not know of any who have returned to this abomination. If there are problems, they are caused by people who have come from elsewhere to live free of their conscience and to cause trouble. With this exception it is one of the better missions between here and Mexico City. I have not seen a trace of drunkenness, except in two pueblos, and even then it was not much. This is particularly noteworthy considering that they have great freedom to do whatever they please without any restraint. Therefore, everything they do is for my edification.

One maiden [20] (which is what they call a married woman who does not yet have children) possessed such virtue that, through her words and admonitions, she was able to bring me six important persons to be baptized. [247] Another woman who was also well instructed in the matters of Our Lord brought me her parents, who were very opposed to Baptism. However, she told them that because she was a Christian and would go to heaven, it would not be right for them to go to hell when they died. So that they could all rest together, she told them that they needed to come to ask me for Baptism. They came and were baptized, and these parents and their daughter are some of the most devout [Christians] in the pueblo.

Although they are new to the Faith, the Mayo very carefully keep the Commandments of God and the Church. There was an Indian woman who, right after she was baptized, asked me, "When is Sunday?" When I asked her why she wanted to know, she told me that she was making a blanket and did not want to work on Sunday, as God commanded. Because they did not have a Christian division of days into Friday or Saturday, they ask me many questions of this nature concerning the commandments, especially about the days when they must abstain from eating the game that they hunt in the monte.

On All Saints' Day, Our Lord interceded to break the most resistant chains that remained in this nation—those of the two most important principales on this river. One of them had three wives, two of whom were sisters; the other had six wives. The truth of the matter is that they would have agreed to my baptizing them if they did not have to put aside all those women. But it was very difficult to get them to do as God commands. Therefore, when I did not baptize them because of their unwillingness to do what was necessary, they did a lot of damage and frightened the people. For this reason I asked the captain to impose his authority—to order them to stop causing trouble. In order to confound my feeble trust, Our Lord willed that very day to prepare one of them so quickly that I had not even received a response yet [from the captain]. This principal cast aside two of his wives, whom he ordered to be baptized and married to other men. He himself was then baptized and married to the woman to whom he had the greatest obligation, to the joy of everyone on the river.

The same day Our Lord also willed to add another soul to the number of His saints. They had brought him to me the day before at the pueblo, and he was very near the end of his life. It was very unusual how when I arrived the principal looked at me with terrified eyes, as though he was looking at a terrible monster. The first words he said to me were, "Go away, I do not want to be baptized." But after I spoke to him gently and compassionately about his suffering, he turned to me and asked me if I was the priest. I told him I was, and that I had come to save him. "Well then, Father, baptize me," he said. He heard all the catechism and had a very clear understanding of the matters of our Holy Faith, and to my great satisfaction he was baptized. In a gesture of farewell and thanksgiving he put his arms around me with great tenderness and affection, and that same day—All Saints' Day—he died. It is a great consolation that frequently when I am out visiting all the pueblos, baptizing the sick, I find on my return trip that Our Lord has taken most if not all of them. Blessed be His name forever, which secures their souls.

After the fortunate Baptism of the principal who had three wives I proceeded to the pueblo of the principal who had six wives. There Our Lord intervened in the following way. The cacique himself put aside all his wives, and the most important ones he ordered baptized and married to other men. So that no traces of affection might remain in him and so that he might not be tempted in any way, he ordered them to go with their husbands to other pueblos where they had relatives. There Our Lord also broke some lesser chains of [248] other Indian topiles or *aguaciles*,[21] some of whom had two or three wives; all were baptized and married.

From there I went to another pueblo where there was a topil who was also a very important principal. He had four wives and had been one of those most opposed [to conversion] at the outset. He scoffed at those who were

20. *Doncella*.

21. Méndez appears to use the terms topiles and aguaciles here as referents for native elites of lesser and major importance, respectively. Presumably some of these elites were war captains, whose power and influence was more circumscribed, whereas others were heads of lineages or clans.

baptized, saying that he wasn't a child who needed to be baptized. But this time Our Lord arranged it so that in my presence the principal cast aside the women he had most loved; he then had them married [to someone else] and baptized. Then he married the woman to whom he had the greatest obligation. When he noticed that I was concerned about a woman he had in a distant pueblo, because of whom I had delayed registering him with the others for catechism, he came to me and made the argument that I should make sure that his soul was not lost. He also said that he had already given abundant proof of his good intentions by going to such-and-such a pueblo for the sole purpose of requesting Baptism, and that he had ordered the woman he loved best to be baptized. For these reasons I should not deny him Baptism and salvation. He had nearly decided that if I did not baptize him along with the others, then he was going to eat a poisonous herb or take his own life in some other way. He could no longer endure the shame and remorse that his soul suffered for not being a Christian. He said this with tears in his eyes. My own eyes filled to the brim and I put my arms around him. Right then and there I registered him for Baptism, giving thanks to Our Lord, whose Faith makes such an impression on barbarous peoples who have been raised all their lives in customs that are so contrary.

I will not omit relating something that happened to me during the days I spent here, which it seems to me is one of the strangest things that has happened to me since I have been in the Indies. It caused me to trust in the Lord and to believe that one should not lose hope of anyone's salvation as long as he is still alive. It happened that in the beginning when churches were being built here, a gentile Indian principal was working on one of them. Either from excessive exertion or because Our Lord wanted to save him in this way, this man became very sick and subsequently ordered his people to take him to a hill more than a league from the pueblo. His condition worsened, and I went three times with the fiscales of the church and this principal's relatives to try to save him. Because his illness arose from

the work he had done on the church, he had become so soured with hatred for everything that had to do with the Church, the Faith, and its sacraments that dealing with him was like coming up against hard stone. The pangs of hell seemed like flowers to him, and he condemned himself to them along with his parents, while turning his nose up at the glories of heaven. Nevertheless, in the face of such hardness Our Lord always gave me confidence from within that this soul for whom He had shed His blood and whose salvation I so greatly desired would not be lost.

I finally left him and went to visit all my pueblos. When I returned I warily inquired about the sick man. They told me that he was still alive but that he was very near the end. I sent a certain person to him, ordering him to do his job well. The sick man ordered that I be called, and he received me with great joy. He sat up in his modest bed, which was nothing more than a bit of sand, and he heard all the catechism with notable lucidity, solace, and demonstrations of faith. Then with great remorse for his sins and past hardness he was baptized. I bid him farewell and returned to the pueblo, where there was no lesser edification, for two days later around midnight news arrived of his joyous death. The fiscal then took six or eight Christian Indian youths, and in the cold of the early morning, they brought him to the pueblo, where at dawn we buried him *cum honore*.[22]

I close, [249] but not without giving infinite thanks to Our Lord. His mercy alone has allowed me, before I die, to enjoy in this land nearly a year of harvest of souls that is proportionate to my desire.

Thus ends the letter of this religious minister to the Mayo, among whom evangelical law was introduced with far less trouble than in other nations. In the cases that have been recorded here it can clearly be seen the frequent and particular means by which Our Lord selects His predestined souls from among these poor people.

---

22. 'With honor'.

CHAPTER V Another priest comes to help in the Mayo mission; the Baptism of the entire nation is completed and churches are built; an explanation is given for the decrease in the Indian population

Father Pedro Méndez worked courageously to found and establish Christianity among the Mayo. Although a large part of the nation had already been baptized, this nation was very large and some of them remained obstinate and were slow to request Baptism. Furthermore, the pueblos where the people had settled were many. Therefore, a helper for the mission was needed. For this purpose the superiors sent Father Diego de la Cruz, who a short time earlier had arrived in Sinaloa from Mexico City. He applied himself to learning the [Cáhita] language and took charge of three [Mayo] pueblos.[23] With his help the Baptism of the Mayo nation was completed. They were settled in five pueblos along the river,[24] all the way to the sea for a distance of ten leagues. In each pueblo there were five hundred to six hundred male heads-of-household, and in some, more than one thousand. Around 1620 these pueblos all together had about thirty thousand Christian souls.

Already at this time these new Christians came with great fervor to religious instruction and Mass — even on weekdays. The boys and young men from the choirs came to learn to sing, read, write, and celebrate the feast days and the rest of the practices that are observed in these missions. Every morning the boys and girls divided into groups to learn the catechism. Here I will add something about devotion at this age. One day the priest found the children placing little Crosses in the ground in front of where each of them was seated. When he asked why, they answered with the Christian innocence of their youth that it was to scare off the devil so that he would not take from their memories the prayers they were learning. It was a great pleasure for the priest who had engendered them in Christ to hear the children speak [in this manner].

Thus it seemed the time had come to build proper churches in the pueblos, which were very populous and where the spiritual exercises were very well attended. The priests discussed the construction with the Indians, who gladly agreed to build churches like the other baptized nations. They set to work with great fervor and joy. There were times when there were a thousand men, women, and children working on the construction. This, together with the fact that the pueblos were large and populous, made it possible to complete the churches more quickly than in other places. They were dedicated with the same solemn ceremonies and celebrations that have been described among other nations.

The Mayo were enormously happy to see themselves Christian and to see their pueblos take the same form that they had seen in other Christian nations. Later, it was necessary to add a third missionary[25] and divide the pueblos of this nation into three districts. There would have been enough for yet another three priests. Through the priests' industriousness, and even by spending their [250] stipends from the king,[26] which are supposed to be for their own sustenance, they have been able to decorate their churches with retablos, vessels, musical instruments, and other precious things for the greater ornamentation of divine worship. All these greatly aid the devotion of these people and make them more appreciative of divine things.

Afterwards, general Communions were introduced in all the pueblos, for this Divine Sacrament (as has been said) is the sustenance of those who are mature in the Faith. The devotion to the Most Holy Virgin and to her Rosary have also been introduced, along with other devotions that are necessary to nourish and preserve the piety of the faithful. The evangelical laborers

---

23. La Cruz came to Sinaloa in 1615 and began working among the Mayo in late 1615 or early 1616. The anua of 1616 contains his first report to Martín Pérez, the rector of the Sinaloa mission.

24. Etchohoja, Curimpo, Navajoa, Camoa, and Tesia.

25. Apparently 1620, as the anua for that year notes that seven priests came to Sinaloa in 1619. One of the priests was an Irishman named Michael Wadding or Miguel Godínez who was sent to the upper Río Mayo.

26. The stipend varied somewhat but generally amounted to 250 pesos.

of these missions never rest or cease in this, remaining constantly vigilant so as to advance them in the Faith and Christian works.

The Mayo pueblos continue in their Christianity at present, although their population has decreased somewhat from its original number. This presents the opportunity to write, albeit briefly, about a topic and events that have been generally observed in almost all the provinces of the Western Indies. This is the decrease in the native population, which has coincided with an increase in the number of Spaniards in almost all the pueblos and cities of the Indies. I will now discuss this topic because it has in part affected the nations that are dealt with here. It is pertinent for this history to declare what is truthful in this regard so that rumors do not exceed the limits of their reality.

The first thing I will say is that I find two immediate causes for the decrease in these peoples' population. One is general and is very well known throughout the Western Indies: the many illnesses that they call cocolitzles.[27] These are particular to the Indians and are like a plague to them. Through this kind of illness Our Lord, in His highest judgment, has willed to diminish the populations of almost all the nations discovered in the New World. Today there are probably not even half the Indians left of those countless numbers who existed when the Gospel arrived.

I want to put an end here to the argument or complaint that it has been the Spaniards' employment of these peoples for their farming, mining, and other work that has contributed to the decrease. Although this is true in part, certainly this has not been the entire cause of the decline in population. One proof of this, among others, is what is happening in our Province of Sinaloa, where populous nations that are very isolated from Spaniards and thus free from personal work service have nevertheless decreased. Therefore, the aforementioned argument and complaint does not hold.

The same can be said of some other places in the Indies, where the Indians have been freer from Spanish labor demands and where the plague has nevertheless affected them. And if human judgment is free to humbly inquire after the higher designs of divine providence, what we can understand is that these peoples deserved this punishment because of their sins, idola-

tries, murders, sorceries, etc. In a single year the most populous Mexican nation [the Mexica or Aztec] sacrificed to devils and their idols twenty thousand of their enemy. This cruelty, as well as the other vices that consumed Sodom, also existed among these peoples. Because of them the Indians deserved to be done away with by God, just as He depopulated the Promised Land so He could introduce His [own] people. Such people deserved to be wiped from the face of the earth by God, as is pondered in Chapters X through XII of the Book of Wisdom, which concludes [251] with this most supreme maxim: *Quis stabit contra iuditium tuum, aut quis in conspectu tuo veniet vindex iniquorum hominum, aut quis tibi imputabit, si perierint Nationes quas tu fecisti?*[28]

With these words the sacred writer[29] refuted all possible human discourse and complaint about the God who punishes and ravages nations that are the work of His own hands and which He Himself has created and multiplied. To this we can and should add that He also redeemed them with His precious blood. Therefore, if He does away with them, we should understand that He has the right to do so and that He proceeds most justly.

If on the one hand God is wiping out the peoples that we are discussing here and is administering the punishment they deserved, [it is also true that] He has mercifully tempered and guided the execution of this punishment. He has not wanted for them to all perish eternally in their unfaithfulness; rather, He has waited for them first to be converted to God by the preaching of the Gospel. Therefore, [even] if they have had to die a temporal death, He has wished to spare them eternal suffering by granting them the time and means to achieve salvation for their souls and to have the remedy of the Holy Sacraments. And if punishment was to take the form of a plague or sudden destruction by fire, as was merited by the infidelity and evil of those other wretched and abominable cities [Sodom and Gomora], God willed that the punishment of these peoples should be gentler, tempered with clemency and mercy.

Let us remember King David's minor sin of pleasing himself by counting the large number of warriors in his kingdom. God punished this sin with the sentence that King David, who had already acknowledged

---

27. A hispanized form of the Nahuatl cocoliztli. As noted earlier this term meant "the great sickness" or "the great dying" and was used as a referent for the unprecedented epidemics of Old World disease that were coincident with the invasion of Mexico.

28. Book of Wisdom 12:12: "Thy acts who shall question, thy doom who shall gainsay? Will some champion arise to challenge thee on behalf of these rebels, tax thee with unmaking the peoples thou hast made?" (Knox 1956:582).

29. Solomon, who is thought to have authored the Book of Wisdom in the Old Testament.

his arrogance and guilt, found to be the most merciful. Even then God's punishment was a plague that, although it lasted only three days, took the lives of seventy thousand men.[30] The population decline has not come so quickly among the nations that we are discussing here. Rather, it has come over time, providing the Indians with the opportunity to prepare for their eternal salvation. They usually leave many assurances of their salvation for the missionaries who are there to help them. Not the least of reasons for this hope is the fact that these peoples' sins and guilt are more worthy of leniency and pardon, or less unworthy, as compared with the sins of other nations in the world. These people are born largely in ignorance and weakness—circumstances that diminish the gravity of their sins.

The issue [of Indian depopulation] has been greatly noticed in the conversions of the nations of this New World and has caused pious hearts to ache at seeing so many pueblos reduced in numbers and ravaged by illnesses, even after they have converted to the Faith. Because I have already touched upon this issue, and in order to assuage those regrets, I will add here something that can largely temper them. The Indian population of the Indies has in fact decreased, and looking at the ruins of the pueblos, it seems that the numbers of those that have been devastated are great. Upon closer consideration, however, the decline is not as great as it seems (I can speak as an eyewitness because of my position and because I have traveled across Nueva España more than a few times).

The reason for this is that since the Spaniards arrived, thousands of cattle ranches, farms, haciendas, mines, and sugar mills have been established that were absent in gentile times. Today there is an Indian pueblo at each one of these places. If these Indians returned to their former pueblos, they would not be as diminished in number as they appear. The practice of going to live at these ranches and places is very well established in the Indies; it is very good for the native inhabitants because they have lands and other conveniences if they want to farm. They also have a secure food supply. Because the owners of these properties [252] need the Indians to work for them, they take better care of the Indians in sickness and in health than the Indians do themselves,

for the latter are very careless about this. Their food and rations are very secure, and for their work they also receive wages with which to clothe themselves. As a result the Indians easily adapt to living in these farms and ranches. This has been a major cause of the apparent decrease they have undergone, for there are undoubtedly many people presently distributed among the ranches.

Although it is true that we cannot always exculpate all the Spaniards of their harsh treatment of the Indians, it is also true that many of them deal kindly and humanely with the Indians, and we must not blame them all. In addition, there is the singular concern for the Indians' preservation demonstrated by all the Catholic monarchs through the laws they have decreed to protect and shelter the Indians, which it is most advantageous to observe.

The last reason [for native population decline], and the best response to the questions raised, is that decisions of divine providence are most just and holy, and human discourse, which cannot comprehend them, should revere them as such. Through these things God shows Himself for what He is, for if at one point in time He chooses to reduce some nations, He is later able to multiply others, [even] those that He has previously diminished. Human judgment must subject all doubts to His just, albeit hidden, objectives.

On more than a few occasions in these missions and endeavors it is very necessary to resort to this sound consideration and reasoning. This is true when a large number of infants are baptized and then subsequently taken by God in throngs, and the sorcerers spread blasphemies against Holy Baptism, saying that it kills whoever receives it. Nevertheless, God wanted lambs for heaven; He is Lord and Master and He knows very well what He does; it is mankind's duty to cover its head and bow to His orders.

With this let us return to our Mayo, whose population decline obliged me to digress somewhat so as to offer an explanation for this decrease in other provinces. The decrease in the Mayo has occurred not only because of illnesses (although there have been many) and because they have moved to Spaniards' ranches and haciendas, of which there are very few in Sinaloa, and they do not offer much work for the Mayo. It is due also to the fact that they are remarkably fond of traveling and are curious about other lands. It seems that they poured out of the province like the currents of a swollen river when a dam breaks. As was noted, they were so isolated in their heathenism and cut off [from others] that, when they were free and had access to a way out, they left the

---

30. *Margin Note*: 2. Reg. C. 24. The referent here is 2 Samuel 24:10–15, which recounts how David, after boastfully counting his warriors, received a messenger from God, offering him his choice of punishment: three years of famine, three months of pursuit by enemies, or three days of plague.

confinement of their pueblos in droves. They set out to see the world and to seek clothing with which to cover and adorn themselves—clothing which today they are never without. Because they are very good workers, it has also happened that there are a lot of Mayo scattered throughout nearly all the pueblos of Nueva España.

In spite of everything that has been said, at the present time a good number of Christian Mayo remain. They are a very good example of perseverance and have never denied or turned their backs on their [good Christian] beginnings. Nor have they ever given any signs of revolt or uprising, as has happened in other nations. They always have been loyal to the Spaniards. With this we conclude the account of this prosperous Christianity. We will now proceed to the discussion of surrounding nations and how, to the greater glory of God, they celebrated their Baptism with new offspring that daily were born to the Holy Church.

CHAPTER VI The reduction and conversion to our Holy Faith of the mountain nations called Tepahue and Conicari

Once the Mayo nation was settled in the manner we have just described, their example and the light of the Gospel penetrated their nearest neighboring nations. These were not as populous as the Mayo nation, for flatland nations are generally more populous than mountain nations, which is what the two nations are that are discussed in this chapter.[31] Despite their [size] they were not scorned by divine providence, which protects and provides for the birds of the field.[32]

One of these nations is the Tepahue, an ally of the Tehueco, to whom the latter withdrew during the uprising that we wrote about in Chapter XIX of Book III. The captain entered their lands with his army and punished the leaders of the rebellion. As a result of this punishment and because the Tepahue saw the peace and pleasure that the Gospel had brought their neighbors, the Mayo (who were their enemies when they were gentiles), the Tepahue talked to the captain about establishing peace under the king's protection and about reducing themselves to a large settlement at a convenient location, leaving their former rancherías and ravines.[33] They also discussed requesting a priest who would come to instruct and baptize them.

The captain (as we said) desired that the light of the Gospel reach all those nations, and as soon as one reduction was completed he set his eyes on the next. He gladly accepted the Tepahue's proposal [253] and discussed with the priests the conversion and instruction of this nation. This happened at a good time [1619–20],[34] because four priests had been sent by the superiors to help their brothers in the fields that were expanding throughout the Province of Sinaloa. The priests were pleased with the Tepahue's positive attitude toward receiving Christ's law, particularly as they were so spirited and warlike. [For example], once when the captain entered their lands for war, an Indian from this nation

31. Relatively little is known about the Tepahue and Conicari, who are thought to have been Cáhita speakers. Both groups ceased to exist as distinct cultural entities by the early eighteenth century. The Conicari and Macoyahui occupied the lower foothill region of the Río Mayo; the Tepahue were centered in the Cedros Valley, which flows into the Río Mayo from the north (see Beals 1943; Sauer 1934).

32. Pérez de Ribas appears to allude here either to Matthew 6:26: "See how the birds of the air never sow, or reap, or gather grain into barns, and yet your heavenly Father feeds them; have you not an excellence beyond theirs?" (Knox 1956:6); or to Luke 12:24: "see how the ravens never sow or reap, have neither storehouse nor barn, and yet God feeds them; have you not an excellence far beyond theirs?" (Knox 1956:70).

33. La Cruz's letter in the anua of 1616 mentions a cacique from a nation near the Mayo (Conicari?) who requested baptism for his people and similar requests from the Tepahue.

34. Note that the anua of 1620 indicates that seven priests arrived in Sinaloa in 1619. Pérez de Ribas says four were sent to help their brothers in the field, so it may be that only four of the seven went to work in new missions and the other three were assigned to the Jesuit college in San Felipe, where large numbers of native children were being educated because of the rapid expansion of the mission frontier.

seized a Spaniard's sword during a skirmish, and even though he had not been trained to use it, he handled it so skillfully that when he struck the Spaniard, he dealt him such a severe blow that if the Spaniard's allies had not helped him, he would have died; no skilled Spanish swordsman could have fought any better.

The Tepahue settlement was agreed upon, and they set out to populate a flat place five leagues up the Río Mayo along a stream that flows into it, where they built a pueblo with approximately six hundred families and two thousand persons of all ages.[35] A priest[36] came to begin instruction, preaching the Gospel and its divine mysteries and precepts, which they gladly received, applying themselves to their observance. After completing the Baptism of about five hundred infants, the priest prepared the adults for Baptism. There were many cases of edification, just as in the many other new Christian communities that have been discussed. After baptizing all the adults he persuaded them to build a proper church. This is an important means by which these pueblos become more firmly established in the Faith and civility, and by which these new peoples come to belong to the Church. The Tepahue built a very good and spacious church, which is still very well attended by these Christians. They have not relapsed, and there have been none of those rebellions that the devil attempts to cause in new conversions. [254] God does not always allow him that license, but when He does (and we have clear knowledge of this), it is to obtain good results. The evangelical laborers are consoled by this sweetest providence whenever they find themselves surrounded by disturbances and riots in these new conversions.

The other mountain nation that followed the Christian example of the Mayo was their neighbor, the Conicari. Although this nation was less populous, it [still] had about two hundred families. They asked for Holy Baptism and a missionary to make them Christian. This enterprise was assigned to the priest who served the Tepahue. They chose a very peaceful and pleasant place in which to settle. Their pueblo was on a stream of good water very close to the Río Mayo. About six hundred people, young and old, were baptized. They built a very spacious and durable church, where today lie the bodies of two holy missionaries who died at the hand of the Guazápare for preaching the Holy Gospel.

The Christian Conicari have demonstrated their Christianity in their religious practices, feast day celebrations, reception of the Holy Sacraments, divine worship, etc. They possess a natural inclination toward civilized life and government; in this regard they have surpassed other nations. Lastly, this nation is a flock from which Christ has taken and will take predestined souls to increase those in heaven. However, it is necessary to leave these two nations [for now] and discuss those in the interior of these lower mountains, before this history moves on to the great conversion of the Río Yaqui and its populous and valiant nation (which follows the Mayo in the plains of the Province of Sinaloa). We will traverse the lands of several fierce nations, whose reduction to the Holy Faith of Christ Our Lord cost two missionaries their lives, which they gave to this glorious endeavor, [dying] shot full of arrows.

35. Note the small family size (under four) implied by these numbers.

36. De la Cruz appears to have initiated baptisms and religious instruction in the new mission pueblos of Tepahue and Conicari. Shortly thereafter, in 1620, Michael Wadding, otherwise known as Miguel Godínez, assumed this responsibility.

CHAPTER VII The reduction and Baptism of other nations that inhabit the interior of this same mountain range

From the time the sons of the Company [of Jesus] began to preach the Gospel in the Province of Sinaloa, its course and extension in all directions have not ceased. And it cannot be denied that this was due to the very favorable and unique compassion of divine goodness. In the fifty-three years since the preaching of the Gospel was begun among these people, there has not been a single nation that has not produced an abundant harvest of souls converted to Christ. They have been baptized and joined to the Holy Church, even in the midst of great dangers and uprisings caused by the enemy of the human race. The total number of converts will be recorded in the following book of this history. Even though the fruit of the flock, or herds of domesticated beasts, recorded in this chapter was not as copious as was hoped, divine providence nevertheless had its harvest. [The Lord] selected many innocent lambs, which were children, to go to praise Him eternally in blessedness, as well as some predestined adults, whom God usually selects and removes from the midst of those condemned to hell.

The fierce peoples recorded in this chapter lived in rancherías spread out along the width and recesses of the mountain range that falls to the north, [255] between the Río Sinaloa and Río Mayo. These are the nations whose reduction we began to discuss in the last chapter of the preceding book. The priest who cared for the Sinaloa [37] visited these other peoples and left them prepared for the time when another minister would arrive from Mexico City to take charge of them. They are called the Chínipa, the Guazápare, the Témori, the Ihío, and the Varohío.

These last people are fiercer and harder to communicate with than the other nations of the province. Even though they are such, their ferocity did not intimidate the apostolic spirit of the minister whom God selected for this enterprise. This was Father Julio Pascual, whom holy obedience entrusted with this new mission as soon as he arrived at our college in Sinaloa from Mexico City. [38] He set out for this mission with a great desire to completely submit himself to this glorious conquest and with fervent enthusiasm to spare no effort, labor, or act to remove from the clutches of the devil these souls that were created for heavenly bliss. This enterprise cost him his life.

This apostolic man arrived [in Sinaloa] with three other priests who were also going to labor in these missions. The first time I saw and spoke to him I was struck by the sanctity that shone in his face. This was subsequently attested to by his works and admirable virtues, which will be discussed later.

Father Julio reached his mission district and established his first mission in the Chínipa nation and pueblo, which was the quietest and most orderly of all the nations in terms of human customs. He then began to learn their language, which is the instrument of conversion, and baptized a good number of infants, the first fruit by which God savors the pleasure of these fervent missionaries, who come with a great hunger for converting souls.

This hunger is such that it spoke even to the Son of God, who was tired and sitting by the well in Samaria when the Apostles said to him *Rabi manduca*. [39] The Divine Master, who was in need of corporal sustenance,

---

37. Recall that Juan Castini, who was working among the Sinaloa and Zoe, traveled to the sierras to visit the Chínipa and their neighbors in 1621 and 1624. Sometime during this period Miguel Godínez also paid the Chínipa a visit, apparently during the epidemic of 1623–25, which killed at least ten thousand Indians in Sinaloa (Reff 1991b:160–68). Pascual's entrada, which is the subject of this chapter, was preceded in January 1626 by a Chínipa delegation that came begging for a priest, because "many of them were dying" (AGN 1626:148). When Pascual began working among the Chínipa in March, he noted that sixty of the eighty children that had been previously baptized by Godínez had died and that more than a third of those baptized by Castini were dead (AGN 1626:148–49).

38. Pascual arrived at San Felipe in 1624 but did not begin his permanent mission to the Chínipa until March 1626. As Pérez de Ribas notes in Chapter 13 Pascual spent 1624–25 substituting for other priests who became ill or were exhausted during the epidemic that raged at this time.

39. *Margin Note*: Ioan. 4. John 4:31: "Master, take some food" (Knox 1956:90).

answered, *Ego cibum habeo manducare, quem vos nescitis.*[40] The hunger that speaks to me, even though all of you ignore it, is the salvation and winning over of the poor little Samaritan woman to whom I have preached, despite being fatigued from the journey. Our Lord communicated much of this His divine spirit and desire to convert souls to His servant Father Pascual.

Enticed by the pleasant morsels from the Baptism of infants, he then completed the Baptism of the Chínipa nation, whom we left well prepared in Book III. They had been assisted by an Indian catechist who was teaching them the Christian doctrine. The Chínipa assimilated the catechism extremely well and all were gathered into one pueblo with five hundred male heads-of-household. They erected a very beautiful church, for by that time there were skilled tradesmen in Sinaloa.[41] The first Christian Chínipa began to live much more civilly than they had in the beginning. This pueblo served the priest as a type of fortress whence he could conquer the other fierce nations that he had sighted.

With the good Chínipa's assistance, he began to cultivate the wildest fields of the neighboring nations, the Guazápare, the Témori, the Ihío, and the Varohío.[42] He congregated these nations, whose rancherías were spread throughout those mountains, into two pueblos, where about fourteen hundred families gathered. They built two churches from wood and straw, wherein he completed the Baptism of the remaining infants, thereby bringing the total to more than a thousand.

Once these infants were baptized he began fervently preparing the adults so that all might receive the sacrament of health and new life. He continually gave talks and preached about the necessity of Holy Baptism so that they would not perish forever. He also preached to them about the principal mysteries of our Holy [256] Faith. The divine word, which was powerful enough to break through the rock that was the spirit of these barbarous people, did not cease yielding fruit. In the end almost all the adults were prepared and received Holy Baptism. The law of God was being introduced to them, as were holy customs. They were leaving behind their barbarous vices of drunken revels, a multiplicity of wives, and others from their heathenism, attending with pleasure to the Christian exercises.

These fruits that the evangelical laborer was now gathering from this vineyard encouraged him to labor tirelessly. But there were more than a few risks to his health and life in this calling; he finally did lose his life, as we shall soon see.

40. John 4:32: "but he told them, 'I have food to eat of which you know nothing' (Knox 1956:90).

41. The Jesuits had limited success attracting craftsmen and architects to the northern frontier, as noted in reports from 1638 and 1657 (Reff 1991b:257).

42. At the end of 1626 Pascual received permission from his superior at San Felipe to begin reducing the Guazápare, Ihío, Varohío, and Témori.

CHAPTER VIII A bellicose Indian advocates murdering Father Julio Pascual; he summons accomplices, attempting to create a general uprising in these nations[43]

Father Julio lived very happily cultivating the tender grapevine that he had planted for the Church, whence God was harvesting His fruits —the souls of children and adults whom He took to Himself before the storm arrived that nearly destroyed this new Christianity. The devil (whom the holy Prophet Daniel called a singularly wild beast)[44] was bellowing and looking for ways to completely destroy it. For four years this apostolic man had cultivated this vineyard all by himself, enduring great hardship, fatigue, deprivation, and danger in places that were very far from the garrison of the province.

When the fury of that infernal beast boiled over, he stirred up the blood of restless Indians, drafting the fiercest persons from among these nations. [He incited them] to wage war against the Gospel and the minister who preached it. For the execution of his plan he found the willing spirit of the Indian cacique named Cobameai, who was mentioned in the previous book. This Indian was reminded of the free and former barbarous life in which he had been raised and the vices that he once enjoyed, without recognition of any law that would prohibit them. And because a licentious life goes hand in hand with a depraved nature, the devil did not need much to persuade him to plot with others like him to kill the priest. By doing so they would revive their vices and entertainments and eradicate the Church, religious instruction, and Christianity, which is what the devil has set his eyes upon.

Cobameai began to summon people and communicate his secret to the most depraved Indians and those in whom Christ's Faith had made less of an impression. He went from one ranchería to another, pouring out the venom that burned hidden within his heart. He was a great orator and speaker, and those who heard him were by their nature easily [convinced]. So accomplices began arriving from his own Guazápare nation, which was itself fierce, warlike, and rebellious.

They held their illicit meetings, toasting in their fashion with the little reeds that they fill with tobacco. Intoxicated with this barbarous smoke, and with Satan stoking the fire, sparks flew in the form of words full of anger and rage. They said that it was a very heavy burden to enter the church and listen to the catechism and to live bound to a law and customs that were so alien to those in which they had been reared. The discussion concluded with a decision to kill the priest who had introduced such laws and had changed the people's old ways. [257]

Some good Christians (for there are always some in the midst of evil) recognized the gentle and loving treatment that the priest had shown them. He also offered them help at all times not only in the spiritual matters of their souls, but also in the worldly matters of their bodies (the priest truly showed the heart of a loving father toward the children he had engendered in Christ). When these loyal Indians learned of the others' treason and perverse intentions they warned the priest. The holy minister, with the heart of an innocent dove and without the bitterness of malice, paid little heed to what they told him about those bloodthirsty wolves who wanted to drink his blood. Nevertheless, when the rumors concerning this unrest reached the priests in other districts and the superior in the college in the Villa de San Felipe, [they understood] that Father Julio Pascual was in grave danger. The superior asked the captain of the garrison[45] (which the king maintained on the frontier for just such occasions) to send soldiers to accompany the priest. They were to protect the church and the Christians who were peaceful in case the rebel faction should attempt to do harm or evil.

The captain dispatched six armed soldiers to protect the priest from whatever danger might arise. The

---

43. The events of this chapter date from 1630–31.
44. Daniel 7:19.

45. Hurdaide died early in 1626 and was replaced by Pedro de Perea.

zealous but docile minister of Christ, who desired the peace and salvation of these people, especially the principal leader of the conspiracy, attempted to calm the depraved and misled spirits, both collectively and privately. He used fervent prayers and gentle words and admonitions, setting out the Christian obligations of those who had already heard the divine word. These bellicose Indians were somewhat quieted, but as was later seen, it turned out to be more a pretense than a true change of heart, because they postponed their evil plans for a later time. They realized that the priest was protected by the soldiers and other faithful Christians who recognized and had experienced the priest's great love and kindness. The priest trusted them, and thinking that the storm had already passed, he sent his escort of soldiers back to the fort, leaving only the Lord as his protector. He had spent four years alone in God's company with these beasts, many if not all of whom he tamed. And so the soldiers returned to the fort at Carapoa [46] and God continued to make arrangements to award the martyr's crown not only to Father Julio Pascual, but also to another priest who was his companion in the endeavor, as will be told.

CHAPTER IX Barbarian apostates murder Father Julio Pascual and another priest who came from Mexico City to assist him

As noted in the previous chapter) the rumors concerning the uprising, mainly by the Guazápare nation and their fierce cacique and leader, Cobameai, appeared to have ceased. Thus it appeared that Father Julio Pascal was safe for the time being. In fact, however, in His great providence God was delaying things until another priest could arrive. He wished to crown the two ministers together with the glorious triumph of death for the preaching of His Gospel and the glory of His holy name. This happened as follows. [258]

Another nation [the Varohío], which was a neighbor to those we have discussed [the Guazápare], was friendly and communicated with apostate Tepehuan rebels, who only a short time before [1616] had cruelly taken the lives of eight priests from our Company of Jesus (as will be duly written).[47] The gentile Varohío were persuaded by the Tepehuan to make friends with their neighbors, the Guazápare, so that they could concur—like the scoundrel gentiles and Jews who killed Christ—in the murders and martyrdom of these two priests. Both the Tepehuan and Varohío encouraged and exhorted the baptized Guazápare to murder their priest, who forced them to go to church, pray, and hear Mass and sermons, with which he was tiring them. With these and other similar arguments they encouraged the Guazápare to carry out this sacrilegious act. They added that just as the Tepehuan had gotten their way and had been victorious, eliminating their priests and killing many other Spaniards, they could expect the same result. Moreover, they noted that Fort Montesclaros and its captain and soldiers were very far away, and the Guazápare lived among the mountain peaks, which were easily defended, even when the Spaniards were right there on top of them.

It did not take much for the devil to ignite the flames that seemed to have gone out, for their old evil spirits returned once again. In order to gather more accomplices in their treason and to help defend against any Spanish reprisal for their intended crime, they summoned other gentiles from neighboring rancherías. They sent them handfuls of little reeds [filled with] tobacco, which is their usual invitation to barbarous attacks. These rancherías received the messages of treason and the invitation with pleasure. Like Pilates and Herods, it did not take very much pleading to get those

46. Fort Montesclaros, which was near the former Villa de San Juan de Carapoa.

47. Book 10, Chapters 15, 18, 20, and 21.

who were incited by the devil against Christ and His ministers to forge their alliances. They set the date and the most appropriate location to carry out their sacrilegious endeavor. They chose the town of the Varohío, which must have had around seven hundred heads-of-households.

Because the would-be murderers were apostate traitors to their God and His Law, they called the priest who preached it to give Extreme Unction to a sick man who was on the verge of dying. The priest, who always looked out for his lambs without concern for hardship or danger, left his Chínipa pueblo for Varohío. He anointed the sick man with the holy oils, and without stopping, as his would-be killers had hoped, he quickly returned to his pueblo of faithful children and very good Christian Chínipa, where he was awaiting the arrival of his assigned companion, Father Manuel Martínez.

The new missionary finally arrived and was received with great happiness by the Chínipa pueblo and even greater happiness by Father Julio Pascual, who had spent those four years in solitude, domesticating the beasts of those barbarous nations.[48] After [the new priest] had rested for three or four days in this pueblo, the two religious priests, whom God had joined so that they could offer their lives for His love, said Sunday Mass; the date was January 25, 1632. They then set out for the pueblo of Varohío (the place of their triumph and victory).

The Varohío received them with many signs of joy and with arches and flowers—all the time hiding poison in their hearts. They masked their faces for the next [259] four days. On Thursday a very loyal Indian choirmaster, whom Father Julio had reared to be very Christian, came to warn him that he had learned that the Guazápare were very rebellious and had decided to join the Varohío and murder the priests, who were now together. He added that the apostate Guazápare had [already] killed a Chínipa temachtiano, or teacher of the doctrine, along with his brother, even though the former was married to a Guazápare woman.

Good Father Julio did not really believe what this teacher of the catechism was telling him, nor was he convinced that the Guazápare uprising had advanced as far as it had. Neither did he wish to frighten his new missionary companion (even though both of them had many premonitions and warnings from heaven that the ends of their lives were drawing near). For the time

being Father Julio ignored [these warnings] until he could see clearer signs of the uprising.

The following day two other loyal Christian Varohío arrived. God had led them by His hand from among so many evildoers, and with tears in their eyes they told the priest that the plotters had decided to kill him that night. When Father Julio realized that the rumor of the uprising was being confirmed, he felt that he needed to forestall the danger that threatened his life and that of his companion, as well as the church and Christianity. He quickly sent a message to his loyal Chínipa, asking them to come to the defense of Christianity, hoping thereby to prevent all these dangers and an uprising by the Guazápare and Varohío rebels.

The messenger reached the pueblo of the Chínipa at a time when few of the people were there. Those who were there took up their weapons to defend the priests, the church, and Christianity. When they had traveled halfway along the road they got news that the number of enemies who had gathered was great. Because they, the loyal Indians, would not be strong enough to resist them, they were obliged to turn back to their pueblo, retreating from danger. Given the strength and number of the enemy, it was considered certain that all the Chínipa would have perished if they had entered the rebel pueblo.

When Saturday morning came and the priests were gathered in their small house, the rebels surrounded it and set fire to both it and the church, which is the target of the devil and his cohorts. Their intention to kill the missionaries was thus revealed. When the priests found themselves in such a terrible situation, surrounded by fire and bloodthirsty wolves who wanted to tear them to pieces, they confessed, consoled, and encouraged each other to joyfully give their lives for Christ and to aid in the salvation of those poor souls. They prayed fervently to God, who kept at bay the fury of the mob of ferocious beasts who tried to break in and murder the two gentle and unprotected lambs.

Divine providence determined that Father Julio Pascual would have enough time to prepare the faithful Christians who were with him to suffer death. There were nine carpenters and tradesmen who were there to construct the church that he was planning to build, plus eight little Indian choirboys who served in the church. He understood that the fury of those apostates and gentiles was such that they would not spare those who were loyal to Christ and His ministers. The priest heard their confessions and consoled all of them for the death that they were to suffer because they were Chris-

48. Martínez reached the pueblo of Chínipa on January 23, 1632.

tians [260] and kept the Lord's commandments. He comforted them with the hope that they would go to heaven, dying as they did for this cause. Nevertheless, he told them to try to escape if they could.

When this was done the priests left the chambers, where they had gathered with their flock, and went to the patio of the house, for now the fire and smoke pressed down on them. There they heard the thousands of insults and affronts that those crazed and furious enemies of Christ spat at His servants. Two of the choirboys escaped by hiding. Father Julio hid one of them in a cupboard and the other under an altar in his house. They later recounted how the priests frequently dropped to their knees, and raising their hearts and eyes to heaven, they accepted the will of God, which had placed them in that mortal danger. And as they were overcome by smoke and fire, they vomited up everything their bodies contained.

Father Julio Pascual, who was so skillful in the language of those fierce barbarians, attempted to calm them with loving words, calling to them from the house to desist in such a terrible crime and offering them whatever he had in the way of clothing, hatchets, and knives. These are things from which they benefited and which he often gave them out of his affection. The ingrates responded that they only wanted to kill him and to live as they wished; when he was dead they would take whatever they wanted.

The priests spent Saturday evening and night in this torment, thus extending their martyrdom. On Sunday morning the force behind the rebellion and the governor of the Guazápare, the apostate Cobameai, gathered all his accomplices and allies and invited them to participate in the murder of the blessed priests. He made this speech to them: "Let us kill this deceiver now (he was referring to Father Julio Pascual, who had preached them the word of God). He forbids us from keeping many wives and commands us to enter the church. Let us also kill the other priest who came from far away to do the same thing. If we kill them now, more priests will not come to our land. What do we want priests for? Let us kill them and be free, without anyone to oppose our desires. Let the captain come: we have our peaks and mountain ranges, where no one can attack us." This said, in a great uproar the scoundrels attacked the priests' house with devilish fury. Some climbed over the walls of the patio, while another group surrounded the house. They opened the portals and began shooting arrows inside so no one could escape. One arrow hit Father Julio Pascal in the stomach, at which point Father Manuel Martínez said: "Let us not die for Christ sadly and with cowardice." Then he emerged from the house, at which point they furiously shot more arrows, pinning Father Martínez's arms to his torso. Father Julio Pascual followed, even though his stomach was pierced by an arrow. Full of devotion and with their rosaries in their hands (I myself have one of these, all covered with blood), they both fell to their knees and asked Our Lord for His favor and grace. They began to be struck by thousands of arrows covered with a poisonous herb. These rained upon their bodies until they became two Saint Sebastians,[49] and within a short time they fell to the ground.

Their murders were concluded with several forms of cruelty by an apostate named Diego Notiomeai, who saw their fallen bodies and came and dragged them to a beam, where he laid their heads. He and some of his companions proceeded to furiously beat and maul these heads, leaving their faces [261] bruised and disfigured. These beasts were not satisfied with the blood of these dead lambs of Christ. One of the Guazápare called to his companions and said, "We should have killed him in our pueblo, where this man preached to us." They then began shooting the dead bodies full of arrows again and slashing them with knives. All this was done so that the priests would resemble their captain, Christ Jesus, who was not spared the lance [even] after He was dead.

While still alive and [even] after they were dead these blessed priests were tortured by fire, smoke, and insults as well as wounds from arrows, knives, and maces. They endured all this until they reached glory. The other circumstances worthy of being remembered that followed the death of these apostolic men are left for the following chapter.

---

49. Fourth-century Roman martyr who was ordered shot to death with arrows by the emperor Diocletian for aiding other Christian martyrs (Farmer 1992:429).

CHAPTER X The unique circumstances surrounding the holy deaths of the two blessed priests

I will summarize in this chapter the circumstances of the most holy death of these two apostolic evangelical ministers. These are noteworthy and unusual and, as such, deserve to be included in this history and will undoubtedly make it illustrious. At the same time they will provide testimony that divine goodness wanted to crown these chosen servants with such a fortunate end and prepare them for their martyrdom.

The first circumstance and testimony of the aforesaid shall be given by the Indian faithful who were eyewitnesses to a marvelous case that took place some days before these joyous deaths occurred. Father Julio Pascual received word that the man who would be his companion in the mission had reached the Villa de San Felipe from Mexico City and that he was already on his way to his district. He greatly desired to see his beloved companion. One Sunday fifteen days before his death, while he was saying Mass in his faithful Chínipa pueblo with all the people listening, he raised the Holy Host the second time and suddenly found that the corporals[50] on the altar seemed to be stained with fine, fresh blood, which appeared to have been spilled onto them. This sudden and strange case amazed and stunned the priest. In order not to detain the people or cause confusion in those who were of little [intellectual] capacity and so new in the Faith, he dissimilated this event for the time being, even though he was filled with various thoughts concerning this wondrous event. He folded the corporals, continued, and finished Mass. When he went into the sacristy, he studied them again and found that the bloodstains were still there. He showed them to the Indian who had assisted him with Mass, who had already noticed the red stain while the priest was washing the chalice.[51]

Seeing the corporals a second time with the same wondrous [stain], the religious priest folded them and began to give thanks and to ask Our Lord for light to understand what He wanted to teach him through that extraordinary event. He arose from this prayer, and still mindful of the wondrous sign of that marvelous event, he withdrew to an oratory in his house, taking those

holy and wondrous corporals with him. He unfolded them once again, and finding them still bloodstained, he showed them to three of his most faithful Christian Indians. Their names were Gaspar Sobori, who was the choirmaster, Ventura Manu, and Andrés Bariu. He showed them the stains, telling them that he thought that through that marvelous event God was declaring some [262] great hardship in the world or that someone was plotting his death. These Indians, being simple people, did not know what to say, other than to express amazement at what they saw and to revere the priest's words.

He stored the corporals, and when he unfolded them the following day he found that they had been restored to their former cleanliness. He told the Indians whom the day before he had shown these bloodstained corporals. All [three of] these Indians strongly and simply affirmed this in their testimonies to the two priests who diligently investigated the case following Father Julio Pascual's death. In the end it was clearly revealed to this priest there on the altar that Our Lord was signaling him that his violent death was approaching and that he would shed his blood for the Lord, who on that bloody altar, the Cross, had spilled His own blood for the priest.

The foregoing is further confirmed by the fact that on the day this happened the priest ordered that all the newborns in the pueblo of Chínipa, which is where the case happened, be assembled so that he might perfectly comply with his ministry to those souls entrusted to him by God. He baptized them, and then on the last page of the baptismal register—because he did not know how or [precisely] when he was going to die—he added a note asking the superiors to distribute some of his stipend to those whose names he recorded there. He did this in exchange for their having served him faithfully, thus making them deserving of that reward and payment. It was later found that this passage had been written on the same day as the incident with the corporals. These were all signs that God was telling this, His faithful servant, about the death through which He was going to glorify him. At the same time God was preparing him for it; because many times one comes close to death before actually suffering it—for God does not work His marvels randomly.

This is not the first time that something similar has

---

50. A linen cloth on which the Eucharistic elements are placed.

51. The ceremonial cleansing of the chalice occurs during the final part of the Mass, after Communion.

happened for these purposes to the evangelical ministers and missionaries of the Company of Jesus. The case published in the life and death of that apostolic man, Father Gonzalo Silveira of our order, was very similar.[52] As he was saying Mass those who watched him noticed that his hands were bloody. Within a few days the enemies of the Faith took his life for preaching the Gospel in the Kingdom of Monoriotapa [Mozambique]. These are divine favors by which it seems God likens His servants to His Most Holy Son, to whom the angel revealed the chalice of His blood just before it was spilled for the glory of His eternal Father and for the welfare of souls.[53]

Returning to Father Julio Pascual, as proof and testimony that he offered his life and blood for God, one can also offer something else that happened on this occasion. A good and faithful Christian Indian by the name of Nicolás Caulori, who was of the same nation as the rebellious Varohío, saw that the priest was in danger. As the enemies' fury was being aroused but before they had attacked the priest's house, this Indian thought it would be a good [idea] for Father Julio and the other priest to leave the pueblo by night to escape this danger. To this Father Julio responded that he no longer felt that it was the time to flee. If God had arranged for his death, he thought it best to welcome it in his own home, without fleeing or turning his back on the enemy. In doing so he was imitating Christ Our Lord, who did not flee but instead offered Himself up when the hour arrived that His eternal Father had chosen for His death. In our case the faithful Indian still insisted that his good Father [Julio], whom he dearly loved, seek safety. The priest responded to this with regret: "It seems to me, Nicolás, that you are more frightened than I am, even though I have neither bow nor arrows." To this the steadfast Christian answered with fervent spirit, "Father, [263] it is not my own death that I fear, but rather yours, which is what grieves me. So that you will not think that I am afraid, I will die first and give my life for you." This is how much this faithful Christian valued the life of the man who preached the divine word to them and who taught them the way to salvation.

And he did indeed confirm his words by deeds, for later when he saw that the enemy was gathering with war cries to execute their sacrilegious intent he sent his wife and children to the faithful pueblo of Chínipa to seek safety. He said that he himself wanted to rescue the priests, who were saints, and to die with them. He took his bow and arrows and when he reached the priests' house, which was already in flames, he saw the insolent and furious people surrounding it, some of whom were his relatives. He began speaking to them, ignited by Christian zeal, and explained how wrong they were to take the life of those who were innocent, who were loving fathers to them and preached to them and taught them the divine word. He took Christian liberty in reprehending them for their evildoings. This speech had the same effect as the speech given by the most holy proto-martyr Stephen when he preached about Christ. After he reprehended his audience for their rebelliousness and the hardness of their hearts, they raged against him. The Holy Scripture says that *stridebant dentibus in eum*,[54] they wanted to eat him alive. The infuriated Indians did the same thing as they listened to the faithful Christian Nicolás speak, for they began to grab hold of him with their cruel mouths and hands.

On this occasion, like the good shepherd who cared for the sheep that the wolves were seizing to tear to pieces,[55] good Father Julio (who had already withdrawn to his house, which was in flames, and had commended himself to God) imitated the Supreme Shepherd: When the Jews were about to seize Him, He ordered them not to touch any of His people.[56] In the same way Father Julio—paying no heed to danger and placing himself in plain view of those fierce Indians—came to the door of his house, hoping to aid his Christian Nicolás in life or death. He began to calm them with gentle reasoning, begging them not to take the life of one who had so many relatives and acquaintances among them and who had never done them wrong. These obstinate Indians were not softened by such humble and gentle pleas. Rather, they signaled a fierce Indian who was nearby to kill faithful Nicolás. This Indian released such a fierce blow on Nicolás' head with his macana that he knocked him to the ground. Father Julio encouraged him to suffer death for Christ, and with the two of them saying the sweet name of JESUS together, Nicolás gave his soul to God. This was the fulfillment of what this faithful Christian, full of fervor, had stated only a little while earlier, namely that he would give his life in de-

---

52. Silveira was a missionary and martyr in Mozambique. He received his death notice while saying Mass, noticing suddenly that his hands were covered with blood (Dunne 1951:137).

53. Luke 22:39–46.

54. *Margin Note*: Actorum. cap. 7. Acts 7:54:"At hearing this, they were cut to the heart, and began to gnash their teeth at him" (Knox 1956:122).

55. Note how this language parallels John 10:1–16.

56. John 18:8:"If I am the man you are looking for, let these others go free" (Knox 1956:108).

fense of the priests. This is when they shot an arrow at Father Julio, and as we said, it hit him in the stomach.

The good Christian Indian, who had bid farewell to his wife and children when he could have fled with them, had instead wished to enter the fray against the enemies of Christ. Thus, in his own way he could say that which the Church sings about martyrs: *Loquebar de testimonijs tuis in conspectu Regum, & non confundebar.*[57] Even though there were no kings or visible tyrants in the theater of evil where this blessed Christian preached, there was no lack of invisible ones, which the Apostle calls 'princes and potentates of hell'.[58] They are the ones who inspired to rage so many apostates and gentiles, by way of whom they attempted to uproot the Christianity that had been planted in these nations.

The perverse intentions of the enemies of Christ and the Holy Faith were clearly demonstrated, [264] for once they had finished cruelly taking the lives of the blessed priests, they set upon the flock of Christians who accompanied them, almost all of whom served in the church. With barbarous cruelty they took their lives, save a few who, as we said, were hidden, for God wanted them to escape so that they might serve as witnesses to what had happened. The rebel Indians ripped the priests' cassocks to pieces and divided them amongst themselves.[59] One Indian made a hooded cape out of the part that he received. They took the vessels and two holy chalices, profaning everything and using them to celebrate their barbarous dances, congratulating themselves on their sacrilege.

Because the devil's infernal hatred is manifested principally against the churches where the word of God is preached and where the trickery and deceptions by which he misleads these peoples are undone, once they had completed this accursed act and had finished burning down the church of this faithless pueblo of Varohío, they went in fury to the other pueblo of Guazápare and set fire to the church and the priests' house. They took whatever they found inside, just as they had done in Varohío, and this is how they concluded their devilish and fierce attack. The results of this attack and its punishment will be recorded once we have concluded that which pertains to the evangelical ministers who therein terminated the course of their holy lives.

CHAPTER XI How the remains of the bodies of the apostolic ministers were found, recovered, and interred

The preceding case was cause for great reflection. It even amazed those who were familiar with the nature of these ferocious peoples. As has been pointed out in other parts of this history, one of their unwavering customs is to sever and tear off the heads of those whom they kill. They then take the skulls to celebrate their barbarous dances. In light of this custom [it is surprising] that the Indians did not sever and remove the heads of these holy priests to celebrate their triumph, even though they had murdered them slowly and very cruelly. Some of the priests in these missions, who were quite familiar with these Indians' nature, attributed their restraint to some fear and internal horror that came over them when they realized their own wickedness and saw at their feet such innocent and saintly men from whom they had received so many benefits, particularly from Father Julio Pascual, their illustrious benefactor.

In the end, no sooner had the evil deed been perpetrated than the aggressors were intimidated by the clamors of innocent blood. With reprehension this

---

57. "I was speaking about your martyrs in the presence of kings, and I was not troubled."

58. Ephesians 6:12.

59. Pérez de Ribas seems to be drawing an implicit parallel here with the Gospel accounts of the Roman soldiers' casting lots to see who would get to keep Christ's clothing (Matthew 27:35; Mark 15:24; Luke 23:24; John 19:23–24).

blood denounced their atrocities, just as fratricide was denounced by the spilled blood of the innocent Abel.[60] Finally, this blood or (what is more certain) divine will itself—which many times kept the claws of lions and the fangs of hungry wolves from touching the bodies of martyrs—appears to have contained these ferocious Indians, who refrained from severing the heads, which were now relics of holy men. God had arranged safe-keeping for these holy bodies. It also appears that with particular favor from heaven, [265] without which this would have been impossible, the Indians who saved the priests' bodies also escaped danger.

It was the case that a loyal Christian named Crisanto Sivemeai, one of those whom the priest had in his company, saw the damage that those beasts were inflicting on the priests' [bodies] and was overcome by anger and zeal. This Indian had returned to [the murder scene] to defend both his life and that of the priests or their bodies. While the enemy was still raging he took his bow and arrows, and with his back to a beam of a house for protection, he began shooting arrows. He fought with so much courage that he killed five of the enemy and kept the others from getting closer to the [priests'] bodies. His escape from such fierce rivals was considered miraculous. When he was later asked how he was able to escape, he answered that the enemy had been frightened when they saw his courage and resolve. But God protected him so that the outrages that those impious Indians were committing against the saintly bodies would cease. This Indian remained there until Sunday evening, when the perpetrators of the evil deed departed.

The news of the priests' death quickly spread to the pueblo of Chínipa. They greatly grieved the death of those whom they loved so much, as they demonstrated on this occasion. Although their priests were no longer alive, they still went to look for them. A group of them took their bows and arrows, and at risk to their lives they set out for the pueblo of the Varohío, which they found already somewhat abandoned. As was already told, after the priests were killed the murderers went to Guazápare to destroy the church, just as they had done in Varohío. The Chínipa found the bodies of the blessed priests lying on the ground in the plaza in front of the burned house. It was very significant that the many dogs that the Indians raise did not eat the bodies the preceding night.

The Chínipa collected the bodies and took them to their pueblo. Because there was no minister who could bury them, the good Chínipa made two deep graves next to the high altar of their church. In each they placed four wooden planks in the form of a box. The Indians deposited the bodies and covered them with the mats they use, grieving greatly over the loss of the priests. However, we can say that they [really] did not lose them, but rather that they became their intercessors in heaven. It has been noted that ever since that time, the priests have taken care of this flock of loyal Chínipa. Indeed, their great Christianity has always persevered and they have been steadfast in their Faith. They have continued to make great progress, even though they were persecuted, as we will see later.

Father Marcos Gómez, who was in charge of the instruction of the Conicari and whose pueblo was some sixteen leagues from Chínipa, received news of the event. Because the pueblo of Chínipa was destitute of a priest and faced the risk of surprise attacks by the rebels, he decided to remove the blessed bodies from Chínipa to Conicari. He did so to the great sorrow of the Chínipa, who were happy with their relics,[61] especially those of Father Julio Pascual, who had engendered them in Christ. I will not omit here what could serve as consolation to all missionary priests, particularly those whom God chooses and appoints for the difficult task of converting new nations. Namely, these nations develop a particular and special love for the ministers who baptize them and transform them from barbarians [266] into Christians. This was especially apparent in the case of the Chínipa and Father Julio.

In the end Father Marcos took the bodies of the two blessed priests from the church of Chínipa to Conicari. The following day, February 14, 1632, the priests who were nearby were summoned to celebrate the funeral of their two brothers who had glorified God by their deaths, leaving them the example of their evangelical zeal for the conversion of these gentiles. The rite was celebrated with the choir from Conicari. Those venerable remains, which had been pierced by arrows, beaten with macanas and clubs, and wounded with knives and hatchets—all happily suffered for Christ and His Gospel—were interred.

In order to benefit from some of these very blessed relics, the [Jesuit] college in Mexico City has requested the heads of these two priests, which those barbari-

---

60. Genesis 4:10: "The blood of thy brother has found a voice that cries out to me from the ground" (Knox 1956:4).

61. *Prendas.*

ans beat and wounded on that beam.[62] Having lived and studied in that college, these priests were its sons. What good fortune it has been for this famous seminary to have been the school where so many apostolic men, including the eleven missionaries who have died in this province for preaching our Holy Faith, obtained wisdom from heaven and [then went on to] shed their

blood for Christ. The glorious martyr Saint Philip of Jesus,[63] of the seraphic Order of Saint Francis, who suffered martyrdom in Japan and whom the illustrious City of Mexico has as its patron, also studied at this school. What glorious fortune to have been the holiest mother of these and other distinguished men.

CHAPTER XII The condition of the Chínipa mission following the rebels' patricide

Our Lord willed that the violent tempest that razed and burned the churches, altars, and sacred ornaments—killing two holy ministers—did not spread to other places or Christian nations. These all remained calm, grieving deeply the unfortunate events, particularly, and rightfully so, the loyal Chínipa who had lost fourteen or sixteen of their sons with the priests. They died a glorious death from arrows because they followed the doctrine of Christ and His most Holy Faith, which they had been taught. If they had renounced it and had become part of the faction that persecuted and committed the crime, they undoubtedly would have been spared their cruel death. But they were unwavering in the Holy Faith that they had learned from the priests. Through the Holy Sacrament of Confession they were prepared (as was told) to give their life for the Faith that they professed. We read in the Roman *Martyrology*[64] the celebration of the deaths inflicted by tyrants upon the saints because they were followers and pro-

claimers of Christ's [message], or perhaps because one of them gave a jar of water as refreshment to one of the confessors. However, I make no judgment here of the deaths of those whom I am discussing; I only provide a narrative record of their circumstances, which will undoubtedly make them illustrious.[65]

The Chínipa were deeply grieved by the deaths of their sons and relatives, who were from the same district and mission as the [267] apostate Guazápare and Varohío. The latter felt great animosity and rage toward the Chínipa not only because they refused to act as accomplices in their sacrilegious undertaking, but because the Chínipa had tried by all possible means to stop it. For this reason, on the day following the priests' murder the Chínipa kept watch and waited day and night with their weapons, ready for a surprise attack by the enemy.

The loyal Chínipa were so advanced in the Faith that following the death of the priests who had instructed them, the principales of the pueblo went to the Villa de San Felipe to insistently ask the Father Rector of the missions for another priest to care for them and their Christianity. He granted their pious request, sending another priest [Father Juan Varela] who was not very busy and could minister to this very Christian pueblo. The priest was also ordered to help Father Francisco Torices, who had under his care the Sinaloa mission, which included all those who had settled there [principally Zoe and Huite].

---

62. The heads were in fact severed and apparently sent to Mexico City as relics, as excavation of the priests' bodies in 1907 revealed two skeletons without skulls (Dunne 1940:261, f.14).

63. In 1597 the emperor Tagcosama became convinced that Jesuit and Franciscan missionaries who had been working in Japan for more than thirty years were a fifth column of sorts, preparing the way for a European invasion. The emperor had three Jesuits and six Franciscans crucified in Nagasaki. Among the Franciscans was Saint Philip de las Casas, who was born in Mexico City (Thurston and Attwater 1956:1:259).

64. This is a liturgical book first published by order of Pope Gregory XIII (1572–85), which lists for each day of the year the martyrs and saints whose feasts are commemorated, with notes about the individual(s) (Attwater 1949:310).

65. Pérez de Ribas is covering himself here, anticipating critics who might accuse him of violating papal edicts prohibiting authors from declaring someone a saint.

The captain of the garrison at that time was a gentleman by the name of Don Pedro de Perea. When he got news of this event he felt great sorrow and grief for what had happened. In the interim, while he considered his responsibilities and the appropriate punishment, he gave orders that the priest who was destined for Chínipa take an escort of six soldiers for protection and defense against any new rebel attacks.

The Chínipa were very grateful for this favor, and like loyal and fervent Christians they obeyed their new priest. They carefully guarded their minister, because the insolent Guazápare rebels and their consorts gave them reason for concern. The Chínipa frequently received word that these Indians had held several sacrilegious meetings, during which they had decided to kill all the Chínipa and the newly arrived priest and his soldier escort. Some of the same Guazápare who had remained loyal during the uprising warned the Chínipa of this decision. In fact, early one evening a gang of rebels attacked the pueblo, but when the Chínipa learned of this attack they came out and drove them back with great courage, capturing some of the rebels. Because they were now Christians, they did not cut off the heads of those whom they captured, even though they were their enemies. Instead, they imprisoned them until they could hand them over to the captain, thereby deferring vengeance and punishment to the king's ministers of justice.

The assaults and constant fear under which the Chínipa lived forced them and the priests, who tenderly loved them, to consider moving the pueblo to a safer and quieter place where they could peacefully attend church and Christian exercises and live happily. To realize this goal, they had to abandon (with great sadness) their very beautiful church, which had cost them a lot of sweat and toil. Because of their love of Christianity, they left this place and their lands and houses and settled in the Christian pueblos of their neighbors, the Sinaloa.[66] It seems reasonable for us to say that these loyal Chínipa were exiled for Christ; in order to confess their Faith, they abandoned their beloved lands and houses where they were born and raised, which is all that an Indian can leave and renounce. These Christians persevere today among the aforementioned Sinaloa as very good examples.

We will now continue with the end [268] met by the rebels who killed the blessed ministers of the Gospel. The punishment of this crime is the responsibility of the captain of the garrison, who as was previously noted, has orders from the king to punish such outrages and to insure Christianity on the frontier. The man who was captain at that time, Don Pedro de Perea, did not dally on this occasion.[67] Rather, he and his soldiers diligently departed with armored horses and a great number of allied Indians in search of the enemy. All of them were determined to punish and avenge the affronts to God and His churches and ministers. They reached the lands and pueblos of the Guazápare and Varohío, where they engaged in several battles. The outcome was fortunate for them but disastrous for the rebels. The latter employed their mountains as a fortress, confident that the Spaniards' horses would be ineffective. But with valor and courage the allied Indians, protected by the Spaniards, caught up with the rebels. They caused more damage than was desirable, for it is already known how difficult it is to repress military furor during war. Approximately eight hundred of the enemy died. This was due to the pretensions of the devil—the enemy of mankind—who creates rebellions against Christianity. The eighty or so rebel families that remained [after the battles] thought better [of their situation], and with the diligent efforts of Father Francisco Torices these lost sheep were reduced. They were affectionately brought back to his Sinaloa pueblos, where they became reconciled with God and His Church, which they attend today as good Christians.

Not all the seed that this evangelical laborer planted bore fruit (as was taught by the Son of God). A few obstinate outlaws and their gentile accomplices remained. Nevertheless, in the end Father Julio Pascual and his holy companion harvested a sizable crop in this labor and enterprise. Even though his sudden death did not give him the opportunity to cultivate this vineyard, he harvested a fair amount of fruit for himself with the crown of martyrdom. He left this entire Christianity watered with his blood, and it has been bearing fruit and growing ever since the death of these holy men.

As I promised, I will conclude this book with the lives and noteworthy examples of such men. In the following book I will relate the most populous of all the conquests and evangelical enterprises accomplished in this province.

---

66. This exodus apparently occurred in 1637 or 1638 (Bannon 1939:19, f.28).

67. Pérez de Ribas is alluding here to Perea's hesitancy and mishandling of a disturbance among the Nébome in 1626 that led to an attempt on the life of Father Diego Bandersipe (discussed in Book 6).

CHAPTER XIII The religious and remarkable virtues of the blessed Father Julio Pascual, killed at the hands of infidels for preaching the Gospel[68]

I t is the law and duty of history that deals with the temporal conquests of barbarous peoples or enemy strongholds to record the bravery, efforts, and valor of the captains and soldiers who overcame and conquered them. This is particularly true when the conquest has been at the cost of blood and lives. In such a case the merits of these types of enterprises justly demand not to be buried in oblivion. The same law must be obeyed when one is writing of spiritual conquests and enterprises, which are more glorious due to their spiritual [nature]. In these [enterprises] one is fighting against the powers of hell and gaining heaven for the souls that will live there for all eternity. Accordingly, then, I will record here the heroic virtues and unique examples of religiousness with which God prepared the two evangelical laborers that He selected for the arduous and difficult enterprise of preaching His Holy Gospel among these barbarous peoples and [269] subjugating them to the sweet yoke of Christ at the cost of their [own] blood.

The first was the great servant of God, Father Julio Pascual, who was born in the city of Bresa in the seigniory of Venice. His parents were very honorable and well endowed with worldly goods, but they were richer in their Christianity and were quite devoted to the Holy Order of our Company of Jesus. In spite of the laws of that republic,[69] they sent their son to Parma and then to Mantua so that he could study in the Company's schools. There he excelled so much in virtue and letters that he was a noteworthy example to other youths of modesty, tranquility, reserve, devotion, and innocence.

Once he had finished his studies in arts and letters he wished to enter our Company. Because of the great virtue he was judged to possess, he was accepted into the Company in 1611. During his novitiate and then the year of seminary and the study of Humanities, the virtues that sprouted in his youthful age took very deep root. Brother Julio's solid virtue prompted the Father

Provincial to send him to the city of Faenza to teach grammar. Brother Julio carried out this ministry with exceeding edification and approval on the part of the priests at the college. His students excelled so much in virtue that the people of the city took a special liking to him during the three years in which holy obedience occupied him in this ministry.

At the end of those three years the Father Procurator of the Mexican province,[70] Nicolás de Arnaya, arrived in Rome to ask our Father General to select some individuals to aid their brothers in the conversion of the Indians in Nueva España, where every day the missions were expanding, offering new evangelical enterprises. Brother Julio had impulses and callings from heaven to go to the Indies, even though his leaning was primarily toward the missions of the Orient and Japan. He wanted to spend his whole life and self in the missions. If necessary, he was willing to spill his blood in the name of preaching Christ's Faith to the gentiles who had been discovered. As is common practice in our Company, he gave our Father General an account of these desires sent to him from Our Lord.[71] And as God governs with His great providence matters pertaining to His supreme ends, He arranged that the news that our Father General received about Brother Julio's wishes should serve to assign him to the mission and post where God had the crown and glorious conclusion of his life awaiting him. Thus, our Father General told him to join the others who were going to Nueva España [in 1614].

Our most obedient Brother Julio accepted this order with unique fervor and satisfaction, as if it had come from heaven. He left Italy for Spain in the company of two other priests who were destined for the same enterprise. During their trip to Sevilla he was of par-

---

68. Pérez de Ribas draws heavily here from a lengthy account of Pascual's life and career in the anua of 1632.

69. The government of Venice was at the time embroiled in a dispute with Pope Paul V, and as a result the Jesuits were banned from the city.

70. The Procurator (at the provincial level) was elected by a vote of the professed members of a province and was entrusted with conveying in person to the father general in Rome the petitions of a particular province.

71. The father general at the time was Mutius Vitelleschi. Jesuit archives at the Vatican contain thousands of letters written by Jesuits requesting a missionary assignment, although relatively speaking only a minority of Jesuits favored such a ministry (see Cohen 1974; de Guibert 1964).

ticular comfort, relief, edification, and even amazement to his companions, as they themselves testified. They departed from Spain, and when they reached the college in Mexico City Brother Julio spent three years finishing his studies in theology. He did not waver a single bit in his religious fervor, and not only grew in his virtues, but also excelled in letters.

When he finished his studies he was ordained a priest. Then holy obedience selected him for his glorious work, which even though it might not seem glorious in the eyes and estimation of men, was very precious in the eyes of God. This is what Father Julio had been longing for with such lively and fruitful hopes since Italy. Through good fortune this great and diligent evangelical minister was assigned to the Province of Sinaloa. It bears repeating here that divine providence has shown unique favor in forming this province and its missions [270] and in selecting outstanding, apostolic men to labor and teach here, most especially Father Julio, of whom we are now speaking. All the vineyards and young vines of the new Christian communities found there benefited from the irrigation, labor, and toil of such an attentive and charitable laborer. It seems that it was an order from heaven for him to substitute in the districts of the province's ministers on the occasion of illnesses that they endured. He assisted in the missions of the Zuaque, Tehueco, Sinaloa, and Yaqui before he was given his own mission. In these nations he acted with fervent and untiring charity for a period of two years. Then the superiors placed him in charge of the mission and conversion of the nations that would cost him his life.

Even though he was exemplary of all virtue throughout his lifetime, the great and excellent examples of holiness with which he had been adorned by divine goodness increased greatly during the years he spent in the missions. The first example, and the greatest that can be given concerning this most religious missionary, was all those virtues that his apostolic, evangelical, and religious profession demanded. These virtues shone in him. I will examine each of them in detail, beginning with that which is the foundation of all holiness, humility.

Father Julio was very careful to construct his perfection upon the foundation of this virtue, and he made it very much a part of himself. And even though this virtue is so opposed to the tendencies of human nature, which always covets esteem and excellence, he warded off that hunger by practicing acts of humiliation. Consequently, he despised all things concerning his own esteem and honor and considered all others superior [to himself].

His love for this holy virtue of humility became so deeply rooted in him that it seemed to be a natural part [of him]. He demonstrated this in his words and deeds not only with those who were greater or equal to him, but with those who were inferior, and even the Indians, to the extent that reason and prudence allowed. When traveling this most humble priest insisted on taking charge of saddling his companions' horses, bridling them, carrying the saddlebags, and seeing to all the most humble tasks that might arise. He did this with such great insistence that his companions could not stop him or lend him a hand. Rather, they had to give in and, in order to please him, they let him continue in these practices. At dangerous passes along rivers and trails he always went ahead of his brothers. If there was any difficulty, it would befall him; the others would thus be spared. He always took the worst mount for himself.

When Father Julio was headed for Mexico City from the port at Veracruz with the rest of his companions, the mule on which one of our brothers was riding ran away. This was in Old Veracruz, by a river with many crocodiles and a thick monte. Our charitable Brother Julio (for whom an opportunity to practice his humility and charity was like a major feast day) went running after his companion's mount. The mule ran into the monte, and he spent the whole afternoon and evening looking for it. At dawn he returned with the mule to the inn, where the other priests had been quite worried, thinking that their poor brother had gotten lost or had died. When they saw and heard him they realized that God had worked a miracle by allowing Brother Julio to cross that river without being harmed. Because he had been unable to find a way out [of the monte], he had spent the night in prayer and had had celestial visitations. It is a very well-known custom for God to send such visitations to the humble, which Father Julio was to an excellent degree.

On one occasion another priest who was a friend of Father Julio's surprised him as he was seated at his [271] table absorbed in a paper, which served as a journal of his devotions. In it were these words from Isaiah: *Ad quem autem respiciam, nisi ad pauperculu & tremetem sermones meos.*[72] This was his continual and savory meditation. He was very careful to conceal whenever possible the splendors of his natural talents, his supernatural gifts, and the deeds of his excellent

---

72. *Margin Note*: Isaí. cap. 66. Isaiah 66:2: "Patient he must be and humbled, one who stands in dread of my warnings" (Knox 1956:680).

virtues. He was never seen to persistently argue or do what he deemed best unless he was obliged to do so by honor for God or the welfare of his fellow man. He was persistent in practicing acts of humiliation, engaging his words and effectiveness in pondering and focusing on his stubbornness, not on his talents or gifts. When he was studying at the college in Mexico City he was obliged, or (to put it more clearly) he obliged himself, to undertake all the humble tasks that might arise.

Because the foundation of this holy man's virtues had been so deep and solid, all those virtues built on this foundation were strong and steadfast, extending all the way to heaven. The virtue that most directly exalts the soul is that of prayer and discourse with God. In this celestial virtue God raised Father Julio's soul so permanently and to such a high level that it seemed he lived and breathed it. The time that he did in fact spend in prayer was the amount that Saint Augustine indicated for the most highly contemplative, saying, *Otium sanctum quaerit charitas, veritatis negotium iustum suscipit necessitas charitatis, quam sarcinam si nullus imponit intuenti, vacandum est veritati.*[73]

Blessed Father Julio spoke with God whenever he had time remaining from his most holy occupation of helping others and fulfilling his obligations. In addition to the hour of prayer in the morning, which is the practice in our Company and where one could always find him before dawn, he was also very disciplined in spiritual examinations and readings, even if he was in the desert or the wilderness. During the canonical hours[74] he usually knelt to pray with singular attentiveness in the church. If he was in his district, he would withdraw and close himself in his room. When he was present at a gathering of priests he would first listen to all of their Masses. Once he was prepared by this long prayer and meditation he would say his own Mass after everyone else, very slowly and with great devotion. This would be followed by another long period of time in which he would withdraw to give thanks. For the rest of the day, apart from the necessary occupations of helping others, he would withdraw to his little house to busy himself in prayer, meditation, and reading holy books. He read these books with such attention that those who knew and lived with him for a period of time called his reading 'prayer and meditation'. For the Hail Marys he would return to his resting place, where he would spend entire hours in prayer, and sometimes they would find him at midnight still praying.

Through this holy practice he received favors and gifts from heaven. Even though our most humble Father Julio tried to conceal them, the impetus and force of the spirit that burned in his breast did not always allow him to do so. When he was alone he was often heard breaking into sobs, canticles, or divine praises to relieve the ardor of his spirit. From the high points of this sweet relationship [with God] he had many [spiritual] remnants to [sustain him] when he was on the road or busy dealing with his fellow man.

He introduced the topic of God pleasantly, without being boring or bothersome. One priest, who said this often, claimed that Father Julio enjoyed the good fortune of this life, which consists of the continual memory of God, and the union and pleasure of living in His love and company by fulfilling {272} to the letter the precept and advice of the Apostle Saint Paul: *Sine intermissione orate,*[75] which was like saying, "Release the leisure and toil of this life to the rest and delights of talking with God." This act of joining action and contemplation, an eminent state within the Church, has been an art among apostolic men who have been taught by their Divine Master.

Other unique and fervent devotions performed by this most religious priest should also be reduced and attributed to this holy life and practice of prayer. He was very fervent in his practice of the Most Holy Sacrament, and this fervor moved him to request permission from superiors to keep this Supreme Sacrament in his inner oratory in his house in the pueblo of the Chínipa, which was very safe and calm.[76] He had carefully set up this oratory in a suitable place and had adorned it with silk draperies purchased with his stipend. The soldiers who sometimes escorted him spoke with admiration and edification of how often he prayed at the oratory. The superiors granted his request because they recognized the holy affection with which he had made it and

---

73. *Margin Note.* lib. 9. de la ciudad de Dios, cap. 19. Book 19 (not 9), chapter 19 of Augustine's *City of God* (Dods 1948:2:330). Pérez de Ribas paraphrases Augustine's observation "holy leisure is longed for by the love of truth; but it is the necessity of love to undertake requisite business. If no one imposes this burden upon us, we are free to sift and contemplate truth."

74. The canonical hours refers to specified times during the day when the Divine Office (prayers, psalms, hymns, etc.) is recited (Attwater 1949:72, 152).

75. *Margin Note*: I. adThes. 5. 1 Thessalonians 5:17: "Never cease praying" (Knox 1956:213).

76. Because the consecrated Host was considered the body and blood of Christ, the Jesuits (and devout Catholics more generally) deemed it inappropriate or sacrilegious to remove and venerate it outside the church, where it might be accidentally or intentionally violated.

the decency in which he would maintain the Lord in his company. He spent much of the night and a portion of the day at the oratory. When it was impossible for him to enjoy that continual presence because of his travels, he never failed to daily celebrate the most holy sacrifice of Mass, always taking along the necessary vessels so as not to deprive himself of that heavenly delicacy.

He took special pains to celebrate the feast day, procession, and festival of this Divine Mystery, especially on Holy Thursday and during Holy Week services. One year, because of a great famine the people of the pueblo were spread throughout the monte looking for food and sustenance and were therefore unable to attend this solemn celebration. Given that it was impossible for the devout priest to celebrate the exposition of the Holy Sacrament with the required continual presence of the faithful, he placed it in the sacristy and, in order to comply with this devotion, he himself spent that day and night with the Holy Sacrament, making up for the absence of his entire flock.

The care he took in building, adorning, and arranging the home, temple, and altar of this Divine Mystery also shows his devotion. He himself decorated it with bouquets of flowers and other little things. It was said that Father Julio was only covetous in matters concerning the church and its adornment, whence was born the frugality that he imposed on himself, spending his stipend from the king on the church and its adornment rather than his own sustenance. Every year Father Julio spent as much as possible on things pertaining to divine worship, musical instruments, and singers. In this way he made his churches particularly bright and ornate. He was very diligent and expended great labor and care on their construction, especially in Chínipa. Although it was very difficult to bring beams down out of the steep mountains, he oversaw all of this. The Chínipa church turned out to be very attractive and spacious, and it was covered with a beautiful ceiling and roof. These were all works that cost a lot of sweat in these deserts, among peoples who were so ignorant of this type of labor and construction. However, because they were very important, nothing discouraged Father Julio Pascual's fervent devotion.

Along with devotion to the Most Holy Sacrament of the Altar, devotion to the Sovereign Queen of the Angels is also very dear to the sons of the Catholic Church. This most religious priest displayed both of these. With the Virgin the filial gifts were heavenly discussions and communication. In his fervor for this angelic devotion Father Julio was unable to contain himself,

and he overflowed, [273] igniting others and thereby making them fervent also. Among his Christian faithful, especially the Chínipa, he introduced this devotion in such a fashion that in place of the jewelry they wore around their necks in their heathenism, which was made of little snail and conch shells, they all now wore the Virgin's rosary, which they all prayed in chorus at church, at home, on the road, or in the fields. Through such holy devotions and familiar discourse with God, and through the anointing of the Holy Spirit that was communicated to him as a result, the virtues of this outstanding religious were perfected and purified.

In those virtues that pertain more to the religious profession, he went to great lengths and achieved noteworthy results, attending to their perfection with most exceptional care. In all matters—be they low, humble, difficult, arduous, and even life threatening—his obedience to superiors was always prompt, joyful, humble, and submissive. Only once, for other reasons, did he espouse an opinion different than the one willed by obedience. He did so in the submissive and dispassionate manner that his self-control allowed. This act, which was at odds with the perfect surrender of will and understanding so professed by the Company, was a thorn that caused him such pain that he could not request enough pardon for it in his letters to his superiors. Even though in this case he had not exceeded the limits of obedience, he was nevertheless afflicted with the shadows of disobedience. His desire was like that of those who obeyed perfectly, showing no inclination for one opinion or another. Rather, as our father Saint Ignatius teaches his sons in his rules, he tried to be as a corpse, which allows itself to be taken wherever and treated however.[77] This perfect resignation was maintained and grew in Father Julio's soul by considering (as he did) the person of Christ to be represented by and present in his superiors. He obeyed all of them and loved them as Christ, even those who were his companions in the missions. To those who were officially his superiors, according to the rules of the Company, he had to provide an especially careful account of the matters of his own soul as well as those of the rest of the district. He did this in person whenever he met with them, or by letter when they were not present. This was

77. Ignatius composed a famous "Letter on Obedience" in 1533, which led to subsequent celebration of obedience as a religious virtue in Jesuit writings and the Jesuit Constitutions. The latter uses the corpse metaphor, which apparently originated with Bonaventure's *Life of Francis of Assisi* (O'Malley 1993a:353).

done with a desire to benefit from their guidance, as if it came from Christ Himself. Last of all it can be said that this holy man carried out his obedience perfectly, admirably, and heroically.

Religious poverty had greatly stripped him of his own will, which is what has the greatest authority over mankind. But it was not difficult for him to observe this [vow] of poverty and to love it as he would his own mother. His consolation was to practice that holy virtue in his attire, which he rarely wished to replace; a poor old habit was what he wished and sought for himself. Whenever his habit needed to be mended he did it himself, and he was quite content with the worst habit in the house. The food in the missions is poor, but he made it even poorer through his efforts not to have or request anything of relief or comfort, and he never had chocolate (which is commonly consumed in this kingdom). He never had any curious or valuable objects, even if they were for devotions. When he was studying at the college it was noted that he used the same single writing quill for a long time, not wanting to allow [himself] anything more. This is how carefully he observed religious poverty, but this did not stem from a stinginess of spirit on Father Julio's part, for he was most generous in giving all that he had. I could better say that he did not have anything of his own nor did he spare anything he was given. In this way he would not fail in his charity toward others. When he received whatever was offered him he had to register it with his superiors, no matter how small.

The celestial virtue of chastity, which religious observe, shone [274] in this servant of God like bright enamels.[78] I will declare this in brief, saying that a priest who dealt with him in religious matters for a long time and heard his confessions for many years affirmed that he did not doubt that Father Julio had died a virgin.[79] He found in him not the slightest venial sin whatsoever, not even in this respect. In addition, Father Julio was a mirror of purity with respect to his appearance, manner, and words, and this purity of his soul shone through the exterior man. Therefore, such a clearness of purity and devotion shone in his face, conversation, and manner that it spread to those who spoke and looked upon him, all of whom considered him a saint. In the end the splendor of that celestial virtue is so admirable and fragrant that it always emits the odors of heaven.

CHAPTER XIV The fervent charity and holy zeal with which Father Julio Pascual exercised his apostolic ministry

Although the previous chapter recorded the remarkable religious virtues that shone in Father Julio Pascual, those that pertain more specifically to the apostolic ministry of a missionary of the Company of Jesus have yet to be discussed. Such missionaries work for the good of souls, setting them on the road to the heavenly bliss for which God created them. This was an enterprise for which the blessed priest had taken a special vow when, already in the missions, he professed the four solemn vows of the Company. In the execution of this ministry his actions and virtues were no less heroic or illustrious than the religious ones already recorded. Eloquent testimony of the burning zeal of this apostolic man has been recorded by a priest who was his mission companion for some time. He claimed that he did not know how to explain Father Julio's holy and fervent zeal for the good of souls except to affirm that it was so constant that he was sure there never was an occasion or means with which to help souls that he did not put into practice, and that he focused all his thoughts on looking for ways to win them to God.

As soon as he reached his district (as was told in

---

78. The vitreous varnish that often was added to metal objects (often of gold or silver), particularly religious ornaments.

79. Pascual's confessor apparently was his fellow missionary, Juan Castini.

Chapter VIII) he settled in the pueblo of the Chínipa, where his fervent zeal had a fortunate effect. Such
a blooming Christianity was established there, as has
been told, that after one year these people appeared to
be long-time Christians. This is something that cannot
always be achieved in other nations, but here the gentle
nature of the Chínipa was joined with the fervent zeal
of the minister whom God had sent them.

When Christianity had been established in that
pueblo, Father Julio set himself with great spirit to the
difficult task of the spiritual conquest of other [nearby]
fierce nations. This same spirit overcame the horrible
conditions that God had set before him; he was not intimidated by the immense hardships of traveling over
rough and dangerous paths, nor by the solitude, exile,
or other difficulties that we have mentioned. We can
truly call exile the time he spent among those nations
in a district very far from the others. The great Doctor of the Church, Saint [John] Chrysostom, wrote to
Pope Innocent about the exile he endured among the
fierce and intractable people of Pontus,[80] calling it an
unspeakable solitude.

Father Julio, who had been exiled for Christ in that
solitude, reduced the fierce Guazápare, Ihío, Varohío,
and Témori nations to two conveniently located, large
settlements. He removed them from their [275] steep
mountains and introduced them to civilized life, taming many of them and affectionately subjugating them
to the gentle yoke of Christ. Although there were quite
a few who failed in the Faith and cast off the gentle
yoke, the numbers of those who persevered and were
reduced to it were considerable, not counting the many
children and infants who went to heaven after having
received Holy Baptism from the blessed priest.

Whenever possible he gave talks about the catechism in the pueblos that he visited. He never tired of
[hearing] confessions (particularly during Lent, when
the numbers are large). Indeed, it was necessary to restrain him so that he would not undermine his health
and his life.[81] When the time came to teach the children
and the elderly it was unusually edifying to see the hu-

mility and peacefulness with which he taught them and
showed them affection. He made himself like a child
with the children or like an old man with the elderly,
as the Apostle Saint Paul said, *Omnibus omnia factus ut
omnes lucrifaceret.*[82] Their rough manners did not tire
him, nor did he become angry when they [bothered
him] with their problems. And after he had spent a day
taking care of such matters he would return at night to
his house, very comforted, and there look for some gift
or morsel to succor the bodies and souls of his disciples
and children in Christ.

His charity shone even brighter with the sick. He
was not satisfied with administering the Holy Sacraments, in which he was most diligent. He frequently
visited the sick, consoling them and speaking to them
about matters of heaven and of Christ Our Lord and
His Most Holy Mother. Whenever he was in the pueblo,
he tended particularly to those who were near death.
This served as a consolation not only to the sick, but
also to their relatives, for when the former died he gave
the latter reassurances that they were now enjoying
the glory of heaven, a concept that was new for these
peoples.

The desire he had to help these souls in that critical
moment by all means possible led him to invent yet
another [strategy] for this purpose. When someone was
near the moment on which eternal happiness hinges he
would order a bell to be rung in the pueblo, so that
everyone would kneel and commend the dying person's
soul to Our Lord. To this the priest added penances
and prayers on his behalf. He also took special care
to have a bell rung at dusk for the souls in purgatory
so that everyone would pray for them in their homes.
This practice was also introduced at Fort Montesclaros,
where the sentinel of the garrison was in charge of ringing the bell. The soldiers remember this so well that
they call it Father Julio Pascual's bell.

But returning to his charity with the sick, this
was so great that some of them miraculously recovered their health. Some very unusual cases were noted
in which those who were witnesses believed that God
had miraculously restored the health of the terminally
ill through Father Julio's prayers. And although other
cases could be reported, I will select only one, which
was related to me by an honorable soldier who served
for some years at the garrison in Sinaloa. His name was

---

80. Saint John Chrysostom (347–407) led a drive for moral reform
among the elite of Constantinople, alienating Empress Eudoxia and the
hierarchy of the Eastern Church, which conspired to have him exiled to
Pontus in 404, where he died from forced travel in bad weather (Farmer
1992:260–61).

81. One wonders whether Pascual's apparent devotion to confession
was the cause of his difference of opinion with superiors, who apparently
found it necessary to "restrain him."

82. I Corinthians 9:22: "I have been everything by turns to everybody, to bring everybody salvation" (Knox 1956:172).

Cristóbal Martínez de Hurdaide, a relative [the son] of Captain Hurdaide, who has been mentioned so frequently in this history. In my presence he retold under oath what he had written, and I will report the case here using the words that he wrote. He says:

I am pleased to have the opportunity to recount the event that happened to me with Father Julio Pascual, [276] a man who lived an apostolic life. I feel that God worked a miracle with me through this blessed priest before he died, for God knows well how to work them on behalf of His servants. One morning when I got up very early to go on a journey with some other soldiers, under orders from my lord the captain, a bad air caught me and twisted my mouth up to my ear. My forehead became contorted, one of my eyes sank into the socket, and the other remained covered by the eyelid. I removed my hat and my fellow soldiers began to laugh, telling me that I was making very ugly and terrible grimaces.[83] I tried to spit and spewed saliva onto my cheek. I spent the night alone at the fort, and at ten o'clock, as I lay suffering terribly in my bed, more because of how ugly I had become than because of my sins, I imagined and told myself that if I saw Father Julio Pascual, who was a saint, he would cure me instantly. Before this idea could be dismissed I heard the noise of hooves and they notified me that Father Julio Pascual was arriving. I thought this strange, because the following day was not a feast day, which is when the priests ordinarily come to the fort to say Mass, provided there are soldiers there. I got up and dressed so that I could go and meet him. He received me with the same words that I imagined in my fantasy, saying, "Señor Cristóbal (he told me), if I were a saint you would be cured." "My sins (I answered) have done this to me, my Father." Then the priest said, "Get down on your knees." I did and the priest made the sign of the Cross over me, uttering a Gospel [verse], and within four days I was healed, without any injury whatsoever.

And I will add that it was with special grace from Our Lord that this soldier was cured in such a short time from a sickness and ailment that leaves men afflicted for the rest of their lives with their sides and members paralyzed.

Knowing of this priest's holiness, some people wrote to him for the sole purpose of obtaining his signature to relieve their ailments. This priest practiced the same charity that he used to cure this soldier with the troops that were assigned to him as an escort, sometimes out of need and sometimes because superiors thought an escort necessary. Because his district was so far from the garrison and because the nations that he was in

charge of were so warlike and fierce, at times he had to be given an escort of four or six soldiers. He aided them with special charity and love in the spiritual matters of their souls as well as in the temporal matters of their sustenance, spending all that he had on them.

He was so generous with his compassion that it extended to the residents of the Villa de San Felipe and to all the Indians of the other districts and nations. This holy zeal, which is characteristic of a minister, shone especially in the priest and was particularly constant towards his Indians, for whom he was always father and mother in the spiritual and temporal sense. He spent his entire stipend from the king on them. When someone asked for something that the priest did not have, he would find something else to give instead, for his charitable heart could not bear for anyone to leave his presence without succor. During barren years and in times of famine he obtained food for his Indians at the places where it was available. He bought this food so he would have some to give to his faithful followers in their time of need, buying it with the clothing that he was sent from Mexico City. By this means his followers could remain in their pueblos and churches and would not need to wander scattered among the montes looking for food. Whenever he finished eating he would give them a portion of maize from his own hand at his own house. There were times when those who benefited from this assistance numbered more than three hundred persons, [277] in addition to the boys and girls to whom he gave food separately and who ate in his presence. He would even feed the little ones so that they would love the doctrine that he taught them; such was his maternal charity.

One can well imagine how much someone who showed such great concern for the temporal matters of his faithful would be concerned about the spiritual and eternal matters of their souls. He was so persevering and zealous in this matter that in less than a year he formed and established the great Christianity of the Chínipa, which could have been accomplished only through the fervor of this holy missionary. He achieved a great deal even with the fierce Guazápare, Témori, and Varohío nations. And even though such universal fruits were not produced among these as compared with other [nations], he nevertheless obtained his crown and martyrdom among them. In addition to having cost him his life, the taming and instruction of these nations involved unspeakable hardships. He often traveled over very rough roads from Chínipa to

83. It would appear from these and other comments below that Hurdaide suffered a minor stroke.

these nations, through ravines, mountains, cliffs, and dangerous passes. The soldiers who had accompanied him claimed that it was impossible, or a miracle, to have traveled over them so many times without going over the edge on the mount that he rode. In this regard they talk about miraculous events that happened to him when the mule tumbled and he was pinned under it, or other times when he raised his hands to heaven, whence came his aid. Another difficulty was the turbulent river that he often had to cross. A missionary priest who accompanied him on this route told admiringly of the ruggedness and danger of good Father Julio's usual route. He spoke with no less admiration about the peaceful and long-suffering manner in which [the father] adapted to such contrary and varied climates as those of the nations where he traveled. It is very hot in the land of the Chínipa; the land of the Guazápare is so cold that Mass could not be said in May or June until very late in the day. Sometimes the snowfall was so deep that the trees were uprooted from the weight of it. Furthermore, in such widely varying climates this blessed priest constantly endured sharp and dangerous aches and pains. He suffered these for the good of his fellow man and found in his God his medicine and relief from fatigue and labor.

As relief for these hardships, and also in aid of souls, his apostolic zeal conquered the learning of barbarous languages, to which he devoted special attention. He also experienced divine favor in this matter, for he learned four totally different [Indian] languages. In fact, when he met his joyous death he was [in the process of] learning a fifth language. This is such a great and demanding labor that it seems an entire lifetime was needed just to be able to practice so many languages. This apostolic man actually spoke seven different languages: three European ones—his maternal Italian tongue as well as Latin and Castilian—plus the four barbarous languages that were mentioned.

I will not enumerate here his rigorous and constant penances, which he willingly added, because from what I have said it can be clearly seen that his life was a continual penance. Let the account of the heroic virtues of this most religious priest and fervent evangelical minister be crowned by that which is the life and crown of them all: charity and love of God. The degree to which this holy soul had increased and ignited this divine fire is evident in the practice of heroic virtues and holy works that he exercised with such great constancy for so many [278] years. These are the fuels that lead this divine fire to burst into enduring flames. His

meditation and continued communication with God and his mortification, humility, interior and external modesty, and charity toward his fellow man continued without ever being interrupted. This charity and love of his God and his desire to be with his beloved called him so strongly that Father Juan Castini, who knew him best and was the closest neighboring missionary in his district, said that when he communicated with him during these last years [of his life] he found him so inflamed with the desire to die and go to heaven to meet his God that he could not distract him from such leanings, even though he tried to do so. It seemed to Father Castini that it would be a great service to the Lord for a man of such virtues and holiness to live for many years in the labor of helping souls. He added that he never perceived this holy man to show aversion to anything except the life of this world.

The main reason that Father Pascual, in whatever way he could, sought to be assigned to the fierce nations that he instructed, rather than being assigned to tamer ones that had already been reduced in the province, was that he hoped to find among them the occasion of his martyrdom. When the marvelous case of the bloodied corporals took place fifteen days before his death, he could have sent notice for an escort of soldiers to come to his aid, but he refused to do so, either out of humility or because he felt that God wished to satisfy his desire for martyrdom. For the same reason, at other times when the escort was sent to him, he accepted them only reluctantly. He had long ago left his life and death up to God. This was noted in a paper that was found signed by his own hand in which, with rare inspiration from heaven, he offered his life to God. As a reminder he wrote that he especially vowed to give and spill his blood for his love, if the occasion presented itself. Therefore, with this desire for heaven, joyous death caught up with him and this holy man passed on to glory.

Many have commended themselves to him, considering him to have attained a high level of glory. His aforementioned missionary companion, Juan Castini, affirmed that he had received aid and favors from heaven through his faithful companion following his blessed passing. Even during his lifetime everyone who talked and dealt with him venerated him as a holy man. The name by which they usually referred to him was Holy Father Julio. It must be understood that this special title was one of personal and private veneration, for as is known, the common and public declaration of holiness pertains only to the Supreme Vicar of Christ Our Lord.

Father Julio Pascual's joyous death occurred on February 1, 1632. He was thirty-two years old and had spent twenty-two years in the Company of Jesus. With this, we will now sum up the very quick manner in which God rewarded the other priest with joyous death. He was fortunate to accompany and receive the crown [of martyrdom] with Father Julio Pascual. [279]

CHAPTER XV The religious life and joyous death of Father Manuel Martínez, companion of Father Julio Pascual

There is good reason to include together in this history the remarkable virtues of those whom God wished to accompany [each other] in death, receiving their crowns as they entered heaven, victorious and triumphant. The events of Father Manuel Martínez's life and the way in which divine kindness prepared him to share with his holy companion in martyrdom and the labors of an evangelical missionary were much briefer than they were for Father Julio Pascual. All the same it was admirable how divine providence prepared the way leading to the glorious crown that he attained.

I can write about his virtues as an eyewitness, or (as they say) as someone who touched them with his own hands. I can also vouch for the gifts and talents with which God prepared him for the glorious end of his illustrious life. I can speak with certainty in this matter because I was fortunate enough to be his Novice Master, and subsequently during his third year of probation he was also under my care.[84] The Company uses this one-year period to allow those who have completed their studies and have been ordained to withdraw to prepare for the evangelical tasks in which they [will spend] the rest of their lives.

This blessed priest was Portuguese by birth, a native of the city of Tabira in Algarve. His father was Jorge Martínez and his mother María Farela, of the house of Bullones and the glorious bloodline of Saint Anthony of Padua.[85] He was born around 1600 and completed his early education in his own country. He then went to Nueva España as a layman in 1619, under the protection of his uncle, who was in the city of Los Angeles [Puebla, Mexico]. There he studied grammar and was an example of great virtue in our schools. He had such a pleasant countenance that he suffered terrible attacks from the enemy of chastity, who tried to rob him of it. But Our Lord saved him through the blessed Virgin Mary, Mother of Purity, to whom he was extremely devoted, particularly later in his life. After his studies of grammar he applied for admission to the Company. Because of his good record he was accepted in 1620. During his novitiate, which he spent in the pueblo of Tepotzotlán, he very fervently exercised all the virtues that are professed by novices. When his novitiate was completed he went on to higher studies at our college in Mexico City.[86] He studied there with the diligence that the Company requires, even though at that time he was overtaken by a serious illness that nearly took his life. But God freed him from that danger because He had predestined him for a more glorious event, in which he would give his life out of love for Him. This helped the priest to make greater and more fervent progress in his virtue, as was noted after he had recovered from that illness.

During the twelve years that he was a religious in the Company he was very faithful to its rules and truly diligent in their observance. In fact, the individual in charge of lighting the lamps for the members of the

---

84. Pérez de Ribas was rector of the novitiate at Tepotzotlán from 1620 to 1623, during Martínez's two-year novitiate and one year of probation (Dunne 1951).

85. Saint Anthony of Padua (ca. 1193–1231) was a charismatic Franciscan friar noted for his preaching and work with the poor (Farmer 1992:26–27).

86. The Colegio Máximo, where Jesuits received advanced training in theology and philosophy.

Company when they rose for morning prayers noted that Father Manuel was always up and dressed when he came to wake him. For this priest one toll of the bell was enough, for he never missed this spiritual exercise unless he was sick. At times [280] they would find him already in prayer well ahead of the community.

His penances were very continuous and rigorous. Most days he disciplined himself so rigorously that he left the walls splattered with blood. Sometimes he used a small scourge so as not to be heard. To these penances he added hair shirts, sleeping on a board, fasting, and [other forms of] mortification. Before he was ordained he took Communion twice a week; he was remarkable in his affection for the Supreme Sacrament of the Altar and would spend long hours kneeling in its divine presence.

He was exceptionally devoted to the Queen of Angels and said her Rosary very affectionately. As a sign of his affection for her he wore the rosary as a precious jewel around his neck under his cassock. He also prayed the office of her Immaculate Conception. On Saturdays and the eve of her feast days he would go to the refectory for public discipline. He also busied himself in the kitchen scrubbing dishes, a practice that he never missed in the twelve years that he lived the life of a religious.

When his studies [for the novitiate] were completed he went on to the college in Tepotzotlán for his third year of probation. There the examples of his virtue and fervor were so outstanding that the favors, aid, and grace that he received from the hand of God spread to his companions. In this way God prepared this outstanding servant for the death that awaited him in Sinaloa, of which he had many premonitions. In accordance with the Company's rule, when he talked to me about matters of his soul and reached the topic of the holy desire that God inspired in him to work in Indian missions, I noticed that he spoke with such tenderness and affection that tears of devotion filled his eyes.

At the end of his third year of probation he received the order of holy obedience to go to the Province of Sinaloa, where he would be assigned a mission. He received this news with great joy and happiness. As he set out on his journey, bidding farewell to devout persons in the pueblo of Tepotzotlán, he explicitly told them with great firmness that he was going to die for preaching the Gospel. To one person who had begged him to send word frequently about his health, he replied: "That will be impossible because the first news that you will have of me is that they have killed me for Christ." Therefore, he very joyfully undertook his journey.

He reached our college in Sinaloa at the time when Father Julio Pascual was experiencing great difficulties alone in his district. This district was very large and extensive, and it was also very isolated from those of the other priests. Father Julio was in charge of peoples whose instruction required fervor and holy zeal for the good of souls, and this was what brought the worker who had just arrived. They assigned him to be Father Julio Pascual's companion, an assignment that good Father Manuel accepted very willingly, as if it were sent to him from heaven. In truth it did come from heaven, through obedience, the sure compass for the religious.

Setting out from the Villa de San Felipe for his mission, he came to the pueblos of the Tehueco, which were on the way. There some priests from different districts met to greet the new companion that God was sending them. Because these priests live in such remote places as if in exile in this hidden province, when one of their brothers arrives from Mexico City it is as if he has come from another world. Therefore, to converse and take comfort in a new companion is a day of rejoicing for them, like a major feast day. Some of the priests [later] recalled that things happened at this holy meeting that they noticed were unusual. [281] It seemed that through them God was foretelling the joyous death that awaited Father Manuel Martínez.

One of the priests who was there was a holy and veteran missionary named Vicente de Aguila, of whom honorary mention was made earlier. When he welcomed Father Manuel he seemed to be compelled by heaven to kiss his robe with special reverence, saying that he did so because he appeared destined for a great, albeit difficult and dangerous mission. He was greeted with nearly the same reverence by Father Pedro Zambrano, a veteran missionary. This priest claimed that he had felt an inner urge to throw himself at Father Manuel Martínez's feet and kiss them (an act practiced by the faithful of the early church with the confessors of Christ who were in jails sentenced to martyrdom). This was because it seemed to him that Father Manuel was to die soon, spilling his blood for Christ.

Their discussions of the difficult enterprise that awaited the neophyte missionary might have saddened or frightened him, but Our Lord had so prepared him with the holy desire to serve Him and offer up his life for Him that he responded that he was consoled to enter a pueblo and mission where there were hardships and dangers to be endured for Christ, and that because he trusted in Him, they did not frighten him. Furthermore, before he knew the name of the companion to whom he was to be assigned in the missions he said to a priest who was his confidante, "Father Julio Pascual has been in the missions for many years without achieving the martyr's crown that he has so desired. The truth is that until I arrive his wish will not be fulfilled." These are all proofs that Our Lord was preparing the spirit of this His servant for the death that awaited him. Moreover, once he had left Tehueco and was headed for his assigned mission, he received a letter from the blessed Father Julio Pascual. As if in premonition of what was about to happen, he wrote to his new companion in a tone full of affection and comfort. These are the words that Father Martínez received four days before he reached his district, "Come, my Reverend Father, be my companion and comfort. Let us be companions in this mission until God wills that we be together in heavenly bliss." With this letter Father Manuel became more enthusiastic. He was also comforted by his fortune of having such an apostolic companion as Father Julio.

Even though he understood that there were some rumors of trouble among those fierce peoples, he enthusiastically proceeded to the pueblo of Chínipa. There he was received with feasting and joy, as was previously stated. Those who ten or twelve days later would enter heaven together in glorious triumph greeted each other with religious embraces. When they had rested for three or four days in Chínipa they set out for the pueblo of the Varohío, where God had prepared the martyr's crown and death for them in the way that was previously told.

Blessed Father Manuel prepared for death with a generous spirit. When the moment came for him to offer his life and die at the hands of those cruel barbarians, the enemies of Christ, to whom he was going to give the spiritual life of their souls, and when he saw that neither their fury nor the flames engulfing the house would abate, he said with great fervor, "Let us not die here sadly, nor let it be thought that we offer our lives with sadness." And even though he realized that when he left the house he would fall into the hands of those beasts and their arrows, macanas, clubs, and whatever {282} torments they wanted to inflict, he still joined his holy companion Father Julio Pascual. Kneeling at his side, he received the thousands of arrows that rained down upon him, as well as the rest of the cruelties that those barbarians inflicted on the priests' holy bodies.

God made these two blessed companions equal in their triumph, considering acceptable the hardships that this new missionary, Father Manuel Martínez, had wished to endure. He was martyred only ten days after he reached this district. This is the courageous spirit that Christ JESUS, whose company this is, has communicated to His sons through His mercy. This can be proclaimed on this occasion for the glory of this very same Lord. His divine kindness has given them the courage and determination to spill their blood for the exaltation of His most holy name in each and every part of the world. On the seas two ships full of evangelical laborers who were bound for Brazil to preach the Gospel to those people fell into the hands of Calvinist heretics. After being abused and cruelly wounded they were thrown into the sea so that their glorious triumph could be consummated in the water.[87] A great many more sons of the Company have died at the hands of heretics in England and other provinces, hanged from the gallows for proclaiming the Roman Catholic Faith.[88] Another great number of fervent laborers who have achieved the glorious martyr's crown in Japan and other places have been burned alive by fire.[89] In places all over the earth many others have died by exquisite tortures, torn to pieces for the glory of Christ and for making Him known to all the peoples of the world. It is an illustrious vow taken by the sons of the Company of Jesus, who are well instructed by so many of their holy brothers that when the time comes to give their lives for the profession of that glorious name and the aid of souls, which He redeemed with His blood, they spare no labor, danger, torment, or life until [they have] attained such a noble and glorious objective. These are the accomplishments of the two holy missionaries whom we have just discussed—many more will be added to their number in the course of this history.

END OF BOOK IV {283}

87. Six Jesuits were sent to Brazil in 1549, less than a decade after the founding of the order.

88. At least two dozen Jesuits were among the hundreds of martyrs of England and Wales between 1535 and 1681 (Thurston and Attwater 1956:2:225–26).

89. In 1614 Japanese rulers ushered in several decades of persecution of Jesuit and Franciscan missionaries and their Japanese converts. During the Great Martyrdom at Nagasaki in August 1622 some thirty thousand spectators witnessed the burning alive of two Jesuits and more than one hundred of their Japanese converts. At least several dozen more missionaries and thousands of Japanese Christians were burned or otherwise tortured to death in the 1630s and 1640s (Boxer 1951:344–45, 390; Thurston and Attwater 1956:2:445–51).

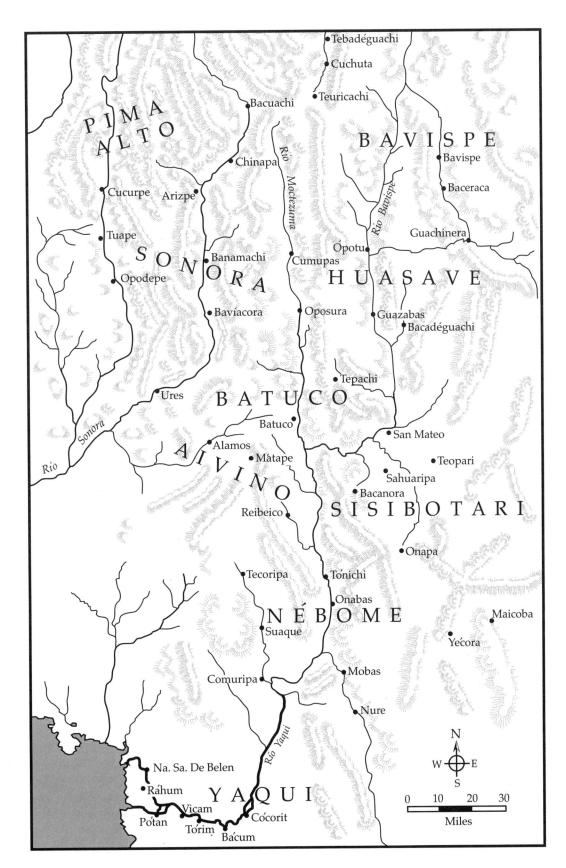

MAP 2. Jesuit Missions of Southern Sonora to 1645

BOOK V

The Spaniards' Wars with the Yaqui Nation and Their Subsequent Baptism and Reduction to Our Holy Faith

CHAPTER I A description of the Río Yaqui and the lands it waters; the people living along its banks and their particular customs

We will now record as history the conversion to our Holy Faith and Christian religion of the most populous nation in the Province of Sinaloa. Before they received the Faith the Yaqui had several confrontations and battles with Spaniards, including some of the most pitched campaigns since the discovery of this province. In truth these wars waged by the Spaniards were justified because the Yaqui had harbored and defended rebellious Christian Indians. But through His supreme providence God was arranging these battles for the most blessed purpose of reducing the large number of souls that received the light of His Holy Gospel.

It has been observed in these enterprises and conversions that a nation that has received the Faith has on occasion backslid because of the influence of bad Christians or because of a gentile uprising. However, from these evils God was able to achieve many good things (as He usually does), because when one nation

backslid, subsequently others would be reduced. Even though this has [already] been noted in another part of this history, it is repeated here, for on no occasion has divine providence shone brighter than in the conversion of the valiant Yaqui. Because they were so far from the [284] Villa de San Felipe and fifty leagues from the garrison [at Fort Montesclaros], and also because they were such a populous, bellicose, and arrogant nation — a nation that had never had dealings or friendship with Spaniards or any other nation — they were not prepared to receive the teaching of the Gospel. Nor would there have been any means of dealing with them at that time if God had not arranged the opportunity recorded here. Although the Mayo, who were in part their neighbors, were at that time [1605-10] attempting to become Christians, these Indians were the Yaqui's principal enemy and were continually at war with them. Still, in the end, to open the door for the Gospel in Yaqui territory God caused the Ocoroni and some other restless Indians to rebel and retreat to Yaqui [lands].[1] In trying to recover these rebellious Christians, a great number of souls were won over to Christianity, and one of the devil's greatest strongholds among these people was overcome. In this way that which was elegantly sung in a hymn by the erudite Saint Ennodius was fulfilled *Christus dedit quot bella, tot victorias*.[2] We will see all of this throughout the course of this book, where I will speak as an eyewitness. From the Zuaque mission, which was under my care and was recorded earlier, holy obedience (fortunately for me) sent me to teach and baptize the Yaqui and to establish their Christianity.

The Río Yaqui, which is one of the largest in the Province of Sinaloa, is almost as strong and fast as the Guadalquivir in Andalucía. Its headwaters are found in the high sierras of Topia, as are those of all the other rivers in that province. It is fifty leagues from the Spaniards' Villa de San Felipe, at thirty degrees north. From the point where the river emerges from the mountains it runs through the plains and some hills for a distance of thirty leagues, where it then empties into the Sea of California. Along the last twelve leagues leading to the sea it is populated by the famous Yaqui nation, who benefit from its many valleys, groves, lands, and fields.

When the river rises and overflows, which ordinarily happens almost every year, the fields are irrigated so that summer planting is possible. Rainfall is therefore not needed for their crops to ripen and for them to enjoy abundant harvests. The Indians have already harvested one crop [by the time] the river overflows, which is usually at the beginning of July. This crop is their main harvest, but nevertheless, during the rainy season some of them plant again, although this harvest is of less importance; their main sustenance comes from the summer crop. This harvest generally produces an abundance of maize, beans, squash, cotton, and other things that they cultivate. At times they also make use of the fruit of the *tepehuaje*,[3] or mesquite tree, of which there are many in their lands. The fruit of this tree is a little carob bean which, when ground in large wooden mortars, produces a tasty flour that is somewhat sweet. They use this for both food and beverage.

Although all the people are farmers and their principal sustenance comes from planting, they also use game from the monte, which is abundant. Those who live near the sea have large fishing grounds, where they catch a great abundance of many species of fish. When the Yaqui lived along this river in their gentile state it was in the form of rancherías spread along the banks and next to their fields. The number of these rancherías would have been about eighty, with thirty thousand souls.[4] Even though this would be a very small number of people for a European nation, in these barbarous provinces nations do not have such a large number of people. They are divided into much smaller groups, and they are separated and have no [285] contact, except to kill one another.

The Yaqui nation was considered to be the bravest and most daring and bellicose of all the nations in the province. Antonio de Herrera, chronicler general of the Indies, writes in his Fifth Decade, Book I, Chapter VIII, of an exploration in which Nuño de Guzmán, governor of the Kingdom of [Nueva] Galicia, participated.[5] He says that when Guzmán reached the Yaqui nation the Castilians in the squadron he was leading swore that up to that time in the whole wide Kingdom of Nueva España they had never encountered any Indians who were so daring and brave. This was confirmed by the brave Captain Diego Martínez de Hurdaide, who after a skirmish and battle with the Yaqui (which we will record later), said that he had never seen a nation fight with as much courage. This was because they did not become faint like others when they saw their comrades' corpses spread all over the field. Rather, they planted their feet firmly on these bodies and arched their bows with even greater fury, saying, "Kill, for we are many." And they did not weaken one bit in the fight.

To this can be added another thing I noticed when I went to baptize this nation. I found hardly a single Indian who did not have a name derived from or signifying the murders he had committed, such as he-

---

1. Recall that in the winter of 1603–4, four hundred Ocoroni fled their mission settlements, seeking refuge with various Cáhita speakers. Some forty families were taken in by the Yaqui.

2. "As many wars as Christ has given, [he has also given] so many victories." This quote apparently is from one of two hymns of praise by Ennodius (A.D. 521), who was bishop of Pavia and a student of Saint Epiphanius (Thurston and Attwater 1956:3:127).

3. David Yetman (personal communication) has pointed out that although the tepehuaje (*Lysiloma watsonii*) is similar in appearance to a mesquite, it does not produce edible fruit.

4. During the decades prior to the founding of missions the Yaqui may well have lost upwards of half their population in various epidemics that affected northern Sinaloa and southern Sonora between 1593 and 1617. Aboriginally—that is, in 1533—the Yaqui may have numbered closer to sixty thousand (Reff 1991b:214–18).

5. It was actually Guzmán's nephew, Diego de Guzmán, who led a foray north to the Río Yaqui in 1533, where the Spaniards experienced the Yaqui's bravery and military prowess (Hedrick and Riley 1976:48).

who-killed-four or -five or -ten, he-who-killed-in-the-monte or -on-the-road or -in-the-field. Similar names also existed in other nations, but there were not nearly as many. When the people of these other nations were baptized they adopted a new name in their language to serve as a surname for their new Christian one. Otherwise, one would not be able to distinguish so many Peters, Johns, etc. However, when an effort was made at the time of Holy Baptism to strip the Yaqui of these barbarous reminders it could not be done because all their names were associated with death and there were no others in their language with which to replace them. I have noted this so that it might be understood how bellicose and warlike this nation always has been. In spite of the Yaqui's ferocity I can affirm that I found many who were of good character, grateful, and loyal, as will later be seen.

The same gentile customs were present in this nation as among the other nations we have recorded—drunken revels, barbarous dances with enemy heads, polygamy, extensive sorcery and great numbers of sorcerers, and other similar customs. These Indians are generally taller and more robust than those of other nations. They speak loudly, with unusual zest, and they are extremely arrogant. When I entered their lands they came to greet me in their manner, and they spoke in such a loud voice that I found it strange. It seemed to me that this was a sign of arrogance not used by the other nations I had known. In order to repress and moderate it, I thought I should tell them that it was not necessary for them to speak in that brash tone if it was in peace that they came to greet the priest who was coming to teach them the word of God. This is because these nations generally speak reverently to priests, even though their languages do not have the terms of honor that the Spanish language does but instead are like Latin.[6] Their response was, "Do you not see that I am a Yaqui?" They said this because that word and name means 'he who speaks loudly', which allows one to understand these people's spirit.

The men all went naked, except for one or two principales who wore a manta made from the hides of deer, lions, or tigers, or from cotton, which the women know how to weave and work very well. The women themselves used grasses for covering their bodies, except for one or two wives of some principal Indians, who wore a cotton manta. It is true that the Yaqui women [286] did such a good job weaving the grasses, reeds, and leaves with which they normally covered themselves down to the knee that they were able to maintain greater modesty than other nations, who used [only] very small mantas of cotton or agave fiber. Now that they are Christians they are very careful about their attire and they weave large mantas, for the Yaqui women are great weavers. They tattooed their chins and arms in the fashion of the Moorish women of Barbary and adorned their eyes with kohl.[7] They adorned their ears by piercing the edge of the ear and hanging some little charms from ribbons of blue cotton thread. Even the men did this, in addition to hanging some small, valuable emerald-like stones [turquoise?] from the cartilage of their nose, which is pierced when they are young boys. In all other respects they were very similar to the other nations already recorded. Therefore, these [characteristics] will not be repeated here.

6. Latin attaches suffixes to nouns to mark the vocative declension, which serves to indicate the person who is being addressed. Spanish, on the other hand, uses terms such as 'Your Grace', etc. Although Buelna's (1891) vocabulary of Cáhita does not mention suffixes, it also has no Cáhita terms of honor comparable to say, principal or cacique. Among the Opata, whose language (Teguima) and culture were generally related to those of the Yaqui and other Cáhita speakers, suffixes were attached to nouns and kinship terms as qualifiers, although it is not known whether there were honorific suffixes (Johnson 1950:28). We are tempted to give Pérez de Ribas the benefit of the doubt, inasmuch as he lived for sixteen years among Cáhita speakers, apparently mastering their language.

7. This is a cosmetic used to stain the eyelids among Moorish and Arabic women.

CHAPTER II The origin and cause of the Spaniards' wars with the Yaqui

Before discussing the unusual conversion to Christianity of this populous nation, an account must be given of the encounters and military expeditions undertaken by Captain Diego Martínez de Hurdaide, who is mentioned frequently in this history. These were carried out with a greater display of weapons and people than all the other expeditions in Sinaloa. They began when the already-Christianized pueblo of Ocoroni fled and rebelled while the captain was in Mexico City talking with the viceroy about matters related to this province. Upon returning from Mexico City he found the Christian pueblo of Ocoroni in rebellion, as was recorded in Book II. The captain tried immediately to reduce them peacefully, but being unable to do so, he found himself forced to resort to the use of weapons. He was notified that the Ocoroni, who were led by some gentiles and other corrupted Christians claiming freedom of conscience, had headed far into the interior, to live freely with gentiles in their [old] customs.

The principal instigator and leader of the Ocoroni's flight and retreat to the Yaqui nation was an Indian of the Sinaloa nation named Juan Lautaro,[8] who pretended to be a Christian. He left Sinaloa and ended up in the mining camp at San Andrés.[9] After he had been there for some time among Christians he returned to his land of Sinaloa. This Indian was astute, cunning, and very crafty. Because he did not like the Church or its doctrine, he avoided all those places where it was [taught] or where he could learn it. Therefore, he went into the interior. He spent some time with the Mayo before their reduction, trying to pervert and incite them against the Spaniards, but he was not able to infect them with his poison. As a demonstration of their loyalty, the Mayo sent some of the Ocoroni fugitives to the captain. The truth [of the matter] is that some of these Ocoroni had been taken by force by these perverse and restless people [Juan Lautaro and other rebels], and so they returned to their pueblo of Ocoroni.

Seeing that he had not been very successful in getting the Mayo to take up arms in defense of the Ocoroni, the Indian Lautaro gathered forty Ocoroni families and proceeded to the Río Yaqui. He spread harmful lies about the captain, the soldiers, and the other Christians, which were born of his depraved heart, itself possessed by the devil. With these lies he stirred up the Yaqui. At the same time he taught them how to defend themselves from the captain when he reached [287] their lands and how to escape musket shots. He also taught them other schemes and tricks.

With things in this state the captain was forced to remedy the unrest, which he feared might spread to other Christian and gentile nations in the province. Thus, he armed his soldiers, drafted some Indian allies, and set out in pursuit of the Ocoroni and their guide.[10] He did not realize that Lautaro's flight had taken him so far into the interior and that he would have to follow him all the way to the Río Yaqui, which, as we said, is fifty leagues from the Villa de San Felipe. The Ocoroni had settled among this nation, in spite of the fact that the Yaqui had never seen or dealt with them before. In payment for the Yaqui's taking them in and protecting them, the Ocoroni had given the Yaqui their daughters as well as their mantas and clothing.

The captain was always of the opinion that pernicious and rebellious Indians should not believe that there was a lair that the Spaniards could not enter in order to punish misdeeds.

Although the captain soon ran short of supplies, he decided to forge ahead to the Río Yaqui. He would first deal with them by peaceful means to get them to surrender the outlaws, so that the latter would return to their pueblo and church. If this did not work, he would resort to arms, even though he had never done so against this bellicose and populous nation, which could assemble eight thousand Indian archers.

Having decided to proceed in this manner, he reached the river and set up his camp. The Yaqui were

---

8. Note that Juan Lautaro was the name of an Araucanian (Mapuche) Indian warrior celebrated for his valor in Alonso de Ercilla y Zúñiga's great epic poem *La Araucana*, which was published in three parts in 1569, 1578, and 1589 (Lerner and Moríningo 1979).

9. This mining camp was founded in 1581 in the heart of the Sierra Madre, in the lands of the Xixime.

10. This initial entrada was in 1607–8.

in plain sight with their weapons at hand. They did not attack, nor did the captain, for he wished to establish peace and friendship with them, both to prepare them for the light of the Gospel and to remove those renegades from their asylum. The Yaqui did not approach the camp, so he sent messages with Indians who spoke their language, which is the most widely spoken in Sinaloa. He asked them to hand over the Christian Ocoroni so that they could return to their lands. He also asked for the Indian Lautaro, leader of the rebels, so that he could be punished. If they did as he asked, then everyone would be at peace, he and his troops would return to the Villa de San Felipe, and trade and commerce would be initiated between the Yaqui and the Spaniards.

The captain presented these and other advantages of peace to the Yaqui, but the Indian Lautaro had spoken so negatively about the Spaniards and had so contaminated the Yaqui's spirit against dealings with them that on this occasion they refused his offers of peace as well as any discussion of working things out. They answered that they refused to surrender the rebels, that they had no desire for friendship with Spaniards, and that they had their bows and arrows at hand. The captain did not feel that this was an opportune moment for starting a conflict, first of all because he did not have enough people, and second because he wanted to renew his efforts at peace upon returning to the Villa de San Felipe.

All the nations of this province, gentile as well as Christian, watched with great interest the Spaniards' and the captain's dealings with the Yaqui. A successful outcome was of great concern to the Gospel missionaries as well as the captain; the former discussed it with the latter in accordance with the captain's orders from the king (as was mentioned previously). They all hoped to find the best means of establishing peace and tranquility in the province so that its hard-won Christianity would not be endangered and so that the expansion of the Holy Gospel would not be hindered. The priests offered sacrifices and prayers to Our Lord so that by His hand He would make these efforts successful.

To further justify these efforts, it was decided that the Yaqui should be sent new offers of peace on the condition that they surrender the renegade Indians who were causing unrest. On this occasion these proposals sat well with some of the Yaqui. Eventually they sent [288] Anabailutei, one of their principal caciques, to the captain and the Villa de San Felipe, offering peace. At the same time they offered to surrender the outlaws,

provided that the captain sent Christian Indians to the Río Yaqui to get them. The captain agreed to do so, and after treating the cacique well he sent him off with a number of loyal Christian Tehueco Indians to fulfill the agreement. He also sent two female Yaqui Indians from the Villa de San Felipe who had been captured during the first expedition and who had been baptized and had become Christian. They would aid in the implementation of the peace that their nation was now proposing.

But this (as it turned out) was a well-planned act of treason. As soon as the Tehueco reached the Yaqui, the latter took the Christian women, killed most of the messengers, and stole their horses, clothing, and everything [else] they had. The Tehueco were extremely upset and demanded satisfaction and revenge from the captain. The captain was forced to take up arms to repair the damage, which would be a threat if left unpunished. He also wanted to maintain the Spaniards' reputation for bravery—a matter of great importance among these nations.

The captain armed his soldiers and readied forty armored horses, together with Spanish servants bearing water jugs.[11] He also drafted two thousand Indian allies, many of whom were Mayo that were still gentiles and had not yet been catechized. Before he marched with his people to the Río Yaqui he sent spies ahead to hide along the road, to insure that word of the army's approach did not reach the Yaqui and they would not have the opportunity to assemble six thousand to eight thousand warriors. When they reached the river he set up camp close to some Yaqui rancherías and sent renewed demands for peace.

The Yaqui's answer came at dawn the following day when, with great fury and clamor, a large number of armed Indians attacked the Spaniards' camp and the Indian allies. The battle lasted almost the entire day and many Yaqui died; many men and women also were captured. Another large number escaped to the monte. Some of our Spaniards were badly wounded, and others, by the time they reached the villa, were in danger of dying because the poison from their arrow wounds had begun to take effect. Many of the Indian allies died on the field, particularly among the Tehueco and Mayo; there were many others who were wounded.

Because the wounded needed to be treated and because there were too few provisions to continue the expedition, the captain was forced to leave the Río Yaqui

---

11. This second entrada apparently was during the winter of 1608–9.

and return to the Villa de San Felipe. He needed a larger army to punish and reduce this nation so that it could no longer serve as a refuge for rebel renegades. He broke camp and returned to the villa with the Yaqui prisoners he had taken, whom he treated well so that they could later serve as hostages and a means of [achieving] peace.

CHAPTER III Captain Hurdaide's third expedition to the Río Yaqui

Great determination was demonstrated by the captain, the Spaniards, and the Indian nations who helped during this last expedition to the Río Yaqui, principally the Tehueco and the Mayo, many of whom had died in battle. Peace in the province ran a great risk of being lost as long as the Yaqui and those who had taken refuge among them continued to rebel. All this was a cause for concern and demanded a solution. In the end it was necessary to undertake a third expedition, which was bolstered by [289] gathering the largest possible number of warriors as well as stores and ammunition. In addition to the soldiers from his garrison, the captain decided to take other Spaniards from the Villa de San Miguel de Culiacán, who had always been good brothers-in-arms to the Spaniards in Sinaloa. Altogether he equipped about fifty soldiers and the same number of armored horses. He gathered about four thousand Indians and large stores and supplies from allied Christian and gentile nations. After assigning some soldiers and residents to watch the villa, and after asking the priests to commend the expedition to God, he set off for the Río Yaqui.[12]

This nation could not feel safe from attack by the captain, because they knew that he did not leave business unfinished. Therefore, they prepared themselves by stockpiling bows and arrows, and they always kept a sentry posted so that they would not be taken by surprise. Their desire was to get their hands on the captain's head the next time he entered their lands, and to dance with it and celebrate their triumph, just as the fugitive Lautaro had promised. This was the subject of their barbarous sermons, which were accompanied by their ritual smoking of tobacco.

12. Apparently in the summer of 1609.

This is the state in which the captain found the Yaqui when he reached their river. Once he had set up camp he sent them renewed demands for peace, telling them again to turn over the delinquent troublemakers. To pressure them even more, he sent them a paper with the seals that were mentioned earlier. He used these seals with the nations of Sinaloa as a sign of a desire for peace and of punishment should they disrupt the peace. The messengers left camp and [soon] found that the Yaqui nation was so arrogant and haughty that they refused to listen to any discussion of peace. Indeed, they took the captain's message and tied it to a string, and then an Indian dragged it along behind him, making a mockery of it right before the Spaniards' eyes.

All that day and the following night the Yaqui encouraged their people to fight. This alerted the Spaniards to take precautions for the outbreak of war. At the break of dawn all the Yaqui from those eighty rancherías or villages that we said were found among this nation had assembled. They attacked our army as one, with such a great thrust of bows and arrows and screaming that our camp was in great danger. The combat lasted for some time, and many people from both sides were wounded and some were killed. The Yaqui persisted in their anger and fury, having the river in their favor, for it was swollen and the waters had risen. They easily passed from one bank to the other, depending on what best suited their offense or defense. The Spaniards' position was not favorable for combat using their armored horses, and the allied Indians began to lose heart. All this forced the captain to give the order to break camp and retreat, for he saw the danger he was in of perishing there with almost all of his people.

The retreat was effected, and it was no small thing for the captain and his men to defend themselves while the supplies were being gathered so that they could depart in as orderly a fashion as possible. At the captain's order the commander, who was acting as sergeant,[13] withdrew with a few Spanish soldiers in order to detain the Indian allies and make sure that they did not run away. They were instead to continue fighting as they withdrew, defending themselves in as orderly a fashion as possible. The captain would stay behind with the others in the rear guard, where the enemy would focus its attack. With this they began to break camp and withdraw.

The retreat route was very dangerous because it passed through a densely wooded plain where there was no place to make use of the armored horses. When the Yaqui saw the troops crossing this plain they unleashed a great volley of arrows. From the cover of [290] the trees they fired with such fury that the allied Indians stopped, turned around, and began to flee. At that moment the Spaniards under the commander who was leading the retreat thought that the captain (who had only twenty-two soldiers) had been killed, and therefore they cut the armor off the horses they were riding and fled, following the Indian allies. Thus they abandoned their captain, who was then left with only those twenty-two soldiers, plus one allied Indian whom they had kept from fleeing. The captain and his small company of soldiers were in clear danger of being killed by the Indians, and the whole province was at the greatest risk ever seen of having its Christianity completely destroyed.

The enemy attack on the abandoned captain and his twenty-two soldiers left many of them wounded; the captain himself [suffered] five arrow wounds to his face and hands. Later I heard him reflecting upon the hardness of the Indian arrow points, which were made from fire-hardened wood, as well as the bravery with which they used this weapon. He said that one of the wounds he had suffered to his face was from the point of an arrow that had been shot with such force that it penetrated the visor of his helmet, which was made of collared chain mail. This is the strongest type [of mail], and it was doubled. At that dangerous moment the brave captain did not lose heart. Instead, with the [same] courage he always possessed he found a nearby hill that was clear of trees. He turned to his little squad, and with great spirit and friendly words he said to them, "Onward, my sons, my Spaniards, let's go up there and fight like Spaniards. Use your harquebuses and your remaining gunpowder wisely. Don't everybody shoot at once—I'll tell you when to shoot." The captain gave this order because he realized that the enemy had taken all their stores and supplies, including their gunpowder. The Spaniards had only the charges they ordinarily carried in their saddlebags[14] on the day of battle.

The Spaniards gathered in this place where they could barely make use of the armored horses, which were tired from fighting and in some cases had been wounded. They were one and a half leagues from the river and it was already well into the morning when, during the summer, the very hot sun beats down on this land. Finding themselves in such straits, the valiant soldiers and their companions nevertheless encouraged one another to fight and defend themselves from the seven thousand warriors surrounding them. It can clearly be seen that if God had not favored them on this occasion—as His paternal providence normally does in these enterprises where the fighting is in defense of His Gospel—then this little squad of Christian soldiers would have died right there and the Christianity of Sinaloa would have been placed in great danger and nearly wiped out. But in the end on this and many other occasions, God takes this Christianity under His care and protection, repressing the enemy and sometimes blinding them so that they are unable to make full use of their military strength.

The mass of seven thousand Yaqui surrounded the little squad and attacked in small groups from whatever vantage point best enabled them to rain arrows down on the captain and his men. However, the shots from the harquebuses reached farther. Thus, the arrows and shots volleyed back and forth. God saw to it on this occasion that the [Spaniards'] shots were right on target and effective against the enemy. As for the arrows that the others were shooting, the captain gave orders to the one Indian [ally] who was left to gather the arrows that fell near the squad and break them so that the enemy's munitions would thus be spent. This was an extreme measure taken to weaken their forces.

Then the Yaqui [291] attempted another battle strategy. When they saw that the place to which the Spaniards had retreated was full of weeds and was like a dry field of straw (which are found in these hot lands, especially when it is summer, which it was), they set fire to the field at the point where the wind was blowing so that the Spaniards would either be burned up or would

---

13. *Sargento*. An individual in charge of several squads (Naylor and Polzer 1986:28).

14. *Burujacas*. This apparently is a Guaraní term! It is not known how or why it became part of Pérez de Ribas' vocabulary (Corominas and Pascual 1989–1991:1:701).

abandon their post. If they did the latter, the [Yaqui] would attack them. As soon as they started the fire with the little sticks that they use in place of flint, tinder, and steel, the captain, who was very skillful in undoing these nations' stratagems, ordered for fire to be taken from the flint of a harquebus and used to set fire to a nearby field of straw. After it quickly burned the captain moved into the clearing with his men and horses. Thus, when the fire started by the enemy reached the Spaniards there was no longer any field to burn and the opponents' scheme was ruined. Still, they persisted in their attacks and shower of arrows.

By this time—now it was later in the day—the sun was extremely hot and the Spaniards were waging battle in the open field. They were afflicted by the heat and by their chain mail armor, which becomes very hot under the strength of the sun. They were also notably tired from thirst, for the river was half a league away. Their only relief was to carry the lead shot in their mouths, a practice Spaniards rely on in these lands. Although the enemy had their refuge in the shade of the trees, they were nevertheless so fatigued that they ordered their women to bring them jugs of water with which to cool themselves, and with this relief they renewed their attacks.

The Spaniards used their harquebuses very cautiously so as not to use up all their powder. As we said, God favored them in that the shots they fired hit their mark. There was one shot in particular that hit an Indian just right, while he was shielding himself with the lid from a box that he had taken from the [Spaniards'] stores. He dared to come closer than the others he was leading and was hit by such a well-timed harquebus shot that he was left there in plain sight of his companions, nearly dead—hanging onto a splinter from the lid with which he had shielded himself.

Then the enemy began to withdraw, for they were being lured away by their desire to enjoy a part of the spoils from all they had taken from the [Spaniards'] supplies, which included all the captain's and the soldiers' clothing and even the silver pieces and the mules' harnesses. They tore everything to pieces and killed many of the horses and mules. Night finally began to fall, and some Indians still remained surrounding the Spaniards so they could warn their companions if the Spaniards tried to execute the scheme and plan thought up by the captain, and especially by God, who helped him. He and his soldiers decided that once it was dark they would release some of the wounded horses. Once the horses were free they would run to the river, just as they normally do when they are thirsty. However, before the Spaniards freed them they would have the strongest of the remaining horses readied so they could depart in as orderly a fashion as possible. The captain was certain that when the enemy heard the pounding of the horses' hooves they would think that the Spaniards were headed for the river, tired from thirst, whereupon the troop of Indians would fire on them. Thus, the Spaniards would have a good opportunity to take off.

Once night fell this plan was carried out. It worked out well, for as soon as the wounded horses were released they took off galloping and whinnying toward the river, where there were some other horses from the [Spaniards'] baggage train. The troop of Indians followed in the horses' wake to ambush them. In this [292] brief period of time the Spaniards mounted their horses and got organized. They took whatever weapons their tired horses could carry and headed for the Villa de San Felipe, which was fifty leagues away. God detained and befuddled the enemy so that they could not attack the Spaniards, whom He wanted to protect. He busied the other Indians in dividing the spoils of clothing and horses that they had taken.

CHAPTER IV What happened to the soldiers who deserted during the battle with the Yaqui; the captain returns to the Villa de San Felipe with the soldiers who remained with him

Before describing what happened following the defeat and retreat of the captain and his remaining squadron, I will write about the others who had deserted the rear guard. They reached the Villa de San Felipe announcing the deaths of the captain and the twenty-two Spaniards who had remained with him, in addition to the other Christian Indians. Such unhappy news caused great sadness and wailing. Everyone grieved: the women who became widows in such a desolate land; the children who were left fatherless; and the province, having lost the best soldiers on that frontier. With the death of the captain, who was the terror of rebellious nations, Christianity was exposed to the obvious risk of being lost. It was felt that nothing was safe in the entire province because of the great victory of the gentile and bellicose Yaqui.

Father Martín Pérez, superior of the missionary priests and cofounder with the blessed Father Gonzalo de Tapia of the Sinaloa Christianity, spilled tears of compassion and sorrow when he realized the risk to all that had been so hard-won. He was at the Villa de San Felipe when the sad news arrived; he immediately dispatched letters and messengers to the priests who were distributed among the Christian nations, notifying us of what was happening. He also ordered us to withdraw to the college in the villa, so that we and the remaining Spaniards could discuss how stability could be restored and how Christianity could be preserved at a time when this province had no governing figure of political authority.

This news and these orders reached me while I was in the Zuaque pueblos, which I was instructing. In compliance I immediately departed for the villa, where we eight religious of our Company congregated. The following day we said Mass for the captain, who was greatly loved and esteemed, and for the other soldiers who we presumed had died in battle. I need to confess a premonition that was also shared by other priests. We were not completely convinced that the captain had been killed, for we knew him to be very valiant, in-

genious, and cautious. Also, when the soldiers who had deserted were interrogated about the place and manner of the death of their captain, whom they should not have abandoned without first seeing him dead, their answers did not coincide. They provided no other detail than to say that the Indian attack fell upon him with great force and that they thought him dead.

They were right about the former: It was later learned that upon seeing the enemies' fury one of the soldiers accompanying the captain asked him to exchange arms with him at an appropriate spot, because the Indians recognized the captain by his distinctive arms and horse. This soldier thereby demonstrated the excellence of his loyalty, wanting to bewilder the enemy in order to insure this life that was of such great importance to the province. What great loyalty was shown by this soldier who, even though he had dark skin, was honorable. The valiant captain did not permit this exchange, but instead (because he could not use his harquebus [293] here) used his sword to constantly defend himself from the Indian troop that pursued him. Given this danger and difficulty, those who had deserted concluded that he was dead and announced it in the villa.

That afternoon the religious were in a state of confusion, suspense, and sadness, when the loyal soldier whom I mentioned entered the villa, shouting with happiness, "Our captain is coming with the soldiers who stayed with him; we are alive." This news revived everyone in the villa. The soldier reached our college and gave the Father Rector a torn piece of paper, which had been used as wadding in a harquebus. The following day the captain had taken it and written to the Father Rector using a twig and ink made from gunpowder: "God forgive those men who abandoned me and thus placed the whole province in danger. Although wounded, I and the other soldiers who stayed with me are alive. We continue traveling slowly due to the fatigue of the horses and the wounded. In order to avoid an uprising in the province as a result of the news that those other soldiers might have brought, I am sending posthaste this soldier, who has been very loyal to me."

When the Father Rector received this happy news he wanted to go meet the captain on the road. I went with him, and we met that small and brave squadron of Spanish soldiers, who were freed from such a large number of enemies by God's miraculous providence. He freed them for the good of the many souls and nations that God brought to His Church through this means, as will later be seen.

The captain and the soldiers told us of the grave danger to which they had been exposed in the midst of so numerous and furious an enemy. Despite unrelenting skirmishes the [Indians] had not taken the head of any Christian soldier with which to celebrate their triumph, which is what they want as payment for the many heads they lose. The soldiers also said that when they reached the Río Mayo and then the Río Tehueco, they were amazed to see that the Indians whom they had thought to be dead were alive.

The Father Rector did not tire of thanking God for seeing and hearing about such a marvelous event. He employed the compassion of his religious vocation on behalf of those who had lost courage in battle and immediately implored the captain to forgive the soldiers who had abandoned him. As soon as they heard the good news of the captain's arrival with his companions, these soldiers hid and did not dare to appear in public. In my presence the captain responded to the Father Rector's intercession with great serenity, "As far as I am concerned, may Your Reverence's will be done."

The captain held up his end [of the deal], but when Don Francisco de Ordiñola, governor of Nueva Vizcaya, whose jurisdiction included the Province of Sinaloa, later received news of the event, he ordered an official inquiry into this desertion. He intended for the soldiers to be garroted for having failed in their duty. When our valorous and prudent captain heard this he dispatched a messenger to the governor requesting that he dismiss the charges. The reason he gave was that if the Indian allies who had deserted with the Spaniards thought the latter would be tried and punished, then they would fear the same thing befalling their own heads. Indeed, it might lead to a rebellion in the province. This argument made a strong impact on the governor and forced him to terminate the inquiry.

It was time to deal with no other cause than the most important one in the province—how to solve the problem of the bellicose Yaqui nation. They were very

insolent and arrogant, having destroyed the greatest army yet assembled [294] by the Spaniards. They celebrated their triumphs with the best spoils they had seen in their lives—horse saddles, bits, stirrups, clothing, etc., which for them were great riches. However, all the same they were frightened and astonished to realize that all of the Spaniards had escaped. They wanted to dance and celebrate their victory with the Spaniards' heads, particularly the captain's, whom they repeatedly called by the name 'sorcerer'. This was a title that was feared and renowned among them because it meant that because the captain was still alive, they were not safe in their land. Because of their past experiences with Captain Hurdaide, they knew that he would not desist until the delinquent troublemakers were duly punished.

This is what was going through the minds of the Yaqui, despite the fact that some bellicose principal caciques announced in their sermons that they hoped the captain would return so that they could fight him. They promised he would not leave their lands alive. For this purpose they came up with a new battle tactic. They said that the most daring Indians should grab machetes taken from the Spaniards and throw themselves beneath the horses' legs, where there is no armor, and cut their hamstrings. This is where all the force of war lies, because when a soldier falls to the ground he is lost under the weight of his weapons.

The captain got wind of all this at the villa from Indian allies whom he had won over and who had penetrated Yaqui territory. This—in addition to the settlement and pacification of a province that had cost him so dearly—caused the captain great concern. On the one hand, he realized that he could not undertake another expedition or equip a new army without permission and financial assistance from the viceroy. He had undertaken the first expeditions at his own expense and had very little money left. Furthermore, he had been informed that the governor of Nueva Vizcaya had not praised his efforts with the populous and bellicose Yaqui nation. The captain—always zealous in doing what he understood would be of service to God, his king, and the Spaniards' good name—did not know where to turn but to his tactics and stratagems (which he knew how to plan extremely well in these wars). He also used threats that were very effective and that were known to come from someone who was accustomed to acting on them.

As was mentioned earlier[15] a ship happened to enter through the Gulf of California around this time

---

15. In Chapter 10 of Book 3; the time was the fall of 1609.

and approached the coast of Sinaloa, astonishing and frightening these nations. Word of the sighting reached the Yaqui. The captain called some Indians who were neighbors of the Yaqui, and referring to the ship, he expressed great anger, telling them that he had given orders for the execution of a punishment unlike any the Yaqui had ever seen before. He said that the Yaqui's pueblos were to be razed and exterminated by three captains and squadrons, which were to invade the Río Yaqui at the same time and from three different directions. Thus, the Yaqui would be unable to unite and help one another and would not escape his hands. He noted that the Yaqui had already seen how the Spaniards could travel on the sea. He told them that one squadron would come from the sea and attack the lower pueblos, which were the most arrogant; another captain would attack the rancherías on the upper river; and finally, he himself would confront those along the middle [of the river], where he would mete out a notable punishment. In truth the scenario painted by the captain was plausible, even though he could not [in fact] carry it out. The captain further commented that the allied nations who had accompanied him in previous military expeditions would now avenge their relatives who had died in past battles.

All these arguments [295] were passed along to the Yaqui by those who traveled to their river and by those who subsequently came to find out what was going on in neighboring nations. All of this caused concern among the Yaqui because they knew that the captain kept his word. All this had an effect on the Yaqui, who reached a decision that will be recorded in the following chapter. It could be called miraculous because it was the beginning of the reduction and conversion of the Yaqui nation, along with many others who subsequently followed their example.

CHAPTER V The singular manner in which the Yaqui nation was reduced to peace and friendship with the Spaniards

The reduction and victory that were achieved among this large and bellicose nation were nearly miraculous, due more to the hand of God than to weapons. This can be seen clearly from the defeat that was suffered by the captain and his four thousand Indian allies. I have decided to write about this here based on public records and authentic information that I have in my possession. The governor of Nueva Vizcaya ordered this [investigation] because some people misrepresented Captain Hurdaide's expedition to the Yaqui (as those who speak from afar often do). These critics had no knowledge of what actually happened. Some of them condemned Captain Hurdaide's expedition as reckless because it had endangered the entire province and its Christianity.[16] Others spread the rumor that nothing had been gained from his expeditions and battles (which have already been recorded). They did not consider the fact that if the captain had not undertaken these expeditions, the province would have been exposed to great danger. Nevertheless, on these and other occasions God favored the brave Christian zeal with which this captain executed great and justifiable enterprises, thereby establishing peace in Sinaloa with the many nations that have been recorded here.

This present peace was achieved in a singular manner: the Yaqui saw that they had not been able to take the head of the captain nor even the head of one of his soldiers, contrary to what the rebellious outlaws had promised them. When the threats of this brave man, of whom they had heard a great deal, reached their ears from the villa, some of the caciques of the nation decided to negotiate peace with him and the Christians. However, there were several obstacles to their going to discuss peace with the captain. The route [to the villa]

16. Hurdaide's critics are unknown; they may well have been encomenderos in Sinaloa who were required to accompany the captain's expeditions to the Yaqui.

was through the lands of their enemy, the Mayo, of whom they had killed many in past skirmishes. Beyond them were the Tehueco, who were upset because of the death of some of their people.

To insure their safe passage, one of the Yaqui caciques named Conibomeai, who was one of those who most desired peace (I later baptized him and he assisted greatly in establishing this Christianity), decided to risk the life of a woman from his group. He sent her to meet with two caciques of the Río Mayo, whom he knew to be principales of that nation: one was called Osameai and the other, Boothisuame. She was to learn from them about the captain's state of mind and his intentions. She was also to ask the Mayo to help the Yaqui sue for peace at the villa, so that they might be under the captain's protection and friendship, like the Mayo. If the courageous woman who departed with this message [296] did not return within four days with a reply indicating the success of her commission, they would assume that she had been killed by the Mayo.

God inspired this woman to walk eleven leagues and to enter the midst of her enemies. She reached the Mayo and met with the two caciques, to whom she gave the message. The Mayo Indians (as has been previously written) are of good character and had cemented a good and loyal friendship with the captain. They heard the message of peace with pleasure. They told the woman to tell the Yaqui that they would help, provided the Yaqui really and truly were pursuing peace and friendship. They said that if the Yaqui were intent on that goal, they should send [additional] word of this. Because these peoples were constantly at war, they trusted each other very little. Then the two Mayo caciques sent the Yaqui woman back. For her greater safety they and some of their people accompanied her so that others would not kill her before she reached safety.

The woman reached her [own] land and communicated the Mayo's reply to the cacique, Conibomeai, who had sent her. He and some other caciques listened to the woman with great joy and decided to send a second delegation to the Mayo caciques. Because the latter had offered to help the Yaqui negotiate peace with the captain, the Yaqui asked them to show their good heart by going to see him to find out whether he was willing to [negotiate]. The Yaqui sent this second delegation with the same woman who had conducted the first one. They provided her with two female companions, one of whom had either been captured years before from the Mayo nation or for some other reason

had gone to the Yaqui. She was the wife of a cacique called Otauaco (sometimes these Indians value a wife or concubine from an alien nation). The three women reached the Mayo and met with the caciques Osameai and Boothisuame. They heard the Yaqui's message with such great pleasure that they [immediately] set out on the forty leagues' journey to the villa, leaving the three women in the safekeeping of their relatives in Mayo territory. They were going to notify the captain of what was happening, of the positive resolution that the Yaqui were taking to insure peace and friendship, and how the three women had remained with the Mayo in order to report his decision to their own people.

The captain and the priests were very happy to hear this news, for they all desired the settlement of a nation that caused such concern to the province and had placed it at such risk. He dispatched the Mayo caciques, ordering them to immediately return to their lands, taking a reply in his name to the Yaqui women and to any of the caciques they happened to meet from that nation. Some of their principal Indians should come to see him at the villa, where they would be received in peace. The conditions for their settlement would be discussed as well as their stability, service to God and king, and anything else that the Yaqui wished to discuss. So that the Yaqui would be able to travel more safely, without harm from the nations through whose lands they had to pass in their coming and going, the captain sent a paper with a seal, just as he usually did with other nations, so that they would be well received by all. In addition, and at his own expense, he ordered the Mayo Indians to provide food and provisions to the Yaqui who were on their way to see him when they reached Mayo lands.

The Mayo departed with this message for the three women who had remained in their lands. However, not far from the villa they encountered the three women and a group of nearly forty [297] Mayo Indians. In view of the high hopes that these women had been given of being well received, and because of the Mayo's own desire to see this peace effected, the latter had decided not to wait for an answer. Instead, they were bringing these women to the captain, before whom that entire group appeared. The women conveyed their mission, saying that their relatives, the Yaqui, regretted the war against the captain, the Mayo, and the rest of the Christians. They lived in their rancherías and along their river in constant fear of dawn attacks and ambushes by the Spaniards. Their fear was so great that it went with them even when they went to draw water from the river. At dusk and at dawn they could hear the sound of the iron bows (this is what they call the harquebuses and muskets).

Here I want to report a suspicion of mine, which is not lacking in credibility. I lived among them for some years, and several times I heard the warlike Yaqui talk about this sound and the fear that it struck in them. I suspected that by chance this frightful sound was caused by the [guardian] angels of this nation, who sought to conquer and subject the Yaqui to peace and the reception of the Gospel. The truth is that, given the defeat they had handed the captain and his troops in the last battle, they could have been much more daring and arrogant than they had been in the beginning. As has already been recorded, they attacked and routed the captain's troops three times, killing many of his people. However, now they requested the peace they had once rejected.

When the women who had come with the squad of Mayo had been heard, the captain asked them whether it was true that they made their request on behalf of the entire nation and all its rancherías and caciques. At that point the women wavered a little, responding that when they had held their meetings about the peace talks some of the spirited young people had protested, saying that they wanted war with the fierce captain, not peace. But the caciques Conibomeai and Hinsiamei, who were some of the eldest on the river, had restrained these restless young people by telling them they should not speak in the presence of their elders, which had silenced them. All these circumstances show that this nation was reduced through the work of God.

The captain ordered that all these people be treated well. After a few days he dispatched the women messengers, instructing the Mayo to return them safely to their lands. He gave each of the women a horse to ride and a dress, and he ordered the Mayo to treat them well on their return journey to the Río Yaqui. When the women reached their land they were to notify other caciques and Yaqui people to come and see him. The captain also ordered that when the Yaqui came through Mayo territory they should be given safe passage and provisions for their journey at the captain's expense. Last of all the women were to tell their Yaqui caciques and rancherías that in order to negotiate peace, men, not women,[17] should come, including some of the prin-

cipal caciques, who would be well received. In order to demonstrate how sincere they were about negotiating peace, those who requested it with a good heart should reduce themselves to pueblos. In this way the captain would know who the real rebels were and he would go after them. Although this might appear to be an inappropriate threat, the captain knew from his great experience that it was necessary to use vigorous methods with such people. Finally, he told the women that they should assure their caciques that even if they came and did not accept the peace conditions [298] they were offered, they would nevertheless be protected until they had returned safely to their lands.

The women were dispatched with this message, and when they reached their land they were received to the general delight of all. They reported to their people what had happened, and many of them were happy to hear the captain's answer. Nevertheless, because they were people accustomed to a barbarous lack of loyalty among themselves, they sent two of their caciques to verify the women's message.

These caciques appeared before the captain, and he asked them several questions about their past wars and about why they had been so stubborn in not accepting peace when it was offered to them. They answered that the Indians Lautaro and Babilonio, the ringleaders of the outlaws who had taken refuge in their lands, persuaded their people and the Yaqui nation to take up arms and declare war for the following reasons: The Spaniards were not courageous—their Zuaque relatives had killed many of them (a topic written about in Book I); when the Spaniards entered Yaqui territory the outlaws would show them how to defend themselves from their harquebuses and how to kill them; the Spaniards tired quickly in battle, and in the time required for one harquebus shot the Yaqui could fire many shots with their bows and arrows; and finally, they assured them that they would have the heads of the captain and his soldiers to dance with and they would live freely in their drunken revels, with as many women as they wanted.

The two Yaqui caciques said they had been tricked by these and other promises. Nothing had been fulfilled. Rather, many of their people had been wounded or killed in battle. At the same time these caciques recognized that their neighbors, the Mayo, and other

17. It is interesting to note how Pérez de Ribas' account suggests that although women could function as messengers, undertaking crucial

and dangerous missions, the Spaniards apparently did not consider them appropriate mediators.

Christian nations were at peace, happy, and content—protected by the captain and cared for by the priests, who treated them as their children. Thus, they wished for the same. This was the reason the Yaqui gave for their mission.

After they had rested a few days the captain sent them off with the Mayo Indians who had accompanied them. He gave some of them horses and others clothing, knives, blankets, and other things that they value. He also promised them peace and safe passage, under the following conditions. First, a good number of their principal caciques would have to come to honor this peace. Second, they would no longer wage war on their neighbors, the Mayo, nor on any other Christian or gentile nation that had been placed under the king's protection. If any of those troublesome and rebellious nations should seek refuge at their river and nation, they were not to protect them. Instead, they were to arrest them and turn them over to whomever was captain of that province. Third, although the captain pardoned their shooting and killing of many horses, they had to turn over those horses that were still alive as well as all the Spaniards' silver plates, jars, and weapons. The fourth and final condition was that they apprehend the leaders of the previous uprisings who were still living among them. In the event that there was no sure way of capturing them they were to kill them during some drunken revel or however else they could. He added that in the event that some other nation should attack them the captain would protect the Yaqui and aid in their defense.

With this he sent them off, [299] having treated them quite well. The two Yaqui caciques requested a period of twenty-six days[18] in which to return with their people's final decision. The captain gave them an additional ten days, and with this they returned very happily to their lands.

Before I write about how this peace was attained I want to relate the good influence this peace had on other nations who learned that the Yaqui, who had previously warred with the Spaniards, had now submitted. To achieve this end, there is no doubt that God had marvelously favored the Spaniards in their dangerous expeditions against this nation. When others saw that a nation as famous and brave as the Yaqui had surrendered and asked for peace, they also went to discuss peace with the captain; to congratulate him and his

soldiers for having survived; and to request friendship, instruction, and priests. For this purpose groups of Indians came with their caciques from eight, ten, and twelve days' journey into the interior. This included the Nure, the Nébome, and others who were later instructed, as is told in the following book.[19]

These were the fruits of the captain's last expedition against the Yaqui, whose reduction was finally achieved in the following manner. After the two Yaqui caciques and the women whom God had inspired to travel so far in order to obtain peace had reached their land, a great crowd of people gathered to hear the answer they brought, which was a message of great friendship toward their nation. The two cacique ambassadors told them about the captain and how well he had received them. As testimony of this the Yaqui now saw that the caciques who had gone to see the captain had horses and other gifts that he had given them. They saw the women messengers dressed like the women of [central] Mexico, with *huipiles*[20] or blouses and shifts of bright colors and feathers, a novelty that they had never seen before. Moreover, they heard their report about how life was enjoyable and peaceful in the Christian pueblos through which they had passed, how the pueblos had churches, how the captain insured the people's peace and protection, and how the priests loved those whom they were instructing. All this made a strong impression on the spirits of many of those who previously had clamored for renewed war and fighting with the captain; they were moved to change their minds and join those who proposed peace.

There were still a number of rebels and troublesome persons, particularly the sorcerers, who were ministers of Satan and enemies of Christ and His evangelical law. However, God had willed that the time had finally come for this nation to escape the power of the devil, who possessed it, and pass into the glorious kingdom of Christ. Therefore, the lovers of peace prevailed. A good number of caciques and Indians of importance assembled, including the two aforementioned principales from this river, who later helped the Christianity of this nation a great deal. They decided that they themselves, with a good number of their people, would go to the Villa de San Felipe. There, with the captain and

18. It seems more likely that the caciques requested what amounted to the passage of a lunar cycle.

19. The groups came to the villa in 1610. The Nébome and Nure, in particular, apparently fared poorly in their wars with the Yaqui even before the arrival of Spaniards in the New World.

20. The woven and brightly embroidered blouse or tunic worn by women throughout Mesoamerica and still worn in Mexico today.

the priests, they would conclude their negotiations for peace, offering the silver plates and Spanish weapons that they had taken as booty in the last conflict. Moreover, so that their seriousness in seeking peace and their will to receive the instruction of the Gospel and become Christians would be understood, they decided to take with them a good number of their sons to serve as pledges of peace and to remain in the priests' custody with boys from other nations in the seminary and school at our college, where they would learn the Christian doctrine. [300] When the priests [eventually] went to preach among the Yaqui these boys would accompany them and could teach the doctrine in their pueblos.

The Yaqui agreed within a few days to all these proposals, and with the captain's assurance of safe conduct through nations along the way a group of 150 people set out for the villa. When they arrived the captain and the priests received them all with a great show of friendship and happiness, as did the entire province, which witnessed such a successful conclusion to such bitter and dangerous wars.[21] The Yaqui handed over the silver and the rest of the booty, [which they had] adorned with feathers. They excused themselves for failing to return the remaining horses [saying] that they were so high-spirited from [pasturing on] the grass along the river that they could not catch them. However, they [promised to] hand them over when they had ropes or leather straps with which to tie them.

The Yaqui stayed for several days to rest, and the priests entertained them in their house, as did the captain in his. They visited the Christian pueblos and churches that were close to the villa. They were happy to see them so peaceful and to see the love and affection with which they were treated. They offered to reduce their rancherías to large pueblos, where they could build churches when the priests came to instruct them. To the principal caciques, who were largely responsible for the peace settlement, the captain distributed some clothing plus some colts, which are very highly prized by these peoples. Finally, official testimony was taken in the form of a request to the viceroy to send priests to instruct this nation in our Holy Faith and to baptize them (they were given firm hopes that this would be

done in good time). The Yaqui were then supplied with provisions for their journey home, and they took their leave to return to their land. They were very happy and intent upon sustaining the established friendship and communication. From time to time some of their people came to the villa, just as the captain and the priests had asked them to do.

When they reached their lands the delegation reported how well things had gone. They held many meetings in their usual manner in their pueblos. Many sermons were preached, exhorting and informing them about how good it would be for them to live like the other Christians of the province, how good the Spaniards' friendship was, and how very different things were from the lies concerning mistreatment that had been told them by those who had come into their lands as outlaws. They concluded from all this that they must again insist on priests coming to their lands to preach to them, so that the nation would finally be settled to enjoy perpetual peace.

Most of the Yaqui were so happy with these talks that whole groups of them left their lands to go to the villa to communicate with the Christians, the captain, and the priests. They carried out one of the conditions that had been requested of them and which they had promised to fulfill. They captured the Indians who had been the ringleaders and authors of past disturbances, particularly the leaders and outlaws, Lautaro and Babilonio. They brought them under heavy guard and handed them over to the captain, who ordered them to be executed. God Our Lord willed to show them the light to recognize their crimes and to ask for pardon and Holy Baptism at the hour of their deaths. They received [this sacrament] with such goodwill that the priest who helped and baptized them was quite satisfied [that they were saved].

The rest of the Christian allies who had deserted [the captain] were pardoned and returned to their pueblos, where thereafter they set a very good example. [301] This time the devil came out quite badly, and the commotion and storm with which he had attempted to destroy Christianity in Sinaloa was dispelled.

---

21. The delegation arrived at the villa in late April 1610, and celebrated the peace agreement on April 25.

CHAPTER VI The captain and priests decide that one of the latter will go to Mexico City to report on the state of the Yaqui nation; the difficulties that were overcome to secure a mission for the Yaqui

There were several reasons why it was necessary for someone to go to Mexico City to report to the viceroy, who was captain general of all the provinces of Nueva España, about the expeditions to the Río Yaqui by the captain and garrison of Sinaloa. These expeditions had been discussed [in Mexico City], and although some approved of them, others did not. Public actions are [often] subject to heated discussion, particularly when they occur in distant places such as the Province of Sinaloa, and even more so along the Río Yaqui, which was 350 leagues from Mexico City. The goodwill of the Yaqui nation [also] required that a Christian mission be hastened before the present opportunity was lost. (As was previously pointed out) this cannot be accomplished without the permission of the viceroy who, in the name of the king, places converted nations under his protection. He also appoints missionaries to instruct them, because His Majesty is also the patron of all these churches.

To deal with such important matters the priests consulted and it was agreed that one of them should go to Mexico City to meet with the viceroy and the Father Provincial of the Company, the latter being the one responsible for assigning religious to missionary endeavors. This meeting took place in our college at the Villa de San Felipe and was attended by a good number of missionary priests.[22] There the very religious priests decided that I should make the journey to Mexico City to discuss the matter of a mission to the Yaqui. They deemed it fortuitous that I had been in the Sinaloa missions for years and had a knowledge of them and the nations discussed herein. They felt I could provide superiors with an extensive and accurate account of everything.

In fulfillment of holy obedience, traveling by way of Durango, I went to relate these matters to the governor of Nueva Vizcaya, who at that time was Don Gaspar de Alvear, a knight of the Order of Santiago. I will take the time to recount my journey in order to make known the ways in which divine providence directed the light of His Gospel to the Yaqui. The governor, who was new in that position,[23] disapproved of the captain's expeditions. He also felt that the Yaqui, who fell within his jurisdiction, were not ready to receive religious instruction. I nevertheless continued onward to Mexico City to discuss this matter—which was of great service to God and the king—with the viceroy of Nueva España, the marquis of Guadalcazar.[24] The Río Yaqui and the establishment of a mission there were matters that actually fell [more] within his jurisdiction.[25]

As soon as I arrived I presented my mission to His Excellency, who listened carefully and with great piety. He was very pleased with my report on the Province of Sinaloa, and he greatly appreciated the bravery that Captain Hurdaide demonstrated in his encounters with the Yaqui, particularly as they resulted in a request for priests and religious instruction. He ordered me to make a written request for whatever was in the best interest of that province and the expansion of the Holy Gospel. Then, in His divine [302] clemency, God—

---

22. Pérez de Ribas neglects to point out here that six years elapsed between the time the Yaqui "surrendered" (April 1610) and the time of this meeting, which took place in 1616. It was in September of this year that Pérez de Ribas went south to petition the viceroy and Jesuit provincial for a mission to the Yaqui.

23. Gaspar de Alvear y Salazar succeeded Francisco de Urdiñola (a strong supporter of Captain Hurdaide's) as governor in 1613, retaining the office until 1618 (Polzer, Barnes, and Naylor 1977:106).

24. Diego Fernández de Córdoba (1612–21).

25. Pérez de Ribas apparently is alluding here to a jurisdictional argument that could have been made to the effect that the Río Yaqui fell beyond the northern limit of the original boundary of the Province of Nueva Vizcaya and thus was the responsibility of the Audiencia de México and the viceroy. The sixteenth century saw a long quarrel over jurisdiction between Nueva Galicia and Nueva Vizcaya.

wanting to bring a large number of souls in darkness to know Him—moved the viceroy's spirit. After consulting with the members of the chancellery[26] he decreed that peace and friendship with the Yaqui should be maintained and that the captain should preserve them under the protection of Our Lord the king. He also decreed that two priests from our Company should go and prepare them to receive Gospel instruction. Father Provincial Rodrigo de Cabredo was notified to appoint these priests. In addition, the viceroy ordered royal officials to give each of the two priests an entire set of ornaments for the altar, as well as numerous bells and some musical instruments.[27] This was all done according to the great Catholic piety with which our monarchs administer the extensive Christianity of the New World. They were granted this royal patronage by God and His Vicar [the Pope].

The viceroy refrained at this time from sending more than two missionaries to a nation as populous [as the Yaqui], who required a larger number of laborers. This was in part because the governor of [Nueva] Vizcaya did not support this cause. Furthermore, the viceroy had learned that some caciques in the Yaqui nation were still hostile and not very committed to peace. Therefore, he was waiting to have more news of these people's stability—because by nature they tend to be very inconstant—before sending more missionaries.

The Father Provincial received the viceroy's order to assign two priests [to the Yaqui]. His Reverence decided that I would be one of them because I had some experience dealing with Indians and knew the Yaqui language, which was the same as that spoken by the Zuaque, to whom I had ministered. I considered this a very fortunate assignment, which befell me through holy obedience. His Reverence gave me as a companion a priest named Tomás Basilio. He had just arrived from Spain with others who had come on orders from His Majesty for the missions of the Indies.

After we departed Mexico City we encountered one detour along the way, which appeared to be an attempt by the devil to disrupt and frustrate this enterprise for the greater glory of God and the good of the many souls that we were attempting to reduce to His Church.

Having traveled 140 leagues from Mexico City, we reached a stopping point near Durango. There we received the sad news that six days earlier [on November 16, 1616] the fierce Tepehuan nation had rebelled and renounced the Faith. This occurred in the same area through which we were to travel. There the rebels had cruelly killed eight missionaries from our Company and burned churches and greatly damaged Spanish haciendas.[28] More of this revolt will be recounted at the proper time [in Book X].

Understandably, we were very upset and confused by this news. Our journey was seemingly at an end, given that we were supposed to travel through the lands of the Tepehuan. We also feared that the rebellion and disturbance—being the handiwork of the devil—would spread to our Province of Sinaloa, which borders the sierra to which the Tepehuan had withdrawn, whence they might impede the conversion of the Yaqui.

This news stopped us from continuing our journey, and if it were not for the special providence of Our Lord, who detained us at various places along the way for some eight days, the Tepehuan would certainly have [303] captured us as well and we would have met the same good fortune as our brothers, dying for the preaching of the Holy Gospel. We were also delayed by the Spaniards in those ranches where we stopped because we received word not to go on to the city of Durango. Neither the city nor its Spanish residents were safe from the Tepehuan's daily assaults and albazos (which is what they call their dawn attacks). We had to turn around and make a detour of another one hundred leagues to reach Sinaloa.[29] In some places and pueblos we found great fear of enemy attack, as I will relate in more detail at the appropriate time.

Finally, we continued on our dangerous journey, and it was not without some fear that we might find Sinaloa in rebellion because of the Tepehuan or one of their allied neighboring nations. It was God's will to guide us safely on our journey, for the captain of Sinaloa sent us an escort of six soldiers and armored horses.

---

26. *Chancillería*. A supreme court of appeals (Haring 1947:74, f.8).

27. Dunne (1951:49) gives a good idea of what each set of ornaments probably included: amice, alb, cincture, vestments (including five sets of differently colored chasubles, maniples, and stoles), chalice and paten, three altarcloths, corporal, purificator, pall, water vessel, vases, candlesticks, pictures, and a crucifix.

28. Ranching "complexes;" that is, large tracts of land homesteaded by Spaniards (but staffed largely by Indians, mestizos, and black slaves) that were devoted principally to raising cattle, horses, and mules. The jerking of beef, leather working, the distillation of mescal, and limited farming (usually of wheat) also took place at many haciendas (see Griffen 1979).

29. The two priests apparently retraced their steps to the Río San Pedro, following it down to the coast, where they then headed northward to the Villa de San Miguel de Culiacán (Dunne 1951:52).

We found the province peaceful and the Yaqui firm in their good intentions to accept priests to instruct them and make them Christians. They had not changed their minds and remained friendly toward Spaniards. In the following chapter I will relate their resolution to begin religious instruction, which the enemy of humankind had so attempted to block.

CHAPTER VII The Father Visitor[30] decides that the two priests sent from Mexico City to Sinaloa should found a mission among the Yaqui; the founding of the mission is described

The two missionaries who were to found a mission among the Yaqui, which was carried out in the face of great obstacles, reached Sinaloa at a time of extreme difficulty and danger. The captain and his soldiers from the garrison were on continual alert, ready to respond to any attempt by the Tepehuan to foment rebellion in the pueblos and nations of Sinaloa. The [Tepehuan] later attempted to recruit some nations from this province as allies. Another difficulty was that the Yaqui were still gentiles and their friendship with the Spaniards, with whom they had had so many skirmishes and battles, was still quite new. Furthermore, some Yaqui were not very happy with the friendship that had been established. Nevertheless, after lengthy consultation it was decided that at least it should be determined whether the Yaqui were still interested in having priests. And so they were notified that two had arrived from Mexico City to provide them with instruction, just as they had requested and had been promised.

When the caciques received this information, some of them came to the villa, where they expressed joy at seeing us. They offered to bring their rancherías together in the form of pueblos and to make enramadas for churches, just as other nations had done to receive us. When the captain and priests heard this offer they conferred about the problems and difficulties that might still exist for both parties. On the one hand, as long as the war with the Tepehuan continued, there was no assurance of peace among the Yaqui. On the other hand, if the present opportunity was lost, there might not be another suitable occasion to instruct the Yaqui, because the war with the Tepehuan was going to last a long time. It would be good to take immediate possession of the Yaqui nation for the Church.

It was finally agreed [304] that we two priests would go and found a mission among this nation. God apparently had a hand in this decision, because as time went on the apostate Tepehuan rebels persisted and the expense to the king in punishing and reducing them increased. If Christianity had not been established at this time among the Yaqui, their reduction and that of the other nations that followed them would have been delayed for a very long time, perhaps forever. Once the decision [to proceed] was made I was ordered by the Father Visitor, under the precept of holy obedience (an assurance for me of the favor that I could expect from Our Lord, who commanded it), to set out with Father Tomás Basilio, who had been brought from Italy to the Indies by a burning desire for missionary work. The Father Visitor also ordered us to stay for a few days with the Mayo, who were already Christians and whose towns bordered the Yaqui along a distance of some eleven leagues. There we were to acquire an interpreter and information concerning the Yaqui's state of readiness, which we were then to report [to the Father Visitor].

These delays should not be considered too many or too long. Rather, they are important for beginning Gospel instruction at the appropriate time. Such delays were clearly insinuated by the wisdom of the Son of

30. Vicente de Aguila (former missionary in Sinaloa).

God, for when the felicitous time had arrived for sending His Apostles forth to preach the Holy Gospel and convert souls, He gave them that noteworthy maxim, *Videte Regiones, quia albesunt ad messem.*[31] I have not revealed until the appropriate time my command to preach my doctrine—when the regions where you are to preach and the crops you are to harvest are ripe. This was duly considered through the efforts and precautions undertaken in catechizing this new and unstable nation.

Finally, carrying out our superior's order, we reached the Mayo nation [in the spring of 1617], whence we sent word to the Yaqui of our arrival. When some of the caciques who had been the most constant in negotiating peace and who had requested priests for their pueblos heard this news, they came to the Mayo nation to welcome us and to show their pleasure at seeing us so close to their lands. They were accompanied by many commoners who had never seen the Christians' fathers, which is what they call the missionaries of the doctrine. A rumor had spread among these people, started by some troublesome Indians from the lower Yaqui pueblos. They asked, "Is the priest's blood like that of the Spanish soldiers?" They also asked, "Why are priests, who have no bows and arrows, coming here? Let the captain, who is courageous, return with his soldiers and their iron bows." It was clear from these statements that these people were not yet ready to receive Gospel instruction. Just as the devil strongly resists the exorcisms that the Church daily employs to expel him from human bodies, so he made every effort to keep from being expelled from these poor souls, who are his strongholds.

We reported to our superior the state in which we found the Yaqui. With inspiration from the Holy Spirit, as was understood from what subsequently happened, he finally ordered us to proceed and initiate that very important and longed-for mission. When we received this order the friendliest of the Yaqui caciques were notified to come and accompany us with some of their people. They were to guide us along the unfamiliar way, thereby initiating an enterprise that was now under God's care. When they received this message the two most important principales of the entire river came to Mayo territory with some of their people to accompany us. Thus we departed for our mission.

CHAPTER VIII The priests reach the Río Yaqui and begin the religious instruction and Baptism of the nation[32]

Here I relate the founding of the mission and Christianity of the Yaqui nation. In the first chapters of this book I portrayed them as very bellicose and rebellious against God, His Gospel, and those who preached it, as well as against the Spaniards and Christians who protected it. From here on we shall see how divine goodness began to demonstrate the nature of its mercy, smoothing over many difficulties, working an admirable change in this nation and forming one of the most noteworthy Christian communities that has [ever] been seen among gentile and barbarous nations. I refer to this change because it may serve to encourage those whom Our Lord deigns to employ in similar enterprises, even though they may appear to be full of unconquerable difficulties.

The group of Indians who had come with two of their caciques to accompany us had reached Mayo

---

31. *Margin Note*: Ioan. c. 4. John 4:35: "look at the fields, they are white with the promise of harvest already" (Knox 1956:90).

32. Pérez de Ribas wrote a letter, dated June 13, 1617, informing the Jesuit provincial of this first, six-week-long entrada. Significantly, in the letter Pérez de Ribas notes that the entrada occurred at the time of an epidemic (the cocoliztli) that claimed the lives of many of the sixteen hundred infants whom he and Basilio baptized (HHB 1617; Reff 1991b:158). Interestingly, the epidemic and its consequences are only hinted at in this and the three succeeding chapters, which deal with this first entrada.

[lands]. On the feast day of the Lord's Ascension,[33] 1617, we two priests set off without the company of an escort of soldiers or any other Spaniards. All the soldiers of the garrison were busy protecting the province and the [305] Villa de San Felipe, which was experiencing daily attacks and assaults by the Tepehuan. Only four Christian Zuaque Indians, to whom I had been ministering, decided to accompany us to aid in the offices of the church and the administration of sacraments, and to serve as godparents to those who were to be baptized. They showed great loyalty and love in wanting to accompany us to a nation where many of them suspected that any of us Christians might be killed. In fact, the priest who was instructing the Mayo,[34] who accompanied us for two leagues, was later amazed by God's good works and said that when he took leave of us along the way he went away saying to himself, "These priests have their heads on the block." He added that later, every morning when he opened the door of his house, he was afraid he would find someone there who had come to tell him that the Yaqui had done away with the priests and the Christians who were with them. But God ordered things to turn out quite differently, for we continued on our way for the eleven leagues between the Río Mayo and Río Yaqui.

We told our caciques that we would begin our mission and visitation in the pueblos along the upper part of the river. On the one hand, [this was] because they were the ones who had most desired peace. On the other, the two caciques who were with us were from those pueblos. Before we reached the first pueblo [probably Cócorit], which was the smallest, with about two hundred male heads-of-household, some large groups of Indians came out to meet us with their children and wives.

Let something be said at this point concerning an unusual thing that is more specific to this nation than to any other in the province. This was very comforting to those of us who were going to preach to them about God being crucified for the redemption of the world. All those [306] who came out to meet us in this and the other pueblos, young and old, and even the children who were carried in their mothers' arms, were carrying little Crosses made from reeds. When they reached the enramada that was to serve as the church they would stick these Crosses between the branches. This seems to be a sign of the victory that Christ Our Lord was achieving in this nation over which the devil held such great power. The glorious banner of Christ was being raised on high, a reassurance that through Holy Baptism we would see the entire nation marked with that divine sign.

In the first pueblo a large number of people had gathered, including not only the residents but people from many other pueblos and rancherías. They came to see the priests of whom they had so often heard but had never seen, and who had preached to so many nations and made them Christian. We were welcomed with arches that were triumphant and joyful, albeit humble, for they were made from tree branches. Having greeted them in their manner, placing our hands upon their heads, I had all those people sit down inside the enramada in the plaza of the pueblo. Three or four rancherías from the area had congregated there. This was a comforting sign to us that they wanted to establish peace and hear the teachings of our Holy Faith. They moved [their households], abandoning the places where they were born and raised and had their fields right at hand. They gave up these conveniences to come and live where they later planned to build churches. Let it be stated here that those in the next ten pueblos downriver did the same, even though many of the people in the pueblos farthest downriver were not as malleable or prepared for peace and Christianity. Many of them were still reticent and remained in their rancherías and homesteads.

When that large crowd of people who had come from several [different] places was seated we spoke to them. We declared our motives for coming to lands and people who were so remote and far removed, leaving behind others that were rich and powerful, where we had grown up and whence we had come at the cost of great effort. But [we told them] that we considered all this worthwhile for [the sake of] their souls, which were immortal. We added (because this was the first time we had instructed this nation) that they should be aware that after this life there is yet another one, and that the one true God who had created us will demand that we account for our life and deeds here on earth. We also told them that He gave His only Son so that we might live well and enjoy the bliss of heaven. We included further arguments appropriate to these beginnings. Of course these all had to be explained to them, because this nation had been so remote and inaccessible that it had had no dealings with Christians. Therefore, they

---

33. Ascension Day generally falls in May. In a letter dated January 23, 1618 Father Basilio noted that he and Pérez de Ribas entered the first Yaqui pueblo on May 1, 1617 (Burrus and Zubillaga 1962:40).

34. Pedro Méndez and Diego de la Cruz were working at the time among the Mayo.

needed this instruction more than others that have had greater contact with Christians before being baptized.

The Yaqui were continually impressed by what they heard, for the divine word in and of itself has the strength to move mountains. The Yaqui understood well the two fundamental articles of our Holy Faith, namely, that one God and Lord created all things and that the soul is immortal. In the end, through the natural light [of reason] some people understood these things, just as the royal Prophet [David] sang: *Signatum est super nos lumen vultus tui, Domine.*[35] The Yaqui experienced a few glimpses of this, especially concerning the immortality of the soul.

Once these first foundations were laid I gave them a talk. (My companion, who had just arrived from Italy, did not know the language, even though later he was a great minister and has persevered to this day in establishing a great Christian community [307] in this nation.) I told them about the necessity of the Sacrament of Holy Baptism for the salvation of souls. I also told them that innumerable Christian nations of this world were receiving it. (It was necessary to clarify this, for they were unaware that there were any other populated provinces outside of Sinaloa.) This is no wonder, because for thousands of years all the Old World was unaware of the existence of these nations of which we have been speaking. Finally, to conclude my talk, I told them I would begin the Christian instruction they had requested, first baptizing their small children, just as had been done in the other nations in that province that had become Christian.

All this was said and done, for I had told the caciques who had come to visit us in Mayo [lands] that upon my arrival the pueblos were to have their children assembled for Baptism. I told the mothers to get in line with them. Then I donned a surplice, a stole, and a white damask choral cape that I had for these occasions, and the Baptism of the Yaqui was begun. About two hundred children ages seven and under were assembled. Then with great pleasure on their parents' part and even greater pleasure on my own, they were baptized, and thus were concluded the acts of this blessed day. My vestments and the ceremonies in which they saw their children baptized caused fright and veneration in the Yaqui. They understood that this divine bath was not like the ordinary ones they took in their river.

Night fell and my companion and I retired to our ramada. There were large groups of Indians there who had come due to the novelty of seeing priests in their lands, and they would not go away and leave us alone. They brought us some small items of food made from squash and maize, which are their greatest gifts. Then they began their feasts and shared tobacco in the caciques' homes. In the plaza of the pueblo there was also a great deal of noisemaking and sermons by the most principal Indians, as well as gatherings of people celebrating our arrival in their land and preaching about the benefits of peace. They did this all night long, in such loud voices that even though we dearly needed to rest, it was impossible to do so. Nor was it prudent for us to prevent these festivities. In the end they helped these [people] receive well those who came to preach to them God's word, whose arrival in their lands they were heralding.

But the devil, the enemy of the human race who is always on the lookout for ways of foiling good works, saw that this nation — his fortress and stronghold, where he had been ensconced for so many years — was succumbing. He also saw that the little lambs that had been baptized that day were being snatched from his clutches. He roared like a lion whose cubs were being taken away, fearing and foreseeing in the remaining pueblos the highly fecund births of children who would be reborn in Christ and His Church. On this occasion, then, he mounted one of the greatest persecutions ever endured during the early days of this Christianity. In my opinion this was portrayed in Saint John's famous vision of the Apocalypse, when he was shown the persecutions of the early Church, represented by a beautiful woman about to give birth to the child in her womb. He said that the gentiles were represented by the child, which was being stalked by the dragon. *Draco stetit ante mulierem, quae erat partitura, ut cum peperisset filium eius devoraret.*[36]

A similar case occurred with the new swarms and flocks of our Yaqui children, who were to be born in the Church that was established among these gentiles. That same night after the first Baptism of infants was celebrated in this [308] first pueblo the devil perverted the spirit of a Mayo Indian sorcerer. Without our knowledge he had accompanied us, and when the good-hearted Indians were congratulating one another for having had their children baptized, he planted that

---

35. *Margin Note*: Psalm 4. Psalm 4:7: "do thou, then, Lord, shew us the sunshine of thy favour" (Knox 1956:480).

36. *Margin Note*: Apocal 12. Apocalypse 12:4: "And [the dragon] stood fronting the woman who was in childbirth, ready to swallow up the child as soon as she bore it" (Knox 1956:268).

seed of the devil's doctrine that is often repeated by these bedeviled sorcerers. He told them that the Baptism performed by the priests takes the lives of the children and anyone else who receives it. Therefore, if they did not want to expose their children to death and lose them, then they should not offer them for Baptism.

The Indian was so clever with his diabolical trick that word quickly spread. The following day when I tried to speak with the principales of the pueblo about celebrating the Baptism of the remaining children (because it is impossible to gather them all for the first Baptism), they answered me with great regret that the mothers who had not yet brought their children to be baptized had withdrawn with their children to their fields and montes. These women had been terrified by the speeches of the Mayo sorcerer, who had fled without the caciques having caught him. They promised me that the next time I came they would assemble the children who had been hidden and bring them for Baptism. I was greatly upset by this early persecution. The caciques in the remaining pueblos were waiting for me and they had asked me to hurry. They had promised that upon my arrival they would have their children gathered for Baptism. Thus, I thought it best to move ahead without further delay.

CHAPTER IX The priests leave the first Yaqui pueblo and visit the next three, where Baptisms are celebrated

We stayed for only three days in the first pueblo of this nation. In this chapter an account will be given of the visits to the next three [pueblos], which were all similar. More than one thousand families gathered in these three pueblos. All of their caciques were very agreeable and happy about seeing us in their lands; they desired to see their children baptized as soon as possible. Large groups of people, young and old, came from all the pueblos to greet us on the road. Each of them carried the aforementioned emblem, the holy Cross. Nevertheless, like the venom of the infernal serpent, the pernicious sermon and talk given by the Indian sorcerer had already penetrated these pueblos. The good caciques went to great lengths to counteract it, persuading the people to ignore the lies and tricks of that Mayo liar. Still, the venom had some effect on the timid spirits of the women. Although barbarians, they still loved their children to an extreme and felt as threatened as wild beasts do by the death of [their little ones]. But in the end the sermons and efforts of the good caciques were effective and all the mothers gathered with [their infants] to have them baptized.

As soon as we reached the pueblo, talks about Christianity were given before the people could disperse. They listened with pleasure, enjoying the fact that a foreign priest whom they had never seen before could speak their language. This is something that comforts these people's spirits. Through these talks we attempted [309] to undo the tricks and lies of those who had inculcated the fear that Holy Baptism takes the lives of those who receive it. They began to lose their apprehension and two hundred or more infants were baptized in turn and born into the Church.

I nevertheless noticed something unusual during these Baptisms. During the holy ceremony, when the blessed salt was placed in the mouth of the person being baptized, some mothers rushed to clean it from the mouth and tongue of their child. In this way they showed that they still had some fear that we priests were casting a spell over the baptized infants, using salt in the same manner as their sorcerers used other things to take human lives. This was done by the most timid of the mothers. The caciques who accompanied me, as well as the few Christian Zuaque whom I had brought with me (who served as godparents, each of them gathering a flock of Christian infants), changed these timid mothers' minds about the death of their children.

We stayed longer in these pueblos than in the first one. First, this was so we could get to know them and win them over by treating them well. All day long they sat in large groups around our ramadas, amazed to see things that were so new to them. I would add that the bothersome curiosity of this nation was much greater than that of others. It reached such extremes that these groups of Yaqui never let us out of their sight, even when the time came for us to eat some maize tortillas and squash, which they gave us. This meal was held in the open ramada that they had built in the plaza of the pueblo. There, flocks of Indians watched us [eat].

All this had to be tolerated because they were very sensitive about any attempt to dismiss them, no matter how mild. It happened once that some Indians from the lower Yaqui pueblos came to see me, and because I was trying to do something, I told them to step back a bit. They turned around, saying, "Let's go back to our pueblos—this priest does not have a good heart," which was the same as saying that I was not well disposed nor did I love them. Although minor, these events are noted [here] because they illustrate the maternal nature, love, and benevolence that these people's ministers are required to show, as if to small children, without tiring of their childishness. [This is] especially true at the beginning of their conversion.

The caciques confided in me the motives for their past wars with the captain and the Spaniards. The reason they had not turned in the renegades who had withdrawn to their lands was because the renegades had told them a thousand evil things about the Span-iards. They also told them that because they, the Yaqui, were so numerous and valiant, it would be very easy for them to kill the [Spaniards] when they entered Yaqui territory. Then the good caciques declared that they now saw the truth and were very happy to see priests in their lands and to see their children baptized. This not-withstanding, it was evident from their words that the hearts of some caciques from the lower pueblos were not very well intentioned or totally serene, although most of them came to see me at these pueblos. I tried to send them back won over and well treated.

I was detained here because I had to answer questions and remind the mothers of the baptized infants (who were many) of their children's Christian names. They came back to ask about the names, which were so new to their pronunciation and language. There were so many that there were often twenty Johns and as many more Peters, etc. It was necessary to keep the book of Baptisms at hand and to refer to the gentile names of their parents, which must [310] be recorded in order to identify their children. In addition to these infants, some sick adults were baptized in these three pueblos. The gravity of their illnesses required that their Baptisms be hastened. During this first entrada to these four pueblos, between the sick adults and the infants, some one thousand people were baptized. For this reason alone this visit could be considered fruitful, even though it was undertaken at the cost of great dangers and toil. But thanks to Our Lord many thousands more were baptized, although not without great effort.

CHAPTER X The priests continue their first entrada to the Yaqui pueblos and are saved by Our Lord from grave danger and treason

The next pueblo to be visited was the fifth of the eleven to which almost all the Yaqui people had been reduced. The friendly caciques (particularly the two previously mentioned who had gone to the villa to speak with the captain about peace) accompanied us to all the nation's pueblos. These caciques were some of the most important ones in the nation. They possessed great spirit and were respected for their bravery. When we reached the fifth pueblo they mentioned that from that point on it was not very safe. However, although they were uneasy about this, they did not say much. They [apparently] had some confidence in the principal cacique of the next pueblo, who was of their faction and had a very good heart.

As we approached the pueblo named Abasorin, a great multitude of Indians from the other lower pueblos gathered in [groups] of six hundred, eight hundred, and one thousand. At the moment we dismounted something happened that alerted us [to the fact] that the devil was already furious and wanted to prevent the Baptism of the great number of children whose souls God was taking for His own. The devil almost got what he wanted. I had charged the people in the pueblos to notify me (as is common practice) of anyone who was extremely ill so I could insure his salvation, given the ready accessibility of Holy Baptism. The devil wished to make use of this means of [salvation] for his own wicked intentions, so he inspired the spirits of some Indians who were similarly depraved—his familiars and sorcerers—to kill those whom Our Lord had sent to plant this Christianity. As part of their [plan] they notified me that there was a very sick Indian who was on the verge of dying in his milpa,[37] or field, about half a league away. They informed us of this as we were dismounting in the plaza of the pueblo, where a large number of women had brought their small children to be baptized.

I confess that this event perplexed us a great deal.

On the one hand, we wanted to help the Indian whom they had told us was near death. At the same time I realized that if I went to instruct and prepare him for Holy Baptism (my companion did not speak the [Cáhita] language), those who had gathered with their children would disperse immediately, before I could baptize them. Some of them would die before I could return and gather them together again for Baptism. Moreover, [if I did go], then all those who had assembled for the customary speech would have to be entertained, because they are restless and impatient by nature.

Finding ourselves in this predicament, my companion and I decided that because he could not speak the language well enough to be understood by the large crowd who had gathered, and because the Indians show a greater appreciation [311] and understanding when they are spoken to in their own tongue, then he would go and determine how much danger the sick person was in. He was to be accompanied by a Christian Zuaque Indian whom we had brought with us. This Indian was well instructed in the catechism and could teach it in his own language. Once the sick person understood the principal mysteries [of the Faith][38] and confessed his sins, the priest would baptize him, provided he was in danger [of dying]. I would remain behind to welcome and talk with the multitude who had congregated and to baptize the children. This is how the dilemma that had perplexed us was resolved.

The priest departed with the good Christian Indian and some Yaqui, including those who were tricking him and deceiving the both of us. They belonged to the faction that was not very happy with our entrada. They planned to kill the priest without risk to themselves the moment he reached the field of the person who was feigning illness. There, the priest could not be defended by the good caciques and the people who favored peace and Christian instruction. With the death of the one priest and the [resulting] clamor and tumult they un-

37. Here Pérez de Ribas appears to use this Nahuatl term for maize field as a referent for what is today called a *temporal*—a small plot of dry-farmed land devoted to corn. A milpa or temporal differs from a field that is naturally irrigated (in the floodplain of the river) or irrigated using canals, which Pérez de Ribas generally refers to as a *sementera*.

38. In Book 7, Chapter 2, Pérez de Ribas suggests that these principal mysteries included Christ's incarnation and resurrection (God was made man and died for our sins, thus making possible our salvation).

doubtedly would have killed the other priest as well as the Christians who had accompanied them. Thus, they would have put an end to religious instruction and Christianity.

It seems that it was the enemy of mankind who had planned and executed this treason. But God, with the particular providence that He has for His own, did not allow the devil to get away with this. The principal cacique of the pueblo whence the priest had departed to baptize the sick person had learned from Indian friends that the traitors had taken the priest to a place where they could kill him without jeopardizing themselves. As soon as he received this news the good Indian sped off. He caught up with the priest along the way and told the Christian Indian who was with him, "Take the father back to the pueblo, now." He gave no other reason than that he had learned that the sick person was not in danger and did not require Baptism; he said the priest could visit him at a later date. As he said this he grabbed the priest's mule by the bit and brought them back to the pueblo where I was.

The loyal Indian who had learned of the traitors' plot said nothing more in public about the priest's return than that the sick person was not in danger of

death. But later he called me aside with dissimulation to an enramada, where he told me about the ambush. He said that he spoke in secret because his life would be in danger if the enemy Yaqui learned that he had revealed their harmful intent. He was always a loyal and peaceable Indian, and (as will be told later) he showed great fidelity on other dangerous occasions, of which there were many at the beginning [of the missionization] of this spirited and bellicose nation. This Indian assisted greatly in establishing Christianity, even before he was baptized. When he was baptized I named him Don Ignacio. As will be told later, after he became a Christian he again saved the same priest from grave danger when he was shot by an arrow.

After this trap that the devil had set was foiled by divine favor, a good number of Baptisms—more than two hundred children—were quietly celebrated in this pueblo. We remained here several days to get to know the people. They appeared warm and friendly, and the women often came to us to ask their baptized children's names. Nevertheless, because of what had happened we were forced to consider whether to continue our visit to the remaining pueblos to baptize [312] the children. The friendly caciques advised against it.

CHAPTER XI The priests continue their entrada to the Yaqui pueblos

The time came to continue our visit and Baptisms in the pueblos that remained along the lower Río Yaqui. I had been told that these pueblos were very densely populated and had more people than those I had already visited. However, the loyal and friendly caciques tried to persuade me to return to the pueblos along the upper river—to be content with those that I had baptized. They wanted us priests to spend some time with them and their people and to baptize their remaining children. [They suggested that we] visit the pueblos along the lower river at a later date. Although they did not say so, it was clear that what these faithful Indians wanted sprang from their mistrust of some of the principales of the lower pueblos. Not all of them (as I said above) were

very pleased about our entrada to their pueblos. There was fresh evidence from the previously mentioned case that not all Yaqui spirits were well intentioned (in this nation the devil had a great number of sorcerer familiars—enemies of Christ and His holy law). These considerations caused more than slight deliberation over whether to proceed or follow what might be the better advice of the friendly caciques. All the same there were other reasons not to interrupt the course of missionization, which up until now Our Lord had favored. If our trip were halted, then the differences that already existed between the caciques of the upper and lower pueblos might be heightened. From the outset I had promised various caciques that I would visit all their pueblos. In addition, they had to understand that the priests were not afraid to enter their pueblos; fear undermines a missionary's authority among these people.

Because this cause was Our Lord's, we decided to continue our first entrada. I tried to encourage the friendly caciques so that we could proceed, pointing out what they already knew—some people from the lower pueblos had shown a good heart and had come to visit me. The faithful caciques agreed with this opinion, adding that for their part some of their people would accompany us to aid in any dangerous situation. Thus, we departed for the following, or sixth pueblo, called Torim, which had more than one thousand families. Many of them had not yet congregated there and were still in their rancherías, which were not very far away. Although the people of this pueblo were the most warlike on the river, it is also true that our friends who went with us had won over one of their most principal caciques.

We reached Torim and a great crowd of Indians gathered in that place and field, receiving us with signs of joy. I preached to them, speaking with special affection in an effort to win over those who were still opposed to priests and religious instruction. From that pueblo on the friendly caciques called some of their own preachers to the plaza to speak in their fashion. With great and loud fervor they spoke positively of peace and of listening to God's word, [313] which so many nations in Sinaloa had received. Moreover, there is something in this matter that is worthy of God's special providence in protecting this enterprise, which should not be omitted. Some of these preachers were not only gentiles, but I also knew them to be famous sorcerers. In spite of everything, they preached in favor of the law of God that we, the ministers of the Gospel, were preaching. A very similar case is celebrated in the Holy Scripture, in the Book of Numbers [22–24]. When the gentile King Balak called the Prophet Balaam to curse God's people and to cast spells on them Balaam instead was obliged to divulge and prophesy God's blessings upon his people. This is similar to what occurred with the sermons of the Yaqui preachers who, although still gentiles, loudly preached a thousand good wishes for God's law and those who came to preach it. These were the same sorcerers who in their gatherings, sermons, and talks had previously blasphemed Christ's law. Nevertheless, on this occasion everything they preached was the opposite. Many times when I heard them I noticed God's unique providence in moving the hearts of Indians whom I knew to be fierce and bellicose to preach

and exhort these pueblos to receive peace and the word of God that had reached their lands.

This method was quite effective, because even though not many infants had been assembled for Baptism, considering the size of the pueblo, still three hundred were baptized. The example of such a principal pueblo helped us so much that the remaining four pueblos followed suit; there great crowds also gathered. After we had spent several days here and had pleaded with those who had not resettled themselves to come with their belongings and their relatives and in-laws, we continued on to the remaining pueblos.

An unusual thing happened while we were traveling, which confirms these people's annoying curiosity. Whenever we left one pueblo to go to another we were followed by the crowd that had come to see us and watch the celebration of Baptisms. They stuck so close to the train of horsemen and came in such great throngs that they covered the entire field. If I asked them why they tired themselves by walking to other pueblos, given that we had already spent several days with them, they answered, "We wish to travel in your company to see the rest of the Baptisms and how the pueblos where you are going receive you. It pleases us very much to see you." I do not know whether all of them said it sincerely, because I noticed that some of them still carried their bows and arrows—a sign of their lack of confidence. Nonetheless, in the pueblos that followed we found the same willingness, and large flocks of lambs were baptized. Thus, during our first entrada more than three thousand children were imprinted with the marks of Christ and Holy Baptism. During the next entrada those who still remained to be baptized would be gathered into the flock of the Church, as the caciques and Indians of greatest authority assured me.

I attempted to win over these lower river pueblos with some modest trinkets that they valued, telling them to come to visit me in the upriver pueblos, where I would be glad to see them. And so our first entrada ended. The caciques of the upper pueblos who had accompanied us were very happy, and even astonished that so much had been accomplished without any of the trouble or hostility that they had feared.

With this we prepared to return to their pueblos, which were more disposed to the establishment of missions. When we returned we were received with great joy by these peaceful and docile people. [314] It was a great consolation to see the people leaving their milpas to greet us along the road and as we entered the pueblos, and to see the women who had already had their children baptized. They came out of their houses and approached us with these children in their arms. Then, as they placed the priest's hand on the child's head, they said with great joy, "See, here are your baptized children." This was an act of kindness for them, which according to their custom meant that those youngsters were the children of the minister who had baptized them and were for him to favor. They were right to think this, because the priest had conferred a status upon their being that was higher than their corporeal one.

Once this new Yaqui mission was off to a good start the captain and the priests in the villa were sent word. They had been greatly concerned about the outcome of this first entrada to a nation fifty leagues away, where two priests had gone alone. There was general and unusual joy when they received the news of its successful outcome.

CHAPTER XII The priests return to the upper pueblos, where they establish a mission and baptize some principal Indians

Once the Church and its Holy Groom, Christ, had taken possession of the eleven large settlements of the Yaqui nation through the Baptism of its children, it was time to begin teaching the holy Christian doctrine in the pueblos and to erect large xacales, which as previously mentioned, were made of poles. These are used until all the people have been baptized, at which point permanent churches can be built. Unlike other nations the Yaqui did not build xacales before priests entered their lands, because there had not been a consensus to receive the Holy Gospel. But divine providence had willed that the Gospel should be preached promptly to this nation.

While the churches were being built, requiring a lot of wood to be cut and hauled to the site, an enramada was erected by driving poles into the ground in the plaza, or field, in the pueblo. There the people gathered for religious instruction and to hear Mass. When the mothers heard that all Christians hear Mass many of them brought their small baptized children to the xacales. Moreover, during these early days they even brought little Crosses made of reeds. When they entered the enramada they set the little Cross in the ground in front of their seated children. These childish things gave us great pleasure, for some of them were holy signs that the doctrine of Christ's Cross

was being firmly planted among these people. We allowed the gentile mothers to attend Mass with their Christian children, because if we prevented them from doing so, they would have stopped coming to religious instruction. The children who were not baptized during the first visit were brought to the second Baptism (there were still quite a few of them, due to the Indian sorcerer's lies).

The older people in the pueblo gathered for instruction very punctually, both morning and evening. The Christian Zuaque Indians whom we had brought along with us served as temachtianos, or teachers of the doctrine. So did other bright young men from among the Yaqui, who quickly learned the catechism, as well as some of those who had been in the seminary in the villa.[39] There were many Indians of good character in this nation, [315] in spite of the fact that it had been

---

39. Recall that at the time the Yaqui sued for peace in 1610, they volunteered some of their children for training at the Jesuit college in the villa, or what Pérez de Ribas here refers to as the "seminary." This was not a seminary in the strict sense of the word—that is, a school where Indian boys and adolescents were trained for the priesthood—it was more of a boarding school. Although at the outset of their mission enterprise the Jesuits advocated the training of Indians for the priesthood (see Zubillaga 1968:3:328–38), the idea was too radical for the Catholic Church as a whole (and, arguably, for many Jesuits as well) (see Poole 1981).

bellicose, and some of these were being identified and instructed.

We wanted one of the first adults to be baptized to be from among the principal caciques, so that others would then follow his example. Our cacique friends who had accompanied us were inclined to [be baptized] immediately. They invited their other relatives and acquaintances to accompany them in receiving Holy Baptism. Each chose a wife of his own, because the ones they had were not permanent. A good number of them gathered together and learned the catechism very well. To the great joy of their pueblos the Baptism of adults was begun with those of the two principal caciques who accompanied us. The first was named Don Pablo Hinsiamei and the other one Don Gerónimo Conibomeai. Because these men were among the first Christians, they had the pleasure of being godparents to those who were subsequently baptized, of which there were a good number in these upper pueblos. Once these caciques were Christian they preached in their fashion with greater fervor, in favor of the holy law they had accepted and against their former drunken revels and barbarous customs.

A great change—which was enough to make even the angels rejoice—was observed with the frequent preaching of the divine word at the church. Although the majority in these pueblos were still gentiles, their principal caciques began to threaten to punish anyone who openly provided wine for communal revels. This was a very difficult thing [to prevent] in a nation that was so fierce, for they had been reared in this deeply rooted vice, which was being uprooted.

The caciques and others who had been baptized wanted to go to the villa to see the captain, the priests, and the Christians in the [nearby] pueblos so that they could congratulate one another as companions and friends. They went, and everyone was glad to finally see the Yaqui as Christians like themselves. The priests at our college treated them well, and the captain distributed colts and clothing to them. They returned quite contented to their pueblos, where they made many speeches, telling their people about the many benefits of Christianity.

The Indians and principales in the lower pueblos paid very careful attention to these events. Although it is true that the changes [that had occurred] among those of their same nation made an impression on them, and that some became docile and showed an inclination to imitate the others, more than a few people continued to be obstinate and wanted to kill the priests and those

who accompanied them. I learned of how some very loyal Indians responded to these threats: "If we must die defending the priests, we will do so." When I told them that it was time to go back to visit the lower pueblos they realized that not all the pueblos were ready for such a visit, and they answered me with arguments that were truly moving: "Our Father (they said), be content for now with us and our children that you have baptized. Little by little those lower pueblos will come to their senses, their heart will become one with ours, and you will be able to baptize them." I replied on this occasion with a subtle threat, which was not really directed at them. I imagined that they would pass it along to those who were lazy and resistant, recognizing the mercy that God had shown them by sending priests to teach them the way to salvation and a captain to protect them whenever necessary. One must sometimes treat these people like children, and at other times like wild animals, but always with priestly authority. I threatened them by saying I would leave them and return to my Zuaque pueblos, where [316] I had churches and my Zuaque children who loved me and came to religious instruction, and where I lived with and instructed the Zuaque in peace, happiness, and safety.

This argument upset them, but because I remained unmoved, they believed it. Many of the Yaqui were very familiar with and had seen with their own eyes the beautiful churches the Zuaque had built and the peace and order of their Christian pueblos, etc. If I had threatened to return to Mexico City or Spain, where there were churches, riches, and an abundance of everything, it would not have made the same impression as that which they had seen with their own eyes. They responded to these threats just as I had hoped they would; their reply was similar to that previously quoted: "Father, could your heart bear to leave the many children whom you have baptized? Wait a while and you will see how everyone is converted."

I write about these circumstances because they can provide useful information for those whom Our Lord chooses for these conversions. Also, God's sweetest providence often uses circumstances as minor as these for works that come only from His almighty hand, as in the conversion of the Yaqui.

I turn now to the entrada to the lower Yaqui pueblos, which were still somewhat rebellious. I placed my trust in the Christian caciques and others who had been baptized and, more importantly, in the favor of God, Our Lord. Thus, I decided at this time once again to visit the lower pueblos. I was accompanied by our faithful caciques, who were very attentive to my security. Even though I had not asked them to do so, at nightfall they would come and sleep with their bows and arrows around my ramada, prepared for whatever might happen. There they gave sermons that were very much in favor of Christianity and peace.

During these visits the people continued to be won over and all the remaining infants and newborns were finally baptized. Thus, within six months [by the end of 1617] more than four thousand Yaqui children were baptized, and from among these God harvested His first fruits for heaven. Those who had lived among wild beasts and barbarians (who remained under the devil's power) found themselves in God's divine presence and suddenly, by pure grace, in the company of angels, and there is no doubt that they will aid their relatives and nation through their intercession. These favors from heaven began to manifest themselves, because some principal Indians from the lower pueblos decided to go to the villa to see the captain and the Christians, whom they had not yet seen. They returned from their journey well treated, and they were encouraged in the pursuit of their objective by the peace and harmony they observed in the Christian pueblos, thereby becoming desirous of the same for their own pueblos.

CHAPTER XIII Wooden churches are built in all the pueblos and the reduction of the entire population is finally completed; many adult Baptisms are celebrated, including one that proved dangerous

During these first months the priests were greatly inconvenienced in some pueblos by a lack of churches in which to say Mass, give religious instruction, and perform other ministries. The enramadas that served as both churches and the priests' homes left them exposed to the sun, wind, and rain. Up to the present the priests had devoted all their time to baptizing the children and sick adults who, because some of them had not yet been reduced, were scattered among milpas, fields, and homesteads. [Reducing them] required care and patience, because the Indians find it very painful to leave the security of the place where they have been born [317] and raised, almost as much as a European who leaves his homeland.

Because the infants were now baptized, however, and the number of people was increasing, as each day more congregated in the pueblos, we proposed the construction of churches, albeit of wood and impermanent. Our Yaqui responded very favorably to this proposal.

They eagerly cut and gathered wood and did everything else that was necessary. Later we proposed that the elderly be baptized, although [at first] we selected those who most often came to church and religious instruction. Good-sized groups came to be baptized and then married according to Christian law. By accepting holy matrimony they agreed to have but one wife from whom they could not separate at will.

When I reflect upon what transpired with these Baptisms I confess that I had no doubt that they had become true Christians through divine grace. Many times I saw young Indian males who had two or three attractive wives or women of the same age; in some cases these women had very young children. Nevertheless, these men subjected themselves to the laws of Christ Our Lord and His Holy Church, separating and divorcing themselves from what had become their own flesh and blood. It was something to see how they carried out these divorces. Sometimes they asked me to help them marry these women, with whom they had been close and who had borne them children, to other men. This [change] could not have originated from flesh and blood, but rather only from Christ's grace, which was at work here. This was confirmed when it was seen that they cut their long hair, which many valued when they were gentiles as an adornment and a sign of courage. Before they received the water of Holy Baptism they cut their hair, which they used to let grow down to their waist, thereafter keeping it trimmed to the shoulder.

Another very singular change followed Baptism that I would judge very difficult to understand had I not seen it many times myself. Generally speaking (I am speaking of the ordinary and common and do not want to exaggerate or go beyond what is certain and truthful), the change wrought by Holy Baptism among those who received it was like changing a wolf or lion into a sheep or lamb. This was apparent in the way the Indians approached the priests, how they treated them, and how they behaved in their presence, obeyed their commands, spent time in church, and forgot their fierce customs. Many enjoyed hearing Mass not only on Sundays, but on weekdays. They also enjoyed listening to the sermons every Sunday, particularly when these dealt with the miracles of Christ Our Lord and His most holy life. They ordinarily greeted one another with, "Jesus Christ be praised." With each day the article of faith concerning eternal life was becoming more firmly imprinted in their minds. They were careful to call the priests to hear the confessions of those who became sick. They also informed him of newborn infants and gentiles who became sick so that they would not die without Baptism. They handled all these concerns responsibly. Accordingly, three or four fiscales were chosen for this purpose from among the barrios[40] in each pueblo. There was so much to do in this respect that it was necessary to keep moving continually in this holy occupation.

In spite of all this we should not assume that the entire Yaqui nation had been subjected to Christ, His law, and His ministers. The infernal enemy bellowed at seeing so many of his prey taken from his jaws. Thus, there was no shortage of difficulties, dangers, schemes, and obstacles with which he armed himself. Even though sorcery had been somewhat repressed, there were still demonic speeches given by a great number of sorcerers who had not yet been entirely extinguished. On the contrary, they set off [318] quite a few sparks, but

Our Lord extinguished them through his special providence, which merits mention here.

At this time I was in one of the upper pueblos, whence I was called to one of the lower pueblos, called Torim. As I said, this pueblo had more than one thousand male heads-of-household in its environs. They wanted me to baptize a sick person who was near death. Although some principal Indians had already been baptized in these [lower] Yaqui pueblos, there was still some concern about how safe it was to visit them. Thus, it was necessary on this occasion to find a loyal Indian to accompany me. In addition to two boys from the church, I was accompanied by two Christian Indians who possessed authority, one of whom was a fiscal in the church.

We reached the sick man, who was in a milpa half a league from the pueblo of Torim. The sick man was old and the size of a giant, and when he saw us he eyed the priest who had come to baptize him with displeasure. Next to him was his son, who apparently was a sorcerer. These are the ministers whom the devil sends to those who fall ill, so that they do not escape him. As I started to get off my mule the sick man said to me with great disdain, "What did you come here for, to kill people? Is that what you are up to?" Although the words he spoke did not reflect kindness or a willingness for Holy Baptism, I dismounted, as did my three companions. I approached the sick man and started talking to him with tenderness, asking him how he was. He answered me disdainfully, gesturing and telling me to go away. I took note of his negative disposition and rudeness, something that these nations do not ordinarily display toward priests because the Indians know that the priests are valued and esteemed by the captain and other Spaniards. One of the boys from the church who had come with me was near the sick person and said to him, "How dare you talk like that to the father?" The man answered that he would kill the boy as well as the priest. Because I perceived that the man was thoroughly [hostile], I said to him with some authority (as is necessary on these occasions), "Well, my son, is that any way to talk to the priest who comes to teach you God's word?" At that moment the sick man's son, who was as fierce as his father and who had been sitting next to him looking dejected, got up with a ferocious look on his face. He ran to his hut there in his field to grab his bow and arrows. At this point one of the principal Indians who had accompanied me got up to seize the bow and stop the son, who clearly intended to create an

40. These subdivisions or "neighborhoods" presumably were composed of patrilineal descent groups and clans.

incident. While the two were fighting, the Indian fiscal, who was next to me, said, "Father, get on your mule fast, and let's get out of here." Because I felt that my stay would not be beneficial, I mounted my mule, as did the Indian fiscal and the boys from the church. At that moment the obstinate Indian freed himself from the Indian who was holding him and shot an arrow. Because God did not want harm to befall anyone who had come to do this good work, the arrow was diverted.

We rode directly to the pueblo of Torim which, as I said, was about half a league away. There I found the principal cacique, who was called Don Mateo; he was a loyal and baptized friend. I reported to him what had happened so that he would be advised and could prevent similar incidents and the great harm that could arise at any moment. The cacique was very distressed to hear what had happened. My companions and I took leave of him and returned to the pueblo whence we had come. There the people, who were loyal, showed great sorrow over these events. That night the cacique Don Mateo held a meeting in his house, where all the people gathered. After the customary tobacco he spoke of the ugly incident. He could not punish it, for one thing because the Indian who shot the arrow was [319] not yet reduced to his kin group.[41] Moreover, these caciques (as was previously mentioned) do not have authority over their people to punish them for the offenses they commit. Still he proposed and his people agreed that no one communicate with or go near that Indian who had disturbed and insulted them. And if the case became known in the villa and the captain sent for him or had people try to capture him, no one was to shelter or defend him.

Without waiting the Christian Indian who had ac-companied me and who had fought with and been injured by the Indian who unleashed the arrow went to notify the captain at Fort Montesclaros. The captain thanked the Indian for what he had done in defense of the priest, and he gave him some clothes as a reward for his loyalty. He also gave the Indian a handful of arrows that another nation had just presented him as a sign of friendship. The captain ordered him to take the arrows to the pueblo of Torim, where first he was to thank the cacique Don Mateo for having spoken to his people about the disturbing incident. He was then to place the handful of arrows in the middle of the plaza. He told the Indian to speak on his behalf to those who were not of the cacique Don Mateo's kin group, telling them that he was sending them arrows so that they would be prepared to shoot when he came after the Indian who had shot {at the priest}.

The captain's orders were carried out and the arrows were taken and placed in the plaza, although no Indian in the pueblo or from its environs dared to touch them. And so they remained there in that plaza. These people already feared the many caciques and people of the upper pueblos who were being baptized and receiving Christian doctrine. One of them was the cacique of Torim, Don Mateo, who was an Indian who possessed great authority and extensive kin ties. With this the Indian who had executed that evil deed became intimidated and quite fearful.

Finally, some time later during one of the captain's visits to the Yaqui the priest interceded on the Indian's behalf, and he was pardoned. As will be seen this was not the last dangerous incident in the conversion of this and other nations. These we can count as the happy fruits of these undertakings.

41. *Parcialidad*. We have translated this term as kin group; it may well have encompassed a number of lineages or what in effect was a clan, or it may have referred to the territory that pertained to a kin group.

CHAPTER XIV The lower Yaqui pueblos are visited; more Baptisms are celebrated; an account is given of some singular cases

There were still quite a few rebellious and hardened Indians in the lower pueblos and even some who harbored hard feelings toward the priests. Nevertheless, there were others with good hearts who had already been baptized. In order to win over the former and preserve the latter, Father Tomás Basilio and I continued to visit and talk with them. In this way they became more docile with each passing day. Nevertheless, at that time unrest arose from the following case.

There was a small ranchería of Indians from a nation called the Guayama[42] who wished to settle in a mission with the Yaqui. Although the Yaqui were their enemies, one of their women came to live among them, placing her trust in the fact that there was already a missionary among the Yaqui. She took as her husband a principal Yaqui Indian; both of them were gentiles. One morning the barbarous furor that is characteristic of the Indians' nature flared up in a group of troublemakers who did not much care for mission life. Or perhaps they were drunk from one of the revels they usually celebrate at that time of day. They attacked the poor Guayama woman and cut her to pieces, ignoring the law of loyalty in which {320} she had placed her trust when she took a Yaqui principal as her husband.

They immediately came to me in another pueblo one league away to tell me what had happened. They said that even though she had been shot full of arrows, she might still be alive and be baptized. I called a few Indians to accompany me and went to see whether I could help this poor gentile woman with Holy Baptism. When I entered the pueblo where the attack had taken place, which was the last of the Yaqui pueblos, a cacique friend who was already baptized came out to meet me. He insistently asked me to turn back; the woman was already dead and the people were in an uproar. [He told me that] I should not approach or say anything.

This Indian spoke the truth and behaved quite faithfully, because the rebels were in such a rage that at that very moment they were splitting the body of the woman into bits so that they could dance with it in several different rancherías, as they usually do. Those who were truly inhuman would raise these bits and pieces of human flesh on spikes in the midst of the dance.

I realized that my presence among such a group of enraged gentiles would be to no advantage. They were so bellicose that as I began to speak to those who had met me at the entrance to the pueblo—reproaching them for their act of disloyalty against a woman who had trusted them and reminding them that they had priests among them who were teaching the word of God—the Christian cacique cut me off, saying, "Father, now is not the time for you to speak about that. Go back, my father."

Thus I was obliged to return to the pueblo whence I had come, where there were a few Christians, but the rest were still gentiles. At nightfall I heard the rhythm of a barbarous dance in the plaza. I went out to see what it was and I found a piece of the woman's flesh raised on a pole. With it they were singing their barbarous triumph. I made them take that piece of human flesh down from the pole and bury it. I reminded them of what it was, which convinced those savages to desist in their outrage.

There was another case that took place at this time [1618–19] when I was in another of this nation's pueblos. Both this case and the previous one were invented and encouraged by the devil through his Indian familiars. He wished to disrupt the peace that the Gospel was introducing among these people. In both cases God's great compassion is demonstrated for conquering and subjugating such a fierce nation to His holy law. In this second case some Indians from the Nébome nation, which has already been mentioned in this history, came to see me [in 1618]. They wanted to become Christians and to have priests in their lands. They knew that the Yaqui already had priests who were preaching them God's word. (These peoples consider this fact to be a

---

42. Little is known about the Guayama beyond the fact that they lived along the coast north of the mouth of the Río Yaqui. During the seventeenth century they were assimilated by the Yaqui.

guarantee that they need not fear any danger among those who in the past had been their enemies, as the Yaqui and Nébome had been.)

The Nébome dared to come and see me from their pueblos, which were ten leagues from where I was. As they were traveling through Yaqui territory an Indian with evil intentions came out of his field. In betrayal he started shooting arrows at the trusting Nébome. When they found themselves betrayed in this attack in a land with such a great number of their bellicose enemy, the Nébome turned and ran. One of their principal Indians, who was at the head of the party, saw that he was being cut off and was afraid to proceed. So instead he hurried along the way to the pueblo where I was, knowing that it was nearby.

God willed that he should happen upon a faithful Yaqui, who sheltered him and brought him to me. He was very upset by what had happened, and the Nébome Indian was even more upset. He complained of the fact that he and his companions should be treated like that [321] in lands where a priest was teaching Christians. I received him with the pleasure that his good intentions deserved. But I feared that the restless Indians from the kin group that had shot the arrows might create a disturbance, so I kept the Nébome cacique safe inside my house. Then some of the faithful Yaqui caciques from the pueblo, which was large, came to see what was happening. They were very upset over what had happened, and they promised to try and find out who the arrogant traitor was who had insulted the Nébome with such an unseemly act. In this way he could be punished and their nation could be given satisfaction.

They spoke with affection and demonstrations of love to the Indian whom I had befriended. They promised to return him in complete safety to his lands. I doubted that this could be achieved in such a time of unrest. However, one of the faithful caciques reassured me, and he himself devised a plan. He said to me, "Father, don't worry. I will take this Nébome on my horse. He can ride in the saddle and I will ride in back, holding on to him. No one will shoot at him for fear of injuring me." This was a safe plan, for these people are very careful not to wound an Indian from their own nation, especially when he is a principal.

The plan was executed, and it worked out well. In this way the faithful Indians accompanied this Nébome Indian and took him to the border of his lands. Later they made an attempt to discover which Indian had shot those arrows at the Nébome, and they reproached him for what had happened, for in the pueblo where this took place there were a good number of Christians. The Indian made excuses for himself, saying that on that occasion he had recalled that the Nébome had killed one of his brothers during their former wars. It was the custom of these people not to rest until they had avenged the death of an Indian from their nation who had been killed by their enemy. The man who had attempted this revenge was still a gentile.

I attempted to confirm peace and friendship between these two nations, and God willed it to be achieved through a unique means provided by the offended Nébome. Along the border of the two nations the Nébome erected a Cross. They waited there for the Yaqui, [to see] whether they had a good heart (this is a term they use to signify kindness and love). With this symbol of the peace that exists between heaven and earth these two nations made their peace.

There are two reasons why I wanted to write about these two cases of the Yaqui's fierceness. The first was so that Christ's grace, which is powerful enough to tame such wild beasts, might be recognized and shine more [brightly] and so that the illustrious change subsequently wrought in them by the divine word might be known. Second, in the midst of similar tribulations, I wanted the ministers of the Gospel not to lose hope of patiently harvesting fruits, in accordance with Christ's promise to His first Gospel ministers: *In patientia vestra possidebitis animas vestras.*[43] Although this interpretation of Holy Scripture may seem strange, it can be understood to refer not only to the fruit of one's own soul, but to those they win to God and, thus, can claim as their own fruit and reward. An important author of Holy Scripture called 'souls of Abraham' those whom the great father and patriarch of all the believers in Haran converted from gentiles to the knowledge of the true God. The Holy Book says, *Animas quas fecerat in Haran.*[44]

Returning to the mission of our bellicose Yaqui, after those early days, when there were cases like those that I have recounted and others that I omit for the sake of brevity, I say that in the midst of those troubles and [322] disturbances there were many Yaqui who listened to the divine word. They did so fruitfully, even in

---

43. *Margin Note*: Luc. c. 21. Luke 21:19: "It is by endurance that you will secure possession of your souls" (Knox 1956:80).

44. *Margin Note*: Gen. 12. Genesis 12:5: "and all the retainers born in their service [in Haran]" (Knox 1956:9).

the lower pueblos, which were the least ripe. There the newborns were baptized along with some adults. Because the people in the upper pueblos gathered every afternoon for religious instruction, it was decided that the same would be done in the lower pueblos. They admitted anyone who wished to attend, which amounted to quite a few people.

Even though the devil grumbled through his sorcerers and familiars, many souls were nevertheless snatched from his claws. The rancherías and the stubborn Indians in their fields were being reduced to pueblos, where they were building wooden xacales for churches. In this way this visit was concluded and we returned to the upper pueblos that had been reduced and tamed [earlier].

In contrast to the adverse events that have been recounted, which occurred in pueblos that were less submissive, I will record [here] a favorable and edifying case that took place in a docile pueblo called Tesamo. Some Mayo Indians from the neighboring river who were already Christian came to see me to complain about the Yaqui. Although many Yaqui were already Christian and had a priest who preached God's word, it was rumored that they nevertheless still kept some scalps of Mayo Indians whom they had killed when they were gentiles. They bragged about still having them to celebrate their triumphs, which are so foreign to the Christian friendship that they should now be professing. The Mayo affirmed that they themselves had already burned these [reminders of their] former gentile barbarism.

I ordered two Yaqui principales in this pueblo to come and respond to the Mayo's complaint. I said that they were justified in their complaint, and because they dealt with one another in Christian friendship and brotherhood, which demands that they forget hatred and war, it was wrong to hang on to such things from the past. The Yaqui principales responded that it had been a long time since they had heard of any dances with Mayo or any other scalps. Nevertheless, they said they would find out whether anybody still had scalps, which they would bring to me so I could burn them. They carried this out so well that in searching the houses where they suspected there were still traces of these barbarous relics, they gathered a large number of articles of superstition besides scalps. They made a bonfire in the middle of the plaza and all those diabolical instruments were burned, along with their author, the devil. The Mayo returned [to their lands] satisfied in their complaint and confirmed in the Christian friendship that

they had established with the Yaqui, who demonstrated quite well how much they had welcomed Christianity.

The satisfaction that these same Yaqui gave for their [heinous] act against the Guayama woman should also be told. She had trusted that, because there was a priest among the Yaqui, she could safely come and marry a Yaqui Indian. The Yaqui nevertheless cut her to pieces. The satisfaction they gave was to reconcile themselves with the Guayama nation, who lived among the marshes [by the coast]. In addition, they allowed the Guayama to come to their pueblos and they gave them land to sow, so that they could receive religious instruction and Holy Baptism. A good number of these people were catechized and baptized, despite the fact that there were many sorcerers among them. Through their art of diabolical healing they opposed the Holy Gospel. In this art there was a well-known pact that the devil had established with the sorcerers, so I will record it here.

When these sorcerers had to cure some sick person they placed a long stick that they carried with them in the sick person's mouth. They led the sick person to believe that the {323} stick reached all the way to the stomach, whence the illness was drawn from the body. Some sick people were convinced that it did go all the way to their stomach. Through magic that he worked on that stick, the devil made it seem to them that it went all the way to the stomach, which it did or appeared to do through the diabolical arts that the devil knows well. Through these tricks the devil fooled those who were cured as well as the healers, who stripped the sick people of all they had in exchange for a cure. [However] through the light of the Gospel the Guayama all came to recognize these pacts and dealings with the enemy of humankind. When they were baptized they renounced and abandoned these practices and remained with the baptized Yaqui, with whom I am principally concerned in this chapter.

Finally, I will record another case in which the Yaqui gave a good account of themselves in the midst of adverse events. At the time [1617] other gentile nations near the apostate and rebellious Tepehuan nation invited the Yaqui to follow them and break off their friendship with the captain and the Spaniards. They even promised them mules, horses, and other things that had been stolen from the Spaniards whom the Tepehuan had killed. The Yaqui would not hear of such things. Instead, they came to inform the captain and me so that the former could prevent any damage and unrest that might result. Among the Yaqui there were still some people who were restless and inconstant, but there were already a great number of them who were happy with peace and were preparing to receive Holy Baptism.

Captain Diego Martínez de Hurdaide decided to visit this nation in peace to win them over with affection and friendship and to establish political government in their numerous pueblos. These were people against whom less than two years earlier he had fought pitched battles, as has been recorded. He set out from the villa—prepared for anything that might happen—with thirty soldiers and armored horses, plus a small number of servants. He sent word ahead to the faithful Yaqui caciques so that they could tell the rest of their people that he was coming on their behalf and that he would be pleased to visit their pueblos, as he usually did when he made expeditions to Christian pueblos. He always distributed some things that they value and he usually did so with Christian zeal in order to win these people over to Christianity.

He reached the pueblos of the upper river, where he was welcomed with signs of great joy. The lower pueblos followed this example. He visited all the pueblos as far as the sea, even though he and his soldiers were on the lookout day and night. The soldiers were amazed by the number of people in the Yaqui pueblos, which they had never seen before except in campaigns, when the Yaqui shot innumerable arrows. Now they saw them without weapons, with their wives and children, many of them happily saying the prayers of the catechism.

In order to introduce some type of government and civility, the captain appointed governors and alcaldes for their pueblos. All this helped to prepare them to receive with pleasure and esteem that which the priests preached to them. With great Christian zeal the captain spoke through his interpreter to the large number of people who gathered to see him in the pueblos. He made them understand how he himself, being a captain, and his soldiers, who were brave (which is what is valued among these nations), listened to the priests and obeyed their teachings and revered them as God's ministers.

In the end this visit was peaceful, even though there were still a few concerns that war might break out because of troublemakers and sorcerers. [324] But Our Lord did not allow this to happen at that time, even though further ahead there will be other cases. Thus, the captain and his soldiers returned to the villa very relieved. At this point [1619] in the conversion of this nation the number of baptized children reached forty-nine hundred, with three thousand baptized adults. This truly shows that in the midst of difficulties and enemy opposition and, conversely, with the aid of divine favor, the very precious and valuable fruits harvested in these nations are unceasing.

CHAPTER XV Another priest comes to assist with the instruction of the Yaqui nation; rebel Indians try to kill one of the priests; other singular events

Three years had passed since 1617, when I and the very religious Father Tomás Basilio founded Christianity among the Yaqui. Then, after sixteen years of good fortune spent in these Sinaloa missions Our Lord willed through holy obedience that I should leave for another ministry and occupation near Mexico City.[45] The superiors ordered Father Cristóbal de Villalta, who was in charge of the Sinaloa nation, as was written in Book III, to carry on the Yaqui's conversion with Father Tomás Basilio. The Christianity of Sinaloa owes a great deal to these evangelical ministers. Before his death[46] Father Cristóbal de Villalta cultivated and preached the Gospel for more than twenty years in the several languages and nations of this province. Father Tomás Basilio [did the same][47] for more than thirty years, harvesting the greatest abundance of fruit in the Yaqui mission, where he baptized a great number of souls who have grown up in great Christianity. For several years he was superior of the priests and missions of the interior,[48] which he visited regularly from his district. After I left I always received accounts from these two very religious priests about what was being done in the Sinaloa missions. They knew the esteem in which I held the evangelical tasks of that province, because I had been an eyewitness [to them] in the past. Thus entered Father Villalta, who had an excellent command of the languages of the Yaqui and the Sinaloa, whom he had catechized.

These two fervent ministers applied themselves to expanding this mission and Christianity. [As a result] adult Baptisms increased throughout all the nation's pueblos, the people came more frequently to instruction, and everything prospered with each passing day. But this aroused and inflamed Satan, the enemy of our health and prosperity, who sowed discord. He will continue to do this until the end of the world, just as the Son of God warned His holy Apostles, founders of the Christianities of the universe. He caused them to understand that the gates of hell would open up, thereby unleashing the persecutors of the Church: *Porta inferi non praevalebunt.*[49] The Lord said this so that cases such as the following would not frighten and intimidate us.

As we said, at the beginning of the Yaqui mission Father Tomás Basilio was in a pueblo whence he was suddenly called away under [325] false pretenses to catechize a sick person, with the intention of killing him. One night [several years later, in 1622] as he was sitting at the door of his poor little house, someone shot an arrow at him from outside. Because it was dark, it was not known who had tried to kill him. The arrow pierced his chest, but it entered at an angle. If it had gone straight in, or if the herb covering it had been fresh, he would have died, for it opened a wound that was more than six inches in length.[50] When the priest was struck he cried, "Jesus [save me], I've been shot." When the boys in the nearby church heard his cry they came quickly, and the evildoer disappeared.

The boys went to notify the loyal cacique Don Ignacio, who had earlier saved the priest from another danger, as was told. He ran to the priest's house, and after he had pulled out the arrow he immediately managed to suck the poison from the wound (like a very loyal friend), which is what they use as a surefire remedy. The cacique and his men, who were very good Christians,

---

45. Because of poor health and his leadership qualities, Pérez de Ribas was recalled to Mexico City late in 1619 and appointed rector of the Jesuit college at Tepotzotlán.

46. Three years after he succeeded Pérez de Ribas among the Yaqui Villalta was appointed rector of the Jesuit college in Guatemala. He died en route to his assignment in 1623.

47. Basilio died in 1654.

48. In 1620 the Rectorado de Nuestra Padre San Ignacio del Río Mayo y Río Yaqui was created, which included some eighty thousand Indian converts in fourteen districts and fifty-five pueblos. Basilio succeeded Villalta in 1623 as superior or rector of this large administrative subdivision of the Sinaloa mission (which retained a superior). The cabecera or headquarters for the rectorate was Torim, which was also Basilio's mission district.

49. *Margin Note*: Math. 16. Matthew 16:18: "and the gates of hell shall not prevail against [the Church]" (Knox 1956:17).

50. *Xeme*—approximately six inches.

were greatly saddened [by this incident]. They guarded the priest until they could find out whether there were many people involved in this crime. Some others went to notify Father Villalta, who was in another pueblo. He came immediately to aid his good companion and brother in life or in death.

The cacique [Don] Ignacio, who had pulled the arrow from the priest's chest, carefully retained this arrow to identify the aggressor. He made great efforts to find out who he was, using clues [from the arrow]. He finally managed to learn the identity of the person who had owned and shot the arrow by means of a particular trick, which I will relate. This showed the love this Indian had for the Faith, the catechism, and the priest who had instructed him.

In their games it is the custom of these Indians to wager their bows, arrows, and other small items that they value, in the same way that Europeans gamble money. They do this especially when they play *patole* or *cañuelas*, which I wrote about in Book I. The cacique attempted to find out who had brought that arrow to the game by showing it to the people of the pueblo. The Indians are so knowledgeable in this matter that they can identify any arrow they have ever used from among others, even when this arrow has had other owners or a long time has passed. I observed this many times during the games that the young people play on important feast days, when they shot hundreds of arrows at a target. Although the arrows all landed in the same place, each boy knew which one was his, even though they had no [readily] distinguishing marks.

At last through these diligent efforts the Indian Don Ignacio learned the identity of the owner of the arrow that had pierced and wounded the priest. When he tried to arrest him, he learned that the Indian had disappeared and gone off into the monte, which confirmed his suspicions. [However], Don Ignacio did not rest until the culprit was captured. Once he had succeeded he dispatched his prisoner to the captain in the villa, where [the prisoner] made a full confession. The captain learned that because he was a Christian, the priest had forbidden his involvement with a lover; therefore, he had tried to kill Father Basilio. In addition, the captain discovered that this Indian had been incited by his uncle, who was a person of great authority. Although the uncle was baptized, he was one of those that the Apostle [Saint Paul] called false brothers, adding that in the midst of such people he found himself in great danger: *Periculis in falsis fratribus.*[51] It was discovered that the uncle, together with the devil, intended not only to murder the priest but to create an incident that would lead to a general uprising among the Yaqui and to the death of other missionary priests [326] who might come [in the future].

When this Indian's uncle[52] learned about the inquiries being conducted concerning the shooting, he fled to the Nébome nation. These people had already established peace with the captain, who sent them an order commanding them to locate the man and take him prisoner. The Nébome captured the delinquent who had stirred up trouble. They found him in a little house to which he had retreated. There they tied him up and dispatched him with a guard of forty Nébome to the captain at the villa, which was sixty leagues away. This prejudicial Indian was so obstinate that when they stopped along the road, he grabbed a poison arrow from one of his guards, and with diabolical desperation he stuck it into his thigh. When the Indians saw what had happened and the danger in which this wretched man found himself, his guards immediately sent a message to the missionary among the Mayo [Diego de la Cruz], who was nearby, so that he could come and prepare him in case he should die. Although the Nébome were still gentiles, they had already asked for a priest to make them Christians, and they knew that in that crucial moment the priests helped those who were in real danger.

When the priest got this message he came running. He found the Indian so obstinate and desperate that he refused to confess as a Christian, nor would he even speak. Within twenty-four hours the rebellious Indian died the death that he deserved. It was dealt by his own hand, just like Judas; the man who had attempted to kill the preacher of the Gospel with a poison arrow died by a poison arrow. The captain sentenced his nephew, who had shot the arrow, to hang. God willed that he died a better death than his uncle, who was the author and instigator of an even greater crime, which it was God's will to frustrate.

---

51. *Margin Note*: 2. ad. Corint. 11. 2 Corinthians 11:26: "danger among false brethren" (Knox 1956:189).

52. In the anua of 1622 the Indian is identified as Juan Suca; he fled to the Nébome pueblo of Tecoripa.

CHAPTER XVI Other priests come to assist with the instruction of the Yaqui, fervently expanding this Christianity

I n the previous chapter we left Father Tomás Basilio badly wounded by an arrow—the result of tending to his duties as vigilant shepherd of the souls that had been entrusted to him. Although he suffered from this wound for a long time, it was eventually Our Lord's will that he should recover and live to continue preserving and advancing the Christianity that he initiated among the Yaqui nation, just as he does today. These religious ministers were very zealous of God's glory and the welfare of souls because they were soldiers of the Militia and Company of Jesus. Through Christ's divine grace and in the midst of so many dangers, they were not intimidated nor did they retreat a single step in the fight. Like that Prince of Shepherds (as Saint Peter called Him), they risked their lives for the lambs that had been entrusted to them. They began anew their Baptism of the many gentiles that were being reduced each day to His Holy Church. With their intrepid spirit and example they encouraged many of their brothers to aid them in these endeavors. Therefore, a short time following the shooting of Father Basilio[53] the superiors realized that two missionary priests were not enough for the great number of Yaqui that were being converted. Therefore, they sent another four priests to help them. These were Father Juan de Ardeñas, who worked for many years [327] in these missions; Father Diego Bandersipe, who also was shot while instructing another nation, as will be seen later; Father Pedro Méndez; and Father Angelo Balestra. All these evangelical laborers considered themselves very fortunate, and so they came with great fervor and worked hard. After two years thirty thousand Yaqui souls had been bathed in the waters of Holy Baptism and marked with the sign of a Christian—the holy Cross. (As I said at the beginning) they carried this as a herald when they came to welcome us during our first entrada.

I will not omit an account of the spirit and pleasure with which these priests worked in this Yaqui mission, assisting and instructing these souls. This will be illustrated by a letter that I received from one of these priests, who gave an account of this Christianity's prosperity, adding:

> I have often wondered and asked other priests in these missions, "Where do we get so much love for these gentiles, among whom there are so many barbarians and ingrates for whom we do so much good?" We live in little pole huts among sorcerers, without an escort of soldiers, and our lives are always in danger and at God's mercy. Nevertheless, we have peace of mind. As proof of the love that God provides these peoples, I have totaled all the stipends that the king has given us and those given to me during all these years for food and clothing, and I find that I have not spent even a third of these funds on myself; two-thirds have been spent on churches, ornaments, and food and clothing for the Indians during their [times] of famine and illness. It is true that these nations could not have been conquered by arms alone, which are so scarce, but instead [required] the power of the divine word and our priests' kindness, Christian love, and patience.
>
> Finally, I wish to relate something that happened to me that is testimony to God's divine providence toward his ministers. In 1632 I left the Yaqui for our college in Sinaloa, which I had not seen for twelve years. After I had enjoyed the company of our priests I returned to the Yaqui to be with them during the first days of Lent. [I wanted] to return quickly to hear confessions and conduct Lenten services, so I chose a new route that seemed shorter, which I had never traveled before. Along the way, in the darkness of the night, I got separated from the Indians who were accompanying me. Not knowing where I was, I stopped at a desolate place with the one boy who was still with me. I got so thirsty and hungry that I began to pull up bitter roots from the ground to eat and to moisten my mouth. While I was in this desperate situation, one of the Indians from whom I had become separated appeared. It was around midnight and he brought with him a little basket of roasted fish. He was guided (he said) by some hand or inner force that separated him from the others. Without knowing where he was going, he was led to me. Thus, the following day I was able to proceed.
>
> The next day I found my Indians, who were also dying of hunger. We all had to continue on to the Río Mayo, where we could find help. As we were all traveling together along a narrow path between steep mountains, God willed that we should find a half-dead hare lying on the ground. I told my Indians to pick it up and take it along. We had barely walked another one hundred paces when an eagle dropped another large hare from above; [328] it landed so close to

53. The anua of 1620 indicates that the priests took up their new mission stations that year, two years before Basilio was shot.

me that the mule I was riding bolted. I told the Indians to grab what God had sent us to eat. We continued on our way, looking for a spring. That night we reached a somewhat salty puddle, and I told the Indians to roast the two hares. The good Christians argued that it would be a sin to eat them because it was Lent. I enlightened them, saying that they were not obliged to observe the Holy Church's precept in a moment of such dire necessity, and that it would not be a sin to eat the meat when there was nothing else and they were dying of hunger. They were thus persuaded to eat, although I went without supper. God willed that the following day I should happen upon a roasted mescal plant. (It was stated earlier that this is the trunk of a plant that the Indians eat roasted.) That night after we had eaten, we reached a Mayo pueblo.

Along the same road the pack animal carrying the supplies I was taking to my district ran into a swamp because he had gone for two days without water. He sank up to his ears because he was so loaded down; no human means could be found to get him out of that swamp. The harder he tried to get out, the deeper he sank. I took hold of his halter and said, "In the name of Saint John the Evangelist, my great namesake, come out of that water and mire!" Suddenly, the old mule gave a leap and pulled himself out. This was a favor from my saint. (This priest's name was Juan de Ardeñas.)

The priest concludes his letter by recounting many other similar things that happened during these evangelical pilgrimages. They demonstrated the succor that the most gentle providence of God Our Lord provides for His servants and ministers, even down to the smallest things used in this mission. At the beginning of this very religious priest's letter he attributed the favors shown by God's sweetest mercy toward His evangelical missionaries to this very same providence, which has now deigned to communicate the ways and means to salvation to such poor abandoned souls as the Yaqui.

For the purpose of making known His divine protection I will add here, without getting sidetracked, something concerning the fierce and bellicose Yaqui nation while it was in its most unrefined state. We two priests who entered at the beginning to establish its Christianity and mission were eyewitnesses to this. We lived among them night and day in pole shelters, without a door, sentry, or defense, except for the two or three boys from the church who slept by the light of a candle at the door, as was their custom. Countless times it amazed us to see that they let us live, knowing that there were innumerable sorcerers who wanted to drink our blood. All the Yaqui knew that they could come into the house or ramada at any time. There they had us at their mercy, and they could cut us to bits for having deprived them of their diabolical profits and having revealed their frauds and obstructed their drunken revels. They also knew and saw with their own eyes that they could call us at any hour of the night on behalf of a sick person; many times they led us out on roads thick with brambles. Those with evil intentions could have easily shot us full of arrows without being detected or recognized behind the brush. And yet they did not do so, despite there being many occasions when these wild beasts could very well have inflicted their barbarity. We found no other answer [329] to our astonishment in such cases than the one given by this priest in his letter: God wanted to be merciful toward these barbarous souls and peoples, so that they could come to know Him. For this reason He bound their hands and closed their mouths so they could not chop us to bits and eat us. May this be useful to this Sovereign Lord's ministers who, for His love and the welfare of souls, abandon the sweet company of their brothers and exile themselves among such peoples. They should understand that they will not lack His divine favor and protection, and if God sometimes left His [ministers] in enemy hands, it was to crown them with copious glory.

CHAPTER XVII The fruits harvested in the Yaqui Christianity following the Baptism of the entire nation, including some unique cases

This chapter will confirm that those who plow and cultivate fields as wild as the Yaqui nation do not labor in vain, nor are the dangers and tribulations they endure a waste. After additional priests arrived and diligently set to work among the Yaqui, almost the entire nation was instructed and baptized. Christian life, customs, and laws were successfully introduced among all the Yaqui pueblos. Therefore, in this chapter and those that follow I will no longer make a distinction between the upper and lower pueblos. In all of them, their acceptance of the Faith and the law of Christ Our Lord and their love (generally speaking) for the priests who preached it to them went hand in hand. In spite of this, we need not dismiss the continual warfare and sieges that the Apostle Saint Peter wrote about in his Canon,[54] where the infernal lion paces and circles, hoping to devour those who are Christian and, perhaps even more so, those who are close to God. I provide this warning here so that the cases I am about to record will not appear to be contradicted by events that will be related later.

It was with great fervor and punctuality that the Yaqui attended religious instruction, Mass, and the priests' sermons. At the first sound of the bell both young and old came running from their little houses, both throughout the week and on feast days. It amazed the Spanish soldiers who sometimes came to barter with the Yaqui for fruits of the harvest to see the latter so changed; they had known the Yaqui from past wars to be very bellicose and fierce.

At times it was necessary to preach to the Yaqui outdoors, because the crowd was so large that they could not all fit in the church. They listened so attentively to the sermon that no one spoke a word. This is noteworthy among people so new to the Faith and by nature restless, as these barbarous Indians are. [In comparison to the Yaqui] the Mexica are calm. The church fiscales made sure that no one made noise and that everyone remained on their knees throughout Mass—even if they were on their bare knees on the ground. This was a difficult and unusual custom for them, but it is now well established. Their interest in hearing Mass has reached the point that when a priest goes to the coast or into the monte to help those who are sick, or on any of the other occasions of famine and need, the Yaqui's first concern is to erect a ramada and altar, so that the priest can say Mass and they can hear it. And all this is in the place where they once held their notorious drunken revels. [330] The joy with which they listen to sermons is such that when the priest leaves the church following a sermon, some greet him saying, "Father, while you were speaking, it was as if my heart were on fire." Others said, "May God reward you, Father, for having preached to us."

To this can be added the fact that their barbarous vices and customs were being uprooted, especially their drunken revels, of which I often have spoken because this is something that is so common and deeply rooted among them. It was most miraculous to have extinguished and uprooted this custom, which had contributed so much to this nation's wars. The Yaqui were fifty leagues from the arm of secular law, which generally must assist the ecclesiastical arm in punishing and extirpating the pernicious vice of drunkenness. This is especially true when the community partakes, and entire families and neighborhoods gather and become enraged.

In some instances God Our Lord also assisted with His divine providence, arranging it so that these people would fear breaking the holy law that they had received. On one occasion the priest was preaching the day before the Feast of the Most Holy Assumption of the Virgin.[55] He spoke to them about that holy day just as the priests normally do in their parishes, reminding them that they were obliged to go to Mass. The priest added (as if receiving special impulses from heaven, as was later shown by what happened) that God would punish anyone who violated that precept. To his detriment one Indian dared to ignore the priest and spent the morning in his field instead of at Mass. And because the feet normally follow the head, this man's wife and

---

54. Peter I 5:8.

55. The Feast of the Assumption is August 15.

children followed his bad example and stayed home, missing Mass. Then, while the entire pueblo was in church—on what was a clear day—a bolt of lightning struck the man's house, badly injuring his daughter-in-law, his little grandson, and his wife. Everyone took note of these events and recognized them as a punishment from heaven. The man and his relatives told the priest that from then on they would fear the threats he made in church, for they saw that what he had preached had come true.

It is nothing new for God to rigorously punish those new to the Faith who transgress His law. One reads in the holy Book of Numbers of a man who dared to leave camp on a feast day to gather firewood in the desert. God sentenced him [to death] through Aaron and Moses, who had consulted with Him: *Morte moriatur homo iste, obruat cum lapidibus omnis turba*.[56] The sentence was: Let such a man be stoned to death by the entire pueblo. Saint Peter, the first Sovereign Pontiff of the Church, sentenced to death Ananias and Sapphira, the first people to transgress the evangelical perfection they had professed.[57]

Although God punished Yaqui transgressors, as recounted here and elsewhere, He also worked acts of mercy, especially through the intercession of His Most Holy Mother, whose feast day was violated by the Yaqui Indian. On one occasion during a great drought, the fields belonging to the pueblo of Torim began to dry up. This prompted the children to hold a scourging procession to a shrine of Our Lady that they had erected on a little hill near their pueblo. Because of these little innocents' prayers and in honor of His Most Blessed Mother, Our Lord let abundant rain fall on the fields of the pueblo; no rain fell on the fields of other nearby pueblos. The Indians were amazed, and the neighboring pueblos became fond of imitating the people of Torim in their devotion to the [331] Most Holy Virgin.

In another pueblo called Vicam the following events took place. The principal cacique, whose Christian name was Don Fernando, died. He left behind a son, who served in the church. He possessed very good character and was quite docile, just like many other boys his age. One night as he was passing the cemetery, his father appeared to him and said, "Look, son, in comparison to

the other life, everything here on earth is trash and excrement," and with this he disappeared. The frightened child went to the priest to tell him what had happened. The priest considered the apparition to be real and not some trick by the devil. Those were not words that the devil would use, nor would he come to relate the joys of the next life to the child, who was known to be sincere and well behaved. This is the type of person with whom divine wisdom likes to communicate. To this was added the fact that the deceased Don Fernando was a very good Christian from the day he was converted. I can add that at the beginning of the Yaqui conversion, he was one of the first to be baptized. He assisted me most faithfully and with extreme diligence. It seemed that God wanted to pay him for his loyalty by allowing him to give his son the light and good news about the other life that he was enjoying, so that his beloved son might be confirmed in the Faith that he had received.

Like others who are new to the Faith, the Yaqui were somewhat horrified by the Holy Sacrament of Extreme Unction. This horror reigns even among some long-time Christians who have been born within the arms of the Church. The Yaqui's fear stemmed from the fact that the priests administered the sacrament (as it should be done) at the very end of a person's life. It appeared to the Yaqui that the anointing was a spell that cast them into the other life, which they feared. But Our Lord was served that they should lose this fear. He arranged this through His divine goodness. By virtue of receiving this sacrament many whom the sorcerers had given up on almost miraculously regained their health. Afterwards, they lost their vain suspicions and persistently requested that sacrament; they usually bring [those who are near death] from their houses or fields to the church to receive it.

I have left discussion of the Divine Sacrament of the Altar for last, because it is the one that requires the greatest preparation; it should not be given to those who lack this preparation. This is why the ministers of the doctrine in these new Christian communities go over this part [of the catechism] very carefully. Thus, when they began to introduce it among the Yaqui, they did so not all at once but slowly, selecting [appropriate] recipients. In this way those who were admitted to Holy Communion considered it a great favor. They received noteworthy preparation in the form of a talk in which the supreme nature of this mystery was declared to them as well as the purity of conscience with which it should be received. They were also told of the fasting that should be observed beforehand, abstaining from

---

56. *Margin Note*: Numer. cap. 15. Numbers 15:35: "His life must pay for it; he must be stoned by the whole multitude" (Knox 1956:128).

57. Acts 5 (the fraud of Ananias and Sapphira). This couple was scolded by Peter for thinking that they could deceive God by withholding from the apostles the full proceeds of a property sale, whereupon they died instantly.

food as well as drink. All this helped them to achieve a greater understanding of such a Supreme Sacrament. The Yaqui listened and carried this out with very noteworthy diligence. It was to their advantage to receive such a divine delicacy. Experience demonstrated well that those who were admitted to Holy Communion were those in whom the greatest change in lifestyle and customs were subsequently observed, as well as a greater faithfulness and example. With each passing day this Christianity was made manifest and grew.

CHAPTER XVIII The superstitions and pacts with the devil that predominated among this nation; how a sorcerer endangered this Christianity and was punished

Although I have written about the topic [of sorcery] on many previous occasions, I do so here with trepidation because it was so prevalent in [332] this Yaqui nation. It seemed that the devil had established a university chair in sorcery among these people, whom he so controlled. This abominable vice compels me to take up the subject again more purposefully.

This nation was so entombed in darkness that a woman who had been enlightened by the teaching of the Gospel declared and so stated to one of the priests who preached the Gospel, "Father, look across the river; do you see all those hills, mountains, peaks, and heights there? Well, we revered all of them and there we practiced and celebrated our superstitions." The old women certified that the devil appeared to them in the form of dogs, toads, coyotes, and snakes—forms that correspond to what he is. Indian principales and fiscales declared as a fact widely accepted among them that at night the sorceresses used to attend certain dances and gatherings with demons and that they returned through the air. One priest who ministered to this nation established for himself the goal of reading that erudite book in which Father del Río exposed the diabolical lies of magic.[58] This priest found that nearly all of these lies had been introduced to this nation by the devil, who deceived some people himself and others through his sorcerers. In one pueblo another priest worked with the [Indian] governor to try to correct some Indian sorcerers, as a lesson to the others. But they themselves said, "Father, don't bother to assemble us [for a sermon], because more or less half of the people in the pueblo (which was large) are just like us."

One can see that the battle and war waged by the ministers of the Gospel are against all the rabble and troops of the demons of hell. It can also be seen that the "triumphs of the Faith" and Christ's Law with which I have entitled this history were glorious. These were achieved in nations in which the Prince of Darkness had fortified himself as nowhere else. Let the reader judge whether the Gospel is victorious when those who preach it survive among so many visible and invisible enemies. If I remember correctly, I have already written about the priest who formerly instructed the Mayo nation. He acknowledged that each morning when he opened the door of his house he expected to receive news that all the priests working among the Yaqui had been killed by the sorcerers. In confirmation of this I will include here testimonies and truths about this topic that God Our Lord forced the devil, the father of lies, to confess through his sorcerers and familiars.

On one occasion[59] a pueblo was stricken with smallpox, which for them is like the plague. The priest

---

58. Pérez de Ribas is referring here to *Disquisitionum magicarum libri sex in tres tomos partiti* (Six Books of Research on Magic Divided into Three Volumes), which was written by a fellow Jesuit, Martín del Río.

59. This was apparently during the epidemic of 1620 (AGN 1620; Reff 1991b:161).

ordered a very famous sorcerer to be brought before him. This Indian had boasted that he had brought on this illness and that it would not end until he desired and commanded it to do so. With these [boasts and threats] he was able to collect from the fearful residents whatever gifts they had, which are the wages of these diabolical liars. The priest subsequently made inquiries and discovered other similar [beliefs] regarding the devil and how he adopted the form of various animals, speaking to them and teaching them how to kill their enemies. This is a fitting and long-standing pretense of the father of lies, who encourages acts of vengeance and rage. The priest asked some sorcerers, "Why don't you kill me?" A famous sorceress answered, "We do not have the power to kill you because you say Mass." Many others confirmed this statement. When the same priest went to preach, the good Christians came to him and said, "Father, we love you very much because you do us a lot of good. However, because you always reprimand the sorcerers in your sermons, revealing their tricks, they hate you [333] and would like to kill you with spells, but they cannot do so because you say Mass."

This discussion of sorcery will be concluded with another case where the devil thought he was victorious but just the opposite was true.[60] There was a principal Indian who as a gentile had been a sorcerer and a great preacher in their fashion. After he was baptized he even helped others to be baptized, preaching sermons in support of Holy Baptism and the Christian doctrine. This sorcerer was encouraged by the devil (who never ceases in his attacks) to revert [to heathenism] and direct a war against the Yaqui Christianity, which was flourishing at the time. He was supposed to destroy it (if he could). The principal solicited and brought together groups of baptized Christians and revived their gentile dances. He told them that he wanted to undo the spells the priests had cast over them during Baptism. Because he was very persuasive, the principal promptly perverted the spirits of some people with this diabolical doctrine. During their secret meetings, in which they smoked tobacco, he preached that the Christians' Faith was pure fiction and that no one should listen to what the priests said; the heavenly bliss they spoke of was a lie. He knew that Christian souls went not to heaven but rather below the earth. It wouldn't matter whether the Yaqui gave themselves over to all forms of vice, because they would still be very happy in the next life. The principal preached these and similar deceits of the infernal master of all

lies, which were given greater substance by a diabolical apparition. On this occasion the devil appeared to these deceived people near their river in the form of an old man, whose words have great force and authority among these nations. He said to them, "Take a good look at me, I am an old man. Tomorrow after I bathe in the river you will see that I am young. The same thing can happen to all of you." The following day he enacted his fiction, appearing to them as if he were twenty years old.

All these tricks helped beguile and pervert the deceived group that the principal had gathered, and a very dangerous fire was ignited. In order to beat back the flames and remove the one who was the source of this blaze, Captain Hurdaide had to be informed. With the force of the secular arm he could remove this weed from that field and halt the fire that was engulfing it. Finding himself obliged to halt and remedy this urgent danger, the captain set out with a good number of soldiers and armored horses for the Christian communities of the Río Yaqui. He drafted only a few Indian allies, in part to avoid rumors of war and in part because he knew that there were many good Yaqui who wanted peace and friendship and who were on the side of Christianity.

The captain reached the Río Yaqui and was well received in the first pueblos. However, while he was traveling through a wooded area to another pueblo two arrows were suddenly fired at him. Because he was so knowledgeable about uprisings and these people's assaults, he judged that this was not an action plotted by the entire nation (and in fact it was not). Therefore, he pretended not to have noticed. He ordered those who were with him not to fire their harquebuses or bows and to continue marching until they reached a pueblo that he knew was located nearby. When he got there he set up camp and arranged for the army's safety. As previously noted, there certainly was no safety among this populous and bellicose nation, which had not yet changed significantly with the preaching of the Gospel.

The captain immediately sought out the Indians who had disturbed Gospel preaching, [334] and he captured their leader, the sorcerer cacique who, as I said, had perverted the others. He questioned [the cacique], who confessed that he had been encouraged by the devil, who spoke to him each day from a poplar tree in the form of a crow. The devil persuaded and advised him to kill the priests, to throw in the river the bells that were used to call the people to catechism, to burn the churches, to use the heat of a fire to sweat out the consecrated oil with which the priest anointed them during Baptism, and finally, to try and put an end to Yaqui

60. This case occurred in 1622.

Christianity as well as the lives of the captain and the Spaniards, thus returning his nation to its gentile life.

After substantiating the charges [against him] the captain sentenced this extremely pernicious Indian to be hanged along with two or three of his most guilty accomplices. At the same time he pardoned the others who had been deceived. After this sentence had been pronounced, a priest who was a good interpreter came to prepare those who were to be executed. Divine mercy disabused and prepared them well for death, for they acknowledged their guilt and confessed their sins with great remorse, particularly the delinquent principal cacique. He told the priest that it helped to have the priest who had baptized him at the foot of the gallows—he who had brought Christianity to the Yaqui (calling me by my name) and who had baptized one of his dead sons. His consolation was that he was going to die baptized, believing the word of Christ. His hope was to see his son in heaven, because he had died with Holy Baptism. Like a true Christian, he added other arguments as well. And one may well imagine that he would realize his wish, because Our Lord gave him time at the moment of death to acknowledge remorse for his guilt and sins and to repent.

After the punishment had been carried out and the scandal removed, the Yaqui along the entire river were quieted. The Indians who had believed that deceptive sorcerer were ashamed and they reformed, and others learned a lesson. The devil was even more humiliated, because (as can be believed) that sorcerer was won over for heaven by the same means through which the devil had intended to beguile him and thereby destroy Christianity. As will be seen in the following chapter the Yaqui were more enlightened and with each passing day their Christianity flourished.

CHAPTER XIX The pueblos build churches; the priests complete the establishment of Yaqui Christianity; cases confirming the mysteries of our Holy Faith

Up until this time the priests had been very busy administering general Baptisms in numerous heavily populated pueblos and visiting the sick in their former rancherías along the seacoast or in the monte. [There were also] many other ministries in which these religious busied themselves during the time of this primitive church. All this work had not afforded an opportunity to arrange for the residents to construct the large, fine, permanent temples that are needed in such populous pueblos. These were necessary for celebrating the sacred mysteries. A place was also needed where other residents could congregate, especially during their celebrations of the major feast days and those of the patron saints of their pueblos.

Churches like these cannot be built unless the priests themselves act not only as foremen, but also as architects. They even actively participate in the construction, assigning tasks and [335] even preparing meals for the people, for (as has been said) there are often six hundred or more people working at a time. Large numbers of people are needed for cutting beams and carrying them on their shoulders, for they have no oxen or mules to pull them, and to gather stone and [make] adobes. These are holy tasks for these very religious priests, and I know for certain that they labor with great joy for the good of these souls and the exaltation of the mysteries of our Holy Faith.

Each of these priests encouraged the people of his district to construct [a church]. The Yaqui were enthusiastic, because just as they had prided themselves in the past on being more spirited and courageous in war than all the other nations, now that they were Christians they did not want the others to surpass them in

Christian matters. Thus, they wanted to have churches that were just as beautiful and handsome as those of other nations. They accepted the proposed [construction] with pleasure and immediately set to work building [their churches].

The pueblo of Torim was the most populous and also where the people were most inclined to being wild and rebellious.[61] This was the birthplace of the woman whose testimony was recorded earlier—the woman who pointed out all the hills surrounding the pueblo and others that were more distant where the people of Torim used to celebrate and communicate with the devil. In this pueblo they were not satisfied with building [only] the main church. They also built a very devout shrine to the Queen of Angels on a little hill overlooking the river, as a special devotion to this Sovereign Lady. They did this so that the piety and worship of the Christian religion would prevail where malice and superstition had [once] abounded.[62]

In the end all the churches in the eight reduced pueblos turned out to be beautiful and spacious.[63] As each one was completed it was dedicated with great solemnity, celebrations, dances, and feasting, which is of great importance to these people. The neighboring peoples that attended were extremely happy to see such a change along the now-peaceful Río Yaqui. They could now go there safely in times of need to trade for maize and the other things that they value, interacting with those whom they used to kill.

When the churches were completed the priests decorated them with handsome vessels, images, and silk banners. They paid for these things out of the stipends they were given by the king for food and clothing. These very religious ministers consider this money well spent because it greatly assists the people in coming to understand divine matters, much more than one might think.

For the shrine mentioned previously, one of the priests that administered these missions sent to Mexico City for a retablo, upon which was painted the Last Judgment. It showed Christ Our Lord, the Judge of the Living and the Dead, with His Most Holy Mother at His side, in glory. Everything else that is usually represented as a proclamation of what will happen on that remarkable day was also depicted. It portrayed the people whom the angels take to heaven as well as the condemned that the demons drag off to hell. The Yaqui enjoyed listening to preaching on this topic. When they saw it painted on the retablo it made a great impression on them. As their priest wrote, the retablo struck such fear and panic in them that its memory has been powerful enough to deliver them from many temptations and close calls with sin, especially sins of the flesh and adultery, in which the change and improvement of the Yaqui nation have been remarkable.

Singing and music in church are also pertinent to religion and divine worship. Although attention was paid to this in the beginning, no progress could be made because it was necessary first to teach reading and writing, and then to teach the musicians the musical notes and how to harmonize. In time all this was accomplished and [336] young men and boys were found who had great talent for this service. Many principales took pride in their sons' employment in the service of the Church, and they gladly handed them over for these ministries. After these clever children were trained, long-time Christians who taught voice were brought to the Río Yaqui, where very talented choirs were established in each of the districts. Feast days are now celebrated there to the sound of the organ and other musical instruments such as the bassoon, sackbut, flageolet, and the flute, all of which they have learned to play skillfully.[64] During their renowned celebrations they are now ashamed to dance in their former barbarous fashion, preferring instead the civilized Spanish dances.[65]

In one case an Indian whom the devil attempted to deceive and trap became [instead] more confirmed in the mysteries of our Holy Faith. This Indian had been sick, and on the eve of the feast day of [the patron saint of] his pueblo, the devil appeared to him, saying, "I feel very sorry for you and your relatives, for you are dying without anyone to cure and heal you." He gave this sick Indian some medicinal herbs and told him to use them to cure himself. Then to treat him even

---

61. The adjective used here for the inhabitants of Torim is *cimarrona*, which often was used as a referent for escaped slaves who resisted capture by fleeing to remote areas that Spaniards were reluctant to enter.

62. It was a long-standing Iberian tradition to build over or on top of the remains of temples or other places of worship belonging to conquered peoples. In Andalucía the Romans erected temples on top of Iberian structures; the Goths built shrines over Roman ruins; Muslims built mosques (often using stone cut by the Romans) where Catholic churches stood; and the latter supplanted or remodeled Muslim structures to serve as churches. The replacement of pagan idols with relics or crosses was also the favored strategy of missionaries and monks in early medieval Europe (Flint 1991).

63. The eight pueblos (note there were eleven a few years earlier) were: Ráhum, Pótam, Vicam, Abasorin, Torim, Báhcum, Cócorit, and Huírivis.

64. A sackbut was a medieval trombone, and a flageolet, a type of flute resembling a treble recorder.

65. Presumably courtly dancing.

better, he added, "Tomorrow is a feast day; be happy and dance, for I will join you in the dance." This Indian, who was already baptized, said, "Don't you see (he said to the devil) that we will be dancing in the church? Do you dare to go in there?" "Yes, I will go in," answered the devil, "and I will dance before your [eyes]." So it was that on the following day the devil danced visibly in the procession, although only the Indian could see him. When the procession had ended and it was time for Mass to begin, the infernal enemy took his leave, saying to his familiar, "You stay; I am leaving and cannot remain here." Thus, God forces even the father of lies—as evil as he is—to sometimes confess the truth.

The Indian noted that when Mass was being said the devil fled, not daring to remain. He was remorseful that he had erred in returning to dealings with such a trickster. He had already heard (because he was baptized) that the devil was frightened off by the Cross, so he frequently made the sign of the Cross and went to church. The devil appeared to him again but did not dare to get very close; he must have been afraid of the sign of the holy Cross. He said to the Indian, "Look, I have not come in vain. If you want to live happily, you must surrender your soul to me and stop going to church and making the sign of the Cross so frequently." But the deceived Indian now had a greater knowledge of the mysteries of the Holy Faith, so he responded to the devil, "You told me that you were not afraid of the church, but now you are trying to persuade me not to go there. Well, it won't do. I regret that I [ever] listened to your reasoning. The priest will come and hear my confession, and I will tell him what has happened with you, for I truly want to be a Christian." Now the devil was furious and said to him, "Don't do any such thing or I will tear you to pieces." The Indian (who was now even more confirmed in the Faith) responded, "Do whatever you want, because God will help me. There is no way you can harm me."

Nevertheless, that night the Lord allowed the devil to physically beat him. This was a punishment for his sin of having conversed with the devil. The beating was so harsh that the poor Indian was unable to move for two weeks. Having learned his lesson, he confessed to the priest, telling him, "Father, the devil wanted my soul, and this is how he has treated me! Not any more, because from now on I will try to be a good Christian." And so he did for a month, but finally God wished to remove this soul from these dangers. He sent him a mortal illness, and after he had once again confessed {337} his life on earth ended. This Indian left assurances that he was going to enjoy the eternal life that God had mercifully granted his soul by freeing him from the devil's snares, just as the Yaqui nation, as we have noted, benefited from Christianity. They now celebrate all their weddings according to Christian customs and have abandoned and forgotten their gentile ones.

CHAPTER XX Other [religious] practices and cases of edification in this new Christian community

The Lenten season always brought the greatest joy and celebration to the missionary priests in these new Christian communities. During this time the priests could clearly see and touch with their own hands (as they say) what the Faith was planting and working in these souls. This is exactly what happened in the new Yaqui Christianity that we have been discussing. Extremely clear evidence of this was the sorrow [the Yaqui felt] for their sins and for having offended the true God, whom they now knew. Also, those who previously knew not God nor law nor king, and who had lived in the freedom of a depraved nature, now confessed and revealed their sins to the priest. To this can be added their penance and blood scourging, which were widely practiced during Lent, even by the children. They also attended church services both day and night.

In the midst of all these holy ministries God began gathering a good number of souls for heaven. If one were to record here the unusual cases of Baptisms of children who had just been born or of sick adults who had just willingly confessed—all of whom we can imagine went to heaven—we would never stop counting. So that these cases are not all forgotten, I will record a few that will serve as examples of those that are omitted.

A certain Indian was returning to his pueblo when he came down with such a high fever that he could go no farther. One of his companions went to cut wood to build a fire so that they could spend the night there. The sick man, who had been left alone, heard a voice saying to him, "Arise." Terrified, the Indian raised his head and saw among the branches of a tree a youth who looked like the angels they usually paint in the churches. The youth said to him, "The Lord has given you this illness as a punishment for your sins, because you refuse to live as the priest has taught you. Arise healed and go to the pueblo. Confess all your sins to the priest and lead a good life from now on."

The Indian was immediately cured and set out for the pueblo, telling his confessor what had happened. He told him that he thought it was the guardian angel to whom he had been entrusted, for he had heard it said that every Christian had an angel to protect him from the devil. It is well known that the holy angels had once been frightened away from these nations, which were besieged and possessed by devils. When they see that these nations have become Christian, these divine ministers once more draw near and happily favor and accompany them.

It is also worth noting, as the priests do, that at the same time the people are baptized the devils unwillingly flee. They withdraw to gentile nations, where there seem to be hordes of devils and demonic sorcerers. In a pueblo that was friendly to the Yaqui and where they spoke the same language, there was an Indian who, as a gentile, had dealings with and was a familiar of the devil. When he became Christian the priest gave him the Most Holy Virgin's Rosary for greater protection against such [338] a bothersome and stubborn enemy. This Indian became sick, and because that is when this infernal beast intensifies his fury, he appeared to the Indian one night with a ferocious countenance. He threw himself upon the poor sick man and grabbed him tightly, saying to him, "Because you once gave yourself to me, I must now take you." The distressed sick man, trying as best he could, took the rosary in his hands and began to say, "Jesus [save me]." Immediately, the devil fled, fearing the sound of that sweetest name and the presence of the Holy Rosary and devotion to His Most Holy Mother. That enemy was so terrified that he disappeared and never again dared to appear to or bother the sick man.

As the following case will illustrate, there are even greater signs that the enemy of humankind fears, flees, and distances himself from the evangelical ministers who instruct these peoples. An Indian was walking in a state of some desperation towards the monte when the devil stepped into his path, inviting him to [come] to a land of plenty that was free from labor. This would be the land of heathenism, where one lives as he pleases and to which the devil flees, as I said. The Indian started to follow, but when he felt that he was losing control of his senses, he feared this disturbing change and he turned to go home. His enemy was still with him, however, and the poor Indian, being so distressed, went into a cave that he found there in the field. There he howled and bellowed like a bull.

When the priest got word of this event he ordered the Indian to be bound and brought to him. He prepared him to make a good confession and ordered him to hear Mass every day. When the Indian regained his senses he found himself free from the devil, who never appeared to him again. The Indian later said that the devil had never completely let go of him until he was within fifty paces of the priest's house. When he reached that point he noticed that the enemy who so persecutes these poor people turned around and threw himself into a ravine out of desperation. This was proof of the strength and virtue that Our Lord places in His ministers for making the demons flee from these conversions, for that infernal beast fled at a distance of fifty paces.

In one of these pueblos a young gentile woman became sick. When the priest was notified he went to help and heal that poor soul through Holy Baptism. As he was about to administer it the woman's mother (who was an infidel) became so furious and bedeviled that she took a pole down from the ramada, which they usually have in their houses, and with it she attempted to kill the priest. She would have succeeded if the fiscales from the church had not been there to prevent it. But her diabolical fury did not end there. She grabbed her daughter by the hair, and to get her away from that Holy Sacrament she dragged her into the thick brush nearby. The priest knew that the poor girl wanted to become a Christian and that God wanted to save her, so he had the evil mother taken away. Then he instructed the sick daughter and baptized her. The following day God took her to heaven and punished the perverse mother. Within a year this woman and her husband plus all the people in their household had died, to the horror of the entire pueblo.

The punishment did not end there, for it was also noted that God took the lives of other principal Indians who were obstacles to the teaching of the Gospel. He finished them off, to the amazement of others. But at the same time these nations have seen and noticed that the priests among them live long lives. They generally enjoy good health, in spite of the fact that they are destitute of doctors and medicines, [339] for these are completely lacking in these remote lands. These are all favors by which divine providence protects these Christian communities, especially those of the Yaqui and its ministers, who are the farthest from the Villa de San Felipe and our college.

CHAPTER XXI How the political and temporal life of this nation has been changed and improved; the state in which it perseveres today

Civilized and human existence presupposes in part a divine and spiritual [presence], as suggested by the words of the Apostle, *Priusque animale est.*[66] It is nevertheless certain that the introduction of the Faith and divine law to these people not only made them Christians, but also taught them a rational and human way of life. Because this is also fruit won by these evangelical ministers, it is worthwhile that we write about it here. Although the change wrought in part by Christian doctrine among other nations was described earlier, it is nevertheless true that the Yaqui nation provides the greatest and clearest evidence of this change.

This nation was more corrupted and steeped in their gentile customs and vices than other nations. And yet the Yaqui's bravery and ability to reason exceeded that of many [others], and with cultivation, their moral and political life have improved greatly. In all of their pueblos there are governors, alcaldes, church fiscales, and their own ministers of justice. These individuals govern with order, respect, and obedience. Some of these officials are appointed by the captain, although

66. "One is first an animal."

he is more than fifty leagues away. The missionaries appoint the fiscales of the church. The latter are responsible for keeping the priest informed of all matters that pertain to the church (as has been described previously), including marriages that Christians wish to contract, newborns who need to be baptized, the celebration of feast days, and those who become ill and are in need of the sacraments. The fiscal accompanies the priest in the pueblo or when it is necessary to go to another [pueblo] to administer the sacraments. They also notify the priest of sins that have become public knowledge or a scandalous violation of Christian law or custom. The civil governors likewise inform the captain of matters that require his attention. Because the missionary is right there and everyone regards him as a father, the people normally go to him with everyday complaints, which usually concern land or similar things. The priest settles these disputes, and they obey him and are satisfied.

The people live in well-planned pueblos; nobody resides permanently in his fields or former rancherías. Many of their houses have walls of adobe with flat roofs. The [Indian] governors have even more ample houses. The priests, who in the beginning endured so many hardships, now have reasonable houses that are sufficient for their ministerial duties and for their regular meetings and religious observances. The Yaqui also enjoy having many ministers gather in their pueblos—pueblos that before did not want to admit a single priest. [In these pueblos] there are Indian sacristans who carefully tend to the appearance of their churches, sweeping them and decorating them with branches, especially on feast days.

With the fruits of their labor many Yaqui have purchased horses, using them for travel and to transport loads. Indeed, they covet horses to the point that they increase the amount of land they farm. Their valley produces so abundantly that in years of scarcity Spaniards and Indians from other nations bring goods to trade for Yaqui crop [surpluses]. [340] This is what they call bartering.

There has been a great change in their attitude toward clothing, which they desire and procure. For this reason they have become more involved in growing cotton. Moreover, to correct their barbarousness, which made them indifferent toward covering themselves, the priests brought sheep to Sinaloa so that the Indians could weave mantas of wool with which to clothe themselves. Once they are made to wear clothing they get to like it so much that some become obsessed with it. Indeed, in order to obtain clothing, or more precisely, to

be elegantly dressed, they sometimes leave their homes and women and travel fifty leagues or more to [find] work outside the province. [This] in part explains why the Yaqui population has decreased, as has the Mayo, as was noted earlier. Although some return to their pueblos, others reside permanently among Spaniards or in the mining centers, where daily wages are higher and they can obtain more elegant clothing. As mentioned previously, disease has also contributed to population decline. As I have discussed at length, God chooses to diminish these populations by carrying many of these people off to heaven. Still, at the time this history is being written the Yaqui nation is divided among eight pueblos with about three hundred, five hundred, and seven hundred male heads-of-household, who are administered by four priests.

These Indians are now very tame and recognize their Creator and Redeemer. They have raised the glorious standard of the holy Cross and are obedient to its divine laws; the laws and darkness introduced by the devil are forgotten. The ousted tyrant has been deprived of those he possessed; newborns are [now] reared with the milk and doctrine of the Gospel. Once [Our Lord] was served by the conversion of this nation, which the devil had so endeavored to retain under his dominion, the door was opened and the strength was found to conquer many other nations, who with the example of the Yaqui have since been joined to the Holy Church. Moreover, when there have been uprisings and the captain and other Spaniards have needed help and have drafted people to pacify rebellious nations, they have found the Yaqui, who are known for their bravery, to be loyal and responsive.

Before concluding this book and moving on to the conversion of other nations, I will fulfill my promise to write about the lives and joyous deaths of those who worked longest in these enterprises. These men were chosen through a special calling from Our Lord who, when He bid farewell to His disciples, assured them that He would be with His Church until the end of the world. And until that time His divine promise will be kept, for He will continue to send apostolic laborers, as He is presently doing, to cultivate and expand [this vineyard] by means of the glorious Catholic monarchs of [all] the Spains, who tend to this matter in the New World by using their royal patronage.[67]

---

67. Royal patronage refers to the rights and responsibilities that were ceded to the Spanish crown by the Vatican for the establishment of Catholicism in the New World.

CHAPTER XXII The life and death of Father Martín Pérez, founder of the Sinaloa Christianity

The Province of Sinaloa, its extensive Christianity, and thus, this history, should recognize the great debt they owe Father Martín Pérez. He was cofounder of this entire Christianity, along with the blessed martyr, Father Gonzalo de Tapia. He was also the first in this province, at the far ends of the earth, to proclaim the Gospel, raising his voice in song in accordance with what the psalmist said.[68] [341] This apostolic man sowed the seed of the Gospel in this ignorant and savage land, and after he cultivated it and endured immense hardships, it has borne the ripened fruit that the Church militant and triumphant has subsequently stored in its granaries for heaven and earth to enjoy. Before this illustrious evangelical laborer died he enjoyed seeing Christianity spread more than one hundred leagues, to almost all the nations of the Province of Sinaloa, as we have mentioned. For all these reasons this history is obliged to relate the holy life and death and the religious virtues of such an outstanding man, beginning with his birth and childhood and the early days of his exemplary life.

Father Martín Pérez was born in Nueva España, in a villa called San Martín in the Province of Nueva Vizcaya. At one time this villa was quite well known and well thought of because of the wealth it provided Nueva España.[69] He was the son of important people, some of the greatest landholders in that region. His father was very concerned about his son's welfare, and even though he was the firstborn and heir to all his riches, when he was still very young his father sent him to Mexico City, where all manner of learning flourishes. There he was to acquire virtue and learning, and because of his keen intelligence and calling for a religious life, he was to become a worthy minister of the Holy Church.

Very early in his studies he showed signs of singular genius. He finished his course work in *Latinidad*[70] or Latin Studies in just fourteen months, at which point he went on to higher studies in philosophy and letters. He was a student of the distinguished Professor and Doctor Father Pedro de Ortigosa, who was a member of our Company and recognized throughout Nueva España as the Master General of the Kingdom.[71]

Young Martín made clear progress in his study of philosophy, and just as he finished his first course in this subject the Lord called him to the Company so that he could study a much higher form of philosophy, that of religious humility. He was received [into the order] in June 1577. As a novice he showed the same concern for learning the basic rudiments of the spirit that he showed during the fourteen months in which he learned Latin. In fifteen months he had advanced so far in his courses on the spirit that the superiors decided he knew enough to teach others about virtue and letters. Therefore, they sent him to teach humanities at the recently founded college in the city of Puebla de los Angeles. He was subsequently employed at the college in Mexico City, where he demonstrated wisdom, good sense, and a maturity that seemed to surpass his young age. Because of this, even though he was only twenty-one, the superiors had enough confidence in him to turn over [to him] the governance of the college seminary—a responsibility the Company takes seriously. At that time this seminary was called San Pedro; it is now called San Ildefonso and it has flourished in Mexico City [as a center] of virtue and letters. He governed the college for two years, and then, when he was still very young, he became a minister at the college in Puebla. This is how great his sense and maturity were, which he demonstrated from a very young age.

Although it might appear from what has been said that he could [best] serve Our Lord and the Company in the area of administration, God arranged for him to take a different route. This was a route that is very

68. Particularly in the Psalms of the Kingship of God, e.g., Psalms 95 and 97 (Knox 1956:517–18).

69. San Martín was one of a handful of mining centers founded between 1554 and 1562 by Francisco de Ibarra; by the turn of the seventeenth century it was no longer a major producer of silver.

70. A multi-year program involving the mastery of Latin and then the reading of the classics of the Ancient World and the composition of verse and prose in Latin. Toward the end of this regime the student devoted himself to systematic philosophy. One indication of Pérez's ap-

parent brilliance is the fact that his mission companion, Gonzalo de Tapia, took five years to complete the course work in Latinidad (Shiels 1934:36–37).

71. Pedro de Ortigosa served as rector of the Colegio Máximo and was a noted and much-respected Jesuit theologian. Bishop Pedro Moya de Contreras undertook private study in systematic theology with Ortigosa (Poole 1987:45; Zambrano 1961–1977:2:566).

glorious for the sons of the Company of Jesus, which greatly esteems the apostolic exercise of missions. This priest busied himself as a missionary in several different areas of Nueva España, in particular among the Chichimec Indians, whom the Spaniards had great difficulty conquering and reducing. [342] These missions were rehearsals for the glorious tasks that awaited Father Martín Pérez in Sinaloa. He was chosen for this spiritual conquest in 1590, which is when he left for Sinaloa. Reference has already been made in Book II of this history to the wretched state of this land, where there were few Christians and outbreaks of war disturbed the province. The people here were wild and barbarous, living and dying in misery under Satan's heavy yoke where everything necessary for human life was lacking. I will add only that the daily living conditions of this land were such that Father Martín Pérez's food at times consisted of wild fruits, bitter roots, and even locusts.

Despite these and other discomforts that necessarily accompany the first entradas of the Gospel into such distant and far-flung lands, Father Martín Pérez and his companion, the holy martyr Father Gonzalo de Tapia, founded the missions of Sinaloa. From the outset these two priests were a source of great religious [piety], which inspired apostolic and evangelical virtue in those religious who subsequently worked in these missions. These are all fruits of those outstanding missionaries whom God chose for His greater glory and who were the first men chosen by the Company for the conversion of the barbarous peoples in the Kingdom of Nueva España.

When the Indians killed Father Gonzalo de Tapia (as was stated earlier) Father Martín Pérez was left with the responsibility of the [entire] Province of Sinaloa, [which meant] visiting, instructing, and baptizing a large number of souls. These pueblos were very far apart, and today they are attended to by six priests. Father Martín Pérez visited them all by himself, although it is certainly true that he was unable to provide them with what is now demanded of their ministers, who do not have enough strength to meet all their needs. He brought wild Indians out of the inaccessible thickets, reducing them to pueblos where they lived a civilized life. He instructed them in the mysteries of our Holy Faith and inculcated in them the practice of the Holy Sacraments. He built churches for the administration of these sacraments, although in the beginning, because of the difficulty involved and a lack of materials, the churches were made of wood. But after some time Father Martín Pérez was one of the first to

attempt to build more permanent structures. In those days this was a task which, although not comparable to the enormous task of erecting great structures in large and populous cities, was still quite an undertaking. If one carefully considers or knows from experience the poverty of this land, the rustic nature of its people, the evangelical minister's many occupations, and the near total absence of tools that are required for building, then one would no doubt consider it a greater feat to have raised four earthen walls with a flat roof, which was safe from water and fire, than to have raised those other great buildings that require great expenditures of time and money. For buildings such as the latter there were expert craftsmen and an abundance of tools, power, and riches. In Sinaloa, especially at that time, the priest's only aid was his zeal; the only craftsmen were the plans invented by his love; the only energy the fervent desires and personal labor of the priest who did the building, laying his own hands to the task.

Father Martín Pérez was just as careful and attentive to the spiritual building of the souls that [343] he instructed as he was to the churches that he constructed. After establishing urban and political order among these rough souls he erected a structure of Christian and moral virtues. This minister's efforts are worthy of mention because they resulted in notable changes in the Indians' old and new customs; he uprooted the former and planted the latter. We should mention and apply to them what Teodoreto stated concerning the changes that Saint John Chrysostom wrought among the barbarous nations that he taught, leading them out of darkness. Because this is similar to what happened in Sinaloa, it is worthwhile to ponder this case. *Habes hanc* (says Teodoreto) *cum Apostolis cognationem; primus apud Scytas aras erexisti, & barbarus didicit genuflectere, & ad pauimentum incuruari; & qui captiuorum lachrymis non mouetur, didicit pro peccatis flere.*[72] If we were to change only the word *Scytas* [Scythians], it would seem that Teodoreto was writing about the Indians of Sinaloa and their devotion to their churches and reverence for their ministers. Their former cruelty toward the priests and other gentiles was exchanged for knowledge and the tears

72. *Margin Note*: Teodor. li. 5 in laud. Chrisostom. Apud Bibliothec Phoc. The referent here is to an apparent collection of works by the Church Fathers containing Theodore's Book 5 in Praise [of Saint John] Chrysostom. "You have this (says Theodoric) relationship with the apostles; you are the first to have erected altars among the Scythians; and a barbarian has learned how to bend at the knee, and to bow to the pavement; and those who are not moved by the tears of captives have learned how to weep because of their sins."

they shed for their sins in their frequent confessions, which Father Martín Pérez taught them to make in the many pueblos where he gave religious instruction. *Quin etiam* (Teodoreto continues) *iaculatore Persam vulnerans, predicatione, & ferrei didicerunt crucifixum adorare, vicit tua lingua Chaldaeorum, & Magorum imposturas, & Persarum inculta natio Templa germinauit, non amplius Babylon pietate adversa est, haec te similim Apostolis fecerunt.*[73] It would seem that Teodoreto was referring here to the tricks of the sorcerers whom we have discussed.

All these passages agree to the letter with the apostolic exercises of Father Martín Pérez, who labored among the barbarous nations of Sinaloa for twenty-six years, some of which he spent as superior of the missions.[74] At the end of this time he was overcome by very frequent bouts of illness, which were brought on by his neglect of his health, his fervent practice of his ministry, and the province's complete lack of medicines and doctors. Thus, when the priest became quite ill there was no other remedy than to repeatedly bleed him,[75] which left him completely debilitated. On one occasion Father Pérez was suddenly in need of another bloodletting, and there was nobody around who knew how or had the instruments to do it. He found a Spaniard and asked him for the love of God to use the point of a knife to open one of his veins.

Father Pérez later developed new and different problems: he was unable to use his feet, his hearing failed, his vision dimmed, and he found it hard to speak because his tongue had become clumsy. Although it was impossible for him to get around with so many illnesses, they did not affect his spirit and will to assist others. Thus, he retired to the college in Sinaloa to converse with his God, concentrating only on matters of great benefit to his spirit. He never missed saying Mass during the first nine years of his painful and meritorious illnesses. In the last year of his life they took him in a chair, although with great effort, to an oratory within the house, where he said Mass and ordinarily received Holy Communion. Sometimes he walked on his own to the oratory, although he would fall and bruise his face because his body would fail him. The strength of his spirit was nevertheless so great that he attended by himself to whatever his body and his poor cell needed, as humble as it was. He swept it out, taking water to wash it down, and he exercised other more humble acts from which he could justifiably have excused himself because of his limited strength {344} and the many years that he had spent in the service of God and the spiritual benefit of others. This continued until he was ordered by the superior to accept help with tasks that he insisted on doing, even though he should have been excused from them.

While he was thus withdrawn from his duties and enjoying holy leisure for his spirit, it pleased the Lord to call him home. He sent him a fever that lasted for three months, which left him bedridden. He was so tormented and thin that he was forced to remain almost entirely immobile, unable to turn from one side to the other. He bore this with such patience that it amazed those who saw him. He received all the Holy Sacraments, and later, even though he lost his senses for three days, he still did not lose his ability to raise his heart to the Lord, murmuring the verses of the psalms, in accordance with his habit, which had almost become a natural part of him. But little by little Father Martín Pérez was losing his strength and drawing closer to the reward for his holy and prolonged works. He fell asleep in the Lord on April 24, 1626, at the age of sixty-five. He spent forty-nine years in the Company, thirty-one as a professed priest. He spent more than thirty years in the missions, where he exercised heroic acts and outstanding virtues, which have been recorded here because of their greatness. These acts and virtues would appear to sufficiently illustrate the life of a man who was so apostolic. However, as I noted at the beginning, because Father Pérez was a founder of these missions, this history cannot ignore the heroic virtues that he exercised in such an exalted ministry.

The first and most excellent virtue, and the one that strengthens all others, is charity. One can judge how many carats of this virtue this venerable man possessed by using the measure that Christ Our Lord gave us, saying, *Maiorem hac dilectionem nemo habet, quam ut amimam suam ponat quis pro amicis suis.*[76] It is well understood that one does not apply this measure of love only when a life is lost, but also when it is risked and offered for a

---

73. "But also (Teodoreto continues) wounding Perse with a javelin, [and] by means of proclamation, [the people] of iron have learned how to worship the crucifix. Through your preaching the Chaldeans and the deceits of the Magi (learned Persians) have been conquered, the uncultivated nation of Persia has sprouted forth temples, and Babylon is no more opposed to piety. These things have made you like apostles."

74. Pérez became superior upon the death of Tapia in 1594.

75. European medicine held that illness stemmed from an imbalance(s) in the humors of the body; bloodletting was thought to restore balance to the blood or circulatory system.

76. *Margin Note*: Ioan. c. 15. John 15:13: "This is the greatest love a man can show, that he should lay down his life for his friends" (Knox 1956:106).

loved one. And yet it is not for mankind to try to attain that greatest perfection of charity because, although it is your life to risk, it is not your place to oblige someone to take it from you.

During the thirty-three years that Father Martín Pérez spent among these barbarous peoples he risked his life on innumerable occasions for the honor of God and the welfare of others. The danger in which he found himself when his companion, Father Gonzalo de Tapia, was martyred is testimony to this truth. The killers wanted to finish off Father Martín Pérez as well, but Our Lord miraculously saved him for His exalted ends. Witness to this are the many occasions at the beginning [of the Sinaloa mission] when he came close to being shot with arrows for reprehending and correcting barbarous and inhuman vices that in those early days inflamed those free nations who had never before been subjugated. Also witness are the many trips that he made every year to instruct a few Spaniards living in a mining camp called Baimoa,[77] which was forty leagues inland, in the mountain range. These Spaniards had no other spiritual aid than the burning charity of this zealous minister of the Gospel. He used to say that the weather during these trips was so variable and unhealthy that on some days he could not take a single step because of the excessive heat, yet the following morning the water would be frozen. These are all occasions that manifest the innumerable times when this servant of God risked his life and his delicate and fragile constitution [345] for the Lord he loved. The events that finally led to his death will be seen to confirm all that has been said.

Once when he had taken a purge they called him that same day to administer Extreme Unction to a sick man. Despite his own grave illness and the obvious danger to which he exposed himself, he was more concerned with attending to another in [grave] need than with his own worldly life. Therefore, he paid little heed to his own health and went to administer that Holy Sacrament. This is the act that initiated the illness that led to his death. For this reason we can call this apostolic man a martyr of charity—this being the [virtue] for which he offered his life. Later he wrote to Mexico City, asking for advice about what he should do in a case such as this, and the answer was found among his papers after his days [had ended].

The Apostle of the People, Saint Paul, noted that the virtue of patience was a direct result and close companion of charity. Our Lord strongly charged His evangelical ministers to be patient, as did Saint Paul, who said, *Charitas patiens est.*[78] These two virtues are so closely united that Saint Cyprian said, *Tolle charitati patientiam, & desolata non durat: tolle sustinendi tolerandique substantium, & nullis radicibus, ac viribus perseuerat.*[79] It seems as if Saint Cyprian were looking upon this venerable man, who for so many years demonstrated enduring patience with delicate matters and uncommon hardships, which he endured and overcame. He stood so firm in the midst of hardship that—even on the numerous occasions when the Indians, and sometimes even the soldiers who escorted him, gave him sufficient reason to be impatient—he remained steadfast; he did not voice the slightest complaint or even change the expression on his face. The soldiers themselves spoke of this in admiration of Father Martín Pérez.

A further proof of his patience and suffering was the continuous nature of his travels, which was such that the Indians called him in their language 'the priest who walks a lot'. It would be impossible to count the number of times he visited the pueblos under his charge, going from one pueblo to another. Then there were the countless leagues and days that he spent traveling during his many years [as a missionary]. He did this without rest and without protection from the sun, rain, heat, cold, and other inclement conditions, for he barely brought along enough to cover himself.

Finally, the suffering that he endured late in life is the ultimate proof of his patience. He suffered from so many and such grave illnesses that it seems each part of his body had its own particular pain. Yet no one ever heard him complain or sigh when he opened his lips to take a breath—this despite a lack of relief from his many illnesses and sores, which because of his great modesty he kept covered. He also had sores on his back that came from lying in bed. These sores oozed so much that it was necessary to wipe him off with a cloth, which tormented him and renewed his pain. What was most amazing was that so many pains did not alter his spirit, but instead seemed to cause the opposite effect,

---

78. *Margin Note*: I Corn. 13. 1 Corinthians 13:4: "Charity is patient, is kind" (Knox 1956:175).

79. *Margin Note: Lib. de bono patient. De bono patientiae* ("Concerning the Good of Patience") is one of thirteen extant treatises by Saint Cyprian of Carthage; it was written around A.D. 256 and focuses, as the title suggests, on Christian patience (Laurance 1984:168–70). "Take up the burden of charity, for it does not harden those desolate [places]; take up the essence of holding up and enduring and when there are no roots or strength, it perseveres."

---

77. This small mining center was in the mountains northwest of Topia.

as evidenced by the joy on his face and the calmness of his expression. This frightened the brother who attended to him. At times when he entered the priest's room he found that he had fallen and injured himself and was unable to move, stuck between the door and the wall. As he helped [the priest] to his feet he would ask if he had hurt himself. To this, [Father Pérez] would answer with a laugh, saying that he had not. This was also [346] his usual answer to anyone who asked him whether he needed anything. If they insisted on asking a second time, he would answer that [he needed for them] to commend him to Our Lord. Finally, if they insisted a third time, with a desire to alleviate the suffering of such a holy man, he would answer, "Beg Our Lord to be served by taking me home, for I am of no use here." With all these responses he demonstrated how deeply rooted in his heart the admirable virtue of patience was. As a final example of this I have left that which is usually rare in persons who are ill, especially if they have been sick for a prolonged period. He never showed signs of craving anything special, nor did he complain if they did not attend to his needs.

Along with his unusual patience this man of God had a serene gentleness that comes from charity. *Benigna est*,[80] added the Apostle [Saint Paul]. The priest gave many examples of this virtue while acting as superior for many years in these missions in Sinaloa. He was kind to all, accommodating himself to the condition of each individual. But his kindness was not remiss nor did it encourage mistakes. Rather, his gentleness was active and effective, geared toward religious observance, which he maintained in his subjects the entire time that they were under his charge. He showed this kindness not only toward the religious of the Company of Jesus, who were his sons and brothers, but also toward the Indians he instructed. He lovingly pardoned them for their ignorance, caressing them like his own children with tender words and trying to win over their spirit and will to Christ.

The evangelical poverty that this Gospel minister demonstrated was very much on target not only in its affection, but also in its effect. This was apparent from the outset when he became a religious and, in the name of Christ, shunned the many things he could hope to inherit from his parents. He embraced holy poverty so closely that all his possessions emitted the odor of this virtue. In the beginning his meager food consisted of maize, squash, and legumes. Later, when things were

more established, and even when he was superior at the college in Sinaloa, he was happy with the poorest of foods—slices of beef cooked in water without any other seasoning or sauce. However, this was done with the great consolation and enjoyment of his professed poverty. Once around Easter time, when we priests gathered together in the refectory at the college in Sinaloa, I sat beside the holy old Father Martín Pérez. In celebration of that feast day and season of the year each priest received a little square of wheat bread; otherwise we always ate maize tortillas. I offered my part to the holy old [priest], saying that I was young and would be fine with the maize tortillas. Smiling, he answered, "Well, Father, I confess of course that when there is bread, naturally my hand goes to the bread on which we were raised." This was an answer which, although it may seem of little significance, reflects the great forbearance with which this servant of God for thirty years deprived his inherent appetite of the bread on which he had been raised—bread that even those in the most distant deserts do not lack.[81] He removed from his own mouth the bread he liked, and did so quite joyfully. When the superiors invited him to go to rest in Mexico City, where he could find this bread in abundance, this man who loved poverty would not agree to do so because [he preferred to] distribute the spiritual [bread] to his children.

The amount that he spent on clothing can be inferred from the fact that he continued to wear the same habit until it was torn to shreds and barely covered his skin. He went without asking for a doublet until finally [347] those who lived in the house noticed this and helped him. His outward attire was ordinarily very poor and old, because he totally disregarded matters of appearance. He wouldn't even use a little mattress until the superiors ordered him to do so. His lack of conceit kept pace with his disinterest in worldly goods, as can be seen from the fact that during his life he concealed his many talents for letters and government, through which he could have shone greatly in the province. In addition to his erudition, he was a man of great wisdom and mature judgment. On those many difficult occasions that arose in Sinaloa his opinion was very comprehensive and correct, although very cautious in its wording. This arose from his great understanding of such issues, and even more so from the virtue of silence. This shone in the priest in such a way that one never

---

80. Repetition of a portion of 1 Corinthians 13:4: "[Charity] is kind."

81. This lack of wheat bread often was mentioned by the Jesuits, despite the fact that some (if not many) came to appreciate if not prefer maize tortillas (Reff 1991b:255–56).

heard a word from him that could be considered point-less or exaggerated. The same was true of his letters in which he presented his reasoning, where the words he used were measured.

Although he had great advice for others, he him-self wished to be taught by everyone else. He had such great humility that even when he asked an easy ques-tion of another priest, he would use the expression, either written or spoken: "Your Reverence, instruct me about this and tell me what I should do." He made himself like a child, in accordance with Christ's advice about how to gain the kingdom of heaven. It is easy to understand how he who became like a child with his equals and inferiors would have acted toward his su-periors. He always saw the person of Christ Our Lord in them, so he obeyed and respected them. The insinua-tion of obedience, even in the most difficult matters, was for him like explicit obedience. When he was in the presence of his superior he remained standing [with-out his cap] until he was ordered to sit down and put his [cap] on. Shortly before he died the Father Rector came in to see him, and even though he was exhausted, he removed the cap on his head and remained that way until his superior made him put it back on. It is easy to understand how much someone who throughout his life was so concerned about such minor things would have cared about more important things.

Finally, he completed the perfection of his humility and obedience by not being tempted by the illustrious positions he could have obtained. Rather, he remained hidden in the farthest corners of the province, at the college in Sinaloa, where ordinarily there is only one priest, because the other priests must attend to their own faithful and pueblos. It was notable how this mis-sionary accepted this pilgrimage and holy exile to such a distant land, leaving the companionship and commu-nication he had with his brothers, as well as the colleges and positions where he could have been more comfort-ably employed as a religious. Nevertheless, from the time he was assigned to the remote Sinaloa mission among barbarous peoples he never requested or wished for his beloved exile to be interrupted, not even in the final years of his life. He wanted to die there for Christ, for whom he preached His Holy Gospel in the desert of this heathenism, which had been so forgotten by the world. He desired not to be known by the world, but rather to be like the most withdrawn hermit in the most remote solitude of the desert.

This spiritual man, Father Martín Pérez, found just such a desert. There he established intimate dealings with God, as well as devotion and Spiritual Exercises, in which he spent a great deal of time. Because he was by nature withdrawn, he saved himself from convers-ing with human beings, giving himself over completely to heavenly communication, in which he spent [348] entire days and a large part of his nights. This was especially true in the last ten years [of his life], when he could barely leave the room to which he withdrew, never leaving [even] to find relief from the great heat of this land. Not only did he not ask for the news sent from Spain and Mexico City—which for that land is like [news] from the Indies is for Spain—but he didn't even ask about the missions he had planted. What is more he never even asked what was happening in the college where he lived. For those who visited him he had only two answers, one to the greeting that charity required, and the other to the question of how he was. When he was not asked he did not speak. It was under-stood from this silence that he did not like conversing with human beings, but instead entertained himself in continual conversation with his God.

One of Father Martín Pérez's superiors, a man of great spirit, said that in him he venerated Paul or Hilarion.[82] Many others from the Company agreed with this opinion, saying that upon seeing Father Martín Pérez they had satisfied their desire to see the lives of the ancient, contemplative, and solitary holy fathers, who were dead to the things of this world. Once when Captain Diego Martínez de Hurdaide was governing the province he came to visit Father Pérez at the college. He sent a soldier on his behalf to tell him he was there. The priest responded to the soldier, "Your Grace, tell the captain that I am saying my office." The captain was not upset by this answer because he knew and esteemed this very religious priest, who at that time enjoyed only his retreat with God. Thus, the captain returned quite edified, and the priest continued in his holy devotion.

In his devotion of spiritual readings he was also quite punctual, attentive, and steadfast. In the book that he used for this devotion many papers and notes were found concerning spiritual matters that the priest had written down so as to fix them more vividly in his memory. Had his silence not concealed them, there is no doubt that we could say a lot about the favors and gifts that he received as a result of his continual deal-ings with God. However, for this same reason we can

82. Paul [of Thebes] was considered the first Christian hermit. Hilarion (ca. 291–371) was a monk and contemporary of Paul who was noted for his life of austerity (Farmer 1992:229, 383).

make an inference in accord with the rule of that very spiritual Doctor, Saint Peter Damian. Speaking of the contemplative man, he said, *Tanto successus in altiora sustollitur, quanto per silentij custodiam circunclusase se extrinsecus fundere prohibetur.*[83]

Finally, as a result of all these heroic virtues and admirable exercises and works that have been briefly noted, Father Martín Pérez was rewarded by God with the title of faithful minister of His Gospel. He was esteemed within the Company as an outstanding missionary and an upright and most observant religious. Among those in the Province of Sinaloa he was awarded

the title of Father and revered as a saint, which is how they venerated him in all that land. He won all this by introducing the first light of our Holy Faith and the first rays of its divine mysteries.

He was the cofounder of this Christianity, along with the blessed Father Gonzalo de Tapia. Thus, we can say that it was founded by a martyr and a holy confessor. Because of their diligence, it has become very widespread, as has already been seen and will be later told. There is no doubt that Father Martín Pérez has been greatly rewarded with venerable glory for the subsequent increase in Christianity. [349]

CHAPTER XXIII The life and death of the very religious Father Hernando de Villafañe, who worked for thirty years in the Sinaloa mission, where his holy life happily ended

The life and death of the very religious Father Hernando de Villafañe is very pertinent to this history, particularly as it appears that he had been chosen since childhood by divine providence to become one of His honorable ministers and to cultivate His vineyard in the extensive fields of the Sinaloa mission. He was adorned with talents that made him an outstanding apostolic missionary. Those of our Company will find his regular observance[84] and untir-

ing fervor for extending our Holy Faith a model to imitate. Father Hernando de Villafañe knew marvelously well how to combine the responsibilities of a perfect religious with those of a diligent evangelical worker. [He demonstrated this] in the various posts, occupations, and offices in which he was employed by holy obedience, particularly in the Sinaloa missions, where he labored for thirty years and where his life ended.

Father Hernando de Villafañe was born to noble parents in the City of León, in Castilla la Vieja. As a child his parents gave him a very Christian education, raising him with particular care and encouraging his study of Latin and virtues, in which he demonstrated his keen mind. Afterwards they sent him to [the University of] Salamanca to study law. But God had greater plans and He endowed him with talents that would assure their realization, for Hernando excelled in modesty and prudence of action even more than in his studies.

He was a singular example of composure and hon-

---

83. *Margin Note*: Lib. 7. c. 6. Apparently Chapter 6 of *De perfectione monachorum* [On the Perfection of Monks] (McNulty 1959:27–28). The first edited volume of Damian's writings was put together by Dom Costantino Gaetani in the early seventeenth century (between 1606 and 1640); a more recent edition by Migne (1844–1864; vols. 144 and 145 of the *Patrologiae Latina*) includes the "Epistolae," "Sermones," and "Vitae Sanctorum" of Damian. Saint Peter Damian (1007–72) was a bishop, monk, and cardinal who returned to the life of a monk after his episcopal duties. Damian's writings are strewn with references to the contemplative and ascetic lives, and he was one of the first and greatest advocates of the regular canonical life (McNulty 1959:25–26); Peter Damian (although no particular work) is on the recommended reading list for Jesuits (de Guibert 1964:217). "Those who are inflamed and raised to higher levels are likewise the watch guard of silence, keeping it to themselves."

84. *De Regular Observancia*. Meaning Villafañe acknowledged and

rarely deviated from the precepts and rules of the Jesuit order, which Pérez de Ribas discusses in detail in Book 7 (see also Polzer 1976).

esty to those at the university, and from this they could see the light of prudence and sanctity that would later shine in him. Our Lord illuminated not only his understanding of letters, in which he excelled, but even more his understanding of the world's deceptive vanities. Contemplation of this matter weighed so heavily on his soul that he decided to leave the [secular] world which, because of his parents' great wealth and nobility, promised so much leisure and ease. He sincerely confided in Our Lord, asking Him to approve his wishes provided He found them agreeable. Divine Goodness granted this wish, facilitating his entrance into our Company, where he was admitted with unanimous approval.

Once in the novitiate he fervently began to imprint religious virtues on his soul. He greatly valued the institution to which God had called him, employing himself in the exercises that would aptly prepare and form him for his ministerial profession. He made a great effort to imitate the most devout of his fellow novices, whom he considered more virtuous and worthy of imitation. His superiors were so impressed with his perseverance and virtue that they sent him to his own country and native city of León to study philosophy, even though he was [still] a novice. He was fortunate to have as a teacher Father Luis de la Puente[85]—a man who was known around the world for his knowledge, sanctity, and writings. Our brother was very happy to have such a teacher, and their closeness and dealings furthered his desire for greater perfection. Here was fulfilled the maxim of Saint Ambrose, who said, *Discendi ardor nobilitas est Magistri*[86]—the student is stimulated by the teacher's ideas and example.

From La Puente he learned [350] philosophy,[87] in which he became very proficient. In spiritual discussions he was similarly informed about matters of devotion and virtue; La Puente's writings on these subjects

were firmly stamped on his soul. He preserved for life the spiritual maxims and opinions that he had heard, referring to them frequently with notable affection and esteem. During long trips he would bring one of Father La Puente's books to read as he rode along.[88] He spent a lot of time on the road reading and praying. I was an eyewitness to this, because I traveled in the priest's company for many leagues.

Through these means God arranged for the welfare of many souls, preparing Hernando to become a missionary, even though he was [still only] a brother in the Company. He was already full of divine thoughts and an appreciation for the salvation of his fellow man. He was not content with these thoughts, but contemplated going to the Indies for the conversion of very many gentile peoples, whom he considered devoted to the worship of the devil. He shared his desires with his superior, who acknowledged his great virtue and true calling. He was sent to the Province of Nueva España with Father Francisco Váez when the latter returned from Rome as Procurator of Mexico. When Hernando arrived at the college in Mexico City, the [superiors] learned about the holy desires that had brought him from Spain and immediately gave him something in which to exercise his desire to be a missionary. Before he finished his studies and received the Holy Orders his superiors sent him to the college in Pátzcuaro to learn the native language of that extensive Province of Michoacán. Holy obedience found him very willing, for as soon as he arrived he very enthusiastically began learning the Tarascan language common among all those Indians.

Although he had to return to Mexico City to complete his studies and receive Holy Orders, as soon as he did so he returned to Michoacán, where he worked for several years for the betterment of the native people, fervently exercising the ministries of our Company. He steadfastly gave them the bread of the divine word, effectively exhorting them to be virtuous and abandon their vices. He heard their confessions and instructed them in piety and devotion. To achieve this he truthfully tried to improve himself in the language. [His knowledge] was so great that many years later, after having learned other barbarous languages, he not only remembered Tarascan, but could still speak it eloquently. Whenever he encountered Indians from Michoacán while traveling he would stop to talk and

85. La Puente (born in 1552) was a student of Francisco Suárez and began his tertianship under Baltasar Alvarez, another intellectual giant of the time. La Puente taught philosophy and theology and began a productive career as a writer in 1605. His two-volume *Meditaciones de los misterios de la Santa Fe* (1605) was his best known work. La Puente was a contemplative who was concerned in part with the different forms of God's presence and how God unites with men. In 1759 Pope Clement XIII proclaimed the heroicity of La Puente, bestowing on him the title of Venerable (see de Guibert 1964:253–57).

86. "Passion for learning is a teacher's nobility." Ambrose (A.D. 397) is one of the four great Doctors of the Western Church (Thurston and Attwater 1956:4:509–16).

87. *Las Artes*. The "arts" as such included philosophy (logic, dialectics, physics, astronomy, metaphysics, ethics, psychology) and other subjects based largely on the works of Aristotle (O'Malley 1993a:244–45).

88. Perhaps La Puente's *Meditaciones de los misterios de la Santa Fe* (1605) or his *De la perfección del cristiano* (1612).

recite the catechism that he had taught them, even if it meant delaying our travel plans. While he was at the college in Pátzcuaro he was chosen by his superior to be the Rector, an office that he exercised with much prudence and vigilance. He attended to the needs of his subjects as well as those of the many Spaniards and Indians in the community, helping everyone with his frequent sermons in their languages.

While he was employed in this ministry he received news of Father Gonzalo de Tapia's joyous death preaching the Gospel. Father Tapia was also from the city of León and was loved by Father Villafañe, who shared his holy friendship when they sailed together to the Kingdom of Nueva España,[89] as well as virtues of zeal and fervor similar to his own. Although Father Villafañe found more reason to envy than to mourn Father Tapia's martyrdom, [351] he still felt great sorrow for those barbarous gentiles who were left abandoned as a result of his death.

Around this time Father Villafañe received frequent impulses from heaven, calling him to the enterprise of extending [Christianity] in the Province of Sinaloa. Despite the difficulties and dangers, his spirit had been ignited and he desired to see himself employed there. He communicated his desires to the Father Provincial. The latter wished equally to send someone with knowledge, religion, and talent to promote and stabilize this mission that was of such glory to God, yet which was being persecuted at that time by the devil and his accomplices, who were trying to destroy it. The Father Provincial accepted the priest's offer, judging that it came from God. He promised himself great fruit because of the holy zeal for the welfare of souls that God had placed in Father Villafañe, and he was not disappointed. Thus, Father Villafañe was sent to the mission and Province of Sinaloa [in 1598].

When he arrived he saw what type of heathenism and field God wanted him to cultivate. However, he was not frightened by the difficulties or hardships, nor by the horror of the dense forests of infidel and barbarous nations that remained to be tamed. On the contrary, he was encouraged to see himself cultivating [Christianity] among people who greatly benefit from piety and divine mercy, as was noted with spiritual insight by Saint Gregory the Great, who explained the mysterious clouds announced in the Book of holy Job:[90]

Nubes lustrant per circuitum; in quocumque loco misericordiae suae eas iusserit inveniri.[91] The holy Doctor explained this by saying *locus misericordiae Dei, est ipsa gentilitas.*[92] In order for God to fertilize with His special providence the lands and places inhabited by gentile peoples, especially when they are as distant and remote as those of which we are speaking, He calls and takes the clouds from one end of the world to another, spiritually and divinely enriching the soil with the celestial waters of Holy Baptism and the divine doctrine. He is most indulgent with His mercy when He sends real clouds to the dry wilderness, which when irrigated, produces flora and sustenance for the animals. On numerous and varied occasions I heard Father Hernando de Villafañe speak highly and with great fondness of his glorious employment for the sanctification of forsaken gentiles, whose souls were purified with the water of Holy Baptism, and how they were thus introduced to the house and family of God and His Church. These were words that sprang from ideas that Our Lord placed in his soul.

It is clear from his special sermons[93] to other religious that Father Villafañe understood very well how God visibly demonstrated in these places His mercy toward gentiles, sending them His spiritual clouds. During thirty years of distinguished service—beginning the day he arrived in Sinaloa—this burgeoning cloud, filled with holy thoughts and wishes, gave heavenly instruction. His zeal for the salvation of souls was so admirable that it appeared like a banner, hoisted high above his other virtues. He was kept busy in the Province of Sinaloa by the very populous Guasave nation. As a true shepherd and father he nourished them spiritually with religious instruction during the thirty years of his apostolic mission, suffering innumerable and unending hardships and even risking his life to convert these gentiles. [352] He preached, administered the Holy Sacraments, established churches, and reduced to a republic those who were so estranged from civilized life. In doing so he obtained great fruit for his holy labor.

Because he realized that he could not communicate the water of celestial doctrine without knowing the languages of the nations that he ministered to, he made an

---

89. The two priests were part of a contingent of twenty-three Jesuits who sailed for Nueva España in 1584 (Shiels 1934:49).

90. Pérez de Ribas alludes here to Saint Gregory the Great's *Expositio libri Job* (Commentary on the Book of Job).

91. *Margin Note*: cap. 37. Job 37:12–13: "this way and that they turn . . . among distant tribes, or here in his own land, let his mercy bid them appear where it may" (Knox 1956:475).

92. "The place for the mercy of God is gentility itself."

93. *Pláticas*. The term plática, or 'chat', 'talk', or 'discussion', often referred to sermons delivered to priests or religious at spiritual conferences or retreats (Smith 1978:42–43). Apparently Villafañe often was asked by the superior of the Sinaloa mission to address the other priests during their semiannual convocations.

extraordinary effort to learn them. Although this was difficult, his holy efforts overcame these obstacles and he attained a perfect command of them. This achievement was all the more meritorious because these languages require more work than those that are learned with little or no effort. I heard him say that in order to explain the mysteries of our Holy Faith, he tried to learn with complete exactness particular and specific Indian ways of speaking. Because these languages were so unusual, he spent considerable time disciplining himself and praying, asking for light from heaven to learn them. He was the first person to compose rules and a grammar for the Guasave language, which was spoken along the entire coast of Sinaloa. Arguably, this apostolic man learned the languages through the fire of the Holy Spirit—in the same way that they were communicated by the Holy Spirit. He learned them not for the applause of the world, but rather to irrigate and enrich it with the water of the divine word.

For thirty years he watered his plants without fail, preaching every Sunday, except when he was ill. In addition, he frequently gave talks about Christian doctrine, explaining its mysteries. He did this every day, immediately after he finished celebrating [Mass] and giving thanks [to God]. He and his Indians sang the Christian doctrine in church with admirable perseverance, and the fruit [of his labor] was a sight to behold, because the Guasave knew this doctrine as well as the well-instructed Christian communities of Spain.

He showed this same zeal when he conducted entradas to the Sinaloa missions, of which he was the superior, as well as on two different visits to the other four missions[94] that the Company has outside that province. He very fervently encouraged the missionaries to value the apostolic ministry that God had given them. When he visited the districts he made sure that each one had catechisms and grammars in their respective native languages, which is the only way to develop and strengthen Christianity in the Indians. He requested and made a special effort to locate items for the ornamentation of [the church] and divine worship. He was especially attentive to cleaning and arranging the altars and adorning his churches, because it is through the exterior that these nations come to appreciate the spiritual.

This was what moved him to be one of the first in the Province of Sinaloa to undertake the building of permanent churches in the pueblos. He supervised construction and even laid his own hands to the task. One might add that he spent a great deal of energy [building] the first three beautiful churches [in Sinaloa], which were destroyed by a flood just as they were about to be dedicated (as was mentioned before). When the pueblos that he had congregated and settled at great effort were also inundated, he received this blow with the same attitude and words that the holy Job used when that destructive whirlwind grabbed hold of the four corners of his house and dashed it to the ground.[95] When the raging flood destroyed Father Villafañe's prized churches, on which he had worked so hard, he said with the quietness of his spirit, *sicut Domino placuit, ita factum est, sit nomen Domini* [353] *benedictum*.[96] His spirit was not broken; rather, he started anew with the same spirit with which he had built the first churches. He and his Christian pueblos finished and dedicated the second ones with great solemnity, thus encouraging neighboring nations to undertake similar works for divine worship, which were of such importance to this evangelical minister. Long-time missionaries used to say, "Let's visit Father Hernando de Villafañe's district so we can learn what to do in our own."

The material improvement of the missions was also the result of his zeal. Viceroys and governors granted his requests, which cost him many hardships and journeys to Mexico City. Whatever the Spanish residents of the province have—be it cattle or sheep ranches, the establishment of a garrison, salaries for the soldiers, benefits for the captain—almost all of this is due to this priest's diligence. He also endeavored to insure that money from the crown was spent on necessary and beneficial things. This is why the viceroys and governors greatly respected this person and also favored his requests. When they saw the signature of Father Villafañe (although he himself was not present) on revenue requests, they granted them without delay and with pleasure, because they were repaid by his great prudence and religion. They knew that the priest's intentions were to secure the stability and safety of the province and its Christianity. The aforementioned Captain Diego Martínez de Hurdaide, who undertook so many successful enterprises, always sought out and

---

94. Villafañe appears to have alternated with Martín Pérez as superior of the Sinaloa mission during the early seventeenth century (Dunne 1940:153). In 1622 Villafañe held the post of Jesuit visitor, conducting an "inspection" of the northern missions.

95. Pérez de Ribas is referring here to Chapter 1 of the book of Job: the "lesson" referred to is that God and his designs are inscrutable and that faith must prevail.

96. "Because it was pleasing to God, therefore has it been done. May the name of the Lord be blessed."

conferred with Father Hernando de Villafañe, wherever he might be.

In matters of the Holy Faith he was also appreciated by the Inquisitors of Mexico. To demonstrate this even more, they made him Commissary of the Holy Office[97] for the two distant Provinces of Culiacán and Sinaloa. To the great satisfaction of the Holy Tribunal he held this post until his death.

Finally, he who was so fervent and careful with matters that did not concern him directly was clearly even more so with matters related to his own profession. With respect to the day-to-day life of a religious, he closely observed his superiors' orders, obeying them with exactitude. He was always the first to execute their orders and to set the example, which always made the orders easier to obey. Father Hernando de Villafañe always considered his North [Star] to be the holy virtue of obedience, which is so valued by the sons of the Company. He used its light to guide his life, which is why he succeeded in difficult enterprises. When he was a student he was ordered to halt his studies to go to Michoacán to learn the Indians' language. He gladly obeyed and earnestly applied himself to the study of [Tarascan]. After he became a priest his superiors ordered him to return to the same province. He went back with the same happiness as the first time. From there he was moved to the Sinaloa mission, three hundred leagues away. He was not only delighted to go, but went with apostolic fervor. Then in a new order he was asked to return to Mexico City as Rector of our college,[98] which is the workshop where [missionaries] for the entire province [of Nueva España] serve their apprenticeship. He came with sadness to oversee the college because he had to leave his beloved, albeit demanding missions. [354]

After he fulfilled his job as Rector the province elected him to be their Procurator in Rome.[99] He accepted this position and journey of several thousand leagues, just as he had walked as many leagues during his many years in the [Sinaloa] mission, where he was continually traveling. After he returned from his long trip to Rome, without resting, he returned to his beloved Sinaloa mission. Once there he was [then] ordered by the Father Provincial to return to Mexico City to attend the meeting of the Provincial Congregation, which required his presence. Although he could have legitimately excused himself because of his old age, attacks of gout, and his fatigue from traveling, he nevertheless undertook the trip of three hundred leagues to attend the congregation. After it was over he returned to his mission, where he could freely enjoy the tranquility, rest, and zeal that burned in his spirit to aid the souls of others. One religious asked him how he could make such long journeys, given his advanced age and his attacks of gout. He responded, "God is the one who calls me, and because I must obey Him, He gives me health and strength for these trips; besides, I am obliged by my promise of obedience and by my duty to God—and I want to travel, even if I am weak. Let us pay with love what love is owed. There is a big difference between obeying when you will suffer and obeying when you will not." It was with this spirit that this very religious priests spoke and labored.

With respect to the vow of poverty taken by the religious, Father Villafañe provided exceptional examples. He was not only offended by the use of vain and superfluous things, but he also abstained from the use of curious items for devotions when it seemed to him that they exceeded [the bounds] of what his [religious] state required. This is the reason why he never kept expensive illustrations or an unusual reliquary, even though he could easily have obtained such luxuries when he went to Rome as Procurator for the province. Being a spiritual man, this priest knew that devotion could sometimes be deceptive and that devotion is appropriately manifested through affection. He was so careful with respect to matters of religious poverty that he did not dare to distribute any of his own sermons without first requesting permission from his superiors.[100]

He was always extremely vigilant in his observance of complete purity and chastity. He lived for thirty years with great prudence in the midst of naked people. He continually mortified his senses so that no specter

97. Because of limited personnel, the Holy Office frequently appointed parish priests in outlying areas—or, as in Villafañe's case, missionaries on the frontier—as *comisarios*, to gather information and occasionally act on behalf of the Inquisition (Kamen 1985:143).

98. This was apparently in 1618.

99. This was in November 1619, during the ninth provincial congregation. The Jesuit Constitutions require that each province convene every three years a meeting of all professed Jesuits. The congregations formulate requests to be presented to the father general in Rome by elected delegates, who while in Rome also participate in a "general" congregation attended by representatives of all Jesuit provinces (worldwide). The delegates consider and vote on matters of importance to the order (Dunne 1951:139). Villafañe and Juan Lorencio were elected by their fellow professed to be Nueva España's representatives to Rome and Madrid (Alegre 1956–1960:2:321).

100. The Inquisition forbade priests from sharing their unpublished (and thus unexamined) sermons with other priests. The prohibition was apparently ignored by significant numbers of priests (Smith 1978:35–36).

could enter through those doors and tarnish its beauty. To protect it, he also performed acts of reconciliation whenever he had a copy of the priest's manual with him.[101] This is how continually concerned he was with the purity of his soul.

This extremely religious priest strengthened his virtues through the holy exercise of prayer. He was always very inclined to prayer and nourished [himself] throughout the day with frequent short prayers and supplications to God. When his gout forced him to remain in bed it was as if he were in prison, because he could not attend to the ministries of teaching and preaching the Gospel, of which he was very fond throughout his life. Thus freed, however, he would devote himself to meditation on eternal matters and the recitation of devout songs. The latter he composed as praise to the Holy Sacrament [of Communion] and the Holy Virgin, thus invigorating his love and devotion for them. As mentioned, his great relief and entertainment when he traveled was to read devout books in solitude, which aroused holy feelings in him. This was a means by which his spirit was uplifted to a greater awareness of divinity. These readings bathed his soul with great sweetness and were a relief not only to the devout priest, but also to those who sometimes traveled in his company.

The priest accompanied the [355] practice of prayer with its loyal companion, mortification and penitence. When his health and age allowed him he undertook rigorous penance to tame the flesh. The priest pursued bodily suffering with this same spirit and was so intent that sometimes superiors had to moderate his fervor and restrain him.

Although he was severe and rigorous with himself, he was amiable and merciful with others, particularly the soldiers who accompanied him during times of danger and otherwise. They were pleased to accompany him because of his concern for them and the gifts he gave them in such a poor and needy land. He showed even greater kindness toward the poor Indians, with whom he spoke very gently in order to win them over to Christ and gain their affection. He was very generous toward them with material things that they lacked,

kindly sharing with them whatever he had. When they became ill he nourished and took care of them. The love he showed toward the little Indian children to get them to sit with him at the table was amazing. He gave them morsels from his own plate, showering them with attention and treating them with as much love as if each one were his own child. In this way he imitated the kindness of our most pious Lord, who told His Apostles not to keep the children from Him.[102] With this kindness Father Villafañe won the Indians over so that they loved him dearly.

The Spaniards admired this [quality] in a man of his age, authority, and occupation—a man who could have lived a more leisurely life as Rector of [the college in] Mexico City, Procurator to Rome, and Commissary of the Holy Office. He devoted himself with great pleasure to these modest ministries, and because he valued them, he made them into his most illustrious achievements. What Spaniards found most edifying was how much attention he paid to the spiritual welfare of his parishioners. At all hours of the night, in fair weather or in the intense heat so common in this land, he would promptly go to hear the confessions of those who were ill, comfort those who were sad, or care for those who were afflicted. He used all the arts of love to reduce them to God's laws and [to instill] virtue.

This account of Father Hernando de Villafañe's virtues will be brought to a close by noting the special devotion he had for the Most Holy Sacrament and the sacrosanct mystery of the Mass. He celebrated Mass every day, even when he was traveling; never could he recall missing it because he anticipated the impediments that might have prevented him from this, his heartfelt devotion. When he went to Rome as Procurator he made sure that during the journey there was a place where he would have the solace of enjoying this celestial Viaticum and nourishment. To go without celebrating Mass during the voyage (at that time saying Mass [aboard ship] was not the established practice that it is today) was the most painful and difficult part of the voyage. When it came time to return to Nueva España he made numerous inquiries about celebrating [Mass] aboard ship, inquiring of erudite men. Although he was given extremely contradictory [opinions], he departed with his wishes fulfilled; he was the first to facilitate and introduce the holy sacrifice of Mass during the voyage to the West Indies.

If he was unable to say Mass because of gout, he had

101. Pérez de Ribas—in keeping with his likening of Villafañe unto a church—is using "acts of reconciliation" here as a metaphor for penance and mortification. A consecrated church that has been violated must be reconciled or purified by a bishop or his deputy using Gregorian water (Attwater 1949:420). The "priest's manual" presumably is a breviary—the book containing all the prayers, hymns, lessons, etc., needed to recite the Divine Office.

102. Matthew 19:14.

himself taken to church to hear it, receiving the Host with great devotion. When this illness forced him to stay in bed he procured a bedroom from his superiors with a wall that had a window overlooking the church. Although racked by pain, he heard Mass from his bed, to the great consolation of his spirit. When he himself celebrated Mass he prepared [beforehand] with special prayers {356} and daily confession; when possible he would assist at all the Masses he could.

The last Lenten season of his life his superior noticed his frail health and lack of strength from old age, so he asked him to stay and rest at the college in the Villa de San Felipe, rather than return to his mission district, where there was a fellow priest who could attend to matters in his absence. Although the priest appreciated this charitable offer, he nevertheless requested permission to return to his mission and holy occupation, which was calling him. He preached and heard confessions with such renewed enthusiasm that he later said he had never felt the same energy and desire to help souls as he felt following that Lenten season.

I know that I have not referred here to this apostolic man's wonderful {works} and miracles. However, I am satisfied that I have related this evangelical minister's solid and perfect virtues. They were exercised with great constancy and tireless perseverance in the face of immense labors and hardships during the founding of the Sinaloa mission. On numerous occasions this very religious priest found himself sentenced to death. Fortunately, all of this toil—thirty years of this priest's life that were consumed for God's glory—merits more as an offering to God than other great works and miracles that in a brief moment would have brought one to the brink of death. It appears that Father Villafañe was repeating what the glorious Father Saint Bernard wrote: *Iam seni requies, iam corona debebatur emerito, et certé tanquam novus in Christo miles, nova iterum tibi excitas bella, provocas adversarium, et rerum fortium proesumit Jesus senex.*[103]

During the last years of his life Father Hernando de Villafañe continued to labor for God's glory. When the time came for his life to end he went out in style,

especially considering how weak he had grown. He was forced to accept this weakened state, and once he did, within a few days he became ill and bedridden. So that he could be taken better care of, he was taken to the college in the Villa de San Felipe. Because it was apparent that his illness was mortal, he made a general confession, as he had done on other occasions. He had been very carefully preparing himself for death during the previous seven years, although this matter still concerned him. When he realized that the time was drawing near when the doors to eternity would open, he said to the Father Rector in the presence of the other priests, "Truly, Father Rector, I give many thanks to God for the favor He shows me by taking me now, when death will find me prepared. I carry out [religious] exercises as best I can, and I appreciate that He gave me this illness while I was preaching to my Indians." As his condition worsened everyone affectionately began to cry, mourning his [impending] absence. With the death of the priest the missions would be missing the main column that sustained them. As a father he had loved them, as a Prelate he had governed them, and as a saint he had edified them with his examples. God did not forget, however, to provide them with other illustrious ministers who would spill their blood on their behalf, as we will shall see.

The hour of death finally came for Father Hernando de Villafañe who, after receiving the Holy Sacraments, departed with great calm and peace. The cloud that God sent from the far corners of Spain to the ends of the province and missions of Sinaloa consumed itself, in accordance with what we said at the beginning regarding Job. And we can say {357} that the observations on Job by the famous lecturer, Father Juan de Pineda, were fulfilled to the letter: *Nubes se totas impedunt, et super impedunt, atque adeó consumuntur, et pereunt*[104]—the clouds expend themselves, doing good by consuming their [very] being and communicating it to the land and its plants. Father Hernando de Villafañe consumed his life, health, strength, and talents cultivating the plants and fields that God had entrusted to him. Therefore, he would enjoy their fruit and compensation for his work. We have good reason to believe that he has attained abundant glory and his own eternal bliss, along with those whom he helped to enter heaven.

---

103. "Now to an old man, rest, now a well-earned crown was owed, and although certainly still a soldier in Christ, you again are raising up for yourself new wars, calling forth your adversary, and because of powerful things, Jesus the elder takes it to himself." Bernard of Clairvaux (1090–1153) was a respected monk who, as in this quote, emphasized the divine presence in human affairs. Bernard authored more than five hundred extant letters and numerous sermons and texts on humility and pride, grace and free will, and related subjects of theological import (Casey 1988).

104. "Clouds expend themselves completely, and they expend [themselves] above, and so they are consumed, and perish." Luis de Pineda was a respected Jesuit theologian who published commentaries on Scripture (Martin 1993:81–82), including Job 37:11–13.

BOOK VI

Of the Sinaloa Missions
The Last Nations in the Province to Receive
Our Holy Faith

CHAPTER I The lands and settlements of the nations and pueblos recorded in this book

I have previously written of the most extraordinary benefits of divine clemency in the Province of Sinaloa. Since the preaching of the Holy Gospel [358] was begun there, it has unceasingly continued its course throughout all the nations that were and are being discovered, without a backward step for a period of sixty years. Thus, in every nation six thousand or eight thousand souls have been baptized, and in some as many as ten thousand. According to the baptismal books and reports that missionary priests send to their superiors, three hundred thousand souls, both infants and adults, have already been baptized.[1]

Although the nations that I will discuss in this book are the ones that have most recently received the Holy Gospel, they are not the last ones in this province. They are bordered by other gentile nations whom God will gather into the flock of His Church. Those whose conversion will be recorded here inhabit the northernmost part [of the Province of Sinaloa]. Their settlements are between the flanks of the mountain ranges, along the banks of four streams, which are not powerful rivers. The streams are located at thirty-two and thirty-three degrees north latitude, some running toward the east

and others toward the west. Here the heat that we have written about is more moderate than in other areas of this province. These nations are called the Upper and Lower Nébome. The pueblos of the Upper Nébome are Movas, Onavas, and Nure,[2] whereas the pueblos of the Lower Nébome are Comoripa, Tecoripa, and Zuaque. The [people of the] latter pueblo are different from the Zuaque nation discussed in Book III, which has the same name and is eighty leagues away. Beyond the Nébome are the Aivino, the Sisibotari, the Batuco, the Ures, and finally, the Sonora nation;[3] the last is 130 leagues from the Villa de San Felipe and 140 leagues from the southern border of the province.

These nations have been reduced to about twenty pueblos and are divided among four districts, which are cared for by four or five missionaries. There are 3,500 heads-of-household or families, speaking four major languages that are different from all the other languages in Sinaloa.[4] This difficulty is being overcome by these

---

1. Note that this figure was compiled around 1637, as the following year it was used (along with other data) by Pérez de Ribas in a report submitted to the crown (AHH 1638; Hackett 1923–1937; Reff 1991b:186).

2. As Pérez de Ribas later points out the Nure were not in fact Nébome or Pima speakers, rather they were Cáhita speakers.

3. The Aivino, Sisibotari, Batuco, and Sonora spoke related languages or dialects (Teguima and Eudeve) and formed the southern and western portions of a larger culture known collectively as the Opata. The Ures were Pima speakers, like the Nébome (Johnson 1950; Pennington 1979; Reff 1991b).

4. Again, this household figure is based on Jesuit reports from around 1637. The four languages included Cáhita (Nure), Pima (Né-

most zealous priests, who become like little children for Christ's glory so that they can proclaim His name in those languages. The great harvest that divine kindness is revealing to the sons of the Company in this part of the New World has to be declared here. Although this book focuses on the last nations to be reduced to Christianity, I will not omit others that lie beyond them. They have been brought within sight of those whom God will choose to carry forward this glorious conquest, when these gentiles are ripe for hearing the good news of the Holy Gospel. [Specifically] the Nacámeri and the Nacosura border the Ures [on the north]. The latter are followed by the Hímeri,[5] a most ferocious and barbarous nation that has refused to have any dealings or friendship with its neighbors and is greatly feared by them. It is very numerous and extends as far as is known along the banks of a river as powerful as the Yaqui,[6] which flows toward the west and into the sea. It is forty leagues from some plains, whence there are rumors of another populous nation called the Seri. This nation is extremely wild, without pueblos, houses, or even cultivated fields. They have no rivers or streams, and drink from some small pools and puddles of water. They sustain themselves on game, although at the time of the maize harvest they come with deer hides and salt, which they gather from the sea, [359] to barter with other nations. The members of this nation who live closest to the sea also sustain themselves on fish. It is said that there is an island in the sea [Tiburón Island] inhabited by other members of this same nation, whose language is considered to be extremely difficult.

To the north [of the Nébome] is the Batuco nation, which borders many allied gentile nations: the Cumupa, the Guasave, and the Babispe. Still farther to the east, on the slopes [of the mountains], are the Suma. Beyond them in the same direction the land extends as far as Nuevo México, where priests from the Holy Order of Saint Francis have been for many years.[7] To

the east beyond the Sisibotari are other gentile mountain peoples, who live among the peaks [of the Sierra Madre Occidental].[8] Finally, other barbarous people are to be found along the borders of the Sonora nation.[9]

These are the various nations that God has placed along the [mission] frontier of the sons of the Company [of Jesus]. These nations have the same qualities as those to whom God sent swift angels, preaching through the mouth of the Prophet Isaiah: *Ite angeli veloces ad gentem convulsam, & dilaceratam ad populum terribilem.*[10] Such qualities and ferocity are [inherent] to these nations, and accordingly God proclaimed He would send diligent laborers as swift as winged angels. God wanted these laborers to preach the divine word of the Gospel of Christ, just as the holy King David had prophesied that his dominion and empire would extend *a mari usque ad mare, & a flumine usque ad terminos Orbis terrarum.*[11] As the great Augustine wrote,[12] this had not yet been fulfilled at the time of the reign of Solomon, although the psalm bears his name. It was reserved instead for the coming of Christ's kingdom. His eternal Father promised to place at His feet all the peoples of the world. This is fulfilled according to God's divine providence, which out of goodness has used the sons of the Company to extend this divine empire to all the nations that have been discussed. God has provided evidence that they will receive His favor and protection, in order to reduce the remaining nations that are so close at hand and to subject the others that I have mentioned in this chapter to Christ's gentle yoke. In the following chapters I will write about the nations that are already converted, relating what is specific to each. It should be understood that in other respects these nations conform in general terms with what has been written about others and their gentile customs. Recalling what has been previously set down, I wish to be precise in what I write. Those whom I call nations should not be understood to

---

bome), Eudeve (Aivino, Batuco), and Teguima or Opata proper (Sisibotari, Sonora, Babispe, Cumupa).

5. The Ures, Nacámeri, and Hímeri all spoke the same language as the Nébome (Pima) and have been referred to by anthropologists as the Pima Alto or Upper Pima (see Pennington 1980).

6. Pérez de Ribas is referring here to the Colorado River and its tributaries, the Gila and Salt Rivers.

7. Franciscan missionaries, beginning with Fray Marcos de Niza (1539), were key figures in the exploration of New Mexico (Ahern 1995a, b; Reff 1991a). The friars were an important part of Oñate's colonization of New Mexico in 1598 and subsequently established missions throughout the region (Kessell 1979; Reff 1994).

8. These mountain people were the Jova, who apparently were related to the Tarahumara.

9. Apparently the Jocome and perhaps the Apache, who at this time (ca. 1640) were expanding southward into southern Arizona and northeastern Sonora.

10. *Margin Note*: Isai. 18. Isaiah 18:2: "Ay, speed on your errand, but to a people far away, sundered from you by leagues of travel, dreaded people at the end of the earth" (Knox 1956:642).

11. *Margin Note*: Psal. 71. Psalm 71:8: "From sea to sea, from the great river to the ends of the earth" (Knox 1956:506).

12. *Margin Note*: lib. 18 de civit. c. 8. The referent here is Augustine's *City of God*, although Pérez de Ribas is in error; the correct citation is Book 17, Chapter 8 (Dods 1948:2:189).

be as populous as the different nations of our Europe. Although there are more of these barbarous nations, they have fewer people, and at the same time have many more languages. They do not have commerce with one another, but rather only continual warfare over division of lands and areas that each nation claims as its own.

CHAPTER II The Nébome's lands, rancherías, and particular customs

I wrote about the Nébome nation at the very beginning of this history, in Book I, where I discussed the first exploration of the Province of Sinaloa. There I said that a large group of these Indians traveled with Cabeza de Vaca [360] and his companions, who had come from La Florida. These Nébome settled along the Río Sinaloa near the Villa de San Felipe. I noted in Book II that they were joined years later by another group of about three hundred from this nation.[13] They were encouraged [to come south] by the good news that they had received from their relatives regarding how well they were doing as Christians. Thus, they journeyed some eighty leagues from their land to Bamoa, where upon arrival they requested Baptism. Both of these groups came from the same nation as the one I will write about here. And so it was that a long time ago divine mercy arranged to finally convert all of this nation to our Holy Faith. Indians from this nation had traversed the lands of other gentiles on several occasions to request that priests come and settle in their lands and make them Christians.[14] However, this could not be accomplished until the nations in between were secure and reduced to Christianity. Before I describe how Christianity was introduced to this nation I will record the details of their heathenism.

The Nébome lived along the banks of good flowing streams.[15] Their houses were better and more permanent than those of other nations because they had walls made from large mud adobes and were covered with flat earthen roofs.[16] Some of these were built much larger, specifically for the purpose of gathering the people of the pueblo inside during an enemy attack. These houses had small windows like those in a fort, which allowed them to make use of their bows and arrows.[17] Almost all the people were farmers and recognized each other's lands. They sowed the seeds that we have said to be common among the Indians. In some places with a good lay of land they had irrigated fields, using ditches to bring the water from their arroyo. In addition to this, they planted next to their houses a vineyard of sorts with a plant that the Spaniards call *lechuguilla*, because it is similar to leaf lettuce in shape but its leaves are much firmer.[18] It takes one or two years for it to grow and mature. Once it is ripe they cut it and roast the root with a few of the leaves, which serves them as food. It is flavorful and sweet and they grind it up to make a type of preserve. When one of the roots is cut new shoots will sprout from it. Therefore, once this vineyard of sorts is planted it lasts them for many years. The Nébome also hunted the game that abounds in their montes, especially deer. They are very skillful in shooting these, as well as birds of the air, which are plentiful.

In their dress they are the best attired of all the nations in Sinaloa. This was due to the fact that they had a large number of deer hides, which they knew how to

---

13. This group came to the villa in 1615; 174 Nébome came south the following year, as did another group, who were asked to return to their lands because there was no room for them at Bamoa.

14. The earliest of these visits was in 1610.

15. Pérez de Ribas uses the word *arroyo* here, although the Río Tecoripa and Río Chico were permanent or semipermanent streams; most arroyos, by definition, are ephemeral rather than permanent.

16. "Large adobes" is an apparent reference to adobe that was "poured" in courses or layers, rather than to actual bricks, which was the preferred method introduced by Spaniards.

17. As Dobyns (1988) has suggested, these structures appear to be similar to the "great houses" of the Classic Hohokam/Upper Pima.

18. Pennington (1980:186) has identified this "little lettuce" as *Agave bovicornuta* (see also Dobyns 1988). David Yetman (personal communication) has suggested *Agave murphyi* or possibly *Agave angustifolia*.

tan to make very good, durable buckskin. These serve the women as a covering, in the manner of a skirt. They are so long that they drag on the ground, and among these women this was considered to be very fashionable. The young women also decorated these buckskins with red ocher. They covered their upper torsos with mantas woven from cotton or fibers from another plant such as agave. Although most men wore no clothing, some covered themselves with these mantas. But these were worn so that they could easily be removed whenever they wanted, and they did so without thinking because they were so accustomed to it.

Just as these women's modesty in their dress exceeded that of other nations, so did the modesty of their countenance. I can confirm this by relating what happened one time when I was traveling with the captain and his garrison on a visit to the Yaqui. At the Nébome's request he had gone to see [361] some of their pueblos because, although they were gentiles, they were allies and confederates. A large number of people of all ages came out to greet us. We reciprocated this act of friendship by placing our hands on their heads. When the women approached, especially the young ones, I saw that they bowed their heads so low that their hair hung in their faces so that they would not be seen. Thus, their gentile vices were not as savage as in other nations. Their nature is gentler and not as harsh or fierce as that of other nations, nor are they as bellicose. Nevertheless, there was still a great deal to combat in people reared in the wilderness of heathenism, and a great deal to endure in cultivating and sowing the good seed in such wild fields, as will later be seen.

There were about three thousand Nébome souls whom God wished to gather into the flock of His Church.[19] He had spilled His divine blood for each one of these souls and had irrigated them with that blood through the Divine Sacraments. For this reason, this young vine has unceasingly produced blessed fruit. Nevertheless, these fruits were also at the cost of the blood of one of His ministers, as will later be seen.

CHAPTER III Nébome efforts to obtain religious instruction

The Nébome nation saw that missions had already been established among the Mayo and the Yaqui, who had priests to teach and baptize them. They also saw that they would be the next nation to receive the Christian Faith, which they had so desired, because the first Nébome pueblos are only fourteen leagues from the Yaqui. They renewed their efforts with the captain and priests to have their wishes fulfilled. One principal Indian, who was one of the long-time Christians of this nation, greatly implored them. Some of them came to see me when I was instructing the Yaqui nation, saying that they wanted to begin building a church and house for the time when a priest would come to give them religious instruction. In anticipation of this they sought construction workers so that the priests could fulfill their promises when the time came. Even though there was no priest free at that time who could effectively take charge of this enterprise, it was decided that the priest who was in charge of the Nébome pueblo [Bamoa] near the Villa de San Felipe should go and baptize the infants (who run a great risk of dying without Baptism) and those who were sick.[20] He was to take possession of and begin the establishment of this Christian community, which was work of great service to God and the welfare of these souls, and which would satisfy the Nébome.

This enterprise was undertaken by Father Diego de Guzmán, a great, veteran missionary who spent many

19. This is an early (ca. 1625) enumeration of the Indians who were baptized in the Nébome Alto district (Onavas, Movas, and Nure) (see Reff 1991b:218–20).

20. This entrada by Father Diego de Guzmán occurred in June 1619, at a time when the Yaqui, Nébome, and other native peoples in southern Sonora were experiencing yet another epidemic. During his brief visit (several months) Guzmán baptized 1,516 adults and 5,096 infants (Alegre 1956–1960:2:321).

years in the missions of Sinaloa and was a [Father] Visitor.[21] He baptized some five hundred children, aided the sick, and left the Nébome consoled, even though their wishes were not fulfilled until they had a permanent minister to attend to their religious instruction. At that time some priests from our Company came to Sinaloa from Mexico City. From time to time superiors send us priests to aid their brothers, and the good fortune of the new enterprise among the Nébome fell to the very religious Father Diego de Bandersipe, of Flemish nationality.[22] His glorious efforts to permanently found this Christian community and aid others will be recorded here.

He set out from the Villa de San Felipe in fulfillment of [holy] obedience and arrived in Nébome lands. These people had reduced their rancherías [362] to something like pueblos,[23] and had erected xacales to be used as churches and lodging for the priest. Father Bandersipe was welcomed with the same demonstrations of joy and festivity that have been described for other nations. We therefore make no mention of them here so as not to repeat things. The infants who were not baptized during the first visit were gathered along with the newborns. They were all baptized to the great joy of this nation. The priest took great concern in learning their language, and did so quickly. He began to fervently instruct the older people in order to prepare them for Holy Baptism. Many of these people had communicated with Christian relatives from the pueblo near the Villa de San Felipe. Therefore, Christian teachings and customs were more easily introduced, and the priest was able to baptize many of them, who were good about coming to church, Mass, and religious instruction.

The Christian doctrine took a great hold of these people. When some who were already Christian were on their way to another district, one of them found a gentile woman from an enemy nation alongside the road. She was so sick that she was about to die. The man who found her—who at one time would have cut her head off and taken the scalp to dance with (which is how they used to celebrate)—instead acted very much like a Christian and as one who had understood Christ's supreme doctrine to love one's enemies. He gathered this stray lamb and the Supreme Shepherd thereby made her a part of His fold. This Indian carried her to a ramada where the priest was resting. The priest ordered some refreshment be brought to the poor woman, and as she regained consciousness she focused on the priest. He asked her whether she wanted to be baptized like the Christians, and she answered that she did. He catechized her as quickly as time and urgency allowed. He baptized her and gave her the sweetest name of Mary. When the Virgin's Most Holy Son saw her marked with His Mother's name, it seemed He wanted to take her to heaven, for she died shortly thereafter. We can understand that He who arranged for that Baptism under such unique circumstances and softened the heart of that Nébome Indian, who carried a former enemy on his shoulders (as if he were a shepherd), arranged all this for the salvation of that soul.

The reader can certainly understand that there are innumerable such cases that take place in these missions. This one was recorded to illustrate how well the doctrine was taught to the Nébome by their Father Minister Diego de Bandersipe. Nevertheless, both he and his faithful were persecuted, just as all the Church's faithful have been persecuted since its earliest days.

21. Guzmán was visitor in 1628.

22. Bandersipe was one of a handful of priests who came to Sinaloa in 1619. That winter (1619–20) he went to work among the Nébome Alto.

23. Prior to Bandersipe's entrada Father Diego de Guzmán reported that the Nébome, with whom he apparently lumped the Aivino of the Mátape Valley and the Opata of the Sahuaripa Valley (Sisibotari Opata), lived in ninety *rancherías grandes o pueblos* (AGN 1615).

CHAPTER IV Some Nébome Indians shoot Father Diego de Bandersipe with an arrow

The devil became upset at seeing himself stripped of the Nébome nation. Thus, he raised his defenses and began looking for an opportunity to fire his artillery against this and other new Christian communities within the Province of Sinaloa. He devised the plan that I will describe here. Around that time [1626] the remarkable Captain Hurdaide, whom I have mentioned so many times in this history, passed away in the Villa de San Felipe. At the same time Our Lord (who has always shown His favor toward Christianity in Sinaloa) arranged for his successor, Don Pedro Perea—who was a brave and daring soldier—to reach the villa. The Indian governors and principales of the entire province had been sent word [363] of the captain's death and of the arrival of his replacement, and they all came to see and acknowledge him. This included the Nébome principales, who were accompanied by some other Indians from their nation who had heard that there were other Indians farther inland who, with Captain Hurdaide's death, were planning a general uprising among the most distant nations in Sinaloa. As a sign of this intention they had sent the customary reeds filled with tobacco. However, some of these nations remained loyal and refused to accept the tobacco.

When the captain, Don Pedro, heard these rumors he conducted an investigation of the matter as he deemed necessary. He detained the Nébome for some time to verify the facts, suspecting that the Nébome themselves were participating in the conspiracy. He arrested a few of them and subsequently received a letter from their priest, who wrote that he saw no trace of an uprising among his Nébome. Because he could find no evidence of their guilt, he asked the captain to return them to their lands, for [the captain] had been holding them for a month at the villa, which upset their relatives. In the investigation of this case it seems that the captain found one Indian to be particularly guilty. He was not a native of the Nébome of whom we are speaking, but rather of another neighboring nation. After finding him guilty the captain ordered the Indian to be hanged.

One day during all this coming and going, two old men came to the priest and said to him, "Look, Father, if those from our nation who went to the villa do not come back in five days, these people have decided to kill you." The priest did not pay much attention to what the two old men said because he saw that the people were quiet in the upper Nébome pueblos where he was. But the Indians who were the relatives of the Indian who was sentenced to hang did not wait the full five days. They went to a pueblo while the priest was away, and because they could not take him prisoner as they had planned, they set fire to his house. Then they tried to set fire to the church, but faithful Indians prevented them from doing so.

The diabolical spirit that angered them was not quieted, and after three days they took up their bows and poisoned arrows and went to the priest's house. It was morning, and he was saying his prayers and was not on guard. They shot two arrows at him; the one that missed was shot with such fury and force that it went almost a palm's depth into a wall. The other arrow struck the priest in the chest, although at an angle. One of the boys from the church arrived at the moment the Indian was drawing his bow, and the boy took a stick that he found nearby and struck the bowstring. This deflected the arrow, but the point, which was made of flint and had been covered with that [poisonous] herb, struck the priest in the chest and his blood began to flow. The boy began to scream, "They're killing the priest!" Many people came [running] because of the screaming, including those who were Christians and loved their priest, and who were greatly upset by what had happened. Even though they were unable to remove the flint arrowhead, they sucked on his wound to extract the poison. These Indians place the arrowhead on the shaft so skillfully that even if the rest of the arrow is removed, the flint tip remains in the wound.

The priest feared he was going to die from the strong poison. He comforted those who gathered around him, saying that he would willingly die for Jesus Christ, of whom he preached for their salvation and the good of their souls. He wrote the same thing to the priest who was closest to his district. Using the following words, he bid him farewell and told him what had happened: "My Father, I willingly die for the love of God. Commend me to God." Like someone who was taking leave of his life, he charged the faithful Indians who were with him—his beloved children from the pueblo of Onavas, where these events took place—to persevere in the Faith and religious instruction [364] that he had given them, to remain steadfast and calm, and not to follow those who had evil intentions. In doing so they would remain free of guilt and would not be jeopardized by the restless disturbers of the peace.

God willed that this, His faithful servant—whom He wished to protect for the good of the many souls he would help to go to heaven (as he does today)—should soon recover somewhat. Nevertheless, he still expected to die, so he set out to comfort himself and confess to his nearest companion, who was ten leagues away. This was Father Francisco Oliñano, who at that time was escorted by six soldiers. The captain had sent this escort when he heard that this was the area where the rumors of an uprising had originated. This was true, as will be seen when the conversion of the district of the Lower Nébome is recorded. The wounded and fatigued priest set out with an escort of many faithful Indians. He reached Father Oliñano's pueblo and was relieved to see him. The soldiers began to treat him, but they had little knowledge of how to treat such a poisonous herb,[24] which caused such torment and was so powerful that at times it caused him to lose consciousness.

The soldiers had given him up for dead, but God willed that after a month and a half in Father Oliñano's pueblo he regained sufficient health to walk a distance of almost one hundred leagues to our college in the Villa de San Felipe. He spent many days there recuperating, because the flint tip still had not come out. God willed that His evangelical minister and confessor should suffer for quite a few years from the torment of the wound and its healing. This wound in and of itself would have been enough to take his life if God's majesty had not preserved him, even though during this time the wound constantly emitted a foul-smelling pus.

Once this brave soldier of Christ's militia felt somewhat improved, he did not flee from battle nor did he request or desire to leave Sinaloa and his missions. It seemed to the father superior[25] that our good Father Banderspe had engendered in Christ many Indians and children in his district who dearly loved him. Nevertheless, he feared that the priest might again be attacked by the relatives and allies of those who had tried earlier to kill him and who had burned the church and disturbed the nation; these Indians still needed to be brought to justice by the captain. Thus, the superior decided to remove him from this danger and employ his holy zeal in aiding the Christian community on the Río Yaqui. This priest—unwavering in his holy fervor—has helped the Yaqui and continues to labor today in the religious instruction of a very populous district in their nation. He has also governed the missions of the interior. I could say many things concerning his virtues and apostolic fervor were I not prevented from doing so by the dictum of the Holy Spirit, which is well known.

The [attempt to] kill the priest and the burning of the church had their origins in a general uprising that was planned by the Lower Nébome, whom Father Oliñano was instructing. Therefore, an account of the punishment that the captain decided on for the aggressors (according to his orders from the king) will be discussed later, when the expedition he and his garrison undertook for this purpose is amply recorded. We will now continue with the conversion and Christianity of the Upper Nébome, to whom Father Diego de Banderspe had begun to give religious instruction. [365]

24. Apparently the famed *yerba de flecha*—made from species of Euphorbiaceae (*Euphorbia biloculare, Sebastiania appendiculatum*), small trees that grow at higher elevations on the slopes of the sierras. The trees produce a sticky substance or *goma* that was used for arrow points as well as fish stupefaction (Nentvig 1980:50; Pennington 1980:218).

25. Father Juan Varela, who was superior of the Rectorado de San Ignacio.

CHAPTER V The progress of Christianity among the Upper Nébome following the arrival of another priest who continued their religious instruction

As was previously explained, it did not seem wise for Father Diego de Bandersipe to remain in the mission where he had laid a good foundation for Christianity and had baptized a great number of infants and adults. They persevered in their fidelity and asked for another minister, because the first one—to their deep regret—was not coming back. Father Blas de Paredes was appointed to replace Father Bandersipe. He had recently come to Sinaloa from Mexico City to work as a missionary. This was a holy ministry that he held in high regard. He had come from Spain to the Indies with the desire to devote his entire life to such employment. He was a religious of great spiritual fervor, and he enthusiastically accepted his appointment to this mission. Because he was not frightened by the enterprise that had so wounded and injured his brother, he set out for the pueblos of the Upper Nébome without a military escort. To everyone's delight he was joyously welcomed by these faithful Indians, who had erected peace arches of branches along the road and knelt with Crosses in their hands. There were nevertheless quite a few Indians from the restless faction that wanted to kill all ministers of the Gospel. Because the faithful Nébome showed great care in guarding their priest and church, the priest wrote the captain, telling him that he did not need an escort of soldiers from the garrison. Without a doubt he experienced divine [assistance], because he persevered by himself for six years, never failing in his ministerial duties. Because there was no other priest who was free to help him, he did the work of two, traveling difficult roads to the distant pueblos that were under his care. Then, most unexpectedly, Our Lord deigned to take him home when he was less than thirty years of age.[26] He had said Mass earlier on the day when Our Lord called him to his reward for such holy works. He died in the same pueblo and arena where he had worked; there was no time to go to our college in the villa to

be healed or aided by his missionary brothers. But we can well imagine that he was assisted by the Lord who guided him to this vineyard—the Lord he loved and for whom he had exiled himself from the colleges, renouncing the sweet company of his brothers.

God chose this loyal minister for the Nébome, who had persevered in their Faith. When he reached their district he promptly learned their two languages.[27] Then he began to sow God's divine word in the good soil that had already been watered with the blood of a loyal confessor of Christ. He baptized the remaining people, and they all began to progress and grow in their Faith and devotion, attending punctually all the Christian exercises. Because specific cases reflect better than words the stability that our holy religion develops in these people—even if they [are still only] children in the Faith—several will be recounted here. [Of course] it would be impossible to relate them all.

One time the priest had preached to them about the most hidden, [366] secret mystery of our Holy Faith, the sacrosanct sacrifice of the Mass and the Sacrament of the Altar. After he spoke the principal Indians of the pueblo came to ask him if he could take his time when raising the Most Holy Sacrament during Mass so that God Our Lord, who was present therein, could be adored for a longer period of time. One of the Indians added, "Maybe our priest does not want us to view the Host for very long because he thinks that we do not believe, like the Spaniards do, that God is present there. But just like them, we do believe and adore Him." Long-time Christians who hurry the priest to say a short and even hasty Mass should be shamed by the faith of these new Christians, who yesterday were barbarians—lacking the light of the Holy Faith and quite unlike those who have been nursed on it.

The case that follows is no less edifying proof of their faith. A young Indian became gravely ill, so the priest went to visit him and hear his confession. Judging that

---

26. Paredes died in 1636 or 1637 (Zambrano 1961–1977:3:88).

27. Pima and Cáhita; the latter was spoken by the people of Nure.

he was in grave danger, the priest administered the holy oils. His parents and relatives cried over this, because among these and other nations there reigned the fear that administering the Sacrament of Extreme Unction is the same thing as casting someone into the grave. The sick person, noticing that his parents were upset, got up as best he could and said, "Why are you crying? Haven't you seen that the priest has given me the sacraments in the name of God? I depart very consoled and happy. I trust in the Lord, who created me, and in Jesus Christ, who redeemed me, that my soul will go to heaven. Take me to the church, which is God's house, because I want to die there and give my soul to Him who created it." He died shortly thereafter, leaving many assurances of his salvation and proof of what the Redeemer of the World preached when He assured us that His Father was powerful enough to resurrect from stones the sons of Abraham, father of believers.[28] Miracles such as these are seen each day among these people.

CHAPTER VI The conversion of the Upper Nébome is completed; the state of their Christianity

Here I will briefly recount what was accomplished by the word of the Divine Gospel in the three Upper Nébome pueblos. I will not dally on topics that are similar to those I have already related concerning other conversions. Divine mercy wrought in this nation everything positive and fortunate that has been said about other nations in this history. The first fruits of the Gospel, which were harvested by the handful from among these people, were the great numbers of children and adults who, once baptized, went to heaven with baptismal grace.[29] The abuses, idolatry, superstition, and sorcery that existed to a greater or lesser degree among all these peoples were destroyed. Drunkenness and the custom of having many wives, which were their delights, were uprooted and nearly forgotten. Their wars and raids upon their enemies, during which they cut off their heads, [and] their forays into the montes or fields for this same purpose, just as one goes out to hunt deer, so that they could use their enemies' heads to celebrate their barbarous dances and inhuman triumphs—all these things came to an end in this nation. Where once there were wild fields full of weeds that bore the fruit of sin and abomination, there continue to be very abundant harvests from the seed of the divine word that was sown in this evangelical field.

As proof of what has been said concerning this nation's similarities [with the others recorded in this history], I will say that one of the priests working in these holy missions [367] wrote that of eighty children who had been baptized in several different rancherías, sixty had died with baptismal grace. Among another sizable number baptized by a different priest more than a third had died with the same [baptismal] grace.[30] These are all early fruits that the Lord savors. Where once there were gentile rites and superstitions introduced by Satan, one now sees only the observance of holy Christian laws and customs. These include daily attendance at catechism by young and old alike, who also hear Mass and the sermon every Sunday and on feast days. They do so with such frequency and punctuality that it is rare for one of these natives to miss this

---

28. In Romans 4:21 Paul recalls Abraham's faith that God will give him and his wife, Sarah, a child, despite their advanced ages.

29. Pérez de Ribas is alluding here to thousands of Pima Bajo who died during the epidemics of 1619–20 and 1623–25; with respect to the latter Father Juan Lorencio noted that more than 8,600 Indians died with the sacraments in Sinaloa and Sonora. Countless others perished in the monte without the sacraments (AGN 1625:137; Reff 1991b:160–68).

30. Pérez de Ribas appears to err here in suggesting that these figures pertain to the Nébome. The anua of 1626 (AGN 1626:148–49) quotes a letter written by Julio Pascual, which gives the same infant mortality rates (sixty out of eighty; more than a third) for the Chínipa not the Nébome.

holy service. Many of them travel several leagues from where they live to hear Mass, even on weekdays. Where once there were drunken revels and the licentious custom of having many wives—whom they used to cast aside whenever they wished—one now finds only the Christian rite of marriage and the observance of chastity that those divine laws command. This is confirmed by what a priest who visited this nation wrote, saying that the devil had been unable to force many young men and the young women they pursued to commit this sin on those occasions sought by that unclean spirit. They remembered (the priest says) what they had heard in church, that they should not stain their bodies and souls with such vices. This is the degree to which the holy fear of God has become rooted in their souls.

I will now relate two other holy customs that demonstrate the improvement in the Nébome's Faith. One is their devotion to the Holy Rosary of Our Lady the Virgin. All of them pray the Rosary very punctually, either at church or in their homes. The other custom is the great grief they express if a child happens to die without Baptism. They say that it is very painful to see their children die as they once did when they were gentiles. Where once there were barbarous celebrations with the decapitated heads of enemy men, women, and even children, there is now only peace, friendship, and brotherhood with other Christian nations. They invite and persuade their gentile neighbors to become Christians, hear the word of God, and ask for religious to come to their lands and baptize them so they can enjoy the peace that exists among others. Their gentile celebrations have been replaced by Christian ones, and there is especially great celebration and rejoicing on the feast days of the patron saints of their pueblos and churches. They invite not only other Christians to these celebrations, but also their gentile neighbors, so that they can become fond of our holy religion. It can clearly be seen that these are not merely blossoms, but rather very ripe and flavorful fruits for God, His angels, and mankind.

With things in such a good state the time finally arrived to build beautiful permanent churches, which physically represent the Majesty of God, who is worshiped therein. They call their churches 'God's houses', which they are. It was not difficult to convince these Nébome to build a permanent church, first of all because they had received our Holy Faith with great enthusiasm, and second because of the example of the many other churches in the province. They built churches, which was unfamiliar labor, because it made

them happy for the reasons I have mentioned. The churches were dedicated with great celebrations. The priests decorated them with as much ornamentation as possible, sparing no expense on tools and craftsmen, which [expense] was great in a place so distant from commerce. Today, they enjoy their churches, adoring God, their Redeemer, like true and loyal Christians.

I have left for now the holiest sovereign mystery and practice of our Christian religion, [368] which is Holy Communion. To institute and celebrate this sacrament, Christ Our Lord sent His two greatest Apostles [Peter and John] to find a place of majesty and adornment: *Coenaculum magnum stratum*.[31] There, the Lord of Majesty washed their feet so that they could receive Communion. To make the teaching and practice of such a divine sacrament more familiar, the priests began to introduce it to select persons. This was so successful that they considered it a great favor to be chosen to receive Holy Communion. And thus they prepared diligently for confession; some of them [even] made general confessions. Then with great appreciation they came to receive that celestial bread.

A major improvement in the lives and customs of those who had begun to take Communion was clearly seen. Just to see their names written on the list of the communicants is enough to make them very attentive to the order and harmony of their souls. Now when the devil launches an attack on these people through some lost soul, their answer is, "Would I, a person who takes Communion, commit such a sin?" This will be seen clearly in the penance of a person who failed and was disobedient. He was a young man who had been chosen to come to the sacred table. Before the time came for him to take Communion others accused him of not setting a good example in the matter of chastity. Because he made no effort to correct his [bad] example, he was told that he would not be allowed to partake of Holy Communion until he gave public satisfaction for this scandal. This threat made such an impression on this young man that one day when the entire pueblo was assembled in church, he came and publicly scourged himself, showing great remorse for his sin and begging forgiveness for the scandal he had caused. All of the events mentioned [here] are very clear demonstrations of how well established the profession of Christian life had become in these pueblos. Today these missions per-

---

31. *Margin Note*: Lucas c. 22. Luke 22:12: "And he will shew you a large upper room, furnished; it is there that you are to make ready" (Knox 1956:1726).

severe in their Christianity, continually improving and growing.

There is a type of plant in the Indies called the banana tree, which is very well known among all those who come here. This tree bears fruit year-round, and when the fruit ripens on a single branch, it ripens all at once, with a bunch of thirty, forty, and [sometimes even] more bananas. This bunch is then removed, along with the branch that bloomed and bore it, leaving behind many other branches growing out of the same tree trunk. Some of these branches are larger and others are smaller; they mature successively and continually bear fruit. In this way this fruit is enjoyed throughout the year. The same thing happens with respect to the spirituality of these missions and nations. When one is converted and joins the Church, it bears the ripened fruits of the Christian religion. God cuts some branches from the converted nation and takes the bunches of fruit to heaven. Then another trunk starts to grow, and once it has matured another nearby nation begins to sprout so that it [too] can bear new fruit. We will see this in the following chapter, where we discuss the Nure. The same thing happens in each of these nations: once the first converts have ripened they bear the fruit of life—

namely the children who are baptized and grow in Christian fervor from that day forward. Then new buds sprout, bearing the most delicate fruits, for they are born in a land cultivated and watered by the rain and irrigation of continual religious instruction, in which the apostolic men employed here continually labor.

So as not to limit this discussion only to the spiritual [dimension] of our Upper Nébome, [it should also be mentioned that] it was easier to settle temporal and political matters in their pueblos than in other nations. Even in their heathenism (as was [369] stated at the outset), the Nébome surpassed other nations in their dress, the chastity of their women, their houses, their irrigated fields, etc. All this was improved when they were reduced to larger pueblos with governors and alcaldes to govern them. Seminaries were also founded for the boys, as were choirs, the members of which became skilled at singing and playing all [manner of] musical instruments. We will now leave these fortunate pueblos with joy and canticles of praise to their Creator, moving forward to discuss the conversion of their companions and neighbors, the Nure, whose pueblo pertains to this mission and district.

CHAPTER VII The Nure's location, settlements, and state; how they were reduced to our Holy Faith

The settlements of the Nure, who are of a different nation and language than the nearby Upper Nébome, are found farther within the sierra, along the banks of an arroyo[32] whose waters they take advantage of [for farming]. The divine goodness of the light of the Gospel reached the Nure through the example of the nearby Christian Nébome. The fragrant aroma of the Nébome's pacific and joyful Christian life attracted their neighbors to friendship and prompted them to request a priest to make them Christians. The Nébome advised the Nure that this could be achieved more easily if they reduced themselves to a principal place (which they did), abandoning their rancherías, which were dispersed among the mountain peaks. The Nure established a pueblo of more than two hundred male heads-of-household; this figure does not include others who are said to be dispersed farther within the sierra. When the superiors saw the good disposition of this small flock they ordered the priest[33] who cared for the Nébome to carry out the same duties

---

32. This arroyo is the Río Chico. Very little is known about the Nure, although they apparently were Cáhita speakers.

33. Diego de Bandersipe, who apparently began working among the Nure in 1621.

among the Nure. This consoled the Nure greatly. The priest went to this pueblo, where he was received quite well. He started his mission, performing the same tasks as he did with the Nébome, despite the fact that the Nure were fiercer and more hostile. But with God's favor the fruits were of a very similar quality as those [harvested] in the Nébome Christianity. Because I have just related what these were, I will not repeat them here for the Nure. There were nevertheless difficulties that had to be overcome, as is the case in many enterprises. I am not referring to the difficult and extremely steep routes that the religious minister was obliged to travel frequently in order to visit his pueblo. [Rather, I refer to] other disturbances by the devil, who tried to prevent the divine word from bearing fruit when it was first sown. The truth, however, is that it is a waste of time for this enemy to rise up against God, as will be seen in the following case.

When the Nure were being reduced to a pueblo, one of their caciques stayed in his ranchería, stubborn and obstinate. The others' example was not reason enough for him to move or [even] be baptized. But one of his sons, a young man, knew that his father had been deceived, so he left his father behind in the sierra with others of the same mind and came to [settle in] the pueblo. He was fond of the Christian catechism, which he steadfastly attended. He asked to be baptized, and to everyone's edification he received Holy Baptism. He was married according to Christian law and lived by this law with such great joy that his good example rubbed off on the others. He endeavored to bring them to Holy Baptism so that they [too] might enjoy the benefits that he had received. [However,] his father persevered in his obstinacy and hardness, which caused his good son great sorrow. [370] He was concerned for his father's salvation, and on several occasions he visited him, pleading with him to settle in the mission and change his life. He persevered in his efforts until he succeeded, for God willed that this [cacique's] hard heart should be softened by his son's loving reasoning. In this way he convinced his father to receive religious instruction and Baptism, which he did. God finally eliminated the bad example and impediment of this hardened old man, whom the devil attempted to use to block the progress of this Christianity.

Greater evil befell another old man, with whom

God employed the rigor of His divine justice. This happened during the rainy season, when [there is] more lightning than usual. This lightning fell upon those rancherías, along with great windstorms and hurricanes. The storms were so severe that they destroyed what [crops] had been sown, which were already drying up because of a lack of rain. On this occasion this old man, who was a sorcerer, called together some of his sorcerer friends. As a solution to their problems, they arranged the celebration of a famous drunken revel and barbarous dance to placate the storms. The author of these gentile abuses is just like the exercises he teaches them to perform. Although they fooled some Christians who were still tender in the Faith into agreeing to participate in this celebration, God undid the devil's tricks, preventing any [real] damage. While the old liar, their minister, was busy arranging matters, God suddenly took his life, leaving him no time to correct his error or be baptized. The diabolical means by which he had attempted to end the storms and lightning bolts being cast down from the sky were also unsuccessful, because the storms and lightning continued. Even the gentiles took note of this, and more so the Christians who had been tricked into attending the barbarous dance. Regretful and embarrassed, they learned their lesson well and were more resolute in the Holy Faith they had received. From then on they were more careful about attending church and Christian exercises. The gentiles were greatly disabused of their former errors and blindness and especially abstained from their former drunken revels. These cases of mercy or justice are all similar to others that I will omit. Although not outstanding, they [nevertheless] serve divine goodness, and it is seen in these missions that through these cases God calls these people to recognize Him.

All the Nure were finally baptized, and all the Christian customs and exercises that flourished among their neighbors, the Nébome, were established in their pueblo. They built their church, which was adorned just like the others. With this everything has been said that is particularly noteworthy about this new flock of Christ, which today perseveres very much as His own. We will [now] move on to the conversion of the Lower Nébome, among whom the Gospel emerged victorious, even though there were greater storms and unrest than in the previously discussed pueblos.

CHAPTER VIII The lands, rancherías, and pueblos of the Lower Nébome; the outcome of an uprising and war

The Indians who pertain to this part of the mission are called the Lower Nébome because many of them are related to the people in the upper pueblos [Onavas and Movas], which are the principal ones in this nation. The Upper Nébome live higher within the sierra than the Lower Nébome, of whom I am now writing. The latter are reduced to the pueblos of Comoripa, Tecoripa, Zuaque, and Aivino.[34] In [these pueblos] there are some three thousand to four thousand people. [371] Some of them are quite wild and have difficulty settling in one place. They live off game from the monte more than off the fruits of the fields that they cultivate. These are people who are very hard to reduce to civilized life, and therefore to Christian life. However, we have already presented evidence that there is hope that these souls will receive the divine mercy of Our Lord, who spilled His blood for them.

The Indians reduced to these pueblos were mostly farmers who made use of the water from their arroyos to irrigate their fields. Their houses were terraced and of adobe.[35] In all other respects they were similar to the other principal [pueblos] of the Upper Nébome, by whose example, and almost simultaneously, they requested priests to provide them with religious instruction.

The first to begin this mission was Father Martín Burgensio, a very fervent religious. His zeal and desire to see these souls reduced to God and placed on the road to salvation caused him to hasten the Baptism of a few people more than he should have, as was demonstrated by later events.[36] In the very beginning of this conver-

sion [1620] the Aivino and some of the other wild Indians became rebellious, for they were people who had not yet forgotten their barbarous custom of celebrating by taking the lives of those whom they considered their enemy. These barbarians killed an Indian who was a fiscal in the church and some other converted Nébome Christians with whom they had had some skirmishes in the past. Not content with this, they threatened to kill the priests who were instructing both the Upper and Lower Nébome, and they prevented them from attending to their ministries and communicating with each other. These barbarians withdrew to the monte, where they continued their rebellion, taking [control of] the roads in order to carry out their evil plan. There was one time when they even set fire to the house where the two priests were. But Our Lord saved them by means of the faithful Indians who were with them.

Captain Hurdaide, who was still living [at this time], heard about this, and in order to restrain these insolent Indians, he set out with his soldiers from the garrison at the Villa de San Felipe, drafting one thousand pacific Indians along the way.[37] He gathered provisions and proceeded to Aivino territory, which was almost one hundred leagues from the villa. He sent spies ahead to find out where the enemy had fortified themselves; they returned having discovered signs of an Aivino ambush, which they had prevented. When the Aivino discovered the captain's troop they sent word to their people that the captain was not accompanied by many men, and that they could lure them to a certain spot by employing one of their military strategies (which they know how to plan well). They lit bonfires, thinking that the captain would head in the direction of the smoke while they lay in ambush. They planned to attack at a place that was well protected by [a thorn] forest and

34. The first three settlements were inhabited by Nébome or Pima Bajo; Aivino was an Eudeve Opata settlement. In the winter of 1618–19 Captain Hurdaide (accompanied by Pérez de Ribas) visited the Nébome and Aivino and arranged a peace between them.

35. *Adobes y terrados*. Here terrados seems to mean 'terraced'; that is, the houses were multiple-room structures with roofs (and floors) at different levels.

36. Burgensio, who apparently was from the Netherlands and changed his name from de Bruges, began working among the Nébome Bajo in the winter of 1619–20. Within a year or so he was replaced by Francisco Oliñano, apparently because of incompetence. This is suggested by Pérez de Ribas' comment that Burgensio hastened the baptism of "a few people" and the implicit suggestion that Burgensio was respon-

sible for the Aivino Rebellion. Correspondence between Jesuit superiors in Nueva España and Rome suggest that the former tried, without success, to have Burgensio transferred to the Philippines or Japan (Zambrano 1961–1977:4:353–55).

37. This was in the spring of 1621. Beginning with Cortés' conquest of the Mexica, Spanish military action was carried out in large part by indigenous auxiliaries (see Ahern 1995c).

rock-strewn hills, which were common in their land. However, our spies sent word that a larger number of people had fortified themselves in their pueblo,[38] in houses with adobe walls. One of these houses served as a fortress; it was large and had small windows. During times of war the women and small children withdrew to this house where, because of the small windows, they were safe from enemy arrows.

When the captain and his soldiers attacked the fortified house the Indians inside came out fighting with great bravery. They were joined by the other Indians [who had lain in ambush] and totaled almost two thousand. They rained a shower of arrows upon our Christian troops, killing some of the allied Indians. The enemies' women also participated in the skirmish, furiously hurling stones as fast as if they were men. The captain and his soldiers closed in on them, [372] and after he had killed eleven of the enemy, the latter withdrew once again to their fortress. The captain and his soldiers attacked, trying to gain entry, but the Indians placed their small shields over the windows. The enemy bravely defended themselves, wounding two Spanish soldiers and several more Indian allies. Then the captain ordered flaming arrows to be fired through the windows into the [fortified] house. At that point quite a few of the enemy died from the flames and smoke.

The captain, who attempted to prevent Indian bloodshed whenever possible, saw them in these [dire] straits and ordered that a paper with his seal, which he frequently used, be sent through one of the little windows. He sent them a message saying that enough people had died, proposing peace, and offering to pardon them for their past crimes provided they surrendered. The enemy saw the difficult situation they were in and agreed to the [captain's] offer. As a sign of peace they sent out mantas, arrows, bows, and the feathers they use. Then the captain ordered the Indian allies to withdraw, for they were furious, attacking even the women and children.[39] The people from the pueblo and fortified house gathered together in the plaza, where they asked the captain not to allow the Indian allies to take their people prisoner and also to pardon them for their crimes. The captain ordered that the captives be

released. However, a large supply of beans and maize that they had taken into the fort-house did not escape the fire.

The excuse they gave for their rebellion and resistance was that their sorcerers and other rebels had promised them a great victory over the Spaniards. They now realized that they had been tricked and that the promised victory was a lie. Having been disabused of this, they wanted to be like the Nébome and have priests in their pueblos who would provide protection and religious instruction. They would thus enjoy the same peace as those nations that were [already] Christian.

The captain promised all this and remained for a short time among the Aivino to rest. During this time some neighboring nations came to see him. These nations were very attentive to what was happening. Moved by what they had heard, some other Indians came, saying that they had come to see the children of the sun. This is the name that they give the Spaniards, who are the only ones who have come to this province from the east, as has been previously stated.[40] They asked the captain for the paper that he normally gives as a sign of [his] friendship and protection so that other nations would not wage war on them. The captain gave them this paper, and in this way the people from these nations were prepared to receive the Holy Gospel and Baptism, as will be told later.

When this was finished the captain left this pueblo and proceeded with his people to Tecoripa and Comoripa, where the priest was ministering to the Lower Nébome, with whom the captain relocated some of the former rebels and outlaws. He left these people settled, ordering them to live quietly and at peace with the Aivino. As usual, the captain distributed gifts to the Indians who had been faithful. Then he returned to the Villa de San Felipe.

With great fervor and zeal Father Francisco Oliñano took charge of Christianity in all these lower pueblos,[41] where there were more than three thousand souls. And so fruit began to be harvested, as will later be seen. [373]

---

38. It is not clear whether this was Teopa, Mátape, or Aivino itself.

39. At times the Spaniards could not control their allies, who had their own code of war practices, particularly in regard to captives or to ethnic groups who were traditional enemies.

40. Recall that in the 1530s Cabeza de Vaca and his companions were hailed as "Children of the Sun." Alarcón and the members of the Rodríguez-Chamuscado expedition also represented themselves or were hailed in the same fashion (Ahern 1993, 1994, 1995a).

41. Apparently in the fall of 1621, when Burgensio departed.

CHAPTER IX A priest undertakes an entrada to the Aivino to establish a mission; the joyous welcome he received

Once the storm and squall recorded [in the last chapter] had passed, the weather cleared a bit and these pueblos were more disposed to the establishment of Christianity. It often happens that a thunderstorm with heavy rains passes over fields and lands, so improving their condition that they yield more abundant fruit. The same thing often happens in spiritual matters. Father Francisco Oliñano, a worthy minister in this new Christian community, has instructed them for more than twenty years, from the early days up to the present. He will now speak in a personal letter to his superior about his first entrada to the Aivino and the celebration with which he was welcomed. He says:

Father Tomás Basilio and I reached the Aivino on July 1, 1624.[42] Because this nation is located to the north, we experienced a great deal of cold. These Indians inhabit hilltops and high foothills in order to defend themselves from their enemies, against whom they waged war in their heathenism. We entered the first pueblo, and there, as well as in the others, we were consoled by the people's good disposition. In front of the enramada that was [to serve as] the church they had erected a very tall painted Cross. They made these enramadas quite large and adorned the entrance to the church and the interior near the altar with a variety of fragrant herbs. Everyone came out with Crosses in their hands and knelt outside the triumphal arches that they had built for us in their fashion. They did all this in a very orderly manner, with the men on one side and the women on the other, as if they were long-time Christians. They lined up quietly in the same orderly fashion, with the women first and then the men, and came very humbly to greet us, showing no fear. With joyful endearment on their tongues almost all of them spoke these words: "Father, you are most welcome here in our lands; stay with us so that we can enjoy your presence." As far as good character goes, I feel certain that one could not find any better among the Indians.

We spent two days in each of the three pueblos, where we baptized 402 infants under the age of four, as Your Reverence had ordered. Then we inquired about the sick, of whom there were only six that we baptized. We brought them to our house; that is, the enramada where we were attending [to these people]. With the help of his relatives a sick Indian principal came of his own free will to be baptized, slowly making his way from a ranchería that was half a league from

the pueblo of Teopa. This man came because he knew that the priests baptized those who were sick. When we left this pueblo called Teopa for Aivino, some women came out with infants who had not been previously baptized, because their mothers were absent when we baptized the others.

The people of these pueblos are settled and do not make their homes in their milpas or fields, like other nations do. If anyone does stand guard over his milpa or fields during the day, at night everyone returns to the pueblo. There are two languages spoken in all this interior region.[43] May the Lord someday send [evangelical] laborers to these people to provide them with religious instruction.

This was Father Oliñano's letter. [374] There was a case at this time that clearly demonstrates the affection these people showed toward religious instruction and having their children baptized.[44] Some of these Indians had set out from their lands to see and visit some of their allies or relatives who were about twelve leagues away. They had to pass through the lands of enemies [the Lower Nébome] with whom they had once been at war. They set out from their lands with no weapons, trusting only in the security that they now had through their baptized children. In spite of this the enemy (who were fugitive outlaws) came out to meet them with the intention of shooting arrows at them. The Indian travelers retreated from this attack, and even though they could have retaliated once they were back in their own lands, as was their custom when they were still gentiles, this time they held back, saying, "Our children are Christians now, and we have a church and a house for the priests. Let's not declare war, for if we do, then perhaps the priest will not shelter us, and he might abandon us. Let's leave this matter to the captain. He will come on our behalf."[45]

One can clearly see from all this the virtue and strength of the Gospel, whose first rays of light illuminated these barbarous people's intellect, thereby taming their fierceness.

---

42. Pérez de Ribas is in error here—Oliñano's letter, which appears in the anua of 1622 (AGN 1622), was written in 1622 not 1624.

43. Eudeve, spoken by the Aivino, and Pima, spoken by the Aivinos' former enemies, the Pima Bajo or Nébome.

44. This incident occurred in 1623 and is related in another of Oliñano's letters in the anua from that year (AGN 1623).

45. Pérez de Ribas paraphrases the direct discourse reported by Oliñano, although he does so without deviating significantly from the discourse's meaning in the original letter (AGN 1623).

CHAPTER X Baptisms are begun in this Christian community; some unusual cases are recounted

ather Oliñano began to clear this wilderness and at the same time to sow the seed of the Holy Gospel. In order to carry out such a holy ministry and to give them the bread of the divine word, he learned these people's two languages quite well. Once he had baptized a large number of infants he then began baptizing the adults. He overcame the difficulties that normally arise because of the devil and the adults' inherent depravity. These difficulties stemmed from battles against the sorcerers' doctrine. Our common enemy continually sows weeds [to choke out] the Christian religion and its holy customs of marriage to a single wife and abstention from drunken revels and the other vices that were common among these gentiles. Through divine favor many victories are achieved and many souls are snatched from the claws of that infernal beast.

One unique abuse was found among the Aivino that was almost a form of idolatry. This was found in no other nation except the Aivino and one of the neighboring gentile nations.[46] The superstition existed that those who wanted to be safe from lightning (which is very common in these lands) should make an offering or give gifts to one of their deceased, an Indian principal who had died a few years earlier after being struck by lightning.[47] They had buried or enclosed him in a type of tomb, where the cadaver was seated. In order to show him [even] greater reverence, they had erected an enramada right in the cave. There they would hang some type of votive or offering, such as the white beads made from little sea snails [olivella shells?] with which they adorn themselves. They also offered mantas, colored feathers, and other things that they value. They thought that in this way they would not be killed by lightning.

46. The Batuco, who were also Eudeve speakers.

47. Although Pérez de Ribas implies that this "unique abuse" was discovered by Oliñano during his first few years working with the Aivino, the practice actually was discovered ca. 1630 by Lorenzo de Cárdenas, shortly after the latter was assigned to the Aivino as their first resident missionary. The practice and the incident that follows, involving a woman killed by lightning, were reported by a fellow Jesuit working among the Batuco, Martín de Azpilcueta, in a letter dated December 3, 1630 (AGN 1630).

The priest learned of this superstition (it is God's providence that there are always Christian faithful in the midst of sorcerers and liars who report anything that is contrary to the Holy Faith that they have received). He gathered [375] a good number of the faithful at the place where this superstition [was practiced]. There he knocked over the cadaver and dismantled the superstition so that no trace of that type of idolatry and deception would remain. He spoke to them with regard to this matter, explaining to them that only God has dominion over people's lives, the clouds, and the lightning bolts that they emit. With this the faithful were more strongly confirmed in the Faith and were happy with its truths. But the devil and his familiars were not pleased about what had taken place, and we shall soon see how they bellowed.

I confess that I record this case somewhat cautiously. It took place in the same district that I have just discussed, where the devil's trick to save them from being struck by lightning was undone. [I am cautious] because I am entering into a discussion of a case of someone being struck by lightning on the important and unique occasion of Holy Baptism. The enemy of humankind was able to make use of this occasion to increase the blasphemy that he spreads against this Holy Sacrament, broadcasting through his sorcerers that it takes lives, even though it is this sacrament that gives life to the souls that receive it. In the end I decided not to leave it out, because I am writing for the faithful, who are familiar with and should venerate and adore God's judgment, especially when it concerns an individual's predestination, in which case it is extremely deep and mysterious.

This case was extremely unusual. The missionary priest had just finished baptizing a large number of adults. These people were all gathered in the plaza in front of the church so that they could be recorded in the baptismal register, as is common practice. The sky was somewhat cloudy, and suddenly, with no rainfall, a cloud unleashed a bolt of lightning that killed a woman who had just been baptized, leaving alive and unharmed the infant that she was holding in her arms. Let us now consider this, along with the religious instruction that we just said the priest had given the Indians: to turn to God, the author of life, who grants His Divine Majesty to those who come to Him and proclaim Him as such, in order to be saved from being struck by lightning. Let us also include what the sorcerers were said to preach against Holy Baptism: that it takes the lives of those who receive it. We will find that God's supreme counsel should be adored, and that it should be believed that He wished to safeguard that soul through baptismal grace, as should be understood from the good disposition with which this woman requested and received Holy Baptism. If she had not died on this occasion, perhaps her salvation would have been placed at risk.

This case nevertheless provided the sorcerers with something to discredit this Holy Sacrament, as they did. They said that those who received Baptism were [subsequently] dragged off to die. In this way they frightened others away from Baptism and made their own false doctrine more appealing. But if one thinks about it, it was even more unusual that God should allow His Most Holy Son to die in such a humiliating fashion upon a Cross, blasphemed by the Jews, without preventing His death, which was for the life and welfare of mankind. This very same Lord did not deflect the bolt of lightning through which, fortunately, the baptized woman most certainly gained eternal life, even though the bedeviled sorcerers blasphemed Holy Baptism.

This case still upset some people, but when the priest noticed this he took charge and spoke to them. With reasoning appropriate to their level of understanding he explained to them that everything that happens on earth takes place because of divine judgment and disposition, which we human beings should revere. [He also explained] that in believing that Baptism had been the cause of this woman's death, they had drawn an erroneous conclusion. [376] Many other people who had been baptized along with her were still alive, including even the baby she was carrying in her arms. As a result of this and other reasoning, they began to calm down.

Our Lord, who through this case wished to promulgate the Faith in some, also was served at this time by another case that was favorable to Holy Baptism. A gentile Indian was being catechized specifically in order to be baptized. This Indian had become ill, and when the priest visited him he found him quite spent. He realized that the severity of the illness left no time for waiting until [the Indian] could be baptized in the church, and also that his soul was in danger of being condemned. He asked the Indian whether he wanted to be baptized. The fear of Baptism caused by the sorcerers was so great that the sick Indian responded very adamantly that he did not, so the priest went away, saddened by the sick man's negative response and disposition. He had barely reached his house when the [Indian's] illness became so severe that he began losing consciousness. They called the priest again, who came and asked the Indian whether he wanted at last to be baptized. The priest found that the Indian had changed his mind, for he answered that he did. The priest prepared and baptized him, and the instant he received Holy Baptism he was miraculously healed in body and soul. The following day he awoke free of illness.

This case amazed this entire new Christian community, which now believed what the priest had taught them: that this Holy Sacrament does not take lives. Indeed, it had miraculously given life to this sick man when he was in danger of dying. This was also confirmation that even though in His supreme judgment God sometimes arranges for or allows cases that give the devil and his followers the opportunity to challenge the Faith and its ministers, at the same time He does not forget to favor these ministers with other cases of unique providence that support and confirm the Faith, and these [He gives] in greater number and quality.

With these and other positive results the number of baptized people began to grow, and Christian exercises flourished in both the church and the mission. But the devil, who is always envious of anything that has to do with human happiness, renewed his attack on this new Christian community, as we will see in the following chapter.

CHAPTER XI The devil uses a new disturbance and uprising to try to halt and destroy Christianity among the Lower Nébome

In relating so many disturbances and battles I do not mean [to imply] that the holy word does not flourish among these nations and that its ministers cannot enjoy peace in these holy missions. Rather, I mean only [to point out] what characterizes the establishment of new missions. This should not seem strange to those who are very familiar with what experience has demonstrated [to be necessary] to dislodge the devil from the souls and bodies that he possesses. Even the Son of God Himself had to use His power when He was preaching to the world. Once the enemy was anathematized by His most holy name, the devil responded with rejection and resistance. For if he tries to hold on to the bodies that he possesses, he tries even harder to retain the souls of his captives. When I talk about disturbances and battles among these newly converted nations I do not mean that it happens among all of them. And when they do occur [377] God grants the [priests] victory. Whoever reads the first part of the history of the holy Order of Saint Dominic[48] will see how for seven years that holy patriarch struggled and suffered, availing himself of both the ecclesiastical and lay arm of the Church to fight the Albigensian heretics in France. He won most illustrious victories over visible and invisible enemies of the Faith, using the sword of the divine word in sermons, disputations, and speeches, together with the sword and weapons provided by the count of Montfort. Saint Dominic did not think it strange to combine the weapons of iron and fire with the divine word and the preaching of the Catholic Faith in order to repress those who rebelled against God and His Church.

Whoever reads this [history] will not be surprised to see that in our mission conquests the devil tries to use disturbances, uprisings, and wars to obstruct the preaching of the holy word. I will describe a tempest and storm which, like the previous ones, was caused by sorcerers who especially wanted to destroy Christianity when it was growing substantially.[49] [Specifi-

cally], some of the wild, fugitive Indians who were previously identified as Lower Nébome, along with others who had been baptized, [were] ill advised by their sorcerers to kill a long-time Christian Indian who was the governor of a Nébome pueblo. The Indian had zealously helped the priests with the religious instruction of this nation, and for this reason the rebels abhorred him. But Our Lord rewarded this good Christian for the fervor and zeal with which he served Him. Although he suffered and died in great pain from poisonous arrows, God willed that this man would have time to receive all the sacraments as a reward for the death he would suffer for his Faith.

These Indians were allied to the ones who shot Father Bandersipe with an arrow, as was previously mentioned. As if this were not enough, the same people raided and set fire to a Christian pueblo and its church [in Father Oliñano's district]. They robbed and severely abused the Christians, and would have killed Father Francisco Oliñano were it not for his faithful Indians, who protected him. These attacks continued for some time,[50] being launched from the mountains, to which the rebels had withdrawn. While the captain of the garrison was preparing an expedition to punish these outrages, he dispatched eight soldiers to accompany the faithful Indians who were escorting the priest [Father Oliñano]. They were all exposed to great danger, assaults, and difficulties, until the captain, obliged to remedy such great harm, sent a corporal and some [additional] soldiers and Indian allies to protect the priest. The soldiers and Indians, together with the Christian Lower Nébome, formed a large squadron, and in several battles with the rebels they captured fourteen of the guiltiest ones who had taken part in the burning of the churches and in the general uprising.[51] They exe-

---

48. Pérez de Ribas apparently is referring to Gerad of Fracheto's (ca. 1189–1265) *Chronica ordinis* (Goodich 1982:53).

49. This occurred in 1626 in Oliñano's Nébome Bajo district and

led within a few months to an attempt on the life of Bandersipe in his Nébome Alto district (described in Chapter 4).

50. The anua from Sinaloa for the years 1625–26 indicates disturbances continued throughout the year 1626 (AGN 1626).

51. Pérez de Ribas makes it seem in this paragraph that Captain Perea did not get involved in quelling the rebellion. However, after Perea sent additional troops to guard Oliñano he himself took to the

cuted them and pardoned all the rest. The Indian who shot Father Diego Bandersipe also was captured and received a noteworthy punishment. The faithful Christian Nébome were so angry that, even after the man had been hanged, they could not be restrained from shooting two thousand arrows into his body [in payment for] that one arrow he had shot at the priest. Although God had saved the priest, the faithful Nébome considered the Indian's attempt to be patricide, because he had attempted to kill the priest, whom all considered to be their father. The other Indian who shot the arrow [378] that penetrated the wall [of Father Bandersipe's house] was not captured during this battle with the rebels.

However, a few days after the soldiers left the man was caught by surprise by his relatives, who cut off his head and sent it to the captain at the Villa de San Felipe.

The punishment described here, which took four months to carry out, proved just and agreeable to God. Afterwards, conditions for Christianity improved in this district, and other neighboring nations ceased to resist receiving God's word. After seeing what happened to the Christian Nébome, they insistently asked for priests to preach the divine word to them. The priests did as they requested, as I will later describe once I have finished discussing the establishment and perfection of this Lower Nébome mission.

CHAPTER XII These people's advances in the Faith and Christian practices

Once the weeds that choked this field were uprooted and the scandals against God caused by the outlaws and rebels were suppressed, wonderful progress followed in this new Christianity. It continued to grow each day, as new infants and adults overcame the fear instilled in them by the sorcerers and begged to be baptized. Thus, there was an amazing increase in [the number of] Christians in this year of 1634 among these last nations of Sinaloa, which includes the district I have described. The number of baptized persons included 2,740 infants and 870 adults.[52] There were 990 couples married in facie Ecclesiae, which means that the abuse of having many wives was diminishing, and this was no less a battle or victory in these enterprises.

Although in later years the number of Baptisms surpassed the figure previously mentioned, I nevertheless want to emphasize how abundant the harvest was during these stormy times. The fugitive Indians, who were still hiding in the mountains, had been terrorized by the punishment meted out to those who were hanged. However, through great affection and gentleness Father Oliñano began reducing them to a Christian pueblo. They were all baptized along with others of the district and became fervent members of the Church.

Among these nations there was an abuse or superstition that the devil had introduced through his sorcerers. The latter had persuaded the people to walk through the monte for four nights in the moonlight. The devil would appear and give them a little stone that granted them the power to heal the sick and bewitch whomever they wished.[53] The priests preached against this abuse and deception which, like others, was practiced by a large number of people. They succeeded in extirpating this fraud so well that the Indians now avoid it, as they do other former abuses.

After baptizing all these people the priest[54] began to improve their Christianity. He carried out all the re-

---

field with a large expedition; it was the captain and his forces that subdued, captured, and hung the fourteen rebels. With peace restored Perea headed back to the villa. While en route, he was sent the head of the other assailant of Father Bandersipe. Jesuit superiors were irked by Perea's slowness in responding to Nébome threats to Oliñano. This may be why Pérez de Ribas slighted Perea's role in finally quelling the revolt.

52. Note that these figures are for the entire Rectorado de San Ignacio not just the district of the Nébome Bajo.

53. Presumably quartz crystals, which have been recovered from archaeological sites in Sonora. One can well imagine partially exposed crystals embedded in arroyo banks or the ground reflecting light during moonlit treks.

54. Oliñano remained in charge of the Nébome Bajo until 1647 (Pennington 1980:379).

quired ministries: administering the sacraments; celebrating feast days, Easter, Pentecost, Christmas, and Epiphany; celebrating Holy Week ceremonies, as well as the corresponding penance; [distributing] Communion to those who were the most advanced [in the Faith]; and [overseeing] devotion to the Virgin's Holy Rosary. All of these became well established among these people.

I would simply be repeating what happened in other conversions if I were to write here about particular cases of the conversion of these people; for example, about sick infants and adults [379] who went to heaven as soon as they were baptized and other cases where the grace of predestination stands out. In all of them divine goodness never ceases to manifest the mercy that *ab eterno*[55] it had planned to confer upon these poor people. So that this mission's share in those mercies does not remain entirely hidden, I will relate here some specific cases of edification concerning their sweet devotion to the Rosary of Our Most Holy Virgin, Mother of God. This is the milk that nourishes the children of the Church; it is what those who are young in the Faith need. Because they are so young, there is no doubt that Our Lady dearly protects them from the infernal serpent.

A sixteen-year-old youth who found himself lost in the monte forgot that he was a Christian. Because he had been born and reared among bedeviled sorcerers, he called the devil to rescue him from that danger. The devil immediately appeared to him, and although he was in human form, he still looked horrifying. This should have been sufficient to frighten this Indian, although it did not. Instead, he stopped to listen to him, and the first thing the devil did was to tell the youth that he would have to give him his soul if he wanted his help. The foolish youth agreed to this, and the devil led him out of the monte. Then for a period of two months the devil continued to appear to the Indian, keeping him company and throwing him food. However, he always did so from a distance and without drawing near. One day the devil told the Indian why he did not get closer. From a distance he said, "If you want a closer relationship and you want me to continue giving you all that I have, throw away the rosary that you are wearing — it bothers me." The youth responded, "I won't do that — it is the dearest and most valuable thing I have." The devil then replied, "Remember, you already belong to me." He then threatened to take the youth's life if he did not

do as he said. The youth became frightened and terrified and began to run away, saying, "Because of this rosary you have yet to harm me — and you can't harm me now."

The terrified Indian immediately ran to the priest and, exhausted, he related what had happened. The priest exhorted him to make a good confession, which he did. This is how he was warned away from the devil's trap. From then on the lad was protected by his love of and devotion to the Holy Rosary, which helped him escape the devil's snares.

The Holy Rosary was just as useful in the following case. One time an Indian was out in the field and started saying the Rosary. The same enemy appeared, this time in the form of a serpent. Hissing, he said to him, "Don't talk like that. Stop using those words with which the priests kill." In fact, this serpent's head throbbed and ached when he heard the Ave Marias, as God had threatened from the beginning of creation. At the same time the devout Indian was already hearing the following (presumably from his guardian angel): "Make the sign of the Cross and fervently pray those words." With this the devil became confused and disappeared, and the Indian remained even more confirmed in his devotion to the Holy Rosary. All these natives, young and old, are now very affectionately devoted to it. This and other Christian exercises clearly showed that the devil was fleeing from those whom he had previously overpowered.

This clever enemy tried to separate another Indian from the Church. He took him down one road after another, senselessly confused. One day his people noticed his absence and started looking for him. Finally, on Sunday, [380] right after High Mass, they found him among some thorns. When they asked him where he had been he answered that he didn't know. He had only noticed that, at the hour at which Mass begins on Sundays and feast days, he would disappear with the devil. When he regained consciousness he remembered that he disappeared about the time the priest would have started saying Mass. The people took him to the priest, who exhorted him to make a good confession. The Indian did so and placed a Cross around his neck, which prevented that beast from appearing again.

After all these Christian exercises [had been introduced] and the people were ready and willing, the priest introduced the most perfect and saintly exercise of Holy Communion. This took a firm hold and enabled these new plants to produce delicious fruit. In order to receive it, some made a general confession, having already attained a greater understanding of the

---

55. "Since the beginning of time."

parts and fruits of that Holy Sacrament. Once the spirituality of this Christianity was established its dedicated minister began to build churches and sacred temples so that Christianity could reach {both} its spiritual and material perfection. Because man has both a body and a soul, he should worship his Creator with the interior of his soul and the exterior of his body. The people willingly initiated this enterprise, building their churches with pleasure, and rejoicing and showing the customary solemnity of other nations at their dedication. They also built a house for their minister; ever since the early days of the conversion of these people {such a house was lacking and} the priests had to endure many discomforts, which they offered up to God.

The captain appointed the governors and alcaldes in this nation, which now enjoys the political and spiritual serenity that is the result only of divine power and the strength of the divine word. We will leave these four pueblos[56] in this felicitous state—having been previously racked by uprisings and rebellions. We will now move on to other pueblos that were also saved from the devil's power by the zealous missionaries whom God has provided the Province of Sinaloa.

CHAPTER XIII The Sisibotari [of] Sahuaripa and the Batuco nation ask for the divine word to be preached to them; two unusual cases are recounted concerning this matter

As we record the inland advance of the Gospel doctrine our history of the missions of the Province of Sinaloa draws closer to its gentile frontiers. The mission that borders the one discussed in the previous chapter pertains to those who are called the Sisibotari and the Batuco.[57] The first nation took its name from a very principal Indian who was renowned among these nations. His name was Sisibotari, and I observed him in person when Captain Hurdaide, who has been mentioned previously, carried out an expedition to this nation before the time of its reduction.[58] This Indian came from his lands to see us. I confess that among the many and various caciques and interpreters with whom I have dealt in these barbarous nations, I never found any who in appearance, character, and dress showed themselves to be as principal, noble, and lordly in their fashion as this Indian, nor anyone who demonstrated lordship, capacity, and noble conduct like he did. He was still young, and he was very good-natured. He wore a long manta tied at the shoulder like a cloak. He also wore another manta wrapped tightly around his waist, as do other Indians in this nation. For protection when shooting arrows he had a beautiful martin pelt wrapped around his left wrist, which holds the bow [381] while the right hand snaps the bowstring. Others use pelts of common animals for this purpose. If the archer has a strong arm, when the arrow is shot the two ends of the bow nearly meet. The bowstring snaps with such great force and violence that it would bruise the wrist if it were bare and lacked protection. This principal cacique's bow and quiver of arrows were carried by another Indian who was like his squire. Both pieces were beautifully carved in their fashion. The cacique brought with him a good number of his vassals, who looked upon and treated him with great respect and reverence.

56. Tecoripa, Comoripa, Suaque, and Mátape. Note that in 1629 Mátape was one of several Aivino settlements that formed a separate mission district cared for by Lorenzo de Cárdenas.

57. Both groups were Opata and spoke different dialects; the Batuco (like the Aivino) spoke Eudeve, whereas the Sisibotari of the Sahuaripa Valley (and most other Opata groups) spoke Teguima. In the middle of the eighteenth century Father Juan Nentvig (1980) commented that the difference between Eudeve and Teguima was analogous to the difference between Portuguese and Spanish or Provencal and French.

58. Pérez de Ribas accompanied Hurdaide on this expedition to the Nébome in search of food during the winter of 1618–19.

I had to deal with this Indian cacique through an interpreter in a language that I knew but which was not his own. He welcomed me at a place near his lands and settlements. Although we did not visit them, they could be seen in the distance. He showed us his valley and pueblos and invited us to visit, expressing his desire for priests to come to his lands to teach them the word of God. I spent a long time talking with him, asking him many questions about his people, his rancherías, and other things that they like to discuss. He gave such a good account of everything that I was forced to take note of such an orderly way of speaking for an Indian who had been reared among such barbarous people. But I have previously pointed out that among these people one finds more than a few who have very good [intellectual] capacity, especially when one educates them and deals with them in their own language.

I treated the cacique Sisibotari as affectionately as I could, giving thanks to God for the door that was being opened for the Gospel. I gave him and his sons (which is what his vassals are called) a few little things that they like, letting him know that from time to time he or some of his people should come and see me in the Christian district to which I was attending, as he later did. When he had said goodbye to the captain and me he returned to his lands and pueblos, which as I said, took the name Sisibotari from this Indian, who was famous among all those nations. He was antonomastically called 'Gran Sisibotari'.

This cacique did not forget his good intentions. After some time [in 1620] he set out from his lands, which are one hundred leagues from the Villa de San Felipe. He assembled and brought with him some allied caciques[59] to the villa to see the captain and the priests. He requested that one of them come to his pueblos to make them Christians and to teach them God's law, which they wished to receive. To better secure and accomplish his objectives, he brought eleven boys from his nation, whom he offered in pledge[60] of his loyalty and request. They were to remain at the Indian children's seminary at our college in the villa. There they would learn all manner of good doctrine, and afterwards they could teach it to their pueblos. He [also] brought a large,

live royal eagle to the father superior at the college.[61] Such game is rarely captured, and through it, it seems that this Indian was showing the spirit of a nobleman. He could have caught other kinds of game that he had in his lands, but he contented himself with presenting nothing less than the symbol of nobility and generosity.

An unusual deed carried out by these Sisibotari people will now be recorded to make known how much they desired to have ministers to baptize and catechize them. They had asked the captain (as he who governed the province) to receive them under his protection so that they could become Christian. In a time of need[62] the captain had [382] dispatched his drove of mules to bring back maize from Sisibotari lands. When the drove of mules reached Sisibotari lands the [Indians] stopped and detained them, saying that they wanted to see the captain [himself] in their lands; [only] then would they give him whatever he needed. The captain understood very well the loyal and benevolent spirit with which they requested that he make this journey. Because he always professed that he would help and favor those who wanted to be Christians, he did not delay in making this trip to please those who had sent him a message that he knew had been born out of kindness. He set out on his journey and reached their pueblos. They celebrated his arrival with many demonstrations of happiness and willingly gave him all they had, offering aid in the form of maize. He returned to the villa, leaving them consoled with the promise that he would soon make an effort and act as their procurator with the priests so that they would send them someone to make them Christians as they desired. The actions of such a willing nation obliged [the priests] to grant their request, as was later done.

Before [recounting] the [first] entrada by a priest to the Sisibotari I must recount a case that pained the entire province. I would not relate it if it were not for the fact that the laws of history require that the negative as well as the positive be recorded.[63] Just as the latter moves and exalts the spirit to give thanks to God, adverse and unfortunate events also teach us to praise God's judgments, which are always just, even though

---

59. The anua of 1627 (AGN 1627) mentions the caciques of the Batucos, Aivinos, Matapas, and Toapas (the last three being individual Aivino pueblos).

60. *Rehenes*. This word, which in contemporary Spanish means 'hostages', derives from the vulgar Arabic *rahan*, which means a pledge or guarantee (cf. Corominas and Pascual 1989–1991:4:855.).

61. The anua of 1620 (AGN 1620) speaks of three eagles; the father superior at the time was Diego de Guzmán.

62. Apparently that same year, 1620.

63. Pérez de Ribas here reflects his understanding of the Renaissance ideal of history—the telling of things as they happened, be they good or bad. However, as the following lines indicate, Pérez de Ribas still gave precedence to invisible truths.

human discourse may not always fathom their purpose and exalted ends.

This cacique of whom I have spoken had insistently requested Gospel instruction and had trudged over a great many miles, as I have recounted, so that this doctrine might be communicated to his people and they might all be guided along the path to heavenly bliss. This cacique returned to his pueblo from what would be his last journey to the villa to obtain what he so desired. He was very happy with the news that a priest would soon come to care for that mission. Unfortunately, death assaulted him so suddenly that there was no time to notify the nearest priest so that he could be baptized.[64] He died without the salvation of the sacrament that opens the doors of heaven to mankind—a happiness and joy that the Sovereign Redeemer of the World has conceded and continues to concede daily to many people in these missions, who have gone to heaven immediately after being baptized. These very people made no previous effort to be baptized nor did they call for a priest to baptize them. God simply sent them a minister who taught them the mysteries of our Holy Faith and then baptized them because they were on the verge of dying in their fields, montes, or along the seacoast. Then, as soon as they were baptized, they ascended into heaven from amongst thickets or sand dunes.

But the cacique of whom we are speaking did not attain this, which was greatly regretted by all. There are many people who have taken some consolation for this sorrow in believing that Our Lord God somehow considered this Indian's desire and efforts as a *bautismo flamminis*,[65] and that in this way he was fortunately saved. This is the term that the theologian uses to refer to the Baptism that comes from the efforts one makes to actually obtain the Sacrament and holy water of Baptism. Moreover, given the many occasions when this Indian talked to priests and Christians he must have heard about and believed the articles and mysteries of our Holy Faith. This must have been the source of his intense desire to receive the Divine Sacrament of water. If this was not sufficient, one can only revere and adore God's judgment, which is most just in administering His grace and glory.

In order to temper the sadness of the preceding case,

and before referring to the entrada made by the minister who was assigned to this nation's mission, I will record the following case, [383] even though doing so might be jumping ahead. At a settlement called Comoripa, not far from [the lands of the] Sisibotari, there was a principal Indian who was a gentile, just like all the other people of his nation. He heard the news that the Sisibotari already had a priest in their lands teaching them God's word. He also had heard that no one could be saved or go to heaven without first receiving Holy Baptism and Christian law. He became very sick, and so he sent his own son and some of his other people to ask the priest to come quickly to his pueblo so he could teach him the way to heaven and salvation, for he was on the verge of dying. The priest responded to this pious act, and when he reached the sick man's pueblo he catechized and instructed him in the articles of the Faith, which the [Indian] listened to with great joy and a very sharp mind. The priest baptized him, and shortly thereafter he died.

The priest had strong evidence of his predestination, for God had spared him long enough to allow him to obtain the means necessary for his salvation. Later, when the priest investigated the life of this fortunate Indian, he found that he had lived very much according to natural law,[66] without ever having gotten drunk or ever having stained himself with this vice, which was so widespread among these peoples. Nor had he ever done anyone wrong or killed anyone, which is quite a feat in the midst of these people's great number of enemies. He contented himself with a single wife and distanced himself from all the other vices found in these nations. From this it can be inferred that God had chosen him to go to heaven, even though he had been born and raised in such distant and remote lands, where it was so difficult to obtain the means necessary for salvation.

Through His divine kindness God prepared the way to this man's [salvation]. But for reasons known only to His Majesty the other cacique did not obtain this means. This should frighten men into living with a concern for the matter of their salvation. With this we will move on to discuss the entrada that the priest made to found the Sisibotari's Christianity.

---

64. The anua of 1628 notes that Gran Sisibotari died four years earlier; this would have been at the height of the epidemic of 1623–25, which apparently spread to the Sisibotari (Reff 1991b:160–68).

65. Baptism by virtue of one's burning desire for salvation.

66. As discussed in the "Critical Introduction," the Jesuits agreed with Thomas Aquinas, who argued that human beings who had not been exposed to the word of God could nevertheless come to a knowledge of God (albeit limited) simply through natural reason—by reflecting on the complexity and wonder of life. Such knowledge of God also implied an ability to distinguish what pleased and offended God.

CHAPTER XIV Father Méndez establishes religious instruction and Christianity among the Sisibotari and the Batuco; the particular customs of each nation

Much could be said here about the apostolic, veteran missionary Father Pedro Méndez. He was fortunate to have been given this mission—and the mission was fortunate to have him as minister. Later I will devote a chapter to [his] holy life, which was prolonged in these glorious tasks. When this evangelical missionary was more than seventy years old, and after he had worked for more than thirty years in these missions, he took charge of establishing Christianity among the Sisibotari.[67] He undertook this felicitous task as if he were a young missionary. I will begin writing about this mission by citing a letter that this priest wrote. In it he demonstrates, on the one hand, the enjoyment and comfort with which God rewarded his labors, and on the other (according to the custom in our Company) how superiors were informed of his first entrada to this mission.[68] At the beginning of his letter he speaks of the welcome he received in the Indian pueblos that he had previously instructed and engendered in Christ. I wanted to copy his letter [384] because it expresses the love and esteem that these people come to have for those who communicate the light of our Holy Faith to them, giving them the first milk of the Gospel. His letter, dated 1628, says:

> I set out from the Villa de San Felipe and arrived at my first district of Ocoroni. One league before I reached the pueblo I found arches all along the way. [I was greeted by] all the topiles and fiscales, with trumpets, flutes, dancers, and masks. They accompanied me to the pueblo, where all the men and women were assembled with Crosses and candles.[69] I entered the church as the music and celebration continued, and after they had [formally] welcomed me and I had thanked them for their demonstration of such great affection, they regaled us that day as best they could. From there we went to Tehueco, my second district,[70] which is

now [under the care] of Father Otón. The improvement in this pueblo is equal to the large number of people I found congregated there before Our Lord, all waiting for me on their knees next to the church, with their Cross well decorated, and singing in the Mexican style and manner.[71] In the choir loft, there were trumpets, flutes, and drums, all of which comforted my soul. This was especially true of a little preacher[72] who was up on a plank in the highest part of the church, whence he energetically proclaimed a thousand joys.

> From here we set out for Baciroa, which is between Tehueco and the [Río] Mayo. The general,[73] who wants to establish an inn there for travelers, was waiting for me, together with many of my former Mayo people, who had gathered on a small hill with all his soldiers. From there we set out for the Río Mayo, which was forty leagues away. It was amazing how groups of men and women came to greet me all along the way, bringing with them whatever gifts they had. They had erected decorated ramadas and Crosses and accompanied me with such affection that they did not take their eyes off me, constantly telling me how happy they were [to see me]. When I urged my companions to hurry to escape a severe rainstorm that was approaching, they ran beside me the entire three leagues; if it were not for them, we would have suffered a great deal more [during the journey]. We reached the Río Mayo, where the priests had congregated. They welcomed me with kindness and took great comfort in my presence.

Up to here [I have been citing] the first part of a letter [written] by the most religious Father Pedro Méndez before he had even reached his mission. Later in the letter he describes how he was welcomed by the Sisibotari:

> I arrived here (he says) on May 15, [1628] with some Spanish-speaking Indians that I had brought with me. As soon as the Sisibotari learned that I was coming, they began to prepare the reception that they are accustomed to giving. They erected arches of decorated branches for many

---

67. Méndez was transferred from the Yaqui mission of Potam.

68. Méndez's letter is in the anua of 1628 (AGN 1628); Pérez de Ribas copies it almost verbatim.

69. *Ciriales.* These "candles" probably were torches made of dried branches of the pitahaya cactus.

70. Recall that Méndez was forced to leave Tehueco more than a decade earlier because of threats to his life.

71. The Indians of central Mexico were noted for their chanting in Latin and singing in Nahuatl, accompanied by drums, flutes, and other traditional instruments.

72. *Predicadorcito.* It is not clear whether this preacher was a child or an adult of small stature.

73. The identity of this "general" is not known, nor are his plans for an inn or whether they were ever realized.

leagues and on each they raised a large, beautiful Cross. The people crowded together in the pueblos and got down on their knees with Crosses in their hands; men, women, and children received me with extraordinary displays of delight and joy. They accompanied me in this manner to the church, which they had already erected.

I certify to Your Reverence that even if I had been [made of] stone, I would have been moved to tears by the sight of so much kindness and devotion among such a barbarous and infidel people. When I went to the Mayo the first time there was not half the display of joy that there was among these people. This devotion continues, and it will grow stronger each day once they have become Christians. From my point of view there is not a nation today in this province that has a better understanding [385] of the matters of our Holy Faith. This is because of the good character that I am finding among them. There is no idolatry among this nation; sorcery is very scarce. They are spirited in war, but otherwise they are not malicious. They practice drunkenness like other nations, but with the grace of Our Lord they have so corrected themselves that in the six months that I have been here I have not detected any [drunken revels].

At the outset, when I had just arrived, one of these pueblos five leagues away held a drunken revel, during which a woman was shot with arrows. She was so badly wounded that her life was in danger. I got news of this, so I went to the pueblo and baptized this woman, but the Lord willed that she should live. I let the Indians know how upset I was, and as they were kneeling in the church I severely scolded all of them. I reprimanded them for that vice and explained how offensive it was to God Our Lord. They took this [talk] so seriously that there has never been another trace of this vice.

When I began this mission there was nothing I feared as much as the nocturnal dances that these people hold, which are the occasion for a great many offenses against God. But this has been corrected, because I know of no nation that enjoys the same calm as these pueblos do. I have congregated three pueblos [Sahuaripa, Arivechi, and Bacanora] with Crosses and churches, and these are located in two very fertile valleys that produce maize and various legumes. They skillfully irrigate their fields with fresh and healthful waters drawn from streams; it appears that these people never suffer from the hunger that affects other nations. Their diet is most moderate, and their principal sustenance is a little bit of ground maize dissolved in water. Perhaps it is this moderation that explains why they enjoy such good health, as there are very few sick among them.

Some have thought that these were mountain people because their land is surrounded by gentle hills and mountains, but this is not the case. Their pueblos and cultivated fields are situated in level valleys and all the inhabitants are very peaceable. In their dress they are very different from the Yaqui and the Mayo, among whom the men barely cover themselves with a manta and the women are nearly naked. It is exactly the opposite among the Sisibotari. The men cover what is necessary with a small painted manta that extends from the waist to the ankle. When it is cold they wear large mantas woven of cotton and pita. The women wear even

more clothing, and they make as much noise as Spanish women when they enter the church. Their skirts hang to the ground and are made of worked and colorfully painted deer hides that are as soft as silk. Alternatively, these skirts are made of cotton or pita, which are abundant in these pueblos. For even greater modesty they wear an apron from the waist down. This is often black, which makes them look like nuns with their scapularies. The young women in particular wear highly decorated doublets, and when it is cold they cover these with an additional garment like a rochet or ecclesiastical garment to keep themselves warm. Thus, they are all extremely modest. Those women who have entered into the [holy] state of marriage never betray their husbands.

When the [Sisibotari] are baptized they become so devoted to Mass that they never miss it. They hear it kneeling down, with all reverence and devotion, and they do not leave the church until I have taken off my vestments and given thanks. Then they ask me for [my] blessing and take their leave by genuflecting. What has most amazed me about the kindness and good disposition of these people is that they have dismantled their rancherías in the mountains, which contained some twenty or thirty houses full of food, supplies, and their valuables. They did so without any violence or [show of] force from the captain or soldiers. Rather, they have come down [of their own accord] with their families and belongings to live in the pueblo. There they established their homes next to the church, building them with flat earthen roofs using the beams from their dismantled homes.74 [386]

In the six months that I have been here they have built three churches which, although they are not the largest, are the best and most beautiful that I have had in all the districts where I have served as a missionary. They worked so hard on them that often when I sent them to rest, they wanted to continue working until the job was finished. Their houses are made of coursed earth 75 the way the best adobe is made, only better because, although the mud is not mixed with straw, they stamp it with their feet and prepare it so that it becomes as hard as rock. Then they cover it with strong, well-dressed beams.

In one of the three churches that I have mentioned, which was dedicated to our glorious Apostle Saint Francis Xavier, Our Lord showed great compassion to the recently baptized governor of the pueblo, who is a very good Indian. As he was taking down a large beam the rope got away from the people who were carrying it, and the beam suddenly fell on top of him. Our Lord willed that it should not strike him directly, but rather that it should only graze him, bruising his body and wounding him on the head, which bled profusely. I was present, and I cannot express how

---

74. Note that if this practice of reusing beams was common, then it would have profound consequences for our understanding of late prehistory, inasmuch as archaeologists generally assume that the beams they recover and then use for carbon 14 and dendrochronological dating were *not* reused by prehistoric peoples. In point of fact components and sites that are thought to data to, say, A.D. 1300 may date much later (Reff 1991a).

75. *Barro y de terrado.* Méndez appears to be describing coursed adobe structures, explained previously.

upset I was. But Our Lord willed that the injury was not serious. Three days later I found the governor working very happily on the church once again. This was [another] case of the devil trying to stir up people who were so new to the Faith.

It is amazing to see how happily they cut their hair and removed their ear ornaments and all other emblems of their heathenism. Both young and old attend catechism very enthusiastically, without having to be called. It is likewise unnecessary to expend any effort gathering them for this holy exercise. So far I have baptized nine hundred people, and although they all want and insistently request Baptism, because I am alone here and one has to proceed slowly catechizing and instructing them, it has not been possible for me to baptize all of them.

This is what Father Méndez wrote. I will only add here what a priest[76] wrote me when he went to visit this nation (while they were still gentile) concerning their modesty: "I went," he says, "to the Sahuaripa, or Sisibotari, in the year 1621, at the beginning of their instruction. Among the good things that we noticed about them was the way they danced. Although they had never had priests to teach them, as the men and women danced together to express their joy, they did not speak nor did they touch hands: instead, they grasped each other's mantas. In this way they demonstrated the modesty and reserve that they maintained through nothing but the light of natural [reason] that we find in these and other nations."

CHAPTER XV Some cases and instances where the devil attempted to obstruct these nations' Christianity

Before I write about the successful establishment of Christianity in this well-prepared flock I will write about the devil's resistance to Christianity and how he tried to obstruct the preaching of the Gospel, thus making the victory that much more illustrious.[77]

There were two old sorcerers who had become aged in their diabolical art. They were gentiles and lived among nations that bordered the Batuco.[78] When the latter welcomed a missionary to their land, the devil, with the help of his sorcerers, [387] planted his own

doctrine in those gentile pueblos. He warned that the Batuco would lose their lands because they welcomed a priest. He added that the priest and others like him killed people with Baptism, and that they bewitched and ate men. Thus, because a priest already resided with their neighbors the Batuco, they should fear that another priest would soon come to their lands, at which point all those evils and harms foretold by these two sorcerers would rain down upon them. The sorcerers were so effective with their devilish sermons that they persuaded their own people, who loved and respected them, to assemble an armed band to attack the Batuco and kill the priest they had welcomed in their pueblo. When the priest learned that this group of scoundrels was approaching the pueblo, he encouraged the Batuco not to be afraid and to stay put rather than go out to meet the enemy. The priest was encouraged by his hope that God (for whose cause he found himself in those straits) would favor him with the vigor and zeal [necessary to uphold] His honor. He told the Batuco not to take up arms unless their pueblo was actually attacked. At the same time he dispatched some loyal Indians with a message for the enemy; he chastised

76. This priest is the same Pedro Méndez. In 1621 he was asked by his superior, Nicolás de Arnaya, to visit the Sisibotari (Alegre 1956–1960:2:328).

77. These cases involving Father Martín de Azpilcueta, who in 1629 went to work among the Batuco, were recounted by a friend and fellow missionary, Lorenzo de Cárdenas, in his "Account of the Life and Death of Father Martín de Azpilcueta" (Pérez de Ribas 1896:2:501–13; Zambrano 1961–1977:3:797–808).

78. The Batuco were concentrated along the lower Río Moctezuma, which flows into the Río Yaqui. The gentile nations referred to here were the Sonora in the Valle del Río Sonora to the northeast. The Batuco and Sonora shared the same Opata culture but spoke different dialects of Opata (Eudeve and Teguima, respectively).

them for their actions and for being deceived by the devil and their sorcerers, who were exposing them to great risk and harm. This message caused such fear that the enemy halted, believing as they did that an army was coming to meet them.[79] With great panic they turned and headed for their homeland.

It is worth emphasizing here that which often has been noted concerning these missions: God's gentle providence, through various and illustrious means, has freed His preachers from innumerable dangers among these people. And if on some occasions He permits the enemy to attack, it is in order to crown His preachers. This dispensation comes from a Lord who knows how to give His servants the strength to scorn death out of love for Him. He is always attentive to whatever affects them, and they are very much under His care and protection. This is of singular consolation to evangelical laborers.

In the present case the warning sent by this poor religious, who was among unknown nations, was very effective, as has been told. Within a few days those who had intended to attack the priest who was baptizing the Batuco, as well as the Batuco themselves, for wanting to become Christian, now began to regret the mistake they had made in allowing themselves to be tricked by their sorcerers. Therefore, they sent a message to the priest, saying that they wanted to be forgiven and to make peace with the Christians. They added that from then on they would respectfully obey the words and orders of the Batuco's father. As a pledge and sign of this they sent four of their very own sons to be baptized, reared, and instructed by the priest. They said that when another priest came to their lands the boys could help the priest in his ministry and the teaching of the Christian doctrine. After all this those who wanted to kill the priest came with much love to visit him. In the end they carried out what they had promised, because in time another missionary priest came to give these people religious instruction and Baptism. Thus, with their conversion God freed their souls from the sorcerers' stratagems.

Another consequence of considerable importance

and value was that the devil was given a good thrashing. [388] This occurred when it was revealed that the prophecies sown by the sorcerers were false. They had said that the ministers of the Gospel killed people and other such lies. These sorcerers lost much of their credibility among their people and their spells began to decrease, as did the vices introduced through them.

There was another lie that the sorcerers tried to introduce among the Batuco. Because they had failed to persuade them to refuse Baptism, they taught and persuaded those who had been baptized and married as Christians that they could separate from their legitimate wives and take up with others, as they had done in their heathenism. At first the priest did not realize what was happening, and this heretic and wicked doctrine began to spread, particularly with the bad example of a lowly woman who was the daughter of a bellicose Indian principal. She had separated from her legitimate husband and was so determined to remain separated that it was impossible to make her return to her former life with him. The missionary priest called the obstinate woman's father and made him understand the obligation of Christian matrimony. He asked him to persuade his daughter, who had been baptized, to fulfill the obligations of Christianity's holy law. The priest's diligent efforts paid off, and the woman came to recognize the mistake she had been led to make by the sorcerers. She returned to married life with her husband, and the error that the devil was trying to introduce was prevented. As a result those who were being baptized were convinced of the duties and perpetuity of holy Christian matrimony.

In one of these pueblos [there was an incident that] strengthened the people's love and reverence for the holy Cross. The infernal enemy visibly appeared to some Indians and began bothering and harassing them. The priest advised the Indians to wear a rosary around their necks and to raise a Cross wherever the enemy appeared to them. The remedy of the sign of our redemption was so effective that our adversary was defeated; the devil disappeared and the Indians became more devoted to the holy Cross.

---

79. Pérez de Ribas neglects to mention that Azpilcueta threatened the Sonora in his "message" with harquebuses, which only Spanish soldiers possessed; thus, there was an implied threat of a counterattack by the Batuco together with Spanish soldiers (AGN 1630).

CHAPTER XVI Father Pedro Méndez fully establishes Christianity among these pueblos;[80] how on one occasion he faced the great danger of being killed on the altar while saying Mass

The great zeal for the salvation of souls that burned in the breast of the apostolic missionary Father Pedro Méndez kept him from slacking off even the slightest bit in the vineyard God had entrusted to him. He was always busy giving talks, teaching the catechism, and performing all other ministries to expand this vineyard. Thus, in four years' time, with no assistance from anyone other than God, he himself had baptized all these people and had established such a brilliant Christianity in them that when the priest who succeeded him, Father Bartolomé Castaño,[81] saw these Indians so developed and so well acquainted with matters of God's law and its mysteries, he said, full of amazement, "It can clearly be seen that Father Pedro Méndez has been here."

Because Father Méndez was now nearly eighty years old and his strength was almost gone as a result of the many hardships he had endured, his superiors felt that mercy begged for him to be brought to Mexico City to rest, as was done. I will recount here a very unusual case that happened to Father Pedro Méndez toward the end of the four years that he spent instructing these people and establishing a great Christianity. At the time there was still a traitorous Judas among them, and this case exemplifies the dangers and risks that Father Méndez experienced in this Christian community, as well as those that our [389] evangelical missionaries are exposed to while enduring hardships for these souls. This is the case with even the most well-behaved nations—those with the best character—such as the Sisibotari, of whom we have been speaking, who received Gospel instruction very well. Finally, it will also be seen that these precious fruits are not harvested by unstained hands, for not even the holy Apostles or their Divine

Master harvested fruits without spilling their precious blood for them.

This good priest had reared a young man to help him with the ministries of the church. Although he seemed to Father Méndez to be of good character and understanding, he gave the devil opportunities for scheming and temptation. He began to change and go bad, causing scandals through his sins and vices. Accordingly, the priest cast him aside, no longer associating with him. The young man became so indignant that he tried to kill the one who had raised him like his own son. The people in another pueblo called Arivechi, which was three leagues away, heard something about this Indian's evil intentions. Fearing some treachery, they set out that night to protect their minister. They ordered the capture of that impious and angry Indian. Once he was captured they tied him up and placed him inside the priest's house.

The following day, as the holy priest was saying Mass before the entire pueblo, the Indian got free and proceeded in a rage to the church. There he attacked Father Méndez on the altar with two butcher knives. He furiously grabbed hold of the priest by his sacred vestments and threw him to the floor. Just as he was about to stab the priest with the knives, the boy who was assisting with Mass leaped forward and threw himself at the Indian. This allowed a nearby Christian Indian principal named Juan de la Cruz Nesúe to remove the beast's claws from the lamb of Christ. Although this good Indian managed to free the priest from death, it was not completely without risk to his own life. He received a few wounds as he snatched the aggressor's prey from his hands. This faithful Christian valued these wounds and displayed them proudly because he had received them in defense of a minister and preacher of the Holy Gospel.

The priest stood up and quickly swallowed the Host that he had consecrated, as well as the chalice [of wine], so that they would suffer no indecency during the dis-

---

80. The pueblos of the Sisibotari and the Batuco.

81. Castaño succeeded Méndez among the Sisibotari in 1635; Méndez spent the remaining eight years of his life in retirement at the Casa Profesa in Mexico City.

turbance. Then the other Christian faithful gathered around and protected their priest. They tied up the one who had been so unfaithful to him and to the holy doctrine that he had received. Without delay they set off for the Villa de San Felipe to turn the Indian over to the captain. They did so in conformance with his order that they should bring him any criminals who were disturbing Christians. The captain considered what had happened, and once he understood the great severity of the crime and the scandal that this Indian had caused among the many nations who heard about the case, he sentenced him to hang. To instill greater fear in [those who might] dare to do something similar, he ordered a corporal and several soldiers to take the delinquent Indian back to Sisibotari lands, and there to carry out the sentence. The Indian confessed and was greatly repentant and aware of his sin when he died. In spite of this fact, the faithful Indians' distress over such a great sacrilege against their priest, Mass, and altar was so great that even after he was dead they continued to shoot arrows at the man on the gallows.

These events did not diminish in the slightest the spirit and fervor with which the Batuco received the doctrine of our Holy Faith. [390] Rather, they seemed to grow even more fervent. Father Bartolomé Castaño, who succeeded Father Pedro Méndez and made a great effort to imitate his fervor and zeal, continued the work of fully establishing this Christianity with its customs and exercises. Within a short time the number of Christians who were worthy and capable of receiving Holy Communion reached three hundred. Considering that these people were so new [to the Faith] and that the priests gave great care to the examination and preparation [of these people] for the receipt of this Supreme Sacrament, it was amazing that so many of them were already taking Communion. Some of them did so even throughout the year, requesting this sacrament out of their great faith and devotion. The children were taught to sing in their language some of the hymns of the Most Holy Sacrament during Communion and also as Mass was being said. Devotion to the Rosary of the Most Holy Virgin was first established in the little ones, who were the tender children of the Sovereign Mother of Mercy. They pray the Rosary as a group in the church, antiphonally, with the little boys saying one part of the Ave Maria and the little girls the next. This devotion was very agreeable to the children, and their parents became so fond of it that in order to enjoy it and to accompany their children, they pray it with them daily. On Saturdays this devotion is celebrated with even greater solemnity by the entire pueblo. An image of the Virgin is placed on a separate altar, with all the adornment that is possible in such poor and distant lands. The little children add to the decoration by gathering all the beautiful flowers that they can find in their montes and fields. Between each decade of the Ave Maria the singers play musical instruments and the little children sing some hymns to the Virgin in their language. Who could doubt that the Holy Virgin receives with particular pleasure these first fruits of her Son's Gospel among these new Christians?

As proof of this I will record a case that took place around this time. The Feast of the Most Holy Sacrament was approaching[82] and many people had assembled. The superior of the missions was [also] there on a visit. The main chapel had been draped and the church had been decorated. The afternoon before the eve of the festival, the sky began to darken and it began to rain in the surrounding hills. The rain began to approach the church, which was not of the permanent kind usually built once Christianity is established. Nor was their church well covered. Rather, the great downpour threatened by the clouds posed a risk of drenching the church and damaging all the decorations, thereby ruining the celebration. On this occasion the priest rang the bell for all the little children to gather in the church. He began to pray the Rosary with them, asking the Virgin not to impede the festival that they wanted to joyously celebrate. Then something marvelous happened, and some considered it a miracle: the threatening clouds that had begun to release water immediately lifted. The Most Holy Virgin kept them from sending more rain than was necessary to water the earth and cool things off, for it was extremely hot. The cool weather lasted until the following morning, when the feast day was celebrated with great joy. The Queen of Heaven made it known with her favors how pleased She was with the prayers of her devout children. [391]

---

82. Corpus Christi, which generally falls in June.

CHAPTER XVII The present state of Christianity in the Sisibotari pueblos

In the previous chapter I discussed the many customs and Christian laws that were proof of how our holy religion took a firm hold in these pueblos. The present state of Christianity will be recorded in this chapter, completing the discussion [of the Sisibotari].

Christ's Holy Passion, which is celebrated during Holy Week, is one of the Christian exercises and ministries that generally becomes well established among these nations, as it is worthy of being remembered by those who have been redeemed by Christ's blood. These people assiduously attend these divine services with great care and devotion. Those for whom [the thought of] repenting their sins was so foreign—because they neither recognized nor feared them—now hold processions and perform blood scourges. They recognize their sins and are devoted to doing penance, especially during Lent, when they very calmly and serenely perform their blood scourges and processions. The priest participates in these processions, carrying a Cross and preaching in their language about the Passion and how God's Son suffered for their sake and for the sins of the world. This is something that becomes notably imprinted in their memory, remaining with them throughout the year.

Once these customs were established these people responded quite well to the labor of building decent churches in which to celebrate their feast days. Like other nations, they devoted themselves with great pleasure to building, dedicating, and adorning the churches, which they never tired of looking at once they were erected in their pueblos. They take singular pleasure in gazing at their churches; the very sight of them keeps them from abandoning their pueblos or even thinking about their former rancherías or rustic huts. They [now] have their houses arranged in an orderly fashion in pueblos, where they appear to stand guard around what they call God's house. What were once deserts inhabited by wild beasts are populated today by tabernacles that are more worthy of veneration than those which the children of Israel, God's [chosen] people, carried through the desert on their way to the Promised Land. The point that I am making here is noteworthy and believable, because there have been Spaniards who at times, upon reaching these distant and far-flung

lands, have reacted with joy at the sight of such a large number of churches in the many pueblos of these missions, among montes and thickets and in formerly unpopulated deserts. Because we are nearing the end of [our discussion] of the conversion of the peoples of the Province of Sinaloa, I [will] add that up to the present time a minimum of fifty beautiful whitewashed temples have been built and adorned with as many glistening ornaments and riches as is possible in such remote lands. That which is most pleasing to God is the great number of people from the pueblos who gather at the churches to adore their one true God—a God they previously did not know. The people of whom I am presently writing care a great deal about [the adoration of their God], as is further evidenced by the choirs that have been established and the musical instruments that have been introduced in these pueblos.

I do not want to omit an edifying case that involved one of the priests who worked [392] in these last missions. This will provide an indication of how pleased the Lord is with His ministers' efforts to erect churches, even if they are poor buildings that lack expensive columns and are not made of stone. This case occurred at a time when the priest was trying to erect a church [dedicated] to the Immaculate Conception of the Virgin.[83] The chief carpenter had cut and dressed the wood for the church as carefully as he could, but before he had finished he was struck with a serious illness that brought him to the brink of death. The priest was notified and came to administer the holy oils. He was greatly saddened to see that the church was going to lose such a skilled craftsman, one who could put the final touches on the church. The priest, who deemed this Indian very important for such a holy task, begged Our Lord for his son's good health. He said to the sick man, "I am sure, my son, that I won't have to administer the holy oils, because if you die, there will be no one to finish the Virgin's church. You have served her, so ask her to give you good health so that you can finish the work that remains." The Mother of Mercy heard this plea and gave this hopelessly sick man his health. He got up and continued his work on the church, which

---

83. Presumably Our Lady of the Angels of Sahuaripa.

was completed and dedicated in honor of Our Lady. The good health of this sick man, who had been so close to death, was attributed to the favor of she who is the Mother of those in need. Accordingly, all these new Christians are greatly devoted to her.

To conclude the discussion of these pueblos and move on to another converted nation, I say that the Sisibotari persevere today in a state of great peace and continue to be a source of great examples of Christianity. Politically speaking, they are very happy with their caciques, who are chosen from among the most exemplary Christians.

CHAPTER XVIII The people of the Valle de Sonora request priests and religious instruction; the location, Baptism, and settlement of this nation

We have reached the last nation in the Province of Sinaloa to have received the good news of the Holy Gospel. Although they have been reduced to our Holy Faith and added to Christ's Holy Church, they are not the last of the barbarous peoples; as was previously noted, others are found beyond the borders of this province, where the light of the Holy Gospel is [now] beginning to shine.

The Valle de Sonora was known to the first explorers of the Province of Sinaloa, who corrupted the name and called it the 'Valle de Señora'.[84] It is on the northern frontier, 130 leagues from the Villa de San Felipe. A mission was begun here around 1638. This valley is quite fertile and has beautiful lands that are irrigated by water from its arroyos. The people who live here are of the same nature as the Sisibotari and share the same customs and dress.[85] Their houses are more permanent and orderly than those of other nations.

It was with great insistence that the Sonora requested religious instruction and a priest to baptize them and make them Christian.[86] They showed the same great desire to become Christians as did other nations in the province. With His divine clemency God attracted this nation through several means, particularly the gentleness and bonds of His sweetest charity, which He promised through His Prophet Hosea *In vinculis charitatis*.[87] Although He had subdued other nations with punishing blows from His staff, this nation was served by His divine kindness, which overcame them with gentleness and sweetness. The Sonora and their households were reduced [393] to large, convenient settlements; three pueblos were established,[88] where one thousand male heads-of-household would be gathered (some people who remained outside the

---

and baptism appears to have stemmed from a belief that baptism provided some protection from disease. Although Pérez de Ribas indicates that a mission was begun among the Sonora in 1638, Father Lorenzo de Cárdenas spent time in the Sonora Valley in 1636, baptizing a large but indeterminate number of infants and apparently adults (Bannon 1955:65–66). The fact that Cárdenas made such a visit before a mission actually was approved suggests that the Opata of the Sonora Valley were in fact dying from disease and, thus, souls were being lost for want of someone to baptize them (see Reff 1991b:168–70).

87. Hosea 11:4: "with leading-strings of love" (Knox 1956:815).

88. Baviácora, Aconchi, and Banámachi; a fourth settlement, Huepac, was constituted around 1640 with the reduction of those who "remained outside the pueblos" in 1638. Note that archaeological evidence indicates that the Opata of the Sonora Valley were living in nucleated settlements with upwards of several hundred houses prior the arrival of the Jesuits, who Pérez de Ribas credits with the creation of pueblos (Pailes 1978; Reff 1981). Apparently in the wake of disease in 1636, many Opata had fled their nucleated settlements, only to be recongregated by Cárdenas and later Castaño.

---

84. Cabeza de Vaca (1536), Coronado (1540), and Ibarra (1566) (see Reff 1981).

85. Both the Sisibotari and Sonora spoke Teguima or Opata proper.

86. In the anua of 1635 (AGN 1635:263) the superior of the Rectorado de San Ignacio, Tomás Basilio, noted that many infants and children were dying each day without baptism beyond the mission frontier, among groups such as the Sonora. The Sonora's insistence for priests

pueblos would eventually follow). With great joy and haste they executed this reduction, which in and of itself is difficult. They [even] invited one another to play the running-stick game that we discussed in Book I. This accelerated the reduction process and pressured priests to come to their lands so that they might benefit from religious instruction.

Father Bartolomé Castaño was appointed missionary to the Sonora,[89] who had already interacted with him when he was instructing their neighbors, the Sisibotari, where he was replaced by another priest. Thus, this new mission had an experienced minister and interpreter, which is what these new Christian communities need. He began with the Baptism of infants, whom he baptized by the hundreds. Then he began his talks concerning the divine catechism and holy laws that they would have to obey. These teachings were welcomed and took such a firm hold that the priest never tired of giving thanks to Our Lord for His grace and aid in preparing these people. For this reason a great deal was accomplished in a short time. Within a year almost all the adults were baptized, numbering three to four thousand people.

Because he saw that these people were so devoted to Christian exercises, the priest made use of a particular strategy to maintain their fervor. He divided the people into decuries,[90] or groups of ten male or female pupils; each decurie of men was led by a man and each group of women by a woman. The leaders were to make sure that all the members of the group attended Christian exercises and became well versed in the mysteries and doctrine of our Holy Faith. Each of these decuries had a specific place in church, which made it easy to keep track of those who attended. These were all means

that resulted from the holy zeal of these faithful ministers. Christ Our Lord demonstrated this same strategy when He performed the miracle of providing bread for five thousand people in the desert, ordering His holy Apostles to distribute the bread in the manner of decuries: *Facite illos discumbere quinquagenos.*[91] And Saint Mark said, *Discubuerunt in partes.*[92] God favors order; He does not like mobs and confusion. Instead, He wants things to proceed harmoniously, following a numbered order. In other nations this duty is carried out by the church fiscales. [The duty of] caring for the pueblo is distributed among three, four, or more of those who hold this position, according to the number of residents.

The division into decuries worked well among our Sonora. They attended very carefully to all their Christian duties. They distanced themselves from gentile customs, which reign in all these nations no matter how well behaved and tame they are, because they live in darkness. This is particularly true regarding the vice that has been so frequently repeated in this history, that of drunken revels, which tainted them all. The Sonora abandoned this vice at the very outset of their religious instruction. There were many other gentiles in the area beyond them—within plain sight—with whom the Sonora maintained trade. Although the Sonora were invited to their toasts and celebrations, they never again had anything to do with such things; they overcame the temptation of this deeply rooted vice.

Once everyone was baptized the priest discussed the matter of building churches. The Sonora erected a very beautiful church in each of their three pueblos. Once these were dedicated this Christianity was perfected and attained the state that will be recorded in the following chapter. [394]

---

89. As noted, this was in 1638. Castaño was joined within a year by Father Pedro Pantoja. The two priests together baptized the 4,000 people whom Pérez de Ribas attributes to Castaño alone (AGN 1639).

90. From *decurio*, a Roman officer in charge of ten men.

91. *Margin Note:* Lucas c. 9. Luke 9:14: "Make them sit down by companies of fifty" (Knox 1956:65).

92. *Margin Note:* Marc. Mark 6:40: "and they took their places in rows" (Knox 1956:39).

CHAPTER XIX The spiritual fruits harvested from the mission among the Sonora and the other nations of Sinaloa

here is a great deal that can be said with respect to cases of edification and the wonderful results obtained when gentiles were converted in their dying hours. As was previously noted, substantial fruits are often harvested from among those who are first converted — instances in which sick people have been saved or have similarly benefited from baptismal grace. All this was corroborated in a letter that I will copy here. This letter was written by a very religious and important individual, so we can be sure of its truth and accuracy. Its author was Father Luis de Bonifaz, Provincial of the Province of Nueva España, who died a holy death while serving in this post.[93] The missions of Sinaloa will always be indebted to him for his twenty-four years of service, most of which he spent fluently preaching the Holy Gospel in the language of the Indians he ministered to. During those years [when he acted as a Rector and Visitor] he governed and visited with great learning and prudence not only the Sinaloa missions, but also the other principal missions and districts that will be discussed later in this history. When he had finished visiting all the districts and pueblos of Sinaloa he reported the state of the missions to the Father Provincial, an office which he subsequently held. He wrote the following letter,[94] in which it should be noted that, although he speaks about all the Sinaloa missions, he refers particularly to the missions of the interior, farthest to the north, which encompass a good part of the Sonora nation, which is the subject of this chapter. The letter states:

Many thanks must be given to Our Lord for this Christian community, which is so isolated. I have just finished visiting the rivers [of the north], and as an eyewitness and one who

has examined, experienced, and carefully observed them, I can affirm that it is one of the best and most glorious enterprises that the Company has undertaken. I observed that all the priests were very dedicated to their ministry; they all very effectively preached two or three sermons in the Indians' languages. Their audiences kept their eyes raised and remained attentive to the preacher during the entire sermon.

There was another exercise of Christian doctrine that would have been enviable even in the most ancient cities of Spain. Children, the elderly, and men and women of all ages responded to questions concerning Christian doctrine. They did so taking turns and using words not found in the catechism. They answered quickly and resolutely not only to questions about the catechism, but to many others concerning matters that had been preached to them. These questions concerned those places under the earth where sins are punished, the purpose of having images in [our] temples, and what to do if someone falls ill and is in a state of sin but does not have a copy of the confessional. The latter situation arises frequently among these people, who wander through the montes and marshes. These Indians also responded quickly and resolutely to questions about the resurrection of the dead, Judgment Day, and similar topics. Because I knew some of these languages, I could bear witness to how well they responded, even some who I knew had never lived in settlements but only in the fields. I can also add that there was an elder among them who was more than one hundred years old; he answered the questions as though he were a well-trained youth.

There was one boy among the children [395] who particularly stood out. When another boy, who was a gentile, came with his parents to be baptized, this child, who was his relative, took him aside and taught him the catechism and mysteries of the Faith. He was such a good teacher that when the time came to baptize the boy [he demonstrated a knowledge of] the mysteries of our Holy Faith that was characteristic of a long-time Christian. It amazed those who were present to see [such intellectual] capacity at such an age among both the catechist and the catechized.

It was people of this type who filled the churches, which are very ample and well built, decorated with various paintings of the mysteries of the Faith. Not only are the children well instructed in it, as noted, but they also are reared with good manners. It is a sight to see how they genuflect in the Spanish fashion when they pass in front of an image or the priest.[95] In some districts the custom has

93. Bonifaz died in 1644. He succeeded Pérez de Ribas as provincial in 1641. In 1640 Bonifaz served as Jesuit visitor to the missions of the north.

94. Bonifaz's letter or report was written in 1640 to Pérez de Ribas, who at the time was Jesuit provincial and who had instructed Bonifaz to conduct an inspection of the northernmost missions, principally among the Opata (Zambrano 1961–1977:4:240). As Pérez de Ribas implies in the opening sentences of this paragraph, Bonifaz's visit coincided with an epidemic among the Sonora, which lasted from November 1639 to April 1640 (Reff 1991b:171–72).

95. The modern custom is to genuflect when passing in front of the central altar and tabernacle, which houses the Eucharist and "body of

been introduced of having the children sing special songs in their own language about matters of the Faith. The songs are frequently heard in the barrios of their pueblos. This has produced two positive results: the first is that the adults have learned the lines sung by the children; the second is that they have forgotten their gentile songs.

All the men as well as the women wear rosaries around their necks. Indeed, I don't think that I saw a single person in all those crowds who was not wearing one. I will make two comments regarding this devotion which, although they may seem minor, are not so at this stage [of their Christianity]. One day I said Mass in one of these pueblos, and I found a great number of rosaries lying on the altar to be blessed. After I had blessed them I watched to see whose they were. When Mass was over a crowd of boys and girls came to collect their rosaries. They came forward very silently, and each one selected his own and took it away.

During times of illness they experience divine aid with the Rosary. This was especially true of one boy who was near death, who completely recovered once his mother—with great faith and devotion—placed the holy rosary on his body. One day [I also observed] the body of one boy being taken for burial to the accompaniment of the prayers of many boys and girls with rosaries in their hands. The adults also accept this devotion quite [well]. In some pueblos it is [so well] established that after they say the Rosary [in their homes], all the families come outside their houses at the appointed time and say it out loud on their knees; the entire pueblo becomes like an oratory. They say they do this even when the missionary priests are absent [from the pueblo], when they are out in their fields, and when traveling. When they are sick they call upon the Most Holy Virgin with such great affection that some of our religious priests who visited these pueblos related that they had been greatly moved by the Indians' devotion.

Their devotion to Mass is also a sign of their Faith; they never miss weekday Mass, attending it as if it were Sunday. When I was with one of the priests an old Indian came to him. According to the custom of the poor in this land, he wore no more clothing than what natural modesty required. He asked the priest to say a High Mass for his deceased daughter. No matter how poor they are, they are able to make this request because they know that our priests cannot receive a stipend for saying Mass.[96] I noticed the same thing in another pueblo where the priests assured me that all the relatives [of the deceased] bring offerings to these Masses; from their poverty they donate maize and other legumes to be given to the poor. This is done by the fiscales.

I found myself in one of these pueblos (which, because it was the most distant and most recently settled, will serve as a good example of the others) one Saturday at

the [appointed time for reciting] the Salve [Regina].[97] I saw more than forty people [396] of all ages scourging themselves. The priest assured me that he had not suggested this but, rather, that they had accepted this good custom so willingly that they turn out for it without having to be called. The disciplines of Holy Week are full of people and blood. One priest in particular wrote to me this year relating that more than fifteen hundred people had turned out for scourging. He said that it was a sight to see them proceed with such great modesty and solemnity. In some places the people scourged their backs three times a week throughout Lent. This was accompanied by organ music and the singing of the Miserere.

The same devotion is shown on All Souls' Day. When the bell is rung for the litany of souls they get down on their knees, and in loud voices heard throughout the pueblo they pray ten Hail Marys and one Our Father.

The priests have told me of the many general confessions that they have heard during these past two years and how the people benefit from everything that is said and repeated to them, [particularly] the need for an authentic confession and remorse for one's sins. Some set a good example of scruples, as in the many cases of men who [once they have dissolved their polygamous marriages] return their wives' dowries so as not to keep them [unjustly]. More than two hundred people usually confess and take Holy Communion on the major feast days of the year and those dedicated to the Most Holy Virgin and the other saints.

Extreme Unction used to horrify them because they believed it to be a sure foretelling of death, but now it is understood and the sick insistently request it. The Lord has willed that many anointed persons who had been given up for dead have been restored to health. During my visit there was a sick man who called for the priest, who had heard his confession but was away at the time visiting other pueblos. Even though this man had already lost his sight by the time the priest returned, he still said to the priest, "You've come right in the nick of time, Father, for now I will die in peace—I will die having received the holy oils." He was comforted and anointed, at which point Our Lord took him to heaven. Another Indian who was dying received the Holy Sacraments. Then he sat up and, taking the rosary in his hands, he began to utter very moving words to Our Lord. He performed a very fervent Act of Contrition, and while he was saying Our Lady's Rosary he expired, leaving great reassurances of his salvation.

The people of this nation had placed their confidence in a large number of sorcerers, who were their former doctors and healers. In the past they believed that they could not live without these sorcerers. However, now they dislike them so much that they do not even like to hear the word sorcerer. They have exchanged their custom of calling upon the sorcerers in their afflictions for coming to church, where they

---

Christ." Apparently, the Indians understood genuflection as a sign of respect for the priest and what was symbolized by the image of the crucified Christ.

96. The Jesuit Constitutions prohibited a priest from receiving alms for saying Mass or distributing the sacraments.

97. This prayer to Mary, which is second only to the Hail Mary, is known in English as "Hail, Holy Queen."

receive the priest's blessing and have him recite a [passage from the] Gospels.

The boys' schools are very well organized. Because the seminarians turn out to be skillful at everything, Masses are solemnly celebrated with singing and [musical] instruments. They are building many houses of adobe where [before] there were only houses made from woven reed mats. Some who are building adobe houses did not even have these mats before, and lived instead in their fields.

Up to this point [I have been citing] the letter of this very religious, prudent, and vigilant Prelate and Visitor of these missions. As an eyewitness and someone who was always careful and discreet in speaking about these things, he narrates how the light of Christianity flourished among these newly converted nations. It must certainly be understood that, just as is the case in all the Christian communities of Sinaloa, these people are very steadfast in their observance of the Christian exercises in which the priests train them and in which they

train themselves. Indeed, they emulate what is praiseworthy in others to the point that they are always trying to keep up with one another. [397]

The Sonora have been one of the most receptive nations with respect to our Holy Faith. There I find the doctrine of the Gospel ready to yield the most abundant fruit that has [yet] been written about. As a final [observation, I add that] they built many beautiful churches and established three pueblos, in which there are more than one thousand heads-of-household and [their] families. They govern themselves very peaceably. Because this nation is the most recently converted to our Holy Faith, they are bordered on the north by gentiles. At the time this [history] is being written the Sonora have been baptized and reduced for only five years. Our Lord shall will that one day the joyful and divine light of the Gospel will reach those nations on their [northern] border.

CHAPTER XX The virtues, ministries, and evangelical labors of Father Vicente de Aguila of the Company of Jesus in the Sinaloa missions

The great religiosity, works, and holy zeal of Father Vicente de Aguila must be recognized by the Province of Sinaloa and its missions and Christian communities. This very religious priest spent the better part of his life—nearly forty years—cultivating and extending Christianity. He labored gloriously in the fields of the evangelical word, where he harvested the most felicitous fruits. It was in this glorious enterprise that his life came to an end. Here I will relate what was written by Father Leonardo Játino,[98] who at the time was Visitor of the Sinaloa missions. (As is the custom of the Company) he gave an account of the virtues, life, and death of Father Vicente de Aguila. The entire province is thus informed whenever someone passes from this life so that all can aid

the deceased with the usual observances we are accustomed to hold.[99] Father Játino's account was longer than usual, in part because of the individual and in part because of the remoteness of the place and the enterprise in which his life ended.

> Today, Tuesday (Játino writes) March 5, [1641] Our Lord was served to summon from these Sinaloa missions Father Vicente de Aguila, who was sixty years old. He was a religious for forty-three years, having professed the four vows of our Company twenty-six years earlier. The priest died at age sixty of a high fever, or *tabardillo*,[100] which did

98. Pérez de Ribas refers to Játino as Xatini. Játino served as visitor in 1639.

99. Jesuit archives in Rome, Spain, and Mexico contain many of these *cartas necrológicas* or *de edificación*. This letter by Játino is in the AGN (Historia, Tomo 308) and is reproduced by Zambrano (1961–1977:3:90–95).

100. In the late fifteenth century typhus, called *tabardillo*, appeared for the first time in Spain. Those who survive the original onslaught of rickettsia can retain the disease for many years, suffering recurrent bouts of fever. It is possible, however, that Aguila suffered instead from malaria, which can also produce "malignant fevers" (Reff 1991b:170–72).

not respond to the remedies of these poor and spare lands. He prepared himself very well for death, maintaining his senses and lucidity until the moment of death. He received the Holy Sacraments with great devotion, affection, and tenderness. Toward the end of his illness he made a general confession. He died as though he were someone who had done nothing else during his life except prepare for a good death.

I find myself obliged to say something here for our edification and consolation concerning this priest's virtue and holy life. However, no one should doubt the zeal with which I begin this task. Father Aguila was so highly thought of—with the fame of a saint—by the native people and Spaniards, both lay and religious, that no matter how much I wish to say about this joyous death (which, perforce, must be brief), I have no doubt that those who knew and dealt with him will find that my comments are insufficient and fall short in terms of praise. Indeed (as pointed out by Saint John Chrysostom), our praise can never do justice to the admirable virtues of a saint: *Quando quide haet est pracipua laudie dius paras, quod fact is* [398] *verba equiparare non possint*.[101] I happily confess (although I am only too happy to offer this praise) that no matter what I say or wish to say, it will fall short.

Father Vicente entered the Company at Alacalá de Henares in the Province of Toledo, where he graduated from that university with the degree of bachelor of arts. He had studied with his brother, Doctor Juan de Aguila, a man of great virtue and learning, who died as the Bishop-elect of Lugo. Father Vicente completed his novitiate at Villarejo de Fuentes, under the discipline and praiseworthy teaching of Father Nicolás de Almazán, who subsequently died while serving in Rome as the assistant [to the Procurator] from Spain. When he began his life in the Company Father Vicente gave signs of what he would later become: a perfect religious. He continually improved himself until the moment of his joyous death.

He was a student of theology when he came to this Province of Nueva España, where he was ordained a priest. Throughout the remainder of his life, which totaled some thirty-five or thirty-six years, he was gloriously employed in the missions. He spent the first two years in San Luis de la Paz and the remainder in this province. The missions of Sinaloa were fortunate to have this man for many reasons, not the least of which were his many construction projects. He was a teacher not only of Indians, but also of Spaniards. He was a missionary, a subject, a superior, and for four years a Visitor.[102] Above all, however, he was a teacher of his fellow missionary priests. When he died he was the eldest among them; he had continuously and untiringly labored in these missions almost since the [day] they were founded. [He worked] with such perseverance in his old age that he

exceeded and demonstrated more energy than a beginner, edifying those who wished to imitate him. Because his only employment as a priest was as a missionary of the Company, I judge as his highest praise (or better to say, all his praise) [the fact] that he became such a good one, which is something that is very difficult, worthy, and glorious.

Without a doubt what is most worthy of admiration in this priest is the perfect combination of a most observant religious and an illustrious missionary. He was a most punctual observer of the rules, exercises, and laudable customs of a cloistered religious; the religious life was his only concern, along with the work, diversion, and varied occupation of a great missionary who was obliged to watch over the bodies and souls of so many [people]. As exemplary as he was as a novice, once he became a priest he could not have been more observant and punctual in getting up at the customary time. For him [the rule of rising] when dawn broke was unbreakable. When someone rang a bell for him at that time, he promptly obeyed. [It was the same with] his morning prayers, the two examinations that are conducted at noon and at night, and the spiritual lessons that lasted half an hour (at least) at the quarter hour of *Contemptus mundi*, which was also the appointed time for [reciting] the litanies.[103] At the designated time he also said the Rosary of the Virgin. He had many [such] devotions, and he [observed] the instructions of the rules until the last days of his life, in the midst of the most demanding challenges. In this regard he was a singular [source] of edification and an example to those who had the closest contact with him. They knew from experience how difficult this [observance] was; but how difficult could this have been for Father de Aguila, who always kept before his eyes the vigilant candle of an entirely scrupulous conscience and a supreme and living rule of interior charity and love of God? He had so refined this rule that he no longer had to concern himself with venial or mortal sins, but rather only with freeing his thoughts, words, and deeds from the slightest imperfection. One would sometimes overhear him say, "Jesus, could I have done something to violate the rule?"

He was likewise punctual and perfect in all the other virtues of a holy religious. He was so obedient that it was as if he had no willpower or intellect to differ with what he was ordered [to do]. He never raised even the slightest objection to his superiors' governance; rather, he was always [399] consoling and edifying. He was an enemy of doing his own will and was so open to suggestions that he could never decide on anything himself. Instead, he always looked to and attempted to follow the opinion of others. This was a virtue that was of great merit and importance with respect to the scruples that he continuously observed throughout his life. (As he told one priest), he would have lost his reason many years ago if he had not adapted so easily to what his confessor, or spiritual father, told him, even if it were totally contrary to what he felt. This is a truth that was well

---

101. *Margin Note:* Homil. de B. Philogo. The referent here apparently is one of numerous homilies written by Saint John Chrysostom (d. 407), archbishop of Constantinople and a Doctor of the Church (Thurston and Attwater 1956:1:178–83). "Because this is particularly true of praise, that words cannot compare with deeds."

102. Aguila held the office in 1616 and again in 1636–37.

103. *Contemptus mundi* is "contempt for the world," perhaps 3 P.M., the hour of Christ's death. Here "litanies" probably refers to the Litany of the Saints (Attwater 1949:293).

attested by the royal Prophet, David, who commented that in stormy times that are without scruples, one's own counsel or wisdom is not sufficient: *Sapientia eorum deborata est.*[104]

His very great and well-known humility was undoubtedly another consequence of his acceptance of this truth. His humility did not allow him to trust himself, although it is true that he knew [his abilities] well, because he had earned excellent grades in all the courses in liberal arts[105] and could easily have held, to everyone's satisfaction, any major university chair. He especially shone in moral [theology], so much so that whenever they wanted to convince him through reasoning and authority, he responded with an equal number of arguments either in favor of or against a position. Indeed, it was jokingly said of Father Vicente de Aguila that he had no scruples except when he wanted. He ordinarily phrased his questions in the following humble manner, "Tell me, Your Reverence, with respect to this particular matter, can one do this or not? Is it a sin or not?" With a simple answer to this question he would be soothed and consoled. This humility shone in the priest's works, words, deeds, and labors. Indeed, it was his maxim, even with the Indians and those who served him, that not even the most minor punishment should be inflicted on Indians, even if they had repeatedly failed to obey and serve him. He preserved and encouraged this humility with gentle religious simplicity, without any kind of duplicity, falsehood, or flattery. Indeed, using even the most ordinary compliments bothered his conscience when it seemed to him they did not reflect reality.

The priest's poverty was that which could be expected from such a humble religious. He was very frugal with his allowances and spent little on personal things, at times exceeding what was required by the dignity of his status and occupation. For many years he wore a cassock made of coarse woven serge that was stained from use and [contact with] the unwashed Indians. His household furnishings were all very poor, and he set a very sparse and rustic table. Once he stated simply that he lived like an Indian. This was in part due to his mortification and penance, which he always loved and exercised until the very last years of his difficult life. Although it would appear that he was very strong, physically he was not; rather, he was small and frail. [Nevertheless], he was very fervent when scourging himself, wearing a spiked undergarment[106] and performing other acts of penance and mortification. Some of these [he practiced] so rigorously that, even when for various reasons he was not obliged to do [penance], all he could think about was whether his penance and mortification were sufficient.

Because he was such a mortified, poor, humble, and religious man, who could doubt his chastity? He undoubtedly was chaste. He was such a great example of extraordinary prudence that he greatly edified his Indians, providing them with an example and thus teaching them to correct their own vices. His chastity was heightened and made beautiful by the gift of virginity, which was verified by his confessor, to whom he made a general confession of his entire life [in preparation for] death. His virginity was so certain that, even if the priest had not said it, his eyes, face, modesty, and prudence proclaimed it, even though it was concealed by his humility. Never over a distance of one thousand leagues was he heard to utter a single word that could be interpreted as anything less than pure. When he dealt with this subject [of chastity], even with all necessary modesty and decency, his face turned redder than the face of the most pure and cloistered maiden. [400] After such protracted and close contact and communication with so many women for the purpose of teaching, confession, and governance, in a district where he had spent twenty-four years, he barely recognized them by sight, and even this became a matter of scruples.

It should not seem that we are straying from our central concern if we discuss what a good missionary he was for the Company. I do not think I have strayed [in this respect], because what has been said about him up to now was undoubtedly what made him such a good missionary. His obedience was so continuous and laudable that when, after some years, he wanted to leave the missions (as he related to [another] priest), he was so circumspect and timid in saying so—in order not to diminish his perfect obedience in any way—that one could not tell whether he wanted to leave them or not. His humility also contributed to this, for he considered himself useless for any other task. After much was said [he finally acknowledged that] perhaps he could do a good job teaching one of the lesser disciplines. This same humility made him so kind and gentle with the Indians that they loved and esteemed him greatly. His poverty and lack of concern for his own person enabled him to give a great deal to the Indians, as well as to the churches that he decorated and enriched, which thus became the most adorned in the missions. Finally, the great charity and love of God that shone in the priest, and which governed his daily life, enhanced all his other virtues. This love of God was the sole beginning and the true mother of that second charity—love for his fellow man—that so completely occupied the priest in all his ministries as a missionary. Indeed, it seemed that he never seemed to know how nor could have been born to do anything else. There was no difficult problem or task that could have prevented him from perfectly fulfilling his apostolic ministry.

While he was ministering to his pueblos he fell and broke a leg. Because he could not stand and go to hear a sick person's confession, he had himself carried in a woven litter so that he could hear confessions and console his faithful. He did so without sparing himself labor or pain. This charity made him a constant and untiring preacher and teacher of the Faith and its mysteries *Opportune & importun*—opportune or not—at any time, on all occasions, collectively or individually, for mestizos, ladinos, black slaves,[107] and his own Indians—or whoever else he might see. It was as though to him alone Saint Gregory the Great had offered

---

104. Isaiah 29:14: "Bereft of wisdom their wise men shall be, cunning of their counselors vanish," (Knox 1956:651); also repeated by Saint Paul in 1 Corinthians 1:19.
105. *Belle lettres.*
106. *Silicios.*

107. *Bozales.*

this counsel: If preaching to them as a group does not provide them with a thorough understanding, then the preacher should teach each one individually. *Considerandum est nobis (the Saint says) ut qui una cadem que exhortationis voce no sufficit simul cunctos admonere; studeat singulos in quantum valet instruere, privatis locutionibus aedificare.*[108] Our missionary did this quite well with all the Indians of the province, calling them whenever the occasion arose, catechizing them very slowly, and providing them with an easy way of memorizing and recounting the mysteries of the Faith. This care also extended to attending to the spiritual needs of the Spaniards [at the Villa de San Felipe] during the time when this priest was superior.[109] In addition, he also compiled a brief summary of the mysteries of the Faith, which he had printed in Mexico City at his own expense, making sure that everyone in the land had [a copy of] it. This love caused the priest to dedicate himself entirely to [learning] the two languages[110] in which he instructed the native peoples for many years. Indeed, he became a master in both languages, compiling grammars, vocabularies, collections of sermons and parables, short and long catechisms, procedures for confession, guides, and even poems to be sung in church that summarized and repeated the mysteries of the Faith, which were always his principal concern.[111] Undoubtedly, all his efforts [yielded] many fruits, even after his death. [401]

This love also made him diligently seek and employ as many means as possible to help the souls of his children in Christ, particularly with regard to the true Faith, which native peoples generally desired yet which is so difficult to find alive and constant among them in the beginning. For this reason he went to great lengths in his veneration and public worship of God and His Most Holy Mother, Our Lady, and, most especially, the Most Holy Sacrament. He made sure to celebrate their feast days and processions with the greatest possible solemnity and spectacle. He even designed some triumphal floats that were made in the Indians' fashion and other more elaborate and magnificent ways of displaying the Most Holy Sacrament,[112] as he had heard was being done in Mexico City, Sevilla, and Toledo. With regard to this public worship he busied himself adorning the church and the sacristy with altars, retablos, vessels, centerpieces, angels, flowers, and other decorations. He did this to the extent that it seemed to be his only concern. To realize this same goal, he began to erect strong, spacious, and beautiful churches so that the [one] true God could be worshiped. He was still working on this when God called him home. When he died he was in the process of roofing two of the best churches in the Province of Sinaloa. I cannot help but think that God led him to the pueblo of Ahome to die,

arranging it so that his body would be interred in the half-roofed church there. This was the same place where there had been a tremendous flood a few years earlier [apparently in 1630], which destroyed another church that had just been built, roofed, and whitewashed. The priest was painting and beautifully decorating it for its dedication, and (as he told a confidant) its destruction was the greatest mortification of his life. [It was] as though Divine Majesty was letting us know how much He was pleased with the priest's work, and even more so with the patience and conformity with which he bore that mortification. Further, it is as if God wanted the priest's body to ascend from that place where he had so gloriously labored so that he could enjoy the reward and great praise that awaited him.

Finally, this priest's love for [his] fellow man extended from souls to bodies. He was always soliciting many things to give to his children, helping them as much as possible in their hunger and need. He learned various simple remedies for their illnesses, dismissing them completely from work [when they were ill], as was his prerogative. His Indians and all those who knew him in the many other districts loved him greatly because of the aid and instruction he gave them. He was likewise loved and venerated by the Spaniards, particularly by all the other priests. He was loved even more by God, who not only wanted to summon him to eternal rest but, of course, also wanted to reveal to us how much the priest's most scrupulous life had pleased Him, and for which he had earned his crown [of glory]. In the final days of his life God gave him such great serenity, peace, and tranquility of conscience that it was as though he had always understood fear, doubt, and scruples. It also seemed that he saw with the eyes of the soul and with a great hope the reward in God to which he was being called. Although his holy life and conversation have entirely persuaded us, still in order to fulfill my obligations, I beg Your Reverence to order that ceremonies for a deceased missionary of our order be conducted in the holy colleges, and that Your Reverence not forget me in his prayers and in the holy sacrifices you offer. Sinaloa, March 5, 1641. [402]

This is what the Father Visitor of the Sinaloa missions wrote, and I can add (as someone who for several years enjoyed the most religious company of Father Vicente de Aguila while ministering in the same mission and pueblos[113]) that I always saw in him an angel from heaven and an apostolic missionary; I was an eyewitness to all the virtues described herein.

---

108. *Margin Note*: S. Greg Hommil. 17 in Luca 10. The referent here apparently is Saint Gregory the Great's Homily 17 on Luke 10. "We must consider thoroughly" (the Saint says) "that it does not suffice to admonish all at the same time with one voice; let him be eager to instruct individuals on how to be good with edifying private speeches."

109. Aguila became superior of the Sinaloa mission in 1631 and held the post until his death in 1641 (Zambrano 1961–1977:3:79–129).

110. Aguila spent many years with the Ahome and Zuaque, who spoke Guasave and Cáhita, respectively.

111. Father Játino neglects to mention here that Aguila also wrote a short history of the Jesuit missions of Sinaloa, apparently in 1613, which Pérez de Ribas drew from for his own history (Zambrano 1961–1977:3:132).

112. Corpus Christi celebrations in Spain and the New World usually involved processions that included arches and floats where the Eucharist (kept safe in a monstrance) was escorted throughout the pueblo, in a sense blessing or purifying the physical space in which the people of the community lived out their lives.

113. In 1617 when Pérez de Ribas (and Tomás Basilio) went to found

CHAPTER XXI The life and death of the very religious Father Gerónimo Ramírez, a member of the Company of Jesus who labored in several Indian missions in Nueva España

I f I were to continue as I should, recounting in chronological order the events and lives of the illustrious men who were outstanding missionaries to these gentile nations, I would now relate the life of Father Pedro Méndez, who did so much in terms of cultivating the nations discussed here in Book VI. I have been unable to follow that order, however, because at the time I left Mexico to represent that nation in Rome,[114] Father Pedro Méndez was still alive, although quite old. It was while I was here at this court in Madrid, where this book is in press, and on my way to Rome, that I received the news that the Lord had given holy Father Méndez a death {on July 23, 1643} as holy as his life and that an account of his life would soon be sent to me. Due to the fact that the presses could not be stopped, the present chapter will deal with Father Gerónimo Ramírez,[115] who was an illustrious missionary to other nations that I will discuss later. If space allows later on,[116] Father Méndez will be accorded the treatment that corresponds to an apostolic man who labored for forty years cultivating the nations of Sinaloa.

Father Andrés Cazorla, who is today one of the oldest members in the [Jesuit] Province of Andalucía and who is well known for his great faith, gave me a signed account of the first glimpses of Father Gerónimo Ramírez's outstanding virtues. These two men were already close friends when they entered the Company.[117] Father Cazorla speaks as a witness to the young but mature and perfect virtue that Our Lord provided this, His evangelical minister (even from his early years).

Gerónimo was born in 1557 in the city of Sevilla, the son of honorable parents. He was raised from an early age within the household of the duchess of Alcalá. When she noticed his great virtue and good disposition she gave him to her relative, the holy Bishop of Cádiz, Don García de Haro. The Bishop thought very highly of Gerónimo, and he remained with him until he was sent for higher education to Córdoba, where the schools are well known for their [courses in] letters and the competence of their students. Gerónimo was not only an outstanding example of common virtue, but he rigorously sought perfection. He regularly wore a spiked undergarment and performed exercises of mortification, penance, and scourging. Our Lord greatly blessed his frequent prayers. On his days off he went into the countryside to instill fervor in his heart. He and his companions would seek one another out and spend the afternoon together joyfully praising God through His creatures. In this way he was moved and became more fervent. As a consequence all those students who aspired to virtue came to seek his counsel, hanging on his words of advice. [403] This fervent young man's devotion consisted at this time not only of words, but also of deeds of mortification and humility.

The holy Bishop gave Gerónimo whatever support he needed. In addition, he also enjoyed a scholarship [118] from the church of Tarifa. However, in order to mortify himself and imitate Christ's poverty, he used to go to convents and the doorways of religious houses where, with his poor man's bowl, he would receive the soup and other alms that were distributed, just like all the other poor. He dearly loved the poor because for him they represented Christ. On one

---

the Yaqui mission, Aguila took over Pérez de Ribas' responsibilities as missionary to the Ahome and Zuaque. During the next three years, until Pérez de Ribas was recalled to Mexico City, the two priests undoubtedly communicated, sharing their common experience as missionaries to the Ahome and Zuaque.

114. In 1643 Pérez de Ribas was chosen by his fellow Jesuits in Nueva España to travel to Rome as Procurator—to advise and petition the father general on behalf of the Jesuit province of Nueva España.

115. The actual printing of the eight hundred-plus pages of the *Historia* must have taken at least several months. This statement about not being able to stop the presses suggests that, had he received information on Méndez before the printing was far enough along, Pérez de Ribas would have had a chance to include a biography of his fellow missionary. If so, one wonders whether the additional chapter would have had to have been approved by censors and Jesuit superiors.

116. Pérez de Ribas never included a biography of Méndez in the *Historia*. However, he did fulfill his promise and devote a chapter to Méndez in a subsequent work, his *Corónica*, which was completed in 1654 but not published until 1896 (Pérez de Ribas 1896:1:378–99).

117. Pérez de Ribas is alluding here to an account of Ramírez's early years as a Jesuit written by Cazorla, entitled *Relación de los primeros resplandores y ejemplos señalados de virtud del P. Gerónimo Ramírez* (Zambrano 1961–1977:5:144).

118. *Beneficio*. Although this term generally referred to the salary or stipend that secular clergy received for ministerial duties, Ramírez was a student at the time, not a priest. Thus we have translated the term as scholarship.

particular feast day for the patron saints of Córdoba, Saint Acisclos and Saint Victoria, he saw a beggar in the street with a festering and seeping wound on one of his legs. Moved by the fervor of his devotion, he knelt down and kissed the beggar's leg, bathing his lips in that foul pus. He considered it a precious ointment, because in that poor man he saw the wounded Christ. Those who witnessed this virtuous young man's action and devotion were amazed.

In the same way he was strengthening his other virtues—modesty, prudence, suffering, patience when it was required, and conversations with God Our Lord—during the entire two years he spent in Córdoba before entering the Company. In fact, we can say that before he entered the school of perfection, he had already advanced in this respect to a heroic degree.

This was the signed testimony of the aforementioned Father Andrés de Cazorla, who was a Rector and spiritual teacher at several colleges in Andalucía. He adds that when Brother Gerónimo was accepted into the Company as a novice, and later during his years of study, he was steadfast in his pursuit of perfection. Indeed, all his study was aimed at molding his life in accordance with the lesson taught by the golden book, *Contemptus mundi*,[119] which he continually read for spiritual insight. Although the entire book discusses and teaches the highest form of the spirit and Christian perfection, Chapter XXIII of Book III stands out in this regard. It deals with the extreme perfection of four things which, because they are so outstanding, caused the chapter to be entitled "The Four Things."[120] One day this fervent youth asked his theology teacher, Father Ignacio Yáñez, "How can such perfection exist in those four things when, through Our Lord's goodness, I possess those four things and yet I am imperfect and sinful?" The very religious brother confessed this with complete sincerity, and we can understand that it was true.

Father Gerónimo Ramírez entered the Company in 1577, when he was twenty years old. He was a member of the Company for forty-three years, [demonstrating] remarkable perfection and sanctity. From the outset of his novitiate he was well known for his great religiosity, devotion, humility, obedience, introspection, and inclination to silence, which he combined with his peaceable

and affable treatment of everyone. His conversation usually concerned the Lord and related matters, for which he quoted the sayings and deeds of the saints, as well as anecdotes. However, what seems to have made him stand out more than anything else was his holy exercise of prayer. For him the hours allotted daily for this were insufficient, so each day he got up an hour before the scheduled time when the rest of the community rose for prayer. He used all his available time to serve the Lord—all the while remaining obedient. Even when he traveled, no matter how tired he was, he observed the exercise he loved, dedicating himself even more to prayer. He always [404] carried a little crucifix, and whenever he was alone he would take it out and talk to it sweetly. He remained very devoted to the Passion of Christ, Our Lord, who always gave him peace and happiness during times of difficulty and need. Last but not least, he was similarly [devoted] to the Most Holy Virgin, whom he always considered his Mother.

His zeal for helping souls was incomparable and among the rarest ever seen. It was apparent even when he was a novice. When he was still a student of philosophy and letters in Córdoba he fervently gave religious instruction to the urchins or vagabonds, reaping abundant fruit among these poor and defenseless people. After two years of theology, in 1584, he traveled from Spain to the Province of Mexico with Father Provincial Antonio de Mendoza. As soon as he arrived in Nueva España, he was sent to the college in Pátzcuaro to learn the language of that province. This province has one of the largest Indian populations in all of Nueva España. At the same time he was given the responsibility of teaching reading and writing to the young children who attended the school at the college. Brother Gerónimo did everything with continuous fervor and care. In fact, he learned the language well enough to give religious instruction as well as preach in the plaza of the city, where there always were crowds of Indians. He took great consolation in employing his fervent zeal in aiding the souls of both these Indians and the little Spanish children from the school. Then he returned to Mexico City to very successfully complete his studies. At the same time (as somebody who knew how to make good use of his time) he learned the Mexican language [Nahuatl]. He acquired and practiced this language very well in order to become an instrument of the Lord and to aid souls.

When he finished his studies and was ordained a priest, he returned to Pátzcuaro [in 1587 or 1588]. With his command of languages and his position as a minister

---

119. Pérez de Ribas is referring here to Thomas à Kempis' *The Imitation of Christ* (1955), which was completed in 1427 and which gives voice to the notion of *contempus mundi*, that is, despising the world in order to draw nearer to God. The Jesuits were extremely fond of Kempis' work, which they considered a "Jesuit text" (Aizpuru 1989:173).

120. Actually, "Of Four Things That Bring Peace to the Soul," namely (1) study to do another man's will rather than your own, (2) seek poverty, (3) seek humility and subordination, and (4) desire and pray that the will of God will be wholly done in you.

of the Holy Spirit, he heard confessions and preached to the Indians and Spaniards. He did so to everyone's edification and with very fruitful results. Still, his thirst to see souls go to heaven was not quenched, so he undertook missions in the districts of this province that had many benefices and curates. There, he exercised all the ministries of love that the Company uses. He undertook one mission in particular that lasted eight months. Despite many difficulties caused by an epidemic of influenza [121] that attacked many people, causing death in some cases, he traveled extensively through very hot lands and along the coasts of Colima, Zacatula, and other provinces, to the extraordinary benefit of the souls there. When this loving priest went untiringly to see those who were sick and infected, he not only provided them with the Holy Sacrament, but he lovingly gave whatever he had in an effort to cure them. In the pueblos he visited he heard almost everyone's confession, as if it were Holy Week. In order to console them all, he had to work until ten in the evening hearing their confessions. Still, the following morning before dawn the church was again full of people waiting for confession.

The fervor of the sermons preached in that unusual language by holy Father Ramírez worked to his advantage and helped him accomplish his holy task among the people of this distant land, who had rarely benefited from sermons. He usually preached two sermons daily, one in the morning and another in the afternoon. Everyone attended the frequent solemn processions in which the doctrine was sung. After conducting catechism drills and distributing prizes to the children he would then preach to the others, sometimes in two or three languages because of the great variety of people who attended. And such a great occupation could not fail to be accompanied [405] by the other that he always greatly esteemed and loved, that of prayer and other Spiritual Exercises. This allowed him very little sleep and even obliged him to forgo food and other necessities. In a land where there was a lack of sustenance and where there was excessive heat, he nevertheless continually fasted and remained penitent. He lived in this same manner for many years in all his missions. It would take too long to recount all the fruits that he obtained: general confessions, changed lives, and customs and vices that were banned—such as drinking, idolatry, and superstitions, which Indians tend to keep even after they have been baptized. Everything was

improved in God's favor; the holy labor of His servant produced a plentiful harvest.

After three years at the college in Pátzcuaro in the Province of Michoacán, Father Ramírez went to the city and mining center of Zacatecas.[122] There [he obtained] no less significant fruits with his solemn religious instruction, processions, exhortations, and sermons. He preached in Spanish, Mexican, and Tarascan, which is the language spoken in Michoacán, where he had been before. Many people who spoke those languages went to work at this famous mining center.[123] Because the Indians particularly feared and respected him, and because of the fervor with which he preached to them, Father Ramírez obtained great results. This did not prevent him from continually assisting and ministering to Spaniards, because he extended his zealous charity to everyone.

Because the college in Zacatecas was closest to the Tepehuan and [Irritilla] of Parras, whose missions we will deal with later, he undertook the conversion of those two gentile nations.[124] The superiors chose Father Gerónimo because of his fervent spirit, knowing how willing he was to suffer great hardships for Christ and the welfare of souls. For that reason the superiors chose him for all potentially difficult enterprises. He considered it very fortunate that they should turn to him for such tasks. Later, when I discuss the history of these two missions, I will discuss in more detail his extensive work in clearing these gentile forests and sowing the Gospel doctrine in places where it had never been heard, and the fruit he gathered there. [For the present] it will be sufficient to note that he learned their languages and domesticated Indians who were more barbarous than the ferocious wild beasts of the fields; he pacified and transformed them into gentle lambs of Christ. He baptized a good number of people and brought them into the flock of the Holy Church, many times risking his life in the process.

121. *Catarro pestilencial*. This was in 1588 (Reff 1991b:127).

122. This was in 1591 or 1592, a year or so after Visitor Diego de Avellaneda approved a permanent Jesuit residence in Zacatecas (Dunne 1944:21).

123. Zacatecas had been a magnet for free Indian labor from central Mexico since the silver strike of 1546. In 1581 there were some 6,000 African slaves and Indians, mostly from central Mexico, working in the mines of Nueva Vizcaya, principally in and around the city of Zacatecas (Paso y Troncoso 1940:15:53). Some of these Mexica and Tarascan Indians had fought in the north with Spanish soldiers against the Zacateco and Guachichile (Ahern 1995c).

124. Ramírez began working with the Zacateco and Irritilla in 1594 and in 1596 founded a permanent mission among the Tepehuan.

Following such difficult labors and pilgrimages, Father Gerónimo, under [the orders of] holy obedience, was sent to found the [Jesuit] college in Guatemala, four hundred leagues from the Tepehuan.[125] This was another no less demanding and consuming task. His superiors knew of Father Ramírez's capacity and ability to save souls from sin, so they sent him to attend to the needs of that very noble city and kingdom. When he arrived in Guatemala he found that the Bishop, Don Fray Juan Ramírez of the holy Order of Saint Dominic, was away visiting his bishopric. He had left strict orders not to let the new preacher administer the Holy Sacraments or even say Mass in his churches.[126] At that time the Company did not have any churches in Guatemala. As soon as Father Gerónimo learned of the Bishop's orders, he set out with his companion to find the Bishop, who was very far away. He traveled day and night, without rest and enduring great hardship, until he reached his destination. At first he was not made to feel very welcome [406] because he belonged to a religious [order] that was new to that city and province (even though the city had requested that the Company establish itself there). The Bishop began to test the priest, [first] with a very difficult moral case and then by asking him to explain a passage from [the Book of] Job, which was equally difficult. The priest managed to handle these matters very well, satisfactorily answering everything. Then he humbly and submissively explained to His Eminence why holy obedience had sent him there. The Bishop was satisfied with his learnedness, zeal, and talent to win souls [to God], so he gave the priest full license to exercise all the ministries of the Company. And that was not all—His Eminence honored the priest by attending the religious instruction he conducted. The Prelate's example remarkably edified the entire city, and the priest's sermons and religious instruction changed it as never before; thus, everyone expressed love for the sanctity that he radiated.

Not satisfied with the fruits that he had harvested, with his usual fervor Father Ramírez visited some neighboring pueblos in the region. The fruits [harvested] there were equally considerable, and they involved some unusual cases in which he aided souls in times of danger. It seems that God provided him with particular light and knowledge for this. Late one night as he was traveling with a young nobleman who later entered the Company, the two of them lost their way. The priest saw a hut in the distance and said to the young man, "Let's go, we're really needed there." When they got there they found a sick woman all alone. She was so near death that as soon as she confessed she died. Once she was buried the priest and the young nobleman continued on their way. The following night, after they found an inn, Father Ramírez said his usual prayers in one small room while the young man [did the same] in another. Late that night the priest's young companion was lying in bed having licentious thoughts. It seems that the Lord revealed this to the priest, who rushed into the young man's room and told him to stop thinking about such things and to make more of an effort to fend them off. The young man paid heed to this.

Father Ramírez had to deal with very similar cases among the collegians at the Royal College of San Ildefonso in Mexico City,[127] which the Company has in its charge. After founding a Jesuit college in Guatemala City he was transferred to San Ildefonso to instill virtue in that large number of noble youth.[128] While he was Rector he endeavored to build character and instill virtue in his large family [of students]. It seemed that God exposed the hearts of the collegians under his care; it was as if their chests were made of crystal and he could see perfectly what was happening inside. Sometimes it happened that they asked him for permission to leave the house, and he would reveal [his knowledge of] their disturbing and harmful intentions. He would then exhort them to repent their intended offenses against God. Their holy Rector's warning penetrated their consciences and some became so distraught that they went immediately to the feet of their confessor, amazed at the priest's timely reprimand. The Rector's opinion was the most valued in the college because he knew the secrets of their hearts. Those who were not at peace with their conscience hid from the Rector, even though he treated them with paternal love. This helped him maintain harmony and order in the college, which seemed more like a religious novitiate. [407]

---

125. This was in 1606 (Pérez de Ribas 1896:2:260–62).

126. Priests who wanted to say Mass, preach, or administer the sacraments required the permission of the bishop of the diocese, unless these functions took place in a church or residence belonging to a religious order.

127. The Royal College of San Ildefonso was one of two "lesser" Jesuit schools (the other, San Gregorio, was for Indians) where students (mostly the sons of Mexico's elite) received introductory and intermediate training in Latin and the Classics. As the name suggests, the premier Jesuit institution in Mexico City was the *Colegio Máximo*, where Jesuits received advanced training in philosophy and theology (Jacobsen 1938).

128. Ramírez became rector of San Ildefonso in 1614, retaining the post until 1618 (Zambrano 1961–1977:5:388).

The Lord had reserved yet another assignment for Father Ramírez in which, once again, he was to use his knowledge of languages and his fervent talent and desire to aid the souls of these poor Indians, which ever since his youth had been communicated to him by divine goodness. In fact, he was to conclude the course of his life in this enterprise. The reason for his transfer stemmed from the fact that, in 1617, Father Juan Ferro died in Pátzcuaro. This priest was a great missionary in the Tarascan language of Michoacán, and he demonstrated a singular faith and zeal for the welfare of the Indians. The superiors decided to appoint Father Gerónimo Ramírez to fill this great void, despite the fact that he had not spoken Tarascan or worked as a missionary in Michoacán for nearly twenty-seven years; for (as was previously mentioned) he worked there during the first years of his priesthood. Once he reached Michoacán his preaching produced the usual good results. He spoke Tarascan just as well as the best translators. Each day priests who had benefices came to hear two or three of his sermons. They were amazed by his eloquence, his appropriate use of the language, and the fruitful results he generally obtained despite his advanced age. He did this in the city of Pátzcuaro as well as in the continual missions he undertook. The priests who had benefices competed to see who could get him to come to their districts. In the Indies it is customary for a benefice to encompass three, four, or more pueblos.

Like a lodestone drawn to a magnet, which as it draws closer gains momentum, the closer the priest felt to God, the stronger his desire was to serve God and aid souls in reaching heaven. During the last three years of his life he traveled throughout the Bishopric of Michoacán, with its varied hot and cold climes. He did not miss a single village, mining camp, or ranch; in all of them he gave religious instruction, preached, and heard confessions, obtaining notable and fruitful results everywhere, and freeing innumerable souls from sin. During the last year of his life at age seventy-three, he reached his final mission, which was located in a hot

clime. He said he feared, or knew, that he would die that year, but his invincible spirit encouraged him not to fear death. As a result of the immense labor and discomforts that he voluntarily accepted for his God he became ill. As soon as the Father Rector learned that he was ill, he sent Father Gerónimo de Santiago, also a great missionary who spoke the Tarascan language, to assist him at the Indian pueblo where he fell ill; this was twenty leagues from Pátzcuaro. Father Ramírez became gravely ill and was given the Holy Sacraments, which he received with great joy in his soul because he understood that Our Lord was calling him. Just before he died divine goodness sent him a marvelous rapture. The last words that he said to Father Santiago were, "Your Reverence, wait and *videbis mirabilia!*"[129] He then lost his ability to speak and shortly thereafter, on January 12, 1621, this saintly and apostolic man died at the age of seventy-three. He served forty-three years in the Company, thirty-six of them as an evangelical missionary in all the provinces of Nueva España. Who could doubt that he who deserves so much will appear before the Lord laden with rewards? With such strength and for so many years he won so many souls to His Majesty. His body was buried in the church of that pueblo, where it is greatly esteemed by the natives. They, along with their beneficiary, felt blessed to have in their church the body of he whom they considered a saint. Later (in the face of great opposition on the part of the Indians) his body was transferred to the college in Pátzcuaro. [There it will remain] until the glorious day arrives when his body will be reunited with his soul to enjoy eternal glory.

I met this blessed priest and dealt with him personally. Although our encounter was brief I nevertheless recognized the same great religiosity [408] and sanctity recorded here that Father Gerónimo de Santiago discussed in his account. He was present at Father Ramírez's death, and the two were also close companions in the holy ministries that I will discuss in greater detail in the following book. [409]

---

129. 'You will see wondrous things!'

BOOK VII

The Particular Characteristics of Missions to Fierce and Barbarous Peoples and the Fruit That They Ordinarily Produce

CHAPTER I Proof that the labors of the evangelical ministers among these barbarous peoples are no less valuable or meritorious than missions among more noble and civilized nations

In the preceding six books I have followed the course of evangelical preaching, recounting the conversion of each of the nations in the Province of Sinaloa. I have reserved for this, Book VII, some general observations about the missions that I have discussed thus far, as well as those that will follow. I intend for these particular chapters to serve as a declaration of what the apostolic labor of missions is among fierce and barbarous peoples. I have decided to present this declaration here because the peoples recorded throughout this history are precisely that—fierce and barbarous. In addition to discussing the qualities of these missions, this subject matter can also serve as consolation and encouragement to the evangelical ministers who labor therein, to whom this work is primarily addressed.

My motivation for writing this treatise [410] was augmented by the fact that I learned that a modern-day heretic had published a treatise against the Company,[1]

saying that its missionary sons seek out and choose ministries only among the richest, noblest, and most powerful peoples and republics, such as China, Japan, and other similar nations. I do not want to ignore these slanderous verses that were published in an effort to further the persecution of the Company of Jesus, which is a squadron and battalion that resists and thwarts these enemies of God and His Church. When they are unable to violently lay their bloody hands upon the soldiers of Jesus Christ (in spite of the fact that they have done so many times), they gear all their efforts, speeches, and writings toward discrediting them in the eyes of the rest of the world. Thanks to the Lord, under whose name His Company is protected, He has caused His sons to be the object of the same insults that He suffered under the Pharisees and the same glory that the two major luminaries of the Church, Saint Augustine and Saint Jerome, enjoyed when they were persecuted by heretics.

From a book published in a foreign nation I have

---

1. This is apparently John Barclay's popular work of fiction that poked fun at the Jesuits, entitled *Euphormionis lusinini satyricon* (Euphormio's Satyricon). *Satyricon* was published in two parts in Paris in 1605 and 1607. Fleming (1973:ix) has described *Satyricon* as the most important work of fiction (aside from *Don Quijote*) from the seventeenth century.

temconsequatar. Titulo en que el mis. moi Apostol fundaua el otro, de que se gloria con los que auia engendrado en Christo, y regalandose con ellos les dezia: *Et si debem millia pedagogorum babeatis in Christo ; sed nõ multos patres, nam in Christo Iesu per Euangelium ego vos genui.* Aunque tengais despues de mi muchos ayos y pedagogos, que os crien en la doctrina que yo os enseñè; poro ninguno me quitarà la gloria ce aueros yo engendrado en Christo y plantado la doctrina cõ que vosotros, y vuestros hijes; y decendientes se hã de criar: frutos son todos essos de mis trabajos que padéci por ganarlos, y ellos me deuen reconocer por Padre. De lo qual se infierẽ dos cosas de singular consuelo para los Ministros destas Naciones, que trabajan en ellas al principio de su conuersion. La primera, que el fruto de la saluacion de las almas, no se ha de medir con solo el que se coge de presente, que esse aun en Naciones populosas, politicas, y sabias, muchas vezes parecera muy corto El mismo san Pablo no dexaua cõuertidas todas, ni todos los de las Naciones dõde predicaua en el Areopago de Athenas, por fruto muy precioso se escriue, q̃ conuirtiò a Dionisio, y vna muger llamada Damaris: y la demas gẽte se quedaua riẽdo, y escandalizada de q̃ les huuiesse predicado la Resurrecciõ de Christo, y de nuestros cuerpos. Otra vez cuenta san Lucas, que oyéron, y recibieron la doctrina del mismo Apostol vnas buenas mugetes, que auian concurrido a la ribera de vn rio; que el zelosissimo Predicador de Christo, no aguardaua a tener numerosos auditorios, ni de ilustres oyentes, para sembrar la doctrina del Euangelio: porque estaua cierto, que los pocos granos que sembraua, y mas si caîan en buena tierra, prohijariañ, y darian fruto a centenares, como predico Christo nuestro Señor en su

I. ad Corin. cap. 4.

Actor. 16.

las Espanas Santiago, ya sabemos por nuestras Historias que fuero muy pocos los que conuirtio de presente pero despues los Catolicos Españoles, que por muchos centenares de años han nacido; y criadose en España antigna, y nueua, y todo el nueuo Orbe descubierto, reconocen por su Padre al glorioso Patron Santiago, y en êl Cielo està coronado con la Fè; y frutos heroicos que los Catolicos Espa. noles con ella han cogido; y el se les ha mostrado Padre desde el Crelo; y en el rezo Eclesiastico, se le aplica aquel trofeo de que se gloriaua san Pablo respeto de los Corintios. *Per Evangelium ego vos genui* Siempre me quedo cõ la gloria de auer sido el primero q̃ plàto la Fè en España: rebaños sois, hijos mios Españoles, que yo gane para Christo, y su Iglesia. Rebaños son los que recogen nuestros Euangelicos Missioneros, que aunque no cõparables con la Nacion Española, que Dios nuestro Señor sublimò en el mũdo; con todo auiendo sido apreciados con sangre de Christo; en ellos ha hecho ostentaciõ de su misericerdia. Y ocasiones huuo, en que con otros menores emplearon su predicacion los sagrados Apostoles, sin saber si tendriã vida; o tiẽpo de predicar a otros mas populosos: dando por muy bien empleados sus Apostolicos talentos en aquello que Dios les ofrecia, de presente. Los hijos de la Cõpañia de Iesus, a centenares y millaradas bautizã, y doctrinan en estas Naciones; demas del fruto futuro q̃ les queda de q̃ gozar, que lo ordinario es ser mas perfecto y abundante. Es cierto, que con admiracion cuentan los Padres que doctrinan Naciones ya bautizadas, y assentadas, las niuestras y mejoras de Christiandad con que procedẽ: el cõcepto mayor de las cosas de la Fè, q̃ cada dia crece en ellos: la estima, y amor de los primeros Ministros que los hi-

taken the satirical verses with which they slander the present-day members of the Company. It says, *Opulentas civitates: ubi sunt commoditates: quaerunt semper isti Patres.*[2] To refute these heretics' slander one need only offer as proof the continuous missions carried out by the sons of the Company among the rustic peoples in small pueblos and hamlets as well as in the prisons and hospitals of the heavily populated cities of Europe, which are visited with great frequency and where all the ministries and duties professed by Christian piety are exercised. The falsity of this slander is further demonstrated by everything recorded in this history—the hardships, dangers, and deaths suffered by our religious among these barbarous, wretched, and miserable people. And even though they are such, our missionaries would not even think of despising them. In fact, they devote their apostolic ministries and lives to them. They abandon their homelands every day and cross wide seas, traveling far from their parents and relatives and from the schools and religious houses of their brothers, friends, and companions. They live in mountains, forests, and valleys—in the midst of fierce peoples—in order to win their souls to Christ and His Holy Church. However, beyond all that has been mentioned—and in order to show how vain this slander is—I will add and prove that the sons of the Company would not even think of abandoning their evangelical work among humble and downtrodden peoples—those who are without civilization. They value very highly these ministries among poor and barbarous peoples, and they consider them just as meritorious as those among the world's most civilized and noblest peoples and nations. They are ruled by the spirit of Saint Paul, who gloried in saying, *Graecis, & barbaris, sapientibus, & insipientibus, debitor sum.*[3] The members of the Company also consider this to be their duty. To fulfill the vow that they have professed of working in these types of enterprises, they can and should say, along with the Apostle Saint Paul, *Debitores sumus.*[4]

I will now examine what I proposed to speak about in this chapter, which is the doubt that might arise in human discourse and thought upon hearing that the Gospel is being preached in these missions to peoples who are as uncivilized, ignorant,[5] and downtrodden as those described herein. It may seem that these missions do not possess the same degree of worth, or that one cannot expect the same fruits as those produced in missions to the world's noble, famous, and civilized nations. [411] The same thoughts could conceivably overtake those who are suffering the immense hardships and innumerable dangers that are recorded throughout this entire history, dampening the spirit they need for these most glorious enterprises. The object of my efforts here is to prove that the very same circumstances and characteristics that appear to tarnish, humiliate, and debase our missions actually exalt them and substantially increase their value in the eyes of God, who is never deceived. This proposition will be clarified by cataloging a list of the aforesaid circumstances and by responding immediately with a careful examination of each of them. This will be accomplished without diverging from our history, for pertinent matters will be touched upon along the way.

3. *Margin Note:* AdRom. c. 1. Romans 1:14: "I have the same duty to all, Greek and barbarian, learned and simple" (Knox 1956:148).

4. "We have an obligation."

5. *Incapazes.* Here as elsewhere we have translated this term as ignorant rather than simple or stupid (implying a lack of intelligence), because the thrust of Pérez de Ribas' argument throughout is that the Indians were capable of grasping Christian truths.

2. "These priests are always seeking opulent states where they can be comfortable."

CHAPTER II An examination and declaration of the capacity of these barbarous peoples to receive the doctrine of our Holy Faith

At first glance what seems to undermine these nations is their limited [intellectual] capacity, which is demonstrated by their inhuman and barbarous customs and their lack of any type of the order that is found in a republic, because they have neither kings nor government. Consequently, one would not expect any fruits—or very limited ones—from the preaching of the divine evangelical doctrine and holy laws to people who seem to have lost even the natural laws that survived among other civilized peoples.

As a way of responding to this and other concerns that will later be raised, we must assume principles and truths which, in the light of reason and faith, cannot be doubted. The first truth is that Christ the Redeemer ordered His Gospel to be preached throughout the world. We will find that He entrusted every nation on this earth—large and small, lofty and humble—to His holy Apostles and those who succeeded these sacred captains in this holy office once the former went to heaven. It is true that the love that Christ Our Lord had for the Church, His holy bride, was not limited to the time when He or His first disciples walked the earth, for His Church will persevere until the end of the world. Christ gave orders to His Apostles and their successors to preach His Gospel, saying, *Euntes in mundum universum, predicate Evangelium omni creature.*[6] These words encompass all types of people throughout the universe; the educated and the uneducated, the rich and the poor, the known, and the oppressed[7] who have yet to be discovered. If this were not the case, what would become of the peasant and those in their hamlets? What would become of the poor old lady whose alms are acknowledged and praised by the Son of God more than the alms of the rich and powerful?[8] The first people in the world to be preached to and to receive the good news of the Gospel were neither scribes nor wise men, but rather shepherds who were reared to care for their sheep. We know the rustic nature of these people who, like our Indians, reside in the countryside. They do not know how to read, and they understand nothing more than raising their little lambs, using their shepherd's crooks, and working their sheepskins. They show no wit with regard to the matters in which the philosophers and politicians of the world have busied themselves.

There was another aspect of the preaching of the Gospel to these poor and rustic shepherds that was even more remarkable than the manner in which the three wise men were so informed. God was content to instruct the latter through the sign of a star, which learned men have greatly honored by saying that it was governed by an angel. However, to teach those poor and simple shepherds, He dispatched an army of wise and great angels from His court to give them the good news and to catechize them in the principal mysteries of our Holy Faith, which is what we ministers teach our barbarous catechumens. The shepherds were given the news that God had become man and was born of the Virgin and that He came to save mankind: *Ecce evangelizo vobis gaudium magnum, quod erit omni populo, qua natus est vobis bodie. Saluatuor, que est Christus Dominus.*[9] Although these words are few, they bear the principal doctrine of our holy religion. When His time came to preach here on earth, the Lord Himself once deliberately stopped to catechize and teach the highest mysteries [of the Faith] to a lowly and ignorant Samaritan woman. He even taught her to pray *in spiritu & veritate*[10] (as the Lord Himself referred to this very delicate matter). She lived a life that was just as bad as that of the Indians, who live with many women, casting them aside at will. This lowly woman had lived with a great many men. The Son of the Lord counted five, not including the man with whom she was currently living, who was not really hers inasmuch as she had taken him from another

---

6. Mark 16:15: "Go out all over the world and preach the gospel to the whole of creation" (Knox 1956:52).

7. In Pérez de Ribas' mind those yet to be discovered and lacking the word of God necessarily are oppressed by the devil.

8. Pérez de Ribas is perhaps alluding here to "the widow's mite" (Mark 13:41–44) and "the poor widow's gift" (Luke 1–4).

9. *Margin Note*: Luc. c. 2. Luke 2:10–11: "I bring you good news of a great rejoicing for the whole people. This day, in the city of David, a savior has been born for you, the Lord Christ himself" (Knox 1956:55).

10. John 4:23–24: "in spirit and in truth."

woman. Christ stopped to teach this woman the mystery of our redemption, explaining it to her with greater clarity than [He did to] anyone else in the entire Gospel. He explained to her that the Messiah, He who was to redeem and teach the world, was He Himself. He expressed it in these words: *Ego sum, qui loquorter*.[11] With this the following truth was established: Christ Our Lord willed, ordered, and taught that the doctrine of our Holy Faith be preached to rough, ignorant, and rustic peoples, no matter what their condition or state.

Let us now examine and respond specifically to the question of the limited capacity of our barbarians. In doing so, we should examine this matter at two different points in time and at two different stages [of the Indians' development]. We will find that at both stages the Indians have quite sufficient capacity to learn and attain the understanding required by Christ with respect to the concepts of His Holy Faith. The first stage is when these peoples are still gentiles and the Gospel is first being preached to them; the second stage comes after these nations have been instructed and cultivated. During the first stage they are not altogether lacking in judgment. On the contrary, they mock anyone among them who is a fool and lacks understanding. For this reason the Lord finds them to have sufficient capacity to be justly condemned for their sins and atrocities against natural law. They demonstrate this capacity first and foremost in their wars, employing clever stratagems and feigned ambushes, as when they light fires to trick the enemy into coming to look for them. (This is a signal that the Spaniards watch for.) Then, when it is least expected, at some dangerous place hundreds of Indians rush from the monte to destroy the enemy. They sow the roads with wooden points covered with poison in order to puncture the feet of their Indian enemies, who ordinarily go barefoot. In their council meetings and public sermons they are very capable of pointing out the advantages that they might obtain from establishing peace with Spaniards or other nations. Their weapons are very well made, even though they did not have iron instruments to carve and polish their bows, arrows, macanas, and lances, which are made of what they call brazilwood. Their adornments for war were quite beautiful, particularly those used for their heads, which they adorned with beautiful feathers intertwined with ribbons in their hair. They are very good at their version of the art of agriculture, given the weather, the quality of the land, and the crops they grow. The women were quite skilled at spinning and weaving (even though they lacked looms). Some even decorated their mantas with interwoven designs [412] and various colors. They did the same with the sashes[12] that they made for their newborn infants.

These people have sufficient capacity for all that has been related, as well as for many other things which, because they are of lesser significance, I will not mention here. Nor will I discuss other unimportant customs, including some decent ones that I have already mentioned. Among these are customs that, although not preserved in codes of written laws, which they lack, are nevertheless more closely observed than the customs of some civilized republics that have archives and books. Thus, who can doubt that, like Europeans in the midst of Christianity—the farmer in his field, the old woman in her home, the clerk in his shop—these nations possess the same capacity for learning and understanding that most supreme mystery: that there is one Creator of everything and that this Creator is three and one? Would we want to exclude from our Faith and Christ's grace many of the aforementioned Europeans simply because they lack [intellectual] capacity? May God be given infinite thanks for not requiring us to understand His supreme mysteries, but rather only to believe them. In the final analysis this is what must be accepted by those who dispute these matters.

The tender mystery of the Incarnation—that God became man and died for him at such a young age—is like a volcano spewing the fire of love. There is no question that the Indians hear and receive [the message of this mystery] with remarkable attention. It makes wonderful sense to their sincere and plain hearts; they offer no haughty pharisaical arguments, nor do they engage in the politics of wise men. As Saint Paul noted, the wise men were appalled [by the idea] that God had become man, although the Pharisees considered this a necessary thing.[13] That is not the case with our poor

---

11. *Margin Note*: Ioan 4:26. John 4:26: "I, who speak to thee, am the Christ" (Knox 1956:90).

12. *Fajas*. It is not clear whether these were sashes that might have been worn to bind the mother's abdomen after giving birth or sashes that were wrapped around the infant to cover the umbilicus. The term might also refer to a sling worn by the mother in which the infant was carried.

13. Acts 23:8: "The Sadducees will have it that there is no resurrection, that there are no angels or spirits, whereas the Pharisees believe in both" (Knox 1956:141). In Jerusalem at the time of the early Christian church the high priest's council (the "wise men") was made up of Sadducees (see Acts 4:1–2; Acts 5:17). The latter taught that God alone is spirit, and that hummans' souls were material, just like their bodies. Thus, for the Sadducees there was no resurrection, and reward and punishment took place in the present life.

Indians, who receive this article with a faith that does not require them to comprehend these mysteries.

The other article that should first be taught to these gentiles, who are quasi-atheists, concerns the immortality of the soul. They had many, albeit confusing, principles or truths concerning immortality that conform quite well to the truth of rewarding those who are good and punishing those who are evil.

I turn now to the second stage at which I said it was possible to consider [the capacity of] these nations. If sufficient intellectual capacity can be found during the first stage—even before they were cultivated—what capacity will be found at the second? If human art is powerful enough to take a rough, thorny, and horrible tree trunk and shape it into a carved image beautiful to behold, how much more powerful would it be once Christ's grace has been imparted to these souls, along with talks, the catechism, and instruction in the doctrine of the Gospel? This is especially the case when the children learn how to read and write with our alphabet (as they do) and to read in their language some simple lessons concerning Christian doctrine. That maxim recorded in the works of Horace, Book I, Epistle I, is relevant here: *Nemo adeo ferus est, qui non mitescere possit. Si modo cultura patientem accomodet autem.*[14]

We must openly confess that before they were introduced to the divine Faith they had neither civil order nor the government of a republic. They differed in this regard from the Hebrews, Greeks, and Romans, as well as the kingdoms of Japan and Greater China. Nevertheless, it can be clearly seen that they learn and value the truths of our Holy Faith.

By listening carefully when the mysteries and truths of the Holy Faith are preached, they abandon their errors. If they did not comprehend these truths and the other things they hear, then we would be ignored by thousands of Indians, who are restless by nature [413] and who do not know how to sit still and be quiet, except when they are playing their game of reeds. How is it possible that such people are now able to quietly listen to religious instruction for an hour each day? The large enramadas that were once used as churches are no longer large enough to accommodate the crowds that assemble. If they did not understand what was being preached to them, then why would they come every day to listen to the preaching of a foreign priest?

They are pleased when a priest can preach to them in their language. Once he has learned a bit of it they say, "Father, we are so happy that you can speak to us in our language and we can understand you." If they did not understand the things they are taught, they would be like the person who does not know Greek, who says, *Graecum est, non legitur.*[15] The Indians who listen to our preachers would say, "We hear your words, but we cannot understand what you are trying to teach us."

It is not their words pronounced by our tongues that these Indians enjoy hearing, but rather the truths they are taught, of which they were once ignorant. These truths are what captures their attention; it is not simply hearing the words of their language spoken by a foreigner. Indeed, even though they had their own preachers who spoke their language better, these individuals did not preach the same doctrine as the evangelical ministers, nor were their preachers paid the same attention. Furthermore, the doctrine they preached was not powerful enough to change the vices and customs in which these nations were reared. Given the innumerable vices that have now been eradicated and the holy customs that have been introduced through the doctrine of the Holy Gospel, it is impossible that these people did not understand [what the evangelical ministers preached].

It has already been proven that no matter how barbarous the Indians might be, if they are well instructed, then their observance of the laws of our Holy Faith is just as exemplary—and at times freer of the vices—as that of long-time Christians in populous cities and places [in Europe]. Our evangelical laborers do not have to fear that the fruits harvested among these people are inferior to those harvested in other lands with rich and learned peoples who, out of arrogance, opposed the Gospel.

There is another difficult circumstance related to the previous one, which also needs to be discussed. This is the variety and multiplicity of totally distinct languages that are found among these peoples. These languages have no letters, characters, grammars, or books to ease this difficulty or to supplement these nations' limited capacity. I will briefly reply that with the favor of divine grace that was sung by David, *Dabit verbum Evangeli-*

---

14. "No one is so wild, who cannot become mild. However, if only culture would be patient." A modern translation of Horace reads: "no-one's vice is too savage to become tamer, if he only lends a patient ear to instruction" (Horace 1986:4). Horace's Epistles date to around 20 B.C.

15. "It's not readable, it's in Greek."

zantibus virtute multa,[16] [the Jesuit] experience has had positive results. To their great merit our priests have clearly overcome the difficulties posed by these native languages. Not only have they been able to declare the supreme mysteries of our Holy Faith, but by composing grammars, glossaries, speeches, and treatises they have also cleared the way for those ministers of the doctrine who later come to these missions. These writings are read not only by the ministers sent to these missions, but also by some of the children of these nations. These means, which are so intrinsic to evangelical charity, have banished the deep shadows that reigned in these souls.

We can add that these missionaries achieved a glorious victory over the devil, who had introduced this confusion of languages. And we can say that for the many languages that these faithful evangelical ministers learn, which is generally two or three each, they have earned an equal number of triumphs and crowns as their assured singular reward. [414] If [learning these languages earns one] a crown and glory (as is undoubtedly the case for someone who composes a book of holy instructions, which takes time and labor, even though there may already be many other writings in that same language concerning the same subject matter), we must also recognize that this is a way of bringing to light the holy doctrine and introducing Christ and teaching His holy law in a new and unheard-of tongue—a tongue in which His glorious name was unknown. This is how one obtains that triumph for Christ that was celebrated by Saint Paul: *Omnis lingua confireatur, quia Dominus Iesus Christus in gloria est Dei Patris*.[17]

In further addressing this issue, I can testify that our laborers usually require three months of study to learn one of these languages [well enough] to teach the catechism and hear confessions. Then, with time and closer contact with the Indians one acquires the skill needed to preach and illuminate these peoples, who have been blind since birth. Who can deny that it was a more illustrious miracle for Christ to restore the sight of a man who had been blind since birth than to do the same for others who had become blind as the result of some accident and whose healing would not have been so difficult? The blind man himself confessed this, saying, *A saeculo non est auditum, quia quis aperuit oculos caeci nati*.[18] Who can deny then that it is more illustrious for these evangelical ministers to preach in an unknown language and to bring the celestial light of the Faith to these people, who were born blind, than to do so for others who did not suffer from such permanent and severe blindness? Those whom God has chosen for these glorious enterprises have no reason to feel discouraged; it is certain that they will find many blind persons who, illuminated by the light of their preaching, will regain their sight and consequently the salvation of their souls.

---

16. *Margin Note*: Psalm. 63. Psalm 63:11: "they are ever blessed who take their vows in his name" (Knox 1956:502).

17. *Margin Note*: AdPhilip. 2. Philippians 2:11: "and every tongue must confess Jesus Christ as the Lord, dwelling in the glory of God the Father" (Knox 1956:204).

18. *Margin Note*: Ioann. c. 9. John 9:32: "That a man should open the eyes of one born blind is something unheard of since the world began" (Knox 1956:98).

CHAPTER III A response to other concerns about the loss of the lives of those who preach the Gospel to fierce and barbarous peoples[19]

One of the apparent difficulties of the enterprise that we are discussing is the barbarous custom of continual warfare in which these peoples have been reared. The people of one nation sometimes kill [those of] another for no greater reason than the taking of human heads. They spare neither women nor children, whom we find in natural history often were spared by other wild peoples.[20] But the peoples we are discussing here are truly fierce, and although they are human beings, some nevertheless murdered other human beings for no other reason than to feed on their flesh and to hold dances and barbarous celebrations, which were their greatest triumphs and entertainment. Because of this, one might draw a conclusion which, if not energetically refuted, could greatly impede and dampen the spirits of zealous evangelical preachers to risk their lives and to expose themselves to the innumerable dangers with which they are constantly besieged.

What ameliorates these dangers and can even make them desirable is the hope for martyrdom, which can only take place when blood is shed and life is lost for the glory of God and His Most Holy Faith. Martyrdom is not due to the whim of a barbarian who has cut off a head or shot a minister of souls full of arrows simply because of his habit of taking the lives of all those who are not of his nation, whom he considers his enemies. Indeed, it would be extremely sad if—once a religious had abandoned his own country, acquaintances, and friends, [415] as well as the sweet company of his brothers, and had suffered so many laborious and tiring journeys over land and sea—that all this should lead to death at the hands of a barbarian, as though he were a deer or a beast of the field or an enemy encountered in the countryside whom this Indian shot with arrows.

I trust in Our Lord that this objection will not stand, for it will be a serious obstacle if left as is. Rather, an effective response must be found; one must demonstrate the triumph that these ministers of the Gospel achieve and the glorious cause for which they die and give up their lives.

First, consider the usual attitude of the Holy Church as expressed in its martyrologies.[21] There it celebrates as martyrs those who died while laboring in a task of charity as great as that of curing and serving those who are sick with contagious diseases. These sick people did not attempt to take these charitable ministers' lives; rather, the ministers exposed themselves to this danger in order to carry out the charity that was so fervently mandated by Christ. We also know that the Holy Church celebrates as martyrs those who died in the defense of a Christian and evangelical virtue—such as chastity or virginity—or those who died because they had gathered up the blood, bones, and relics of those whom they considered to be saints so that they could venerate them; or some faithful Christians who gave a jug of water to someone who was going to his death, having been condemned for the Faith.

I now come to our evangelical ministers. In order to win these people over to God and show them the way to their salvation, thereby rescuing them from the clutches of the devil and the darkness in which he had entombed them, and also to extend the Catholic Church, these ministers exposed themselves to life-threatening dangers and self-exile, dying from the blows and wounds of macanas and clubs and poisoned arrows. Do they perform deeds that are any less heroic than those performed by individuals who died because they exercised other virtues of healing sick people who were contagious,[22] or because they observed chastity or gave a jug

---

19. Eleven Jesuits had been killed in various Indian uprisings between 1594 and 1643. Many other missionaries, indeed the majority, were either wounded or had one or more brushes with death, owing to apostate Indians.

20. Pérez de Ribas apparently is alluding here to works by authors such as Isidore of Sevilla and perhaps classical authors such as Lucian or Livy, all of whom wrote of barbarian invasions and wars.

21. In 1643—while Pérez de Ribas was in Madrid composing the *Historia*—the Jesuits at Antwerp under Jean Bolland began the systematic compilation and critical assessment of thousands of *vitae* and *passiones* dating back to the early Christian era, which recounted the lives and acts of Christian martyrs and saints (Musurillo 1972).

22. Large numbers of Jesuits in Europe gave their lives caring for the sick during epidemics in the sixteenth and seventeenth centuries, particularly during the 1630s (de Guibert 1964; O'Malley 1993a:171).

of water to someone who was being taken to be martyred? I point out here that I am not trying to qualify any particular person as a martyr. That pertains only to Christ's Supreme Vicar here on earth. I simply consider the causes and circumstances that must co-occur in order for a martyrdom to be saintly and for the death suffered to become a glorious crown for the person who endured it. Finally, I declare that all these motives and causes are usually found in our missionaries when they conclude the course of their lives, which have been spent teaching these barbarous peoples and making known to them Christ Our Lord and His redemption and Gospel.

Another circumstance cannot be omitted here that especially occurs with the religious of the Company of Jesus and confers upon their missions the glorious title of 'apostolic'. The violent deaths they suffer for preaching the Holy Gospel are crowned very illustriously with the title of having been endured for the virtue of holy obedience. The members of the Company take a special vow to obey the Supreme Pontiff in whatever enterprise His Holiness assigns them, be it among the faithful or infidels.[23] They do so without requesting recompense, even though it might mean exposing themselves to all the risks and life-threatening dangers that should happen to arise in the fulfillment of that most holy vow and sacrifice. From this it can be inferred that the religious preachers of the Gospel—with full knowledge and recognition of the hardships and the obvious life-threatening dangers that have occurred and continue to occur with our missionaries—enter these nations with apostolic spirit to procure the Indians' salvation and the glory of Christ's name, exposing themselves to the dangers of this quest, and thereby, to losing their lives. [416]

We can rightfully call these deaths 'exiles' and 'deaths suffered for holy obedience'. This is precisely how the Apostle of the People, Saint Paul, referred to the glorious death of Christ, the very first and prime example of martyrdom, *Factus obediens visque ad mortem*,[24] which meant that Christ died for the holy virtue of obedience to His eternal Father. There should be no doubt that our missionaries, who have the good fortune of dying at the hands of barbarians while preaching the word of God, die out of obedience to the Supreme Pontiff and to God in him. It should be pointed out that

when the Supreme Great Shepherd of the Church does not directly assign (as he sometimes does) those who are to go and preach to infidels, he always does so through our Father General (which amounts to the same thing), because for this purpose His Holiness has given him his proxy.[25] This is a great consolation to anyone who by risking his life has lost it, thereby winning the eternal crown through observance of his vow of obedience.

I will not be satisfied with having declared the causes and circumstances of these deaths. For even though each of these causes would be sufficient to make these deaths glorious, all of these circumstances together make them precious in the eyes of God. I will examine the most immediate circumstance that, according to the teachings of the Doctors of the Church, should concur in a true and authentic martyrdom. This requires that the martyr die in defense of our Holy Catholic Faith and that he receive and suffer death like a Christian, either by order of or at the hands of someone who is killing him out of hatred of the Holy Faith. In narrative fashion, and without deviating from our history, I will relate the fundamental facts that demonstrate that those soldiers of Christ's militia who exposed themselves to preaching the Gospel to these barbarous peoples and subsequently died were executed because of these peoples' hatred of our Holy Faith and because of their attempts to persecute it and, if they could, eradicate it.

It is true that these nations have not followed the style of the ancient tyrants who brought the martyrs to their tribunals,[26] therein examining the Faith they professed and then sentencing them to death for it, at times accusing them of other crimes of which they were innocent. Even though these peoples did not use this kind of legal system or tribunals, it is most certainly true that they had their own style of tribunal: the meetings of their sorcerers and others with depraved customs, sometimes even apostates of the Faith. They (being the greatest enemies the Gospel has) were always the promoters of the cruel deaths of those who preached the Gospel in their lands. This was because the ministers preached an evangelical law that forbade their drunken revels, their barbarous vices, and their unrestrained sexuality in having many wives or concubines, whom

---

23. This is the "fourth vow" that professed members take, obliging themselves to undertake missions anywhere at any time.

24. Philippians 2:8: "accepted an obedience which brought him to death" (Knox 1956:204).

25. In point of fact most missionary assignments were made by the father general not the pope, although the latter could and did request particular enterprises.

26. Pérez de Ribas is referring here to the *Acts of the Roman Martyrs* (dating mostly to the fourth and fifth centuries), which recount the persecution of Christians by various governors, emperors, and other officials of the Roman Empire prior to the reign of Constantine.

they cast aside or changed at will. Or perhaps it was because these sorcerers state and declare that by administering Baptism the priests take the lives of those who receive it. In the end all these reasons led them to sentence to death anyone who tries to establish Christ's laws and teach the Holy Faith, which is precisely what is needed for salvation. What more is needed for such a death sentence than a hatred of our holy religion?

I will [now] present additional circumstances ordinarily found that clearly demonstrate the spirit of these glorious deaths. When an evangelical minister is sentenced to death all that is holy is simultaneously condemned to destruction. Thus, the decision is made to set fire to the church or enramada where those who are baptized and who want to be baptized gather. Crosses are likewise torn down, holy images are burned, sacred vestments are defiled, and [417] there are a thousand other acts of destruction, savagery, and rage.

The devil has always attempted by means of his familiars to eradicate, if he could, our holy religion and to simultaneously condemn to death those who preach it and sometimes [even] those from among their own nation who have received it, as is told at different points throughout this history. From all this we infer that, once religious have tamed these fierce peoples, reducing them to our Holy Faith and placing their lives in the priests' hands, the latter are not frustrated in their hope of the glorious crown of martyrdom, for which they offered themselves from the moment they went amongst these peoples to communicate the light of the Holy Gospel and later to preserve it in the face of such clear and obvious dangers. The truth of this is borne out quite well by the signs that some of these holy religious left behind at the moment of their deaths. Even though they are recounted in detail elsewhere, I will briefly summarize them here. They will demonstrate that these priests died for the cause of Christ's Faith, and even though it may appear that they bear witness to their own cause, they are faithful and worthy of total credibility.

The venerable Father Gonzalo de Tapia was the first to introduce a very great Christianity among the nations of Sinaloa. He died at their hands for this cause. Immediately after his head had been split open by macanas

he staggered out of the hut that had been erected in front of the church, and there he received many more blows, thus ending his life. Only the trunk of his body was left, for his head and left arm had been cut off. But with his right arm raised and the fingers of his hand set in the sign of the Cross, he lay there on the ground in testimony that he died for having uplifted and preached that divine triumph to those nations. These very same enemies confessed that they took his life because of the doctrine he taught and because he preached against and reproached their gentile vices. The glorious precursor of Christ [Saint John the Baptist], to whose incomparable holiness it would not occur to me to compare our ministers, is venerated by the Holy Church as a martyr because he died for reprimanding Herod's concubinage.[27]

The other two apostolic men, Father Julio Pascual and Father Manuel Martínez, who as I have related, were killed by the Guazápare nation, met their deaths shot full of arrows as they knelt with their rosaries in hand.[28] This was just after the blessed Father Pascual had preached Christ's doctrine in a language that he knew extremely well. A very good Christian who was a fiscal in the church and a native of that nation also exhorted his people not to commit a crime as grievous as taking the lives of those who were teaching them God's word, and he, too, was cruelly killed.

In these and many similar incidents that took place with the ministers in these enterprises, it clearly can be seen that these deaths are not executed randomly, nor did the Indians kill them like wild animals or enemies that they encountered in the monte or along the road. Rather, these deaths were extensively deliberated and discussed in the diabolical councils of their sorcerers who, instigated by the devil, oppose and persecute our Holy Faith and divine law. This will also be found in other joyous deaths that will be recorded later. Thus, we finally come to infer that these deaths to which the zealous evangelical laborers expose themselves among these nations offer the hope of the same martyrdom that other servants of God have achieved at the hands of other, more civilized peoples who persecuted our Christian Faith and Religion.

---

27. Matthew 14; Mark 6:14–29.

28. Pérez de Ribas seems to be making an implicit comparison here with Saint Sebastian, who also was shot full of arrows.

CHAPTER IV Discussion of other qualities and circumstances of these missions that prove that they are not inferior to missions among more urban and civilized peoples

[418] I turn now to a discussion of other features intrinsic to missions to fierce peoples. It cannot be denied that these peoples differ a great deal from civilized and wealthy nations. In the latter there is human interaction and dialogue and the people live in settlements with [public] buildings and adorned houses. Furthermore, the minister who goes to preach in these nations finds shelter and people with whom he can converse. But in these barbarous nations one lives in isolation from mankind, in the company of wild beasts who inhabit hovels along the seashore or in montes, forests, and deep canyons. In the final analysis, to live among them is to experience a kind of perpetual exile (even though one's life is not lost). The cost of all these continuous and acknowledged hardships would appear to debase dealings with these peoples and to discourage any rational person from undertaking such an enterprise. Although we will not deny that these evangelical ministers suffer, at the same time we will prove that these qualities do not diminish apostolic labor among these people, but instead enhance it. All this suffering that is endured for the glory of Christ and His redeemed souls provides an equal amount of consolation to our religious missionaries, who sacrifice and dedicate their lives to God by laboring in exile, free from dross, dust, and straw.[29] By reducing fierce and barbarous nations to Christ, they enjoy the great assurance that all their labors are fruitful. These will be crowned with reward and glory because they are free of the human concerns that are more characteristic of dealings with civilized peoples.

It is not my intention here to diminish in the least the glory (which is so apparent) of great evangelical endeavors among said civilized and illustrious peoples. Rather, I wish to further declare the glory (albeit hidden and less known) found in the enterprises among our barbarous Indians, in which there are no fewer instances deserving of rewards and crowns. I am not referring to the precious and abundant fruit of converted souls, which will be discussed later on, but rather to the reward for apostolic labors endured for Christ in which the Apostle of the People, Saint Paul, took special pride. Even though this great Apostle had converted the greatest and most civilized provinces in the world and had won them over to Christ, it must be noted that he did not aggrandize his glorious enterprises by focusing on these conversions. Instead, he [simply] pointed out that he had worked harder than the other holy Apostles: *Abundantius illis omnibus laboravi*[30]—nobody surpasses me in the suffering [that I have] endured for the welfare of souls and to make Christ known. And the Son of God Himself—He who came down in person from His royal throne of heaven to convert Saul—told Ananias that the glorious task for which He had chosen Saul was this: *Ego estendam illi quanta opporteat eam pro nomine meo pati.*[31] This means "I have chosen Saul to be one of my Apostles—he will reveal that he is an Apostle by his great suffering for the sake of my glory. That which is unusual, admirable, and precious about my selection of Saul will be seen in the many and varied difficulties that he will endure for the sake of my name."

Let us now examine what motivates the missionaries of whom we are speaking to endure hardship. I ask, what motive or [419] human consideration can or should move these ministers of God to labor among these inhuman peoples? What motive can take them from their colleges and lead them to exchange their dwelling places and companions for warlike Indians?

---

29. "Dross, dust, and straw" presumably is a metaphor for modern society—the "progressive," machine-age society that was emerging in capitalist Europe at the time (dross being 'slag', a byproduct of reducing a metallic ore to pure metal).

30. *Margin Note*: I. Cor. 15. 1 Corinthians 15:10: "I have worked harder than all of them" (Knox 1956:177). Note that Pérez de Ribas omits the remainder of I Corinthians 15:10, where Paul gives credit to God for the success of his undertakings: "only, by God's grace, I am what I am, and the grace he has shown me has not been without fruit; I have worked harder than all of them, or rather, it was not I, but the grace of God working with me" (Knox 1956:177).

31. *Margin Note*: Actor. 9. Acts 9:16: "I have yet to tell [Saul] how much suffering he will have to undergo for my name's sake" (Knox 1956:124).

Or what reason can induce them to search for [converts] along harsh and difficult roads, rather than in cities, towns, and inns? Their sustenance is frequently roots and wild fruit from the fields. They often are exposed to inclement weather, with no house to shelter them from either the cold or the burning heat of the sun. They often have to travel and spend the night in terrain full of poisonous lizards, snakes, and serpents. All the above are found in part or in whole in all of these missions. And I ask, what else could motivate these religious ministers in the midst of such hardships but an ardent and burning love for Christ and the welfare of these souls?

It clearly follows from this that the evangelical and apostolic status of these missions is elevated by the very qualities and circumstances that should debase and demean them. In this regard they are not inferior to missions to powerful and illustrious peoples, for these servants of God receive a consolation of their own. Even though they do not all achieve the triumph of glorious martyrdom (which belongs only to those for whom God supremely reserves that crown), anyone who risks himself in all these glorious works has the hope of some type of crown and martyrdom. This may not come from the occasional, sudden shedding of blood, but it is nevertheless a kind of triumph and victory that comes from innumerable and prolonged labors, a type of martyrdom that is endured over a period of many years.

Much could be added with respect to this issue if I were not concerned about spending more time on this topic than history demands. This has already been discussed with erudition and piety in all the writings of the very religious and erudite Father [Juan] Euse-bio Nieremberg, particularly in his *Ascetical Doctrines*, Book 1, Doctrine 10, Chapter 95.[32] Citing the doctrine and authority of the holy Doctors of the Church, he offers proofs concerning the degrees of glory and the crowns awarded to those servants of God who did not suffer violent deaths from tyrants. They instead endured hardships in His name that were comparable to, and at times exceeded, the death that the holy Prophet Elijah ultimately hoped for, rather than endure the persecution of the unholy Jezebel.[33] He refers to such authorities as Saint John Chrysostom, Saint Augustine, and Saint Ambrose, each of whom celebrated and gave the title of martyr to men who endured great hardship for Christ's glory. Although they did not endure bloodshed, nor were they lacking the will to do so, they exposed themselves to suffering that was equivalent to and more prolonged than death itself.

Much of the same will be found in our missionaries who live among barbarous and fierce peoples. That which Christ Our Lord confided to His first missionaries and Apostles is verified to the letter with respect to these peoples. He said, *Ecce ego mitto vos, sicut oues inter lupos.*[34] The threats and death sentences that our ministers hear among these wolves are countless, especially when the missions are newly founded. From the day they accept [a missionary assignment] these apostolic men are exposed to the risks of death. Thus, carefully examining this issue, we find that for these missionaries the excessive difficulties of these enterprises result in an increased and enriched love of Christ and their fellow man. [420]

32. Nieremberg was perhaps the best-known Jesuit spiritual writer of the seventeenth century. The *Ascetical Doctrines* (*Doctrinae asceticae*) was published in 1643 and was a general treatise on spirituality (de Guibert 1964:318–19).

33. Pérez de Ribas is referring here to I Kings 19, which relates how Elijah put all the prophets to the sword and Jezebel subsequently threatened him with the same. Elijah fled to the desert, where he called on God to take his life so he would not have to face Jezebel (Knox 1956:245–46).

34. Luke 10:3: "I am sending you out to be like lambs among wolves" (Knox 1956:67).

CHAPTER V Other hardships found in missions to barbarous peoples that make them more meritorious; these are discussed in a letter that is copied here

Let us now discuss in more detail the greater portion of those hardships for which Christ Our Lord said He had chosen Saul, and which also befall our missionaries. Once Saul became known as Paul, he considered these hardships emblematic of his apostolate, and he enumerated them to the Corinthians: *In intincribus saepè, periculis fluminum, periculis latronum, periculis ex genere, periculus ex gentibus, periculus in civitate, periculus in solitudine, periculus in falsis fratribus.*[35] May thanks be given to Our Lord who has presented our missionaries with many of these same hardships, providing at the same time the strength to endure them.

[Our missionaries] travel innumerable dangerous routes, one of which will be discussed in the mission to Topia and San Andrés. The Spaniards named this route 'The Trembler' because one trembled when walking it due to the risk of falling nearly one thousand *estados* [1,600 meters] into a deep gorge. In fact, one of our religious missionaries, Father Alonso Gómez Cervantes, fell into this canyon with his mount. The Indians who were with him thought he had been killed and dashed to pieces. They could not determine where his body had come to rest because of the depth of the gorge. However, a little dog who was with Father Gómez provided a sign. This faithful little animal, who had jumped into the gorge following its owner, began barking as if calling for someone to help its master. This made it possible for the Indians, albeit with great difficulty, to come to the aid of their minister, whom they found nearly dead. Although he was taken out alive, he suffered from his injuries for the rest of his life.

When one wants to avoid the route spoken of here, which they call 'The Heights', it is necessary to take others that are just as difficult. In these missions one travels through canyons and along the rivers that run through them, crossing back and forth as many times as there are days in the year, as our Spaniards have noted. And although the missions of Sinaloa are free of such rough trails—the land being almost all level— one nevertheless has to travel through thorn forests and rock-strewn hills to reach these peoples' settlements. The priests have found it necessary each year to clear brush, sometimes cutting and bloodying their faces, to be able to travel through the thickets. But this is not the greatest danger for the minister of the doctrine; rather, it is being called at prime, or midnight, to administer the Sacraments of Confession and the holy oils to sick Christians or to baptize a gentile in a pueblo that is four, six, or more leagues away. These people frequently fall ill while hunting in a thicket or in a sand dune while fishing along the coast. These are all cases that can serve as proof that these servants of God are not spared hardship or danger.

I will add here another major risk that one runs while traveling these roads: being [shot] full of sorcerers' arrows. These nations teem with sorcerers who, with prompting from the devil, are always desirous of killing those who are the enemy of their diabolical art. They can freely execute their plan wherever there are no faithful Christians to oppose them. By hiding at night in the brambles along the road, undetected and unrecognized, they can shoot the missionary full of arrows without anyone realizing it or identifying the author of the crime. [421] I recount these hardships and dangers here without concern that they might frighten those whom Our Lord calls to these enterprises because I am sure that, having been drawn by His divine providence and a zeal for the salvation of souls, they will say the same thing that the Apostle [Saint Paul] did concerning this matter: *Charitas Christi urget nos.*[36]

Having recounted the hardship and danger of travel, let us move on to other difficulties listed by the holy

---

35. *Margin Note*: 2. Cor. 11. 2 Corinthians 11:26: "What journeys I have undertaken, in danger from rivers, in danger from robbers, in danger from my own people, in danger from the Gentiles; danger in cities; danger in the wilderness, . . . danger among false brethren!" (Knox 1956:189).

36. *Margin Note*: I Cor. 5. 2 Corinthians 5:14: "With us, Christ's love is a compelling motive" (Knox 1956:184).

Apostle in which our missionaries can be found to be joyfully employed. Saint Paul continues: *In vigilis multis in fame, et siti, in ieiuniis multis, in frigore et nuditate*.[37] There is no shortage of vigils for those who happen to spend many nights out in the open and on the roads I have just mentioned. One of our brother coadjutors humorously commented that there were many Christmas Eves in Sinaloa. He was alluding to the night when the Redeemer of the World was born, when the faithful stay awake and keep watch, celebrating that divine birth. It seemed to the good brother that one could also call glorious the nights that a shepherd of these souls spends (as is often done) aiding a soul and returning a sheep to the flock—a sheep that cost the Redeemer of the World His blood. Thus, these too were holy vigils.

With regard to the other hardships indicated by the Apostle—discomfort, lack of food and drink, fasting, being cold, and lacking clothing—one will clearly see that the great lot of these things befell our ministers. They lived and traveled among the peoples whom we have recounted, [in a land] where everything is unusual and unknown to them. Traveling through cities and populous areas of human beings and civilized persons, the Holy Apostle Saint Paul encountered many of these hardships. (It is not my intention to equate those he experienced with these lesser hardships.) How many of these types [of hardships] are endured by our ministers who work among such fierce and intractable people—people lacking any kind of political order and whose sustenance and customs are so foreign? These evangelical ministers have frequently been obliged to live off squash, beans, and maize, which is the best sustenance to be found in these lands. Even then, it is cooked in water without any type of seasoning (as there are none).[38]

The Indians often have presented [us] with a gift of some ears of young maize that have been roasted over coals. On numerous occasions bread made from wheat flower or grape wine for the holy altar have been so scarce that it has been impossible to consecrate and celebrate the sacred mystery of the Mass. Everything is brought to Sinaloa in carts over great distances and at great cost. In fact, when they are so fortunate and an abundant supply of provisions reaches them, a *cuar-*

tillo of wine [still] costs eight *reales de plata*.[39] The same is true regarding other things that sustain human life. From this it can be concluded that in these lands and enterprises [our ministers] suffer the better part of the various types of hardships related by the Holy Apostle [Saint Paul]. I do not want to deny that over time many of these needs and hardships have to some degree abated, particularly once these people are converted and organized politically. Nevertheless, we are always left with a good number of hardships to offer up to Our Lord, particularly when assistance is delayed from Mexico City, which is three hundred leagues away, whence almost all our necessities are carted each year.

Finally, as proof of the hardships endured in these missions, it seemed to me appropriate to stress this point by copying a letter written by a missionary to his superior, giving an account of the state of his mission and district, as is the practice of these [422] obedient religious.[40] This letter is representative of many other letters that could be copied here that speak of the same matters. For the sake of brevity these will not be cited. Note that the district discussed in this letter, called Guasave, is one of the closest to the Spanish Villa de San Felipe. The people are some of the easiest to deal with in the entire Province of Sinaloa, and their district is located such that it offers far fewer hardships than more remote and distant places. This section of the letter refers to a time of disease and hunger, which also occur frequently in other districts. Having already dealt with other matters, the letter says:

> What has caused me the greatest sadness and pain at this time of disease is the suffering of the maritime people who, forced by hunger, headed for the beaches to rest and search for whatever shellfish they could find. It was there that they fell sick and died. When I learned of this I was in the pueblo of Guasave, and I immediately set out to aid them with some maize. After traveling a league I came across an Indian in the monte who had died of either disease or hunger. I had some young men who were with me take the Indian to the church for burial. I continued traveling for nearly four leagues, and because night had begun to fall and neither I nor those who were with me knew where the sick were, I cautiously and fearfully proceeded until Our Lord finally

---

37. 2 Corinthians 11:27: "hungry and thirsty; so often denied myself food, gone cold and naked" (Knox 1956:189).

38. No seasonings from Europe, perhaps; the Indians used the *chiltepin* pepper, cholla buds, and many other spices and flavorings.

39. A cuartillo equaled 0.456 liters. At the beginning of the colonization of the New World the real de plata was valued at thirty-four maravedís (Polzer, Barnes, and Naylor 1977:35–37, 44). By way of comparison the *Historia* sold for 1,005 maravedís (roughly the cost of two liters of wine on the northern frontier!).

40. The letter was written during an epidemic in 1617 by Father Alberto Clerici, who had been working among the Guasave since 1611 (Alegre 1956–1960: vol. 2).

led us to them. They were all in pain, and only one of them could stand; the rest had fallen naked where they were, stretched out on the cold sand. They had but a small fire and were exposed to the cruel north winds of the sea. The worst thing was that they were almost dead from hunger. Indeed, such a spectacle of misery made our company start to cry. The starving Indians were nevertheless pleased to see me, and I encouraged them as much as I could. I immediately asked about the sick who were in the greatest danger of dying. I heard their confessions and administered the holy oils to them. Among them was a woman who had scarcely received absolution before she died. I distributed the maize that I had brought and got those who were stronger to make atole, a gruel made of ground corn, for the weaker ones. I asked about the dead and was told of two dead women who were nearby. Because it was night, I went searching for them with torches made from burning pitahaya branches. The young men and I recovered the bodies and dug a grave and buried them; the young men also helped by saying the prayer responses.

It was after midnight before I was able to briefly rest. At dawn I heard the confessions of those who remained, numbering around thirty. After hearing confessions I distributed the remaining maize. I then went to another place, arriving around noon, and there I found another group of sick people, to whom I gave some food. Four of them who were in better condition took me to another ranchería, where I heard the confessions of those who were sick. I also anointed five of those whose confessions I had heard, including a cacique who lay ill on a petate, or woven reed mat. Beside him was a pole that had been driven into the ground, with many little Crosses hanging from it. Because he was about to die, I told his relatives that they could bury him there in the monte, inasmuch as it would be a great inconvenience to carry him back to the pueblo, which was eight leagues away. But the cacique expressly commanded his kin not to leave him there but to take his body to the church for burial. At the same ranchería I also found a newborn, so I baptized him and then he went to heaven.

From there I was taken to other rancherías, where I spent part of the night. Then after assisting the people I returned to the place whence I had begun my visits. The following day [423] I assembled the people for religious instruction and a talk. Although it was Sunday, I could not say Mass for them because of difficulties presented by the fierce winds. After hearing confessions and distributing the remaining maize I instructed them to pray, because of their illness they could not return to their pueblo and church. With this I returned to the pueblos of Guasave, Nío, and Tamazula, where I learned that a good number of people had fallen ill among the other estuaries of Toroaca. They had gone to help a Spaniard with his fishing[41] and had been stricken by the illness. I set out from the pueblo around midnight, sending some maize ahead of me. I arrived at a field where some Indians had been overtaken by the sickness and were unable to proceed. I found them half-dead from fatigue as well as from sickness and hunger. I found it necessary to remain there a while because the sickness continued to overtake people along the road. Thus, women could not care for their husbands nor could children care for their parents. Indeed, it was necessary for those who accompanied me to gather all the stricken, whom they then brought to me on horseback. I gathered and aided them, but the following day six of them died. Leaving the survivors with a good supply of maize, I returned to the pueblo [of Guasave]. I continued my efforts there until Eastertide, when it pleased the Lord that the sickness abated, and little by little ill persons began to recover and attendance at church returned to what it was before.

Here I terminate my citation of this missionary priest's letter. It clearly demonstrates the abundance of exercises of apostolic charity and [other] acts of holy virtue that are presented to the evangelical ministers among these people, as well as the hardships they endure. These are good indicators of their apostolic ministry.

41. During the second half of the sixteenth century Spaniards built or assumed control of native weirs and other devices along the coast of Sinaloa. Each year tons of dried fish, shrimp, and oysters were exported to central Mexico (see Mota y Escobar 1940:87–88; Reff 1991b:121–22).

CHAPTER VI The abundant spiritual fruit that has been harvested by those who labor among these barbarous nations, preaching and instructing them in the Holy Gospel

The labors that have been recounted [here] would be fruitless if it were not for the principal and primary fruit of evangelical preaching: placing souls on the road to salvation and attaining their eternal bliss. If the fruit of preaching the Gospel amounted only to suffering numerous hardships for Christ, then those who labor in the vineyard of the Father of Evangelical Families would merit a great prize. However, such a prize would always be lacking because it is necessary for the vineyard to produce fruit once the laborers' hardships have ended. It is in the hope of these fruits that these laborers sweat, dig, and prune, assuming the costs and expenses of tending this vineyard. When the Redeemer of this World sent the first laborers—captains of the spiritual conquest of souls—on their evangelical mission, He first encouraged them, telling them that they would not only suffer hardship, but also that the fields were ripe for the harvest and promised abundant fruit. *Levate oculus vestros* (He said to them) *& videte Regiones, quia albae sunt iam ad messem.*[42] Look to the fields—they invite you with their fruits and grains.

It follows from this that we can now proclaim the principal fruit of the harvest that is being gathered among these people. In doing so, the close link between labor and fruit can be understood. If, as we have suggested, these tasks are great and not inferior to those among civilized peoples, then we can consider the labor itself to be fruit—a fruit that is dear to those who endure it [424] for Christ. If we wish, we can also count those who can be called the fruit of Christ Our Lord and His Church; that is, the people among these gentile nations in Nueva España of which I am writing who have received Holy Baptism and whom the Company of Jesus has instructed. According to baptismal registers, this number has reached three hundred thousand, not including those who each day enter the net of

the Holy Gospel. The harvest count should include not only those who are presently becoming Christians, who in the beginning are often quite few in number, but also those who will later follow. In addition to the aforementioned, one should also count as fruit the change in lifestyle and customs that our missionaries' instruction has wrought among these people. With the aid of divine grace they changed wild and barbarous customs into holy, Christian ones. These included dealings and familiarity with demons, idolatry, and diabolical superstitions. [They underwent this change] out of recognition of and reverence for the one God, Creator of the Universe, and His Most Holy Son, the Redeemer of the World. They were also transformed because of the practice of the Divine Sacraments and their love for the ministers who minister to them and preach to them.

These were all marvelous changes and glorious triumphs for the Faith and the Gospel, which is how I have titled this history. And because these were achieved in every one of these nations, I will summarize them here. Let us first consider the one that was wrought in the early Church through evangelical preaching and discussed by Saint Luke. He said, *Multi credentium veniebant confitentes, & annuntantes actus suos: multi autem ex eis, qui fuerant curiosa sectati, contulerunt libros, & combuserunt coram omnibus.*[43] As an illustrious victory of Gospel preaching, Saint Luke recounts that many of the recent converts came and confessed their crimes and sins as well as their superstitions, black magic, and deceptive and vain arts. Once they were disabused they abominated and detested these things, as they clearly demonstrated by bringing forward the books that had been written concerning these diabolical fables and lies and burning them in public. The changes that have been wrought by Christ's doctrine are evident among the innumerable sorcerers in Sinaloa and in other mis-

---

42. *Margin Note:* Ioan. c. 4. John 4:35: "Why, lift up your eyes, I tell you, and look at the fields, they are white with the promise of harvest already" (Knox 1956:90).

43. *Margin Note:* Actor. c. 19. Acts 19:18–19: "Many believers came forward, confessing their evil practices and giving a full account of them; and a number of those who followed magic arts made their books into a heap and burned them in public" (Knox 1956:136).

sions that will be discussed later. Although they did not have books to burn concerning their bedeviled arts—indeed, they did not [even] have an alphabet—once they received the Holy Faith and Baptism, they sentenced and cast into public bonfires the items that they valued even more than the books used by the sorcerers discussed by Saint Luke. The Indian sorcerers loved these items in the same way that Catholic Christians love their holy and sacred relics. They threw into the fire items with which they had established pacts and familiar dealings with the devil in order to cast effective spells and to heal or kill whomever they wanted. These items included little sticks, thorns, human bones, and small animal skins that had unusual little stones wrapped inside. They used all these things for their deceptive healing or to kill whomever they wanted. These sorcerers were quite revered or quite feared by one and all, and they commanded authority as well as material benefits. Nevertheless, they renounced all these things, receiving in their place the truth of our Holy Faith and the adoration of Christ's Cross.

On other occasions they brought forth to throw into the fire some stone or wooden figurines that represented the form in which the devil appeared to them. These figurines were always extremely ugly, but all the same the sorcerers were deceived and revered them. When they performed their barbarous dances they adorned their heads by wearing something similar to a turban with these figurines on it. [425] I unintentionally turned up at one of these dances with two other priests. There existed the danger that this celebration would end with the Indians taking our lives. Many gentiles had gathered, and there were a great many people dancing. They only practice this collectively, with hundreds of them dancing together in a circle. We had been watching these figures, but we did not yet understand what they meant. They were unusual and took on the appearance of fish or unknown wild animals never seen before. In fact, they were a very good likeness of the ugliness of demons. God willed that the chance to observe them should turn out well. With the help of some good Christian Indians who were present one of these priests, who had an excellent command of the language, preached to them effectively and calmly about the lies and deceit of the enemy of mankind and how he was misleading them. After this speech they surrendered all those figurines and offered to burn them in a bonfire built in the middle of that field. They were burned to ashes, and the devil, against whom this and other victories were achieved, was left perpetually

wailing. Evangelical instruction was so victorious that these very same peoples have now converted all these celebrations into holy Christian ones. They celebrate them, especially those of the holy namesakes of their churches, with more joy than their former barbarous ones. The name they commonly give to these celebrations is 'Pascuas', because 'Pascuas' are celebrated in all of Christendom with the same great solemnity and joy used by these Indians to celebrate these festivals.[44]

What has been said here concerning this matter will be sufficient, for a great deal has already been recorded throughout this history. But one cannot fail to include something concerning the other change in those early Christians celebrated by Saint Luke. He says that they began to confess and reveal their sins, crimes, and deceit, *Confitentes & annunciantes actus suos*.[45] It is a heroic act for people to confess and indict themselves for the crimes and abominations that they committed in secret. These peoples have revealed such sins, indicting themselves in the process. Although their sins are not as abominable as those that have been found in other parts of the world, it is still equally or more difficult for the people of these nations to reveal them, given their character and disposition. In the past they would not denounce their sins, even when tortured. This being the case, they now receive the Holy Sacrament of Confession with such esteem that as soon as someone falls ill, they send for the priest to come to their pueblo, even if he is leagues away. No matter how near or far, they want the priest to come and hear the confession of the sick person, or to baptize him if he is [still] a gentile. The fact that they worry about dying without the sacraments whenever they are in danger is a good sign that many of these souls will attain salvation.

In this regard I cannot help but consider an unusual and appropriate circumstance that is common to the sins of all these peoples. This diminishes their sins, making them more venial and less deserving of punishment when compared with the vices and sins of the peoples of this world who are considered to be wise and powerful. The Indians' vices and sins ordinarily stem from ignorance and weakness. For this very reason the Son of God Himself asked forgiveness for those who crucified Him: *Pater, dimitte illis, non enim sciunt quid*

---

44. Pascuas generally refers to the Christian celebrations of Christmas, Epiphany, Easter, and Pentecost. The Yaqui's Easter celebrations still incorporate some elements of earlier ritual, such as the deer dance.

45. Acts 19:18: "confessing their evil acts and giving a full account of them" (Knox 1956:136).

faciunt[46]—Forgive them (cried the beloved Son to His Most Holy Father), they do not know what they are doing, even though the crime they commit is so great, taking the life of Your only Son. The crimes committed by these poor Indians are not so great: they are more ignorant than those who were able to see [426] the Son of God's miracles and wonders with their own eyes and who heard the doctrine that He preached with their own ears. For what greater reason can we say of the Indians: *No sciunt quid faciunt?*[47] They were born and raised in the deepest darkness, ignorant of both divine and human matters. They were unaware that there were wise and civilized people in the world, and that there was a Lord who had created them. Even after the light of the Gospel reaches them, they hear it from a poor and unfamiliar priest who comes to their lands as if he had fallen from the clouds. When these people falter and break one of the Church's divine precepts that has been preached to them, what greater cause is there to say that they do not know what they are doing and, therefore, that divine goodness should show them greater compassion, pardoning their sins, which stem from such great ignorance and are much fewer than those normally committed by wise and civilized nations? The barbarous nations that we are dealing with totally lack any illicit dealings, profiteering, swearing, blasphemy, slandering, or any other vice that shows a great deal of malice. These things usually abound in wealthy nations that consider themselves or claim to be wise.

It can be inferred from all this that because these new Christians are so concerned about benefiting from the Holy Sacraments, which are the instruments of our salvation, and also given that their sin is venial and not in as great a need of being pardoned, there are many reasons to believe (as wise and experienced men understand) that many of these Indians' souls are saved and attain eternal bliss. This is the principal fruit toward which our missions are directed among civilized as well as barbarous peoples. Achieving this blissful end is very important, even if it entails the salvation of but a single soul. This is a well-known and evident [truth] established by the Doctors of the Church. There have been cases in which a missionary has been obliged to risk his own life to administer Holy Baptism to a mere tiny infant, in order to obtain its eternal bliss. What greater fortune could an evangelical minister have than to be employed and to lose his life rescuing the souls of the many infants and adults who are [now] in a state of grace among these nations?

There is sure to be an abundant harvest and first fruits of innocent lambs who join the company of the Lamb of God in eternity. At the beginning of these conversions divine goodness, through baptismal grace, joyfully takes flocks of these lambs to heaven, despite the barking of bedeviled sorcerers, who try to defame Holy Baptism by saying that it takes the lives of those who receive it. Although it is true that at times the priests who engender these people in Christ could not help but feel natural sorrow over seeing so many children die, and also over the fact that the sorcerers accused them of killing them, nevertheless they have found some consolation in the fact that these souls nevertheless have been saved. There is something else that can be added as a further consolation to these ministers, who work so hard for the salvation of these souls: We can imagine that when these children suddenly found themselves in God's presence and in such bliss, their first act of understanding and reason was to see God clearly, and at the same time to recognize their benefactors, who offered themselves at great risk and danger so that these infants could be placed in this state of great happiness. Because these missionaries administered them the sacrament that is necessary to attain this state, these infants will be eternally grateful; they will always [427] recognize that they owe more to the missionaries than to their own biological parents. This is why Saint Francis Xavier, the Holy Apostle to India (as he is called in his *vita*), commended himself to the eternally blissful souls of these blessed children.

The certain harvest among the nations with which we are dealing is not always obtained in other populous and wealthy nations. It is now an established practice of great consolation that when these peoples request a priest to go to their lands to teach them the Christian doctrine, they offer as a condition, to which they comply, that beforehand [they will gather] their children, and when the priest arrives he will baptize them. These Baptisms are celebrated by the hundreds, in groups of two hundred at a time and sometimes more. This is to the great joy and consolation of their fathers and mothers, who bring them to receive the divine bath by which they are washed in Christ's blood. The Christian religion is marvelously imprinted on those infants who do not die, many of whom become the foundation of the highly useful seminaries that were discussed earlier.

46. *Margin Note*: Lucae 23. Luke 23:34: "Father, forgive them: they do not know what it is they are doing" (Knox 1956:84).

47. "They do not know what it is they are doing."

CHAPTER VII Other changes in customs and the triumphs of the Faith achieved among these peoples

I have not yet finished telling about how these nations, barbarous as they might be, have benefited from divine fruit and how the virtue and strength of our Holy Faith has affected the wild and deep-rooted customs that they inherited from their ancestors. These peoples have forgotten these customs and replaced them with others that were [once] repugnant to their depraved taste for flesh and blood and the free life that once predominated among them. If the power of grace and the light of the divine word could not overcome these customs, they would be impossible to conquer. Who can deny that it is a marvelous change when a barbarian who is baptized and becomes a Christian denies the love he has for his wives and children, leaving those who were once at his side and keeping only one wife? Add to this the clamor raised by the wives who have been cast aside. The first threat they make against their husband when he throws them out is that he will never again see those babes-in-arms and toddlers, for they will take these children to live in other pueblos and among other nations. It is law among these peoples, just as it is among others, that the young must follow their mother.

One can imagine that in [the hearts of] these peoples there reigns a love for their children that is just as strong as in other nations, and that they value having many children. The reason for this (in addition to the nature found in wild peoples) is that the power and authority of the principales and caciques stem mainly from having many children, relatives, and descendants. The Indian who receives the Faith and Baptism deprives himself of these things, at times casting aside in one fell swoop two or three wives or concubines and sometimes three, four, or more children. On innumerable occasions I saw with my own eyes and heard [with my own ears] the angry clamor of those women who had been cast aside. As he was being baptized, the Indian would respond to them by turning to me and saying: "Father, marry these women to other husbands. I am going to keep only this one wife." Here it can clearly be seen that it was not nature at work, but rather grace.

On many occasions the women who had been cast aside turned their clamor against me, because it seemed to them that the priest who married their husbands to only one wife was the cause of their widowhood. I could find no better answer than to tell each of them to forget about her husband's indifference, inasmuch as he did not consider or choose her as the one he loved most. [428] I told them I would marry them in the Christian fashion to someone who would love them. This was carried out, for many of them were young and attractive. Other men took them as wives because it was not considered a disgrace that they had been cast aside by someone who had become a Christian.

What has also been marvelous is the change we mentioned with respect to the Indians' surrendering and subjecting themselves to having their prized hair cut off once they are baptized. Because their hair protected them from the heat of the sun, they did not cut it down to the scalp. However, they at least cut it shoulder length, in a ponytail like one now sees in Spain. All the same it still takes a great deal to get them to sacrifice their hair, for they value it highly and consider growing it long to be a sign of gallantry and bravery. Experience has shown that once they cut their hair they lose much of their wildness and barbarism. Moreover, when an Indian who has been baptized and has given up his hair starts to let it grow again, this is a sign—as experience has shown—that his loyalty is in question. Good Christians show their faithfulness by always concerning themselves with keeping their ponytail well trimmed. This also serves as a way of distinguishing Christians from gentiles when an entire nation has not yet been baptized. Sampson experienced great difficulty in explaining to his beloved Delilah that all of his strength and bravery resided in his hair, so it is no wonder that it upset these Indians to submit their hair to the scissors, for they considered it a sign of their gallantry and bravery. It is also their hair that they adorn most when they go into battle. Thus, surrendering their hair was a sign that they were abandoning and surrendering their weapons.

Another unique change that was a consequence of these others, and which was thought to have been a hindrance and an obstacle to these nations' receiving the Faith and Christian laws, has in fact helped many people hasten their steps toward Holy Baptism. As proof of this, it should be noted that the most common way in which these nations contracted matrimony as gentiles, especially when they had many wives, was for both men and women to go off and marry somebody else whenever they saw fit, regardless of whether or not this upset their partner. It followed from this that, according to natural law, these were not true marriage contracts, as Christ Our Lord made clear when He said: *Erunt duo in carne una.*[48] He did not say three or four, but rather only two in one flesh. To the opposing license of the Indians the Lord responded that it had been permitted by Moses: *Moysis ad duritiam cordis vestri permisit vobis dimittere uxores vestras, ab initia non fuit sic.*[49] The Indians took this same license in their marriages, or concubinage, which evangelical law does not allow. At first it was feared that depriving the Indian men of the freedom of casting aside any woman that displeased them or made them unhappy, or depriving the women of being able to choose another man who was more to their liking, would hinder their subjugation to the law of Christian matrimony. But this is not what has happened, for divine providence has worked admirably well. The state of holy matrimony — of being married to only one wife or husband, without being able to abandon one's spouse — has caused many of these people to hasten their requests for Holy Baptism. Men and women no longer fear being cast aside. Many times it has happened that those who desire perpetuity in their marriage — at times the husband, at other times the wife — have bombarded their spouses and the priest, pestering him to baptize them and then immediately marry them as Christians. With this [429] both of them are secure. Therefore, what was thought to be a hindrance has in fact been a help in getting them to seek Holy Baptism. With their submission to its laws, the Faith has been triumphant over their former barbarous customs.

The Gospel and Holy Baptism have also wrought a change in the savage names that were used by these nations when they were gentiles. They valued these names that made them feared and renowned amongst their people in the same way that nobles display their coats of arms. When they were gentiles many of these people took their names from murders and homicides that they or their ancestors had committed. In the Spanish language these are equivalent to 'he-who-killed-three', 'he-who-killed-five', 'he-who-killed-along-the-routes or -in-the-montes or -fields', 'he-who-killed-the-one-with-long-hair',

I will [now] tell of an even greater change that we will encounter among some of the nations in this history. When the priests went to preach to them the Holy Gospel, they found thousands of human skulls and bones in their rancherías and houses. These bones belonged to their enemies, whom they had killed and whose flesh they had eaten. They kept them as [a sign of] victory. They abandon and forget all these wild and barbarous things, and one no longer hears these names, but rather those of the saints that they are given when they are baptized. They glory in these names, in fulfillment of the prophecy of Isaiah. This is particularly true of the preaching of the Gospel among these nations, more so than in others: *Lupus, & agnus pascetur simul; leo & bos comedet paloas: non nocebunt neque occident, in omni monte sancto meo.*[50] Men are no longer murdered in the montes or along the roads or in the fields. Instead, they travel without bows and arrows. After they are baptized, when they go to the pueblos of those whom they used to kill, they go like gentle lambs into the church for catechism with their former enemies. They also find friendly lodging and meals in their homes. The same thing happens when they come to the Spaniards' villa, where people from all nations and languages come together, especially on feast days and at Christmas and Easter. They go in complete friendship to see the Spaniards, entering the doorways and homes of those whom they once feared and considered their enemy.

These peoples have changed in another way that is important with respect to both spiritual and temporal or human affairs. [When they were still gentiles] they were the most idle people in the world, unaccustomed to working for more than three or four hours during the growing season. After working in the fields an Indian would return home and entertain himself by playing the reed game, sleeping, or going hunting in the monte for deer or honeycombs; they had no other concern or occupation throughout [the remainder of] the year.

48. *Margin Note*: Matt. c. 19. Matthew 19:5: "and the two will become one flesh" (Knox 1956:19).

49. Matthew 19:8: "It was to suit your hard hearts that Moses allowed you to put your wives away; it was not so at the beginning of things" (Knox 1956:19).

50. *Margin Note*: Isaia. cap. 65. Isaiah 65:25: "Wolf and lamb shall feed together, lion and ox eat straw side by side, . . . all over this mountain, my sanctuary, there shall be no hurt done, . . . , no life shall be forfeit" (Knox 1956:679).

Now when the time comes to build their large, permanent churches which, even though they are usually made of mud, still require large amounts of wood and other materials for the roof, both men and women, boys and girls, all joyfully join in the work in whatever tasks and duties their strength and age allow. There are usually five hundred or more people involved in this effort. Care is taken in the beginning not to tire them out in tasks to which they are not accustomed, and the workday does not go beyond four or five hours. Later, when they are more accustomed, they can be much more easily employed in this labor, and they become anxious to see their churches finished and dedicated. This they celebrate with a festival with great solemnity and rejoicing, to which foreign nations are invited, as has been recorded. When they see these buildings finally completed, they never tire of looking at them, glorying in the fact that they have them in their pueblos. These churches also invite them to settle there more permanently; those who were used to living in the montes now usually build their houses close to the church. [430] The most valuable fruit produced by these churches is that every morning at the sound of the bell some of these people come to hear Mass, even on weekdays. With a second tolling of the bell everyone comes to catechism. On feast days there is no one—young or old—who is absent. Sometimes this devotion even brings them from pueblos that are two or three leagues away. On several occasions when the churches were in danger of being burned down by wicked and rebellious people, the good Christians defended them from fire and their enemies, risking their own lives. If the churches happened to burn down, they built new ones that were just as good as the first ones, if not better. These are the marvelous effects that Christian doctrine has on these peoples.

I will now recount another equally or more marvelous change that has come from God's almighty hand. In the beginning the first priests in these missions doubted that this change could be effected. It involved uprooting that frequently mentioned and well-established Indian vice of continual drunken revels. These were celebrated communally, one day in one neighborhood, the next day in their neighbor's house. These people never drank alone in their homes or at mealtime the way other people in the world do. Rather, a large number of people gathered together: friends, acquaintances, and sometimes rancherías and entire pueblos, especially when this celebration of wine was to declare war on some other nation. In these latter celebrations there was a greater number of the large

earthen jars in which they made that terrible drink. At every one of these celebrations all the wine had to be drunk and there could be no leftovers, for they already had the following day's drink prepared at their neighbor's house in the same pueblo or at somebody else's in a neighboring pueblo. They neither prepared nor served any food with this drink, for their sole intention was that vice and delight of losing their senses, which the devil had caused to become so widespread among these peoples. For this reason it seemed nearly impossible to uproot this vice and to clear up their misunderstanding and thereby bring them to the light of reason. Infinite thanks are due to God, because what has been impossible to achieve in other nations in the world that are much more civilized, and even among long-time Christians, has been achieved among these nations. In the Mexican nation, which was much more civilized as gentiles and which has been Christian now for more than one hundred years, this vice predominates more than one would like. But in our barbarous nations that have just recently received the evangelical doctrine and been baptized, this vice has been so completely uprooted and eliminated that one no longer sees or hears of a drunken Indian. The catechism they have been taught has taken such a great hold that their very own Indian preachers, who were present when they were still gentiles, have since the early days of their conversion frequently given sermons in the plazas and councils of their pueblos [against drinking]. They detest this pestilential vice of drunkenness, and they [now] exhort their people to total sobriety, ridiculing a custom to which they used to be so attached.

I will recount here a minor but entertaining case that confirms what has been said. I had gone to give notice of our Holy Faith and Christian religion to the brave Yaqui nation, as has been recorded. The infants had been baptized, as were a fair number of adults. In order to begin the construction of churches and dwelling places, I chose as carpenters and masons (the minister is in charge of all these things) some of the most skilled of all the young men who had been baptized. [431] These young men accompanied me from pueblo to pueblo doing construction. One night after these workers had eaten at a home near my enramada, for entertainment and as a farce, they very joyfully and loudly mimicked the drunken revels that their nation used to celebrate. There were still many gentile Yaqui, and the young men ridiculed this custom right before their very eyes. They acted out the gestures and faces as well as the sayings and deafening screams that were mispronounced by the drunkards. They concluded this farce with great laughter that rang throughout the entire plaza, and they did this to ridicule that mad and savage vice. I felt that the joke was on the devil, the author of that vice, who thought that it was very deeply rooted among these subjugated people and that there was no power on earth that could uproot it. In spite of the fact that the joke made me happy, I was still concerned and frightened that these young men would suffer harm at the hands of those in this nation who had not yet been baptized, some of whom were not very fond of the Christian doctrine. It is nothing new, especially in the beginning, for there to be some people who do not enjoy listening to someone preach against their barbarous vices. But God's desire was such that the Yaqui, who were more inclined to drunkenness than any other nation, did not become upset by the public joke made of this vice. Rather, they were quite changed, and as with other nations, this vice was completely eliminated. I can certainly call these and the other changes recorded throughout this history, 'triumphs of Christ's Faith'.

Finally, we can [also] add to these changes in customs the one that has taken place concerning these peoples' barbarous nudity. When our father, Adam, saw himself naked after he had sinned, he was so ashamed and humiliated that he immediately sought a way to remedy his nudity, even if it was only with leaves from the trees. All nations where there is still some reason have tried to amend this condition. Although the women in the nations we are discussing showed some concern for their nudity, the men paid no mind to it whatsoever. Today, in Christian fashion with modesty and propriety they all cover themselves with clothing. If they are extremely poor and can find no clothing with which to adorn themselves, they leave the province to find work in order to obtain some, going forty or fifty leagues or more. In order for an Indian to return to his lands with clothing for himself and his wife, he will spend half a year or more working in some mining camp or at one of the Spaniards' settlements, especially if the clothing is at all elegant, which they like. This is the degree to which nudity has been uprooted, along with the other barbarous customs that predominated in these peoples.

CHAPTER VIII The marvelous deeds or miracles that the Lord has wrought in these missions through the preaching of the Gospel

I am not qualified to judge what are true miracles; this falls under the higher authority of the Church. Rather, I can only provide a historical narrative of the extraordinary acts of singular and divine providence that have shone in the conversion of these peoples. I will begin with that greatest miracle and testimony of our most Holy Faith given with outstanding genius and wisdom by Saint Augustine. He noted that promulgating our most Holy Faith involved preaching and introducing laws that truly oppose flesh and blood and that eliminate all the vices and pleasures that burden the sons of Adam. He nevertheless noted that the doctrine of our Holy Faith had such superior and divine power that it subjugated all the peoples of the world, overcoming [432] their vices, laws, privileges, and indomitable customs, replacing them with calm, holy, and celestial ones unknown to these nations. In this regard there have been many marvelous changes, and as proof of this, I can speak personally about the aforementioned Yaqui nation. This was the most fierce and populous of all the nations reduced in these enterprises. Once these bellicose Indians had been baptized they began to tell the priest who was instructing them about their past wars with the Spaniards and their continual wars with other peoples. Comparing the present to the past, they would ordinarily say, "Father, we are no longer what we used to be. It seems that the water you used for baptizing us has taken away our fierceness and spirit. Now we have reason, which we previously lacked." These and other similar statements manifested the change wrought by Holy Baptism.

There is another wonder, divine above all the others, that we experience daily in these nations, and it proves what Saint Augustine said. When a religious minister comes to their lands to give them religious instruction, these people are persuaded that they will have to abandon the deep-rooted customs in which they have been reared. Thus, they must abandon their dwellings and rancherías and go to newly founded, populous pueblos that are established for facilitating religious instruction. In spite of all these conditions, they often come themselves to ask us to preach and to teach them the doctrine. Thus, they relinquish the place where they were born, as well as their licentious life filled with vices. In addition to this insistence upon having Christ's doctrine preached to them, they sometimes bring their children and leave them with the ministers to be instructed so that they can learn to teach their parents and relatives when religious come to instruct them. This is not true of the entire nation, however, for there are always some bedeviled sorcerers who oppose it. But even in this case, divine providence has been evident in not allowing them to prevail, favoring instead the followers of the Faith, which has been victorious.

There are some who think that the Indians are baptized en masse, as they say, without any understanding or choice on their part nor on the part of he who is baptizing them. It is thought that the Indians do not understand what they are receiving and the laws to which they are submitting themselves. Such persons are wrong, and it would be a mistake for anyone to think this (I speak from experience). One must be convinced that God's virtue and the virtue of His Holy Gospel are what have wrought the wonderful effects that we have just mentioned.

Let us now examine in detail what was experienced in the conversions of these peoples and the type of miracles that were promised by God's Son to those who are new in the Faith. As He was about to ascend [into heaven] He charged the Apostles with preaching the Holy Gospel to the entire world: *Signa autem eos, qui crediderint, haec sequentur: Daemonia eijciunt, linguis loquentur nouis, serpentes tollent, & si quid mortiferum bibent non eis nocebit, super aegros, manus imponent, & bene habebunt.*[51]

I refer anyone interested in learning about which of these wonders has occurred in these missions to the entire course of this history. One will find a great number of clear cases in which demons were expelled, although not so much from bodies as, more importantly, from the souls of innumerable sorcerers who had intimate and familiar dealings with these enemies of the [433] human race. The demons had a stronger hold on the souls than on the bodies of the possessed in whom they dwelled.

The grace that comes from this *Linguis loquentur nouis*[52] has shone and been wrought in many ways in these missions. Moved by a love for Christ and a zeal for preaching His Gospel, these ministers have overcome the difficulty of the innumerable new languages of the New World, acquiring the most complex and unusual languages discovered in the universe. By making these languages tractable and familiar, it appears that they strip them of their fierceness and barbarity. They made the highest mysteries of our Holy Faith understood by the natives in the latter's own language. These priests speak so eloquently that the Indians (as they themselves have confessed) sound like babbling children in comparison to their priest-interpreters, who in all matters are their teachers. There have been even more outstanding cases in which divine grace has assisted these servants in learning to speak these languages almost immediately when necessary. However, for the sake of brevity I will not expound upon this point.

With respect to the next marvelous event, *Serpents tollent*,[53] I say that it is more dangerous for these religious missionaries to be among these ferocious Indians than the snakes and poisonous serpents of the earth. Snakes can be seen and will flee, but the Indians are often deceptive and traitorous in spilling their poison. However, Christ's grace wrought a divine metamorphosis even among them, as they lost the venom with which they used to kill. One can see wrought in them the same great miracle that is told concerning the serpents on the island of Malta. After one of them had bitten the Apostle Saint Paul on the hand, as is related in the Acts of the Apostles, it became legend that the rest of the serpents lost their venom.[54] It is of no less wonder—indeed, we could consider it of even greater

---

51. *Margin Note*: Marc. c. 16 Mark 16:17–18: "Where believers go, these signs shall go with them; they will cast out devils in my name; they

will speak in tongues that are strange to them; they will take up serpents in their hands, and drink poisonous draughts without harm; they will lay their hands upon the sick and make them recover" (Knox 1956:52).

52. "They will speak in tongues that are strange to them."

53. "They will take up serpents in their hands."

54. Acts 28:1–6.

esteem—that these ferocious Indians, whose only purpose was to kill people, now love one another with a Christian charity that is closely observed among all these converted nations.

The next miracle listed by Saint Mark states that the Apostles will not be harmed should they happen to drink poison. These Indians certainly had poisonous herbs close at hand near their houses. Induced by the devil and out of desperation, they often took their own lives using these herbs, as is related elsewhere in this history. This barbarous custom is now forgotten. It is an even greater miracle that, out of their hatred for the religious instruction given by their priests and evangelical ministers, none of these barbarians has given them this poison in their food or drink. They could do so very easily, for whatever sustenance these priests obtain—their bread or maize tortillas, their boiled or roasted squash, the honeycombs they are sometimes given, the water carried from the river—this all comes straight from the Indians' hands, and they have had the opportunity to kill the priests with poison. This being the case, who can doubt that it is a great wonder to see the priests as free from danger as if they had drunk poison and remained unharmed? The fact that God broke the arms and hands of so many barbarians so that they would not give the ministers food or drink containing any of the poisons they have so close at hand is no less a favor than if He had broken the cup that held the beverage. We can call this a miracle that has continued for many years, because, of the seventy-five missionary priests assigned at any given time to instruct these people—and an [434] even greater number when one counts all those who have labored here—not a single one has ever been endangered by poison.

To confirm and expound upon this wonder as well as the next on Saint Mark's list, which says, *Super agros manus imponent, & bene habebunt*,[55] I can add that these servants of God have cured innumerable sick people, sometimes by applying relics of saints to them or by reciting Gospel verses over them. At other times when they are ill the priests assist them with Christian charity, providing food and care as well as medicines that they bring from Mexico City. If this is carefully considered, we can say that their merit is greater than if they had cured with miracles. If it were only God's virtue at work, their merit would be less. Instead, the faithful and loving minister complements that divine virtue with his labor and his diligence, often depriving himself of sustenance and rest in order to perform for his brothers these charitable acts of love for Christ. So that these precious acts of charity might be performed, we can further understand that God often chooses not to perform or make use of those sudden miracles of healing referred to by Christ Our Lord in the Gospel. We can also add that the health of which the Gospel speaks is spiritual and is verified as the health of souls, as many saints have understood. In this sense two things are true: first, curing a soul of mortal sin is a greater deed than curing all those who are crippled, maimed, leprous, and all the sick laying in hospitals the world over. Although it would be truly extraordinary if one were to revive all the dead with a single word, it is a far greater deed to heal or revive a soul that is dead because of sin. This claim is certain, and it is equally true that committing any mortal sin is not permissible, even if doing so were to lead to the resurrection of all the dead, past and future, from the beginning to the end of the world. To avoid committing a single mortal sin, a man should, if necessary, sacrifice his own life as well as those of his parents, friends, relatives, and indeed the lives of all men, if their fate were in his hands. All these people should be offered to the knife, the flames, the rack, and [any other instruments of] torture if doing so would prevent one single mortal sin from being committed. To give health to and liberate the soul from the mortal wound of a serious sin is more wonderful than curing the lame, the blind, the maimed, and the leprous. With regard to the Son of God's promise to His disciples concerning the miraculous healing of the sick, it is certain that Christ's principle aim, and what was to be the principle aim of His disciples, was the health of souls. It is the opinion of nearly all the holy Doctors that when the Redeemer of the World healed people's bodies, He also cured their souls. It would have been an insufficient redemption if the Lord, who came down from heaven to redeem the world, had provided these people with only corporal health, leaving their souls deceased. To achieve His goals, He deigned to have collaborators in that divine redemption (that is how Saint Paul referred to them: *Dei sumus coadiutores*),[56] not so much for them to cure the bodies of those who were blind, maimed, and disabled as to have them revive their souls and liberate them from the death of sin.

Who could count the innumerable supreme and precious miracles of this kind that [435] our evangeli-

---

55. "They will lay their hands upon the sick and make them recover."

56. *Margin Note*: I. Cor 3. I Corinthians 3:9: "We are only his assistants" (Knox 1956:166).

cal preachers have performed and continue to perform daily in these missions? Who can count the number of individuals now revived to the life of grace who before were not merely blind or mortally wounded, but existed in a spiritual darkness the likes of which had never been seen among mortals, wounded by unheard of, fierce, inhuman, and barbarous vices? They now possess the heavenly inner glow of the Faith and are cured of their inclination to their barbarous customs, which they now abhor, having replaced them instead with a love for Christ's laws. These miracles will not remain so hidden as to be invisible to our eyes, and because this is what makes corporeal miracles stand out, this grace will also be found in the miracles wrought among these peoples. They, too, manifest themselves, being revealed so frequently that the ministers of the doctrine as well as the soldiers and [other] Spaniards observe them daily. As has been recorded at several points throughout this history, when these Spaniards are present during the holy celebration of feast days in the pueblos of these new Christians, they praise with admiration their Communions and confessions, as well as the crowds that gather at their churches. Thus, we can conclude that there have been a great number of similar important miracles that have enhanced the preaching of the Gospel among these peoples, no matter how barbarous or uncivilized they might be.

CHAPTER IX How spiritual matters are governed in this entire province, and the favors received from the patron saints to whom these missions have been dedicated

Having recounted the felicitous fruits harvested and enjoyed in our missions among barbarous peoples, I will write in this chapter about how they are distributed and governed, in order that their fruit will continue and ripen. I will also write about the difficulties that have been overcome as well as the blood spilled by the members of our Company of Jesus to attain the current successful state of the missions. I have no doubt that this news will please their brothers who are elsewhere.

All these missions are grouped into districts of two or three pueblos, depending on their location and the number of people in them. One missionary priest cares for each district, aiding and protecting the flock that Christ Our Lord has given him. Although these missionaries are obliged to be far away from one another so they can aid the souls under their care, they are very united in the Lord's love, and they do all they can to be able to enjoy the pleasant company of their brothers. Nobody can deny that although they lack the company they would have had in their colleges and religious houses, these servants have much to offer God. Only the welfare and salvation of souls could separate them from such solace and religious joy, which is why JESUS Christ chose them for His Company. Although it is impossible to have this solace [of living with other religious] and still attend to their faithful, [436] they compensate for this through their correspondence with and governance by their superiors, who reside in the three mission headquarters to which all the missions of Sinaloa and their ministers pertain.[57] Each superior visits the districts of his rectorate, lending his comforting presence so that these ministers of God have the chance to communicate in their mother tongue. Sometimes there is nobody with whom to speak Spanish during an entire year, except when the priests visit each other to

---

57. In 1620 or thereabouts the missions of Sinaloa were divided into two rectorates: San Felipe y Santiago and San Ignacio. In 1639 the Rectorado de San Francisco Xavier was created, encompassing chiefly the Nébome of the upper Río Yaqui and the Aivino and other Opata along the Río Matape, Río Sahuaripa, and Río Sonora.

hear confession or whenever there are enough ministers for two to be together. Therefore, the visits by superiors prevent them from forgetting their own language.

The Father Rector of our College of San Felipe y Santiago is in charge of the missions on the first four rivers of Sinaloa [Mocorito, Sinaloa, Ocoroni, and Zuaque]. Another superior is in charge of the missions on the Río Mayo and the Río Yaqui, as well as those in the surrounding foothills. This residence and headquarters, with its missions, is named for and protected by our father, Saint Ignatius. Another superior is in charge of all the missions and priests scattered throughout the interior, as was previously mentioned. This third residence enjoys the name and protection of the new Apostle of the Indies, Saint Francis Xavier.

Without deviating from our history, it is to the glory of those saints and the solace of their sons to herein discuss some of the unusual favors from these glorious saints that have been experienced by these new Christian communities and those who administer them. These are in addition to those already mentioned in this history, where these holy protectors demonstrated their concern for our ministers. All these nations have learned very well from these experiences, acquiring a particular devotion to these saints, whom they call upon in their time of need. Through their intercession they have received great favors, especially from our patriarch, Saint Ignatius, to whom they frequently and successfully turn for rain. In times of severe drought, on the very same day that they have brought his image out for a procession the heavens have showered abundant rain on their lands and fields.

Our patriarch also worked a special favor on behalf of a woman from the pueblo of Mochicahue [58] who could not deliver her child because it was stuck inside her for four days. She was in danger of losing her own life as well as that of the baby. This woman's worried husband came to the priest on her behalf and asked him for the blessed image of our saint. The priest gave it to him, saying, "Tell your wife to hang this image of Saint Ignatius around her neck and to commend herself to him, offering to attend a Mass for him and to have her child named for him." The suffering woman did so, and as soon as she had put the image around her neck, she delivered the child very calmly. In this regard this saint's favors have been experienced continually, and many babies who were born sickly have recuperated.

Another favor from this saint happened to a priest at the pueblo of Cacalotlán. A woman was dying from the sudden onset of a hemorrhage. The priest had just arrived at this pueblo from another that was far away, where he had heard the confession of another sick person. When they told him about this sick woman's condition he went to her hut and asked her whether she wanted to confess. He found that she was unable to talk and that her eyes had already begun to bleed.[59] He gave her absolution because the other Indians testified that she had expressed that desire when she had learned that the priest was coming to their pueblo. The priest also administered the holy oils. However, after he had returned to his house he thought that it would do her good to send her a medal of Saint Ignatius. [437] They brought it to her just in time, because her chest had already begun to swell. The priest asked them to place the medal upon her chest and to whisper into her ear to commend herself to the saint whose image was engraved on it. Then a marvelous thing happened, because the blood stopped flowing immediately and she soon began to feel better. She who was on the verge of death recovered so quickly that she was able to sit up and eat that very same day. She finally recuperated, and ever since she has acknowledged the saint who favored her in her hour of travail.

I must not omit what Saint Ignatius' holy companion, our father Saint Francis Xavier, has wrought in the most recently founded Christian communities that were dedicated to his name.[60] There it seems he has taken the banner from the hands of his father, Saint Ignatius, just as he did when he set out for the Indies of the Orient. The glorious patriarch [Saint Ignatius] has now introduced the banner of the Faith through the efforts of his sons throughout one hundred leagues of the Province of Sinaloa. He encouraged his sons to place themselves under the protection of his felicitous companion, Saint Francis Xavier, who bore the banner of the Gospel throughout the Orient. Saint Ignatius has encouraged them now to take this same banner to the countless nations of the west, whose boundaries remain unknown, as was mentioned earlier. What is considered to have been a singular favor from Saint Francis in these western nations is the fact that they have been converted with less trouble and fewer wars and disturbances than other

---

58. One of the two Zuaque pueblos along the Río Fuerte.

59. The woman may well have been suffering from typhus, which reached epidemic proportions on several occasions in Sinaloa (at least as early as 1611). Hemorrhaging (*pujamiento de sangre*) was a common symptom of the disease.

60. In 1622 Pope Gregory XV canonized both Ignatius of Loyola and Francis Xavier.

nations. Fortunately, a robust Christianity and change have been attained from the Most High. When Saint Francis Xavier traveled through the Orient he founded marvelous Christian communities, and now that he is in heaven he has not lost his desire to make known the name of Christ Jesus, *Ab ortu Solis, usque occasum*.[61]

As proof of these patron saints' favors, I can write that during the years following these most recent conversions there have been prosperous and abundant Baptisms of infants and adults, amounting to six thousand or seven thousand each year.[62] No one can doubt that for this corner of the world (in addition to other wide fields cultivated by the sons of Saint Ignatius and Saint Francis Xavier), this is a successful harvest for the Holy Church and a source of continuous labor for these evangelical workers. There is no end to the nations that are being discovered in these parts, including those along the coast opposite Sinaloa in the land of the Californias [Baja California], which is also populated by these kinds of people. Moreover, it is established practice among our missionary priests that whenever one finds himself in a nation bordering gentiles, in addition to caring for his own Christian community, he also takes great care to win over the nation that God has set before his eyes. This requires a display of great love on the part of these missionary priests, who are inspired by a burning desire to save souls. Sometimes they invite these gentiles to take part in the celebrations of the converted Christians. At other times they give them little presents. Then, when they are partially won over, they ask them to bring some of their children to be reared in the church with other youngsters so that they can be instructed and perhaps baptized. There are times when Our Lord moves the adults to request Holy Baptism before the priests enter their lands. This is conceded on the condition that the people in gentile pueblos attend services in the Christian pueblos at the specific times designated for Christian exercises, and the Indians comply. [438] All these means produce such successful results among these people that in the end the entire nation willingly requests the light of the Gospel.

CHAPTER X The political government of this entire province and what is judged to be most advantageous for its preservation and extension

At the beginning of this history, particularly in Book I, I wrote about the great barbarity in which this entire province was entombed both politically and culturally. I should discuss the great change that has taken place in this respect throughout the entire province following the arrival of the doctrine of the Gospel. The civil governance of this entire province is under the jurisdiction of the governor of Nueva Vizcaya, whose seat is in the city of Guadiana, or Durango; thus the Province of Sinaloa falls within this jurisdiction. I particularly specified civil government because all matters concerning war, garrisons of soldiers, the pacification of new nations, expenses and payment of the militia, and everything else are in the hands of the viceroy of Nueva España. He is the captain general of this entire kingdom and its provinces and governments. Although the governor of Nueva Vizcaya is actually responsible for civil justice, for the past fifty years—ever since the founding of the Sinaloa missions—this has been administered by the same person who was captain of the militia, who was appointed by the viceroy. This was always considered very advantageous, not only because it avoided the multiplication of political offices in such a distant province, but also because it avoided burdening the Indians and prevented disputes concerning jurisdictions, which ordinarily are a hotbed

---

61. Psalm 112:3: "From the sun's rising to the sun's setting" (Knox 1956:525).

62. Beginning around 1619 (when the Yaqui were largely incorporated into the mission system), Jesuit baptisms exceeded seven thousand annually (except for the lean years, 1626–29, following the destructive epidemic of 1623–25).

of legal controversy. Furthermore, with this additional authority the captain, who is in charge of the garrison, has even greater power to keep the entire province at peace and well governed. This way of doing things was specifically maintained during the thirty years that Diego Martínez de Hurdaide was captain (he has been mentioned at various points throughout this history). Since his death, however, this strategy has not been consistently employed, as the governors of Nueva Vizcaya have entrusted the office of the governor's deputy[63] to persons other than the captain. As recently as a few years ago, a gentleman who had served the king in this office in Sinaloa[64] attempted to divide the garrison. At the Royal Council of the Indies, he tried to get the king to grant him the favor of the title of 'Captain and Founder', with all pertinent privileges, for the region north of the Río Yaqui. He made this request under the pretense of having served the king by pacifying the nations of the interior while at the same time being obliged to sustain twenty-five soldiers to safeguard and protect new Christian communities. This captain and settler made his home in the Valle de Sonora [in Banamachi] (which was recorded in the final chapters of the preceding book). From all this arose the disadvantages of differences and disputes over jurisdictions that I said occur when there are too many political offices.

I will omit other disadvantages that are not pertinent at this point. However, because these matters are closely linked to the spiritual enterprise of converting these people, and because I have observed things during the many years that I have spent among them—having traversed the Province of Sinaloa several times—all this provides me with the opportunity and some license to record here that which can serve to inform those [439] whose duty it is to make such important information available to the service of both the Divine and human Majesties. With this license I will declare here what those ministers—who are spread throughout the entire Province of Sinaloa and who are experienced, zealous, and religious—have desired and consider to be the only means of government free of disputes and discord in new and distant lands, not only for their preservation, but also for their extension to lands that are still being discovered. What these highly zealous priests consider of service to both the human and Divine Majesties and to the expansion of the Holy Gospel is that the garrison now at Fort Montesclaros should be moved further inland so that it can serve the same purpose it has during the last fifty years: securing the way for the Gospel and maintaining peace in the nations that are receiving it and placing themselves under His Majesty's protection as his vassals. This cannot be achieved if the garrison remains where it is today, so far away. The new nations that are now being converted are more than one hundred leagues from its shelter and protection. In addition, the garrison is not needed in the Spaniards' Villa de San Felipe or by the nations that we have left better secured and domesticated. The gentile nations that follow will also become more domesticated and secure as the garrison is brought closer to them. In this way the need for a new captain and government in the province can be avoided and at the same time a new expense to His Majesty is forgone, as are burdens on the Indians. Just as the Gospel has been preserved and has unceasingly expanded in past years with only one captain and garrison, so will it forge ahead and be amplified among the new people who are being reduced to the Church and who are now subjects of both the Divine and Catholic Majesties. For this reason I have been moved to touch upon this topic, without having deviated from my professed intention.

63. *Justicia mayor*. An individual appointed by the governor to act as his deputy in each town council within the governor's jurisdiction (Polzer, Barnes, and Naylor 1977:143).

64. In 1636 Don Pedro de Perea, who a decade earlier had succeeded Hurdaide as captain of the Sinaloa garrison, petitioned the viceroy for the right to settle and create a new province called Nueva Andalucía, encompassing much of present-day Sonora, Mexico, north of the Río Yaqui. The Jesuits had eyed this region since the early 1620s and were loathe to see Perea monopolize the area and its native population. Fortunately for the Jesuits, Perea died rather suddenly in October 1645 from an apparent bout with malaria (Bannon 1955; Polzer 1972; Reff 1991b:173).

CHAPTER XI The conclusion of the manifesto that I have tried to advance here in Book [VII]

The principal intention of the manifesto [that has been the focus] of the chapters of this book has been to make known how thoroughly evangelical preaching has accomplished its goal among these people, no matter how fierce and barbarous they might be. The goal is to show that these conquests are just as successful and abundant in spiritual fruit as those carried out in those nations of the world that are of greater renown and more illustrious and noble. Among these barbarous nations one still finds crowns of blood shed for Christ and His Gospel and unspeakable toil suffered for His glory. All this was to make His Gospel known to those who at that time were the most oppressed and dispirited peoples in the entire world. Our Lord, however, bought with His blood those who were more possessed by the devil than any others on earth. The tyrant who possessed them has been defeated, along with the vices and savage and inhuman customs that he had introduced among those who were created for heaven. Finally, we can say that Babylon has been converted and changed into Jerusalem, where the citizens now travel the road to heaven. They wish to obtain bliss, and through Christ's grace many of them have.

This is the glorious cause that was professed by the Apostle to the People, Saint Paul. It encouraged him to endure great hardships and dangers for the salvation of souls: *Omnia substineo propter electos, ut & ipsi salutem consequatur*.[65] [440] It was on this basis that Saint Paul took glory in those whom he had engendered in Christ, rejoicing in them and saying, *Et si decem millia pedagogorum habeatis; sed no multis patres, nam in Christo Iesu per Evangelium ego vos genui*,[66] although you may all have many other tutors and teachers after me who will rear you in the doctrine that I have taught you, none will take from me the glory of having engendered you in Christ and of having planted among you the doctrine in which you and your children and descendants

shall be raised. These are all fruits that I have won through the hardships I have endured, and I should be acknowledged as their father.

From this can be inferred two things that are of special solace to the ministers who labor in these nations at the beginning of their conversion. The first is that the fruit of the salvation of these souls should not be measured only in terms of the present harvest, because even in populous, civilized, and wise nations this fruit often seems limited. Saint Paul himself did not convert all the nations and peoples to whom he preached. In the Areopagus [supreme tribunal] of Athens the conversions of Dionisius and a woman called Damaris were recorded as very precious fruit, but the rest of those present laughed and were scandalized by the fact that Saint Paul had preached to them about Christ's resurrection and the resurrection of their own bodies.[67] On a different occasion Saint Luke says that there were some good women who had gathered on the shores of a river, where they heard and received the doctrine from the very same Apostle.[68] Christ's most zealous preacher did not wait to have a large and illustrious audience in order to sow the doctrine of the Gospel. He was certain that the few grains he sowed would produce and yield fruit by the hundreds, especially if they fell on good soil, as Christ Our Lord preached in His parable.[69] We already know from our histories that there were very few who were converted during the time of our great patron of the many Spains, Saint James.[70] Nevertheless, the glorious Saint James is the patron of [the many] Spanish Catholics who have been born and raised over the course of many hundreds of years in both the old and new Spains and throughout the entire New World that has been discovered. He is in heaven, crowned with the Faith, and through it, with the heroic fruit harvested by Spanish Catholics. From heaven he has acted as their father, and in ecclesiastical prayers Saint James is awarded

---

65. *Margin Note*: 2. AdTimot. c. 2. 2 Timothy 2:10: "I am ready to undergo anything; for love of the elect, that they, like us, may win salvation" (Knox 1956:223).

66. *Margin Note*: I. adCorin. cap. 4. 1 Corinthians 4:15: "Yes, you may have ten thousand schoolmasters in Christ, but not more than one father; it was I that begot you in Jesus Christ" (Knox 1956:167).

67. Acts 17:16–34.

68. *Margin Note*: Actor. 16. Acts 16:13.

69. Matthew 13:3–9; Luke 8:5–8.

70. Pérez de Ribas appears to acknowledge here the fact that theologians questioned what was at the time an ancient tradition to the effect that the apostle James preached in Spain, building the first Christian sanctuary on the Ebro River, where the Virgin Mary purportedly appeared.

the same trophy that Saint Paul received for his work among the Corinthians: *Per Evangelium ego vos genui*,[71] You, my Spanish children, are the flocks that I won over to Christ and His Church. I will always have the glory of having been the first to plant the Faith in Spain.

Those whom our evangelical missionaries are gathering are also flocks, and although they are not comparable to the Spanish nation, which God Our Lord has exalted on earth, they have all been redeemed by Christ's blood and He has visibly shown them mercy. There were times when the holy Apostles preached to smaller flocks, not knowing whether they would live to preach to other more populous ones. Still they believed that their apostolic talents were very well employed in what God was offering them at that moment in time.

The sons of the Company of Jesus baptize and catechize these nations by the hundreds and thousands. In addition, there are still future fruits to be enjoyed, and these are generally more abundant and perfect. It is true that the priests who instruct the nations that have already been baptized and settled recount with amazement the signs of Christianity and the continuing improvement of these nations. The [Indians] have a great understanding of matters of the Faith and it increases daily. They admire and love the first ministers who made them Christians and they live with the solace and peace [441] of that most holy law.

I will [now] conclude the manifesto that I have tried to present in this chapter for the glory of God and the consolation of those whom His divine goodness has chosen and will choose in the future for these apostolic enterprises and ministries among the most scorned and humble people in the world. I will close this treatise with the promise that God made through His Prophet Isaiah, who was the one person who particularly celebrated the marvelous effects of evangelical law in the world. Through him God presented these effects to His blessed preachers so many years ago, encouraging them with the hope of abundant fruit from their enterprises. It seems that Isaiah's comments about these enterprises agree completely with what I am now discussing in this history. He says, *Electi mei non laborabunt frustra, neque, generabunt in conturbatione*,[72] let those to whom I choose to preach my Gospel be certain that the exhaustion and fatigue they suffer in planting the Faith will not be in vain. In this enterprise, they will engender many children for My greater glory and their hardships will be well worthwhile.

These illustrious promises (along with others given by the same Prophet in the same chapter) are well kept by divine mercy, and we benefit from them in our missions. This can be seen in the approximately fifty churches that have now been built. The Indians (as has been mentioned) call their church a *teopan*, meaning 'house of God'. Three hundred thousand souls who just yesterday (as they say) were gentiles have now been baptized in these churches. The Prince of Darkness has been driven from these, his former castles, and many of them now enjoy God in the Church triumphant, for which they were created and redeemed by the blood of the Lamb. A new flock has also been added to the Church militant, increasing and multiplying its children. Many abundant fruits are harvested in the vineyard that Our Lord planted in the lands of barbarous nations and humble and oppressed Indians. Finally, celebrating the triumphs of our Holy Faith, which is the title of this history, the following chapter will give an account of other nations that are now being prepared.

---

71. 1 Corinthians 4:15: "it was I that begot you in Jesus Christ, when I preached the gospel to you" (Knox 1956:167).

72. *Margin Note*: Isaias. c. 65. Isaiah 65:23: "Not in vain shall they toil, these, my chosen, nor beget children to see them overwhelmed by calamity" (Knox 1956:679).

CHAPTER XII The door that is now being opened to the extension of the Gospel from the Province of Sinaloa into the Province of California to provide those people with religious instruction

In the preceding chapter I discussed the care taken by the missionary priests in the Province of Sinaloa to win over neighboring gentile nations to Christ and His church. Some of these gentiles live on the opposite shore of the Gulf of California, which I have mentioned on several occasions in this history. To conclude this discussion of the Sinaloa missions, and before moving on to others, I want to copy a letter from one of the priests who not long ago crossed the gulf that separates Sinaloa and [Baja] California.[73] He surveyed this land and its people, whom it appears God is preparing to receive the light of the Gospel. The author of the letter is Father Jacinto Cortés,[74] who has worked in the Sinaloa missions for nearly sixteen years. In compliance with the request of Captain Luis Cestín de Cañas,[75] who governed this province and its garrison, he accompanied him in a small ship. Some Spaniards had explored these lands earlier in large ships, sailing from the South Sea coast of Nueva España. Because these lands lay so close to the captain's own jurisdiction, he had orders to go and explore the lay of the land and determine the nature of its people. He carried out this order in 1642, taking soldiers from the garrison at Sinaloa as well as Father Jacinto Cortés, who wrote this letter to the Father Provincial, [442] giving an account of his journey. He says:

Following my lengthy pilgrimages, I accompanied the captain to the Californias, following the orders that Your Reverence sent me. We spent the entire month of July there, and after we had seen those islands of California we quickly set sail to return in order to avoid crosscurrents and winds. We started out [on this journey] from Baibachilato, and as we were headed up the coast toward the port of San Ignacio, we came upon an outcropping or little hill in the middle of the sea, no more than twenty leagues from San Ignacio. We continued westward, and before we had lost sight of Sinaloa we saw the land of the Californias. We disembarked at the port that is called San José,[76] where there are some friendly Indians. We continued [northward] along those inlets for some forty leagues until we reached La Paz. All the Indians gathered [and greeted us] with as much friendliness as if they were from Sinaloa.

Along this coast as far as San Bernabé there must be, according to what they say, some one thousand Indians, all of them fishermen. They have no other sustenance than seafood. They are a simple people with good habits; they have no drunken revels, nor do they have more than one wife. They live in peace and go to war only with those Indians called the Guaycura, who live in the interior and on the opposite shore. The Guaycura want to expel these Indians from their lands, so they come looking for them at the port of La Paz, which adjoins the Guaycura mainland.[77] These Indians fear the Guaycura, who are a very spirited people.

For weapons the Indians of the Californias use large bows and arrows with stone points. Although the poisonous herb exists there, they are unfamiliar with it and do not use it. Therefore, any war that might arise against them is less difficult. They also use some fire-hardened darts, which they throw with an instrument that makes them fly like an arrow.[78] The Spaniards who have explored this land over the years have aided these Indians in their battles against the Guaycura. Thus, when Spaniards come to their inlets, they come out to meet them bringing fish and the fruits of the pitahaya. They ask the Spaniards to fire their harquebuses against the Guaycura, which (when they do so) greatly pleases them. For this reason the Indians joined us in a procession in which we carried [an image of] the Most Holy Virgin and sang all her litanies. More than two hundred women and men joined in with their bows and arrows because they thought we were going to war against the Guaycura.

73. As is more apparent at the end of the following chapter, Pérez de Ribas' rather lengthy discussion of California in the midst of what is ostensibly a summation of the Jesuit experience in Sinaloa is intended to convince the Crown and Jesuit superiors in Rome to continue their support for the missions of Nueva España. In this regard California and its promise of souls and material riches was worth dangling before the eyes of supporters (and also potential critics).

74. Cortés was working at the time among the Sinaloa of the Río Fuerte and had been recommended to Cañas by the Jesuit provincial, Father Luis de Bonifaz (Alegre 1956–1960:2:12).

75. Luis Cestín de Cañas became alcalde mayor of Sinaloa in 1637.

76. San José del Cabo, at the very southern tip of Baja California.

77. La Paz is on a peninsula, thus Cortés' statement "which adjoins the Guaycura mainland."

78. Apparently an *atlatl*, a shaft of wood or bone with a worked base for holding and launching a spear. The atlatl may well have been used by the first Americans, eleven thousand years before Cortés observed its use in California.

These islands,[79] where water and sustenance are scarce, are made up of little bare hills where there are only a few wells and one pool of drinking water. Before these islands can be settled it will be necessary to first find lands that can be settled on the Guaycura mainland. That is where one finds all the shellfish and pearl beds that can sustain the islands. At the time of our visit only a few pearls were recovered, and the captain is sending them to His Excellency so that he may see the fruits of this land. The reason only a few were recovered is that the Indians had withdrawn to their caves, fleeing the rising waters.

We had been there a month, and then we returned [to Sinaloa]. My feelings about this land are that it seems to be quite extensive, enough for another new world and another Nueva España. If God should arrange for these people to be converted, I offer myself for the task; this and no other desire is what brought me from the college in Mexico City. May Our Lord bless and keep Your Reverence for the good of the entire province.

This was Father Jacinto Cortés' letter. What can be added is that when this visit (albeit brief) was made to the Californias, there was still no knowledge in Sinaloa of what was ordered the following year by His Most Catholic [Majesty], Our Lord King Philip IV. May Divine Majesty grant him many years during which his Faith can be expanded in the New World so that all the nations living here can be reduced. [443] The king's royal order and provision were that Admiral Don Pedro Portel de Casanate was to explore the land and islands of California, the people who lived there, and the shellfish and pearl beds. Ultimately, he was to establish Spanish settlements and arrange for those people to receive the light of the Gospel. The admiral came to Nueva España with these royal orders and presented them to the viceroy, who at present is the count of Salvatierra.[80] His Excellency arranged for everything to be carried out as His Majesty had ordered. In order to round out this enterprise, the admiral wanted to make use of and take along some men from our Company of Jesus, who are so close by in the Province of Sinaloa. Toward this end the admiral asked the viceroy, as administrator of the king's patronage in the Indies, to order the Father Provincial to select religious for this enterprise, which was of such great service to both the human and Divine Majesties. In accordance with this request the viceroy wrote the Father Provincial the letter that I will set forth here, of which I possess an authentic copy. It reads as follows:

His Majesty (may God keep him) saw fit to favor Admiral Don Pedro Portel de Casanate by placing the exploration of California under his care and diligence. This is something that many others have attempted without success. Due to this gentlemen's great experience in sailing and other fields, there is no doubt that his journey and efforts will be successful, especially because he is taking along priests from the Company of Jesus. The latter pleases me greatly, and I therefore predict very good results. So that he can achieve such success, I would greatly appreciate it if Your Most Reverend Father would assist in whatever he asks of you and that you give orders for the same to be done in the houses and missions of your Company for all that is beneficial to the service of God and His Majesty. Your Reverend Father knows that I will rely on your favor for whatever help you can give. Therefore, I beg that you consider this cause and show Don Pedro Portel de Casanate your complete favor. October 13, 1643.

Once this matter was taken care of the admiral attempted to proceed to one of the ports on the South Sea to prepare his ship and enterprise for the journey up the coast of Sinaloa. Father Luis de Bonifaz, Father Provincial of the Company, who as was stated earlier, worked for many years in the missions of this province and governed them, wrote the following letter to the Father Visitor of the Sinaloa missions [Pedro Pantoja], in compliance with the viceroy's order.

The Royal Council of the Indies has placed the Lord Admiral Don Pedro Portel de Casanate in charge of exploring both coasts of California. He has been given this charge so completely and with such great favor that all that has been established and accomplished by others up to this time is now revoked, regardless of their authority. He has been granted full authority to establish settlements, fortresses, and anything else that might be necessary for this exploration. His Majesty has also based his [decision] on the services that the admiral has provided his royal crown, for which he has been twice knighted. He wears one of these awards on his chest and the other he freely displays through his great intelligence concerning matters of the sea, cosmography, and all the mathematics pertinent to this subject, on which he has written and published books.

Although the admiral's principal goal was to fulfill His Majesty's order to extend his royal crown, out of respect and fondness for His Majesty his first concern is assisting in the salvation of the large number of souls found on those two coasts as well as in whatever is discovered and established on the mainland. It should be understood that this is [444] the lord admiral's motivation. Likewise, according to its Institute, the Company has its principal concern in cultivating the greatest number of souls. Because of this gentleman's fondness for the Company and his knowledge of its profession and its promise of success in his good intentions, His Lordship has wished to make use of the Company for this enterprise. The lord viceroy, count of

79. Apparently off the east coast of Baja California.
80. García Sarmiento de Sotomayor, viceroy from November 1642 to May 1648.

Salvatierra, agreed strongly that the priests should be from the Company, not only because he saw the admiral leaning in that direction, but also because of the love and respect he has for the Company. He demonstrated this in a letter in which His Excellency expressed how glad he was that the Company is participating in this enterprise. Thus, we [now] have in our hands this great enterprise, which many people have desired for a very long time and have attempted on numerous occasions without significant results. None of these [previous] attempts were as well supported as this one, nor were they as strongly desired by His Majesty and his Royal Council.

It is necessary that on this occasion the sons of the Company, whose vocation is to extend the Holy Gospel throughout the entire world, show ourselves to be the sons of just such a vocation, sons of the spirit of our father Saint Ignatius, to whom many worlds seemed too few, and sons of our father Saint Francis Xavier, who carried his father's spirit to the Indies. Also, many of the sons of the Company have very strong impulses for extending God's glory. Therefore, let us help and cooperate in these holy endeavors, which are largely motivated by God Our Lord, His Majesty Our Lord the king, and his Royal Council. For this purpose I desire Your Reverence's cooperation in spreading their good spirit and well-known zeal. In whatever way possible may the lord admiral be granted all possible aid in those missions. For the time being two priests will be required. Choose those who seem best suited. They will each need their own ornaments, which for now can be the ones they are currently using in their own districts. I am also sending two other individuals in their place (so that nothing that is obligatory will go unattended). By the time this letter reaches Your Reverence they will already be in the province. I truly and dearly hope that the lord admiral will be provided whatever he needs with respect to any sustenance that can be obtained in that land. That coast [of California] should be a colony of our coast [of Sinaloa]; they should be two sisters who greatly aid each other.

I now conclude this [letter] by strongly begging Your Reverence to take this, my charge, very seriously. For greater merit and obedience I leave its execution to Your Reverence's prudence and religiousness, in accordance with the present circumstances. May Our Lord keep Your Reverence for many years. From Mexico City, October 15, 1643.

From the letters recorded in this chapter one can clearly see the abundant fields of new peoples that God is preparing at this time so that the boundaries of the Church can be extended. Even though these peoples are barbarous, divine clemency does not scorn them, nor are the hardships endured by the evangelical ministers and the fruits they harvest without purpose. This is clearly manifested by what has been recorded up to now and by what will follow. Unusual testimony that confirms this is presented in the following chapter. [445]

CHAPTER XIII The unusual testimony of the glorious virgin Saint Teresa of Jesus [of Avila], which manifests how esteemed and precious the fruits are that are harvested among these barbarous peoples

It is my good fortune to be able to adorn this history and support nearly everything that is written herein, particularly in the present book, with one of the singular reasoned argumentations and teachings of the illustrious Saint Teresa of Jesus [of Avila]. She was a great spiritual teacher who was enlightened by God in our time with singular light from heaven. I wish to make this work more illustrious with her authority because it relates so directly and appropriately to the topic that I am dealing with here and because it took place under such unusual circumstances. The case is recounted in detail by Friar Father Francisco de Santa María in his very devout *Historia de la Reforma del Carmen*, in Book II, Chapter I, which says:

On this occasion a Franciscan friar by the name of Father Alonso Maldonado, a devout servant of God, arrived from the Indies. He addressed Saint Teresa and her [religious] sisters, encouraging them to penitence. In the course of this he told them how many millions of souls there were in those distant provinces that were being lost due to the lack of religious instruction and light. This sorrowful fact pierced the saint's heart in such a way that she could think of nothing else.[81] She always spoke of this to her [spiritual] daughters, requesting their prayers for the salvation of those souls. She declared to them how pleasing these wishes were to the Lord and how appropriate they were for her daughters and His brides. She stated this in the following manner: "I was so distressed by the loss of so many souls that I could not contain myself. I went to a shrine and tearfully called upon Our Lord, begging Him to provide some way in which I could [do] something to win just one soul to His service, for the devil was taking so many. I also asked to be able to achieve something through prayer, for I could do nothing more. I envied greatly those who were able to labor for the

love of God in this [endeavor], even though they might suffer a thousand deaths. And so it happens with me, for when we read in the lives of the saints that they converted souls, this evokes in me even greater devotion, affection, and envy than all the martyrdoms they suffered. It seems to me that Our Lord places greater value on a soul that we have won through our prayers, by means of His mercy, than on all the services we can render Him."

Here I have cited Father Maldonado, who quotes Saint Teresa. These words are worth pondering not only because they themselves are contemplative, but also because they were uttered by someone who was so favored and instructed by God. It was a very special consolation for me that this lesson by this very holy and wise spiritual teacher should be born of the occasion of hearing about the souls of the Indians that are dealt with throughout this history, of whom the priest who came from the Indies spoke. These labors among poor souls produced such esteem in the saint's heart that she obliged her nuns to aid them with their prayers so that the triumphs that are sought in these endeavors might be achieved. If the saint could have labored here herself, she would not have considered it any less worthy (as her words clearly express) than to have been alone in the desert, nor would the favors that she hoped [to receive] from God have been any less than if she had received the calling and had been able to go and work in person in this glorious enterprise. The words and deeds of such a holy and equally wise teacher are so remarkable that they merit contemplation, and we will not be satisfied with merely recounting them here.

The first thing that Father Maldonado notes is that the thought and consideration of the salvation of the souls of the Indians of whom she had heard that religious speak caused her such [446] sorrow and pain that she could think of nothing else. We can deduce from this that even though the saint had the most lofty and celestial contemplations, the thought of aiding souls stole her heart and soul. The second proposition con-

---

81. In his very popular *Memorial of 1634* Fray Alonso de Benavides noted how Sister María Jesús de Agreda, a cloistered nun of some renown in Spain, favored the Franciscan missions of New Mexico by transporting herself to New Mexico and appearing to the Jumano Indians, encouraging them to convert (Reff 1994). Pérez de Ribas appears to be following a similar tack here, invoking the patronage of no less than Saint Teresa of Jesus of Avila.

firms the first, when she says of herself that she cried out to Our Lord, begging Him tearfully to provide a way for her to win [over just] one of the many souls that were being lost. What would she who so highly valued helping to win but a single soul say when, through great hardships, not one but many souls are saved? The third proposition follows from the first two and is no less worthy of contemplation. She was greatly envious of those who could perform this labor for the love of God, even though they might suffer and it might cost them a thousand deaths. She who acknowledges this makes it clear that she, too, would employ a thousand lives to do so.

Beyond this glorious saint's remarkable sorrow, with which she has shown with heavenly spirit the esteem in which she held these ministries and labors among our poor Indians, which is what that religious servant of God who came from the Indies discussed with her, the most remarkable sentiment and that which merits greatest contemplation is the one that she states in the following words: "With me (she says) it happens that when we read in the lives of the saints that they converted souls, this evokes greater devotion, affection, and envy than all the martyrdoms they suffered." Here the saint said a great deal, for in addition to the services they rendered to God, the saints have many other virtues to envy. Nevertheless, of all these services and virtues, and even the crowns of their martyrdom, it is affirmed that what caused her the greatest devotion, affection, and holy envy was that they had converted souls. She strongly supports this teaching with her final proposition: "It seems to me that Our Lord places much greater value on a soul that we have won through our prayers, by means of His mercy, than on all the services we can render Him." This, she said, was what caused her the greatest affection and devotion of all that she had read concerning the saints, for this glorious saint knew and had been well instructed by the Lord that true devotion consists of and is found in the fulfillment of what is most pleasing to His divine will, and that His Majesty offers and communicates this devotion to those who are employed in aiding souls. And just as He is generous with the gifts that He gives abundantly to those who are cloistered, He also has no shortage of gifts with which to enrich and favor those who with their prayer and contemplation join in the pursuit of the salvation and welfare of the souls redeemed by His divine blood. And they labored out of their love for Him and because of the orders of holy obedience. These are all circumstances that (as has been proven) are found in our missions among barbarous peoples, thereby strongly confirming the intentions of this book.

The life and profession [of a missionary] in and of itself requires great virtue and holiness. It is a life exposed to greater difficulties, dangers, and hardships than the cloistered life. Therefore, one will find that ever since Christ's Church was founded, the greatest sanctity that His divine kindness has granted His saints in heaven and on earth has been to those who joined their own virtue and sanctity with the procurement of their fellow man's welfare. Such were the lives of the Son of God, His holy Apostles, and the greatest saints of evangelical law. It was in the same fashion that all the saints of the Old Testament excelled, as did all those who later were luminaries in Christ's Church and the *crème de la crème* of sanctity: Church Doctors, the patriarchs [447] of the holy orders who have embellished the Church with many martyrs, and the great saints. These individuals all joined the contemplative life with the life of action, forging a single life from both of these, which is the most excellent life of all.

These illustrious saints' intense desire for their fellow man's welfare in no way diminished their virtue and sanctity. On the contrary, these things grew within them and elevated them to greater degrees of holiness. This is why such an illustrious saint envied these kinds of enterprises, and it is with her authority that the intentions of this book are made more illustrious. The orders and particular means by which the evangelical ministers of our missions have been able to combine their own benefit with that of their fellow man will now follow.

CHAPTER XIV Special rules that govern the religious of the Company of Jesus who labor in these missions among barbarous nations

In the previous chapters of this book I discussed the manner in which these people and missions are governed by our evangelical ministers. I decided that it would be no less edifying, and also a guide for those who will be working in these enterprises, to write here about the particular rules that govern our religious, who join their own spiritual welfare with that of their fellow man. It is through our religious, who can be considered intermediaries, that the felicitous fruit discussed [up to this point] and those yet to be discussed have been produced. Through God's mercy the sons of the Company of Jesus have been able to tend without difficulty to their own spiritual welfare as well as that of their fellow man. This has been demonstrated throughout this history and it will be further illustrated by the examples that will follow later.

Before writing about these particular rules I will say that our missionary priests are very attentive to the one rule that is common to all of them. This is the first rule of the Company of Jesus and its holy Institute,[82] and it says, "The objective of the members of this Company [is] not only to attend to the salvation and perfection of their own souls through divine grace, but also to strive with the same intensity for the salvation and perfection of their fellow man."

In addition to this rule, [the members of the Company] heed and practice the rule that the Apostle Saint Paul gave his disciple Timothy, who was employed in the conversion of the gentiles. Saint Paul sent him instructions about preaching the Gospel, saying, *Attende tibi, & doctrinae: insta in illis: hoc enim facies, & te ipsum, salvum facies, & eos qui te audiunt.*[83] This is a rule and doctrine that is very celebrated by the holy fathers in their writings and I will not pause here to ponder it. I know how much it is kept in mind by those who work in these missions, away from the community of a college. Because they live outside of colleges, they find it more necessary to observe this rule, because it is for [the sake of] divine mercy that it is observed by the sons of the Company. If they did not observe this rule, they would not have produced the felicitous fruit in themselves and their fellow man that this history has recounted.

Notwithstanding what has been said, the practice and implementation of the doctrine of evangelical perfection demand that one accommodate oneself in particular to a variety of climates, locations, and ministries. For this reason the superiors judged it convenient and necessary to set down particular rules and regulations to help those who work and travel among these barbarous and newly found peoples of the world. By placing these peoples on the road to heaven, these missionaries simultaneously earn great crowns of glory for themselves and [448] also attain the elevated goal for which these missions are established. Father Rodrigo de Cabredo,[84] a man of great zeal and prudence who served as Provincial of our Province of Nueva España, compiled these rules when he was Visitor. He had consulted with all the superiors of these missions, who for many years had labored and practiced in the apostolic ministry of preaching the Gospel. These rules are as follows:

1. To the degree possible in these missions our [priests] will work in pairs, with one being subordinate to the other. In an enterprise as holy as aiding these souls they will help each other with fraternal charity and the love of Christ, in accordance with the instructions of he who is in charge of the [mission] district. In the event that there are not enough ministers to

---

82. "Institute" refers to the foundational document, "The Formula" (later expanded and revised somewhat and referred to as the constitution[s]) drawn up in 1539–40 by Ignatius Loyola and his followers, which laid out the Jesuit style of ministry (O'Malley 1993a:4–7).

83. *Margin Note*: I. adTimos. c. 4. 1 Timothy 4:16: "Two things claim thy attention, thyself and the teaching of the faith; spend thy care on them; so wilt thou and those who listen to thee achieve salvation" (Knox 1956:219).

84. Rodrigo de Cabredo served as visitor general to Nueva España from 1609 to 1611 and as Father provincial of Nueva España from 1611 to 1616. During this time he drew up the rules discussed in the present chapter; see Polzer (1976:14–32, 61) for a discussion of these rules and their implementation.

have them work in pairs, the priests in neighboring districts shall at a minimum arrange to meet occasionally, to counsel and comfort one other and to discuss in holy solitude matters concerning their souls.

2. The purpose of this rule is to ensure the successful governance of the evangelical enterprise, the objectives of which are greater glory for God Our Lord and the salvation of these many souls. To insure that prosperous results are achieved with the guidance of holy obedience, our priests are charged to consult with their superior or Rector, even if the latter is not present, securing his permission in matters of importance to their district and pueblos. This would apply to the entradas undertaken to give religious instruction to gentile nations that are presently being reduced to our Holy Faith. This should not be done without first communicating with one's superior, informing him of the readiness of such a nation to receive the Gospel, so that all may be done with his approval and that of his advisors. The same holds true whenever a church or house is to be built for this purpose in a pueblo and it is going to be costly. Whenever it is beneficial for religious instruction to reduce pueblos, the people should be gently moved and reduced with as little violence as possible. The Indians must be enticed with invitations and kindness, particularly from the people of the pueblos in which they will be residing, with whom an agreement must be made concerning the distribution of land in said district.

3. If at any time it should be necessary for one of our [priests] to exercise spiritual jurisdiction in public affairs in places far removed from the Lord Bishops, which is why Their Eminences usually permit religious superiors to exercise such jurisdiction in these missions, then in such cases our [priests] will strive to exercise said office with the least possible offense to the guilty party. They will do so in such a way that it will be understood that he is obliged to perform this public act for reasons of his office and for edification. The same will hold when Indians must be punished; it is well known that cases arise in which punishment is necessary, as the holy canons demonstrate. Such punish-

ment will be administered by those who govern the pueblo, such as the fiscal of the church or his appointees, making sure that the Indian understands his guilt.

4. When, as is presently the case, there are Spaniards residing in mining camps near the lands of nations that our priests administer or there are garrisons of soldiers, both of which have their own curates and priests, our ministers may assist them in their ministry, provided they do not neglect their own flocks and pueblos, which are their first concern. They shall inform the superior of the mission [449] so that he can assign another minister during this absence.

5. With regard to the Spaniards who reside in ranches, farms, or settlements within our mission districts and the soldiers who escort our priests in times of danger, these priests will minister to them with all due charity and kindness, both spiritually and materially, to the degree that is possible so that they will not be a bother to the native people. The purpose of these soldiers will be to provide assistance and defense against uprisings caused by the Indians and, through his familiars, by the devil. They will also aid us in removing these obstacles to the preaching of the Gospel, thereby opening the way for sowing the seed of the divine word.

6. Inasmuch as the mission districts encompass several pueblos, the [priests] will strive to continually visit them, stopping in each one for an appropriate number of days so that all can enjoy the bread of the divine word as well as other ministries. They will also leave clear instructions for the fiscales of the churches and the temachtianos, or catechism teachers, to insure that the people attend [instruction], particularly the children. The fiscales must be very prompt in reporting the sick so that the priest can aid them with the Holy Sacraments. In emergencies when the priest happens to be absent each pueblo will have the best-trained and most capable person who knows the [rite of] Baptism baptize those who are in danger of dying at birth. He will then inform the priest of all that has taken place so that he can review these actions that are of such importance to the salvation of a soul.

7. The missionary priests will carefully introduce

the practice of receiving Holy Communion at regular intervals to those Christians who are most advanced in the Faith, even though they may be recent converts. [He will] prepare them for this by giving them special talks, explaining this most profound mystery to them in such a way that they come to esteem this most holy and important sacrament to the degree allowed by their [intellectual] capacity. Most especially, the priests must see to it that the sick are not deprived of the Holy Viaticum, which is of such great importance in that moment of need.

8. For this reason, and for the consolation and devotion of the pueblos and even more so the missionary priests themselves, tabernacles will be installed in those pueblos where Christianity has been most firmly established and where there are already suitable churches. The Most Holy Sacrament will be placed in these tabernacles with decency and guarded there on those days when the priest is present in the pueblo.

9. In the principal pueblo of each district great care will be taken to establish schools for Indian boys so that they can be reared in Christian doctrine and virtue. They will learn to read and write, to sing and serve in the church, and to provide an example of complete virtue to all the other pueblos. This has been a very successful means of establishing Christianity and preserving peace in these nations. Therefore, it is good to maintain these schools, especially where a royal stipend is assigned for this purpose.

10. Whenever a priest is assigned to a mission, he will endeavor to learn the language spoken by the natives of that mission. To do so, he should spend several months in the company of another priest who [already] knows the language. If this is a new language, as sometimes happens, he will [seek] the aid of those Indians who have the best command of Spanish.[85] He will reduce to rules all that he has noted so that eventually a grammar [450] can be composed that subsequent priests can use to learn the said language. Experience has demonstrated that this is a very important step in preaching the divine word to these people, in making them understand the mysteries of our Holy Faith,

in winning them over, and in getting them to dedicate themselves to the Christian life.[86]

11. When the superior of the entire mission makes his yearly visits to the priests in their assigned districts, the latter will provide him with a report on the state of their districts, commenting on everything, both spiritual and material, pertaining to their own greater benefit and that of their fellow man, which is our duty. We shall endeavor in everything (as our father Saint Ignatius teaches us) to be guided by our superiors, who govern us in the place of Christ Our Lord. Whenever communication is required with those who govern the political and material [lives] of these peoples—such as the governor of the province or the lord viceroy of Nueva España, who are generally quite far away—and it is judged necessary to inform him or request some course of action from him, this will not be done without the consultation and approval of the mission superior, nor without notifying the Father Provincial in Mexico City so that he or the priest he has appointed can discuss these matters with His Excellency. This will allow an appropriate solution to be found for such important matters as arranging peace or the reduction of new peoples to our Holy Faith. It will also insure that all the concerned parties suffer the least possible offense.

12. Our ministers should exhort and induce the Indians to productive work. This will rid them of laziness, which is the root and mother of all vices. At the same time it will make their lives more civilized, providing them with clothing as well as food on which to sustain themselves. The Indians must not be forced, however, but instead gently encouraged to work so that they do not become frustrated and so that other gentile nations do not get the wrong impression that Christian life is all work or a form of slavery. Thus, under no circumstances should our ministers assign the Indians to labor on the ranches of Spaniards in their districts; it should be left up to the Indians whether they wish to hire themselves out to Spaniards. Wherever there are judges who have been appointed to

---

85. *Más ladinos.*

86. This sentence does not appear to be in the version of the rules copied by Polzer (1976:63).

oversee labor assignments, the priest should advise them to carry out their job with as little offense to the Indians as possible. It is our experience that when indigenous peoples are little offended they apply themselves to and become fond of working, which makes them less prone to restlessness and uprisings.

13. If Indians or Spaniards who are in some of our districts should offer a stipend for [Masses] for the dead or at other times of the year, this stipend will be applied to the church and those who serve therein, thus observing the purity of the Institute and rules of the Company, because we priests cannot receive payment for our services, as we have always professed.

14. The priests of each mission, who will be governed by a superior at the mission's headquarters, will meet with their superior two times a year at a convenient place so that all can attend without having to travel too far from their districts. The priests will spend a period of at least eight days together. During this time they will strictly observe communal rules and the religious distribution [of activities and responsibilities] followed in the Company's colleges. The priests will examine and discuss the means by which Christianity can be better promoted among these peoples. They will confer about what has worked in the past and what might be useful in these conversions, because these means are often quite unusual and are not discussed in great detail in the [works of the Church] Doctors. In addition, one priest will be designated by the superior to give a talk to the community [451] about religious observance and perfection, and the fervor that comes from doing these things when they are joined with the exercise of our ministries, which requires a holy life. At this meeting the priests will also indicate any material needs that they have, such as vestments, wine for Mass, medicine for the sick, etc. In this way the needs of such poor and remote places can be met by the stipends that Our Lord the king has assigned to the Royal Treasury in Mexico City. Being the poor religious that we are and wishing for all to proceed with the blessing of obedience, a list of these items will be sent with the superior's signature to the Procurator General of Mexico.

15. If there is an epidemic or some other misfortune in a priest's district and he is therefore unable to meet with the others at one of the two gatherings that must be held each year, he will make certain not to miss the next convocation. In this way each priest will be certain to attend at least one meeting per year. In addition, each priest must come on his own to undertake an eight-day retreat, performing the exercises of our father Saint Ignatius in compliance with our Company's rule. They can do this at the house that is the headquarters of the mission, where the superior usually attends to them. During this absence the priest will entrust his district to the nearest neighboring priest. He will inform him of anyone who is ill so that this priest can aid them with the Holy Sacraments lest there should be a failure to fulfill such a strict obligation.

16 and final: Over and above the rules that are common to our religion, on which our apostolic and religious ministers always remain focused, these particular rules will govern them in such a way that they may live outside the communities and colleges just as if they were [living] within them. It is holy obedience that has placed them in these enterprises and missions that are of such glory to God and are so proper to the apostolic Institute of our Company. All the aforementioned means by which religious perfection is preserved will aid in the salvation of souls, without hindering the attainment of the two goals for which God instituted the Company, calling its [members] the soldiers of His militia. They travel throughout these missions for as long as they are commanded by holy obedience; they cannot leave without orders from the Father Provincial. When he is advised that for reasons of poor health or lack of strength for the labor of these missions it is appropriate to replace a priest, the Father Provincial may do so. His Reverence may do the same when someone who has worked for several years wishes to return to the company of his brothers in the colleges and our houses.

Up to this point I have cited the particular rules that govern the missionary priests in the five main missions of our Company of Jesus in the Kingdom of

Nueva España. They number sixty-five religious (as has been said), not counting those who have recently been requested to preach the Holy Gospel in the land of the Californias and in other new lands that are daily being discovered. There our evangelical ministers, who are governed by such holy regulations and observances, can expect to attain through divine grace the same fruit and triumphs as their brothers. This is in spite of the fact that their labors are among poor and humble Indians, whom the Company does not scorn, as will be understood by the following vita, with which this book will be concluded. [452]

CHAPTER XV The outstanding examples of virtue given by Father Juan de Ledesma of the Company of Jesus, professor of advanced theology at our college in Mexico City and also a distinguished laborer in the ministry to the Indians

In the title of this excellent man's vita I state why I have included here the life and admirable examples of virtue of this teacher, who held university professorships, expertly taught the sciences, and filled posts that are ordinarily considered to be more lofty and illustrious than the ministry of laboring among poor Indians. Even though this history records the lives of those whose principal occupation was among nations of poor and humble Indians, I include Father Juan de Ledesma because this was precisely how he demonstrated his excellent virtues. In this man one observed the unusual combination of that which is high and mighty and that which is humble and less illustrious. Although the former of these virtues might beg to have this outstanding man included in their history, the latter beg for his vita to be recorded here. He devoted his life most sincerely to ministering to the humble, as will be seen in the account I will provide, which has been summarized from the records concerning this highly respected teacher that were printed at the request of important people in Mexico City. For this reason I will be obliged to write more extensively than usual about this matter. The esteem in which the sons of the Company hold the ministry to the Indians (a point that is discussed throughout this book) will also be demonstrated and confirmed.

Father Juan de Ledesma was born in the most noble city of Mexico, of noble parents who were well known there. Of even greater advantage is the fact that they were people of great virtue and piety, as the churches and poor who benefited from their generosity and alms bear witness. Father Ledesma entered the Company at the age of fifteen and henceforth was an unusual example of virtue, which continued to grow. As a novice his master was Father Gregorio López, a man of outstanding spirit who went on to found and govern the Province of the Philippines.[87] Referring to Brother Juan, he said that he was the model of the perfect novice.

As Brother Juan continued his studies the splendor of his virtues grew, as did those qualities that are required of a student by the rules of the Company—letters, modesty, devotion, and diligence. These are the means by which he became a talented philosopher and theologian. He gave signs of this in all the academic proceedings used by the Company, including summations, readings, rebuttals, and examinations. Despite the fact that holy obedience interrupted his studies of philosophy and theology, assigning him to a position

87. López was an influential and much respected Jesuit theologian in Mexico during the last quarter of the sixteenth century (see Ocaranza 1944). As Pérez de Ribas notes, López was instrumental in the founding of the Jesuit missions to the Philippines, which actually were administered from Mexico.

teaching literature and rhetoric, he produced talented students of these subjects.

Once he was ordained a priest he held the position of minister in the novitiate at Tepotzotlán. He filled this post with such humility that the only thing he wanted for himself was to personally serve everyone, particularly the sick, and to perform other humbler duties that are normally attended to by our brothers. During his many years as a religious this was the only occasion when he accepted an administrative position. His humble abhorrence of such positions prevented superiors from making more such assignments; he considered himself incapable and was so persistent and effective in arguing as much that he convinced his superiors of the same. Actually, what persuaded them was their desire not to bother him or violate his humble intentions. [453]

Having completed his courses in arts and sciences and theology, and after he fulfilled other duties to which [holy] obedience obliged him during those first years, he demonstrated completely his wisdom and religiosity, insuring that they would shine like a torch when placed in the candelabra of a professorship of advanced courses. He first taught arts and sciences and then went on to teach introductory theology at the well-known college in Mexico City.[88] He was there at the same time as his own professor of arts and sciences, Father Diego de Santisteban. The latter was teaching advanced theology and was so outstanding that he later became prefect and regent for many years at colleges in Mexico City; Lima, Peru; and eventually Sevilla. He traveled to all these places at the request of the viceroys of the Indies, who called upon Father Santisteban's great learning and prudence to assist them in their governance. I wanted to recount this here as testimony to the understanding of letters and doctrine that Father Ledesma possessed. The following cases will illustrate this quite well.

Father Santisteban was lecturing on a difficult subject and twice cited Father Ledesma, who at that time was teaching introductory theology. In the end Father Santisteban deferred to what Father Ledesma had written concerning such matters. This is a case in which both priests deserved a great deal of praise: the disciple because of the authority granted him by his teacher, who had referred to him in his lectures; and the teacher, not only for his humility but also for the authority he gained by training a student and disciple to whom

he could defer. This is similar to the case of Ausonius Gallo and his disciple, Saint Paulinus, as can be seen in Ausonius' own writings.[89]

Thus, Father Juan Ledesma succeeded Father Santisteban in the position of professor of advanced theology. He attained such great authority in letters in the Kingdom [of Nueva España] that his opinion was always given great consideration and weight in tribunals. The Lord Bishop of Guadalajara, Don Fray Francisco de Ribera, who later became Bishop of Valladolid in the Province of Michoacán, was a Prelate of great wisdom who had been Father General of the holy Order of Our Lady of Mercy. In his tribunal in Guadalajara he found against a litigant who had presented him with various opinions. He said that one of his reasons for deciding that this case had no merit was that among the signatures of all those other theologians he had not seen Father Ledesma's. He assumed, therefore, that Father Ledesma had not wanted to sign that document because he did not find this man's case to be reasonable and just. This same opinion was held by the extremely just tribunal of the Holy Office of the Inquisition, which would not deal with any matter of importance that was not first referred to Father Ledesma. Those men placed great trust in his recommendations and most sorrowfully affirmed that his death had cost the Holy Tribunal a great minister. He possessed the same authority not only in the kingdoms of Nueva España, but also in the others with which they had contractual dealings. Many contracts from Peru, China, the Philippines, and Sevilla were submitted to Father Juan Ledesma for his approval or disapproval. The parties to the contracts agreed to his opinions with great satisfaction. His rebuttals at public proceedings and at the university were awaited and applauded by the audience.

If Juan de Ledesma's learning possessed the authority that we have stated, then his unusual and heroic virtues were of no lesser quality. What was of greater esteem [454] and more amazing is that he combined all this learning, wisdom, and greatness of virtue with uncommon humility. I will first state how much he

---

88. Presumably the Colegio Máximo, the premier Jesuit institution in Mexico.

89. Paulinus, bishop of Nola was born in Gaul in A.D. 355 and died in 431. A generous and wealthy man, at age forty or so he sold his and his wife's property and became a religious and took up a life of monastic asceticism. The author of numerous letters and an esteemed poet, Paulinus became one of the most respected men of his age, eulogized by the likes of Ambrose, Augustine, and the famous poet Ausonius, who was Paulinus' teacher of rhetoric and poetry (Lienhard 1977; Thurston and Attwater 1956:2:615–16). Before they had a falling out over Paulinus' asceticism, Ausonius praised Paulinus' eloquence (Thurston and Attwater 1956:2:615; White 1951:1:xxiv, 87–91).

demonstrated this in letters, and then in other matters. Never did he allow himself to be carried away by the desire that others usually have of printing and publishing the works they produce and write. It cannot be denied that in the eyes of God it is a virtuous and meritorious act for learned persons to publish their works. This is because they benefit others and provide splendor for the entire Church, as is demonstrated by the pens and works of the very great Doctors of our times. It is also known that there have been extremely learned and sublimely virtuous men who have refused to publish their own works because of their humility. In his *Epistola ad Pamachium* Saint Jerome noted this very same thing with respect to the extremely wise martyr, Saint Pamphilus.[90] So did the great Doctor Saint Augustine in his Epistle 34,[91] where he wrote to the extremely wise Saint Paulinus, Bishop of Nola, begging him to make his writings known. Both the petitioners' zeal and the writers' humility were most holy.

Father Ledesma showed great affection for this holy humility. His breadth and competence in divine and humane letters as well as in scholastic, moral, and expository theology were great enough and well enough known that he could have had his works published. He was asked to do so by very important people who held great power in the kingdom. Although some even accused him of being lazy or of lacking interest, he responded that he did not feel capable of such an enterprise, even though everyone else thought just the opposite. The subjects that he taught in his university professorship, which were recorded by his own hand in fourteen volumes complete with indices, were always greatly respected in the opinions of very erudite people. There was a prebendary who was a university professor at the Archbishopric in Mexico City who discovered that Horace Cardón,[92] the famous French printer, had

written to the priest asking him to send him his works. Cardón had become a friend of Father Ledesma's when he went to Rome in the company of Father Francisco Báez, Procurator of our Province of Mexico. He told Father Ledesma that he would publish his works without asking for any money for the printing and that he would even send him volumes for his own personal use. The prebendary visited Father Ledesma to beg him to follow this advice, offering him money for scribes and the shipping [of his manuscripts] to Spain and France. He declared that Father Ledesma replied, nearly in tears, that nobody could understand that he could not undertake an effort that required such great competence in letters. His regret clearly demonstrated the humility of a teacher who, according to the opinions of very learned men, was just as accomplished as other highly illustrious teachers, from humane letters all the way up to the most advanced divine and theological ones. In the end, after Father Ledesma died, the Province of Mexico asked our Father General to have these works published, which His Reverence was pleased to do.[93]

Father Ledesma spent nearly thirty years teaching philosophy and theology and acting as regent of our schools in Mexico City. During the last six years of his life he gave up teaching, but he was kept even busier with studies because of the many moral cases for which his opinion was sought. These came to him from the Holy Tribunal of the Inquisition. He was also obliged to attend academic proceedings at the college, of which he was prefect. During all this time his humble manner of proceeding was always the same. It served him as an anchor {455} with which to steady a ship so full of rich merchandise, allowing him to ply the waves of that sea of studies, professorships, and lecturing, where such swollen typhoons and such dangerous hurricanes ordinarily arise. He was greatly talented in the pulpit and his sermons displayed great learning, with the authority of both Scripture and the holy Doctors. He presented very strong arguments pondered with great authority and mastery. He was pestered by Prelates and [other] persons of great authority to preach sermons on solemn occasions and on very important feast days. These sermons were later printed by his followers, al-

---

90. "Letter to Pammachius"; the latter was a Roman senator and patrician (the son-in-law of Saint Paula, Jerome's benefactor) to whom Jerome wrote in 397 (Hughes 1923). Pamphilus (d. 309) was the greatest biblical scholar of his age, noted for his humility and martyred by the emperor Firmilian. He was later praised by Jerome for his "style and taste" as a writer (Brady and Olin 1992:76; Thurston and Attwater 1956:2:437–38).

91. Augustine actually wrote several letters to Paulinus between A.D. 395 and 397, in which he asked or implied that Paulinus should write more and share it with others (see Schaff 1994:248–50, 260). What Pérez de Ribas refers to as Epistle 24 is apparently Epistle 42 (A.D. 397) following the modern Benedictine chronological rearrangement of the letters. The letter was addressed to Brother Paulinus as well as a Sister Therasia; in it Augustine begs Paulinus to send him the book that Paulinus was writing on paganism.

92. Horace and his brother, Jacque, were the foremost publishers of

books on law and theology in Lyons, which nearly rivaled Paris as the center of the book trade in France (Martin 1993:213).

93. This request to publish Ledesma's works on theology and philosophy was one of ten petitions or *postulados* that were drawn up by the provincial congregation held in Mexico in November 1637 (Zambrano 1961–1977:5:236–37). It is not known whether Ledesma's works were ever published.

though Father Ledesma did not want this. One can infer that humility was indeed the most outstanding and singular thing about this highly talented man. This is also why I said that his life was pertinent to this history of ministers who worked with the poor Indians.

I have presented more than enough arguments on how the virtue of humility was resplendent in Father Ledesma. It might be questioned whether the following arguments are examples of humility or of mercy and zeal for the welfare of souls, for they pertain to both these virtues. The priest excelled so greatly in his virtue of mercy toward the Indians that it detracted from the acts that resulted from his other virtues. It also seemed that he thought of nothing more than sympathizing with the Indians, favoring and assisting them as if he were dedicated entirely to that ministry. At a minimum it can be said that he built, dedicated, and enlarged the renowned Indian school of San Gregorio in Mexico City. Even though it was the Company [of Jesus] that founded this school when they came to Nueva España, it improved in every aspect once Father Juan Ledesma dedicated himself to it. Therefore, we can call him its founder. The great improvements it has experienced and the fruits that have been and are today being harvested from this school are the fruits of his saintly labors and ministries.

[We can] begin with the more spiritual fruits, those that more immediately touch upon the souls of these scorned Indians. Every morning Father Ledesma said Mass at the church of San Gregorio. He chose this church out of devotion, even though the beautiful temple at our college, where he lived, was closer at hand. He was drawn by his affection for the Indians to [the church of] San Gregorio, where he had his own key for coming and going. There he said Mass very early in the morning. Once he had given thanks he would sit in a low chair in the main part of the church. He would wait there for any Indian who wanted to confess, especially the sick. When they are ill these natives often come to church for the Holy Sacraments, as long as they are not too weak. Father Ledesma had ordinary license[94] to administer these sacraments, even the Viaticum and Extreme Unction. Once they had confessed he himself administered them Holy Communion, and if their illness was serious, he also administered the holy oils. He spent the largest part of his mornings in this ministration. Because the Indians knew that they could find

him there ready and waiting, many of them came to receive this charity. When they called him to go to some Indian's home to hear confession, he immediately got dressed and went to console the sick person, no matter how far away the Indian lived. He was so attentive to this that when he taught theology—during which there were [supposed] to be no messages or other distractions, no matter how serious—he gave orders that they should not fail to notify him if there was an Indian in spiritual need. Even though these Indians are naturally timid, they dared to enter the classroom and approach the podium from which he was lecturing to give him these messages. Then stepping down from the podium, he would gather his cloak and go to hear the confession of the sick person.

He would do the same thing at any hour of the night when he got word of a sick Indian who had called for him. He made a special effort to hear them, because his cell was right over the [456] little bell at the entryway. [When someone called] He would immediately get dressed and go to console the sick person. He did this for all the cases that arose in the most distant neighborhoods of Mexico City as well as in the hermitages at the end of the paved road, which extended quite a distance. Many times it was raining, windy, or cold, but neither the weather nor the distance made any difference to him, even when those who accompanied him (who were usually young and strong) turned back. They themselves were tired and worn out and notably amazed and edified by the untiring fervor of the charity of someone who was himself weak, aged, and ailing. He nevertheless favored and assisted these poor Indians with all his strength.

For many years Father Ledesma suffered from an ulcer on his leg. It had four openings and fistulas that finally led to his death (as we will later see). Furthermore, he had open, seeping wounds on his arms. It was for this reason that the doctors did not dare to try to close the ulcer on his leg. Even though this was an impediment to walking, it was not so bad that it made it impossible to forget about his own wounds and walk a long way, sometimes limping, showing great spirit for long journeys that benefited the Indians and enabled him to continue his holy exercises. There was one learned man who dealt with Father Ledesma a great deal and knew him well. He felt that the words from [the Book] of Ecclesiastes, which spoke of the tender and compassionate love that a father has for his children, suited Father Ledesma quite well: *Pro animabus filiorum (it says) colligabit vulnera sua, & super omnem vocem*

---

94. Meaning a license from the bishop.

turbabuntur viscera eius,[95] he will be so concerned about his children's lives that no matter how much more injured and wounded he himself might be, his wounds will not be an impediment or prevent him from attending to his children when they are sick; he will bandage his own sores in order to forget about them and tend to his children's needs, and the tiniest teardrop or whimper from a child will suffice to move his heart and soul.

Many of us saw how, the minute an Indian arrived seeking consolation, Father Ledesma immediately *turbabantur viscera eius, alligabat vulnera sua pro animabus filiorum?*[96] This man of nearly sixty years of age would bandage his own wounds and limp out to help the Indian. There was no father who so desired his children's welfare and no mother who so lovingly became one with them as this loving priest did with these poor Indians. He wished for their welfare, their aid, and their improvement, both in word and in deed.

I write as an eyewitness to these matters. Because of my duties, I had Father Juan Ledesma under my charge for several years.[97] During times when there were many confessions to be heard, such as Lent and the Jubilee days[98] that the Indians at [the church of] San Gregorio enjoy, he would spend the entire day hearing the women's confessions and then stay at the church until nine o'clock in the evening hearing those of the men. Sometimes he would spend nearly the entire night there. I told him that he was killing himself and endangering what little strength he had left. This charitable priest's answer was to smile and make it understood that this was his consolation.

The case that I will now add is extremely noteworthy and serves as a declaration of the holy affection for scorned Indians that Our Lord had bestowed upon this, His servant. Many important Spanish señoras wanted him as their confessor, but his duties and concern for the Indians left no room for this. There was nothing that could sway him in this regard, and when the señoras saw this, they said, "Let's dress like Indian women in huipiles so that Father Ledesma will hear our confessions." But when he was hearing confessions and a Spanish woman reached his feet, he would immediately send her to the confessors who had been appointed for people of that rank.

This man was [457] naturally serious and grave, even inclined to being cold, although not to the point of being offensive. Christ's grace and charity were remarkable in overcoming this temperament when he was dealing with poor Indians. Father Ledesma treated them with special affection, never tiring of them or becoming angry with them, and going to their humble homes to visit. The latter is quite admirable, given that this priest made very few visits to important people. Nevertheless, because they were important and because of their great respect for him and his knowledge, he was obliged to visit them. Still, he gave his all to consoling and serving poor humble people. The truth of this easily disproves the false libel that I mentioned the heretics spread about the members of the Company [of Jesus]. They said that our ministers worked only with the rich and illustrious. Father Ledesma, however, is one of innumerable examples [that demonstrate the opposite to be true].

Father Juan de Ledesma's charity, humility, and mercy with his Indians were illuminated on two different occasions that must be mentioned here. The first took place around 1629 or 1630. There was an illness spreading like a plague among the Indians, and it was so devastating that they fell sick and died in great numbers.[99] On this occasion what we said earlier was indeed verified, that *pro animabus filiorum colligabit vulnera sua*.[100] To care for them he continually placed his own life in danger, without hesitating to do all he could for them. He went to visit them every day, walking among their miserable little houses, or *bohíos*,[101] which were always filled with smoke and foul odors. Not only did

95. *Margin Note*: Ecles. c. 30. Ecclesiasticus 30:7: "Let a man pamper his children, binding up every wound, his heart wrung by every cry" (Knox 1956:612). Note that the general tone of Ecclesiasticus 30 hardly seems to suggest that a father should be kind or compassionate toward his children; Ecclesiasticus 30:8 continues, "and he shall find a spoilt son headstrong and stubborn as a horse unbroken." Note also the footnote concerning Ecclesiasticus 30:7 in the Knox translation of the Vulgate, which says, "The sense given here is that of the Greek; the Latin version, apparently through misunderstanding a rare word in the Greek, gives us the meaningless phrase, 'he will bind up his own wounds for the souls of his sons.'")

96. A repetition of Ecclesiasticus 30:7 with a transposition of the first and second clauses, as well as a change from *colligabit* to *alligabit*.

97. This was presumably when Pérez de Ribas was head of the Colegio Máximo (1626–32, 1637).

98. Popes often granted plenary indulgences (a remittance of temporal punishment for one's sins) during announced "holy years," which were generally celebrated every twenty-five years. Although to receive this indulgence one generally had to make a pilgrimage to Rome to make confession, receive Communion, and pray for the pope's intentions, the Indians of Mexico could apparently receive the indulgence by fulfilling its requirements at San Gregorio (see Attwater 1949:269).

99. An epidemic of cocoliztli claimed many lives in the region around Mexico City between 1629 and 1631 (Gibson 1964:449).

100. Ecclesiasticus 30:7: "binding up every wound."

101. *Bohío* was taken from an Antillean Arauac dialect during the early colonial period (Corominas and Pascual 1989–1991:1:613).

he hear their confessions, he also brought them as much corporal assistance as he could, feeding them with his own hands. He had learned what medicines could be administered for this illness and made arrangements with apothecaries who would give him these medicines at the lowest price. He also sought alms with which to pay for them. One of these apothecaries was edified by this fact and realized the difficulties the priest faced in finding funds. Therefore, he offered to give for free whatever was necessary from his apothecary shop to all the Indians that he learned were sick. This act of charity on the part of this pious Christian was born out of the charity personally practiced by a person of such great stature as Father Ledesma toward people who were so humble and helpless. He placed these people before all the other more important ones, speaking more willingly with them than with lords and princes.

The second occasion when Father Ledesma spent the remainder of his charity on the Indians also benefited poor Spaniards. This is because everyone was affected by the great calamity that took place in Mexico City when its lake flooded.[102] This started around 1625, when the water rose more than a vara above the level of the city and destroyed more than half the houses, especially those of the Indians, the poor, and all those houses that were not made of stone and mortar in the modern fashion. Some of the people were forced to abandon their homes, and those who remained were marooned and in need of somebody to aid them with food and sustenance. This flood was not caused by a river, which recedes once it has crested; rather, it involved a standing lake with no current. Therefore, this hardship lasted a long time before the waters began to subside and recede. Means were found to drain the lake and prevent flooding, and these have since been implemented.

At the time of this calamity the Father Rector of the college in Mexico City[103] demonstrated his charity by generously sending alms of bread and meat to the most severely flooded neighborhoods, where those suffering from the greatest need were Indians. The instrument of this most pious work [458] was Father Juan de Ledesma, who at that time was teaching his seminar on advanced theology. He finished his lesson at half past ten, which is when the sun beats down most intensely and its rays are reflected off the water, thus doubling the heat. The priest got in a little boat that they call a canoe, in which he carried the needed pots of meat and baskets of bread. Upon entering the little houses, which were full of water, he himself took the meat out of the pots and distributed it to the needy, who were living on little platforms. He also gave them other alms, spending the hottest part of the day in this task. He would not return to the college to eat until one or two in the afternoon; these were considered feast days of great pleasure for this servant of God. Those who accompanied him took turns doing so, either because they became sick or because the work was so hard. Father Ledesma, however, never missed a day, nor did he weaken during the long period of the worst part of the flood. Likewise, he did not allow any discussion of trading this extremely pious and difficult exercise with someone else. So that his fervent charity could shine, Our Lord allowed him to hear some coarse and inconsiderate statements that were made by ungrateful people who were the recipients of those alms, but none of this was enough to cause him to relent in the least.

With all this there is still so much left to say about the saintly acts and virtues of this outstanding gentleman that any historian would have plenty of material with which to employ his eloquence. I will summarize them in the following chapter so as not to draw this one out too much. The account given there will serve as the second of the two vitae [I said I] would record [at the end of each book], because his most outstanding life is worth [as much as] two.

102. This was the most devastating flood in colonial history; thirty thousand Indians were said to have died, although many probably succumbed to typhoid, typhus, or dysentery, which were coincident with the flood (Alegre 1956–1960; Gibson 1964:239).

103. Pérez de Ribas is apparently referring to himself, as he was the head of the college at this time.

CHAPTER XVI The spiritual and temporal progress made by Father Juan de Ledesma at the seminary for Indians of San Gregorio; his holy death

Later [in Book XII] there will be an occasion to write about the holy ministries that are undertaken for the service of Our Lord at the Company's school for Indians in Mexico City. It is called San Gregorio and is located next to the Colegio Máximo de San Pedro y San Pablo. Here [we] will relate how Father Ledesma's holy zeal contributed to its growth in both its physical appearance and in the personal, spiritual matters of the soul, toward which the former was directed. He was thoroughly convinced that the physical appearance of a church attracts both Indians and non-Indians, for being both body and soul, man must revere his God in both these realms.

When Father Ledesma began to apply his great talent and learning to aid those poor natives, the church of San Gregorio was little more than a wooden hut thatched with straw. Although it was very ample and great crowds of Indians gathered there to hear sermons and [receive] the sacraments, everything was very crude. It was particularly lacking in adornments for the feast days, such that these had to be brought from the main sacristy of the college. The little Indian students were and still are maintained largely by donations to the college itself. However, everything was increased and improved by the efforts and charity of this priest, who amazed those who observed him. They declared that God had aided [him] with unusual favors with his raising and completion of a structure [459] that in the eyes of everyone provided extraordinary fruit and was an example to the republic. Although this church is dedicated to Indians, many important individuals and Bishops attain consolation and devotion by visiting it on feast days. The priest built [a] wide [building] of limestone and mortar, with three naves. He decorated it with beautiful gilded retablos and bedecked it with rich ornaments made of precious cloth and sacred vessels of gold and silver. For Holy Week, he had a very unusual float [104] built, one of the largest and most ostentatious of all those found in the churches of this wealthy city.

He was greatly aided in the construction of all these things by the goodwill of the Indian craftsmen, who all venerated and dearly loved their Father Ledesma. Nevertheless, in the rendering of his accounts following his death it was discovered that he had spent 17,500 pieces of eight [105] on just the sacristy and its ornaments which, together with what was spent on the actual construction of the church itself, added up to a very large sum. This all came from private donations, to which he even added money from his own pocket. This was noticed on the occasion when one of our priests was obliged to give up one thousand pesos of the money he had coming to him. This was at the time when everyone was wanting Father Ledesma to publish his writings. This priest offered him his one thousand pesos to help with that cost, but Father Ledesma responded, "Father, I would appreciate it if this donation were applied to the church of San Gregorio or to the needs of the Indians."

Wise people felt that the things Father Ledesma did at [the church of] San Gregorio were miraculous. At a minimum some events were unusual, a result of his trust in God, who clearly aided him in his holy labor on behalf of the Indians. One Saturday when the church was being built the priest was very short on money to meet the payroll for the craftsmen. He had stayed late, kneeling in front of the main altar, when a Spaniard of very fine countenance entered the church. He asked the church's Indian fiscal who it was that received donations for the building. When the fiscal went to get the priest, the Spaniard, whom the priest did not know, came forward to speak to him and to leave a substantial donation that was enough to meet the payroll plus a little extra. The Spaniard took his leave and the priest once again knelt down, but then it occurred to him that it would be good to know who the donor was, even though he knew all the important people in Mexico City (one of whom the donor appeared to be), inasmuch as [Ledesma] had been born there and had served there for so many years. As the man who had left the donation

---

104. *Un monumento*, presumably a float like those used in Holy Week processions throughout the Spanish-speaking world. These typically bear a statue of the Virgin Mary or of Christ during some part of the Passion.

105. *Reales de ocho*. The common silver standard for coinage was the piece of eight, which was valued at 275 maravedís. It subsequently came to be known as the *peso de plata* (Polzer, Barnes, and Naylor 1977:36).

was going out the main door of the church, the priest called out to the fiscal to ask him his name. Although the fiscal hurried to carry out this order, he could not find the man, nor did others on the street know anything about him. The fiscal and the other Indians from [the church of] San Gregorio reported this case and testified with amazement to what had happened.

Another noteworthy thing happened to Father Ledesma as he was preparing to dedicate the church of San Gregorio with its beautiful retablo. All the wood had to be painted white, which left the priest penniless. He knew of no one who could lend him money so that he could have the remaining wood sized and gilded. He wrestled with this and decided to go ahead and celebrate the church's dedication without the retablo. He set out from [our] house [at the college] not knowing for sure where he was headed, speaking all the while with his companion about this matter. Then, coming up the street he saw Don Juan, an amusing simpleton who was well known in the city. This man was never offensive to anyone and came from a very honorable family. When he saw Father Ledesma he addressed him, [460] saying as he approached, "Potens est Deus, Father Ledesma, Potens est Deus." [106] The priest understood that these words were commanding him to trust in God, and this so encouraged him that he went straight to a person who did work in gold leaf and begged him to begin gilding the retablo, asking him to extend him credit for a brief period. The craftsman very willingly agreed to do so, and within a short time the priest unexpectedly received a large donation to pay for his project.

A similar and equally unusual case involved this same simpleton, who learned that the priest had commissioned some silver processional candlesticks. The priest was on his way to the silversmith's with no money or idea of how he was going to pay for them, when he came upon this simpleton, who said to him, "Your Reverence should go get the candlesticks. You will be able to bring them back with you and you will not have to pay for them." And that is what happened, for as the priest was entering the silversmith's shop he encountered an individual who was very fond of him. This man unexpectedly said, "Father Juan de Ledesma, those candlesticks are truly very nice. Your Reverence is to order them to be delivered [to the church of San Gregorio]; they have already been paid for." The priest was stunned and amazed, and after the man who had made the donation departed he charged his companion

not to say anything about what had happened because he had no part in what was clearly [a work] of God.

On a similar occasion when he was worried about funds, the same thing happened to him on another street with this same Don Juan. Therefore, Father Ledesma used to laughingly say that Don Juan was his crazy prophet.

With regard to this same matter of the assistance with which God favored the holy efforts of His servant, who sought to improve divine worship at the church for his Indians, we can include the following case. One afternoon he was at the silversmith's discussing a piece [of silverwork] for the church, having no money with which to pay for it. A gentleman arrived and, having greeted the priest, he asked him why he was there. The priest attempted to change the subject because he was naturally shy about asking for money and did not like to bother people. The silversmith, however, replied that he was discussing the aforementioned piece [of silverwork]. The gentleman ordered one of his servants, who was carrying a sack full of money, to pay that craftsman the entire sum, and then he ordered the priest to take his purchase.

One could record here many other similar acts of singular providence through which God demonstrated how pleased He was with the care taken by this, His minister, who was so fond of ministering to the humble Indians.

Although God gave Father Ledesma talents and honorific titles for which he could think highly of himself, he forgot all of them, esteeming only one: being sacristan of the Indians' church of San Gregorio. He fulfilled this duty with his own hands, going to the church every day at one thirty instead of resting as a person of his age and poor health should have done at that time of day. There he would lay out the frontal, [107] changing the color according to the [ecclesiastical] calendar. He himself cleaned the altars and swept the presbytery [108] every day, even when the church was full of people. Ordinarily, on major feast days when the church was crowded he would sweep the front entrance after he had laid out the frontal. He did so uninhibited by the presence of very important people with whom he normally dealt in important matters. Their presence did not keep him from placing the candelabras on the altar, adorning them and being seen in public to trim or snuff out the candles. He never let any of the other sacristans

---

106. "God is all powerful."

107. A cloth that hangs over the front of the altar.
108. That part of the church reserved for the clergy.

take this job from him. When learned people who had been his disciples attended on feast days and saw him so steadfastly fulfilling this duty, exercising these ministries with great devotion and esteem, they said that it was the Old [Testament] law that moved him to busy himself in these duties [461]: *Adolebit incensum suum super altar Aaron mane, quando componet lucernas, incendit illud, & quando collocabit eas ad vesperum.*[109] [According to this law] no one other than the high priest was allowed to light the candles. Father Ledesma wanted to carry out that task and service according to the law of grace, wherein the sweet perfume[110] that is offered to God on His altars is incomparably divine and precious. Thus, he wanted to be the priest dedicated to caring for His torches. He made this clear through the steadfastness, affection, and tenderness with which he exercised this duty, which [actually] was the Indians' responsibility. He would get up out of his seat and straighten the torches if they were crooked or replace them when they burned out, as happens during the forty-hours devotion [to the Holy Sacrament]. He would also always extinguish the torches, which caused great devotion and edification in very important people, sometimes even the Bishops who came to enjoy these celebrations, which were highly renowned. One time the Father Prepositus[111] from our professed house enjoyed one of these celebrations with other important priests. As he was taking leave of Father Ledesma, he told him that everything he had seen in the church had pleased him (for he had prepared it with such ornamentation and splendor). What had pleased him even more, however, was watching Father Juan de Ledesma. This is what people of importance and authority usually said as they departed.

We can add something else that took place during these celebrations, which was combined with these many virtuous acts of humility, devotion, and piety. Father Ledesma sometimes invited a young priest, including at times one of his current disciples, to sing Mass, which is always celebrated by the splendid chapel choir of San Gregorio. Acting as vice-deacon, Father Ledesma would sing the epistle, making sure that [it was understood that he did so] not out of humility, but because the deacon had just been ordained, and this was

his first time singing the Gospel.[112] He said other discreet things that ultimately stemmed from his true and solid virtue, his devotion to serving God in the Indians' humble church, and his great esteem for that ministry.

He was especially careful about the Indians' instruction in the Christian doctrine and also about [following] the superiors' orders that during Advent and Lent public instruction and sermons be given in the plazas and marketplaces that the Indians call *tiangues*.[113] Likewise, under no circumstances were these sermons and instructions to be skipped or interrupted at the church of San Gregorio. When the priests from Mexico City who were translators became ill or busy, Father Ledesma would bring someone from Tepotzotlán or some other college. Even though he knew the Mexican language well, he was happy to use it [only] in the confessional, where the amount of time and labor required were greater. Nevertheless, around the time that God took him to heaven he was determined to preach to his Indians in the Mexican language if nobody else was available to do so because his heart could not bear a single lapse in this respect.

It is true that in order to record that which this person of such great attributes uniquely exercised with great care, we are skipping over other religious acts and virtues of great importance that would be outstanding in any religious and spiritual man. Father Ledesma's style of preaching emulated Saint Gregory of Nyssa's prayer concerning the holy martyr Theodore: *Communibus relictis, peculiarem sancti Theodoreti sermonem inflituamus est enim suum cuique gratum, & acceptum.*[114] What he wanted to say is that although there are some virtues that are common to all of God's saints and servants, each saint exemplifies a particular virtue. For example, when mention is made of the virtue of alms, everybody says, "That is the virtue [462] of Saint John of Antioch, the almsgiver." If it is the virtue of poverty, they say, "That is Saint Francis' virtue." If it concerns zeal for God's greater glory, they say, "That is the patriarch Saint Igna-

---

109. *Margin Note*: Exod. 30. Exodus 30:7–8: "Aaron, when he trims the lamps each morning, shall burn fragrant incense on it, and again when he lights them at evening he shall burn incense in the Lord's presence" (Knox 1956:77).

110. *El timiama*: aromatic incense used in Jewish religious services (Simon and Schuster 1973:1539).

111. Rector or superior.

112. The reading of the epistle (often a letter of an apostle or prophet) is said to invoke one of God's messengers, whereas the reading of the Gospel invokes the life of Jesus and his message.

113. This is a Nahuatl term for market. Variants in use today are *tiánguez* and *tianguis* (Simon and Schuster 1973:1538).

114. "When common [things] are abandoned, one denies that the speech belongs to Saint Theodore; indeed, his [speech] is pleasing and welcomed by everyone." Theodore of Heraclea was a legendary soldier-martyr beheaded for his faith; Gregory of Nyssa, a "Father of the Fathers," wrote his panegyric on Theodore around the turn of the fifth century (Thurston and Attwater 1956:1:269, 533–34).

tius' virtue: *Est enim suum cuique gratum, & acceptum.*[115] In this fashion, when it came to love and mercy for the poor, humble, and defenseless Indians, everybody who knew Father Ledesma would say, "That is Father Juan de Ledesma's virtue." We can say that there was not a moment or hour of his life when he did not provide an example of this unique love and mercy, showing it not only in spiritual matters, but also in the earthly concerns of the Indians. Even though he avoided visits from illustrious people who greatly esteemed speaking with him, his continual station was at the Archbishop's court, where he solicited favor for Indian causes from the *Provisor* [Vicar General]. From there he would go to the jails to get the Indians released and to resolve any problems that might have arisen concerning their cases. Once he had finished with this he would go to visit and treat the sick. On the feast days that we mentioned, when he would retire to the sacristy at San Gregorio, he would stand by the main door of the church and grab poor Indian beggars as they passed by on the street. No matter how disgusting they were, he would take them to the sacristy, where he had some water ready. He would seat the Indian in a chair and wash his feet and then kiss them. Then he would give him some gifts of food and a *tilma*, or manta, with which to keep warm. He would then take him back out to the street again. Even though Father Ledesma tried to do this without attracting attention, a member of the choir of San Gregorio, of whom the priest was especially fond, caught him in these saintly acts and spread the word.

In order to provide others with alms, this servant of God became like a beggar, asking for alms from one person and then another. This was a lot for his integrity [to bear], as was the possibility of being subjected to disdain, apathy, and retorts. He bore all this with love, a love for his Indian children and, better said, for Christ Our Lord, who was represented in them. He became a beggar to enhance these poor people's renowned Christmas celebrations at San Gregorio and so that the poor would have warm clothing for the rest of the year. That which outstanding men of an [earlier] time celebrated in their congratulatory letters concerning that illustrious and most merciful gentlemen Alesio, who was Saint Paula's[116] son-in-law, was verified in Father

Ledesma. Alesio held a great party for all the poor in Rome, serving them a very fine banquet in Saint Peter's Basilica. Saint Paulinus, who had been Roman consul, writes of Alesio, among others, in his Epistle 33: *Tecum in peuperibus suis Christus recumbit, & habet in te filius hominis, ubi caput suum reclinet.*[117] Those of us who observed Father Ledesma could say the same thing of his talents, which were entirely given over to merciful feasts for the poor Indians at San Gregorio as well as elsewhere. If he were walking down the street and either heard or thought he heard somebody mistreating someone (as happens with the defenseless poor), at the mere thought of what might be happening he would hasten his steps to help them. As soon as Father Ledesma appeared those who were offending or bothering the Indian desisted. There was one occasion when the priest rescued an Indian and was told by the disrespectful [assailant] that he would kick him, too. The priest paid no heed whatsoever to this discourtesy, nor did he display any anger. He did nothing but continue his defense until he was satisfied that his poor Indian was safe.

I will omit many other cases concerning this subject in order to leave room for other virtues that shone in this outstanding [463] religious; his unique mercy for these humble people and his zeal for their salvation did not stand alone. His [own self-imposed] penance was great, in addition to the penance he suffered from his open sores and ailments. The walls of his living quarters bore witness to this, [for they were] spattered with blood from his rigorous scourging. The books that were all around [his room] had to be sent to a bookstore to have the blood scraped off. A brother who used to stop by his quarters caught him sometimes using hot water to wash the whip he used to scourge himself. [Ledesma] was fearful that others would learn of this practice and he begged him not to tell anyone about it.[118] The well-worn spiked cilices[119] that were found following his death also bore witness [to his great penance]. Some of them were large enough to go all the way around his chest and back. For a long time he spent many nights sleeping only on planks, having removed the

---

115. "Indeed his is pleasing and welcome to everyone."

116. Saint Paula (d. 404) was wealthy and from a respected family. Late in her life she became a religious, using her wealth to found a monastery and convent in Bethlehem and to support Jerome in his studies and writing (Farmer 1992:383).

117. "Christ reclines with you in his poverty, and the son of man has in you [a place] where he may lean back his head."

118. Ignatius Loyola discouraged his followers from excessive mortification. Loyola believed that once an individual had established a close relationship with God it was unnecessary to scourge or otherwise violate one's body, particularly if such acts undermined a person's health and thus the ability to assist other souls.

119. *Cilicios de rallos*, a garment of iron spikes worn by penitents (Simon and Schuster 1973:1046).

bedclothes. The only time he failed in this practice was because of his ailments. During Holy Week in particular he never undressed, nor did he go to bed from Holy Wednesday to Saturday. Instead, he slept in a chair, for during that time he heard innumerable Indian confessions, as we stated [earlier]. On Maundy Thursday he remained with those who were participating very early Friday morning in the blood procession, letting them know that he would be there to hear the confession of anyone who wished to participate in that procession. He always fasted on Fridays and Saturdays throughout the year. In general his food was so meager that it could be called perpetual fasting.

The grand and heroic virtues of this great servant of God were sustained by his exercises of devotion and prayer. These were not only the practices established by the rules and precepts [of the Company], but also others that he added himself. He spent a great deal of time kneeling in the side chapels and at the altars of his church of San Gregorio, where he took joy in God.

Our students celebrate the eight days of Corpus Christi with great solemnity at the church at our college. The Holy Sacrament is revealed to the accompaniment of music and candles, and Communion is distributed to one or two classes each day. Father Juan de Ledesma used to spend all this time in the choir kneeling in prayer with whatever devotional he happened to have with him. He dedicated these days entirely to God. It caused devotion and sometimes amazement to see a man who was so old and weak from Spiritual Exercises and studies there on his knees for such a long time. It can also be added that he said the Divine Office on his knees, as well as the Rosary of the Most Holy Virgin. He [also] recited many other offices to which he was particularly devoted, including the Office of the Immaculate Conception,[120] always demonstrating his fondness for that mystery in his sermons and writings. He also recited offices that he had written himself concerning the guardian angel and Saint Joseph. One of his colleagues who used to visit his living quarters inherited one of these because of Father Ledesma's respect for him. There were many educated people who, upon pondering how much Father Ledesma wrote and the great amount of time he spent on matters of devotion and the other exercises that we have recorded, said that he must have gained a great deal of his knowledge by an infusion [of the Holy Spirit], for they did not

know how else he could have found the time to acquire it. Although this was nothing more than a pious consideration, it is nevertheless clear that Our Lord greatly favored this very religious priest's holy works.

It would also be wrong to remain silent about his devotion to our holy fathers Saint Ignatius, Saint Francis Xavier, and Saint Luis Gonzaga.[121] His devotion to them was very loving and unique, and on their feast days he made special efforts to adorn their altars [464] and retablos in his church of San Gregorio. He himself sang the Mass with great solemnity, and the acts of fervor that he displayed on those days were apparent. During the last feast day that he celebrated for our holy patriarch Saint Ignatius, his particular affection and love for him were especially apparent. He was not satisfied with performing this solemn celebration at the altar to Saint Ignatius in the church. Instead, he placed the saint's image on the high altar, bearing a large, new medallion adorned with precious stones and other ornamentation, which he had commissioned. He also did something that had not been done on other occasions: he led a procession around the church, with such a great number of torches, dances, and music that it seemed that he had foreseen that this would be his last celebration for Saint Ignatius here on earth. Thus, he wanted to spare nothing.

I will conclude this account with his holy death which, although it came very suddenly, found him very well prepared because of the heroic virtues with which we leave him adorned. In addition to the ailments from which Father Juan de Ledesma usually suffered, he was also overcome by edema. He refused treatment and, whenever possible, continued to travel by foot in his usual ministries. The doctors, however, felt that he would be endangering his life if he did not seek some cure. As the easiest and most effective treatment, they ordered him to bathe at the springs located half a league from Mexico City, where there is a high rock that rises out of the middle of the lake; these waters are considered to be very beneficial. As someone who was truly obedient, and in order to comply with that rule, the priest yielded to the medical doctors' decision, even though he was apprehensive about risking his life, as he in fact did, already having given a great many signs

---

120. Prayers, psalms, and other devotions honoring Mary's sanctifying grace at birth.

121. Gonzaga (1568–91) is perhaps the least known of these three Jesuits. He died prematurely as a result of his selfless efforts on behalf of the sick during an outbreak of plague in Spain in 1591. Although Pérez de Ribas refers to him as a saint, his cult was only approved in 1621 and he was not canonized until 1726 (Farmer 1992:209).

that he was going to die. The Father Rector of the college selected a priest and a brother to accompany Father Ledesma in order to attend to whatever might be necessary at the baths. There the spring water flows through rooms, which is where those who go to be cured bathe. Because of his great modesty and chastity, the priest did not permit either of his companions to enter the room with him. They remained in another room nearby in order to help him with whatever might be necessary.

When he went to take his second bath it seemed that he was going in to die. Even though his companions told him to forget about the bath, he responded that those were the doctors' orders. Once he had gotten into the bath they overheard him reciting several psalms and prayers, in particular the Miserere. With great affection and love he repeated the [following] verse several times: *Tibi soli pecaui*,[122] like someone performing the Act of Contrition[123] in preparation for death. He must have taken this from the great Church Doctor Saint Augustine, whose writings he had so carefully studied. It is said in this saint's biography that he performed the [same] acts when he died. Father Ledesma gave signs of his [own] death as he entered the water that second time, and when his companions heard him from without they entered the room and found him unconscious. They had barely removed him from the waters when he who had prepared so well during his lifetime for this act of obedience expired, turning his soul over to God.

Here, we can say that he did not wait for death to come for him, but instead went out to meet it. When he disembarked in the middle of the lake at the rock where the springs are located, they noticed that he remarked with deliberation that even though he had been born in Mexico City, he had never been to the springs before, despite the fact that they were so close. This meant that he had waited until the time of his death. He indicated the very same thing on many other occasions and in many other words, thus making it clear that he was prepared [465] to meet death. As he set out from his quarters for the baths, the brother who was attending him asked what he wanted him to have ready when he returned and he responded that he wanted a shroud. The day before he told the priest who was in charge of the seminary of San Gregorio, which he so

loved, devoting himself to it entirely, that he wanted to pay the college's debts, as if he knew that he would not be back to pay them. Several days earlier he repeated that he had already registered his death.

When as a part of my duties I entered Father Ledesma's quarters following his death, I was amazed to see how orderly were his accounts for San Gregorio as well as his records concerning other matters that were under his care. Only someone who was certain of his death could work and plan with that degree of diligence, clarity, and attention to detail. From his holy life one can certainly believe that through special impulses God had prepared him for this. He died on October 12, 1636, at the age of sixty-three. He had spent forty-eight years in the Company, having professed the four vows thirty years earlier. Father Juan de Ledesma's profession of his fourth vow was officiated by our Father General Claudio Aquaviva who, among others, wished to perform this favor for Father Ledesma when he came to Rome. The Father General was pleased by his religious life and good attributes.

When the news of Father Ledesma's death at the springs reached Mexico City, it immediately caused great sorrow among the Indians, who left their homes and went running to the lake to recover the body. They clamored for their priest and lamented his unexpected death and their irreparable loss. From eight o'clock in the morning on the day of his death until the following day when he was buried, Indian men and women remained in the church of San Gregorio, weeping bitterly. As soon as the rest of the city learned of his death the *cabildo eclesiastico*[124] offered to come to his burial, which they did; not a single member was absent. Archdeacon and Commissary General of the Holy Tribunal of the Crusade[125] Doctor Lope Altamirano immediately sent word that he would officiate the ceremony, singing the Mass to the accompaniment of the chapel [choir] from the cathedral. The *cabildo seglar*[126] and the city's nobility also attended, as did the religious orders by community. When they reached our college they sang their responses in the special chapel for students, where the body was placed before it was taken to be buried in

---

122. "I have sinned against you alone." From Psalm 50:6: "Thee only my sins have offended" (Knox 1956:498).

123. A prayer said at the conclusion of confession and at times of impending death to acknowledge one's sins, love of God, and intention to lead a better life.

124. The chief clergy of the diocese who advise the bishop.

125. A papal bull issued during the time of the crusades granted an indulgence to all those in the kingdoms of Spain who were doing battle against infidels. This indulgence was overseen and administered by the members of the Tribunal of the Holy Crusade, which was headed by a commissary general (Real Academia Española 1969:667–68).

126. Presumably the city council, which was in charge of local government.

our church. The love and affection that the clergy of the city and Father Ledesma's disciples had for him were so great that they came to the church at six o'clock in the morning to sing a Mass for him. This was celebrated in the chapel before he was taken to the church for the solemn High Funeral Mass. A great many people turned out for the recitation of prayers and the other ceremonies that took place one after another throughout the entire morning. The Indian men and women piled up in a crowd in the street outside; the women were not allowed to enter the chapel because it was inside the cloister. Their great sorrow could be seen in the abundant tears they shed as they waited for his holy body to be brought into the church. Once it was placed in the church the Indians rushed up to kiss his hand, even two-and three-year-old children and infants in their mothers' arms. Although it is true that children normally fear the dead, they did not run away; amazingly, they insisted on being allowed to touch him and kiss his hand. The ceremony was considered [466] one of the most solemn funerals ever seen in that city.

The following day the brotherhoods from the church of San Gregorio requested the Father Provincial's permission to perform solemn honors for him there. These were preceded by nine successive High Masses, which many of the most important university Doctors and clergy insisted on celebrating, for they had all had Father Ledesma as a mentor or teacher of letters. These

honors were carried out with great solemnity, with many candles on a sumptuous bier that was carried by his Indian children from San Gregorio. The walls of the church were adorned with many placards from his devotees, with eulogies, hieroglyphics, elegies, and funereal epigrams. Even though the celebration took place at a church for Indians, people of higher class were present, for all the devotees of the deceased wanted to show how much they respected him. The final Mass was sung by the senior canon [127] from the cathedral in Mexico City, who was also professor of advanced theology at the university and today holds the office of archdeacon of that holy church.

These are all signs of the universal respect for Father Juan de Ledesma's religion, holiness, and erudition, and this is all very clear proof of how much the sons of the Company esteem their ministries to poor Indians, which has been the focus of this entire book. Before moving on to the remaining books, which deal with the Company's other missions among barbarous peoples outside the Province of Sinaloa, I want to record one of the clever epitaphs that adorned the venerable Father Juan de Ledesma's bier. Even though it may seem to have been written with excessive affection, it demonstrates very well the esteem in which this servant of God was held. He was a great scholar and at the same time a great minister to humble Indians.

Ingenio Thomas, calamo Augustinus, amore
Bernardus, Paulus senore, morte Scotus.
Franciscus nibilo, latis patentur Iobus,
Ignaztius zelo, Religione Xavier.
Nomine, reque simul (scruteris) uterque Ioannes,
Munere, Pauperie, More, Pudicitia.
Hic iacet: O maerens lachrymas compesce viator;
Clausaque sit mortis, ne tibi causa, lege.
Iustus erat: iste solofulsit, que is turba viatrix:
Fulgeat ergo, quibus turba Beata, Polo.[128] [467]

---

127. The senior canon would have been the highest ranking of the clergy among the members of the cathedral chapter, all of whom were appointed by the bishop and served as his advisors.

128.

In temperament, Thomas; with the pen, Augustine; in love, Bernard;
    Paul in indebtedness; in death, Scotus.
In his nihilism, Francis; in enduring patience, Job; Ignatius in zeal;
    in religion, Xavier.

In name, and at the same time, in life (see for yourself), both Johns.
    In Office, Poverty, Custom, Sense of Shame.
Here he lies: O grieving traveler, restrain your tears; Read [what]
    the end of death is, lest there be [another] reason for you.
He shone forth on earth with the same qualities as the crowd that
    passes by.
Therefore let him shine forth from heaven with the same qualities as the
    blessed crowd.

MAP 3. Jesuit Missions of the Sierras and Parras to 1645

PART II

Of the [History of the] Missions of the Company of Jesus to the Barbarous Peoples of the Kingdom of Nueva España

This second part will recount the preaching of the Gospel to other nations, which although as fierce and uncivilized as the nations of Sinaloa discussed in the seven books of Part I, nevertheless differed significantly in some of their customs and the particular lands [that they inhabit]. There were differences as well with respect to their peaceful settlement and reduction to Christianity, which followed armed uprisings when the devil (the cruel enemy of mankind) attempted to block the preaching of the Holy Gospel.

There are four principal missions, each with its own districts, that will be discussed in the four books of this second part. These are Topia, San Andrés, Tepehuan—which [encompasses some of] the neighboring Tarahumara nation—and finally, the mission of Parras and the Laguna Grande de San Pedro. In an appendix at the end of this history there is an account of other missions to various Indian nations and lands, where the sons of the Company have practiced the ministries of their profession. As in other provinces of the New and Old Worlds, they have taken whatever route was necessary to aid in the salvation of the Indians of the Kingdom of Nueva España.

As was the case in Sinaloa, God granted success to these enterprises, where eight of our missionaries spilled their blood while preaching. They were murdered with arrows, clubs, and [other] barbarous weapons by the enemies of Christ and His holy law. Although they did not achieve the martyr's crown, many illustrious men merited rewards for their evangelical work in the Lord's vineyard. They irrigated the vineyard with their sweat, rather than with their blood, and they tilled it for many years through religious instruction and other works, harvesting abundant fruits, as will be subsequently recorded in this history. [468]

BOOK VIII

The Topia Mission

The Reduction and Conversion to Our Holy Faith of
the Nations That Inhabit These Mountains

CHAPTER I Description of the mountains, rivers, canyons, silver mines, and climate of Topia; how the region was settled by Spaniards[1]

This very high mountain range [the Sierra Madre Occidental] is one of the most famous in the Western Indies and the newly discovered world, owing to its height, deep gorges, rivers, and the tall forests of pine and other trees that cover its peaks and summit. It is also famous for its rich mineral ores and silver. I will speak of it as one who on several occasions has crossed its peaks en route to the Province of Sinaloa, which is on its western flanks (as has been written). The heart of this mountain range is more than thirty leagues from the city of Guadiana, or Durango. It falls within the diocese of Durango and the jurisdiction of Nueva Vizcaya. Lastly, this mountain range is some two hundred leagues from the great City of Mexico, the seat of the entire realm.

In order to describe how steep these famous mountains are, one must say that their peaks are nearly inaccessible to birds.[2] The Spaniards could not have scaled them were it not for the lure of silver, which spurs men to cross the great waves and gulfs of the ocean sea. The gorges of this mountain range are such that I was astounded [469] that men had been able to penetrate and settle them. Let us say that the devil had guided and hidden the natives therein, to possess them without difficulty in places so hidden and isolated that even the light of the Gospel could not reach them. The highest mountains in Spain look like pygmies in comparison to those found here, and even though the mountains of Topia are that tall, they are dwarfed by other peaks farther to the north, which must also be scaled in order to reach the silver deposits that have been discovered therein. There are slopes that rise and descend from three to six leagues, constituting a rough terrain of sharp mountain peaks and passes. As I said before the Spaniards have given them names like 'The Trembler' and 'The Sliver' because traveling through these mountains is so dangerous. Nevertheless, with time and experience the difficulties of these trails have been overcome somewhat. The major gorge [of Topia] will be described later when I discuss the Indians that inhabit it. This mountain range runs for more than 150 leagues from north to south, nearly from Nuevo México to the city of Guadalajara. It is forty leagues at its widest point. Great rivers have their origins in its highest peaks. Some run

1. Much of this chapter is based on letters from Father Hernando de Santarén, the superior of the Topia mission, to Jesuit Provincial Ildefonso de Castro, which were copied and included in the Jesuit anuas of 1602 and 1604 (see Alegre 1956–1960:2:498–512, 542–49).

2. The high peaks of the Sierra Madre Occidental range in elevation from approximately 8,500 to 12,000 feet.

toward the west and flow into the South Sea [Pacific Ocean]. Others flow through the eastern range into the North Sea [Gulf of Mexico]. Some end in the Laguna Grande [de San Pedro], which will merit more mention when I write about the Parras mission [in Book XI]. The rivers that empty into the Laguna are called the Nazas, Papasquiaro, and Ahorcados [Río Tepehuanes]. The water and flow of these rivers are increased by the great amount of snow that falls on the mountain heights during the winter. Often the high roads are covered for more than a month with snow that is two varas deep. When the snow melts the rivers rise and overflow their banks for two or three leagues (as was noted in the discussion of the Province of Sinaloa). The same thing happens to other rivers that flow through Culiacán, Chiametla, and Acaponeta. All these provinces are sustained and fertilized by these rivers, which have abundant fish. The rains in these mountains fall from the month of June until September. The rain is so frequent, particularly at higher elevations, that there is barely a day when it does not rain in the afternoon. Many of the showers are accompanied by such strong thunder and lightning that more than a few pines bear witness to it. I was amazed by the many trees I saw on those heights that had been felled or reduced to splinters. One saw with one's own eyes what the Prophet said, *Vox Domini contringentis cedros Libani*.[3] It also moved one to praise divine power to see those lofty mountains with pine groves that are so thick that in some places the rays of the sun do not reach the ground, and where the trees are so high that their crowns rise into the clouds. I said the heights because from the mid-slopes downward, where the climate is not so cold, the land is populated and the rocky slopes are full of other kinds of trees that are characteristic of warmer regions. The valleys are so deep that the heat of Africa and Libya cannot be greater; to this one must add that the mosquitoes are very bothersome.[4] It is understood that the climate of this mountain range is not uniform, but rather varies by location in terms of temperature and in other ways. Although the climate is not actually unhealthy, nevertheless it is to their great credit that the [470] ministers of the Gospel regularly travel through these mountains.

Some of the trees in the forests bear fruit which, although wild, still may be used as food by humans and animals. There are *guacamayas*,[5] which are birds of very bright plumage, much larger than parrots but very similar to them. At the time when the pine cones open they come in flocks to feed on them. Other birds, which the Spaniards call carpenter birds and are as large as starlings, use the trunks of the pines as cupboards,[6] where they store their food so that it will not spoil. They drill two thousand little holes in the large trunk of a dry pine tree. In each one they place an acorn that they have picked ripe, fitting it into the hole so snugly that it is very difficult for a person to pick it out with ten fingers. God gave this little bird the industry to store [acorns] so they would not rot on the ground, and so that they could take them out and eat them as needed. Many other birds come [here] and are seen in these pine forests, particularly the ones the Spaniards call native hens and cocks, which in Spain are known as tom and hen turkeys. However, the wild hens and cocks of these mountains are larger than the domestic ones in Spain. There are also some royal eagles as well as many other varieties of birds that fly in the valleys. The wild animals found in these mountains, which the Indians hunt, are bears, lions, and tigers, whose pelts they wear as they do those of other, abundant wild animals, particularly several kinds of squirrels.

The Author of Nature, divine providence, enriched these mountains so that they could be of holy use to His Catholic monarchs. He created a great quantity of silver ore, which He kept hidden in the bowels of these mountains for many thousands of years, to be discovered by Spaniards for the defense of the Catholic Church and the extension of the Gospel in these remote provinces.[7] The Indians were not aware of these deposits nor did they use them except [to extract] stones or soil of various colors, which they mixed with worms to form a paste they used to decorate their faces and bodies. This is one of the ways that Spaniards locate ore deposits, by noting what kind of paint the Indians wear. The ore in this mountain chain has been extraor-

---

3. *Margin Note*: Psalm. 28. Psalm 28:5: "The Lord's voice, that breaks the cedars; the Lord breaks the cedars of Lebanon" (Knox 1956:489).

4. As this statement suggests, most Acaxee were canyon dwellers, living in the canyon bottoms or on the lower slopes of the canyons (one to two thousand feet below the mountain peaks); in the bottomlands the climate and plant communities are similar to those found along the coast of Sinaloa (Beals 1933; Sauer 1935).

5. Apparently either thick-billed parrots or military macaws; the latter sometimes frequent pine forests (David Yetman, personal communication).

6. *Alholies, o alacena*. The former is an Arabic word for 'granary' or 'salt box' (Corominas and Pascual 1989-1991:1:156); *alacena*, also of Arabic origin, is a cupboard with mesh panels and shelves for storing food so it will not spoil.

7. The initial discovery of rich ore deposits was at Zacatecas in 1546; miners, mostly Basques, subsequently flocked to the northern frontier, where they established mines to the north and northwest of Zacatecas.

dinarily rich and of very high grade.[8] It was so rich, in fact, that when the silver was extracted using mercury[9] they found that a *quintal* of ore yielded a *marco* or more of very pure silver.[10] When the silver alloy from these mountains is taken to be smelted, the silver yield is even higher.[11] It is well known that the method used to extract silver depends on the quality of the ore.

It was the high grade of ore that attracted Spaniards to these mountains, which they penetrated, overcoming almost invincible obstacles. They endured great hardships, ascending these peaks, scaling the cliffs, and descending into the deepest of gorges. The veins these miners [work] are found in all these places. God, in His highest providence (as someone else cleverly said) gave this silver to these impoverished and barbarous peoples as a dowry, to attract civilized Christians who would enter into friendship and peace with these fierce people, who were accustomed to feeding on the flesh of those who were not of their nation (as will later be discussed in more detail). [471]

Once they learned of these ore deposits, Spaniards who accompanied the governor of Nueva Vizcaya, Francisco de Ibarra, founded mining camps in these mountains and along their flanks.[12] It should be noted here that these mining centers are more for the milling of silver ore than for farming. The mining center of Topia, which we are presently discussing, also is the principal settlement of one of the Indian nations of the region that are receiving religious instruction. It took its name from a legend of some very ancient Indians. The tradition among them was that there was a woman named Topia, which is the same as a *xicara*,[13] or a vessel made of tightly woven straw. Because of her sins, this woman was turned into a stone that was venerated for a long time by the barbarous Indians from the main valley of this mountain chain of Topia. The mining camp that the Spaniards established three leagues away has the same name of Topia, as does the main pueblo of the Indian mission of the region, which is called the Topia mission. This mining camp and its population originally had been extremely prosperous, but it has been on the decline. The purity of its ore has been decreasing. It is also in a very deep gorge, far from [centers of supply and] commerce. It is very expensive to run because of a scarcity of clothing and [other] supplies required for mining. If the mine and its ore were located in a more convenient place, closer to Mexico City, it would be very rich. Perhaps God has saved it for a time when His Majesty sees fit. Such changes frequently are observed in Nueva España and the rest of the Indies, where God has reactivated and resuscitated abandoned mining camps. The discovery of new or better quality veins of ore and many [similar such] signs are a daily occurrence. May the Lord grant these mines be put to His holy service.

8. By 1643 the silver mines in the Sierra Madre Occidental had generated more than twenty-nine million pesos in "taxes" (*quinto* or royal fifth) for the crown (Mecham 1927:46). These mines provided half or more of the silver that flowed from the New World to Spain during the colonial period.

9. Pérez de Ribas is referring here to the amalgamation process, which involved mixing finely crushed ore with water and several reagents (salt, mercury, copper sulfate) in a enclosed courtyard (*patio*). The mixture was then removed and allowed to stand for weeks or months, during which time the silver chemically separated from its compounds. The residual amalgam was then pressed into bars (see West 1949:32–37).

10. A quintal equaled 101.5 pounds and a marco, eight ounces.

11. The silver bars resulting from the amalgamation process contained mercury. When smelted by cupellation, the mercury was burned up, leaving pure silver-gold alloy (West 1949:27).

12. In 1564–65 the recently appointed governor of the new Province of Nueva Vizcaya, Francisco de Ibarra, led an army of mostly Basque followers and Indian allies from Durango northward to the valley of Topia, subduing the Acaxee inhabitants. Within a decade or so Spanish miners were working silver deposits in and around what became the Real de Topia as well as at San Martín, Fresnillo, Indé, and Santa Bárbara (Deeds 1989; Griffen 1979; Hammond and Rey 1928; Mecham 1927; West 1949).

13. Xicara is a Nahuatl term that generally refers to a hemispherical gourd bowl.

CHAPTER 11 The particular customs of the nations that inhabited these mountains

The Indians who inhabited the broadest portion of this sierra were and [still] are many.[14] Here I will discuss only those who were reduced to the central mission of Topia. I will save the others for my discussion of the neighboring missions of San Andrés and Tepehuan.

The Acaxee are the principal nation that inhabits the region around the mining center of Topia. Their rancherías and small pueblos were in the form of aldeas,[15] at lower elevations sheltered by the hillsides rather than in the highest pine forests, where it was too cold. They were usually on knolls or peaks that were difficult to climb and served as a fortress for defense against enemy attacks. They built their small houses on these knolls out of stone and mud; others were made of undressed trees from the forest, with roofs of straw. In some pueblos they also built larger communal houses, the doors of which were so small that one had to bend over and stoop to enter them. These houses served as a fortress during enemy attacks.[16] They would open the narrow windows and shoot their arrows at the enemy, without themselves being wounded.

There must be from twelve to sixteen thousand souls in all the rancherías of this nation, not counting those that later will be reduced.[17] Maize and beans were the main sustenance of these people, all of whom were farmers. [472] They also planted seeds of other plants that they consider delicacies, which are different from European plants. They have a great abundance of several varieties of squash that are different from those

of Castilla and are good tasting and commonly used in their dishes. Their bread is made of maize that they grind with a stone hand mortar, which they all have in their houses. This was strictly a woman's job because a man would be insulted if he had to grind maize. They also ate wild fruits from trees, such as the plums that they call *zapotes*, and the guamuchiles that grow in the mountains or gorges through which their arroyos and rivers flow. They always built their pueblos near some spring or stream where water and fields were close at hand. God gave these people another gift, without any effort on their part and of no benefit to Himself. This is the sweetest honey, white as snow, which is found in the hollows of the holm oak.[18] It is not found in honeycombs (although they are not lacking in these combs, as is the case in the Province of Sinaloa), but rather it is deposited in the hollows of these trees. A type of large bee makes little balls of wax that are full of honey, which are piled one on top of another like eggs. They enjoy an abundance of this sweet liquid as well as wax for [candles for] their altars.

The clothing these people wore was as minimal and simple as that recorded for other nations, although it is true that these mountain women make more use of mantas woven of pita, which serve as skirts. The men also wear them over their shoulders, taking them on and off as they please. Some of these mantas were woven of cotton, of which there is little [here]. From the time they were very small they all wore belts made of thin twine or ribbons, from which some of them hung little tassels or a fringe that covered them to some extent. This is what they wore when they were gentiles. Now that they have received the Faith and have begun to work in the mines, everything is improved and changed. They grew and kept their hair long, which they greatly esteemed. Both men and women braided it with ribbons. The females, and even more so the males, adorned themselves with great strings of small, white snail shells. These were highly esteemed and were sought out or bought from maritime peoples.[19] They

14. Note that, based on Santarén's letters, Pérez de Ribas is here describing the Acaxee as they were in 1600 rather than ca. 1643. By 1643 the Acaxee, Xixime, Tepehuan, and other mountain groups all had declined in population by upwards of 75 percent (Reff 1991b:203–9).

15. By this statement Pérez de Ribas seems to imply that most Acaxee settlements were relatively small, yet more than a haphazard collection of dwellings. Like the Xixime, the Acaxee appear to have arranged their houses around patios or courtyards connected by wing-walls.

16. These structures were first described by Obregón, who accompanied Ibarra in 1564 (Hammond and Rey 1928:62–65). They appear to have been similar to the compound-enclosed structures described for the Aivino and Nébome in Part 1 of the *Historia* and also documented archaeologically for the Classic Period Hohokam of southern Arizona (Dobyns 1988).

17. Note here Pérez de Ribas' use of the future tense ("that later will be reduced"), reflecting the fact that he is largely paraphrasing Santarén's letter in the anua of 1604.

18. *Encina*.

19. Obregón (Hammond and Rey 1928:67) implied that the Acaxee in the valley of Topia traded with the Indians of Culiacán; presumably

also wore charms on their arms and ears and in the cartilage of their noses, which was pierced for this purpose when they were young. For show they also wore some bands on their legs and others around the insteps of their feet, which they made out of strips of leather from deer that they had killed. They said that these bands gave them strength to travel through their mountains and along rough trails. If they became tired, they sometimes sought relief by bleeding their legs, piercing them with a very sharp arrow. At other times [they pierced] their temples and their head when it ached.

These peoples are of medium stature, much smaller than the Sinaloans, and their skin is yellowish brown. As laborers they are strong, particularly when climbing up slopes, hills, and cliffs. Because they are fast, they are feared by the nations of the [coastal] plains, who did not dare to enter their lands, for the mountain people are very quick while the others are very slow and clumsy. Their women are excellent at carrying loads, even the heavy ones they carry on their backs in a large basket. The basket is supported by some cords or sashes that hang from their heads or foreheads. An Indian woman can carry a fanega of maize in this basket, together with her swaddled baby and her household equipment of pots and jars. With this load and sometimes even the parrots and birds that she raises, she scales the hills and crags with a short staff in her hand, traveling four leagues or more through these mountains. They are accustomed to doing this from the time they are little girls.

These people are high-spirited and happy, not sad or melancholy. Therefore, {473} they converse affably with the priests and the Spaniards. The food they prepare in their houses is kept at the door for anyone who might stop by, except their enemies, even if they are from another pueblo. Their intellectual ability is not limited, for it frequently happens that in a single day they can learn in their own language the Our Father, the Hail Mary, and the Creed. They are very persevering in whatever they begin. Frequently the catechumens who were to be baptized were there from dawn to dusk for several days, forgetting to go and eat. They demonstrated the same perseverance in an uprising that I will later recount. For fifteen days straight they besieged some Spaniards who had fortified themselves in a church, maintaining [a shower of] arrows.

I will now write about the perpetual wars that they

the latter were the source of shells, salt, and other items traded into the interior.

once waged with enemy nations, including some who were even of the same language. This vice, which was passed on from father to son, was firmly established among these people by the devil, in order to whisk them off to hell. Some of these wars involved communities and large groups that would go out to face the enemy in battle. Others were in the manner of surprise attacks along the roads and fields, when they would seek out an enemy to eat, just like someone who goes out to hunt a deer. The way they waged war and the weapons they used are the same as those recorded concerning other nations: a bow, a lion-skin quiver full of arrows, a macana, a club, and short lances of red brazilwood. As a defensive weapon some of them carried shields made out of animal hides. They decorate themselves for war by wearing as much of their finery—strings of snail shells and feathers—as they can. Another special and barbarous adornment that these people wore was an emblem like a long tail, made of many strips of buckskin dyed in various colors. The tail hung across the back from a cord or ribbon that they wrapped around their torso. The purpose of these wars and raids was to bring back the bodies of dead men to eat, which for them was the attainment of victory. When they had achieved this end, they sent word to their wives and children a half a league before they reached their pueblo with their booty. Just as lions show their cubs the prey [that they have killed] in the forest, so these Indians showed their children [their human prey]. They fattened and fed the children on human flesh to make them ferocious and inhuman toward these prisoners. When they brought back a human body, they carried it either whole or cut up, handing the pieces over to their elders. After these persons had been cut into pieces at the joints they were thrown into huge pots, which they had for just this purpose. They were cooked along with beans that served as chickpeas. They carefully roasted and cooked the flesh all through the night until they could remove the bare bones, which they kept as victory trophies. When all the people of the valley were assembled, they distributed this inhuman stew to everyone, along with wine that they had made. The first dish was given to the person who had taken the prisoner and killed the enemy. They also made a small hole below his lip, if he did not already have one from his youth. In it they placed a small bone from the dead person, whereby he was marked as a courageous man among those of his nation. This savage banquet was followed by their barbarous dance, during which the elders celebrated with speeches and sermons, exhorting and encouraging the young men to achieve similar triumphs and victories, and reminding them of their relatives and allies who had died at the hands of their enemies. The devil played his part in this celebration; indeed, one could very well say that it was all his doing, as he captured and took the souls of those who celebrated it. More specifically, they distributed a bowl or small cup of that inhuman stew and offered it to the idol [474] that some of them ordinarily had in their houses so that he would give them victory in their wars. Before they went to war they would begin a fast, which they entrusted to just one woman, usually a virgin. This fast was very rigorous, for it had to last the entire time they were at war. The food during this fast was very sparse, [consisting] of only a little bit of toasted maize and nothing salted. This woman had to remain alone and withdrawn and could neither touch nor speak to anyone. Finally, to understand the extreme cruelty of these banquets and inhuman slaughters, which the devil had introduced among these people, I affirm that

when the priests arrived to instruct one of these mountain nations, they counted 1,724 skulls of people who had been killed and eaten, which hung from people's houses. This figure did not include those skulls that had disintegrated with time nor other innumerable bones that were hung for display, for their cruelty spared no one. More or less the same thing happened in the rest of the nations in these sierras, among whom reigned this fierce vice, which has been described in detail so that the change wrought by the preaching of the Gospel can be more clearly seen. Once the [people] receive the Gospel, this ferocious custom ceases and is forgotten and abhorred. This is the fruit that the ministers of Christ's doctrine harvest from their preaching. Even if there were no other fruit than having rescued the lives of so many men, women, and children who were falling into the hands and jaws of these wild beasts, they would have obtained a very pious redemption of human lives. And thanks to divine goodness, at the same time eternal life has been attained for their souls.

CHAPTER III How the lives of these mountain people were dominated by superstitious idolatry; other customs[20]

Because of the victory over the devil, who deceived these Indians by speaking and appearing to them through countless little idols, the fruit that has been harvested [among the Acaxee] is not of lesser but rather greater esteem as compared with other [missions]. At one house the Indians handed over to the priest a dozen baskets full of little idols of their household gods.[21] The sorcerers, who were the devils' familiars, were the principal mediators between these idols and the devil. Usually they were false healers of illness to whom everyone paid tribute; for this reason they were the ones who were always

the most opposed to the preaching of the Gospel. But thanks to Jesus Christ, these same familiars and their infernal powers have been overcome and redeemed by the power of the divine word. A great many of these idols and figures have been cast into the flames. Countless thousands of these idols have been smashed to bits and burnt to ashes by the priests who instruct these mountain nations.

The Indians had idols from whom they requested victories in war, protection for their fields from wild animals, and rain or good fishing in their rivers. All these idols had diverse shapes that had never been seen before. At times they even lacked features, and amounted to nothing more than some unusual stones or rocks. Through them the devil deceived the [Indians], frequently talking with them in their homes or outdoors. He taught them that his name was Meyuncame,

20. In this chapter Pérez de Ribas continues to draw from Santarén's lengthy account of the Acaxee in the anuas of 1602 and 1604.

21. *Penates.* See Beals (1933) for a summary of Jesuit and other observations on Acaxee idols and fetishes.

which is [475] to say, 'He Who Is All-Powerful'. He was still consumed by his cursed arrogance and old pretension of being revered as God. He deceived these peoples not through his power—as he had none—but rather through mockery and devilish tricks. In one pueblo there was a huge knife of local flint, which they revered; they would touch the flint tips of their arrows to the knife to insure that their arrows would hit their mark. These mountain peoples make their arrowheads with a barb, so that when it strikes its target it hooks into it; when an attempt is made to remove the arrow, the tip remains in the flesh—it cannot be removed without tearing the wound.

Some of these idols they erect in the form of altars or shrines[22] that consist of piled-up stones and dirt. There the people leave offerings. When nothing else is available they place a stone on the pile, setting it in place with straw and grass. They do so in the same way that Christian travelers place a stone at the foot of the holy Cross, reflecting their reverence and desire to make more secure this holy sign upon which Christ paid for and insured our redemption (as Saint Paul said).

At other times they invoked [the devil] with a celebration that took place at dusk in some dark house. The people who gathered inside were seated along with those who served as priests. The latter, in particular, held rattles in their hands and uttered strange words with which they invoked the devil. He appeared to them in human form and at other times in the form of various animals, although he was always ferocious looking, which he has been since the time he disobeyed God. There they petitioned the devil and received his responses, which were lies and in some cases the cause of cruel and barbarous acts.

I will conclude the customs of these peoples by briefly discussing some that were naturally good and others that were of no consequence. A good and praiseworthy custom of these people, who [otherwise] were so blind and deceived, was that they were not given to stealing or lying. They considered stealing a vice of childhood. If someone had this fault, it was not necessary to search for witnesses to convince the delinquent to confess, even if it cost the Indian dearly. Because they did not close their doors or lock anything up, those guilty of some petty theft might be obliged as punishment to leave the settlement or pueblo. These people were not very lustful. There was no way that someone would marry a woman who was known to have been

bad in the past. Married couples generally live very peaceably without any offense to the fidelity that they owe each other.

With respect to innocuous customs; that is, games and entertainment, these happy mountain people have as many as those previously described for the nations of Sinaloa. The rubber ball game, however, is much more celebrated and popular among these people. As noted, the ball is propelled using the shoulders or a yoke at the waist. When the ball is propelled along the ground, they swiftly and very forcefully throw themselves to the ground in order to return it. The Acaxee kept the plaza where the game was played clean and very orderly; encircling the plaza was a wall that they built in the manner of bricks. Often one ranchería would challenge another to a game. The pueblo that challenged would send a wager, which the other pueblo answered by putting up goods of comparable value. The wagers involved their most valued possessions. After they began working in the silver mines that were discovered they sometimes wagered clothes or finery worth five hundred pieces of eight. They knew very well how to obtain what they call *pepenas*. Let me here explain what this term means, [476] so that it will be understood how Indians who labor in the mines can win such large sums. It is principally ladino or Spanish-speaking Indians who know metal ores and who are the bar drivers in the mines, breaking open veins of ore with bars. Besides their daily salary, which is at least four pieces of eight, these key workers have the right and permission to take for themselves one basket of ore, which they call a *tenate*. Because they are the ones who locate the deposits, each day when they break one open they choose—even before their masters—a basket of the most valuable ore, which is set aside for them. This practice cannot be changed, because if one were to do so the Indians would immediately abandon the mine and it would be lost for them and their masters. The basket of ore that the Indian extracts is usually worth four, six, and sometimes ten or more pieces of eight. This is what are called pepenas; they are very common in the mining camps of Nueva España and probably in the other kingdoms of the Indies. Thus the Indians who are skilled miners go around beautifully dressed and adorned, and these rewards, as I mentioned, are wagered in their ball games, where sometimes the bet amounts to five hundred pesos or pieces of eight.

This game was particularly popular among the mountain peoples. For three nights prior to the day set for the game everyone in the challenging pueblo

22. *Humilladeros.*

got together. Groups of women came to the pueblo as though it were a war celebration and danced for two or three hours each night. In the same plaza, or batei, the women loudly sang, celebrating the combatants' spirit and swiftness in the game and reminding them of the joy and honor that would come with victory. The night before the game the women busied themselves preparing a great banquet. If the opposing team won, they were fed. If their team won, the opposing team was given nothing; the feast was only for the winning pueblo. The challenging pueblo usually fielded a team of six or eight players. The side that was challenged did not have any set number of players. Rather those Indians who wanted to play simply entered the batei

and returned the ball. At times people who didn't have anything else would wager their eyelashes, and when they lost they plucked them out three or four at a time. Sometimes some of them wept when this happened and others laughed and were entertained. These entertainments continued even after these people were baptized as Christians, because they were not found to be an obstacle nor is there any reason to cease [such] legitimate diversions. The same is true of other games that only women played, which I will not discuss here, so that I can continue with the main topic of this history, which is the work of the evangelical ministers and the conversion of these peoples to Christianity.

CHAPTER IV Priests of the Company go to preach the Gospel to these mountain people

As I wrote previously, in Chapter IV of Book II of this history, around 1590 the honorable Father Gonzalo de Tapia began religious instruction in the great mission that he founded in the Province of Sinaloa.[23] A short time before, Spaniards had founded the mining center [477] of Topia. They begged Father Gonzalo de Tapia to visit their mining center and, on the way, the large number of gentile Indians in the mountains, who would benefit as much from the light of the Gospel as the Indians of Sinaloa. It is true that wherever they have gone Catholic Spaniards have never lost their zeal to make every nation in the world know their God. This apostolic man, who gave up his life at the hands of the enemies of our Holy Faith while exercising this evangelic ministry, was moved by the Spaniards' request to visit the mining camp. Afterwards, he descended into the valley of the Acaxee to exercise the ministries of Faith. He gave some talks and prepared them for a more opportune time, because he could not leave for too long the mission of Sinaloa that he had just started.

Some time went by and the Spaniards at Topia

and other mining camps insistently requested that the priests in Sinaloa send one of their members to establish a mission for the mines of Topia, San Andrés, and others that were being discovered daily. They asked the priests to help them and others who were joining them with the Christian ministries of religious instruction and the sacraments. In addition to the Spaniards, [these mining camps have] black slaves and Indians called laborios,[24] who are established Christians and know about mining and metal ores. As soon as word spreads of the discovery of a new mine, especially if it is of good quality, they arrive in great numbers to work, because of the good salaries and benefits they obtain.

Many of these kinds of people had flocked to these mining sites, where settlements were barely formed and spiritual aid was needed. Given this state of affairs, [Spaniards] again insisted that religious of our Company go and console these souls. On their way they could also provide religious instruction for the many rancherías of gentile Indians in the region. It undoubt-

---

23. Tapia and Pérez actually arrived in Sinaloa in 1591, having spent part of the previous year working as itinerant ministers in Durango.

24. These were free Indian laborers, principally Nahuas and Tarascans who, beginning around 1579, were encouraged to migrate northward by the thousands to work in the mines, where there was a shortage of labor (Deeds 1989; Powell 1952; West 1949).

edly would seem that the order had finally come from divine providence and with it the time that God had set aside for rescuing so many souls from the shadows of their heathenism. He placed this enterprise in the hands of Father Hernando de Santarén (luckily, and by order of holy obedience), who was appointed [to the Topia mission], and who was at the time in the Province of Sinaloa.[25] From here on he will be very noteworthy and it will be our duty to mention him often in all the missions and conversions of the Indians that he founded in these mountains. He finally ended his life with his blood being shed at the hands of the enemies of Christ, as will be related in its proper place. This very fervent man, who so zealously sought to help and save souls, left Sinaloa to start this glorious spiritual enterprise, which was fraught with very many difficulties, as will later be revealed.

Father Santarén began exercising his ministries among Christians in the mining camps, which were the principal [Spanish] settlements in the region, where some gentiles had begun to have dealings with Spaniards. He arrived at the mining camp of San Andrés during Lent and was busy there until Passion Sunday, because the laborers and other people insisted that he stay. Their insistence grew to the point that they threatened to desert the mines if he did not give in to their request. They didn't stop with this threat (which, if carried out, would have greatly harmed the haciendas of that mining camp), [478] and one day after he had finished preaching, more than two hundred people threw themselves at his feet, crying and begging for him to stay for another week. They said that they would not stand up until he agreed. That's why Father Santarén had to stay longer than he had planned. From this mining camp he moved on to the one at Topia, whose residents had the same desire as those of San Andrés. As previously mentioned, at Topia he harvested the same fruit among the Spaniards, Indians, and blacks. Particularly noteworthy is the fact that he eradicated drunkenness among the laborers, except in four or five Indians who backslid and were reprimanded by the priest. That evening the rest of the Indians came to the mining camp and scourged their backs. This was observed by gentile Acaxee from the region who came to see the Christian exercises of that blessed season. The visit made a very positive impression on them and they acquired a liking for Christian life. More than one thousand people came down to see a scourging procession. They carried torches of burning resin, which is abundant in their mountains, illuminating the procession of scourgers. The night seemed as bright as day. These gentiles gave very good signs of receiving our Holy Faith. They asked the priest to descend to their pueblos [in the canyon bottoms] and give them religious instruction, which the priest desired more than they did. In the meantime, he decided to prepare them and win them over to God with loving deeds.

25. Santarén left Sinaloa for Topia in 1599.

CHAPTER V Father Hernando de Santarén begins the reduction of the Acaxee nation to our Holy Faith; cases of edification

After Father Santarén had carried out his first Christian ministries among the [Spaniards], who were his brothers and were close at hand, he dedicated all his energies to the new harvest of gentile Indians.[26] However, he continued to visit the mining camps regularly and never abandoned the [Indian mine workers who were] longtime Christians. He untiringly helped in every way possible to insure the well-being of their souls. The Spaniards and the mine workers loved him for this reason. They often sought him out or took him from the Indian settlements so that he could console them with religious instruction and the Holy Sacraments.

The priest descended to the nearest Indian rancherías. The Indians welcomed him with pleasure and, because some of them already had been to the mines and had dealt with him, the priest had already gained their goodwill. He began to erect enramadas as primitive churches in their rancherías. In front of them he erected the glorious standard of the holy Cross, in order to defeat and destroy the endless number of little idols that the devil had introduced to these blind people, as will be mentioned later. He began his mission by baptizing the infants that were willingly offered for that divine bath, with which they were reborn in Christ. He established religious instruction and the catechism, which he translated into their language. Although this work of translation is at first very difficult, [479] this fervent priest overcame the difficulties with hard work. He managed to accomplish this superbly. With his translation he has been able to win more and more souls each day. God helped him by giving him some able young men who, with perseverance, quickly learned the catechism. They then taught it to others and were called temachtianos of the church. They were the first adults who were baptized, and [they] were followed by their

relatives. They took their learning of the prayers and catechism so seriously that they spent entire days without even thinking of eating (particularly during the eight days before their Baptism). From early morning to evening they did not interrupt their instruction. To facilitate memorization in their circles and groups, they used a native mnemonic strategy of placing little stones in a circle. They arranged the stones in order according to the words or prayers that they afterwards repeated. The one who was the most skillful in religious instruction pointed at them with a little rod that he held in his hand, gladly correcting anyone who made a mistake. They applied themselves to this task so well, especially when someone was sick and could not attend church, that one would find the little stones [to aid] their memory and instruction at the doorways of many homes. The angels must have inspired such an invention adapted to the [intellectual] capacity of these nations, who had neither letters nor characters that would have helped the ministers of the Gospel. God granted them this highly efficient method. When the priest went to baptize sick people who had not been able to learn the catechism in church, he would find them so well prepared and instructed that he could baptize them quickly.

When the priest was called from these rancherías to others he likewise [began by] baptizing the infants. He administered this Divine Sacrament to thousands and got the Indians off to a good start with Christian instruction. The good impression that the priest and the Company left in these first rancherías prompted neighboring ones to ask him to visit and instruct them. And as a way of obliging him to come they set up Crosses in their settlements. At one ranchería where it seemed that the priest was staying too long, ten Indians came to ask him to baptize them immediately. Although he spent several days instructing them, he could not hurriedly baptize them because he had to determine whether the people had impediments stemming from polygamy (which was still somewhat present in this nation). He had to console them by telling them that he would soon visit their settlement, when he could spend more time teaching and preparing them for Baptism. They insisted

---

26. In this chapter Pérez de Ribas summarizes Santarén's missionary work in February and later December 1600. Santarén, with the help of Captain Diego de Avila, brought 1,700 Acaxee together in ten pueblos, baptized close to 300 Indians, and visited numerous dispersed rancherías that were said to have some 1,200 Acaxee residents (see DHM 1600).

that he at least baptize one of them who was gravely ill. They also asked him to send them a skilled Christian instructor to teach them in their ranchería. The priest very willingly granted them both requests and they returned consoled to their pueblo to await the priest.

The priest reached another pueblo called San Bartolomé, where the principal Indian had his people so well prepared and instructed that fifty of them were quickly baptized and married in facie Ecclesiae. They gave up their idols very easily and burned them in the presence of the entire pueblo. In order to be baptized they agreed to cut their long hair, of which they were very fond as gentiles. Those who were not baptized showed a great desire to learn the doctrine in order to receive the sacrament.

Other rancherías also called the priest, [480] but, because he was alone and the rancherías were dispersed throughout the mountains, he could not visit all of them. He had to wait until more priests arrived from Mexico City to help him toil in this vineyard. Some of these people cleared trails through the dense growth and rocks to open the way to their rancherías.

The priest went to another ranchería, where he stayed briefly because he had to hurry to many places. Just as he was about to leave (through God's special providence), he was detained by an intense rainstorm, during which he learned of a little girl who was sick and close to dying. He baptized her and she went to heaven. When he left this pueblo for another, he was told along the way of an old man who was one hundred years old. The priest instructed and baptized him at this final stage of his life; God then took him with the grace of that Holy Sacrament. These cases and signs of predestination are abundant and they encourage the ministers to joyfully accept the innumerable difficulties of their way and ministry. I am noting only a sample of these difficulties. The case that follows is one in point.

Among the gentile Indians who had come from the mountains to settlements where they could receive instruction was a young man and his sister. They were anxious to be baptized because they had heard that the ones who died without Baptism went to hell. Through the light and fear that God had given them, they learned the catechism so carefully that they were baptized very quickly. They were still not satisfied with this benefit to their souls. Like good children, they sought to obtain it for their mother, who was very old. They very sincerely persuaded her also to become Christian. The old woman was very resistant [at first], and the most that her persevering and zealous children could do was to get her to come down from the mountains to live with them in the pueblo. The priest also tried to persuade the old woman to receive religious instruction and be baptized. But she remained resistant until Our Lord, who seemed to have predestined her, sent her a grave illness. When the pain became very sharp she called the priest and asked him insistently to teach her all that was necessary for her soul to be saved, now that her body could not be healed. The priest instructed and then baptized her, and ten hours later she left for the blessedness for which God had marked her and kept her for one hundred years, which was her age.

God favored the beginnings of the conversion of the mountain people of Topia with these fortunate cases and many others, which for the sake of brevity I will not relate here. Father Hernando de Santarén noted the need for more companions to help him among settlements that were so dispersed and hard to reach. He asked his superiors for the aid of new and fervent laborers who could assist him in such a glorious enterprise. The results of this petition will be related in the next chapter.

CHAPTER VI Other priests reach this mission from Mexico City; how they endeavored to reduce the Indians to accessible pueblos; an unusual letter that tells of their difficult travels

Father Hernando de Santarén urgently requested that the Father Provincial of the Company in Mexico City send aid in the form of companions for his new mission, which promised such great spiritual as well as temporal fruits. [481] The latter would come from the rich veins of silver that were daily being discovered. It was very important for the security of these mines that peace be established with the Acaxee nation, in whose lands the mines were located. Indeed, Spaniards had written to the viceroy of Nueva España about the spiritual and temporal advantages of this cause, asking His Excellency to order that ministers be sent to aid with the conversion of these mountain nations, who had showed such a great willingness to receive our Holy Faith. Through many royal decrees our Catholic monarchs have placed the viceroy in charge of the expansion of the Holy Gospel, especially among nations that are being discovered. The viceroy happily welcomed this proposal from Spanish miners and the governor of Nueva Vizcaya, in whose district these mining camps are located. According to the Royal Patronage of the Indies, it is the viceroy's duty to help convert and protect nations, providing them with capable ministers and supporting the priests with stipends from the Royal Treasury. In all the laws of the Holy Church there are no subsidies during the early stages of the conversion of these extremely poor nations, as there are for established benefices.

And so the viceroy spoke with the Father Provincial about sending some priests to assist the one who had founded the new mission of Topia. At the same time he ordered the officers of the Royal Treasury to send ornaments for the ministers as well as the churches that would be erected in this new Christianity. With this order from the viceroy the Father Provincial in 1602 sent two more priests to help Father Hernando de Santarén.[27]

This fervent minister and religious was visibly happy with the arrival of the two priests. Father Santarén became the superior of the others, and they all joyfully prepared for the enterprise. They divided the Indians' settlements and little pueblos amongst themselves. The religious instruction that had been initiated continued and efforts were made to finish baptizing all the infants. These infants were spread out among small and isolated rancherías. They especially tried to get all the people to reduce themselves to pueblos and accessible places, so that they could all receive religious instruction and churches could be built. The priests usually proceed with great care in this matter so that the Indians are not violently uprooted from the place where they were born and where their beloved trees are nearby,[28] together with an accessible food supply and pleasant recreation spots[29] in the nearby mountains.

I have left till now a more suitable description of one of the obstacles characteristic of this mission. It appears that the devil encouraged this obstacle in order to keep the light of the Gospel from reaching these people. However, through a second obstacle God converted the first into glorious rewards for the ministers who have overcome it with fervor from heaven. Specifically, as I mentioned at the outset, the Spaniards had to overcome steep mountains in their exploration for mines. There was another equally great and more constant difficulty that the priests had to overcome in order to visit and instruct the many pueblos in this mission and administer the Holy Sacrament at all times and on all occasions. The difficulty was having to traverse the renowned gorge that they call Topia and ford its river.[30]

---

27. One of the priests, Alonso Ruiz, actually joined Santarén late in 1601 (AGN 1601a). The second priest, Father Andrés Tutino, arrived in 1602.

28. This statement appears to be a veiled reference to Acaxee "worship" of several trees, including the zapote and jitote (turpentine tree) (Beals 1933:29). We know little about this "worship"; it may well be that the trees were significant to the Acaxee by virtue of their origin myth. Among the Pueblos the pine has a sacred meaning because it furnished passage from the underworld.

29. *Aranjuez*, 'pleasant recreation spot' (Covarrubias 1943:138).

30. West and Parsons (1941) provide an excellent overview of travel in the gorge of Topia.

It is necessary to cross this river more than 360 times. To pass through the gorge just once, Spaniards have noted the river must be forded as many times as there are days in the year. Who could count the number of times, over the course of so many years, that ministers of this mission have passed through this gorge, including those many nights and other times when they least expected it and got caught in a downpour, which are fairly common. [482] What these servants of God have suffered and continue to suffer on these occasions will be told in a letter that I have saved for this point in the history. It was written by a serious priest from this mission, who worked here for seven years and later became Provincial of Nueva España. His name was Father Florián de Ayerve, and he was writing to his superior.[31]

I was obliged (he says) to comply with what Your Reverence ordered me to write concerning what is happening in this undertaking and district, particularly what is happening now, and not only what had happened previously. Even though these events afflict the body more, they are of greater benefit to the soul. My Father, I arrived in Colura after we separated following our meeting. I had been visiting Acaxee pueblos in the midst of downpours that began on the fourteenth of December [1606]. Now it is the twelfth of January and it has hardly stopped raining, except for intervals of a few days. The level of the [river in the] gorge has remained so high that it is impossible to cross it. I spent Christmas Day in a pueblo where, because of a shortage of Hosts and wine, I said Mass only once, and this was with only a small wafer. On New Year's Day and Epiphany [January 6] I spent the entire time in the narrows [of the mountains], with no other sustenance than a few beans and a maize tortilla. I had no way of sending to Topia for relief, because even at the highest elevations there were ravines between the mountains. Because the Indians' little houses are all made of straw and small poles, they were completely filled with water, and I was forced to spend the entire day on a little platform, for I could not set foot on the ground. There was no part of the roof that did not leak, and I had no way of consoling myself by saying Mass. But this is the great thing that brings us here from Spain, and now that I am actually in the missions of the Indies I give a thousand thanks to Our Lord, who has made me a son of the Company of Jesus. Our Lord wanted some fruit to be harvested from tears, and for me the fact that he sent these poor barbarians an illness from which almost no one escapes has been fruitful. Some of those who were Christians confessed and then went to heaven. I walked from the narrows to the upper region to console those of Aguas Blancas. This was a journey of two leagues, which took from seven in the morning to three in the afternoon. Because the vegetation was so thick, I was forced to wrap myself up in my cloak and let myself roll downhill. Three Indians went with me, clearing the way. During this epidemic I have removed more than fifty idols and many deeply rooted superstitions. Four or five times I thought I was going to drown while trying to reach these places. During many river crossings the water was all the way up to the mule's haunches, and (as Your Reverence knows), one must cross this gorge more than 360 times when visiting these pueblos. My prayer books got wet, and I lost my papers and was unable to recover them. At one of these crossings the Indians who were going ahead of me halted and refused to cross, either on foot or horseback. To encourage them, I went ahead of them, jumping into the water with my mule. With my first step the both of us sank into the depths [of the water]. In the middle and deepest [part of the river], between two big rocks, the mule's hooves got stuck and one of my legs was trapped between the mule and one of the rocks. Today, my leg is still in pretty bad shape. The mule pulled so hard that it freed itself and me in the process. If I had fallen in the water, I would have drowned without God's help.

When I was in Atotonilco, twelve naked barbarians came with their bows and arrows and asked me to come to their pueblo to baptize them because they wanted to be Christians. Then they presented me with a difficulty: I could not get there without going through a narrow pass between two boulders, and from there down to the river, which then flows into the Humaya. At that time the river was very deep and was running very swiftly. [483] But if I did not cross it then, I would not be able to do so for another three months. I told them that I would go later and that they should go back and tell this to their pueblo. They refused to do so unless I baptized them first. They took to learning the doctrine and catechism with such desire that I was able to baptize them within eight days and I gave them the names of the twelve Apostles. They departed quite happy, and when I [finally] was able to go to their pueblo, it took me two days of walking through mountains that ascend into the heavens. When I got to the river, it was so deep that I had to cross on a raft, which four Indians supported with their heads. If one of them had turned his head, it would have been the end of me. On the other side of the river I found more than fifty Indians waiting for me. They guided me upriver to a nice flat area near some very high mountains. There I found more than seven hundred Indians—men, women, boys, and girls. [They came forward] in four processions, crowned with their wreaths of bulrushes and with palms in their hands. They sang in their language, "I believe in God the Father Almighty, etc.," on their knees. I was amazed to see them, and even more amazed to hear them. I asked them how they knew those things. I discovered that the twelve Indians who insisted that I baptize them had been good temachtianos, or teachers, and had taught them all the catechism. Therefore, during the few days I spent in that place, where I had a church built of brush, the Indians built more than one hundred houses and I baptized 482 people. I gathered all the people of the gorge and river and established a large pueblo. I spent several days with my baptized Indians. They

31. Ayerve served as the provincial of Nueva España from 1633 to 1637; Ayerve's letter to his superior, Father Alonso Ruiz, was written towards the end of April 1607. As the letter indicates, it was at the time of an epidemic (Alegre 1956–1960:2:158–61; Reff 1991b).

frequently asked me questions in their fashion, which were of considerable substance. They asked how I had dared to come there all alone, to such harsh lands where no Christian had ever been before. What would happen if they killed me and ate me? I answered that I had come because of my desire to take them to heaven, where there is great glory, etc., and so that they would not be damned to hell, where there is great suffering and everlasting fire. Would I want the company of anyone other than God? I had came from a distant land across the sea to bring them something of great benefit. If they killed me, I would be very happy whereas they would be very wretched, because God would punish them and the Christians would destroy their homes and fields. They responded that they thought it very fair that I wanted nothing more of them than their salvation.

That very same night at midnight I was [suffering] with my *quartana* [malaria], which has lasted all year. I heard a noise and the pounding of the feet of many people who came running towards my hut screaming loudly. I stood up with my cassock on and a crucifix in my hand and went out the door to meet them. I expected to die, for I had started thinking the day before that they were going to kill me. Two very young boys, who served in the church and had come with me, hid behind my back, crying. The troop of people from the pueblo passed me screaming, and I realized they weren't going to kill me. At that point I saw that a little house was on fire. Because these houses are made of straw and palms, they were afraid that all the houses would burn down. They had come to prevent this from happening. Later, on a different day, my boys brought me a human head with long hair, which had been placed in a net next to my little house. I asked the Indians whose it was. They told me that it was their enemy's and that they kept it for dancing at night. I told them how contrary this was to God's law and that they were not to do it anymore. They promised me [they would not] and they threw the head in the river. According to my own count, in this pueblo and others I have probably baptized some fourteen hundred people. They have attended punctually the lessons on Christian doctrine, and I am consoled to see them late [484] at night and before the day has begun sitting in their circles praying. In all those gorges one heard nothing other than the [Apostles'] Creed, the Our Father, and the Hail Mary.

Later, I went to the Villa de San Miguel de Culiacán, as Your Reverence had ordered. I took many Indians with me so that they could see how the Christians celebrate the Passion of Our Lord Jesus Christ.[32] It was of great importance to have brought them down to the villa. The vicar and the alcalde mayor gave them the best seats in the church, intending with Christian piety to endear these people to Christianity on the day of the Passion. On Maundy Thursday[33] they saw me administer Communion to the pueblo, who were all on their knees; I was the only one standing. When I spoke, they were all quiet and cried and beat themselves on the chest. The following day, Good Friday, I was the only one to speak from the pulpit to all the people of the pueblo. From this [experience] these Indians formed such an opinion of me that it became necessary to partially undo it. Every morning they waited for me at my door, down on their knees, to kiss my hand. I asked them their reason for doing this. They responded that because the Spanish Christians, who are so brave, did this, why shouldn't they? I taught them that the Spaniards performed this honor only for Our Lord God, for whom I was a servant and minister. [I told them that] from then on it would be sufficient to kiss my hand without kneeling.

While en route to Culiacán, the new Christians whom I said I managed to get to come down to the villa were told some nonsense by a mulatto, who tried to persuade them not to proceed and to return to their pueblos. He told them that I had sent him to teach them the Christian doctrine and to show them an image of Our Lady, the Most Holy Virgin. Many of them refused to go back, and when they reached me they told me what had happened. When I heard about the false mulatto's trick,[34] I immediately sent Indians to capture him. They went but never found him, and he never appeared. This case became widely known in the Villa de San Miguel, and it was rumored that the devil had wanted to prevent the Indians from coming to Culiacán for Maundy Thursday. The residents there were amazed to see such barbarous people who were at the same time so pious and showed such great devotion and affection for matters of God.

I removed from this new mission some three hundred idols, which they most willingly brought to me. Some of them we broke into pieces and others we burned, to the great amazement of those who, up to that time, had adored them as God.

All these pueblos from the mountain peaks and gorges have been brought together. When I have gone to search them out, I have found old people hidden in caves who were on the verge of dying. They turn their idols over to me and, at their request, I baptize them; they then die in my arms. One of these old people was in a high cave where I could not get to him.[35] I sent word to him to come down because he was dying and should be baptized. He answered that they had told him earlier that if he was baptized, he would immediately die. I told him that even though it was true that he would unfortunately die soon, because he was so old, it would not be because of Baptism. Rather, by being baptized he would be saved and go to heaven. I also sent him my rosary. He kissed it and the image on it. Finally, I got him to come down. I instructed him as best I could, and then he died. There are quite a few cases like this that I omit here for fear that I already have gone on too long.

---

32. Easter Sunday this year, 1607, fell on April 15 (Alegre 1956–1960:2:159, f.17).

33. This is the Thursday before Easter, also called Holy Thursday, honoring the Holy Eucharist; it is also the occasion of the ceremonial washing of the feet of the poor.

34. The Jesuits understood this "false mulatto" to be the devil who, as noted, was frequently portrayed as black.

35. A Franciscan missionary writing in the 1700s commented that "in every part of the mountains one encounters caves full of human remains" (Sheridan and Naylor 1979:115).

To this point I have been citing this letter that portrays so well the difficulties encountered in this mountainous region as well as the fruits harvested by God's servants. I could record other similar hardships, of which there are a great many. Indeed, some people remain in pueblos where, in order to reach them, it is still necessary today to cross the same canyons and its river hundreds of times. Only the pure love of Christ Our Lord can sustain His servants in this hardship. [485]

CHAPTER VII The priests continue with the reduction of the Indians to pueblos; the barbarous customs that they uprooted

With affection, gifts, and favors the priests tried to win over first the caciques and captains of the rancherías, and then the others, so that they would finally be reduced to settlements appropriate for their religious instruction. As history shows, benevolence defeats the fiercest nations in the world, and even beasts and lions. These ministers, who are so zealous when it comes to the welfare of souls, spared no effort in this regard. They felt that everything their poverty allowed was well spent on this goal. They spent a large portion of the stipend that they received from the king on hatchets, knives (which these Indians highly prize), small blankets, and items of clothing that were brought from Mexico City, [which they distributed] especially to those who care for the mission and who build and serve in the church. They also acquired medicine for the sick, which tames and completely wins them over. During the early days [of the mission] some devout Spaniards from the mines also contributed.[36] With this the majority of the Acaxee who were near the Spaniards and Topia mining camp were reduced to a good number of pueblos where they could be instructed and some type of churches erected.

As has been stated, in the early days it was necessary to make these churches provisional, out of poles and straw. Both gentiles and Christians already had begun to gather in these churches in greater numbers and with greater fervor for the catechism and sermons. The Christians also came punctually to hear Mass. The number of baptized adults also increased. With this their gentile customs began to be uprooted, as did those of their many sorcerers, and even more so, their idols and other diabolical instruments of superstition. The priests found a great deal of these items in all the houses. The light of the Holy Gospel begins to disperse and dispel all this darkness, whenever and wherever it goes. It is necessary to record a few cases and examples of this.

The Indians' manner and fashion of burying their dead were that as soon as they expired, before the body became stiff, they would double it up, with the knees meeting the mouth. Once the body was made into a ball like this, they would place it in a cave or under an overhang of rock, without covering it with soil. They would leave the deceased with some food for sustenance on the journey that they thought the dead had to make. They would also leave the [dead] Indian his bow and arrows, in case he needed them on his trip. Then they would close up the cave and leave the body there. In the end, through this custom, they showed signs [of understanding] that even though people die, they still have another life.

The priests disabused them of the errors they committed and introduced them to the Christian way of burial. They also taught them the truths of the Faith concerning the other life and the deceased who passed on to it, all of which the Indians received well. In other places the type of altars that we have said they used were being knocked over and destroyed. The Indians greatly feared demolishing them because the devil had

---

36. The most notable of these Spaniards was Captain Diego de Avila, who appears to have been as supportive of the Jesuits of Topia and San Andrés as Captain Hurdaide was to Pérez de Ribas and other Jesuits in Sinaloa.

convinced them that they would die if they did. Nevertheless, this difficulty was gradually overcome, and the devil was unseated from his throne. Another barbarous custom was remedied by a priest when he went to a ranchería. He found an Indian there who impiously wanted to kill twins to whom his wife had given birth. [486] Because the delivery had killed the mother, the barbarian wanted to avenge her death through those whom he perceived to be the cause of it. The priest told him that those little babies were not to blame for their mother's death and that he should not commit that cruel act against those who were his own children. This Indian was persuaded, and to insure the infants' safety, the priest asked the Indian to give them to him so that he could baptize them and give them to somebody who could care for and raise them. This barbarous father gave them over to the man who spiritually was more truly their father. Once he had baptized those little babies, he entrusted them to a good old woman who was a long-time Christian. She took what the priest had entrusted to her so seriously that with great concern she went from house to house looking for women who could nurse the babies. In this way these two little innocents were freed from both corporal and spiritual death.

The priest reached another pueblo and found the people playing the ball game that has already been described. On one side of the batei, or playing field, there was an idol in the form of a man; on the other side there was the root called peyote, which is of great renown among the Indians in Nueva España.[37] Even though this root is medicinal, its use involves many superstitions, which the Holy Tribunal of the Inquisition sometimes has to punish. When the priest saw those Indians' idolatry and superstition, he gave them a talk. He told them that there was only one God, whom we should worship as such, and that they should abhor the tricks of our enemy, the devil. The speech had a good effect, for they received it well and destroyed the idol and the devil within. The game was concluded by all of them kneeling and adoring our one true God and Lord.

These cases are recorded so that these people's blindness and barbarism can be understood. Divine goodness wished to bring them out of that darkness. Through these entradas many pueblos were being founded and instructed among this nation, and in them many prosperous fruits of the doctrine of the Holy Gospel were being harvested. The fierce, infernal enemy saw himself being stripped of a great many souls that he had planned to hurl into hell. He was upset and rabid with this dispossession and stirred up the storm and tempest that will be recorded in the following chapters. He threatened this Christian community with destruction, along with all the mining camps that had been established by the Spaniards and the other Christians who worked in them. God, however, did not want this, nor did He allow the devil to succeed.

---

37. The apparent association here of an idol, the ball game, and peyote (*Lephophora williamsi*) are suggestive of some form of worship or recognition of Xochipilli (or a syncretic Acaxee variant of the same), the Mesoamerican god of youth, music, and games (Soustelle 1961:22).

CHAPTER VIII The scheming of a famous sorcerer leads to an uprising and rebellion among the Acaxee[38]

There were several furious storms during the early days of the establishment of Christ Our Lord's Church. During one storm the protomartyr, Saint Stephen, was stoned and murdered.[39] On another occasion James the Less, Bishop of Jerusalem, was cast out of the temple.[40] During yet another storm Simon the Magician, who was head of the heretics and whose greed made him evil, fooled the city of Rome, which was the leading city of the world.[41] He portrayed himself as divine and said that he would fly off to heaven. The one who deposed him of his insanity was the Prince of the Apostles, Saint Peter.

Thus it is a very ancient custom for the Prince of Darkness to use his diabolical arts and tricks to try to uproot and extinguish the light of the Gospel. This is what the devil attempted using somewhat similar wiles in the general uprising of the [487] Acaxee nation, whose mission, religious instruction, and Christianity we have been discussing. The devil himself invented this scheme, which was carried out by one of his familiars, who was his instrument. He was a lying Indian sorcerer who was a great speaker and resembled Simon the Magician. With his schemes and lies he attained great authority among his nation. This Indian also was ruled by greed to the extent that it is allowed by the limited capacity of these people.[42] Not only did he attempt to gain honor and authority, but he wanted everyone to donate their valuables to him. Lastly, he was the most renowned liar and sorcerer to have been

discovered among these peoples. His arrogance was so great that he posed as their Bishop. This was on the occasion when Don Alonso de Escobar y la Mota visited his Bishopric in Guadalajara.[43] At that time the adjoining mountain range of Topia, which is now in the diocese of Durango, was part of his diocese. The false and diabolical liar began making speeches (they call these speeches tlatollis) to the rest of the Indians against the doctrine preached by the missionary priests. At other times he persuaded them that he himself preached the same doctrine as the priests. Throughout the land they addressed him as "Bishop." He rebaptized the Indians that had already been baptized by the priests. On other occasions he would divorce them from the wives whom they had married as Christians and remarry them with other women as he pleased. These diabolical hoaxes led to yet another hundred thousand errors.

The purpose of all of this was to get the Indians to do away with the churches, the Christian doctrine, the priests who preached to them, and all the Spaniards and mining camps in that mountain range. The devil's ultimate intention was to completely uproot and destroy the Christianity that was being established among the Acaxee nation and to return them to their former idolatries, superstitions, and barbarity in which he had kept them entombed for so many years. This false bishop, who was a true sorcerer, had no lack of accomplices. About fifty people came to him and fanned the infernal fire that this Indian had ignited. More than five thousand of those who had been reduced revolted, which finally led to the lamentable destruction of nearly forty churches, which had [barely] begun to take form. Almost the entire nation retreated to the most inaccessible mountains and peaks. They took the lives of five Spaniards whom they found alone in their mountains. They then set out to attack all the mining camps in the region, in particular the one at Topia and those at San Andrés, plus another called Las Vírgenes. They set fire to mills that were used for grinding ore and made a pact and sworn agreement in their fashion to persevere until

38. This rebellion began on September 8, 1601. Like the Tepehuan Revolt in 1616, the Acaxee uprising recounted in this and the following chapter has all the earmarks of a "revitalization movement" (Reff 1995; Wallace 1956). Much of Pérez de Ribas' discussion of the revolt is based on accounts of the revolt in the ánuas of 1602 and 1604 (AGN 1602; Alegre 1956–1960, vol. 2).

39. Stephen (d. 35) was one of seven deacons appointed by the apostles; he was stoned to death for blasphemy after scolding a crowd of listeners for having killed Christ. His life is recounted in Acts 6–7.

40. The apostle James the Less (d. 62) supposedly was the brother of Christ and was beaten to death with a club (Farmer 1992:251).

41. As recounted in Acts 8.

42. Pérez de Ribas appears to imply here that intelligent people (i.e., Europeans) were more prone to greed, presumably because with more intelligence one was more likely to scheme at others expense.

43. This was in 1601, shortly before the Acaxee Revolt.

death or victory, when all Spaniards would be dead. They unleashed their anger against some groups who did not participate in their harmful plot and who had shown loyalty and friendship toward the priests and the Spaniards. They burned down their churches and killed those who opposed them. When the Spaniards and priests realized that a storm was brewing, they gathered together at the mining centers of Topia and San Andrés to combat the enemy. The Acaxee, however, burned the mining center at Las Vírgenes to the ground, along with as many Christians as they could get their hands on. The enemy then attacked with greater force the San Andrés mining camp. They [appeared] almost out of nowhere and shot several Spaniards and a large number of [Christian] Indians. About forty [Christians] retreated and gathered at their church, [488] along with Father Alonso Ruiz, who had instructed some of these Indian pueblos. He was a religious of great virtue and bravery and was the first one to come to this mission to assist Father Hernando de Santarén.

The Spaniards and [Christian] Indians at San Andrés were surrounded by eight hundred enemies for fifteen days. The siege was maintained by frequent volleys of arrows, which enabled other Indians to join the siege. The Spaniards found themselves with a shortage of weapons and war supplies because they had not anticipated this attack. Some of them were badly wounded, and all were feeling desperate, even though they at times ventured out to confront the furious rebels and ward them off as best they could. During one of the final attacks, which was carried out with great force, Father Alonso Ruiz, who undoubtedly was inspired by heaven (as was seen by the outcome), with great spirit and courage took a crucifix in his hands and left the church, encouraging the Spaniards to fight to the death against the enemies of Christ and His holy law. He placed himself in full view of that entire rabble, whom the devil marshaled and inflamed with fury. It was amazing that even though they shot many arrows at him, not one struck him. Thus, the battle relented, although the siege still continued.

The next morning the priest gathered his Christian Spaniards in the church. He began to say Mass, trusting in God that he would have time to finish. Once they had confessed he gave them all Communion in preparation for death—just in case the enemy attack resumed. Even though the battle had subsided, they feared renewed and prolonged attacks by the rebels. And this is what the rebels would have done had God not helped the Spaniards, for at that moment ammunition and soldiers arrived that had been sent by the governor of Nueva Vizcaya.[44] The besieged had [found] a way to send word to Durango, which was sixty leagues away, of the straits they were in and how everything would be destroyed, including the new Christianity, if help did not arrive soon. The governor hastened this aid and, as recounted in the following chapter, took expedient measures to calm and put an end to this storm.

44. The governor at the time was Rodrigo de Vivero (1600–3).

CHAPTER IX Governor Francisco de Urdiñola enters the mountains of Topia with Spanish troops and Indian allies;[45] the measures taken to reduce the rebels and make peace

With all the haste that the occasion required the governor gathered together sixty well-armed Spaniards. In these remote provinces there are too few men to draft for a large company. The governor sent orders to draft Indians from the pueblos at Laguna Grande de San Pedro (whose mission we will mention), who were famous as great archers. He marched quickly with his troops and ascended the Topia mountain range. As soon as the Indians at San Andrés learned of his approach, they raised their siege of the mining camp, which they had maintained up until that time. The enemy withdrew to the highest peaks, which are their fortresses. And it is indeed true that if the powerful arm of God had not aided His Catholic Spaniards in this conquest as well as other more important conquests in the New World, they would not have been victorious. God [has] favored the Catholic zeal that burns in their souls, [489] protecting them and supporting the spread of our Holy Faith and Religion throughout the entire world. I have been an eyewitness to this on many occasions, and also to the fact that Spaniards have not taken up arms to violently subject nations; they have done so only when attacked and for their just self-defense, as their monarchs have commanded them.

To return to the matter of the governor's expedition, he brought together his Spanish troops and [loyal Christian] Indians from the mining camps and mountains. The missionary priests who had begun to instruct the Acaxee and who worked closely with them also joined the governor. There were still many Indians who, although they had gotten caught up in the rebellion, nevertheless were fond of these holy religious, from whom they had received instruction and kindness. In a meeting that was convened by the governor, the main strategy that was agreed upon was to try to make peace with the rebels and to gather in pueblos and doctrinas those who had already been baptized. Because Father Hernando de Santarén was the person best known to the Acaxee, it was decided that he should go see them and try to calm them down and peacefully reduce them. Although the priest had from the very beginning won over most of the nation, the governor wanted him to take an escort of soldiers, in case the rebels should act imprudently.

And so the priest left for the mountain heights to beg the rebels to lay down their arms and not be fooled by that deceitful sorcerer who had incited them and their women to rebellion. He told them that the Spaniards had done them no wrong by entering their mountains and working the mines, which they did not use or know how to work. [He told them] that they had obtained many benefits from their dealings in the Spaniards' mining camps; they had clothing and iron axes that they did not have before and with which they were able to cultivate the rock-strewn ground. Other items would become available to them if their friendship was forthcoming. Finally, they should understand that if they persevered in these wars and uprisings, the Spaniards would not lay down their arms, but rather would take revenge for the insults that they had received.

Father Santarén did not have any success this first time with the Indians and, indeed, he escaped at great risk to his life. However, because the rebels were encamped in different locations, he tried again with a different group. He went ten leagues farther into the gorge, where he encountered a squadron of rebels who had intercepted a mule train from Culiacán that was bringing help and supplies to the mining camp at Topia. When the priest arrived he found that the Indians had shot a Spaniard who was with the mule train and had killed a black and the other mule drivers who were Christian Indians. They even vented their anger on the mules. The priest from a distance shouted to them in their language that he wanted to talk to them, hoping

---

45. Urdiñola did not succeed Rodrigo de Vivero as governor until June 1603. It was the latter rather than Urdiñola who led the expedition recounted in this chapter, which led to the capitulation of most Acaxee, save the Sobaibo, who rebelled during the winter of 1602–3.

to calm their ferocity. They asked that the soldiers who accompanied the priest withdraw, and then they would talk to him alone. Although not without risk, he approached them. He told them that, whatever else, he was their father and that he would look out for them as his beloved children. The answer they gave was that they were no longer his children, and with that they sent him back out of that dangerous and tremendously deep gorge.

Sometime later when Father Santarén and I walked through that same gorge,[46] he himself told me that it was a miracle that he got out alive without being chopped to pieces, given how the Indians' thirst for blood had been so aroused by the prey that they had captured [490]. On that occasion God saved the priest for another time when he would give his life for the sake of other souls.

Father Santarén returned alive with his escort of soldiers, who were too few in number to have engaged so many enemy. However, the fatherly love of the priest for his children, who had been so difficult to regenerate in Christ, did not cease. Neither did his efforts to bring them back into his flock; he never lost confidence that he would achieve this through divine favor. He sought out a faithful and brave Indian and gave him a Cross with a white flag. He sent him to the same Indians he had met in the gorge, with a new message, begging them to abandon their rebellious ways and return to their pueblos. He would always be their father, and as such he would protect them.

At the same time Señor Don Alonso de la Mota, Bishop of Guadalajara (as I mentioned), also came to beg these Indians to make peace. This Prelate, who later became a Prelate in the city of Pueblo de los Angeles, was a very learned and prudent person. When he reached the Villa and Province of Culiacán, bordering on the mountains of Topia, he learned of the damage that the mountain-dwelling Acaxee had wrought throughout the region and their zeal for the destruction of that new Christian community. The Bishop sent a message and an envoy to the Acaxee, together with his white miter, which was held high upon a standard. It was a sign that he would intercede on their behalf with the governor if they would decide (as he begged them) to return to their pueblos, settle down in peace, and continue to be instructed by the priests who had preached to them and whom they had so gladly received. [He sent the message to them that] he was their true Bishop and not the false one who was deceiving them. Although Father Santarén had softened [these Indians] somewhat, this embassage helped. As a symbol and remembrance of the Lord Bishop's efforts, his miter afterward hung as a peace trophy at the side of the main altar in the church in Culiacán.

Now the rebels sent a more positive message with the faithful Indian whom Father Santarén had dispatched. This message was that, on an appointed day, the father himself should go to a place that they had chosen, where they would wait for him to determine what might be done. The Spaniards did not want the priest to go alone because they did not trust the Indians, nor did they want to entrust to them their priest, whose instruction and ministries they had enjoyed at their mining camps. Thus, ten well-armed soldiers decided to accompany the priest in case anything happened. When he reached the agreed-upon place he found the Indians of that faction well disposed. He stayed with them until eleven groups had assembled, whom he managed to convince to accompany him. He took them with him to the mining camp at Topia, which they entered peacefully and happily. They declared their obedience to the governor and were feted by him and the Spaniards. They were then sent back to their pueblos. This time these groups remained quiet and at peace. They continued with their instruction and all their people were baptized, as will be told later. First, however, I will recount how the other more obstinate groups were reduced. The fires that the devil ignites are not easily extinguished, nor is there any shortage of opportunities for rewards for apostolic missionaries. [491]

---

46. This was apparently in the fall of 1616, shortly before the Tepehuan Revolt, when Pérez de Ribas traveled from Sinaloa to Mexico City, passing through the mountains of Topia and visiting with Santarén there in his mission.

CHAPTER X New means and efforts are made to reduce the entire Acaxee nation; the leaders of the uprising are punished

The Sobaibo Indians were part of the Acaxee nation and spoke the same language.[47] These Indians, who had not yet been reduced, had been the most perverted by the false bishop, who had boasted of being God their Father. Both he and the Sobaibo were truly obstinate. As he had done with other Acaxee, Father Hernando de Santarén sent the Sobaibo several messages of peace and love. This went on for two months, during which time the Indians ignored his offers. Although the governor desired a general and bloodless peace and the settlement of this nation, he was forced to enter those mountains with his soldiers.[48] The settlements of the rebellious Sobaibo were very inaccessible. The governor, nevertheless, battled the rebels and captured a good number of their women. Rather than harm them, he returned them safely to the Sobaibo, together with an invitation to make peace. This softened the spirits of these obstinate people, who had so strongly resisted and opposed [the Spaniards] and who had publicly sworn not to make peace. They were the ones who burned the churches of the pueblos that wanted to keep the peace. They even killed some of the Indians who opposed them. They had also been discussing among themselves whether they were going to kill Father Hernando de Santarén. Although most did not want to take his life (because they had not forgotten his love and how he benefited them), many others disagreed. Among the latter there was a clever Indian who stood up and said that the priest had to die. "If he lives," he said, "he alone could force us to make peace. And so we should kill him."

Although they remained at war, the governor's wise decision to return the rebels' captured women softened the rebels' hearts. These people are not of such limited capacity that they do not appreciate good deeds. So [now that they were] better disposed, they sent a message to Father Santarén, asking him to come to their settlements and rancherías. Despite the considerable risk, he went for the sake of his children. Four allied soldiers accompanied the priest, rather than abandon him at such a time of danger. Our Lord granted them good fortune because it was for His cause as well as that of the Gospel.

The Sobaibo welcomed them to their rancherías. The priest exercised the same office as he had previously done with the groups that were already reduced, pointing out the benefits of peace. They told him that they had previously determined to kill every Spaniard who was in their land. They added that when they found out that Bishop Don Alonso de Escobar y la Mota was coming to Culiacán, they had decided to kill him one night, even though he was accompanied by an escort of forty soldiers. However, in the end they decided to take the priest's advice to lay down their weapons, make peace, and return to their pueblos and rebuild their churches.

Father Santarén at this time [the fall of 1603] brought nine groups down from the mountaintops, rescuing them from the devil's control. They became as well settled, peaceful, and steadfast as the other groups. This caused great joy in the Spanish mining camps, which now with peace [492] could begin to rebuild and work the rich silver mines that God had given the Spaniards. The joy of the evangelical ministers was even greater, because it had been so difficult to found this new Christianity. They had spiritual mines, which were more precious than the veins of silver that had been discovered by the miners. They were infinitely grateful to God for having calmed that storm, disposing those people toward the ministries of our Holy Faith, so that Christian religion could be continued, as we will relate later on.

We have written about the end of the false bishop, who was truly a diabolical liar. He was the devil's principal means of destroying (if possible) the Christianity of those mountain people, intending to leave not even a trace of it. Besides burning pueblos and churches, the

47. The Sobaibo lived in the mountains above the Villa de San Miguel de Culiacán. In 1602 the people of the Culiacán River valley suffered an epidemic that began the previous year among the Jesuit missions to the north along the Río Sinaloa (AGN 1602; Reff 1991b:146). The consequences of the epidemic may have contributed to Sobaibo "unrest" and the apparent revitalization movement discussed in this chapter.

48. Urdiñola took to the field in the early summer of 1603.

common enemy sought to kill as many Spaniards as possible, for they protected this Christianity. They also tried to kill the priests who preached the holy law of Christ. The end that befell the perverted Indian who had lit the fire was very much a matter of divine mercy. After he was captured the governor sentenced him to death for his serious crimes. With this sentence he began to recognize his evil deeds. He had time to ask God and man for forgiveness, strongly suggesting that he achieved salvation. Although his good counsel could not save him from corporal death, Father Hernando de Santarén helped prepare the principal author of the rebellion as well as his accomplices for a good death before they were hanged. One of the false bishop's accomplices publicly confessed that he had pretended to be Saint James because he had heard the Spaniards say that this saint was their patron and captain. I regret that I do not have the original text of the confession that the false bishop made when he was taken to be executed. But they say that it was eight pages long, and in it he declared various frauds through which he misled those poor and ignorant people. They became totally disabused of them and acquired a strong desire for peace.

In order to keep peace in those pueblos, a loyal Indian governor of good disposition whose authority was recognized by the Indians was given a position usually reserved for Spaniards. When he learned that another Indian had rebelled and was reviving the old restlessness, he arrested him and sentenced him to a severe and immediate punishment. Without consulting any Spanish judicial authorities, as the Indian governors are ordered to do, this governor ordered that the agitator's body be cut in half and hung from a tree. Through such means the entire Acaxee nation was completely pacified. They repaired their churches and pueblos, and Christian religious instruction was re-established. The Spaniards [meanwhile] repaired their mills for grinding the ore that was extracted from the silver mines. Everything about this mission began to bloom again and yield spiritual fruits that we will later mention.

CHAPTER XI The Indians who have been reduced form pueblos; the governor asks the viceroy to send more ministers to the mountains; other events concerning the establishment of Christianity

When the tempest that had destroyed the pueblos and rustic churches subsided, [493] Father Santarén, who was superior of this mission, and his companions refocused their efforts, which had been put on hold during the storm. They set to work repairing the damage that had been done to this new Christianity. Religious instruction and [recitation of the] catechism, which had declined, were begun anew. At the same time those infants who had been born in the mountains during the uprising were baptized. The priests also began preparing the adults for the same. Father Santarén himself (in one of his letters to the Father Provincial of Mexico) describes the work that was carried out at this time [1604] in this mission. He writes as follows:

> God Our Lord wished to send the members of the Company to rescue these people from their darkness and idolatry, and to reduce them to the flock of His Holy Church. The first thing we did was congregate them in large pueblos and build temporary churches of straw. The Indians established their houses close to these churches to receive religious instruction. Today, more than five thousand people [have been reduced]. They attend church and religious instruction with such fervor that until now thirty-seven hundred people have been baptized during this year following the uprising.

Of these, more than four hundred are infants; the rest are adults. More than six hundred couples have been married in facie Ecclesiae. The rest of the people are eager to learn the doctrine. When Lent came, more than three hundred people went to confession and participated in Holy Week services. Spaniards who were present were moved by the Indians' devotion. On Mondays, Tuesdays, and Wednesdays, special scourgings were held at the church. On Holy Thursday there was a large blood procession.[49] On Friday there were three processions because there were not enough gowns or scourges for everyone. This way they could take turns using what they had. These people, who the year before could not get enough Spanish blood, [now] shed their own with great sorrow for their sins and a desire to repent their deeds.

Just before he returned to Durango Governor Francisco de Urdiñola emphasized to the Indians that they must revere the priests who gave them religious instruction just as they revered him. Thus, when a priest arrives at some of these pueblos, men, women, and children come out to receive him at a designated place, carrying a Cross and singing the catechism in their language. Then they go with him to the church where they sing it again. Unless [the need] is urgent, no Indian leaves while the priest is in the pueblo. The priests even announce in advance when they will arrive at a pueblo. Many of [the Indians] have left their inaccessible settlements and dwellings and have settled in pueblos that are readily accessible, generally along rivers, where there is an abundance of several kinds of fish. These people can gather some four hundred arrobas of fish by spreading barbasco on the water. All this keeps these people happy.

This was the letter of Father Hernando de Santarén. After peace was established he [wrote] to his superiors in Mexico City, urging them to send new laborers to work in the vineyard, where the once-thick weeds and thorns had already been uprooted. The governor of Nueva Vizcaya, Francisco de Urdiñola, helped a great deal with this request. He had seen with his own eyes the great hardships that the priests endured, traveling the rough roads to visit the settlements of this nation and providing them with religious instruction. He also saw that more and more pueblos were being established. He wrote to the viceroy about the need to increase the number of ministers to instruct this nation, which was now at peace and ready to serve the two Majesties. He added that, with more priests, they could continue preaching the Gospel to those nations [494] in the mountains that had not yet been reduced. This would be very beneficial to the king and his vassals in existing as well as future mining centers. These great mountains have always been famous for their rich silver ore. It has

always been said that they are the source of the best-quality and richest silver deposits in Nueva España. Because we are dealing with the richest mountain chain in Nueva España, one can perfectly say that the silver lodes or veins are like trees — trees whose roots send out many shoots. When God sees fit, these will be discovered and worked on each side [of the Sierra Madre Occidental].

Returning to the governor's petition, he asked the viceroy not only for more ministers, but for whatever was needed in the way of ornaments, images, and vessels for the altars of the new churches that were being constructed. All [the existing churches] had been destroyed during the uprising. Finally, he added that, to establish lasting peace among these mountain peoples whom he had pacified and known in their natural state, it was important both spiritually and politically to provide a stipend from the Royal Treasury for a school where the sons of the Indian elite could be reared to serve the church, and later, when they were grown, to maintain loyalty and good Christian customs in their pueblos. The governor proposed this with affection and goodwill toward the Acaxee, of whom he became fond when he first went to pacify this nation. He recognized these Indians' good nature and interest in peace and the establishment of missions.

The viceroy reacted very favorably to the governor's proposal. He gave orders for everything to be carried out, because they were in accord with the royal orders governing such matters. The viceroy charged the Father Provincial of the Company to send four more priests to help the ones who were instructing the Indians in the mountains of Topia. Four new ministers were sent [in 1606 and 1607], together with some ornaments, painted pictures in frames, and bells for the churches, which the Indians like because they think they are better than the barbarous drums that they used in their former celebrations. They also took some musical instruments, flutes, flageolets, bassoons, and trumpets. The Indians quickly learn music and joyfully celebrate their Christian feasts and the divine mysteries that are preached to them. All this is the result of the Catholic kings of the Spanish monarchy and their magnificent support for pious deeds. Although the kings' great and constant generosity will never be sufficiently recognized—even though I have written about it—it will be rewarded throughout eternity. This generosity also has inspired those religious priests who are exiled to work and travel so many difficult and exhausting trails. This is a very holy exile, because they are fervently employed

49. Christian (1981:189) provides an excellent discussion of these Holy Week processions in sixteenth-century Spain.

in a new Christian community, permanently separated from their brothers and the frequent commerce and celebrations that they once enjoyed in Christian cities.

The new soldiers of Christ arrived at Topia to help in the spiritual conquest of these mountain people.

They were welcomed with great joy, as much by their brothers as by the Indians. And so the total number of ministers of religious instruction in this mission was increased to eight. [495]

CHAPTER XII The priests divide the pueblos of this mission among themselves for the purposes of religious instruction; the remainder of the Acaxee are reduced; some unusual cases of sorcery

The four new laborers who were sent under holy obedience from Mexico City were so desirous of aiding souls that they could hardly wait to begin their work. To proceed in the most orderly fashion, which is what greatly helps the success of these enterprises, they divided amongst themselves the care of the pueblos that had been reduced. Each priest was assigned what was considered an appropriate number so that all the people could have frequent instruction and receive the sacraments.[50] Although, as noted, the hardships and roughness of the trails were great, [the priests] reduced the population to three districts, which were under the jurisdiction of the mission headquarters [at Topia]. Then [the priests] attempted to reduce those Indians who, because they were less tame than the others, had yet to leave the mountains to join the flocks in settled pueblos. This was made difficult by some gentiles who lived in an inaccessible place who were so opposed to our Holy Faith and the priests who preached it that they threatened to kill all those who wanted to join the Church. They arrogantly

and barbarously boasted that the Church was like a woman who had neither bow nor arrow (it is foolish how these barbarians trust in their weapons). The Church (they said) cannot offend us or defend itself, and it does not have to be feared. They likewise did not fear the Spaniards' weapons; for it seemed to them that they were safe and defended by their inaccessible peaks.

Among these Indians were long-time rebels who did not hesitate to encourage this opposition. At one time they had received religious instruction and were more or less Christians, although false ones. They subsequently decided to withdraw and go live with these people in the mountains. This pained the priest who wanted to reduce them more than the danger of death with which they threatened him, as he himself wrote. However, God in His mercy wished to console him, and so He gave him more souls than those that the devil had taken from him. For soon about 250 rebels came and were reduced, and there was reason to believe an equal number would follow. Moreover, about five hundred other gentiles (some of them relatives of those who were baptized) sent the priest a message that they wanted to leave [their homes] and resettle. They and their wives and children wanted to become Christians, enjoying the instruction that their relatives and friends received. This offer did not remain mere words; all these people came out [of the mountains] and a very sizable pueblo was established. A church was erected, where they attended instruction so conscientiously that in a short time they were all able to be baptized. They

50. The Mission of Topia and San Andrés, which was still one unit (it was divided in 1610), was headed by Alonso Ruiz, who worked on the Acaxee-Xixime border in the mission of San Gregorio, assisted by Father Alonso Gómez and Andrés Tutino. Gerónimo de San Clemente was in charge of the central Acaxee missions of Topia and San Andrés; Florián de Ayerve and Hernando de Santarén were in charge of Baimoa and the Sierra de Carantapa, respectively; José de Lomas was entrusted with Atotonilco; Diego González de Cueto was entrusted with the Sobaibo (Alegre 1956–1960:2:155–56).

took matters of piety, the devotions, and Christian exercises so seriously that when Holy Week came they did their blood scourging as though they were very solid Christians. At Lent [51] they were given some talks, introducing them to the Sacrament of Penance. They took the confession of their sins so seriously that they even confessed sins that they had committed before they were baptized. Even though they were informed that those [sins] had been pardoned by Holy Baptism, they replied that they still found [confession] comforting. At a minimum it was a good sign of how firmly the preaching of the Faith had taken root in them.

On several occasions a gentile came down from his mountain lair, to which he had retreated, [496] to ask the priest for Baptism. Each time the priest did not grant his wish, first because the Indian did not know the catechism well, and second because he did not leave his home on the mountaintops. The Indian then went to a blind man who knew the catechism and paid him very well for religious instruction; the two of them shut themselves up for eight days [reviewing the catechism]. Afterwards, the man presented himself to the priest for examination and Baptism, which he received, along with a warning to bring his household and resettle with his Christian brothers. All this he did without protest. He went to the mountains and got his wife and his children and they all were baptized.

In that mission there were some Indian sorcerers who had an explicit pact with the devil. We necessarily encounter many of these bedeviled persons who are discovered by the light of the Gospel, just as was the case when Christ Our Lord preached in the world, driving great numbers of demons from their caves. The [devil] wrought remarkable damage through his familiars among these people. The sorcerers preached and persuaded the rest of them that it was in their power to do good or evil, to give or take away health or sickness, work or rest, abundant or barren years, and life or death. They actually killed with diabolical spells, which terrified and confused people.

The priests attempted with talks to reveal such lies and to mend the great harm [done in the past]. They informed the pueblo of such frauds, declaring the power of God over all. In addition, they had the Indian governors punish the most pernicious sorcerers whom they could identify. Both of these things served to enlighten the pueblo.

But sparks and smoke always remain from the fire

that one attempts to extinguish. It happened that the wife of one of these sorcerers died. Her husband got together with another sorcerer and prepared some charms, which he placed on the breasts of her dead body. She was buried with these on the pretense that the charms would empower her to leave her grave at night and kill very horribly and frightfully whomever she encountered, but especially children. Because this perverse Indian was now filled with the spirit of the devil, with whom he dealt, he said that he was envious of the children who had mothers to rear them and love them, whereas his own children were now without a mother. This cursed vice takes hold of so many of these familiars of the demons that, if they see that the fields of other persons are greener and clearer than their own, they use the power of spells to dry them up and destroy them within an hour.

However, in the end, through his secret judgment, or in order to more fully demonstrate the power of the Gospel to destroy such diabolical tricks, God allowed the dead woman or a diabolical phantom to arise from the grave. She appeared for two or three nights, terrorizing four or five people who immediately fell speechless to the ground. The people got so upset about this that even in the daytime they did not dare to enter the church; still other people tried to flee to the most inaccessible mountaintops. The priest, who learned of this unrest while in another pueblo, set out for the pueblo with great caution and wariness of such pernicious frauds. When the sorcerer learned that the priest was coming, he stopped or released the spells that he had placed on those who had fallen speechless. They regained their senses but nevertheless remained as frail as though they had come through a grave or powerful illness. The sorcerer, however, did not lift the spell or charms from the body of the dead woman. Rather, that very same night the same phantom appeared to an old man of about sixty years of age, who was struck dumb. He became so stiff that the priest and [497] two other Indians could not even bend his arm.

When the priest saw this, he summoned the entire pueblo to the church. He gave them a fervent speech, condemning their dealings with demons—those capital enemies of men—whose pretensions and desires were only to retain them as companions in their condemnation. This condemnation was the objective of the devil's dealings and pacts with his familiars. [After this speech] the priest learned who was the most responsible for the unrest. To insure that they did not disappear and later foment more unrest, he had the individuals immediately punished by the Indian alcaldes. He exhorted the rest of them to truly commend themselves to God Our Lord while he said Mass, asking the Powerful Majesty to undo those spells and diabolical apparitions. Our Lord heard him and received this powerful and divine sacrifice that counters all the furies of hell. From then on the false apparitions and frightening events ceased. The people were comforted and encouraged to continue in peace, [learning] the Christian doctrine. The sorcerers meanwhile were expelled and corrected in their errors.

With this case and other similar ones the truth and virtue of our Holy Faith was confirmed, as was Our Lord's favor and protection of those who preach with such marvelous effects as these. The priests, assisted with such favors from heaven, worked diligently at the reduction of other recalcitrant and obstinate Indians. They happily achieved the reduction of all the people of the region who now pertain to this mission. Later [we will] tell about others that were added to it.

CHAPTER XIII All the people are baptized, permanent churches are erected, and Christianity advances

After the priests had finished reducing [these people], including the most errant Indians from these mountains and gorges, they were able to baptize all the people. This was followed by the construction of permanent churches. Although this task requires great effort on the part of these poor missionaries, it is understood that it is of great importance to the stability and steadfastness of Christianity (as has been noted). As long as there are no permanent churches in the pueblos where people are resettled, it seems that everything is disposable and makeshift, as they say. These buildings are highly esteemed [by the Indians], although [others] elsewhere might consider them rustic. They provide form for the pueblos and Christianity, making it possible to introduce Christian practices and ministries. These are all fruits that encourage these priests, who are zealous for God's service and glory, to participate in these holy labors.

After the priests in this mission of Topia completed the Baptism of adults, they carefully constructed churches in their pueblos. Next they introduced all the Christian exercises, concluding with the sacraments and other customs of the Holy Church. Because it is something that new ministers should understand, I note here that the ministers who work in these missions often find that [498] not everything can be accomplished at once.

Not even the holy Apostles immediately burdened the faithful with ecclesiastical precepts, which subsequently were set down on various occasions in the councils that were held by the Apostles and by the Holy Church. Before those who are to be baptized receive that Holy Sacrament, through which they become subjects of the Church, they are instructed in the observance of God's law and agree to obey it. Nevertheless, their practice of this law is introduced and established over time. This is particularly the case with the communion of the body of Our Lord Jesus Christ, which requires the greatest preparation because it is such a Divine Sacrament.

This sacrament was introduced, as were the devotion of the Rosary of the Most Holy Virgin and the celebration of the feast days of the principal mysteries of our Holy Faith. I have already described the one means that was particularly helpful in all this, namely the [founding of] schools for the brightest and best-behaved boys and young men. There they learn to read, write, and sing, so that they can serve in the church and at Christian festivities, playing music and singing. This is a divine means of preserving the people's faith and devotion.

All these things were established in this Christian community through the aid of Our Lord. Because this can only be made known through particular cases, it will be necessary to recount some so that the fruits of the Gospel among these people may be better understood. During one feast day celebration, some old Indians asked the priest if they could make a little wine (this was no small request on the part of those who not too long ago used that drink very licentiously, taking great liberties and being dissolute). To obtain the priest's permission, they added that they would consume the wine in moderation. To accommodate a bit these people who were so new [to the Faith], the priest agreed to their request on the condition that they had offered. Although they went a little too far [with their drinking], the priest discovered on his way to church the next day that all those Indians who had drunk to excess were on their knees in front of the [church] door, begging pardon with great remorse and vowing to make up for their sin. The priest exhorted them to do so and indicated that he expected them to [change their behavior]. In the meantime he was consoled by the fact that they were at least able to recognize the damage done by their deeply rooted vice. The Lord, who has never rejected those who are remorseful, would, of course, pardon them.

Many Indians showed great devotion to Mass, even though it often was very difficult for them to attend. Today they often travel five, six, or even more leagues from their pueblos to hear Mass. When many Masses are celebrated, such as on a feast day of the namesake of a pueblo or when the priests [in a mission] assemble as they are required [to do],[52] the Indians attend all the Masses out of devotion. Sometimes the priest and the fiscal of the church have to tell those who have already heard one or two Masses that they can go home and rest and take some refreshment. The Indians respond that they have nothing to do at home that is as important as hearing Mass. If one says Mass in their pueblo, even though they may be sick and are therefore not obliged to attend, some of them are so devout that they order themselves to be carried to the church so that they can enjoy Mass. They attend religious instruction with the same punctuality and fervor, even on days when the priest is busy in another pueblo; they are hesitant to miss even then.

The devotion to the Rosary of the Most Holy Virgin is very pleasing to them, as is the Virgin herself, together with the milk with which this most pleas-

ant Lady sweetly nourishes the Church and its faithful. These people whom we are discussing consider it very fortunate to have the Rosary, and ordinarily they recite this holy devotion in unison. (Because it is so beneficial) the priests attempt to introduce this devotion with [499] very special care.

Regarding their devotion to the Holy Sacrament of Confession, and in confirmation of that which has been related, I will include here a letter that one of the fathers wrote four years after the end of this nation's rebellion.[53] Although it does not relate extraordinary feats, nevertheless it shows the progress of people so new to the Christian Faith as well as the favors with which Our Lord consoles His servants who labor in the ministry of the salvation of these poor souls. The letter reads as follows:

Affection for confession and devotion to the Rosary of Our Lady shines strongest in two pueblos, where it seems Our Lord has sprinkled them with most abundant blessings. All the men and women continually pray the Rosary together. When they confess it is with such affection and sorrow for their sins that when I reach these pueblos (doing so is very difficult and the place is also very hot), the Lord sends me such singular comfort and relief from hardship that I become very upset when I must take leave of them. I was at one of these pueblos during a time of heavy rains, when the waters were raging. The current ran so fast between the rocky cliffs that I could not cross the great swell of the river, nor could the [people of the pueblo] cross over to where I was. Nevertheless, an Indian dared to venture into the water. As a result, he was very badly bruised, and when he reached me, he said, "My only motive in crossing the river, Father, was to confess. That's why God kept me from drowning." He confessed and then returned to his pueblo, with the great consolations of having achieved what he so desired as well as safety from the danger to which he had exposed himself in order to pursue such good intentions.

At the same time one of the most principal Indians of all that land fell sick. He had good character and was notably fond of matters concerning God. He was eager to learn these things and continually asked questions about them. Then he would go and repeat everything to his children, who therefore had an advantage over the rest of the Christians. In spite of these good qualities, the poor Indian was very much given to weaknesses of the flesh. Although he had been stripped of some concubines, it was impossible to get him to give up two who were sisters. Our Lord inflicted him with an illness that was so grave that after a few hours he became unconscious. I reached his pueblo and learned of this soul's needs. I did everything I could to bring him

52. Pérez de Ribas is alluding here to Jesuit rules that prescribed that the priests working in a mission such as Topia assemble at least once, and preferably, twice a year, in part to make the Spiritual Exercises and to consult with one another about matters relating to their own spirituality and that of their neophytes (Cabredo 1611; Polzer 1976).

53. As Pérez de Ribas indicates later in this chapter, this letter was written by Father Diego González de Cueto; it describes his work among the Sobaibo in 1607. A portion of the same letter was copied by Alegre (1956–1960:2:157–58).

back to consciousness, which God willed to happen. He was greatly frightened by what he had seen of the other life, as is well demonstrated by his change. He made a good and lengthy confession, and I gave him the Holy Sacrament in the form of the Viaticum as well as Extreme Unction. I told him that what remained of his life should be spent at the feet of Our Lord Jesus Christ and His Most Holy Mother, begging them for mercy and forgiveness. He did so and it worked for him, for God gave him complete health. He expelled the two sisters from his pueblo, and he [now] lives in great modesty. He says that when the devil now tempts him, he immediately remembers what he saw and this keeps him from sinning.

I asked another person in the same pueblo what prayers he said. He told me of his many devotions to each of the divine persons, to Our Lady and her devout saints for the souls in purgatory, and for acquaintances, both living and dead. It seemed to me that in prayer the most devout religious novice did not even come close to him. There are several such people here, women as well as men, which is even more [impressive]. There are nevertheless others who have been the cause of many hardships, owing to their rusticity, obstinacy, and subjection to the devil for so many years.

The land we are speaking about also offers many opportunities to suffer and earn rewards because of its [500] extremes of weather and its crude and limited sustenance.

However, there is no denying that we receive a very tangible reward in the form of fruit so palpable. When I recall that during those years I baptized with my own hands nearly one thousand children who died—children who were not old enough to sin—it seems to me that I have no right to ask God for any greater reward for my labor in this life; the consolation is that abundant. Faith tells us that after [receiving] payment in this life, eternal life and greatness await us in the kingdom of heaven, provided we do as we teach. May God Our Lord, who deigned to call the most wretched of the earth, grant them perseverance in the Faith till the end, so that they may be saved. [May He also grant us] inner light to communicate with them and the esteem appropriate to such a holy and noble occupation so that following our labors we can rest with these and many other [peoples], Amen.

To this point I have been quoting the letter of the devout Father Diego González de Cueto, who after laboring very fervently for many years in this mission went to found another, which later will be discussed.[54] In this letter he tells us about the condition and fruits of this new Christian community of Topia, which each of the other priests was individually perfecting in the same way.

CHAPTER XIV Other Christian practices that are exercised with great care by the Acaxee nation

It remains for me to discuss here an unusual devotion that was established among this new Christianity during its very early days. I made mention of it earlier with reference to several particular pueblos. The pious Holy Week devotion and penance grew and became so widespread that they deserve more detailed discussion here. Because what happened in one pueblo or another occurred precisely in all of them, I will thus content myself with one illustration of this devotion.

At that time the offices of Holy Week were celebrated in a pueblo called Las Vegas. This pueblo had been selected because it had the greatest abundance of provisions and was no more than four leagues from a mining camp called Las Vírgenes. Las Vegas was also relatively close to Culiacán, whence Spaniards enjoyed

coming to watch the new Christians' celebrations. A large number of people came from both Culiacán and Las Vírgenes to join the Indians of this pueblo. The Indians performed two blood processions involving more than a thousand people with scourges. These processions were held at night and were illuminated by crude torches which, although they were poorly made, at the same time were indicative of these poor people's devotion. The Lord, who knew of their affection and devotion, would not cast them aside because their poverty did not permit them to have torches that were

54. Pérez de Ribas is alluding here to Diego González de Cueto's entrada to the Hina in 1620, which was followed a decade later by his establishment of a mission among this group, which apparently was a subgroup of Xixime (see Chapters 15 and 16 of Book 9).

anything more than those that they made out of handfuls of dried reeds from their fertile plains. Many in the procession shed tears of devotion, which shone ever more brightly in God's eyes, just as they did in the eyes of those who were present, who saw the change in those once barbarous infidels. They were so transformed that they ripped open their own flesh and asked God for mercy and pardon for their sins. One Spaniard who was there wrote that he had been more moved by this procession—with two poorly carved wooden Crosses and a similarly carved humble box that carried the Most Holy Sacrament, [501] which was adorned with four wretched cotton mantas—than by the great and rich adornments and fittings that he had seen displayed during Holy Week in wealthy Mexico City. It cannot be denied that these first fruits of this new Christianity were most pleasing to Our Lord, as were these people's tears of devotion. To be able to gather these fruits among people who were still rebellious seemed as great a miracle as drawing water from a rock, and of even greater esteem and worth.

In another pueblo where the same solemn Holy Week celebrations were held, another priest wrote that he had given them a talk concerning the penance that they must do for their sins. They accepted this so wholeheartedly that five hundred people participated in a scourging procession. They executed this penance with such fervor that the marks on their backs remained with them for many days. This could easily be seen because their backs were bare. This procession was accompanied by tears of devotion and caused the Indians to become so devout that in their speeches and councils they themselves celebrated and confessed that they felt their souls had benefited greatly from Holy Week exercises. More than one thousand people—young and old—went to confession during this time. In doing so they showed great sorrow [for their sins] and met the other sacramental requirements of truthfulness, integrity, and worthiness. To insure that the advances made by this Christian community in all these matters are proclaimed, I add the following. During a time of famine a priest had given a speech on the charity and alms that Christ Our Redeemer charged us to show towards all those who are needy and poor. This doctrine took such a strong hold that, because many people had gathered in this pueblo due to their reasonably good harvest, the people here began to open their hands and their homes to all the poor guests who came. Many of them stayed for a long time, and they were all satisfied and well fed the entire time they were there. The poorest took enough food home with them to remedy their needs. [The residents of] this pueblo, which was called Otatitlán, became so fond of this labor of mercy that they decided to do the same thing every year and to plant enough to be able to share [their food] with the poor. Our Lord showed how pleased He was with these charitable Indians' offer by providing them with a very abundant harvest the following year so that they could carry out their saintly proposition. We will now leave these people to discuss the reduction of more isolated Indians who joined this mission of Topia, which remains our topic of discussion.

CHAPTER XV The priests journey to rancherías and pueblos outside the Topia gorge, initiating and providing religious instruction

The fervor and desire of the missionary priests in Topia were not enclosed by or confined to that gorge and the settlements that were in the area surrounding the Topia mining camp. Nor were they limited to merely gathering the flocks from the pueblos that they had already congregated. Rather, like soldiers for Christ, they set out on their campaign, or better said, to the corners of that mountain range, to find the strongholds of the Prince of Darkness, as the Apostle Saint Paul calls the devil. Beyond the Topia gorge, on one side of the mountains, this enemy had under his dominion some rancherías and pueblos near the former Villa de San Miguel de Culiacán,[55] which was mentioned earlier. Even though the light of the Gospel had surrounded these Indians on all sides, they were still in [502] darkness under the devil's power. The priests attacked in order to remove them from his clutches so that they might benefit along with the others from Christ Our Lord's redemption. Their enterprise was successful, for when one of the missionary priests from Topia [Diego González de Cueto] went to these pueblos, he reduced them and administered to them the same good services that [he had administered] to the others.

All the people were congregated in three pueblos, called Vadirabato, Conimeto, and Alicamac. They built their churches and a school for boys, who would serve in the church, learn to sing, and occupy themselves with all the other tasks in which they are employed in these schools, as we mentioned earlier. This school was needed here because this district was far from the school in Topia. In the end a very good Christian community was established here, which became part of the mission of Topia, under the care of its superior. This all led to an increase in the number of Christians and a rebirth of children for the Holy Church.

The fervor of God's faithful ministers did not end here. They got word that deeper in the mountains,

on the slopes facing Sinaloa, there were many other gentiles scattered among places that were harsh and difficult to reach. Nevertheless, these priests penetrated the deepest valleys; they were like the unbending rays of the sun, to which the Son of God compared those whom he sent out into the world to preach, saying to them, *Vos estis lux mundi*.[56] These Gospel ministers fulfilled the same duty and decided to take the light to these people, even though they lived among the crags, for this part of the mountains (called Carantapa) is very vast and rough. The Spaniards, who never relent in their search for silver, had heard that there were rich ores here, so they went in search of them and established a mining camp with this same name [in 1603–4]. Although the Spaniards extracted a lot of wealth, the mines quickly declined. This was not the case, however, with the spiritual prosperity of the souls that the priests went in search of. These priests faced great difficulties gathering and adding to the Church people who were scattered among the mountains, which severely lacked land that was well situated for planting fields or forming populous pueblos. Still, they dismissed no effort or great danger to reduce and convert these souls, of whom thousands were baptized in our Holy Faith.

Their principal pueblo was called Tecuchuapa. Its Christianity persevered and was more steadfast than the material mines at Carantapa. What happened here in the beginning is recorded in a letter from Father Hernando de Santarén. After he had founded the mission at Topia and worked there for years, he went on with the same fervor to found the mission at Carantapa.[57] Because this job was in his hands, he can relate this enterprise better than I. After first offering many thanks to his superior for having sent him a second priest to help him, his letter reads:[58]

---

55. This apparently is the original Villa de San Miguel, which was near Navito on the Río San Lorenzo; sometime prior to 1560 it was relocated to the Río Culiacán (Gerhard 1982:261).

56. Matthew 5:14: "You are light for the world" (Knox 1956:4).

57. It was apparently in September 1606 that Santarén and Florián de Ayerve began working among the Acaxee of the Sierra de Carantapa region.

58. Santarén's letter apparently was written in 1607. According to Dunne (1944:70), at this time Father Florián de Ayerve, who had been working with Santarén, became ill and was replaced by Father José de Lomas.

Father José de Lomas reached this pueblo of Tecuchuapa, where we subsequently spent fifteen days. It was a great consolation to my soul to see a priest from the Company with whom I could console myself in lands as remote as these. After we separated and set out for different pueblos— I having made one day's journey—two extremely upset Indians came to me. They had been sent by the cacique of the pueblo whence I had departed. They begged me to return immediately to help and encourage them to defend the church and my house, such as it was, from the Tepehuan. The latter had killed everyone they could find in a ranchería. Only one person had escaped, who had brought news of the attack. He said that the Tepehuan were moving upriver, killing whomever they encountered, [503] and were determined to burn down the church and the [priest's] house.

Before Father José de Lomas and I had left this pueblo we had learned that two Tepehuan Indians had taken three young maidens from their parents, after threatening to kill the latter if they did not turn their daughters over to them. We sent for the Tepehuan so that Father Lomas, who knows their language, could calm them down and persuade them to return the young women to their parents. They refused to come; instead they persuaded the Indians in those rancherías not to go to church or obey the priests who instructed them, and gave other such diabolical advice. Father Lomas then sent thirty Indians to recover the three captives. They bravely accomplished this mission, even though the Tepehuan drove them off with a hail of arrows. This made the Tepehuan angry, and they called together others of their nation, who carried out the aforementioned destruction. Just months before they had killed a cacique in one of our pueblos and at the same time had tried to kill me.

This is the danger that I have faced during the entire month of September. I keep watch and ordinarily guard the church with fifty archers. The taste of death is very strong, because my house is made entirely of straw. Still, those Indians who are faithful show themselves to be so loyal that many of them guard me. This is the case even when I go from one pueblo to another, defending each with my presence rather than abandoning them, even if it costs me my life. May Your Reverence and the priests commend me to God.

The Indians of Baimoa, which is thirty leagues from this pueblo of Tecuchuapa, have come to call on me, wanting to become Christians. To obligate me even more, they went for a third time to see the captain of the mining camp at Carantapa, presenting him with metal ore from their lands. I have excused myself for the time being, making them understand that because they lived so far away I could not go and instruct them and abandon the work that was now in my hands, especially in its present state. They greatly regretted this and thus decided to abandon their lands and come seek the waters of Holy Baptism. During May, 150 people came to this pueblo of Tecuchuapa. I do not doubt that anyone would cry tears of joy and would be inspired to serve Our Lord at the sight of them and their entire rancherías pulling up stakes. Men come loaded down with their little children; women with their most valuable possessions and their food; and others with the old and the blind, who could not walk. This was not just one day's journey; rather, it took fifteen days, for their mountain range is the highest and extends for twenty leagues. These people made this journey not in search of silver or gold, but rather in search of salvation and the requisite water of Holy Baptism. I trust in God that some of those who have died have attained this salvation, for once they received religious instruction and were baptized they settled in peace. The rest who have come are content and calm, and none has gone back. Rather, they have clamored so much for their companions who stayed behind in their mountain range, wanting them to participate in the benefits that they have, that I was forced to go there in person, along with the captain from the mining camp. The journey took seven days because we had to travel thirty leagues through the steepest mountains. The day we made five leagues was considered good. I spoke with about 150 Indians, and of these more than twenty came back with me. Others gave me their word that they would come once the rainy season had passed; I am waiting for them.

So far I have been citing the letter of this minister who demonstrated such great spirit for the welfare of these souls, who dearly cost him so many hardships and dangers as well as his life, as later will be recorded [504]. The fruits of his journey to Carantapa and the founding and results of this new mission are discussed in the following chapter.

CHAPTER XVI Other Indians who left their rancherías to receive religious instruction; the fate of the mission at Carantapa

The example provided by the Baimoa of leaving their lands to search for the means to salvation and communication with Christians, whom they now had so close by and who were so closely related to some of them, encouraged others to leave their settlements as well. Sixty Sicuraba Indians came to give Father Santarén this happy news. He wanted to find out the number of people who would be coming so that he could assign them a place where they could congregate. The Indians counted (with kernels of maize, as they normally do) nine hundred people. The messengers came with such a great willingness and desire for religious instruction that they spent three days with the priest, learning the catechism. With these good beginnings they returned to their settlements. As it was harvest time, they waited until they had harvested their fields before they left [their lands] and moved to the closest Christian pueblo. Our Lord began to expand this Christianity in such a way that, once Baptisms were begun, twelve hundred people were baptized that year [1607] in this pueblo. There were also four hundred couples who were wed in the Holy Christian Sacrament of Matrimony. Before they were baptized they were asked to give up their little idols, for it was known that the devil still had many of these objects among these peoples. They turned them over and more than two hundred were burned. Some were made of stone, in the form of people, which either they themselves had made or which the devil had carved for them. Others were like big knives made from the flint that they use for their arrows. It appears that it is in this flint that the devil established his pact with them for success in war. Some of these idols were even made from deer bezoar, which provided them good fortune in hunting, to which these nations are so inclined.

Even though these people's Christianity was growing with the aforesaid prosperity, there were nevertheless attacks by enemies. Because they are invisible, the Apostle [Paul] taught that they should be even more feared, for they do not tire, nor do they relent in battle.[59] But in the end God wills that their plots be revealed, and He aids His chosen ones with His grace so that the devil may be overcome.

During a time of a deadly plague of smallpox which struck these pueblos [apparently in 1607], a great number of sorcerers in one pueblo called all the people together in one of the houses. Men and women, young and old, gathered to ask the devil to free them from their illness and affliction. There was one man who remained outside the house, hidden in some nearby bushes. He was an Indian from another nation who was a long-time Christian. The priest had brought him along to serve as these people's temachtiano and teacher of the catechism.

Once the people had gathered in the house, a great sorcerer began to invoke and call on the devil with his diabolical arts. He appeared to them, and after they requested his aid in this affliction the demon promised to help. They then invoked another demon, and these two then called upon others. In the end there were five or six demons. In plain view and earshot of all those people all these evil spirits spoke to the principal sorcerer. Upon seeing and hearing so many devils the Indian temachtiano could not contain his fright and fear. He began screaming [505], repeatedly invoking the holy name of JESUS. Immediately, a great clap of thunder resounded, and that infernal group disappeared in a stampede. The house was shaking and swaying and so were those inside.

This is the degree of familiarity that these people have with the devil. This will be proclaimed in a portion of a letter that was written by Father Diego de Acevedo.[60] He spent a great deal of time and suffered many hardships instructing these people. He says:

I have discovered that the devil lives and resides among these people and that for many years he has gone around in human form from one rancheria to another. His size and height are always like that of a child of ten or twelve

59. Pérez de Ribas is referring here to Ephesians 6:10–20.
60. Acevedo began working among the Acaxee in 1611. His letter was written at the time (1612–13) of an epidemic of what appears to have been in part typhus (Reff 1991b:154–58).

years of age. He orders himself to be carried around on the Indians' shoulders, and does all he can to preach to them and exhort them to return to their former drunken revels, for he knows from experience all the sins that result from these celebrations. Our common adversary is not content with doing this among the Indians who roam these peaks and canyons. In human form, dressed in red, he also appears in the pueblos to those who are sick. He persuades them to go into the mountains to die, for their ancestors did not have the custom of being buried in the priests' churches. The devil does all this so that they will die without confession and he can carry them off to hell. I understood this to be the case one day when an old man who was very sick sent for me to hear his confession (even though he died, he left me consoled by the fact that he had been well prepared). After I did so two of his sons noted that he had died as soon as I had left him. They concluded that I had been the cause of his death, so they shouted throughout the pueblo that I was a sorcerer, that whenever I spoke to sick people they died, and that they should go to the sierra, where they would live longer and more happily. Fooled by Satan, they left and took their mother with them. She died a few days after they had reached the mountains, and with her death they realized that they had been fooled. Because she had been baptized, they brought her to be buried at the church. The governor of the pueblo asked them how it was that their mother had died so suddenly, without being seen by the priest whom they had called a sorcerer. The sons had no response; they realized that they had made a mistake. Afterwards, they continued to live in the pueblo, where, thanks be to God, they have remained very quiet and calm.[61]

I will omit for the time being other cases and include here a joyous one that involved two young maidens from among these people. God well knows how to pick roses from among the thorns. This was the case during a time of illness when, with Holy Baptism, God harvested infants as His first fruits for heaven. Although there were quite a few others who were saved through His divine kindness, there were two young maidens in particular whom he took in their prime. One of them was eight years old and the other thirteen. The latter exercised great care in attending church and catechism. After she had become seriously ill and was experiencing seizures that were bringing her closer and closer to death, her parents came and melted into tears, holding her so that she could die in their arms. After one of her seizures, when she regained consciousness, she said to her parents, in front of many other people: "Why are you crying? Don't you see that I am going to heaven? Don't cry, you're not my parents. A Lady came to me

with a white *tilma* (this is what they call the white manta that the women wear) and that Lady told me that she was my Mother and that my Father was in heaven waiting for me. She was a very beautiful Lady, and I want to go there." Repeating this and a few things from the Christian doctrine that she had learned, she died, giving these good assurances of her salvation. The other, younger girl, also commented before she died that she was not concerned about dying because she was going to heaven. [506] This greatly reassured the priest that these two sincere souls, whom he had instructed, would be saved. He was especially consoled to see with his own eyes how the Lord frequently worked in these souls who were new to the Faith. Through the souls of these little ones Our Lord prepared—as He usually does—the way [for the Gospel].

Also, we must not forget the fruits that this mission produced at the mining camp among the Spaniards and other long-time Christian [Indians] as well as [gentile] Indians and black laborers. Because this mining camp had only recently been founded and the mines were located in the harshest part of the mountains, they did not have their own secular priest. For that reason a priest [of the Company] went there that year to celebrate Holy Week. Besides providing the Holy Sacraments to such destitute people, he attended to the needs of a good number of Indian gentiles and new Christians who came to observe how the Spaniards celebrated Holy Week. The latter performed their blood scourges along with the camp laborers. This both horrified and edified the new Christians, who desired to celebrate in the same way in their own pueblos.

Returning to the settlements at [the mission at] Carantapa, I can say that Christianity flourished there. The people built beautiful churches, including one that appeared to be the work of a master Spanish craftsman. As construction was proceeding on this church, a furious storm suddenly arose. If this tempest did not completely destroy this church, it certainly damaged it severely. [Later] these people suffered greatly during several attacks by Tepehuan rebels,[62] whom we will discuss when we reach their mission. The rebels had hoped to provoke them and win them over to their cause. On several occasions the missionaries and the Spaniards from the mining camp were surrounded by these ferocious people and their lives were in great danger. They would have perished if they had not been

---

61. Pérez de Ribas appears here to terminate his quotation of Acevedo's letter.

62. During the Tepehuan Revolt in 1616.

rescued by the captain and soldiers from Sinaloa. After several encounters and skirmishes, as a final resolution, these mines were almost entirely abandoned. Some of the Indian pueblos that had received religious instruction were reduced to other Christian pueblos in the Province of Sinaloa, which was not far away. The remaining pueblos were reduced to those that pertained to the Topia mission. Even though the Carantapa mission was eliminated, in the end there were very good fruits harvested from the labors invested in this conversion. We will now leave and conclude [this discussion of] the Topia mission, to which the former pertained.

CHAPTER XVII   The present state of Christianity in the mission of Topia

The number of people at the mission seat of Topia increased with the addition of the flocks from the pueblos near the Villa de San Miguel de Culiacán and those of Carantapa, of which we have spoken. Although the population today is less than what it was in their heathenism, this lesser number is much more pleasing to God than the greater number that previously existed. Concerning this, one can say what the Prophet Isaiah said, *Multiplicasti gentem sed non magnificasti laetitiam.*[63] These are also God's words in Ecclesiastes, *Non concupiscit multitudinem filiorum infidelium & inutilium.*[64] Having multiplied these barbarous nations in their heathenism, God was not pleased to lose them. Now His Sovereign Majesty is much happier seeing the people from the ravine of Topia with others beyond it who have been reduced. Even if they are not increased in number (for with illnesses He has taken to Him many who were aided by the sacraments), those who remain are flourishing in their Christianity. They have persevered very firmly and with so many [edifying] examples [507] that their spiritual fruits greatly console the six religious priests from our Company who ordinarily minister to them. Since 1600, when this mission was begun, until 1644, when this history is being written, some fifty thousand souls have been baptized in these ravines and mountains. The Indians who are still alive today have now completely forgotten their former barbarous customs.[65] Innumerable idols have been overturned and very beautiful churches have been erected in their pueblos that were once subject to surprise attacks. The priests have adorned the churches with very beautiful ornaments, sacred vases, and tabernacles where the Most Holy Sacrament is kept secure. On feast days as well as throughout the year these Indians attend the Divine Sacrament of Holy Communion, which is joyously celebrated with music and singers from the schools of this mission. Some of these priests have even obtained organs for their churches, for they desire to make use of all possible means of aiding the spiritual well-being of these peoples. They have also found organists to play and to teach some of the local Indians, who learn to play well and with pleasure. Finally, in social and political matters they are totally different from before. The attire of the people of this mission as well as their very good behavior, homes, and affable treatment of Spaniards have become an example and lure for many other gentiles from this large mountain range who have settled at this mission and been converted.

We can say that the Topia mountain range was the first and most important stronghold to be won over from the infernal enemy. Others are also being conquered, as will be told in the following book. The religious ministers of this Christian community recognize and are governed by a superior in this mission and residence. They all gather at least once a year at one of their homes to discuss their own spiritual development

---

63. *Margin Note*: Isaias 9:3. Isaiah 9:3: "Their number thou didst increase, but gave them no joy of it" (Knox 1956:636).

64. *Margin Note*: Eccles. 15.22. Ecclesiasticus 15:22: "A brood of disloyal sons and worthless, how should this be the Lord's desire?" (Knox 1956:600).

65. By 1644 the Acaxee were in fact on the verge of disappearing as a distinct culture.

as well as that of their faithful. During these gatherings they usually celebrate the principal feast day of the saint for whom the pueblo was named. This is done with great solemnity and a large number of priests in attendance, whom everyone enjoys seeing. All of this helps these Indian converts better understand Christian perfection.

To complete the account of this mission and the fruits that the sons of the Company of Jesus have harvested here with the favor of divine grace, I will say that they never had their own permanent residence at the Spaniards' mining camp, because the Indians were the principal ones for whom they were destined by holy obedience. In spite of this, their charity always extended to those who were their brothers by blood and nationality. The Most Holy Apostle Paul was so moved by such affection that he was led to proclaim that highly celebrated verse that has been so studied by the saints: *Optabam ego ipse anathema esse a Christo pro fratribus meis, qui sunt cognati mei secundum carnem.*[66] As long as fondness for one's own flesh and blood is joined with a fondness for the spirit, no contradiction exists between them. This holy Apostle's charitable affection for those of his own blood and nation was never lacking in these religious priests [who cared for] fellow Spaniards,

even though they were busy with the health and religious instruction of these Indians. On all the principal feast days throughout the year and when other needs arose concerning illnesses, etc., the people of the Topia mining camp always found them very close at hand to preach to them, hear their confessions, and resolve their disagreements, differences, and disputes. There are quite a few occasions like this that crop up in mining camps. In the end, in these and many other [508] matters, these missionaries always carried out all the offices of charity. Today they work at the Topia mining camp to the great spiritual benefit of the miners and the people in their service. Although this mining camp is now greatly diminished both in terms of silver and people, there are still some Spaniards there who harbor hopes of great prosperity. We will leave them with these hopes in order to move on to new enterprises. I will first conclude this book, as was my intention, with the life of Father Hernando Santarén and the martyrdom that consumed and crowned it. He was mentioned many times in previous chapters and was founder of this mission. Although his apostolic labors were not concluded here, this is where they had their glorious beginnings.

CHAPTER XVIII The life and martyrdom of Father Hernando de Santarén, founder of the missions of the mountains of Topia

The mission enterprises that I just related in this book are followed in their proper place by an account of the life, glorious labors, and martyrdom of the apostolic minister, Father Hernando de Santarén. He established Christianity in nearly all the nations of the wide mountain range of Topia and in the neighboring mountains. In the second volume of *The Illustrious Men of the Company of Jesus*[67] the very religious Father Eusebio Nieremberg has published an account of the life and joyous death of the venerable Father Santarén. As an eyewitness to his apostolic virtues it is my duty to write about his life and recount the history of his enterprises. I can add that I worked closely and communicated with him when he was my superior in the Province of Sinaloa and Rector of its college and missions. Although his holy labors were many and the circumstances of his holy death while preaching the Holy Gospel were blessed,

---

66. *Margin note*: Roman. 9.3. Romans 9:3: "and how it has ever been my wish that I myself might be doomed to separation from Christ, if that would benefit my brethren, my own kinsmen by race" (Knox 1956:156).

67. The referent here is Juan E. Nieremberg's *Varones illustres de la Compañía de Jesus*, a modern edition of which was published in 1889.

this topic must be left until later. In Book X, which deals with the Tepehuan mission, I will discuss his martyrdom and that of his blessed companions. Here I will discuss Father Hernando de Santarén's holy life, because his principal and most extensive labors were dedicated to the glorious founding of Christianity in the mountains of Topia, about which we have just written.

Father Hernando was born of noble parents in the city of Huete, in the Bishopric of Cuenca. His father, Juan González de Santarén, held a lifetime appointment as a councilor[68] of that City; his mother was Doña María Ortiz de Montalvo. His uncle was Esteban Ortiz, who founded the college of our Company in Huete. Our Hernando was one of the first fruits to be harvested at this very religious college, where he began his studies at a very young age. When he was fifteen years old he was received into the Company. His Novice Master was Father Nicolás de Almazán, and he spent his novitiate at Villarejo de Fuentes. From there he went on to study philosophy at the college in Belmonte. During all his studies, he gave evidence of being a most true son of his religion, chosen by God for a great evangelical mission. On one occasion I heard him say that when he was a young man, busy at his studies, God seemed to fill him with a burning desire to travel and work in the Indies for the salvation of the poor Indians. He never lost this burning desire, [509] and because he was called by divine kindness, he could not wait to realize his goal. Thus he volunteered to his superior to go to the Indies of Nueva España. His [petition] was granted in 1588.

He traveled to the Indies in the company of Father Dr. Pedro de Ortigosa, an individual who honored the Kingdom of Nueva España as much through his holiness as his excellence as a teacher. He was universal master of theology in Nueva España. Brother Hernando studied the first four courses of theology under him in the city of Puebla de los Angeles. However, God called him to do and suffer more in His divine service, filling him with a burning desire to win gentile souls [for heaven]. And so he was sent to the recently founded Sinaloa mission. Although he worked there for only two years, he suffered and endangered his life working with those gentiles, helping to place them on the road to salvation, as is told in Book II of this history. This was not the principal harvest that God had chosen for this illustrious laborer. Shortly after Spaniards had established the two mining camps of Topia and San Andrés, which were in the midst of several gentile

68. *Regidor perpetua.*

nations that populated that great mountain range, they asked the Father Provincial to send some religious to convert such a large number of souls and to minister at the same time to the Catholic Spaniards of that isolated land, which was so difficult to reach and so in need of help. At that time the mining camp at San Andrés still did not have a parish priest of its own. Thus Father Santarén was ordered to leave Sinaloa for this glorious enterprise. He received this order with great pleasure, as though it were sent from heaven.

This history would indeed be very long if I were to narrate the heroic actions of this apostolic man. He endured immense hardships and on innumerable occasions was in danger of losing his life at the hands of infidels. For twenty-three years—until he died, spilling his blood while preaching the Gospel—he persevered with firmness and fervor of spirit. Thus, I will attempt to be brief in summarizing his life as a missionary. In order for my statements to be more clearly understood, one must keep in mind what kind of place and station God had earmarked for this brave soldier of His militia. It is one of the most difficult [regions] to penetrate in all the New World. This is because of the steep mountains, high peaks, inaccessible cliffs, and the depths of its valleys and canyons. As previously mentioned, the trails are extremely dangerous and there are innumerable river crossings in the mission of Topia. Later I will discuss the mission of San Andrés, with its extreme cold and intolerable heat. All these discomforts this apostolic man had to endure in order to gather Christ's lambs that were separated from the flock and scattered. At the beginning of his mission, when he was alone and the people needed [additional] ministers, his burning fervor extended to all the places where he could help souls. It seemed incredible that a human being whose body was so fragile could endure so many hardships. At the Lenten season, especially during those first years, it is said that he walked five hundred leagues. At the mining camp of San Andrés, he preached [510] three sermons on Sundays to the Spaniards, to their slaves and servants in the mines, and to the Indian laborers who spoke the Mexican language. The priest had learned this language when he studied in Mexico City. Because he was preparing himself for the holy ministry to which God called him, he made sure from the outset that he became an apt instrument for sowing the divine word.

The same day he preached these three sermons, he would set out from San Andrés for the Spanish Villa de San Miguel de Culiacán, thirty leagues away. At times he traveled by foot over cliffs that dropped more than one thousand estados. He preached on Wednesdays in this villa and then—without stopping to rest—he would depart to preach and hear confessions at the mining camp at Topia, another thirty leagues away. He made some three hundred or more crossings of that gorge, each hour offering himself to Our Lord, for whose love he exposed himself to such dangers. On Fridays he preached as many sermons in the mining camp of Topia as he had at San Andrés. The following week he would leave and begin the same cycle.

This was the beginning of his early mission [in the mountains], where he aided Spaniards and people of other Christian nations. The glorious works of this evangelical minister were innumerable with respect to the gentiles who were converted in the areas surrounding [the mining centers]. Father Santarén established, increased, and maintained Christianity among the Acaxee, Xixime, and other nations throughout the mountains of Topia and San Andrés. These were fields and peoples that were so spread out that, even though he had only begun to cultivate them, the later harvest was [enough] to keep fourteen missionaries busy. It is not easy to summarize with a pen the heroic works that this zealous and holy missionary undertook and achieved, the almost invincible dangers and difficulties that he overcame, and the most abundant fruits that he harvested.

He erected more than forty churches, some of them in practically inaccessible places. Some were on mountain peaks and cliffs, others were in areas where heat and swarms of mosquitoes were a terrible affliction. So as not to upset the people who had grown up in these places, he was happy to suffer with them. I can certify as an eyewitness that I was amazed when I traveled through this land and saw in the distance the churches. On the one hand, I was moved by the sight of the Cross of Christ Our Lord and [the fact that] his Gospel had penetrated such places, as evident by the churches that had been erected. And although some churches eventually were relocated, more than a few churches that were erected by Father Hernando de Santarén endured. The [number of] souls of infants and adults that he baptized is about fifty thousand, the majority of whom were resettled and converted to the Faith. He destroyed innumerable idols and superstitions, replacing them with the Cross of Christ.

I have previously written a little about the dangers that he faced from uprisings and rebellions. However, it is impossible to count all the [dangers] that he endured over so many years, in so many settlements, and

during so many expeditions for which he was always the first to volunteer. [He did this] with such unusual fervor and joy—even at times of great danger—that he stimulated others to volunteer. One could add to this list of dangers the great risk he ran of being dashed to bits in the very deep gorges or drowned during the innumerable fordings of the swollen rivers that he had to cross to visit and collect four or five gentile Indians who remained [511] ensconced in the cliffs and far from the flock. One could add as well the times that he went with the Holy Sacrament to aid some sick person in any number of settlements that he had under his care. [He did all this] with untiring perseverance and fervor, while enduring discomfort and hunger in that land among such poor people. Many times it was necessary for him to get along on squash and boiled or toasted maize that had been ground into flour. The latter served as his usual food while traveling.

In confirmation of this I will insert here a portion of a letter written after Father Santarén's death by Father Andrés Tutino, superior of the mission of San Andrés, concerning Father Santarén. It reads as follows:

> Our Lord led Father Hernando de Santarén, through a special inner movement, down the road where he met the joyous martyrdom that was to crown his many productive years. I do not know that there is anyone in these missions who has suffered as he has, nor whether there is a person of more courage or years who could endure the suffering of that poor priest, who was so worn out health-wise. When he was gravely ill, I went to see him in a district of the Xixime. The pueblo was very difficult to reach, on such steep slopes and surrounded by such fearful gorges and cliffs that I said that, if I should die in that place and leave a will, I would add a clause concerning my burial in which I would request that, even though I were dead, I be removed from that place because it seemed to me to be hell in terms of its harshness and human discomforts. But Father Hernando de Santarén was as happy there as if he were in Madrid or Toledo. Indeed, he used to say that this place was his Mexico City and [had all] its delights.

These are the words of Father Tutino. I can confirm that Father Santarén was not a man who was frightened by difficult trails. Indeed, the trails he traveled to and from his pueblos and district crossed the roughest and steepest mountains; everyone who traveled them was astounded at where the fervent Father Hernando de Santarén lived. The above is sufficient indication of the difficulties that this subject of God endured because of his divine love for Him and his fellow man. I will now narrate the talents with which he was endowed by divine kindness, and the virtues that he acquired and enhanced, aided by divine favor.

God Our Lord conferred upon Father Hernando from his earliest years a pleasant and pacific disposition and manner, which captivated those who dealt with him. Later [in his life] this disposition enabled him to fulfill his desire to aid his fellow man. Even during the ocean crossing to Nueva España, he was so smitten by the desire to save souls and send them to heaven that he did not wait to see the Indians. He began to talk about salvation with captains, soldiers, sailors, and passengers, and even the cabin boys, who were the scum of [the ship]. He persuaded them in conversation and through Christian doctrine to reform their habits, avoid their vices, and receive the Holy Sacraments. He did this so charmingly that he managed to win the affection of everyone. He humbly served everyone as best he could in whatever task. But his amiable manner harvested its greatest fruits during many years in the missions and mining camps, where there are usually many quarrels, conflicts, and arguments about mining claims and mineral ores. The lust for silver was always a seedbed of dissent and conflict. [512] However, Father Hernando de Santarén won them all over with his happy and joyful disposition and his willingness to help everyone save their souls. They [often] sought him out to settle disputes and conflicts. Everyone yielded to him and was pleased that he could settle matters. This is what [happened] with the Spaniards.

Although the Indians were poor, wretched gentiles, he went to extremes to attend to them and win them for God. I once witnessed an occasion when the priest was returning from a long journey and an old and unfortunate Indian came to meet him along the way. He first embraced the poor and unfortunate Indian, warmly placing his venerable cheek against the old man's face. A loving father could do no more if he were finally seeing his own beloved son after many years. Then he asked him about his people and their health, telling him how happy he was to be able to come see them after being absent for days. This was the tone that he used when he visited the sick, no matter how repugnant they were. This loving and affable manner was not limited to mere words and gestures. Rather, it extended to works of charity, for he gave the Indians whatever he had. One time he even gave a needy person the shirt off his back. The priests who were his comrades in the missions affirmed that if he had wanted to do so, he could have saved for himself and his own people a substantial amount of money that he was offered by wealthy miners and other Spaniards who loved him. However, he never spent the money on himself, but instead distributed it

as alms to the poor. This money, which amounted to more than forty thousand pesos or reales de ocho, included money from Spaniards and the stipend that the king gave each year for the support of ministers.[69] He satisfied himself with a worn habit. His food was often squash, beans, and maize, which were cooked in unsalted water, as was mentioned. When some of Father Santarén's comrades noted how happy he was at times with such poor and unusual food, they jokingly said to him: "Father, who could eat that [stuff]?" And he replied with the joy that he always displayed on his face: "Won't you have some? We've always got plenty of it." Actually he was very happy to eat this poor and unusual food, whether on the trail or in the [Indian] settlements. This servant of God was not satisfied with what really was the continual penance of such a life. He added to it a harsh, nail-studded belt, which he often wore. He was no less severe in his scourging. As if that were not enough, [he thought] it best to receive the scourging at the hands of others who would show him no pity, lest he feel sorry for himself. Once, on the trail, he went into the thicket and ordered the Indians to tie him to a tree. He bared his shoulders and ordered them to whip him as they liked, without showing him pity. These events were witnessed by two Spaniards, Captain Gerónimo de los Reyes and Lieutenant Encinas. Both were astounded by this, and rightly so. This is not ordinarily to be imitated, because it does not enhance a minister's authority nor the Indians' limited capacity. This is particularly true when they are so new to the Faith, have not yet formed a concept of humility and Christian penance, and are [still] cruel by nature. Indeed, ministers must maintain authority. The actions of Father Santarén in this case were an exception because they were born of the impetus of the spirit and he was moved by God. Rather than lose respect for him, the barbarous Indians loved him because of this and many other acts of [513] humility.

In this life of penance he kept good company with God through regular conversation, that is, through the holy exercise of apostolic prayer, which he practiced while he was traveling and while ministering to these peoples in their pueblos. He was very attentive—as prescribed by the Company—to the hour of prayer at dawn and in the evening. He extended this practice while crossing deserts and on many trails, enjoying many tender tears of affection for Christ. Once I heard him say

69. Santarén's liberality with his stipend actually raised concerns with Jesuit superiors (Decorme 1941:2:93).

(because he was humble, honest, and of the most sincere spirit, he was very far from hypocrisy) that one time on a desert trail the mules got away from him. He stopped along the road (as often happens where there are no inns or places to rest) and sent the boy who accompanied him to look for the mules. The priest was alone for a day and a night, which he spent in continual praise of God. He consoled himself that it was one of the best times in his life—there alone and defenseless in the desert.

Although he mentioned only this one occasion, there must have been many similar ones during so very many years of travel. For there were [many] nights that he spent on the trail in the wilderness, and still others when his way was blocked by rivers and snowfall or when he did not know which trail to take. There were other times as well when he endured the heat and sun, hiking through deep valleys. On these occasions his countenance demonstrated the consolation that Our Lord communicated to him, because no one ever saw him sad, only happy. He demonstrated this joy that sprang from his soul to Spaniards in the mining camps and to the soldiers who escorted him during times of danger, while on expeditions to pacify rebel nations. He [displayed this joy] to the mule drivers and travelers whom he met. He always seemed to enjoy the variable climate, adjusting to it without becoming annoyed, like Saint Paul and also our father and missionary guide, Saint Francis Xavier, whom he strove to imitate.

The outstanding elements of Father Santarén's temperament were revealed in his sermons as well as his daily dealings with his fellow man. Through them God gave him grace to set ablaze the hearts of others. Those who saw him were struck by the way he moved his listeners to tears, no matter how hardened they were. He was aided in this by the pleasantly resonant voice that God had given him. When added to the ardor of his spirit, it swept away the listeners' attention. He was also aided by his physical appearance, size, height, and face. He was one of the most handsomely proportioned men in the kingdom. His composure was that of serious modesty, yet his gestures were [always] pleasant. When he preached, all the people of the pueblos [were able to] understand him; his sermons wrought many outstanding changes and improvements in the lives and hearts of sinners and people who had fallen away [from God]. His sermons usually focused on the gravity of sin, the sorry condition of the sinner, and the harm that sins caused. He emphasized the importance of availing ourselves right now of God's mercy. He quoted Scripture and the saints with great ease and affection. He

continually meditated on them while on the trail, and even more so while praying, whence he obtained marvelous fruits. He used to say humorously that when Spaniards asked him to preach, he would prepare his sermon [514] from topics he had [written down] on slips of paper that he kept under the table, which read, "Choose me, Choose me." This holy preacher considered prayers and meditation on the Holy Scriptures to be relief and entertainment while on the trail.

In the midst of all these ministries and dealings with people of such diverse backgrounds and callings as are to be found in settlements where the most reverend father traveled, he was very dedicated to keeping his heart, soul, and body free of any stain. This was particularly true with regard to matters of purity. Indeed, he was horrified by this sin ever since his very earliest years. It was common knowledge that he lived and died a virgin. The reports that were made after his martyrdom include testimony from a Spaniard who had invited Father Santarén to lodge at his home in the mining camp, where we had no house of our own. The Spaniard affirmed that over the course of twenty years, whenever the priest stayed at his house, the priest never looked his maiden daughter in the face. He would not even tolerate a single word or gesture that hinted of the slightest offense against purity. Rather, his exemplary behavior and fragrance of purity won people over to a chaste life.

If I were to write in detail about the examples of the other virtues of obedience, poverty, and humility that shone in this evangelical missionary, it would be a very long story indeed. He was, however, dominated by and practiced extreme and (heroic) virtues, which were born of an untiring zeal to gain souls for Christ and spread His most holy name to blind people. His spirit was invincible and intrepid with regard to this highest objective because he was confident that he had been marked and chosen by Our Lord. Thus, he had no fear of death. In the midst of constant danger to his life, which he risked among infidels and perverted Christians, as evident in the uprisings and disturbances of nations, he never tried to abandon those he had engendered in Christ nor their churches. On the contrary, he was resolved to die a thousand deaths rather than leave them exposed to wolves and infernal enemies.

He was in no lesser danger during epidemics. He ignored contamination and death to care for those who were sick in body and soul, attending to them and healing them himself. He often bled them with his own hands when he felt that was necessary and there was no one else who could do it. He had learned how to do this for just such occasions, in such remote lands, destitute of remedies. Finally, he helped the dying obtain a holy death. The greatest difficulty and adversity seemed to invigorate and uplift his spirit. When some [of the Indians] begged him to flee from these dangers, he chided them—with his usual constant smile—for what he considered to be their excessive fear, telling them to trust in God. Because I have just written about this subject in [those chapters on] the missions of Topia and San Andrés, where the blessed priest carried out most of his work, I will not say anything more. Rather I will close this account with a letter of Father Santarén's that was written in the last years of his life [in June of 1613]. The letter was addressed to the Father Provincial who, being a charitable and compassionate father, had invited Father Hernando de Santarén, for his own solace, to take a rest from such prolific labors at the college in Mexico. [Father Santarén] answered him with the clarity and directness that he owed his superior, whom he sought to serve in the place of Christ Our Lord. His reply will confirm what I have previously narrated. [The letter] reads as follows:

> Although I feel old and tired, I do not want [515] the health of the souls in these missions to suffer because of my absence, nor will I ask to leave them. However, I will not close the door on holy obedience [and the right] to dispose of my person as though it were a corpse. It would be terrible if, after nineteen years [in this] mission with its [many] difficulties, I had not acquired the stoicism that our father Saint Ignatius requests of us. Although now I may have less talent [for that] at least I can offer myself once again: *Ecce ego non recuso laborem, fiat voluntas Domini.*[70] In Mexico City I will not feel the joy and contentment that Our Lord communicates when He is served by those who work in missions. Rather, the Lord sometimes confers more to those who travel in solitude around a bend of the trail—to find themselves at the foot of mountain, in the midst of a snowstorm, caught out in the open on a dark night, or in a rainstorm without shelter—than in long hours of prayer and retreat. The consolation that the Lord grants me in the midst of these difficulties is very great. Moreover, it seems to me that to leave the Indians is to turn one's back on God and to leave Christ Our Lord alone, with His Cross on His back. The thought that His Divine Majesty will confront me with this causes me not to ask to leave here. *In hoc positus sum.*[71] I will consider myself fortunate when death reaches me here, as I will esteem dying alone on the battlefield with my weapons in the midst of these barbarians as [much as] dying surrounded by my fathers and brothers. I will have the protection of Our Lord, for whom this solitude is endured.

70. "Behold, I do not object to any labor, if the Lord's will may be done."

71. "Here is my place."

I write at a time when I am very tired, for I have not sat down for even a little while during three days. Because there is no one else to do so, I have been bleeding the sick with my own hands. I have baptized and instructed more than seventy people who are currently receiving and keeping the Faith, and they constantly call me. May the Lord Our God grant health to these poor people and heaven to those who die; may He grant Your Reverence many workers for His vineyard; and may He grant me His courage to obey like a true son of the Company of JESUS. God keep Your Reverence.

This is the letter of this staunch soldier of the Company and the Militia of JESUS, who wished to die in battle in the service of its Divine Captain. His Majesty granted him this wish when his superior called on him to undertake a new entrada to instruct a nation in the Province of Sinaloa that was considered ready for conversion. As we will discuss in the following book, he left the Xixime, whom he was instructing, and set out for a meeting with the governor of Nueva Vizcaya. He passed through Durango and the lands and pueblos of the apostate Tepehuan. When he approached the pueblo of Tenerapa he fell into the hands of the rebels, who killed him, as will be told in detail. He welcomed [this death] as though it came from the hand of God. Many times he was heard to say that he would consider himself deprived and unfortunate if he should die in bed, dreaming, rather than bleeding like those who entered heaven by spilling their blood for Christ. His Majesty granted him this joyous death. When the Indians knocked him off the mule he was riding, in order to kill him more easily and with greater cruelty, he asked them, "My sons, why do you kill me? I have helped you in every way possible. How have I wronged you?" He could truly say this because he was well known among them. His district bordered theirs, and he had done them many good deeds and was beloved by all those nations. The apostate Indians replied, "We are not killing you because you have done us wrong, but because you are a priest." When he saw that he was to die for such a glorious cause, he joyfully responded, [516] "If that is the reason, now is the time." They struck such a blow to the blessed priest with a club that his head broke open. They then beat him with many clubs, [causing] other wounds from which he expired, invoking the sweetest name of JESUS. He died on November 20, 1616.

With this glorious closure the apostolic man, Father Hernando de Santarén, ended his life at age forty-nine. He was chosen by God at the age of fifteen for these glorious enterprises. He had spent thirty-four years in the Company; twelve of these years followed his profession of the four vows. He worked for thirty-three years in the missions, governing them as superior for fourteen years. He learned several languages spoken by the barbarous nations among whom he continually lived. He also lived among fellow Spaniards, who loved him dearly. He resided among them, however, only when they needed the help of his ministries. Both Indians and Spaniards considered him a man of great holiness who had lived a pure life. There is abundant evidence that he obtained the very resplendent crown of a martyr with many degrees of glory.

The death of this blessed man was greatly regretted even by the barbarous women who were the wives of the Tepehuan murderers. He was mourned even more throughout the Kingdom of Nueva Vizcaya, where these missions were and where his name and his memory were very famous. Today, his devout [followers] invoke his name in their hour of need. Captain Diego Dávila, who is well known in the kingdom, made a sworn declaration before an ecclesiastical judge[72] that he had been miraculously saved by God as a result of the

intercession of Father Santarén. The captain entrusted himself to him during two or three life-threatening situations. It also seemed that this priest, once in heaven, favored and protected the Xixime Indians whom he was instructing when he died. The holy doctrine that he had imparted to them was so well established that they remained firm in the Faith even though the apostate Tepehuan begged and induced them with promises and threats to abandon the Faith. They persevered then and are exemplary Christians today.

The city of Huete, birthplace of our blessed father, petitioned the Father General to send them the remains of his body. However, very few remains were found where he died. Among them, a bone was taken in 1631 to the college in Huete by Father Gerónimo Díaz, who was Procurator to Rome for the Province of Nueva España. Later, when I write of the history of the [Tepehuan] mission and uprising, I will discuss more of the circumstances of the joyous death of Father Hernando de Santarén.

CHAPTER XIX The very religious virtues and martyrdom of Father Hernando de Tovar, of the Company of JESUS

The blessed Father Hernando de Santarén, of whom we have just been speaking, was accompanied in his joyous death by another brother in his profession and religion from the Company. His name was Father Hernando de Tovar, and he also died at the hands of the apostate Tepehuan. Although he did not die in the same place as Father Santarén, he died for the same reason—because he was an evangelical minister. Father Tovar was coming down from the Sierra de Topia, of which we have spoken,

out of holy obedience, and was [also] headed for the city of Durango. These are all reasons why it is necessary to record here together these two holy lives and joyous deaths. Some of the specific circumstances are left for a later time, as are the deaths that six of their brothers [517] suffered for ministering the doctrine of our Holy Faith among the Tepehuan. When these Indians rebelled against God and His Holy Law, and against the Catholic king under whose protection they had been placed, their first diabolical attack of fury was unleashed on the highly religious Father Hernando de Tovar (as will be later told in greater detail). Here will be recorded the life of this most holy religious, who also was called by God to the labor of evangelical missions that is the focus of this history.

This blessed man was born in the noble Villa de

San Miguel de Culiacán, which is one of the oldest in the Kingdom of Nueva España and which borders on Sinaloa. He was the only child of very noble parents, Don Luis de los Ríos Proaño, who was very well known because of his nobility, and Doña Isabel de Guzmán y Tovar, daughter of Don Pedro de Tovar,[73] nephew of Don Antonio de Mendoza, the first viceroy of Nueva España. He was the grandson of Don Sancho de Tovar, lord of Villa Martín, and Doña Elvira de Rojas y Sandoval, sister of the cardinal duke of Lerma. Father Hernando enhanced this illustrious bloodline by dedicating himself to God and the life of a religious. In the end he consecrated his life to Christ Our Lord, spilling his blood for no other cause than to be a minister and priest of Christ. This noble youth did not value the prospect of worldly importance, and he renounced positions to which he could easily have succeeded because of his lineage. Because he was their only child, his parents reared him with all measure of blessings and comforts. They sent him to Mexico City to study, where he learned grammar. Then at age seventeen he requested to be received into the Company, which he entered in 1598. It was as if he had been called by a unique light and realization of truth sent from heaven. From the time of his novitiate he completely gave himself over to God and to the virtues of a religious. These virtues took such a strong hold in his angelic character that he earned the nickname of 'Angel', which is what everyone called him. He was meticulous in [exercising] the virtues of humility and obedience as well as all the other virtues of a religious. [And yet] he considered himself the least of all those in the house of God.

He left the novitiate and continued his studies in philosophy and theology. Because of his great genius, he made tremendous progress. He had also received great God-given talents as a preacher, speaking gracefully from the pulpit to Spaniards. He won them over to God with such energy and elegance that they listened to him gladly. These talents shone very brightly in this holy youth. Indeed, shortly before he was martyred, a layperson who knew him but not his holy intentions—which are so foreign to what is sought after in this world—came to him and said, "Now, Your Reverence, you will get a miter,[74] because you are such a

close relative of the duke of Lerma, who can give and take [as he pleases]." This humble religious, who was extremely observant (as he always was) of the rules of his order, smiled and said, "Sir, I value teaching these poor little Indians the way to heaven more highly than all the world's grandeur."[75]

As a religious, he never emitted any scent of vanity or conceit concerning his talents, his [noble] bloodline, or family; nor did he ever mention these things in conversation. His silence and modesty in these matters nevertheless inspired outsiders as well as those within the [Jesuit] residence who knew about his attributes, talents, and great virtue. He was considered a most outstanding example of and benefit to [fellow] religious. When those of more importance spoke of him, they said, "Father Hernando, what a great man!" His manner was that of a highly spiritual religious. He regularly talked with God through his holy practice [518] of prayer as well as through mortification and penance, which provides prayer with admirable and safe company. The loving devotion, tears, and sighs that sometimes escaped him—no matter how hard he tried to suppress them—manifested the special favors and gifts that he received from Our Lord through this exercise. He possessed great and tender devotion for the saints, particularly for the Most Holy Virgin. He celebrated this devotion by daily reciting her office, Rosary, and litanies. He also fasted and carried out other singular acts of penance in preparation for her feast days. He attempted to imitate her in her angelic purity of body and mind. These shone in him in such a way that those who dealt with him called him 'Angel'. He tried to maintain this purity through prudence and circumspection in his behavior so that there would not be the slightest stain in this respect. The fragrance of this purity bore witness to the fact that he died a virgin, as those who knew and dealt with him believed to be true.

Father Hernando's virtues and talents made him a very apt candidate for the colleges and the Company's ministries therein. However, great virtue and learning are no less necessary for the apostolic endeavors of the missions, where one lives outside the religious community. In addition, God called Father Hernando to help the poor Indians. Thus, the superiors were obliged to send him to this ministry. God was acting through them and leading Father Hernando to the martyrdom that he had glimpsed at a very young age, as we will later see.

---

73. The names Proaño, Guzmán, and Tovar belong to some of the first Spanish explorers and colonists of Nueva Galicia; Diego de Proaño, for instance, served until 1533 as the first alcalde mayor of San Miguel de Culiacán; Don Pedro de Tovar was an officer on the Coronado expedition.

74. A headdress worn by bishops and abbots.

75. Tovar's respect for the Indians was such that he became a vocal advocate of training Indians for the priesthood.

He spent some time in the mission at Parras, which will later be recorded, and there he suffered the same hardships that are experienced in all these missions. He assisted in the instruction and salvation of the Indians, and the same pleasantness and affability that he showed in all his occupations and positions shone in these as well. [While he was working in the mission of Parras] his mother, who had become a religious, endeavored to have her son nearby. After she had been widowed and had offered her only son to God she decided to offer herself to Him as well. She traveled three hundred leagues from Culiacán to Mexico City and withdrew into the Convent of San Lorenzo. In the company of a young maiden who was her niece and whom she had raised, she took the vows of a religious, and there the two of them led holy lives. They did not die until after their son and cousin had been martyred. Before her son died this woman lovingly pleaded with the Father Provincial to bring him from Parras to Mexico City for her consolation. There he could also serve Our Lord and the Company. Father Hernando, however, had already spoken with the superiors, asking and begging them to govern him for the greater glory of God, to whom he had dedicated himself, without the interference of laypeople or anyone associated with him. However, because this saintly matron's home in Culiacán had been the refuge of all the missionary priests of Sinaloa and Topia, and because she now lived as a great example of holiness, the Father Provincial, to console her, decided that it was advantageous and proper to grant her extremely pious request. At the same time he assured her son that he was not being removed from his post simply because of his family's insistence. Rather, he also had another position for him in Mexico City that it would be beneficial for him to fill at that time.

In the meantime the Father Rector of Durango had sent Father Hernando to the Topia mining camp to carry out an act of piety. It was on his return that the hour of his joyous death arrived, in the pueblo of Santa Catalina. This pueblo was inhabited by some of the most bellicose and insolent Tepehuan Indians. Their first attacks and cruelties were inflicted on this blessed priest. They were incited and moved by a [519] bedeviled idol that caused this nation to rebel, forcefully speaking and persuading the Tepehuan first to kill all the priests who preached and taught them the Holy Faith of the Christians. The first one they came across was Father Hernando; he received the first blows of apostasy and cruelty. They shot him with arrows and wounded him with a spear. It was from the latter that he finally fell, with great serenity of spirit, raising his heart to heaven. He was traveling with a Spanish muleteer, and when the latter realized how furious the barbarians were, he mounted his horse and escaped, yelling at Father Hernando to do the same. When this holy priest saw that the enemies of Christ were upon him, he answered very resolutely, "Now is not the time for that. Rather, it is time to welcome death in the holy name of the Lord who sends it upon us." Then the apostates executed this death under circumstances that will later be recorded. They are omitted here in order to avoid repetition, but one cannot omit those circumstances that proclaim the depraved and infidel spirit in which they took his life, nor the reason why the priest accepted his death so peacefully, particularly when he saw that they were killing him out of a hatred and loathing for Christ's ministers and those who taught His holy law. Father Hernando was the one at whom they hurled their apostate insults and as they were killing him, they said, "These priests think there is nothing more than teaching [us] 'Our Father Who Art in Heaven,' 'Ave Maria,' etc. Let's see how this holy man's God resurrects him."

It was in the midst of these blasphemies, which we can say made his martyrdom more illustrious, that the blessed Father Hernando de Tovar was killed. Now I will recount how from his earliest years this blessed soul was informed by God that he would pass on to glory with the martyr's crown. When Hernando was very young, Father Gonzalo de Tapia was martyred in Sinaloa, which neighbored and bordered on Culiacán, where this child was born and lived. The martyrdom of this outstanding man has already been discussed at length. Father Martín Peláez, who had gone to the Province of Sinaloa as Father Visitor, was returning to Mexico City with the head of the holy man. En route he stopped at the Villa de San Miguel de Culiacán, where he was a guest in the house of Doña Isabel de Tovar, for the Company had no house of its own there. This lady knew that Father Peláez was carrying what she considered to be a precious relic and she wanted to see it. In order to show this skull devotion and greater reverence, she wanted to accommodate it in the richest coffer that she had for her jewels. However, when the time came to place the skull in the coffer, it turned out to be too small. At this point the little boy Hernando, who was watching, said something that stuck with his mother forever: "This coffer is much too small for the head of such a great saint as Father Tapia. Save it for my head, for I am destined to die a martyr."

The little boy's comment became widely celebrated,

even more so after he had been martyred. Following the holy death of her son, I heard his holy mother say that, although she regretted it with the tenderness that a mother feels for her only son, she considered the death, which had first been announced during his very early years, a blessed sacrifice for the glory of Christ. In a very flattering letter our Father General Mutius Vitelleschi consoled this woman as someone who was the mother of a martyr and a son whom she had very willingly offered for the religious life, and whom she had now seen sacrificed for Christ.

I will now add some outstanding testimony of this martyr's glory as well as the martyrdom suffered by his holy companions, which will be relevant later when we record their lives. The priest [520] and Doctor Pedro de Ortigosa was a person of great authority and devotion in our Company. For many years he taught the university course on advanced theology[76] in Mexico City. Father Hernando de Tovar always respected and acknowledged him very much like his own father. Doctor Ortigosa had been [Tovar's] professor of theology, and he valued this disciple with special affection because in him he saw such beautiful character and virtue. Once the news that eight priests had been killed at the hands of Tepehuan apostates reached Mexico City, a tiny, shiny little cloud appeared to Father Pedro de Ortigosa in his dreams. In this cloud there were some doves, but he could not count how many. They flew toward him from the west, which is the direction in which the priests died, relative to Mexico City. The priest had a burning desire for them to sit in his hand, and they immediately came and lit upon his arms. They were very tame and they pleased him with their words, saying, "Praise be to the Lord of all." After they had been with him for some time, bringing him great consolation, the one who was directly in front of him showed his very beautiful face, which he recognized as that of Father Hernando de Tovar. This dove drew close, as if he were going to give the priest the sign of peace, and then they all flew off, leaving him very happy and devout.

Father Ortigosa was firmly persuaded that this had been the representation of the eight martyred priests' souls, even though he had only recognized the first of them to die, Father Hernando de Tovar. This vision was confirmed *in verbo Sacerdotis*[77] by a person of great authority, namely Father Pedro de Ortigosa. And a no lesser vision was recounted and affirmed by Father Francisco de Arista, superior of the mission at Parras, where Father Hernando had worked. He appeared to Father Francisco de Arista in his dreams. At first he had the face of a dead man, which concerned and frightened Father Arista. He wanted to know about the condition of Father Hernando's soul, so he asked him, "What is this, Father Hernando? Where are you?" The blessed priest's appearance suddenly changed and he now appeared happy. Glowing, he said, "I am in heaven, Father Francisco de Arista, where I have everything." The vision that had appeared to him disappeared, leaving the priest greatly consoled.

The vision a priest of Italian nationality[78] had was somewhat different but of no lesser consolation. The priest had heard of blessed Father Tovar's beautiful virtues from the accounts [of Father Tovar's life] sent to our Father General in Rome. He became extremely fond of Father Tovar and was so moved from within that it was as if he had seen him in a vision from heaven. He made a request to come to the Indies, which was granted, and he was a most exemplary laborer in these holy missions. It has been observed in our Province of Nueva España (and the same can rightfully be said of the others) that Our Lord has favored our missionaries with special providence. He has called and chosen for these provinces men of great religion and sanctity, men like our blessed Father Hernando de Tovar. He died at the age of thirty-five, having professed the four vows. He spent eighteen years in the Company; these will be followed for all eternity by the crown of glory that we firmly believe on such strong evidence he is now enjoying in heaven. [521]

---

76. *Prima.*

77. "in the words of a priest"
78. The identity of this priest is unknown.

BOOK IX

The Mission of San Andrés and Its Nations

CHAPTER I The location of the mission of San Andrés and its pueblos and people. The establishment of its Christianity by the venerable Father Alonso Ruiz; the hardships he suffered and his joyous death

This mission took its name from a Spanish settlement in the most interior part of the mountains of Topia. The Spaniards had heard of the great wealth of silver deposits there, and so they went to locate and work them. They set up grinding mills and established a mining camp named for San Andrés.[1] It is customary for Spaniards, out of devotion, to name the settlements that they found after their favorite saints or their homeland, prefacing the name with 'New', as did the first Spaniards who populated Mexico. They undoubtedly did so with the approval of the glorious Spanish monarchs, who wanted that first kingdom of this [new] world to be called Nueva España. The pueblos of the region took to calling themselves the mission of San Andrés, after the mining camp of San Andrés. Even though the members of the Company have not had their own house at this mining camp, just as they have not had one at Topia (as has

been stated), these religious nevertheless have attended to both mining centers with all possible charitable services, paying no mind to the great hardships that they have endured in the process. These mining camps are usually located in the roughest part of the sierra, in very deep canyons, like those one has to cross in order to reach the mining camp of San Andrés, where they have extracted and worked [522] very high-grade ores. Although the mines to this day produce ore, it is not as abundant nor as rich [as previously]. Perhaps someday when it serves His Majesty, God will revive these mines for these individuals, as He has done with many other rich silver mines.

Until I discuss the Xixime, who later came to join the Acaxee, it will not be necessary to comment further about the rancherías, pueblos, and customs of the Indians of this mission. The people in the pueblos of San Andrés are similar in all respects to the people in Topia and speak the same Acaxee language. In [discussing] the establishment of this mission center, we cannot omit the glory of its founder, the aforementioned Father Hernando de Santarén, who founded other mis-

---

1. The mines of San Andrés were opened a short time after those of Topia and were being worked when the Jesuits arrived on the scene in 1598.

sions in this sierra. It has been recorded how he made many journeys, visiting the mining camp of San Andrés when they had neither their own parish nor a priest; how he preached many sermons to all kinds of people who gathered there from nearby rancherías: Spaniards, Indians, and black slaves. Although this is all true, it was Father Alonso Ruiz, who was Father Hernando de Santarén's first companion,[2] who succeeded Father Santarén and established a mission among the local Indians. He was an individual of excellent virtue and religion, worthy of being remembered in this history. His memory left a long-lasting impression upon even the rocks of these mountains (shall we say), as well as upon the Indians, and even more so, on the miners at San Andrés. He was the one who saved them during the previously recorded uprising and rebellion, when the Indians laid siege to the church where the Spaniards had fortified themselves. Father Alonso Ruiz was the one who urged and encouraged the Spaniards, staying with them until they were freed. He was the first one to go out to face the barbarians with a crucifix in hand, reprimanding them for their ferocity.

When Father Santarén became busy with the great harvest of Indians around Topia, he put Father Alonso Ruiz in charge of the people in the area around the mining camp of San Andrés. This saintly man suffered and endured immense hardships during these early days of instruction and education. During his quest for the welfare and salvation of these poor blind souls he endured very rough trails as well as hunger, exhaustion, and danger to his [own] life. God miraculously saved him during the aforementioned Acaxee Rebellion and uprising, because the people and rancherías of San Andrés were the most rebellious. Father Alonso Ruiz was the first person they attempted to kill, as they had agreed upon in their councils. This was not because he had ever given them the least little reason to do so, for he was like a loving father to them. Rather, it was because, as usual, the devil and his sorcerer familiars presided over these meetings. Both the devil and the sorcerers always target the Gospel ministers first, because it is they who wage war against them.

The Indians and the devil would have achieved their goal on this occasion if Our Lord had not prevented the attack with His singular providence. As it happened, there was a faithful Indian whom the priest had baptized who had given his son to the priest to rear in virtue. He got word of the rebels' perverse intentions

and sent his son with a message to the priest, warning him that if he did not protect himself, it might be the last night of his life. To avoid such great impending danger, the priest set out immediately, almost at nightfall, to warn the Spaniards at the San Andrés mining camp. The rebels [in the meantime] had divided into two squadrons, agreeing that one would go to the pueblo called San Miguel, where [523] they would kill the priest. The others were to guard the routes leading to San Andrés so that nobody could get through to warn the Spaniards at the mining camp, for they wanted to take them by surprise and finish them off. Due to the warning he received from the faithful Indian, Father Ruiz was not caught and killed in the pueblo. He still could have fallen into the hands of the second squad of Indians and their spies. God Our Lord, however, prevented this by a singular [act of] providence. Without the priest even noticing or realizing it the mule he was riding went off the main path and took another narrow trail through the crags, which took him to the San Andrés mining camp, where he arrived around midnight.

At the first mining hacienda, which belonged to a Spaniard named Martín de Gastelú, he warned the Spaniards of the danger they were in. Gastelú then gathered up his belongings and his servants, who usually are numerous in these mining haciendas, and they all went immediately to the church, where everybody was saved by Our Lord's singular providence. Thus, the intentions of both enemy squadrons were thwarted. They were so outraged that the priest had escaped that the following day they went to his humble little house, which in the early days (as I said before) was usually made of sticks and straw. They set fire to Father Ruiz's house, which contained his meager personal belongings, and also burned the church to the ground. From there they proceeded to lay siege to the mining camp, as was recorded earlier.

At this point I wish to note the hardships, exhaustion, and life-threatening dangers that the most holy Father Alonso Ruiz endured in order to establish Christianity in this mission at San Andrés, which I have [just] begun to discuss and where the good priest's holy deeds were successful (even in the midst of disturbances and confrontations). During all these times he instructed and baptized thousands of souls, the number of which increased over time. He founded six or seven of the major pueblos in this mission [district]— San Gregorio, San Pedro, Coapa, Tecaya, and others. Once the uprising was quelled, they were joined by

2. Ruiz joined Santarén in 1600.

other pueblos, which were entrusted to our missionary priests in Topia by the aforementioned Prelate, Don Alonso de la Mota y Escobar.[3] These were the pueblos of Las Vegas, Llexupa, Chacala, and others, which some clerics had previously taken charge of but which over time had been abandoned. This very zealous Prelate and shepherd [Mota y Escobar] always tended to the well-being of the poor Indians; with special affection he looked after these sheep who had strayed so far. Thus, he placed them under the care of the shepherds of the Company, whom he observed to be so highly dedicated to these holy ministries.

The first person to take charge of these pueblos was Father Alonso Ruiz. God willed to take him to heaven just a few years after he had established this mission. He died in the very same place where he had worked so hard because of his love for and desire to help these poor souls. I will record here his joyous death, which came to him as he was giving religious instruction. In doing so, it can be said that it was the many hardships that he endured that finished him off. Both these and his death deserve to be remembered here because they will serve as edification for his brothers and the sons of the Company of Jesus, to whom (as I have stated) this history is addressed.

In order to help his dear and faithful [524] Christians, this servant of God did not avoid traveling, no matter how far or rough the trails. Nor did he concern himself with the sun and excessive heat. He attended to everyone at all hours, seeking to heal souls—all the while he ignored his own bodily well-being. This caused considerable harm to his health and so ravaged him that he became seriously ill at the pueblo of San Gregorio. When those in the San Andrés mining camp learned of his illness they decided it must be serious, because it had forced Father Ruiz—a person who had been made for enduring great hardship—to remain in bed. Considering the great scarcity of medicines and the lack of anyone to administer them in that Indian pueblo, they decided to bring him to the mining camp, whether voluntarily or not, so that they could care for him out of their own charity.

One of the principal miners, Captain Diego de Avila,[4] was particularly concerned about Father Ruiz.

He was devoted to the priest and was a notable benefactor of the missionaries. He personally set out with some of his people. When they reached Father Ruiz they found him weak and gaunt. With great pleas and insistence the captain succeeded in getting the priest to go to the Spaniards' mining camp to be healed. The Spaniards loved him like a father; he loved them as well as the children he had reared through religious instruction. Once they finally convinced him to leave, they set out from San Gregorio for the captain's hacienda, where the priest's illness seized him and God's servant, faithful minister, and diligent laborer ended his temporal life to go to enjoy eternal life.[5] Neither time nor his illness afforded the opportunity to send word to other missionaries in their [own] districts, so that they could administer the Holy Sacraments. He had nevertheless said Mass the day before the illness seized him. Moreover, he had always prepared himself and lived as a vigilant servant of the Lord; he was an exemplary man of great religion, as evident by the blazing light of his holy works.

Father Ruiz's charitable caregivers were notably distressed by the death of he whom they had hoped to cure and comfort—he who was their father, teacher, and spiritual guide in these distant lands. Because they had been unable to restore his health, they wanted to have him again with them at their mining camp, in the church where the priest had worked so hard to help his children and his brothers in Christ. They were afraid that when Father Andrés Tutino and Father Pedro Gravina, who were also ministers of religious instruction in this mission, learned of his passing, they would come for his body to bury it at the church in San Gregorio. They realized at the same time that they were prevented from taking his body to their mining camp at San Andrés because they would have to cross a river that at the time was overflowing its banks. Although there was great fear of the river's strong current, the love they felt for their priest overcame their fear of losing his body in the river, and they decided that four people should venture into the water with the litter. They crossed the river despite the dangerous force of the currents due to a special act of God's providence, or the miracle that it was. For when they were crossing the river with the body, the current was restrained or the waters slowed down. Once they had crossed, the currents came rushing down again

3. Note that because these pueblos at the time fell within the Diocese of Guadalajara, Bishop Mota y Escobar had authority over the assignment of priests and religious ministries (preaching, sacraments) in the pueblos.

4. Captain Diego de Avila was an encomendero and leading mine operator in San Andrés; for years he had worked closely with the Jesuits,

encouraging the Indians to accept mission ways of life and to work as free laborers in his and other mines (DHM 1600; McShane 1945).

5. Ruiz apparently died during the winter of 1607–8 and before Lent of the latter year.

so strongly that those who had remained on the other side and wanted to swim across could barely combat the force of the water with the strength of their own arms.

Great notice was taken of this unusual case in the San Andrés mining camp, where it was sworn to by an eyewitness whose testimony should not be doubted, lest an entirely credible person be offended. [525] Through piety we can understand that God Our Lord wanted Father Alonso Ruiz's body to rest at the church, which His servant had defended at such great risk, when with a crucifix in hand [he sought] to repress the sacrilegious fury with which the barbarians wanted to burn the church to the ground with all the Christians inside.

When they finally reached the mining camp with Father Ruiz's body, accompanied by many torch bearers, he was welcomed and buried with many tears.

These were tempered by the fact that they were able to keep such a cherished treasure, which they buried on the Gospel side of the altar. They have defended it with such vigilance that, during all the years that we have forcefully pleaded with them, they have not agreed to turn the body over to the priests of our Company. Their respect and esteem for this apostolic missionary is so great that, even today, when they speak of him they refer to him as blessed Father Alonso Ruiz.

This honorary mention has been presented here in order to write about this priest at the beginning of the Christianity and mission of San Andrés. Although this evangelical minister spent only a few years here, he founded this mission and labored and endured suffering equivalent to the labor of many, achieving great success, as we will see in the following chapters.

CHAPTER 11 Father Andrés Tutino continues caring for this Christianity; a letter giving an account of its progress

Father Andrés Tutino succeeded the late Father Alonso Ruiz as the administrator of these pueblos [apparently in 1608]. He had already come from Mexico City to work in this mission of San Andrés, where he labored for more than twenty years, providing outstanding examples of his religion from the very beginning. He was superior of this mission for some years, and improved and maintained it with much diligence, fervor, and dedication in the midst of difficulties and revolutions, which later will be discussed. This priest was encouraged by the fruits harvested in this new Christianity, which he reported in a letter to the Father Provincial in Mexico City. I have transcribed and included it here, as follows:

The people of this pueblo of San Gregorio have built a church, which could be considered to be a good one anywhere in this province. We invited the Spanish residents of San Andrés and San Hipólito to the dedicatory Mass. They considered the occasion so important that fifty well-armed Spaniards, which is normally how they go about in this region, gathered for the celebration, which lasted eight days. During the first three days, High Masses were sung

by deacons, and sermons were preached at each one, and each day there was a solemn procession with music. The church was festively decorated according to the possibilities of such newly discovered and remote lands. In addition to the volleys from the Spaniards' harquebuses, there were fireworks amounting to two arrobas of gunpowder. The Indians who had gathered [for the celebration] from more than thirty leagues away were made aware (because they were new to our Faith) that this was all done to honor the true God, Lord of heaven and earth. They also were encouraged to honor Him by building good churches in their lands and pueblos.

All the guests were given food during the eight-day [526] celebration, which included many colorful dances that went on day and night. The Spaniards wanted to outdo the Indians, and so the most important Spaniards performed a religious play or comedy that was composed for the occasion, with much humor, music, and fine costumes. They also gave a demonstration of the game of cañas on horseback, to show their joy at seeing these new nations reduced to our Faith.

The blacks and long-time Christian laborers also performed another play and fine dances. Our Lord wanted everyone to rejoice and honor His house without problems and to the edification of the new Christians and great admiration of some gentile Indians of the Xixime nation who came to the solemn celebration. All of them were inspired and moved to worship God in their celebrations and to build churches.

Because the pueblo of San Gregorio was the head of this district, the church was very large. It was centrally located and where everyone came for major religious feasts or pascuas, especially during Lent. This year [1608] it was a happy and edifying sight to watch more than four hundred Indians—who were once idolaters and slaves of the devil—gather to celebrate Holy Thursday. They scourged themselves with as much fervor as Spaniards, while their women held torches to provide them with light. During another procession that was held later for the Feast of the Solitude of the Most Holy Virgin and the Burial of Christ, more than four hundred people scourged themselves. About two thousand confessed and those who were more advanced in the Faith were allowed to receive Communion. On Easter Sunday morning they celebrated the Feast of the Resurrection with dances and a great procession, after which they heard Mass and returned happily to their pueblos.

The Indians attend religious instruction punctually and follow Christian burial customs, praying over the graves of their dead. They observe the wake, keeping vigil all night, with some praying and others singing the doctrine for the souls of their departed. The women of the pueblos in this district are most modest and discreet. When some soldiers who had gone there with lustful intentions saw how modest the women were, remaining on their knees as they said the Rosary, the Spaniards—seeing how these converted barbarians behaved—became ashamed and repented, determining to reform their own lives.

I will tell you about a particular case that happened one day during Holy Week, when all the people of a pueblo attended the service of Tenebrae,[6] which was sung as best it could be. So many people attended that the church barely held them all. A Spaniard happened to be standing next to a woman who was making her confession, and he noticed that she did so with such sobbing and tears that she could hardly talk or confess her sins. This so moved the Spaniard that the eyes of his soul were opened and he gave himself up to what God wanted from him. Talking to himself, he was perplexed and said, "Is it possible that this barbarous Acaxee woman who has gone so long without knowing God can confess her sins with such feeling, and yet my sins do not oblige me to do the same?" When the woman finished he immediately went to the priest and told him this with as much emotion and tears as the woman. He repented and made a general confession for the great benefit of his soul.

The following day two other Spaniards gave an [edifying] example. [527] After the priest had given the Indians a talk about the commandment to wash the feet [of others], as Christ Our Lord had done,[7] the priest began to wash the feet of twelve poor Indians. Two other Indians helped to carry an empty container and another that was full of water. Although they were barbarians, these Indians were so pious in their actions that two Spaniards who had come from the mining camps broke into tears of devotion when they saw the Indians. Rather than be outdone, the Spaniards laid aside their harquebuses and shields and, getting down on their knees, they also helped to wash the feet of those poor Indians, whom they consider to be very inferior.

To this point I have quoted the letter of the priest who instructed this pueblo. Although long-time Christian Catholic nations might not consider these great deeds, miracles, or unusual events, nevertheless they are precious fruits of Christianity. Those who were once gentiles trapped in the error of their ways now are forgetting their fierce and barbarous customs and affectionately receiving other customs. These examples illustrate the progress that has been made in this mission of San Andrés, for as the Faith has spread similar events have occurred in the other pueblos of this mission.

6. This is a reference to the Roman Catholic service known in Spanish as *Oficio de Tinieblas* (celebration/rite of darkness). It is observed at the end of Holy Week and commemorates Christ's suffering and death. As part of the ritual, the candles in the church are gradually extinguished until only one remains lit. Special matins and lauds are sung and there is a reading from Lamentations, the Old Testament book attributed to the prophet Jeremiah.

7. See John 13:14.

CHAPTER III The hardships endured by the priests during an epidemic[8] that struck these pueblos; the fruits of this illness

In order to harvest the abundant, ripening fruit in its prime (as I will later relate), Our Lord, for his supreme ends, sent these people an epidemic of measles and smallpox. Once again the priests faced innumerable hardships, although undoubtedly there were innumerable rewards as well. They found themselves forced to work day and night without pause, perpetually moving from pueblo to pueblo and house to house. In one hand they carried the holy oil, which they administered to these people along with the other sacraments for healing souls. In the other hand they carried all the medicines and aids that they could find to heal and mend bodies. The other hardship was one that I referred to earlier—the rough trails they had to travel over hills and deep gorges. What was even more dangerous were the swift rivers that they had to cross in order to rescue these souls. On one occasion the water was so high that two priests almost drowned when they were swept downriver. Their response to those who reprimanded them for daring to place themselves in such evident danger was that they had not acted out of fear or bravery, but rather to care for the children they loved. This type of penance, suffered by these servants of God in His apostolic ministry in these mountain missions, was quite common and ever-present. Accordingly, I cannot fail to give a more detailed account of it, citing a few cases that took place at this time in addition to those already discussed.

On an occasion similar to the one previously mentioned, the priests were stranded for eight days between two rivers, with no way out. There were others who were snowed in for five days, with no other nourishment than bitter acorns. To neutralize some of the bitterness, they mixed in a little flour made from the toasted maize that they happened to have with them. This was the most luxurious of their provisions during this early conversion. Although today this lack of basic necessities for human life [528] is somewhat ameliorated, every day these servants of God endure difficult journeys, steep hills and valleys, and dangerous rivers. It is impossible to remedy this situation—to move the mountains, flatten their peaks, or change the land that God has given them. The suffering that these missionary priests endured in these mountains was discussed in a letter that their superior wrote to the priests in Mexico City.[9] I will copy the letter here:

> Two priests (he says) departed the pueblo of Ocotlán, where we had all gathered for our meeting. It rained on them for three days, and then they were forced to wait six days for the water to subside in a branch of a river they had to ford. When they did cross, the force of the water swept away the mule that was carrying their clothing and books. Unfortunately, all the books, papers, and everything else got wet; they were lucky to get the mule out of the river quickly. Then one of the priests tried to cross and the current hit him so hard that it carried him along for quite some distance. When he realized the danger he was in, he decided that he had a better chance of saving himself if he jumped off the mule and into the water, which is what he did. The current carried him along as if he were a piece of straw, repeatedly pulling him under the waves. If a brave Indian who was a skilled swimmer had not jumped in and grabbed the priest, pulling him to the bank of the river, he would have drowned then and there. He was very fortunate to have come out of this [alive], even though he became deaf and got soaking wet. The priest's cloak, his breviary, and his papers were [all] lost. The priests' relief from this suffering came in the form of another storm, during which it rained for twenty-four hours without stopping. They spent that day, which was a Sunday, under a blanket without saying Mass. If neighboring Indians had not heard about them and immediately come to their rescue with some of their meager food, the priests would have died then and there from hunger, because they had almost no sustenance and had not been able to cross the river for more than fifteen days. In the end the Indians got them out by taking them over some peaks. They traveled part of the way on foot and part of the way on horseback until they reached their pueblo, where they spent a few days. They were unable to go on to some of the other pueblos that they needed to visit (these are the unavoidable dangers these priests often confront). The two who found themselves in the danger that I have recounted here were relieved to see

---

8. This epidemic occurred in 1607, before Ruiz's death and his replacement as superior by Tutino (Reff 1991b:151).

9. This letter was written by Alonso Ruiz, superior of the mission of San Gregorio, and relates events from around Lent, 1607 (Alegre 1956–1960:2:156).

the joy and concern of the Christians in the pueblo. They attended church and catechism, singing the latter along with other devout prayers in honor of the Mother of God, for whom they have a loving affection.

Up to here I have cited this letter that proclaims the hardships and difficulties of this mission, which these apostolic men have overcome and continue to [overcome] daily, in order to communicate the light of the Gospel to these poor people. Although there are at times other hardships, these priests continually travel over difficult paths to visit the two or three pueblos, the minimum that each has under his care. The charity of Christ Our Lord has taught them to suffer, and many of them have been employed for many years and continue to labor in these doctrinas and missions. Even though efforts have been made to see to it that their pueblos and districts are free of shortages, it has been impossible to remedy them all.

I turn now to the fruits that were harvested amidst the hardship of the epidemic that obliged the priests to frequently travel these trails. The first fruits that Our Lord took were more than eight hundred children. They received the water of Holy Baptism, and before they could sin, died from the illness and, thus, could go to dwell in heaven. This harvest and such blessed first fruits are alone sufficient to consider the toils suffered worthwhile. The saints celebrate as a work of great piety what [529] God did for those newborn infants who were deprived of their temporal lives by the cruel and ambitious King Herod. Through His clemency God arranged for them to have another happier and more blessed life. All priests and the Church refer to these children that were taken by God as budding fruits because they had not yet committed any sin. The same thing happened with the children in our mission, who were assured salvation. If they had stayed in their mountains here on earth, they may well have endangered their place in heaven, because they would have remained subject to many grave sins. This is a consideration that tempers the regret and tenderness that the priests cannot help but feel when they see so many of their children perish—children they most certainly love more than do the children's biological parents.

Another eight hundred or more adults died from the illness. It was rare for anyone from this multitude of widely dispersed rancherías and pueblos to die without having received the Holy Sacraments of Confession and Extreme Unction. The priests declared another fruit among those who escaped with their lives after being deathly ill, for in this state the Lord opened the eyes of their souls. He did so in such a way that the priests no longer saw their former customs or the vestiges of deeply rooted vices that usually remain, especially drunkenness. Those who did not contract the illness considered this to be a special favor and benefit from Our Lord, whom they acknowledged and thanked. They became more careful and cognizant of their need to prepare themselves for the next life, of the reward or punishment that awaited them there, and of the fact that they had lived in utter ignorance when they were gentiles. In spite of what has been said, at that time there was no shortage of the bad seed about which the Son of God preached. The enemy of the salvation of souls was sowing this bad seed even in the midst of the good seed, as will be told in the following chapter.

CHAPTER IV A perverted, deceitful, lying Indian delivers a speech to Christian Indians to keep them from building churches; another gentile is moved by God to come with his family to join the Church

Although several pueblos had been formed, they did not as yet have durable, permanent churches. This only comes with time and a certain readiness—when all or most of the Indians are baptized and are fond of our Holy Faith. The ministers of the doctrine must also have time to supervise such an undertaking, which (as I have often mentioned), frequently requires great effort on the part of the priests, including actual participation in construction.

The time finally came when the priests were no longer busy performing Baptisms and the Indians were very well prepared and ready to build a church. However, [before they could do so] an evil and perverse Christian got together with some gentiles and began preaching diabolical lies to them and other simple and ignorant people.[10] This liar, who had not abandoned his dealings with the devil or, if he had, had gone back to them, was a great rhetorician and public speaker. He persuaded the people that he had spoken with their priest and that now the priest believed what the liar preached about the afterlife. Pointing with his finger [to the church cemetery], the liar said that the dead and their souls remained where they had been buried and that the church was [the source of] cocoliztli (which is what they call epidemic disease). He told them that the priests and other Spaniards who taught about an afterlife were the cause of sickness and hunger. Thus, their desire to build churches was like calling forth sickness and hunger to [530] wipe them out. Continuing, he told them not to believe a thing the priest said about the afterlife because it was not true. The priest had tearfully told the liar in confidence that he had successfully deceived the people.

Here the devil made use of lies that were spread at this time by heretics. On many occasions heretics have published lies, convincing Catholic preachers and writers of falsehoods.[11] Christ Our Lord suffered even more from such falsehoods when He walked the earth—when the Pharisees attributed His works and evangelical doctrine to Beelzebub.

In the end this Indian heretic and his cursed doctrine infected the souls of many, not only in terms of opposition to building churches, but in terms of fomenting hatred for Spaniards and the priests. He fanned a fire among one group that spread so far as to threaten the lives of a priest and several Spaniards at the mining camp of San Hipólito. God Our Lord was watching over His chosen ones and He stopped the fire from spreading. Once the priest got word of the heretic, he sent a faithful Christian Indian to talk with the rebels and troublemakers. God made him so effective that he persuaded them to desist from their intended uprising. However, he was not able to persuade them to build churches, as they still believed what they had been told by their lying rhetorician. The latter and his companions roamed the land, threatening to kill those who wished to build churches. Thus, the priests reconsidered their plans for the time being, awaiting a more opportune moment. As we will later see, the time did come when these and other churches were built.

Around this same time God lifted the spirits of other good Christians who wanted to build churches. He also lifted the spirits of gentiles who wanted to receive religious instruction. The goodness of these gentiles exceeded the malice of the perverse. God awakened one man to the point where, even though he was a gentile, he spoke endlessly day and night, dissuading the people of the doctrine that had been sown by the devil through

---

10. This happened in 1610 (AGN 1610), which is when the San Andrés mission was separated from Topia, each with its own superior. This and the next few chapters relate to the Xixime Revolt of 1610.

11. Pérez de Ribas presumably is referring here to Luther, Calvin, and other leaders of the Reformation.

that other lying [Indian]. He spoke of God, the Creator of all things, and of matters pertaining to the afterlife. He spoke with such efficacy, particularly about the punishment that sinners endure, that he was admired by even the most ladino and well-instructed Christians. The latter said that there was nothing that they could add or say [that superseded what this Indian preached].

This Indian was very steadfast in what he preached and in his desire to be a Christian. He saw, however, that his life was in danger where he lived because he opposed the Indian liar, who was still making trouble. Accordingly, [the faithful] Indian and some of his followers gathered their households and went to live near some Christians. There they sowed new fields, which was a clear indication that he wanted to be a Christian. He was so serious that after a while he attempted to build a church and opened a trail to his settlement so that the priest could more easily come to baptize him and his children. He told them that he was a Christian at heart even before he became one and that he had not allowed anything to stop him, neither his home nor his trees nor his mesquite and prickly pear fields

(plants which, as we have previously noted, they greatly esteem). This Indian, now enlightened by God, added that if the Creator of all that he possessed rewarded him when he was unfaithful, he would now certainly be better rewarded because of his acknowledgment of and desire to totally serve Him.

This outstanding Xixime Indian and his Baptism, which became famous, {531} will be recounted later. It can clearly be seen in this case how God and His divine providence watches over these people, however barbarous they may be. Here, as elsewhere, whereas some falter others are aided by God. When the devil and his accomplices try to demolish and destroy our Holy Faith, Our Lord Himself supports it, opening new doors for it to spread.

This then was the state of this new Christianity. I leave the greatest improvements for later, when I will speak of other reductions that were incorporated into this mission, particularly the conversion of the most bellicose nation in these mountains, which cost great labor and bloodshed.

CHAPTER V The Xixime's fierce customs and inaccessible lands; Francisco de Urdiñola, governor of Nueva Vizcaya, decides to undertake an expedition to punish this nation's effrontery

The Xixime nation was the wildest, most inhuman, and rebellious of all those that lived in the broadest portion of these mountains. These Indians lived in the steepest and most difficult locations. Both their neighbors, the Acaxee, and the Spaniards from all those mining camps in the interior of the sierra were already aware of this. To reduce them to our Holy Faith and secure their friendship with Spaniards caused unspeakable hardships and conflict. This nation lived in the heart of this mountain range, fortified and protected by its most inaccessible peaks. Because of the height of the mountains and the depths of their gorges, they could not be reached, and

thus, it was impossible to deal with or tame them. Moreover, what made them even more impossible to deal with was their inhuman custom of regularly consuming human flesh. This custom had been more deeply ingrained in them than in any other nation that has been discovered in Nueva España. They came down out of their mountains and gorges only to search for their neighbors, the Acaxee, whom they cooked in pots full of flesh, which they gorge on. They take their bones and skulls to celebrate their triumphs and to adorn their walls and doors; they hang them as well on the trees outside their homes.

As a result of these victories and celebrations, they

became so proud, insolent, and daring that with each day they launched new and more frequent attacks. In this way they were eliminating especially the Acaxee, which is the principal nation in the missions of Topia and San Andrés that form a border on the north with these barbarous and inhuman Xixime. On several occasions the Acaxee, with the assistance of some Spaniards, attacked the Xixime, but this resulted in a loss of their people as well as their reputation. The Xixime relied on the inaccessibility of their mountains as well as the fact that they were so adept at climbing. Thus, they entered these confrontations very haughtily, causing their competitors to retreat and even lose some of their people.

At this time the Acaxee Indians were almost all Christians. As vassals of the king, they were under his protection. In an effort to protect the children whom they so loved, the missionary priests intervened on behalf of the Acaxee, asking the governor of Nueva Vizcaya to remedy the many problems and great harm [caused by the Xixime]. The governor felt that the Acaxee's request was just and reasonable, and so he immediately instructed them to mount an attack to capture one or more Xixime.[12] They were to bring them to him [532] so that he could have an interpreter and could arrange for peace with such remote and cruel people.

The Acaxee were fortunate to capture two Xixime, although one of them died shortly thereafter from a wound that he had received when he was captured. The other Xixime reached the governor safe and sound. He did not employ force with the Indian, but rather attempted to deal with him affectionately. He detained him for several days so that he could become familiar with Spaniards. Then he dispatched him to tell his people that things were not as they had been led to believe; the Spaniards were friendly and kind, and they should give up their attacks and assaults and be at peace with the Christians. As a final note he said that if they did not do so, he personally would lead a powerful army into their very lands—no matter how steep the mountains might be—to mete out an unforgettable punishment.

The Indian was dispatched with this message, quite content and honored with the suit of clothes that the governor had given him. To insure the Xixime's safety, the governor asked one of the priests who was instructing the Acaxee to please accompany the Indian to the

mining camp at San Hipólito, which was on the border between the Acaxee and the Xixime. He also ordered the captain, in the name of His Majesty, to receive the obedience and peace of those barbarians, should they come to offer it. He was also to pardon the murders and insults that they had committed up to that time.

This was all carried out; the captain dispatched this Indian from his garrison, and he reached his people safely. There he was well received, for they saw that he was very content with the good treatment he had received. They heard his message and decided that all the heads or caciques from their pueblos would go to the mining camp at San Hipólito and, in the name of the entire nation, establish peace with the captain. They did this according to the governor's specifications, collectively yielding their obedience to Our Lord the king and pledging themselves as his vassals from that time forward.

The Xixime maintained this peace for some time [1607–10], visiting the Christian Acaxee's pueblos, communicating with Spaniards in those mining camps, and demonstrating their kindness. Nevertheless, just when it seemed that they were ready to receive the light of the Gospel, for no reason whatsoever (even though any occasion is sufficient for the devil), this nation rebelled with great and diabolical fury. They struck simultaneously in four different places, taking the lives of all the Christians they could find in order to eat them, as they used to do. When the Christian Acaxee saw themselves in such dire straits, they once again asked the governor of Nueva Vizcaya to defend and protect them. If he did not, they would abandon their homes and churches and would settle elsewhere. They also notified His Lordship that the Xixime were inviting them to become their allies against the Spaniards, and that the Xixime would finish them off if they did not do so. As proof of this, they sent him as a prisoner the Xixime Indian who had brought them the offer of an alliance.

Governor Francisco de Urdiñola was a great soldier and an expert in wars with the fierce nations of the provinces of Nueva Vizcaya and Nueva Galicia. Nevertheless, to avoid bloodshed and expense to the king, he ordered the captain of the garrison at San Hipólito to renew his efforts to pacify the Xixime. The captain accomplished this through the previously mentioned Xixime cacique. This cacique had left his own people and had come with twenty of his followers to settle near the Christian Acaxee. On various occasions the Xixime rebels [533] resolved to kill them because they were so

---

12. Pérez de Ribas is here recounting events from 1607 (see Dunne (1944:100).

friendly toward the Spaniards and the Church. It was by God's special providence that they did not do so on this occasion, when the cacique took them this message from the captain of the garrison at San Hipólito. Arrogantly, they responded that the cacique was to tell the captain and his Spanish soldiers that they did not want peace with them, but rather war, and that they should immediately come and fight them. If they did not, then the Xixime themselves would soon find them, wherever they were. They would kill and eat them, for they liked the taste of their flesh.

Immediately, a large squadron of people joined together and set out for the mining camp known as Las Vírgenes, with the intention of destroying it and killing everyone there. Their arrogant determination and pride were such that they killed a Spaniard whom they found in his hacienda, along with his son and five Christian Indians and their wives. Only one person escaped to bring this news. The rebels took the bodies of the dead to eat, leaving behind their entrails as witness to what they had done.

This incident caused the entire region to revolt. When the governor got word of this he dispatched a letter to the viceroy of Nueva España, who is captain general of all the provinces of Nueva España. The governor provided him with an account of what was happening there and in the Sierra de San Andrés, in order that His Excellency could order what should be done and provide a remedy and funds for war. At that time the marquis of Salinas was viceroy.[13] To this day he is still remembered in the Indies for his sound government.

A council was held of religious theologians and the judges of the Real Audiencia to certify this cause and the punishment demanded by such acts of extreme insolence. It was resolved that the governor of Nueva Vizcaya himself should draft Spaniards as well as allied Indians and punish the crimes, reining in such a haughty and insolent nation and defending and protecting the Christianity of that mountain region. In compliance with this order the governor assembled two companies, each with a hundred Spanish soldiers as well as troops of Christian Indians, who in total numbered eleven hundred infantrymen. He set out with his people for the mining camp at San Hipólito. Once he was there he selected twenty Spanish soldiers to stay behind to guard the Acaxee pueblos and the priests who were instructing them in case some troop of Xixime Indians should decide to attack them during the war, because these Xixime run and climb like deer in those mountains.

With this precaution taken he set out with his people for the Xixime's lands and high mountains. He took along as advisors two priests who were providing religious instruction in these missions and who had great knowledge of these lands. During this extremely dangerous expedition the priests assisted the army spiritually. The events of this enterprise will be told in the following chapter.

13. The marquis of Salinas, Luis de Velasco II, was viceroy from 1607–11.

CHAPTER VI Governor Francisco Urdiñola's punitive expedition to the rebellious Xixime nation

Before I discuss this expedition I wish to forewarn the reader of two or three circumstances pertinent to this and the other expeditions in this history. It is my intention to be completely accurate, without [534] passing things off as having greater worth than they actually do. In the matters that we are presently discussing it is certain that neither the nations that are fought nor the armies that are raised are comparable in number and quality to the numerous European armies and nations at this time. Nevertheless, it is also certain that the difficulties of these conquests and battles are—as fate would have it—not proportionately inferior. Although only one thousand Indians from a single nation might be conquered, they still make use of lands and strongholds that are by nature more impenetrable than those that are skillfully erected. This will be seen in the following case.

Because this history is so public and might come into the hands of foreign nations, the second thing that I wish to point out (and I am speaking on the basis of a great deal of information and personal experience) is that our Spaniards do not take up arms against these people, no matter how barbarous they may be, unless they are forced to do so by these Indians, for very good reasons. The third and most important thing about these enterprises is that the title of 'Catholic Monarchs' enjoyed by the Spanish king and queen shines here. At the expense of their own possessions and wealth they gloriously tend to the obligations and concerns that God has given them of spreading His Most Holy Faith throughout the entire world. They do so without neglecting any nation or people, no matter how barbarous and low they might be. Lastly, the fruits harvested among these nations are precious to the one who is both the King of Kings and the Savior of the World. Having made this clear, I will move on to write about the governor's expedition to the fierce Xixime nation.

I can find no better, safer, or certain way to tell what happened during this difficult enterprise than to present here a letter from one of the two priests who accompanied the governor and his army.[14] This priest gives the Father Provincial of Mexico, who was his superior, an account of the course and events of this expedition. He speaks as an eyewitness, saying:

> The Xixime Indians were divided among two settlements. One of them was called Xocotilma and the other Guapijuxe. The governor did not want to split up our army and be at a disadvantage. Rather, he wanted us all to attack Xocotilma, where it was said the greatest number of enemies were located. We suffered a great deal along the way, for it was necessary to open most of the trail by hand; traveling on foot.
>
> We descended into extremely deep canyons, climbing back up and over steep hills and mountains. We forded very strong rivers and cleared and burned our way through thickets. Through God's favor we at last reached the Xixime lands, very tired and having suffered greatly. We first won from them some of their important crags and peaks. With this they began to be frightened, and they sent word to one another that they were being attacked by a large number of Spaniards and Christian Indians. With this news some of the Xixime decided to come and see the governor. He welcomed them with kindness and treated them well, assuring them that he had not come to harm their nation, but rather to punish the delinquents among them who were inciting rebellion and to firmly establish the peace agreements that they had broken. He ordered them to go and tell this to their comrades, and also to tell them that on the following day, which was the Feast of Saint Luke [October 18, 1610], they were all to gather in their pueblo of Xocotilma, where he planned to speak to them and give them a more detailed account of his intentions. With this the Indians departed to tell their people what had happened.
>
> On the feast day of Saint Luke we reached Xocotilma, which was the best and [535] happiest day that we had on this journey. Not only did we reach this difficult place, but we found the land so beautiful and green that it was as if it were covered in basil. Here the soldiers put on their armor, but under all that weight it was hard for them to walk along the trail. The entire army prepared itself for possible battle. As everyone was slowly descending we came upon 150 fierce Indians, ready and aligned for battle. Some of them bore the lances and shields that they use, whereas others had bows

14. The two priests were Francisco de Vera and Alonso Gómez; Pérez de Ribas here quotes Gómez's letter, copied in the anua of 1610 (AGN 1610).

and quivers with a large supply of arrows. Still others had macanas, hatchets, and knives. Their hair was long and finely braided with ribbons of several different colors. Some of them had their faces painted. In this fashion they came one by one to see the governor, who received them in friendship. He told them that, considering the multitude of people he knew to be in Xocotilma and its rancherías, he did not see very many of them. For this reason he had no intention of telling them why he had come. He would wait until they all were gathered, for which he gave them two more days' time. These two days passed, then on the Day of the Eleven Thousand Virgins [October 21][15] many Indian men and women began to descend [into the canyon], along with a numerous rabble of children.

Before the men could approach the governor to speak with him the captain from San Hipólito had them leave behind their weapons. Once they reached the governor, disarmed, he ordered them to sit down, which they did, with the Spanish soldiers all around them. Thus seated, the governor told them that he had come for their good and for the peace and quiet of their lands. In spite of the past deaths and the fact that they had broken the peace agreements that they had made, he wanted once again to establish peace. However, to do this, it would be necessary for them to call together that very day the many Indians who were still missing. In order to force them to comply, he would have to keep three or four of them as hostages. He implored them not to rebel or be upset by this, for once those three or four had been chosen, the others could go freely to look for their companions. The first one whom the governor named was a wicked Indian who was responsible for many deaths. The governor must have known who he was going to select, because he had the Indian under close surveillance. This Indian quietly was taken into custody.

Then the governor selected the second one, who resisted the soldiers' attempts to subdue him, and immediately all the others then got upset and rioted. They were encouraged to do so by an old Indian who stood up and, shouting, exhorted them to be killed rather than bound. They immediately tried to break through the barrier of Spaniards and their Indian allies who had encircled them. They were so desperate that they ran straight into the tips of the swords of the soldiers who were detaining and threatening them. They tried to defend themselves with their hatchets and knives, which they had kept hidden. The Spaniards realized that they could not calm them down or detain them, so they charged upon those who were most intent on getting away. They forcefully detained them, which resulted in a few deaths. Many of them were taken prisoner, and many others who were badly wounded later died.

The priest who was my companion and I rushed to prepare these injured Indians, with a desire that they should not die without Holy Baptism and salvation for their souls.

God willed that they should receive this counseling well and they were prepared for death with instruction and Baptism.

After the others who had been captured were taken prisoner the governor ordered that the entire army move to a more suitable location. [536] There he carried out an investigation to find out who had been the most responsible for the past disturbances and especially for the death of the Spaniard whom they had killed a few days earlier, after having broken their peace accord. He discovered that eleven of those who had been taken prisoner were the most highly implicated in that crime. They confessed to this in their statements. They also proclaimed that they and the other Xixime who had come in peace to welcome the governor had really intended to kill the governor and then his soldiers, shooting them with arrows as they fled through the narrowest and most difficult passes through which they had allowed them to enter their lands. The investigation was concluded and the governor condemned these eleven Indians to death. He notified them of this sentence, and God willed that they should recognize their crimes and accept the sentence with a good disposition. Then the other priest and I went to prepare them for death, exhorting them to receive Holy Baptism, through which they would insure the salvation of their souls and die as Christians and without which they could not partake of the joys of heaven. God was served and they accepted this speech well. In this way we prepared them as well as we could in the time we were given. They were baptized at the foot of the trees where they were to be hanged; nine of them died like good Christians, leaving us assurances of their predestination and eternal salvation.

The tenth to die was the old man who had incited them to riot when the governor tried to keep three or four of them as hostages. By chance Our Lord allowed this evil old man who had been the cause of these events to die as he did: desperate, without any way of getting him to receive the water of Holy Baptism (in spite of all the efforts that were made). Thus he was hanged and all the Indian allies, who were upset by his obstinacy, shot him full of arrows in such a way that he looked like a hedgehog from hell. The eleventh of those who were condemned to die was spared his life at the plea of Father Francisco de Vera, who interceded with the governor on his behalf not only because he was a boy, but because there was little evidence that he did more than accompany the killers.

Here I must add something more. The Xixime cacique, who was one of our allies and had left his people to come and live among some Christian Acaxee, was there with his wife to see the punishment of those delinquents. He scolded the prisoners for the harm they caused by breaking the peace agreement and killing so many Christians. They had paid no heed to the good advice that he given them, and as a result they now found (and rightfully so) some of their own people dead and others in miserable condition.

This Indian, who was of very sound judgment, knew that we wanted to proceed from Xocotilma to Guapijuxe in search of the remaining rebels, and so he insistently asked us to baptize him and his wife and marry them as Christians.

---

15. The feast day honors a fabulously estimated group of maidens, led by Saint Ursula, who died as martyrs in Cologne prior to the fourth century (Attwater 1949:166).

To insure that their wishes were granted, he argued that they already knew the prayers and principal elements of our Holy Faith. It was also the case that because they had been friends with the Spaniards and allowed them to pass through their lands, there was a clear danger that the Indians who had withdrawn into the mountains might suddenly attack and kill them before they had become Christians. It seemed to us that the Indian was right in making this request, and we questioned both him and his wife concerning the catechism, prayers, etc. They responded well to everything, and so Father Francisco de Vera, who was there as superior, baptized and married them. Governor Francisco de Urdiñola honored them by acting as their sponsor [537] and made the man take the name Don Francisco and the woman Doña María. As the Baptism was being performed, the Spanish soldiers shot off a salute with their harquebuses and the Indian allies celebrated with their drums and trumpets. The governor gave them his word that he would celebrate their Baptism with greater festivity when a solemn Baptism ceremony was later held at the church at San Hipólito and they were anointed with the chrism.[16] Lastly, he sent this cacique who was now a Christian (to the great joy and

applause of the entire army) back to the place he had chosen for himself and his relatives. He pardoned and freed any of the Xixime Indians who wanted to go with him, on the condition that they live in peace. This was the case even with those who had been found guilty and implicated in the deaths, robberies, and uprisings. This Christian cacique was dispatched quite content. The governor then set out to find the rebellious Xixime of Guapijuxe. However, before he broke camp the soldiers burned and razed the pueblo and rancherías of Xocotilma so that the rebels could no longer take refuge there. The soldiers found hanging in the houses more than one thousand skulls of men who had been eaten by those inhuman barbarians. Many other things were found that had been taken from Spaniards, such as harquebuses, swords, etc.

To this point I have been citing the letter of one of the priests who accompanied the governor and his army on the expedition. Because this letter is long, it will be concluded in the following chapter, together with the events of this expedition.

CHAPTER VII   The account of this expedition continues; the reduction of the Xixime

This priest's letter continues:

With the end of the events that I have related we headed for Guapijuxe, overcoming the same difficulties that we encountered on the way to Xocotilma. When [we] came to the [rebels'] principal rancherías, the governor sent an Indian prisoner with the same message that he had sent to the Indians at Xocotilma. This Indian was dismissed with a volley of arrows and fled for protection to the Spaniards, who were seizing some places to prevent the rebels' advance. They frightened the Indians out of one ranchería with shots from their harquebuses. When they reached the center of this ranchería, they found a spectacle that caused us all great horror and sorrow. There were some pots on the fire that contained human flesh and there was a human heart on a small roasting spit. The [person's] eyes had been gouged out and were placed on a maize husk. The skull had been stripped clean and was hanging with the rest of the bones from a stake that they had placed in the middle of the plaza for that purpose.

Here the governor took another Indian prisoner and sent him with a message to one of those petty Guapijuxe kings

whom the Indians considered to be God. They revered him as such because of the tricks that they saw him perform through the devil's wiles. He was begged to come in peace to see the governor, with the assurance that neither he nor anyone else who came with him would be harmed. This was an important message because the ambassador found the petty king holding a war council with his people, weighing whether to attack the Spaniards. When he heard the governor's message, he dismissed his advisors and came to see His Lordship, who treated him and those who had come with him as well as possible. When the governor asked him whether he wished to re-establish the peace that his people had broken, the petty king replied that he and seventeen [538] rancherías that were under his command were at peace and that they had never broken it, even though at the present moment they were all very apprehensive because of what had happened at Xocotilma. Then he pointed toward some rocky promontories to which his people had fled and ensconced themselves when they had seen so many Spaniards with their Indian allies in their land.

The soldiers then set out for [those heights], despite the difficult terrain, but when they arrived they found the houses and ranchos abandoned. The Indians had retreated to the highest points and peaks. Then a Xixime Indian

16. Consecrated olive oil mixed with balsam (Attwater 1949:93).

appeared at the top of a very high peak, whence he shouted that one of our men should come to him. When this request was conveyed to the governor, he ordered two Spaniards to go to see him, accompanied by two more of that petty king's followers. The four of them climbed up to where the Indian who had shouted was, and the latter asked to see the governor. He came and was well received, confirming what that petty king had previously said, [namely] that if His Lordship wanted to pardon them, then all the people would descend, little by little. The governor promised to pardon them, adding that if they were afraid to come down all at once with the women and children, then the leaders of the pueblos and rancherías could come down and make peace on behalf of the rest of their people, and he would be satisfied with that. This reassured them and a throng of people descended, who were well received by both the governor and the priests. To confirm their desire for lasting peace, they promptly erected two enramadas in the fashion of churches and asked the priests to instruct them like they did the rest of the Christians, for they also wanted to be baptized. They made altars and erected Crosses in the churches, where we said Mass on the days that we were there.

The Xixime Indians of Xocotilma learned of these events from their spies and they sent twenty of their people to also ask the governor's pardon for what had happened. They said they would be pleased to settle wherever he wanted and that they would congregate and build churches there, for they wanted to become Christians. However, because there were only a few of them left at Xocotilma, they asked that the governor favor them by freeing all those who were still prisoners, so that they could join them. They also asked that he send them priests to teach them the law of God. On this occasion Father Vera and I insistently asked the governor to do as they requested, offering to go ourselves to instruct them.

With great generosity and a Christian heart the governor ordered [the prisoners] released. He told them that they should thank the priests for their freedom, because if it were not for the priests' petition, he would not have freed them as well as their children and relatives. Therefore, they were to behave like other Christians, loving us dearly and obeying us when we returned to organize pueblos and erect churches. The Indians promised to do this, and then they all thanked us for interceding on their behalf, kissing our hands and embracing us.

The devil must have greatly regretted this peace and the freedom granted these prisoners, as many souls were freed from his harsh bondage. All those Xixime who were dispersed among more than sixty-five rancherías, not counting the other little ranchos and houses that they have

in their peaks and gorges, are now peacefully settled. They have been reduced to five good pueblos, with five to six thousand people. The governor entrusted them all to the members of the Company so that we could supervise their religious instruction. Thus, this expedition ended.

Although it comes at the end, I do not want to omit what happened at the beginning of the Xixime uprising in some peaceful Acaxee pueblos. [539] The situation was as follows: When the news of the Xixime uprising and rebellion reached Topia, it was rumored that two of the Acaxee Indian pueblos closest to the Xixime wanted to join the rebellion against the Spaniards. When three of the priests who were near the Topia mining camp heard about this, they went with some Spaniards to find out what was happening. When they were in sight of the first pueblo, the Indians saw them and let out such strange screams and yells that the priests and Spaniards became very fearful and distressed, believing that the rumors were true that the Acaxee had joined the uprising. With great courage and bravery one of the soldiers who was with the priests broke through more than two hundred Indians, who were all painted as if they were going to fight. God willed that they were all pretending to be at war, when they were actually at peace. They said that they had made all that noise and commotion of war to show the pleasure it gave them to learn of the priests' coming to their pueblos. The priests entered the pueblo, which they found full of women and children who were sick with smallpox. The priests heard their confessions and attended to them as best they could. One of the soldiers bled those who had fevers.

Thus it was that through this false rumor Our Lord willed that the bodies and souls of those poor people should be healed. Then God wished to take from among them a boy and an older woman. The latter was so well prepared that the priest who heard her confession barely found anything to prevent him from granting her absolution, so careful was she about the purity of her soul. During the days that the priests remained there, they found these people to be more charitable and benevolent than ever. [This was true] not only of those who were already baptized Christians, but also of the catechumens who wished to be baptized.

Thus ends the letter of Father Alonso Gómez Cervantes, who labored apostolically for many years in these missions. I will conclude this chapter so as to move ahead to the establishment of religious instruction among the Xixime nation. These Indians were very fierce and inhuman, as has been told, and their reduction came at the cost of great hardships and danger.

CHAPTER VIII Pueblos are established and religious instruction is begun among the Xixime; other events at this time

It was with great fervor that priests of our order, who were entrusted with [this task] by holy obedience, began cultivating this nation, whose gentile customs we have just described. The most important of these priests was the founder of these mountain missions, Father Hernando de Santarén. His life and martyrdom were described at the end of the previous book concerning the mission of Topia, which was the first mission that he founded. Because this apostolic man had instructed the Acaxee, who are close neighbors of the Xixime, he was acquainted with both nations. He continually endeavored to convert the Xixime, and it was in the process of instructing them that his life was consumed in glorious triumph and violent death. However, he did not die at the hands of the Xixime, but rather at the hands of their neighbors, those apostates of the Faith, the Tepehuan, whom I will discuss in detail in the following book.

After the blessed priest took charge of the conversion of the Xixime,[17] which he had so dearly longed for, his superiors sent him priests as companions to help cultivate such harsh and dispersed fields. The first thing they did was establish pueblos in specified locations and open roads through the steep mountains, which are full of peaks and ravines. By bringing the people together [540] the ministers of the doctrine could regularly visit and serve these pueblos at all times. It was not possible to do this uniformly, because there are usually many Indians who love their mountains dearly and are reluctant to give up their barbarous way of life. Some even obstruct the reception of the law of the Gospel, which must be accepted freely and spontaneously.

It was in the midst of such early difficulties [in 1611] that Our Lord quickly favored Father Hernando de Santarén through a special case that is worthy of comment. Among these Xixime there was a great sorcerer who was more than eighty years old. His people both respected and feared him, revering him as a God of

heaven and earth. The priest was very desirous of converting this old man, in part because his conversion would be a clear and noteworthy example for the others of his nation to follow. Also, if he was not baptized he could do a great deal of harm, both in word and deed, particularly as the devil was his familiar. Our Lord heard the pleas of His servant who worked so hard for the good of souls, and He sent the old man a grave and dangerous illness. When the priest learned of this, he immediately went to visit and attend to the man as best he could. At the same time that he cured his body he healed his soul, telling him about the mysteries of our Holy Faith, particularly about the one God, the Creator of all things. The priest had learned that this Indian had many idols of devilish form in his pueblo. Luckily, God favored the priest, who managed to convince the old man and everyone in his pueblo to surrender all the idols; within six days they all were burned in the presence of the [inhabitants]. The great sorcerer surrendered to his true God and requested Baptism, which he received. Our Lord was additionally compassionate, because through Holy Baptism he was healed in body as well as soul. The Indian himself appreciated this and was very grateful to God for this singular favor. The priest showed him an image of the Child Jesus in the temple at the age of twelve, which the priest devoutly carried with him. He told the Indian that it was the image of the Lord, who had come down to earth from heaven to redeem us. The old man immediately got down on his knees, and joining his hands, he exclaimed with remarkable affection and feeling, "Lord, I have made you my Lord and I recognize you as my Father. I want only you as my God. Give me life to serve You."

From that day forward this Indian was sensitive to the affection that God had imprinted upon him through that most holy image. During the days that the priest was there in the pueblo, the old man would go to his house at dawn and in person renew his original vow and prayer to God. A few days after he was baptized he was going along a trail and fell into a river. He would have drowned if God had not miraculously

---

17. This was in 1611; Santarén was assisted in his work among the Xixime by Alonso Gómez.

delivered him. He himself declared to the priest, "God aided and saved me; He took me by the arm and removed me from that danger."

The conversion of this remarkable Indian was a matter of much joy for the priests. There was another edifying case where these people were disabused of one of their vices, which involved an Indian who had a small idol of a stone like crystal. Either the crystal or the devil who was inside it forced the Indian to fast for as long as planting season lasted and for several months afterwards. He fasted so rigorously that he did not allow himself to eat more than raw grasses and maize, just like a horse. When the priest found out about this, with prudent reasoning and words [541] he disabused him of that fraud, freeing him from the love for and devotion to that little idol, which he turned over to the priest. The priest persuaded him that he had been duped and that he should forget about such fasting, because it was worthless. In the end the Indian was freed from such superstitions and he was well instructed and then baptized.

This superstition of rigorous fasting was very well established among these Indians. It was practiced by many young boys for as long as the growing season lasted. If the maize harvest was not good, they blamed and punished those who fasted. They said that they must have slipped up and eaten meat or something besides maize and wild grass; otherwise there would have been an abundant harvest. The devil wished to be honored—as God is in His Church—by these penances and ceremonies. However, thanks to His most Holy Son, who willed to remove these wretched people from their blindness, the Xixime were delivered from it. Thus, after the priests had translated the catechism into the Xixime's own language, they began praying it every day, just as was done in other Christian pueblos, where the people punctually and joyfully attend church.

After thousands of Xixime infants had been baptized the priests began instructing the adults. A great many begged for and joyfully received instruction. Even happier were their ministers, who were glad to see the Xixime transformed into gentle lambs. They traveled among them and through the mountains without a military escort, despite the danger from remaining wolves. However, these shepherds were not about to neglect Christ's flock of lambs, nor did they fear being abandoned, inasmuch as Our Lord announced to them that He would send them like lambs among wolves. This will be seen in the unusual case that I will here

relate, which also shows how the teaching of the Gospel improved the customs of some and did away with the rebelliousness of others.

Specifically, after the Xixime had made peace, three of them who still harbored a taste for human flesh encountered two Christians by a river, a husband and a wife, together with their four children. That cruel enemy of humankind, the devil, had placed them there as a temptation. He persuaded the three Xixime to kill the five of them, which is what they did. When the principales were informed of what had happened, they searched for and captured the delinquents and handed them over to the Spanish captain. The principales begged the captain to hang the delinquents. The captain was obliged to apply this deserved punishment because the principales of their same nation had requested it and also in order to obtain satisfaction for the Christians who had been violated and had been under royal protection. Because all those who were to be executed were gentiles, the captain sent for a priest to prepare them for death and Baptism. All three received Holy Baptism well and were then hanged. A boy who was also involved in the murders was retained as a prisoner. Because he was so young, the priest pleaded with the Xixime principales to pardon the boy. The principal cacique responded in a way that was quite intelligent for a gentile and barbarian: "Father, we don't want to pardon him (the Indian said); we would rather he die with the others because, even though he is a boy, he committed a crime and sin. He behaved as an adult and he should pay as an adult; he will serve as an example for the young people of his age."

I wish to be precise, but I don't know for a fact whether the boy was executed. However, I do know that the Xixime caciques, besides requesting this punishment, begged the captain to notify them [542] of any crime that was committed by these people. They [themselves] would immediately turn over anyone who disturbed the peace, because it was not fair that those who lived peaceably should suffer for the acts of three or four wrongdoers. This last request was a good example of how well these people received Christian law and justice.

It happened that along with the punishment of hanging, another punishment of flogging was carried out on an Indian from the mining camp because he had stolen another Indian's wife. This man was already a Christian and a ladino who spoke Spanish. The Xixime who observed this punishment commented that they never punished criminals when they were gentiles. The most they did was scold them in their fashion. They thought flogging was a good punishment for taking another man's wife, because it was in fact stealing another's property. In the end these people, even though they were barbarians, were pleased with that which was just and reasonable.

CHAPTER IX The material benefits of peace and the instruction of the Xixime

Before discussing how the planting of the Faith among this nation took root, sending out shoots and producing spiritual fruit—all of which demanded such great labor of Spaniards and was a great expense to the king—I will first briefly describe how the deserved punishment and reduction [of the Xixime] was spiritually and materially beneficial. I already mentioned in the prologue to this history that human actions were entwined with divine will in the conversion of these peoples. These actions cannot and should not be separated from one another. Accordingly, I can say that the greatest benefit of the punishment and resettlement of the Xixime nation was that once they were at peace, many silver mines in their lands could begin to be worked along with other mines that Spaniards previously had not been able to reach or exploit. Another major problem that was resolved concerned the Acaxee, who had been converted to the Faith and thus placed under royal protection and who had been in extreme danger of being eaten and eliminated, including their women and children. The Xixime would have realized this goal had His Majesty the king not helped and protected the Acaxee. Alteratively, the Acaxee would have died of starvation, because they did not dare to leave their houses and pueblos to work their lands for fear of being attacked and killed by their enemies. The danger was so grave that the Acaxee were obliged to make a final plea to the governor to defend them; otherwise they were going to abandon their land or join the enemy. Both possibilities posed a great threat to the Spaniards who populated the mining camps in those mountains, because [if the Acaxee were destroyed or their settlements abandoned] the Spaniards would not have a place to buy food for themselves or their workers.

All these dangers ceased with the peace and reduction of the Xixime. When this was achieved there was collective joy in the entire Kingdom of Nueva Vizcaya, where these lands and nations were located. The joy was even greater among the Christian Acaxee and the missionary priests who provided them with religious instruction. This is declared in a portion of a letter from one of [the priests] who wrote to our Father Provincial about the happy [543] news. The letter reads as follows:[18]

> The peace of the Xixime has been a source of great happiness in this land; may God allow it to prosper. Because we are secure in this peace, our Christian children are able to leave the pueblos to search up and down the river for shellfish. This was not possible before, when I let them leave to work their land only with an escort. Such was the fear caused by so many disastrous deaths. Because they were hemmed in and deprived of their lands and the fish in their rivers, they became worried and sick. But now with the peace they can enjoy the rivers and lands at their leisure.
>
> For two months this canyon has been as populated as the pueblos themselves. Everyone who travels this way thanks God that fear and surprise attacks have been replaced with great security and happiness. One old Indian man was so happy that he no longer had to fear ambush or violent death from his enemies that he decided to plant [crops along] the riverbanks so that his children and people would have enough to eat. He carried this out so thoroughly that from a pueblo called Guejupa to another called Otatitlán, which were separated by ten leagues, he did not leave a single plot unplanted, particularly with squash. The [fields] yielded so much food that two pueblos were needed to harvest the plots—places that they had never frequented before without soldiers. There was enough squash for the men, women, and children, and even for the pack animals of the travelers who

18. This letter apparently was written by Santarén in 1611.

carried supplies to the mining camps. The main thing was that these gentiles had become Christians.

Here ends that portion of the letter relating the material results of peace among the Xixime. Although these matters may seem trivial, there are others related to them that are of great importance, because once the Christian Acaxee could enjoy their lands and live securely in their pueblos, their Christianity increased. They provided food for the mining camps and helped the Spaniards to work the mines. With their earnings the Acaxee purchased clothing and food for themselves and their families. Lastly, the land was at peace, although we should keep in mind that the battle with invisible enemies will continue to the end.

CHAPTER X Other means that were used to establish peace among the Xixime nation

In this chapter I will further discuss what was considered necessary to establish peace with a nation like the Xixime, who had broken the peace so many times and who were neighbors to the Tepehuan (whose ferocity will be seen later). The viceroy issued a decree that ordered the building of a fort at the mining camp of San Hipólito.[19] A captain and sixteen soldiers were assigned to guard it and to restrain any group of outlaws who might attempt an uprising, which is what the devil often tries to do in these new Christian communities. Moreover, in the event of an uprising such as the Tepehuan Revolt, the fort, which still stands, would provide Spaniards and peaceful Indians with a refuge and place where they could await help from Durango, which is sixty leagues away. [544] I cannot omit a matter that was recorded elsewhere [in Book II] but that is nevertheless pertinent to what is now being discussed. For one thing this information may be useful to many people who are entrusted with zealously guarding the Royal Treasury. We, the king's vassals, must watch over that which belongs to His Majesty and which is used for the proper defense of the Catholic Faith throughout the world. I dare to broach this topic because I have witnessed events in various parts of Nueva España where the Faith is practiced. The point is that some people have noted that the conversion of these barbarous peoples costs the king a great deal, which is spent on missionaries, churches, and garrisons (although few) that are necessary to keep the Indians peaceful and lawful. These nations are so poor and of so little benefit for His Majesty that, generally speaking, they do not have anything to pay in tribute. It is indeed true that these people do not have anything with which to pay, especially when they are newly converted and have just established civil government. However, it should be understood that the material benefits for His Majesty and his vassals of keeping these people in peace and Christianity are far more important and far surpass the tribute that is due him as sovereign. The king Our Lord defends them from their enemies who kill them and their women and children. He supplies them with missionaries who bring them eternal salvation and lead them to heaven. If Christ Our Lord pronounced the unusual sentence, *Reddite qua sunt Cesaris Cesari*[20] in favor of the tyrannical emperor, Caesar, who subjected God's people of Judea, what would the Lord pronounce for a Catholic king who uses his wealth to expand the Catholic Church — His treasured and beloved kingdom? The answer is clear, as are the reasons why these recently converted nations are placed under our king's protection. If they had property and income of their own, then they should help with the expenses of their king. However, it is nevertheless very important — even from a monetary perspective — to keep them peaceful. This peace has greater value than any personal tribute that these or other peoples might be able to pay. If these nations were not at peace, it is very certain that it would be impossible to maintain the mining camps that are so rich in silver in the

---

19. The fort was completed by 1611.

20. *Margin Note*: Luc. c. 20. Luke 20:25: "give back to Caesar what is Caesar's" (Knox 1956:79).

surrounding areas as well as others located within their lands. Nor would it be possible to maintain investments in livestock and cultivated land, which provide for the needs of the mining camps. If the Indians were to riot or revolt (which is what the devil tries his best to make happen), then they would burn and destroy everything, as they have done on occasion. In addition, these domesticated Indians (if treated well) accustom themselves to work and to desire clothes (which they become very eager to have, once they wear them). Once they are converted, they apply themselves to work and to labor in the mines. The latter, regardless of how rich they are, would decline if it were not for the Indian labor. When they are won over and well treated, the Indians themselves have revealed the mines that were hidden or unknown in their lands. Who can doubt that the material benefits of this {545} (and other benefits that I omit for the sake of brevity) are of greater advantage than the limited tribute that they could pay and yet cannot at present pay because of their poverty? If the tribute were imposed at the beginning of their reduction, they would rebel, and this would result in a much greater expense for the Royal Treasury. Thanks to His Majesty who, as far as I know, has not yet imposed this in Nueva Vizcaya.[21] Experience has demonstrated that treating these newly converted people well produces much better results than strict enforcement of *repartimientos* of Indians as labor in the mines.[22]

I will conclude this chapter, which has dealt with the material benefits of peace among the Xixime nation, by relating something that beautifully supersedes that which has been said. It concerns royal piety and generosity toward this nation for its material and spiritual well-being. Even though this has been discussed with respect to other missions, I say that it should be repeated here because the piety of Our Lord the king has been repeated. Thus it was that the viceroy rejoiced when he learned from the governor of Nueva Vizcaya, Francisco de Urdiñola, that the Xixime nation was well prepared to receive religious instruction. The viceroy provided stipends from the Royal Treasury for four priests who would minister to the Xixime nation, as well as [providing funds] for vessels, images, and bells. He did this in accordance with the orders and decrees that Their Excellencies have received, in the name of His Majesty, for the building of churches and the support of the preaching of the Gospel. All this helped to pacify this nation. He authorized an additional stipend, as important as the first, in the amount of three hundred pesos for food and clothing for a seminary where the young sons of Indian principales would be raised. They would serve as examples in the church as well as the government of the pueblos. With this help and their unfailing diligence the priests and the people who were already baptized continued to labor for the increase of this new Christianity.

CHAPTER XI The spiritual fruits harvested with the conversion of the Xixime to our Holy Faith

Although there were great temporal benefits of peace with the Xixime, who were ensconced in the mountaintops, there were far greater [spiritual] benefits resulting from the preaching of the doctrine of our Holy Faith. The Christianity that was established among this nation, which had been so inhuman and fierce, was just as splendid as that which was seen in the missions of other friendlier and more domesticated nations. Indeed, more can be said about the goodness and prosperity of this nation as compared with the other nations I have written about. To wit, thousands of adults have been baptized and instructed, and a great many of them have been married in the holy rite of the Church. They have shown their missionaries great love and goodwill, treating them with more love and affection than the missionaries ever imagined possible. There was a great deal of all this in this new Christian community, but I

21. Pérez de Ribas' usage here ("as far as I know") may reflect the fact that he wrote portions of the *Historia*, including apparently part of Book 10, after he reached Spain in 1643.

22. A labor supply system in which Spaniards would draft Indians for specific periods and tasks, and pay them appropriately in return.

will record only a few such cases and events to serve as examples of their progress. So that this can be better understood, it seemed to me a good idea to include here a letter written by one of the priests who administered this mission. He says:

The majority of the Xixime who remained after the killing and punishment carried out by Governor Francisco de Urdiñola when he entered Xocotilma [546] have always been very peaceful. They have been very steadfast in matters concerning our Holy Faith, even though they had so many and such clear opportunities to lose their faith, owing to the bad example set by their neighbors, the Tepehuan rebels who surround them. Nevertheless, they always have shown great affection for matters concerning divine worship and the welfare of their souls. They recite the Christian doctrine and many other prayers on their knees, showing great reverence for the temples and sacred things. As a result, they do not speak in church unless it is absolutely necessary. One day it happened that one of them went to speak with the priest after he had finished sweeping and straightening the church, which was being readied for the celebration of a feast day. In the middle of the conversation this Indian left without saying goodbye. When he returned the priest asked him where he had gone. He answered that he had gone outside to spit. Such was the respect shown the church by this Indian, who just yesterday was a barbarian. Saint Gregory the Nicene celebrates the [same] act of illustrious piety by his holy sister, Saint Gorgonia.[23] He wrote that her reverence for God's temple became so great that she did not dare to spit inside it; this Xixime Indian felt the same way.

The affection they have for the holy images and the rosary is remarkable. They make these things themselves, carving them with their knives. One can clearly see that their faith springs from the heart and is not just external appearance. For example, some old Indian men and women came to the priest to tell him that in the past when they were baptized, they did not know as much about matters concerning our Faith, so they did not know what they were receiving, nor had they respected it as they should. Some of them were so scrupulous and so convinced of their former ignorance that they had to be taught the catechism and baptized again. Furthermore, the gentiles who led the uprisings have been reduced and changed from Sauls to Pauls. Through their good example they have brought and continue to bring others [to the Faith]. In general, they all give very good examples, observing the law of God very closely. They have no outstanding vices; there are no drunken revels, nor have there [ever] been any. This vice is not even mentioned, as if it did not exist in the world. Nor is there scandalous concubinage. If there happens to be any as the result of mere weakness, it is easily dissolved with good penance and admonitions. In days past there was a case that showed how much Our Lord has been served by communicating with these people. It happened that an Indian cacique violated a married woman. When the wronged husband found out about it, he sought out one of the priests of those missions. He was very upset, and as soon as he found the priest he told him of his affliction and sorrow. The priest consoled him and calmed him down as much as he could. He told the husband to take a letter to the pueblo of the delinquent cacique and to tell the cacique, in turn, to take the letter to Father Pedro de Gravina. This religious was highly respected by these people. The cacique was to tell Father Gravina of his offense and confess and do penance for his sin.

The letter and instructions reached the cacique at a time when one of his daughters was on the verge of dying. He nevertheless left her and walked all night to the pueblo where he expected to find Father Gravina, who was not there. The cacique left the letter and a message that said that he was going back to be with his daughter who was very close to dying. After having walked thirty leagues round-trip, he found his daughter about to die. After she was dead and had been buried he set out again in search of Father Gravina. He found him along the way and told him of the crime that he had committed. To the priest's great consolation the cacique confessed with great remorse for his sins. [547] The priest was amazed to see such submissiveness in a barbarian who was a principal among his people and a recent convert. The cacique never relapsed into the crime he had committed.

In accordance with their good lives, Our Lord grants the Xixime death with notable peace in their souls. They request the Holy Sacraments, surrendering themselves into God's hands with great resignation. An Indian who had been very bellicose as a gentile was baptized and later lived as such a good Christian that there was barely any matter in his confessions requiring absolution. He was very loyal to the priests and the Spaniards and was the first to warn them during uprisings. One day one of the priests was in dire straits and in great danger of losing his life, as frequently happens among these peoples. When this Indian noticed the priest's fear, he approached and knelt before him. With remarkable affection he let the priest know how upset he was at the priest's own sorrow, suggesting many ways in which he would defend the priest's life. He told the priest that, even in the event that this kingdom should be lost, all his people—of whom there was not one who sided with the rebels—would die first, before the priest, in whose defense he and all his people would offer their lives. It could clearly be seen that this loyal Indian was speaking truthfully. When he got sick and the hour of his death was near, he prepared himself well. He was not content with having confessed many times, so he sent for the priest to give him Extreme Unction, which he received with all his faculties. The priest asked him if he much regretted dying, and he answered that he did not because he trusted in God. Even though he had been a great sinner in the past and confessed that he had harmed the priests, God would pardon his sins.

This is the end of the letter that illustrates the first fruits of this Christianity.

23. The author is referring here to Saint Gregory Nazianzen's panegyric to his sister, Saint Gorgonia (ca. 372) (Thurston and Attwater 1956:524–25).

CHAPTER XII The Xixime build churches; some cases of edification

Once the majority of the Xixime Indians had been baptized, they began to build more permanent churches. This was a task that they generally undertook with pleasure. In one of the principal pueblos of this nation the Indians' desire to hear Mass and be consoled in their own church was so great that the dedication of their church had to be celebrated even before its construction was completed. This took place on the feast day of Our Lord's Transfiguration [August 6]. Many Spaniards from the region attended this celebration, as did the lieutenant governor. The Indians celebrated and adorned this festivity with many arches made from fresh, fragrant flowers and grasses from their thick montes. The Spaniards [added] gunfire from their harquebuses to the procession and Mass. The importance of their temple and house of God was explained to the new Christians in a sermon. They were so happy that they could not stop congratulating and exuberantly greeting one another in Christian fashion.

Once churches were erected in their pueblos, the use of the Holy Sacraments was introduced. They not only complied with the Church's precept of partaking of the Sacraments once a year, but many Indians frequented the divine remedy for their salvation on various feast days throughout the year. Let us add here something that these Indians did very punctually: when they became sick, they would send word to the priest, no matter where he was, even if it was at a distance of quite a few leagues, so that he would come to hear their confessions. On many occasions they would repent very minor sins, [548] being very far from having fallen into serious ones. Those who only a short time earlier did not recognize as sins their idolatry, dealings with the devil, and living off human flesh and blood, now were greatly concerned about the integrity of their confessions and doing penance for their sins. Of the many cases of this type about which I could write I will content myself with recounting one of them so as not to draw out this history. The following case I will recount with the very words of one of the missionary priests who wrote about it:

> They called me (he says) to a sick man, who I thought wanted to confess. It was a time of great rains, and it was difficult coming and going through the mountains to the pueblo, which was three leagues away. The route was very rough and dangerous. When I reached the sick man's house, I found an Indian who was just skin and bones lying on the floor. I asked him his name, thinking that he had [already] been baptized. I found out that he had not been. He told me that when he fell ill he traveled five leagues [to this pueblo] from a gorge where there were other people who had fled Holy Baptism. He, however, had been disabused and was desirous of salvation, and so he had come to be baptized before he died.
>
> I instructed and baptized him with great joy in my soul, and there he died in my arms, thus going to heaven. Then I understood the meaning of the strong feeling in my heart, which Our Lord had sent me when they called me to this sick man. This call obliged me to set out in the rain along such a rough path which, as I have said, I did with such great consolation and strength that I did not feel the least bit tired during my journey. Other people in these locales have been no less fortunate, for having fallen sick, their very own wives have brought them from three or four leagues away, carrying them in a type of woven litter in the form of a sling. After receiving the Holy Sacraments they have gone on to rejoice in God, as we expect.

Up to here [I have been citing] the priest whom God encouraged with a special impulse, enabling him to overcome so many hardships in order to aid these souls whom God wanted to save. All these examples taken together illustrate Our Lord's singular providence in rescuing some of these predestined souls. There are innumerable such cases that are experienced in these holy missions. This is very much in accordance with the apostolic missions, where the missionaries were Christ's Apostles. Saint Luke recounts a talk given to Jews and gentiles by the great preacher of the people, Saint Paul, who said to his audience, *Crediderunt quotquot erant praeordinati ad vitam aeternam*.[24] Those who were chosen for eternal life believed and accepted this doctrine, and we can say that this sick man was among that number. He left that cave of gentile outlaws, to which they had fled from the only means of their salvation. In the end he who was sick and weakened in body and blind in spirit was divinely moved to seek the light of the Gospel and his eternal salvation. The letter [quoted above] was written on the occasion of an epidemic that will be discussed in the following chapter.[25]

---

24. *Margin Note*: Actor. 13. 48. Acts 13:48: "and they found faith, all those who were destined to eternal life" (Knox 1956:129).

25. This letter is testimony to how Old World diseases spread be-

CHAPTER XIII An illness strikes these people, and other events

At this time [1613] Our Lord sent a deadly sickness to this newly baptized nation. It was not smallpox, like the one previously related, but one that caused bloody stools, which affected many people.[26] Thus, as previously noted [in Book IV], God applied the same policy His Majesty applied to almost all the other [549] nations of the New World, taking as first fruits thousands of baptized infants and adults who had been converted to the Faith. The same thing occurred at this time [in this mission], where the course of human events has had the same results. I will note the increased merit of the ministers and shepherds of these souls who, as noted, endured great suffering on such rough roads, attending to great numbers of people who fell ill outside their pueblos and ranchos. The widely scattered bodies and souls obliged one priest to turn his house into an infirmary. There he brought the sick, attending to them as priest, nurse, and doctor. He also attended others who were gravely ill and could not come to him. The other priests did the same thing in their districts.

God consoled the priests with some unusual cases that eased their burden. A very good Christian Indian learned that there was a woman who was a great idol worshiper and devotee of an idol that she had kept hidden in the most secret part of her house. A good Christian went to the house of this woman to disabuse her of her error and to try as best he could to obtain that diabolical possession and deliver her from the power of Satan. When he began his talk, the woman obstinately replied, "How can I abandon and scorn this stone, which I have had for twenty-one years, ever since my father died? I inherited it from him and with its help I have enjoyed abundant harvests each year from my fields. Get out of here, because if I were to give you my idol, I would perish from hunger."

The diligent Christian did not give up, although he saw that the woman was becoming infuriated. Instead, he advanced more arguments so that she would realize

that she had been deceived. God willed that heavenly light should strike the understanding and will of this Indian idolatress with such force that right then she took out the idol, threw it to the ground and kicked and smashed it to bits. She did not stop there; she went to look for the priest of her doctrina, [expressing] great regret and sorrow for the deceit and blindness in which she had lived. She confessed her sins and was baptized and reconciled with God and healed in body and soul. She was happy, she confessed, that God had freed her from the cruel torments that her soul had suffered, and she was confidant that she would be saved. With these and other examples the Christianity of the Xixime was perfected and purified. However, we will leave the Xixime with a discussion of that which was most resplendent among them — the devotion with which they celebrated and participated in Holy Week exercises.

Although the practice of scourging has been discussed with regard to other nations, among the Xixime it was particularly singular and remarkable. These Indians have applied themselves to it with such devotion that nearly all of them undertake scourging during Holy Week. In addition to the scourgings that are practiced every Friday during Lent in the church — even when the priest is not present — others carry the Cross on their shoulders. It happened one time that a priest who was visiting the pueblos of his district found a shrine that was made of branches in which a very large Cross had been erected. At the foot of the Cross were scourges, which had been bathed in blood during the procession that the Indians had just voluntarily conducted. It seems that those Indians were [inspired] by heaven to place their scourges — bathed in their own blood — at the foot of the holy Cross. These trophies symbolized how profoundly the Indians had been changed, a fact that never ceased to amaze the priests. The Xixime had been so bloodthirsty for human flesh and blood that it used to be said — by the Xixime [550] and by those in the mining camps — that the Xixime had a saying that the flesh of Indians tasted like ordinary beef; the flesh of blacks tasted like bacon; and best of all was the flesh of Spaniards, which tasted like mutton. These barbarians celebrated feasts where they ate the flesh of all those they killed who worked in and traveled to and from the mines.

---

yond the mission frontier, affecting even those who fled the Jesuits and Christian Indians.

26. During the previous year the same or similar maladies, including typhus and typhoid or dysentery ("bloody stools"), reached epidemic proportions in Sinaloa and southern Sonora (AGN 1612; Reff 1991b:153–58). The smallpox epidemic referred to occurred in 1610.

They [who once] delighted in the flesh and blood of others now view the shedding of their own blood as a penance for their sins. Their inhuman and deeply rooted vice is so forgotten that not a trace of it remains, except the abhorrence with which they confront the ferocity and blindness of their previous state. This was [one of the] triumphs of the Cross of Christ; through the spilling of His innocent blood these Indians have abandoned and forgotten their barbarous customs. Today a very brilliant Christianity flourishes among them. If there are not as many people here as there were in the beginning (for the reasons that I have noted), they [nevertheless] are in a much happier state than before. Now many [more] souls go to heaven as compared to previously, when they all went to hell. Today, nearly all of them go to glory. These conversions and reductions with which God wished to multiply this mission of San Andrés have not been concluded. In the following chapter I will relate what happened around the year 1624.

CHAPTER XIV The priests undertake a new entrada to reduce and convert to our Holy Faith the pueblos and rancherías of the Hina[27]

It was noted earlier that this mountain range (in which we still remain) covers many leagues in both length and breadth. Many nations of barbarous people lived hidden among its canyons. In spite of this, they were not so hidden nor was this mountain range so great that they did not experience the evangelic ministers' charity. Due to it, these [priests] were able to travel through these mountains and valleys as swiftly as deer (as I stated in the prologue), moved and inspired by Christ's charity to seek out these souls and bring them to His flock, thus placing them on the road to salvation.

These nations are called the Hina and the Humi, and they were especially known for their remarkable bellicosity. They were spread out among many rancherías, some of them close to a very strong river called Piaxtla, which begins in the upper reaches of this mountain range. Still other rancherías were farther in the mountains. Because of this and also because of their reputed ferocity, Spaniards had not set foot in their lands, although they surrounded them on all four sides. For sixty years these nations had been quite close to long-time Christian settlements within the jurisdiction of Nueva Vizcaya and Nueva Galicia, which were populated by Spaniards. His Eminence Don Gonzalo de Hermosillo, the first Bishop of Durango[28] (who was mentioned earlier, when I wrote about the missions of Sinaloa) had knowledge of the loss of these souls. He asked Father Luis de Bonifaz, who at that time was Visitor of the missions, to send Father Diego [551] González de Cueto to visit these people, because he was a long-time missionary in these mountains. The Bishop had heard a lot about him and about the holy zeal and grace that God had given him for attracting and reducing the Indians—no matter how fierce and barbarous they might be—to the gentle yoke of Christ Our Lord. Many real difficulties and dangers were encountered in this enterprise. Nevertheless, this was a very pious cause in the service of both the Divine and human Majesties. It was a cause in the service of the Divine Majesty because of the salvation of those souls; the royal, human Majesty was served by the reduction of these people and the elimination of an asylum and den of outlaws who disturbed the neighboring mining camps and other Christian nations that were already subjects of the king.

For all these reasons the Father Visitor was obliged to find a way to overcome the obstacles to the Hina's

27. Little is known about the Hina and the Humi. One of the earliest Jesuit commentaries on the two groups, written by Alonso del Valle (DHM 1618), suggests that they were related to the Xixime. The Humi lived near the headwaters of the Río Piaxtla; the Hina lived farther downstream in the famous Devil's Canyon. Apparently Cueto's first entrada discussed in this chapter took place in 1622.

28. Hermosillo was bishop of Durango from 1621 to 1631.

conversion. Therefore, he decided upon Father Cueto's visit, despite the fact that some missionary priests were of the opinion that a person like Father Cueto, who was of such great benefit to those mountain [nations] where he had suffered so much, should not be exposed to such clear danger. If it were time to do so, [which it is not, because] this venerable priest is still alive, I could say a great deal here concerning the great hardships that he has endured in his holy and untiring zeal for helping poor Indians, in which he [still] perseveres to this day. Perhaps another occasion will arise in which to do so. In the end this religious priest accepted willingly, joyously, and with pleasure his entrada to a region with such fierce and cannibalistic people, one where other troublemakers and outlaws had gone to live in barbarous freedom. It was for this reason that Father Cueto was ordered to go only to the first pueblo, called Guaimino, whence he was to try to aid these Hina people, without going farther inland. I will first write about these Hina people, leaving the Humi for later.

The priest reached the settlement of Guaimino, whence he sent messages into the mountains, requesting that some of their principales come to see him. Six of them came down by themselves. The priest treated them well (which he knew how to do with grace and skill). Through these six principales he was able to communicate with the rest [of the principales], to whom the Lord Bishop's message was explained. They all made excuses as to why they would not come to the settlement at Guaimino. It was later understood that this was because they feared that the priest was accompanied by Spanish soldiers who came to execute outlaws (because there were some guilty individuals among them). Even though they were disabused when they saw no Spanish soldiers, their final reply, nevertheless, was that if he came by himself and wanted to talk to them, it would have to be in another pueblo called Iztlán, four leagues farther inland, up the river. They would all wait for him there, and if that was not satisfactory, he was to turn back and never set eyes on them again.

The good priest was greatly perplexed. On one hand, he did not want to overstep the boundaries of obedience nor the limits of the settlement to which he had been assigned. On the other hand, he realized that he faced the same life-threatening danger in the settlement of Guaimino as in the one that the Indians had designated. He felt that much would be lost if he allowed this opportunity to pass him by. Furthermore, he had brought along none of the soldiers whom the Indians feared. Therefore, placing the welfare of these souls above the risk of losing his own life, he decided to go to the pueblo of Iztlán, which today is dedicated to Saint Francis Xavier. These religious missionaries consider this glorious saint their great protector, for he was the founder of the missions of the Indies of the East, as well as captain and guide of the missionaries of the Company.

When Father Cueto reached the pueblo of Iztlán, he found only its inhabitants. The remaining Hina were at three other rancherías in the highest and most interior reaches of the mountains, waiting for a final decision to be made. [552] When the priest heard this, he tore into three pieces a small red taffeta drape that he was carrying along with the chalice for saying Mass. The drape served as a backing for the image of the Most Holy Virgin, in whose presence he celebrated Mass every day. He wrapped his rosary in the first piece [of taffeta], a reliquary in the second, and the aforementioned tiny image [of the Most Holy Virgin] in the third. He sent one object to each of the three rancherías, hoping to negotiate the impossible by means of those holy relics. They all came back from these three places with the same answer, asking the priest to advance ten leagues farther inland to the place they called Oveibos, which in Nahuatl is called Quilitlán. Today this pueblo is dedicated to the glorious Apostle Saint James. They promised that without fail they would all be waiting for him there. When one priest who was a comrade of Father Cueto's wrote about this entrada, he justifiably exclaimed (and he would have had even greater reason to have done so later on, as we shall see), "My God," he says, "what patience and willpower one needs to accomplish great things, especially among such barbarous people! Who would not unscrupulously turn back after so many delays, meeting places, and deceptions? And who would not run from those who were so rebellious?" Father Diego González de Cueto did not. Instead, he was convinced that if he were already trapped between two doors (as they say), the life-threatening dangers where he was were as great as those ten leagues farther inland.

Commending this cause to Our Lord, to whom it pertained, he sent word that he would set out immediately and that they should expect him the following day. The outcome of this journey will be told in the following chapter.

CHAPTER XV Father Diego de Cueto continues his entrada to reduce the Hina

Because the journey was long, Father Diego de Cueto stopped along the trail to rest for the night. At that place more than three hundred young warriors, armed for battle, began to descend. They were not accompanied by women or children, which served to warn the priest to place his trust in divine protection. His cause for concern was particularly strong because his long experience had taught him that their intentions are not good when they hide their children and women. He spent a sleepless night in holy conversation, fearful of barbarous attacks and wondering how his labors would end. At dawn he set out on the road for Quilitlán, accompanied by the Indians who had descended the previous night as well as by others who were joining them. At a wide, sandy stretch of a riverbank, he found three stakes from which hung the taffeta cloth, the rosary, and the image and the reliquary. However, there was nobody guarding them. All this increased the priest's fear of what might occur, given such evident danger. He picked up his holy objects and knelt down, kissing them and shedding many tears. On the one hand, he cried at the joy and happiness of such an obvious risk of losing his life for spreading the Holy Gospel and introducing Christ Our Lord to these blind people. On the other hand, he cried because he lamented the enormous difficulties that threatened his [attempts] to achieve his objective.

On this occasion Our Lord wanted to show how pleased He was with the patience [553] and suffering of His evangelical ministers. When the priest looked more carefully, he saw that a good number of people had slowly begun to descend. They had been waiting to see whether the priest came alone or with soldiers. Once they realized that he came alone, more than a thousand men, women, and children gathered before nightfall. Everybody rested that night, and the following morning after saying Mass the priest spoke to the Indians in the name of the Bishop. He knew how to do this so elegantly that with the [aid] of divine providence they all decided to resettle.

The first thing they built was a small church with walls and a roof of straw, similar to the poor palace where God chose to be born into this world. The priest called it the Church of the Holy Spirit, so that such a patron would enlighten these hearts and lead them out of their blindness. He baptized more than 150 infants to the great delight of their parents. He gave them hope that once he reported to the Bishop, he would return to see them and they might then be able to settle permanently with other people.

The priest returned to his district of Otatitlán and gave an account of these very happy events to His Lordship the Bishop and the Father Visitor, Luis de Bonifaz. The continuation of this work was delayed for a long time for reasons and causes that were not the priest's doing, which need not be related here.[29] Thus, the complete establishment of the doctrine could not be accomplished at that time. Fortunately, divine providence was at work and saw to it that these people, who by nature are not easy to tame, were better prepared. The time came when God moved some of these people's Indian principales to request that the Father Provincial and superior of the mission of San Andrés return to them their Father Diego de Cueto. His peaceful manner was known to them and they wanted him to instruct them and make them Christians. When the Bishop, who was a vigilant and good shepherd, heard the good news about the people's readiness, he arranged with the Father Provincial to have Father Cueto again take up this enterprise. Father Cueto was in Durango, where it seems he had been sent by God so that he could quickly accomplish such a beneficial task for the glory of His Divine Majesty. The Father Provincial, Father Gerónimo Díaz, dispatched Father Cueto, who received the blessing of the Bishop who, as will be seen in the following chapters, entrusted this new community to the Company for religious instruction.[30]

---

29. Pérez de Ribas may be alluding here to the epidemic of 1623–25 and a shortage of missionaries that limited mission expansion during the late 1620s.

30. Gerónimo Díaz was provincial from 1628 to 1631. The Hina region apparently fell within the Diocese of Durango, and accordingly the Jesuits or other religious had to have the bishop's permission to preach and administer the sacraments and otherwise attend spiritually to the Hina.

CHAPTER XVI Father Diego de Cueto returns to the Hina; the difficulties that arose in their reduction

Father Diego de Cueto initiated his mission to the Hina in 1630 by establishing a base station of sorts at the pueblo of San Sebastián de Guaimino. There he carefully gathered the Indians whom he had dealt with earlier and many others from the region with whom he had communicated. Nevertheless, he again encountered great difficulties, as usually happens in these enterprises. Although on the one hand it was easy to reduce the leaders, who were willing to receive Holy Baptism, there still were many elderly people who continued to resist and who had withdrawn to the interior of the mountains, taking with them their vices, drunkenness, and superstitions. No less disturbing were the interventions of a Tepehuan Indian [554] from the pueblo of Tunal, in [the Diocese of] Durango, who had also withdrawn to these mountains because of the crimes that he had committed during the Tepehuan Revolt. He had taken the people of Tunal with him. In the following book I will give a full accounting of the Tepehuan Revolt; my intention in this book is to discuss all the missions and conversions that pertain to the mission of San Andrés. Therefore, let us return to the restless and perverse Tepehuan who tried to take good Father Cueto's life.

Because cowardice ordinarily accompanies treason, this Indian sought out accomplices for his crime, which he would have undoubtedly succeeded in executing were it not for the Indians of a Christian pueblo called Tepustla. After he tried to recruit them to his harmful cause the Indians instead told the captain of the fort at San Sebastián, who warned the priest to be alert. He also told the alcalde mayor of that district so that he could take the appropriate measures, which is in fact what he did, arresting the Tepehuan Indian and placing him in shackles in the aforementioned fort. His imprisonment calmed the spirits of those who wanted to be reduced, who soon came from their rancherías at the priest's calling. However, there were still other disturbances created by some Indians who were lukewarm to [the idea of] congregating and accepting the Church. When the governor of Nueva Vizcaya heard about this, he gave orders for the alcalde mayor of that jurisdiction to take a small troop of soldiers composed of encomenderos (in accordance with the terms of their encomiendas) and carry out a campaign to restore peace and calm the rebels. Here one can clearly see the many advantages of having forts, as was discussed at length in Book II. Forts are not needed to forcefully introduce Holy Baptism; that has never been done. Rather, they are only to suppress rebels who disturb Holy Baptism and obstruct those who wish to establish peace with God and the king. And this was the case with the alcalde mayor's campaign.

As a result of Father Cueto's blandishments and gentleness as well as the many gifts that he gave them, including a large number of donated cows, these well-intentioned Indians finally came down to the plains. They built churches and established settlements with almost two thousand people. It seems that through these diligent acts the devil had been deprived of his prey and many other souls. Still, much fighting remains against the powers of hell before these spiritual conquests achieve the necessary victory.

Owing to his age and the merits of his suffering, Father Diego de Cueto was assigned an assistant, Father Diego Jiménez, who was also a spirited minister of the doctrine. He arrived at a time of drought and famine [in 1633], which forced those who had congregated to go into the mountains in search of roots and other sources of sustenance. The priests sent word of this to the governor of Nueva Vizcaya, Don Gonzalo Gómez de Cervantes, who was a gentleman of great piety, which he exercised with these poor people. To calm and win over the Indians, he ordered that they be given one hundred fanegas of maize. Although it could be said *quid inter tantos?*[31] it at least provided them with seeds for planting so that they would not perish the following year. Despite all the benefits [that would be realized] at harvest time, those with restless and perverted spirits attempted once again to take the people back to their former settlements. If this were the only damage done, there would have been nothing to fear. However, this

---

31. "Is that all?"

depraved spirit went so far as to want to kill the priests and halt religious instruction and Christianity.

With the positive zeal that Our Lord communicated to them these two fervent ministers faced up to these fearful rumors. They continued visiting their pueblos, giving them sound talks and exhortations, and instructing the adults and baptizing the infants. Nevertheless, the unrest did not cease; the threats became so serious that it was rumored and recognized that some of the Indians were preparing their arrows in order to declare war against the Spaniards. Once the rumors became this [555] serious, the priests were forced to warn the governor of Nueva Vizcaya, so that he would have time to prevent the impending danger and drive the den of outlaws from the land. Because these outlaws were close to the city of Durango, they posed a threat to the city and even more so to neighboring Christian communities.

The governor immediately tried to remedy the situation and ordered the captain of the fort at San Hipólito to take his soldiers and pacify that land and punish the rebels. This took nearly a year, during which time Father Diego de Cueto's spirit and zeal for the glory of God never ceased. He sacrificed his own temporal life for the greater wealth of the spiritual lives of those whom he so loved. He sent the restless gentiles additional gifts and new messages of kindness, convincing some to descend and form a settlement and mission. He founded the sixth pueblo of this mission, which was dedicated to our patron saint of all the Spains, the Apostle Santiago. Nevertheless, because matters [of the Faith] were not taking hold nor was peace certain, the final measure had to be taken. The governor ordered Captain Bartolomé Suárez de Villalba to take his soldiers from the fort at San Hipólito with some allied Christian Indians and pacify the land; he was not to return until the land was free of those who disturbed and disrupted the peace. This outstanding captain's valor, prudence, and Christian zeal deserve an honorable mention here. He held the post of captain for more than twenty consecutive years, demonstrating great zeal serving both [the Divine and human] Majesties. During these years he protected the mining camps and helped to reduce all the nations of the extensive mountains of Topia and San Andrés. His deeds were some of the most courageous of all those by captains who have battled fierce and barbarous Indians in the Kingdom of Nueva Vizcaya. Because his labors were extensive in the campaign that we are now discussing, we will leave them for the following chapter.

CHAPTER XVII The expedition of Captain Bartolomé Suárez to the Hina nation[32]

The account of this expedition will be given by an eyewitness and companion of Father Diego de Cueto, Father Diego Jiménez. He received an order from his superiors to accompany the expedition as chaplain, attending as best he could to the spiritual needs of Captain Suárez and his troops. Therefore I will here insert the account that he wrote to our Father Provincial, which reads as follows:

Captain Bartolomé Suárez, who was lieutenant general of all these lands, had commanded the leaders of the Hina nation to come to see him at the pueblo of Yamoriba. We reached the pueblo on November 18, 1633. There we found no news of the arrival of the caciques; rather, we found only a warning from Father Juan de Mallen, superior of the mission of San Andrés, telling the captain to proceed carefully. He had learned from several local people that the elders among the Hina were readying themselves to defend [556] their rancherías and lands. This warning was validated by the fact that it was already the twentieth of the month and the caciques had not arrived.

The captain, who did not wish to enter their lands by spilling blood, was greatly worried. However, his concern became moot when another letter from Father Diego de Cueto arrived that very day. The letter indicated that the caciques would reach the pueblo that afternoon. As a reception and to instill fear in any who might rebel or start fighting, the captain ordered his commander to instruct the Indian allies from Santa María de Utaís, San Pedro, San

32. Suárez was a lieutenant captain general, meaning that he was acting on behalf of the captain general, which in this case would have been the governor of Nueva Vizcaya. In the long letter by Jiménez quoted in this and subsequent chapters, Jiménez refers to Suárez as both the general as well as the captain. Suárez's expedition took place in the fall of 1633.

Miguel, Santiago Basio, and others who were well armed and equipped for war, to meet the Hina at the entrance of the pueblo. The more than thirty Spaniards from the garrison would remain inside the pueblo. The Indian allies aligned themselves in the form of a half moon and received the Hina in the center. At that point the soldiers with their harquebuses came out and completed the circle. Some had muskets that were loaded with so much [gunpowder] that when they fired I think the new guests trembled. The captain was also very well armed and gallant.

The commander ordered the Hinas to put away their weapons, and once they had done so the captain explained the reason why he had brought them together. This was to reaffirm the peace agreement that they had agreed to previously, when the Indians came and swore to honor their obligations. As a sign of confederation and friendship, Captain and Lieutenant General Bartolomé Suárez gave the Indians bullets; they in turn gave him arrows. After a thunderous volley from the harquebuses they all embraced.

After the general had played his part, I played mine. I arranged for the entire army to go in procession to the church, singing prayers in their language while the soldiers fired volleys from their guns. The Salve Regina was sung to the accompaniment of an organ, because now we had someone to play it. Afterwards, for the edification of the Indians and to demonstrate greater humility and the authority of its ministers, the general got down on his knees, and to my great consternation, without my being able to stop him, he kissed my feet, cleaning them with his venerable gray locks. This act not only aroused emotions in me, but it moved the Spaniards and the Indians in a very singular way. Afterwards a generous number of bags of food and meat were distributed among these people, who had come in fear and trembling at the name of Suárez, knowing the remarkable punishments that he had inflicted upon scandalous Indians who spread trouble in this mountain range. That night the Indians were in such a good mood that during the splendid dancing that more than four hundred of them performed, they sang songs of praise and thanks for Captain Suárez. The next day the captain dispatched five Hina caciques and their followers, retaining two other caciques. Although he said he was retaining them so they could serve as his guides, they were really hostages for his safety.

The trails were cleared and on the Feast of San Pedro Alexander [November 26] we reached a flat area where there was a tranquil river, stretches of which are hidden like the Río Guadiana in Spain. When I saw this pleasant place, which was given the name of San Pedro del Río, I ordered a Cross to be made, which the general and I together erected. Because no Spaniard had ever set foot in these lands, we took possession of them for Our Lord the king, in the name of Nueva Vizcaya.

From this place we walked for two or three days until we sighted a low place in the mountains. When our guides reached this place they were fainting from the roughness and steepness of the tremendously deep gorges and vertical cliffs. They said it was impossible to go any farther. [557] This bad news made the general very upset, and the next morning at

dawn he assembled a meeting with the caciques to discuss the trail. He threatened to hang the chief guide who had brought us thus far, not knowing the terrain (he said). He had led us to a place whence it was almost impossible to extricate ourselves. I interceded for this man to give him time to find a solution; he consulted with the others about the problem. Although some mules were lost, finally he led us out through a trail that was broken by much hard work and digging with pikes and spades. The general was such a gentleman that he took some of his own mules and gave them to those who lost mules.

On the feast day of San Andrés [November 30] we came upon the fields of the Hinas. Although the allies who accompanied us needed food and threw themselves upon them, the general had the bugle sounded and gave an order that no one should enter those fields on pain of death. This order won the Hina over; one of their caciques came out to meet us with twenty cargas [33] of maize, which provided no small relief.

After another day's travel, late in the afternoon, we reached the first pueblo, called Santiago. Its inhabitants did not trust the captain and had withdrawn. We found only a few whom Father Diego de Cueto gathered after calling to them several times and promising them that the captain absolutely would not harm them. They came out to meet us in procession with Crosses in their hands, men and women, young and old, Christians and gentiles. Among them was an Indian who bore the same emblem of the holy Cross that a few years before, during the Tepehuan Revolt, was [involved in] a miracle. When this Indian and some Tepehuan reached the mines called Pánuco, they burned the haciendas and the church and everything in it. Moreover they set fire to a beautiful Cross that had been erected in the cemetery. Our Lord, who had arranged for the youths in Babylon to be saved from the fiery ovens,[34] extinguished the fire at the foot of the Cross. No matter how much they fanned the fire it would not consume the Cross, nor was the holy wood even singed. The Indian perpetrator of this sacrilege became so agitated—which should have served him as a warning of the evil that he was committing—that he charged the holy Cross with demonic anger and tried to knock it down by kicking it. But with his first kick the tendons of that arrogant foot tightened so much that from that moment until now he has not been able to set his foot down.

This fellow came in the procession with the Cross in his hands. Because he was crippled, at every step he made a thousand genuflections and sweeping bows before the Cross, which he had sacrilegiously persecuted in the past. He shamed the devil who had wanted to use him to destroy Christ's holy standard. From then on, God made the Cross of Pánuco famous through many marvelous signs.

That night on the eve of the feast day of our Father Saint Francis Xavier [December 3], all those frightened [people] gathered together in the pueblo of La Concepción de la Santísima Virgen, eight leagues from Santiago. The next day we sang the Mass of the Saints as we crossed the river,

33. A carga equaled 138 kilos.
34. Shadrach, Meshach, and Abed-Nego (Daniel 3).

near the pueblo. There we found all the people gathered together in the church. We gave thanks to Our Lord for such a populous pueblo, which is one of the largest in all the mountains. None of them exceed it in number of residents, and it surpasses all of them in the pleasantness of its location on the wide plains.

The general thanked them for the elaborate reception that they gave him. [558] The next day around nine o'clock we went on ahead and reached the pueblo of Santa Apolonia, which is two leagues from the said pueblo of Concepción.

There the general rested, much to the pleasure of the Indian residents of the pueblo, who now saw how peaceable and human he was.

The preceding is from a report of Father Diego Jiménez. Because it was so long, as was the expedition, we will continue quoting the report in the following chapters.

CHAPTER XVIII Captain Suárez continues his entrada to these mountain people

Up to this point Father Diego Jiménez has spoken of the expedition that Captain Suárez undertook to give greater permanence to the pueblos that Father Diego de Cueto had managed to congregate and reduce to our Holy Faith at the cost of great danger and hardship. The enemies of the Faith did not cease in disturbing and disrupting these pueblos. The captain, likewise, did not desist in his journey or in procuring aid for this evangelical minister, who suffered greatly to spread the glory of Christ and for the good of the souls that had been entrusted to him.

Now follows Father Diego Jiménez's account. We had left him and Captain Suárez's expedition in the pueblo of Concepción. The captain did not stop until he reached the place chosen by Father Diego de Cueto and Father Jiménez. The account continues as follows:

The troops set out for the pueblo of San Ignacio. After a little more than a league and a half we found a most beautiful ramada. All the residents of the pueblo at Iztlán, which is named after my father, Saint Francis Xavier, and those from another pueblo called San Gerónimo de Ahoya, held Crosses in their hands. Still others wore Crosses made of palm fronds around their necks. Although these pueblos were poor, as a sign of joy at his arrival the inhabitants presented the general with a great gift: the entire three leagues leading to this pueblo of San Ignacio, where Father Diego de Cueto was waiting, were lined with triumphal arches, Crosses, and sedge.

We entered the pueblo in splendid military order at about five o'clock in the afternoon. The allies saluted with their customary unnerving screams while the Spaniards fired their harquebuses. The church responded with a great ringing of bells as well as with music from instruments that the priest had acquired throughout his many years as a missionary. To see Father Diego de Cueto, whom the captain revered, was especially comforting. At the same time our hearts all were pierced at the sight of the crippled priest. His advanced age, frailty, and frostbite made it impossible for him to walk.

When these two elderly men first saw each other, they each tried to outdo the other with courtesies. This ended with both of them in tears. For the priest these were tears of gratitude that the captain had come to help in that enterprise of the Faith—to favor the faithful and to restrain those who were obstructing it. For the general the tears were of sorrow and grief at the sight of the priest's serious ailments.

Then the commander ordered all the allies and gentiles to pay attention to what the general was doing. Clinging to his staff, he got down on his knees and tried to convince the priest with a thousand pleas to allow him to kiss his feet. Because of his great humility, the priest refused, and so the general then kissed the hands and feet of the two of us priests. Then, turning to those who were present, he gave a very Christian speech, charging them to revere and greatly respect the priests, especially Father Diego [559] de Cueto who, in order to ransom them from darkness, had suffered great hunger, toil, nakedness, sweat, danger, and other hardships. As they could see, this had notably damaged his health. And because he—the captain whom the Tepehuan, Xixime, Acaxee, and other nations feared—laid his lips and eyes at the feet of the priest, they should hold him in the highest esteem.

Father Diego de Cueto was so moved by these words that he could not respond except with tears, which streamed from his eyes. He took the captain to his lodgings, which were well appointed, considering the rusticity of this land.

He repaid the captain for the expense and labor of the expedition with repeated thanks and with other major deeds that his great poverty permitted. The troops spent thirty-seven days here, during which time discussions were held concerning the complete and total settlement of these peoples.

On the *Dominica infra octavam*[35] of the Virgin's Immaculate Conception, all the people gathered to celebrate it. A very orderly procession was organized, which set out from the church with an image of the Virgin's Immaculate Conception, which was carried on a very nicely decorated bier. Although it was not adorned with rich jewels, it had many lovely flowers and was accompanied by music, flutes, and more than thirteen hundred people. The procession went to where the general and his military escort were encamped. The general, his infantry, and the more than three hundred allies that he had brought with him came out to meet the procession. After the harquebuses had fired a joyful salute he put down his cane and took up a flag. He unfurled and waved it and then laid it before the Most Holy Virgin. Worshiping her with three well-timed genuflections, he humbly kissed the bier. Those present were moved by the sight of such unusual (albeit proper) piety in a soldier, who [generally are] more inclined to the haughty and arrogant spirits produced by drums and bugles than humble ceremonies.

The image was placed on an altar that had been prepared in a field. There, in the Mexican language, the remarkable Suárez de Villalba gave a solemn speech adjusted to the Indians' intellectual capacity. He was permitted to do so because, even though he was not an ecclesiastical minister, his speech aided those who were, and he was acting as a minister of the king, who supported them.[36] He was very clever at making himself understood by way of comparisons and similes, which he had learned from his lengthy experience in dealing with Indians. He charged them to maintain the peace, attend [church] in their pueblos, frequent religious instruction, and love and respect their minister. The trails to their rancherías, pueblos, and fields were now open; thus, if they did not do as he instructed, he would return, not as their kind and gentle father, but rather as a lion that would tear them to bits, setting fire to their homes and everything therein. This threat was intended for those who might cause trouble and sow unrest or induce rebellion in this Christianity. A skilled interpreter translated this talk for them into their language, for which they were very happy and grateful.

I will now recount a case that took place at that time. The inhabitants of the pueblo of San Xavier (led by their cacique, who had set a bad example a few days before the captain arrived) had held a communal drunken revel. It was celebrated with a joyful dance for an idol that had been carved from the widest part of a macana, a weapon of war, into [the shape of] a human head. Father Cueto had reprehended them for this idolatry, and even though he made an effort to obtain the idol, he was never able to get his hands on it. Taking advantage of the present occasion, he commanded them to bring it to him immediately, saying that the captain wanted it and that under no circumstances (on pain of severe punishment) were they to hide it. This frightening demand sufficed for the idol to come into the general's possession. [560] At the end of his speech he took it out and cast it before the Most Holy Virgin, notably angered at those who revered that stick of wood. He undoubtedly would have beaten them with it had Father Diego de Cueto not intervened. He felt what was done was sufficient to resolve the problem. The captain concluded his talk by going on a most Christian tirade against the idol. He then ordered those very people who adored it to stomp and spit on it, thereby ending the scandal in this Christianity.

In the following chapter this account will continue, recounting other events.

---

35. "Sunday during the octave" of the Feast of the Immaculate Conception, which is commemorated over eight days, culminating on December 8.

36. Again, because the lands of the Hina fell within the Diocese of Durango, the bishop's permission was required for a priest, or in this case a soldier, to preach.

CHAPTER XIX Some singular cases in these pueblos; the conclusion of Lieutenant Captain General Bartolomé Suárez's expedition

Because we are discussing the Holy Virgin (Father Jiménez continues) let us not return her to the church until we recount an unusual case that was considered miraculous. It took place in June of this year [1633] at the pueblo of San Juan Bautista and was witnessed by Father Diego de Cueto, another religious from [the Order of] Saint Augustine, and others who were present. One day as Father Cueto was finishing up his regular visit to that pueblo, a ladino Indian said to him very furtively: "Look, Father, even though these idiots claim to be very happy, I fear something bad is going to happen to you. Two of the oldest Indians from this pueblo (naming them) are full brothers, and they have told me that one night their deceased mother appeared to them. She exhorted them in a thousand different ways to leave this pueblo where they are living and return to the place where she gave birth to them. She also told them to plant their fields there. If they did not do so, they should not expect rain or good harvests. Rather, they and their priest would die from sheer hunger." The Indian added that some of them had said, "We are all leaving this place—and fast."

These are Satan's lies, for he attempts to obstruct the reduction and conversion of these people in whatever way he can. This warning caused the priest great concern, for the Indians who were the authors of this lie were old and one of them was known to be a famous sorcerer. Therefore, with the consent of the Indian who had revealed this to him he summoned all the people to the church to tell them what he had been told. Turning to these two brothers with great sorrow, he asked how they could possibly believe that their mother, who had been dead for more than forty years and was burning in hell because she did not want to be a Christian, was hurting their hearts (an expression that the Indians use). It was not their mother, but rather the devil, who was angry to see them as Christians. He wanted to deceive them so that they would return to the mountains, turning their backs on God and thus losing their souls. There on the altar was a painting of the Most Holy Virgin that Father Gerónimo Díaz had presented to this new mission when he was Provincial. Pointing to this painting, the priest added, "My sons, do not allow yourselves to be deceived. Recognize that the only mother you have is that Lady whom you see here in her beautiful image. Even though she is the Mother of God, she is also yours, to aid you through God, her Son. Ask her to help and support you. Do not leave the church for the mountains. God will make it rain so that you can plant and harvest fertile crops."

After he encouraged them with this speech he mounted his horse. Although the sky was clear with no more trace of clouds than those seen by the servant of the Prophet Elijah,[37] suddenly the weather changed and the sun darkened and it began to storm. The sky filled with extremely dense clouds, and [561] there followed great thunder and lightning. Although the weather was frightening, the priest gave thanks to Our Lord for having validated his sermon and teaching by fulfilling the words that he had spoken while trusting in God's mercy. So much rain fell that it was not until he reached his house that he was able to take shelter and kneel and give thanks.

Although the rainfall was copious in that region, in that pueblo [of San Juan Bautista] the winds were particularly strong, so much so that they ripped the roof off the straw church and strewed it over the fields. The wind carried the holy image to a lake that was more than a hundred paces away. In spite of the fact that it was a painting, when they found it two days later it was whole. The varnish had not been damaged and the colors were so bright that when we saw them it was as if the painting had just come from the hands of the artist. Although it seems worth considering that God allowed the image of His Most Holy Mother to be overturned by the tornado and cast into a swamp, we can interpret this as a demonstration of those cold and lukewarm infidels' lack of faith and reverence. At the same time God did show His concern for the reverence of the image of His Most Holy Mother in not allowing the water or mud from the lake to harm it, for when it was removed [from the lake] it was very beautiful. Furthermore, He comforted those who were truly faithful with the water from heaven that was needed in their lands. Our Lord has continued for a very long time to validate what the priest said. He also has given them very abundant harvests, which on the occasion of this entrada generously sustained us Spaniards and our more than three hundred allies. Indeed, not even a dent was made in their granaries.

Let us now return to the procession that we left behind at the point when they were returning the Most Holy Virgin to their church. Let us listen to the hymn Ave Maria Stella or Hail Mary Guiding Star, which was sung to her with solemn music as a farewell. The shots of the harquebuses provided one of the most joyful salutes that has ever been heard here.

Above the pueblo of Santiago there were some rancherías that had never yielded to the priests' many pleas. The general now summoned them by way of a squadron of Indian allies, asking them not to force him to come after

37. See I Kings 18:43.

them. They all came with their entire families, asking and begging for Holy Baptism and saying that they desired to be carefully instructed in our Holy Faith and to live together as Christians. It seemed appropriate to baptize more than seventy-five souls on the first and second days of the Feast of Christmas, and to marry in facie Ecclesiae those who as gentiles had been married to three and sometimes four women. (This is not usually done so hastily, but on this occasion it must have been wise [to do so] in order to gain these people's loyalty.) There were many from these rancherías still missing, so the general decided to found a new pueblo, which he did. [It had] a very beautiful church, where Mass was said and I baptized their cacique, naming him Don Luis. This was the name of the man who had been governor of Nueva Vizcaya, and the new pueblo was called San Luis.[38]

Just as the general was about to return to his garrison, Indians arrived from another nine, smaller rancherías. They had not been summoned because no one knew about them. They came with the very good news that they also wanted to become Christians and receive the water of Holy Baptism. They were very well received and were treated well by the captain. The priest began to prepare them to receive Holy Baptism and, through it, the grace of the Holy Spirit. May this same Holy Spirit give him the courage and strength to complete that which he had initiated with such great difficulty.

In concluding this letter I say that this expedition has been very important [562] because it resulted in the establishment of these pueblos. Those who have been baptized live peacefully, and disturbances and bad examples have been eliminated. Their friendship with the Spaniards has been strengthened. The trails have become so safe that I and the two little Indians who ordinarily accompany me travel in and out of these lands as safely and with as much hospitality as if I were traveling through Castilla.

This is the letter in which Father Diego Jiménez recorded his eyewitness account of Captain Suárez's expedition. Father Diego de Cueto also confirmed the importance of this expedition, saying that only someone with the captain's spirit could have overcome such dangers and difficult trails. As a result, something very important had been accomplished, including the reduction of 120 of the most bellicose Indians in the region. They had been so fierce that neither the benefits of peace nor any other means had persuaded them even to stay in a pueblo.

The priest added that the dangers of this expedition had been so great that one of the Indian allies, who [generally] are the best at detecting danger, approached the priest who was traveling with the troops and said to him, "Father, turn back; they are going to cut your head off." But the Lord, for whom this expedition was undertaken, moved the hearts of those who were most rebellious in such a way that when they reached the pueblo where they anticipated trouble that afternoon, God willed that they should find the people gathered together and kneeling before a Cross that they had erected. All their ferocious threats were transformed into the first requests from these rancherías for peace, friendship, a church, and Baptism. Therefore, we will move ahead to others. Divine mercy does not cease to show kindness towards these poor peoples, for once this conversion had taken place, around 1631 or 1632, the following year the people referred to in the next chapter joined them.

38. Luis de Velasco was governor of Nueva Vizcaya in 1630–31.

CHAPTER XX The priests' subsequent entrada and new mission to the Humi Indians

The Humi Indians had their rancherías about nine leagues from the pueblo of Quilitlán, in the highest part of these mountains, toward the east. This name alludes to two steep cliffs and sharp peaks where they live. Forty years earlier [ca. 1594] Spaniards had undertaken an expedition to these lands in search of mines. However, these were abandoned either because the veins were not pure enough or because the terrain was too rough. Some of these Indians had come down to Christian lands and pueblos at different times and had spoken with some of the priests who ministered to the Tepehuan. They were well treated and returned to their lands with an inclination toward becoming Christians. But the difficulties presented by their lands and the fact that the ministers were busy with other nations left no time for arranging for these Indians' instruction. They also made no effort to abandon their inaccessible lands, until the time arrived when divine mercy and the fervor of its ministers overcame these difficulties.

Lord Bishop Don Francisco de Hermosillo was happy with the Hina's recent conversion. These Humi bordered the Hina on the other side of the sierra, and thus had some knowledge of religious instruction and the benefits of priests. The Bishop therefore desired and asked that the Company take charge of saving these poor gentiles and conveying to them the light of the Gospel. Father Pedro Gravina, whose holy life is recorded in the following chapter, was appointed for this enterprise in 1633. The priest underwent very great hardships in this mission up until the time he gave his life.[39] The trails {563} were rough enough to take the life of even a person who was much more robust in years and strength. He baptized a good number of infants and instructed and then baptized some adults. Through his fervent and continual speeches he was preparing the people so that they could all be baptized. However, his holy death cut short his saintly desires. The following year Father Diego Jiménez, who was mentioned in the previous chapter, took charge of this mission. Because he gave us such an accurate account of the last mission

of the Hina, I will record here the brief account he wrote to his superiors concerning the Humi's progress.

All around these two pueblos (he says), which are ten leagues apart, many gentiles have settled with their families of fifteen or twenty people. In all, their number amounts to more than three hundred. On many occasions I tried to get them to reduce themselves to one of these pueblos. Although they did not refuse to do so, a year passed and they still had done nothing [and they remained] in their mountains, which were the steepest and most rugged in the entire region. When the Tepehuan rebelled they withdrew to these mountains with their commander, Gogoxito, as one would withdraw to a stone castle. Along the way they picked up a multitude of livestock, mares, mules, and anything else they came across. They kept the sheep—large flocks of which now roam free—because they could use the wool for weaving. Of the larger livestock a large portion fled to the upper reaches of the mountains, and the rest they killed so mercilessly that the trail is littered with their bones for more than two leagues. This was in spite of the pardon given in the name of Our Lord the king to the entire Tepehuan nation, whom it was impossible to conquer by physical force. The principal apostate delinquents, who had committed the most renowned insults, came to live near one another amongst these crags and some of them married gentiles from other nations, even though they themselves were Christian turncoats. In addition, other Indian outlaws from Spanish pueblos have found such a secure reception here that no one other than God Our Lord can take it from them.

I suffered for these souls and feared that such a horrible mixing of apostates, gentiles, outlaws, and bandits would cause my new Christians to become upset or infected by the mortal poison of conversation and proximity to these people. This was especially true given that it was such an uphill battle for the Humi to abandon their lands, which were very good and produced fertile harvests of maize and sugarcane, which grows so lush that it sometimes reaches a height of more than ten spans of a hand.[40] I agreed that when they chose an appropriate place and gathered there I would administer to them the teachings of the Holy Gospel. They did this, even if it was not all of them.

Because the terrain was so rough, it was necessary to spend six months or more opening a trail. The trails nevertheless are so dangerous that one has to spend a good deal of time on foot. I settled 250 people at a place that they selected on the other side of the river that flows down

---

39. Gravina actually began working among the Humi in January 1634 and died one year later, on January 15, 1635.

40. Sugarcane was introduced by Spaniards and apparently grew very well in the subtropical microclimates of the canyon bottoms of the Sierra Madre Occidental.

to Mazatlán [the Río Quezala or Presidio]. This pueblo was called San Pablo because it is twelve leagues from San Pedro de Guarizame, although only three by air. It has been no small deed to gently eliminate the practice of having many wives, leaving them contented in holy matrimony with only one. To the Spaniards' notable amazement and edification, the vice of drunkenness has been uprooted in all of the missions in this mountain range, owing to the good efforts of their ministers. Christianity is putting down deep roots among those who recently have been settled, despite their proximity to the Tepehuan, who are a very disruptive people, which concerns us.[41] A visit by the captain to these parts would be very beneficial for reining in the bold ones and removing the other outlaws that remain in the place that they call the Rincón de Zamora. May Our Lord in His infinite mercy grant that they all be brought to His flock so that it may become *unum ouile, & unus Pastor*.[42]

Up to here I have cited the letter of Father Diego Jiménez, who perseveres today in this [564] mission. Father Diego de Cueto also suffered many hardships from which abundant fruits have been harvested. He still perseveres with the same fervor with which he started this mission. There are now six pueblos of people, who previously seemed like wild beasts of the fields. Thousands of souls have been baptized who today live in peace. They regularly attend religious instruction, Mass, sermons, and festivals that are neither gentile nor barbarous, but rather Christian and holy. I will not stop here to recount particular cases of the conver-

sion of these people; of Our Lord's unusual providence, which transformed those Indians who had grown old in their vices; or of the Baptisms carried out and arranged by that same divine providence so that God could take to heaven from this gentile wilderness some predestined old people and infants. I have written a great deal concerning other wildernesses, and the same things should be understood to have happened in this one. I will only note that in adding this new and final mountain Christian community to the head mission called San Andrés (which has been discussed throughout this book), this mission has thus been expanded. Today there are at least eight priests from the Company of Jesus working here in some sixteen churches. This does not include the superior, who from time to time visits these churches and their ministers and subjects. Such visits serve these, God's servants, as consolation and companionship in the remote loneliness that they most joyfully suffer for Christ, so that these souls may partake of His Divine Redemption. As I have proposed, this book will be concluded with the exemplary life and death of a man who was an illustrious missionary in these mountain Christian communities. Even though he did not surrender his life through a violent death, he died after having suffered tremendous hardships for many years in these glorious enterprises, which are worthy of memory.

CHAPTER XXI Father Pedro Gravina's life, exemplary religious virtue, and evangelical labors

God has displayed His amazing and divine providence in all His works. Even so, He has principally demonstrated this by selecting and preparing ministers for the souls He has redeemed and laborers for the vineyard that He planted in His Church. This was very clearly manifested by the parable that He preached from His own mouth, portraying for us the Lord of the vine-

yard—[laboring] either early at sunrise, at the hour of prime, or at the third, sixth, or eleventh hour, when the sun's rays beat down the strongest—unceasingly to provide beneficial ministers and laborers for the vineyard that had cost Him so dearly. Among these we can undoubtedly include the most religious Father Pedro Gravina. God selected him and led him from his native Italy [43] to the remote and lofty mountains of the Xixime, of whom we have been speaking. For a period of nearly thirty years he worked at cultivating this hea-

---

41. Jiménez may be referring here to unrest caused by a Tepehuan cacique at El Zape (AGN 1638).

42. "One flock and one shepherd."

43. Gravina was born in Terme, Sicily.

thenism and planting in it one of the most successful Christian communities found among these barbarous peoples. It is true (as has been recorded) that during the last three years of his life, before he was martyred, the blessed Father Hernando de Santarén worked here. However, this Christianity was subsequently extended, sustained, and perfected during the aforesaid years by Father Pedro Gravina, who suffered tremendous hardship in this enterprise. His life and heroic virtues will be told by Father Francisco de Ibarra, who was superior to Father Gravina and the entire mission of San Andrés. He also provided the Father Provincial with an account of this holy missionary's death, as is common practice in the Company. He says: [565]

On the fifteenth of January in this year of 1635, Our Lord was served by taking to Himself Father Pedro Gravina, who was sixty years old. He was a religious for thirty years. Only one of these was spent in the novitiate, the remaining twenty-nine having been spent in these mountain missions. His rank in the Company was that of one who had professed three solemn vows.[44] He was ordained a priest in the Company and showed very great signs of the fervent calling that he had received from Our Lord. He showed a complete resignation to the will of his superior, which the Father Provincial realized came from this novice's mature and developed virtue. He had such a strong foundation that it was as if he were someone who had lived as a religious for many years. It seemed to the Father Provincial that the words spoken by the Holy Spirit were befitting of Father Gravina: *Consummatus in brebi expleuerat tempora multa.*[45] What is most important is that through a special impulse from heaven Father Gravina's superior sent him to work in these missions after only one year in the novitiate. This is not a common practice in the Company; ordinarily novices spend two years in the novitiate before undergoing many other tests, especially if they are to be employed in missions. However, in this case God was at work arranging things, as was clearly confirmed by experience and events.

This novice complied with obedience, setting out with great joy in his heart and a desire to spend his entire life instructing poor Indians, as he did. When he reached the missions [in 1613], the superiors sent him to serve as a companion to a priest who was administering the district of San Gregorio. When this priest saw that Father Gravina was still a novice he, being a religious of strict observance, wanted to test him to see whether he possessed enough virtue for the job for which he had been chosen. He busied him in the most humble exercises that he could find, both within and without the house. This good novice priest attended to all these tasks with great joy, speed, and

promptness. In addition, as a novice he bore reprimands and advice with great spiritual serenity, without getting upset; he did this to the great edification of all those who saw him being so submissive and humble.

In time [his] superiors placed him in charge of the missions and district of the Xixime, whose harsh trails, lands, mountains, gorges, and rivers are notorious. Father Gravina walked and traveled throughout their lands almost continuously for a period of nearly thirty years. His fervor for helping others was indescribable. He spared no labor nor did he avoid difficulty in order to lead others to heaven. For this reason the hardships suffered by this evangelical minister for God and his brothers can be said to be greater and more general. To better aid his brothers, Father Gravina learned as many languages as necessary to distribute the bread of the divine word to those who were under his care. He learned Spanish, for he arrived from Italy being quite clumsy at it. He needed this [language in order to be able to speak to] the Spaniards at the mining camps. He also needed to learn Nahuatl to assist the Indian laborers who worked in the mines. He learned as well two other languages of the nations that he settled and instructed. These were the Acaxee and the Xixime, whose languages he learned with such fluency that he knew them better than many native speakers. He composed a most perfect Xixime grammar and vocabulary. Those who have since come to instruct these people have been guided by this work.

Father Gravina suffered a great many discomforts and hardships along the harsh and difficult trails that he continually traversed in these destitute lands impoverished of sustenance. His life and health were almost continually endangered by the extreme heat in some places and the extreme cold and snow in others. This was equivalent to [566] the most rigorous penance in the desert. Nevertheless, the priest added to this penance with continual blood scourging and by wearing a studded belt. He also slept on a flat board or cowhide. Whenever he reached a place where there were Spaniards and they forced him to rest on a bed, he would comply in order to disguise his mortification. However, he would not actually use the bed, but rather left it untouched. He was notably austere in what he ate; his ordinary sustenance being what is called *ezquite*, which is toasted maize. He also ate the Indians' stews, herbs, and meager, crude delicacies. If there was any time when he ate meat or fish, it was on the occasion of a meeting, when it was necessary to avoid calling attention to himself and to fit in with his brothers.

Although his life consisted of perpetual fasting, he was especially meticulous in this exercise during Advent, on Saturdays, and throughout the year on the eves of the feast days of the Most Holy Virgin, to whom he was especially devoted, as he also was to the Most Holy Sacrament. When councils were held at this time (which all the priests of the mission attend), he would hear all the other priests' Masses first; always waiting to be last to say his Mass. During his travels, when ailments caused his mule to tire, he would dismount and go on foot while the Indians who were with him continued on horseback. They noticed that he would stop every once in a while and get down on his knees to

---

44. Meaning that Gravina was a spiritual coadjutor, a rank below professed (four vows) yet superior to temporal coadjutors.

45. Book of Wisdom 4:13: "With him, early achievement counted for long apprenticeship" (Knox 1956:576).

pray. When he was riding the mule, the Indians and some soldiers who accompanied him confirmed that he went along with his eyes raised to heaven, turning his heart to God in contemplation. In doing so, he allowed his mount to go in whatever direction it wanted, and as a result his face was usually all bruised and scratched by the branches and thorns that he ran into. He was warned to travel carefully with his mule over these rough trails and steep slopes, which had so many dangerous cliffs, for he was also told that someday he would lose his life on one of them. Nevertheless, the great fervor and inspiration that burned in his breast left no time for heeding these warnings. God assumed the responsibility of guiding and freeing him from many great dangers, as we will later see.

I will first speak of the gift of prayer that God granted to this, His servant. Father Pedro Gravina was intense and steadfast in this holy exercise of prayer and talking with God, just as Christ Our Lord and His Apostle Saint Paul, commanded us. He was not happy with the amount of time established by the Rule for daily prayer.[46] Instead, he desired to continue praying all day and all night. When the Indians or other laypeople were looking for him and came to discuss their concerns with him, which impeded him, he would abandon his prayers (for in all their afflictions he was their refuge). However, once he had carried out this act of charity which, as such, he did not refuse to perform, the flame in his heart would rise anew and he would go to his God, with whom he would discuss the concerns of his fellow human beings as well as his own.

He spent almost the entire night awake, praying on his knees without undressing or lying down until he was overcome by sleep. Then, with regret and sadness that he was being overcome by this natural need, he would throw himself to the floor. Having thus broken somewhat his drowsiness—which he considered his enemy—he would return to his prayers.

It is clear that someone who was so familiar in his dialogue with God—the source of all virtue—would not be lacking in all other virtues. These virtues would be highly developed in such a person: zeal for the salvation of others, works and exercises of charity on their behalf, patience and humility, and all the other virtues that are common to apostolic men, even when they have not withdrawn into the desert. Therefore, I will not detain myself here with particular examples of these virtues, of which a great deal could be written. I will conclude the account of the life of this evangelical missionary with the [567] unusual and marvelous cases through which Our Lord favored him in the travels and evangelical steps that were his life's work. There were reliable witnesses who affirmed these cases, and it seems that all those who dealt with Father Pedro are

sufficiently convinced of the sanctity of his life. They called him by no other name than Holy Father Pedro.

Captain Bartolomé Suárez was in charge of the garrison of soldiers that existed for the peace and calm of the various nations of these mountains. He was a very brave commander and showed great wisdom in times of war, and he was of great assistance to these people's Christianity. His garrison was stationed at the fort at San Hipólito, only a few leagues from Father Gravina's district. Therefore, these two men had very friendly dealings with each other for many years. The captain added to this friendship his great respect for the priest's sanctity, especially after a case occurred that he told about, which I will recount here along with the others.

On one of the many occasions when Father Gravina went to visit the soldiers at the garrison to exercise his ministries of charity, he stayed at the home of the captain, who was a bachelor. There were some young servant boys in a little room outside. At a late hour he heard the boys shouting, "Father Pedro's lodgings are on fire." One of the boys, who had become very upset, tried to get into the priest's room. In doing so he realized that the great light and brightness that they were all seeing was not from a fire, but rather emanated from within the priest, who was on his knees praying but had risen off the ground. They went to tell the captain, who refused to disturb the priest. These events did not surprise him because of what he believed concerning the priest's holiness, which he had already experienced.

This very reliable witness told of another case that was no less unusual, when orders were issued by the governor of Nueva Vizcaya to [initiate] a campaign to punish the Tepehuan rebels. In 1616 the Tepehuan committed notorious temporal and divine acts of destruction (these will be recorded at length in the following book). To insure the success of his mission, the captain sought the aid of his good friend (as he said), holy [Father] Pedro. He asked him for help [in the form] of his prayers, which would be worth a great deal more than a few soldiers from the fort. He set out with his soldiers and came to a pueblo called Tenerapa. A large number of people from several nations had congregated there, whence they were going to attack and raze the city of Durango. When the captain launched his first attack on the Indians, he and his people were in great danger of being killed, for the enemy was much greater in number and very bellicose. The two sides fought from sunrise until four in the afternoon, each side beating against the other like waves. Neither could get the upper hand, and our army was in dire straits. The captain feared defeat, but then he remembered (as he said) the answer that Father Pedro had given him—that he should trust in God that he would achieve victory, and that until the captain returned Father Pedro would not stop scourging himself and praying for the captain's success. As soon as the captain remembered this promise and saw himself in these straits, he lifted the chain mail visor that is used by these soldiers and he cried out to heaven (as he said), asking for help against those who had betrayed the Holy Faith and destroyed sacred objects. God must have been the one who moved him to raise his visor, for he need not have done so to ask for [568] divine aid. Indeed, this was a dangerous thing to do when the sky was

46. Ignatius Loyola steadfastly refused to prescribe a set duration of time that fully formed Jesuits were to pray; he recommended one hour of daily prayer for scholastics. In the seventeenth century fully formed Jesuits such as Gravina probably were obliged to one hour of mental prayer in the morning and a fifteen-minute examination of conscience at noon and at night (de Guibert 1964:221–29, 554; Ganss 1991:458, 469–70, 546; O'Malley 1993a:359).

raining enemy arrows. It seems that this happened so that the captain could see with his own eyes how much God's servant, Pedro, was helping him in that conflict. As soon as he raised his visor, he saw the image of Father Gravina himself on that field. Not only was he raising his hands to heaven like Moses, he was also kneeling with a crucifix raised in one hand and a scourge with which he was flogging himself in the other. The captain considered this a sure sign of his victory. Closing his visor, he shouted to his soldiers with great bravery, repeating, "Men, the victory is ours, the victory is ours." He encouraged his people with his shouting and they attacked the enemy with renewed vigor. At this point they began to bear down on them and finally destroyed them. A large number of people were captured, together with the belongings that they had taken from the Spaniards' destroyed farms and haciendas. At the moment when the destruction of the city was feared Captain Suárez entered Durango triumphant with his prisoners. After he returned to his fort in the mountains he visited his benefactor and helper, Father Pedro Gravina. Without revealing what had happened and what he had seen with his own eyes, he asked Father Gravina if he had fulfilled his promise of helping him with his prayers. The priest answered that he had. Then the captain revealed to him what had taken place. The priest affectionately begged him not to publicize it or say anything to anyone. But the captain so highly esteemed this priest's holiness, which he had experienced for a very long time, that he could neither keep silent nor refrain from constantly referring to it.

In his home the captain had a woman servant by the name of Mencia. She was on the verge of death, racked by illness. He sent someone to go as quickly as possible for Father Pedro, who was fifteen leagues away in the pueblo of Basís.[47] When the priest received word, he set out with the same diligence and speed as he normally did in these types of cases. When he arrived he found the sick woman so close to death that she had been unable to speak for twelve hours. It greatly upset this charitable minister to see that there was no way he could hear her confession. He shouted at her, but she did not respond. Therefore, he decided through his words and deeds to turn matters over to God. He told those who were present to go outside and leave him alone with the sick woman, for she was dying. They obeyed, and within a short time, they heard him scourging himself. From time to time the blows of the scourge could be heard; he also seemed to be praying. After some time he called the people in. There, in the presence of many, he called the sick woman by name. She responded, "Father" (and she was right in calling him that, for he was the one who had gone to such lengths to give life to her soul). The priest answered back, "My daughter, do you want to confess?" The sick woman responded that she did, and as soon as he had confessed and absolved her, she immediately died in his arms. It seems that God had saved her to demonstrate the value of His loving servant's prayers.

As further testimony of what other people in these

mountains proclaimed concerning Father Pedro's great virtue, I will record here what Lieutenant Gerónimo de Acosta affirmed about this priest. He knew him for twenty-seven years in these missions. Once when he was serving as an escort for the blessed Father Hernando de Santarén (who, as we said, died at the hands of infidels), this priest spoke the following words concerning Father Pedro, who had been his companion, "Señor Gerónimo de Acosta, revere Father Pedro greatly, for the Holy Spirit resides in his soul. Let proof of this be the fact that I woke up very late one night and saw a light coming from his lodgings. Thinking that it was a candle, I called a little Indian boy named Juan Gamuza [569] to go and light a candle for me from Father Pedro's candle. When the boy got there, he could not find the light. Father Pedro dismissed him, saying, 'Go away. I don't have any light.' Once he had dismissed him, he closed his door, and I once again saw the same light as before. The following morning I went to visit him and I clearly saw from the candle that they had taken to Father Gravina during the night that it was not this light that had appeared in the night, but rather a light from heaven, through which God illuminates the prayers of this, His servant."

Not only the living, but also the dead came to seek the aid of Father Gravina's prayers. There was a Spanish woman named Catalina González [who lived] in those mountains in the pueblo of Santa María Utaís. Late one sleepless night as she was commending herself to God because of a serious illness, she saw a figure come into her room. It looked like a man who was known in her household. The sick woman told him to go to bed and asked him what his intentions were in coming there at that hour. With this the figure disappeared and the sick woman began to regain her senses. Not understanding what had happened, she became frightened and started to yell, telling them to call Father Pedro, who was in the pueblo. The priest went to the disturbed, sick woman and soothingly said to her, "Don't be afraid, the man who came to you was so-and-so" (naming him by his real name). This person had died only a short time earlier and had come to request the priest's prayers. The priest added, "Pray to God for this person, just as I am doing." This calmed the sick woman.

If these were marvelous demonstrations with which He favored and manifested the worth of this, Our Lord's servant, then those with which He protected and freed him from many dangers while traveling were no less numerous or marvelous. The priest did not relent in his frequent travels through the horrible roughness of those mountains and gorges, traversing rivers. It was amazing to see Father Gravina come out alive. Those who witnessed this considered it to be at least a miracle, and they spoke of it as such.

47. Basís was along the headwaters of the Río Remedios.

The priest was passing through some extremely harsh mountains [on his way] from the place that they call Banome to the pueblo of San Gregorio. He came to a terrible gorge and a tremendously deep pass. When he tried to proceed, the mule he was riding reared back on two feet and made a complete turn, knocking the priest from the saddle and leaving him hanging from a stirrup. Then the mule turned around again in mid-air, flinging the priest safely to the other side of the gorge. The strap of the mule's stirrup looked as if it had been cut by a knife, but the priest suffered no injury whatsoever. Eyewitnesses who recounted this case to Gerónimo de Acosta considered it to be miraculous.

The very same people witnessed the following cases, which were even more miraculous. Gerónimo de Acosta himself recounted one occasion when Father Pedro was supposed to visit the pueblo of Coapa. He was preparing to walk, but then it happened that a mule came by and kicked him twice, knocking him to the ground. Those who were there thought that he was dead. When they went to help him he got up, saying, "I don't need any help. Thanks to God, it was nothing." This is the extent to which he remained free from harm, which those present thought had taken his life.

They called him on another occasion at a late hour of the night to go to another pueblo [to hear] a confession. He got one of the Indians who was with him to quickly round up the mules on which they were going to travel. Because the night was so dark the Indian did not realize that one of the mules taken from among the others was wild and unbroken. He thought that he had saddled one of the mules that was accustomed to being ridden. The untamed mule stood still and let itself be saddled and bridled [570] (trainers are well aware that this is unusual and that it is dangerous to try to saddle and mount an unbroken mule). The mule was saddled and calm, and the priest mounted it and rode all the way to the confession and back as if he were traveling on an extremely tame animal. After he got back and they went to remove the mule's saddle and bridle, it began to buck and ran off with the bridle still in place. Once it was daylight Father Gravina ordered that the mules be rounded up and the bridle removed from the mule that had fled. [It was] then that they realized that the mule Father Gravina had ridden so securely was the wild one. They were amazed and gave thanks to God for such an uncommon and unusual case.

The case told by a soldier named Francisco de la Bría was similar. He was in the fort at San Hipólito, whence the priest set out for one of his pueblos. The mule that the priest was about to mount was very spirited, so the soldier tried to walk it around first to calm it down. That way the priest would not wind up in any danger (for they all loved him and wanted him to stay alive). The soldier got on the mule, which bucked so much that it threw him to the ground. He was injured in the fall and the mule ran loose. Then the priest came up to them and said, "Stand back, let me catch it. It's as tame as a lamb." And for God's servant, it was. It stood still and let him mount, and he made his journey without any danger.

These cases are recounted here as demonstrations of Our Lord's special providence in protecting this, His servant, keeping him from the dangers to which he exposed himself for His love. In the same way that these dangers were so continual, so was divine mercy in protecting him from them, and everyone had something to tell. Another soldier named Sebastián Gómez recounted that once when he was traveling with the priest at night to the pueblo of Basís, they came to a pass called Puertezuelo.[48] This pass was so difficult to get through that when the priest got down from his mule and tried to go through on foot, he tripped and fell. In order to detain the mule, which was loose, the soldier followed it. However, before the priest could get up off the ground, the mule stepped on his neck and started choking him. The soldier dismounted and pulled on the mule, which was still standing on the priest, suffocating him. He got it to move, and Father Pedro stood up with no injury whatsoever. The soldier recounted this case as miraculous. But these are the kinds of things that God does to favor His servants, who place themselves in so many dangerous situations in order to save souls.

There were other ways in which God favored Father Pedro. It also seems that He illuminated him with the gift of prophecy in cases of holy ministries that arose for the good and consolation of souls. A Spanish woman named Catalina González came to the priest upset (everyone came to him to escape their troubles). She told him about the displeasure she was experiencing because of one of her sons-in-law. He wanted to leave the land, which would have posed a great problem for his wife and his mother-in-law. The priest consoled her with these few words, "Madam, your son-in-law will not go away. Our Lord is just testing you with these hardships. Later, you will be at great peace with him." God fulfilled what the priest had said.

His Indians also were upset that their spiritual father had to attend to so many pueblos and be absent from

48. Meaning 'difficult or steep pass or gateway'.

them. Father Gravina consoled them by saying (when this was still unknown) that a young priest would come as his companion, and he would learn their language and love them just as he did. In time the priest came who was the very servant of God that [Father Gravina] had described, and one day, while he was studying the Indians' language using the grammar that Father Gravina had written, the Indians came to him and said, "In you, Father, [571] we see what our Father had told us about, when he spoke of he who would come to help us."

When a mining camp called Guapijuxe was being abandoned and some people were upset about it, Father Gravina said to them, "It will not be abandoned, for they will find great wealth there, although there will be a lot of fighting over it." And this is what happened following Father Pedro Gravina's death.

The blessed priest's passing was brought on by a pain in his side that increased from the continual hardships and journeys that he made at all hours to visit the needy in his pueblos. God wanted to remove him from these pueblos and reward him for the many hardships he [suffered], from which he eventually died. He was traveling through a place near nightfall when he fell into a river. He spent the entire night with his clothing soaking wet. When he reached one of his pueblos called Yamoriba, the pain in his side got worse. He realized that the day of his blessed passing was drawing near, so he prepared himself by receiving all the Holy Sacraments. He dispatched someone to bring him a holy crucifix, which he had kept out of devotion in the pueblo of Santa María Utaís. Before the person who

was bringing it had returned, he told those who were there to go out and welcome the Holy Christ who was coming to their pueblo. The Lord whom he had so often embraced must have sent him word that He was on His way to attend and help him at [the hour of] his death. Once the crucifix arrived, they placed it in his hands, and with sweet murmuring full of devotion he turned his soul over to the hands of God, who had reared him for His own greater glory.

Throughout that entire mountain region, as far as Durango, this saintly and apostolic man was called by no other name than Holy Father Pedro. Those who lived far away commended themselves to his prayers, and out of their special devotion, they sought some relics for themselves when he died. His body was taken to be buried in the church at Santa María de Utaís, despite the fact that it was two and a half days' journey from the place where this holy priest had died. He had requested this out of the great devotion he always had to that church where he now rests, which he built and dedicated to the Most Holy Virgin.

Divine goodness has granted these missions and enterprises the favor of giving them ministers who lead holy and apostolic lives. With this we will move on to record another mission, which was fortunate to have received other ministers who were no less illustrious, and who shed their blood for Christ and His Holy Gospel. Their lives will be recorded at the end of the following book. Because there are many lives that will be recounted, we will omit here one that should accompany the life of Father Pedro Gravina. [572]

BOOK X

The Conversion of the Tepehuan to Our Holy Faith and Their Subsequent Rebellion and Apostasy

CHAPTER 1 The Tepehuan's lands, rancherías, and customs

Many chapters will be required to narrate the enterprise that I am about to present. Although it was a spiritual one dedicated to the preaching of the Holy Gospel, it also involved very difficult and bloody temporal wars and battles. I should note at the outset that Spaniards were not looking for a reason to wage war, but legitimately took up arms to defend themselves; their women, children, and ranches; and above all else the Catholic Faith of Christ Our Lord and His Holy Church. Satan, that long-time common enemy of humankind, tried to destroy everything. He employed the most diabolical and ferocious strategies and tricks, causing one of the worst disasters ever seen in the Western Indies and the greatest ever seen in the Kingdom of Nueva España. He destroyed churches, images, and sacred ornaments, and caused the cruel deaths of religious, other Spaniards, and faithful Indians. Finally, he tried to destroy and wipe out the entire province that is called Nueva Vizcaya. All this happened in the mission that I am about to discuss, among the nation that is called Tepehuan. Although this mission was not as populous as other Christian provinces (whose populations I previously discussed), [573] the people were hostile and fierce. Here, Satan was able to cause

the aforementioned ravages, in part because there were only a few Spaniards living in the region.

Something must be said about the location, population, and customs of this gentile nation. It must also be told how the Holy Gospel was first introduced and the resistance it encountered from the enemies of the Faith. Even though they caused lamentable damage, divine goodness did not allow them to accomplish their harmful and final objectives, as will be recorded in the concluding chapters of this book.

The ferocity of the Tepehuan nation is inscribed in its name, which comes from the Mexican word *teptl*, which means 'mountain', or from the derivative *tetl*,[1] which means 'rock' or 'cliff'. Both suit the Tepehuan equally well, for they live among mountains and cliffs. They are of a hardened and rough nature, like the tall oaks among which they are raised. Nevertheless, the most wonderful thing is that God had some of those people [who dwell] among these cliffs predestined for heaven.

When they were gentiles they lived in rancherías; now they have pueblos that are partly along the plains and partly along the flanks of the Topia and San Andrés

---

1. See Pennington (1969:3) for a discussion of the etymology of 'Tepehuan'.

mountain ranges, which we have already mentioned. On the western slopes they border the Xixime and Acaxee and even those Sinaloans who live inland. We have already noted that although this is not a populous nation, it has one of the most extensive territories in Nueva España, extending as [far north] as Nuevo México.[2] It lies within the jurisdiction and government of Nueva Vizcaya and the bishopric of its principal city, Durango.

The Tepehuan pueblos begin thirty leagues outside of Durango. The first of them is Santiago Papasquiaro, which is two hundred leagues from the great city of Mexico. Since leaving Sinaloa, where I began this history for the reasons mentioned,[3] we have been approaching this pueblo.[4] In the process of exploring for silver veins and mines, Spaniards settled lands within Tepehuan territory, some of which were deserted. Many mines have been found and many others of good quality are being discovered daily. In addition to those previously worked at Guanaceví, Indé, and elsewhere, they have recently [in 1631] discovered veins of silver at Parral, where there is a considerable population of Spaniards who have extracted ore that has made them very rich. Every day new discoveries are made in this region. Spaniards have also been attracted to Tepehuan lands because they possess beautiful, spacious fields and very fertile, thick pastures for livestock, especially cattle and horses, of which there are great herds and ranches. All this has not offended the local Indians, who instead have benefited from them because they had not previously exploited the mineral deposits or raised livestock to sustain themselves.[5] Ever since the Spaniards settled here, there has been an abundance of food, clothing, riches, and other material comforts.

These are all reasons why Spaniards were able to peacefully settle the land. Nevertheless, they were mindful to bear arms for self-defense because they were among fierce, newly discovered people whose fidelity could be little trusted. During these early years, the Tepehuan threatened the Spaniards, who tried their best to avoid war and treated the Tepehuan with affection in order to [574] soften their natural roughness and win over some of their caciques and captains. No matter how barbarous they may be, there are always some among them who are easier to deal with and are more trustworthy.

The Tepehuan always were poor subjects because of their hostile and warlike nature. They boasted of subjugating and instilling fear in neighboring nations, particularly the Acaxee, Tarahumara, and others, all of whom were intimidated. The Tepehuan felt so superior that a small number of them would enter their neighbors' settlements, and without any one daring to resist them, they would take women and girls and return to their lands, where they tyrannically abused them.

In their gentile state these Indians used the same weapons as those described for other nations: bows, arrows, macanas, and clubs of brazilwood. After the Spaniards arrived and warred with them, the Tepehuan became very skillful horsemen and learned how to use a lance or goad for driving cattle. When they had access to these weapons, they used them as effectively as Spanish horsemen. They even learned how to use firearms and harquebuses, which they took from Spaniards, although their use of these weapons is limited by the fact that they do not know how to make gunpowder. This is all there is to say regarding their weapons and warfare.

The common food of these Indians was corn and other native grains that they sowed. Most of them were farmers, but they did not plant large fields. When they lacked crops they sustained themselves on the same wild fruits as other nations. They also hunted game and fowl, which abounded in their lands. Their clothing was like that of other nations in the mountains. Many of them wear mantas made of cotton, which they cultivate, as well as of fiber from plants that grow in their montes. The women wear a type of skirt made from the same material. They made wine from the mescal plant and other wild fruits, and they frequently celebrated the drunkenness that the devil had introduced to all these nations. Their houses were made either of wood and poles from the monte or of mud and stones. Their settlements were rancherías of little houses built close to their main springs, brooks, and rivers. The main settlement was at Santiago Papasquiaro, their principal pueblo. Here, as in other nations, the infernal enemy

---

2. Pérez de Ribas is perhaps alluding here to the fact that the Tepehuan and Pima languages are closely related and form a continuous south-to-north distribution, extending northward from Durango into what is today southern Arizona, which in 1645 was considered part of New Mexico.

3. That is, because the Sinaloa mission was the first Jesuit mission in the north.

4. By this statement Pérez de Ribas appears to equate his writing the history of the northern missions with the actual journey he often made from Sinaloa to Mexico City; the journey as such began in Sinaloa, went through Topia, and then through the lands of the Tepehuan.

5. This is not quite true, as one of the first places settled by Spanish miners was Indé, where the Indians resented and opposed Spanish encroachment on their lands.

introduced other gentile customs, particularly sorcery. He made himself more of a lord among these people, however, because he found them by nature fierce and cruel, which is how he clothed himself following his fall from heaven in order to pursue men and drag them off with him to eternal torment.

CHAPTER II The priests of the Company of Jesus go to preach the Holy Gospel to the Tepehuan nation

The aforementioned qualities and customs of the Tepehuan did not frighten the ministers of the doctrine into forsaking the dangerous and risky task of taming and domesticating such indomitable wild beasts. They expected nothing less than to be ripped and clawed to death, [575] as they eventually were. Strengthened by divine favor, however, they undertook this enterprise in the name of the Lord, to whom they are dedicated by the special vow that the sons of the Company of Jesus take to shed their own blood in this glorious quest.

The priests who were residing in the Jesuit house in Durango (which today is a chartered college) considered this task very much their own. And so they decided to send a priest to some of the Tepehuan's rancherías to preach and begin instructing the people, preparing them to receive the Faith and Holy Baptism. This good fortune befell Father Gerónimo Ramírez, whose life was recounted at the end of Book VI. He was truly an apostolic man, in whom there burned an untiring desire for the salvation of Indian souls, for which he endured great hardship. The hardness and ferocity of the Tepehuan nation required just such a fervent spirit.

Confident in divine aid, Father Ramírez undertook his entrada without an escort of soldiers or anyone else. Although at times a military escort is advisable (as previously noted), on this occasion the priest was intent only upon talking with the Indians about their souls and the Holy Faith so that they would voluntarily request religious instruction. [He also went to] confirm the peace they had previously established with the Spaniards. Thus, it seemed better to go alone rather than create a disturbance with soldiers.

En route to the Indians' rancherías, he stopped at all the Spanish settlements, ranches, and mines that he came across, providing the people with services and instruction. In addition to Spaniards, these settlements usually have many servants who have come from other parts [of Nueva España]. Although they generally are long-time Christians, because they live in such remote lands they are in need of spiritual aid, due to the fact that during these early years some of these places lacked their own priest.

The first ranch that Father Ramírez came to in the lands of the Tepehuan was called La Sauceda. There he found some gentiles who nevertheless had dealings with Christians. With both groups he exercised charity and holy ministries. Old and young enthusiastically attended the instruction and talks that he gave. The gentiles also listened to him with pleasure.

The priest was there for the Feast of the Holy Spirit, the very day [that honors the occasion when] the holy Apostles began preaching. This feast day was celebrated with notable joy by both Spaniards and Indians; the latter's devotion was very evident in their change of customs, because they usually celebrated this and other feast days with wine and drunken orgies. The priest threatened that he would immediately leave if any of them got out of hand. This threat was so effective that not a single Indian drank to excess.[6]

During the three days of this feast he heard many

---

6. Pérez de Ribas neglects to mention here that it was common for Spaniards in Spain to celebrate religious feast days with dancing and drunkenness, which led to "lewd and enormous sins" (Christian 1981:164).

people's confessions and preached daily not only to Spaniards in their language, but also to the Indians in several of their languages. This is the same gift that the Holy Spirit granted the holy Apostles on this day, and although the priest did not receive it instantaneously in the same manner as the Apostles, God had granted it to him earlier so he could learn languages. He knew quite well two of the most widely spoken languages of Nueva España, Mexican and Tarascan. He had also begun to learn Tepehuan so his instruction could reach all the Indians. They were so pleased and benefited so much from this that they insisted that the priest [576] stay with them for the Feast of Corpus Christi, which they wanted to celebrate with as much solemnity as possible. It seemed that God was doing everything possible to see to it that the gentile Tepehuan could learn about Christian mysteries and see how they were celebrated, and thus that they would become more fond of them. This is in fact what happened, when the Feast of the Most Holy Sacrament was celebrated with great solemnity in that barren place. To liven up the procession, Indians from various lands and nations performed seven dances and displays of rejoicing. The Tepehuan gentiles also tried to imitate this procession with [one of] their own, which was very indicative of the barbarous state of their souls. They covered their bodies with a kind of grass that was like wool and carried deer antlers in their hands. In sum, they looked like wild animals that were being lured and tamed by the law of Christ Our Lord, which these barbarians were now beginning to like. Although this behavior is of little importance, I wanted to recount it here because it was the beginning of this nation's conversion.

From this pueblo the priest went to other Spanish mining settlements. There he offered the same services and ministries of charity that he had exercised at La Sauceda, enjoying the same success. The priest was so encouraged by the good beginnings of this mission that he continued on to the rancherías of the Tepehuan, which were his principal focus. He notified them of his coming and they received him with great pleasure, coming from many leagues away to meet him. When he reached their rancherías, he found that a large group had assembled out of curiosity. He announced to them that he had come to their lands and homes to obtain the salvation of their immortal souls. He told them about the rewards and punishments of the next life, their need for the doctrine he had come to teach them, and their need to know the true God worshiped by the Christian Spaniards. He also spoke of the other benefits of living in peace with the Spaniards, etc.

The Indians listened to all of this, and generally speaking they received it well. Nevertheless, as has always been common in the preaching of the Gospel, some hear and receive it while others remain deaf and rebellious. The same thing happened on this occasion. At one ranchería where the priest found a great willingness among old and young to hear and submit to the divine word, there was an old man who was so stubborn and hardened that he bragged that he would not become a Christian and that the priest would be unable to change his mind. The priest took the old man's resistance and outburst very seriously, realizing that the old man's example and authority could become an obstacle to his fruitful labor among these people. As subsequent events demonstrated, Our Lord favored the priest's holy efforts almost miraculously. The priest affectionately attempted to make the old man understand how important it was to listen to and accept what he was teaching concerning the divine word and to prepare himself to receive the Christians' Holy Baptism, which had the virtue of cleansing the soul of sin. With this the old man—who was still blind in his understanding—responded in almost the same way as that other leper, Naman, whom the Prophet commanded to bathe in the River Jordan to cure his leprosy.[7] His reply is well known, and the old man in our case uttered something very similar. [He said] that he regularly bathed in the river and did not need any other bath. The priest replied that such baths in the river [577] would not protect him from the eternal flames of hell; that required becoming a Christian. At this point the old man, still persevering in his blindness, revealed another even greater deception, saying that he was immortal and would never die. When the priest heard such stubbornness and realized how the devil and his familiars, the sorcerers, had deceived and defrauded this old man, he called on everyone present to be a witness. (With impulses from heaven it seems) he again warned the old man about the swift punishment of hell that God would deliver. The old man stood up and walked away laughing, paying no heed to this warning. Although what the priest had warned was not carried out as rigorously as he had said it would be, it was in fact executed just as swiftly as he had promised, albeit more kindly in a manner proper to divine clemency. The following

7. See II Kings 5:10–12.

morning when the people gathered for instruction, the poor Indian humbly appeared before the others with his flesh torn and bleeding. Turning to the priest, he said, "I know {now} that you speak the truth, Father, and that I have lived my life being deceived. Now I know from experience that I am mortal like the others. Even though the devil promised me that I would not get sick or suffer any other accident, last night a wild animal attacked me and almost killed me; I would have died were it not for God, who favored and saved me. As testimony to this you {can} see the wounds on my body."

It was not known whether a wild animal had actually exacted that punishment, but what was certain was that it was executed by the Lord's command. The wounded and disabused Indian added, "I beg you to baptize me, Father, so I will not lose my soul." The priest embraced the remorseful penitent and took great care to teach him the truths of our Holy Faith. He freed him from the great troubles and dealings he had with his demon familiar, and later he was baptized with great joy. This man who had been so obstinate became the means by which others left the shadows of heathenism to come to know the light of the truth Faith.

[This was] the fruit of these first rancherías, the good news of which the priest shared upon his return to his college in Durango. He brought with him samples from the lands he had gone to explore, leaving its inhabitants well disposed toward his return and their spiritual conquest. Even though he had clearly seen the difficulties of this enterprise, including the ferocity of the people and their settlements, of which he had learned a great deal, he was not daunted, like that other explorer of the promised land. He did not return saying that it was inhabited by men who were giants, even though he could have done so due to the Tepehuan's ferocity; instead, like that other courageous explorer, he placed his confidence in God. Thus, Father Gerónimo Ramírez returned very encouraged and intent upon the enterprise of establishing Christianity in a field so full of the weeds of sorcerers and sorcery, which abounded in this nation. In time eight priests from our Company and many other Christians were to die at their hands, but not without harvesting fruit from the same fierce Tepehuan whose conversion we are presently discussing. All this will be seen in the course of this book and mission.

CHAPTER III   Father Gerónimo Ramírez returns and visits other Tepehuan rancherías, founding the pueblos of Santiago Papasquiaro and Santa Catalina; other events at this time

[578] When Father Ramírez gave the Father Rector of the college in Durango the good news about the success of his first entrada, expressing at the same time his hope and desire to return and continue his work among the Tepehuan, the Father Rector sent him back after only a few days' rest. Because the Tepehuan mission was still in its early stages, there were no superior and no missionaries formally assigned to it by the viceroy or Father Provincial. Indeed, the Jesuit residence in Durango had only recently been founded. The priests never forgot, however, the Institute of their holy religious order, which required them to aid souls wherever they might be, using all the means indicated in their rule, in particular that of missions. Thus, the Father Rector ordered Father Ramírez to return to the Tepehuan and to resume more purposefully the mission he had started, visiting other rancherías and endeavoring to reduce them to congregations and pueblos where they could be more easily and fruitfully instructed. If things went well, he was also to begin erecting churches, even if they were only of thatch and wood; in time more permanent structures could be built.

Father Ramírez willingly accepted this charge and departed with the blessing of obedience, which always leads to success for the individual who complies. At the first Tepehuan ranchería he was greeted by the old sorcerer whom he had converted during his previous entrada. The remarkable conversion of this old man, who at first had been so obstinate, was truly an act of heaven. When he saw the man who had cured him of his blindness and recognized (although a barbarian) the benefit he had received, he went to the priest and, with a great show of happiness, said, "For years I have been dealing with Spaniards and they have never cared about me. You are the only one who has appreciated me, rescuing me with the water of Holy Baptism and giving me your own name, Gerónimo Ramírez. I do as I am commanded and pray to God, calling out to Him when I am alone in the fields, begging Him with all my heart to forgive my sins and save my soul." The comments of the old man, who was now a Christian, aptly demonstrated that he had gained an understanding of our Holy Faith and that he had truly received it. This was a great consolation for the priest.

Something else that was no less significant also happened at this ranchería during this second entrada. It was on a Sunday morning when the Indians and some Spaniards from the mines came to hear Mass. Among them was a gentile maiden who was accompanied by her relatives. She was dressed in the more formal Mexican style [8] and had traveled six leagues to request Holy Baptism. The priest at first questioned her sincerity, thinking that because she was so young she was requesting Baptism capriciously or because of its novelty. He told her that he would gladly baptize her, provided that she first learned the prayers and the catechism and joined the other catechumens who met to study and prepare for Baptism. The prudent maiden insistently replied that she wanted to be baptized that very day. She said that she had greatly desired this and that she had come [579] prepared to receive the Holy Sacrament. As proof she was prepared to answer any questions the priest might choose to pose. The priest found that she was so knowledgeable about the prayers and catechism that she did not err in a single question. So that very afternoon he baptized her along with the others at that ranchería who had prepared themselves to receive the sacrament. Although she was baptized to the great joy of everyone, some were ashamed that a

girl from a foreign nation had surpassed them in learning the catechism and was baptized before they were. Thus, they were inspired and became very eager to learn it. Meanwhile, the young woman, who was now a Christian, returned very happily to her pueblo, with her soul like the roses that God often plucks from these harsh fields, which are filled with thorns.

These felicitous events encouraged the evangelical minister to continue on to the ranchería of the girl whom he had baptized. All the people of the ranchería joyfully came out to meet him, demonstrating their desire to learn the catechism and to receive our Holy Christian Faith. The priest got the people off to a good start and promised to return later and fulfill their wishes.

To insure greater esteem for Holy Baptism, it is important for the priest to proceed [slowly] with these people, making sure that they distinguish between Baptism and the baths they ordinarily take in their rivers. This was the case with the previously mentioned old man as well as with some wild Indians who lived in other rancherías and in the mountaintops and cliffs. It seems that through drought and hunger God compelled them to search for more suitable and accessible places [to live], where He could communicate to them the light of the Gospel. At the time of Father Ramírez's second visit some of these people had already come down out of the mountains to this well-situated place, which today is the principal Tepehuan pueblo of Santiago Papasquiaro. And it is fitting that this pueblo should become noteworthy, for God had chosen it as the place where blood would be shed for our Holy Faith by both the religious who preached it and by many other Spaniards who died with them.

This settlement is located in a beautiful valley, with a river abundant in water and fish; along the banks of the river there is land well suited for farming. Drawn by these lands, some of the wilder Indians had come down to work them. When the priest learned of this, he went to visit them and initiate a settlement with a good number of people, as he had been ordered to do. When the few Indians who had gathered there learned that the priest was on his way, they came to meet him along the trail. They came without their bows and arrows, which was no small thing for the Tepehuan, who usually do not go anywhere without them. Instead, they welcomed him in a very friendly and peaceful manner. When the priest saw how well situated the place was, he begged them to gather there and form a pueblo. He promised to help them and to see to it that the Spaniards who had

8. Presumably in a blue or multicolored skirt and blouse of cotton and perhaps an ornate cloak of cotton (see Soustelle 1961:134–39).

settled in nearby ranches would not mistreat them, but instead would aid them in whatever needs they had for clothing and food for themselves and their women and children. He also told them that for all this it would be useful to have his friendship and continued contact, particularly for holding religious instruction there so that they could become Christians and be saved.

The priest's offer was well received by these first Tepehuan settlers, and thus were established the beginnings of this pueblo. Other Indians as well as Spaniards and mestizos also settled here because it is at the foot of a mountain pass that merchants and other travelers must use to reach the mining camps in the mountains and surrounding countryside. [580] For the same reason the priest decided to take this trail to the next ranchería, which was seven leagues away. There he intended to establish another pueblo and begin religious instruction. The people of this ranchería were known to be the most hostile and bellicose and the least trustworthy of all the Tepehuan. Knowing this themselves, the Indians of Santiago Papasquiaro decided to provide the priest with a friendly escort. They took their bows and arrows with them to defend him in case some Tepehuan should become unruly or there was an uprising or disturbance. This is recorded here so that the reader will understand these people and the spirited and holy zeal with which these religious ministers of the Gospel enter in their midst for the salvation of such fierce souls. Although on this occasion the Indians did not demonstrate their ferocity, later the Indians of this ranchería, which subsequently became a pueblo called Santa Catalina, were the instigators of the Tepehuan Rebellion, as will be told later on. It was here that they took the life of the first priest to die in the rebellion, Hernando de Tovar.

Returning to Father Ramírez's first visit to this ranchería, when he reached the settlement and all the people had gathered, he explained to them why he had come. He was there simply for their salvation, so that they could enjoy the same benefits he had brought to other nations and so they could receive the divine word and with it live together as Christians, receiving the instruction that had been introduced to other nations. At this point in the priest's remarks a poor old woman spoke up. It appeared to her that the audience was very lukewarm or resistant to the priest's arguments. Thus the woman raised her voice among those fierce Tepehuan. *Extollens vocem*: she raised her voice, just like that other poor woman of the Gospel who listened to Christ Our Lord's celestial words spoken to a crowd of hardened Pharisees.[9] He did not cease preaching His divine sermon because of them; in fact, he was satisfied with the fruit of that one poor woman who benefited from it. Our poor old woman imitated her, raising her voice among these fierce Tepehuan who were listening to the priest in either a lukewarm or a rebellious manner. With great zeal, which undoubtedly had been sent from heaven, she said to them, "Because you are rebellious, none of you are willing to do what the priest preaches and begs of you. How can you be convinced to heed him? Are you willing to go hunting for deer in the mountains and valleys, and yet unwilling to gather here to listen to the priest's religious instruction concerning your salvation and how you can get to heaven? Don't be angry with me because I speak so freely, because although I am just a mere woman, I have the heart and spirit to obey the priest, and I will be the first to do so."

This happened on the evening that could be called the eve of the triumph of the holy Cross. The speeches made by the priest and the Indian woman were a portent of the victory that would occur at this place on the following day, which was the Feast of the Holy Cross.[10] They had been so moved by these two speeches that all the people in the surrounding area decided to congregate there in two barrios. In each barrio they erected a Cross, and as a pledge that they would gather there and learn the catechism and become Christians, they offered some of their children for Baptism. These Baptisms were performed, and the pueblo was founded and given the name of Santa Catalina, apparently because of a special devotion to this saint on the part of the priest or the Spaniards who had settled in the nearby ranches or mining camps.

9. See Luke 11:27.
10. The Feast of the Exaltation of the Cross is celebrated on September 14 (Attwater 1949:231).

CHAPTER IV Another missionary priest assists with the reduction and conversion of the Tepehuan; an unusual case of an Indian sorcerer and his idol

[581] The Tepehuan mission got off to a successful start with Father Ramírez's visit to several of their rancherías. However, there were many others farther away that remained to be visited and attended to, without abandoning those that were already receiving religious instruction. The Father Rector of Durango felt that the situation called for additional laborers. While superiors in Mexico City were selecting those who would officially take charge of this mission, the Father Rector appointed another priest to help Father Ramírez.[11] These two priests, each working alone, cared for this new flock, attempting to bring them into the Church. Although this was not a very populous flock, it would nevertheless be wrong to fail to record the glorious things that divine goodness wrought among them. One should also record the things that His servants have accomplished with His aid in winning the Indians over to God and in the service of His Catholic Majesty and his Spanish vassals. The peace and tranquility of these people, particularly the Tepehuan, were very important, because the latter were widely dispersed in these lands, which were rich in silver mines and promised still greater discoveries.

The priests continued their spiritual and evangelical endeavors, taking the light of the Gospel to these highly misguided souls in their rancherías. At that time [1602] there were already two or three settlements or pueblos, each with some two hundred male heads-of-household. As best they could, they had erected some rustic straw churches. Some infants were baptized in these churches and the adults were being prepared for Holy Baptism. As he always did, the devil [promptly] began trying to block all routes to the preaching of the Gospel. At that time there was an Indian in one of those settlements who was about sixty years old. He had spent forty years of his life as a great sorcerer and familiar of the devil, who had dealings with all these gentiles. The devil protected this Indian by means of a little idol, which the Indian kept well hidden. He revered this idol with

such dread that he had convinced the others that if they happened to look upon it, they would fall dead. Thus, no one dared to look at it. The priest got word of this diabolical idol and wanted to disabuse the sorcerer of the errors and lies with which he and the other people had been blinded. Although the priest did not know where to find the old man or the idol, God willed that the sorcerer should be found, and joyful of having encountered the prey that Satan clutched so tightly, [the priest] lovingly began to win the Indian over, endeavoring to bring him out of darkness. He kept the Indian with him for two days, instructing him in the truths of our Holy Faith and in the news of one God, Lord and Creator, whom alone we should adore and fear. He taught him other truths of Christian doctrine, especially the punishment that awaited him in the other life if he did not abominate the superstitions that he practiced.

During this first encounter the Indian was stubborn and refused to reveal or abandon his idol. Although he had not achieved victory in this first battle, the priest did not lose courage. On the eve of [the feast day of] Christ's forerunner, Saint John the Baptist [June 24], whose duty it was to prepare the way for the light of Our Redeemer, the priest sought out the old sorcerer and brought him to the church, where the people had gathered for religious instruction. There he began to try a new strategy, begging the old sorcerer to reveal [582] the false god in whom he placed such great trust and who had so misled him. He who is Lord and the true God willed that this time the Indian's heart should soften. The Indian promised to get his idol for the priest to see, and he immediately set off to retrieve it. The priest asked some faithful Indians to accompany him. Although they still harbored some of the fear that the idolater had instilled in them of looking upon the idol, in the end they went with him. He brought his idol out of his house or hut, and to protect those who were present, he had it wrapped and covered. He took it to the priest, warning bystanders to remain outside if they did not want to be struck dead on the spot. The

11. This was in 1601; the new priest's identity is not known.

minister of God, however, through His favor, did not fear the powers of hell. Thus he unwrapped the idol in the presence of its familiar, and to undo the false fear that had been instilled in the others, he threw it to the ground, spat on it, and then kicked it. The Indians who witnessed this act did not dare to look at the little idol; they trembled at the thought of what might happen to them. The old sorcerer was sweating and waiting for the priest to fall dead. When the people saw that he still lived, however, they began to lose their fear, so much so that they themselves began to execute the same acts as the priest, trampling the devil in what was his image.

When they turned the idol over to reveal its face, it was impossible to see anything. Out of curiosity some Spaniards who happened to be there unwrapped that diabolical lie that had been so feared. It was covered with three or four very soft coverings, which they decided were membranes from human brains. These covered a round stone that was like jasper, a little larger than an apple. It is nothing new for the devil to use this and other lesser and more vile tricks to trap even people of great and civilized nations, using images of bats, rats, and other creatures. As long as he succeeds, it matters not the least bit to him whether the idol is small or large.

The way the devil [won over and] misled this Indian (as he himself confessed) was as follows: One time when he was seated in the company of others, he saw this stone rolling toward him. He took it in his hands and a voice issued forth, telling him to keep and cherish it, for in it was the power to cause and cure illness. In addition, in this stone lay the devil's strength, which he gave to those who went into battle. The Indian who trusted in this stone, taking it along, could [confidently] go to war against his enemies. These were the first talks and dealings that the devil had with this Indian by way of his idol. Later, after some time, the devil became more friendly to him, warning him about particular things that were going to happen. When war was going to erupt the stone became stained with blood. Sometimes the stone would disappear from the Indian's house for several days and then it would reappear, making him believe that the stone was doing him a favor by return-

ing. However, the Indian did not always come out of this singing praises, for not only did he lose his soul as the price for those favors, but whenever he felt like it, the devil also afflicted his body, which is often what happens to those who are bedeviled. The Indian's dealings with the infernal spirit were clearly evident in that he was left debilitated and powerless and horrendously ugly. When the wretched Indian at last saw himself freed from this master, however, he was very happy, although he still showed some traces of fear of renewed injuries from that tyrant, whom he now scorned. The priest freed him of this fear, or better said, it was banished by a crucifix blessed by Saint Toribio, which the priest placed around the Indian's neck. With this the Lord who died on that Cross freed the Indian, just as He had freed from that tyrant all the bedeviled people discussed by the holy Evangelists. [583] The above case has been recounted at such great length because it resembles those cases and is the fruit of the preaching that is now carried out with their Holy Gospel.

In order not to omit the end met by this diabolical idol, about which the devil so strongly boasted, I note that the priest waited until the day after the feast day of Saint John the Baptist to disabuse these people. So that the victory would be more renowned and public, and so that they would all see that he who sold himself to them as the god of strength was in fact powerless, the priest arranged for a Spaniard to beat the idol to dust with a sledge hammer and an iron anvil. The dust was then thrown into a bonfire that the Indians themselves had built. Thus, on this occasion the devil's haughtiness was foiled and Christ's glory and that of His holy Cross were revered and adored by these barbarians. With these happy events many were converted during these early days. Although later the very same devil used another idol and sorcerer to ignite another great fire and persecution, these were all signs of how upset he was to be cast out of his strongholds among this nation. They were also signs of how great God's glory was in this extremely difficult enterprise, undertaken and executed by the soldiers of JESUS.

CHAPTER V The establishment of the pueblo of El Zape

From the ranchería discussed in the preceding chapter one of the priests continued on to another farther inland called El Zape, which was on the banks of a river that runs along the base of a high cliff. Due to the large number of stone idols, figures, ruins, and traces of houses larger than those ordinarily built by these Indians,[12] as well as from other reliable evidence, it was believed that the ancient Mexica had come here from very distant lands. They brought along an idol, and with it the devil, just as God's people brought along the Ark of the Covenant. And just as in their own manner the nation of Israel built ornate temples and resting places along their way to the Promised Land, so did the Mexica on their way to the lake where they settled [Tenochtitlan]. This story is recounted at length by the chroniclers of the Indies.

Returning to our history, idols, columns, and other signs of treasures that pertained to the Mexica were found at the cliff at El Zape. Because it was fertile and well situated, when the priest saw that the Tepehuan were interested in settling there, he approved of them doing so, hoping that more would gather there and in the surrounding area, where they could [eventually] be instructed. This is what happened. During the first entradas the priests laid the foundations for religious instruction, preparing to teach it and baptizing those infants whom the Indians offered for Holy Baptism. Through this holy and necessary sacrament, they also aided the sick whom they prepared to receive it. They performed all the other ministries that could be of aid to these souls, as time and the people's disposition allowed. Because this nation was so dispersed and was not as docile and friendly by nature as others,

it was impossible to employ the same approach with them as with the other [nations] that were previously discussed. This was particularly true of Sinaloa, whose nations were more unified and settled. Their conversion and Baptism were more sweeping and renowned, but that is no reason for omitting the remarkable cases that took place in this nation.

In El Zape the priest had another encounter with sorcerers [584] and the infernal spirits that govern them. The Apostle Saint Paul said that the air is filled with these spirits,[13] and this was especially true in the midst of these people's darkness. There was an Indian here who was known for his spells and his dealings with the devil. At the time when the missionary priest was establishing a mission in this pueblo, it happened that in another pueblo not too far away, later to be called San Ignacio, an illness struck, affecting many people. The sorcerer and healer (for as we have said, these two occupations always went together) went to this pueblo, and the first thing he did when he got there was spread the word that the priest who was teaching the Christian doctrine had brought the illness. When the priest heard about the illness, however, he went to cure the souls of those gentiles, preparing those who were in danger [of dying] so that they could receive Holy Baptism. He was not content with that single act of charity, but extended it to their bodies by seeing to it that food was prepared for the sick in a little straw house that he had [in the pueblo]. He himself took it to them in their homes, attending to them as best he could in such a poor and needy land. His charity was especially focused on an old man [and sorcerer] whose condition was worsening. He wanted to win him over to Christ so that he would not die without Baptism. The devil, however, was careful not to release that old man, whom he had held as a prisoner for so many years. As a result of the speech by the other sorcerer, the old man claimed that it was the priest's food that was killing him and bringing him to the brink of death. This rumor subsequently spread among the other sick people. It made such an impression on them that they no longer wanted the food that the priest was giving them or the Baptism that he was

---

12. Pérez de Ribas is referring here to the remains of the "Chalchihuites culture," an archaeologically defined culture dating to A.D. 1000–1450. The Chalchihuites are thought to have been a Mesoamerican group who colonized Zacatecas and Durango for the purpose of mining turquoise, chert, and other minerals. Archaeological surveys and limited excavation at Chalchihuites sites, which range as far north as Zape, have revealed pyramids, ballcourts, platforms with stairways, masonry architecture, and a wide range of luxury items characteristic of Mesoamerica. The Chalchihuites culture is thought to have abandoned northern Mexico sometime prior to the Spanish conquest (Brand 1939; Foster 1978; Kelley 1980; Reff 1991b:89–95; Weigand 1981) and migrated south to the valley of Mexico.

13. See Ephesians 6:10–13.

advising them [to receive], nor did they want him to continue with his acts of charity. In effect, they were all convinced that he was killing them with spells.

It is not unusual for Christ's ministers to encounter such difficulties and speeches when they are preaching the truth of the Gospel, particularly at the outset. In confirmation of this truth, when the Lord was preaching and casting out demons His enemies spread the word that He was doing this by virtue of Beelzebub,[14] with whom they claimed He had dealings and communication.

In spite of the lie that was being spread, our religious priest did not lose heart. Although he suffered a [temporary] setback with the sick [Indian] who was dying on him, he did not cease his efforts to get him to listen to the catechism and be baptized. He finally succeeded in teaching the sick man the holy catechism, whereupon

the latter received Holy Baptism, healing his body and soul so quickly and thoroughly that the following morning he walked to the church and proclaimed that Baptism had restored his health. As confirmation of the fact that he no longer believed the lie that the priest was killing sick people with food, he asked the priest to give him food right there in the church, which he would very gladly eat. This amazed the other sorcerer who had been the author of that lie. He too was disabused and came to the priest, asking to become a catechumen and to learn the doctrine and be baptized. With this change in both of these men, the people of this ranchería became very excited about coming to church to learn the catechism and become Christians, which is what happened. As we will see, however, this was not the final encounter with demons, nor was it the last victory of Christ's Faith over them. [585]

CHAPTER VI The priests continue to visit new rancherías; they banish gentile abuses; other cases

The author of all the cruel and barbarous abuses that are found among gentile nations, which are subject to the devil, had introduced among the Tepehuan a cruel practice that was carried out by their elders and sorcerers. When sickness spread among them, in order to free a specific person or persons from it, they would kill one or more children so that through these innocents the disease would be consumed. The priests endeavored to redeem the blood of these innocents by making these people understand how much this abuse went against the laws of nature and human charity. Although they eventually convinced the Indians of this in the [mission] settlements that were established, there were many other weeds to uproot. Through singular cases Our Lord favored the enterprise that His ministers had undertaken for the glory of His holy name, for which they endured immense hardships. And although the difficulties recorded in other missions were many and great, in the instruction of this nation they were multiplied. God

Our Lord was served, however, to temper this labor with prosperous results that paid them in kind.

Such was the case with a very young son of a cacique. When the child became ill and his parents could not find a way to cure him and restore his health, they decided to take him to the church to have him baptized. With great pleasure the priest administered that Holy Sacrament to the innocent child. When he received the holy baptismal water, he became so healthy and free of illness that he joyfully walked around the church. His parents, who were gentiles, were moved to conversion by this event. They made an effort to learn the catechism and did not cease until they were baptized and had become Christians.

Our Lord showed similar mercy to another Indian who was not a child, but rather a one hundred-year-old woman. When she was on the verge of dying, she called her family so that she could say goodbye to them and they could watch her die. But God inspired and prepared her so that she also called for the priest to baptize her. The priest went and instructed and baptized her, and that woman—who had been so close to

14. See Luke 11:14–22.

death that she had said farewell to her relatives — immediately sat up in bed, healthy and sound. She then cheerfully dismissed those who had come to witness her gentile death. With these examples of mercy Our Lord favored His laborers' ministries. At other times He demonstrated His justice by punishing rebels, which all aided the cause.

One night when a priest was in one of these rancherías, a good Christian woman came to him. She had been baptized when the Spaniards [first] came to this land. Crying, she complained about her gentile husband, who did not allow her to attend church, learn the catechism, or do anything that was for the well-being of her soul. Above all, he beat her; for this reason she came to ask for help. The priest had the Indian brought before him and scolded him for his tyranny. He explained to him what a great sin he was committing by preventing his wife from seeking what was important for her salvation, even if he did not care about his own [soul]. The priest threatened him with God's punishment for that sin. Even though he acted to the contrary, the ferocious Indian was not mollified by the priest's reasoning. [586] Indeed, after he left the priest's ranchería his anger and rage erupted and he violently grabbed hold of his wife and took off, without anyone being able to stop him (even though the poor woman cried out and asked for help). He carried her to a cave among some cliffs where they had their little house and left her there imprisoned, thus we could say she was a prisoner of the Faith. The Lord, however, did not delay in freeing her or in punishing the one who was persecuting her. On that same night the miserable husband died suddenly, which freed the faithful Christian woman and punished the tyrant who tormented her.

There are many noteworthy ways in which God selects those who are predestined among these people. Indians from other, more distant rancherías called the priests because they were famous for their instruction and the friendliness with which they treated the Indians. One of these priests went to visit the rancherías, and the Indians came out to receive him two leagues before he reached the first settlement. Some three hundred people came up to him so that he could put his hand on the heads of the young and old, as a sign of kindness and respect. They had erected Crosses in their ranchos because they already knew that this is a sign that is venerated by Christians. The priest preached to them about the mysteries of our Holy Faith and initiated religious instruction by choosing a capable and

docile Indian to begin teaching the rest of the Indians [the catechism]. The priest left the caciques and principales contented, promising that a minister would return to their lands to teach them the word of God and His holy law so that they could achieve salvation. They were very pleased and promised to carry out whatever was asked of them when a minister of the doctrine arrived.

This chapter will be concluded with one particular case that occurred during this entrada that confirms what I said about God's special providence in saving some of these souls, which He did not ignore, for His heaven. During the priest's evangelical pilgrimage, he had seen a man who was so elderly that he was certain to die soon. It worried the priest that the old man would proceed to the next life without having secured salvation. One day in particular he felt especially moved to go and seek out the old man, who lived very far away. Although he did not know how close the old gentile was to dying, the priest followed his impulse, which seemed to have been sent from heaven. He found the old man so sick that he had very little life left. The priest began to teach him the catechism, but the old man was so hardened and resistant that there was no way to convince him that there was a God who punished sins and wickedness and rewarded good works in the next life. "I believe," said the old atheist, "in what I see on earth. I do not see this God whom you preach is in heaven. I see [only] deer and fields of corn on earth."

With this rebellious spirit the hardened old man dismissed the priest. The next day, however, the priest persevered with his charity and his desire to help that soul, and once again he visited him to see whether he could draw water from that stone. He began to assail him with new arguments and to frighten the old man with the punishment that awaited him. *Compelle eos intrare, ut impletur domus mea discumbentium*,[15] thus spoke the Lord to that other servant who was gathering people for heaven. The religious priest urged the sick man, first with threats and the punishment of hell, and then with the rewards of glory that are enjoyed by those who receive the Faith and the law of Jesus Christ. God willed that his latter efforts should begin to soften the Indian's hardened heart, and he finally yielded to the doctrine proposed to him. He prepared himself well for Baptism, and a day and a half after the priest administered that

---

15. Luke 14:23: "and give them no choice but to come in, so that my house may be filled" (Knox 1956:73). This passage was uttered by a master to a servant in the parable of the great banquet, in Luke 14:15–24.

sacrament of health, this man departed this life with particular peace. [587] The priest was consoled as well, due to the many assurances he had of the salvation of a soul that had displayed so many signs of predestination.

No less unusual was another case through which God carried to heaven the soul of a boy who was in serious danger of remaining in Limbo. The priest arrived at a ranchería where once again he found some old people who, at the devil's urging, had decided to sacrifice this boy. To achieve health, as we mentioned earlier, they were going to put into practice that which had been taught to them by that cruel enemy. The priest learned of their intention and decried this inhumane and diabolical deed. He then endeavored to have them bring him the lamb they wanted to sacrifice to the devil. They brought the boy to him, and he offered

[the boy] to the Lamb of God. With no resistance on their part the priest baptized him, fearing that if he turned his back on them, they would carry out their evil intentions and the boy would be deprived of glory. God freed him from all this and from the hands of those butchers, because as soon as he was baptized, he died and God carried him away to His heaven.

He was not alone, for there were others just like him whom the Indians wanted to sacrifice who also died of illness. They had been recently baptized, however, and were thus saved from eternal death. Through other similar cases that I will not mention here, God was saving some of these people at the time of their conversion, before they became corrupted. [In the next chapter] I continue my discussion of the early years [preceding the Tepehuan Revolt].

CHAPTER VII A request is made to the viceroy for a greater number of missionaries for the Tepehuan nation; the reductions and cases of edification increase

With the aid of divine favor the religious working in this mission brought this nation to such a state that other laborers were needed to help with the establishment of the doctrine and the reduction and congregation of so many widely dispersed rancherías. Even though the doctrine had already been established in some of these rancherías, there were others still to be reduced. Those [people] who were already reduced required greater assistance from their ministers so that they could be baptized and their Christianity sustained in peace. All this called for a greater number of ministers. The Father Rector of Durango gave an account of this to the superiors in Mexico City and, at the same time, an account of how important the total conversion of the Tepehuan was to that land. With these reports and by the viceroy's order and accord, the Father Provincial sent religious to take charge of this enterprise.

For this task they took along ornaments for the church and vestments for the priests, which as noted, are ordered by Our Lord the king to be given at the outset [of a mission]. These said priests reached their mission, which for the majority of these blessed religious would be the place of their triumph and martyrdom. Father Juan Fonte went as their superior and as superior of the mission, which was removed from the governance of [the Jesuit superior] in Durango. He was a religious who had great fervor and zeal for the welfare of souls, and there will be much to say later concerning his virtue and the hardships he suffered in this conversion. Those who went in great brotherhood in Christ divided amongst themselves the places and districts inhabited by this nation. Each of them very enthusiastically took to heart the care of his respective flock. No matter how much effort was made to congregate the people, it could not be done in such a way that each priest had any less than two or three pueblos under his care. Thousands of infants were baptized. God had begun taking to the safety of heaven a good number of infants, as well as adults and {588} sick people who had been baptized. The priests had begun to establish the doctrine in their pueblos, selecting the most advanced and faithful youths with the best character to be temachtianos and teachers of the doctrine. Some of these youths already knew enough to fill this post. They built more adequate churches in their pueblos and selected fiscales. The latter were in charge of gathering the people together for catechism and informing the priests of those who were sick and of any adults who wanted to be baptized. Lastly, they began to establish the type of civil order and government that was possible among these people, who were so free {both} inherently and in their gentile state. But God did not fail to send some Indian helpers who possessed intelligence, good manners, and an affable character. Although these people were generally always bellicose, on the other hand, they also always possessed a lively and enthusiastic intelligence. The priests noticed this in some of them who upon applying themselves to the catechism were able to memorize it in one or two days, such that they were then able to teach it to others. This was in spite of the fact that these matters {of the Faith} were very strange to them because they had never heard of or learned them before. Once religious instruction was established, the people came frequently to hear it, as well as the speeches and sermons of the priests, who had already learned the Indians' language. With this the older people were prepared to receive the Faith, and the general Baptism of adults could be celebrated.

The obstacles to marriage according to Christian law were not as numerous here as in other nations. Not many men had multiple wives on a permanent basis, nor were they as dissolute in this vice as they could have been. Ordinarily in this regard, the husband would not take back his wife if she failed him in fidelity; nor could she find anyone else to marry, {and the same was true of} a maiden who had lost her virginity. Nor did they steal or rob from their people. The way in which the devil enjoyed perverting and blinding them, which was sufficient for him to destroy them, was through sorcery, superstition, and idolatry. Furthermore, the Tepehuan were very inclined to warring with and stealing from other nations. They boasted of this, considering it to be their glory.

In one pueblo the priests found an idol that was highly renowned among these people. It was made of stone and was forty inches tall.[16] It had the head of a man, and the rest was like a column. It was placed on the top of a little hill in their pueblo. Next to it they had placed many offerings of arrows, animal bones, pots, herbs, tree branches, and beads, which they use for adornment. Another little stone idol in the shape of a snail was placed next to the larger one. When the priest at first came upon this superstition, he pretended to overlook it, awaiting a better opportunity to destroy it, when doing so would have a better effect. He gathered the people together and preached to them about the adoration of only one God, Creator of all things, and of the true doctrine of the Christians, which [was what] they should become. He waited for the appointed day to celebrate the Baptisms of some of those who were well instructed. Before he began he went with some of his catechumens to the place where the idol was. [He told them] Satan existed in this idol, and those who were going to be baptized had to openly renounce him, according to the holy rites of the Church. The cacique of the pueblo was prepared to knock the idol over, so he hurled that demon down the hill and it landed at the bottom of the river. There it remained buried and covered over. The catechumens returned with great joy because of the deed that they had carried out. The priest's joy was even greater, for he had demolished the devil's dominion over these people, who returned to celebrate their Baptism. Once the new Christians had received Baptism—they thus being already marked with Christ's Cross—they {589} assembled a very large Cross and placed branches on it and adorned it with flowers and carried it in a procession. So that this procession would be even more solemn, they also placed branches in the plaza of the pueblo and sang the creed in their language, thus professing the Faith that they had received. They reached the place where the idol had been and in its place they erected the beautiful Cross that they were carrying. They raised that sacred trophy that always triumphed over idolatry, and the pueblo that before had belonged to the devil was named Santa Cruz. From then on it belonged to Christ, who had redeemed their pueblo.

This is what happened in this pueblo; in the others that the priests cared for they were [also] successful in introducing religious instruction, Baptism, and other Christian practices. This was especially true in the first and principal pueblo, which was called San-

---

16. *Cinco palmos.* A palmo equaled 8.23 inches (Polzer, Barnes, and Naylor 1977:39).

tiago Papasquiaro. Some long-time Christian Indians that usually work in the mines were being added to this pueblo, particularly some Mexicans and Tarascans.[17] They serve as guides, leading barbarous nations in the way of Christian practices. They are always important to these enterprises, as will be declared by the following case, even if it seems minor. These Christian Indians wanted to celebrate the eve of Our Redeemer's birth. They planned on their own, without the priest's knowledge, a devout portrayal of the shepherds who came to adore the Christ Child. It was so well per-formed that it amazed those who were present. They appeared in the church dressed as shepherds. Some of them were old men, who usually are not very disposed to this type of youthful entertainment. They all arrived and offered gifts to the Christ Child. One of them who had nothing with which to make his offering ended by offering the most precious thing possible: as he knelt, he offered his soul, with such great faith and devotion that he instilled the same in the others, particularly the Tepehuan. Because of this example, they all became more fond of our Christian Faith and Religion.

CHAPTER VIII The remaining practices of our Holy Mother Church are introduced to this nation

Before recording what is promised by the title of this chapter, I will point out two things, because although [the practices I refer to pre-viously] are discussed elsewhere, not everyone will read the history chapter by chapter. Moreover, the topic that claims this space should not be considered repetitious. First of all, not all Christian practices can be introduced to these people when they are being baptized. This is the case because not all of them are obligatory; some require a readiness and understanding on the part of the Indians that takes time [to instill] before they can be beneficially introduced. Second, be-cause this history deals with spiritual enterprises among new nations, the fruits that the Gospel has produced in them should be mentioned. Even though such fruits might not be unusual among nations that were Chris-tian at birth (as they say), among those who were born and raised as gentiles and barbarians, foreign to any type of civil order and religious instruction, it is amaz-ing suddenly to see fruits appear that took many years to introduce in the Holy Universal Church. With this assumption I will continue with spiritual matters—a welcome change from the temporal wars and battles with this nation.

The celebration of the mysteries of our redemption are very important to these peoples, and with regard to the people of whom we are speaking they produced marvelous effects. In a pueblo in the valley that they call [590] Atotonilco, a priest celebrated the first Holy Week that they had ever seen. Some Spaniards from neighboring ranches came and joined in this celebra-tion. The Indians were amazed at the Christian prac-tices that they saw being performed, which also elicited devotion. On each day the meaning of the holy cere-monies of the Church were preached and declared to the new Christians: the blessing of palms, Tenebrae, the monument or [decorated] float, and the veiling and un-veiling of the Most Holy Sacrament. As they were very concerned about having all the accoutrements, Span-iards from the ranches assisted with tapestries, jewels, and silk for decorating the monument. Many Spaniards and Indians confessed, and Communion was received by the Spaniards as well as those Indians who were most advanced in the Faith. Following the [re-enactment of the] decree [issued by Pontius Pilate], a blood scourg-ing procession was organized, in which the Spaniards wished to set a good example for these people, for it is certain that this Catholic nation does not know how to dissimulate the zeal that God has granted it in matters of the Faith. There were many people from both groups who used scourges in the procession. The women ac-companied them with torches of resin from their thorn

17. As early as 1579 Spanish miners had successfully petitioned the crown to bring 1,000 Tarascan and Tlaxcalan Indians to the mining frontier to work as free laborers (Mecham 1927:230–32).

thickets, which although rustic, gave off more light than those made from wax. Because these were still new lands on a frontier of war with gentiles, some soldiers went along with their harquebuses to escort the procession, together with two squads of well-equipped Indian archers. Men from both parties took turns that night guarding the Most Holy Sacrament. On Good Friday it was a great consolation to finally see the wild barbarians come tamed and kneeling to adore the holy Cross, in which they and all of us were redeemed. The morning of the Resurrection and Christ's glorious triumph was celebrated with no less solemnity. Everyone attended the procession, which was performed with the Most Holy Sacrament displayed. The native people joined in with garlands of flowers, which they carried in their hands together with lit candles; there was music as well from their trumpets and dancing in their fashion and tradition. The priest had arranged for the Baptism of several children and adults who had been instructed in order to resurrect their souls with Christ that day. It cannot be doubted that this would be just as pleasing to the Lord as it would be to bring souls out of Limbo, for He was removing them from a state of greater danger than those who were awaiting His Holy Coming. The catechumens came out dressed in white and adorned with the beads and feathers that they use. Their godparents wore the same attire, and this is how this feast day was celebrated and concluded. Something very similar to what has been recounted here took place in the districts of the other priests. There were remarkable Baptisms as well as the partaking of the sacraments, especially Confession, by those who were already baptized. It was not easy for members of such a free and arrogant nation to reveal to the confessor their vices and sins. Some women who overcame this great and inherent obstacle and revealed their sins did so only to faint at the feet of their confessor.

CHAPTER IX Through an unusual act of providence, God Our Lord frees a priest from the danger of being killed

Christianity was progressing with the prosperity that has been portrayed in the settled pueblos. Nevertheless, in the more distant rancherías that always remain at the borders of these nations, the Gospel ministers had no lack of difficulties and dangers to overcome, from which God helped them emerge victorious. In one of these rancherías the priest was trying [591] to save the soul of an old man who, in spite of his advanced age, was carrying on an affair with one of his long-time concubines. Even though the priest sought this man's salvation gently and tenderly, the old man was very distraught over being deprived of his entrenched pleasure. And so he decided to withdraw to the mountains after first killing the priest. Night fell and he sat down where he would be within an arrow's shot of the priest. He prepared seven arrows, in case the priest did not fall dead from the first one. When the Indian attempted to use his bow to execute his evil deed, he found that as light as the bow was, he could barely lift it because he trembled so. These bows are nothing more than a long piece of very hard wood. They know how to draw and shoot them with the same force as a good crossbow. These people did not use crossbows, but they loaded their [own] bows and fired their arrows with [even] greater ease. The perturbed Indian finally gave up on carrying out his evil deed, but not his harmful intentions. He came back before sunrise the following morning, more angry than the first time, not only with himself, but with the man who desired the salvation of his soul and who was perhaps at that moment commending it to God. Through His divine and paternal providence God freed His servant from this second danger in the same way as He had from the first. The Indian sat with his weapons in the same place as before, and found himself similarly perturbed and weak. This case was brought to the attention of a few Indian faithful, and they told the priest about it so that he would be cautious. But they did not feel satisfied or safe with this, so that night they came to stand guard over the priest with their bows and arrows. They spent the night keeping watch at the door of the little house, which was illuminated by a torch of the type that they use.

The priest made an effort to see, speak with, and tame this Indian who was being so fierce. They brought the Indian to him, and {the priest} made him see how wrong he was and the danger in which he was placing his soul. God wished to show piety for this soul, and the old man cast aside his temptation and became fond of the priest and his teachings. From then on he attended church and religious instruction more carefully than before, and he became tame and did not try to return to the mountains. This is the same as walking among basilisks and not being bitten, which is what God promised his Gospel preachers. With this and other examples, many other old people finally began to attend Christian exercises, and their children came every day for catechism.

This careful priest and shepherd set out for another ranchería because he had learned that those who lived nearby had never wanted to go into the church. He gathered the people together to find out the cause of their rebelliousness and found that they were dissuaded by the fear that they would not be safe inside what they called the house of the dead. They gave this name to the church because they saw dead Christians buried there. The priest disabused them of this delusion and vain fear, and spoke to them about the truths that are taught by our Holy Faith and the matters of the other life, which they listened to with pleasure. He gave them a Cross to erect in the midst of their huts as well as a boy who was well instructed to teach them the catechism. They were quite satisfied with this and placed this Cross in the midst of their homes. They gathered there twice a day to learn their prayers, and thereby this flock was won over. Another larger flock will be told of in the following chapter.

CHAPTER X The priests attempt a new entrada to reduce the Tarahumara nation; how the devil tried to prevent this and how the priests quelled the uprising

[592] The fervor with which these apostolic men pursued the salvation of souls was not confined to the Tepehuan's borders. Another and more populous nation, called the Tarahumara, who spoke a different language, bordered the Tepehuan. Their rancherías were well hidden and farther inland. Because our common adversary who reigned in these nations is also the enemy of peace, he always sowed discord between these peoples, who engaged each other in wars and assaults. The priests wanted to establish peace between these two nations in order to introduce the Gospel, which would bring true peace to the Tarahumara. God offered a good oppor-tunity for this on the occasion of a threatened war [in 1607], when the Tepehuan neighboring the Tarahumara in the Valle del Aguila requested that other Tepehuan pueblos assist them in their attack on the Tarahumara.

As there were already a good number of Christians among the Tepehuan, both Christians and gentiles consulted as to whether to send aid. They decided that one of their principales should go to discuss the matter with their minister of the doctrine, who would advise both Christians and gentiles. They [had] already demonstrated esteem and obedience toward their ministers and priests. The priest took control and successfully resolved the differences by peaceful means. Thus the Tepehuan and the Tarahumara were won over and the former were more disposed to show the latter the light of the Gospel. However, as usual, the devil was already arming himself to oppose divine preaching, rather than be robbed of the souls that he possessed. For this he invented a way to disturb these people using an old sorcerer whom he persuaded to kill a principal Indian who was a catechumen. This Indian was a relative of one of the caciques from a settlement in the Valle de San Pablo, close to the Tarahumara.

Persuaded by the devil, the sorcerer carried out this deed. He took ten fierce Indians with him and executed his wicked plan, killing the catechumen. The [soul of the] latter may have been saved because he was learning the Christian doctrine and died at the hands of the devil and an enemy of Christ, [a murder] carried out due to hatred for the holy law. The relatives of the dead man were so angry and outraged that they prepared to go after the killers to take revenge. The only thing that stopped them was a fear that stemmed from the love they had for the priests. Two of the priests were at that time giving religious instruction in the settlements of this valley. They were afraid that the killers would ally themselves with other fierce Indians who were their friends. They also feared that [the killers] would come back to overtake [the priests] and kill them, or that they would invade the pueblos that they were instructing and the priests would not be able to defend themselves or the Indians.

These are the difficulties and dangers in which these servants of God place themselves in order to win these souls. [593] Evangelical preaching, nonetheless, bore its fruit in spite of these difficulties and dangers. Fearing for the priests' safety, faithful Indians persuaded the priests to move for the time being to safer pueblos and other places. Although it was imperative that they do this, the priests felt great sorrow at leaving [those Indians] that they loved so much. They expected, however, to see them again soon, when they would renew Christ

[in them]. The priests left for a somewhat distant but safer pueblo. When the priests left the people prepared for war, in case the enemy should attack. At the same time they sent a son of the cacique of San Pablo, along with twelve brave Indians, to Durango to ask the governor to defend them and punish the murderous sorcerer who, with his group of followers, prevented them from becoming Christians. At the time the governor was already leading an expedition of Spanish troops to punish the Xixime, as was previously recorded. Either moved by fear or (most certainly) moved by divine impulse, the troublemaking Indian sorcerer went to find one of the priests. He asked him, with an insistence that came from his heart, to give him religious instruction and baptize him. The priest fulfilled his request, and after giving him careful religious instruction, he baptized the Indian. The Indian then went to see the governor, whom he encountered along the way. He threw himself at the governor's feet and asked him to forgive him for what he had done. He was now a Christian and wanted to live as such, and would henceforth change his life.

The governor received him well and pardoned him on the condition that he would keep his word and neither he nor his people would disturb those who wanted to become Christians. He fulfilled this condition, and the Tepehuan of the Valle de San Pablo asked their ministers to return to instruct and baptize them, which the priests did. Father Juan Fonte (who was a true and tireless evangelical minister) congregated and baptized a good number of people in this valley. He used all the possible means that his charity allowed to win these souls and prepare them to be instructed. Because many of them were recent arrivals, he told them how to irrigate their fields by taking water from the river through channels. This was something they had neither used nor known before.[18] These means won these people over and they began to congregate. The entrada to the Tarahumara followed, which will be recorded in the next chapter.

18. It seems highly unlikely that the natives knew nothing of irrigation (see Mecham 1927:81).

CHAPTER XI A letter from Father Juan Fonte in which he relates his entrada to the Tarahumara nation[19]

Although the Tepehuan Rebellion, which is drawing near, cut short the establishment of missions among the Tarahumara, I will not omit writing about an entrada to this nation, which served to prepare some of them to receive Holy Baptism and which had other good results. Father Juan Fonte gave an account of his entrada to the Father Provincial in Mexico City, requesting the assistance of laborers for the new field that was being prepared to receive the Gospel. His letter reads:

After the rains were over I journeyed to the rancherías of the Tarahumara, in order to learn about the people of that land and along the way to bring them news of God Our Lord. It was also my intention to congregate as many people as possible in the Valle de San Pablo. This is what they had requested. [594] Moreover, the location was favorable, peaceful, and ample. I was accompanied by four caciques and some other persons, among whom only two had been baptized; one was a boy who assisted me at Mass and the other was a cacique who had recently become a Christian.

I arrived at the rancherías of these Indians, which are some eighteen leagues from the Valle de San Pablo. The road was in reasonable condition, but the Indians say that [the Tarahumara live in] canyons that horses cannot cross. Many people dwell in the caves that are plentiful in this land. Some are so spacious that they accommodate an entire extended family; interior divisions of the caves are occupied by separate households. The [men] wear clothing consisting of mantas made from hemp, which is very well woven by the women, who also wear mantas of the same material. The [women] are very reserved and neither sit nor mix with the men. Their burial customs differ from other nations in that they have designated a separate place that is like a cemetery. They bury the dead with all their clothing and some food for the journey. The home of the deceased was burned or totally abandoned; relatives would mourn the dead by cutting their hair.

These people are by nature more gentle and docile than the Tepehuan. The manner in which they received me was that they would send two watchmen two leagues from the pueblo to look for my approach, whereupon they would run back to the pueblo to notify all the people. Then the men, women, and children would form lines to come and welcome me. The cacique led the others, carrying his lance or mace, adorned with feathers and other ornaments. A good distance from the pueblo they would meet me, and each one would then ask me to place my hand on his head. They then accompanied me to their settlement, where I would give a talk, letting them know how pleased I was to see them and how my great love for them had brought me to their lands. Then I would say goodbye, at which point they immediately provided me and my companions with maize and other things. I cannot describe the happiness they expressed at seeing me again. Although during the first entrada the women were shy because it was something new for them, when they saw the men speak to me without fear and saw that I spoke to them as a father speaks to his children, they also came to speak to me as a father. Both men and women added that they wanted me to return to their lands.

I usually preached something about how we all needed to be saved by Holy Baptism. One Indian told me about his son who was dying. I went to visit his cave and because he was so close to death I instructed him. He already knew something of the Faith from his Christian neighbors, so I baptized him. I learned there were four sick infants, and to their parents' great joy I baptized them as well. Are these not acts that God has reserved for the salvation of these souls?

As I was baptizing these children, a woman and her husband brought their son to me in their arms. He was very sick with smallpox.[20] They asked me to baptize him, which I did to the great pleasure of all of us.

Before leaving this land I wanted to take note of the number of people in this nation. From the account they gave me I calculate 3,170 people, not including those in isolated rancherías, which I could not visit. I picked four Indians who seemed most suitable to act as fiscales, assigning to each one of them a district so that [595] from time to time they will come to see me at Christian pueblos in order that I may get to know and deal with the people and prepare them for instruction, and also so that they may become disposed to settling in suitable places, as many of them already wish to do. May God and the protection of the Apostle of the People, Saint Paul, whom I have named patron of this mission, help them accomplish their goals.

Upon my departure from their pueblos, men and women have accompanied me for a good distance. The caciques and some of their people even accompanied me as far as the next

---

19. This entrada took place during the winter of 1607–8 (Reff 1991b:152).

20. Note that the fact that the child's parents had not contracted smallpox suggests that the Tarahumara had been exposed to the disease previously (probably in 1604), acquiring some immunity in the process (Reff 1991b:153).

pueblo and did not return to their own pueblo until I had departed the one I had gone to. The Tarahumara practice this type of benevolence whenever I travel from the Valle de San Pablo to their lands or to others. Without my requesting it, the caciques send eight or ten of their Indians, one of whom is designated as captain, to accompany me. When I had to go to the distant Spanish pueblo of Santa Bárbara to discuss with them the matter of making peace with the Tarahumara, they sent me a cacique with thirty men armed with bows and arrows. When I said that I did not need an escort, the sensible Indians replied that the Spaniards needed to see how much the Tarahumara appreciated the man whom they considered their father. For this trip they prepared food for me and everyone else.

They showed me so much love that late one day, when I was hurrying to avoid a pouring rainstorm and could not find a place to spend the night, the cacique sent seven men to accompany me. Such was his diligence and attention to the welfare of the priest. I have found much faithfulness and affability in these people. The caciques came to see me every day, ready to help with anything I asked. There was one old man among them who was so superstitious that he suffocated his grandson with his own hands, simply because his mother, the old man's daughter, had died from an illness. This man must have been inspired by the devil.

However, God has been favored by the winning over and domestication of such a fierce Indian. Now that he has been disabused and is being instructed, he has led some of his people down into the valley. He also has accompanied me on some trips and has been so helpful that he has become like my own hands and feet. He is among those who have most helped the people of the Valle de San Pablo. As the son of a Tepehuan man and a Tarahumara woman he speaks both languages, and thus has made efforts to gather people of both groups.

Thus did I arrive in Durango to discuss with the governor of [Nueva] Vizcaya the religious instruction of these well-disposed people. He agreed and assigned this instruction to the Company of Jesus. He asked me to send him a report about the pueblos and His Eminence also said he would ask the viceroy to order the dispatch of priests as well as ornaments for the churches. All this will open the door for us to a great conversion.

This is the conclusion of Father Juan Fonte's letter, which describes how the Tarahumara nation was prepared to receive the Gospel. We will put this aside for the time being, to relate other adverse and painful events that impeded the conversion of the Tarahumara.

CHAPTER XII The state of the Tepehuan nation and Christianity at the time of their uprising and apostasy, foretelling the revolt

It is first necessary to record the state of this Christian community in order to understand the damaging fire [596] that the devil ignited to raze and destroy it. The ministers to this nation had established Christianity through infinite hardships and tireless diligence. And by divine permission they defeated the furies of hell, for ends known [only] to God Our Lord. These ends are always just, and it is for them that God has permitted innumerable persecutions, which we read also were experienced by Christ's Holy Gospel and His Church, from the early days of the founding of Christianity in the universe. The persecution that we are discussing here was more excessively fierce than all the other persecutions that have been overcome in the other missions. The nations of those other missions [afterwards] remained calm and stable in their Chris-

tianity, but here nearly everything was destroyed. To make this more clearly understood, I will record the state of each of the principal settlements and places where the fires raged the fiercest and where the damage was most extensive. It must be understood that the devil had ignited the fire several months beforehand.

The Indians of the pueblo of Santiago Papasquiaro, which was the first in which the catechism was established, were just as assimilated to civil life and matters of the Faith as any other nation in Nueva España. They celebrated their Christian feast days and solemnities, and the exercise of the Holy Sacraments had already been introduced. There was a seminary for boys and young men, who learned everything that is ordinarily taught in seminaries concerning doctrine, reading, writing, singing, and worship. They had [also] nearly completed the construction of a beautiful church. Some Indians from other nations who were long-time Christians had joined them at this pueblo, and they served as examples to the others in their frequent partaking of the sacraments. The settlement was so well situated that some Spaniards were already living there with their families. In addition, there were others who lived in ranches in the region, to which they had brought livestock and where they had [planted] fields.

The people in the neighboring pueblo of Santa Catalina had always been the wildest of the Tepehuan. Nevertheless, the priests had taken special care to tame them, and they had already lost much of their fierceness, or were hiding it. They had built a church, and everyone in this pueblo was baptized and attended church as well as religious instruction. Some sparks of these people's natural fierceness still flew. These people were the first aggressors and produced one of the principal captains of the revolt. The priests tried to extinguish these sparks through all the gentle means that were available to them. They did not fail to send several warnings of [impending] danger to the governor of Nueva Vizcaya so that he could formulate the most effective solution, which this nation most desperately needed. But he was not convinced of this until it was too late, as was eventually seen. The eight religious priests from our Company who were employed in the different districts of this mission had already baptized nearly everyone. They continued using all the means available to them in their missions and pueblos to tend to their sheep. Even though they could already hear the roars of the infernal lion that wanted to devour both them and their sheep, they did not abandon them. And even though many barbarous customs had been uprooted, those associated with the sorcerers still had their roots. These were the predominant barbarous customs in this nation, and they are the most difficult to uproot, having become entrenched over the course of so many years. Even though they were weeds that did not allow the good seed to grow, the priests tried to carefully uproot them so that the good field would not be harmed.

I will record here that to which I was an eyewitness. This was about two months before the unleashing of the fury of the Tepehuan Revolt, [597] when some forewarning could already be sensed and when some of the Indians had started to go bad. At that time I was travel-

ing from Sinaloa to Mexico City to ask His Eminence the viceroy to give orders to send religious ministers to give instruction to the populous Yaqui nation, as was recorded in its appropriate place. I passed through the Tepehuan nation and was there with some priests who were giving the Tepehuan religious instruction. They took me to see some of their pueblos. Two things impressed me. First of all was these people's newness [to the Faith], as reflected in their lack (generally speaking) of affection for the Church, which I had experienced in our Christian nations in Sinaloa. [Second], they neither possessed nor demonstrated that trace of Christianity — nor any of the affable dealings with the priests, their ministers — that was seen in other nations. I said something about what I had noticed to the priest who accompanied me, and he responded, "I do not know what hellish idol has been erected among these people that has changed them and made them restless. The other priests and I spare no effort to quiet and subdue them." This was the answer that Father Bernardo de Cisneros gave me. He was one of the eight priests who died two months later at the hands of the Tepehuan apostates. I was notably edified by his remarkable charity and zeal in seeking the salvation of souls that seemed to be so hostile. But there were some souls among these people that God wanted to save. These people were not as stubborn as the others, and for their sake both God and the priests suffered the other Tepehuan's rebelliousness. Later, when it is more appropriate, I will recount the rest of what happened to me with Father Bernardo de Cisneros, along with the life of this great servant of God. I will conclude here the forewarning of restlessness among the corrupted Tepehuan and the outbreak of war that was feared from them. These signs were also noticed at the Spaniards' mining camps and other haciendas in the region, even though they did not believe them to be as well founded as was later seen [to be the case]. Therefore, they did not prepare for them, and commerce and the shipment of clothing and other goods to the mining camps continued while the Tepehuan plotted the execution of their rebellion and apostasy. The Tepehuan had already been deceived by the devil and they used all the means that Satan was teaching them. Their revolt was initiated in the manner related in the following chapter.

CHAPTER XIII The devil's plan that was the cause of the Tepehuan nation's rebellion and apostasy

Before writing about the fierce, barbarous, and infidel decision made by this nation, I must explain the motive and cause of this—one of the greatest uprisings, disturbances, and ravages of war in Nueva España. We could even say that this was the greatest [rebellion] since the conquest. It is true that after the Mexican Empire was conquered the Spaniards fought for a long period of time with the very renowned and fierce Chichimec nation, of which something will be mentioned later in Book XII of this history. Nevertheless, the Chichimec nation never caused as much destruction as the Tepehuan. Thus, we must record here that which was well known concerning the Tepehuan nation, namely that they could not allege that the Spaniards, far less their missionary priests, had mistreated [598] or maligned them in such a way that they should have any reason to fail in the Faith that was their duty to God. Nor did they have reason to break the peace that they had established with the Spaniards and their king, under whose protection they had placed themselves. There was only one cause of what happened here—it was a scheme invented by Satan and welcomed by these blind people. [The scheme] enraged their spirits to take up arms against the Faith of Christ and all things Christian. They demonstrated this in the many deeds that they executed during their destructive attack. This was demonstrated even more clearly by the principal instigators and authors of the uprising—the diabolical sorcerers who had familiar dealings with the devil. I will record here what happened, abbreviating two authentic reports, one of which was prepared by the governor of Nueva Vizcaya,[21] with concurring witnesses. The other report was submitted by the Episcopal Vicar of the city of Durango[22] on behalf of his order and Church, as was required of him.

There were also letters from other priests who were in the region at the time of the uprising.

The case began in the following way. There was an old Indian in this nation who was a great sorcerer and had very intimate dealings with the devil. Although he had been baptized, he only pretended to renounce that diabolical pact. Or perhaps he truly did renounce it and subsequently backslid, just as many other heretics in the world have done. He apostatized, taking along with him an idol, which was like his oracle and the means by which he communicated with the devil. When he entered the pueblos of Santiago, Tunal, and Tenerapa, which were all near Durango, he preached perversely against our Holy Faith, with the harmful intention of inciting those people to abandon their Faith and rebel against God and the king. The governor of Nueva Vizcaya received some news of Indian unrest in Durango. He investigated the case and determined that it was nothing more than one of these people's ancient diabolical superstitions. He ordered the usual punishment for this Indian and his accomplices: that they be flogged for the scandal they had caused in those pueblos. This sorcerer was astute and bedeviled, and in order to disguise his intentions (in which he still persisted, as was later demonstrated), he found an image of our holy crucifix and displayed it to some people. He told them that this was the God whom he and his companions worshiped. Afterwards, however, he went to the aforementioned pueblo of baptized Tepehuan, called Tenerapa, which was not far from Santiago Papasquiaro. There he ordered that his idol be worshiped, and through his lies and tricks he convinced these Indians that he, through his idol, was God. He also convinced them that both he and the idol were angry and offended because he had assigned the Spaniards a homeland in kingdoms on the other side of the ocean in Spain, and yet they had come to these parts without his permission, settling in his lands and introducing the Christian law. He wished to free them of this, and in order to do so, as well as to placate their true gods, they would have to cut the throats of all long-time Christians, particularly the

21. Gaspar de Alvear y Salazar was governor and captain general of Nueva Vizcaya from 1613 to 1618 (Naylor and Polzer 1986:247). An English translation of his *Relación breve y succinta de los sucessos que ha tenido de los Tepehuanes* . . . can be found in Hackett (1923–1937, vol. 2).

22. It is not known which report Pérez de Ribas is referring to here.

priests and fathers who instructed them, as well as all the Spaniards in the region. If they did not do so, they would receive a terrible punishment in the form of illnesses, plagues, and famine. But if they obeyed him, he promised them safety for their own lives, their women and children, and victory over the Spaniards. Even if some of them should die in battle, he promised them that within seven days they would be resurrected. He who is the father of deception and was this Indian's own familiar demon heaped one lie on top of another. [599] He added that once they had achieved the promised victory, all the old men and women would be made young again. The devil is aware of how strong this desire is in mankind, who do not want even to appear to be old. On this occasion he used this and other lengthy arguments to pervert [these] ignorant people, just as he has done many other times for similar ends with other people of greater [intellectual] capacity.

This trickster did not desist in his lies and false promises. He assured the Tepehuan that they would wipe out the Spaniards in the region, and that afterwards he, [acting] as God through his idol, would create storms at sea, sinking the Spaniards' ships and thus preventing additional Spaniards from reaching these lands. In confirmation of this diabolical hoax and to further terrorize and frighten these people, he gave them an example [of his power], which some said actually occurred. Even if there was some truth to what was said to have happened, owing to the fact that God, for His reasons, allowed it to happen, the Indian trickster nevertheless misled the people. That notwithstanding, some Indians confessed that an Indian named Sebastián, who was a native of Tenerapa, and a woman named Justina, a native of Papasquiaro, were both swallowed up when the earth opened on the order of the sorcerer, who punished them for disobeying him. The same thing had happened to another Indian in another pueblo called Cacaria.

By secretly and repeatedly sowing his diabolical doctrine in various places, the bedeviled Indian kept these people demented and fooled. This was ultimately the true origin and cause of this uprising and revolt and the tragic apostasy of the Tepehuan nation.

CHAPTER XIV The bedeviled sorcerer encourages other nations to rebel; he plots the execution of this conspiracy with fellow Tepehuan

This Indian sorcerer, or the devil in disguise, was not content with his efforts among the Tepehuan nation. He went to the neighboring Acaxee and Xixime nations, which were already Christian, and tried to stir them up as well. He added new wiles to frighten them, trying to get them to rebel. This old Indian appeared to the Xixime as a youth, with a bow and two arrows in his hand. He also had a stone idol that was half a vara high and could speak all languages. The old man appeared in an aura of light and interpreted the stone for the Xixime. This fraud by the devil is not a new one, for Saint Paul wrote to the Corinthians that the devil transforms himself into the Angel of Light. This is to better corrupt those who are loyal to Christ's true Faith, which is what the holy Apostle was discussing in that letter.

The devil appeared to others of the Acaxee nation in the form of a young man with a glass like a mirror on his stomach, which they said spoke elegantly in all languages.[23] The words were spoken so loudly that to the Indians they felt like blows, or they perceived them thus, so that it was impossible not to do what they were commanded. We could say that this was an Antichrist, like those whom Saint John the Evangelist said existed

23. Perhaps this apparition was somehow related to the Mesoamerican conception of and worship of Tezcatlipoca, the god of young men and a wizard who saw all in his obsidian mirror (Soustelle 1961:42, 102–3).

in his time: *Nunc Antichristi multi facti sunt*.[24] It is certain that this perverse sorcerer conducted himself as an Antichrist in his nation, and I am not sure whether the famed one who is called Antichrist by Athanasius[25] will do any greater harm to the nations of the world than this perverse Indian [600] did in his own and neighboring nations.

The news spread among the Spaniards of the region that the devil disguised as this old man was the same one who was involved in a famous case that was recounted in Chapter XXXV of Book II. [This case] occurred among the Guasave nation, when the devil was cast out of a woman by a missionary priest through exorcism on the feast day of our father, Saint Ignatius. The demon emerged spewing threats, saying that even though he was leaving, he would go someplace where he would make the priests pay. It was not very long before he made good on this threat, turning the wretched Tepehuan against their blessed priests. Furthermore, with the aforementioned spells or bedeviled tricks, which lasted for several months, this wizard began to pervert and confuse the spirits of some people and then others. He did this in such a way that his lies went undetected, which were many more than those detected by the governor of Nueva Vizcaya, who did not think that the flames of the conspiracy had spread very far. For the finishing touch this Indian sorcerer persuaded his Tepehuan people to rebel, and then he and his followers set to work planning their treason.

The plan was as follows. All the pueblos were to arm themselves so that they could simultaneously attack the Spaniards in their settlements and the nearby mining camps. On the feast day of Our Lady,[26] which was rapidly approaching, all the Spaniards as well as the priests in their lands were to be killed. The feast day ordinarily was celebrated with great solemnity in the pueblo of El Zape (which was dedicated to the Virgin). The crowds would be larger that year because people knew that her image had been brought from Mexico City and was to be installed on the altar. (This news reached these apostates because they were being instructed in the Christian mysteries.) [The Tepehuan reasoned that] because the priests did not believe that the people had become all that corrupted, they would continue instructing the Tepehuan. However, on that day all the Tepehuan would rise up as one and attack, destroying everything. They reassured themselves by saying that the Spaniards who would congregate in El Zape would be unarmed and unprepared to counterattack. [With the Spaniards] having left their settlements and mining camps unprotected, the Tepehuan could split up and attack each location, killing whomever they found and destroying everything by blood and fire.

This was the conspiracy agreed upon in this final council between Satan and his ministers and plotted against Christ and His priests, [who were] Christs for Our Lord. The devil unleashed his greatest fury on them as well as on the churches, holy images, and everything [else] that was sacred. As discussed below, everything was razed and burned during the apostasy of the Tepehuan.

---

24. *Margin Note*: I. Cant. c.2. 1 John 2:18: "many Antichrists have appeared" (Knox 1956:254).

25. *Antomasia*. Athanasius was the archbishop of Alexandria in the late fourth century and subsequently became a Doctor of the Church.

26. November 21, the Feast of the Presentation of the Blessed Virgin Mary.

CHAPTER XV The Indians of Santa Catalina prematurely rebel and murder Father Hernando de Tovar of the Company, Father Juan Gutiérrez of the Order of Saint Francis, and many other Christians

All the Tepehuan pueblos had agreed to execute their conspiracy and general uprising on November 21, 1616. However, the Indians in the pueblo of Santa Catalina, whom we have said were the most ferocious of this nation, rebelled five days in advance, on the occasion that I will now relate. It happened that a mule driver [601] who brought clothing and goods to the mining camps stopped to unload clothing at a house in the pueblo of Santa Catalina. At the same time another mule driver arrived there, accompanied by Father Hernando de Tovar, one of our religious, who was returning from the Villa de Culiacán, his native city, and the mining camp at San Andrés, where he had gone on business by order of holy obedience. The Indians saw that this was a good opportunity to steal the clothing and merchandise that the first mule driver had left in their pueblo and also to take the life of the priest who was passing through. Even though he was not their missionary, he had instructed other Indians and was like the missionaries in the Tepehuan mission, against whom the fury of the devil was always [directed]. And so they executed their plan ahead of time.

When the priest was about to mount his mule to continue on his way, the Tepehuan came toward him, armed and displaying great ferocity. When the priest's Spanish companion recognized what was happening, he jumped on his horse and shouted to Father Tovar to get on his mule and escape before the mob got hold of him. Here this servant of God responded, "If the hour has come, let us receive what God sends us." He had had very many premonitions, which we have noted in our discussion of his life in Chapter XIX of Book IX [Book VIII]; we will not include them now in order to avoid repetition. The enraged Tepehuan attacked him furiously with arrows. They grabbed the religious priest and held him, blasphemously shouting, "Let's see how his God resurrects this man who is said to be a saint! These priests think the only thing worthwhile

is teaching 'Our Father Who Art in Heaven' and 'Hail Mary.'" With a brave and firm spirit, the holy priest began preaching the Holy Christian faith to counter such blasphemy. But such rabid wolves were not to be tamed. The devil had greatly infuriated them and they very hungrily wanted to devour their prey. Without further discussion, one of them pierced the priest through the chest with a lance while he was preaching. The priest quickly died, commending himself with great affection to God Our Lord and calling upon Him for help. This happened on November 16, in the year mentioned above.

A Christian Mexica Indian who was a servant of the Spaniards and who had been tied up by the Tepehuan only to escape saw the blessed father stripped of all his clothes before he died. He made his way to Durango, where he swore to the account given above. The Spaniard who was accompanying the priest was quicker getting onto his horse than the priest, who was being attacked by arrows. He spurred his horse and took off at a gallop so that the enemy could not catch him, leaving behind the pack train with the goods. He ended up at a nearby Spanish ranch called Atotonilco, where he found the people from the region already gathered together. The priests who were in Papasquiaro had warned them of the Indian uprising and they had gathered at that ranch to safeguard themselves from enemy attack. At the same time and for the same reason, a Franciscan priest, Fray Pedro Gutiérrez, arrived at the ranch. Now there were about two hundred persons, old and young, gathered there.

On the day after the Indians from Santa Catalina killed Father Hernando de Tovar, they arrived with the same fury and laid siege to the ranch house where the Spaniards had taken refuge. Then the battle began with barbaric screeching and bragging. They unleashed such a rain of arrows, stones, and fire [602] that they knocked down several gates and broke through the roof of the house. They then threw [into the house] burning torches with chile, which in Spain are called peppers, trying to do away with everyone inside. The people suffered terribly from the strong fumes, which caused such violent coughing that many spit up their guts. Some [even] died from this torture.

The Spaniards had very little gunpowder and even less in the way of defensive weapons. When they saw themselves so besieged, they decided to go up to the roof to fight and defend themselves as best they could. But the tragedy was that their gunpowder ran out and they finally were forced to surrender. The barbarians, enraged by the devil, rejected all peace offers and instead inflicted atrocities upon the men, women, and children. All two hundred persons were cruelly murdered, except for two persons whom I will mention later. Those who died prepared themselves by repeatedly confessing their sins. It seemed that God had sent for this purpose the blessed father Fray Pedro

Gutiérrez, whom they also killed. When the Indians opened fire this holy religious came out with a crucifix in his hand, preaching to them and begging them to calm down and to desist from such an evil crime. However, their fury did not subside and they shot him with an arrow that pierced his stomach, killing him. A Spanish boy who was only fourteen years of age [went out and] picked up the holy crucifix that the religious priest was carrying. The boy, who was very virtuous and had studied in Mexico City, was called Pedro Ignacio because he and his parents had received special favors from our patriarch, Saint Ignatius. God willed that he should end his life at such a young age, dying like a martyr. He died with the crucifix in his hands, proclaiming our Holy Faith, which is [precisely] why the apostates persecuted and finally killed him. Because the course of this persecution is long and the cases and the places where they occurred are many, it will be necessary to divide the events into shorter chapters.

CHAPTER XVI How two Spaniards escaped from the aforementioned fury at Atotonilco; the enemy attacks others gathered at Guatimapé

In the previous chapter I mentioned briefly that two Spaniards escaped from the general and regrettable massacre at Atotonilco. God willed that these men should escape so that there would be witnesses to what happened and so word could reach Durango of the general uprising of the Tepehuan nation. One of these two Spaniards was Lucas Benítez, who escaped by hiding in a hole in a wall where he went undetected by the Indians. The other Spaniard was Cristóbal Martínez de Hurdaide, who was the son of the captain of Sinaloa and who had spent many years among the Tepehuan nation. On this occasion he relied on a Tepehuan Indian with whom he had been friendly in the past and whom he begged to protect him. The Indian remained loyal [603] but pretended otherwise because he was afraid of his Tepehuan companions and kinsmen. He grabbed hold of Hurdaide, saying that he wanted the Spaniard [all for himself] and he was going

to drown him in the river. He then quickly separated him from the others and took him to a place where the fortunate Spaniard remained hidden until nightfall, at which point he fled. Although the Indian feared that his kinsmen would kill him for what he had done, they never found out about it. They were too busy unleashing their fury, killing all the others, pillaging the [priests'] house, and destroying everything.

The two Spaniards who had escaped traveled some twelve leagues, staying away from the road, until they reached Durango, naked and nearly dead from hunger. There they recounted the disastrous events that had taken place at Atotonilco. On the same day as the massacre other Spaniards who had withdrawn to a place called Guatimapé were more fortunate, due to the special providence of Our Lord. Another squad of Tepehuan was attacking them with brazilwood clubs, arrows, hatchets, some stolen spuds, or iron bars, that are used in mining, and even some harquebuses, which because the rebels had contact with Spaniards, they knew how to fire. Some thirty Spanish men had retreated to this ranch when the enemy began their onslaught. Those Spaniards who happened to have harquebuses countered this attack from the rooftop of the house. However, the Indians were firing their arrows so furiously that they badly wounded some of the Spaniards. They were thus able to capture the rooftop, which they broke through, casting fire inside the house. To escape, the Spaniards used mining spuds to break holes in the walls and to move from one part of the house to another. In addition to the rooftop, the Indians had also taken control of a corral with twenty saddled mares that had been prepared for battle. The enemy attack had been so sudden that the Spaniards had not been able to employ the horses. This placed them in very dire straits, with little defense and few munitions. If God had not favored them in this predicament through a special act of providence, they would have been killed then and there. His Majesty conveyed

this favor in a singular fashion: there were many colts that were raised on this ranch, and on this occasion a large herd of them came together and headed down the Camino Real, perhaps guided by some angel. They raised such a cloud of dust that the Indians thought the colts were Spaniards coming to the aid of their besieged [brothers]. They raised the siege and fled, leaving the Spaniards safe and sound. None of them died, whereas a number of Tepehuan were killed.

This was a most singular event, and {it was} not the first nor the only one through which God has favored His Catholic Spaniards, who defend His Faith. He has frequently freed them from danger among these barbarous peoples, just as he did on this occasion. And if He fails to do so on all occasions, as we will see in the following chapter, this is for the supreme ends of His divine providence, of which the very wise King Solomon (and, through him, the Holy Spirit) said, *Omnia in mensura, & numero, & pondere disposuisti*:[27] He planned all things in accordance with His supreme wisdom.

CHAPTER XVII The pueblo of Santiago receives word of the Tepehuan Rebellion; the people take refuge in the church and send to Durango for help

While the events that I have recounted were taking place, the Tepehuan [604] rebels focused their principal fury on their main pueblo of Santiago Papasquiaro. There two priests resided, Fathers Bernardo de Cisneros and Diego de Orozco, who were in charge of the mission and other pueblos in the district. When Father Cisneros learned that the Indians were plotting a rebellion, he attempted to prevent this through one of the principal caciques, who was called Don Francisco Campos, and two other faithful Indians who were not among the conspirators. The priest asked them to inform him about the plan of the troublemakers and go to try to quiet them down and persuade them with better counsel. The three Indians offered to do this by going to a pueblo four leagues from Santiago, which

was the main seat of the conspirators. The devil had so infuriated {the conspirators} that when one of the three messengers who had come to discuss peace arrived, they grabbed Don Francisco, and without a word they flogged him and a companion to death. The third one escaped to bring back the sad news.

The previous evening the teniente alcalde mayor of the Spaniards in Santiago had been warned in the following way. Two unrecognizable hooded men arrived who were friendly Indians whom the conspirators had not killed because they had hidden themselves. They told the teniente that he had better defend himself be-

27. *Margin Note*: Sap. cap.II. Book of Wisdom 11:21: "all thou doest is done in exact measure, all is nicely calculated and weighed" (Knox 1956:581).

cause the Tepehuan were planning to rebel. This news preceded the death of faithful Don Francisco (who died on November 15, one day before those at Santa Catalina killed Father Tovar). The teniente and the priests ordered all the Spanish women and children and the long-time Christian Indians who resided in the pueblo to take refuge in the church, which was made of stone, and the priests' house, which was made of bricks and attached to the church. There they could all take refuge from the impending danger. Then they received word that two hundred Tepehuan, who were excellent riders, were approaching on foot and on horseback. On the day that the Santa Catalina Indians killed Father Tovar this force reached the pueblo of Santiago, where the people had already taken refuge in the church and the priests' house.

The Tepehuan laid siege to the place and no one could escape. The tragedy was that very few of the besieged Spaniards had sufficient or appropriate weapons of attack or defense to venture out to confront so many furious foes. Despite the Indians' vigilance, a plan was devised and a messenger was dispatched to the governor of [Nueva] Vizcaya, twenty-seven leagues away in Durango, begging for help and describing the desperate situation. The message arrived on Thursday, November 17, at eleven o'clock in the morning. Aid was enlisted immediately, and then another message arrived that same day. It was hastily written and lacked a signature and simply said: "Help, Help, Help, Lord Governor, we are about to die."

The governor ordered the royal storehouse opened, and he distributed whatever he could find in the way of gunpowder, harquebuses, chain mail, arms, and other weapons. Although there was not enough to go around, twenty-six Spaniards and some of their servants were quickly armed. I have already advised those who do not know about these remote lands that there are not as many Spaniards here as there are in the populous cities of Spain, [605] where in a very short time one can draft many people. Spaniards reside largely in the central part of Nueva España, in the large cities of Mexico, Puebla de los Angeles, and many others that are two hundred leagues distant from this very remote region. Finally, because of this and for other reasons, it was not possible to arm a larger force than this, which was led by Captain Martín de Olivas, who was a rich miner from Topia and who was well versed in the terrain. However, this was to no avail, because while the rescue force was being hurriedly assembled in Durango the fury of the enemy who besieged the church in Papasquiaro went unabated. Before the captain reached Papasquiaro the enemy killed everyone and committed insolent thefts and other atrocities, both in the pueblo as well as on the royal road to the mines, where they had destroyed everything. This sad news prompted Captain Olivas and his troops to retreat to a place where they could resist the enemy onslaught, as will be told later, after recounting the dreadful disaster at Papasquiaro.

CHAPTER XVIII The enemy tightens the noose with reinforcements and then murders two priests of the Company and all the Christians who had taken refuge in the church

The enemy fiercely attacked and twice set fire to the portals of the church, which the besieged Spaniards tried as best they could to extinguish. [At the same time] they watched the Indians furiously remove an image of Our Lady from a shrine that was near the church. While one Indian held it in the air, two others flogged it (clear testimony of the hatred of the Faith that the devil had ignited in the fierce spirits of these people, inciting them to such impious, horrendous, and sacrilegious acts). It broke the hearts of those inside the church to watch [the flogging of the image], which they could not aid or defend. The demonic apostates also took a crucifix from a house. After dragging it along the ground they threw it in a corner, spewing infernal and insolent blasphemies — calling it a thief, a drunkard, and a thousand other insults, like those that our divine Lord of the Jews and gentiles suffered when he spoke to them while imprisoned in the garden: *Haec est hora vestra, & potestas tenebrarum.*[28] Here these insults were inflicted anew upon His most holy image. He gave those who were possessed by the devil free rein to inflict upon His sacred image what the others had inflicted upon His person.

They were no less ferocious toward a great Cross that was erected in the plaza of the pueblo and church cemetery. Their fury and diabolical rage was always vented against anything that was sacred, and thus they invented another new outrage against the holy Cross: because they were horsemen — used to jousting with lances and hamstringing, with their patrons at their sides — they played with the Cross as though it were a dummy, striking it until they smashed it to pieces. Their heretical acts did not cease here. From the shrine they took out two floats that were used to display the holy images during feast day processions and placed two women on them who had most applauded their uprising. They then paraded them around in a sacrile-

gious procession and offered to them as a prize, instead of incense, the spoils that they had plundered. Meanwhile, the distressed and besieged [606] Spaniards defended themselves and the church throughout that entire Thursday, using the few harquebuses and munitions that remained. During the attacks on the church some of the enemy were killed. Some Spaniards were also wounded by arrows while waiting for help to arrive from Durango.

On Friday Indian reinforcements arrived. These were Indians from Santa Catalina, who had killed Father Tovar and those who were with him. Approximately five hundred men on foot and horseback then attacked the church and the priests' house and all those who had taken refuge there. With renewed vigor they attempted to destroy everything; they burned all the houses in the pueblo and set fire to as many parts of the church as possible. When it was finally burning and there was no hope of extinguishing the blaze, an Indian apostate named Miguel shouted to those inside that he and his companions were Christian Indians who wanted to restore friendship and peace with the Spaniards, provided the latter came out of the church and surrendered their weapons. This treasonous Indian, who had once served one of the besieged Spaniards, hoped to take the Spaniards alive in order to commit greater atrocities than the fire.

It was very difficult [to comply] with this Indian's request, but after weighing various options and pressed by the fire and such [a large] number of enemy, the Spaniards decided to negotiate with the Indians. They sent out an Indian with a simple request to be allowed safe passage to the city of Durango. The traitors replied that they should come out immediately. So those people who were already in dire straits and perishing in the fire prepared to leave the church. Perhaps it would have been better if they had died, consumed by the burning flames, rather than suffer at the hands of those who despised the Holy Faith of Jesus Christ. We cannot, however, judge the will of God in such cases. He may want

---

28. *Margin Note*: Luc. 22. Luke 22:53: "But your time has come now, and darkness has its will" (Knox 1956:82).

His servants and faithful to die in the way arranged by His esteemed providence. We must not condemn acts that, although they do not appear to be appropriate, are in and of themselves good and holy. This warning is necessary with respect to the pitiful events that I must narrate in order to observe the rules of history.

Because this church that was besieged by the foe was in Santiago Papasquiaro—a pueblo of Christian Indians, the first among the Tepehuan that converted, and one in which some Spaniards resided—it had the Holy Sacrament in its tabernacle and monstrance. At the time that the barbarians laid siege to the church, the priests did not consume the Host as it seems they should have so no irreverent action or outrage should befall such a supreme mystery. Their own devotion and that of those Catholic Christians who wanted to confess and take Communion under those dangerous circumstances in which they found themselves must have inspired them to preserve [the Holy Sacrament] in order to have the protection of that Lord and Redeemer of the World in their affliction. They were also waiting for the aid they had requested from Durango. Furthermore, they were not persuaded that the arrogance of those who had been Christians (although false ones) and who now promised them peace, showing signs of contrition, was so daring that it would reach the unholy and horrendous levels that it did.

Finally, without consuming the Sovereign Sacrament, which they took with them, they left the church in the form of a procession, ready to die like faithful Christians, professing the Faith that the apostates persecuted. [607] Father Diego de Orozco, who instructed these people, came out with the monstrance in his hands; the teniente alcalde mayor, Juan de Castilla, carried the image of Our Lady in his hands; and all the rest of the men and women filed out in an orderly procession. When they saw the Spaniards walking out of the church, the Tepehuan betrayed their promise of safe conduct and reconciliation and approached the monstrance, getting down on their knees and worshiping it. With this act the Catholic Christians regained some hope that their lives would be spared. However, the Indians wanted [only] to carry out their plan unimpeded. When they saw that some Spaniards still had their harquebuses, they told them to hand them over, at the same time allaying the Spaniards' fear by pointing out that they did not have any gunpowder with which to use them. The Spaniards, finding themselves surrounded by so many of the enemy and without gun-

powder, which had run out, were forced to hand over their weapons. They did so, as they say, playing the good thief. An Indian came up to a captain who still had his sword at his waist and took it without resistance. This was not the moment for that Catholic Spaniard to expend his life or jeopardize the lives of the young people and women.

When the procession reached the middle of the cemetery, Father Orozco, who was carrying the Holy Sacrament, spoke like a loving father to the rebels. With the gentle and loving words of a missionary and shepherd of souls, he tried to calm them and have them listen to better advice. [He told them] that they should not forget the divine doctrine that he had taught them; he pointed out that he was carrying the Lord who had created and redeemed them. If they did not calm down and correct what they had done, great harm might come to them, for God would punish them for the insults that he and the Christians had received. When they reached [the cemetery], the hellish fury that had been planned for such a long time by the sorcerer and his diabolical idol was unleashed. A cry arose from among the misled Indians, who with one voice shouted that the priest spoke lies. [They said] that the God of the Christians did not speak like their god, who had told them that all the Christians had to die that very day. If God permitted the idol to tell them this and allowed them to [actually] do it, it was to make known how such a hatred of Christ's Faith and Divine Sacrament could lead to the death of so many men and women, simply because they were Christians.

As they spewed forth those blasphemies, they attacked the monstrance and the holy body of Our Redeemer, who wished to suffer in His Sacrament what He had suffered in mortal flesh. They snatched the holy monstrance from the priest's hands and dashed it to the ground. Uttering horrendous blasphemies, they kicked and trod upon the Awesome Sacrament. They tore to bits the image of Our Lady that a Spaniard carried and finally they brutally killed all the Spaniards, who must have numbered approximately one hundred, including men and women.

Because he was a priest of Christ who carried the holy monstrance, the misled Indians vented their greatest fury and cruelty upon Father Diego de Orozco, a young, very devout, and very kind religious. Before they killed him eight Indians raised him in the air, mocking him with the words that they had heard in Mass: *Dominus vobiscum*, while others answered, *Et cum spiritu tuo.*[29] As they carried him in this way, from a distance they shot an arrow that passed through one side of his torso to the other. Then—so that his death would be crueler—three of them grabbed him and two of them held him by his arms in the form of the Cross, so that he would die like His Lord and Our Redeemer, Jesus Christ. The third Indian split open his body from top to bottom with an ax. [608] Before he expired the blessed priest said, "Do with me what you will, my sons, for I die for my God," and with this he gave his soul to God in sweetest holocaust.[30]

They [also] killed Father Bernardo de Cisneros, who instructed these people along with Father Orozco. He died quickly from a lance thrust and a blow to the head delivered with a macana, which is a weapon like a mace. I have noted that this blessed priest two months earlier had told me that he had observed that his Tepehuan were restless. This was because of the tlatollis and lies of an Indian who carried a devilish idol with which he had deceived these people. Although Father Cisneros had attempted to enlighten them, God wanted him to have a glorious end to his life and his labors, which he endured for the salvation of souls.

Only three Spaniards and three children who were hidden in a confessional escaped the fierce massacre at the church. The enemy had not noticed them because when they had concluded, they celebrated their barbarous and sacrilegious victory by getting drunk in their gentile fashion on the wine that they had stolen from the Spaniards' houses and pack animals. Thus they concluded this act, which was not their last one.

CHAPTER XIX The survivors of the destruction of Santiago Papasquiaro reach the ranch of La Sauceda

Those who escaped the fury of the Tepehuan at Santiago Papasquiaro set out at midnight, traveling off the road through mountains and canyons. They were guided by two young Spaniards who had been raised in these lands. Some of them went to Durango and others to a ranch that was along the road just before one reaches La Sauceda. They were all very exhausted from the journey. A little farther ahead Captain Olivas was marching with a few Spaniards from Durango to aid [the people of Santiago Papasquiaro]. They met up with the survivors at that ranch. When they heard the news concerning the great ravage caused by the enemy at Santiago Papasquiaro, and how many of them there were and how infuriated they were, the captain decided to go back to La Sauceda to seek protection in the house there, where there were some provisions. From there he sent word to the governor to arrange whatever means he could to end the uprising and to help the priests in the other missions as well. The captain knew the danger they were in because he had talked [with people] throughout the region. At that time the Father Rector of Durango arrived. When he heard the rumors of the uprising, he had set out to aid his sons. He and the captain had barely reached the ranch when the enemy attacked. The captain went out several times with his men to fend them off, but these skirmishes did not cause much damage to either side. Captain Olivas stalled until additional help could arrive from Durango. God sent a group led by Captain Gordejuela, who had a prosperous livestock ranch near Durango. He brought along a good number of soldiers. He himself was very courageous and experienced in wars against barbarous Indians. Thus, he set out to provide this very important assistance against the Indians. Other Spaniards from the region also came. They had been defeated and were seeking shelter at this

29. "The Lord be with you," "and with thy spirit."

30. See Ahern (1999) for a discussion of this "sweetest holocaust" in terms of the construction of Jesuit martyrdom in the *Historia*.

settlement. The enemy had very good reinforcements in terms of both foot soldiers and horsemen, [609] who joined them. They attacked the house four times. It was necessary to protect the house because there were women, children, and provisions inside. During these attacks the enemy suffered some damage from the harquebuses and were forced to retreat. Our [men] were not greatly harmed by the enemies' arrows.

The captains remained here with their people for forty-two days. During this time they went out on several occasions to fight the enemy in the open field. The enemy was encouraged by the deaths of some of the Spaniards and the spoils that they had collected. For these reasons, and also because they were in their own lands and had food, they were able to sustain the battle, even though they sometimes retreated. During these retreats Captain Olivas went in search of them with whatever people he could, without abandoning his fortification. He surprised the enemy with dawn attacks on some [of their] rancherías. The Spaniards managed to slit the throats of some of the principal aggressors in the destruction of Santiago Papasquiaro. Many weapons that had been stolen from the Spaniards were recovered: harquebuses, leather armor, and swords. In addition to these things, they also recovered sacred ornaments used in divine worship, such as frontals, albs, and other things. Even some livestock that the Indians had taken for their sustenance was recovered. The captain burned their houses and did not lose a single soldier. He returned to his post at La Sauceda, where about four hundred of our people had gathered, many of whom were women and children. Because it was no longer

necessary to maintain this settlement, and because it was necessary to make more specific preparations for war and the punishment of this nation, the two captains decided to move the people who had gathered at the ranch to a safer location. Thus, they formed an escort with their soldiers and took them to safety at Durango.

In order that it be understood how the Tepehuan had been so thoroughly convinced by their diabolical idol and sorcerer that all the Spaniards in this land and their Christianity would be destroyed, I will recount here a case that took place after the Spaniards had gathered at the ranch at La Sauceda. [There were] two Tepehuan Indians who either had not been at Sauceda or did not know what had happened at this settlement. Thinking that the Spaniards had been finished off, as was the case at Santiago Papasquiaro, they came through the gates looking for spoils, unprotected by their bows and arrows. The Spaniards captured them, and once they were captives their confession was taken. They declared that their aim was to destroy everything, even the city and jurisdiction of Durango itself. What is certain, as we will later see, is that [the people of this city] were very concerned about its ruination and destruction. After hearing this confession the Spaniards decided to rid themselves of these enemies, so they hanged them, thereby no longer having to defend themselves from them. This brought to an end the skirmishes and attacks on La Sauceda. We are still left to recount, however, the many other attacks that took place throughout the region with unfortunate consequences and the death of religious priests and Spaniards.

CHAPTER XX The destruction caused by the Tepehuan in the pueblo of El Zape; the murder of four Jesuits along with other Spaniards; what happened at the mining camp at Guanaceví

On the same day of the outrages and destruction wrought by the rebels in the pueblo of Santiago Papasquiaro—where nothing human or divine was spared—another squad of Tepehuan [610] took charge of the destruction of the pueblo of El Zape, which bore the name of San Ignacio. This squad did just as much damage as the first group had done at Santiago Papasquiaro. Even though Christ Our Lord in His Divine Sacrament did not suffer as He had in Santiago Papasquiaro, an image of His Most Holy Mother did. Christ also suffered through the four priests who were His ministers of the doctrine to this rebellious, apostate nation. These were the venerable Fathers Juan Fonte, the superior of the others, Juan del Valle, Luis de Alavés, and Gerónimo de Moranta. There will be much to say later at the appropriate time concerning these priests and their saintly lives. Nineteen Spaniards and more than sixty blacks and other Spanish servants also died. All these Christian people had come to El Zape to celebrate the installation of an image of Our Lady which, as we have said, had been brought from Mexico City. This image caused great devotion to the Most Holy Virgin. Spaniards and their slaves and [other] people from the mining camp at Guanaceví (these mines are very rich) came to El Zape to help with the decorations for the celebration. They were unaware of the impending disastrous event because things happened much more suddenly here than they had at Santiago Papasquiaro. This is what occurred: when the people were congregated in the church for the celebration, an enemy army suddenly attacked. They killed everyone and executed the most cruel acts, which they had been taught by the devil. With diabolical fury they placed their sacrilegious hands on all that was sacred, destroying and profaning everything they found. The two priests, Juan del Valle and Luis de Alavés, died here. The following day their two companions, Juan Fonte and Gerónimo de Moranta, were coming to the celebration. They had been unable to come earlier from the settlements where

they were. A quarter of a league before they reached this destroyed settlement, the enemies of Christ and His holy law attacked and killed these two holy priests. This took place under unusual circumstances that will be told in their vitae and those of their holy companions. These Indians did not even spare the life of Father Juan Fonte, who during the sixteen years following the founding of this mission had provided this nation with innumerable benefits. More details of this disaster will be given later in an eyewitness account by the governor of [Nueva] Vizcaya, who went with several companies of soldiers to punish this rebel nation.

Only one boy escaped from El Zape while the Indians were busy killing the Spaniards. He told the people of the mining camp at Guanaceví what had happened. The alcalde mayor, Don Juan de Alvear, immediately readied twelve soldiers and set out with them to verify what had happened. Before they reached the pueblo they found the corpse of a Spanish acquaintance. His hands had been cut off and his stomach had been ripped open. It was nighttime when they reached the church, where in the moonlight they found the bodies of Spaniards scattered throughout the cemetery. They were naked and had been killed with the same cruelty. From a distance they saw other similarly [mutilated] corpses inside the church. They did not dare dismount, and so they yelled to see whether there was anyone still left in hiding who had escaped the fury. However, nobody answered. Because there were too few soldiers to meet the threat of an enemy troop, who because of their fury might attack at any time, they returned to the mining camp at Guanaceví so that it would be better protected.

The troop that they feared [611] caught up with them along the way. Some of the Indians were traveling on foot and others on horseback. Some were wearing the clothes and caps of the priests whom they had killed. They followed the Spaniards for a distance of two leagues, while the latter continued in their retreat, maintaining great order and spirit. They stopped from time to time, facing the enemy and firing their harquebuses. They were unable to avoid some arrow wounds, even though none of the Spaniards was in any real danger during this skirmish. The Indians killed the alcalde mayor's horse. A Mexica Indian who worked in the mines was so loyal that he got off his own horse and made the alcalde mayor ride it. This was the loyalty of a faithful servant who almost lost his life. Even though he was built for running fast, just as all the Indians are, he was nevertheless struck by some arrows. His wounds were so serious that they left him for dead. But later he showed up at the mining camp at Guanaceví, where he was healed. As soon as the alcalde mayor arrived with his men, he ordered everyone to withdraw to the church, where five hundred people gathered. All those who could fight and had weapons, which were not that many, because they were unprepared [for war], positioned themselves to defend the church in the event of an enemy attack. They were waiting for some assistance from Durango, where the people already had heard about the uprising. Before that aid arrived the enemies attacked the mining camp. They did not harm the people because the Spaniards courageously defended themselves. However, they did cause a great deal of damage to property, setting fire to the mining equipment and whatever else they found. This is how the solemn celebration that was supposed to take place at El Zape was concluded, ending in disastrous tragedy.

CHAPTER XXI The Tepehuan kill Father Hernando de Santarén in the pueblo of Tenerapa; events at the mines at Indé

Because the death of Father Hernando de Santarén occurred on the day of that unfortunate celebration at El Zape, I will relate here this event as well as his holy life. When the priests at El Zape learned that Father Hernando de Santarén, who was instructing the Tepehuan's neighbors, the Xixime, was coming to Durango on a matter of obedience, they invited him to take part in the famous feast of the Most Holy Virgin. Shortly after Father Santarén had departed for the celebrations, Father Andrés Tutino, a long-time missionary, sent him a warning that the Tepehuan were restless. Although several messages were sent on foot and on horseback, telling Father Santarén to turn back because he was in danger, God did not will that any of the messages should reach him. He wanted to grant him the glorious death he received. Once I heard him say that he desired it.

Father Santarén arrived at a Tepehuan pueblo called Tenerapa, unaware of what was happening. He wanted to say Mass, so as soon as he arrived, he requested that the bell be tolled. It is customary in Indian pueblos [whenever the priest is absent] to toll the bell to summon the person left in charge to provide travelers with information. When he found nobody around Father Santarén began summoning aloud the fiscal of the church. Then he entered the church, finding it terribly desecrated. The altar had been split into pieces and the images had been knocked down and disfigured. There were other signs as well of how lost these people were and how they had insulted the Faith of Christ that they now persecuted. [612]

Father Santarén got back on his mule to continue to Durango, but the Indians who had remained in that unfaithful pueblo were watching the priest. When he reached an arroyo not far from the pueblo, they overtook him and knocked him off his mule, dashing him to the ground. The priest, who knew their language, asked them what harm he had caused them and why they wanted to kill him. The apostates answered that they needed no other reason than the fact that he was a priest. No sooner did they say this than they fiercely struck blows to his head until it split open and his brains spilled onto the ground. They struck more blows that made the blessed father invoke the sweet name of JESUS and blissfully end his journey. It was later learned that his body lay naked in that gulch but there was no way of recovering or burying it [at that time] because the entire land was at war and the Tepehuan were committing other cruel deeds. It was also learned, however, that the Tepehuan women cried over the death of this blessed priest, who often had passed through their lands. They recognized the love and affability with which he used to treat the Indians. Some faithful Tepehuan women were distressed at the sight of their husbands' cruelty toward the priests who had so peacefully and kindly given them religious instruction.

Shortly before this tragic event at El Zape, Father Andrés López received the warning that God had not allowed Father Santarén to receive. Father López was also a missionary to the Tepehuan and a companion of the priests who died. God did not want him to accompany them in their death. As he was ready to depart for the feast day, to which he had been invited, he received a letter from the priests. They wrote that they saw signs of unrest and uneasiness in the Indians who were participating in the celebration, but they nevertheless had decided not to interrupt the celebration, unaware that the rebellion was about to erupt. Still, they told Father Andrés López to cancel his trip. The priest received additional warnings that the people had rebelled, and so he retreated to the mining camp of Indé, where some thirty Spaniards who lived nearby had gathered and barricaded themselves in a house. They had very few weapons and only enough ammunition for about twenty harquebus [shots]. They were thus ready, although still in great danger from the enemy squads that were in sight. Father Andrés López and the many others who had gathered at this settlement sustained themselves until they were rescued by people sent by the governor. At the time of this widespread rebellion Father Andrés López wrote a letter from this settlement of Indé to the Father Provincial, giving an account of what had happened. It was a brief letter that reads as follows:

My Father Provincial, I wish I could send better news to Your Reverence. Still, divine kindness has decided that I, who am unworthy of such goodness, should be the one to transmit the news of the martyrdom of my fellow priests, whom God has taken to His kingdom. On November 18 the Tepehuan rebels killed the priests who had gathered at El Zape. Because I was warned that the snow was too deep and the celebration had been postponed, I waited. God saw that the fruit was not ripe and that I did not deserve the glory that our priests who spilled their blood for Him [613] have earned through their naked, bloodstained bodies, which are said to remain there on the ground. They cannot be buried because the Indians have taken over all the [mountain] passes. Those of us who are still here are in obvious danger. At present I am at the mining camp of Indé, where I am ready to die with my blessed companions. In life or death I will not abandon the land that they irrigated with their blood. Only a few of the Indians under my charge have rebelled and the rest are still peaceful. May God grant I survive.

This is the end of the letter, which in a couple of days was followed by another:

I have written many letters to Your Reverence giving an account of what has happened here, fearing that the messengers might have been attacked by the enemy, as happened to four messengers fifteen days ago four leagues from this mining camp. I am writing this letter at the request of the people of this settlement, where I have spent the Lenten season, to inform Your Reverence. A thousand thanks are due God for the remarkable fruit of five hundred confessions that have been made here, where I have cared for the blacks, Indian laborers, and a ranchería of people who have not rebelled. Along with this letter I am sending Your Reverence a cap that belonged to Father Cisneros. It is bloodstained and torn from the blow that was struck to his head with a stone or scythe. Father Luis de Alavés was found [still wearing] a studded belt. [The cadaver of] Father Valle was found with one hand making the sign of the Cross and the other covering his private parts.

This is the end of the letter recounting events in this settlement. The following chapters will relate what happened elsewhere.

CHAPTER XXII The uprising spreads to the Acaxee; Captain Suárez executes the Indian principales whose diabolical machinations caused the Acaxee to rebel

Many sparks flew from the great fire that the devil lit in the Tepehuan nation and in many other Indian nations and Christian communities, which he tried to destroy and burn to the ground. These fires must be made known, along with the great and mortal danger that was endured by the priests of our Company, their brothers, and many other Spaniards living in this extensive region. This history must cross this entire land before reaching the city of Durango, which was also in danger of being lost, even though the governor later set out from there with his people to travel across and bring aid to the land.

Father Andrés Tutino was instructing the Acaxee nation, which bordered on the Tepehuan (of whom an account already has been given). After he had received news of the Tepehuan Revolt he was the first to dispatch the messages mentioned [earlier], which never reached Father Hernando de Santarén. On the same day as the disasters in Santa Catalina and Santiago Papasquiaro, at ten o'clock at night, he dispatched another warning to all the mining camps in the region so that they could prepare for any nearby uprising. Because of the same worries and concerns, which increased with every hour, he decided to visit his entire district, fearing that the people in his flock might become upset or contaminated by their neighbors. This decision was important for stemming the anxiety and unrest [614] that already threatened all those lands.

When he reached the pueblo that was closest to the Tepehuan, called Coapa, he discovered that two Indians principales named Don Pedro and Juan Gordo had begun to sow discord among the loyal people. The priest had perceived very little loyalty in these two, despite the fact that they were baptized. They [now] intended to gather the people of this mission to go to Papasquiaro to help the Tepehuan against the Spaniards, telling them to pay no mind to the aforementioned brave Captain Suárez, who was at the fort near San Hipólito. To make the people of Coapa even more

enthusiastic about his diabolical intentions, the Indian Juan Gordo described to them some visions of the other life, which he told them he himself had experienced. This was all a devilish lie or trick. Still, some affirmed what the sorcerer and principal author of the uprising had preached, namely that if some of them happened to die in the revolt, they would be resurrected. These cases cannot be ignored because they are a manifestation of the great fire that the devil had started through that Indian sorcerer. From the beginning he planned to destroy the Christianity of all the nations that had been converted to our Holy Faith in the entire province.

Thus, the perverse Juan Gordo told the people of Father Tutino's pueblo that one night as he passed by the church those [who had been killed] called out to him. He was frightened the first and second times this happened and did not dare to go inside. However, the third time he gathered his courage, and inside the church he saw an Indian named Diego Morido floating in the air. This Indian had died just a few days earlier. He told Juan Gordo to come closer and not to be afraid, and to send word to his wife that he was not dead and that she should not remarry, because once his father and lord god, whom they awaited, came to that pueblo the dead man would be resurrected and he would live with her in greater harmony and pleasure than before. This was the speech made by this diabolical Indian.

The priest learned at this time that there were several meetings and councils held in the aforementioned pueblo of Coapa that threatened unrest. Because things had become so dangerous, the priest was himself forced to send a warning to Captain Suárez, who at that time was quite far away. (It has already been noted what a great soldier he was and how many barbarous nations he had restrained with his great bravery, which he displayed on numerous occasions.) When he received the warning, this highly conscientious captain acted with such diligence that in a single night and half a day, he traveled fifty leagues over the steep, rough mountains. He and Father Tutino traveled to the pueblo of Coapa, where they tried to calm the unrest. Father Pedro de Gravina, who had been instructing the Xixime, arrived at the same time, bringing word that the Tepehuan also were actively entreating the Xixime to join the rebellion. Even though some of them joined the rebels, there were others, two pueblos in particular, that remained very loyal and steadfast in the Faith that they had received. The captain took the [two] priests along with him and went to one of the pueblos where the unrest had begun, in order to calm them down. They arrived at midnight and the people welcomed them in peace, with many lit torches. Then the captain called together the Indian principales from the pueblos where the unrest had started. Once he had them all together, he spoke to them, encouraging and exhorting them to keep their peace and loyalty and not to let themselves be deceived by the disloyal and misled Tepehuan.

With this exhortation and another offered by the priests, [615] it seemed that the Indians would, at least for the time being, remain calm. However, subsequent events showed that this was not the case. The captain realized that more effective means were needed to stem the various rumors that were spreading among the mountain nations, which were in the captain's charge. He decided to return to the pueblo of Coapa and punish the two Indians who were disturbing the peace with their deceptions and spells; he also discovered they had in fact aided the Tepehuan. He took Father Tutino as well as a few soldiers, and they arrived at night. In the morning (completely unaware of the captain's plans)

the priest said his Mass and delivered a sermon to the people who had gathered in the church (who were quite a few), which was appropriate for the occasion and about peace and steadfastness in the Faith. After [the priest] had finished the sermon, the captain ordered all the people to gather together, as if he wanted to take his leave of them. Indians came from several pueblos and among them were the two pernicious troublemakers, Don Pedro and Juan Gordo. The captain unexpectedly ordered them to be bound. He then proclaimed that he would pardon all those who had followed their lead (concerning which he already had a great deal of information) because their guilt was more the fault of the two prisoners. They were the ones who had stirred up the people; he knew them well from having punished their crimes on other occasions. Furthermore, he proclaimed that the two would pay right then and there, without resort to the pleas that on other occasions the priests had made on their behalf. He asked the priest who was there to forgive him, for he had to fulfill his duty and see to the public welfare of that entire land. And no sooner said than done, he ordered them to be garroted. Because there were many faithful among those people, not all of whom had gone bad, this punishment did not cause a riot. Rather, it was beneficial to that faction [of loyal Christians], whom we will leave here in order to move on to others, and to other dangers in which the priests in these missions found themselves during these rebellious times.

CHAPTER XXIII The Tepehuan cause some Xixime pueblos to rebel; the destruction and danger in which the priests found themselves

The Tepehuan, and through them the devil, did not cease their efforts to get all the neighboring Christian nations to rebel. Thus, there was continued harm and unrest. A few days after the two Acaxee Indians were punished, as was told in the preceding chapter, a group of Xixime who had not learned their lesson and who had been solicited by the Tepehuan enlisted their allies and attacked three peaceful Christian pueblos of their own Xixime nation. The rebels intended to kill Father Pedro Gravina and Father Juan de Mallen. The priests, however, got word the day before and withdrew to the fort at San Hipólito. Because the rebels could not satisfy their desire to kill the two priests, they burned the three churches to the ground, together with the altarpieces and other ornaments that the priests had left hidden. But many faithful Indians gathered afterward and went after the rebels. And even though they were from the very same nation, they wounded many of the rebels, cutting off some of their heads, which they brought to the fort at San Hipólito. Had the loyal Xixime not been hampered by snowfall in the mountains, they would have achieved [616] a more complete victory.

The loyalty and steadfast charity of these Indians were attributed to the religious instruction that they had received from the blessed Father Hernando de Santarén, who had baptized them. Even though the rebels had tried very hard to get these Indians to join the uprising—making them great promises of freedom if they would revolt and threatening them with war if they did not—they remained steadfast, responding that they were willing to give their lives for their Christian Faith and Church. This loyalty was so important to the priests that they wrote that the entire Christian community of Nueva Vizcaya, including Sinaloa, should be grateful to these faithful Indians, especially those of Guapijuxe whom Father Santarén instructed and who put out the fire that was being ignited by these very warlike nations.

The missionaries working among the Xixime were nevertheless in great danger because of the endless solicitations of the neighboring Tepehuan rebels. During these unsettled times the priests were occasionally forced to take refuge in the fort at San Hipólito. They did not abandon their flocks, however, nor did the death of their brothers frighten them to the point that they discontinued their enterprise. Indeed, a new enthusiasm was seen at this time in the missionary priests, all of whom longed to give their lives for their God, helping the souls that they were instructing. At the time of these persecutions they wrote several letters to the Father Provincial, asking him to leave them where they were, even though danger and hardship were so close at hand. Because the worthy offers made by these apostolic men are all very similar, I will record here only one passage from a letter written by Father Andrés Tutino,[31] whom I mentioned before. Before he died he spent nearly thirty years in these mountain missions. In his letter he writes of the dangers confronting the priests, of whom he was the superior. He says:

> I give infinite thanks to God to find myself in such circumstances, for I never thought my coming to the Indies was as useful as I do now. It is true that my failings and sins are so numerous that I doubt I will ever attain a joyous death, but at least I will spend my life with the extraordinary consolation of the aroma of a memory as sweet as the one left by our brothers who have so gloriously shed their own blood. Blessed are they and those who, with divine grace, hope to follow them. May it please His Majesty to be served by my spilling my blood as they did theirs for His honor and His Most Holy Faith.

To this point I have been citing Father Tutino. The other priests individually wrote the same thing. To make known as well the Catholic spirit of the Spanish soldiers who, when necessary, help with their weapons in these Christian enterprises, [I will cite] a brief note written by Captain Suárez that speaks for all Spanish soldiers. At the time he wrote this letter to the superior of these missions, the captain and a very small number of his soldiers were resisting the enemy's fury. He says:

> Father Andrés González and I are in the pueblo of Las Vegas, where each night we await our deaths. Although the Indians for the time being seem fairly quiet, because of the

---

31. At the time of the Tepehuan Revolt Tutino was working among the Acaxee of Coapa, bordering the lands of the Tepehuan.

doctrine of the false god of the Tepehuan we do not know how long this calm will last. We remain vigilant, and if Our Lord's most holy will is for us to die, our lives will never have been put to better use; may His Divine Majesty be served by them and by our prompt [617] willingness to die just as our priests have for their Holy Faith.

This quote demonstrates this captain's Catholic zeal. He was one of those who bravely worked until this uprising was crushed, calming the disturbances of wicked Indians, defending those who were pacific and faithful, and punishing the delinquents. Because I have recorded the intrepid spirit of the zealous missionary priests and the Catholic captain who risked their lives in the defense of our Holy Faith, I do not want to omit the testimony of the devil himself. The devil experienced both the priests' and captain's spirited opposition when he tried to execute his diabolical plans to destroy the entire Christian community. This was confessed by both men and women rebels who were captured (as will later be told). They confessed that the Tepehuan had built a shrine a short distance from their houses, in which they placed their infamous idol, or the devil, who had been its inventor and the author of the bedeviled revolt. They turned to this idol as if it were their oracle to receive its forecast of [their luck] in battle. On one such occasion they complained about the fact that the promises that the idol had made to them in the beginning were not coming true, namely that those who died in the uprising would be resurrected within seven

or ten days. This time had already passed and he had not resurrected any dead; they had been fooled. The father of this lie told them to continue with the war, for if they abandoned it, they would perish. He also said that he could not help them anymore because of the resistance of those of the crown, by which he meant the priests; with this he sent them away.

We might think that those whom that enemy called 'those of the crown' were the priests who survived in these missions, undoing the devil's lies and working and suffering great hardships and dangers in order to maintain the peace and the faith of Christ Our Lord. But we have equal if not greater reason to believe that he was speaking of the priests and holy religious who had been killed and went to heaven with a crown of glory. Without a doubt they pled with God on behalf of this Christian community, which had cost them so dearly. I should add here that the entire province of the Company of JESUS in Nueva España, and even in other provinces, was very far from faltering or being frightened by the deaths of so many of their brothers. In addition to those in the Province of Nueva España who offered to carry this enterprise forward, the Father Provincial wrote to our Father General, asking him to send aid in the form of additional priests, so that all of them could risk their lives and be part of such a glorious effort. And there were some from very remote provinces who offered themselves for this enterprise.

CHAPTER XXIV The spread of the Tepehuan Revolt to the Topia mining camp and other places

We have not yet finished traveling with this history to all the places that were reached by the fire of rebellion lit by the Tepehuan. The Spaniards at the Topia mining camp thought that the danger had been eliminated with the punishment that Captain Suárez had administered to the two Indians who had [618] begun to ignite revolt in the towns between the Tepehuan and Topia. There was nevertheless continued unrest on the part of some Indians who had gone bad. Because

of this unrest, and in case the Tepehuan (who did not cease raiding those lands) should attack the mining center, which was populated with mining haciendas, the alcalde mayor and captain, Don Sebastián de Alvear, took steps to protect the church and plaza by constructing as quickly as he could three turrets to enclose them. He also prepared sixty horsemen with harquebuses to confront the enemy. Although they felt somewhat reassured with this protection, they still found themselves with the same shortage of gunpowder that was being experienced elsewhere. Thus, some soldiers were forced to try their luck at traveling through enemy lands on horseback to bring [back] small sacks of gunpowder.

In two Acaxee pueblos very close to Topia the enemy revolted. Corrupted and encouraged by the Tepehuan's fury, the Acaxee planned to attack the Topia mining camp on Epiphany [January 6]. Their primary intention was to kill Father Juan Acacio, superior of the mission, and Father Juan Alvarez, both of whom were instructing them. However, because there were also loyal Indians, they sent word to Topia of the treason from which God miraculously freed the two priests. Once the alcalde mayor captured and executed the two leaders who had planned the evil attack, the restless and rebellious Tepehuan no longer dared to attack the Topia mining camp; they realized that it was too well defended. And so they attacked from a different angle, stirring up the new Christian pueblos of Tecuchuapa and Carantapa, which were mentioned earlier and bordered on Sinaloa. Father Diego de Acevedo, who was instructing these pueblos, ascertained from rumors that were circulating that the unrest and danger were now very close. The captain and the Father Visitor of the missions [Vicente de Aguila] also had sent him a warning from the Villa de San Felipe in Sinaloa. They had heard the same rumors that Father Acevedo's life was in danger, and they told him to withdraw to the villa immediately to wait out the storm. The priest understood this to be Our Lord's will, and so he withdrew to Sinaloa. This advice turned out to be right on the mark, for around this time the Tepehuan arrived in these pueblos, where they gathered together the principal Indians and admonished them to follow the new god of whom they preached (as they called their idol). They forced them to rebel with the same rewards and threats that they had used elsewhere, implying a thousand lies and promises to those who would revolt with them and horrendous punishments to those who did not join their faction. The Tepehuan asked many times about the priest who had been instructing the pueblos, saying that they had very strict orders to immediately take his life. The treacherous Tepehuan were not satisfied with perverting these new Christians in the pueblos of Tecuchuapa, and so they took some of them to Santiago Papasquiaro to see firsthand the Tepehuan's victory and the priests' and Spaniards' corpses lying all over the ground. All this was intended to horrify and frighten them so that they would be reduced to becoming partners in their conspiracy.

These people continued to be harangued by the perverse admonitions of the apostate Tepehuan, despite the fact that the people at that time showed no interest in rebelling or harming their churches. Going after the churches is the first thing that these people do when they are fooled by the devil. Thus, it seemed a good idea to Father Acevedo to be [619] with his flock, and so he set out from Sinaloa for his mission district. Before he left, the captain of that province, Hurdaide, of whom honorific mention has already been made, suggested that six Spanish soldiers and seventy Indian allies go along to serve as a garrison. They were to set up a little fort with supplies for their sustenance, where they could withdraw to await help and defend themselves during any enemy invasion. Even though the Indians in Tecuchuapa showed their loyalty, it was later discovered that some of them had been perverted by the Tepehuan's speeches and were determined to kill Father Diego de Acevedo and his companion, Father Gaspar de Nájara. Because Captain Hurdaide had a lot of experience and therefore did not much trust these people's loyalty, he developed a good plan that would enable the priest and his escort to determine whether they were in the midst of friends or enemies. They were to persuade the Indians that, because the Tepehuan were coming to disturb and agitate their homes and pueblos and had declared themselves to be so much [in favor] of the persecution of Christianity, they should go to the nearest rancherías of these enemies and wage war on them, destroying them or making them abandon that place. In doing so they would demonstrate that they were not allied with them, but rather that they would willingly and purposefully defend their church and priests and maintain friendship with the Spaniards. The plan worked well, for 130 Indian gandules, or warriors, took up arms and attacked their Tepehuan neighbors when they least expected it. Some of them fled and others were killed and their heads brought back as a sign of victory. They also brought back a gentile woman who had been badly injured in the skirmish. She died after she was baptized, having declared that her Tepehuan [kinsmen] had refrained from planned attacks on these pueblos because they were waiting for a large number of people to help them destroy whatever they found. These pueblos were freed from this danger because of the captain's plan, or God's plan through the captain.

At the same time notable signs from both heaven and earth were experienced in this place, which are worthy of being recounted here. Through these it seems that heaven was pointing out the danger to this Christian community, which was being persecuted by hell.

Comets appeared in the sky and the earth trembled, things which had never been seen here before. One day it trembled seven times. In addition to this, bellowing in the form of frightening thunder was heard coming from the area where the Tepehuan nation lives. And yet the heavens were serene and clear. The priests and Spaniards asked God for the same thing that those from Jerusalem requested during Antioch's impious persecution, when they saw different signs in the heavens *rogabant in bonum monstra conuerti*.[32] Let the threats be turned against the enemy. The missionaries were in great danger here, as were others in various parts of Sinaloa where [the Tepehuan] sought to stir up the land and destroy all of Christendom. The priests all looked after and guarded their flocks, rather than abandon-

ing their missions. Those in Tecuchuapa remained with their Indians, and even though some of them went bad, others were steadfast in their Christianity. Finally, having been persecuted during several attacks by the Tepehuan and their allies, those who were still loyal abandoned this place and joined Christian pueblos in Sinaloa, as has already been recounted.

So as not to accumulate too many uprisings and too much apostate restlessness caused by the Tepehuan nation, I will leave what happened in the nation and mission of Parras for the following book. [620] We will now move on to the seat of government, the city of Durango, and what happened there during the Tepehuan Revolt.

CHAPTER XXV How the city of Durango was endangered during the Tepehuan Revolt; the punishment that was administered to [the rebels] and the precautions that were taken

The city of Durango is the seat of the government of the Province of Nueva Vizcaya. Although the city does not have many Spanish residents, there are many Spaniards in the surrounding region because of the many mining camps. Durango is 160 leagues from the seat of the realm, Mexico City, whence come all its people and commerce. Part of Durango borders on the lands of the Tepehuan, who are no more than fourteen or sixteen leagues away. If God, through His divine providence, had not spared this city, it would have been endangered along with the other places that were attacked by the enemy. The situation was that the Tepehuan had entreated all the pueblos in the region to join their conspiracy and general uprising. Among these pueblos they had summoned the people of Tunal, which was

no more than two leagues from the city. The Indians of Tunal were corrupted, and prepared their weapons and a great number of arrows to accompany the Tepehuan at the appointed and agreed upon time. However, for the reasons previously mentioned, the people from Santa Catalina anticipated the outbreak of war and rebellion. Word reached Durango of what had happened in Santa Catalina, the death of Father Tovar, etc. However, because God so willed it, the people of Tunal were completely unaware of events at Santa Catalina.

Once the governor of Nueva Vizcaya had received news of the uprising in Durango, he tried to erect defenses for the city in case the Tepehuan should attack. He did not realize that the people of Tunal were the Tepehuan's depraved consorts. And so with complete assurance he sent for the people of Tunal to help supply [laborers]·to blockade some of the city's streets, all of which were open, and to dig some trenches and [erect] turrets for protection. As they were working at this task, a religious of [the Order of] Saint John of God (which

32. *Margin Note*: 2. Machab.5. 2 Maccabees 5:4: "the prayer was on all men's lips, good not ill such high visions might portend" (Knox 1956:893).

has a hospital in Durango) overheard what one of them said (the Indians could not see him), "Go ahead, make us hurry along today, tomorrow you'll see." When the governor learned of this, [which confirmed] his suspicions and concerns about the Indians' restlessness and their stockpiling of weapons, he ordered that they be placed in prison and that their principales be tortured until the truth of what was going on was discovered. As this case was being investigated, a cry and uproar suddenly arose in the city. The alarm was sounded, signaling that the enemy was at hand and killing Spaniards. The soldiers who were guarding the prisoners heard the shout, "Draw your weapons, draw your weapons!" and doing so, they drew their swords and daggers and stabbed the prisoners to death. Some people attributed this cry to some Spaniard who falsely signaled the attack because it seemed to him that the interrogation [of the prisoners] was taking too much time and the city was in imminent danger of being destroyed. They also [questioned] waiting for an attack by Indian rebels who might join with those who were already in the city, even if they were prisoners. It seems most certain that it was celestial providence [that sounded the alarm], for two of the wounded [prisoners] [621] loudly confessed before they died that they had been allied with the rebel Tepehuan and that they were expecting their help soon so that they could attack the city and destroy it and finish off all its residents.

Later, this plot became more clearly understood, for it was learned that even though the Indians use trumpets extensively under the guise of the festivals that they celebrate, they were [actually] sounding the call to arms. During those days it was understood that this was to prepare for war, calling people to the agreed rebellion. In addition to this, a crown of rich plumage was found in the home of an Indian from one of these pueblos whom they had chosen to be the king of Durango and its province. The governor later captured him, along with nearly seventy other Indians from the same pueblos, most of whom were caciques and governors. He ordered them all to be hung around the periphery of the city. Once he had learned that the rebel Tepehuan's designs were focused on attacking the city with a large number of people, he arranged for more protection. He posted garrisons of soldiers in four places, with four captains, and also issued a decree of general pardon to any Spaniards, mestizos, or mulattos who had committed any crimes, provided they came to serve the king in aid of the city. He dispatched ammu-

nition, gunpowder, and supplies to Guanaceví, Indé, and the other places within his jurisdiction. Most of the lesser people of Durango, the women and children, withdrew to the church of the Company of JESUS, which was the strongest and most spacious in the city. Others went to the church at the Convent of San Francisco and some to fortified houses. There they remained for several days until help arrived from Mexico City and other places.

Once the city was secure and the governor had people to lead into battle, he sent messengers to Mexico City to inform the viceroy of Nueva España, who also was the captain general, of the general uprising of the Tepehuan nation and the great damage and deaths that they had caused. This event greatly distressed the people of Mexico City, who had commerce with Durango and its mining camps. The viceroy then dispatched orders to draft people in the city of Zacatecas, which was closest to Durango, and to release currency from the royal treasuries of those two cities for necessary expenses. Then he organized a council of the members of the Real Audiencia, other learned men, and members of religious orders. They met to decide on the degree to which war should be waged against the Tepehuan, and to plan accordingly.

I have been an eyewitness to such meetings, when the Spaniards proceed with great care and justification. It is good that other nations realize how cautiously Spaniards proceed and how they pay great heed to their monarchs' orders to justify wars and the taking of Indian life or liberty, no matter how barbarous these nations may be. The justification for this war was decreed and the governor [proclaimed it would be] waged with blood and fire, albeit always mindful that the innocent and least culpable should not be harmed. As this was being decreed in Mexico City, a spy happened to be captured in Durango. After he was placed in prison he confessed that those who had attacked Santiago Papasquiaro had now approached this city and had set up camp two leagues away. The captain of their squad was an Indian named Pablo who had feigned a desire for peace, thus prompting the priests and Spaniards at Santiago Papasquiaro to come out of the church so that he could take their lives. God willed that this traitor should lose his own life and pay for his crime, [622] for when he came back to trace a route by which they could attack the city, he was captured and then hanged by order of the governor, who had been waiting for hours for the aid he needed to go into battle.

CHAPTER XXVI The governor reconnoiters the land and comes upon the corpses of holy religious from the Order of Saint Dominic as well as other Christians

Until now there has not been an appropriate moment to record the spirit and enthusiasm with which the Spaniards set out to avenge the great many offenses committed against God, His sacraments, and His priests, as well as against their relatives, wives, and children, and finally, to punish the nation that had so profaned everything sacred and human. These Spaniards had been violated in so many places, owing to the fact that the attacks came suddenly, or better said, unexpectedly. If history is to recount (as it should) the truth of the matter, and it is good that these things be known for future reference, it is certain that the missionary priests in the Tepehuan nation sent several warnings of impending danger to the governor of Nueva Vizcaya, asking him to take effective action. This seemed unnecessary to the governor, as did incurring expenses for the king. Without giving this any more thought, [I note that] the costs to His Majesty proved incomparably greater. There were even people who said that those warnings were only the fears of the religious seeking unnecessary security for themselves. In order to be brief, I will not pause to refute these arguments.

Instead, I will move on to discuss the strength and bravery with which the governor of Nueva Vizcaya, who at that time was Don Gaspar de Alvear, a knight of the Habit of Santiago, left the city of Durango protected and set out in search of the enemy Tepehuan in order to punish their crimes, in spite of the fact that it was very difficult to catch up with them. These Indians and nations, which are all spread out, are like herds of deer, skipping through mountains and valleys. They don't march in formation, nor do they have any fixed place where they can be attacked, which makes conquering them more difficult. Nevertheless, the governor was obliged on this occasion to overcome the obstacles, no matter how large and invincible they seemed. The numerous difficulties that arise in Europe when attacks are waged against large armies and fortifications are equivalent to capturing these peoples' trails

and mountain peaks. These are, by nature, as difficult to overcome as the artfully constructed forts of Europe.

The governor finally set out with only seventy Spanish soldiers and armored horses, and 120 Indian allies on foot. He took along a large quantity of flour and seven hundred head of cattle for places that were in dire straits. He arrived with this aid at the mines of Indé, and then went on to Guanaceví, where he found dwellings that had been burned to the ground. In the churches they found the chalices, altars, and sacred ornaments smashed to pieces. Even though he encountered some enemies, he could not pursue them until he had distributed the aid that he had brought. Nevertheless, in the skirmishes that took place some of the enemy died, and he exacted five hundred fanegas of maize from them. An even greater amount had to be burned so that they could not make use of it.

When the governor reached a very difficult slope that is called El Gato, which the soldiers had to traverse in single file, an enemy squad attacked, throwing boulders and rocks down on them with such force that {623} they knocked down trees along the way. However, in the end the soldiers set them to flight with their harquebuses, and our people finally captured the top of the hill. There they found the body of the council member[33] from Durango, Pedro Rendón, and a religious from [the Order of] Saint Dominic named Fray Sebastián Montaño, as well as other Christian Indians who had accompanied them. They had all been killed at the beginning of the conspiracy. An outstanding phenomenon worthy of being recorded here was discovered with respect to the body of the holy religious. Even though two months had passed, the body of the holy religious emitted an amazing fragrance. The blood on his tonsure, feet, and the thumb and index finger of the hand with which the consecrated Host is held, was as fresh as if it had just been spilled. The breviary from which he prayed was at his side; it was as perfect and

33. *Regidor.*

whole as if the heavy rains and snow that had fallen the month before had never even touched it. Even though this religious was not in charge of instructing the Indians, he had gone to the mining camp to preach that devotion which is so characteristic of his holy order, the Rosary of the Most Holy Virgin. He was traveling at the time of the sudden Tepehuan uprising.

The governor ordered that the bodies be gathered up to be taken and buried in a decent place, especially the body of the holy religious. He took this corpse with him to Guanaceví, which is where [the religious] had been headed. At that mining camp, which was heavily populated, the governor found all the machinery for extracting silver burned to the ground. All the people were squeezed into the church because of daily enemy attacks. Although the Spaniards had decided to abandon this mining camp, he encouraged them not to forsake such an important place, and with the aid of some soldiers and the ammunition that was given them, they were inspired to defend it.

The governor then set out for battle with only twenty-seven soldiers on armored horses and thirty Indian allies. Because his journey had been long and eventful, it was necessary to pause from time to time. He sent the brave Captain Montaño, who was an expert in these lands, to another area, with twenty-five soldiers and sixty loyal Indians, some of whom were Tepehuan. There were still some Tepehuan, albeit few,

who remained faithful. These Indians served as spies and reconnoitered the lands and holdings of the enemy. Montaño and his people came across a squad of Tepehuan, some of whom they killed. They captured alive an Indian named Antonio, who declared in his confession that he had been present at all the killings and robberies that had taken place. He was the son of the cacique of Santa Catalina, where Father Hernando de Tovar had been attacked and killed. He further confessed that the conspiracy had been so widespread that the Tarahumara, the Ocotlán, some Xixime and Acaxee, and some other more distant nations had all participated. He explicitly declared that the Indians of Tunal—the same ones who we said were stabbed or hanged in Durango—were accomplices and allies. He confessed that they had spies who kept them informed of the Spaniards' intentions. The devil in the Tepehuan idol, who had done such a good job with his plan to destroy all Christianity in the province, could make the same confession that Satan made before God when he was asked whence he had come. He could not deny the truth, and said, *Circuiui terram, & perambulaui eam.*[34] This idol (if it is not the case that it is Satan himself) had roamed throughout the entire [624] Province of Nueva Vizcaya and its new Christian communities in order to destroy them and contaminate everything, as will be seen in all the places and events that follow.

CHAPTER XXVII The governor continues his expedition to several Tepehuan strongholds

The governor dispatched Captain Montaño to explore the land and locate the enemy. He also had orders to go to the pueblo of El Zape, where he was to meet the governor and they would assess the destruction that was said to have taken place there. He followed these orders, and upon reaching El Zape he executed the treacherous Indian, Antonio, who was his prisoner. He ordered him to be hanged from a post in front of the church, which the Indians had profaned and where they had killed the priests. In this place he encountered one of the saddest

spectacles that could be imagined, as well as signs of the cruel deeds that had been carried out there.

The bodies of the blessed priests Juan del Valle and Luis de Alavés lay where they appeared to have been killed—about two steps from their house next to the church. The blessed priests Juan Fonte and Gerónimo de Moranta appeared to have been killed one-quarter league from the pueblo, one in front of the other in

34. *Margin Note*: Iob. 2. Job 2:2: "he had been roaming about the earth, to and fro about the earth" (Knox 1956:454).

the road, on their way to the festival that turned into a tragedy. They were all easily recognizable, as if they had just been killed, just like the others that died, whom we can believe gloriously lost their lives because they were Catholic Christians and were persecuted by apostate heretics out of hatred for the Holy Faith. What other motive could so infuriate the spirits of people who did not pardon even two-year-old children, whose bodies were found on the ground? More than thirty Spaniards had gathered there to celebrate their devotion to the Most Holy Virgin. They were joined by their servants and other long-time Christian Indian men and women, numbering ninety in all. Having gathered for such a holy celebration, they died cruelly. Their bodies were found all together, face down on the ground. Either this was a ceremony of this nation or the devil in the idol taught it to them because he felt tormented by the prayers that came out of their mouths. The church and the priests' house were burned to the ground and plundered. In another house the burned bodies of another thirty Christian Indians—young and old—were found. They thought they could protect themselves there, but not even being Indian was enough to save their lives.

The governor, Don Gaspar de Alvear, was distraught to see such destruction. He ordered that the bodies of all those Catholic Christians, except those of the four priests, be buried in that church, which had been burned because of the Faith. The residents of Guanaceví had requested the priests' bodies out of the devotion they felt toward them and the religious instruction that they had received from them. This is the argument they presented for their claims to the bodies. Nonetheless, the governor, who was very devoted to our Company, wanted to take them with him (as will later be told) to deposit them in our church at the college in Durango, to which they belonged. Taking the blessed bodies along, he went back with his troops to find out all he could about the destroyed pueblo and area around Santa Catalina. There he ordered a search for the body of the blessed Father Hernando de Tovar. Nothing more was found than a little basket with papers and pieces of sacred ornaments. He dispatched two captains, Montaño and Hontiveros, with some soldiers to overtake the enemy, whom he wanted to cut to pieces, [625] having seen with his own eyes the tremendous destruction they had wrought.

The two captains came upon squads of Indians, who fled, [arrogantly shouting to the captains] that they would see them later in Santiago Papasquiaro, although they never showed up. However, as the governor set

out from that place, he was intercepted by an enemy squadron captained by a mestizo named Canelas, who was the son of an [Indian] woman and a Spaniard. He was very famous and renowned in this uprising, even though he made excuses for siding with the Tepehuan. He declared that if he had not done so, the Spaniards would have killed him, and he also said that he did this so that he could turn them over to the Spaniards. Whatever the case might have been, he was serving as captain of this squadron, with which the governor and his people had a few skirmishes. Although they suffered no harm themselves, they killed some of the enemy and took some of their harquebuses. They also stripped them of the horses and mules that they had stolen, and put them to flight. The [enemy] fled because they saw one Indian killed whom they greatly respected. He was the one who under false pretense of peace had made the priests and Spaniards come out of the church where they had gathered in Santiago Papasquiaro. This is how God was punishing and doing away with the traitors and principal apostates of His Holy Faith. Another Indian was taken alive who, when tortured, declared that all the enemy's provisions and their wives and children were in a pueblo called Tenerapa. (This was where they had placed their bedeviled idol and were under the protection of their false god; it had also been the first place where he had been adored and where the uprising was forged.) This pueblo was ten leagues away, and our people had already traveled five that day. The governor convened a council to encourage his troops, even though they all were so enthused that they decided to travel by night and execute a dawn attack the following morning, which they did.

The governor set out quickly with fifty Spanish soldiers, taking along Captain Gordejuela, who had joined him, as well as sixty Indian allies, leaving the rest behind to guard the provisions. At daybreak they came within sight of Tenerapa. Our men were spotted by an Indian who was rounding up the enemy's horses, and he shouted to them that Spaniards were coming. The Spaniards quickly attacked the pueblo. The enemy fled, as did the mestizo Canelas and some women. Nevertheless, thirty people died in the assault and some two hundred Tepehuan women and children were taken prisoner. Among them were two Spanish girls who had been taken prisoner by the Tepehuan. They were the daughters of Juan de Castilla, the lieutenant at Papasquiaro, who died there. They also rescued five mulatto women whom the Indians had captured as well as some of our other people whom they were going to make servants on the day when (they thought) they would became the lords of the land, as their idol had falsely promised them.

The governor ordered some of the old women who had played an important role in the uprising to be hanged. They have great authority among these peoples [and are instrumental in] these types of deeds and plans. The devil makes use of them in all the plots he hatches against Christianity. To reiterate the point that was made earlier about God punishing and taking the lives of these diabolical instruments, it was ordered and willed that two of the women who were hanged were those whom the Tepehuan had carried in their procession on the saints' bier during the aforementioned destruction of Santiago Papasquiaro. Some of the Spaniards' harquebuses, chain mail, leather clothing, and other valuable objects were taken here as spoils. More than 150 mounts were taken—mares and mules—and thus ended this successful endeavor.

The governor set out for Santiago Papasquiaro, where the enemy, unaware of what was [626] going to happen, had dared the Spaniards to fight. Rather than flee, the governor intended to search them out. Thus, he gave orders for the people to follow him with the provisions, and he set out quickly for Santiago. This order was carried out and each group took a different route to Santiago, where upon their arrival they thanked God for their good fortune. However, here they were greatly distressed by signs of evil deeds and atrocious crimes, such as the bones of numerous victims who had been cruelly killed at that place, as was mentioned. The bones were as bare and clean of flesh as if they had been there for many years. It was impossible to recognize to whom they belonged. The bones were buried in the burned church. The priests' house had also been burned and was nothing but a barren and stripped plot of land.

Because the enemy had not shown themselves, the governor set out for Durango, taking as prisoners some 250 of the enemy's less important people, namely their women and children. He also took what he most esteemed, the bodies, found intact, of the four blessed priests who had been killed at El Zape for preaching the Faith of Jesus Christ. Even though the priests at Santiago Papasquiaro gloriously died for the same cause, God did not wish to single them out with this favor, just as has happened in similar cases with many of His other holy martyrs whose bodies He allowed to be burned, whereas others He freed from the flames, not allowing them to be consumed by fire. Incorruptibility has also been granted to some of His holy virgin confessors whereas others, even though they were very holy, were left subject to corruptibility. The reason for this is because their principal and full glory is reserved for them until the day of the universal resurrection. The other is a special favor that God grants according to the motives of His supreme providence. And even though this is a favor, this is not what saintliness consists of, nor is it a necessary sign of that state. Therefore, it is not surprising that the governor had no way of recognizing or picking out the bones and remains of the two priests who died in that place, the way he had identified those who died at El Zape, which he had found intact and had brought back himself on this journey, which was not his last. I will leave the [account of his] other journeys until later; this one will conclude with his arrival in Durango with the Tepehuan captives as his prisoners, as well as the arrival of the bodies and blessed remains of the four priests who triumphed in their deaths suffered in El Zape for preaching the Faith and Gospel of Jesus Christ, as will be told in the following chapter.

CHAPTER XXVIII The governor returns to Durango to bury the bodies of four priests of the Company who died at the hands of the rebel infidels[35]

Governor Don Gaspar de Alvear was a pious and Christian gentleman and a member of the Order of Santiago. He had dealt with some of these holy religious when they worked in his jurisdiction as ministers of the doctrina. He grew very fond of them and came to recognize their many religious virtues. Moreover, from the inquiries he had made as governor and from what he himself had witnessed during the previously mentioned expedition, he realized that the priests had died preaching our Holy Faith. For all these reasons he carefully and reverently gathered up the remains of those men whom he considered holy. When he was met along the road outside Durango by the [627] Father Rector and another priest, the governor's first comment, said with considerable solemnity, was that he had felt very safe and confident in the success of his journey, knowing that he was returning with such holy corpses. Out of respect he had ordered that the bodies be loaded on four of his own mules, which were draped with his coat of arms. Armed and mounted Spanish soldiers marched in rows at the head of the procession. The mules were flanked by two rows of Indian allies—some three hundred Laguneros and Conchos—most of whom were on horseback and were armed with bows and arrows. The governor and the priests followed right behind the mules and holy bodies. At the end of the procession was the baggage train, which included an escort of soldiers and stretched for a quarter of a league.

When the troop reached a point a quarter of a league from the city, the commissioner of the Royal Treasury, Rafael de Guasque, came out to meet it with his carriage, in which the bodies were placed. Although it was late and the sun had set, the people of the city were devoutly waiting along San Francisco Street. The reverend fathers of the Church of San Francisco wanted to keep the bodies until the approaching feast day of Saint Thomas of Aquinas, when they could be taken with respect to our church of the Company of Jesus.

When the governor and those ministers of the Lord 's Gospel reached the city, their arrival was triumphantly signaled by the tolling of bells and many volleys from the soldiers' harquebuses. The soldiers cleared a way through the crowd that had gathered at the Church of San Francisco. As the procession approached, the very devout priests of that religious house came out to welcome it, carrying the Cross on high. They were accompanied by other religious from the region and by singing and organ music. Large numbers of people, including the city's elite, were there to receive the bodies and place them in the church. As a sign of his great devotion to the deceased priests, the commissioner of the Royal Treasury personally distributed candles to the people in attendance. The Father Provincial of San Francisco, Father Juan Gómez, who happened to be there at that time, decided to officiate at the ceremony wearing a great cloak.[36] Although His Reverence wished to celebrate the Vespers of the Martyrs of Christ (as was evident from his eyes filled with tears of devotion), this liturgy is reserved for the Vicar of Christ on earth, the Roman Pontiff. So Father Gómez resigned himself to [arranging] for good music to be included in the celebration.

The bodies were respectfully placed in the main chapel, where they remained from Sunday evening until the following Tuesday. During this time four large torches burned, which had been provided by the general of the army [Captain Suárez]. Four soldiers stood watch, guarding the bodies in shifts. On Monday all of the priests of the Church of San Francisco were present for the Office of the Dead, which was sung by the Father Provincial. Because the deceased priests were

35. This chapter is based in good part on the anua of 1616 in the Ayer Collection at the Newberry Library (Ayer 1616).

36. *Capa de coro.* This may well be "the great cloak" (*cappa magna*), which is a garment of state worn by cardinals and bishops and permitted by privilege to other prelates (see Attwater 1949:74).

thought already to be in heaven, crowned in glory, the office was accompanied by solemn music.[37]

On the following day, Tuesday, when the Church celebrated the feast of its luminary, the Angelical Doctor Saint Thomas Aquinas, our priests of the college of the Company went to retrieve the dear remains of their late brothers and soldiers of Christ's militia, who had died courageously fighting for the honor and glory of JESUS, their captain. Our priests were accompanied by the city's elite as well as 150 [628] militiamen, who fired volleys from their harquebuses. They were followed in turn by the boys from the Company's school in Durango, who were handsomely dressed. Each boy wore a wreath on his head and carried a burning candle. Then came the Episcopal Vicar[38] (at that time this holy church was not yet a cathedral, as it is today) who carried a tall Cross draped in white, and who was accompanied by our priests.

In this fashion [the entourage] made its way to the Church of San Francisco. There the priests of that religious house took the bodies, which were covered with embroidered mantles, and carried them on their shoulders to the Company's church [of Saint Thomas Aquinas]. The latter, though large, was full of people from many walks of life. The Mass for the feast day of Saint Thomas Aquinas was celebrated, during which the bodies of the priests were laid to rest. They had preached to the Tepehuan the Divine Faith that the Angelical Doctor illustrated to the world through his teachings, just as they did through the blood that they spilled. During Mass the bodies of the priests rested on an adorned bier, which was beautifully illuminated by numerous candlesticks. On top of the bodies and embroidered mantles a cassock, a chalice, and a paten

were placed, as is the custom for deceased priests. The floor was covered with rugs and all around there were placards with poems and compositions that celebrated the triumph of the courageous soldiers of Christ, who fought until their death.

After the Gospel was read the homily was preached —the same one that the Son of God had given to His Church for the feast day of its Doctors—namely that they are the salt that preserves the world from the corruption of idolatry and heresy.[39] When the relevance of this teaching to the deceased was pointed out, many in the audience testified to it as they were moved to tears. After the Mass was concluded, the four bodies were laid to rest in a vault that had been made in a side altar dedicated to our holy patriarch, Saint Ignatius, which was located on the Gospel side of the main altar. The bodies, which were in a large wooden casket that bore the titles, names, and date of the priests' deaths, appropriately rest in the shadow of their holy father who engendered them in Christ with the doctrine of his Institute and holy religious [order], in whose observance they gloriously finished their lives, as did their brothers who died for the same cause, preaching the Gospel to the same nation. At the end of this book I will relate at length the example of their outstanding virtues and well-deserved memory. For now we will leave them to rest in this place. As noted, the holy bodies and bones of the other four religious of the Company of Jesus could not be distinguished from the remains of the other faithful Catholics who had died at Santiago Papasquiaro, having confessed and received Holy Communion as Christians. We can expect that the Lord will bring them forth in glory in the company of the others on that day chosen by Him for the glory of His saints.

---

37. In the Roman Catholic rite, organ and other types of music were not permitted at the Office and Mass of the Dead, except with special permission from the bishop (Attwater 1949:336).

38. Pérez de Ribas probably meant vicar general, which is a deputy appointed by a bishop (Attwater 1949:516).

39. Matthew 5:11–13.

CHAPTER XXIX A clarification of what has been written about the Tepehuan Rebellion and the religious who died at the sacrilegious hands of the apostates

The clarification that I have decided to add at this point would not be necessary had I not been obliged by important authors to support what I have said and to account for certain differences between my account and those [of others] who have touched upon the events recounted here. [629] Although the differences concern circumstances rather than matters of substance, they are nevertheless considerable and demand scrutiny and justification. Because close attention to the truth is the heart and soul of history, that which is said here must be supported by both primary and secondary sources. I excuse those authors who wrote things that differ from what has been recounted herein; they relied on accounts that were hurriedly dashed off (as they say) from Mexico to Spain, very early during the Tepehuan Rebellion. At that time it was impossible—even in Mexico City, which is nearly two hundred leagues away—for people to know fully the events of this rebellion. Some months later, however, the governor of Nueva Vizcaya, Don Gaspar de Alvear, went to this land with his soldiers to punish the delinquents. He investigated both the substance and circumstances of this case through eyewitness testimony and official reports. After the completion of this investigation, which involved a case that was not only political but also touched upon many issues of religion and our Holy Mother Church, the Bishop of Durango, to whose flock the Tepehuan belonged, ordered a further investigation. Some thirty witnesses who represented some of the most reliable individuals in the region were examined about these matters. Because these people had been in the midst of the Tepehuan and had had frequent contact with the religious who were instructing them, they possessed a certain amount of knowledge concerning all that had happened. That which was learned from their accounts already has been recorded here. I will use them to discuss what remains concerning these events and to also write about the lives and outstanding virtues of the holy religious who were martyred.

Among those authors who have written about this subject, Fray Marcos de Guadalajara, in the fifth volume of the *Pontifical* [History],[40] Book XI, Chapter X, has complied most fully with [the law of] history. I will now account for what other authors have written, which is inaccurate. When speaking of the joyous death of that holy religious of the Order of Saint Dominic, Fray Sebastián Montaño, who was a native of Madrid and died at the hands of the Tepehuan, the author of *The Greatness of Madrid*[41] says that the marquis of Salinas, who was the viceroy of Nueva España, had sent five hundred married Indians from the city of Tlaxcala to live among the fierce and barbarous Tepehuan in order to tame them. As a result, the Tepehuan's spirits were said to have been disturbed, and during the uprising they killed some of the Tlaxcalans. This is entirely different from what everyone in Nueva España knows to be the truth, especially those who live in Nueva Vizcaya. This is the province where all the events of the uprising occurred and where the motive for the Tepehuan's rebellion was investigated and discovered. And it can be clearly understood that when this history reaches the hands of those who were part of these events, some of whom still live today in this province, they would judge me badly if I were to record anything that was out of line with the truth. Indeed, I can say the same thing about everything else that is told in this history, for it is relatively recent and refers to [630] Nueva España, where this all took place.

Returning to the case at hand, which must be examined, what is certain is that no Indians from the city of Tlaxcala, which is two hundred leagues from the Tepehuan, ever went to live among them. There were some Mexican and Tarascan laborers who of their own free will go to work in the mining camps. However, there is

---

40. Marcos de Guadalajara authored the fifth volume (1605–23) of this six-volume history, entitled *Primera{-sexta} parte de la Historia pontifical y catolica*, . . .

41. The referent here apparently is Gil Gonzalez Davila's *Teatro de las grandezas de la villa de Madrid*, . . . (1623).

no way that Tlaxcalans settling in Tepehuan lands could have caused the Tepehuan Revolt. Rather, the rebellion was caused by the previously recorded bedeviled idol, who spoke to them, and by the famous sorcerer who was in charge of this idol, who corrupted these poor people. Furthermore, it is chronologically inaccurate to state that Viceroy Don Luis de Velasco, the marquis of Salinas, ordered and arranged for the Tlaxcalans to go and settle among the Tepehuan. At the time the Tepehuan rebelled, Don Luis de Velasco had been out of office for years and had returned to Spain to serve as president of the Royal Council of the Indies. At the time of the Tepehuan Revolt the viceroy of Nueva España was Don Diego Fernández de Córdoba, the marquis of Guadalcazar. That account also was misleading in stating that seven priests from the Company had gathered at Santiago Papasquiaro and that all seven had been killed there at the hands of the Tepehuan. There were eight religious from the Company who died, and they were killed in different places—separated by thirty leagues, which is the distance from El Zape to Santiago Papasquiaro. Also, these priests died on different days: this has been recounted at length and will not be repeated here.

That account calls the superior of these priests Luis del Valle, but his name is actually Juan del Valle. It also says that the blessed priest Fray Sebastián Montaño preached to the Indians there, which is impossible. This priest did not know the language of the Tepehuan, who were instructed only by members of the Company. Furthermore, this priest had not spent any time among the Tepehuan and was merely passing through those mountains on his way to preach the devotion of the Holy Rosary at the mining camps and to request alms for the Dominican religious house in Zacatecas, which was more than sixty leagues from the Tepehuan. Likewise, Fray Sebastián did not die at the same place where the apostates committed all the other murders, but rather on the road leading from Guanaceví, near the slope called El Gato. He was traveling with a coun-

cil member from Durango when a squad of treacherous Tepehuan caught up with them, as was previously told.

In no way do I intend for this to mean that this holy religious did not die for his religion and because of the hellish hatred the devil had ignited in the hearts of the apostates, prompting them to persecute and destroy all that had to do with the Christian Religion and Faith, especially those whom they knew to be its ministers and priests. This is sufficient to make someone a martyr, and it was enough to provide this holy Dominican religious with a glorious crown. For this same reason his holy body was later removed to the Dominicans' illustrious religious house in Mexico City. That author also says that it was the Chichimec who killed these holy religious, and although it is true that in Nueva España 'Chichimec' is the name ordinarily given to any barbarous nation, the fact of the matter is that the Chichimec constitute a distinct and separate nation from the Tepehuan, who were the ones who rebelled and martyred these priests.

Regarding these and other minor circumstances which I will omit, the accounts by the aforementioned authors do not correspond to what I have written. Therefore, I felt it necessary to include here the relevant clarifications. [631] These will be read by those from the Province of Nueva Vizcaya, which although it was the arena for calamities also was the arena for glorious martyrdoms. Memories of this are still fresh there, and the report I have recorded thus far and will record later will conform to the truth of what happened and to the testimonies that were given, which should be in the archives of that jurisdiction. Because these fuller investigations were carried out after events that remain to be told, it comes as no surprise that they differ from the first reports to reach Spain from such distant lands.

With this, let us return to the expeditions of Spanish Catholic soldiers who took the field in defense of the Catholic Faith, which the devil and his Tepehuan followers had unceasingly sought to destroy.

CHAPTER XXX The new disturbances created by the Tepehuan at various places throughout the province

We left the bodies of the ministers who gave their lives for the glorious preaching of the Gospel resting in the earth; their souls we left resting in heaven. But the enemy of humanity and of the Gospel itself did not rest in his attempts to uproot the Christianity that remained in the Tepehuan and other nations that had accepted the gentle yoke of Christ's law. This same devil also endeavored to avoid being discredited in the eyes of those whom he had deceived with false promises that they would become lords of the land and that they would finish off all the Spaniards and priests in the province, [thereby] becoming free [to practice] all the superstitions, idolatries, and barbarous and savage customs that he had taught them. It was already becoming apparent how false this was. As a result, he was losing his diabolical reputation among the Indians, for many of his principal supporters were already dead and had not been resurrected. Thus, to regain his false authority, he once again provoked the spirits of the remaining Indians, inciting them to continue their attacks. [His provocation] was such that they neither ceased in their attacks, nor in sending spies to initiate these attacks, nor in trying to convince other nations to join their faction.

The Tepehuan's fury became quite daring. The governor was on his way back to Durango from his expedition, bringing with him the bodies of the holy religious fathers as well as the captives of whom we have written. He had left behind a fair number of enemy dead, and as he approached La Sauceda with the remains, eight leagues from Durango, he was told that the enemy were along that road waiting in ambush to seize his prisoners. He was also told that Spanish soldiers had gone to locate the spies and had killed two of them. In addition to this, the governor received news from other places that the Indians had burned the church in the pueblo of Tunal, five leagues from the Villa del Nombre de Dios. They added that the Tepehuan had robbed and murdered some soldiers that His Lordship had dispatched with three thousand pesos worth of clothing intended for enlisting people in the Province of Chiametla. Also, Spaniards in the Villa de San Sebastián,

eight leagues from the Villa de Chiametla, had withdrawn to their church out of fear of Tepehuan attack.

I now begin to discuss things and events at which I was present. As I was traveling along this road at that time, with three other priests headed for the Province of Sinaloa, we reached the [632] Villa de Chiametla. Although this is several leagues from the lands of the Tepehuan, their attacks were still feared there. They were feared even more in the Villa de San Sebastián, which was closer [to Tepehuan territory]. The Spaniards from both these places asked us newly arrived religious to divide up and accompany them in times of such danger, when surprise attacks were a daily and nightly threat. There were not enough people from these two places, which were small, to withstand the enemy force. At one of those places there was no priest, and at the other there was only one to comfort them in the event of necessity and danger. The priest who was acting as superior charged me with attending to this act of piety in the Villa de San Sebastián. As soon as I arrived there I gave a sermon, preparing the people to receive the Holy Sacraments of Confession and Holy Communion, which are a very secure way to prepare for any event.

The women and children withdrew every night into the church, while the men stayed outside standing guard. A fire was lit where we all stood our watch; rumors were heard daily concerning Tepehuan attacks. We four priests spent some ten days at these places. Then it seemed to us that the rumors had subsided, so we left these people encouraged with the divine word and sacraments and continued on our journey.

We were joined by some Spaniards who were making the same journey, even though there was a danger of attacks along the way from enemy groups that infested that mountain range. Once we had passed through it, these enemies attacked the Villa de San Sebastián as well as the nearby pueblo of long-time Christian Indians called Acaponeta. They also attacked a convent of Franciscan friars, burning their house and church. These Tepehuan rebels disrupted the entire land and placed it in great danger.

Governor Don Gaspar de Alvear received this news

as he was returning from his expedition and approaching Durango. He brought with him the remains of the bodies of those who had died for our Holy Faith, as well as the prisoners who persecuted It. Upon hearing such news it was necessary for him to set out once again on campaign, as will be told in the following chapter.

CHAPTER XXXI The governor again sets out on a campaign; the successful results of his expedition

The many rumors [of impending attack] obliged the governor to undertake another campaign before he returned to Durango. After respectfully escorting the holy bodies to La Sauceda and safely interring them there, he departed with a substantial number of soldiers whom he had recruited to bring an end to the many evils and rebellion created by the devil and his cohorts. As the uprisings of the enemies of Christ and His holy law increased, so did the spirit and courage of the Spaniards to defend it, shed their own blood for it, and punish the unholy and sacrilegious infidels. The governor did not want to reveal where he was going with his armed troops because he suspected that the enemy might somehow be warned. He had become so angry that he set out with the intention of not returning to Durango until the Tepehuan were broken. He resolved to punish those who were guilty and subject the lesser offenders to God and king; otherwise he would destroy them. On an occasion of such mortal danger he took with him and his army a priest from our Company named Alonso de Valencia. [633]

The governor departed with a small number of Spanish soldiers at a time of snowstorms in the mountains [of the Tepehuan], traveling along very steep trails through mountains and gorges. One of these gorges was so deep that it was named El Diablo.[42] It was said that the Tepehuan rabble were gathered here with their women and children. There were places in this gorge that had never been seen before by Spaniards. They were accessible at great risk by descending pole ladders. It was a miracle that they survived all these trails.

42. This gorge is within the Río Piaxtla drainage.

Moreover, besides these dangers, they endured hunger, because their supplies had run out. They got to the point where they ate the soles of their shoes and pieces of leather, which they softened and cooked on the fire. When their horses and mules became so exhausted and thin that they could not proceed, they ate them.

The governor set out for the southern flank of that mountain chain. This was the roughest and steepest part, but it was where the enemy was located. During the daytime the governor and his troops hid in the forests so they would not be seen by the enemy lookouts and spies. They captured a few whom the governor ordered to be tortured so that they would reveal the locations of their people. However, they allowed their joints to be broken and [their flesh] cut to pieces rather than utter a word. This was the kind of people that the Tepehuan were; their idol made them even more diabolical and perverted.

The governor and his troops nevertheless proceeded in search of them until they reached a halting place where the trail divided. As they were trying to decide which route would lead to the enemy, thirty Indians with lances appeared on a hilltop far away. They were coming to get cattle for food because they had consumed all those they had previously stolen. With this the governor halted and awaited the enemy's approach, hiding his squad of Indian allies in ambush. Six of the enemy who were at the forefront detected the ambush and turned back to warn their companions. However, the allied Indians who were hiding in ambush fired such a volley of arrows that the enemy were overcome. God willed that their leader died right there on the spot. He was the one the Tepehuan most esteemed in war because he was their captain and was like a general.[43] He was a very valiant, daring, and astute Indian who spoke Spanish. His name was Francisco Gogoxito and he was famous throughout that territory. He was also the one that the governor most wanted to capture.

Gogoxito's death became very well known throughout the province, as did the war that was undertaken in the name of our Holy Faith to avenge and punish the [Tepehuan] for their insolence and outrages against things sacred. The apostate Gogoxito had publicly worshiped his demonic idol. He was one of the principales who had burned churches and murdered the priests at Papasquiaro, desecrating and destroying holy images. This sacrilegious Indian who had taken Francisco as a baptismal name no longer considered himself to be Francisco, nor did he consider himself baptized. He instead considered himself a gentile named Gogoxito, as he was called throughout the land. On the feast day of the seraphic father [Saint Francis], he desecrated an image of the saint, just as he had desecrated the name that he unworthily bore. He also desecrated another image of the Most Glorious Virgin, the Mother of God.

This was how unholy this man was, and how singular was the punishment by which God signalled that he would continue to pay for his sins in the next life. And so it was that when the Indian allies [lying in ambush] shot their arrows, most of them hit this unholy sacrilegious person. They pierced his body in different places; [634] three arrowheads pierced his mouth—punishment for the blasphemies that he had spewed forth when he publicly denied the true God, blasphemously boasting of his worship of the devil, and ordering the aforementioned unholy acts. Only five other enemy were killed because the rest of them fled on their horses. However, the [Tepehuan] nation was later as sorrowful as they were disheartened by the loss of their principal captain and commander.

Governor Don Gaspar de Alvear, who was a valiant soldier (his bravery and the difficulties that he endured were recorded at length by Father Alonso de Valencia[44]), marched on with his troops. Even though they were tired, they covered two hundred leagues of trails, searching throughout the territory for the enemy. They wreaked great harm and destruction on the [Tepehuan] and their houses and ranches. Captain Suárez (who was previously mentioned) also harassed them to the point that they began to falter in their attacks, losing their daring and becoming afraid. Some of them even asked for peace and pardon, as will be told when this history records the damage caused throughout this land by this conspiracy, which was invented by the devil himself.

CHAPTER XXXII The temporal and spiritual damage caused by the rebellion of the Tepehuan apostates in the Province of Nueva Vizcaya

Although a large part of the damage [caused by this rebellion] was discussed in the preceding chapters, some damage still remains to be mentioned. A summary will be given here of all this damage, so that it can be fully comprehended. [I will] begin with the temporal damage that was readily visible to the eye. In the vicinity of Durango, which is the seat of the province, there were very extensive herds of mares and cows, numbering close to two hundred thousand head. The cows provided provisions and sustenance for many of the major mining camps in Nueva España. From time to time the [ranchers] would send large herds of young bulls as far as Mexico City, even though it was 280 leagues away. All these [ranches] were destroyed and razed by the Tepehuan, who were great cattle ranchers and horsemen. They killed some animals and took others to their

---

43. Presumably meaning that like a captain he led others in battle, and like a general he plotted attacks and counterattacks.

44. Pérez de Ribas here draws from a letter of Father Valencia's; a Spanish transcription and English translation of the entire letter can be found in Naylor and Polzer (1986:245–93).

rancherías for their own use during the time that the uprising and war lasted. Others ran wild and were lost to their owners.

The residents of Durango were ruined by the war, and their commerce with the mining camps came to an end. The mining camps at Indé were abandoned; at other [camps] the mills for grinding ore were burned and destroyed. This important equipment is very costly. The working of silver ceased, and His Majesty thus lost a great sum from his royal fifth.[45] However, this was not the only damage to the royal coffers; even greater damage was suffered by the treasury in Durango. Taking into account what had been spent on the war as well as the punishment of the rebels, the accountant for the *tribunal mayor {de cuentas}*, Don Juan Cervantes Casaus[46] —a gentlemen of proven merit who held many positions in the kingdom—found that 800,000 pesos had been spent from the Royal Treasury. This did not include losses to the king's vassals, who spent great sums in rebuilding their mills for grinding ore and attracting a labor force. Some of the people who had worked there previously had been killed. Others had left or were dispersed by the uprising. There was also immeasurable damage and loss of [other types of] property.

The loss of lives was even greater in this recently settled territory, which had only a small number of Spaniards. [635] To encourage settlement, special royal privileges are granted to the first Spanish settlers of towns or villas in these provinces. More than two hundred Spaniards as well as many more black slaves and Indians who were long-time Christians died in the province. It is my belief that quite a few of the latter died for our Holy Faith. I do not doubt that if they had joined in the unholy Tepehuan apostasy, the Tepehuan would have protected them and taken them into their company. This was especially true of the Indians who, after all, were like the Tepehuan, albeit from different nations such as the Mexican and Tarascan. They nevertheless died like Christians and did not join the Tepehuan apostates.

The damages referred to were those suffered by our side; however, the losses suffered by the enemy were just as great. More than a thousand persons from the Tepehuan nation must have died in the war and from the hunger and harsh life that they endured in the monte. Their houses, pueblos, and fields were all destroyed.

Turning now to the lamentable spiritual damage, which is what the devil most wanted, I will leave for the time being the many religious who experienced glorious deaths like those that have [already] been related. What was most regrettable was to see so many people who had received divine light—and many with great enthusiasm—deceived by diabolical doctrine. These people, who had abandoned the darkness of their gentile state, went back to it and to their idolatries and superstitions. Damage of these types was not confined to the lands of the Tepehuan nation. Instead, sparks flew from this infernal fire, endangering other lands and nations. Indeed, they ignited many people, and it took much time and effort to extinguish them, as we will see below. The reason for recounting all these damages will become clear in the following chapter.

45. From 1548 until 1723 the Spanish crown claimed as a tax or royalty one-fifth of all silver brought by bullion merchants to the royal smeltery (Haring 1947:259–60).

46. Cervantes Casaus was a knight of the Order of Santiago and *contador mayor* of the Real Audiencia; his brother, Gonzalo Cervantes Casaus, was governor of Nueva Vizcaya (1630–33).

CHAPTER XXXIII The spiritual and temporal advantages offered by the conversion of the Tepehuan and other barbarous peoples

Now I must state why I have summarized all the damage done by the Tepehuan—a subject that I could have expanded upon were it not for my concern with the brevity of this history and the [fact that] I have already dealt with the subject (albeit it in passing). My intention is that the advantages of reducing these people to our Holy Faith be made known. First, this is what the Catholic kings have charged in their decrees and provisions, thus faithfully carrying out the responsibility that the Vicars of Christ have entrusted to them for the spiritual as well as temporal good of these people. As is very apparent and has often been remarked in this history, the past and present Majesties have fulfilled this obligation with royal generosity and munificence. The world should know this about these very remote provinces. My intentions, however, do not cease here; I also wish to make it known that it is of great temporal as well as spiritual advantage (for when God gives, it should not be turned down) to keep the peace and preserve the Divine Faith in these nations, continuing to reduce them to the Gospel. This serves both Majesties, not only the Divine, but the human. Certainly, [636] if the Faith of Christ does not reach these peoples, their lands cannot be safely entered nor can their treasure of silver ore be discovered. In this regard it must be noted that the Indians are not harmed by mining, inasmuch as they did not take advantage of the silver deposits [before the conquest] nor did they possess techniques or knowledge of mining. With regard to the advantages of having Spaniards working the [mines], the Indians who are employed in the mines are well treated (as is to be supposed), as they now have the advantages of clothing and live like civilized human beings rather than wild beasts. The Spaniards defend them from other enemy nations and gentiles who [once] killed them. I say this because I know what goes on in Nueva España.

Now, if these peoples were to remain gentiles and were not reduced to our Holy Faith, then it would be impossible to obtain their constant loyalty, which is sustained and nourished in large part by the Faith of Our Lord Jesus Christ. If this should fail, then one can expect daily attacks on Spaniards. Morning attacks will be planned the night before in drunken gentile orgies, which they celebrate for the purpose of working themselves up into a fury. Their sorcery is worked for this purpose and it will persist unless the Faith and the Gospel of Christ destroy it. Where they are lacking, nothing is safe—neither human life or property can survive. The final conclusion to be drawn from all this is that royal funds are gloriously employed in both the human and divine realms to introduce and preserve the Divine Faith among these peoples. And finally, in winning them for Christ, that treasure is found that the divine Lord preached of in this world when He said in His parable that a prudent man would sell everything he has to buy his own field. Besides the spiritual treasure of very many souls who are saved (instead of them all being lost to heathenism), great treasures of silver also are discovered among these nations and their human and divine fields. God preserved this silver for the defense of the Catholic Faith and Church, and so that Faith could spread to the Indies, among even poor and barbarous nations.

I cannot help but mention something that has been observed in Nueva España that confirms this argument of divine providence. It is that the purest and greatest number of silver mines that God has given to Our Lord the king and his vassals in this vast kingdom have their source in the lands of the fiercest and most barbarous peoples that have been discovered. God thus shows that the reason He placed this silver in such places was so that through this means the light of the Gospel might reach and be preserved among peoples who His divine clemency did not scorn. In order not to speak at length and without proof, I will here explain something to which all those in Nueva España can bear witness. Nearly all the major mines of this kingdom are located in the north, among barbarous nations. There are few in the southern and middle regions, where little ore has been found. The most celebrated of these mines is called San Luis Potosí. Its ores are rich in gold, which is mixed with the silver. The ore can be likened to the crystallite of Holy Scripture because, as the miners note, it is composed of two precious metals. The silver from these mines is so rich that the mark or stamp on ingots or silver sheet already subjected to the royal fifth is valued at fourteen or more pesos, whereas under royal law the mark or stamp for the highest-grade ore from other mines is valued at no more than eight pesos and six reales. This high value is due to the gold that is found in the silver lodes, which is not found elsewhere in Nueva España.

The point here is [637] that such rich deposits were discovered in the lands of the fiercest, poorest, and most barbarous nation of the Indies—the famous Chichimec nation. This name is so famous that when one wants to say that an Indian is barbarous, ignorant, and a gentile, one refers to him as a Chichimec. It is a word used not only by the more civilized Mexican nation, but also by our barbarous nations, who consider it an insult to be called Chichimec. The ferocity of the Chichimec was such that no matter how many times the ancient Mexica tried to subjugate them—and the Mexica were very powerful and numerous—the Chichimec proved indomitable. Later, the Spaniards also tried to subjugate them but many died at the hands of the Chichimec. Although a great deal of the king's money was spent trying to subdue them in an effort to gain access to the rich mines in their lands, the Chichimec were not pacified until evangelical ministers began preaching among them. More than a small part was played by the Company of Jesus. This will be seen later when [I write] about the Jesuit residence and mission that were founded there by order of Viceroy Don Luis de Velasco, for the purpose [of bringing] peace to those lands in which God had located the previously mentioned mines of San Luis Potosí.

Thirty leagues inland God created the famous mines of the city of Zacatecas, which have been the richest and steadiest [producers in all] of Nueva España. It would take a long time to count all the wagons that have left here for Mexico City, or the number of ships filled with silver from here that have sailed for Spain. It is widely known that among the many rich miners of Zacatecas some have paid the king five hundred thousand pesos in taxes from their mines. How much must they have made from the bars of silver that were stamped and registered,[47] and from which were taken the crown's tax of a fifth? You figure it out. Here I will state only that God placed these riches in the lands of the wild Zacatecas Indians as a dowry so that the light of the Gospel could be communicated to them.

Let us go northward to the lands of barbarous nations where we find the mines of Parral, Guanaceví, San Andrés, and Topia. These mines are and have been very rich, as have others that are less known, including ones that are [presently] being discovered. God located all of them in the lands of barbarous and poor peoples, particularly in the lands of the Tepehuan, of whom we speak. Divine goodness did so in order that these people would have the means for salvation, as they did. Indeed, although it is the case that the Tepehuan were deceived by the devil and became apostates, many other more populous nations, about whom this history has spoken at length, persevere today in their Christianity. It is true that many of the rebel Tepehuan did not remain firm in their Christianity. However, those who were perverted and who survived the rebellion have been quieted. They have now been disabused of their false and diabolical idol. They have been gathered together and reconciled with their true God, who pardoned Saint Peter, [another] who denied him. Today, these reconciled Tepehuan and the mines in their territory are peaceful vassals and possessions of Our Lord the king, as will be seen in the following chapters.

47. In drawing the reader's attention to this registration process, Pérez de Ribas seems to imply that many or most miners did not register, and thus did not pay taxes on all the silver that they produced.

CHAPTER XXXIV The fathers of the Company once again endeavor to pacify the rebellious Tepehuan; the means employed for this purpose and their effects

[638] Of all the priests who were instructing the Tepehuan nation, only Father Andrés López was spared from death at their hands. As previously noted, God chose to look after him. As one who knew the [Tepehuan] language, Father López was able to keep the infernal wolf from the remainder of the flock, which he had kept together. Now that the lightning bolt of persecution had passed, God wanted Father López to cure and heal all those who were injured and suffering. The father carried out both duties. From his post at Indé, where we left him, he began to make new attempts to pacify his rebellious faithful. Although a good number of them were innocent and were not members of the rebellious faction, they nevertheless were afraid that they would be punished along with everyone else. Seeing that the governor was on a campaign, they fled to the mountains. Father López sent them various assurances of peace in the name of the viceroy and governor, from whom he had orders to offer peace. He wanted to protect these poor, misguided people, particularly those who had not been leaders in the general uprising of this nation.

The priest's first offers and attempts at peace were unsuccessful, because God wanted him to employ a more insignificant but unusually glorifying means which would reflect the application of divine mercy to this nation's ailments. Among the Tepehuan who were captured by the Spaniards there was an old, lame woman who was further weakened by other ailments. This woman offered to help resettle those Indians who had played a lesser role in the rebellion by conveying the priest's message and assurances [of peace]. Although the captain of the town where the woman was being held at first refused to release her, he finally turned her over at the request of the priest. The zealous minister of these people's souls took her to a safe place, where for two days he treated her with charity. He instructed her as well on how to win over those misguided people. At the end of this time he gave her a paper with the commission he had received from the viceroy and governor. As an even greater sign of the security that he prom-

ised them, he gave her his prayer book, which was well recognized by the Indians. He then sent her on her way.

The old, lame woman was accompanied for five leagues, at which point she was left on her own, even though it was obvious to everyone that she was not only incapable of making such a long trip, but also had only a short time to live. God, however, knows how to work with feeble instruments—although they may appear useless, it is this very appearance that makes them effective. Thus God gave this feeble woman the strength to go from ranchería to ranchería for nearly two hundred leagues until she finally came to the Tepehuan for whom she was searching. They listened well to the assurances that she brought from Father López. This occurred at such an opportune moment that a crowd of people offered to follow the woman and enjoy the tranquility and peace that was being offered them. Many of those who stayed behind were nevertheless favorably disposed toward returning to the abandoned pueblos and missions, there to rebuild their churches and live like true Christians. Although not everyone was won over by this first offer of resettlement—some still resisted obstinately (as we will later see)—this was a felicitous beginning for the general resettlement and salvation of a nation that had been so hopelessly lost. Father Andrés López was confident [639] that God was directly responsible for such a good beginning, and he hoped that His divine goodness would carry him forward. With this in mind he wrote to the Father Provincial requesting companions to help him in his undertaking of removing these souls from the claws of the devil, who had ferociously ravaged their souls. The viceroy and governor of [Nueva] Vizcaya wanted to restore this mission, which had been founded by the priests of the Company. Now that peace had returned to the land, one could move about as before; miners could return to mining and other business. The religious of the Company, being soldiers of the militia of Christ and undaunted by their brothers' deaths, generously offered themselves for this undertaking. The Father Provincial gave the assignment to Father José who had served in this mission and knew the Tepehuan language. Although Father José de Lomas was recuperating from difficult duties and ailments, he very enthusiastically offered to risk his health and life and return to the [Tepehuan mission], and so he was dispatched from Mexico City. When the Tepehuan received word that their former priest was returning, a good number of those who (as they say) had a good heart prepared to venture forth to welcome him. As we will see in the following chapter, they welcomed him in the main Tepehuan pueblo of Santiago Papasquiaro, which had been destroyed.

CHAPTER XXXV Father José de Lomas recounts in a letter how he was welcomed by the Tepehuan and their readiness [to embrace Christianity]

The letter that Father José de Lomas wrote to the Father Provincial in Mexico City reads as follows:

I reached the pueblo of [Santiago] Papasquiaro on the eighth of February [1618], where I was received with as much joy as if I were their own father. I nevertheless found everything in ruins and the church burned and destroyed. Only three small rooms of our dwelling were still standing. Since I arrived we have had dangerous snowstorms on three occasions; the winds have howled, and my companions and I have earned merits by enduring hunger.

As soon as I arrived, I led all the people to the Cross in the patio of the church, which had been desecrated. There we sang the prayers of the Christian doctrine. Each day we do the same, encouraging affection for our Holy Faith among those who had been deceived and had therefore abandoned it. In the morning the children return to receive instruction in the catechism and to learn about Confession, and in these matters their progress is evident.

My opinion of the Tepehuan is that, although they have learned their lesson, they are still not entirely reduced to our Holy Faith. Those who are disabused believe the devil—whom they used to see visibly—has not fulfilled his promises to them. The very same places where he had told them they would be most favored are where they have suffered the most. This suffering came in the form of the governor and Captain Suárez, who attacked their settlements, taking their women and children as prisoners. When these disabused people realized this and the falseness of our common enemy, they took the life of the great Quautlatas. He was the one who had the most intimate dealings with the devil, for he was a great sorcerer, somewhat like a priest of their new religion. He was the one who fomented and kept the rebellion going, directing the war. The Tepehuan were not satisfied with killing Quautlatas,

and afterward killed another of their [war] captains who had prevented them from making peace. [640] Yet another great sorcerer, who was considered an oracle and provided them with prophecies, remains at large. He has withdrawn with others who are among the guiltiest, whom I will attempt to reduce with the help of God and the prayers of Your Reverence. Guisivita, one of the captains of the pueblo of Santa Catalina and a great traitor, also is at large. He is camped with his people at a place that they call Boyagame. He has with him many Indians from Tecuchuapa and other nations, who consider him their cacique. He is the one who took in one of the Spanish maidens whom the Tepehuan had spared, although he has handed her back. He boasts that he will never settle peacefully.

I don't think this place is currently safe unless it has a detachment of soldiers. This was demonstrated by events that happened shortly before I arrived. The first case was a drunken revel that took place in Santa Catalina, during which one young man got furious at another and killed his assailant. To avenge that death the relatives of the dead man killed him. I will mention another case that shows how this uprising turned this nation back to its barbarous customs, which was the devil's intention. It happened just before Christmas, when there was a downpour that lasted eight days and the river violently rose as it had never done before. To pacify the river, the Indians took an infant from the arms of a poor woman. The two of them wailed, but nothing could prevent the Indians from throwing the infant into the river to placate it, as they were accustomed to doing in their gentile state. Perhaps this was done to save the life of a sick elder who was about to die, for with the death of a child he might yet live for many years. Spaniards who have traveled in these parts have told me that they had learned that every morning when the morning star shines, these Tepehuan greeted it and offered a very long speech to the sun, which they worshiped as God, along with the moon. These are all designs of the devil, who has owls fly over our house at night, attempting to frighten us with their sad hooting—as if that would scare us.

This is the end of the letter by Father Lomas, who described the state of affairs following the uprising when he was trying to establish peace, which the devil opposed in as many ways as he could. The Indians from the Valle de San Pablo, who were farthest away, unsuc-cessfully tried to kill the two priests who were there, although they did succeed in shooting a faithful Chris-tian woman full of arrows. However, in spite of all this, the fervent ministers of God were not intimidated. They continued their campaign to lead the remaining Tepehuan to their true God and Lord who had created and redeemed them.

CHAPTER XXXVI Four other priests from the Company come to aid in the restoration of the Tepehuan's Christianity; the heralded installation of a remarkable image that was desecrated during the uprising

The Tepehuan nation had been punished by Governor Gaspar de Alvear during his expedi-tion, and the principal leaders of the uprising had been put to death; other punishments also had been meted out by other captains. As a result, the viceroy of Nueva España decided that priests from the Company should attempt to rehabilitate these people. Four more religious were dispatched from Mexico City [in 1620] to help those who had already begun to establish peace. They were to help complete the re-duction of the Tepehuan and assist with their religious instruction and the re-establishment of churches. His Excellency ordered that an appropriate location and house be found where a detachment of several soldiers could be maintained to restrain troublemakers when-ever necessary. The garrison was to remain for as long [641] as it took to pacify and settle this nation.

The four priests who were sent to the Tepehuan mission arrived with great enthusiasm; they all were en-couraged to see themselves working in a land and har-vest that had been fertilized by the blood of martyrs, as the [priests who were killed during the uprising] were and [still] are called today by both the Spaniards and Indians of that region. The [priests] divided amongst themselves three former settlements and pueblos, and each one went his own way, summoning and inviting the people who were scattered throughout the moun-tains. Many of them, tired of the evil and wretched life into which the devil had led them, responded favor-ably to the priests' summons and returned to their pueblos. They began to repair them, along with their churches, which had been destroyed by the Tepehuan's diabolical fury. Their greatest rage and destruction had been inflicted on the holy images of Christ Our Lord and His saints, who were persecuted along with the blessed priests. Some images of the Most Holy Virgin especially suffered. They were desecrated by those be-deviled barbarians with diabolical fury, demonstrating their hellish impiety. These sacrileges were particularly painful to the Spanish miners residing at Guanaceví, who were particularly devoted to this Lady. Because of their ardent devotion and veneration of their Lady, Queen of Angels, they were very anxious to restore her honor and due veneration.

There was one case that most stood out during the restoration of this Christianity and must therefore be recorded here. It was noted previously that on the day when the four priests and Spanish residents of Guanaceví had gathered in the pueblo of El Zape to celebrate the installation of a beautiful image of the Most Holy Virgin, the bedeviled apostates executed their ferocity by taking the lives of the priests as well as the Spaniards and their servants. They did not [even] spare the holy image of the Mother of God. Instead, they dared to seize it with their sacrilegious hands, dashing it to pieces. Thus, one of the first acts by the priests who later came to settle this Christianity was to reinstall the image of this Lady in its [proper] place, restoring her honor. They placed these errant and misled sinners under her care and protection, returning them to the house and grace of her Son, restoring at the same time the appropriate piety due both Mother and Son.

There was a captain at the Guanaceví mining camp who had made a vow to the Virgin at the time of the rebellion that if she spared him from the dangers of war, he would refurbish her holy image and adorn it with the jewels that those infidels had stripped from her. He fulfilled his vow as soon as the storm of the rebellion began to subside, commissioning one of the most beautifully finished images in the kingdom. It was so beautiful that it seemed that God Our Lord had bestowed some special grace on the craftsman in order to restore the glory and honor of His Mother, who had been so disgraced in this pueblo. When this image was finished, her devotees kept it for some time in Guanaceví. Later it was placed in the church at El Zape, where [the original] had been desecrated and destroyed. When the appointed day arrived, many Indians from the three pueblos gathered in El Zape. They, along with the Spaniards, spared no effort, ornaments, or celebration in receiving the Queen of Heaven. She returned to her tabernacle and dwelling place triumphant over the devil and his allies, having been exiled by outrages far greater than those [642] she experienced when she fled with her son into Egypt.

The road from El Zape to Guanaceví was lined for a distance of half a league with triumphal arches, which the [Indians] had erected and decorated with flowers from their fields and mountains. At the place where they had taken the life of the two blessed fathers, Fonte and Moranta, who were on their way to celebrate the feast day, the [Indians] erected an enramada decorated with flowers. It was here that the Virgin was first displayed and where it seems Our Lady wanted to celebrate the triumph of her devotees and their faithful servants who had spilled their blood to honor her and her Most Blessed Son.

There is one thing particularly worth noting here that made this celebration greater and more joyful, and which later was celebrated as a very singular circumstance of this feast day. This was the sight of the converted Tepehuan's fervor. The Spaniards who were present were amazed and astounded by the Tepehuan's devotion and the happiness with which they responded to this celebration and feast day. The Spaniards had never before observed such fervent piety, even before the Tepehuan's apostasy from our Holy Faith. The Spaniards' own devotion was such that, from this enramada to the church where the holy image was to be placed, which was almost half a league, all of them traveled on foot. Many important individuals walked barefoot in this procession, which was celebrated with dances, flutes, and trumpets. When the Virgin entered the pueblo, it seemed to them that she was entering in triumph over her enemies. Like something celestial, it caused them such respect and reverence that they could not describe it. The following chapter will relate the installation of this holy image and the resulting devotion throughout the region.

CHAPTER XXXVII The holy image of the Virgin of the Martyrs is placed in the church of El Zape; the special favors that the faithful have received from her

The day the image of the Most Holy Virgin entered the pueblo of El Zape to be placed on the altar whence her enemies had torn her coincided exactly with the eve of the Feast of her Glorious Ascension, when the Queen of Heaven was placed above the seraphim. Late that afternoon most solemn vespers were sung, and that evening many luminaries were lit and a round of harquebus shots were discharged. There was music as well from bugles. The next day a Mass was sung to the accompaniment of an organ; there was a sermon and some persons shed as many tears as if it were the day of the Passion of Christ. Some of them cried when they remembered the desecration that the Mother of God had endured in that place and the deaths of her servants, four priests and eighty Spaniards of all ages [who were] their relatives, as well as many other Christians who had come to attend the feast. Others shed tears of devotion to see the Virgin return to her place, whence she was their protection and defense. When they took leave of this Lady to return to their homes, they shed tears of devotion anew. The people of this area have great affection for this holy image, which is the best attended and most famous sanctuary in this land. They bring their needs and afflictions to it to be resolved, and they come to her church to fulfill the vows and novenas that her veneration inspires. Many stories are told of miraculous favors that have been received by the gravely ill who have been healed, by women who have been aided during breech births, and by travelers in this region who have been delivered from dire straits after commending themselves to this holy image. In recognition of the favors and graces that the faithful have experienced, they have given her rich gowns and jewels and other ornaments for her altar. [643]

Among those who have become indebted to this sacred Virgin, I will relate here the story of one man whose offering, although not very rich, nevertheless demonstrated his singular devotion. This person was the owner of a large mule train that traveled these roads between the mining camps and the haciendas. The Virgin had rescued him from dangers that he had encountered along the roads, including one time when he was very seriously wounded by a lance thrust by an enemy. By invoking the Virgin of Martyrs he was spared. On another occasion during a snowstorm he and his mules and the goods they were carrying all were on the verge of being lost when he called upon the same Virgin, and they were saved. Immediately this devout traveler dedicated his best mule to the Mother of God. He named her María and handsomely adorned her, fastening a name tag on the mule that read, "Slave of Mary, for whom she labors." Everything that he earned through the mule was spent on the adornment of the Sovereign Virgin, who came to be known throughout this land as the Virgin of the Martyrs. Our Lady thus honored with that glorious title those whom she so esteems—those who died while celebrating her solemn feast in this place.

I will not stop here to relate other cases and favors that have been obtained through devotion to this holy image, which are well known throughout this land. However, one cannot omit noting what has been the most unusual and virtuous relic—the remains of another image that the Tepehuan apostates had destroyed during their rebellion. It is well known that a large number of people have been cured of various illnesses after drinking some of its dust mixed in water. It is believed that all this and more has been worked by the Son of God in honor of His Mother and to repair her honor. Although these favors of the most Holy Virgin and her Son are worthy of great gratitude and remembrance, worthy of even greater esteem are the spiritual favors that have been extended to the souls of the Tepehuan. They have come in peace to settle in this place in greater numbers than prior to the rebellion; they also are much more domesticated than before. They punctually attend religious instruction and the rest of the Christian exercises. On Saturdays, with special joy and devotion, they attend Mass and sing to their patron and restorer, the Virgin. Often Spaniards from Guanaceví come to confess and take Communion; they are attracted by the unusual devotion and miracles that they recognize as such. All the people of the region come from far and wide to attend her feast days.

We can say that the Tepehuan's Christianity, which was so ruined by the devil's wiles, has been repaired and restored by the hand of the Most Holy Virgin. It is no surprise that the false promise of the Tepehuan's idol and false god was not fulfilled—that he would resurrect those who died fighting against the Christians. The Son of God and the Most Holy Virgin counterat-tacked, truly resurrecting the Tepehuan's Christianity. This is true with respect to spiritual as well as temporal matters, for in all things she is the Mother of Mercy. When the uprising and rebellion were over, one of the richest mines of Nueva España was discovered in this land. It is called El Parral, and it has yielded a great treasure in silver. Today it is settled in Tepehuan lands by such a large number of [644] Spaniards that it is one of those most populated by them, as well as by many other laborers from Nueva España.

CHAPTER XXXVIII The Tepehuan nation is settled in peace; the reparation of offenses against holy images; the state of this Christianity

As previously discussed, the sacrileges committed by the Tepehuan against the Divine Sacrament and holy churches greatly offended God the Son and His Most Holy Mother. Nevertheless, He who shed His blood on the Cross [on behalf of] those who spilled it wished to pardon those Indians who had spilled [also] His blood by trampling on His Divine Sacrament throughout this land. God the Son and His Most Holy Mother wanted all the Tepehuan who had survived the uprising to be brought together to live in peace and Christianity, especially the people of the pueblos where the tempest and uprising had been most furious, such as El Zape, of which we have just spoken, and Santa Catalina and Santiago Papasquiaro.

These pueblos were once again settled, and some Spaniards even resettled in Santiago Papasquiaro, where they had lived before. Once the Indians were disabused of the lies and false promises of the sorcerers and devils, they were left more confirmed in the Faith. They built new churches and returned to religious instruction, becoming even better Christians than before. As a result of the havoc that was wreaked on them by the Spaniards, which they truly deserved for their crimes, they became tamer and more domesticated. They gave good testimony of this during the first Lent and Holy Week following the uprising. They celebrated with singular devotion the Christian exercises of that holy season, greatly aided by the good example of Spaniards from the garrison and from nearby settlements that were once again populated. These Spaniards attended all the services, including one that seems to have been arranged by God as reparation for the insults that His Most Holy Mother had received from these people.

As previously mentioned, the apostate Tepehuan had gone from pueblo to pueblo with their idol, making the people adore it. In this way the devil plotted the foretold ravages against all that was sacred, particularly images of the Most Holy Virgin. Once the uprising was over, God moved the hearts of the Indians of the Province of Culiacán, who are great and long-time Christians. Although they are some sixty leagues from the Tepehuan pueblos of Santa Catalina and Santiago, they were overcome by devotion to very reverently carry an image of Our Lady, which they believed worked miracles, through the same pueblos where the diabolical idol had passed. They did so in order to celebrate the woman who was the Mother of the one true God. When they reached the Tepehuan pueblos, they were welcomed with singular rejoicing. People came from sixty leagues away, staying for two or three days in each pueblo, celebrating the holy image with special affection and devotion.

The reparation that had been arranged by the divine

Son in honor of His Most Holy Mother did not end there. He wanted other celebrations to be held at even greater distances. Another image of the Virgin, which had been greatly mistreated by the Tepehuan, was in the possession of a resident of Mexico City, who was an honorable and landed gentleman who had conducted business in the mining camps of Durango. The image had been withdrawn to one of his haciendas two leagues from Mexico City, near a very famous sanctuary in Nueva España, which is known as Our Lady of Hope.[48] [645] There he built his home and dwelling place and a very unusual chapel dedicated to the image, which had been so abused by the Tepehuan. This gentleman had rescued her and had her repaired and adorned with jewels. She is greatly venerated by both him and the faithful when they come to visit that other famous sanctuary for Our Lady of Hope. She is considered to be the Conqueror of Mexico because her image was carried by one of the early Spanish conquerors. Similarly, we can call her the conqueror of the Tepehuan, who are much fiercer than the Mexica.

Those who have read what was recorded earlier concerning the outrage that the Tepehuan committed against the monstrance that contained the Holy Sacrament of the Altar, which was dashed to the ground, might wonder how this offense was repaired. I will briefly note that no sacrosanct relics were found, so angels must have lifted them to heaven, just as it is said that angels collected the blood that was spilled by the Redeemer of the World on Calvary at the hands of Pilate's praetor. The angels gathered the divine blood so that it could be returned to His veins when the Lord was resurrected. In our case the angels must have gathered up the holy relics, which contained the same blood, so that they could be placed in another holy monstrance. Alternatively, they took them to some decent place where the sacramental Species was consumed.

God did not arrange for the reparation of His Holy Sacrament in the same way that He repaired the damage done to images of His Most Holy Mother. Frequently the Most Holy Son has demonstrated that He is more attentive to His Mother's Honor than He is to His own. Nevertheless, the priests who went to work among the Tepehuan following the rebellion were concerned with

repairing the outrages that had been committed against so Sovereign a Sacrament. They once again placed it in the churches, altars, and tabernacles, introducing anew the supreme veneration, celebration, and use of this highly Divine Sacrament. As a result, the Tepehuan are as good Christians [now] as they have ever been, going back to the time when they were gentiles with barbarous customs. They have six priests from the Company of Jesus, who have endured great danger and hardship in order to repair and reinstate the teaching of the catechism, which young and old are learning better than before.

Once the land was quieted, the Lord Bishop of Durango, Don Fray Gonzalo de Hermosillo, of the Holy Order of Saint Augustine, wished to visit this nation and his sheep, who had now been gathered together. He noted in a letter to the Father Provincial of the Company the great joy with which he returned from his visit. He briefly described the state in which he found the Tepehuan, saying:

> I offer a thousand congratulations to Your Paternity for the great success that the priests of the Company have had in these parts, where their religious instruction promises very glorious results. I am very thankful to Our Lord for His countless mercies and good fortune in reducing these people during my time [in office as Bishop]. I respect and have the greatest affection for Your Paternity and the rest of my priests for all their efforts on behalf of these Indians. For my part I will do everything in my power to help and serve them in their missions. May Our Lord keep Your Paternity, etc.

To this point I have quoted the letter of the Bishop, who following this visit undertook a visit to the Province of Sinaloa. As previously discussed, it was during this visit [in 1631] that the Bishop's holy life ended.

I have declared here the state of the Tepehuan mission. In terms of population, it was diminished as a result of the ravages suffered during the rebellion. It nevertheless has improved in terms of its Christianity, in which it perseveres today in great peace. It should be understood as well that many more souls are being saved today as compared to when its population was greater.

48. Apparently Santa María de los Remedios de Totoltepec (see Lockhart 1992:244–45).

CHAPTER XXXIX The state of the Tarahumara nation, neighbors of the Tepehuan, following the establishment of peace

[646] In Chapter X of this book I began to discuss the reduction of the Tarahumara nation to our Holy Faith. This nation has a large population and is a neighbor of the Tepehuan. I interrupted my discussion of their conversion to recount the Tepehuan uprising, which also corrupted the neighboring Tarahumara, despite the fact that they are inherently more pacific, gentle, and docile. The fact is that even today the devil employs many and varied schemes to close the door and prevent the Gospel from reaching these people.

Although prior to the Tepehuan Revolt some Tarahumara had received the Gospel and were baptized, almost all of them today are still gentiles.[49] The Indian principal who saw to it that the people remained gentiles was the most perverse Indian among them; he was a cacique named Oñate. It was said that he had killed with his own hands Father Juan Fonte, who was minister and superior of the Tepehuan mission. Although the governor of Nueva Vizcaya went to great lengths during one of his campaigns to find Oñate, he was unable to get his hands on him. Later, when another captain went with a priest to re-establish peace with the Tarahumara, God willed that the perverse Indian should pay for his evil deeds. God wanted to do away with this instrument of evil whom the devil had relied on to impede the teaching of the Gospel. As a result, the captain devised an ingenious plan to capture him, whereupon Oñate was hanged from a tree that served as a gallows. During the uprising this Indian had used this same tree to hang a long-time Christian Indian who had worked in the mines. While the Indian hung from the tree, Oñate cruelly cut his body in half.

God wanted this Indian to pay for his crime in the very same place, although not with the same cruelty that Oñate had employed. Nor did God punish him with the same rigor with which He judged other leaders of the uprising, who died disastrously in the war. God touched Oñate's heart, and so he acknowledged his guilt. At the foot of the gallows he carefully confessed and, having previously been baptized, he died leaving very good reassurances of his salvation. The blessed Father Juan Fonte, who died at his hands, must have interceded in heaven on Oñate's behalf. In the end this Indian died so disabused that he concluded his life with a speech in which he charged his people to live well and in peace, according to the law of God that they had accepted.

With the death of this Indian God finished punishing and removing from this land the leaders of the rebellion and apostasy. However, there was still one other barbarous Indian extremist who became angry with the priest when the latter began encouraging the people to return to their pueblos so that they could enjoy peace. This Indian persuaded the people to return to the mountains and their licentious lifestyle. God, however, changed this man in such a way that he completely reversed himself, becoming one of the principales who helped gather his people into pueblos for religious instruction.

These are all cases and events that can serve to reassure those who are called to these enterprises by God and His institution. Although they may be besieged by hardship and danger, they will not fail because, through the Lord's favor, they will achieve glorious victories. And even if some of their brothers have lost their temporal lives in this endeavor, they nevertheless have gone to enjoy eternal life with God in heaven. Those who have remained on earth continue to harvest abundant fruits not only of their own, but also fruits from the seed that was sown [647] by those who are now in heaven. A letter that I have saved until now will serve as confirmation of this point. It is from the priest of the Tepehuan mission, who offered to our Father Provincial to go and instruct the Tarahumara, whom we are discussing here.[50] He says:

49. When Pérez de Ribas refers to "today," he means 1639, rather than 1645, when the *Historia* was published. During these intervening years, new missions were founded and thousands of Tarahumara were baptized (Alegre 1956–1960, vols. 2, 3; Dunne 1948).

50. This letter (AGN 1638) apparently was written in 1638 by Gaspar de Contreras to Pérez de Ribas, who at the time was Jesuit provincial.

Many thanks must be given God for the joy with which these people come and assemble for religious instruction. It is apparent that everything has been well arranged, thanks to the merits and great hardship that was endured by our priests who died here: *Alij lavorauerunt, sed nos introuimus in labores eorum.*[51] I ask Your Reverence on bended knee, with all the truth and love in my soul (even though I am unworthy to count myself among the Company's missionaries) to allow me to devote my life and strength to this mission in the Valle de San Pablo. There have been few things in my entire life that I have wanted more. Indeed, I can say that I have had a special devotion and calling for this: I have been so inspired that it seems to me that my entire happiness and salvation rest with this enterprise. All that remains is for Your Reverence to confirm this assignment, which is so removed from human comforts and whose sole purpose is to serve Our Lord and His Company. I will most willingly give my life in this quest.

Up to here I have cited a portion of a letter from this religious and fervent priest, which was written with the desire to go and instruct the gentile Tarahumara. At the time of the writing of this history it has not yet been possible to begin this [mission], owing to certain fortunate or unfortunate events plotted by the devil. As is always the case, his goal is to impede the way of the Gospel and to disrupt the conversion of this nation's almost one thousand families.[52] In spite of this, two of our priests who were sent from Mexico City for this enterprise are standing at the door and waiting to enter.[53]

To conclude my discussion of this entire mission I will record [in the following chapters] the lives and unique circumstances surrounding the deaths of those who watered and fertilized this mission with their blood. These lives will be presented in lieu of the lives of illustrious men—like those recorded at the end of the other books—who, although they did not suffer a violent death for Christ, still spent their lives assisting others with the salvation of their souls.

CHAPTER XL The life and apostolic ministries of the venerable Father Juan Fonte, killed by Tepehuan apostates for preaching our Holy Faith

The joyous deaths suffered for the cause that has been referred to at length throughout this book was sufficient to make illustrious and worthy of remembrance the eight religious from the Company of JESUS who, in order to expand the glory of that most holy name, died at the hands of the impious Tepehuan. Because they lived their lives with such great and heroic virtue, these virtues deserve to be recorded and, thus, their deaths will be made more illustrious. We can very rightfully presume that they live on in the everlasting memory of the righteous.

We will begin with the lives of those who worked for the greatest number of years cultivating the fields and thorny wilderness of the fierce Tepehuan nation—the enterprise that cost them their lives. The first of these will be the venerable Father Juan Fonte, whom I knew and dealt with personally, albeit only briefly. This was many years before this nation rebelled, when I passed through [his mission] on my way to the Province of Sinaloa. I can certify that during those few days that I enjoyed his religious company, I gained a great understanding of the holy, burning zeal and untiring charity with which this venerable man endeavored to lead those lost souls who lived in such inaccessible places—and in the shadow of death [648]—to salvation. His desire to gather and tame them was the same as wanting to remove lions and tigers from their dens and then taming them. On this occasion, when I realized the hardships that this apostolic missionary had endured, I asked a Tepehuan cacique whether his Indians greatly

---

51. "Our labor is that of others who came before us."

52. Pérez de Ribas is alluding here to trouble stirred up in April 1638 by a Tepehuan cacique, which led to the brief suspension of missionary activity among the Tarahumara (AGN 1638).

53. In June 1639 Fathers José Pascual and Gerónimo de Figueroa reached Parral and within a few months began working among the Tarahumara.

loved and respected Father Fonte (this was long before their uprising, when the priest was still busy reducing them). The cacique responded, "Our people love him a great deal; now that he has to go farther inland to people who have not yet been baptized, I will accompany him and help with their reduction."

During the early days of this mission there were a number of people like this who later went back on their word. It is nothing new for those who were once good Christians to become corrupted and to reverse their good beginnings and intentions with respect to the Faith and living virtuous lives. When after three years of preaching the Apostle Saint Paul took leave of the Bishops and priests of Asia, he addressed them with almost continuous tears. The holy Apostle told them that, despite the marvels and miracles that he regularly had worked, a perverse man would arise in their midst who would disrupt and pervert the Lord's flock: *Ego scio, quoniam es vobis ipsis exurgent viri loquentes perversa, ut abducant discipulos post se.*[54] This is a statement that is well worth noting and pondering because of its relevance to what we are now discussing. It is a statement and assertion by the Apostle of the People, who was unceasing in his apostolic preaching. Even though he had right before his eyes those who had received his holy teaching and seen his miracles and tears, some of them would nevertheless go back on their word, indeed to the extent that they would turn into wolves, which is how the Apostle referred to them. They would destroy Christ's flock, which he had gathered by enduring so many hardships.

It is also nothing new for saints to be paid with death for their beneficence toward those who kill them. In this way they resemble their captain, JESUS. The same thing happened to Father Juan Fonte, who had loved, instructed, and favored his Tepehuan. Indeed, when I learned of the destruction wrought by the Tepehuan against their missionaries, I was amazed at their cruelty and the fact that they had not spared the priest who had benefited them for so many years and who had been such a loving father (enduring great hardship for them as well). In the end, God, for whom these hardships had been suffered, wished to reward him with the crown of martyrdom.

Father Juan Fonte was born in Teraza, in Barcelona.

54. *Margin Note*: Act. 20. Acts 20:29–30: "I know . . . there will be men among your own number who will come forward with a false message, and find disciples to follow them" (Knox 1956:138).

He entered the Company in 1593 at the age of nineteen. He came to Nueva España from the Province of Aragón in 1599 with Father Master Pedro Díaz, who was Father Provincial of Nueva España. He then set out for the Tepehuan mission, where he succeeded its founder, Father Gerónimo Ramírez. In 1604 he professed his four vows in the Company. He spent a little more than sixteen years of his life converting the indomitable Tepehuan. For many of them he was their first priest— the one who had given them rebirth in Christ through Holy Baptism. He went to the Tepehuan alone, without an escort of soldiers and with an intrepid spirit, although he trusted in God, being one of His ministers. He traveled fifty leagues inland through the mountains and the solitude of that land of infidels, where no other Gospel minister had ever been before. His home was a little canopy [649] made of sackcloth, in which he would say Mass. In these deserts of intractable peoples, he ordinarily went an entire ten months without seeing another Spaniard. Many times all he ate were some toasted kernels of maize, and when he lacked even this much, he ate plants from the fields. He drank rainwater from puddles. He resembled the desert fathers of antiquity, to whom he was very similar not only in his meager and tattered attire, but also in the venerable beard that he had grown as a result of his lack of a razor or anyone to shave him. This is the way he returned to Christian lands—so thin and unrecognizable that it caused pity to see him in such poor condition. However, this holy man returned each time joyful and contented, having snatched away the devil's prey by continually bringing large numbers of barbarous Indians to the waters of Holy Baptism. After he had them congregated, and in order to make them even more settled, he taught them how to build houses, giving them tools made with his own hands. His charity reached such great lengths that sometimes he would plow their fields and teach them how to till them. He also obtained oxen to oblige them to live as Christians and adopt a civilized life; in one sense he made rational men out of beasts. When they became sick he cured them with his own hands. He would cook their food for them and, with singular love, he would place it in their mouths like a pious mother. The stipend that the king provides ministers for their clothing and sustenance he spent on his Indians; as noted, he himself lived in extreme poverty. His bed frequently was the hard ground or, as a luxury, a buffalo hide or a board. He was not satisfied with such a life of continual penance, and so he added studded belts and frequent and rigorous scourging. His humility was profound and his prayer frequent, both in settlements and in the countryside. He offered the sacrosanct sacrifice of Mass with such preparation and devotion that he frequently endeared those who heard it. Finally, this blessed priest's charity (which is the crown among virtues) shone in him so brightly that it seems that he wanted to take everyone into his heart. His love could very clearly be seen to sprout from the love that he had for the divine Redeemer of the World, who died for these Indians and for everyone. There was no one else, not even here, who was strong enough to summon the spirit to suffer so many hardships and such a prolonged exile. These lasted for so many years that it seems we can compare them with those suffered by the great saints.

Father Fonte had a gift for learning barbarous languages which, although he was not conceited about it, was nevertheless the result of divine favor. He learned Tepehuan with such propriety and distinction that when he spoke he seemed to be one of them. He wrote a grammar and vocabulary of Tepehuan as well as a lengthy catechism. The priests who have since followed [in his footsteps] have learned Tepehuan very easily using these works, and their instruction of this nation has produced great fruit in these souls. In these ministries he united the attributes of a perfect anchorite, praying for the greater glory of God and the honor of His Church while fulfilling the office of an Apostle, providing Him with many thousands of new children and erecting quite a few temples and churches. It sometimes happened that the Indians, led by their natural inconstancy, abandoned their pueblos and the churches that the priest had built with so much labor and at such personal cost. They would say that they were not satisfied with these places. There were times when just one disruptive group or ranchería would cause the abandonment of five pueblos that he had built and congregated. In these instances the humble priest would acquiesce so as not to upset them and in order to make God's law easier on them; he paid no mind to how much each pueblo and church had cost him. Nevertheless, his patience and perseverance were so admirable and constant that he managed to congregate and establish many pueblos. By enduring immense hardship he was able to lead large numbers of naked Indians out of the mountains to Baptism and the Lord's holy law.

While this evangelical minister was occupied in these [650] highly apostolic ministries, he wrote a letter that I will excerpt here. In it blossomed the holy zeal that burned in his heart for the salvation of these souls who cost him such fatigue and sweat.

> When I was in the pueblo of Indé (he writes), so many people came to see me from six or seven leagues farther inland that I was touched and regretted greatly not being able to go with them as they insisted. Therefore, I said to myself, "How I wish I had the power not to have to rely on or turn to the viceroy, and could go to preach the Holy Gospel like our father Saint Francis Xavier! I would do so even if it meant risking my life, for I would make good use of that power for the conversion of souls."

With these brief arguments this servant of God made clear the fervor of his desires. His intention was to bring the fiercest and most remote nation of the world to know God. The last nation he converted was the Indians of what is called the Valle de San Pablo. At one time they were so bloodied that they alone had the entire neighboring Province of Santa Bárbara up in arms. However, this priest domesticated, converted, and baptized them. Some of them—moved by their inherent barbarous freedom and primarily instigated by Satan—were like wild young bulls and would not patiently endure the Christian life and its divine commandments. In order to shirk the gentle yoke of Jesus Christ, they tried many times to take His minister's life. In fact, on two occasions they had him locked up and did not give him anything to eat for a long time so that he would starve to death. However, because his time had not arrived, Our Lord did not give them license for the execution of their sacrilege.

The holy priest never abandoned his apostolic task, despite this ingratitude. If he had wanted, he could have abandoned these many dangers for other duties for which he was very talented. However, he had no desire to abandon those wretched, naked Indians. He preferred helping them over all the university chairs and pomp in the world; they were the reason for his self-imposed exile from Spain. What is certain is that by remaining with these people, this apostolic man did great honor to his religious order and mother, the Company of JESUS. He left great examples of his virtues for his brothers, and these have been recounted here in general, without considering many specific deeds. It would be an endless task to try to recount all the heroic virtues that he exercised. For many years he was superior of the entire Tepehuan mission. He suffered martyrdom at their hands, along with the other priests who were his companions, and this took place in the manner that has been recounted. I will not relate it here because it suffices to know that for his blessed triumph and good fortune he placed himself in that danger and finally ended up spilling his blood for the preaching of the Gospel of Christ Our Lord. This is the same as dying out of love for Him who, in emphasizing the perfection and exhalation of this love, said: *Maiorera hac dilectionem nemo habet, ut animam suam ponat quis pro amicis suis.*[55]

The love of Christ Our Lord brought this, His faithful servant, from Spain to the most remote part of the Indies and this difficult enterprise. And this same love brought him to the brink of death, which he [finally] suffered. Although on this occasion he did not escape death, there were innumerable such occasions throughout his many years [as a missionary]. There were dangerous moments just like his last, when he found himself offering his life to God for the sake of his fellow man. This was not only after he had withdrawn and was out of danger, but when danger stared him right in the eyes and he heard the death sentence pronounced against him. We can say [651] that, by offering to die, Father Juan Fonte many times tasted death, as the excerpt from his letter demonstrates. Because this blessed priest was one of the first to convert these people when they were still naturally wild and ignorant, he necessarily suffered more and experienced greater dangers than later priests.

The blessed hour finally did arrive when he gave the life that he had so often offered for Christ. The governor of Nueva Vizcaya, Don Gaspar de Alvear, who was there when the holy bodies were gathered up, said that each of the priests was recognizable, as they all were intact and without a trace of bad odor. Lying next to the bodies of Father Fonte and Gerónimo de Moranta (whom I will

discuss later) were some papers with sermons written on them. Although they had been there almost an entire month and had been rained and snowed on, they were as undamaged as if they had been kept in a box. During this time some little dogs that the priests kept to guard their mounts in unpopulated areas remained so vigilant guarding the corpses that when the Spaniards arrived, they barked as if to direct them to where their owners lay. This showed that the priests had gotten more loyalty out of these dogs than they had out of those barbarians to whom they had been loving fathers and teachers.

Father Juan Fonte died on November 19, 1616, in the pueblo known as San Ignacio del Zape, at the hands of its inhabitants. The latter were joined by those [Tepehuan] who just the previous day had martyred the other priests in the pueblo of Santiago Papasquiaro. Their leader was the previously mentioned Indian apostate named Francisco de Oñate. Because his concubinage with many women caused a scandal, the priests spoke to him as a parish priest might, reprehending him and giving him good advice. In payment for this and mainly under the influence of their false idol, who they said spoke to them, they killed these servants and ministers of God.

Let it be pointed out here for the account of this man's life, and for those of his companions who also suffered death, that the principal matters recounted herein are in accordance with and taken from authentic accounts obtained by authority of the Bishop of Durango shortly after these priests' deaths. These accounts are kept in the archives of the Province of Mexico.

55. John 15:13: "This is the greatest love a man can shew, that he should lay down his life for his friends" (Knox 1956:106).

CHAPTER XLI The life, remarkable virtues, hardships, and martyrdom of the evangelical minister Father Juan del Valle

After Father Juan Fonte, Father Juan del Valle worked for the greatest number of years as a missionary to the Tepehuan. He tended to their souls with invincible patience and perseverance and was among the others who died at their sacrilegious hands. He was made truly illustrious not only by his martyrdom, which he suffered preaching the Holy Gospel, but through his remarkable and heroic virtues, which characterized his apostolic ministry.

I begin my discussion of his virtues by noting that this great servant of God was born of a noble lineage in the city of Vitoria, Vizcaya. In 1591, at the age of fifteen, he entered the Company in the Province of Castilla. From the outset he was an example of all virtues, which increased each day during his twenty-five years in the Company. He was not only [652] a very observant religious, but one with apostolic desires that continued unabated until he gave his life for God. In 1594 he left Castilla for Nueva España with a burning desire to convert many souls through a knowledge of their Creator, and to die a martyr. After his studies in Mexico, at which he excelled, Father del Valle, who was already a priest and had completed the third [year of] probation in the Company, was appointed to the Tepehuan mission. There he endured many exquisite challenges in the service of God and for the glory of His holy name. This alone was enough to elevate him to the highest level of virtue and to make more apparent its presence in him.

In reviewing his very religious and holy life, we can cite his strict observance of the rules and Institute of our father Saint Ignatius, to which God, to whom he was extremely devoted, had called him. The testimony of several who knew and had dealings with him states that they never saw or noticed anything that would contradict all that was said about such a saintly man and perfect religious. Because of his deep and profound humility he desired to see himself humiliated and defeated on behalf of Christ. He not only desired as much, but actually accepted the lowliest and most humiliating jobs, working like a menial laborer on the construction of churches. In imitation of his holy companion, Father Juan Fonte, he worked for and with the Indians in order to domesticate them, teaching them how to cultivate their lands. Because of his love for them, he denied himself bread and sustenance and became the cook for the barbarians who worked building the church. He distributed among them the stipend that the king generously gave him for his clothing and sustenance. He was happy with just a little toasted maize and frequently ate only plants gathered from the countryside. He treated the Indians with great love and tenderness, as if he were the father of each one of them. This affection was such that it overflowed his heart and was evident in his words. When he referred to them, including those who wanted to kill him, he would say, "They are my children, they are my brothers." Although this manner of speaking is not understood by those of this world, it accorded very well with Christ's laws and teachings, which Father Juan del Valle respected during his life.

One can well imagine that he who labored on behalf of ungrateful barbarians did as much for those who were not his inferiors. And to his greater merit, Our Lord permitted that he should very patiently accept insults not only from Indians, but from high-class Spaniards. At times they added grave lies to the insults—lies that not even the great saints were able to escape. However, Our Lord freed him from this [blasphemy] to the great credit of his sanctity and virtue.

Father del Valle was a man of great resolve who totally divorced himself from the things of this world. Although he could very well have taken an illustrious position in the order, he always wished and chose to work converting the humble Indians. He enjoyed being a missionary so much that he used to say, "[Even] if God Our Lord had given me very great talents and the wisdom of an angel, I would [still] gladly discard everything to be able to help these poor little Tepehuan Indians."

His poverty was so great that he ordinarily wore only an old, mended cassock, which provided little protection in that region. Although he was the superior, he appeared to everyone to be the cook. There are a number of people who have testified that the priest's skin was exposed during very cold weather because of his torn cassock. This was not because he lacked [money to buy clothing], but rather because he was so generous and charitable he shared all he had. Miners and other Spaniards offered and begged him to take silver. Whenever he accepted it, it was to buy clothing for his naked Tepehuan, whom he considered his children. He kept for himself his deep love of holy [653] poverty and a great desire to suffer for Christ. He united a life of religious observance with the apostolic life of evangelical preaching. Although he was very austere and hard on himself, his charity toward others was great. He treated with fatherly affection the Spaniards who came to work the mines in the region, substituting love and affection for the little he could offer in the way of material resources. He always let his guests use his poor bed. Many times his only bed was a plank or a piece of cowhide; this was the case even during the harshest days of winter. He spent eight months of the year in the desert, traveling fifty leagues inland to convert gentiles and living under a tent. In Indian pueblos he stayed in little xacales or cramped and flimsy huts that were made of branches and straw and which had only a mat covering the window and doorway, allowing the cold and wind to enter freely. Some called these blessed priests the hermits of Thebaid,[56] and not without good reason. Not only did these hermits live in poverty and among men who were as fierce as the very beasts of the mountains, but they surpassed the recluses [of antiquity] in their penance by pacifying these wild beasts and converting them into docile sheep so that they could be reduced to Christ's flock.

The above-mentioned exercises did not satisfy Father Juan del Valle, who treated his body as an enemy, punishing it with painful studded belts. He also scourged himself to the point of bleeding. He did this with such frequency that when he traveled with others, he would get up during the night and go into a field where he would discipline himself without being seen. Often he offered to do the penance for sins committed by those whose confessions he heard; on such occasions he would double the penance.

It could be said that this servant of God fasted continuously. He fasted every Friday and Saturday and during vigils to the saints to whom he was devoted. These fasts consisted of bread and water, or alternatively, what is called ezquite, which is made from kernels of roasted [maize] that are mixed with water from the river. When there was no river handy—which often is the case—he would use water from a pool of standing water. In this land there was hardly [enough] wine to say Mass. When he traveled and occasionally stopped at the house or ranch of a Spaniard who invited him to eat, they knew that he would only taste their delicious food, preferring to discreetly leave it so it would later be given to the children who helped him during Mass.

Although it may seem that I have recorded similar, and at times, the same virtues and behavior for other holy men, it should be kept in mind that, because they are holy, I cannot ignore those who gloriously exercised such virtues. Usually they did so in singular ways, further adorning these virtues and behavior, which complement others that are particular to each of these illustrious men.

For twelve years the apostolic Father Juan del Valle preached to Christians and gentiles throughout the Tepehuan province, evidencing humility, extreme poverty, and disdain for things of this world. As we have mentioned, he experienced innumerable difficulties, hunger, thirst, and exhaustion. He risked his life to baptize many thousands of wild beasts, whom he removed from their dens. He founded many churches, which he adorned with ornaments and images, and he destroyed a stone idol that these wretched people worshiped. This so upset the devil that he made the earth tremble, spout fire, and do other strange things. The devil's inventions were not enough, however, to keep this priest [654] from realizing victory in the battle that he undertook for the honor of God.

Father del Valle spoke to others in words that were measured yet had flair and grace. With each word he seemed to throw a dart of fire at men's hearts. He wielded such authority that he was always successful, no matter how hard or difficult the task (as witnesses confirm). He resolved disputes and deadly hatred before they reached the point of dissension and discord. He brought peace wherever he went; everyone put themselves in his hands out of respect and reverence for him. He was so successful that they nicknamed him Father Juan of Peace; he is still known by this name in that province.

Ever since the day that this servant of God consecrated himself to His divine service, he gave himself over to the holy exercise of prayer. He prayed for hours not only during the day, but at night, when he quietly retired with prayer. The countryside and thickets were his oratory. He prayed the Divine Office kneeling down and would say Mass with such devotion that [it

---

56. Thebaid was a great monastic settlement of fourth-century Egypt.

seemed} he was praying to his listeners. His lifetime devotion to the Most Holy Virgin was rare. From this devotion sprung his great virginal integrity and purity, which he guarded from birth to death. In order to preserve this, he relied on an admirable circumspection and control over his senses and powers, thus working in cooperation with the favors he received from Our Lady, the Virgin Mary. When he heard her sweet name, his soul was moved and his eyes filled with tears. He made many vows to serve this Lady and accepted every request made on her behalf. In accordance with his profession, he renewed that vow every day. He signed with his own blood a letter in which he committed himself to be a slave of this Sovereign Princess. Being a prisoner of love, he wore a rosary instead of a chain and every day he knelt and said the Rosary. As tribute from her vassal, he consecrated each day all his thoughts and deeds to the Queen of Heaven. On all of her feast days and the eight days of her octave, he prayed at least seven litanies and would say an additional Rosary in her honor and praise, substituting the following prayer for the Hail Mary: "My soul rejoices in your glory, My Lady; you are the very Holy Virgin Mother of God." He said this Rosary 150 times—every Saturday as well as during vigils and on feast days.

All this affection sprouted from his soul, which was filled with devotion to so sovereign a Mother and Lady. He fasted every Saturday and on the eve of her feast days. Day and night he visited a cherished image [of the Virgin], which the savages shot with arrows and then dropped into a well at the time of his martyrdom. It seemed that the very holy Virgin wanted to honor her devoted son's martyrdom by having her own image suffer—an image that he had devoutly venerated. Father Juan del Valle never acted without consulting and requesting the favor of this divine Lady. He invited everybody from the whole region to her feasts in the pueblos, which were celebrated with great solemnity, devotion, and whatever was possible in terms of elaborate scenic display. He preached the devotion of his slavery throughout that land, founding brotherhoods that were dedicated to her and which yielded a great fruit of souls and honor for this Lady. Her servants were honored to wear the rosary around their neck as a sign of their slavery. This devotion to Our Lady is recognized by the Church when it prays, *Ego diligentes me, diligo.*[57] She truly loves those who truly love and serve her. In accordance with this prayer, the very holy Virgin granted Father Juan del Valle many singular favors, as he confessed in his letter of enslavement. Those who knew him believe that he received the crown of martyrdom as a reward for his singular devotion. [655] This is what he pleaded for when he lifted the Holy Sacrament during Mass. He used to say that he would gladly give his life if it would sow love in the souls of those whom he engendered in Christ. This is what he desired and why he offered to be a martyr, provided that the Indians and the common good did not suffer as a result. His Majesty heard his pleas and fervent wishes and sent signs of his impending martyrdom, as the father himself clearly indicated in a number of letters that he wrote to friends. In the letters he said goodbye and affirmed that he would die at the hands of the Tepehuan in three months' time. And it would seem that he received this precious gift because of his great devotion to Our Lady, because he died celebrating her Feast of the Presentation, which he had prepared with such great solemnity. As previously noted, the very holy Virgin also suffered together with her devotee through her image. It was also well known that one day when he was saying Mass in front of an altar with a statue of Saint Agnes, the palm leaf that was in her hand fell on his head—foretelling the good fortune [that awaited him].

God prepared His servant for martyrdom in a singular manner, presenting him with several occasions when he experienced serious injury and difficulty, which he accepted with admirable patience. On one occasion he had just finished saying Mass in the pueblo of San Ignacio, where he was [later] killed. After arranging everything he headed to the sacristy to undress, carrying the chalice in his hands. On the way he was confronted by a daring and sacrilegious Tepehuan who slapped the holy priest in the face. With his customary humility he said to the Indian, "Well, my son, why did you hit me?" The barbarous Indian responded: "Because you say Mass." "Well, if that is the reason (replied the priest), let it be for the love of God." With that the priest got down on his knees, offering the Indian his other cheek, in accordance with the advice given in the Gospel. When word reached the authorities of such a sacrilegious act, the barbarous Indian was arrested. However, the priest himself saw to it that the Indian was not punished.

While converting these Indians, this priest came to a place along what is called the River of the Hanged Men [Río de los Ahorcados], where he encountered several thieves who were accustomed to doing great harm to passersby. He scolded them for their evil deeds and threatened them with the punishment of God, whom

57. "I love those who love me."

they should fear for leading such an evil life. One of the Indians approached him and slapped the priest so hard that he fell down. The priest's revenge was to kneel before the Indian and say, "Let it be for the love of God; hit me as many times as you like."

Another time an Indian hit Father del Valle with his bow because he had reproached him, like a parish priest, for cohabiting with three women. On yet another occasion an Indian woman slapped him in anger after the priest tried to convince the woman, who had been used by the devil as an instrument of lust, to be chaste.

There were many such offenses and insults that this servant of God endured with notable patience at the hands of this naturally fierce nation. Of all the barbarous nations that are being instructed by the more than sixty priests working in these missions, none has dared to be as insolent as the Tepehuan have in their treatment of this blessed priest. Although, as noted in this history, other nations besides the Tepehuan have killed their ministers, no nation ever showed the same amount of disrespect and shamelessness as this one, particularly toward Father Juan [656] del Valle, whom Our Lord offered such suffering in order to crown him with greater glory. Indeed, there were many occasions when he was in danger of losing his life but was spared by God, who reserved his death for a later hour.

Besides shielding him from the continuous danger that he faced while traveling through both populous and uninhabited areas, God three times protected him from these people in ways that were considered miraculous. On one occasion the priest endeavored to free his flock from the bad example of a man who was cohabiting with two women. When the priest spoke to the man in his customary, soft manner, trying to correct his scandalous behavior, the Indian, who was crazed and drunk with his vice, decided to kill the priest. Three times the Indian went to the priest's house. However, each time the Indian entered God made the priest invisible. When the barbarian realized that the priest was actually inside the house but could not be seen, he told a friend and they both became frightened. In the end the aggressor was changed by this event and recovered his conscience; he went to the same priest and confessed, and afterwards reformed his life.

The time finally came when God Our Lord decided to recognize the hardships and exhaustion that Father Juan del Valle endured, bestowing on him the crown of teacher, because he had preached for so many years the evangelical doctrine and had rescued so many souls who were buried in the darkness, not all of whom were lost. He also deserved the crown of a virgin, as everyone agreed who had known him or had dealings with him. We can also understand that he acquired the crown of martyrdom, inasmuch as he died for the preaching of the Holy Gospel. As previously noted, he suffered along with everything else that was sacred—images, churches, ornaments, and chalices. This destruction is manifest proof of the unfaithful spirit in which these barbarous tyrants persecuted and killed this holy minister of Christ and his companions. The way in which they died was discussed in detail in Chapter XX of this book.

The blessed Father Juan del Valle died on November 18, 1616. The governor and other Spaniards who went to punish the rebels found his uncorrupted body sixty days later. The body was so fresh that it is said that when a gentleman named Don Antonio de Gama, of the Habit of Christ, saw the body he cried out in astonishment, "This priest of the Company is alive!" The governor told Father Luis de Bonifaz (who later was Provincial of Nueva España) the following: "It was amazing to see how Father Juan del Valle was fresh and rosy and had a smile on his face" (he was like that when he was alive). And we can certainly believe that an even greater sight is the eternal glory of that man's soul—a man who devoted so many years to works of heroic virtue.

Father del Valle's body rests next to those of his three companions (as I said before) under an altar on the Gospel side of the church of our college in Durango. The priest carried around his neck a little bag with a relic of the sacred *Ignum Crucis*, or relic of the holy Cross, which Governor Don Gaspar de Alvear (who always kept in touch with Father Juan del Valle, whose sanctity he respected) had asked him for when he last saw him in Durango, shortly before Father del Valle's death. The priest had told him that he would give it to him some other time. Thus did he keep his word even after death. When the governor went into the countryside on the previously mentioned expedition to punish the Tepehuan, he was among the first to find the body [657] of the holy priest. Even though the priest had been stripped of his clothing by those infidels, they had not taken the relic of the holy Cross that was around his neck. This is what these people customarily do, as they are covetous and curious about anything that belongs to Spaniards. It seems that God intended that it would be understood that Father del Valle had died while raising and revering the holy Cross amidst this barbarous nation, just as in fact it has been raised and revered, albeit at the cost of considerable blood.

When the governor found the holy relic, which he

had so desired and which had been promised to him by the priest, who fulfilled his word, he picked it up and kept it with great devotion. It had become an even more precious relic because it had been given to him by a martyr of Christ. Also found with the relic was Father del Valle's letter of enslavement to the Most Holy Virgin and the vows he had made to her.

Other marvelous things were related about this priest that I will not include here in this history because I have not been able to adequately determine their veracity, owing to the fact that I have written this chapter while in Spain and the information was gathered [and remains] in Nueva España.

CHAPTER XLII The life and angelic virtues of Father Luis de Alavés, who was murdered by Tepehuan apostates

I can indeed characterize as angelic the virtues of this priest, who was an angel in his ministry of announcing the word of God and in the way he lived his life, which he offered to God. This angelic minister, who was at the side of his superior, Father Juan del Valle, died in the pueblo of El Zape for the same cause of preaching the Holy Gospel and instructing the Tepehuan nation.

Father Luis de Alavés was a native of the city of Oaxaca in the Kingdom of Nueva España. Despite the newness of this realm, it has provided men who are illustrious in sanctity and learning. The blessed martyr and religious Father Luis de Alavés was no less outstanding. He was born to illustrious parents in 1589. His father was Melchor de Alavés and his mother was Doña Ana de Estrada, respected citizens of the pueblo of Texestistlan. It seems that ever since Baptism God had singled him out as one destined for martyrdom. The priest who administered the divine bath (a holy religious of the Order of Saint Dominic) was inspired to write his name in the baptismal registry in large red letters—the color of the blood that he was to shed for Christ. All the other names in this baptismal book were written in ordinary black letters. This included the name of one of his brothers, who was baptized at the same font; there was no difference in the size of the letters or the handwriting, despite the fact that Father Luis' brother was the firstborn son. After Father Luis was martyred and these unusual circumstances surrounding his name were discovered, efforts were made to learn the reason for it. However, the only reason that could be found was that God must have wanted to signal with his first Baptism Father Luis' second Baptism through holy martyrdom. In this regard it was notable how ever since childhood, God had marked him for this crown.

His parents reared him virtuously, enrolling him at our college in Oaxaca, where he studied grammar and the humanities. He studied philosophy at the Colegio Real de San Ildefonso in Mexico City, earning a bachelor's degree. He then entered the Company on May 21, 1607. After completing his novitiate with great examples of virtue, he went on to study [658] four years of theology, after which he was ordained a priest. He then withdrew for what we in the Company refer to as the third or final year of probation. Afterwards he was assigned to the Tepehuan mission.

In all these occupations Father Luis was an outstanding example of virtue. Father Nicolás de Arnaya, who had been his Novice Master and was Provincial at the time of Father Luis' martyrdom, wrote to our Father General about Father Luis and his virtues. Father Arnaya had been his regular confessor and had tended to his soul for a long time. Among Father Luis' virtues he noted the following:

> We believe that [he] did not lose the grace of Baptism. From the time he was a child he was an example of virtue for others. He was so conscientious that he noted the tiniest faults and sins of omission; he scrupulously kept track of the slightest sins. Even though his modesty and reserve

were unusual, he was always very affable; his countenance was full of religious joy, for which he was beloved by all. He often went about with his eyes raised to heaven. It was noticed that even when he was silent he raised his heart to Our Lord, sending Him mental praise. Sometimes he was overheard without his knowledge to utter tender phrases for the heavenly homeland for which he was reared. Unusual truth and sincerity accompanied his virtue and religion.

This is a brief section of the letter by the solemn father who had such intimate dealings with this angelic youth, who seems to have been born with the same fragrant virtues that God has bestowed upon His other great servants. Witnesses cited in the reports that I have consulted add that, as a missionary, he was very humble and had a great zeal for the honor of God and the well-being of his fellow man. He harvested marvelous fruits with his unusual gift of preaching, which Our Lord had given him. He had a burning desire for martyrdom, for which he had prepared through rigorous penance, scourging, wearing a studded belt, and often sleeping on the hard ground or a board. His poverty was great because he gave to the Indians nearly all his own food and his stipend from the king; he was left to suffer great need. He was so oblivious to the things of this world and so given to prayer and conversation with God that he was seen praying for three or four hours, not only at home but while traveling.

Although he practiced great charity as well as many other heroic virtues, what shone so remarkably in him was his virginal purity, which it is known that he always conserved. This statement is in agreement with what Father Nicolás de Arnaya affirmed; he believed that Father Luis never lost his baptismal grace. Following the [Jesuit] Rule, he imitated angelic purity with cleanliness of body and mind, which he preserved with very chaste behavior. The devout Father Luis strengthened this angelical purity through the unusual devotion that he always had for the Queen of Angels, whom he imitated as much as possible. He was like a seraphim in his love for this Sovereign Lady, with whom he spent many hours in tender conversation and loving petition, begging insistently that she grant him, among other gifts, that of martyrdom. [It is certain that] the most Holy Virgin promised him this, because it was learned that on at least three occasions she had spoken to him, as witnesses declared in sworn testimony.

On one occasion he was saying Mass; another time he was giving thanks; on another occasion he was fulfilling the special devotion that he had of visiting her holy image three times during the night. Those who observed him on these occasions were amazed when they heard him conversing with Our Lady and her most Holy Son about his martyrdom [659] and that of his holy companions. Although they could not hear all the words of the conversation, from the questions that the priest asked they were able to understand what he was talking about. One time when he was celebrating Mass those in attendance heard him say, "Is it possible, Lord, that we must undergo this kind of death?" A short while later he said, "And all of us, Lord? May Your most holy will be done." The people who had heard him later asked him what these conversations had been about, but the humble priest changed the subject.

Various witnesses, including Governor Don Gaspar de Alvear, related the preceding case to Father Luis de Bonifaz when he was in Durango. The governor said that he had verified it while at the mine of Guanaceví, when he undertook his entrada to punish the Tepehuan. On the night following [the incident related] a young Spanish boy who accompanied Father Luis heard the priest talking in a similar fashion. When he asked the priest directly what he had said and to whom he had been speaking, the priest replied, "It was nothing." Then he asked the boy, "Would you have the courage to die as a martyr with me?" The boy answered, "Yes, Father, why not?" This angelic child fulfilled this promise, because when the child, who was at the mining center of Guanaceví, learned that the priest was in mortal danger, he departed for El Zape to be with the priest. Although he could have excused himself, the boy fulfilled the promise he had made to Father Luis.

These revelations occurred a few days before the joyous martyrdom that Father Alavés spoke of with tenderness and delight. A particularly striking instance of this divine favor and forewarning from heaven took place when Father Fray Sebastián Montaño had his confession heard at the church in the mining center of Guanaceví by Father Alavés, who was substituting for the Vicar, Amaro Fernández Pasos. After Father Sebastián, who had come to Guanaceví from Zacatecas seeking alms for his convent, was informed [of his impending martyrdom], he made a record of all the alms that he had collected and where he was leaving them. This record he sent to his superior on November 17. This same day Father Alavés reached his district of San Ignacio de Zape. He had come in great haste, well prepared for the death that Our Lord had announced. Although he could have delayed his arrival and avoided danger, he understood that his time had come. He paid no heed to the pleas of those at the mining center who had requested that he stay and say Mass for them the next day. They could not detain him because the day had arrived which Our Lady had revealed to him—the day when he would achieve the crown of his glorious death, which occurred in the manner that has been told.

His glorious triumph occurred on the November 18, 1616. He was twenty-seven years of age and had spent ten years in the Company. The governor (who recovered his holy body) said that he found it in an unusual posture, with only the chest touching the ground. The rest of the body—the head, feet, and hands—all were raised to heaven, despite the fact that those barbarians, as was their custom, had placed it head down, as they had done with all the other priests and Christians they had killed. The holy young man and religious father was [found] wearing a sharply studded iron belt that pressed into

his flesh, revealing how much he had tightened it. The rest of his body was free of lesions, although one witness testified that he saw fresh blood on one foot, apparently where the barbarians had struck a harsh blow.

Father Luis' cadaver was taken to Durango along with the body of Father Juan del Valle and the other two companions who died at El Zape. There they were received with the solemnity that has been related. One religious who was recognized throughout the province as a great servant of God affirmed that years later, when the grave [660] was opened, the bodies were found to be intact. When Father Luis de Alavés' cadaver was placed upright, it remained standing with only slight pressure from a finger applied to the shoulder. [He also said] that the bodies emitted a very sweet aroma, corresponding to the aroma emitted by their very religious virtues when they were alive.

CHAPTER XLIII The exemplary life and martyrdom of Father Gerónimo de Moranta, missionary to the Tepehuan nation

Father Gerónimo de Moranta and his three companion priests achieved the triumph of their glorious death at the pueblo of San Ignacio. It was through special insight that these three blessed priests gave this pueblo its name, which previously had been Zape. There the four very legitimate sons of the holy patriarch shed their blood because they belonged to the Institute that had conceived and reared them in Christ.

Father Moranta was born in Mallorca in 1575 and entered the Company in 1595. That admirable man of the Company of JESUS, Brother Alonso Rodríguez, requested that he travel to Nueva España. This seemed a good thing to the blessed priest, who had frequent dealings with holy men and was humble, composed, cautious in his use of words, and charitable, and who practiced other heroic virtues. He was the nephew of Father Gerónimo Nadal, who was greatly esteemed

by our father Saint Ignatius.[58] He had communicated personally with Father Ricardo Haller, who was the confessor of the holy Queen Doña Margarita of Austria and was considered a very holy man. By the time he died in Madrid Father Haller had declined a number of major positions within the Church. This remarkable man wrote in his own hand very kind letters to Father Moranta, predicting the latter's glorious martyrdom. The venerable Brother Alonso Rodríguez made the same prediction, as is recounted in his vita.

And so in 1605 Father Moranta came to Nueva España, where he professed the three vows of our order. He was then sent to the Tepehuan mission, where he worked for ten years at the conversion [of the Indi-

58. Nadal was second in importance only to Ignatius in creating the Jesuit esprit de corps and formulating the early Jesuit identity and "way of proceeding" (O'Malley 1993a:11–14).

ans], nearly all of them in the company of Father Juan Fonte. He partook of all the great and glorious hardships that Father Fonte endured during his continuous travels. He was also his companion in martyrdom; his burning desire for that crown having been encouraged by the predictions of those two holy men.

Father Moranta prepared himself for the singular gift that Our Lord grants to those He chooses. For this [martyrdom] he practiced with great care the holy and religious virtues that he had professed. His poverty was such that he generally wore a worn and patched habit, which barely covered him. One time the superior of the entire mission found him endeavoring to reduce some gentile Indians who were thirty leagues distant from the nearest settlement. His only lodging was a flimsy tent where he said Mass. He spent the rest of the day in prayer and holy reading, exposed to the inclement weather. His beard was as long as those depicted on the ancient hermits. His bed was a cowhide. When the priest stopped at the house of Spaniards and they offered him a bed, he pushed it aside and slept on the hard ground. During his frequent travels the priest paid little or no [661] attention to his own comfort. If he had been traveling where there were inns or populated areas, or if the journey had encompassed a single day, as is normally the case in Spain, it would have been no great matter to endure the discomforts that such travel entails. Travel here in the Indies, however, is very different, and the journeys undertaken in the missions and lands of these barbarous people are even more unusual. And such were the travels of this servant of God, who frequently traveled on foot, due to the roughness of the roads. He did so in cold weather, high water, and even at night, when he was called to hear confessions. Even though he had a mount, he still wished to suffer. Accordingly, the mount that he used was a humble nag of little value that had a bad gait.

Like his companion priests, he spent the stipend he received from the king for food on the Indians of his doctrina. His usual food was the same as that of all other missionaries: kernels of maize that were toasted or cooked without salt. He even abstained from this coarse food when he fasted on the days of his devotion. It was noted that when Father Moranta was invited to the homes or lodgings of Spaniards and was offered delicacies [i.e., chocolate], he would quietly dilute them with water to lessen their flavor. This man, who was so austere with himself, was remarkably generous with others. He gave lodging to all in his heart, making sure

that when they passed through his doctrina he welcomed them with all that his poverty allowed. What he lacked in material comforts he made up for with loving charity. His purity, prudence, and chastity greatly endeared him to all those witnesses who met and knew him. He was steadfast in his holy practice of prayer and was seen on his knees for long hours in church. His devotion to the most holy sacrifice of the Mass was singular, for which he received special favors from Our Lord. The same thing was true when he said the Divine Office. Indeed, even when he was out in the fields, he continued the holy practice of prayer.

Although citing these virtues [may seem] repetitious, doing so makes those of Father Moranta and his holy brothers and companions more resplendent. It was the good fortune of these holy religious and their mother, the Company of JESUS, that holy martyrdom should befall sons who were so outstanding in virtue and religion, and that their virtues should be so similar to one another and to those professed by their mother, the Company.

Let us return to Father Moranta and the recourse that he had to God in prayer. Once when he was traveling he withdrew into the bushes with a crucifix in hand and uncovered himself. He then began to scourge himself vigorously, all the while crying so that his tears and blood might together move Our Lord to make him a better preacher to the Indians about conversion; he insistently begged Our Lord to prepare their hearts to receive Him.

The pious pleas of this minister, who so desired the health of the souls in his charge, did not go unheeded. In the settlement called Las Salinas, which was one of the most isolated in this mission, he reduced and converted five hundred gentiles. As a result of many other entradas to other rancherías, he brought a similar number of Indians together to found several pueblos, suffering great hardship in the process. Witnesses gave sworn testimony to this, adding that only someone like this priest, who had a burning love for God and his fellow man, could have undertaken such labor. When they talked to him about it, his answer was that he very happily endured these hardships for the love of God. The hardships were indeed so extreme that they would have been unbearable were it not for a [662] love of Christ. This is what the Apostle of the People, Saint Paul, said motivated him to endure the enormous suffering that he says he endured. The very same thing motivated this blessed priest to do what others described and I have recounted. He was like a slave of the barbarous Indians, making their houses and fields for them, all in an effort to win them over for God.

On the two or three occasions when the Indians tried to rebel and apostatize, this servant of God went at great danger to his life to their homes in the mountaintops and forests. With his example he pacified and calmed them. The great virtue that the Spaniards of this land saw in Father Moranta obliged them to call him the Theatine Saint.[59]

Finally, after a prolonged hardship of ten years, the martyrdom that other servants of God had predicted caught up with Father Moranta. In addition, the Lord himself revealed it to him, according to those who talked with this priest. Although we lack information for a complete report about what happened to those servants of God, owing to the fact that many who had direct dealings with them died also, there were still some witnesses to a very unusual case that involved Father Moranta, which happened not once but five times during the days leading up to his martyrdom. It happened when he was saying Mass at the pueblo called San José, also known as El Tizonazo. At the moment when he elevated the chalice the people who were serving Mass saw a dove suddenly descend, spilling the chalice and spattering blood on his face, the chasuble, the altar, and the base of the altar. Those who were serving Mass were so stunned by this event that they did not dare to ask Father Moranta about its meaning. But later it happened that these same people were as-

sisting him at the settlement called Las Bocas, fifteen leagues from San José, and witnessed the same thing as had happened previously. This time when Mass was over they asked the priest what was the meaning of the dove and the blood that they had seen on three occasions.[60] The priest replied, "My sons, what I understand is that Our Lord wishes me to shed my blood for His love." And so it happened that within a few days he died with the other three priests at the hands of the apostate Tepehuan in the pueblo of El Zape. As noted in detail elsewhere, they died along with 130 Christian Spaniards, Indians, and blacks.

When the body of the blessed priest was found three months later, it was naked but intact and gave off no odor, as was true of his companions. Next to Father Moranta was a chalice that he carried with him to Mass while on the road. It was surprising that the barbarians should have spared it. It was noted that they did not spare a holy [portable] altar, which those sacrilegious people had treated with abominable indecency. The bodies of Father Moranta and Father Juan Fonte, who died at his side, were found wearing cinched studded belts; they did not neglect their usual penance even in death. As has been recorded, the cadavers of the four priests were transferred to the church in Durango, where they await union with their glorious souls on the Day of Resurrection. [Father Moranta] died on November 17, 1616, at the age of forty-one; twenty-one of those years he spent in the Holy Order of the Company of Jesus. [663]

---

59. The Theatines were a religious order founded in the sixteenth century largely to reform Catholic morality.

60. Although Pérez de Ribas has actually recounted only two occasions, the Spanish original here mentions three.

CHAPTER XLIV The apostolic virtues and martyrdom of Father Bernardo de Cisneros and Father Diego de Orozco, both of the Company of JESUS

I call apostolic those virtues that were practiced principally by the holy Apostles by order and commandment of their divine Master. Meditating on the Gospel law and its supreme mysteries and sacraments, they attended not only to their own perfection and sanctity, but to that of their fellow man. They did this in such a way that this divine light radiated to those around them, making them participants in Christ's redemption through their recognition of His holy name; there is no other in whom mankind can be saved. These are the virtues of those who lived and died following the Institute as true sons of the Company. Therefore, I have reason to give these virtues the fame of being apostolic. By the grace of God we Christians enjoy our most illustrious title, which comes from Christ, the Sovereign Son of God. This title is not derived from the Apostles. The virtues of the two very religious priests, Father Bernardo de Cisneros and Father Diego de Orozco, were apostolic. They were crowned with the blessed martyrdom that was recounted at length in Chapter XIII [Chapter XX] of this book. Here I will only add the specific circumstances of the life and death of these two blessed priests, who achieved their triumphant martyrdom in the same place and at the same time, working together to care for some of the same pueblos. These were the principal pueblos of the Tepehuan nation and those where the fire of persecution was greatest, especially Santiago de Papasquiaro.

Fortunately for me, I happened to talk with and enjoy the pleasant company of these servants of God, although I was only passing through Santiago Papasquiaro and was there for only a few days. It was just two months before the barbarians martyred the priests. There were suspicions and many signs of unrest in these people at that time, and these blessed priests were not unaware of these rumors. Rather, they discussed them with me and realized that their lives were in danger. The unrest and the speeches that the Indians call tlatollis were already being heard, especially those of the principal sorcerer who introduced them.

The first thing that the members of this bedeviled profession try to do is to take the lives of the evangelical ministers who undo their old tricks. Nevertheless, even though the valiant soldiers of Christ found themselves in the midst of such dangers, they did not abandon their positions. They did this so as not to be like those of whom the Lord spoke—who because they are not true shepherds but rather hired hands—flee and abandon the sheep that God entrusted to them: *Mercenarius videt lupum venientem, & dimittit oves, & fugit.*[61] These two ministers did not flee. Once they had the news that I recorded in Chapter XIII—that packs of wolves, and even worse, were gathering among the Tepehuan and that their councils were focused on destroying Christ's flock and tearing to pieces the shepherds who pastured them—they were steadfast in preaching the doctrine of heaven, to the point of spilling their blood for it.

As confirmation of this, I present the following case, which happened while I was en route to Mexico City. I accompanied Father Bernardo de Cisneros to some of the pueblos that he was instructing. One day before we were to go our separate ways, this servant of God expressed concern about the obstinacy and hardness that he found in his Tepehuan. He told me that they had him so [664] vexed that he was thinking about sending a letter with me to the Father Provincial, requesting that he assign him to whatever other mission His Reverence wanted, no matter how laborious. He was not trying to avoid hardship but only wanted to be gone from such perverted and rebellious people. However, because God wanted him to be a martyr, the following day at dawn as I was going to say Mass, he changed his original plan. Having entrusted this matter to Our Lord, the religious priest told me that he wanted to conform to the perfection of obedience that is professed in the Company. Therefore, he had changed his mind and did not plan to write the letter. Instead, he would leave himself open

---

61. John 10:12: "the hireling . . . abandons the sheep and takes to flight as soon as he sees the wolf coming" (Knox 1956:99).

to divine will in the post that obedience had chosen for him. In this way he clearly showed how much he wished to conform to this most holy virtue, to which the Apostle Saint Paul specifically attributed the holy death of Christ. And so Father Bernardo, *Factus obediens*, awaited his death, imitating the Lord. On the same occasion his companion, Father Diego de Orozco, told me that he was experiencing very poor health in that post; he was in fact inherently frail. Nevertheless, he waited for a change in post or ministry to come through holy obedience. These were clear demonstrations of the holy motives that persevered in these valiant soldiers of Christ, who did not abandon the battlefield nor flee the enemy's face and imminent mortal wounds. The heroic thing about this outstanding virtue was that they practiced the acts of true fathers and the affection of loving mothers with the very same enemies who were trying to take their lives. It was remarkable to see, as I myself noticed, the sweetness and gentleness with which they treated those Tepehuan and their children, who served as little singers in the church. Notable also were the holy strategies that they used to win over both parents and children to God, plus the labor pains that (as the Apostle of the People said) it cost the priests to give these people rebirth in Christ. These were the virtues practiced by these servants of God, along with the hardships, discomforts, and dangers that all bore with great patience, which made them very similar to the first Gospel ministers, to whom the Lord announced, *Ecce ego mitto vos, ficat agnos inter lupus.*[62] Like gentle sheep among the Tepehuan wolves, whom they heard pronounce death sentences, the priests practiced virtues of Christian perfection not only in meditation and contemplative withdrawal, in which there is no doubt that holy desires are awakened for performing many services for God Our Lord, but also in deed, where very religious and solid virtues are revealed and proved. Spanish miners and other people from the region who had contact with the priests were reliable witnesses to and also gave highly reliable testimony of the virtues of the two priests that I have presented here. It is the case that those who are found in such distant lands and mining camps are ordinarily the type who most censure the lives of the missionaries. They testified that the lives of these two most religious priests were highly exemplary and religious. Having already stated what was common to the two of them, I will now provide the specifics, as

well as the path and unique means by which God prepared each of them so that they could attain the crown of martyrdom, both of them in their prime.

Father Bernardo de Cisneros was of Spanish nationality, a native of Carrión de los Condes, Castilla la Vieja. He was thirty-four years old when he died, which was in 1616. He entered the Company in 1599 and went to Nueva España in 1605. Once he finished his course in philosophy at the college [665] in Mexico City, he studied four years of theology and afterward was ordained. He then moved on to what we can call the spiritual course of the Company, the third year of probation, which we have explained its Institute orders in preparation for the holy enterprises for which its members are reared, particularly missions among barbarians. During all this time, he excelled in his highly religious virtues, the observation of the Company's rules, his composure, his studies, and prayer. His humility was resplendent, as were his great friendliness and modesty, which made him pleasant to those who dealt with him. These talents and virtues persevered and were perfected during the years he spent in the labor of his mission, where he endured continual hardships. He was ever concerned with [instilling] the Christian catechism. In his sermons and ordinary speeches he endeavored with holy zeal to soften and reduce the Tepehuan's hardened hearts, exhorting them to obey the divine commandments and to flee from offenses to God at all cost. These people tested and refined Father Bernardo's gentleness and patience, which were of very high quality and persevered. He continued to suffer great hardships without seeing any fruits, for when this fruit is harvested the suffering endured for preaching the Gospel becomes sweet. The suffering of this evangelical minister among these people reached such extremes that witnesses testify to various cases before his murder when he was beaten with stiff blows from sticks, which he suffered with great silence and patience. I will record only one of these, which was very remarkable.

In the pueblo of Otinapa in his mission district, the priest had destroyed something of a shrine in which a perverse and stubborn Indian had placed an idol. Father Orozco had once before removed this idol from a pueblo where Christ's church had already been erected. But the idolater had erected it again. Father Bernardo (with zeal for God's honor) destroyed it once more, even though it was at risk to his own life. The Indian, inflamed with diabolical fury and anger, went in search of the priest. When he found him, he stabbed him with a knife three times in the chest, next to his heart, and

---

62. Luke 10:3: "I am sending you out to be like lambs among wolves" (Knox 1956:67).

left him for dead. However, Our Lord wished to preserve him in order to crown him later with even greater merits. He sent him to a Spaniard named Simón Alvarez de Sotomayor, who cured his wounds. This case was kept secret through the efforts of this most patient priest, but one day a miner from Guanaceví named Gonzalo Martín de la Mediana, an encomendero of the pueblo of El Zape, noticed that the priest had three holes in his cassock that looked like they were from [knife] wounds, so he asked him what they were. He was not satisfied when God's servant tried to change the subject, and so he became more insistent and pestered the priest to tell him about it. The priest did so in secret, and as he unbuttoned his cassock, the encomendero saw that he still had stitches in the three wounds, which were not yet healed. All of the aforementioned acts of the blessed Father Bernardo were good tests for the martyrdom with which he finally concluded his life.

Father Diego de Orozco, his holy companion, was also his companion in martyrdom (as we stated earlier) and in the profession and labor of the same mission. Furthermore, he also came to the Indies with the same desire of working at the conversion of gentiles, and they had sailed together the same year on the same boat. Father Gerónimo de Moranta, whom we have just discussed, also sailed with them. What a blessed ship to have brought three of Christ's confessors to preach His holy name, and ones who were to shed their blood proclaiming it!

Father Diego de Orozco was a native of the city of Plasencia, the son of noble parents: [666] Doctor Antonio de Orozco, a council member in that city and an attorney for [various] councils, and Doña Isabel de Toro, his wife. His uncle was Rodrigo de Orozco, marquis of Mortara, field marshal and governor of Alexandria de la Palla. With such parents and relatives, the son certainly had promise of achieving highly honorable secular goals. But Our Lord, who had chosen him for more lofty enterprises, prepared him very early on and called him to be a soldier in the Company of JESUS. He did so with a light from within that shone in his understanding from a tender age. This light was so remarkable that as a child he was heard to say that he would go on to study to become a religious in the Company of Jesus and go to the Indies to be a martyr for Christ. I will record a testimony of this truth further ahead.

This holy servant was not lazy in responding to the voices from heaven that resounded within his soul. At the age of fifteen he requested admission into the Com-

pany, and because he had been reared in great virtue and had an angelic nature that he displayed in his appearance and modesty, he easily achieved his wishes and was received [into the Company] in the Province of Castilla la Vieja in 1602. He thus hastened to carry out the desires that heaven sent him. Shortly after he had finished his novitiate in 1605, he requested to go to the Indies. This request was granted, despite the objections of many of his noble relatives, his young age, and his delicate health and natural frailty, all of which were overcome by his steadfastness. Once he arrived in Mexico City, he studied philosophy and theology, in which he so excelled that he could have occupied high positions and taught advanced university courses. Because he was humble and submissive to holy obedience and even though he was drawn by his desires to labor in the conversion of the Indians, he allowed himself to be governed by God through [his] superiors. Therefore, he went to teach grammar in the colleges of the cities of Puebla and Oaxaca. Once he had completed these ministries and the third year of his probation had passed, he had a desire to distance himself even more from his family, even though they were very distant from Nueva España. He unsuccessfully sought an assignment in Japan, promising himself there to obtain the crown of martyrdom for which he felt Our Lord was calling him. God granted this through holy obedience and he was sent to the Tepehuan mission, where His Majesty had Father Diego's martyrdom waiting for him. After having participated in the same labors and exercises of patience as his brothers, his premonitions of and desires for the holy conclusion of his life that the Lord had inspired in him from a young age were fulfilled. In testimony of this I will include here what was recounted by one of our brothers, Marcos de Olea, master of writing at our college in Guatemala City.

The case was that when he was in that city, a certain Don Medrano arrived, who was the governor of the Province of Soconusco, which is not far from Guatemala City; this was an assignment granted by His Majesty in Spain. In his wife's company was a devout young maiden, a native of the city of Plasencia, who had been raised in the home of Father Diego de Orozco when he was a child. When this young maiden saw Brother Marcos, which was long after Father Orozco had gone to Nueva España, she wanted to know about the man who had been reared as an angel in childhood and in her company. She asked the brother what Father Diego de Orozco was doing. When she asked this question it had been a little more than one year since the priest had been killed in the Tepehuan province, which is five hundred leagues from Guatemala City. Thus, news of the priest's death had only recently reached Guatemala City. [667] The brother hesitated, and so she asked him again how Father Orozco was doing. She added the following, "I ask because we grew up together, and ever since he was a child, Diego used to say that he was going to join the Company and go to the Indies and die there as a martyr, shedding his blood for the Faith. Now that two of the three things he used to say have come true, there's only one left." The brother, who knew that it had already been fulfilled, felt unusual consolation to hear that devout young maiden testify that from such a young and tender age Our Lord had prepared Father Diego with such holy desires and heavenly light for the blissful conclusion of his life. He responded that the final favor had already been granted and that the priest had died for Christ. The devout young maiden was greatly moved by this answer and began to spill tears of devotion, thanking God for having fulfilled the pre-monitions with which he had prepared Father Diego de Orozco since his childhood to shed his blood for Christ's glory. It is nothing new for this divine Master to prepare His servants with the light of the labors that they must suffer for His glory. Although Saint Paul was such a great Apostle, the Holy Spirit prepared him, announcing to him in all the cities where he went the tribulations that awaited him in Jerusalem: *Spiritus Sanctus per omnes ciutates mihi protestatur dicens: quoniam vincula, & tribulationes Hierosolimis me manent.*[63] It is no small sign of the angelic virtues of our Father Diego that he was able to guard so secretly throughout his entire life [the fact] that Our Lord had prepared him as someone who was to be raised to become a martyr. Furthermore, it was considered to be certain that he preserved his virginal purity until he died, this being accompanied by all the other virtues that he exercised during the years that he lived among the Tepehuan. Even though these years were few, the corporal and spiritual labors that he suffered were great in number and intensity. His desire was to soften the hearts that he felt were so hardened and misled by the devil, in order to win them over and reduce them to the truth of our Holy Faith. He suffered by living in a place that inherently possessed so many discomforts, as well as from his own delicate health and

having been exiled from the company of his brothers. Even with his fragile constitution, he nevertheless wore a studded belt and frequently scourged himself; he also spent all he had for the benefit of those who took his life.

The day finally arrived when he would complete the course of his holy life and spill his blood. He would do this with the companion whom God had given him for his journey, who was employed in the same work in the same place. Together, on November 18, 1616, the blessed Fathers Bernardo de Cisneros and Diego de Orozco were murdered by the Tepehuan apostates in the pueblo of Santiago Papasquiaro for preaching the name of Christ. The circumstances of the martyrdom of these servants of God [at El Zape] were the same as those related about their brothers. It was suffered not only by a large number of Catholic Spaniards, but also by the sacred images of the crucified Christ and His Most Holy Mother, as well as by the great and Holy Sacrament of the Altar, as was detailed earlier in this book.

The most unique of all these martyrdoms was experienced by the blessed Father Diego de Orozco. He was split open cruelly down the back with a hatchet, while his arms were stretched out in the form of a Cross; rather than being fastened by nails, his arms were held in place by those Indian tyrants. So that this death would resemble Christ's even more, it was accompanied by blasphemy that spewed forth from the infernal mouths of those barbarians. At the same time that they had a hold of him and had his arms stretched out, and while others swung [668] their hatchets, they mocked the words they had heard during Mass, repeating, *Dominus vobiscum. Et cum spiritu tuo.*[64] However, the words that were heard from the blessed priest as he was dying, which imitated the calmness of the Lamb of God, were, "Do with me, my children, what you will, because I die for my God."

These are all very clear demonstrations of the holy spirit with which he offered himself to his Redeemer in this holocaust and, at the same time, of the depraved spirit with which the bedeviled apostates persecuted the Faith of Our Lord Jesus Christ and those who preached it. They gave Father Bernardo de Cisneros a cruel lancing and other blows with their barbarous weapons. The remaining circumstances of these two martyrdoms are recounted at length in their respective places, and are therefore not repeated here.

I now conclude this account of the persecution that

---

63. Acts 20:23: "as I go on from city to city, the Holy Spirit assures me that . . . bondage and affliction await me" (Knox 1956:138).

64. "The Lord be with you. And with your spirit."

the bedeviled idol raised with the hope of destroying the Tepehuan mission. Finally, I note that hell was not successful. Although it took the lives of eight evangelical ministers (I have written about six of them here and the other two at the ends of the preceding books), there were still other religious, their brothers, who with great spirit went to repair this damage. Nor did God allow so much bloodshed to prevent additional fruit, for the remaining Tepehuan were reconciled with God and His holy Church. Even though the remains of the holy bodies of the two priests about whom I have written in this chapter could not be distinguished from those of the other loyal Christians who died with them, a relic remained from the religious instruction given by these two evangelical ministers—the Christianity that is now improved in the Tepehuan. We can understand that in His holy glory God holds as sacred relics the souls of those who preached His doctrine, for which they gave their lives. Eternal glory to God on high for all things. [669]

BOOK XI

The Mission of Parras and Laguna Grande de San Pedro

CHAPTER 1 The location of this mission and the customs of its inhabitants

The religious of the Company in Nueva España have reaped a copious harvest in the principal mission centers and districts that have been recorded thus far. Various gentile nations have been reduced to their Creator and true God, whom they had never known. Sizable flocks of souls have also joined the Church—souls who, as noted earlier, were once lost in the clutches of the infernal wolf.

We have yet to discuss other nations in different lands and settlements, who also lived in the shadow and danger of eternal death. Although to convert these people the soldiers of the Militia of JESUS did not have to travel through mountains and sierras, they still had to cross deserts where there was no water. Through Christ's divine grace, they planted the doctrine of our Holy Faith, harvesting the same precious fruits as in the other missions. Although there was no bloodshed, the ministers still suffered immense hardships, and on many occasions they found their lives in danger in the enterprise of which I will now write.

The people of the mission of Parras and those who are called Lagueneros live along the shores of the lake called Laguna Grande de San Pedro. Some of them live on little islands in the lake itself. The mission center was named Parras by the Spaniards because they found there a type of wild plant that looks like the Castilian grapevine. However, the principal reason for this name is that, although [670] grapevines were unknown

in the Indies until they were introduced by Spaniards, the soil of Parras embraced and welcomed the Castilian grapevine so well that there has been no foreign plant introduced to Nueva España that has repaid this kindness with greater abundance. It is true that these plants are not enjoyed extensively, for the boundaries of this land are limited. Only a short distance away, there are places that are so dry that the only trees that survive are the very wild and thorny ones that grow in the monte. Between this region and the lake where the devil held these wretched people captive, one finds some dry desert plains.

In this first chapter (following the pattern I have adopted thus far), I will write about their particular lands, customs, sustenance, and way of life in the darkness of their heathenism. In this way one can understand the material on which the stamp of evangelical law fell and was imprinted.

The settlement of Laguna Grande is thirty leagues from Durango (the seat of government). Water is so scarce along the road between Durango and Laguna Grande that it is necessary at certain times of the year for passengers and travelers to carry it in barrels. In fact, the road is better between Laguna Grande and the mining center at Zacatecas.

The lake has a perimeter of about forty leagues. During floods this increases to fifty or sixty leagues. I said 'floods' because at certain times of the year, especially when it rains, the great Río Nazas rises and its swift current fills the lake. This river has its headwaters in the mountains of Topia, which have been mentioned often in this history. The lake is at twenty-seven degrees north, two hundred leagues to the northwest of the great city of Mexico. The valley in which the lake is located is very flat and broad and is protected on one side by foothills and mountains. The climate ranges from hot to very hot. The soil is moist and permits the lush cultivation of any type of plant.

The rising and falling waters of the river and lake are very beneficial to those who live there. The high waters bring large numbers of fish, which then remain in the good home provided by the lake. The high waters also spread out and fertilize large tracts of land surrounding the lake. When the waters recede, the Indians are able to sow their crops in the already irrigated land. At the same time, as the water recedes they are able to catch fish more easily and make use of a variety of fish [that remain] in inlets and small pools. This is especially true of a fish called the *matalote*,[1] which is considered a very precious and tasty food; this fish is fattened on the very suitable sustenance provided by God in the lake itself. All these things are a gift of sustenance for mankind, whom God's divine paternal providence has not forgotten, for no matter how barbarous they may be, He has taken care of them.

In addition to the abundant fish, the people who live around the lake consume a great number of ducks that come here to nest. The Indians easily kill these ducks with their arrows. They also use another amusing strategy for duck hunting, which I have heard is also used by the Mexica. Because this is something new to Spain, I will describe it here.

The Indian hunter takes half of the shell of a round gourd and makes some little holes in it to look through. He places it on his head and enters the [671] water, plunging his entire body under except for the gourd shell. He quietly advances toward the unsuspecting flock of ducks swimming on the water, and then this person who looks like a gourd sneaks in among the ducks. They do not find this odd because it is common to see gourds floating on the lake. Sometimes the Indians even intentionally put them there. The Indian moves quietly underwater and begins to grab the ducks' legs, pulling them under, whence they do not return but rather become prey and sustenance for man. God created them for this purpose and therefore left them subject to man's inventions and schemes. It is thus that the Lagunero Indians have this as their usual and abundant sustenance.

In this regard, I will note here what happened to the priests who went to give these people religious instruction and who tried to explain the Church's precept of abstaining from meat on certain days. The priests had difficulty convincing the Laguneros that duck was considered a type of meat rather than fish. The Indians argued that ducks live in water, just like fish, and also hatch their eggs in the water among the bulrushes. They eat and live in the water and should therefore be considered fish. In this, as in many other important matters, the Indians finally submitted to their ministers' doctrine.

Continuing with the sustenance that God has provided these people, there is another [food source] that is most particularly and properly theirs. They themselves consider it very ordinary but tasty, and it comes from the root of a type of bulrush, similar to what in Spain is called cattail.[2] These rushes grow along the lake, and they grind the root and use the flour in beverages and as a very substantial and delicious food source. And although I have heard priests of this mission praise these roots as such, I also believe that they grew to be tasty to those who had no other sustenance in such a destitute land, where their principal pleasure is the salvation of souls. The way in which the Indians benefit from their roots is by grinding them and making them into a dough for cakes or large loaves of bread, which last for many days without going stale. They consider these breads tasty food, and because they have [food] in abundance, they are not as concerned about farming as other nations are. They also make bread and wine from the fruit of the mesquite, which was mentioned earlier. In addition, they have an abundance of fowl, hares, and deer; in some of the latter, they find bezoars, a well-known medication that is highly valued everywhere.

---

1. Matalote is derived from *matalón*, which refers to an old worn-out horse. Perhaps a member of the Catostomidae family (carp, catfish, sucker), whose mouth reminded Spaniards of the face of an old horse.

2. *Anea*.

CHAPTER II These people's other barbarous customs and superstitions

I will begin here with these people's particular barbarous customs. When the wife gives birth, the husband abstains from eating meat and fish for six or seven days. They thought that if they ate these things, the fish and game would be repulsed and would withdraw to the mountains or the deepest part of their rivers and lake. They always kept the heads of the deer they killed, along with the antlers, which were used as a form of idolatry. They expected these heads to bring them success in hunting, so that they could kill many deer. The devil introduced other superstitions through these deer heads, as well as into the heads of the Indians. I omit these superstitions here for the sake of brevity and because of their similarity to those that were previously recorded which the Prince of Darkness had used to blind these people.

In order that the light of the Gospel, [672] which rescued these people from their darkness, might shine ever more brightly, I must not omit the intimate dealings that this enemy had with these people. It is well known from the Indians' oral traditions that the devil, for whom they had their own native term, appeared to them on innumerable occasions. He always appeared in a horrible form, as indeed he is. He would also take the form of a black man who spouted fire through his eyes, or of a black man with blood flowing from his nose and ears.[3] On other occasions the devil would appear in the form of a wild beast that caused fear, horror, and fright. He attempted to terrorize the Indians into obeying his diabolical commands and thus become the base slaves of this cruel tyrant. His command was to take men's lives and sometimes the lives of their own children, particularly firstborn children, or to do away with people who were sick or aged, so that he could whisk them off to hell.[4] Sometimes the devil threatened them with diseases, leading them to believe that he was the lord of life and death.

He would induce them to hold barbarous dances that were always celebrated by a throng of people. The people would form a circle and crown,[5] and keeping the beat with their steps, the entire ring seemed to be one. Because his dances were usually held at night and would last until sunrise, there were bonfires and torches in the middle and all around the dancers. Even when the men and women danced separately, these diversions and festivities were not free from the abuses that the devil promotes. Moreover, these were celebrations of drunkenness, which further deprived the Indians of the scant senses that remained in such heathen darkness.

[The devil also] introduced them to the habit of the weed called peyote, which is very famous among the Indians of Nueva España. Although it is of medicinal value when used in moderation, in excess it makes a person lose his senses and causes diabolical fantasies. In the end the devil links many of his superstitions to this plant.

He also is feared to be present in funnel clouds of dust that rise up on the wind. Everyone who saw them would throw themselves to the ground, saying to one another, "Cachinipa." This is the name they gave to the devil or to whatever they feared or revered in that cloud of dust, because they could not explain what it was.

Later, however, through the doctrine of the Gospel and all its mysteries the ministers give them the news of the sin of the angels. Because of this sin, these angels fell from heaven, and for this reason they are envious of men who go to heaven. This is why they persecute us. The priests also tell them everything else that is necessary concerning this matter. In order to explain original sin to them, [they are told that] Christ Our Lord instituted Holy Baptism as the remedy. (Not everything, however, is declared to them at the outset; later, with time, they are taught more). Because this doctrine is true, the Indians accept it very well, and they easily

---

3. Native oral traditions may have been referring here to black or mulatto mine workers who fled Mapimí and Parras during the typhus epidemic of 1575–81 (Reff 1991b:124–27).

4. The anuas tell of many instances where the Laguneros as well as the Tepehuan abandoned their sick, and in some instances buried them alive for fear of becoming ill and dying (DHM 1596:30, 1598:57). The Jesuits also were shocked and dismayed by the widespread practice of child sacrifice to ward off disease or insure the recovery of adults who became ill (DHM 1598:51). It is not clear, however, that native peoples

made special sacrifice of firstborn children. Parallels from the Bible may have led Pérez de Ribas and other Jesuits to make this inference.

5. A group of people holding hands and dancing in a circle would resemble a crown.

understand the malice of our adversary, the devil, who had fooled them. They develop such ill will toward this infernal enemy that the same dislike on the part of long-time Christians does not exceed that of these nations. When they commit any sin, their normal excuse is, "The devil tricked me."

The traps with which he had deceived the Indians of Parras and Laguna Grande have forced me into this digression. Returning to these Indians' superstitions, I note that they had others that were observed for deaths, burials, and the mourning of their deceased, as well as for other occasions. All this is very similar to what has been recounted throughout this history, particularly in Book I, concerning other nations entombed in darkness. In His infinite clemency, God has deigned to remove them from that darkness and has placed them in the happy state of children of God and His Church through [673] the means and in the manner that will later be declared. I do not want to fail to warn anyone who might think that there is repetition in the matters concerning these enterprises, or that they are very similar to things that happened in other missions. It should be noted that in recounting the history of human enterprises, just because one writes about victories, successful campaigns, the destruction of the enemy, and the taking of enemy territory, that is no reason to ignore the successful or unfortunate events of other conquests, even if the events are similar. This is especially true when they are as glorious to God as those recorded here. Moreover, it is common for some particular circumstance to arise that sets one apart from the others.

CHAPTER III The priests of the Company begin working in the rancherías of the Zacateco Indians; a letter from Father Gerónimo Ramírez discussing the entrada

For the reasons recorded in the previous chapter, particularly the great lack of water en route to the Parras settlements, it was difficult to instruct these people, who were so remote and isolated. Once the priests of the Company in the city of Zacatecas learned of their wretched state, they nevertheless decided with fervent zeal for the good of souls (in accordance with their profession) to initiate a mission among these people. They decided to visit these gentiles and convey to them the light and good news of the Gospel. Two religious priests embarked on this enterprise in 1594. They were Father Gerónimo Ramírez, whose work in the Tepehuan mission has already been discussed, and Father Juan Agustín. Both were priests of notable spirit and religion. Father Agustín concluded his life with a glorious (albeit hastened) death, which came a few years after he began teaching these souls the way to salvation. He did not die violently, but rather from his very apostolic work. Nevertheless, he died in the middle of this gentile wilderness, among the barbarous Indians whom he had sought to lead to heaven and without a nearby brother from the Company to assist him.

These two evangelical ministers were the first to cultivate this vineyard, or forest of thorns and weeds, sowing the seed of the divine word. They gave an account of the land and its people to their superior in order to convince the viceroy of Nueva España of the advantages of providing ministers of the doctrine for these people, who were scattered throughout that extensive land. The priests' account reveals the means by which divine providence directed the relief and salvation of these souls. Although the fruits that were gathered at first seemed few, they became great in the end, which is why I did not want to omit them.

Father Gerónimo Ramírez says the following in his letter:

Our Lord brought me to this pueblo of Quencame, which is located in a pleasant valley, surrounded by somewhat distant mountain ranges. It is also far from the Río Nazas, which enters the Laguna some eight leagues away. The Zacateco Indians inhabit [the land] up to this point. Because they live near the mines, where they have already begun to work, some of these Indians came wearing clothing and on horseback to welcome me to their pueblo. [674] Although there were not many houses and people in the little pueblo, the men and women who were there came in separate groups and welcomed me with great friendliness. Some Indian principales who had received news of my entrada came from the Río [Nazas] and gave me some of the fruits and seeds that they gather. They did so expressing great joy that I had come to their lands. They were even happier when they heard me speak a few words in their language, which I had learned along the way. They housed me in the only adobe dwelling in the place, which belonged to a Tarascan Indian from Michoacán who was a long-time Christian and whom God had brought here to aid us. Although the house was small, under the circumstances it seemed to me to be appropriate for a church. The Indians covered an area in front of the house, which served us as a dwelling.

I have started to learn the language and to prepare the doctrine and catechism. I dare not baptize the people until instruction is better established and they are better prepared.

I have given this sacrament only to one woman *in articulo mortis*[6] and to an old man whom it seemed Our Lord had kept alive just long enough to be baptized. After he listened attentively, understanding the mysteries of our Holy Faith and showing remorse for his sins, he received the Sacrament of Salvation. After doing this, he lost consciousness due to the severity of his illness and died.

I visit other Indians who are sick and bring them holy water and whatever food I can. I tell them Gospel stories to which they attribute the health that God provides them. The Indians are extremely happy, so much so that they tell me if I leave them, they will go with me. I understand clearly that if the viceroy and governor help, it will be easy to attract and congregate the rest, because many of them do not live in pueblos. May God move those who govern to have pity on these poor people.

Up to this point I have cited Father Ramírez's letter, in which he spoke of the Zacateco Indians before the doctrine had been fully established among them. The priests were on their way to the more remote and distant mission of Parras, which they wanted to try to re-establish.[7] In the following chapter Father Juan Agustín will relate his experiences with these people during his first entrada.

CHAPTER IV Father Juan Agustín goes to establish the Parras mission; in a personal letter he records the willingness of these people to receive the Gospel

Although God wished to abbreviate to only a few short years the time that this evangelical minister labored in this undertaking, he was very successful at the outset of this mission in sowing the teachings of heaven. We cannot deny him the glory of being the founder of this Christian community, and even though his death was neither violent nor at the hands of tyrants, it was as if it were, for he suffered great hardships and, with them, death, as will be told at the end of this book. It was also thus because he preached Christ's Gospel to those who were in darkness, providing them with knowledge of His divine re-

demption. We will see from a letter that he wrote to his superiors how he initiated this enterprise and mission:

The first Zacateco Indian pueblo that I reached is situated at the foot of what the Spaniards call Cerro Gordo,[8] due to its large size and its height. Because the cacique knew I was coming, he came out with some of his people to welcome me. When they were still a good distance away from me, [675] they dismounted their horses, which they

6. "At the point of death."

7. Franciscan missionaries established a short-lived mission in the valley of Parras in 1578.

8. 'Fat Hill'.

already possessed because of their proximity to Spaniards, and with great reverence they came to receive my blessing, welcoming me and telling me that they were very happy I had come. I thanked them as well as I could, and because it was already night, I remained with them in that field.

The following day we reached the pueblo or rancherías where all the people had gathered. They came out in a procession to welcome us with demonstrations of great love. Then we went to a manner of church that they had prepared. After I had prayed, asking Our Lord to grant a good start to the welfare of those souls, I sent them away.

The following day, which was Sunday, the humble church was dedicated. A beautiful image of the Assumption of the Virgin was placed within, as were two other images of Saints Peter and Paul, so that under the protection of the Queen of the Angels and these glorious Apostles the spiritual edifice of these souls might grow. We also put up a bell we had brought along, and after having sung some prayers in the Zacateco language, the first Mass was said. This amazed the gentiles, who had never before seen such a thing.

The same day I initiated religious instruction, which everyone joyfully attended, both morning and afternoon. They took their religious instruction so much to heart that at night we could hear them in their houses teaching one another; they even attend Mass every day. I found some Christians here who, due to the closeness of Zacatecas, had been baptized but were Christian in name only. They neither knew nor had any memory of those who had baptized them, nor did they have any written record of it. In their lives and customs, and in their abuses and ceremonies, they were as gentile as the rest. In order to secure and revalidate their Baptisms and marriages, I took the measures that seemed necessary to me.

One of these Indians, who was eighty years old, was the cacique of the pueblo. There were three or four others of the same age, as well as some other younger men, including one who was the son of the cacique. I left them very informed about matters of the Faith and Christian obligations. I did not attempt to baptize the adult gentiles, who were not ready; I baptized only a few very young children. Our Lord has placed in their hearts a great appreciation for the good they expect and that which has come to them by way of the priests. They are of the fine opinion that, because God has already come to visit them and has done them so much good by sending them one of his sons (this is what they call the priest) to teach them and guide them to heaven and make them His children too, then from now on they must lay aside their vices and sins and abandon their dances and drunken revels. Since I have been in this pueblo there has been no trace of these vices and sins.

One of the Christian Indians I mentioned, who was one of the most important in the pueblo, came and asked me to hear his confession. He confessed with great sorrow and remorse, saying, "Father, before we got word that you were coming, I used to get drunk every morning and evening. I would be so out of my mind that, like a lunatic, I would forget about God and the fact that I was a Christian. I also committed a thousand other evil deeds. However, when word arrived that you were coming to this pueblo, I felt

in my heart that they were telling me not to get drunk anymore, because a priest was coming through whom I would be saved. Although it was very difficult, I nevertheless became so determined to abandon my vices and sins that I have not drunk wine or committed any other sin for four months. Therefore, Father, I beg you to look after my soul." I encouraged him, and he is getting along very [676] well.

Word of what was happening in this pueblo spread to Laguna [Grande de San Pedro], and so many caciques came to see me because of the wonder of seeing priests in their land. They insistently asked me to come to their pueblos, particularly three Indian principales from the Río Nazas. They requested that I hasten my departure because there was an epidemic there, and many children and older people were dying. They said that they were not concerned so much that these people might die, but rather that they might die without becoming Christians. If so, they would be unable to save themselves, according to what they had heard. One of them added, "We are well aware that you do not come in search of gold or silver (like the miners), but rather only for the welfare of our souls and to take us to heaven. Because this is your desire, pay no heed to our poverty and our lack of clothing, for our souls are worth more than that." Who would not be convinced by this Indian's reasoning, even if he was a barbarian?

I left in the morning and they sent word ahead of my departure. We reached the little pueblo at sundown. The people, who were visibly happy, came out almost a quarter of a league to welcome us. We all went into the semblance of a church that they had erected, and I baptized seventeen or eighteen boys and girls who were sick. I also heard the confessions of some adult Christians who had retreated there and had never confessed in their lives. They did so with great sorrow and remorse for their sins.

Then some other caciques from neighboring pueblos came to see me, accompanied by their people. Together they told me that they wanted to congregate and form a large pueblo, provided I would settle there. I answered them, giving them high hopes. I remained in this place for three days, teaching them the Christian doctrine in the Zacateco language, which quite amazed them.

I returned to the first pueblo, and even though I had only been gone those three days, they came out to welcome me as if they had not seen me for a long time. I told them that the place whence I had come seemed very suitable to me. The cacique of this pueblo responded that he and all his people would follow me. Although they would be leaving their lands, they considered their salvation more important. This is the willingness that I have found in this land and among these people. May God Our Lord, who has been served through His mercy to give this mission such a fine start, also be served to carry it forward for His greater glory.

To this point I have cited Father Juan Agustín's letter. I was able to say that he was already giving religious instruction in the Zacateco language because he was born to honorable and landed parents and reared in that renowned Spanish silver mining town [Zacatecas] in the lands of the Zacateco Indians, who go there to work. Therefore, Father Juan Agustín had been able to learn their language. Although it is true that one ordinarily goes to the Parras mission and Laguna [Grande de San Pedro] by way of the road through the dry plateau from Durango, under the jurisdiction of which it falls, these places can also be reached from the city and mining center of Zacatecas.

I have begun the account of this mission and doctrina using the priests' letters, which reveal God's particular [acts of] providence and the means He employs to remove those He has predestined from among these people. Now follows an account of the remaining rancherías and settlements and the manner in which religious instruction was introduced to them. [677]

CHAPTER V The number of people living at Laguna [Grande] de San Pedro; the viceroy entrusts the priests of the Company with their religious instruction

The reasons for founding this mission and doctrine have been provided in the preceding letters. This mission was initiated in the region of the mountains of the Zacateco Indians, who border on those of Laguna [Grande de San Pedro] and Parras. I will now record what was accomplished there by the priests of the college at Durango (which from the beginning was recognized as this mission's headquarters). I will also record the number of people in those settlements and the establishment of their mission.

Those who lived around the lake had a great number of rancherías that benefited from the great advantages offered by the lake itself: fresh water and fertile land. There was a great number of souls in all of these rancherías to whom God wanted to extend His mercy. At the lake and in the surrounding area alone there were about twelve thousand people, not counting those at Parras or the [other] people who have continued to come down from the mountains to settle here. The priests have been encouraging these people to hear the doctrine and to live as Christians. This harvest (as will be told ahead) has continued up to the present time. Some families come down from the mountains (which can be seen [from the lake]) in order to remain and live among the Christians. This is a means by which a great many souls have been won over to God. It is nearly impossible for the ministers of the doctrine to reach these settlements in the mountains because of the difficult roads and lack

of water along the way. The Indians supplement their [intake of] water with the juice of a wild plant, [a drink] called mescal, to which they are already accustomed.

The Spaniards established friendship with the Indians of the Valle de Laguna [Grande] after they settled the region of Durango. Securing peace [with the Laguneros] was considered very important for the peace of the [entire] province, for they were the key to making peace with other nations. In addition, the Lagunero Indians were of great aid to the Spaniards, diligently working on Spanish farms, ranches, and mines. Moreover, these people were always quick to learn, enthusiastic, and of a good nature. Although they wore little clothing when they were gentiles, once they became accustomed to doing so, they liked to be well dressed and adorned, so much so that they seek out work in order to be able to buy clothing. The women are particularly concerned about their attire, which was made from the [same] material and cloth—animal hides—that God gave our first parents after they had broken His divine commandment. These women added fringes and tassels as adornments, fashioning them from the same animal hides dyed various colors. They braided their hair stylishly and adorned their necks with strings of shells from little snails and conches. All this has helped these people to receive the Faith, apply themselves to their work, and live a civilized and Christian life.

The men's greatest interest was in their bows, which

are longer than those of other nations. They handle them with great strength and skill and are considered to be more courageous than men of other nations. They are tall and fairly well proportioned and are generous with each other, helping one another with all they have. They keep their houses open and unlocked, and they have no fear of robbery, which is something they abhor. They knew only loyalty and nothing of double-dealing. They always maintained peace with Spaniards, [678] helping them in their wars against other barbarous nations. They did so for the reasons already mentioned, as well as because their reduction and settlement was very important for their security from the neighboring Chichimec.

The Spaniards of the Province of Nueva Vizcaya wanted the Laguneros to receive religious instruction, so they asked the viceroy to assign ministers to go and preach the Gospel to these gentiles. The viceroy ordered the religious of the Company to take charge of this enterprise, and he ordered the royal officials to

provide the ministers with all necessary provisions. As I have previously noted, these nations do not provide subsidies or food, nor does the Company receive these things [from the Indians]. The people cannot support their ministers, nor can they provide materials for building and adorning churches. [All] praise and glory to the Catholic monarchs of Spain, who have dedicated innumerable temples to God in the New World using the riches that divine goodness has granted them here.

Everything was carried out according to the viceroy's orders, and Father Francisco de Arista, a religious of great prudence and apostolic zeal, journeyed through Durango to establish this new Christian community. He, along with the two others who were mentioned, traveled through the Zacatecas mountain range and initiated the reduction of these people, preaching the Gospel in the manner that will be related in the following chapter.

CHAPTER VI Father Francisco de Arista records in a personal letter his entrada and mission to Parras and the beginning of religious instruction

There is no better or more truthful way to recount the means and plans by which the religious priests who entered this mission established the Christian doctrine and laws than [to cite] what they themselves wrote to their superiors concerning this enterprise. Therefore, I will copy here Father Arista's letter, which discusses these matters.[9] He says:

I have been here for three months, and we have made some trips to the rancherías of some caciques who act as ambassadors, bringing the widely scattered Indians together. With these trips and the news that has been circulating about the good treatment that the Indians receive, there is now a large number of them in this settlement; the fruit is greater than was expected. This reduction and congregation has obliged them to uproot themselves and abandon their

settlements. This is so alien to them that, on the one hand, it seems to be an extraordinary act of divine power, and on the other, a great sign of the good that Our Lord intends and that can be expected. Up to this time they have come by the hundreds with their families, and with them have come many other interested parties to sample the new fruit. If they like what they taste, they spread the word in their lands and try to congregate their people. Some of them have already set out, and others are waiting to do the same during the rainy season. It seems that these people's time for healing has finally arrived, according to the [679] schedule established by divine providence. We will deal with others at the appropriate time, but for now let us attend to these good people's spiritual and temporal affairs.

[We are] always trying to gain their goodwill, and from time to time we invite the caciques to dine at our house. On principal feast days we invite the entire pueblo to entertain themselves by holding one of their former communal dances. With respect to divine matters they have endearing Christian tunes in Mexican that we taught them. These celebrations take place in the patio of the church, and it is

9. Arista's letter was copied and included in the anua of 1607, which Pérez de Ribas draws from here.

just as pleasing to us as it is enjoyable to them that we attend and do not forbid their decent celebrations. Even the boys and girls participate, once they have finished their religious instruction in the afternoons. This has all been a good strategy for domesticating them. They already erect Crosses of their own free will in their barrios. There at night they recite their prayers in unison, so loudly that we can joyously listen to them from our house. The procedure followed in the case of people who come to settle in these congregated pueblos is to measure off land for a house, a garden, and a small field, like the ones they used to have next to their [former] homes. This settlement always follows an orderly street plan, as is common in many Mexican pueblos. We visit them to see how their houses are coming along and to find out whether anyone is sick, so that we can attend to him both spiritually and corporally with whatever food possible. In preparation for Holy Baptism, a good number of adults have started learning the catechism, which is taught in two languages. The Indians are also given talks concerning the [doctrine], and in this way they are beginning to understand the Christian religion. There is no one in this pueblo who does not desire or request Holy Baptism, nor is there anyone who dares to do anything improper or perform any ritual or custom that reeks of heathenism. If they want to dance, they say that the music will concern God. As is known, their dances are always accompanied by music, just like those of the Mexica. On some of the principal feast days we form

processions in which all the new Christians carry Crosses made from flowers. They attend the divine rites with such reverence and attention that, with each passing day, they show more and more of their good nature and understanding of the Church's holy matters and ceremonies. For the burial of a baptized child all the Christian children wear wreaths on their heads and sing the prayers in their language. Everyone from the pueblo participates in the burial of adults. These burials in the Christian fashion are very pleasing to them.

This is the good disposition that these good people have shown thus far. May the Lord preserve this willingness and send us comrades to aid in this evangelical labor. They will certainly be needed, because with only the Indians who live in the surrounding area, without considering those who might later join them, more than two thousand male heads-of-household can be reduced to four or five pueblos. We trust that the paternal providence of God Our Lord will not fail these Indians so that this Christian community can be completely established.

Up to this point Father Francisco de Arista has written about the beginnings of this young Christian community, which he cultivated for sixteen years, working to perfect and increase it, as will be seen ahead. [In this regard] the deeds of mature adults should not be expected of those who are still children in the Faith. [680]

CHAPTER VII Some very singular cases of gentile Baptisms

I will not pause to record here the general Baptism of children, who by the hundreds are baptized together at the outset of these doctrinas; they are the delectable first fruits of these missions. I have already written a great deal concerning this elsewhere. Therefore, the same should be understood to have taken place in this mission, and I presuppose this to avoid repeating that which generally happens in all of them. Nevertheless, I do not want to omit some singular cases that demonstrate the special divine providence with which God arranged for the salvation of some souls. Even though these people lived in darkness, He had predestined them for eternal bliss. Just as Christ Our Lord did with His first missionaries, God ordinarily has set aside these early fruits for the missionary priests, especially the new ones; they are a comfort

for the great hardships that beset these priests in the early days of their missions. Saint Luke says[10] that the first missionaries returned from their mission joyful and celebrating, recounting to the Divine Master the marvelous works they had done and telling Him that the demons themselves surrendered to them and became their subjects. From this they drew divine lessons, which I will not ponder, nor will I pause to recount all the cases that take place in our missions, for this would be never-ending. Instead, I will recount some cases that will serve as edification and encouragement for those whom Our Lord might call to these enterprises.

10. *Margin Note.* Luc. 10. Luke 10:17: "And the seventy-two disciples came back rejoicing; Lord, they said, even the devils are made subject to us through thy name" (Knox 1956:67).

[In these missions] the priests attempt first to prepare the older Indians, owing to the danger presented by their advanced age, to receive the means necessary for their salvation. One of these Indians had behaved in a rebellious and adverse manner toward Holy Baptism. He fell ill, and when the priest went to visit him, it seems that God moved the priest to place in the Indian's hands a small image he had with him of the Most Holy Virgin with her precious Son in her arms. The hardened old man looked at it for a long time. In the meantime, the Mother of Mercy did her work, just as the Queen of Heaven always does. The Indian asked the priest to explain the significance of the image. The old man listened attentively and then said that he had had many opportunities to be baptized and become a Christian (it must have been impulses from heaven), yet he had never wanted to do so. But now this Lady had softened his heart and had changed him in such a way that he wanted to hear the doctrine and word of God and be baptized. Even though he was sick and quite old, thereby making it difficult for him to learn, within a few hours he nevertheless learned the catechism so well that he responded with great accuracy to all the questions he was asked. The priest baptized him, and shortly thereafter he died and God took him to heaven. We can clearly understand that it was not in vain that the priest was moved to use that particular means, which is ordinarily not employed, although it is in and of itself so admirable and effective. It is also to be understood that the Virgin's most serene gaze captured the soul of that barbarian and changed his heart, which was so hardened; the Mother of Sinners won his soul and carried it off to heaven.

Just as quickly, if not more so, God took another soul in the case that follows. It happened that there was a gentile burning straw out in the fields when a priest happened by. This Indian had heard about the suffering endured in the other life by those who are bad and die without Baptism, for this is one of the first doctrines [681] taught to peoples who are so profoundly ignorant of the next life. As the Indian watched how quickly the fire consumed the grass and dry straw, he asked the priest, "Is the fire they say is found in hell like this?" The priest responded that the Indian's fire looked like a painted [imitation] by comparison. The Indian then asked him whether it burned out as quickly as that one. He responded that the fire endured by those who were damned was never-ending. Then the Indian answered back, "Well, Father, then what do I need to do to keep from going there?" The answer was

that he should become a Christian and keep the law of God, which is what the priest was preaching to them. At the conclusion of this talk, God, who had initiated it, willed that it should lead to the Indian's final resolution to become a Christian and learn the doctrine so that he could be baptized. He carefully followed through on his intentions, attending catechism for several days. He was baptized on the feast day of [Mary] Magdalene, returned home contented, and the following morning was dead. We can say that he is living in heaven with baptismal grace, which God did not wish that he should lose. He won this soul on the occasion of some burning straw and through deeds proper to His divine measures, which are not thwarted.

A priest was going to visit some sick people who he had been told were in the distant mountains. At nightfall he reached a place where there was water, which (as I stated) is rarely found in this land once one leaves Laguna [Grande de San Pedro]. The Indians who were with him told him that they should stop and spend the night there because the remainder of the journey would be difficult, as they would encounter many marshes. Furthermore, it was two leagues to the place where the sick people were located and along that stretch of trail there was neither pasture for the animals nor water to drink, but rather only the water from the wild magüey, a plant from which the Indians drink the juice to sustain themselves. The priest contemplated the difficulties and decided to overcome them, proceeding on so that no sick person would die without the aid of the Holy Sacraments. He reached this place just as an old woman was about to die. She was in such agony that even though others had spoken to her, she had given no signs of hearing anything. Here they considered it a noteworthy case that as soon as the priest called out and spoke to her, she sat up in her bed and asked him to baptize her. He instructed her and she repeated the catechism twice, demonstrating well that she understood it and was sorry for her sins and the life she had led. Then he baptized her, and in less than an hour she died, leaving the priest with good assurances of her salvation.

In an even shorter space of time and with even greater certainty and signs of divine providence, three souls went to heaven in the case that follows. A missionary had set out from his pueblo for a neighboring district. He and the Indians who were with him had stopped briefly along the way to rest, and they let their mounts loose to pasture in the fields (as is customary). By order of divine providence (as was made clear by what happened), these mounts ran back to the pueblo, thereby forcing the priest to return and abandon his trip. When he arrived he found some gentiles waiting for him; some of their children were with them, on the verge of dying, and they wanted the priest to baptize them. He did so and it seems that God waited no longer to take them to glory, for they died immediately. This is a matter of great consolation to those who labor in aiding these souls, because the number of those whom they send to heaven with their own hands is countless, and there is almost no journey that does not have as its

reward the salvation of one of those who cost God His blood.

May the cases recounted [here] suffice as a sampling of many other similar cases. [682] I omit the cases of one hundred-year-old Indians, whom it seems God kept alive solely for the purpose of their being baptized by the priests in order to pass on to glory. Whenever the priests went to their rancherías, mountains, and thickets and found [any Indians who were] very old and in great need, they would baptize them.

CHAPTER VIII The priests prepare to reduce the Indian rancherías of Laguna and Parras to large pueblos; four more priests arrive and begin religious instruction; the special attention paid to the instruction of young people

The minsters of the doctrine had visited many of the rancherías of Laguna and Parras and had won over many of the caciques and principales who wield authority over these people. Once the [leaders] are won over, so too are their followers and families. The priests then began congregating the people in suitable pueblos and settlements, both for the Indians' temporal well-being as well as for their religious instruction and spiritual welfare. This was successfully accomplished through the priests' diligent efforts and by allowing the Indians to proceed at their own pace. It is a matter of great importance at the beginning of these missions to exercise patience and not to offend the Indians. It is known from experience that when these people are given time, which God grants to sinners, one achieves one's goals, and this is what eventually happened in the reductions of Parras and La Laguna.

Five pueblos were formed and settled, each with two hundred, three hundred, or five hundred households. There were also other small rancherías called visitas, which were very difficult to uproot because they were on islands in the lake. Although very narrow, these

were nonetheless amenable to the Indians. These reductions offered many material and temporal advantages to the Province of Nueva Vizcaya, including peace and laborers for Spaniards living in the province. There were also spiritual advantages, namely the removal of obstacles to the Indians' religious instruction. Mindful of all these good reasons, the viceroy of Nueva España decreed that in certain pueblos the Indians were to be provided a ration of meat and other foodstuffs at royal expense. The principales were also to be given a yearly allotment of clothing, in addition to swords to enhance their authority over their people. The viceroy approved an allocation from the treasury for these expenses, which continued for many years until these people were better established and prospered as a republic. This custom was practiced not only in these nations, but also in others in Nueva España such as among the Chichimec. The viceroy was further informed that two missionary priests were not sufficient to instruct so many people in such a large number of pueblos separated by eight or more leagues. Two missionaries were also too few to provide the Indians with the Holy Sacraments, especially in times of need and for such a large area. All this convinced His Excellency to order the Father Provincial to dispatch four more priests to minister to this new Christianity, bringing the total to six. In addition to this stipend, three hundred pesos were provided each year from the Royal Treasury for a seminary. There young men were reared and trained as singers and acolytes for the Church, and so that later they could govern the pueblos in peace and Christian civility. This royal beneficence, in addition to being very much in keeping with the piety of the Catholic kings of Spain, was well provided for by God. As was [683] previously noted, in this land rich silver mines have been found and continue to be discovered each day.

The four new religious reached Laguna and Parras, and together with the others they prepared to fully establish the Indian settlements, dividing their charges among them. They began instructing the adults for general Baptism. The children, who are the first suckled in this milk, attended with such diligence and speed that they competed to see who would reach the church first and give the best account of what they had learned. Those who were most diligent came to catechism even before daybreak, calling to others from the streets and awakening the people who were asleep. Some even carried tree branches from the monte to sweep the church each morning. Although such behavior may seem childish, it nevertheless engendered esteem for matters of our holy religion that the priests sought to instill in these people. It was also a means of teaching children and winning their affection that was used and esteemed in the East Indies by their Apostle and our father, Saint Francis Xavier. And above all others is He who was and is the Wisdom of God, Christ Our Lord, whose affection for children was remarkable, as the holy writers of the Gospel noted.[11] For this reason I will say no more.

The custom was introduced in this doctrina of naming one of the young Indians as the little fiscal. It was his duty to insure that no one missed catechism. The boy took this position so seriously that he and his squad of companions would go looking for whoever was absent. They would search the fields and thickets, and if they did not find him, the next day at daybreak the junior fiscal would be out looking again. In this way no one escaped catechism, regardless of how wild or rebellious he might be. This pleased not only the children's spiritual fathers but also their parents by birth.

These are all signs of the fervor with which the Christian doctrine was introduced and then embraced by parents and children who had once been barbarians. The duties of the little fiscal included watching over and caring for the manner in which his charges heard Mass. To increase this devotion among the children, who are the principal harvest of these new Christianities, the priests introduced their own celebration, which was held each year on the Day of the Holy Innocents [December 28]. After Mass the priests invited the children to a banquet in the patio of the church, and the little barbarians were served a meal by their religious fathers, who looked upon them as angels. With each course the children were saluted with trumpets, in keeping with the Lord's statement that they would be princes in the kingdom of heaven.[12] The children's parents by birth were amazed, and the children learned the doctrine of Christ very well.

These were all means of winning souls that were invented by the holy zeal of these apostolic men and learned from their divine master. Among these children, some were later chosen to learn to read and write and to learn music and singing, at which they became very skillful. In time the general Baptism of adults was celebrated, which (as has been noted) does not occur until they have learned the catechism and have heard several talks about it. In this way they come to understand the law they are receiving and to which they have subjected themselves.

The people of Laguna and Parras were so well prepared to receive Holy Baptism that both peoples did so with great affection and esteem. Indeed, the happiness of those who were baptized was equaled in sadness by those who were not baptized because they had failed to respond well to instruction, all of which served to quicken the pace with which they prepared to become Christians. [684]

---

11. Mark 10:14: "Let the children come to me, he said, do not keep them back; the kingdom of God belongs to such as these" (Knox 1956:430); see also Matthew 19:14, Luke 18:17.

12. Luke 9:48: "He who welcomes this child in my name, welcomes me; and he who welcomes me welcomes him that sent me. He who is least in all your company is the greatest (Knox 1956:66); see also Matthew 18:4.

CHAPTER IX Abuses and superstitions that were corrected and banished from these people

Although the introduction of Christianity among these people was not attended by difficulties or rebellions, as is usually the case, it is impossible to avoid the inevitable when dealing with nations that have been tyrannized by the devil and who are possessed and governed by him. It is glorious to see them liberated by the doctrine of Christ and, accordingly, that which has been wrought by divine virtue merits recounting, for this victory is the greatest and most precious miracle of Christian law.

There was a deep-rooted abuse that was more common among these people than among other barbarians. When an important person became sick, they would sacrifice a newborn child so that the older person would regain his health. One night not long after the priests had begun this mission, a woman dreamed that some of her relatives, whom she dearly loved, were going to die. Just because of this dream, when she awoke she smothered her newborn baby (a cruel case). Such were the dreams that the cruel enemy of mankind sent to these people, frequently leading to cases like this. This deeply rooted abuse was not amended through a miracle and revelation from heaven like that experienced by the great emperor Constantine. Rather, it was completely eradicated by the divine word, which was conveyed by our priests and ministers of Christ, who played the role of ambassadors from heaven.

The devil persuaded another faction of these people that if they were present when a sick person died, they would all die as well. The fear caused by this superstition and abuse led people to bury the sick before they were dead in order to avoid being present at the hour of death. They also practiced other superstitions so that they would not die. A priest went to visit a woman whom he had learned was ill, and he found her surrounded by deer heads and antlers, which were laid out in an orderly manner. He realized that some diabolical superstition was at work there, so he told some old gentiles who had surrounded the sick woman (there are always sorcerers and ministers of Satan standing by, ready to finish off the soul so that it goes to hell) to throw those deer heads into the fire (which they usually build near the sick). They answered that if the smoke reached them, they would die. Instead, they immedi-

ately began to hide the deer heads. "Well, let's all die," said the priest, and to eradicate that vain fear he immediately threw the remaining deer heads into the fire. The sorcerers departed as quickly as if fleeing death itself, but later they were freed of their deception by seeing that the priest had not died. More importantly, they were freed by the light of the Gospel. Even though this abuse was very common, it too was eradicated.

The mournful verses and dirges that they composed for their dead were famous. Some mornings or evenings the relatives and acquaintances of the dead would gather at the grave, and with their faces blackened the men and the women would each compose their laments. These laments celebrated or lamented the deceased and his deeds—his bravery in war, his greatness as a hunter and provider for his children, and how much they suffered due to his absence. [685] And if these sad, grieving people had known where that soul had ended up, they would have cried much harder. Many longtime Christians today should realize that they also have a lot to cry about, knowing that they did not tend to the salvation of the souls of their dead while they were still alive. Here it is the case that once our new Christians have received the doctrine of heaven, the first thing they are concerned about when they or one of their relatives becomes sick is that they receive the Holy Sacraments.

To conclude writing about these gentiles and their superstitions concerning deer heads, I will note that throughout the year they used to hold some famous dances, during which they would bring out one of these heads that they had very reverently guarded in memory of a person who had died. While they were doing their dance, one of the old men presiding over it would throw into the fire (which they always light for a dance) some pieces of the deer's bones and antlers. He persuaded the people that the flames, which burned brighter when the bones were added, were the soul of the dead person, who had come to call on the others and tell them about his virtue and diligence during [the deer hunt] while he was alive. The old man would add that the dead person was in the drink made from the powder of those bones, which he gave to his sons so that they might be as swift as the deer and have the strength to track and exhaust them when hunting.

At the beginning of this Christianity, when there were still many gentiles, one of the priests found out that on the day of the Feast of Saint John the Baptist [June 24] some people had gotten together to celebrate a superstitious dance like the one I have mentioned. He reproached them for this vain abuse, and they responded so well that when Mass was over, the governor and the Christian fiscales of the pueblo, in the priest's presence, went to all the houses and collected all the deer heads they could find so that they could be burned. In their place they erected holy Crosses that they had made. Thus, Christianity was glorified and this abuse was defeated and banished, along with the devil, who had introduced it.

The same thing happened in the following case. Once when a priest was in one of those pueblos, the Indians heard voices and shouting as though someone were begging for help.[13] The priest went with them to see what it was and realized that the devil was taking an Indian away, like a possessed madman. They followed the trail of voices until finally, with great difficulty, because it was nighttime and the road was steep (the devil usually drags his captives through thickets and scrub), they found him in a place full of caves.[14] It was already infamous because they said that it was there that the infernal beast had his lair, and that the Indians used to see him there, sometimes in the form of a serpent, other times in human form but ugly and frightening. Once he was even seen in the habit and clerical robe of the Company of Jesus. The dragon uses all these forms, some to deceive and others to frighten and terrorize those he is misleading.[15] The Indians declared that the sight of him had killed many people, and in testimony to that, the priest saw a sepulcher with human skulls and bones. The Indians threw piles of rock upon them so that the deceased would not haunt them. The priest also found characters in the shape of letters on the cliff faces and inside the caves, applied in blood and in places so high that only the devil could have placed them there. The characters were so firmly affixed that not even water or wind had faded or erased them.

Finally, they found the Indian there, who was unconscious. Although the priest did all he could to revive him so that he could baptize him, due to the fact that he was a gentile (and it was even said he was a sorcerer), the Indian remained lifeless. In the morning God willed that he should regain consciousness, and the priest exhorted him to renounce [686] his dealings with mankind's most ferocious enemy and instead to listen and believe in the word of God and be baptized. He agreed to this, and because the priest did not want to delay the Holy Sacrament that would free this poor Indian's body and soul from the danger they were in, he baptized him with one hundred other adults that he had prepared for Baptism that day. Then he organized a procession of the new Christians, and carrying a Cross they proceeded to the devil's cavern. There they performed the exorcisms and blessings of the Church, and an altar was erected and the priest said Mass. A holy Cross was placed in the cave, which from then on they called Santiago, because this was the feast day of the great patron saint of the Spaniards [July 25], under whose protection they have planted the Faith and the Catholic Empire in the Indies.

The terror that the devil had caused at the cave was immediately and entirely brought to an end, and at the same time the Indians acquired greater affection for and devotion to the ceremonies of the Holy Church. They were also more confirmed in the Faith they were receiving, and the devil was outsmarted and his tricks undone. This was not, however, the final conflict and battle experienced by the ministers of the Gospel. Just as when the Son of God walked the earth and Our Lord cast the devil out of certain bodies and souls, the devil remained in others so that His divine kindness might work further miracles. Rather than elaborate (which I could) on the gentile superstitions and abuses that were banished, I will omit other cases (all for the glory of God and His divine Gospel) in order to write about the holy Christian customs that replaced gentile customs among these people, and were no less glorious for the Gospel itself.

---

13. The story Pérez de Ribas is about to relate was taken from a letter by Father Francisco de Arista in the anua of 1604, which recounts the Jesuits' success among the Laguneros.

14. This is apparently the cave of Texcalcos, well known to this day by residents of Parras. What follows is a description of a mass burial associated with what was probably a pre-Jesuit epidemic, perhaps the typhus epidemic of 1576–81. Cave burials that logically can be attributed to Old World diseases are also known for neighboring groups such

as the Tarahumara and Tepehuan (Brooks and Brooks 1978; Sheridan and Naylor 1979: 115).

15. Lagunero stories about the devil appearing in a cleric's habit and punishing the natives with disease may refer specifically to typhus that was spread by Franciscan missionaries who established a short-lived mission in the Parras Valley in 1578, at the time of the epidemic of 1576–81 (Dunne 1944: 203, f.20).

CHAPTER X Christian Customs and exercises, particularly the Christmas celebration, are introduced in the Parras mission

By the year 1607, the priests had baptized most of the gentile adults [of Parras]. However, as I will later relate, some people who lived very far away, particularly those in the mountains, are still coming down from their settlements in the steep mountains and are being reduced at the time this history is being written.

As the number of baptized persons increased, Christian feast days and celebrations were introduced. Because these took place in a new Christian community and demonstrate how well Christianity took hold, they will be recorded here. In his district one priest celebrated the joyous Feast of the Nativity of Jesus Christ Our Lord, declaring this pleasing and joyous mystery to the new Christians. This was an organized celebration and was attended by some Spaniards who had haciendas in the region. Because it was a Christmas celebration, and in order that the Indians might rejoice as Christians, the priest invited them to perform a dance in the Christian fashion, as all gentile ceremonies had been banished. They very gladly accepted this invitation, and when the evening [Christmas Eve] arrived—which is appropriately called *Noche Buena* because it is the blissful night that brought heaven to earth—great torches were lit all around the plaza of the pueblo and at the door of the church. Then one of the many and varied groups that attended this celebration began a dance, guided by a cacique of a people called the Irritillá.[16] He was a baptized Indian who clearly demonstrated his great Christianity. After [687] adoring the Christ Child and His Most Holy Mother, whose images had been placed in the church, they went out to the patio, which served as a cemetery. This place provided more room for celebrating the festival which, because of its novelty, had attracted many Christians and gentiles. Here, many other groups and nations from Laguna [Grande de San Pedro] and its environs joined the Irritilla. It has been stated previously that although these nations are not very populous, I call them nations because they dealt with and referred to one another by making the same distinctions as the different nations in Europe. I know of no other way of making this distinction than to call them different nations.

Returning to the festival being celebrated by the priests who were present, they said with special joy that it seemed to them that they were observing the partial fulfillment of that universal prophecy: *Omnes gentes venient, & adorabunt coram te Domine.*[17] All those who came danced, and as was mentioned earlier, these dances involve not simply ten or twelve people, as is the case in Europe, but rather two hundred or more Indians.

Because this history deals with these [dances], I will say briefly that at the celebration in Mexico City of the beatification of our glorious patriarch Saint Ignatius,[18] which the Mexica Indians celebrated in their plaza, there was a dance that they call a mitote which was performed by two or three thousand Indians. They all were adorned with feathers and headdresses and kept step as though there were only ten or twelve [of them] dancing. Some of them carried their unusual little drums, which are made of a special wood, and they marked the time and rhythm of the dance with the beat of these drums.

Let us return to the dance of our barbarians, who are two hundred leagues from the civilized Mexica. When the nations had gathered, as I said, in the pueblo of Parras for the Nativity of the Christ Child, they held their dance. They were adorned with feathers of various colors from guacamayas and other birds. They held arrows in their hands, as was their custom, and sang words that were no longer barbarian but rather Christian, although in the manner dictated by their simple capacity. And this is how they would be welcomed by the Lord, who came down from heaven to earth for them and who deigned to receive the gifts of poor and rude shepherds, accompanied by the songs of blessed spirits. The songs of our Indians, translated from their language, in which they sang, went as follows: "God Our

---

16. Little is known about the Irritilla, who ceased to exist as a distinct culture in the seventeenth century.

17. "All people will come and praise you together, Oh Lord."
18. This was in June 1610 (Dunne 1951:96).

Lord is worthy of praise; the feast of Our Lady makes us happy; let men praise Our Lady and Mother; let us worship the place where Our Lady is found, she who is the Mother of God and Our Lord." These motets were repeated and sung in the tone and rhythm that they use, the same way that one pauses and then repeats the brief verses of a song when accompanied by an organ.

This feast day, which was celebrated in a Christian fashion, was greatly enjoyed by the Spaniards in attendance. They saw occupied in the worship of the true God, the Redeemer of Men, those who just a short time before were dedicated to the worship and reverence of devils. At the appropriate times—at midnight and at dawn—two Masses were said, which all Christians heard with devotion. Afterward the priest had a splendid feast prepared for them, consisting of a yearling bull that a Spaniard had donated from his ranch. The Indians were very grateful and became so fond of the priest who organized the celebration for them that they said they would not let him leave their pueblos even if he wanted to.

They also devoutly celebrated the Feast of the Epiphany, an appropriate celebration for gentiles who had come to recognize Christ Our Lord. A solemn Baptism was reserved for that day for people who had been instructed in the Faith. Those who were Christian [also] confessed that day. [688] This was later followed by the introduction of Holy Week exercises, which (as was previously indicated) generally take very good hold in these converted nations, as a direct result of the blood of Christ shed for the good of men. This was a mystery that did not escape comment by the Apostle of the People, Saint Paul, and even though these people are barbarians, it makes a great impression on them. Thus, on Friday afternoons during Lent, the new Christians of Parras and the people from Laguna [Grande de San Pedro] were introduced to [the practice of] forming a procession and going out into the streets singing the Christian doctrine. On the way back to the church the priest would speak to them about the Passion and he would conclude by singing the Miserere, during which they would scourge themselves. This was not a blood scourging, however, which was reserved for Holy Thursday and Good Friday. They very devoutly attend these latter processions, and the priests tend to the health and material needs of people who are so new to the Faith and have so little adequate clothing. This is done so that they might recognize in their ministers the affection of a father and mother rearing these little ones in Christ.

The above holy exercises of penance were promoted by a devout Christian Indian who was blind and whom God had sent to this nation. On Fridays throughout the year he convinced them to scourge themselves, and he himself would recite the prayers in place of the Miserere. The precept and use of the Holy Sacrament of Confession during Holy Week and when they were ill, hearing the Mass of Our Lady on Saturdays, and other Christian devotions were all becoming established and were increasingly adopted by couples, thereby daily increasing the number of Christians.

CHAPTER XI A means that is very helpful in the establishment of Christian communities; one Indian's singular Baptism and the signs of his predestination

I will] declare and make known here the means that were helpful in this new Christian community, just as they will be in the innumerable others yet to be initiated and settled in the Western Indies,[19] with the [support and] Catholic zeal of Our Lord the king and his governors. For this purpose it should be pointed out that one of these means, which was quite helpful in the conversion and settlement of these people and others whom an attempt was made to domesticate and reduce, was to take some settlers from more civilized Christian nations and have them live in the reductions of the barbarous and uncivilized ones. These Indians who [come to] live among them possess the same qualities they do, but because they are long-time Christians, they are better versed in matters of Christianity. Through these Indians the customs and lifestyle of our holy Christian religion are more easily introduced. For this reason, when the governor of Nueva Vizcaya desired the good settlement and peace of these Indians in Parras and Laguna [Grande de San Pedro], some Mexican and Tlaxcalan Indians were offered rewards and privileges if they would come to live and settle among them. These Indians also were well treated by the priests and helped this Christianity a great deal.[20]

Although at this time [1603 or 1604] almost all the adults had been baptized, the priests had to content themselves with rustic churches. Because of the poverty of these missions in their early days, [689] the priests had nothing more than xacales, or shelters of wood and straw, which as we said, served as churches. Parras was the first pueblo in which the priests set to work building a permanent and durable church. There they erected a beautiful painted church with a very beautiful image of the Most Holy Virgin, with her precious Son in her arms, which the priests had brought from Mexico City. Because of its beautiful handiwork and because it was the first image these Indians had ever seen, it amazed them and they revered it with great joy. As a result, this mission remained under the protection of the Most Holy Virgin; the pueblo was given the name of Santa María de las Parras, and this church and Christ's flock continued to prosper.

I will conclude this chapter with an unusual case that took place at that time. Two priests went together to visit some families who had not yet abandoned their rancherías. They had just arrived when one of the priests asked whether there was anyone who was sick. They told him no; the only person who was sick had recently died. This caused the priest great grief because they had not sent him word and he had not arrived in time to be able to aid that gentile soul. He was prompted by this grief to certify whether the person was really dead, or they only thought he was, which is often the conclusion they reach when someone loses consciousness. He tried two or three times to go and see for himself if this person was really dead, and just as many times the Indians tried to prevent him from doing so. They told him not to tire himself in vain and that he should make more constructive use of the time it would take him to travel to that distant rancho, where the Indian was already dead, by instructing instead those who were there and alive. The more they insisted on detaining the priest, however, the more he felt moved from within to go and see the one they said was dead. Finally, he acted on his intentions. He went to a house, and around back in a field, lying in the sun, he found a very old Indian who was so thin that he was a living portrait of death. There was nothing left of him except the skin clinging to his bones. His eyes were half-open, his teeth were worn down, and he could barely say a word. In that critical moment the priest questioned him several times to see whether he could bring him back to consciousness so that he could give him the news of the mysteries of our Holy Faith, which was absolutely necessary for

19. Here Pérez de Ribas distinguishes the New World from the Indies of Japan, China, and the Philippines, where the Jesuits also labored.

20. The anua of 1596 mentions Tlaxcalan and Mexica Indians settling in the Parras mission.

Baptism. God (who had undoubtedly predestined this soul) willed that he who was already thought to be dead should regain consciousness, and the priest asked him whether he wanted to die as a Christian and receive Holy Baptism. He said that he did, mumbling through his teeth, extremely exhausted and near the end. When the priest heard this, he gave the sick man a drink of the wine he carried for celebrating Mass. This revived the old man a little, and he raised his head. With some help, he tried and was able to sit up. The priest instructed him in the mysteries that were absolutely necessary at that [critical] time, and he listened with pleasure. When the priest exhorted him to renounce his sins and gentile abuses, even reminding him of those into which these Indians usually fall, the Indian responded with great serenity and peace: "Father, in my entire life I have never killed anyone, nor have I wished or done any wrong to anyone, nor have I coveted anyone's wife or belongings, nor have I lost my senses from drinking wine." He recounted in this fashion the way he had lived, which was so upright that the priest was amazed and could find no obstacle to [baptizing him]. He saw that this sick man was now very spirited, and in order to celebrate this unusual Baptism with greater solemnity, he ordered four Indians to gently carry the old man in a manta to the nearby church. There he received Holy Baptism with exceptional reverence and rejoicing in his own soul as well as those of the priest and the Christian and gentile Indians who were present. [690] These gentile Indians were amazed by what they were seeing. Once the priest had baptized this Indian under the unique circumstances that we have described, he asked the baptized man how he had come to believe so quickly and so easily in the mysteries and doctrine of our Holy Faith, and how it was that he had shown such a great desire to be baptized. "Look, Father," the Indian responded, "at the beginning of this illness, two venerable people who had great authority and were very

resplendent came to visit me. They carried me through the skies all the way up to heaven, where we entered into some delightful palaces inhabited by the people of heaven. I saw an empty seat that was so beautiful that it contented me greatly just to look at it. I was even happier when they said it was for me. I told them that I wanted to stay there, but those who had brought me said it was not yet my time. I was not a baptized Christian, so I had to go back to earth and wait for two priests who would soon come to this place. They would teach me the Holy Faith and baptize me. Then those who were speaking to me would take me to enjoy that seat in the company of the other blessed people I had seen."

This is what that good baptized old man said, and that is how the priests knew (as they wrote) that everything had happened just as the Indian had explained. He had barely received the water of Holy Baptism when he expired, leaving the priest—who had been moved by so many impulses to go and baptize him—full of amazement and consolation, as can be imagined from his having seen such remarkable signs of the salvation of this predestined soul. It seems to be like [the case of] those souls considered by the theologians, for if such people reared *in syluis*[21] did not obey natural law, what would God do with them? Let the Doctors consider very carefully what they judge to be most certain in laws and matters of grace, for it appears that here God provided the means for this soul to attain the glory he had awaiting him through special acts of providence. These included leading the priest to that ranchería on that occasion and sending him all those impulses so that he would go visit the one whom they so strongly asserted was dead. Although the priest found him very exhausted and worn out, the man was nevertheless able to receive the sacrament of life for the soul. This is the stuff of divine praises and the kind of events of which I believe we will find many in heaven. In subsequent chapters we will learn of others here on earth.

21. "In the wild." Arguably, "the theologians" refers to Thomas Aquinas in particular.

CHAPTER XII God sends an epidemic to the Indians of this region; several unique cases that took place during the epidemic

In this chapter, as is stated in the title, I attribute to God a general and deadly illness that affected all the Indians of this region, many of whom had been baptized and still others who were not. I intentionally said that God sent this illness. On the one hand, even though during this illness the devil tried to meddle and launch his own attacks, just as he tried to make holy Job lose his patience and perfection during his illness, God sent this illness for His own holy and supreme ends, as the holy [Job] confessed, saying, *Dominus dedit, Dominus abstulit*.[22] This is what happened during the epidemic that God sent to this new Christian community and to those who were still gentiles. The devil attempted to take the latter with him to hell before they could be baptized. In addition, in an effort to defame Holy Baptism, he used his sorcerers to stir up trouble by attributing [691] the general illness and deaths to that Holy Sacrament. The sorcerers proclaimed that the new doctrine that the priests had brought to the land was the reason why the people were dying and [nations were] being finished off. However, God was seeking the fruits that He harvests through these illnesses, a point that I discussed more fully in the second book of this history. I will say more about this further ahead, and I refer the reader to that passage. Here, in particular, I will relate what happened to the people we are presently discussing. Along the way it will be necessary to refer to the great and apostolic hardships—the stuff of which merit is made—that overwhelmed the Gospel ministers at this time. This was in addition to the ordinary difficulties of these enterprises, a topic we should know about.

The type of illness that overcame these people was a mortal one called cocoliztli, or smallpox. With this God took His early harvest of the innocent lambs who were children, conducting many of them to heaven with baptismal grace. And it was of no small edification to see and hear the resignation of many good Christian parents after their spiritual fathers consoled them with the certainty that their baptized children were going to heaven before they could sin. This consoled those who were their parents in the flesh so much that they demonstrated this by taking the children to be buried wearing crowns of roses and flowers.

When the religious ministers took the Holy Sacraments to adult Indians, both Christian and gentile, they usually had fallen ill in pueblos and places that were very far away. The hardship the [priests] suffered was great and continual. There was no time for resting, day or night, but they did not cease. These shepherds who were ministers of the Supreme Shepherd, Christ, extended their charity to caring for bodies as well as souls. They took them food, bringing maize, flour, beef (which they consider a great luxury), and everything else they could acquire using the stipend the king gives them for their own sustenance. They also administered whatever medications they could obtain, because as gentiles these Indians used nothing more than some firebrands made with burning twigs, or they tied a tourniquet around their legs, lancing it with the point of an arrow until they bled.

These priests considered worthwhile anything they could do to help these people, seeing that through such hardships God was also gathering a good harvest of adult souls who were saved once they had been baptized. God wanted this type of first fruit of adults with baptismal grace in heaven, and it must have been for this reason that he sent this illness so soon, before all the people were baptized.

The devil then began to launch his own attack, attempting to gather a harvest for hell. He tried to defame Holy Baptism so that it would not free the sick from eternal damnation. For this purpose he relied on his usual instruments, his gentile sorcerer familiars, who held great dances and mitotes to placate (as these individuals said) the rigor of the epidemic. They affirmed that while they were holding one of these dances, the devil appeared to them for a period of several days, sometimes in the form of fire, other times in the form of a deer or serpent, and on occasion dressed entirely in white, with a fierce and angry countenance. He threatened that he would kill them and finish them off with

22. Job 1:21: "The Lord gave, the Lord has taken away" (Knox 1956:453).

illnesses, which he brought upon them because they were becoming Christians and receiving a doctrine that was different from the one he was teaching them. The fear that this fierce adversary produced in these deceived people with these threats was so great that there were times [692] when he had them dancing three or four days and nights in a row, with nothing to eat, in front of an idol in which he appeared to them, until they were worn out by the labor of the gentile dance and fell to the ground weak and half-dead.

CHAPTER XIII The devil hatches new plots to frighten the Indians away from Holy Baptism

Although the priests had baptized many people, especially those closest to the mission, and had preached to them and extirpated many of their gentile customs (as stated above), it was impossible to uproot simultaneously all the vices of those to whom they were preaching, for not even the holy Apostles were able to achieve that. Indeed, even their Divine Master—being who He was—did not manage to get all those who heard His divine doctrine to receive and benefit from it. And this is what happened among the people we are discussing at present, among whom there still were some who retained heathenism. We should ponder carefully the battles of the ministers of these missions, in which they fight against flocks of demons and, as a result, against hell itself. These enterprises prove to be evangelical and apostolic because the devil persecuted them so. But Our Lord also favored them, and the enemy was unable to benefit from the threats, tricks, and dances through which he had persuaded them that he would prevent this epidemic, because before he could do so, this epidemic wreaked havoc on those who had celebrated this dance. Once they saw themselves in this danger they began asking for Holy Baptism, retreating and taking refuge, as they say, in things sacred, including the church wherever there was one. The grace of Christ Our Lord was befitting of His divine wisdom as He outwitted the devil. The latter had plotted to use this epidemic to frighten these people away from Holy Baptism, threatening that he would kill them if they were baptized, but God turned this very same plot against him. When the Indians saw that even though they had followed the devil and celebrated his diabolical dance, they were still falling ill, they returned disabused to request Baptism, saying that

if they were going to die, they wanted to be baptized to secure their salvation. Even though some of them did not escape temporal death, by way of Holy Baptism they escaped the hands of the devil and eternal death.

The devil did not desist, however, for his rage and obstinacy are unceasing. Other sorcerers similar to the first came forward, telling their followers that they had seen the devil in various forms. They tried to persuade their people to hang large flint knives over the doorways of their houses to free themselves from the illness. Others were told to hang dead hawks or their talons from their doors, along with other deceitful objects. They were reassured that the sickness would not pass through their doors, nor would death enter their houses. Some of them allowed themselves to be fooled by this superstition, but others who were more knowledgeable and rooted in the Faith did not consent to having such superstitions placed on their doors. Instead, in their place they hung Crosses and the Virgin's rosary, trusting that God would give them good health through this holy and devout means. And those for whom God, for His own secret reasons, did not want to free them from corporal death by this means, were better served by it, in that they died as Christians, steadfast in the Faith and free of those diabolical tricks.

Another bedeviled old man rose up, saying that the priests held them in those reductions [693] and pueblos so that they would all be finished off and die, and that this was what they and the Spaniards intended when they were not persecuting them with their weapons. The answer that this diabolical old man received from the good Christians was highly edifying. They told him that they could not run from the wrath of God and that if they were going to die, they wanted to die like the

Christians they were, with the Holy Sacraments and burial in the church.

The devil did not cease in his scheming. And even though he is a wolf, he is able to dress in sheep's clothing; and although a demon, he can transform himself into an angel of light. For this purpose he tried to make use of the holy Cross that the Christians used against him by employing a Cross seen in dreams to try to fool these poor people. A large group of Indians came forward saying that they had dreamed that the Cross that was in front of the church had fallen over and that this meant that God was angry and wanted to finish them off. These Indians had come to settle from a distant place, and because of the deceptive dream, they abandoned the pueblo and went back to their former homes, just as the devil had intended. Once again, however, God, who knows the ways of the devil, did not allow him to succeed. He saw to it that after they had gone eleven leagues, they were overcome by the illness. When a priest got word of what had happened, he set out to aid the souls and bodies of those fugitive children, taking maize and meat with which to sustain them.

He spent several days looking for them before he finally found them in a deep thicket that was so dry that there was not even grass for the priest's mounts. What caused him the greatest grief was that seven or eight of them had died just that day, without the sacraments, and there were others who were dying. Those who still had the energy to do so came out to meet him, asking for the Holy Sacraments, disabused of the idea that the pueblo they had abandoned was the cause of death. The priest aided them with all the ardent charity possible in such a bleak land. This charity is so exemplary that even when it is carried out in a settled area and in a hospital furnished with all human aids and remedies, the Holy Church considers such works so excellent that those who lose their lives in laboring therein are given the title of martyrs. These apostolic men were endangered not only by the illness, but also by the trouble caused by the sorcerers at the devil's bidding. One priest wrote that perverted Indians shot three of the horses that he and his companions were riding, and he was waiting for the moment when they would also take the lives of their riders. And because the other memorable events that took place in this regard were considered on the one hand to be the work of God and, on the other, attempts by the devil to conquer these souls, it is worthwhile that those ministers whom God chooses for the religious instruction of these Indians have notice of this.

CHAPTER XIV More about the epidemic among the Indians; superstitions associated with it

One of the pueblos pertaining to the mission of Parras is called Mapimí. It is one of the most remote and distant pueblos from the head pueblo of this mission, and it is the hottest place, in spite of the fact that it is afflicted by winds and furious dust storms. There is also a mining camp nearby, and all this has meant more work for the priests. One of those priests will now recount in his own letter what [694] happened there at the time of the epidemic, when a comet appeared in the sky. He says:

A comet appeared at the outset of an epidemic, and some Indians from another nation who had been reduced to this pueblo were afraid that the sickness would affect them here.

Therefore, they decided to hold a mitote, their very well-known traditional dance, to favorably dispose the comet, or Satan, whose trickery was encouraging them. The dance was celebrated in the following fashion: First, they came forward in pairs—women and men of all ages, from seven to one hundred years old. All of them carried little baskets in their right hand; in their left hand each held an arrow with the flint point pressed against their heart. Some of their little baskets were full of the dates that they have in this land. Others were full of prickly pears, whereas still others had the fruit they call mescal or *mezquitamal*.[23] Some of them brought field mice, pocket gophers,[24] rabbits, and snakes,

23. Roasted buds of the century plant.
24. See Santamaría (1974:1097) and Nowak (1991:1:617).

all of them dead. At the end of the procession came four old men, all of them painted and each with a leather whip in his hand.

The end of the comet (some of them said) was in the form of plumage; others said it had the form of an animal's tail. For this reason some came with feathers on their heads, and others with a lion's or fox's tail, each of them mimicking the animal he represented. In the middle of the plaza there was a great bonfire into which they threw their baskets along with everything in them. They did this in order to burn up and sacrifice these things, so they would rise up as smoke to the comet. As a result, the comet would have some food during those days and would therefore do them no harm.

As soon as the smoke of that diabolical sacrifice began to rise, the four old men began to shake their whips, ordering the smoke to go straight up to the comet, without being diverted in any other direction. At that moment a light breeze blew up, causing the smoke to disperse rather than ascend straight up. The diabolical old men, who were acting as priests, took this as a bad sign. They thought it meant that the comet was angry, so in order to placate it they came up with another strategy.

They cut the hair of six virgins nearly down to the scalp, much to their distress, and then with some blades the old men began to scrape their own flesh in such a way that they bled freely. The others then followed them in that sacrifice, subjecting to this practice even the newborn babies, who were not spared on this occasion by he who is such a cruel enemy. They collected all the people's blood in some large bowls made from gourds, and using the virgins' hair as an aspergillum,[25] the old men sprinkled the air in all directions with this blood, while at the same time emitting horrendous bellows. As a final step, they threw the remaining blood into the fire and returned to thrashing the smoke with their whips. Seeing that it was going straight up, because the breeze had stopped, they were happy. They felt that they no longer had anything to fear from the comet or the illness, so they ended their diabolical dance.

On the one hand, this is demonstrative of barbarous blindness, and on the other hand it is a source of amusement. But for those whom God, in His great mercy, has reared in the midst of the Church and the light of the Gospel and divine doctrine, this should inspire infinite thanks that He did not cast them aside such that they should find themselves enveloped in the same darkness as these barbarians.

Once this diabolical dance was concluded, the rabble dispersed to their various rancherías. Some of them returned to the pueblo of Mapimí, where the illness finally arrived. This was because God did not want them to believe that the superstitious and diabolical sacrifice in which they had placed their trust would free them from this illness. There was one Indian principal, among others, who came down with the illness, and in order to free him his people [695] resorted to another abuse that I said these people practiced as gentiles: killing and sacrificing a newborn. They went to the mother with deerskins, bowls made from gourds, earthenware cups, and strings of beads and bones. They used these things to barter for or buy the child they wanted to sacrifice. The mother understood their reasons for coming, and that night she fled with her son three leagues from the pueblo.

Armed, the barbarous gentiles went in search of the child. They met with resistance from the relatives of the mother and child, and the two groups came to blows, with arrows flying all over the place. While the skirmish was in progress, the poor afflicted mother escaped with her son to Mapimí. The enemies saw that they had been fooled, but their barbarous fury did not cease. They set fire to a small hut in which there was a sick old man who was the child's relative. They burned him alive and scattered his ashes in the air, saying that with this the illness would proceed no further.

But God did not want for such a cruel act to go unpunished. Later, the epidemic worsened in such a way that so many of these savages died that they had to dig pits in which they were buried in heaps. Some of those who were fleeing farther inland were dying in the countryside. Thus, as I was responding to a call to baptize a sick young man who was nine leagues away, along a stretch less than a quarter of a league long I encountered eleven people dead in the countryside. This was the course that the epidemic ran among these unfortunate people, and a great number of sick Indians died.

---

25. A brush or perforated container held in the hand that is used for sprinkling holy water in religious services.

CHAPTER XV Remarkable cases of God's mercy toward Indians stricken with disease

[Trans. note: The following quotation completes the quotation begun in the previous chapter.]

Even in the midst of His punishment, God willed to bestow on these poor people His ordinary mercy, which is worthy of description. He healed some in their bodies and others in their souls, such that they died baptized, disabused, and leaving behind reassurances of their salvation. One such person was an Indian cacique who was the governor of a pueblo on the Río Nazas. Once he caught the illness, he prepared himself for death with a general confession of his sins since the time he had been baptized. Shortly before he died, he offered a declaration of how truly steadfast he was and how much he valued the Faith that the priests had taught him. He summoned to this declaration all of the pueblo's most important Indians, delivering a very fervent and truly Christian address, admonishing them to be most attentive to the priest's teachings. He admonished them also to be humble and obedient and very thankful to Our Lord for having given them His Holy Faith and having made it known to them.

This same Faith was demonstrated by another little pueblo that we visited near Parras when they were stricken by disease. Just after the illness had begun but before it became severe, they sent for the priest so that instead of turning to the former preventive [measures] and superstitions that others used to save themselves from such illnesses, they could now prepare themselves with the Holy Sacrament of Confession in order to be ready for whatever God had in store for them. They performed this act of devotion with as much fervor and general participation as if it were Holy Week.

In another place there was an old gentile man who was gravely ill. The priest had visited him and made many efforts [to persuade] him to receive Holy Baptism. [696] Nevertheless, the old gentile was obstinate, offering the excuse that Christians did not live long and that some of the children who had been baptized had died. His doctors found his case to be so hopeless that they did not expect him to live, and the priest, trusting in Our Lord, persevered in his desire that this poor soul not be lost. Although the gentile old man continued to resist, the priest promised him good health through Holy Baptism, if he took it to heart and with true faith. The gentile requested this [sacrament] and he was instructed and baptized. Our Lord then provided signs that He would fulfill the promise that his servant had given in His name. Immediately, the sick man began to recover and finally regained complete health.

God showed the virtue of His words not only with this case, but also through other unusual ones, so that these people would be strengthened through His words. One child who had been baptized became so deathly ill with a strong and virulent case of smallpox that he was not able to take even a sip of atole, which is their drink of sustenance when they are sick. While the priest was visiting the sick, the child's father came to him and asked—with more emotion than they usually display—that he recite over his son the prayers that he ordinarily says over the sick (he was trying to refer to the Gospel). The priest did so, and then the boy ate and was well.

Another man of about twenty years of age became afflicted or possessed by a demon, and he became so crazed that he tried to kill the members of his household. When they bound his hands to keep him from committing a crime, he started yelling, telling them to leave him alone. He told them that he wanted to kill himself and go with the demons to hell, and he chewed on his own flesh with great fury. His siblings who were helping him were Christians, and they told the priest about the case (with many tears). They asked him to help them and to bless that young man. He ordered them to bring him thus bound to the church, and there the priest prayed before a very holy image of Our Lady. He then read a passage from the Gospel over the young man, who was so crazed that three or four Indians could barely restrain him, even though his hands were bound. The priest sprinkled him with holy water and then gave him something to drink, with which the young man became quiet and began to laugh with a very mild countenance. The priest asked him if he was feeling better, and he responded affirmatively. The priest had him untied, and the young man returned to his house very calmly with the same people who had brought him, as if nothing had ever happened—and nothing ever did in the future. These are cases that have served to confirm these people in the Faith.

To this point I have quoted one of the fathers of the Parras and Laguna mission. He was there during the outbreak of illness, at a time which clearly proclaims the combat that the ministers of the Faith were waging against the Prince of Darkness and his sorcerers. And now we continue with what happened in another nation which, although distant and isolated, nevertheless forms part of this mission. It requires, however, its own chapter for discussion.

CHAPTER XVI The specific reduction of a mountain people who pertain to the Parras mission

God Our Lord had saved a flock of Indians who live in a mountain range called Quavila in order to add them to this mission and its holy church. These distant mountains were so harsh, steep, and difficult to penetrate that [697] if God had not arranged through His most gentle providence such a unique means for the salvation of these predestined souls, it would appear that they had no hope of receiving the light of the Gospel. What has been even more amazing here is that these same people who were so distant and without hope of salvation have become a source of increased fruits for this mission and its people. Every year new Christians are born to the Church, despite having no church in their lands nor having had any way of establishing one. For all these reasons it seemed to me that I should dedicate a specific chapter to them.

The trail through these mountains is so difficult and without water that during some months of the year, when their natural source of water runs out, travelers find that their only remedy is water distilled from the trunks of a plant that they call magüey. The same thing happens to those who live in some of the rancherías in these mountains. Let it serve as proof [of this statement] that if at any point a priest dared to go and visit the sick there, the first thing they would ask him was whether he had brought them water. One time, for example, one of the religious who ministered to this mission, led by his charity, dared to go help an Indian who had fallen ill quite a few leagues from his district. The Indians who accompanied and guided him took him from hilltop to hilltop for two days without finding a single drop of water. This was during a time of very severe heat, and therefore he was on the verge of perishing had God not almost miraculously aided him. This is the reason why the Spaniards have not wanted to nor have they been able to enter this land. Perhaps some of them dared to try and were murdered by the Indians, who thought the [Spaniards] were coming to subjugate them, or (what is more noteworthy) because they thought they wanted to take them away from their dry, horrible mountains.[26] This is how innate a quality it is for a man to love the land where he was born and raised.

Once the priests from our Company began the mission at Parras, they got word of these people. They were said to be very inaccessible, but the priests made efforts and sent them messages through the Indians from Parras, who at different times of the year would go to trade with the mountain Indians, either loaded down with water-filled gourds or relying on the water from the magüey. They offered an invitation for some of them to come with them to see the fathers of the Christians who were teaching them the word and law of God. These first messengers were fairly well received, and some Indian principales began to come down out of their mountains to visit the priests and see the novelty of the catechism, churches, and everything else that goes along with a new Christian community. The [visits] lasted only a short while, for they soon returned to their lands, which drew them back. But the priests' charity did not end here; they always paid great and special attention to endearing these people through material benefits, using things to win them over to God. Even though they had done this with all the other nations (as has been stated at many points throughout this history), with these very distant mountain people they had a greater need to resort to these means and measures. Christ Our Lord entrusted His Apostles with the same thing, giving them permission and charging them to cure the bodies of those to whom they went to preach the Gospel. It is noteworthy that when the Apostles went to a certain city to preach, the holy Evangelist gave first priority to curing the sick; later they could preach the Gospel: *In quancunque ciuitatem intraueritis, curate infirmos, qui in illa sunt, & dicite: Appropinquauit in vos Regnum Dei.*[27] [698] It is in accordance with this divine doctrine, therefore, that we should make use of material benefits in order to save these people. Furthermore, the first interested parties from the mountains who had come to the Valle de Parras and

---

26. Spanish slave raiders had been busy in the region since the 1570s (Griffen 1979).

27. *Margin Note*: Luc. 10. Luke 10:8–9: "When you enter a city . . . heal those who are sick there, and tell them, the kingdom of God is close at hand" (Knox 1956:67).

to Laguna to see the priests were so well treated and entertained by them that they returned to their mountains quite content, giving excellent reports of their embassy and journey. Throughout all those mountain rancherías they proclaimed the great good that they had seen and heard concerning not only material comforts for their sustenance, but also spiritual comforts for the good of their souls for those who wished to go and settle in the valley with their neighbors. Even though this talk displeased some of the caciques, it displeased the devil even more, for he is always opposed to the spreading of Christ's kingdom. Over time, however, and through greater contact with Christians and their ministers, other caciques came to see them. And even though many of them went back, others have started becoming attached to the place and staying on. The [priests] have begun preparing these latter people for Holy Baptism, never daring to grant that Holy Sacrament to those who went back to their Egypt, in order that they not mix it with their barbarous superstitions.

In spite of the fact that these people are so distant and barbarous, they have been found to possess good character and [intellectual] capacity, and they are not as contaminated by the vices that are found in other nations. And this itself has further ignited the priests' desire to seek out the salvation and remedy of these poor people, and in order to do so, their charity has taken various forms. One, among others, was to ask them to bring some of their older sons to be baptized and reared in the boys' seminary, which they had already established. There in the priests' company, they would be taught the catechism and everything else that the others were learning. They promised them that the [boys] would be very well treated and that their parents could come to see them from time to time. This was a means that (as has already been stated) always had a marvelous effect. Because the mountain Indians had already experienced this good treatment, they had no qualms about selecting and handing over their sons to the religious. The boys did so well and showed themselves to be so skilled in learning the catechism and writing, reading, singing, playing musical instruments, and other honest entertainment, that when the Bishop of Nueva Vizcaya, Don Fray Gonzalo de Hermosillo, happened to see and hear them on the occasion of a visit to this [mission within] his diocese, he was amazed by the little mountain barbarians. He did not think that they would possess this type of grace and ability.

In spite of what has been said, it happened that some apparently were drawn away by their love and natural inclination for the mountains where they were born and raised. But they paid for this escapade in such a way that of the three who made excuses to return, two of them died along the way from thirst and hunger (this is how dry and harsh the trail is). Their bodies were found eaten by wild beasts. What was left of them was brought back and buried at the church, and this served as a lesson to the others.

CHAPTER XVII Cases of edification among the mountain people

From the beginning of this mission up to the present day, God's providence with such distant and inaccessible Indians as those who live in this sierra has been unique. His providence and the priests' efforts have meant that both adults and infants have been baptized and have joined the other Christians who have found the means to salvation. So that the effects of God's divine providence are not silenced, I will recount here some cases of edification.

One cacique named Ilepo had never seen Spaniards, nor had he ever left his sierra. He was a young man in his prime and had decided to [699] descend with fifty of his relatives to see the priests. Fortunately, when he heard the doctrine and law of Christ Our Lord, he became so fond of it that he resolved to stay and learn the catechism and be baptized. In his Baptism he took the name Joseph; his glee and joy at being baptized shone on his face. Nevertheless, it caused him great grief that those who had come with him went back to their steep and inaccessible mountains. He went in search of them, and not only did he convince them to come back and become Christians like himself, he also reduced other mountain people whom he brought back with him and who were baptized. Such are the amazing ways in which God saves souls.

Another singular case involved a priest who was in the pueblo where these newcomers ordinarily gathered. He was supposed to set out to visit another pueblo, and as he was leaving he asked (as these cautious ministers usually do) whether there was anyone else in the pueblo who was sick. Those who cared for the church responded that there was not, but he was not fully satisfied. Moved by God, he insisted again three or four times that the Indians look into this carefully. Finally, they came to tell him that there was a sick woman who was a newcomer, and for that reason they had failed to mention her. She was a gentile, and the priest immediately went to see her. Finding her in danger of dying, he began to prepare her with the doctrine of the catechism so that he could baptize her. At first she greatly resisted receiving the sacrament for her salvation. But Our Lord was served to soften her hardness, and she heard the catechism, sufficiently understood the mysteries of the

Faith, and was baptized. Within a brief time she went to enjoy glory, tenderly repeating the sweetest names of Jesus and Mary. Even though a short time earlier this soul had been so blind and ignorant and others had forgotten to seek out eternal bliss for her, it seems that God had arranged this for her. And He increased His mercies in this case, for once this sick woman was baptized, she turned over her one-year-old son to the priest so that he could baptize him. He was baptized, and two days later he followed his mother to heaven.

Another old man among these infidels asked to be baptized, and once he had obtained his wish, he frequently went to visit the priest who had done him so much good. This Indian was so grateful that he would get down on his knees for a very long time, thanking the priest. Although the priest told him that because he was so old and tired he should not remain kneeling, he nevertheless continued in his devotion and affection. Within a short time his death arrived. God granted him a very good death, with acknowledgment of his sins and with great consolation for his own soul, as well as for the priest's, who was left with many reassurances of his salvation.

These were all means by which divine goodness was selecting individuals from among the distant mountain people whom He had predestined for His heaven. At the time when God sent the general illness we have mentioned upon the Indians of this region for the ends of His secret intentions, about 350 mountain Indians, whom God willed that the illness should not pardon, had come down from the sierra to settle among the Christian Indians at Parras. With some of them He used the sword of justice in this illness, whereas with others He used His mercy. But with all of them, there were many occasions of hardships and merits for their ministers among such new and foreign people. The illness struck them so hard that the majority of the three hundred died. Although on the one hand, the priests were consoled and relieved to see them dying with the beneficial water of Baptism, on the other hand, it caused them great pain to see that with this event the devil was persuading those who were healthy [to believe] his repeated lie that sickness and death were caused by becoming Christian and being baptized. [700] With this lie those who remained returned to their sierra, fleeing illness and Baptism.

This talk was flamed by another similar rumor that circulated among the old people, which was started by an old mountain woman. She was greatly esteemed as a prophetess and claimed that she had dominion over illnesses. Therefore, they had tried to placate her with gifts and offerings. Nevertheless, her rage and anger had not subsided, and she had them all terrified. Nor did the devil omit any means to which he could resort to pervert these souls. The priests tried to use speeches and admonitions to undo these tricks, reminding them of other illnesses that they had suffered as gentiles before the mission and priests had come to their lands. On this occasion it was clearly seen that Christ's grace was fighting against the ruses of he who is the enemy of the health of souls. One cacique saw that those who were left were rapidly becoming ill, and he wanted to flee from the illness and return with his wife to his home in the mountains. In order to get her to follow him, he even tried to resort to the priest's authority. Even though this good woman, whom God wanted to save, was being pressured, she remained so steadfast in resisting this departure that she responded very resolutely that she already saw that she could not escape the illness. What was important to her was to assure her salvation by receiving the sacraments and being where she could be aided by the priest and buried in a holy place, even if it was at risk to her own life. This is remarkable constancy and an outstanding example of the growth in the Faith that this barbarous woman had received only yesterday. She ignored the risk to her life so as not to endanger her salvation, tending to the latter first. We do not always see this in long-time Christians, for in times of epidemic the first thing they do is flee the place where the mortal illness is circulating. This new Christian woman did not do that, and no matter how many efforts were made, she refused to leave the place where she had the remedy of the Holy Sacraments for her salvation. And all this was fulfilled, for God sent her this illness for the good of her soul (as we should understand), and within three days she died, having received the Holy Sacraments that she did not want to miss out on and the good death that God sent her, leaving clear reassurances of the salvation that she had so valued.

CHAPTER XVIII   The illness overtakes some fugitive mountain people; singular events that took place among them and the hardships that the priests endured

The deceived fugitives from the mountains were not served by their flight to their mountains. Instead, many of them wound up in the hands of death and the infernal enemy who guided them. There were so many of them who died along the way that those who were left alive burned them in bonfires so as not to have to stop and dig graves to bury them. This was an occasion of infinite hardships for the priests and shepherds of this mission. In addition to having to attend to such a large number of distant pueblos along almost forty leagues of lake shore, as well as those on islands in the middle of the lake and still others in different areas, the priests found themselves obliged by their great charity to go and aid these fugitive sheep. They would travel for two or three days at a time along routes where there was no water or pasture for the animals, nor water for themselves. One of these priests traveled twenty-three leagues in a single day, encountering Indians who sustained themselves on snakes, serpents, rats, and even [701] the ground bones of dead animals that they found. What can we say about the region around Laguna to which some of these people had retreated? Some of these places were so remote that in order to reach them it was necessary to travel for two or three leagues through swamps where the water came all the way up to the horses' chests. Moreover, it was learned that Father Juan Agustín—who (as I said above) was one of the original founders of this Christianity and who died after only a few short but blissful years in this enterprise—many times stripped off his cassock, and with the water up to his chest waded out to these little islands for the welfare of these souls and to baptize and hear the confession of some Indian in need.

Returning to the people from the mountains who fled the illness, it not only overtook them along the way, but also spread to their lands and distant rancherías in the mountains. It attacked them with such fury that barely one or two people survived in rancherías that previously had a hundred or more people. The few survivors came to give word of what was happening, and as a result many were disabused of the erroneous belief preached by their sorcerers, namely that the illness had struck and killed them because they had been baptized. However, now that God had shed some light on them and they saw that this illness raged in their distant peaks, they were forced to confess that God was very justly using disease to take their lives, as punishment for their sins and for once having taken the lives of many people with their arrows. There were gentiles who, once they were disabused, brought their sick children down from the mountains to be baptized. They arrived half-dead, and upon receiving the water of Holy Baptism, they went to heaven. God did not grant them any more life than what they needed to make it to Parras and from there to be taken to His glory.

What is even more marvelous and worthy of virtue, as well as of the divine mercy that was being wrought here, was that there were some old women who, upon seeing their children falling into such a stupor from the severity of the illness that it prevented them from paying attention to what they were being taught at catechism (for they were of the age that required this), on such occasions they would wake them up and exhort them to pay attention to what the priest was telling them. One of them, who was a gentile and was very ill, got up from her poor bed, upset that her son, who was also ill, was not paying attention as she would have liked. She took him in her arms and admonished him to wake up. She did not stop until he and she were both instructed and baptized; the following day, both went to heaven with baptismal grace. There were many

others like this who, as soon as they saw that they were mortally afflicted, made a Cross out of two little sticks and placed it at the head of their beds. They exhorted one another to heed what the priest taught them in that hour so that he could baptize them.

Among others, mention must be made of a young man from the mountains who died. He was sixteen years old and had been raised for some time in the seminary. He had such a good disposition that he was friendly toward Indians as well as Spaniards in the region. He also possessed as much ability as any Spaniard of the same age. He had learned to play the organ and was also an extremely good cornet player. He was struck by the illness and made a general confession of his sins since the time he had been baptized. He very insistently requested Holy Communion, which he received with unusual devotion. He also demonstrated remarkable devotion to the Most Holy Virgin. The members of his household placed an image of that Sovereign Queen and Mother of Mercy in front of his bed, and as soon as he saw it, he began to recite some prayers that he had learned in the Mexican language [Nahuatl]. These were so tender and informed that it moved and amazed the priest and those present to hear them from the mouth of a young barbarian from the mountains. "Mother of God (he said), [702] pay me now for the Masses I sang to you on the Sabbath and on your feast days. Do not abandon me in this hour, for I am dying and have not done penance for my sins. Now, now is the time for mercy." And repeating, "Now, now," he looked at the priest and those present once again so that they too would beseech the Most Holy Virgin on his behalf. They had no doubt that she who has a heart of sweetness had heard him and had come to his aid in that hour, for he died in such peace and tranquility that those present admired it as much as they envied it. This death was greatly mourned and lamented, not only by the Indians, but also by the Spaniards who have haciendas in that region and sometimes come to hear Mass at the church in Parras.

Another choir boy, a companion of the former, also died from this illness. He was so well prepared and concerned for his salvation that he confessed five or six times, presenting no real sign of mortal sin. He requested Holy Communion with such yearning that, even though he had never received it before, due in part to his young age and in part to the fact that he was new to the Faith, the priests decided that he should not be denied. He received the Holy Sacrament with such reverence that the priest who administered it was moved to tears of devotion by the child's understanding of the Church's Most Holy Sacrament. His illness had been one of the most severe and painful, yet he bore it with great patience. He never complained or said a word that did not concern God or the other sick children who shared the same room. He begged those who were attending them to give them whatever they asked for and to keep them covered. Half an hour before he died, he asked the priest to commend him to God, and the priest recited the commendation of the spirit over this boy. He was so cognizant that when he noticed that there was no one there to give the response to the priest's prayers, he himself responded, assisting as though it were not he who was dying.

These cases are a clear manifestation of God's mercy toward these remote mountain people who had been raised among rocks and brambles. Through them He also consoled and encouraged His loyal ministers. With all the fatigue and effort and the many hardships of traveling, they did not tire in their fervent charity of aiding these souls. Here I charge the reader to keep them in mind and to consider them along with the material presented in Book VII.

CHAPTER XIX The singular wonders wrought by our glorious patriarch Saint Ignatius for the benefit of his sons and their flocks

I should not omit from this history, which throughout deals with the glorious hardships that the sons of our patriarch Saint Ignatius endure in these enterprises, the favors that these beloved sons and their flocks have received from their father. From heaven, this glorious saint favors those who labor in the task that is most central to the Institute he left to them, that of missions, to which he obliged them through a special vow. They make good use of his favor like sons of just such a father.

They were celebrating his feast day [July 31] in San Pedro, one of the principal pueblos of this mission, and among those who had come to this celebration was a cowboy riding a wild mare. A little Indian three or four years of age walked right up to him, and the horse kicked the child so hard in the head that it shattered his skull. As a result, the Indians started to wail loudly (they are notably distressed by anything bad that happens to a member of their own nation). The priest, who was equally upset by what had happened, had the child taken to the home of a Spaniard so that it could be determined if there was any way of saving him. [703] Two or three Spaniards who were there looked him over, and when they examined his head with their fingers, they said that the bone fragments crackled and that there was no sense wasting time on such a hopeless case. Therefore, without treating him, they sent him back to his biological parents and relatives. Because of their great grief, they shot the horse, or mare, full of arrows and spent the entire night in continual wailing. When the priest saw these people's suffering, he comforted them as best he could, telling them that the boy's only hope was in God Our Lord, and that they should seek his healing through the intercession of Saint Ignatius, whose feast day was being celebrated. He told them that he himself would fervently do the same. That night they came to tell the priest that the boy had finally died, and the Indians' screaming and wailing, which is inherently frightening and terrifying, especially when a child has died, was such that the priest was persuaded that the child was in fact dead. The following morning, however, when he went out to see where they were planning to bury him, he came across the boy's father, and his grief and tears were quite changed. He said that his son had improved and was asking for something to eat. The missionary father was immensely happy to hear the news that had so consoled this boy's biological father, confident in the favor he awaited from his father

Saint Ignatius. The following day his joy was increased, as with his own eyes he watched the boy who had been given up for dead come walking in search of his biological father, who was working in the church. On the third day, to the amazement of the Spaniards, this boy was walking and playing in the plaza with all the other children. Everyone attributed that wondrous and supernatural healing to the intercession of our father Saint Ignatius, who on the occasion of his feast day wished to favor his sons who labor in the conversion of these new Christian communities.

The intercession of our father Saint Ignatius was also experienced in the following case. There was a young man who kept a demon continually in his company, to the point that he was always at his side. The demon appeared to him in various forms and gave him whatever he needed, sometimes bringing it out of its hiding place and at other times summoning it from far away. The pact and condition that the infernal enemy had established with his familiar was that he was not to let the priest know anything about this, threatening to kill the young man if he ever did. The Indian, who had been baptized some time earlier, was intimidated by the demon and did not want to confess. God, however, wanted to show him mercy, so He sent him a racking illness, and in dire straits [the Indian] sent for the priest. In doing so, he showed that he feared God more than the devil's death threat. He bared his soul to the priest, who asked him several questions to find out whether this was what was really happening or whether the young man was caught in the snare of a lying Indian, as one ordinarily finds among these blind people. The priest accordingly told him that if it was indeed true that the devil told him about things that happened

in faraway places, then the young man should tell the priest what was going on at a certain time in a specific pueblo thirty leagues away. The Indian said that the devil was telling him that at that moment some Spaniards were playing cards, and as proof of this the stake that they were playing for would appear. Immediately, there appeared a pile of reales. The Indian added that if the priest wanted to see the demon and be more thoroughly convinced, he was right there in another interior room. The demon was very angry at the young man for having exposed him, in spite of his threat. From the noise that the demon was making from within the little house, the priest was satisfied that there was a basis for what the poor Indian was saying. Therefore, he advised the Indian to confess all his sins and denounce those dealings with the devil. For security and protection against the threats made by that enemy he gave him a medallion of our father Saint Ignatius. This enlightened Indian did all he was told to do, and it worked so well that his old familiar, the infernal enemy who had held him captive, never dared to appear to him again. [704]

Through the cases and events that have been recounted in this chapter, one can clearly see the singular and marvelous means by which God harvested for His heaven the first fruits of this new mountain plant, those who even while in the shadow of death, *Ab aeterno praesciuit, & praedestinauit, conformes fieri imagini Filij sui*.[28] This is why in His supreme wisdom He sent the mortal illness that struck these people at such an early point in their conversion, for He wished to have His chosen and predestined individuals from among them. For this they will certainly be grateful throughout all eternity.

---

28. "He knew from eternity and marked beforehand as adopted sons to be made in the image of his own son" (Ephesians 1:5).

CHAPTER XX Christianity is fully established and churches are built in all the pueblos of the mission of Parras

Having recorded the many events of the early years of Christianity among the people of Laguna and Parras, I will now relate the full establishment of its Christianity by the priests following the difficulties, illness, and Baptism of all the older people. Although it cannot be denied that due to God's just and exalted reasons, these people's numbers were greatly diminished, there was no decrease in the fervor with which the sons of the Company of Jesus continued the cultivation and improvement of this vineyard, to which the Lord had led them and in which they are employed up to the present time.

Once they had some relief from the earlier hardships, they set their hand to building permanent churches. Although these are material matters, they are very necessary and beneficial to sustaining spiritual ones and to celebrating with decency the mysteries of our Holy Faith. They also built houses for the ministers, which although modest, were made suitable for religious. Priests and Indians alike worked very willingly to erect handsome churches in these remote lands, which lack the commerce of civilized people because there is no pueblo or city of Spaniards nearby, but rather only a few haciendas. The Spaniards from these haciendas attended the dedications of the new churches. These were celebrated with the same great joy and feasting that has been recorded for other nations in this history, so no further detail is given here.

Once their churches were built, they finished establishing all Christian customs and laws which, although they were introduced at the outset, cannot be completely implanted all at once. In time, however, they established them just as successfully as in other Christian communities. The custom of receiving Holy Communion annually as well as on major feast days and jubilees is practiced by all the most advanced converts and by those raised in the seminaries. They display remarkable devotion to the Most Holy Virgin, whom they view as a most generous mother. They have learned in their own language the catechism as well as the Hail Mary and other little hymns. During Lent they do penance and scourge themselves, some dry and others drawing

blood, just as if they were in the midst of Christianity. Whenever any weak persons have happened to commit a public sin, doing penance has greatly edified these people, who not long ago lived freely and without laws.

I will relate only one case as an example of others of this kind. In a Laguna pueblo there was an Indian who, although still young, was very ladino and who had great authority among them. He was deceived by the devil, [705] who appeared to him in the form of a woman. Although he should not have done so, he began to converse with this enemy in female form (the enemy unceasingly uses women to do battle), and he became very corrupted, as can be imagined concerning someone who would stop to listen to such talk. He added further to this, when the missionary priest was not there, by gathering the people of the pueblo and telling them about part of what the devil had said and about things that were just as abominable as one might expect from one who is a dirty, filthy spirit, as he was called by the Son of God. He terrorized them with threats of death and starvation if any of his listeners told the priest what was going on. Despite his many threats, however, one Christian fiscal did warn the priest about the scandal and scheme that the devil had begun to plot in order to lead those people back to their old idolatry. The minister acted to bring the harm caused by this talk to an end. He went to the pueblo and found the bedeviled Indian charlatan. The Indian displayed a very different temperament from that which he normally possessed, and he paid scant attention to the instruction that the priest was giving him and his comrades. The priest had to punish him in the presence of those people by threatening to abandon those whom he had baptized and made Christians if they returned to their former gentile customs. God willed that this threat and punishment should cause great regret and shame among them, and to expiate their guilt, they decided to do public penance. They held a scourging procession in their pueblo that went from their houses to the church; once this was completed they implored the priest to return to visit and console them. The priest heard with joy the petition of his prodigal and repentant children. They came out to meet him along the road to their pueblo, where they confessed their error and promised to mend their ways. This recognition of and penance for their mistakes would be worthy of admiration even if they were very long-time Christians.

In the end Christianity, piety, and divine worship were so well established here that among all the Indians of the Province of Nueva Vizcaya, those of Parras and Laguna are the most outstanding. In spite of this, the difficulties and persecutions were not over, as we will see.

CHAPTER XXI An extraordinary flood that inundated these pueblos and churches

I hesitated to record this event for fear that it would appear that these missions are characterized by one adversity after another and, thus, undertaking these enterprises would become more frightening. On the other hand, considering that these greater difficulties and hardships make these enterprises more glorious and manifest the courage of the soldiers of Christ who undertake them, I decided not to omit them. Those who write about worldly enterprises do not and should not forget the hardships suffered by soldiers in opening and back-filling trenches, erecting fortifications, etc. Although all those things are done to gain control of a piece of land, these other spiritual hardships are undertaken and embraced in order to cast the devil from his throne and gain heaven for souls.

The event that renewed the priests' hardships and those of this new Christian community involved the Río Nazas (which runs very full and swift, passing through the middle of this mission). As a result of heavy rains, the river overflowed its banks [706] with such great force that the Indians said they had not seen anything like it in thirty years. The water burst through the banks of the river in nine locations, altering the course of the river itself near a pueblo called San Gerónimo, which was endangered by the flood. In another pueblo called San Ignacio the water rose with such great force that it leveled the church and the priests' dwelling place. In the pueblo of San Pedro the river opened a large channel and carried away some of the Indians' houses. It kept on rising until the Indians began to flee out of fear, terrified of a repetition of what had happened earlier under similar circumstances, when many [of them] had drowned. They sent word to two priests

who were there at the time not to endanger themselves any longer. Despite how quickly they worked to gather up the vestments and valuables from the church, they were caught in a thunderstorm on that dark and rainy night. Only two Indians remained, who helped and guided them out of this dangerous situation. They took them through some terrible thickets until they reached some streams that ran so full that when one of the Indians crossed to the other side to get word to some others who were a quarter of a league away, the water came all the way up to his waist. These latter Indians were keeping themselves warm around a bonfire they had made, and they came to help the priests cross the streams. They took them to a forest of mesquite trees, where they were surrounded by a perilous situation for two days, waiting for those floodwaters to recede. Because they were still in danger of drowning, the Indians looked for another safer and more comfortable location. They found one and spent thirteen days there, with such a lack of room and such discomfort that they could barely make an enramada to protect themselves from the continual rainfall. The river finally receded and allowed them to leave these dangers behind, but not entirely with dry feet, for they had to pass through some swampy areas with water up to their knees and through some other places where there was even more water, which they crossed in rafts that the Indians had made out of reeds. They reached a pueblo whose church had been dedicated to the Most Holy Virgin, to whom the priests had entrusted it. They found that the Mother of Mercy had not only protected her house but also that of her devout chaplains. This amazed both the priests and the Indians, for the church was not made of stone and mortar, but rather of mud, which softens very easily. The current had run swiftly against the church for several days, and the water had risen more than a third of the way over the foundation. Nevertheless, the church did not collapse, and they offered great thanks to Our Lady, who provides shelter for the afflicted.

Her Most Holy Son added another favor to the one carried out by His Mother. Through His divine will and providence, He had wished to test the priests and their new Christian faithful with the foregoing tribulations. Along the way He performed for them an unusual benefit, which extended to the entire land. This land is very dry once one moves away from the river, and for this reason both Spaniards and Indians had tried to build a ditch to irrigate their fields. But they had never found a convenient way of doing so. What they had been unable to accomplish over a long period of time and at such great expense, Our Lord did in only a few hours. In one spot where the river overflowed, it opened a channel from which it was easy to draw water for irrigation, as they had wished to do. Our Lord was thereby preparing for the following year, during which the sky produced very little rain, yet there was nevertheless water for the fields and the Indians did not go hungry. If God had not helped them by arranging for the water to be diverted from the river, they would have suffered great famine and need. [707] This benefit was not for that year alone, for the water reached so many and such very good lands that these attracted a good number of gentile Indians who, desirous of them, came to settle and congregate there. As a result, their souls also enjoyed the most precious, celestial, and healing waters of Holy Baptism. All this is arranged by God's most sweet and gentle providence.

I do not know whether there are any settlements where He is seen to be more attentive (as I have mentioned several times) than in these missions, the conversion of these poor people, and the hardships experienced here. Some remarkable cases of this divine providence at this time are worthy of being included here. On one occasion the Río Nazas rose and overflowed, leveling a priest's poor house in a certain pueblo (where he happened to be at the time). He went to the church to rescue the ornaments so that the flood would not destroy them, and just as the priest was going into the church, he suddenly heard a voice. He did not know where it was coming from, but it told him to go outside immediately because the church was going to collapse. The priest obeyed the voice, but despite how quickly he moved he was struck on the shoulder by a chunk from a weakened wall, which had been softened by the water and had fallen. Even though he was only bruised, he realized how close he had come to danger, for this was but a warning from heaven.

God showed no less favor toward the priests in freeing them from the great number of poisonous snakes which, due to the dampness of the ground, happened to emerge right under their feet and sometimes even from under their beds. The number of these fierce poisonous snakes was such that in a single pueblo fifty of them were killed, some of which were 1 3/4 varas in length. God protected the lives of these, His servants, with singular providence, or a miracle (as they themselves judged it to be). He did this so that they could bring spiritual life to many souls.

A good example of Christianity shown by these Indians during the year of the drought should not be omitted. The waters of the lake had receded, and as a result the fish had retreated to some inlets and pools. During times of famine the local Indians resorted to fishing there. Some other, more distant nations also came to fish there when they were in need. When they were gentiles, the Laguneros maintained continual warfare with these nations, taking the lives of many of them with their bows and arrows and preventing their enemies from coming to fish in their lake. At the present time, however, not only did they not prevent their enemies from fishing, they actually invited them like brothers, offering them whatever they had in their homes, even if they themselves were in need. When the priests praised them for these deeds, they responded that when they decided to be baptized and become Christians, they cut the strings of their bows and tossed them to their enemies along with their arrows and quivers. They did this as a sign of friendship and brotherhood, abandoning the weapons that they had once used for their barbarous wars, for they felt a desire to maintain this brotherhood.

These acts reflect the change in these people that was wrought by the Holy Gospel, to which we can add that change celebrated by the Royal Prophet in his psalm: *Arcum conteret, & confriget arma*. We can even add the following: *Exaltabor in gentibus*.[29] Although it seems that the Prophet was speaking about God Our Lord, it is no less marvelous when it is wrought by means of those who were so barbarous and fierce. They themselves confessed that when they used to defend their

---

29. *Margin Note*: Ps. 45. Psalm 45:10: "the bow shivered, the lances shattered," and Psalm 45:11: "claiming empire among the nations, claiming empire over the world" (Knox 1956:496).

estuaries, killing their enemies, they did this so they could eat them, as they in fact did. Now, with such great Christianity, they share their own sustenance with [708] their former enemies.

Once the trials of flood and famine had passed, the people of Laguna and Parras looked for more suit-able spots to rebuild their churches and some of their pueblos, which had been severely damaged. It was from these pueblos that God harvested the fruits that we have recounted here, and the same thing happened in the tribulation that follows.

CHAPTER XXII The trouble caused by the Tepehuan Rebellion among the people and pueblos of the Parras mission

The preceding book discussed at length the Tepehuan Rebellion and the uprisings that it caused among many other nations. The uprising that it caused among the Christians of Laguna and Parras will be recorded here, because both this persecution and the Tepehuan Rebellion pertain to this holy mission. The apostate Tepehuan made a particularly great effort to win the Laguneros over to their side. First, because the Laguneros were known by all to be very skillful and courageous with their weapons, as they indeed were. Second, without these Indians as allies, the Spaniards in Durango would have had no other nation nearby to aid them and supply them with people for combat. It is true that without the Laguneros the Spaniards would have been greatly bereft of this type of soldier (which is very important in Indian enterprises). The uprising that the Tepehuan caused in these people was such that if God in His divine providence had not cut it short, its course could have caused the ruin of this Christianity and the death of all the religious of the Company who ministered to it.

The dangers were recognized immediately, first and foremost because once the Tepehuan bordering on the pueblos of the Parras mission, the Río Nazas, and Mapimí had rebelled, they attacked a mining camp near Mapimí. They did great damage to the Spaniards' ranches, as well as to their houses and church, taking livestock, clothing, and the ornaments from the church. When the Spaniards at Durango learned that some Indians on the Río Nazas had joined and aided the Tepehuan, they executed the ones they managed to apprehend. As a result, some Lagunero Indians (who were truly corrupted) talked of joining the Tepehuan rebels and killing Spanish residents. In their meetings the Indians also proposed killing the priests and doing away with all of Christianity. These corrupted Indians (of which there have always been a few during all the Church's conversions and persecutions throughout the world) added that in other pueblos the Tepehuan had been able to make off with spoils, sacks of clothing, and Spanish livestock, and that by killing Spaniards they had become rich, leaving the Spaniards in Durango fearful and without courage. Actually, [the truth was that] for many days at the beginning of this uprising the Spaniards had not received weapons and troops, so they could not pursue or punish the enemy. This delay was seen as cowardice by the rebels, and it caused greater arrogance among those whose spirits were already corrupted.

The news of these tlatollis, or talks, so worried the governor of Nueva Vizcaya, who was in Durango, that he attempted to send an escort of soldiers to protect and defend the priests at the Parras mission [709] and to lead them to peaceful territory. The delay in sending the escort was due first of all to the fact that the group would have to be large enough for the people to be able to defend themselves from Tepehuan attacks that were feared along the roads, which had all been taken over by the enemy. Furthermore, any Spaniards who might have been sent instead were needed to safeguard the city from other anticipated attacks.

Fear of trouble and an uprising by the pueblos of the

Parras mission did not end here, for on this occasion the devil got his way by means of the sorcerers (there is always some of that bad seed, which continues to sprout until it is eventually exterminated). They raised their voices and renewed their speeches, saying that it was after the priests had come and the people were baptized that they had begun to die. Satan himself again appeared to them, threatening them with sickness and death if they did not do away with the priests, churches, and Christianity. These talks reinforced the similar talks that the famous Tepehuan sorcerer, accompanied by his devilish idol, had given throughout the land.

Satan was confirming these rumors (and although we have already discussed them, it is necessary to go over them again). A Christian Indian woman told a Spanish woman who lived near Parras that she was very concerned because the night before she had overheard her very own father talking with the devil. Listening closely, she heard that enemy making threats and complaining loudly about the fact that the pueblo had become Christian and the people had become subjects of the priests. [He claimed that] all this was good reason for joining the Tepehuan and doing the same thing that they had done with the churches, priests, and Christianity.

The priests were placed in such dire straits by all these rumors and unrest that they were convinced that should the rebel faction prevail, the blessed time would be at hand for their lives to come to an end for the [cause of the] evangelical teachings that they had preached to those people. Thus, at seven in the evening, after the priests had received several warnings of danger, they decided to consume the Blessed Sacrament that they had kept in the pueblo of Parras, where there were more long-time Christians. Then the priests prepared to die for the Lord and His Holy Gospel. They gathered together the faithful of the pueblo and encouraged them to die like Christians and do whatever they could to attempt to put down the rebellion and unrest that the devil was causing in order to harm them. Those who heard this sermon were so encouraged that a faithful Indian principal left the church and went out into the plaza of the pueblo, and with great fervor he gave another talk, admonishing the disturbers of the peace for allowing themselves to be deceived by the sorcerers. Then, of his own volition, he summoned all the people and commanded them to take up arms, and even though it was a rainy night, they placed sentinels around the priests and the church.

This was not the only aid God provided for His ministers, to whom the governor had been unable to send

any assistance. In the meetings that were held in the pueblos of Mapimí and Las Nazas, which were closest to the Tepehuan, the perverse sermons and talks had taken hold, and they were discussing what they would do to the priests if they decided to revolt. Most of them felt that at least they should not take the priests' lives, for no matter how fierce they are, even the most barbarous cannot help but recognize the spiritual and temporal benefits that they receive from these priests. In the end the Indians decided that they would allow the priests to choose between staying with them or leaving for peaceful territory.

Two Indian principales intervened at this point, and through sound arguments they persuaded all of them not to act without thinking and not to get carried away by the deceit of depraved individuals, [710] for things could turn out very badly for them. Many of them were so enlightened by this talk that they went to warn the priests of what was happening, and others offered to stay and die with them rather than allow themselves to be swayed by the arguments of the apostate Tepehuan and those who had joined their band.

These were all measures that divine providence used to quell the hellfire that the devil had attempted to light along so many roads of the Parras and Laguna mission. These Indians remained so faithful that when Governor Don Gaspar de Alvear was drafting people to battle and punish the Tepehuan, he recognized their fidelity—in addition to their great skill with their weapons—by making them the principal squadron of Indians he took with him. These Laguneros conducted themselves valiantly in battle. Their demonstration of Christianity when the draft was carried out in their pueblo is worthy of being remembered. Before they departed the priest warned them of the frequent mortal danger that they would face in the campaign, and that they would do well to go prepared as Christians, having made their confessions. They did so in such great numbers that it seemed like Holy Week. Among all the Indian allies from this province who accompanied the governor on this campaign, the Parras and Laguna Indians were the most noteworthy in battle against the Tepehuan and in searching them out of their mountain lairs. For this the governor and the Spaniards were very grateful. The Parras and Laguna Indians, for their part, returned to their pueblos very happy to have been of help and service, and they have always maintained their perpetual friendship. This was the outcome of the efforts by the Tepehuan rebels and their allies to foment rebellion among this nation.

CHAPTER XXIII The present state of Christianity in the mission of Parras and Laguna Grande de San Pedro

Having discussed the events, hardships, and dangers presented by the conversion of these gentiles to our Holy Faith and Religion, along with the success that was achieved in this enterprise by the sons of the Company—through the aid of Our Lord—the only thing left to recount is their present temporal, political, and spiritual state. Once again it is necessary to acknowledge what I previously made explicit concerning the general decline in the numbers of people and nations in the Indies. This decrease has been particularly felt by those in Parras and Laguna Grande de San Pedro. In the year 1594, when our priests initiated the establishment of this Christianity through their first visits (before they were permanently assigned to this mission), there were probably some sixteen to twenty thousand souls in these pueblos and their surroundings; today this number is greatly decreased.[30]

There are, however, two consolations in this matter. The first and most important is that almost all those who have died have done so with the divine light of our Holy Faith and the only means to salvation, the Holy Sacraments. There are many well-founded reasons to believe that a great number of these native people have reached their final goal of eternal bliss, which was not available to all those who were born and died in their gentile state. Those who remain today and those who are being born, although their numbers are not great, are all reared with the hope of salvation through the doctrine and great Christianity in which they are being raised. The other consolation for the decrease in these people's numbers is that even as God allowed the light of the Gospel to ascend and enter into the inaccessible mountains of the mountain people living near Parras, [711] divine providence provided them with news of the Gospel very close at hand in the Valle de Parras. It reaches even the steepest peaks of their mountain range. Moved by this light, a good number of the mountain people come down each year. The priests invite them to receive

the Faith, and they stay to settle among Christians. The persistence shown by the devil in removing and hiding these souls has been overcome by the love of Christ and His ministers, who search them out and gather them up. These were all divine designs intended to increase the number of Christians here, as is happening today.

In order to better know the means divine providence employs in order to save predestined souls, and how it is able to use the very same tactics by which the devil attempts to destroy them, I will record here a particular case, in addition to those already recorded, involving these mountain peoples. It happened one year that they came down from the mountains in such great numbers that it caused the priests some concern that it might be for the purpose of war. Therefore, they dispatched some faithful Indians to the mountains to reconnoiter the land and the state of these people. Among one of the nearest groups they found a squadron of almost three hundred Indian archers. They had come from another faction, some of them badly wounded, in order to seek healing in Christian pueblos. It was learned that the wars that went on among those peoples was the cause of this; for this reason they had come in search of healing and peace among the Christians. When a priest learned of this, he immediately went to assist the wounded whose lives were in danger. He found a gentile Indian who had been pierced completely through by an arrow and had little hope of survival. [The priest] told him that he should prepare to receive Holy Baptism, and he found him very well disposed to do so. The Indian even added, or God inspired him to add, that through this holy bath he hoped to regain the health of both his body and soul. And that is exactly what happened; without resorting to any of the superstitious cures that they used, once he was instructed and baptized he completely recovered both corporal and spiritual health. These are all cases and means by which God continually calls these mountain people to relocate at the Parras mission, and as they do so the mission continually regains its numbers.

Ordinarily there are six priests from our Company laboring in this doctrina and its pueblos—as well as in a

---

30. By 1645 the Indians of Parras and Laguna Grande numbered perhaps several thousand.

few visitas and Spanish ranches and the mining camp at Mapimí—which all fall within the surrounding region. These ministers of God attend to all these [places] with large quantities of love, instruction, and sacraments. The superior over all of them is located in the pueblo of Parras, which is the mission center where they hold their regular meetings. The churches are very well decorated with sacred ornaments, particularly the one at Parras, which has altarpieces [retablos], a tabernacle with the Holy Sacrament, and music by singers from the seminary. The priests tend to all these things, making use of the stipends they are given by the king for their sustenance, which they spend in order to see divine worship increased among these people. Thus, they complement their exile from the pueblos and inhabited cities of Spaniards by living in very remote places for the good of these poor Indians, whom God redeemed with His

blood. These Indians have become so dedicated to their Christian celebrations that no trace of their old ones remain. They are so attentive to the decoration of the church that for it, and for those who serve in the church, they plant fields so that with the profits gained from them they can maintain and increase them. In political and temporal terms the Parras and Lagunero Indians are those who get along best with Spanish officials. One reason is because they are very hard workers. Another is because they greatly value being neat and well dressed. They are people who are concerned with their salvation; they live good lives and die leaving many reassurances of having obtained eternal bliss. And this is worth much more than the [712] great number of gentiles who once existed. We will conclude this book about their mission and Christianity with the holy life of the priest who successfully laid its foundations.

CHAPTER XXIV The apostolic labor of preaching the Gospel by Father Juan Agustín, founder of the Parras mission, where he ended his holy life

In keeping with my plan of concluding each book of this history with the lives and deaths of illustrious missionaries and apostolic ministers of the Gospel among barbarous nations, I have chosen to conclude this book with the life of the man whom God chose to initiate and found the Parras mission. As I noted at the outset of this book, the most religious Father Juan Agustín was one of the first two missionaries sent to Laguna Grande and Parras, and a very legitimate son of our patriarch Saint Ignatius. To describe his holy virtues, I will cite a letter that Father Juan Agustín himself wrote from his mission to another member of the Company, addressing him familiarly as a brother in Christ of the same profession. I was fortunate to have this letter, written in an apostolic spirit, come into my hands. I will transcribe it here because it reflects the virtue, zeal, and charity of this apostolic minister and it is of edification to those whom God has called to this holy employment and ministry of the salvation of souls. After the usual greetings, the letter reads as follows:

Aside from continuous instruction and catechism, I baptize, hear confessions, marry, and pacify not only the natives, but also foreigners [i.e., black slaves] and Spaniards whenever the occasion arises. I do all this with great passion and pleasure, seeing how the Lord places in my hands the means of serving Him, even though I am poorly prepared to be an instrument of His Divine Majesty for saving souls.

The devil wages a war on me that at times is dreadful. A few days ago I was so full of boredom, sadness, and emptiness that *taedebat iam animam meam vitae mea*.[31] Oh, the patience and confidence in God that these ministries require! What wealth of troubles! What solitude! What difficult travel! What wilderness! What hunger! What filthy and foul-smelling waters! What nights spent out in the open! What sun! What an abundance of mosquitoes! What thorns! What people and how childish they are! What tlatollis and confrontations with sorcerers! But if everything were a bed of roses, Father, what would remain for us to enjoy in heaven? Let the will of the Lord be done in me. I wish to walk in the will of the Lord, not in my own corrupt will; I wish to be in His hands, which He placed

31. "My soul is now weary of my life."

on the Cross, not in my own sinning hands. And so I am encouraged to suffer until the angel arrives who will be my companion. May he come soon. He will suffer much to bring souls to God. He will console, encourage, and aid me, and I will serve, respect, obey, and love him. If only, by the Mercy of God, other souls would help mine reach heaven. Every day I await death, and to receive it I beg my God for an enduring spirit and a contrite and humble heart, for with these the sacrifice made by my soul will be acceptable.

To here I have cited the letter of this blessed priest which, although brief and general, still has his life imprinted on it. His life was such that each day he awaited death; his apostolic spirit is evident in his desire to be a worthy instrument of God, leading souls to heaven. His humility can be seen in the contrite and humble heart that he offers to God; his obedience is evident in his willingness to subject himself, of course, not only to his superiors, [713] but also to the companion that they send him. He exercised evangelical poverty by sustaining himself on barbarous and crude foods such as wild plants, animals, reptiles and, as I have often noted in my discussion of this mission, on water from swamps or the juice of the wild magüey, which is so unusual for human consumption. His zeal for the salvation of souls was so constant and fervent that not even the clear waters of the lake, which he waded into up to his chest to aid a soul (as was told in Chapter XVIII), nor the winds nor the frost of cold nights could discourage him from good deeds. Finally, his perseverance is observed in the fact that neither mountains of hardship nor the dangers of heaven and earth could impede him.

The purity of Father Agustín's life is well known, because he was a person (as he said) who awaited death daily, and he lived with a constant desire to make his life a pure sacrifice that would be pleasing to God. Indeed, beyond what has been quoted in this book, the letter of this servant of God breathes forth a burning charity and love of God and his fellow man that goes beyond paper or words. His charity and love were practiced in his deeds and the risks he took with his own life for his beloved, enduring with much pleasure (as he says) the hardships that the tedium of this same life caused him. The union that this apostolic minister forges in his letter is noteworthy, joining pleasure with tedium, saying that everything he worked on he did with great pleasure for His Divine Majesty, and also that these difficulties were such that *taedebat aninima viate sua.*[32] It seemed to me that these words are not unlike those used by

the Apostle of the People, Saint Paul, when he was describing his own evangelical missions. He commented to the Romans, *Gloriamur in tribulationibus,*[33] and in one of his letters to the Corinthians he said, *Gravati sumus supra virtuten? ita ut taederet nos estavivere.*[34] The severity of the difficulties that Father Agustín endured made his life wearisome, wherein we say that the labors of apostolic men are those that place them in straits that are more trying than death itself, which they would gladly embrace rather than endure these hardships. Thus, life itself, which naturally is pleasant, becomes more difficult than even death or martyrdom. What is miraculous about these evangelical labors is that [even though] they are so difficult, they are joined with a pleasure that the Apostle calls glory. *Gloriamur in tribulationibus.* Such were the tribulations that this evangelical minister, Father Juan Agustín, noted in a letter to his friend and brother in Christ. His constant labors were such that he humbly confessed that *taedebat animam vitae suae.* However, in spite of everything, this labor filled him with great pleasure for His Divine Majesty. He then went on to list them, and although the list is short, it reveals what his brothers endured in this same enterprise and mission. The very religious father was not afraid to enumerate them, and in doing so, to invite his brothers of the Company of Jesus to learn about them without fear. Those in the illustrious college of the great city of Mexico, where one may serve Our Lord well, as is done, were not subject to as many difficulties and trials.

I have not hesitated to write about the difficulties of this mission and the others that I have dealt with in this history because I am very sure that God Our Lord has mercifully communicated to the sons of the Company of Jesus the zeal to make His holy name known. Because such difficulties are a large part of the profession to which they have been called by God, they will not be intimidated by them. Rather, I am sure that they themselves invite and foster them in these conquests because they awaken holy and heroic [714] desires of ending their lives in these enterprises. Thus was the case with the blessed Father Juan Agustín. Although he did not surrender his life to the Indians' arrows and clubs, he endured such difficulties while planting the Faith in this land, which can be called a desert, initiating the Parras

---

32. "His soul is weary of life."

33. *Margin Note*: Rom. 5. Romans 5:2–3: "We are confident in the hope of attaining glory as the sons of God; nay, we are confident even over our afflictions" (Knox 1956:152).

34. *Margin Note*: 2. Ad Cor. I. Corinthians 1:6: "Have we trials to endure? . . . It is so that you may . . . undergo the sufferings we too undergo" (Knox 1956:181).

mission and doctrinas in the neighboring nations. Even though [these difficulties] caught him in the prime of his youth, at thirty years of age and only four years after his evangelical preaching began, they brought him down [on April 27, 1602]. He did not notify any priest to aid and cure him (for in those days the other priests had not yet arrived), and he surrendered his soul to his Creator with a death very similar to those with which the holy men and confessors of Christ ended their lives, exiled for their Holy Faith. In order to preach and extend it, this great servant of God died very abandoned in one of the little pueblos of his Indians, the children he had engendered in Christ, with only a few of them attending him. We can therefore clearly surmise that the souls he had sent to heaven from among the many infants and adults that he had baptized would come forth to welcome him when he entered therein, obliged to give him thanks for the incomparable benefit they had received at his hands. For those who remained on earth, their affection for and memory of the priest were so keen that he was not forgotten. A few years after his death I traveled from the Sinaloa mission via the city of Zacate-

cas, the birthplace of this evangelical missionary and a resting place for the many Spaniards traveling to Parras. The memory of Father Juan Agustín and the aroma of his virtues were so fresh that they had given him the title of 'Angel', which is why I have referred to him as such in this chapter. He had demonstrated great poverty when he was growing up in this city, and because this poverty shone even more brightly in his Parras mission, where he lived and died, he earned the title of 'Angel'.

God cut down this handsome shoot from the Parras mission to graft him to Christ, His vine, which is symbolic of those who were chosen. This was preached by the Son of God himself, who bestowed this title upon His first ministers of the Gospel as He was taking His leave of them. In order to console and encourage them to preach in His name, He said to them, *Ego sum vitis, vos palmites*,[35] which has a more beautiful and complete fulfillment in paradise. Here we will leave the blessed Father Juan Agustín and go on to write about a priest who spent his entire life in ministering to and aiding Indians.

CHAPTER XXV The very religious life and joyous death of Father Hernán Gómez of the Company of JESUS

Although this venerable man did not spend his life in the places and missions that I have discussed up to this point, he nevertheless worked and spent his entire life assisting poor Indians with their salvation. I could have placed this holy life at the end of the following book, where I discuss the places where he labored, but there is no lack of martyrs who can be discussed in Book XII. Let it be noted in passing that this history would be very long indeed if I had to record all the lives and outstanding virtues of the Gospel missionaries whom God has given to these holy missions. I have contented myself with selecting some of those whom I have personally known and dealt with, leaving the others for their own place and time.

The venerable Father Hernán Gómez was born to

noble parents in Arcila, a city in Africa [715] belonging to the Portuguese crown. His family was so wealthy and they were such great Christians that two of his three first cousins founded very outstanding Jesuit colleges. One of them was Esteban Rodríguez, who went to the Philippines and founded our college in the city of Manila, which is the seat of that principality. Esteban's brother, Alvaro Rodríguez de Figueroa, became very wealthy in Mexico and returned to Spain, where he founded our college at Jeréz de la Frontera. The third brother, Juan Rodríguez de Figueroa, was an *aguacil mayor* at the court in Mexico City.

Coming now to our Hernando, when he was eight

---

35. *Margin Note*: Ioann. 15. John 15:5: "I am the vine, you are the branches" (Knox 1956:105).

years old he was taken from Arcila to Lisbon to study and be raised with the discipline and care required by his noble lineage. He was already a remarkable young man when he went to Nueva España, where he could expect to have very wealthy inheritances and prosperous and honorable positions. But, of course, God removed his desire for secular positions and occupations and led him instead toward those of the Church, in which Divine Majesty was to make such good use of him. Following his ordination, he obtained the benefice of Tepotzotlán, and later that of Gueyacocotla. At that time these were two of the most lucrative benefices in the Archbishopric of Mexico. Financially they were very rewarding, and this did not include what he could hope to receive in the future from the viceroy and the Archbishop, who greatly esteemed his noble attributes and virtue, the very difficult language that he had learned, and the successful dealings they had had with him in matters they had entrusted to him.

But all this did not quiet his spirit, for God was calling him to the Company of JESUS, which only a few years earlier had reached Nueva España. He took this pursuit so seriously that he left his district and benefice and set out for Mexico City to pursue admission to the Company. He did this with great humility and fervor, giving clear signs of these virtues. He arrived at our college at the hour when the priests ordinarily sweep the patio of the main entrance. One of them told him (jokingly) to help them, and he took this so seriously that (removing the elegant long cloak that he was wearing and picking up a broom) he immediately took to sweeping in plain view of the many laypeople who were there. They were edified by the humble act of someone who had not yet professed humility.

He was admitted to the Company in 1574, at the age of thirty-two. His fervor in all the virtues with which he began his life as a religious more than lasted him throughout his entire life. In fact, they continued to increase in such a way that it seemed with each day he was starting anew and growing in these virtues. He conformed to the goals, Institute, and rules of the Company in such a way that no lack of consideration was ever noticed on his part. His humility (the basis of all virtue) was not only contemplative, but very profound in practice. He always considered himself inferior to all others. He felt he was the most unworthy of all the members of the professed house, and he behaved accordingly. He never mentioned his family, nor did he discuss them or go to visit them, except on rare occasions when he was obliged by obedience to do so. This

was in spite of the fact that they were very powerful and honorable. Everything in the house that was the most meager and humble had to be for him, be it his attire, sustenance, living quarters, or his position and duties. He spent several years at a ranch belonging to our college in Mexico City, where he was very contented to serve as chaplain for our brothers who cared for the ranch. He also took care of the religious instruction of the few Indians who worked there, whose language he knew. This was someone who could have been lord over parishes and benefices that were densely populated by Indians who would have been under his command, as have been established for the natives of the Indies.

Virtue in the exercise of [716] prayer and conversation with God made all these other virtues very agreeable to Father Hernán Gómez. He offered himself so fully to prayer that to this exercise he devoted all the time remaining after he had attended to his fellow man and his other ministerial obligations. This amounted to many hours a day, and he prayed very deliberately and slowly, sometimes keeping his arms raised in the form of the Cross. Those who knew this were amazed that someone who was so sick and ailing could bear that penance, especially as he grew older. They decided that this was all facilitated by the favors and consolation that Our Lord sent him. But the priest did not communicate these things to anyone, for he was a very withdrawn and silent man who sometimes spent the entire day hearing confessions. His rest at night and relief from the day's labor was prayer, which he performed very purposefully, adding rigorous penance.

Even though this, God's servant, was so inclined to continual and familiar talks with Our Lord, he combined them with zeal for the benefit of his fellow man, as is professed in the Company. Therefore, nearly the entire time that he was in the Company, his superiors employed him in various regions and districts of Indians. This was of great service to God and the welfare of souls, for which he avoided no type of hardship. To aid these souls, he took to learning all the languages he encountered in his missions, even at an advanced age. Our Lord aided him so much in this regard that in a very short time he was hearing confessions and preaching in Nahuatl, Mazave, Matlazinga, and especially Otomí, which is the hardest language in all Nueva España to learn and pronounce. He was the first to attempt to reduce this language to a grammar and rules so as to make it easier for other members of the Company [to learn].

He also left them amazing examples of edification by which they ought to proceed in the ministry of the missions—self-discretion, poverty, strength, and all the other necessary virtues, especially in missions among Indians. Through these virtues he attended not only to the benefit of the Indians, but also to making this benefit as long-lasting as possible for their ministers and parish priests. This included teaching the priests what he knew of the languages in which they were ministering, and making them fond of and facilitating their dealings with the Indians and the holy exercise of prayer, of which he was so fond. He accomplished amazing results with these men and with the benefice priests with whom he dealt. They were so notably edified that they were constantly amazed by Father Gomez's holy zeal and the great examples of his virtues, and thus did they proclaim them.

The principal mission in which Father Hernán Gómez was employed by holy obedience for several years was in the residence that the Company has among the Chichimec Indians in the pueblo of San Luis de la Paz, which will be mentioned in the following book. A colony was founded there to tame the Chichimec, who were extremely fierce. This colony was made up of Otomí Indians, whose language the priest knew with distinction. He ministered, taught, and gave them the catechism in this language, suffering quite a few discomforts, hardships, and dangers among them. At that time this fierce nation was still not entirely peaceful. Because of his many ailments and illnesses, his superiors removed Father Hernán Gómez from this place and sent him to Mexico City, where he concluded his holy life.

I have left for last a kind of martyrdom with which Our Lord wished to test Father Hernán Gómez—a very painful torment that became perpetual for this servant of God. This was the continual test of scruples; even though it did not prevent him from attending to the aid of [717] his fellow man, as has been said, he suffered so much anguish and spiritual affliction that it was like being on a Cross in perpetual torment. He also endured great mortification, which he bore with remarkable patience, without weakening or slackening the least bit in his holy exercises. His only relief was to go and discuss his doubts with his superiors and other spiritual men, who consoled him by telling him that at the hour of his death this barrage would cease and Our Lord would grant his soul great tranquility. This was fulfilled in the final days of his illness, when he found such serenity and calm in his soul that nothing could disturb him. But because this man did not suffer with his illness, God wanted to test him to prove that he was strong. This priest fulfilled what the divine Book of Wisdom said concerning such people: *Certamen forte dedit illi, ut vinceret.*[36] In order that His servants' victories may be more illustrious, God ordinarily prepares them through difficult battles.

Because the battle that this most religious priest had suffered in his soul throughout his entire life had ceased, the Lord willed that he should face another battle in his body so that his life and death would become a Cross, which is what makes saints noteworthy. The afflictions the priest suffered during his final illness were so many and so varied that it is not known which of them brought his life to an end. He had swelling in his legs, gout, asthma, dropsy, sharp pains in his side, continual fever, and other painful ailments, all of which he suffered with great patience, accompanied by his beloved exercise of prayer. Even though he was informed that in such a grave state of illness he could stop praying the Canonical Hours, he omitted them only on the day of his death and one other time before then. Finally, with great peace in his soul, he turned himself over to the hands of his Creator, having received all the sacraments while he still had his complete faculties. Having also heard the commendation of his soul, he reclined his head to the right side of the pillow and gave his spirit to the Lord. His face had a more peaceful look than when he was alive, so much so that one could not even tell that he was dead. This and the softness and flexibility of his hands and the rest of his extremities lasted until they buried him. Everyone considered this to be a sign of the purity and cleanliness that he always maintained in his body and soul. This man led such a holy life, so full of great examples of virtue, that Father Francisco Ramírez, a very important and holy individual in the Province of Mexico and propositus of the professed house there, compiled a few of them. He said that he could write a very long and exemplary history of such a holy man. Father Hernán Gómez died on the first day of September 1610, at the age of sixty-eight, having spent thirty-six years in the Company.

There was another important priest who also had great knowledge of the hidden sanctity of Father Hernán Gómez (a religious who was always very withdrawn and silent). When he saw Father Gómez's corpse, he said that he was convinced that Our Lord would produce some manifestation and demonstration of such

36. *Margin Note*: Sap. c. 10.12. Book of Wisdom 10:12: "kept him safe from his enemies, protected him from their scheming. She would have him wrestle manfully, and prove that there is no strength like the strength of wisdom" (Knox 1956:580).

humble and hidden sanctity. It seemed that later His Majesty wished to fulfill this prediction. Father Fray Bartolomé Moreno, an important and completely trustworthy religious from the Order of Saint Dominic, was a companion of the Lord Archbishop of Mexico. At the moment they began to toll the bells for Father Gómez, which was a little before five in the morning, he opened the window of his room, which was in the tower of the Archbishop's palace and had a view of our college, where the blessed priest had died. Above the bell tower of our church, Father Moreno saw a shining white cloud winding like a [718] stairway and rising toward the east all the way up to heaven. This unique and extraordinary spectacle caused this religious man to take great notice and at the same time provided him with great consolation. Therefore, he stood watching it for a period of almost a quarter of an hour. Because it was something

that had some special meaning, he sent someone to our college to find out for whom the bells tolled. The answer was that they were for a holy religious who had died. Therefore, both he who was a witness to that vision and the other people who learned of the case (who were many) felt certain that God had signaled the sanctity and glory of the venerable Father Hernán Gómez. God wished to glorify Father Gómez's great virtues and thereby reward his labors (even though he himself hoped to hide them). He had worked for very many years ministering to poor Indians, accompanying this with solid and perfect virtues and deeds, placing greater value on these things than on all the material wealth and pretenses to which he could have aspired. With this I bring this book to its happy conclusion, moving on to record what will be the end of this entire history. [719]

BOOK XII

An Appendix to the History of the Missions That the Religious of the Company of Jesus Have Undertaken among These Barbarous and Remote Peoples of Nueva España

CHAPTER I An explanation of what is recorded in this final book

The preceding books have offered a description of the principal missions founded by the evangelical preaching of the religious of the Company of Jesus among barbarous and gentile nations in provinces that are very remote and distant from Mexico City, which is the capital of the extensive Kingdom of Nueva España. To complement this history, which has dealt with the evangelical ministries exercised among Indians, I felt that I should also discuss the sons of the Company who have labored in all of the houses and colleges of Nueva España in Mexico City and other nearby settlements. They have labored not only among those Indians who are long-time Christians, but also among those whom they converted and reduced to our Holy Faith.

I will leave the foundations of the many colleges and other ministries to Spaniards that the Company has undertaken in great service to God Our Lord, receiving His divine favor, to the pen of whoever is entrusted by holy obedience with that greater charge and subject matter of writing the history of these enterprises.[1] In the present history I have endeavored to record only what the Company of Jesus, in accordance with its Institute,

has done in service to the Holy Church for the benefit of Indian natives. Although it is well known that the colleges that the Company has in all the cities inhabited by Spaniards [720] function mainly as schools in which youths are educated and raised with virtue and letters, it is also well known that the ministers in the colleges do not limit themselves to only this, nor do they labor only for the aid and benefit of Spaniards. They work for the spiritual good and betterment of all the various Indian nations that are found intermingled in the Spanish cities and pueblos of the Indies. Because of this, everywhere the Company has a college, there are priest trained in Indian languages who dedicate themselves to the spiritual good of the Indians. From this work the priests have harvested abundant fruits, which will be the subject of this final book. Herein, I will first describe the Company's residence in the town of San Luis de la Paz, which is not far from Mexico City in the land of the Chichimec Indians. Following this, I will write

1. Impressed by the *Historia*, the father general gave Pérez de Ribas this "greater charge," which was realized in Pérez de Ribas' *Corónica*, completed in 1654.

about the Company's only parish benefice[2] in Nueva España, which is in the district of Tepotzotlán. This will be followed by a description of the Company's house, church, brotherhoods, and seminary for the young sons of Indian principales, in the great city of Mexico. I will also write about another church and congregation that the Company has for Indians, in addition to the one for Spaniards, in the city of Puebla de los Angeles. I will conclude this book with the martyrdom suffered by nine priests from the Company at the hands of unfaithful barbarians. These priests were sent to La Florida to preach the Holy Gospel by order and decree of our gloriously remembered Lord, King Philip II.

Although these blessed religious did not convert the gentiles there, they nevertheless attained the palm and crown of apostolic and evangelical men, having risked their lives for such glorious intentions and, in the end, having shed their blood before they had the chance to found a Jesuit mission or college in La Florida, Nueva España, or any other part of the Western Indies. And what is very worthy of noting is that this same land of La Florida where the blessed priests suffered was the starting point for the discovery, conversion, and missions of the Province of Sinaloa, as was related in the first book of this history, which will be concluded with the martyrdom of these apostolic men.

CHAPTER II The fierceness of the Chichimec nation of Nueva España

The ancient and bellicose Chichimec nation is not more than forty leagues to the north of Mexico City. I refer to this nation as ancient because when the first Mexica Indians made their famous journey [south] to found Mexico City, they found the region already populated by the Chichimec. This nation has always been recognized as the most courageous and warlike in Nueva España. Throughout the history of the Mexican Empire, neither the ancient Mexica nor their great emperor, Moctezuma, who subjected and reduced many kings and nations with his armies, could ever subject the Chichimec. When the Mexica were at last victorious over these very courageous people, they considered this to be an outstanding achievement worthy of remembrance. Therefore, the Mexica celebrated this victory in their very solemn and famous songs, which they sang during their mitotes, or public dances. The cruel wars against the Chichimec continued for many years after the Spaniards conquered and subjected the Mexica to the crown of

Castilla and its Catholic [721] kings, creating the Kingdom of Nueva España. As noted, the Chichimec were on a frontier no more than forty leagues from the Spaniards in Mexico City, and they resisted conquest and subjugation more than any other nation. Through their lands passed the royal road to the interior and to the provinces of Nueva Vizcaya and Nueva Galicia, and it was through their lands that one gained access to the mining camps and many settlements where Spaniards labored. Thus, many carts loaded with goods and silver were robbed by these barbarians, who also killed Spanish secular priests and religious who traveled on foot. After this nation was pacified and I crossed their lands, I was filled with admiration and pity when I saw so many Crosses along the roads where people had died.

The reason these fierce Indians were so indomitable had nothing to do with their numbers. The Chichimec were divided into many languages and groups, which traveled in separate bands, in the fashion of the Arabs of Africa. They were not sedentary and had neither houses nor lands and fields that they cultivated. They moved their camps and huts in accordance with the ripening of the wild fruits on which they sustained themselves. The most common of these were the prickly pear, which in Spain they call 'figs of the Indies', in addition to a type of date, not very tasty, that comes from an

---

2. *Beneficio curado.* Note that this benefice was an exception to the Jesuit Constitution (perhaps because it involved Indians who otherwise might not have had a priest to care for them), inasmuch as the constitution prohibited Jesuits from holding salaried appointments, which normally were held by parish priests and, less frequently, by other religious (O'Malley 1993a:73).

unusual palm tree, as well as the fruit of the magüey plant, which I mentioned previously. From these fruits they also made several types of wine on which they got drunk. Drunkenness was such a common vice among these people that one can say that they lived and sustained themselves on these drinks, or beverages, as if they were a daily food and delicacy.

After first discussing the efforts that were made to reduce the Chichimec and the incalculable damage that they caused, I will then discuss what proved to be the only effective way to accomplish these goals. Initially, the viceroys of Nueva España gave orders to build fortified houses along all the royal roads that crossed the Chichimec lands.[3] These were to provide protection for travelers, mule teams, and carts, which regularly travel in groups of fifteen or twenty. In case the enemy should attack the caravan when it was far from a fortified house, one cart was built of planks in the manner of a castle, which provided adequate protection from arrows. Women and children who walked unarmed retreated to this cart for protection. In addition, in order to wage battle against the enemy, a squad of soldiers stationed at each fortified house would escort the caravans from one fortified house to the next. This escort of soldiers was responsible for accompanying the carts and people until they reached the fortified house at the next post and watering hole. This is how one traveled from one fortified house to the next until one reached the last one, whence the soldiers would guard the travelers and carts until they finally reached the city of Zacatecas, which is the most famous mining camp in Nueva España.

In spite of all these efforts and expenditures by the king on forces and squads of soldiers, the fierce Chichimec continued to cause damage. Although travelers in these caravans were usually protected by soldiers, this was not always the case. At times people were killed, and sometimes the enemy took their clothing, also shooting and killing the oxen, mules, and horses. [722] There were also other disasters, and these continued for many years. These barbarians were so insolent as they traveled every day throughout the land on foot or on horseback (which they knew how to do). Some murderers among them boasted and bore as a trophy a bone on which they recorded the number of Spaniards and Indian servants they had killed. Some of these bones had ten marks, others had twenty or thirty. The fact that these barbarians had neither a settled dwelling place nor a king or anyone else who governed them made it very difficult for the Spaniards to conquer these people. Because the Chichimec wandered like savages over a very extensive territory in separate groups, the Spaniards could not go after them to subjugate them. Thus, they persevered in their barbarous freedom, committing all the aforementioned damages and robbery.

These people remained in this state, with no hope of salvation, until the only means to peace was instituted, the introduction of Christ's Gospel. Even though there were many difficulties presented by introducing and planting the Gospel in a forest so full of thorns and weeds and among people as fierce as those we have depicted, and in spite of the fact that unsuccessful efforts to conquer them had already been made, it was nevertheless necessary to resort to this means. The Gospel had to be purposefully introduced, along with other steps taken to finally reduce these fierce people to Christianity. Long after Christianity had spread from one side of Mexico to the other for hundreds of leagues among more civilized and populous nations, this nation, which was right at the borders and gates of Mexico City, had not yet been reduced and subjugated. This should come as no surprise, however, for (as I said) the ancient Mexica and their numerous armies had always found the Chichimec to be a fierce and indomitable enemy, and for more than four hundred years they had been unable to defeat and subjugate them.

3. In 1569 Viceroy Martín Enríquez initiated construction of the first forts along the royal road linking Mexico City and the mining frontier in the north (Naylor and Polzer 1986:34).

CHAPTER III The viceroy of Nueva España gives orders to the religious of the Company to found a pueblo and church in the lands of the Chichimec and to attempt their reduction

By 1594 Don Luis de Velasco I, a gentleman of great prudence, administration, and zeal in the service of both the Divine and Catholic Majesties, governed the great Kingdom of Nueva España as viceroy and captain general. The viceroy realized that a great deal had been spent from the Royal Treasury on fortified houses, military escorts, and other means that had been deemed necessary to defeat the fierce Chichimec nation and subject and reduce them to peace and human civility. Therefore, rather than [construct more] fortresses, he decided to use divine force against the power of hell itself. Churches and Christian temples and the holy doctrine of the Gospel taught therein are sufficient to pacify wild beasts and to reduce a nation as stubborn as the Chichimec, bringing to a halt their continual and onerous damage. To accomplish this goal, the viceroy ordered the establishment of some pueblos and the erection of churches. These would be assigned to religious from the Company, who would attract and reduce these people to the doctrine and law of the Gospel and peace. In fact, in the New World these enterprises have always been entrusted to the sons of holy religious orders, who [723] in these glorious enterprises have always proved to be courageous soldiers for Christ.

With respect to the Chichimec, of whom we are speaking, churches and convents were first established by the Holy Order of the Seraphic Patriarch Saint Francis, whose glory it is that they were the first to plant our Holy Faith in the extensive Kingdom of Nueva España. Although it was years later that the Company began working among the Chichimec, God had reserved for them the glorious part of this conquest that is declared in this history, together with other glories that will be declared at the appropriate place and time. Among them is the role that the Company played in establishing peace among the Chichimec nation.

The viceroy decided that the members of the Company would be in charge of a new pueblo that he wanted to found on the principal frontier of this Chichimec

nation. He asked them to try to invite and pacify this fierce nation, reducing them to the flock of the Holy Church. They located the pueblo on the banks of a river which, although it does not carry a lot of water, nevertheless provides the Indians with good fields and other things that are necessary for human and civilized life. The viceroy wanted this pueblo to be called San Luis, out of devotion to this saint. And because it was being founded for the purpose of pacifying the bellicose Chichimec, he decided it should be called San Luis de la Paz. This pueblo became a stopping place and shelter along the royal road to the provinces of the interior. A good number of Otomí Indian families, who were long-time Christians, were moved from not very far away to the new settlement in order to live with the Chichimec and better establish peace. The viceroy gave privileges and particular exemptions to both the Chichimec and the Otomí in order to win them over. He freed the Otomí from the obligatory royal tribute to the king and gave them land and water for their fields. Those Chichimec who were willing to reduce themselves and settle in the pueblo, and stop roaming the mountains in search of food, were to be given, at royal expense, a weekly ration of maize and meat for themselves and their families. They also received an annual gift of clothing, which particularly benefited their captains and caciques. These orders were executed, and the pueblo of San Luis was founded. The viceroy ordered the royal officers to provide whatever was necessary from the Royal Treasury to build an ample church and provide for the sustenance of its religious ministers and all spiritual needs that pertain to divine worship.

Three religious of our Company went to the settlement of San Luis de la Paz, where they were welcomed by some Chichimec families who had come to look the site over. Although they were people who were not accustomed to this new mode of living, which had not yet been established, the priests attended to and won over those Indians who came down from the mountains. Through them they called to the others who had not yet descended, bringing them down out of the mountains as well. Because they wanted to gather Christ's flock, the priests—like shepherds—went themselves into the interior to gather in those lost lambs. Sometimes they were successful and returned with a good number of people who had been living in isolation like wild beasts in those far mountains and deserts. Other entradas were not successful, owing to the considerable danger that the priests faced of being killed and torn to pieces by the Indians, who are more ferocious than carnivorous wolves. [724] They were so fierce that all that was necessary for trouble was their desire for it, or more certainly, the desire that the devil imprinted upon their hearts. One can well imagine the suffering required to reduce such a people. Nevertheless, with the patience, suffering, and Christian charity that Our Lord communicated to His evangelical laborers, they finally managed to form and congregate a pueblo of three hundred Chichimec families. Thus, that area was secured for travel into the interior and the assaults and robberies that plagued the roads began to cease. The following chapters relate the means that were employed by the priests to better secure this reduction and establish Christianity.

CHAPTER IV The priests begin religious instruction and other means of introducing Christianity in this Chichimec reduction

Once the priests had congregated some people, they tried to learn their language, in which they then began Christian instruction. Some children were baptized, as were other sick and elderly people whose age and illness forced the hastening of their Baptism. Events demonstrated that God had predestined them by protecting them in the midst of their heathenism so that they could receive this Holy Sacrament, which is necessary for the salvation of souls. The priests never failed to find adequate understanding on the part of these mountain people, and in some of them they found signs of sound reasoning and submission to the evangelical ministers' advice. There were several means by which these ministers introduced a steadfast Christianity and civilized life. One such means, the importance of which we have mentioned at several points with regard to various nations in this history, was to organize a seminary for the sons of the Chichimec. Through being raised in our house, they would learn the doctrine, letters, singing, and Christian customs, thereby endearing these things to their parents when they saw them in their sons. In the beginning it was difficult for some parents to give up their sons, for fear that they were being taken as slaves for the Spaniards. Nevertheless, with time they became disabused [of this fear] and turned them over most willingly. They saw for themselves the good treatment and gifts of clothing and food that the children received from their spiritual fathers, who had more love for these sons than did their parents by birth. In order to found this seminary and establish a lifestyle appropriate to it, they took some young students and singers from another seminary that the Company has in the pueblo of Tepotzotlán (which will be spoken of later). The boys from Tepotzotlán were able to instruct these novices in that way of life, and this was a very helpful way to achieve the goals of this new seminary. Virtue, the catechism, reading, writing, and dancing were all very easily learned by these Chichimec boys. They and those who continue here today became so adept that they could read a book in Spanish at mealtime in the refectory just as well as any good reader and student. In addition, they were taught ecclesiastical singing to the accompaniment of the organ, all of which aided in the introduction of Christianity.

A young Chichimec student gave a significant demonstration of Christianity and virtue when another child, who was the daughter of a Chichimec principal and captain, made fun of him. [725] The boy went to her father to complain about his daughter's immodest mockery. On the one hand, her father was edified by this chaste young man's warning. On the other hand, he was regretful of the incident caused by his daughter. For this reason he punished her rigorously, which was something new and unusual in this undisciplined nation.

The boys were so happy with their orderly life and good treatment that even though some of the parents attempted to take them out of the seminary, they hid and resisted going home. They were very happy with the good customs and lifestyle that they enjoyed in the seminary. It should not, however, be understood that these cases of edification applied to all. Among these lambs there were also kid goats who on Judgment Day will be set to the left-hand side.[4] There were also some little wolves among those we are discussing who were drawn back to their mountains. This is no reason for the evangelical laborers and shepherds of these souls to be discouraged, for Christ, the Sovereign Shepherd, said that in search of even one sheep He would traverse mountains and valleys.[5] This is what our missionaries to the Chichimec did, and their efforts were successful.

Once those at San Luis de la Paz were congregated, they dutifully attended church, religious instruction, and catechism. The viceroy desired that this should continue and that the Chichimec should become more settled. Thus, he ordered that comfortable houses be built for them at the king's expense. Although not all of them had yet come down from their mountains and lairs, with each day more of them were arriving and becoming fond of the mission. The priests tried to initiate the general Baptism of those who were first to arrive. I will record here only one of them, which was very well known because it was the first Baptism. The xacal or house that served as the church was adorned with many flowers and bouquets. [To provide] for even greater rejoicing and celebration, the day before this ceremony those who were going to be baptized decided to go with their relatives and friends on a communal hunt for wild turkeys and honeycombs, in order to hold a feast for everyone. The following morning all the people who had learned the doctrine and catechism gathered. Thirty couples were selected for Baptism from among the most advanced of them, leaving the others for the following

Sunday. They received the water of Holy Baptism before Mass, which was sung with as much music as possible. During Mass they received the blessing of Christian matrimony, with which they were all very delighted. The priests were also delighted to see that Christ's flock was beginning to multiply. That night, as a sign of even greater happiness with their new state, they wanted to celebrate with a public dance. They were allowed to do so, provided that they did not dance in their former infidel fashion, but rather in a very orderly and Christian way. They agreed to do this, and once night had fallen a large bonfire was lit in the plaza, which was completely illuminated. They then arranged themselves in the circle that they use in their dances, with each husband leading his wife by the hand. The dance lasted three hours and was accompanied by their drums and singing. This is how the celebration was concluded, and they all returned to their homes extremely happy.

The priests were even happier to see what before had seemed impossible: the Chichimec converted and tamed. Not much earlier, these people's only occupation was that of bandits and murderers of Christians. Indeed, one priest wrote to Mexico City that he had learned for certain that one of the Chichimec who had come to be baptized at this reduction had killed more than thirty Spaniards. When one adds to this number [726] the Christian Indian travelers and servants who died at his hands, the figure totals one hundred. Even so, he was now as obedient as a child, praying and saying the catechism on his knees so that he could be baptized. Once he was baptized, he became one of the most helpful Indians, both in church and with the priests.

These are all good signs of Christianity, as well as of the effectiveness of the divine word. Those who could not be overcome by weapons, harquebuses, and armored wagons surrounded by escorts of soldiers were overcome and transformed by the doctrine of Christ's Gospel. A few poor religious were able to pacify and domesticate those whom squadrons of armed soldiers could not overcome. For those who were already reduced and pacified, the militia was no longer necessary. Nevertheless, for several years the viceroy thought it advisable to keep soldiers at several settlements in the region, for fear that some of those who had withdrawn to the mountains might rebel. Once these fears had passed and everyone had been reduced and was pacified, this garrison was reassigned, the fortified houses were abandoned, and the entire land remained at peace, just as it does today.

---

4. In Matthew 25:31–46 it is explained that on the Day of Judgment Christ will divide the nations just as a shepherd divides the sheep from the goats, with the latter being set to the left-hand side and then sent to everlasting punishment.

5. See Matthew 18:12 and Luke 15:4.

CHAPTER V How some of the Chichimec's customs were changed

So that the account given in the previous chapter does not serve as the only testimony to the changes that took place in this nation and its Christianity, I will add here other edifying cases. Drunkenness was more common and deeply rooted here than among all the other peoples discovered in the Indies. In fact, we could say that these people nourished themselves as much on their wine as other nations did on food. Although it is true that this vice was being uprooted, it was impossible for this to happen all at once; rather, it had to proceed gradually over time so that the medicine that produced such good results would not become distasteful.

The priests began to preach against this vice and point out the dangers it presented. It happened on one occasion that a principal Chichimec named Don Juan, who held the office and title of governor of his people, backslid into drinking. His people did not pardon him this transgression, throwing his guilt back in his face for having fallen into the same vice for which he had scolded them, and for failing to follow the advice he had given them. They even went so far as to slander and insult him. Don Juan was an Indian who if he had met with such affronts when he was a gentile, would have mightily avenged himself with his bow and arrow, for he was considered brave and courageous among them. However, because he was a Christian, he did not use such means. Instead, he went to the priests' house to find out whether they had learned of his lapse. The priests knew why he was coming, so they had the doors closed and sent him a message saying that they did not receive drunkards in their houses, especially those who were supposed to be setting a good example for others. The Indian grieved over the priests' coldness toward him much more than the scorn he had suffered from his own people. He went to the Spaniards' captain and asked him to intercede on his behalf with the priests so that he could regain their friendship and kindness. He was welcomed back by those who had been wishing for the very same thing, despite their initial coldness toward him. He presented himself before them, and because his sin had been public, he was reprimanded in the presence of his people for the bad example he had set. He received this reprimand with tears of re-

pentance and a major change in lifestyle; such are the effects wrought by the virtue of the holy Gospel.

This fierce Chichimec's demonstration of Christianity did not end here. [727] One of his sons was being instructed at the school along with the other boys, and at the time of his father's disgrace he had fled. This Indian had become convinced that the priests had thrown his son out as punishment for his father's sin of drunkenness, so he returned to the priests, saying to them, "My Fathers, I have not really suffered that much from being denied entry to your house, nor because you publicly reprimanded me, because I know that you did those things for my own good. What has caused me great anguish is knowing that because of my sins you have thrown my son out of your house. What blame, my Fathers, does my son have for what I do? If it was I who sinned, I should have been the one to bear the punishment and reprimand, and you should not have cast my son from your company, in which he has been reared. Now he will fall in with other bad people and become delinquent." These heartfelt arguments were given by an Indian who previously had reared his son to be a bandit. The priests proved to him that his son had not been dismissed from the seminary, but rather that he had run away. Immediately, he ordered a diligent search to find him, and when he was found, [the father] returned him to the priests, subjecting him to punishment. This valiant Indian principal's humility and submission amazed the Chichimec. Through his example they became so changed in their drinking that, if one of them backslid, they offered many excuses, saying that they had done so in order that the people could understand the vice in which they had formerly gloried.

Even greater was the crime and penance of another Chichimec captain with regard to this vice. This Indian was so brave and daring during times of war that he had wrought great destruction in that land. He was overcome by temptation, and on Holy Monday [the Monday before Easter] he got drunk. While still under the influence of wine, he attempted to enter the church, where the priest was instructing the people of the pueblo. Twice the priest sent him a message not to enter the church and to go home and settle down. The Indian responded so violently to this message that he furiously shouted to the people, telling them to come out of the church and not to pay any attention to what the priest was telling them, nor to obey him in anything he commanded. This was a case that could have led to great unrest and rebellion among people so inherently free. It was Our Lord's will, however, that the people should pay no heed to the words of this Indian, who was talking nonsense and whom they knew gave them good advice when he was in his right mind and exhorted them to matters of the Faith and Christianity.

The Indian returned to his house, and once his anger had subsided and he realized how bold and scandalous his behavior had been, he decided to go and seek forgiveness. When he felt that the right moment had come, he went and threw himself at the priest's feet, and with great humility and affection he begged his pardon. He told him that he was very sorry for what he had done (this is something rarely spoken by an Indian when he is a gentile, no matter what crime he has committed).

Here one could see what God was working. The Indian continued to repeat that he was very sorry for what he had said and done and that he was prepared to carry out whatever penance he was given. The priest scolded him for his behavior and told him that because his sin had been public and had caused a scandal in the pueblo, his penance would also have to be public. The Indian agreed to this, and on Holy Thursday while the entire pueblo was in the church awaiting the departure of a procession of blood scourging, he publicly confessed his sin and the lack of respect he had shown the priest and their church. He asked them to forgive him, for he had done this when he was not in his right mind. He promised to mend his ways on both counts, and having said this, he began to scourge himself like the others. He did this so zealously that it amazed and edified the Spaniards who were there. [728] They gave thanks to God for the change they saw in the Chichimec Indians, whose name alone had struck fear in people in earlier times.

CHAPTER VI Other ways that the priests of San Luis de la Paz aided souls

Because the Company employs its sons in the aid and welfare of the health of their fellow man — not only in places where it has a house or college, but also everywhere beyond them — it has exercised this same charity from its house and residence in San Luis de la Paz. Peace was established throughout this land with the foundation of this pueblo and the Company's house. The Spaniards shared in this peace and its benefits, founding ranches and settlements that were populated by industrious people, ladino Indians, mulattos, mestizos, and other servants. They also founded mining camps named Los Pozos, Sichu, and that famous one so rich in gold known as San Luis Potosí. God had preserved all these riches in this land of the Chichimec for the Spaniards and their Catholic king. Due to these mining camps, and for their benefit, haciendas were also established to produce charcoal for the smelting of ores. These are inhabited by a large number of people who are destitute of spiritual aid for their souls. Moreover, there are also some parishes and

doctrinas of Otomí and Mexica Indians in the region that are ministered to by priests who have benefices.

The priests of San Luis de la Paz conduct visits to all these places, where they exercise their ministries with great charity. They can do this because, through the grace of God, they have learned the languages required to communicate with the various people who come to their house. These are herdsmen who freely roam the land, rarely seeing the inside of a church or town, or other travelers or people from the countryside.

A brotherhood was established so that its members could strive to make known the Christian doctrine in these settlements, letting people know that knowledge of it was required for admission to Confession and the Sacraments. [The people] took this so seriously that within a short time those who had lived without master or shepherd came to demonstrate that they knew the Christian doctrine and prayed it in their settlements and out in their fields. They built a separate chapel in the church, and there they held their meetings during Holy Week, when they all come to confess and take Communion. The Chichimec joined [the brotherhood] at this time, so this new Christian community was introduced to the practice of penitential scourging. There were large numbers of penitents, and they were so devout that the Spaniards were amazed to see how the Chichimec, in spite of themselves, had transformed the spirit and daring that they had employed in shedding the blood of Spaniards and other Christians. Now they watched them come like docile sheep and as brothers to all. At dawn on Easter Sunday they filed out in another procession, rejoicing and signaling with music, green branches, and adornment in their attire the spiritual joy of seeing Our Lord Jesus Christ risen in their souls. These good customs have endured here up until the present time.

There were many specific cases and signs of special predestination [729] that the priests experienced during their continual journeys through those fields. We can call these fruits of the vineyard of Our Lord, who would not allow the loss of the crumbs of bread that he spread with such abundance in this desert.[6]

At this time a Mexica Indian (who as a child had been captured and reared by the Chichimec) came to inform the priest that in a hut in the country there were two very old and decrepit persons, a man and a woman, who had not been baptized. He said that they wanted to be baptized if someone would visit them, so the priest immediately went to them. He found that between the two of them the sum of their ages was 250, and they looked like the image of death itself. The priest informed them that they had to believe in order to be baptized. Their catechism, however, had to be abbreviated because neither their age nor capacity allowed for much time. Having joyously accepted the priest's proposal without resistance, and comprehending what was required of them, they were baptized, the old woman taking the name of María and the old man the name of Pablo. The following day as the priest was preparing to leave, he wished to stop by the hut of his children [who were] now reborn in Christ. When the old Indian, who was blind from old age, heard his new name of Pablo, he became very happy and frequently and very joyfully repeated the sweetest names of JESUS and MARY, which had been imprinted upon his heart. This is testimony to the interior happiness of his new state. The Indian María died after three days and Pablo died fifteen days later, leaving many reassurances that they had been saved and that, as the good Christians they were, they had gone to the glory which God had prepared for them, even though they had been gentiles for more than 120 years each. Thus is the unfathomable disposition of God and His divine predestination that these two old people died such good Christians, and as such the Indians gave them a solemn burial.

6. See John 6:12.

CHAPTER VII Other cases and singular indications of the predestination of Indian souls. A miraculous case of the intercession of our father Saint Ignatius

Although I have already included in this history some cases and signs of predestination that God has shown Indian souls, these are so worthy of esteem that recording them amounts to glorifying Him. One time a priest was traveling to San Luis Potosí and got lost. Not knowing where he was or on what road he was traveling, he came upon a ranch, where he found a woman who was quite fatigued due not only to illness, but especially to her concern for dying without anyone to hear her confession. The priest comforted her and heard her confession, and soon she died. This religious minister was greatly consoled by what had happened to him because, by becoming lost, he had found the path to eternal heavenly bliss for that soul.

This same priest happened to be passing by a ranch where he found a cowboy who was on the verge of dying. He heard his confession and remained with him throughout the night, aiding him to achieve a good death. As he was reciting the commendation of the soul, the cowboy died, also leaving assurance of his salvation.

There was one sick Indian who walked ten leagues to San Luis in search of a confessor who understood his language, Otomí. When he arrived in San Luis, he confessed and received the Viaticum. Then he died and was taken by God, who had given him the strength to walk ten leagues and had moved and encouraged him to seek the means to his salvation.

On other occasions God used special acts of providence as a means of salvation. [730] Once it happened that a priest trained in Indian languages was passing through a pueblo at a time when the [resident] priest was absent, and there was an Indian who was very sick not only corporally, but especially spiritually. Although this poor Indian knew that the priest of his benefice was not in the pueblo, he did all he could to go from his house to the church to see if God would bring him someone to minister to him. He who had redeemed this soul with His blood had mercy on him and brought this priest to this place. The priest thought that [his arrival] had been purely by chance, but it was not; instead, it was so that he could aid this soul in search of a means to his salvation. The priest led the Indian in making a general confession (which he needed), and then he exhorted him to perform many Acts of Contrition. Then, with the sweetest names of JESUS and MARY, a few hours later he expired.

Although I am omitting other similar cases, I wished to relate these here so that it can be understood that there are many particular benefits wrought by divine kindness among these poor Indians. The number of those who are saved is great, and their ministers' hardships and travels produce abundant fruits in this land and even greater rewards in heaven.

To conclude all these cases, I will close with one that was considered miraculous. It took place in the pueblo of San Luis de la Paz, where there is great devotion to our glorious father Saint Ignatius. He is found in their church in a very handsome gilded image and altarpiece that adorns the side altar. A gentleman who was one of the conquerors of this land and who lived in San Luis de la Paz fell ill from several grave ailments that lasted for six months. He suffered from a foul-smelling hemorrhage for which no remedy could be found to stop the bleeding. The sick man was so drained of blood that, due to this and his other ailments, he was on the verge of dying, so much so that his wife and children were already mourning him as dead. This happened on the feast day of Saint Ignatius, and at nine in the evening they went to call the father superior of that residence to aid this man in his hour of death, for he had already heard his confession. When the priest entered he knelt down, and taking out a medallion of our father Saint Ignatius, he asked those who were present to commend the sick man to the saint, praying five Our Fathers and five Hail Marys. To this the sick man added (as best he could) a personal vow that if through the intercession of our holy patriarch God should grant him health, he and all his household would celebrate the saint's feast day by confessing and taking Communion. With the sick man remaining on his knees, the priest held the medallion against him, saying "In the name of the Most Holy Trinity, Father, Son, and Holy Spirit, may the intercession of our blessed father Saint Ignatius be worthy to Your Majesty, the living and all powerful God." As soon as the priest had said this, the sick man's blood clotted, and he was soon feeling better. He was able to rest that night, and the following day he was almost entirely recovered. On the eighth day following the feast of Saint Ignatius, this man who had been sick for six months came to our church on his own two feet to give thanks to Saint Ignatius, through whose intercession God Our Lord had miraculously restored his health. As a result, devotion to our glorious patriarch remained well established in this pueblo, which is cared for by his sons.

With this and other similar cases, which for the sake of brevity are omitted, Christianity was established in this pueblo, along with frequent reception of the Holy Sacraments and the celebration of feast days. There is a well-organized Indian choir here, with an organ and all kinds of instruments. The church is decorated with very rich ornaments, lamps, and silver vessels. Today this pueblo is used as a resting place by all those traveling to the interior, where some of the [731] Spanish conquerors have their homes. This is a settlement where previously all one saw were numerous Crosses set up in memory of travelers killed at the hands of infidel bandits. It was, however, well deserving of the title it was given—that is, San Luis de la Paz—because it was here the peace originated that is now found throughout this land. Many other Chichimec Indians were resettled in pueblos where religious instruction was being given by the religious fathers of the Seraphic Order of Saint Francis. With this I will move on to other places where the priests from the Company purposefully and permanently carry out their ministries to the Indians.

CHAPTER VIII The religious instruction received by the Indians of the parish benefice in the district of Tepotzotlán, which has been entrusted to the Company

The Company of Jesus has only one Indian doctrina in all of Nueva España that is in the form of a parish benefice. All the missions that we have discussed where the Company carries out its ministries among barbarous Indian nations are ministered to by religious with the jurisdiction and authority of priests. These missions are not set up as parish benefices, however, unlike others in the Indies that belong to secular clerics and other holy religious orders. This is in part because these Christian communities are too new. Also, their people are so poor that they have neither offerings, fruits, nor stipends to give their priests. Furthermore, according to its Institute, the Company cannot accept such ministries [benefices]. The Company has taken charge of only one such benefice, by a special order of Our Lord King Philip III. As patron of all the churches in the Indies, he ordered the very illustrious Archbishop of Mexico, Don Juan de la Serna, to entrust the benefice and district of Tepotzotlán to the Company. At the same time His Majesty ordered the viceroy, the marquis of Guadalcazar, to transfer the secular cleric who was administering this benefice at the time to another suitable and equivalent benefice or vacant prebendary. The order was carried out as His Majesty commanded and the said beneficed priest of Tepotzotlán was promoted to a curate of the cathedral in Mexico City. The Company took charge of this benefice and district in the year 1621, under the order and license of our Father General. The transfer was made because of petitions and pleas from the Indians of that district to Our Lord the king for the reasons mentioned later.

Tepotzotlán, which is the lead pueblo and has three other pueblos within visiting range, is five leagues from Mexico City. After the Company came to Nueva

España, by order of Our Lord King Philip II, it built a residence in this pueblo, which later became a house for novices. In addition to the novices who received their training here, the superiors always took care to have some priests trained in Indian languages resident to hear confessions and preach to the Indians. This is because the Otomí language spoken by these Indians was the most difficult in Nueva España. It has innumerable precepts and rules, particularly regarding pronunciation. The language is guttural and has some aspirations and stress patterns that they use in a very strange manner. Indeed, when they omit them their words change meaning or do not mean anything at all. This language is so difficult that rarely does someone learn it unless he has been raised [732] among these Indians, or (as they say) unless he receives it from his mother's milk.

Through great hardship and many years of practice, some of the first priests of the Company who arrived in Mexico overcame the difficulty of this strange language. The venerable Father Hernán Gómez, whose life and holy death were recorded in the preceding book, labored and was of great aid in the learning of this language. Eventually our priests learned it well enough to reduce it to a grammar, which has not yet been printed because of the great difficulties of its accents and pronunciation. And yet the number of people who need to hear religious instruction in this language is great. Before the ancient Mexica settled here, the Otomí had multiplied and formed a large population, which persists to this day in the region surrounding Mexico City and in other bishoprics. Notwithstanding all the difficulties of this language, the Company always had three or four priests in the pueblo of Tepotzotlán who knew the language, in order to hear confessions and preach in that district and in many others where that language was spoken. Seeing how tremendously helpful these priests were, the Indians of Tepotzotlán begged Our Lord the king to order the priests of the Company to become their own priests and relieve them of the expense of secular priests. This was the occasion and particular reason why His Majesty placed the Company in charge of this benefice; it was on behalf of God Our Lord and His Majesty that [our Company] was entrusted with this benefice, whose language was so strange and difficult to learn. After the Company took possession of it, in order to conform to its Institute, it was ordered that the offerings laid at the foot of the altar should be used for the church and its ornamentation and for the singers who serve there.

In addition to its principal pueblo, this district has three other pueblos and churches within its jurisdiction. Although at the beginning there were numerous people, they have diminished just like the other native peoples in Nueva España. Thus, there are not more than six or seven hundred tribute-payers or families in those pueblos.[7] Because there are many other parish benefices in the region of Tepotzotlán, our priest-interpreters have always tried to aid them in missions. Their ministries to the Indians have provided them with a copious harvest. This reached the point that the Company eventually founded a seminary college for boys in the pueblo of Tepotzotlán, which is the headquarters of the district. The college was in a separate house and dwelling, where one priest and a religious live and administer the school. Usually more than fifty students are raised in this school, many of them the sons of surviving Otomí and Mexica caciques and principales. Their parents usually bring them from many leagues away so that they may be reared in complete virtue and taught how to read, write, sing, and play all types of musical instruments, which can be heard during ecclesiastical feasts. These young men have become such skilled musicians that cathedral churches have called on them and offered them very good positions and salaries to serve in their choirs and chapels, particularly playing various musical instruments, such as the sackbut, bassoon, cornet, and others. Many other pueblos and benefices have greatly desired to have these students from Tepotzotlán as teachers for their chapels and even as governors in their pueblos.

Some of these young men, especially the sons of principales, have shown such skill that once they have completed their grammar studies, they have gone on to Mexico City to study rhetoric in our schools, followed [733] by courses in philosophy. They have been so successful that those who have graduated from this famous university, have had their graduation ceremonies attended by many of Mexico City's Spanish grandees and nobles who, because they were so illustrious, lost none of their dignity by honoring the natives, even though they are Indians. When the Lord Archbishop of Mexico City, Don Francisco Manso, saw how capable and well mannered was one of these bachelor graduates, named Don Gerónimo, he wanted him ordained as a priest (a very rare thing in the Indies). Today Father Gerónimo has a parish benefice in the archbishopric. At his first

---

7. Tribute-payers generally were males between the ages of fifteen and sixty, representing perhaps a quarter of the population.

Mass he was honored by having as his godfather Don Diego de Guevara, the Archbishop of Santo Domingo and Primate of the Indies, who at the time was cantor and governor of the Archbishopric of Mexico City. Another student named Don Fernando, who completed his studies in philosophy in 1642, went on to study sacred theology, a course he is currently pursuing.

We have touched on a matter infrequently discussed yet of great interest among those who have not been to the Indies: Do the native Indians have the capacity to be ordained as priests and ecclesiastical ministers of their own people? I will answer briefly, addressing the reasons that have delayed and prevented the Lord Bishops from ever or rarely granting the Indians sacred orders. It cannot be denied that this issue has been the subject of considerable discussion worthy of these great Prelates' superior knowledge and holy zeal. The reasons given [against ordination] are that the Indians are still neophytes and new to the Faith. The Sovereign Pontiffs call them neophytes in very recent bulls that we have concerning their privileges. One of the instructions that the Apostle Saint Paul gave to his disciple Timothy was not to ordain anyone who was a neophyte: *Non neophitum, ne in superbiam electus, in iuditum incidas diaboli.*[8] Do not let the devil deceive him, as one who is new to the Faith. Although it seems that the Apostle was speaking of episcopal rank, those who study the Scriptures well know that the Apostle also used the word 'bishops' to refer to presbyters and priests. He did not want such men to be neophytes, new to the Faith, as our Indians are today. Moreover, because there are so many Spanish clergy and religious who are well versed in letters and are long-time teachers of the Catholic Faith, there has not been nor is there at present any need to teach the Faith using those who are known to be inferior in character, as is the case of the Indians, especially when it comes to such high ministries as those of the holy priesthood. If this title has been bestowed on those about whom I have written, it was due to very special circumstances: They were the sons of very great caciques; they were reared with extensive religious instruction in seminaries where this is imparted; they were youngsters of advanced skill; and above all, their language was Otomí, which was very difficult, as was stated. It was desirable to have ministers who had mastery of Otomí and could use it to explain the mysteries of the Holy Faith, which are sung in Latin in the church. These Indians could do this with great skill because they had learned Latin extremely well, and they had learned their own language—which presented the greatest difficulty—as their mother tongue. In addition, the natives who receive and listen to the doctrine each day from Spanish priests would receive it with great pleasure from their own people, enjoying this occasionally, even if it were not every day. These were the reasons for this dispensation. Thus, for the time being I believe that I have responded to and satisfied the curiosity and difficulties raised by this matter. [734]

---

8. *Margin Note*: AdThim.?. 3 Timothy 3:6: "He must not be a new convert, or he may be carried away by vanity, and incur Satan's doom" (Knox 1956:218).

CHAPTER IX The fruits of the benefice that the Company administers in the district of Tepotzotlán

We will now continue with the Indian seminarians who are raised in the college of Tepotzotlán and the fruits of this endeavor. One can truly say that these Indian seminarians are the most well mannered and civilized in the entire region around Mexico City, which has very large settlements of Indians and Mexica nobles. The district of Tepotzotlán has very well-organized pueblos, wherein they rebuilt their churches once the Company had taken charge of their religious instruction. The principal pueblo is especially orderly and has a very beautiful church with a vaulted ceiling and recently refurbished paintings and altars with precious golden retablos, rich ornaments, and sacred vessels. The organ in the church was repaired no more than four years ago, and they had another one built that is worth six thousand pesos or ducats. The choir is the best known in Nueva España. Indeed, they frequently have been asked by very important people in Mexico City and many other districts, benefices, and churches of the region to sing at important feast day celebrations. People from all over the region come to enjoy this music and these famous feast days in Tepotzotlán, where some Spaniards live and have their properties and haciendas nearby.

What is of greater esteem and importance here are the spiritual matters related to souls. The monthly jubilees granted by His Holiness for all the churches that the Company has on earth are celebrated here with great pomp and solemnity and with the exposition of the Most Holy Sacrament. On these days many people assemble from pueblos in this and neighboring districts. The Indians very frequently receive Communion, and among them there are people of notable virtue and unusual example. Their work in their brotherhoods and fraternities of the Holy Sacrament and the Souls in Purgatory is carried out with great devotion and care; Holy Week devotions and processions of penance are celebrated all over the region. In addition, this pueblo has other very particular devotions of Christian charity that are observed and carried out twice a year. One of them

is on the Feast of the Holy Innocents[9] and the other is on Holy Thursday. On the first of these feast days, all the Indian children from the neighboring pueblos are invited and brought together. After a large number of those innocents who are seven years old or younger have been gathered and have prayed the doctrine, they are given a splendid feast and lots of leftovers to take home with them. All this is done in honor of those blessed and innocent child martyrs who celebrated with their blood the Son of God's arrival in the world.

The other charitable occasion is on Holy Thursday. Following the washing of feet, which is celebrated with great solemnity, the Father Rector of the college washes the feet of twelve poor Indians, while the governors and principales of the pueblos help him by pouring the water. After this they give a large number of poor Indians clothing with which to cover themselves.

In summary, although the pueblo of Tepotzotlán may not be the most populous, it is known to be the most splendid and remarkable for its Christian exercises and divine and civilized ritual. The settlement is pleasant and in a refreshing location, and it often attracts powerful people from very important tribunals. [735] They go there to rest by listening to music at the church or to make retreats at the novitiate house.

To conclude, the priest-interpreters who reside there have many abundant fields in which to employ the talents and holy zeal that God has given them to aid the souls of these poor Indians. They make many journeys—that is, missions—from this pueblo to other pueblos and districts whenever the clergy of the benefices request their ministries of preaching and hearing confessions in these Indians' languages. These missions are not undertaken on a permanent basis, as are the ones I have described among barbarous and gentile peoples; rather, they are more temporary. Nevertheless, these ministers harvest abundant fruits among the Indians

---

9. This feast day on December 28 commemorates the death of all the children slain by King Herod in an attempt to kill the Christ child (see Matthew 2:16).

and are quite free of any interest in personal benefit. How much more will these ministers be rewarded by the Lord, who said that He would reward the smallest crust of bread given to His poor,[10] if what the Indians are given here is the blood of Christ and the divine treasures of the priests' merits? This will be seen on Judgment Day, when these priests will have no regrets for having gone to the Indies in search of such treasures.

CHAPTER X The ministries exercised by the religious of the Company among the Indians of Mexico City

In this chapter I will speak only of the ministries exercised by the members of the Company among the Indian natives in Mexico City, which is the capital of Nueva España. I will omit the service that they have rendered Spaniards of that great and most noble republic from their four residences in Mexico City and the many colleges that they have founded throughout the kingdom. These are matters for a more eloquent and erudite author.

Our history began with the most distant and isolated of all the Indian nations in Nueva España. Subsequently, I have moved closer and closer to the capital, Mexico City, where the great Moctezuma had the seat of his empire. For this reason, when the Spaniards encountered this city, it was inhabited by an immense number of Indians. Although it is true that this great quantity of people is now greatly diminished for the reasons mentioned earlier, today the number of people living here and in the surrounding area is still very large.

The Company does not have its own particular parish in Mexico City, unlike other religious orders, who administer their parishes with great zeal for the welfare of the Indian natives. The sons of the Company have not, however, neglected their charge to aid the Indians; rather, they have ministered to them everywhere in many ways, pursuing the salvation of these poor souls through all the means available to them. The first and foremost ministry in this great city has been maintaining three or four select priests who speak Nahuatl at the great College of San Pedro and San Pablo. These priest-interpreters are dedicated to minister to the Indians, whom they aid at all hours and in all places, both the sick and the well. In proof of this I refer the reader to the account I have given [in Book VII] of the life of the outstanding laborer among Indians and great master of theology, Father Juan de Ledesma who, to the amazement of the people in this city, managed to combine the great and lofty aspects of theology with the humble aspects of applying this theology with great care, to the aid of the poor and humble Indians near Mexico City.

It should be noted here that in their most refined speech, the Mexica people require the use of what they call the 'reverential' [voice], which is singular in its formation and pronunciation. Their Indian courtiers were always outstanding in their use of this register, and in their manner of speaking with princes or discussing matters that demanded reverence, such as their gods or idols, they were especially careful and notably civilized. This register is very different from that of the [736] spoken Nahuatl that is employed throughout the kingdom. Its usage is such that if our preachers are explaining to the Mexica the supreme mysteries of our Holy Faith and they fail to use the reverential register—even if it is only in a single word or term—the Indians laugh at them. They consider them to be persons who speak their language very coarsely because they do not even understand the respect they should have for things holy and divine when they speak of [those] matters worthy of reverence.

10. Luke 14:13–14: "when thou givest hospitality, invite poor men to come, the cripples, the lame, the blind; so thou shalt win a blessing, for these cannot make thee any return; thy reward will come when the just rise again" (Knox 1956:73).

Although this may lengthen my digression, to avoid discouraging those whom God might call to labor in the instruction of the elegant Mexica, I wanted to add here that the formation of the verbs and nouns in the reverential register is not very difficult. It is true that the singular nature of this register and its associated reverence are not accomplished simply by adding the terms used in Spanish, such as 'Grace, Lordship, or Majesty', depending upon whom is being addressed or referred to, but instead has the reverence incorporated into the word itself. Nevertheless, once one knows the basic language, which is not too difficult, there are very general rules for the formation of the words of reverence. The Mexica are so attentive to this that even a four-year-old girl knows what language [register] she must use when speaking to a priest or an important individual, as opposed to an Indian macehual, which is the same as 'laborer' or 'commoner'. With this I have digressed enough and will now return to the matter at hand.

For the aforementioned reason, the Company always endeavored to have preachers and confessors for the Indians in Mexico City who were highly skilled in their language. One of these priests, Father Antonio del Rincón, became so adept in Nahuatl that he composed a grammar of it that is the most elegant and proper of all those that have been written. This grammar is used by priests in parishes and benefices throughout Nueva España. Father del Rincón was born in Mexico City of a noble bloodline, and his nobility was made even greater by his very religious virtues and his zeal for saving the Indians' souls, at which he labored quite fruitfully.

So that ministries to the Indians in Mexico City would not be disrupted by ministries to the Spaniards and their numerous students, the Company founded a seminary next to its principal college, with its own church and residence for the Indian students. It was named for San Gregorio El Magno [Saint Gregory the Great], who as Supreme Pontiff of the Church did not disdain caring for and personally instructing the young people who would eventually serve in the Church.[11] At this seminary, which is under the protection of this glorious Doctor of the Church, there are usually fifty or more students being reared. Many of them are the sons of Indian principales from the region, who bring

them here so that they can learn all manner of religious doctrine and good habits. They are taught all the same honorable exercises of service to the Church that were discussed in the previous chapter concerning the seminarians at Tepotzotlán. In addition, there is a school of reading and writing. The teacher serves not only these students, but also other Indians and the children of poor Spaniards who lack the means to pay a teacher at a secular school. There is also another skilled teacher at San Gregorio who teaches music, at which the Indians become very adept. Some of them have gone on to serve in the cathedrals of Mexico City and other places; they are particularly skilled at playing all musical instruments.

The Indian church of San Gregorio is quite spacious [and is] adorned with beautifully gilded altarpieces in its three naves. These are needed for the large number of people who come to the feast day [services] and sermons in Nahuatl, which are numerous throughout the year, particularly during Advent and Lent. Toward the end of the sermon [737] silk drapes are removed to reveal floats on which the Indians have placed very cherished images of Our Lord's Passion, which these natives hold very dear. They kneel with great tenderness and devotion, and listen to the rest of the sermon. This is concluded with a Miserere, which is sung accompanied by very beautiful music provided by the students of the seminary. Through special orders from the governing superiors, these students and their families belong to this church and its congregation. These are all means that increase the renown of this church among the Indians, although it is true that there are also many Spanish men and women who are quite fond of and who frequent this famous church, which is so well served and adorned.

The language spoken by the preacher is the thing that most attracts the Indians and produces the greatest fruits. Efforts have always been made to have someone who can preach eloquently in Nahuatl, as the Mexica greatly enjoy hearing their courtly tongue. On the days of a sermon during Lent and Advent, one of the classes of students sets out beforehand in a procession, carrying a Cross and banner and singing the catechism in their language. They are accompanied by some of our religious brothers, and as they travel throughout the city and then return to their plaza, they gather many other Indians, who join in singing the prayers. It often happens that there is not enough room in the church for everyone. On Thursday of Holy Week the same class goes out again and stops in the great plaza of Mexico City, where another sermon is preached in their lan-

11. Pérez de Ribas is perhaps alluding here to an apocryphal account of how Gregory was prompted to undertake a mission to Britain after encountering three captive Angle boys in a market in Rome (Thurston and Attwater 1956:567).

guage to the Indians who gather there, both residents and those from outside Mexico City. This happens during the time of the markets that they call *tiangues*,[12] which attract many people.

In addition to all that has been said, it is very advantageous for the College of San Gregorio to have two congregations of Mexica Indians, who have their own separate chapel where they are given their own particular talks. During Holy Week these two congregations perform two blood scourging processions that are greatly renowned throughout the city. One of them is dedicated to the Seven Effusions of the Blood of Christ Our Redeemer. [The participants] carry the corresponding floats and devout emblems in this procession. They are accompanied by a great number of Indians who perform blood scourges, and by others with wax candles and torches, all of whom are preceded by Indian children dressed as angels (this is a privilege that their parents greatly esteem, and they spend generously in adorning them). The final float in the procession is dedicated to the shedding of Christ's blood on the Cross and is covered by a very rich canopy that is held aloft on twelve gilded poles by twelve students from the Company's Royal College for Spaniards in Mexico City.[13] The remaining sixty students from this college also honor the Mexica Indians with their

participation. This procession is greatly edifying and highly esteemed in Mexico City.

The other procession on Good Friday is dedicated to the burial of Christ Our Lord, who is carried on an adorned float, with His most holy body covered in the richest fabrics. It is deposited in a beautiful bier that is like a mausoleum, which is set up for this purpose in the main church of our college. It remains there with torches that burn until very early in the morning of the Resurrection, when they bring the risen body back out again, and in a very solemn procession, with music and many candles, they return the body to their church of San Gregorio. What is of even greater esteem on this joyous morning is the general celebration of Communion by a large number of Indian men and women. With singular devotion they spend nearly the entire [preceding] night going to confession, owing to their great numbers. They then receive the most holy body of Christ our resurrected Lord.

These are all matters and deeds that I would not have paused [738] to recount in detail if they had not concerned Indians who, after all, are not as old in the Faith as those in Europe, where many of the same kinds of celebrations occur. Other successful fruits [harvested] from the Indians of San Gregorio and their church will be told in the following chapters.

CHAPTER XI   Exercises of Christian edification performed by the Indians

There is one notable act of charity that merits being recorded here. The members of the two brotherhoods at San Gregorio celebrate Easter each year with [services] attended by both men and women. One day during Holy Week all the poor Indians of the city are gathered together to receive a splendid meal, as well as other gifts. Because the

city is so populous, there is a large number of poor who attend, four hundred or more. A suitable place for so many people and servants is needed to hold this celebration for the poor, so it is held in the church of San Gregorio. This feast is very similar to those celebrated in the early Church. On that day the women of the congregation bring the best food and delicacies they can from their homes. Usually these are dishes prepared from their hens, which in Spain are called 'turkeys of the Indies'. All this food is very well prepared.

The poor sit in rows in the middle of the church and the Father Rector comes out, followed by all the religious of the college. They sprinkle holy water on the

---

12. Although thousands were said to visit the marketplace of Tlatelolco each day, every fifth day there was a "great market" when the number of shoppers more than doubled (Soustelle 1961:26).

13. This was the College of San Ildefonso, which provided Spanish youth with an education in Latin.

poor and then the Father Rector blesses them; much music is played throughout the feast. The women fill plates from the dishes they have brought and all the religious serve them to the Indians. The food is so abundant that there is even enough for the poor to take home additional meals. After they finish serving these delicious dishes, the members of the congregation emerge, loaded down with blankets and clothing, which they distribute to the poor, along with some silver coins and cocoa beans, which are used as money by the Indians. When the feast is over, they receive a spiritual talk in their own language on the topic of giving and receiving alms. All of them return very happy to their homes, especially the women who prepared the delicious foods for Christ Our Lord in the person of His poor.

I confess that sometimes I found myself greatly moved by the Christianity of these natives, particularly by the devotion demonstrated by their devout women, who were some of the most important in this nation. The happiness with which they shared the best they had prepared in their homes with the blind, the lepers, the cripples, and the helpless old people—who came in large numbers—makes them all remember the feast and the day when it is held. This is an act of great edification in Mexico City.

We still need to mention the spiritual and celestial feasts of the bread of the angels, Holy Communion. This is offered very frequently in this church of San Gregorio because they have been granted many jubilee celebrations by His Holiness the Pope, particularly the famous Forty Hours celebration that takes place during Carnival time. These days are celebrated very solemnly by the Spaniards at our professed house, and they are celebrated separately in this church for Indians in order to gather in these people, who are generally more uncontrolled and restless at this time. For the Spaniards (through the mercy of God), secular Carnival celebrations have already ceased [739] in Mexico City.

In order to invite the Indians to more fully enjoy the spiritual feasts of Carnival, the collegians at San Gregorio usually present some colloquia on holy matters in their Nahuatl language, along with mitotes, or dances, accompanied by music or singing, which is great entertainment. Here I will make a brief digression and describe the mitote, or festive dance, which is a particularly enjoyable sight and is new both to Spain and other nations. The mitote that the seminarians of San Gregorio celebrate is called the mitote of the emperor Moctezuma. Although in the past it was dedicated to

gentile purposes, now it is a Christian celebration dedicated to the honor of Christ Our Lord, King of Kings.

The first things that are unusual about this feast, when fully celebrated, are the costumes and ornaments worn by the dancers. These resemble the garb of the ancient Mexica princes. The two mantas or shawls are layered; the outer one is transparent, which allows the embroidery and beautiful flowers on the inner one to be seen through it. They wear these hanging from their shoulders, in the fashion of the Roman emperors, fastened on the right shoulder with a knot that forms a handsome rosette. They wear a diadem tied around their heads, raised over the forehead in the shape of a beautiful pyramid. This is adorned with the most precious stones and gold they can find, in the shape of the crown of the Mexica emperors. They also wear a handsome bracelet on their left arm, which clasps a tall cluster of the bright green feathers they wear and value highly. They carry another cluster of feathers in their left hand, which they wave as they follow the rhythm of the dance. In their right hand they carry an instrument called an *ayacaztli*, which is made of some rattles formed from some gold-colored gourds that have seeds in their tips. These, too, are waved to the beat of the music, producing a pleasing sound. The rest of their decoration consists of embroidered doublets and loincloths made of two folded cloths, [in layers] just like the mantas. They also wear richly adorned sandals.

The stage that is assembled for this celebration was strewn with flowers, and at the head of it they placed the seat of the emperor Moctezuma, which was like a short golden stool. On one side of the stage they set a table, placing upon it a little drum called a *teponaztli*, which is very different from the ones used in Europe. It is made of a rare red wood, using two little planks, one spaced in front of the other, which enclose it, forming a hollow. This is struck with the rubber tips of small drumsticks; their beat guides the dancing, accompanied by the rhythm of the rattles that the dancers carry in their hands. The Spaniards have added the harp, cornet, and bassoon to these instruments.

The place of the old men and the Mexica principales was around the drum, for they were the ones who sang the hymns that always accompanied the Mexica dance. This was performed at a slow pace, without much music. The dancers of the festive dance[14] were usually fourteen in number, plus the emperor, who

14. The Spanish text reads *sarao*.

came last. The emperor advances with a considerable show of majesty, wearing the same clothes as the rest of the principales, although his is a richer garment, more finely decorated. A boy follows him with a large fan made of rich feathers. As he dances to the beat like the others, the fan shades the emperor and serves him as a canopy. Two other richly dressed boys proceed on both sides, one step ahead of the emperor, sweeping the way with their feather clusters and occasionally strewing flowers at the emperor's feet. [740] The festive procession emerges from the inner palace, summoned by the music and singing, which in the Spanish and now Christian fashion goes as follows: "Come out, Mexica, and dance the *tocontín*. We have the King of Glory here." The three syllables of this word, 'tocontín', are like the beats kept by the rhythm of the drum; this is why some call this dance by that name. The dancers come out dancing in two rows in the manner of the Spanish *hacha*.[15] The pace is slow and solemn, and they beat out the rhythm with their hands, arms, and feet. They shake their rattles and wave and raise the crests of feathers, which are very long, thin, and golden in color; sometimes they wave a branch of an aromatic tree instead. They then take their places, after which the emperor emerges at a very majestic pace. He takes his seat at the main end of the stage, and immediately, without a signal, the dancers (whose solemn movements never stop) turn toward their prince, bowing to him in unison, positioning their plumes, rattles, and bodies so that it seems as if they wished to cast themselves beneath his feet. When this genuflection is complete, they quicken their movements before the emperor. (Now that Moctezuma is converted, this genuflection is to the Most Holy Sacrament of the Altar). After the dancers have performed the mitote, the emperor rises to dance by himself. The two little boys who, as I said, accompanied him sweep the ground before him with their plumes and sprinkle flowers at his feet while the third boy holds the parasol that serves him as a canopy. Each one follows the movement of their prince so exactly that it seems as though they are part of a single motion. During the time the emperor is dancing, all the rest of the people stay in their places, bowing down

to the ground. When the emperor passes through the two lines, all of the [dancers], in pairs, touch his feet with the instruments in their hands, as a sign of humility. This is accompanied by the constant rhythm of the ayacaztlis. When the emperor has finished making his rounds he takes his seat again, and the two choruses start their dance with new movements, which although not that different from the [previous ones], are very pleasant and not boring. The unceasing vocal music corresponds to the person playing the teponaztli, who has his own chorus, which is hidden behind a curtain or grill, as though this were being sung by two choruses.

The entire dance—with its novelty, adornments, actions and singing—is so pleasant that it has been a great entertainment and diversion for very important people, lords, and Archbishops who have come from Spain. The little Mexica collegians of San Gregorio perform and preserve this dance today. Although the common mitotes are danced by the rest of the people who are macehuales, or vassals, these are very ordinary dances that do not display the same preparation and ceremony as [the dances] performed by these boys, which are often imitated by the sons of the Spanish elites.

I deserve to be pardoned for having tarried in this telling, because this festive dance is now being employed in the service and recognition of the King of Kings, Jesus Christ, Our Sacramental Lord. This was what prompted me to record it here, and the Catholic faithful cannot help but be pleased to see the ancient Mexica heathenism cast down at the feet of their Redeemer, whom before the [gentiles] did not know but now worship and recognize with all possible demonstrations of happiness.

In addition to this mitote, they add the participation of a certain kind of flyers, who come flying down through the air. When the float of the Most Holy Sacrament reaches the plaza, they come flying down in a very unusual manner, sustained on cords tied to a pole that is like the mast of a ship, with some of them shaking rattles or playing other instruments.[16] I will now leave these entertainments, [741] which as such, are always an aid to the Indians' welfare and devotion. In the following chapter I will return to what most concerns us.

---

15. An ancient Spanish dance.

16. A reference to what was sometimes called the "Moctezuma" or "pole-flying dance."

CHAPTER XII More about the spiritual fruits of the seminary for Mexica Indians; the outstanding and unique virtues of one of its seminarians

Up to this point I have spoken of the ministries and aid provided by the Company to the Indians of San Gregorio and its seminary. It should be noted that these ministries are not limited to those who attend this church, but extend to all of Mexico City and anyone who wishes to make use of them. This includes the Indians who live on the outskirts of the city. Despite their great numbers, members of the Company attend to them very willingly and charitably at all hours of the day and night, whenever the Indians become ill and on other occasions of temporal need. So as not to repeat the proof of this, those who desire can turn to Book VII, Chapter XVI. I recorded there Father Juan de Ledesma's efforts and great charity toward the Indians of Mexico City, which other priests have endeavored to imitate.

In addition to the ministries that are exercised by the members of the Company in Mexico City, they have frequently been called or invited to pueblos and benefices in the surrounding areas. Through God's mercy, abundant fruits have been harvested during these missions. The same religious of the Company continue to aid the Indians in the city of Puebla, which is a city of Spaniards and one of the largest and most important in the Indies. It is also a very rich bishopric with a cathedral. I will not include a separate chapter on these ministries, but will simply note that in this city, in addition to the two colleges with very illustrious student bodies made up of Spaniards, the Company also has a church for Indians. There priest-interpreters minister in the same way as the priests in Mexico City and to a similar number of Indians from both Puebla and the surrounding area.

In all parts of Nueva España the sons of the Company always try to help the native poor through all their ministries. They recognize that they are obliged by their profession to pursue these ministries, regardless of the innumerable hardships that arise daily in their holy ministry to the Indians.

I will now write about the outstanding and rare example given by one Indian who was reared in virtue. He himself taught virtue, catechism, and reading and writing in the two Indian seminaries that have been mentioned in this book. Because he died in one of these seminaries, at the time of his death he deserved to be welcomed into our Company as a religious and counted among the unique fruits of our teaching to the Indians. He is therefore worthy of memory in this history, which is entirely dedicated to that subject.

He was born in Mexico City to a very important and noble Mexica lineage and was given the name Lorenzo (he was happy to be referred to by this name alone, and thus he was known and respected by all). When he was very young, he entered the seminary at our college at Tepotzotlán in order to serve in the church and to learn to read and write. He became so proficient in this art that he was able to teach it, doing so with distinction for more than forty years in the [742] aforementioned seminaries of Tepotzotlán and San Gregorio in Mexico City. The most important Indians in the province, descendants of Mexica and Otomí lords, brought their sons to him so that he could instruct them not only in reading and writing, but also in all the virtues. He also taught them Spanish, which he spoke very well. Moreover, he spoke with great distinction the courtly and reverential Nahuatl language, which (as we said) is extremely elegant. Because Lorenzo was of noble lineage, he knew this form of Nahuatl very well. Indeed, missionary preachers asked him to examine their sermons and to correct their Nahuatl so that they could better explain the mysteries of our Holy Faith, which he had pondered and meditated upon at length.

Although our Lorenzo excelled in these faculties, he was even more respected for his outstanding holy virtues, which benefited him more than his intellectual faculties. Among all others, there is one that is rare among Indians: celibacy and moderation. He guarded these states throughout his entire life, never desiring to marry. Because of his nobility and good background, he could have had a very honorable marriage to an important and wealthy woman. He never discussed such matters, however, in the more than sixty years that he lived.

In addition to his previously mentioned duties as teacher, the one occupation to which he dedicated himself with unique affection was serving in the church.

No matter where he was, he would tend to the decoration of the altars, adorning them with beautiful little bouquets of flowers that he raised in a little garden at Tepotzotlán which he had dedicated to this purpose. He did this throughout the year, in such a way that it amazed those who saw roses and other flowers on the altar in spite of the fact that they were out of season and were seen nowhere else in the area. He was careful to plan ahead so that when flowers were not available in the area, he would send for those that grew year-round in warmer regions twelve to fourteen leagues away. This affection was particularly apparent in his devotion to the Supreme Sacrament of the Altar and to the Immaculate Conception of Our Lady, the Virgin. He was extremely devoted to and fond of these mysteries, and he took pleasure in celebrating their feast days with all possible ceremony, especially that of the Most Holy Sacrament. For greater solemnity and so that the natives could achieve a greater understanding of that most supreme mystery, he usually gave talks and directed dramas about the Holy Sacrament, which he composed in the most elegant Nahuatl. On the day of the feast these plays were enacted by his students from the seminary. They did so with great spectacle, costumes, and adornment, in the customary Indian fashion. Large numbers of Spanish authorities also attended, and during the festivities the dance, or famous mitote, of the emperor Montezuma, which was mentioned earlier, was performed. This was introduced as a part of the drama and songs of the Mexica nation in recognition of their Sacramental God, and they now abominate the cruel sacrifice of thousands of people whom the ancient Mexica nation formerly dismembered.

The devotion of our Lorenzo did not end with flowers and words, for he gained much more fruit from his truly outstanding virtues. Throughout his entire life he went to confession and took Communion at least every eight days. His confessions were so exquisitely conscientious that his confessor said that he didn't know how to deal with someone whose life was so geared to perfection and so superior to his station.

With respect to the virtue of holy contemplation and prayer, he was so well practiced at these that we can say that from [743] the time he got up at three o'clock in the morning until seven A.M., he spent the entire time in prayer, either in his cell or before the Most Holy Sacrament while hearing Mass. He left many other devotions for nighttime; some he practiced alone whereas others he carried out with the little Indian seminarians who were always under his care. He would pray the Rosary with them on their knees and assist them with other devotions. Although Lorenzo did not have the obligations of a religious until he was welcomed into the Company at the hour of his death, it cannot be doubted that he exercised all the virtues of a perfect religious. I can speak as an eyewitness, for I had him under my charge for many years at the college in Mexico City. He obeyed the superior of the college and even the other priests who lived there as though he were a novice in the Company. The same was true of the poverty of his attire and sustenance, and although he could have obtained a great deal in the way of gifts and other benefits from many of his disciples, who were the sons of wealthy Indian principales, he never attempted to obtain such comforts, even while suffering and enduring bouts of illness alone and without treatment. If at some time he requested or received something from persons of his nation, he used it to celebrate feast days or for adorning the altars.

What was more unusual—and something that is rarely seen among the Mexica or Indians from other provinces and kingdoms—was that Lorenzo was never contaminated by the vice of drunkenness which, generally speaking, affects all the Indians. He never drank wine, not even when he was very aged, nor did he resort to the drink made from chocolate, which is so widespread in this land and was readily available to him. He steadfastly abstained from these things until the time of his death. He was happy with the meager and religious food that he received as alms at our house. He deserved a very good salary for his duties as schoolteacher, sacristan, and others that he carried out in caring for the students, but this Indian refused even to discuss payment. He also received his attire as alms, and this had to be very modest, made from ordinary linen. He normally wore clothing and a cape in the Spanish style, never dressing like an Indian.

The acts of penance that our good Lorenzo added to his temperance were many, including scourging himself and wearing a cilice [hair shirt]. In this way he maintained his purity and chastity throughout his entire life; not even the slightest error was ever noted in this regard. Rather, he always lived with great and outstanding composure and prudence, in spite of the fact that he spoke and dealt with many female Indian principales who attended church or were the mothers of his students. All these women respected and revered him because of his great virtue. This modesty and composure were edifying to everyone, even when he was going down the street or to the markets that the Indians call tiangues, where he bought food for the little Indian seminarians who were under his care. In everything, he was the example of composure and religious behavior. No religious could be more careful in his attention to that holy virtue. Whenever he noticed some deficiency in his virtue, he sought a way to correct it, albeit humbly and sensibly.

Because Lorenzo was endowed with so many virtues and talents, the superiors made use of them in places where they were needed. Therefore (according to the demands of the times), they moved him from the college in Mexico City to the college in Tepotzotlán, and then back again. He worked for more than forty years in these holy exercises, until he was sixty years old. Then Our Lord wished to reward him, sending him an affliction and pain in his side, from which he soon realized he was dying. His life ended within a few brief days, and he greatly [744] conformed to God's will as

he received all the sacraments with great devotion. Particularly singular was his joy over the favor of having been received into the Company, for which he had very humbly sought the license of the Father Provincial. He was happy to have been granted and to have earned this grace of dying as a religious in the Company, even if it happened only at this last hour. And that is how he died and was buried, with our members celebrating the Office of the Dead with his body lying in state. A great number of Mexica Indians attended this ceremony, and they were happy to see this person from their nation honored as a religious. This is something rarely seen in that kingdom, even though he was very deserving of it. He left a great many assurances that Our Lord would welcome him into the eternal bliss of His heaven, for which He who grants His mercies to all the nations of the world had selected Lorenzo.

CHAPTER XIII An account of the first religious of the Company of JESUS who went to the Western Indies; what happened to nine of them who died at the hands of barbarous Indians in La Florida[17] for preaching our Holy Faith.

In writing this history, which deals with the enterprises among barbarous Indians in which the sons of the Company have labored, I am justified in recording the first of these undertaken by these soldiers of Christ in the Western Indies. It should be assumed as a known fact that the lands of La Florida form part of the same continent as those of Nueva España. La Florida was discovered and even explored by our Spaniards a few years after the conquest of Mexico, or Nueva España, which is one and the same. As stated in Book I of this history, the Province of Sinaloa was discovered

and settled following news that was received about this province and its nations from those three Spaniards who had entered La Florida with General Pánfilo de Narváez. When misfortune destroyed their armada, they headed inland and wound up ten years later in the lands of the Province of Sinaloa, in Nueva España.[18] For this reason I am justified in including the missions of La Florida along with those of Nueva España, and to join the martyrdoms suffered by the sons of the Company in Nueva España with the joyous deaths of nine of their brothers who shed their blood in La Florida

17. In Pérez de Ribas' time 'La Florida' referred to an enormous territory covering the southeastern Atlantic seaboard and Gulf Coast of North America from present-day Virginia to Louisiana.

18. It was actually eight years (1528–36) from the time the Narváez expedition landed in Florida to the time Cabeza de Vaca and fellow survivors encountered Spaniards in southern Sonora.

for the same cause of preaching the Gospel. It is worth noting that even though these holy religious, who were the first from the Company to set foot on the soil of the Western Indies, did not achieve their goal of planting our Holy Faith in the land of La Florida—nevertheless, through the blood they shed for that cause, it seems that by means of unique and divine providence, God opened the way from that very same land for the religious of the company to go to preach the Gospel and convert the large number of gentile nations in the Province of Sinaloa, which are now Christian. These were recorded in the first seven books of this history. The joyous deaths of those who initiated the enterprises that have been discussed throughout the entire course of this history will provide it with a joyous ending.

The account that I will record here is taken from a brief *relación* or report written by Father Juan Rogel, of our Company, who was one of the first to actually come to La Florida from Spain.[19] It happened that in 1566 Pedro Meléndez, adelantado of La Florida and governor of [745] Havana, made an effort to get some religious from the Company to go from Spain to La Florida, where the Spaniards had some ports and some small forts. He wanted them to conduct their ministries not only among Spaniards there, but also among the Indian natives, in an attempt to domesticate them and prepare them to receive our Holy Faith. To initiate this enterprise, Francisco de Borja, father superior and Father General of the Company, received a letter and orders from that great guardian of God's glory, the Catholic king of all the Spains, Philip II. The Father General was charged to select twenty-four religious to go to the Western Indies. His Majesty would supply the provisions for all their needs on the journey. The first selected were Father Pedro Martínez, Father Juan Rogel, and Brother Francisco de Villarreal.

They embarked on a Flemish ship of the type known as a hooker, setting sail in 1566 in the fleet headed for Nueva España. From there they followed a course heading for the port known as Saint Augustine in La Florida, where the adelantado, Pedro Meléndez, awaited them. The pilot of the ship, who had very little experience on those unfamiliar seas, became lost. They traveled up and down that coast in search of the port, but were unable to find it during a period of thirty days. Given

this predicament, Father Pedro Martínez decided to go ashore to obtain an interpreter from among any Indian inhabitants he might happen to find, as well as any news concerning the port where Meléndez awaited them. The squad of Indians that he encountered were fierce and barbarous, and they were not on good terms with the Spaniards from those ports. In addition, they were very inclined to idolatrous superstitions and had a type of temple in the pueblo [fort] they called Carlos. Therefore, when they saw Father Pedro Martínez, without waiting for questions or answers, they attacked him with their weapons, taking the life of this servant of God who had set out from Spain and exposed himself to those hardships and dangers with no goal other than the salvation of those souls and the preaching of the Gospel. This cause glorified his death, as was declared by the Redeemer of the World and recounted by Saint Mark: *Qui perdiderit animam suam propter me, & Evangelium, saluam faciet eam.*[20] Here, the Lord canonizes with His own tongue those who lose their life for serving Him in the preaching of the Gospel, without regard to whether or not they actually managed to preach or plant it. The desire to preach that doctrine brought the blessed Father Pedro Martínez to his death. For that reason we can call his death blessed and joyous.

Because of these unexpected events, the ship in which the priest was traveling went back to Havana, with Father Juan Rogel and Brother Villarreal, to see what Meléndez would arrange concerning that enterprise. In the meantime, things took a turn for the better, so Meléndez asked Father Rogel to return with the soldiers to the fort named Carlos, and for Brother Villarreal to go to another fort on the same coast, where each of them could assist the Spaniards with whatever ministries they needed. They did so with all the charity they could summon, for these two religious possessed remarkable virtue. God protected them so that they could later be the first to minister in Nueva España, as will later be told.

During this time, for the purpose of attending to business matters, Adelantado Meléndez made a trip to Spain. There he met an Indian cacique from La Florida who some religious from the Order of Saint Dominic, who had landed there first, had taken to Nueva España, where he decided to become a Christian. Then for purposes of even greater solemnity and so that later [this cacique] could help in the conversion of his own

---

19. This report was written between 1607 and 1611 by Father Juan Rogel. The Spanish text is in *Monumenta antiquae Floridae* (Zubillaga 1946); excerpts in English translation are in Lewis and Loomie (1953:118–22).

20. *Margin Note*: Marc. 8.35. Mark 8:35: "The man who loses his life for my sake and the Gospel's sake, that will save it" (Knox 1956:41).

people, [746] Viceroy Don Luis de Velasco the Elder was pleased to grant him the favor and honor of acting as his godfather in Baptism. Therefore, this Indian took his name, calling himself Don Luis. He was a very sly and treacherous Indian who spoke Spanish very well. He passed himself off as a lord over many Indians, and through various turns of events he wound up in Spain. There the Catholic King Philip II heard about him, and with his royal piety he ordered that Don Luis be given clothing, rations, and sustenance. Don Luis confessed and took Communion, outwardly appearing to be a very good Christian. It seemed to Meléndez that this Indian could be of great assistance in the conversion of the natives of La Florida and that he could be an interpreter of their language, so he took him along on his return trip to Havana.

Father Francisco de Borja had a burning desire for God's glory to be increased and for those of the Company to labor in the conversion of the Indians. In fulfillment of the royal order, and in spite of the fact that word had already been received of the death of Father Pedro Martínez, he selected Father Juan Bautista de Segura as Vice-Provincial of the seven other priests and brothers who accompanied him in order to continue this enterprise. Father Rogel and Brother Villarreal, whom we left waiting in Havana, were to join up with these eight other religious. With great desires to employ their lives and labors for the love of God and the welfare of the souls of their fellow man, these religious ministers set out from the port of Sanlúcar on the thirteenth day of May 1568. The cacique Don Luis was with them, and they disembarked at the port in La Florida known as Saint Augustine, where they suffered great discomforts and hardships. In the following chapter the events of this most holy journey will be told, as will the fate of those who were going there to preach the Holy Gospel.

CHAPTER XIV The holy deaths of the priests who went to La Florida to preach the Holy Gospel

Adelantado Pedro Meléndez [i.e., Pedro Menéndez de Avila] placed the priests sent to La Florida to preach the Gospel under the protection of the cacique Don Luis. Soon afterward this Indian cacique left the priests, telling them that he was going to a pueblo that was some ten leagues inland, where he had a relative and where he was going to prepare the people for religious instruction. As a result, God's servants suffered so many discomforts and found themselves so lacking human assistance that, without any help at all, they themselves had to erect a small house for shelter and where they could say Mass. Their lack of food became so great that they went into the thickets some leagues distant to look for wild fruits or plants on which to sustain themselves. This situation continued for six months.

It is not clear whether the Indian Don Luis had only pretended to be a good Christian from the outset, or if he had actually been one at some point and then had failed in his loyalty and obedience to the Christian law that he had accepted. Whatever the case, he surrendered to the vice of treachery in such a way that the last thought he had was of returning and helping the priests. Rather, he thought only of taking their lives, as was later seen.

When this Indian delayed so long, the Father Vice-Provincial [Segura] decided to send a priest named Luis de Quirós to meet with the Indian to beg him to return to the priests so that they could plan the entrada for which they had come from Spain. Meléndez had charged the cacique with this enterprise and in return had done him many good deeds. The perverted cacique received [747] this message [from Segura] with dissimulation, telling Father Quirós to return and that he would follow later.

At nightfall the disloyal Don Luis armed himself and took some of his people with him. He followed Father Quirós, overtaking him on the road, where they killed him. From there they went after the rest of the religious, Father Quirós' companions. Father Vice-Provincial [Juan] Bautista de Segura was ill and praying in his rustic bed, very concerned about what might happen. His fellow priests were doing the same, for it seems God was preparing them for what they suspected awaited them. Thus, on the eve of the Feast of the Purification of Our Lady, the Most Holy Virgin {February 2], they made a general confession. It was later learned from an eyewitness [21] that they also took Holy Communion with great affection and devotion. Subsequently, Don Luis and his people, armed with macanas, or bludgeons, and with some sturdy long poles, reached Father Bautista and his companions. The Indians first greeted them as friends, but then, being liars and traitors, they attacked the priests and took their lives. One member of the group, Brother Sancho de Zevallos, had gone to get firewood for their meager food. The barbarians went in search of him and killed him [as well].

This is how the lives of these eight holy religious came to an end. For the glory of God and His Holy Gospel, which they wished to spread, they exposed themselves on land and at sea to all types of dangers and difficulties, uprooting themselves from their own land and becoming pilgrims in the lands of fierce barbarians. These are the very qualities that made them blessed, and because we know that their names are recorded in the book of life, it is proper that they should also be noted here. The names are as follows: Father Vice-Provincial Juan Bautista de Segura. This blessed priest was a native of Toledo, and because of his great religion, he was much loved by the holy Father Francisco de Borja. He insisted on leading this holy enterprise himself, even though another priest had volunteered and, as Vice-Provincial, he could have remained in Havana to govern the other priests. The other priest and his holy companions were Father Luis de Quirós and Brothers Gabriel Gómez, Sancho de Zevallos, Juan Bautista Méndez, Pedro de Linares, Cristóbal Redondo, and Gabriel de Solís. The latter was a relative of the adelantado Meléndez, and he was blessed with the crown of a religious and a martyr. He was enthusiastic about the glorious enterprise that the Company was undertaking and he joyfully asked to be part of it. He thus joined the enterprise in La Florida, and together with his brothers he gave his life for his God.

The barbarous infidels pardoned only one boy named Alonsico, due to his young age. He was the son of a Spaniard who resided at the fort of Santa Elena.[22] The

soldiers had given him to the Father Vice-Provincial so that he could assist the priests with Mass and be raised by them. The young man truly desired to die with the others, but a brother of the perverse Don Luis had kept him locked up in his house. Afterward, Don Luis told the young man to bury the bodies according to Christian custom, and he ordered others to help him. It seems that this was the only trace of Christianity left in this barbarian. They dug a large grave in the chapel where they used to say Mass. There the bodies of these blessed religious men remain today. They are not forgotten by God, however, who has an eternal memory of His chosen ones: *In memoria aeterna erit iustus. Capillus de capite vestro non peribit.*[23]

Those in Havana, which is an island very close to La Florida, did not know what had happened in La Florida for many months. There was no news from La Florida, nor from Fathers Juan Rogel and Antonio [748] Sedeño, nor from Brother Vicente González, all of whom were sent by the Father Vice-Provincial to minister to the Spaniards at the fort at Santa Elena. {The Father Vice-Provincial in Havana] had ordered them to take supplies to their brothers, whom they thought were still alive in La Florida. It had been impossible for many months to dispatch these things because there was no pilot who knew the harbor where the priests had landed. One brother took these supplies in the company of a skilled pilot named Vicente González, and when they reached Axacán,[24] the place where the priests had disembarked, they anchored but did not go ashore. They remained on the ship awaiting some news. When the treacherous Don Luis and his allies saw that the Spaniards were delaying their landing, they pretended that the religious were still alive by having some of the Indians walk around in the black robes of the deceased, while the Indians along the shore gestured, talked, and pretended they were the priests. When Don Luis saw that the Spaniards still hesitated, he sent two Indians out to the ship. The Spaniards had already realized the barbarians' evil intentions, however, because of their poor imitation of the priests. Therefore, the Spaniards captured the two Indians, raised anchor, and returned to Havana. The Indian prisoners refused to confess the truth. One of them, realizing his difficult

---

21. Undoubtedly the boy Alonso de Olmos, from the Santa Elena colony, who was the only survivor of the massacre, rescued in 1572 by Rogel and Menéndez.

22. Located at the site of present-day Tybee Island, Georgia.

23. The first sentence is Psalm 111:6: "men will remember the just forever" (Knox 1956:525), and the second Luke 21:18: "and yet no hair of your head shall perish" (Knox 1956:80).

24. The region around Chesapeake Bay and present-day Virginia, where the missionaries led by Father Segura had tried to establish a mission.

situation, threw himself into the sea as they approached land and escaped.

Adelantado Pedro Meléndez was determined to verify the facts concerning all these events and to punish the guilty. Therefore, he decided to go [north] to the port [at Axacán] in La Florida with a detachment of soldiers. He took along Father Juan Rogel and Brother Villarreal. Once they arrived at the port, the adelantado and some of the soldiers went ashore. They greatly hoped to capture Don Luis and hang him, as long as it could be proved that he had violated his sworn fealty. The adelantado was not able to apprehend him, but he caught eight or ten of his Indian accomplices. He also had the good fortune of finding Alonsico. This boy was lucky; God had spared him so that he could report all that had transpired. After the adelantado had verified that the Indian prisoners had been accomplices in the deaths of the religious, he immediately sentenced them to die. He gave orders for them to be hanged from the long masts of the ship. By good fortune God willed that Father Rogel could work diligently with the condemned men, using Alonsico as an interpreter, so that they would understand the doctrine of our Holy Faith and be baptized. They heard the message and were therefore well instructed and received the water of Holy Baptism. Then they met their deaths, giving assurances of their salvation and eternal life.

We can well imagine that through these Indians' salvation God wished to console in heaven His servants who had died in La Florida. Even though the former were their cruel murderers, the deceased priests would beg God to save them and would thereby achieve their salvation. There can be no doubt that these martyrs' glory and triumph in heaven will increase upon seeing that their prayers and merits have won the souls of their greatest enemies and killers, just as it is to the glory of the Prince of Martyrs, Jesus Christ, that many of those who concurred in spilling His most innocent blood on the Cross are probably in heaven today.

Thus, it was seen that God had taken Father Rogel to La Florida specifically to perform this good deed. He asked the adelantado for an escort of soldiers to go to the burial site of the blessed bodies of those who had died preaching our Holy Faith. [749] This was for the purpose of recovering and gathering up their holy remains, but it did not seem to the adelantado that this was the right time [to attempt that]. Therefore, Father Rogel returned to Havana with his companions, taking Alonsico with him.

Alonsico recounted in great detail a marvelous case that occurred when those barbarians attempted to insult and profane the priests' sacred ornaments. After the [priests] had been killed an Indian who was greedy for spoils went looking for the box that held the ornaments and the holy crucifix for the altar. It happened that when the greedy and insolent Indian opened the box, he fell dead right then and there. The same thing happened to another Indian, and then a third, who received the same punishment from heaven. With this the rest of the Indians were filled with fear and awe, and not one dared to go near the box, which they left lying there. In one of his letters which I have in my possession, Father Rogel says that some old soldiers from La Florida had told him about this case. They had been in the Province of Axacán, where the priests died. [Local] Indians told these soldiers how after forty years the Indians still kept and venerated that box, not daring to approach it.

After Father Juan Rogel had spent some time in Havana, he and two companions were transferred on orders from their superiors to the Province of Nueva España. There he lived a holy life until old age, zealously pursuing the salvation of souls. Through great personal effort he managed to bring along a crucifix from La Florida, which is now guarded and venerated at our college in Oaxaca. Legend has it that those Indians in La Florida who had attempted to violate this very holy image and the sacred ornaments fell dead upon seeing it.

Finally, the joyous deaths of these eight religious men—actually nine if we include Father Pedro Martínez who, as mentioned in the previous chapter, also died in La Florida—were the first blooms of martyrdom from the Company of Jesus in the land of the Western Indies. The desire [of the Company] to sow our Holy Faith continued in Nueva España, as discussed in this history, whence these sweet-smelling flowers have been transplanted to heaven.

CHAPTER XV Epilogue to this history

In conclusion I can say that this history is neither perfect nor complete. One reason for this is that I greatly doubt it is written in the style required by the matters that have been recorded up to this point. The other and principal reason is that the topic it covers continues (thanks to divine mercy), as does the fervor that ignites the hearts of the sons of the Company of Jesus to embrace these holy enterprises and carry them forward. They labor in the salvation of the souls of poor and humble Indians and in traveling to the remaining nations, the most fierce and barbarous in the world, to bring them the good news of Christ's Gospel. They do so even though it means shedding their own blood, because the Redeemer of the World shed His own divine blood for them.

In this history an account has been given of twenty soldiers from this militia who shed their blood in the conquests that have been recorded here, three of them in the Province of Sinaloa, eight in Tepehuan lands in the Province of Nueva Vizcaya, and nine more [in La Florida] related in the previous chapter, bringing the total to twenty. To these we can add two more who shed copious amounts of blood from their arrow wounds. And even though they suffered greatly because of the poison on those arrows, God did not wish their lives to end, but He [750] kept them safe so that they could labor for many more years in their holy ministries in the places where holy obedience had sent them. I could more rightly say that it is Christ's charity and love that detains them. It is easily proven that they are very willing to render obedience in service of this Lord, for without turning back, as soldiers of the Company of Jesus, they continue in the same enterprise today. And they are not the only ones who are spirited and eager, for there are other soldiers of this same militia who, encouraged and strengthened by divine goodness, longingly and eagerly offer to go forth onto the field with their brothers to do battle with the powers of hell and the fiercest nations in the world, in order to remove them from the power of darkness and subject them to their true God and captain, JESUS.

One thing that I cannot fail to ponder here concerning the barbarous, uncivilized, leaderless, and fierce nations and peoples who have been the principal topic of this history is the countless number who are still gentiles, idolaters, and atheists. This includes not only those who have already been discovered, known, or heard about, but also those who are yet to be discovered, those of whom nothing is known, and those who are daily being discovered by our Catholic Spaniards, who have demonstrated themselves truly to be Catholics since the moment they received the Faith of Christ Our Lord through their great patron and leader, the Apostle Santiago. God reserved for them, among all the nations of the world, this glory of introducing that Divine Faith in the New World, where it was unknown, planting it there and raising the sacred standard of the Cross. God also reserved for this, His chosen nation, the glory of bringing the countless numbers of people who are being discovered into the fellowship of the Holy Catholic Church.

In order that this be stated in a non-confusing manner, and so that the truth of the proposal remains more clearly specified, I cannot nor should I fail to declare it here. In Nueva España Our Lord King Philip IV (may Divine Majesty preserve him for many long and happy years) has ordered that the land of the Californias, which as I have written is very extensive, be settled and that all the nations that inhabit this land be reduced to our Holy Faith. In compliance with this royal order, in the present year of 1644, two religious from the Company of Jesus have gone there, as was told, in the company of Admiral Don Pedro Portel de Casanate, to whom His Majesty has entrusted this enterprise. It has been stated at various points throughout this history that in Nueva España, from the northern regions of the Sinaloa mainland to the Sea of California, the discovery of new peoples has not ceased nor has the concern of the sons of the Company of Jesus for reducing them and placing them on the road to salvation. In the Province of Peru, and in Paraguay, an equal number have been reduced and are daily being removed from the darkness of their infidelity. In the extensive provinces and fields of the new kingdom, the harvests in which the laborers of the Company are employed are most abundant. On the Río Paraná a countless number of people have been discovered in the last two years. In the Philippine Islands, which are like a colony of Nueva España, the conversions are unceasing. Finally, in the New World of America there are countless nations of barbarous gentiles, and in Japan and Greater China there are the widest and most unending fields, the latter's grandeur being among that of the greatest nations of the world.

Who has multiplied these peoples if not the Lord and Creator Himself? It is in His hands alone to multiply men. Our Lord made that promise when He declared to [751] His ancient people who it was who had multiplied all the nations of the world and why He had done so: *Faciat te Dominus excelsiorem cunctis gentibus, quas creauit, in laudem, & nomem, & gloriam suam.*[25]

Regarding the Spanish nation, what is noteworthy in this passage (where God spoke of all the nations He has created on earth) is that the illustrious promise made by God to His ancient people, who were undeserving, was fulfilled for all eternity by our Spanish nation. God chose it from among the other nations of the world to carry the light of the Gospel to the New World, there to reveal in our time all the peoples and nations He had propagated. This is a glory through which He raised the Spanish nation above all others in the world, and they should recognize their duty to fulfill it. It is clear that divine clemency did not wish for so many people, regardless of their nature, to remain without salvation. Nor did He wish it to be in vain that He revealed them and placed them before the eyes of Catholic Spaniards and their priests and religious orders, especially before the kings of the Spanish monarchy, who are gloriously crowned by such singular enterprises. This is what the Redeemer of the World said to His disciples: *Videte Regiones, quia albae sunt ad mesem.*[26] This was also in fulfillment of the prophecy and holy and joyous announcement of a Prophet-king [David], who sang of the works and deeds of past and present Catholic monarchs: *Reminiscentur, & convertentur ad Dominum universi fines terrae.*[27]

In this history I have written about the abundant fruits harvested by the sons of the Company in the Kingdom of Nueva España. I have done this to the glory of Our Lord and so that the triumphs wrought by the Catholic and Divine Faith might be made known to confused, present-day heretics, who are abandoning the Faith. This is also in order that anyone whom Our Lord might call to these enterprises should know

how much this very same Lord protects and favors them with successful results in the conversion of various peoples and nations; with martyrdoms suffered for this cause; and with countless churches erected in the wilderness of jungles and mountains, where previously the Prince of Darkness was revered by so many blind and barbarous peoples. These are all triumphs which, because they are of great glory to Our Lord, are worthy of being recorded.

The sons of the Company who are employed in the many other provinces of the Western Indies are in charge of reporting the successful results of the preaching of the Holy Gospel and the fruits of their holy labors. Here I have related only those pertaining to the missions of the Kingdom of Nueva España, which will continue with whatever fruits Our Lord is served to grant to those who at present labor here and to those who will come later. My only goal has been for praise to be given to God for the great mercies He has granted these unknown and forgotten nations of the world, and to make known the glorious triumphs won here by His divine word and Gospel. With this I also wish to alert others (to whom the door is still open) to give us news—which will undoubtedly be very good—of what is being accomplished through the aid of Our Lord by those of the same militia and Company of JESUS, that Divine Captain whose squadrons are distributed throughout the world. There is no doubt that with this favor and protection from Our Lord they will have won glorious victories and triumphs. And it is good that we, the faithful, should take joy in them. It is true that we have been given just such news by those who have written about the missions [752] of the Orient in China and Japan, in histories full of triumphs by martyrs and confessors of Christ, who have labored in the vineyard of the Lord to the great edification of the Holy Church. Nevertheless, there is no doubt that it will be pleasing for the faithful to hear and read what divine mercy has wrought by way of His faithful ministers, and to learn of the propagation of our Holy Faith among the fiercest and most barbarous nations of the extensive kingdoms and provinces of the west.

I cannot help but comment here on another fruit and benefit that results from these histories. I wish and beg the faithful of the Holy Roman Catholic Church (for there is only one Church of the Supreme Shepherd, Jesus Christ: the one founded by its first Vicar, Saint Peter, at its apostolic seat in Rome) that they remember to beg and plead in their devout prayers that God favor these holy apostolic enterprises and that He remove

---

25. *Margin Note* Deut. 26. Deuteronomy 26:19: "his will is to exalt thee high above all other nations he has made, for his own praise and glory and renown" (Knox 1956:170).

26. John 4:35: "and look at the fields, they are white with the promise of harvest already" (Knox 1956:90).

27. *Margin Note*: Psalm 21. Psalms 21:28: "The furthest dwellers on earth will bethink themselves of the Lord, and come back to him" (Knox 1956:487).

this great number of blind and gentile nations from their present darkness. This is a prayer that we find highly commended to us by Our Lord, because on one occasion He charged His holy and beloved disciples not to forget it. The Evangelist Saint Mark made particular note of the memorable occasion on which the Redeemer of the World gave this charge: *Videns turbas misertus est eis, quia erant vexati, & iacentes, sicut oves non habentes pastorem*.[28] He saw hoards and Masses of wretched people living like sheep without a shepherd, and on this occasion He turned to His disciples and said, *Discipulis suis: Rogate Dominum mesis, ut mittat Operarios in mesem suam*.[29] Given the innumerable rancherías, nations, and peoples in this newly discovered world who are lost and blind in the darkness of their heathenism, I know of no other place than the one we are presently discussing that is a better representation of this occasion on which the Son of God charges His disciples to pray that more apostolic workers be sent, in addition to those whom His Majesty had already dispatched, for the salvation of the hoards and squadrons of those lost and shepherdless people. On this occasion it seems that Christ Our Lord is charging His faithful to aid them through their prayers, using the same words He spoke to His disciples: *Rogate Dominum mesis, ut mitt at Operarios in mesem suam*.[30] If His pious heart was moved to give His disciples this charge on that occasion when there were only those crowds before him, what would He say today when we have half a world of wretched people who are perishing? It should be understood that when the Lord asks and charges us to pray for lost souls, He wants to favor not only them, but also those who pray for them. Through their prayers He wants the latter to have a part in this great work of effectively extending Christ's redemption to these peoples.

I do not want it to seem that the words of the Son of God and the prayer He charged were directed only to His holy disciples, because I consider it to be a very important point for the faithful to understand that the Lord was speaking to all of us and charged all of us with this work of such great love. Therefore, I will illustrate here (although restraining myself somewhat) how much the Redeemer of the World commended this to us in the formula and propositions He left to

all us Christians in that most divine prayer, the Our Father. Therein are found those petitions, which being the most important ones, Christ Our Lord placed first, *in capite libri*.[31] These are: *Sanctificetur nomen tuum: adveniat Regnum tuum*.[32] Although the first of these [753] seems to pertain to the glory of God and is greatly due His most holy name, the Lord's immense love did not end there, for He did not want to enjoy the infinite riches of His glory and kingdom alone. Rather, he wanted His souls to enjoy them with Him, and for this reason He added the second proposition: *Adveniat Regnum tuum*.[33] He was already enjoying His kingdom in eternity; now He wants to make men kings along with Him, but He wants them to ask Him for it. Returning to the matter at hand, all this is accomplished and fulfilled when these peoples acknowledge and worship the name of JESUS, which they had never heard before, and when the kingdom of God and His Most Holy Son and the treasures of His sacraments and His heaven pass through these poor peoples' gates. These glorious ends moved Christ's Apostles and countless other apostolic men to leave their homelands for the distant lands of fierce and strange peoples. There—at swordpoint and amidst storms, tempests, flames, and fire—they introduced the sweet and glorious name of JESUS, as well as His kingdom, laws, and celestial doctrine.

Such were the desires of some pure and delicate souls who, due to their condition or state, were unable to labor in these enterprises, yet nevertheless aided them as best they could through continual prayer and penance. The most illustrious holy virgin Saint Teresa of Jesus excelled in this regard, dedicating her religious Institute and obliging her nuns to a continual remembrance in prayers and holy tears of the nations of barbarous Indians discussed in this history. This matter is discussed in detail in Book VII, Chapter XIII, where I dealt with a case of great edification that took place with Saint Teresa on the occasion of her receiving news from a religious who had come from the Indies concerning the souls who were perishing there without salvation. For this reason I did not feel it would be inappropriate to write here about another revelation recounted by the very same saint and also referred to by the very reverend Father Fray Francisco de Santa María, General Historian of the Order of the Reformation of Our Lady

---

28. *Margin Note* Math. 9. Matthew 9:36: "Yet still, when he looked at the multitudes, he was moved with pity for them, seeing them harried and abject, like sheep without a shepherd" (Knox 1956:9).

29. Matthew 9:37–38: "Thereupon he said to his disciples, . . . you must ask the Lord to whom the harvest belongs to send labourers out for the harvesting" (Knox 1956:9).

30. Repetition of Matthew 9:38.

31. "In first position."

32. Matthew 6:9–10: "Hallowed be thy name. Thy kingdom come" (Knox 1956:5).

33. "Hallowed be thy name."

of Mount Carmel. This glorious saint [Teresa] did the Company a great favor through a revelation that she recorded in her book about her admirable life. The reverend Father Fray Francisco also recorded it, tracing it to the Company. I will record it here in the very same words with which this very religious author himself recounts it in Book V of the History of [the Order of] the Reformation [of Our Lady of Mount Carmel],[34] Chapter XXXVI, page 881. I will then state my reasons for having included this in the present history. In Fray Francisco's history, when he discusses the book of the life of the glorious Saint Teresa, he says the following:

> The saint had just recounted what Christ Our Lord had told her to tell the Rector of the Company, Father Salazar, who was her confessor. The published version [of Teresa's life] states: *"I have seen great things concerning a certain order, all of the order together. I saw them in heaven with white banners,"*[35] etc. Because she does not specify here which order it was, there have been many who have attempted to claim this jewel. But as an eyewitness I certify and swear that it pertains to the very religious Company of JESUS, because the [original] text expressly states the following: *"I have seen great things concerning those of this priest's order, which is the Company of Jesus, with all the order together. I saw them in heaven with white banners."* I find no one (continues Fray Francisco) to whom I can attribute such a notable error, unless it is to the printer or the editor. For the same reason, the Prelates of the order cannot be blamed. And because [754] all the writings of our holy mother were so full of praise for this holy order, it would be a foolish and malicious theft to defraud the Company in this matter. Therefore, I most gladly restore to the Company what is known to rightfully belong to it.

Up to this point I have been citing the very religious Father Fray Francisco de Santa María, most worthy author of the history to which his Holy Order of the Reformation [of Our Lady of Mount Carmel] is so greatly devoted. He restored [to the Company] this highly valuable revelation experienced by this outstanding saint, who was favored by such great illuminations from heaven and glorified with the renowned name of JESUS, with which divine kindness also deigned to glorify His Company.

Now I can explain why I have included this revelation and story, in which Saint Teresa discusses the sons of the Company who have labored in the spiritual enterprises among barbarous peoples that I have recorded up to this point. Although sufficient reason for doing so lies in the fact that this illustrious revelation and its restitution pertain to a religious order whose sons are employed in the enterprises and conversions recounted in this history, the arguments concerning this glorious saint's revelation must still be explained and advanced as they bear on our present purposes and objectives.

Saint Teresa says that she saw great things concerning all of the Order of the Company of Jesus, and although she did not explain what all these things were, there was one remarkable fact that she did not want to omit: that she had seen them in heaven with banners that were white. Although such banners could be attributed to varied and excellent virtues, it seems that there can be no doubt that they sit well in the hands of those men who, as brave soldiers of the militia of Jesus, entered into the midst of squadrons of blind and barbarous peoples who were living in darkness, dispersing and banishing this darkness by brandishing the white banners of the celestial light of the Holy Gospel and winning glorious victories over the devil, Prince of Darkness, who possessed these blind peoples. If the Church attributes whiteness and white banners to virgins for having continually battled and overcome the flesh, then the battle against the Prince of Darkness is no less glorious.

Saint Paul, Apostle of the People, emphasized that this battle was not against visible enemies, but rather against the greatest invisible powers.[36] Victory in these battles was signaled with these banners, and there is no lack of reasons for their being white, because they signal victories over Princes of Darkness won by those who preached the Gospel and replaced that darkness by introducing this divine light. The primitive Church dressed its recent converts in white, and on the night when the angels gave the joyful news of the Gospel to the shepherds and again when they gave Mary Magdalene the good news of Christ's resurrection—which is the central tenet of our Holy Faith—they, too, appeared in resplendent whiteness. And to he who mends errors by preaching Christ's doctrine, the Lord promises as a reward during the Apocalypse a white stone or jewel upon which will be written a wondrous name. Therefore, it is not at all unusual that Saint Teresa of JESUS should see the members of the Company of JESUS (whose Institute is based upon bringing people out of darkness and mending their errors through the preaching of the Gospel) in heaven rewarded with emblems that were white, nor is it unexpected that these insignias should be banners, a symbol of victories.

---

34. Santa Maria's *Historia* first appeared in 1630.

35. The two passages italicized in this section appeared in italics in the original 1645 edition.

36. See Ephesians 6:12.

In this history I have recounted (in my simple fashion, for whose faults I ask pardon, for I seek truthfulness and accuracy) the victories that have been achieved among fierce peoples by some of the soldiers of the militia and Holy Order of the Company of JESUS. I have also set out for those who will follow in both these and future glorious enterprises [755] the triumphs won by their brothers and the rewards they earned through

their great and apostolic labors, following their captain, JESUS, who selected and encouraged them in order to lead them through His love. They can be assured of receiving favor in the shadow of the banner of such a divine captain, under whom they have the good fortune of doing battle in this world in order to reign with the Lord throughout all eternity.

CHAPTER XVI The end of the work

IHS[37]

We understand from our sacred Apostles and Scriptures, who declare Your name (Our Lord JESUS), what the final and blessed end is not only for men, but also for the angels and, indeed, for all creatures. They teach us that, in order to succeed in our actions, works, and intentions, we must refer to what is and should be their most happy and blessed end. Lord, Your beloved disciple [John], in the middle of those divine revelations that he was recording, heard a voice from Your divine mouth. You spoke of the beginning and the end with those mysterious Greek letters, alpha and omega, the first and the last letters of that alphabet: *Ego sum A. & O. Principium, & Finis.*[38] This was the statement that Saint John was ordered to write three times, and it is also very relevant to the end to which all our writings, desires, and pretensions should refer and be consecrated. The Apostle [Paul], who was chosen for the conversion of the people, preached and taught that Your divine and eternal Father had You as His end and goal. In His wisdom and with His divine hands, He created for Your glory all creatures and remarkable works. *In ipso condita sunt universa in coelis, & in terra; visibilia, & invisibilia; Throni, sive Dominationes, sive Principatus, sive*

Potestates: omnia per ipsum, & in ipso creat sunt.[39] It says that God created all things visible and invisible for the glory of His Son.

The sovereign name of Jesus, which was given to Our Majesty by His divine Father, has come to be synonymous with the ineffable name of *Jehovah*, together with *Alpha* and *Omega, Principium & Finis.* With this greeting the beloved disciple began and concluded his book about the Apocalypse. He explains to us that the Lord, founder of His Church, would aid the Church until the end of the world.[40] He would make it victorious in its struggles and bloody battles down through the ages, and this provided the argument for the divine book of the Apocalypse and the revelations recorded therein. With that very lofty title and name of Beginning and End, He would encourage and strengthen those who were to labor in such enterprises with confidence in the same Lord who had established His Church and would continue His work until it accomplished its blessed goal, which is Christ Jesus.

Your divine goodness has deigned to make Your Company of Jesus illustrious with this name and also to select soldiers for it. Enlisted under such a banner and with the help of such a divine name they have gone into

---

37. An abbreviation of *Iesus Salvator Hominum* 'Jesus, Savior of Mankind'.

38. *Margin Note:* Apoc. cap. 1, 21, 22. Apocalypse 1:8, 21:6, 22:3: "I am Alpha, I am Omega, the beginning of all things and their end" (Knox 1956:261, 275, 276).

39. Colossians 1:16: "Yes, in him all created things took their being, heavenly and earthly, visible and invisible; what are thrones and dominions, what are princedoms and powers? They were all created through him and in him; he takes precedence of all, and in him all subsist" (Knox 1956:207).

40. *Margin Note: Alcac Super hunclocum.*

combat against the army of hell and uncivilized heathenism that had populated the most hidden recesses and corners of the earth. They did this to make known to all the world the glory of His divine name. They consider this labor their coat of arms, just as it is the coat of arms of divine mercy and compassion to save wretched, downtrodden, and [756] humble souls, the lost sheep of Your flock. Because they were lost, they have been loved by the Majesty of God, and in order to find and shelter them (we can say), that He has turned the whole world upside down, searching for them as if they were very precious, long-lost jewels. Here (Lord) we could well introduce Your divine wisdom preached in that parable about the woman who turned her house upside down looking for a lost jewel, and who lit a lamp and searched until she finally found it.[41] We can say that You (Lord) have turned not a house, but rather the entire earth upside down; You have gone around the entire world searching. In obedience to You so many of Your servants and ministers have circled the globe, traveling to the most remote parts of the world, lighting torches with Your Gospel's celestial light. They do all this in order to find those souls that have been lost, souls that were ignorant of Your blessedness or the road to Your blessed end (which are one, as You alone are Lord). Your servants and ministers have done this so that these souls may find You and know You.

The instruments that Your divine mercy has chosen for such glorious, difficult, and arduous labors and undertakings have been the soldiers of the Company of Jesus. That sovereign name, which belongs to He who is the beginning and the end, has glorified the Company and has encouraged it through Your divine grace. He who is the most lowly of this religious order has written this book, which he offers to You and lays at Your divine feet, recounting in part what has been accomplished by some of his brothers, Your servants and ministers. They have done this in compliance with their profession and by Your divine mandate, under which they labor, set-

ting souls on the road to heaven. When this history was begun, this, Your lowly and humble servant, wanted to have You (Lord) as the beginning and end, and he did not wish to include anything that did not pertain to that blessed end. This history, he who has written it, and the undertakings that it recounts (in order to accomplish its most felicitous goal) are offered and laid at Your divine feet. With myself at Your feet, I now come to its conclusion. I do so imploring Your divine goodness to pardon my defects and to favor the enterprises recorded in this history. I pray for strength for the sons of Your Company so that they may carry these glorious undertakings forward, achieving new victories and fulfilling the desires that have been indicated by Your royal and divine Prophet: *Cognoscamus in terra viam tuam, in omnibus gentibus salutare tuum.*[42] This *salutare tuum* is the same beginning and blessed end that we will all attain, particularly those of the Company of Jesus, if their Master, the owner of that sovereign name Himself, will be present in all our actions and thoughts and in our blessed end.

The martyrdom or violent deaths suffered by evangelical ministers among these barbarous and unfaithful people are discussed in various parts of this history, as are examples of heroic virtues of other religious who labored as preachers of the Gospel. Also recorded are the marvelous works of Our Lord, in confirmation of their preaching. Because of the preceding, I affirm and declare here, as I did at the beginning of this work, that it is not my intent to give more authority to the things to which I refer than that authority which a human account possesses. These things enjoy only the faith that one can place in a human author, with no pretension that they deserve cultic veneration and are infallible, something that can be decided only by the Catholic Church and Christ's Vicar here on earth, the Holy Roman Pontiff. It is to him that the author of this history and the history itself remain subject. The author is like a very obedient son who desires to be governed by the Holy Apostolic See, to whom we, the sons of the Company of Jesus, are dedicated by a special vow.[43]

THE END [757]

---

41. *Margin Note*: Luc. 15. Luke 15:8–10, the parable of the lost drachma (Knox 1956:73).

42. *Margin Note*: Psalms. Psalm 66:3: "make known among all nations thy saving power" (Knox 1956:503). "Thy saving power" is repeated immediately following.

43. In the original 1645 edition this paragraph appears in italics.

Index of Remarkable Events in This History

Missions among barbarous peoples are made more glorious by the hardships suffered therein, 420.

N

Nacabeba, Indian outlaw; his troublemaking; his murder of Father Gonzalo de Tapia; his accomplices and allies, 74. Captured by Spaniards, receives justice, 77.

The fruits of barbarous nations are of no less esteem than in civilized nations, 408 passim.

Nations of the Río Zuaque come to request evangelical ministers in order to receive Holy Baptism, 143.

A ship lands on the coast of Sinaloa, 159.

Nébome come en masse to settle near Christians in order to be baptized, 120. Their rancherías and customs, 359. Their efforts to receive religious instruction, 361. They shoot Father Diego de Bandersipe with an arrow, 362. Father Blas de Paredes goes to the Upper Nébome, 365. Progress of their Christianity, 366. Lower Nébome, their pueblos and rancherías, 370. Outbreak of war, 371. Uprisings, 376.

A very unusual bird's nest, 4.

Nure, their location and conditions. They are reduced to our Holy Faith, 369.

O

Bishops visit their Diocese of Sinaloa; letters of thanks that they wrote, 174.

Bishop Don Fray Gonzalo de Hermosillo visits the Province of Sinaloa, where he dies, 177.

Special ordinances by which the religious of the Company are governed in these missions, 447.

P

Parras, description of the settlement of this nation and the customs of its inhabitants, 669. Other customs and superstitions, 671. The priests enter this mission and report on it, 673. The viceroy assigns the instruction of the people of the Laguna de San Pedro to the priests, 677. The way instruction is established, 678

Unusual cases that occurred with some Baptisms, 680. The priests prepare to reduce the rancherías to large pueblos, four more priests arrive, 682. Doctrinas are established, 683. Holy exercises conducted by the natives, 686. Help for Christian communities, 688.

Sickness and unusual cases that occur, 690. The devil invents tricks to divert people from Holy Baptism, 692. More sickness and superstition, 693. Unusual cases of sick Indians, 695. Another reduction of mountain people who belong to this mission, 696. Unusual cases that occurred among the mountain people, 698. Sickness among the mountain fugitives, events and labors of the priests, 700. Christianity is established among all the pueblos, construction of churches, 704. A disastrous flood, 705. The Tepehuan Rebellion causes restlessness among these people, 696. The present state of their Christianity, 710.

Father Pedro de Gravina, his life and death, 567.

Father Pedro de Velasco goes to instruct the Indians in the mountains of Sinaloa, 110. He baptizes seven thousand souls, 111. He abolishes a superstition practiced by these Indians, 112. They rebel against him, God miraculously saves him from death, 113. Other events and labors of this priest, 114.

Father Pedro Méndez arrives in Sinaloa from Mexico and his reception, 54. Entrada to the Tehueco nation, 171. He reaches the Mayo, 239. [763] He writes a letter about the fervent conversion of the Mayo, 245. He reaches the mission of the Sisibotari and the Batuco, 385. At risk of death when saying Mass, 388.

Garrison of soldiers established in the Villa de Sinaloa, 58. Good results that it produced, 72. Arguments for establishing garrisons in newly converted nations, 61. Arguments that oppose establishment of garrisons and a reply to them, 65. Employment of garrisons does not contradict the apostolic mode of evangelization, 67.

A sign of unusual predestination in an Indian, 689. Other cases and signs of it, 729.

R

Rebellion and uprising of the Acaxee nation, 487.

Rebellion of the Tepehuan, 599 and others.

Forewarning of this rebellion, 623.

A Dominican is killed by the Tepehuan, 623.

The Tepehuan kill a Franciscan, 602.

Rodrigo del Río y Losa, governor of Nueva Vizcaya, is the first to request priests of the Company of Jesus for Sinaloa, 3.

The large Río Sinaloa and the nations that inhabit its lands and valleys, 141.

The Río Mayo that rises in the Topia mountains and empties into the Sea of California, 237.

The Río Yaqui and its settlements, 283.

Elderly persons who die with signs of predestination, 56, 79.

Villa de San Felipe y Santiago in Sinaloa, 128.

X

The Xixime, a wild nation, their customs and remote settlements, 531. The governor decides to punish their insults, 532. Their reduction, 538. Beginnings of their religious instruction and the cases that occurred, 639.

Benefits produced by their peace and instruction, 542. Spiritual fruits resulting from their conversion, 545. Construction of churches and cases of edification, 547. Sickness, 548.

Z

The Zoe nation is reduced to Our Holy Faith and annexed to the Sinaloa nation, 208.

END OF THE INDEX OF REMARKABLE EVENTS

REFERENCE MATERIAL

GLOSSARY

albazo. Dawn attack.

alcalde mayor. Chief magistrate and administrator of a district or province.

aldea. Small village (intermediate between a ranchería and a pueblo) having upwards of several dozen houses and no public architectural features such as a ballcourt.

alférez real. Second lieutenant.

arroba. Liquid measure equal to 11.5 kilos.

arte. Grammatical synthesis of a native language.

atole. Maize gruel.

barbasco. Any of a number of plants thrown into water to stun fish.

barrio. An area ("neighborhood") within a pueblo that was occupied by a distinct kin group.

batei. Prepared plaza or court for playing a Mesoamerican-style ball game.

beneficio. Ecclesiastical office receiving an income.

braza. Linear measure equaling 1.67 meters.

bohío. Hut or field house.

cabildo eclesiastico. Chief clergy of a diocese who advise the bishop.

cabildo seglar. City (or secular) council in charge of local government.

cabo. Corporal.

Canonical Hours. Hours of the day set aside for recital of the Divine Office; namely, matins (*ad Matutinum*) at daybreak; prime (*ad Primam*) at the first hour after sunrise; and vespers (*ad Vesperas*) at dusk.

cañuelas. See *patoli.*

capitán. The supreme military commander within a province, technically a lieutenant captain general.

caudillo. Commander.

chapulines. Locusts.

chicubites. Baskets.

chimales. Shields used by the Mexica or other Nahua groups, which the Spaniards adopted for battle along with their Nahuatl name.

chirimía. Reed flute.

coali (or *serǎ wi*). Tepary bean.

cocoliztli. Nahuatl term for epidemic disease or 'great sickness'; often used as a referent for fulminating smallpox.

cozcates. Glass beads; from *cosca*, 'glass bead' in Cáhitan.

cuartillo. Liquid measure equal to 0.456 liters.

Divine Office. Historically (up until 1971), daily prayers and psalms said at regular intervals ("canonical hours") by religious, generally as a group in choir. The prayers were seen as a necessary complement to the divine worship of the eucharistic sacrifice.

doctrina. The catechism, or a gentile community whose inhabitants were receiving religious instruction and were not fully formed in the faith.

encomienda. Grant of land and Indian labor for which the recipient, or *encomendero*, agreed to protect his charges as well as support their conversion to Christianity.

enramada. Ramada enclosed on three sides with walls of woven mats or brush, which at times were plastered with mud.

entrada. Often used by the Jesuits in the sense of a "formal visit," approved by Jesuit superiors and civil officials.

estado. Linear measure equal to 1.67 meters.

Extreme Unction. A sacrament of the Catholic Church extended to the dying (often referred to as "last rites"), which involved the application of holy oil.

fanega. Dry measure equal to 2.58 bushels.

fiscal. Indian official often entrusted with the care of a church.

gandul. 'Young, bellicose Moor or Indian', deriving from an Arabic term used to refer to a young man of modest means who feigns elegance and attempts to please women, living without working and quick to take up arms.

geme (or *xeme*). Distance between the ends of the thumb and index finger when both were fully separated; approximately six inches.

gobernador. Governor; often an Indian cacique recognized (with a vara or staff) as the leader of a pueblo.

guamúchil. The fruit of a number of trees of the family Fabaceae (e.g., *Pithecellobium dulce*) native to northwestern Mexico and found primarily in the foothills and sierras.

hacienda. Ranching "complex" devoted principally to raising cattle, horses, and mules; it was settled by a Spaniard but generally staffed by Indians, mestizos, and black slaves.

huipiles. Woven and brightly embroidered blouses or tunics worn by women throughout Mesoamerica and still worn in Mexico today.

iztli. Generic term derived from Nahuatl and used to refer to any kind of plant fiber, particularly that of the agave.

jagüey. Indian term, perhaps Cáhitan, for 'little puddles of rainwater.'

jícara. Nahuatl term for a semi-hemispherical bowl made from a gourd.

jornada. A day's work or travel.

juez. Judge.

justicia mayor. An individual who serves at the behest of the governor as his deputy in a given settlement or municipal corporation.

ladino. Spanish-speaking and Hispanicized Indian.

latinidad. Curriculum for young men ("high school") involving mastery of Latin, reading of the classics of the ancient world, and composition of verse and prose in Latin.

lechuguilla. 'Little lettuce' (*Agave bovicornuta*).

league (legua). Linear measurement equaling 4.19 kilometers.

macana. Hard wooden club.

macehual (or *maceual*). Nahuatl term for a commoner or subject of the elite (*macehaul-li* [sing] *macehual-tin* [pl]).

manta. A woven piece of cloth, generally of cotton.

maravedí. Unit of Spanish currency; 275 maravedís equaled a piece of eight.

milpa. Nahuatl term for a dry-farmed field or small plot of land devoted to maize (sometimes referred to as a *temporal*); a milpa differs from a field that is naturally irrigated (in the floodplain of a river) or irrigated using canals, generally referred to as a *sementera*.

Miserere. Psalm 50 of the Vulgate. Historically this psalm has been considered the ultimate psalm of penitence; often it was sung by religious while mortifying themselves.

mitote. Dance made famous by the Nahua involving a large number of people, colorfully adorned, who held hands and danced in a circle around a banner next to which there was a vessel filled with an alcoholic beverage, which was consumed to the point of intoxication.

monte. Refer either to a hill or to the dense, thorny-plant vegetation that abounds in the foothills and near the coast of Sinaloa and Sonora.

ordinario. Ecclesiastical official who exercises jurisdiction in his own name.

pascua. Spanish term used in reference to the Christian holidays of Easter, Christmas, Pentecost, and Epiphany.

patoli (also referred to as *cañuelas*). Game similar to cards or dice involving the use of four short reeds that have been split open, each less than six inches in length.

petate. Woven reed mat, from the Nahuatl *pétlatl*.

piñole. Maize flour.

pita. Fiber extracted from cactus leaves.

principales. Indian elites or respected leaders who exercised vary-ing degrees of power and influence; often heads of lineages or clans.

procurator. Representative or delegate; also an individual entrusted with financial and temporal concerns.

provisor. Ecclesiastical judge and often a vicar general.

pueblo. Generally a referent for a nucleated settlement of several hundred people that also was an economic and political center and had public architectural features.

ranchería. Generally a small settlement of a dozen or more houses.

real de minas. Mining center where crown taxes (*quinto real*) were collected.

real de ocho. Monetary unit worth approximately 275 maravedís; it later came to be known as the peso.

real de plata. Monetary unit; at the beginning of the colonization of the New World the real de plata was valued at thirty-four maravedís.

retablo. Religious painting (often in two dimensions) done on a plaster-covered wooden panel, typically part of a church altar.

tabardillo. Typhus (also used for other diseases involving fever and hemorrhaging).

temachtiano. Catechist (usually a trained Indian).

teopa (or *teepo*). Cáhitan term for a church or a xacal that functioned as such.

tepehuaje. Cáhitan term for a tree similar to the mesquite (and considered as such by Pérez de Ribas).

tiangues. Nahuatl term for markets.

tlatolli. Speech or discourse; from the Nahuatl verb *tlatoa* ('to speak').

ulle. From the Nahuatl *ule*, referring to rubber.

vara. Staff of office; also a linear measure equal to 0.84 meters.

tucuchi. Apparently a corruption of *hutuqui*, a Cáhitan term for any of sixteen trees with edible fruit.

vecino. Resident and generally a property owner; often refers specifically to a male head-of-household.

villa. Technically a municipal corporation; often a referent for a Spanish as opposed to an Indian settlement (pueblo).

visita. Generally a small, outlying ranchería within a mission district, which was visited on a regular basis by a missionary who resided in the largest pueblo (*cabecera*) in the district (*partido*).

visitor. An appointed inspector, as in "father visitor," sent by a Jesuit provincial or the father general to assess the state of a mission or province.

xacal. Nahuatl term for a hut or other perishable structure made of plant material.

zopilotes. Vultures; from the Nahuatl *tzopílotl*, a compound of *tzotl* 'filth, dirt, nastiness' and *piloa* 'to hang'.

BIBLIOGRAPHY

Achebe, Chinua

1988   An Image of Africa: Racism in Conrad's *Heart of Darkness*. In *Heart of Darkness, by Joseph Conrad*, edited by R. Kimbrough, 251–62. New York: Norton and Co.

Acosta, José de

1894 [1590]   *Historia natural y moral de las Indias.* 2 vols. Madrid.

Adorno, Rolena

1986   *Guaman Poma: Writing and Resistance in Colonial Peru.* Austin: University of Texas Press.

AGN (Archivo General de la Nación, Mexico City)

1593   Misiones 25. Anua del año de mil quinientos noventa y tres.

1594a   Historia 15. Memoryas para la historia de la provincia de Synaloa. Anua del año de mil quinientos noventa y quatro.

1594b   Historia 15. Memoryas para la historia de la provincia de Synaloa. Relación de la muerte executada en el Padre Gonzalo de Tapia, por el año de mil quinientos noventa y quatro, en Pueblo de Tovoropa.

1601a   Historia 15. Memoryas para la historia de la provincia de Sinaloa. Anua del año de mil seiscientos y uno.

1601b   Historia 15. Memoryas para la historia de la provincia de Synaloa. Carta del Padre Juan Bautista Velasco del año de mil seiscientos uno.

1602   Historia 15. Memoryas para la historia de la provincia de Synaloa. Anua del año de mil seiscientos y dos.

1604   Historia 15. Memoryas para la historia de la provincia de Synaloa. Anua del año de mil seiscientos y quatro.

1610   Historia 15. Memoryas para la historia de la provincia de Synaloa. Anua del año de mil seiscientos y diez.

1612   Historia 15. Memoryas para la historia de la provincia de Synaloa. Anua del año de mil seiscientos doze.

1615   Historia 15. Memoryas para la historia de la provincia de Synaloa. Carta del Padre Diego de Guzmán al padre provincial de septiembre de mil seiscientos veinte y nuebe. [Note: despite the title, internal evidence indicates that this letter was written in 1615.]

1616   Historia 15. Memoryas para la historia de la provincia de Synaloa. Carta del Padre Martín Pérez, del año de mil seiscientos diez y seis.

1620   Historia 15. Memoryas para la historia de la provincia de Synaloa. Anua del año de mil seiscientos y veinte.

1622   Misiones 25. Carta annua de la provincia de la Compañía de Jesús en Nueva España, 15 de mayo 1623.

1623   Misiones 25. Carta annua de la provincia de la Compañía de Jesús de Nueva España, Juan Lorencio, 16 de mayo 1624.

1625   Misiones 25. Carta annua de la provincia de la Compañía de Jesús de Nueva España, Juan Lorencio.

1626   Misiones 25. Annua del Colegio y Misiones de Cinaloa de los años de 1625 y 26. 2 de junio 1626.

1627   Misiones 25. Carta annua de la provincia de la Compañía de Jesús de Nueva España, Juan Lorencio, 20 de mayo 1627.

1628   Historia 15. Memoryas para la historia de la provincia de Synaloa. Missiones de San Ygnacio en Mayo, Yaqui, Nevomes, Chínipas, y Sisibotaris.

1630   Misiones 25. Carta del Padre Martín de Azpilcueta al Padre Ignacio de Cavala, 3 de deciembre 1630.

1635   Misiones 25. Puntos para el anua del año de 1635, destas misiones de San Ignacio Nuestro Padre en la provincia de Cinaloa, Thomas Basilio, 26 de marzo 1636.

1638   Misiones 25. Copia de una carta del Padre Gaspar de Contreras al padre provincial, Santiago Papasquiaro, 5 de agosto 1638.

1639   Misiones 25. Puntos de anua de la nueba mission de San Francisco Jabier, año de 1639.

Ahern, Maureen

1993   The Cross and the Gourd: The Appropriation of Ritual Signs in the Relaciones of Alvar Núñez Cabeza de Vaca and Fray Marcos de Niza. In *Early Images of the Americas: Transfer and Invention*, edited by J. M. Williams and R. E. Lewis, 215–44. Tucson: University of Arizona Press.

1994   The Articulation of Alterity on the Northern Frontier: *The Relatione della navigatione & scoperta* by Fernando de Alarcón, 1540. In *Coded Encounters: Writing, Gender, and Ethnicity in Colonial Latin America*, edited by F. J. Cevallos-Candau et al., 46–61. Amherst: University of Massachusetts Press.

1995a   La relación como glosa, guía y memoria: Nuevo
         México, 1581–1582. *Revista Iberoamericana. Literatura
         colonial I: Identidades y conquista en América* 41:41–55.

1995b   Testimonio oral, memoria y violencia en el diario de
         Diego Pérez de Luxán: Nuevo México, 1583. *Revista de
         crítica literaria latinoamericana* 21:153–63.

1998   Fronteras mudables: Un informe náhuatl de la Guerra
         Chichimeca, 1563. In *Indigenismo hacia el fin del milenio,*
         ed. Mabel Moraña, 61–76. Pittsburgh: Publicaciones de
         la Revista Iberoamericana.

1999   Visual and Verbal Sites: The Construction of Jesuit
         Martyrdom in Northwest New Spain in Andrés Pérez
         de Ribas' Historia de los Triumphos de nuestra Santa
         Fe (1645). *Colonial Latin American Review* 8: 7–33.

AHH (Archivo Historico de Hacienda, Mexico City)

1638   Temporalidades 2009-1. Memorial al rey para que
         no se recenta la limosna de la misiones: y conserva al
         Señor Palafox en las relaciones a la Compañía, Andrés
         Pérez de Ribas, 12 de septiembre 1638.

Aizpuru, Pilar G.

1989   *La educación popular de los jesuitas.* Mexico City: Univer-
         sidad Iberoamericana.

Alegre, Francisco J., S.J.

1956–1960   *Historia de la provincia de la Compañía de Jesús de
             Nueva España.* 4 vols. New edition edited by E. J.
             Burrus and F. Zubillaga. Rome: Biblioteca Instituti
             Historici Societatis Iesu.

Alonso, Martín

1986   *Diccionario de medieval español.* 2 vols. Salamanca: Uni-
         versidad Pontificia de Salamanca (Imprenta Kadmos).

Alter, Robert

1981   *The Art of Biblical Narrative.* New York: Basic Books.

Amundsen, Darrel W.

1986   The Medieval Catholic Tradition. In *Caring and
         Curing, Health and Medicine in the Western Religious Tra-
         ditions,* ed. by R. L. Numbers, 65–107. New York:
         Macmillan.

Anglo, Sydney, ed.

1977   *The Damned Art: Essays in the Literature of Witchcraft.*
         London: Routledge and Kegan Paul.

Aquinas, Saint Thomas

1945   *Introduction to St. Thomas Aquinas.* Edited by A. C.
         Pegis. New York: Modern Library.

Asad, Talal

1986   The Concept of Cultural Translation in British Social
         Anthropology. In *Writing Culture: The Poetics and Poli-
         tics of Ethnography,* edited by J. Clifford and G. Marcus,
         141–64. Berkeley: University of California Press.

Aspurz, Lazaro de, O.F.M.

1946   *La aportación extranjera a las misiones españolas del
         Patronato Regio.* Madrid: Consejo de la Hispanidad.

Astrain, Antonio, S.J.

1902   *Historia de la Compañía de Jesús en la asistencia de España.*
         7 vols. Madrid.

Attwater, Donald, ed.

1949   *A Catholic Dictionary.* Rev. ed. New York: Macmillan.

Ayer (Ayer Collection, Newberry Library, Chicago)

1616   Carta annua de la provincia de Nueva España del año
         de 1616. Nicolás de Arnaya, 18 mayo de 1617 (ms.
         1036).

Bakewell, Peter J.

1971   *Silver Mining and Society in Colonial Mexico: Zacatecas,
         1546–1700.* Cambridge: Cambridge University Press.

Bakhtin, Mikhail

1968   *Rabelais and His World.* Translated by Helene Iswolsky.
         Cambridge, Mass.: MIT Press.

Bancroft, Hubert Howe

1886   *The Works.* Vol. 15, *History of the North Mexican States
         and Texas.* Vol. 1, *1531–1800.* San Francisco: The
         History Co.

Bannon, John F.

1939   The Conquest of the Chínipas. *Mid-America* (new
         series) 10:2–31.

1955   *The Mission Frontier in Sonora, 1620–1687.* New York:
         United States Catholic Historical Society.

Barnes, Thomas C.

1991   Pagan Perceptions of Christianity. In *Early Christianity:
         Origins and Evolution to A.D. 600,* edited by I. Hazlett,
         231–44. Nashville: Abingdon Press.

Barnes-Karol, Gwendolyn

1992   Religious Oratory in a Culture of Control. In *Culture
         and Control in Counter-Reformation Spain,* edited by A. J.
         Cruz and M. E. Perry, 51–77. Minneapolis: University
         of Minnesota Press.

Barnouw, Jeffrey

1990   The Separation of Reason and Faith in Bacon and
         Hobbes, and Leibniz's Theodicy. In *Philosophy, Religion,
         and Science in the Seventeenth and Eighteenth Centuries,*
         edited by J. W. Yolton, 206–27. Rochester, N.Y.:
         University of Rochester Press.

Barthes, Roland

1987a   *The Pleasure of the Text.* Translated by R. Miller. New
         York: Hill and Wang.

1987b   The Death of the Author. In *Image, Music, Text,* trans-
         lated and edited by S. Heath, 190–215. New York:
         Hill and Wang.

Beals, Ralph L.

1932   *The Comparative Ethnology of Northern Mexico before
         1750.* Ibero-Americana No. 2. Berkeley: University of
         California Press.

1933   *The Acaxee: A Mountain Tribe of Durango and Sina-
         loa.* Ibero-Americana No. 6. Berkeley: University of
         California Press.

1943   *The Aboriginal Culture of the Cáhita Indians.* Ibero-
         Americana No. 19. Berkeley: University of California
         Press.

Bechtel, Edward Ambrose, ed.

1906   *Livy, the War with Hannibal.* Chicago: Scott, Foresman
         and Co.

Benavides, Fray Alonso

1916 [1630]   *The Memorial of Fray Alonso de Benavides.* Trans-
               lated by E. Ayers. Chicago: Privately Published.

Biraben, Jean N., and Jacques Le Goff

1975   The Plague in the Early Middle Ages. In *Biology of
         Man in History,* edited by O. Ranum and E. Forster,
         48–80. Baltimore: Johns Hopkins University Press.

Bolton, Herbert E.
1913   *Guide to the Materials for the History of the United States in the Principal Archives of Mexico.* Washington, D.C.: Carnegie Institution.

Borges Moran, Pedro
1960   *Métodos misionales en la cristianización de América, siglo XVI.* Madrid: Departamento de Misionologia Española.

Boxer, Charles R.
1951   *The Christian Century in Japan.* Berkeley: University of California Press.

Brady, James F., and John C. Olin
1992   *Collected Works of Erasmus.* Toronto: University of Toronto Press.

Brand, Donald B.
1939   Notes on the Geography and Archaeology of Zape, Durango. In *So Live the Works of Men,* edited by D. B. Brand and F. E. Harvey, 75–105. Albuquerque: University of New Mexico Press.

Brooks, Sheila, and Richard B. Brooks
1978   Paleoepidemiology of Multiple Child Burials near Zape Chico, Durango, Mexico. In *Across the Chichimec Sea,* edited by C. Riley and B. C. Hedrick, 96–101. Carbondale: Southern Illinois University Press.

Bruner, Edward M.
1994   Abraham Lincoln as Authentic Reproduction: A Critique of Postmodernism. *American Anthropologist* 96:397–415.

Buelna, Eustaquio
1891   *Arte de la lengua Cáhita.* Mexico City.

Burkhart, Louise M.
1989   *The Slippery Earth: Nahua-Christian Moral Dialogue in Sixteenth-Century Mexico.* Tucson: University of Arizona Press.

Burrus, Ernest J., S.J.
1979   The Language Problem in Spain's Overseas Dominions. *Neue Zeitschrift für Missionswissenschaft* 35:161–70.

Burrus, Ernest J., S.J., and Félix Zubillaga, S.J.
1962   *Misiones mexicanas de la Compañía de Jesús (1618–1745): Cartas e informes conservados en la "Colección Mateu."* Madrid: Porrúa Turanzas.

Cabredo, Rodrigo de
1611   Ordenaciónes del Padre Rodrigo de Cabredo para las missiones, January 1, 1611, Durango. Latin American Manuscripts, Mexico II, Lily Library, Indiana State University.

Cameron, Averil
1991   *Christianity and the Rhetoric of Empire: The Development of Christian Discourse.* Berkeley: University of California Press.

Caraman, Philip
1985   *The Lost Empire: The Story of the Jesuits in Ethiopia, 1555–1634.* London: Sidgwick and Jackson.

Caro Baroja, Julio
1978   *Las formas completas de la vida religiosa. Religión, sociedad y carácter en la España de los siglos XVI y XVII.* Madrid: Akal.

Casey, Michael
1988   *A Thirst for God: Spiritual Desire in Bernard of Clairvaux's Sermons on the Song of Songs.* Kalamazoo: Cistercian Publications.

Casillas, José Gutiérrez, S.J.
1964   *Santarén, conquistador pacífico.* Mexico City: Editorial Jus.

Cervantes, Fernando
1991   *The Idea of the Devil and the Problem of the Indian: The Case of Mexico in the Sixteenth Century.* University of London Institute of Latin American Studies Research Papers No. 4. London: Institute of Latin American Studies.

Chestnut, Glenn F.
1986   *The First Christian Histories: Eusebius, Socrates, Sozomen, Theodoret, and Evagrius.* Paris: Editions Beauchesne.

Christian, William A.
1981   *Local Religion in Sixteenth-Century Spain.* Princeton: Princeton University Press.

Clifford, James
1986   Introduction: Partial Truths. In *Writing Culture: The Poetics and Politics of Ethnography,* edited by J. Clifford and G. Marcus, 1–27. Berkeley: University of California Press.
1988   *The Predicament of Culture.* Cambridge, Mass.: Harvard University Press.

Clifford, James, and George Marcus, eds.
1986   *Writing Culture: The Poetics and Politics of Ethnography.* Berkeley: University of California Press.

Cohen, J. M., trans.
1957   *The Life of Saint Teresa of Avila, by Herself.* Harmondsworth, Eng.: Penguin Books.

Cohen, T. V.
1974   Why the Jesuits Joined. *Historical Papers/Communications Historiques,* 237–59. Toronto: The Canadian Historical Association.

Constable, Giles, ed.
1967   *The Letters of Peter the Venerable.* Vol. 2. Cambridge, Mass.: Harvard University Press.

Cornett, James W.
1987   *Wildlife of the North American Deserts.* Palm Springs, Calif.: Nature Trails Press.

Corominas, Joan, and José Pascual
1989–1991   *Diccionario crítico etimológico castellano e hispánico.* 5 vols. Madrid: Editorial Gredos.

Correia-Afonso, John, S.J.
1969   *Jesuit Letters and Indian History, 1542–1773.* 2d ed. New York: Oxford University Press.

Covarrubias, Sebastián de
1943   *Tesoro de la lengua castellana o española.* Edited by Martín de Riquer and based on Covarrubias' 1611 original and the 1674 edition prepared by Benito Remigio Noydens. Barcelona: Horta.

Cowgill, George
1993   Beyond Criticizing New Archaeology. *American Anthropologist* 95:551–74.

Cox, John D.
1994   Drama, the Devil, and Social Conflict in Late Medieval England. *American Benedictine Review* 45:341–62.

Cramer, Peter
1993   *Baptism and Change in the Early Middle Ages, c. 200–
        c. 1150*. Cambridge: Cambridge University Press.
Crosby, Alfred W.
1997   *The Measure of Reality*. Cambridge: Cambridge University Press.
Cruz, Anne J., and Mary E. Perry, eds.
1992   *Culture and Control in Counter-Reformation Spain*. Minneapolis: University of Minnesota Press.
Cummins, J. S.
1961   Palafox: China and the Chinese Rites. *Revista de historia
        de América* 52:395–427.
de Certeau, Michel
1992   *The Mystic Fable*. Chicago: University of Chicago Press.
Decorme, Gerard, S.J.
1941   *La obra de los Jesuitas mexicanos durante la época colonial,
        1572–1767*. 2 vols. Mexico City: Jose Porrúa e Hijos.
Deeds, Susan
1989   Ritual Work in Nueva Vizcaya: Forms of Labor Coercion on the Periphery. *Hispanic American Historical
        Review* 69:425–49.
Deferrari, Roy J., ed.
1952   *The Fathers of the Church*. Vol. 15, *Early Christian Biographies*. New York: Fathers of the Church.
Defourneaux, Marcelin
1979   *Daily Life in Spain in the Golden Age*. Translated by
        Newton Branch. Stanford: Stanford University Press.
de Guibert, Joseph
1964   *The Jesuits: Their Spiritual Doctrine and Practice; A
        Historical Study*. Chicago: Loyola University Press.
Delehaye, Hippolyte, S.J.
1907   *The Legends of the Saints: An Introduction to Hagiography*.
        Translated by V. M. Crawford. London: Longmans
        Green Co.
Deloria, Vine., Jr.
1992   *God Is Red*. 2d ed. Golden, Colo.: North American
        Press.
Denhardt, Robert M.
1975   *The Horse of the Americas*. Norman: University of Oklahoma Press.
DHM (Documentos para la Historia de México, 1853–57,
        Serie IV)
1596   Anua del año de 1596.
1598   Anua del año de 1598.
1600   Testimonio jurídico de las poblaciones y conversiones
        de los serranos Acaches, hechas por el Capitán Diego
        de Avila y el venerable padre Hernando de Santarén por el año 1600. 4:173–267. (Written by Martín
        Duarte.)
1618   Carta de Alonso del Valle al padre provincial, 9 de
        mayo de 1618.
DiPeso, Charles C.
1979   Prehistory: Southern Periphery. In *Handbook of North
        American Indians*. Vol. 10, *Southwest*, edited by A. Ortiz,
        152–61. Washington, D.C.: Smithsonian Institution.
Dobyns, Henry F.
1988   Piman Indian Historic Agave Cultivation. *Desert Plants*
        9:49–53.

Dods, Marcus, trans. and ed.
1948   *The City of God*, by Saint Augustine. 2 vols. New York:
        Hafner.
Dunne, Peter Masten, S.J.
1940   *Pioneer Black Robes on the West Coast*. Berkeley: University of California Press.
1944   *Pioneer Jesuits in Northern Mexico*. Berkeley: University
        of California Press.
1948   *Early Jesuit Missions in Tarahumara*. Berkeley: University of California Press.
1951   *Andrés Pérez de Ribas*. New York: United States Catholic Historical Society.
Duran, Diego
1971   *Book of the Gods and Rites and the Ancient Calendar*.
        Norman: University of Oklahoma Press.
Ekholm, Gordon F.
1942   *Excavations at Guasave, Sinaloa, Mexico*. Anthropological Papers of the American Museum of Natural History No. 38 (Part II). New York: American Museum
        of Natural History.
Elkin, Judith L.
1993   Imagining Idolatry: Missionaries, Indians, and Jews.
        In *Religion and the Authority of the Past*, edited by
        T. Siebers, 75–99. Ann Arbor: University of Michigan
        Press.
Elliott, A. G.
1987   *Roads to Paradise: Reading the Lives of the Early Saints*.
        Hanover, N.H.: University Press of New England.
Elliott, J. H.
1989   *Spain and Its World, 1500–1700*. New Haven: Yale
        University Press.
Evans-Pritchard, Edward Evans
1940   *The Nuer*. New York: Oxford University Press.
Evennett, Henry O.
1968   *The Spirit of the Counter-Reformation*. Notre Dame:
        Notre Dame Press.
Farmer, David Hugh
1992   *The Oxford Dictionary of Saints*. 3d ed. New York:
        Oxford University Press.
Felger, Richard S., and Mary B. Moser
1985   *People of the Desert and Sea: Ethnobotany of the Seri Indians*. Tucson: University of Arizona Press.
Fleming, David A., trans.
1973   *John Barclay's* Euphormionis Lusinini Satyricon (Euphormio's Satyricon), *1605–7*. Nieuwkoop: B. De
        Graaf.
Flint, Valerie I.
1991   *The Rise of Magic in Early Medieval Europe*. Princeton:
        Princeton University Press.
Foster, Michael Stewart
1978   Loma San Gabriel: A Prehistoric Culture of Northwest Mexico. Ph.D. diss., University of Colorado,
        Boulder.
Foucault, Michel
1970   *The Order of Things*. New York: Random House.
1978   *The History of Sexuality: An Introduction*. Vol. 1. New
        York: Vintage Books.
1987   The Order of Discourse. In *Untying the Text*, edited by
        R. Young, 48–78. London: Routledge.

Gadamer, Hans-Georg
1989   *Truth and Method*. New York: Crossroad.

Ganss, George E., S.J.
1953   *The Fathers of the Church*. Vol. 17, *Saint Peter Chrysologus, Selected Sermons; and Saint Valerian, Homilies*. New York: Fathers of the Church.
1970   *The Constitutions of the Society of Jesus*. St. Louis: Institute of Jesuit Sources.
———, ed.
1991   *Ignatius Loyola: The Spiritual Exercises and Selected Works*. New York: Paulist Press.

Geertz, Clifford
1973   *The Interpretation of Cultures*. New York: Basic Books.
1988   *Works and Lives: The Anthropologist as Author*. Cambridge, Mass.: Polity Press.

Gerhard, Peter
1982   *The North Frontier of New Spain*. Princeton: Princeton University Press.

Gibson, Charles
1964   *The Aztecs under Spanish Rule*. Stanford: Stanford University Press.

Gilchrist, John
1993   The Lord's War as the Proving Ground of Faith: Pope Innocent III and the Propagation of Violence (1198–1216). In *Crusaders and Muslims in Twelfth-Century Syria*, edited by M. Shatzmiller, 65–83. Leiden: Brill.

Gill, Sam D.
1983   Navajo Views of Their Origin. In *Handbook of North American Indians*. Vol. 10, *Southwest*, edited by A. Ortiz, 502–5. Washington, D.C.: Smithsonian Institution.

Gilmont, Jean-Francois, S.J.
1961   *Les ecrits spirituels des premiers Jésuites*. Rome: Institutum Historicum Societatis Iesu.

Glimm, Francis M., M. F. Joseph, S.J., and Gerald G. Walsh, S.J.
1969   *The Fathers of the Church: A New Translation*. Vol. 1, *The Apostolic Fathers*. Washington, D.C.: Catholic University of America Press.

Gómez Canedo, Lino
1977   *Evangelización y conquista: Experiencia franciscana en Hispanoamérica*. Mexico City: Editorial Porrúa.

Gómez Hoyos, Raphael
1961   *La iglesia de América en las Leyes de Indias*. Madrid: Instituto de Cultura Hispánica de Bogotá.

Goodfellow, Peter
1977   *Birds As Builders*. London: David and Charles.

Goodich, Michael
1982   *Vita Perfecta: The Ideal of Sainthood in the Thirteenth Century*. Stuttgart: Anton Hiersemann.

Griffen, William B.
1979   *Indian Assimilation in the Franciscan Area of Nueva Vizcaya*. Anthropological Papers of the University of Arizona No. 33. Tucson: University of Arizona Press.

Gundry, Robert H.
1970   *A Survey of the New Testament*. Grand Rapids, Mich.: Academic Books.

Hackett, Charles W.
1923–1937   Historical Documents Relating to New Mexico, Nueva Vizcaya, and Approaches Thereto, to 1773.

3 vols. Washington, D.C.: Carnegie Institution of Washington.

Hackett, Charles W., and Charmion Clair Shelby
1942   *Revolt of the Pueblo Indians of New Mexico and Otermin's Attempted Reconquest, 1680–1682*. 2 vols. Albuquerque: University of New Mexico Press.

Hammond, George P., and Agapito Rey, trans. and eds.
1928   *Obregón's History of Sixteenth-Century Exploration in Western America*. Los Angeles: Wetzel Publishing Co.
1940   *Narratives of the Coronado Expedition, 1540–1542*. Albuquerque: University of New Mexico Press.

Haring, Clarence H.
1947   *The Spanish Empire in America*. San Diego: Harcourt Brace Jovanovich.

Harnack, Adolf
1981 [1905]   *Militia Christi: The Christian Religion and the Military in the First Three Centuries*. Translated by D. M. Grace. Philadelphia: Fortress Press.

Hedrick, Basil C., and Carroll L. Riley
1974   *The Journey of the Vaca Party*. University Museum Studies No. 2. Carbondale: Southern Illinois University Museum.
1976   *Documents Ancillary to the Vaca Journey*. University Museum Studies No. 5. Carbondale: Southern Illinois University Museum.

Heffernan, Thomas J.
1988   *Sacred Biography: Saints and Their Biographies in the Middle Ages*. New York: Oxford University Press.

Heimann, Peter M.
1990   Voluntarism and Immanence: Conceptions of Nature in Eighteenth-Century Thought. In *Philosophy, Religion, and Science in the Seventeenth and Eighteenth Centuries*, edited by J. W. Yolton, 393–405. Rochester, N.Y.: University of Rochester Press.

Herbert, Christopher
1991   *Culture and Anomie: Ethnographic Imagination in the Nineteenth Century*. Chicago: University of Chicago Press.

HHB (Hubert H. Bancroft Collection, Bancroft Library, University of California, Berkeley)
1617   Carta del Padre Andrés Pérez al padre provincial, 13 de junio 1617.

Hoare, Frederick R., trans. and ed.
1954   *The Western Fathers: Being the Lives of SS. Martin of Tours, Ambrose, Augustine of Hippo, Honoratus of Arles, and Germanus of Auxerre*. New York: Sheed and Ward.

Hodge, Frederick W., George P. Hammond, and Agapito Rey, eds.
1945   *Fray Alonso de Benavides' Revised Memorial of 1634*. Albuquerque: University of New Mexico Press.

Hodgkin, Thomas, ed.
1886   *The Letters of Cassiodorus*. London: Henry Frowde.

Hogden, Margaret
1964   *Early Anthropology in the Sixteenth and Seventeenth Centuries*. Philadelphia: University of Pennsylvania Press.

Horace
1986   *Horace: The Epistles*. Translated with brief comment by Colin MacLeod. Rome: Edizioni dell'Ateneo.

Hughes, L.
1923   *The Christian Church in the Epistles of St. Jerome.* London: Society for Promoting Christian Knowledge.

Huizinga, Johan
1967   *The Waning of the Middle Ages.* New York: St. Martin's Press.

Jackson, Robert H.
1994   *Indian Population Decline: The Missions of Northwestern New Spain, 1687–1840.* Albuquerque: University of New Mexico Press.

Jacobsen, Jerome V.
1938   The Chronicle of Pérez de Ribas. *Mid-America* (new series) 9:81–95.

Johnson, Harry Prescott
1945   Diego Martínez de Hurdaide, Defender of Spain's Pacific Coast Frontier. In *Greater America: Essays in Honor of Herbert Eugene Bolton,* 199–218. Berkeley: University of California Press.

Johnson, Jean B.
1950   *The Opata: An Inland Tribe of Sonora.* University of New Mexico Publications in Anthropology No. 6. Albuquerque: University of New Mexico Press.

Jolly, Karen Louise
1989   Magic, Miracle, and Popular Practice in the Early Medieval West: Anglo-Saxon England. In *Religion, Science, and Magic in Concert and Conflict,* edited by J. Neusner et al., 166–82. New York: Oxford University Press.

Kamen, Henry
1985   *Inquisition and Society in Spain in the Sixteenth and Seventeenth Centuries.* Bloomington: Indiana University Press.

Karttunen, Frances
1983   *An Analytical Dictionary of Nahuatl.* Norman: University of Texas Press.

Keber, James
1988   Sahagún and Hermeneutics: A Christian Ethnographer's Understanding of Aztec Culture. In *The Work of Bernardino de Sahagun: Pioneer Ethnographer of Sixteenth-Century Aztec Mexico,* edited by J. J. Klor de Alva, H. B. Nicholson, and E. Q. Keber, 53–63. SUNY-Albany, Institute for Mesoamerican Studies, Studies on Culture and Society No. 2. Austin: University of Texas Press.

Keen, Benjamin
1990   The European Vision of the Indian in the Sixteenth and Seventeenth Centuries: A Sociological Approach. In *La imagen del indio en la Europa moderna,* edited by J. Pérez, 101–16. Sevilla: Escuela de Estudios Hispano-Americanos.

Keenan, Sr. Mary Emily, S.C.N, trans.
1952   Life of St. Anthony by St. Athanasius. In *The Fathers of the Church.* Vol. 15, *Early Christian Biographies,* edited by R. J. Deferrari, 127–216. New York: Fathers of the Church.

Kelley, Donald R., ed.
1991   *Versions of History: From Antiquity to the Enlightenment.* New Haven: Yale University Press.

Kelley, J. Charles
1980   Discussion of Papers by Plog, Doyel, and Riley. In *Current Issues in Hohokam Prehistory: Proceedings of a Symposium,* edited by D. E. Doyel and F. Plog. Arizona State University Anthropological Research Papers No. 23. Tempe: Arizona State University.

Kempis, Thomas à
1955 [1427]   *The Imitation of Christ.* New York: Doubleday.

Kessell, John L.
1979   *Kiva, Cross, and Crown: The Pecos Indians and New Mexico, 1540–1840.* Washington, D.C.: Department of the Interior, National Park Service.

Kieckhefer, Richard
1987   Major Currents in Late Medieval Devotion. In *World Spirituality.* Vol. 17, *Christian Spirituality,* edited by J. Raitt et al., 75–108. New York: Crossroad.

Kilburn, K., trans.
1958   *Lucian in Eight Volumes.* Cambridge, Mass.: Harvard University Press.

Klor de Alva, J. Jorge
1988   Sahagún and the Birth of Modern Ethnography: Representing, Confessing, and Inscribing the Native Other. In *The Work of Bernardino de Sahagún, Pioneer Ethnographer of Sixteenth-Century Aztec Mexico,* edited by J. J. Klor de Alva, H. B. Nicholson, and E. Q. Keber, 31–51. SUNY-Albany, Institute for Mesoamerican Studies, Studies on Culture and Society No. 2. Austin: University of Texas Press.

Knox, Ronald A., trans.
1956   *The Holy Bible: A Translation from the Latin Vulgate.* New York: Sheed and Ward.

Kramer, Heinrich, and James Sprenger
1971 [1487]   *The Malleus Maleficarum.* Translated with an introduction by Montague Summers. New York: Dover.

Kristeller, Paul O.
1974   *Medieval Aspects of Renaissance Learning.* Translated by E. P. Mahoney. Durham, N.C.: Duke University Press.

LaCapra, Dominick
1983   *Rethinking Intellectual History: Text, Context, Language.* Ithaca, N.Y.: Cornell University Press.

Larousse
1983   *Spanish-English, English-Spanish Dictionary.* Barcelona: Larousse.

Laurance, John D.
1984   *Priest as Type of Christ: The Leader of the Eucharist in Salvation History According to Cyprian of Carthage.* New York: Peter Lang.

Lea, Henry C.
1939   *History of Witchcraft.* 3 vols. Arranged and edited by A. C. Howland. Philadelphia: University of Pennsylvania Press.

Lerner, Isaías, and Marcos A. Morínigo, eds.
1979   *La Araucana, por Alonso de Ercilla.* Madrid: Editorial Castalia.

Lewis, Clifford M., S.J., and Albert J. Loomie, S.J.
1953   *The Spanish Jesuit Mission in Virginia, 1570–1572.* Chapel Hill, N.C.: Virginia Historical Society and the University of North Carolina Press.

Lienhard, Joseph T., S.J.

1977   *Paulinus of Nola and Early Western Monasticism*. Bonn: Peter Hanstein Verlag.

Lockhart, James

1992   *The Nahuas after the Conquest: A Social and Cultural History of the Indians of Central Mexico, Sixteenth through Eighteenth Centuries*. Stanford: Stanford University Press.

López, A.

1976   *The Revolt of the Comuñeros, 1721–1735*. Cambridge, Mass.: Schenkman Publishing Co.

MacCormack, Sabine

1991   *Religion in the Andes*. Princeton: Princeton University Press.

Maravall, José A.

1986   *Culture of the Baroque: Analysis of a Historical Structure*. Minneapolis: University of Minnesota Press.

Marrow, James H.

1979   *Passion Iconography in Northern European Art of the Late Middle Ages and Early Renaissance*. Amsterdam: Van Ghemmert.

Martin, A. Lynn

1988   *The Jesuit Mind: The Mentality of an Elite in Early Modern France*. Ithaca, N.Y.: Cornell University Press.

Martin, Henri-Jean

1993   *Print, Power, and People in Seventeenth-Century France*. Translated by David Gerard. Metuchen, N.J.: Scarecrow Press.

Martin, Janet, ed.

1974   *Peter the Venerable: Selected Letters*. Toronto: Pontifical Institute of Medieval Studies.

Martin, Luis

1968   *The Intellectual Conquest of Peru*. New York: Fordham University Press.

Martin, Malachi

1987   *The Jesuits*. New York: Touchstone Books.

Matarasso, Pauline M., trans.

1969   *The Quest of the Holy Grail*. New York: Penguin Books.

McGrath, Alistair

1988   *Reformation Thought: An Introduction*. Cambridge: Blackwell.

McNaspy, Clement J.

1984   *Conquistador without a Sword*. Chicago: Loyola University Press.

McNeill, William H.

1976   *Plagues and Peoples*. Garden City, N.Y.: Anchor-Doubleday.

McNulty, Patricia, A, trans. and ed.

1959   *Selected Writings on the Spiritual Life*, by St. Pietro Damiani, London: Faber and Faber.

McShane, Catherine Mary, R.S.C.J.

1938   Pueblo Founding in Early Mexico. *Mid-America* (new series) 120:3–14.

1945   Hernando de Santarén, S.J.: Pioneer and Diplomat, 1565–1616. In *Greater America: Essays in Honor of Herbert Eugene Bolton*, 145–62. Berkeley: University of California Press.

Mecham, Lloyd

1927   *Francisco Ibarra and Nueva Vizcaya*. Durham, N.C.: Duke University Press.

Meeus, Jean, and Hermann Mucke

1983   *Canon of Lunar Eclipses – 2002 to +2526*. Vienna: Astonomisches Büro.

Migne, Jacques Paul

1844–1864   *Patrologiae cursus completus*. Series Latina, in qua prodeunt Patres, doctores scriptoresque Ecclesiae Lateinae, a Tertulliano ad Innocentium III. 21 vols. Paris: Garnier Fratres.

Mignolo, Walter

1982   Cartas, crónicas y relaciónes del descubrimiento y la conquista. In *Historia de la literatura hispanoamericana, época colonial*. Vol. 1, edited by L. I. Madrigal, 57–116. Madrid: Cátedra.

Miller, Wick R.

1983   Uto-Aztecan Languages. In *Handbook of North American Indians*. Vol. 10, *Southwest*, edited by A. Ortiz, 113–24. Washington, D.C.: Smithsonian Institution.

Moore, James T.

1982   *Indian and Jesuit*. Chicago: Loyola University Press.

Morner, Magnus

1953   *The Political and Economic Activities of the Jesuits in the La Plata Region: The Hapsburg Era*. Stockholm: Library and Institute of Ibero-American Studies.

Morrison, Toni

1993   *Playing in the Dark: Whiteness and the Literary Imagination*. New York: Vintage Books.

Mota y Escobar, Don Alonso de la

1940 [1604]   *Descripción geográfica de los reinos de Nueva Galicia, Nueva Vizcaya y León*. Mexico City: Editorial Pedro Robredo.

Musurillo, Herbert, ed. and trans.

1972   *The Acts of the Christian Martyrs*. Oxford: Clarendon Press.

Nader, Helen

1990   *Liberty in Absolutist Spain: The Hapsburg Sale of Towns, 1516–1700*. Baltimore: Johns Hopkins University Press.

Nakayama, Antonio, ed.

1974   *Relación de Antonio Ruiz (La Conquista en el Noroeste)*. Mexico City: INAH, Centro Regional del Noroeste.

Naylor, Thomas B., and Charles W. Polzer, S.J., comps. and eds.

1986   *The Presidio and Militia on the Northern Frontier of New Spain: A Documentary History*. Vol. 1, *1500–1700*. Tucson: University of Arizona Press.

Neill, Stephen

1964   *A History of Christian Missions*. London: Penguin Books.

Nelson, William

1973   *Fact or Fiction: The Dilemma of the Renaissance Story-Teller*. Cambridge, Mass.: Harvard University Press.

Nentvig, Juan, S.J.

1980 [1764]   *Rudo Ensayo: A Description of Sonora and Arizona in 1764*. Translated and annotated by A. F. Pradeau and R. R. Rasmussen. Tucson: University of Arizona Press.

Nichols, Stephen G., Jr.

1983   *Romanesque Signs: Early Medieval Narrative and Iconography*. New Haven: Yale University Press.

Nieremberg, Juan E., S.J., with Andrade Cassini
1889 [1666]   *Varones illustres de la Compañía de Jesús.* 3 vols.
              Bilbao.
NJB (The New Jerusalem Bible)
1985   *The New Jerusalem Bible.* New York: Doubleday.
Noel, Charles C.
1985   Missionary Preachers in Spain. *American Historical
        Review* 90:866–93.
Nowak, Ronald
1991   *Walker's Mammals of the World.* 5th ed. Baltimore:
        Johns Hopkins University Press.
Obelkevich, James
1979   Introduction. In *Religion and the People, 800–1700,*
        edited by J. Obelkevich, 1–7. Chapel Hill, N.C.:
        University of North Carolina Press.
O'Brien, John, A.M.
1879   *A History of the Mass and Its Ceremonies in the Eastern and
        Western Church.* New York: Benziger Brothers.
O'Callaghan, Joseph F.
1975   *A History of Medieval Spain.* Ithaca, N.Y.: Cornell
        University Press.
Ocaranza, Fernando
1944   *Vidas Mexicanas: Gregorio Lopez, El Hombre Celestial.*
        Mexico City: Ediciones Xochitl.
O'Gorman, Edmundo, ed.
1967   *Apologética Historia Sumaria,* by Fray Bartolomé de las
        Casas. 2 vols. Mexico City: Instituto de Investigacio-
        nes Históricas, Universidad Naciónal Autónoma de
        México.
Olin, John C.
1994   *Erasmus, Utopia, and the Jesuits.* New York: Fordham
        University Press
O'Malley, John W.
1993a   *The First Jesuits.* Cambridge, Mass.: Harvard University
         Press.
1993b   *Religious Culture in the Sixteenth Century: Preaching, Rhe-
         toric, Spirituality and Reform.* Brookfield, Vt.: Variorum.
O'Meara, Maureen F.
1992   Planting the Lord's Garden in New France: Gabriel
        Sagard's *Le Grand Voyage and Histoire du Canada. Rocky
        Mountain Review of Language and Literature* 46:1–24.
Ortiz, Alfonso
1969   *The Tewa World.* Chicago: University of Chicago Press.
———, ed.
1983   *Handbook of North American Indians.* Vol. 10, *Southwest.*
        Washington, D.C.: Smithsonian Institution.
Pagden, A.
1982   *The Fall of Natural Man.* Cambridge: Cambridge
        University Press.
Pailes, Richard A.
1978   The Río Sonora Culture in Prehistoric Trade Systems.
        In *Across the Chichimec Sea: Papers in Honor of J. Charles
        Kelley,* edited by C. L. Riley and B. C. Hedrick, 20–39.
        Carbondale: Southern Illinois University Press.
Pailes, Richard A., and Daniel T. Reff
1985   Colonial Exchange Systems and the Decline of Pa-
        quime. In *The Archaeology of West and Northwest Meso-
        america,* edited by M. S. Foster and P. C. Weigand,
        353–63. Boulder, Colo.: Westview Press.

Paso y Troncoso, Francisco del
1940   *Epistolario de Nueva España, 1505–1818.* Vol. 15. Mexico
        City: José Porrúa e Hijos.
Paxton, Frederick S.
1991   *Christianizing Death: The Creation of a Ritual Process in
        Early Medieval Europe.* Ithaca, N.Y.: Cornell University
        Press.
Pegis, Anton C., ed.
1948   *Introduction to Saint Thomas Aquinas.* New York: Mod-
        ern Library.
Pennington, Campbell W.
1979   *The Pima Bajo.* Vol. 2, *Vocabulario en la lengua Nevome.*
        Salt Lake City: University of Utah Press.
1980   *The Pima Bajo of Central Sonora, Mexico.* Vol. 1, *Material
        Culture.* Salt Lake City: University of Utah Press.
Pérez de Ribas, Andrés
1645   Historia de los triumphos de nuestra santa fee entre
        gentes las más barbaras y fieras del nuevo Orbe.
        Madrid.
1896 [1653]   *Corónica y historia religiosa de la provincia de la
              Compañía de Jesús de México.* 2 vols. Mexico City:
              Sagrado Corazón.
1944   *Páginas para la historia de Sinaloa y Sonora: {historia de
        los} triunfos de nuestra santa fe entre gentes las más barbaras
        y fieras del Nuevo Orbe.* 3 vols. Mexico City: Editorial
        Layac.
1985   *Páginas para la historia de Sonora: {historia de los} triunfos
        de nuestra santa fe entre gentes las más barbaras y fieras del
        Nuevo Orbe.* 2 vols. Hermosillo: Gobierno del Estado
        de Sonora.
Petersen, Joan
1984   *The Dialogues of Gregory the Great in Their Late Antique
        Cultural Background.* Toronto: Pontifical Institute of
        Medieval Studies.
Phelan, James L.
1970   *The Millennial Kingdom of the Franciscans in the New
        World.* Berkeley: University of California Press.
Polzer, Charles W., S.J.
1972   The Franciscan Entrada into Sonora, 1645–1652: A
        Jesuit Chronicle. *Arizona and the West* 14:253–78.
1976   *Rules and Precepts of the Jesuit Missions of Northwestern
        New Spain, 1600–1767.* Tucson: University of Arizona
        Press.
Polzer, Charles W., S.J., Thomas C. Barnes, and Thomas H.
        Naylor
1977   *The Documentary Relations of the Southwest Project
        Manual.* Tucson: Arizona State Museum.
Poole, Stafford, C.M.
1981   Church Law on the Ordination of Indians and Cas-
        tas in New Spain. *Hispanic American Historical Review*
        61:637–50.
1987   *Pedro Moya de Contreras: Catholic Reform and Royal Power
        in New Spain.* Berkeley: University of California Press.
Powell, Philip Wayne
1952   *Soldiers, Indians, and Silver: The Northward Advance
        of New Spain, 1550–1600.* Berkeley: University of
        California Press.
Pratt, Mary L.
1986   Fieldwork in Common Places. In *Writing Culture: The*

Poetics and Politics of Ethnography, edited by J. Clifford and G. Marcus, 27–50. Berkeley: University of California Press.

Rabinow, Paul
1977   *Reflections on Fieldwork in Morocco*. Berkeley: University of California Press.

Radding, Cynthia
1979   *Las estructuras socio-económicas de las misiones de la Pimería Alta*. Hermosillo: Centro Regional del Noroeste, INAH.

Rades y Andrada, Francisco de
1572 [1980]   *Corónica de las tres Ordenes de Santiago, Calatrava, y Alcantara*. Barcelona: Ediciones El Albir.

Ramge, Sebastián, O.C.D.
1963   *An Introduction to the Writings of Saint Teresa*. Chicago: Henry Regnery Co.

Real Academia Española
1969   *Diccionario de autoridades*. 3 vols. Facsimile reproduction of the 1726 original. Madrid: Editorial Gredos.

Reff, Daniel T.
1981   The Location of Corazones and Senora: Archaeological Evidence from the Río Sonora Valley, Mexico. In *The Protohistoric Period in the American Southwest, A.D. 1450–1700*, edited by D. R. Wilcox and W. B. Masse, 94–112. Arizona State Anthropological Research Papers No. 24. Tempe: Arizona State University.
1991a   Anthropological Analysis of Exploration Texts: Cultural Discourse and the Ethnological Import of Fray Marcos de Niza's Journey to Cibola. *American Anthropologist* 93:636–55.
1991b   *Disease, Depopulation, and Culture Change in Northwestern New Spain, 1518–1764*. Salt Lake City: University of Utah Press.
1993   La representación de la cultura indígena en el discurso jesuita del siglo XVII. In *La Compañia de Jesús en America: Evangelización y Justicia; Siglos XVII y XVIII*, 307–15. Córdoba, Spain: Congreso Internacional de Historia.
1994   Contextualizing Missionary Discourse: The Benavides Memorials of 1630 and 1634. *Journal of Anthropological Research* 50:51–68.
1995   The "Predicament of Culture" and Spanish Missionary Accounts of the Tepehuan and Pueblo Revolts. *Ethnohistory* 42:63–90.
1996   Text and Context: Cures, Miracles, and Fear in the Relación of Alvar Núñez Cabeza de Vaca. *Journal of the Southwest* 38:115–38.
1998   The Jesuit Mission Frontier in Comparative Perspective: The Reductions of the Río de la Plata and the Missions of Northwestern Mexico, 1588–1700. In *Contested Ground: Comparative Frontiers on the Northern and Southern Edges of the Spanish Empire*, edited by D. J. Guy and T. E. Sheridan, 16–31. Tucson: University of Arizona Press.

Ricard, Robert
1966   *The Spiritual Conquest of Mexico: An Essay on the Apostolate and the Evangelizing Methods of the Mendicant Orders in New Spain, 1523–1572*. Berkeley: University of California Press.

Ricoeur, Paul
1980   *Essays on Biblical Interpretation*. Philadelphia: Fortress Press.
1981   *Hermeneutics and the Human Sciences: Essays on Language, Action, and Interpretation*. New York: Cambridge University Press.

Riley, Carroll L.
1987   *The Frontier People: The Greater Southwest in the Prehistoric Period*. Albuquerque: University of New Mexico Press.

Robertson, Duncan
1995   *The Medieval Saints' Lives: Spiritual Renewal and Old French Literature*. Lexington: French Forum Publishers.

Robertson, Tomas A.
1968   *My Life among the Savage Nations of New Spain*. Los Angeles: Ward Ritchie Press.

Rorty, Richard
1989   *Contingency, Irony, and Solidarity*. Cambridge: Cambridge University Press.

Rosaldo, Renato
1986   From the Door of His Tent: The Fieldworker and the Inquisitor. In *Writing Culture: The Poetics and Politics of Ethnography*, edited by J. Clifford and G. Marcus, 77–98. Berkeley: University of California Press.

Rowe, Joseph H.
1964   *Ethnography and Ethnology in the Sixteenth Century*. Kroeber Anthropological Society Papers No. 30. Berkeley: University of California Press.

Ruiz de Montoya, Antonio
1892 [1639]   *Conquista espiritual hecha por los religiosos de la Compañía de Jesús en . . . Paraguay*. Bilbao: Corazón de Jesús.

Russell, Jeffrey B.
1984   *Lucifer: The Devil in the Middle Ages*. Ithaca, N.Y.: Cornell University Press.
1986   *Mephistopheles*. Ithaca, N.Y.: Cornell University Press.

Rylance, Rick
1987   *Debating Texts: A Reader in Twentieth-Century Literary Theory and Method*. Philadelphia: Open University Press.

Sahagún, Fray Bernardino de
1989   *Historia general de las cosas de Nueva España*, edited by A. M. Garibay. Mexico City: Editorial Porrúa.

Sánchez Ortega, María Helena
1992   Woman as Source of "Evil" in Counter-Reformation Spain. In *Culture and Control in Counter-Reformation Spain*, edited by A. J. Cruz and M. E. Parry, 196–215. Minneapolis: University of Minnesota Press.

Santamaría, Francisco J.
1974   *Diccionario de mejicanismos*. 2d ed. Mexico City: Editorial Porrúa.

Sauer, Carl O.
1932   *The Road to Cíbola*. Ibero-Americana No. 1. Berkeley: University of California Press.
1934   *The Distribution of Aboriginal Tribes and Languages in Northwest Mexico*. Ibero-Americana No. 5. Berkeley: University of California Press.
1935   *Aboriginal Population of Northwest Mexico*. Ibero-Americana No. 10. Berkeley: University of California Press.

Scarborough, Vernon L., and David R. Wilcox, eds.

1991   *The Mesoamerican Ballgame.* Tucson: University of
          Arizona Press.

Schaff, Phillip

1994   *Nicene and Post-Nicene Fathers.* Vol. 1, *The Confessions and
          Letters of Augustine, with a Sketch of His Life and Work.*
          Peabody, Mass: Hendrickson Publishers.

Schiebinger, Londa

1993   *Nature's Body.* Boston: Beacon Press.

Schoenhals, Louise C.

1988   *A Spanish–English Glossary of Mexican Flora and Fauna.*
          Mexico City: Summer Institute of Linguistics.

Scholes, Francis

1930   The Supply Service of the New Mexican Missions in
          the Seventeenth Century. *New Mexico Historical Review*
          5:93–115, 186–210, 386–404.

Schroeder, Albert

1956   Southwestern Chronicle: The Cipias and Ypotlapiguas.
          Arizona Quarterly 12:101–11.

Shaul, David L.

1990   The State of the Arte: Ecclesiastical Literature on the
          Northern Frontier of New Spain. *The Kiva* 55:167–75.

Sheridan, Thomas E.

1992   The Limits of Power: The Political Ecology of the
          Spanish Empire in the Greater Southwest. *Antiquity*
          66:153–71.

Sheridan, Thomas E., and Thomas H. Naylor, eds.

1979   *Rarámuri: A Tarahumara Colonial Chronicle 1607–1791.*
          Flagstaff: Northland Press.

Shiels, William E., S.J.

1934   *Gonzalo de Tapia (1561–1594), Founder of the First Perma-
          nent Jesuit Mission in North America.* New York: United
          States Catholic Historical Society.

1939   The Critical Period in Mission History. *Mid-America*
          (new series) 10:97–109.

Shreve, Forrest

1951   *Vegetation of the Sonoran Desert.* Washington, D.C.:
          Carnegie Institution of Washington.

Simmons, Marc

1980   *Witchcraft in the Southwest.* Lincoln: University of
          Nebraska Press.

Simon and Schuster

1973   *English–Spanish and Spanish–English Dictionary.* New
          York: Simon and Schuster.

Smith, Hilary D.

1978   *Preaching in the Spanish Golden Age.* Oxford: Oxford
          University Press.

Soustelle, Jacques

1961   *Daily Life of the Aztecs.* Stanford: Stanford University
          Press.

Spicer, Edward H.

1962   *Cycles of Conquest: The Impact of Spain, Mexico, and the
          United States on Indians of the Southwest, 1533–1960.*
          Tucson: University of Arizona Press.

1980   *The Yaquis: A Cultural History.* Tucson: University of
          Arizona Press.

Stalker, John C., comp.

1986   *The Jesuit Collection in the John J. Burns Library of Boston
          College.* Boston: Boston College Libraries.

Steele, Thomas J.

1974   *Santos and Saints: Essay and Handbook.* Santa Fe: Calvin
          Horn.

Steneck, Nicholas H.

1976   *Science and Creation in the Middle Ages.* Notre Dame:
          University of Notre Dame Press.

Stocking, George W., Jr.

1992   *The Ethnographer's Magic and Other Essays in the His-
          tory of Anthropology.* Madison: University of Wisconsin
          Press.

Thomas, David Hurst

1989   Columbian Consequences: The Spanish Borderlands
          in Cubist Perspective. In *Columbian Consequences.*
          Vol. 3, *The Spanish Borderlands in Pan-American Perspec-
          tive,* edited by D. Thomas, 1–17. Washington, D.C.:
          Smithsonian Institution Press.

Thurston, Herbert, S.J., and Donald Attwater, eds.

1956   *Butler's Lives of the Saints.* 4 vols. London: Burns and
          Oates.

Titiev, Mischa

1944   *Old Oraibi.* Papers of the Peabody Museum of Ameri-
          can Archaeology and Ethnology, vol. 22, no. 1. Cam-
          bridge, Mass.: Harvard University Press.

Treutlein, Theodore E., trans.

1949   *Sonora: A Description of the Province,* by Ignaz Pfeffer-
          korn. Albuquerque: University of New Mexico Press.

Trevor-Roper, Hubert R.

1967   *The European Witch-Craze of the Sixteenth and Seventeenth
          Centuries.* Harmondsworth, Eng.: Penguin Books.

Tylenda, Joseph N., S.J.

1984   *Jesuit Saints and Martyrs.* Chicago: Loyola University
          Press.

Tyler, Stephen

1987   *The Unspeakable: Discourse, Dialogue, and Rhetoric in the
          Postmodern World.* Madison: University of Wisconsin
          Press.

Van Dam, Raymond

1993   *Saints and Their Miracles in Late Antique Gaul.* Prince-
          ton: Princeton University Press.

———, trans.

1988   *Glory of the Martyrs,* by Gregory of Tours. Liverpool:
          University Press.

Wallace, Anthony F.

1956   Revitalization Movements. *American Anthropologist*
          58:264–81.

Ward, Benedicta

1992   *Signs and Wonders: Saints, Miracles and Prayers from
          the Fourth Century to the Fourteenth.* Hampshire, Eng.:
          Variorum.

Weber, Allison

1992   Saint Teresa, Demonologist. In *Culture and Control
          in Counter-Reformation Spain,* edited by A. J. Cruz
          and M. E. Perry, 171–95. Minneapolis: University of
          Minnesota Press.

Weber, David J.

1987   John Francis Bannon and the Historiography of the
          Spanish Borderlands. *Journal of the Southwest* 29:331–
          63.

1992   *The Spanish Frontier in North America*. New Haven: Yale University Press.

Weigand, Phil
1981   Minería y intercambio de minerales en Zacatecas pre-hispánica. In *Zacatecas 3, anuario de historia*, edited by C. Esperanza Sánchez, 138–95. Zacatecas: Universidad Autónoma de Zacatecas.

Weinstein, Donald, and Rudolph M. Bell
1982   *Saints and Society*. Chicago: University of Chicago Press.

West, Robert C.
1949   *The Mining Community in Northwestern New Spain: The Parral Mining District*. Ibero-Americana No. 30. Berkeley: University of California Press.

West, Robert C., and J. L. Parsons
1941   The Topia Road: A Trans-Sierran Trail of Colonial Mexico. *Geographical Review* 31:406–13.

White, Hayden
1973   *Metahistory: The Historical Imagination in Nineteenth-Century Europe*. Baltimore: Johns Hopkins University Press.

1978   *Tropics of Discourse: Essays on Cultural Criticism*. Baltimore: Johns Hopkins University Press.

White, Hugh Evelyn, trans.
1951   *Ausonius*. 2 vols. Cambridge, Mass.: Harvard University Press.

Wilson, Catherine
1990   Visual Surface and Visual Symbol: The Microscope and the Occult in Early Modern Science. In *Philosophy, Religion, and Science in the Seventeenth and Eighteenth Centuries*, edited by J. W. Yolton, 85–108. Rochester, N.Y.: University of Rochester Press.

Wright, A. D.
1982   *The Counter-Reformation: Catholic Europe and the Non-Christian World*. London: Weidenfeld and Nicolson.

1991   *Catholicism and Spanish Society under the Reign of Philip II, 1555–1598, and Philip III, 1598–1621*. Lewiston, Australia: Edwin Mellen Press.

Wuellner, Wilhelm
1979   Greek Rhetoric and Pauline Argumentation. In *Early Christian Literature and the Classical Intellectual Tradition*, edited by W. R. Schoedel and R. L. Wilken, 177–88. Paris: Editions Beauchesne.

Zambrano, P. Francisco, S.J.
1961–1977   *Diccionario bio-bibliográfico de la Compañía de Jesús en México*. 16 vols. Mexico City: Editorial Jus.

Zubillaga, Félix, S.J.
1946   *Monumenta antiquae Floridae (1566–1572)*. Vol. 3 of *Monumenta missionum Societatis Jesu*. Rome: Institum Historicum Societatis Iesu.

1968   *Monumenta mexicana*. Vol. 3, *1585–1590*. Rome: Institum Historicum Societatis Iesu.

1973   *Monumenta mexicana*. Vol. 5, *1592–1596*. Rome: Institum Historicum Societatis Iesu.

INDEX

ABOUT THE TRANSLATORS

DANIEL T. REFF is an anthropologist and Associate Professor of Comparative Studies at The Ohio State University. He is the author of *Disease, Depopulation, and Culture Change in Northwestern New Spain, 1518–1764* (1991). His research on Spanish exploration chronicles, missionary texts, and Spanish-Indian relations in the Greater Southwest also has appeared in numerous journals. In 1997 Professor Reff received the Edward H. Spicer award from the *Journal of the Southwest* for his 1996 article on Cabeza de Vaca's *Relación*. Dr. Reff is currently working on a comparative study of missionary texts and the rise of Christianity in early medieval Europe versus colonial Mexico.

MAUREEN AHERN is Professor of Spanish at The Ohio State University, where she teaches Latin American colonial literature and culture. She has published extensively on the sixteenth-century narratives of first contact on the northern frontiers of New Spain, including essays on the relaciones of Fray Marcos de Niza, Alvar Núñez Cabeza de Vaca, Fernando de Alarcón and the accounts of the Coronado (1540–42), Rodríguez-Chamuscado, and Espejo expeditions (1581–83)

to New Mexico. She is presently working on a study of Jesuit martyrdom in Pérez de Ribas' and other seventeenth-century missionary histories. Among her many translations of Mexican and Peruvian writers are *A Rosario Castellanos Reader* (1988) and *Five Quechua Poets* (1998).

RICHARD K. DANFORD is an assistant professor of Spanish at Marietta College in Ohio. His primary area of specialization is Spanish linguistics, with additional interests in Portuguese and translation studies. His doctoral dissertation addresses the historical development of word order patterns in Spanish as they relate to pronominal reduplication and the organization of information at the sentence level. He has also co-authored an article on parallel subordinate clause constructions in Spanish and Appalachian English. His current research interests include pronominal reduplication phenomena in Andean and Argentine Spanish, as well as the grammars and vocabularies of Amerindian languages written by Spanish and Portuguese missionaries during the colonial period.